Beginning Oracle Programming

Sean Dillon
Christopher Beck
Thomas Kyte
Joel Kallman
Howard Rogers

Apress™

Beginning Oracle Programming

© 2002 Apress

ISBN (pbk): 1-59059-286-7

Printed and bound in the United States of America 45678910

Trademarked names may appear in this book. Rather than use a trademark symbol with every occurrence of a trademarked name, we use the names only in an editorial fashion and to the benefit of the trademark owner, with no intention of infringement of the trademark.

Distributed to the book trade in the United States by Springer-Verlag New York, Inc., 175 Fifth Avenue, New York, NY, 10010 and outside the United States by Springer-Verlag GmbH & Co. KG, Tiergartenstr. 17, 69112 Heidelberg, Germany.

In the United States: phone 1-800-SPRINGER, email orders@springer-ny.com, or visit http://www.springer-ny.com. Outside the United States: fax +49 6221 345229, email orders@springer.de, or visit http://www.springer.de.

For information on translations, please contact Apress directly at 2560 Ninth Street, Suite 219, Berkeley, CA 94710. Phone 510-549-5930, fax 510-549-5939, email info@apress.com, or visit http://www.apress.com.

The information in this book is distributed on an "as is" basis, without warranty. Although every precaution has been taken in the preparation of this work, neither the author(s) nor Apress shall have any liability to any person or entity with respect to any loss or damage caused or alleged to be caused directly or indirectly by the information contained in this work.

The source code for this book is available to readers at http://www.apress.com in the Downloads section.

The image of the Bocca della Verita (Mouth of Truth) in Rome, used as chapter divider, is © 2000 by Lauren Ruth Wiener (http://www.verbing.com/).

Credits

About the Authors

Sean Dillon

Sean Dillon started programming a Commodore Vic 20 back in 1980 at the age of nine. Trying to program sprites and word games in the enormous 3.5KB of user memory was truly a labor of love. Sean grew and so did his love for programming. He began his professional programming career in the United States Marine Corps, shortly after returning from the Gulf War. Sean is now a Senior Technologist, working for Oracle Corporation based in Reston, Virginia. He has nine years of experience specializing in database architecture, database tuning, web application development, XML, and Web Services technologies.

Sean currently lives outside Washington, DC, with his wife Whitney, his sons Jordan and Cameron, and one "bun in the oven".

"Many thanks to my '21-years-old-and-holding' mother, Pat Martakes, for giving me life. My mom taught me what goes around comes around and that life is what you make of it. She is a remarkable woman.

I want to thank my friend and coworker, Tom Kyte, for providing a constant wealth of knowledge that inspires me each day. He has a mind to be envious of and a work ethic to strive for.

Many thanks to my friend, no, my brother Greg Parker, for the camaraderie he has given me over the years and for showing me that a Jarhead can succeed in this high-tech world.

Thanks also to Richard Rood and David Rogers, for showing me that Marines can be just as smart as they are strong; to Gary DeYoung for the welcome mat into Oracle and the leadership once I got on board; to Sandra Duerr for her guidance, her enthusiasm and for taking a chance on me; to Phil Woody and Stan Galanski for the Business 101 lessons; and a sincere thanks to Tim Hoechst for his unparalleled leadership and for hiring me to work with a phenomenal team of technical minds.

Last but not least, I want to thank my best friend and wife, Whitney. She took care of our children when they wanted Daddy to read a book or go outside and play. Whitney kept our household running, while I sat affixed to my monitors working on this book. Without Whitney's unwavering support and motivation, I would not have been able to take on such a monumental task. She is an intelligent teacher, a ferocious editor, a generous friend and a marvelous mother.

To Whitney, Jordan, Cameron and my unborn child, whom I can't wait to meet, I'm proud to say... "The book is finished, Daddy's home" "

Sean Dillon contributed Chapters 1, 2, 3, 4, 5, 7, 9, 10, 19, Case Study 2, and Appendices A, D, and E to this book. Appendix C was jointly contributed with Christopher Beck.

Christopher Beck

Christopher Beck, who holds a BA in Computer Science from Rutgers University, has worked in the industry for 11 years. Starting off as a junior Ada software developer for a government systems integrator, he has spent the last seven years with Oracle Corporation and is now a Principal Technologist. He specializes in core database technologies and web application development. WebView, a "science project" that he and a colleague wrote, became what is now known as Oracle Portal. When Chris is not working at Oracle or enjoying time with his wife and 4 children, he is either tinkering with Java and Linux (he still has a version of Linux circa 1993, encompassing 70+ floppies) or he can be found online enjoying a 'friendly' game of Quake III Arena.

"I would like to thank my good friend and fellow author Sean Dillon for getting me involved in this project (I had nothing better to do with the last 10 months, thanks Sean), Tom Kyte, my boss and friend for most of my career, who has taught me immensely over the years, the folks at Wrox for putting up with my late submissions, and my management at Oracle for allowing me to pursue this endeavor. Most importantly I would like to thank my wife Marta, daughter Samantha, and sons Cameron, Addison, and Sebastian for just being there for me. I love you all."

Christopher Beck contributed Chapters 11, 14, 15, 16, 17, Case Study 1, and Appendix B to this book. Appendix C was jointly contributed with Sean Dillon.

Thomas Kyte

Thomas Kyte writes:

"I have been working *for* Oracle since version 7.0.9 (that's 1993 for people who don't mark time by Oracle versions). However, I've been working *with* Oracle since about version 5.1.5c ($99 single user version for DOS on 360k floppy disks). Before coming to work at Oracle, I worked for over six years as a systems integrator, building large scale, heterogeneous databases and applications, mostly for military and Government customers. These days, I spend a great deal of my time working with the Oracle database and, more specifically, helping people who are using the Oracle database. I work directly with customers, either in specifying and building their systems or, more frequently, helping them rebuild or tune them ('tuning' frequently being a synonym for rebuilding). In addition, I am the Tom behind 'AskTom' in Oracle Magazine, answering people's questions about the Oracle database and tools. On a typical day I receive and answer 30 to 40 questions at http://asktom.oracle.com/. Then, every two months, I publish the 'best of' in the magazine (all of the questions asked are available on the web, stored in an Oracle database of course). Basically, I spend a lot of my time helping people be successful with the Oracle database. Oh yes, in my spare time, I build applications and develop software within Oracle Corporation itself.

In addition to the above, I found the time last year to write another book entitled *Expert One-on-One Oracle* (Wrox Press, ISBN 1861004826). That book is geared towards an intermediate to advanced Oracle developer/DBA and is a good follow-on to this book. It goes into much more depth on the details of how Oracle works, how many of the features are implemented and what they are useful for."

"I would like to thank many people for helping me in the completion of this book. I work with the best and brightest people I have ever known at Oracle and they all have contributed in one way or another. In particular I would like to thank Tim Hoechst and Mike Hichwa with whom I've worked with and known for almost 10 years now – their constant questioning and pushing has help me to discover things I would never have even thought of investigating on my own.

Lastly, but most importantly, I would like to acknowledge my family's continual support. Without the support of my wife Lori, son Alan and daughter Megan, I don't see how I could have finished this."

Thomas Kyte contributed Chapters 6, 12 and 18 to this book.

Joel Kallman

Joel Kallman is a web systems technologist for Oracle Corporation. His background over the past 12 years has centered on database and content management, from SGML databases and publishing systems to text and document management. He is currently developing solutions and tools for customers to easily build database-centric web applications. When he is not consumed by the daily advances in computer technology, he enjoys reading about investment principles as well as working out at the local 'Y'. Joel is a proud alumnus of The Ohio State University, where he received his bachelor's degree in computer engineering. He and his wife Kristin reside in Powell, Ohio.

Joel Kallman contributed Chapter 13 to this book.

Howard Rogers

Howard Rogers works as an Education Consultant for Oracle Corporation in Sydney, Australia, specializing in the DBA curriculum. Born and bored in England, he soon discovered that a History degree from Cambridge University was not much use to anyone, and thus migrated to Australia in the early 1990s. He has spent the last 15 years working in the IT industry as trainer, network and database administrator, consultant, and hired help. He's older and more versatile than he looks. On his occasional days off, he composes truly dire operas, takes an OK photo now and again, and has been known to sing lead tenor in the odd Church and Cathedral choir or two. What he doesn't know about Benjamin Britten probably isn't worth knowing in the first place, and any day now, he'll put his Private Pilot's License to some good use. His work for this book is dedicated to MJO, whose understanding, encouragement and frequent cups of tea made it all possible.

Howard Rogers contributed Chapter 8 to this book.

Table of Contents

Table of Contents

Table of Contents

Table of Contents

Introduction

So you want to learn about Oracle? I liken the task of learning Oracle to my experiences on US Marine Corps Recruit Depot Parris Island. Parris Island is the first stop for young men and women who have joined the United States Marine Corps. It's the place where drill instructors transform recruits into highly motivated, physically fit Marines. The stories of torturous drill and the challenges I was going to face during my three month stay on 'The Rock' filled my head with emotions ranging from exhilaration to outright fear. It seemed an insurmountable task, yet I faced the challenge with a seemingly endless supply of determination and desire to succeed.

Although you aren't going to be doing any pushups, and we won't be yelling at you through the chapters you're going to read in this book, your Oracle learning experience will bear a striking resemblance to that of a recruit on Parris Island (albeit yours will be much more lucrative!). You will be challenged time and again. The learning process will at times seem difficult, and at others it will seem relatively simple.

When I arrived at Parris Island, I had an idea of what to expect – plenty of physical training, Marine Corps customs and traditions, how to clean, fire, clean, assemble, and clean weapons (Did I mention cleaning?). I had no idea how I was going to remember everything. I was worried about being able to keep up with the physical training. I knew there was no way I would be able to fire a weapon from two hundred meters and hit a paper target the size of a computer monitor! But, as my three-month stay progressed my drill instructors taught me things I remember even now, thirteen years later. I had a hard time with the physical training at first, but it was nothing repeated practice couldn't solve. As for firing that rifle not only did I hit the target from *five hundred* meters, I earned the 'expert' rifle badge, the highest achievement you can get on the rifle range.

Starting on your road to mastering Oracle, you will have expectations as well. You know you'll be using a database. You know you'll be writing queries, inserts, and updates. I'm sure you have a slew of preconceived ideas of what to expect as you learn how to use this mountain of a database. The instructors at Parris Island taught us well, drawing from their experience and using practical application as a learning tool. We will use the same approach to teaching in this book. We'll use practical examples, employing the lessons you learn to help teach these concepts to you. By the time you have completed this book, you will have all the knowledge you need to use Oracle databases with confidence.

Why Read This Book?

When you opened the cover of this book, you had a notion of what you would find. With a title like *Beginning Oracle Programming*, it's fairly obvious what this book is all about. Simply put, the purpose of this book is to teach you how to manage data using an Oracle database.

The goal of *Beginning Oracle Programming* is to introduce you to those concepts that are important to understand as a beginning-level Oracle user. You are setting out on the same journey we traveled some years ago. We know the things you are going to run into time and time again. We understand the challenges you are going to meet when you have to develop an application or administer your database. We can guarantee you that the techniques you'll learn in this book are proven and have led us through many successful implementations.

So instead of talking about the things we want to teach you in an abstract kind of way, let's talk specifics. What are the kinds of skills you will learn, exactly? What will you have when you finish this book? Why should you buy it, or, now that you have, why should you **read** it?

Who Is This Book for?

As we write this book, we have no idea what you know or what you don't. You might be a master DBA in SQL Server looking to diversify your resume; maybe you're a Java programmer who has been charged with storing and retrieving your data using Oracle; or perhaps you are a college student who is looking for a nice paying job once 'the best days of your life' are behind you. No matter what your background might be, this book takes a simple approach to teaching you Oracle technology.

Assumptions

The only things we have assumed are that you understand the underlying concepts behind relational databases and have a basic understanding of SQL. If you don't have a grasp of those two things, the lessons in this book may be difficult to understand.

> *If you lack these skills, read this book in conjunction with an introductory SQL book. Examples include Beginning SQL Programming (ISBN 1861001800, Apress) and SQL Queries for Mere Mortals (ISBN 0201433362, Addison Wesley).*

Readers who have not used Oracle before will want to read through the book from front to back. Concepts introduced in the first chapter will be built upon in later chapters. Once you have an understanding of the core concepts of the book you can skip around from chapter to chapter; just keep in mind you may run across unfamiliar terminology or corners of the database that you've not yet used.

DBA vs. Developers

Some of you are looking to become database administrators, whereas others are looking to become database programmers. These different jobs require different personalities. Somebody who likes to explore new technology, is excited by new features, or feels constrained wearing a beeper for work twenty-four hours a day, seven days a week ought **not** to answer that job offer for a database administration position. This person has all the qualities of a programmer. In my experience, I have found most programmers to be the type of person that enjoys learning new languages, new data formats, new protocols, and so on, in order to build solutions. On the other hand, IT professionals who are more confident digging into a particular technology and exploiting everything that it has to offer may want to lean toward database administration.

At Oracle, part of my team's charter is to write web-based applications. We write applications for a variety of reasons, such as showcasing Oracle technology, helping our sales team's productivity, and to have the experience to draw from when making recommendations to our customers. Regardless of why we wrote the applications, we found that after writing a large number of them we were missing one key ingredient: a database administrator!

We decided to hire a database administrator to manage the production applications and make sure they were up 'most of the time' for our users. Even though these applications were not mission-critical at the time, our users came to expect a level of service that we found we simply couldn't maintain without somebody dedicated to administering the systems full-time.

Why did we hire a database administrator? Why didn't one of us just change job responsibilities and take on the administrative role for the applications the other members of the team were producing? Every member of the team has served as a database administrator in the past. We all knew how to do it, for the most part, and anything we didn't know, we had an entire team of experienced administrators to draw knowledge from. Add that to the fact that the systems didn't need twenty-four hour a day, seven day a week uptime, and it should have been a no-brainer. The only problem was, none of us were really cut out to be database administrators.

So we hired Fred, an experienced database administrator from the financial industry where *big* databases require *24 x 7 uptime*. Fred has all of the traits we need in a database administrator:

- ❑ He knows the database architecture like the back of his hand
- ❑ He appreciates the importance of backup and recovery plans
- ❑ He can apply patches and bug fixes to the database at a moment's notice, in order to overcome an issue our users might be encountering
- ❑ He has the patience to monitor the databases performance over time, to help tune the system for response time and ensure the application will scale

This is really just the tip of the iceberg when it comes to good traits of a database administrator, and the qualities Fred brings to the team.

The point is that, even though any person on our team might have been able to administer those databases, nobody could have done it as well as Fred. Fred is *really good* at database administration. With him managing our database servers, we could all concentrate on what we did best, namely writing applications that take advantage of Oracle technology. Everybody wins.

The lesson to take away from this is: give it some time. Cross train. Learn the different facets of not only your job, but also the jobs around you. You may find that the grass really is greener on the other side!

What does this have to do with this book? *Beginning Oracle Programming* is a book for administrators *and* developers, alike. Throughout the book, we have taken an approach to the technology that provides you with the knowledge you need to effectively use an Oracle database. Some material is more appropriate for administrators; other material is targeted for developers. All in all, however, both sets of readers will benefit from the lessons and technology covered in this text.

What's Covered in This Book?

We've tried to arrange the subjects covered in this book to take you from no knowledge to expert, in as logical a manner as possible. We cover topics in the following order:

- ❑ First, we're going to familiarize you with Oracle. We'll look at an overview of terminology and tools that will be used throughout the book, but which you may not have seen before. We'll also talk about the different classes of Oracle databases.

- ❑ Once we have talked about Oracle at a high level, we'll dive right into the database by learning how to write some basic SQL using our tool of choice, SQL*Plus.

- ❑ After you have been introduced to SQL*Plus and have a basic understanding of using SQL data manipulation language (DML), we'll learn how to create and manage users and tables with SQL data definition language (DDL).

- ❑ We'll move on to introduce the sample users provided by Oracle. These sample accounts will be used throughout the book for code samples and in illustrating concepts.

- ❑ At this point in the book, having introduced the basics of Oracle, we'll take a look under the hood of the database, at the architecture of the database and how Oracle operates behind the scenes.

- ❑ Once you have an understanding of how Oracle works, we can start to use Oracle to write applications. We'll learn how to create objects in the database such as tables and indexes.

- ❑ Next, we'll master more SQL*Plus before discussing writing procedural code in the database using PL/SQL. We'll also discuss storing PL/SQL in program units for use in our applications and day-to-day operations.

- ❑ With procedural code covered, we can see how Oracle manages transactions and concurrency.

- ❑ We round out our look at the database internals with chapters on security, views, triggers, and objects.

- ❑ Oracle is capable of some very powerful SQL. We'll look at writing some advanced queries to do things most databases can't do without procedural code.

- ❑ One of the biggest problems with writing database applications is ensuring you are getting the best possible performance out of your database. We will learn how to use some of the tools that come with Oracle for evaluating performance and to assist in the tuning process.

❑   Now that we have quite a bit of SQL, we'll discuss the notion of a SQL Toolkit. This is a collection of useful scripts that you can use in your database. In this section, we will review a number of scripts that the authors have found helpful.

❑   Lastly, we'll finish off with a couple of case studies. These not only show practical uses of the Oracle database, but also talk about why the applications were written the way they were.

What You Need To Use This Book

To work through *Beginning Oracle Programming* you need access to an Oracle database, whether locally or via a network. You need access to the sample schemas, and a DBA account with which to create new database objects.

The book covers functionality found in Oracle 8, Oracle 8*i*, and Oracle 9*i*. Where something is version specific, it is noted in the text. Otherwise, the concepts, examples, and explanations apply to these releases, and to the various classes of the database (Personal, Standard, and Enterprise).

To download a trial version of the latest release of Oracle 9*i*, navigate from http://otn.oracle.com/software/products/Oracle9i/content.html. If downloading 3 CDs worth of software is a little too much for your network connection, you can also buy CD packs of the software for 30-day trial from the Oracle store http://oraclestore.oracle.com.

Conventions

To help you understand what's going on, and in order to maintain consistency, we've used a number of conventions throughout the book:

When we introduce new terms, we **highlight** them.

These boxes hold important information.

Advice, hints, and background information are presented like this.

Words that appear on the screen in menus like the File or Window menu are in a similar font to what you see on screen. URLs are also displayed in this font. Keys that you press on the keyboard, like *Ctrl* and *Enter*, are in italics.

Try It Out

1.   After learning something new, we'll have a Try It Out section, which will demonstrate the concepts learned, and get you working with the technology.

How It Works

After a Try It Out section, there will sometimes be a further explanation, to help you relate what you've done to what you've just learned.

When we're running examples from the command line, we'll show the command and the results like this:

```
SQL> connect scott/tiger
Connected.

SQL> select empno, ename, job from emp where job='MANAGER'
  2  /

    EMPNO ENAME      JOB
---------- ---------- ---------
     7566 JONES      MANAGER
     7698 BLAKE      MANAGER
     7782 CLARK      MANAGER

SQL>
```

The things you need to type are shown in bold.

In the book text, we use a fixed-width font when we talk about code. For example, in the above code, we've used the SELECT statement to extract EMPNO, ENAME, and JOB columns for managers. Filenames, like init.ora, have a similar style.

If you've not seen a block of code before, then we show it as a gray box:

```
if condition then
  my_proc( value1 );
end if;
```

Sometimes you'll see code in a mixture of styles, like this:

```
if condition then
  my_proc( value1 );
else
  my_proc( value2 );
end if;
```

In this case, we want you to focus on the code with the gray background. The code with a white background is code we've already looked at and that we don't wish to examine further.

Additionally, when example code is shown in SQL*Plus format, we may highlight important sections in bold.

```
SQL> declare
  2    l_text varchar2(100);
  3  begin
  4    l_text := 'Hello, World!';
  5    dbms_output.put_line(l_text);
  6  end;
```

```
    7 /
Hello, World!

PL/SQL procedure successfully completed.
```

Customer Support

We always value hearing from our readers, and we want to know what you think about this book: what you liked, what you didn't like, and what you think we can do better next time. You can send us your comments by e-mail to support@apress.com. Please be sure to mention the book title in your message.

How To Download the Sample Code for the Book

When you visit the Apress site, http://www.apress.com/, visit the Downloads area of the site and click on the book's detail page.

The files that are available for download from our site have been archived using WinZip. When you have saved the file to a folder on your hard-drive, you need to extract the files using a decompression program such as WinZip or PKUnzip. When you extract the files, the code is usually extracted into chapter folders. When you start the extraction process, ensure your software is set to use folder names.

Errata

We've made every effort to make sure that there are no errors in the text or in the code in this book. However, no one is perfect and mistakes do occur. If you find an error in one of our books, like a spelling mistake or a faulty piece of code, we would be very grateful for feedback. By sending in errata you may save a future reader hours of frustration, and of course, you will be helping us provide even higher quality information. Simply e-mail the information to support@apress.com, your information will be checked and if correct, posted to the errata page for that title and used in subsequent editions of the book.

To see if there are any errata for this book on the web site, go to http://www.apress.com/, and visit the book's detail page.

E-mail Support

If you wish to directly query a problem in the book with an expert who knows the book in detail then e-mail support@apress.com. A typical e-mail should include the following things:

❏ The **title of the book, last four digits of the ISBN**, and **page number** of the problem in the Subject field.

❏ Your **name, contact information**, and the **problem** in the body of the message.

We *won't* send you junk mail. We need the details to save your time and ours. When you send an e-mail message, it will go through the following chain of support:

- ❑ Customer Support – Your message is delivered to our customer support staff, who are the first people to read it. They have files on most frequently asked questions and will answer anything general about the book or the web site immediately.

- ❑ Editorial – Deeper queries are forwarded to the technical editor responsible for that book. They have experience with the programming language or particular product, and are able to answer detailed technical questions on the subject.

- ❑ The Authors – Finally, in the unlikely event that the editor cannot answer your problem, he or she will forward the request to the author. We do try to protect the author from any distractions to their work; however, we are quite happy to forward specific requests to them. All Apress authors help with the support on their books. They will e-mail the customer and the editor with their response, and again all readers should benefit.

The Apress Support process can only offer support on issues that are directly pertinent to the content of our published title. Support for questions that fall outside the scope of normal book support is provided via the community lists of our http://forums.apress.com.

Getting To Know Oracle

Before we start getting into the nitty-gritty of the chapters to come, there are some core concepts you should understand. In the next few sections, we will discuss concepts that aren't to do with acquiring technical skills, but will be helpful in your pursuit of knowledge of and understanding about Oracle. In this chapter, I will explain:

❑   Fundamentals. What is a database? An instance? A schema? What kind of terminology will you encounter in Oracle that you most likely haven't seen before? What are SYS and SYSTEM? I'll explain some of the basic terminology you should be familiar with before you begin. This will arm you with the 'lingo' you'll need to understand the information you'll encounter throughout the book.

❑   The many flavors of the Oracle database. Oracle has one core database product, but it comes in a couple of different 'classes'. We'll discuss the intent of each class of database, and look at some of the factors that differentiate them.

❑   What you will find throughout this book and some things you should bear in mind as you move through it.

Let's begin with those fundamental terms.

Oracle Fundamental Terms

As you begin your journey of mastering the Oracle database, you will encounter terminology that may be unfamiliar. Additionally, Oracle has its own meanings for a variety of terms you may already feel comfortable with, but that may be confusing when used as Oracle presents them. In this section, we'll take a quick look at some of the terminology and nomenclature of the Oracle database. This section should prepare you for the lessons and the more detailed concepts you will encounter in the rest of the book.

Database

Oracle is the name of the industry's leading relational database management system (RDBMS). Throughout this book, we will also make reference to **Oracle Corporation**, the company that develops the Oracle database, and sometimes we'll refer to the Corporation as Oracle too for brevity, so you will have to be able to distinguish these two meanings through the context of the sentence.

The term **database** refers to all those files necessary to operate Oracle. There are data files, temporary data files, redo log files, control files, and parameter files. When we refer to a database, it is the files we are talking about and we'll discuss them in detail in Chapter 5. When using Oracle, *you* will only infrequently refer to the files that are used to operate the database. Oracle itself, on the other hand, uses the database files continuously.

Instance

The Oracle **instance** encompasses all the processes and memory structures that execute and are allocated in order to operate the database. It is the database invoked into memory and processes so that we can use it. Throughout the book, we will also commonly use the term Oracle to refer to an instance.

There are a wide variety of processes that Oracle (the RDBMS) runs to manage its great number of 'moving parts', and it does this in an instance. In addition, a fairly complex memory architecture must be allocated from your server's available memory and used for performing database operations. These memory structures will be discussed in detail in Chapter 5.

Although we will not be talking about **Oracle Parallel Server** (OPS) in this book, the architecture of OPS deserves mention here. In OPS (known as **Real Application Clusters** (RAC) in Oracle 9*i*), there can be many instances running on different servers all accessing a single database on a shared disk.

Users

Users in Oracle are named accounts that are used to log in to Oracle. When you install Oracle, there are two users created by default, SYS and SYSTEM, which we will discuss in the *Security* section below. Oracle also comes with other user accounts that can be installed as sample schemas. We use these sample schemas to demonstrate the functionality of the database throughout the book.

Schemas

A **schema** in Oracle is a collection of database objects belonging to a particular user. The terms *user* and *schema* are sometimes used interchangeably, although technically they're not the same thing. When you create a database application all the tables, constraints, indexes, triggers, sequences, packages, procedures, functions, dimensions, directories, and other objects that might be needed within your application should be organized into a single user's schema. This is accomplished by creating a user account and making it the owner of all those objects in Oracle. A schema is not an object on its own, it is simply a term used to describe the collection of objects that belongs to a particular user.

We will be using the schemas included with the database throughout this book. There are installation instructions in Appendix D that outline how to create the user accounts and then create all the objects for that user. We refer to these schemas as the **sample schemas**, because when they've been installed they provide a collection of database objects you can use. Chapter 4 discusses, in detail, what you get with the new sample schemas in Oracle 9*i*.

Security

The basic security model in Oracle is based on **privileges**. A privilege is permission to perform specific types of action within the database. If you've not been granted the privilege, you cannot perform the action.

There are **system privileges** that give you the right to perform particular types of actions, and **object privileges** that authorize you to perform an action on a particular object. An example of a system privilege might be to select data from any table in the database (no matter which schema it is in), or to alter some properties of the database itself (a privilege usually reserved for administrators). An example of an object privilege might be the ability to select data from a specific table or to execute procedural code owned by a specific user. These privileges are granted to users to allow them to carry out operations they wouldn't be permitted to perform otherwise.

Users must be granted the CREATE SESSION privilege before they are permitted to connect to the database. Once created in the database, they must be granted the appropriate privileges to create objects. When this has happened, every time they create an object they are automatically granted certain privileges over it, such as permission to alter tables and drop tables. It's what I would describe as a pessimistic privilege model, where you don't have any privileges until an administrator grants them to you.

The only problem with a privilege model is that managing it becomes far too complex. Imagine an application that has one hundred tables. Each person using the applications needs to be able to select, insert, update and delete from those tables. Privileges for each table (or object) must be granted in individual grant statements, so you would have to write one grant statement for each user, for each table. Now we enhance the application, and in the process add ten tables to the schema. Each user must be granted privileges for each of the tables we added. If we then only wanted certain users to delete records, we would have to revoke the delete privilege from all the users who should not be able to perform deletes, for each table. This kind of administration will consume your time, energy, and patience!

To help ease the overhead of privilege administration, Oracle uses **roles**. A role is a database object used to help manage database security. You can grant privileges to a role, and then grant roles to users (or other roles). This makes security management very intuitive and easy to administer. In the scenario above, you would create two roles; one for users who could perform any activity on the tables (including deletes), and another role for users who could select, insert, and update the records. The privileges would then be granted to the roles, and the roles granted to the users. Now when you add tables to the application, role privileges are automatically granted and the users automatically inherit them because they are granted the role. If you add a user to the application, one grant statement gives them the role and they now have access to all the tables they need.

You will read more about privileges, roles, and a plethora of other database security features in Chapter 13, but let's finish our discussion of security here with a look at the SYS and SYSTEM users as they have a great deal of power in your database.

SYS and SYSTEM

These are your administrative accounts and they have unrestricted access to everything in your database. They get this access from the DBA role, which is granted to them during database installation. The DBA role has been granted most of the system privileges in the database.

Many users assume they should use these accounts to administer their databases and perform their day-to-day operations when they start out using Oracle. Although SYS and SYSTEM are certainly powerful enough to handle these tasks, it is generally bad practice to use them in this way. Between them SYS and SYSTEM own a large part of the database. Many underlying objects used during the normal operations of the database rely on other objects owned by SYS and/or SYSTEM. A simple mistake using either of these accounts can do a great deal of damage to your database. For this reason, the Oracle documentation suggests creating a DBA account for yourself and using that account to perform all your administrative tasks in the database. We look at creating users in Chapter 3.

The base tables and the views that make up the data dictionary are all owned by SYS. These tables and views are necessary for successful operation of the database. There is no reason for you to perform inserts, updates, or deletes on the tables owned by SYS. In summary, use your own DBA account for administering the database, and leave the SYS schema to internal operations and data dictionary management only. We talk more about the data dictionary and views later in this chapter.

Tables used to store information for features and options of the database are owned by SYSTEM. Tables supporting replication, Materialized Views, LogMiner, and Advanced Queues are some examples.

Up to and including Oracle 9i 9.0.1, Oracle defaults the password for these accounts to be change_on_install for SYS and manager for SYSTEM. As the first password indicates, these passwords should be changed immediately after you install your database. Not changing them presents a *huge* security risk, as access to either of these accounts means you are handing over the keys to the database.

Using Oracle

Before we get started on building tables, writing functions, and querying data, let's step back for just a minute to look at some of the underlying concepts. We'll talk a little about what you're going to learn in this book and some of the things I feel you need to know to use Oracle effectively – **SQL*Plus** and the **data dictionary**.

SQL*Plus

SQL*Plus is a client tool used by developers and administrators to interact with Oracle databases. It lets you issue SQL statements, compile and execute PL/SQL code, and administer your database from a command-line console connected to Oracle, either on the local server or anywhere on your network.

SQL*Plus has been a favorite tool of mine for years now. But when I started using Oracle, I saw no value whatsoever in SQL*Plus and couldn't understand why Oracle continued to develop the tool. Most of the people I come across feel the same way as I did then – that just because the tool works and you can use it to write SQL doesn't make it effective or useful!

I remember the day my whole world changed.

I had been assigned to a development project where I would be working on a secure, easy-to-use, Internet-based portal for children in schools. The entire application lived inside the database. The interface was all web based. There would be tools for the kids to send and receive e-mail, build web pages, share their work online with not only teachers and other students from their own school, but also with schools in other Counties, States, and Countries.

It was a very advanced application to build, with half-second response times for each and every page that came up and full image/video/audio support on the pages. We were basically showcasing Oracle technology by building something that would be useful to kids all around the world. The programmers I was to be working with were some of the best I had ever met. Building an application like this that had to scale to support millions of kids, all over the world, would have to be a pretty intense project indeed! Very advanced concepts, very advanced technologies, very advanced tools…

The first thing my development manager did was to show me the application. He was demonstrating what the team had already built, and he ran into a bug. "Oh, watch how fast we can fix this", he said. He opened a telnet window to the server, edited the file with vi, and ran SQL*Plus to recompile the module. SQL*Plus?! An advanced project like this and you're running SQL*Plus? At first I thought that the development manager must be the 'dinosaur' of the team who just couldn't let go of old habits… but in time I learned that everybody on the team was using it.

It only took me a few days to really dig into the tool and start seeing the value it held. There is so much you can do from SQL*Plus; so much it offers. Reporting, installing applications, application development, database monitoring, performance tuning, benchmarking; the list goes on and on. It's no coincidence that I use SQL*Plus for almost every example in this book.

As a database developer, or a database administrator, you simply must know this invaluable tool and we'll cover it in detail in Chapters 2 and 9 of this book. Oracle doesn't charge for the licenses anymore: it comes free as a part of the database. By the time you have finished *Beginning Oracle Programming*, you will have an intimate understanding of how to use SQL*Plus.

Data Dictionary

As you create users, tables, indexes, views, stored procedures, and other database objects, your database keeps track of these items in an internal repository called the **data dictionary**. The data dictionary is a meta data repository for all the objects and data stored in an Oracle database. It gives you a central location to find anything you need to know about the contents of your database.

For application developers, the data dictionary is a place where you can find the specifications for procedures, functions, and programmatic interfaces. You can find out the structure of tables into which you intend to insert data, and you can see how an object type is constructed in order to utilize it in your application. You can investigate indexing strategies on tables so the SQL you write against tables can use those indexes when appropriate… and this is only the beginning. Developers building PL/SQL applications that live inside the database, or Java programmers writing J2EE-compliant classes that access Oracle from an application server over the network, will find that the objects in the database are published in the data dictionary.

Database administrators will use the data dictionary even more than application developers. All the information on how the database has been using the host file system's disk, the virtual buckets where tables, indexes, and other data structures are held (known as **tablespaces** in Oracle), and all the meta data you could ever want to see about the database objects, will all be found in the data dictionary. Processes running in the database, the users that are currently connected, what those users are doing, what SQL statements have been executed, and many other types of information are all available to you through querying the data dictionary.

We'll take a look at using the data dictionary in the next chapter. Here you'll see examples of querying the data dictionary and using it to give us practical answers to everyday questions you might have about the database. As you progress through the book, you will find references to data dictionary views along the way. In Chapter 19, *A SQL Toolkit*, we'll explain how to set up a script repository that is readily available to you in SQL*Plus. The scripts you find in the toolkit chapter will use the data dictionary extensively to not only give you examples of using it, but also provide you with useful tools we use in our own day-to-day interaction with Oracle. Finally, Appendix C, *The Data Dictionary*, provides a lookup for the data dictionary. This is the most centralized source of data in the book about dictionary views, the columns in those views, and why you might use them.

Oracle's Way of Doing Things

Not all RDBMSs are created equal. They work differently, and the way they were built determines how they react in different situations. If you are new to database technology, you are arguably better prepared to learn Oracle than somebody who has been using a different relational database product. A person who comes from a Sybase background, for instance, might build their application thinking more than one person inserting into a table or updating a table at the same time is dangerous. Also that users should commit frequently to avoid locking resources that could potentially make other users wait. In Sybase, this is true. They had to build their applications this way because of the way Sybase locks resources in the database.

Many databases in the market today are still plagued by the 'writers block readers' problem. This means if a user (the writer) updates a row in a table, another user (the reader) cannot read that row until the writer saves their work to the database (using something called a commit). Some databases let the reader read the row, with the understanding that the row is wrong. This is what is called a **dirty read**. Oracle suffers from no such problem. In Chapter 12, *Transactions and Concurrency*, you will read how Oracle performs transactions so that writes from one user have no bearing on another user until such time as a commit happens.

The differences don't stop at the locking and concurrency level, however. Oracle is a very robust database engine, and there is a great deal of functionality built into it so developers don't have to do things themselves. I have found programming shops that have written hundreds or even thousands of lines of code to do things that Oracle could have done for them.

One healthcare customer did claims processing inside the Oracle database. They would upload a patient claim into the database, and they inserted data into a job tracking table to signify that the claim had to be processed. Every so often, their operating system would fire up a job (using CRON on Linux, or AT on Windows) to check the job tracking table and look for new claims to be processed. If there were claims to be processed, it would start up a procedure in the database that would process the claim. The processing of the claim would record statistics such as when the processing began, how long it took, and other related information into the job tracking table so they could report on those statistics at a later time.

They ended up with problems somewhere in the thousand or so lines of PL/SQL code and could not figure out how to resolve the issues. When I saw what they were doing, I introduced them to DBMS_JOB, a package of PL/SQL code supplied with the database that did 90% of what they were trying to do (DBMS_JOB and other packages supplied with Oracle are the subject of Appendix B). Not only did this resolve the problem they were having debugging their custom code; it relieved them from having to maintain their own code, and it introduced a wide variety of additional job-related functionality they hadn't had time to build into their application, even though they wanted to.

The underlying theme here is that databases work differently. If you are used to the way your database works or you assume that Oracle is just the place to stick your data and pull it out, you are missing the boat. Oracle isn't the best database on the market simply because of its speed but also its support for applications.

An Approach To Learning

When you use Oracle to write your applications, you shouldn't believe for a second that the only thing you need to understand is how to write SELECT, INSERT, UPDATE, and DELETE statements.

I built a web-based e-mail interface for a project I was working on about a year ago. The e-mail interface was part of a much larger portal application that was built exclusively in PL/SQL in the database. My job was to get e-mail data and include it in one of these PL/SQL-driven dynamic web pages. Whenever we had e-mail bugs, the team building the larger portal application would turn to me to dig into the code to resolve the problem. It was a fairly complex architecture and it was far easier for me to take five minutes to look at the code, find the source of the problem, and fix it.

After the e-mail interface had been built, the development team took control of my code and began figuring it all out for themselves. They had issues from time to time for me to help them with, but for the most part they had become self-sufficient. One day, they came to me with a problem and asked for me to take a look at it. They had spent hours upon hours trying to resolve the problem, and still they couldn't figure it out.

When I started digging in to the code to find the source of the problem, I couldn't find it either. I looked and looked, instrumented the code with debugging statements to tell me what was going on, followed the trail of calls, and after a couple of hours I came up with the problem. A low-level package had been recompiled with a 'new & improved' version. Unfortunately, the 'new & improved' version was not complete, and therefore it couldn't handle the type of HTTP request we were issuing. There was nothing in the new version they needed, they just thought it would be best to run the latest and greatest code. As soon as we recompiled the old version, everything worked fine.

It took me a couple of hours to find what normally might have taken a few minutes to resolve. Why is that? It was because I didn't understand the new architecture. They had changed code, and the innermost workings of the code were unfamiliar to me. Once I knew all the moving parts, once I had a grasp on how everything was working, it was easy to figure out.

This is the same way I approach everything I do with Oracle technology. If you know how everything under the covers works, you are that much better prepared to build a successful solution. When you observe your application or the database exhibiting a particular kind of behavior, you have a better idea of where the problem is originating. Having a better understanding of things such as:

❑   Oracle architecture; the processes, the memory structures, and the files involved (Chapter 5)

❑   how Oracle deals with things such as concurrency control and transactions (Chapter 12)

❑   the workings of Oracle's security model (Chapter 13)

will help to equip you with the knowledge you will need to effectively operate an Oracle database.

Storing and Querying Data Using Oracle

Relational databases have come a long way since the late 1970's when Oracle released their first version of the database. Today, databases provide strong security facilities to prevent unauthorized access to data. They allow you to store and execute business logic in languages such as PL/SQL or Java inside the database. Not only can you store native XML documents inside the database, but you can also dynamically generate XML directly from relational data stored in the columns and rows of your tables. You can make web requests directly from SQL to retrieve web pages from the Internet, which can then be processed inside the database.

With all this exciting functionality it's very easy to lose focus on the core function databases are supposed to provide. Putting data into the database, and subsequently processing it in some way, has always been the core competency of the relational database vendor. Oracle is no different. At the heart of it all, Oracle's best capability is managing any type of data, anywhere, any time. That used to be a sales slogan Oracle used... "*Any Data, Anywhere, Any Time*". Personally, I feel that's one they should have stuck with.

In this book, it will be a constant theme. We are going to talk about database architecture, database security and stored procedural code; but don't let that detract from concentrating on the importance of simply storing and retrieving data from the database. We have included a number of chapters discussing basic querying, advanced querying, tuning your SQL and building a repository of scripts to retrieve data. The first things we talk about are retrieving, storing, and managing your data using Oracle.

Oracle is only as good as you make it. Anybody who can write a SQL statement can have a poorly implemented database. The trick to using the database is to make sure you can squeeze your data for every ounce of value it can give you. You need to know your data and know its value. If you don't understand how to exploit your data, how do you know you need to store it? It is imperative that you understand how your users interact with the data and how they expect to use the data you offer. By knowing what data you are storing, understanding how the data is being put into the database, and constantly adjusting the database based on how users are accessing it, you will already be ahead of the game. Be in tune with your database, and you will succeed. Assume it is going to perform well because the power light is on, and you are doomed to failure.

In Chapter 7, we talk about the different types of tables in Oracle, and why you might use one instead of another. In Chapter 17, we talk about doing some more advanced and pretty nifty stuff with queries of your data. Learn to use the data dictionary for finding out more information about the database. Most people that are intimidated by Oracle feel that way because they don't know how to ask it questions. Don't be intimidated.

Building Applications in the Database

One of the features of Oracle is storing and executing procedural logic inside the database. Back in the Oracle 7 days, Oracle introduced stored procedures to its users. At the time, the language was PL/SQL, a proprietary Oracle language, loosely based on the Ada programming language. In Oracle 8, Oracle built a Java Virtual Machine that allowed Oracle developers to deploy and execute their Java classes that ran inside the database.

The team I work on at Oracle concentrates on database technology. We have built many an application that runs solely in the database. The user interface is a web browser. The web server, Apache, uses an application called MOD_PLSQL to talk to the database (MOD_PLSQL is a modification to Apache that lets the web browser call PL/SQL packages and procedures directly). There's no Java, no C, and no assembler required. The entire application, besides the user interface, runs inside Oracle. Using just the database, we are able to create applications that support tens of thousands of users and record millions of hits per week.

Oracle offers a great deal of functionality for those development houses with the skills necessary to employ it. With the myriad of PL/SQL packages that are supplied with Oracle, and the ability to load just about any JAVA class library into the database, the possibilities are endless. In this book, we'll explore how to write PL/SQL code for use in your databases. You'll be taught the difference between procedures, functions, and packages and why to use one instead of another in Chapter 11. This book isn't going to make you an expert PL/SQL programmer, but by the time you've absorbed this material you'll know how to get the job done.

Practical Uses of the Technology

One last thing you will find in *Beginning Oracle Programming* is a wide array of practical examples to get your familiar with how Oracle works and how it is different from other RDBMS you may have used. As you progress through this book, you are going to learn through concept explanation and practical application. Instead of being given theory and left to figure it out for yourself, plan on encountering real-world examples in the chapters to come. When you understand how concepts are applied to solve real-world problems, your ability to retain them will skyrocket.

A Family of Databases

Oracle is a term this industry uses interchangeably to refer to database products developed by Oracle Corporation. What many people do not understand, however, is that there are a few different classes of the database being distributed by Oracle. Let's have a look at what these are now.

Classes of Databases

There are three classes of the Oracle database available:

- ❑ Standard Edition
- ❑ Enterprise Edition
- ❑ Personal Edition

The **Standard Edition** is Oracle's basic database product, full of most of the features to be found in Oracle's databases. From a single-node departmental implementation through to a multi distributed federated database architecture, the Standard Edition database offers more reliability, scalability, security, and manageability than most other database products on the market. The Standard Edition of Oracle is a multi-user database, and is capable of building large-scale mission-critical applications on almost any server operating system available today. Almost every bit of technology you will encounter throughout this book is available on the Standard Edition of the database.

The **Enterprise Edition** of the database is a superset of the Standard and Personal Editions with added features and the availability of more options. In particular, the Enterprise Edition is much more powerful in the areas of high availability, scalability, security, manageability, and very large database functionality. In general, the Enterprise Edition of the database is used for mission-critical applications that require high-volume transaction processing, query-intensive data warehousing, and large-scale Internet-based applications. In the next section, we will explore the options and features available with the Enterprise Edition of the database that are not available with the Standard Edition.

Personal Edition is Oracle's desktop database. It is fully compatible with the Standard and Enterprise Editions of the database. Personal Edition is typically used by developers to write and test applications and application modules in a controlled environment, so that at a later date the developer can move the functionality to a Standard or Enterprise Edition database. All the features of the Enterprise Edition are available in the Personal Edition, as well. The Personal Edition is available on Windows 98, Windows NT, and Windows 2000. I'm sure Windows XP will be another supported operating system as soon as Oracle gets around to certifying the database on that platform (I've been running Enterprise Edition on XP since it was a Release Candidate).

Don't get the wrong idea about Oracle's database products, though. The databases are all the same software. The **only** difference is in the options and features available in the Standard Edition, when compared to the Personal and Enterprise Editions. Applications written on Standard Edition or Personal Edition will always work seamlessly on Enterprise Edition. Applications written on Personal or Enterprise Edition may require some reworking to be ported to Standard Edition.

Option and Feature Availability

Everybody knows a relational database is capable of storing data in columns and rows. That's what a database is for, right? At the end of the day, that's a pretty accurate description of a database's core competency, but it's also a far cry from the multitude of features and optional components available in Oracle. There are features such as security to eliminate unauthorized access to the data, backup and recovery for ensuring data and transactions will not be lost due to hardware or software failures, the ability to run processes on many CPUs in an SMP-enabled server, and run many database instances across clusters of servers... and that's only the beginning! The options and features available to Oracle databases are many, and understanding what is available in your database will go a long way toward helping you to architect and build a solution for your business.

Options... and features; two terms to describe things that may or may not be a part of your database. There really is a difference between the two terms. An **option** is some type of functionality that you may or may not choose to install into your database. They are typically 'for-cost' options, so they must be licensed for use. A **feature** is functionality that just comes with the database. It is automatically installed as a part of the database and there is no extra licensing necessary.

As indicated above, not all the options and features are available on every class of database. The Personal Edition has almost everything the Enterprise Edition does, except of course things such as Real Application Clusters or Parallel Server with Oracle 8*i*. This is because it just wouldn't make sense to have these options on a single-user desktop database. The Standard Edition has fewer features, simply because it is meant for smaller implementations and systems that do not require the features of the Enterprise Edition. The Enterprise Edition is Oracle's mother ship. In it, you will find every production feature Oracle was able to sharpen before the release date for the version you are working on.

For a detailed list of the options and features available in the different classes of database, refer to Appendix E. It lists options and features from version 8.0.4 up until 9.0.1. This information is included to help you understand the type of functionality that will be supported by each of the three editions. There are a great many people who pay too much for database licenses because they don't know the Standard Edition could satisfy their needs, and there are others who don't know what the Enterprise Edition database can do, making the assumption that Oracle can't handle their needs either.

Summary

In this chapter, we talked about what you will and will not find in this book. Then we learned the basic terminology of Oracle databases We also discussed the different classes of the database, how they work together and where they might not. We investigated the differences between the Standard and Enterprise Edition databases.

Mastering the Oracle database is not an overnight job... it will take time, practice and, to be perfectly honest, a lot of real-world experience. This book sets out to teach you the core concepts behind using the database, to show you how and why they are employed and to give practical examples of how they have been used. Oracle is an extremely powerful relational database management system that, when used properly, will provide a solid foundation upon which to build enterprise scale applications. Let's get to it...

SQL*Plus and Basic Querying

Throughout this book you will find SQL*Plus is the predominant tool used for sample code, learning concepts, and putting Oracle through its paces. In this chapter, we are going to get you acquainted with using SQL*Plus to interface with your Oracle databases. You'll learn the different ways to start it up. You'll learn how to use it to query your database for application data or to get descriptions of your database. You'll learn how to configure SQL*Plus to your needs.

Once we have a grip on using SQL*Plus, we are going to roll up our sleeves and start learning how to use Oracle. We'll take a quick tour of the SQL language and use Oracle to utilize it. In this section of the chapter, we will take an in-depth look at SELECT statements and what all the related SQL constructs are. We'll look at performing different types of queries, such as UNIONs and INTERSECTs. We'll even take a quick look at joining tables in your queries.

After we learn about SQL queries, we'll walk through using INSERT, UPDATE, and DELETE statements to modify the data stored in our databases. By the end of this chapter, you should expect to be comfortable using SQL*Plus to connect to the database, and to play with database objects and the data stored within those objects.

To summarize at this point, you should expect to learn the following in the course of this chapter:

- ❑ How to connect to a database and perform queries using a tool called SQL*Plus
- ❑ How to configure SQL*Plus for formatted query results
- ❑ The different categories of SQL statements
- ❑ The anatomy of a SQL statement
- ❑ How to write queries against the database to view your data
- ❑ How to modify data stored in the database

Introduction To SQL*Plus

SQL*Plus is a tool for interfacing with the Oracle database. Using it, you can connect to either a database located on the same server machine, or a database located on a different server across a network. It is a great tool for working with Oracle, as it has a number of capabilities that cater for Oracle users and administrators, including:

❑ Executing SQL and PL/SQL in the database

❑ Updating data in your database

❑ Performing queries on your data

❑ Formatting the result sets of those queries into reports

❑ Create, edit, retrieve, and execute SQL scripts

❑ Help Oracle users tune their SQL queries

❑ Administer the database

❑ Describe tables and PL/SQL objects in your database

❑ Copy data from one database to another

❑ Send messages to users, and accept input from those users

These are just a few of SQL*Plus's capabilities. We will cover the basics in this chapter, and we will get into more detail in *Chapter 15*.

While there are other tools besides SQL*Plus available for interacting with Oracle, we will use SQL*Plus throughout this book for the following reasons:

1. It's free!

2. Everybody with an Oracle database should have access to SQL*Plus.

3. It lends itself to writing and modifying the examples provided throughout this book to aid your learning.

Differentiating Between SQL, PL/SQL, and SQL*Plus

Structured Query Language, or **SQL**, is the language used to put data into the database, retrieve data from the database, control transactions, and administer your database. We are going to look at using SQL later in this chapter, and in more depth in the next chapter.

PL/SQL is the procedural programming language of Oracle, and with it you can write custom programs and procedural code for execution inside the database. Just as Oracle has a SQL engine, it also has a PL/SQL engine that executes PL/SQL code. PL/SQL programs can be stored inside the database for use in your applications and day-to-day operations. This lets you implement business logic close to your data, in a programming language that was designed and architected with the Oracle database in mind.

SQL*Plus is an interface you can use to write both SQL and PL/SQL scripts. SQL*Plus transmits your input to the Oracle database, where it is processed, and a response returned to SQL*Plus, which then displays any returned data to you.

The following diagram will help you distinguish between SQL*Plus the tool, SQL, and PL/SQL:

Let's break down the screenshot above to help understand what we are looking at. When SQL*Plus is started, it outputs a "version banner", which indicates the version of the SQL*Plus tool you are running. This is followed by the version of the database you are connected to. From the above picture, you can see we are running SQL*Plus version 9.0.1 and we are connected to version 9.0.1 of the Enterprise Edition of the database.

Once the tool is initialized, we can begin submitting SQL and PL/SQL commands. The first line command we enter into SQL*Plus is a SQL query, and looks like this:

```
SQL> select a
        from foo;
```

This SQL query asks the tool to fetch and display information from the database. As you can see, SQL*Plus retrieved the three records from the table FOO, and reported the results:

```
                    A
          ----------
                    1
                    2
                    3
```

The next command you see in the screenshot is a short PL/SQL block. Although we're not going to get into detail about writing PL/SQL right now, you will notice on lines 2 and 3 that we use the same SQL statement as our previous example to query the database. Effectively, this makes a looping structure that will execute line 4 for every record retrieved from our table FOO:

```
SQL> begin
  2     for cur1 in (select a
  3                        from foo) loop
  4        dbms_output.put_line(cur1.a || ' is a value in FOO');
  5     end loop;
  6  end;
  7  /
```

You will notice in our PL/SQL, the first line was BEGIN and the last line was END. These keywords start and stop a block of PL/SQL code. We will talk more about this in Chapter 10. Once the PL/SQL executes in the database, we are presented with the database's response:

```
1 is a value in FOO
2 is a value in FOO
3 is a value in FOO

PL/SQL procedure successfully completed.
```

Now that you understand how to differentiate between SQL*Plus (the tool), SQL (language used to interact with Oracle) and PL/SQL (procedural language used to store and execute processes inside Oracle), let's dig into the tool a little deeper and see how helpful it can be in your interaction with Oracle.

Starting Up SQL*Plus

On the Windows platform, there are two ways to start SQL*Plus. The first way is by using the GUI SQL*Plus tool through the Windows Start menu. The other way is by using the command-line version, through DOS. Both GUI mode and command-line mode start up the tool, but the manner in which you start SQL*Plus is going to depend on personal preference. You should try both methods out, to find out which best suits your needs. On UNIX platforms, you start up SQL*Plus using either an xterm in the X Window System, or in your shell at a console, and it is command-line driven.

SQL*Plus in Command Line Mode

To start SQL*Plus in command-line mode, type sqlplus from DOS or an XTERM on Unix. The sqlplus executable file should be in the following location:

❑   Unix: $ORACLE_HOME/bin/sqlplus

❑   Windows: %ORACLE_HOME%/bin/sqlplus.exe

This directory should be in your PATH environment variable! Once SQL*Plus starts up, you will be prompted for a username and password. If you are unsure about what user account to use, you can use one of the user accounts installed by default:

❏ SYS is the owner of the data dictionary, and should only be used for administrative purposes. This account is basically the "master" DBA account. This account is reserved for particular purposes, and should not be used for everyday operations. SYS's default password is CHANGE_ON_INSTALL.

❏ SYSTEM is an administrator account. The SYSTEM user is the default administrative account created by Oracle when you install the database. If you do not have your own administrative account, you should use the SYSTEM user to create a new user and grant that user the DBA role. This new user will then be your default administrative account. SYSTEM's default password is MANAGER.

❏ SCOTT is a demonstration account, and is typically installed with the database to provide some sample tables and data to play around with. We will see more about SCOTT in Chapter 4. SCOTT's default password is TIGER.

> **NOTE: If this is not your own database, you will need to talk to your database administrator about what user account(s) you may use. SYS and SYSTEM are both very powerful database accounts and as indicated above should not be used for everyday operations.**

Let's now try connecting to Oracle using SQL*Plus.

Try It Out – Connecting To Oracle

1. Open a SQL*Plus session from DOS or an XTERM by typing sqlplus at the prompt.

2. Use the username SCOTT and the password TIGER (it's OK to use a different user account if you know a valid username and password for your database).

```
$ sqlplus

SQL*Plus: Release 8.1.6.0.0 - Production on Mon Jul 23 19:06:00 2001

(c) Copyright 1999 Oracle Corporation.  All rights reserved.

Enter user-name: scott
Enter password:

Connected to:
Oracle 9i Enterprise Edition Release 9.0.1.0.0 - Production
JServer Release 9.0.1.0.0 - Production
```

Those users that are connecting to a database on a different server, must use an Oracle Net Services alias in the connect string. See overleaf for instructions on how to accomplish this.

27

How It Works

Your output might differ from the sample above, depending on the version of SQL*Plus you are using, the version of the database you are connecting to, and the username you are using. If this is your first time wielding the SQL*Plus banner, congratulations! This is your first conquest!

So what have you done? Basically, you have created a new session in the Oracle database. Now that you are connected, you are able to issue queries, execute PL/SQL, run scripts against the database, and a great number of other things! For now, it's enough to know that you are "connected" to Oracle and ready to learn the next lesson.

Connecting Over the Network

Some of you might be connecting to databases that are not located on the same computer as SQL*Plus. In this case, you must connect to the database using Oracle Net Services. (Note that in Oracle 8 and Oracle 8*i* this was known as Oracle Net8, and prior to that it was called SQL*Net). Net Services is Oracle's networking software used by tools such as SQL*Plus to connect to databases across networks. Without Net Services, SQL*Plus could only connect to databases on the same computer.

For the purposes of this discussion, we are going to look into determining what databases our client computer is configured to connect to. Configuring Net Services is well beyond the scope of this chapter, and if your database is on a different machine you most likely have a database administrator who can assist in this area. We will look more at Net Services in Chapter 5.

In order to check the Net Services client configuration, we will use the Oracle Net Configuration Assistant. This is a tool that is included with the Net Services client installation, and if you have SQL*Plus installed on your computer you will most likely have this tool as well. If you do not, you probably don't have the Net Services client installed and you'd be best to talk to a database administrator about getting it installed and configured.

To start the Net Configuration Assistant, click on Start | Programs | Oracle - Ora90Home | Configuration and Migration Tools | Net Client Assistant. The first screen of the Oracle Net Configuration Assistant should look like this:

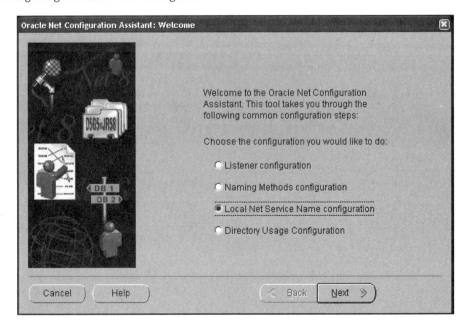

As you can see from the screenshot above, you can configure a Listener, Naming Methods, Directory Usage or Local Net Services. Click the **Local Net Service Name configuration** radio button and click **Next**. The next page gives a number of options for modifying your client's Local Net Services configuration. Click on **Test** and click the **Next** button. The test page shows us all those services that the local computer is configured to use. Each of the services represents some type of connection to a database, either on the local computer or a different computer. You should pick the database service you want to connect to and click **Next**. This will automatically try to connect to that database service using the SCOTT user with the password TIGER. If the connection was unsuccessful for any reason, the error is displayed in a text area on the next page. If the SCOTT user does not exist or the password for SCOTT is not TIGER, you have the option to change the credentials using the **Change Login** button. As an example of this screen, the screenshot below shows a Net Configuration Assistant connecting to a database successfully.

Make sure you remember the service name you selected on the test page. This is the name we will use in SQL*Plus to connect to the remote database.

Now that the local Net Services configuration has been tested and is working properly, you can attempt to log in to the database using SQL*Plus. Open a DOS window or XTERM in Unix to start up SQL*Plus in command line mode. The syntax for connecting to a remote database service is:

```
sqlplus <username>/<password>@<service_name>
```

As an example, here we will connect to the service we just tested:

```
C:\>sqlplus scott/tiger@slaphappy

SQL*Plus: Release 9.0.1.0.1 - Production on Tue Jan 8 23:19:04 2002
```

```
(c) Copyright 2001 Oracle Corporation.  All rights reserved.


Connected to:
Oracle 9i Enterprise Edition Release 9.0.1.0.0 - Production
With the Partitioning option
JServer Release 9.0.1.0.0 - Production

SQL>
```

In the command we used, SCOTT is the username, TIGER is the password, and SLAPHAPPY is my database service name from the Net Configuration Assistant. Now that we can get connected to our database whether it's on the same machine or a different machine, we'll take a look at working with the GUI SQL*Plus tool.

Starting up the GUI SQL*Plus tool

From the Windows Start menu, select Programs I Oracle – OraHome90 I Application Development I SQL Plus. This will open a window entitled Oracle SQL*Plus, and will have a dialog box entitled Log On with fields for User Name, Password, and Host String. Once you specify a username, password, and Net8 alias to connect to a database successfully, the Log On dialog box will go away and your session will begin. The Log On screen looks like this:

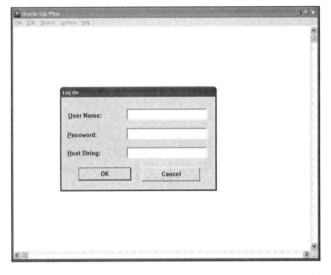

Just as with the command-line mode SQL*Plus tool, we must provide a username and password to connect using the GUI SQL*Plus tool. The host string (database service) is optional, depending on which database on your network you want to connect to. By default, you connect to the local database. Once you have provided a username and password, the SQL*Plus banner is displayed indicating the version of SQL*Plus you are running. If the username/password/host string combination you provide is valid, you'll see the database version banner indicating the version of the database you are connected to, as shown opposite:

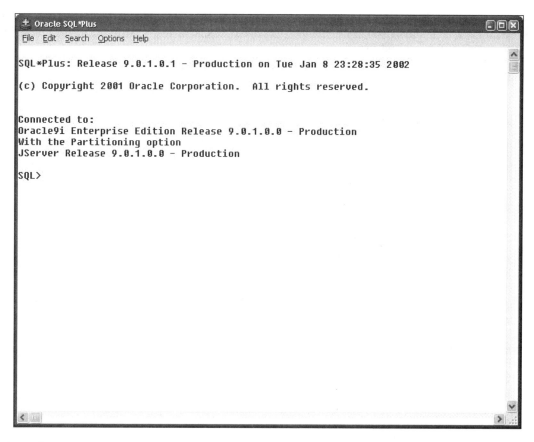

If you've gotten this far, you are now able to use SQL*Plus in both the command-line mode and in GUI mode. Now that we are connected to the database and we feel confident getting into SQL*Plus, let's start using the tool to talk to Oracle.

Quick and simple, Querying the Database

Once you have SQL*Plus started up, the next thing to accomplish is to get acquainted with using it to execute your SQL. When you connect to the database, you are connected as a particular user account. Depending on the privileges given to your user account, you may or may not have access to data that is already stored in the database.

Oracle provides a number of sample schemas (demonstration user accounts) for you to use while learning how to use the database. The first user account we will use is SCOTT. This user account owns a couple of simple tables that you can use to familiarize yourself with using SQL*Plus. You will also be using other schemas from Oracle's sample schemas (such as HR and OE). You can read more about these schemas in Chapter 4 and Appendix D.

Try It Out

First, start up SQL*Plus, and connect to the database as SCOTT using the password TIGER. Once you have connected to the database and are in the SQL*Plus tool, run a simple query using the SQL command SELECT (discussed in more detail later) to find out the names of the tables you own:

```
SQL> select table_name
  2    from user_tables
  3    /
```

The following is the output you should see, listing all the tables belonging to the SCOTT user:

```
TABLE_NAME
-------------------------------
BONUS
DEPT
EMP
SALGRADE
```

How It Works

USER_TABLES is a view in the Oracle data dictionary that can be used to find out information about those tables belonging to the current user. In the example above, we were connected to the database as the user SCOTT, so the results tell us what tables belong to that user:

❑   BONUS

❑   DEPT

❑   EMP

❑   SALGRADE

Now that we know what tables belong to the current user, let's do a quick query to find out what data is stored in the EMP table:

```
SQL> select *
  2    from emp;
```

EMPNO	ENAME	JOB	MGR	HIREDATE	SAL	COMM
DEPTNO	HAIR_COLOR					
7369	SMITH	CLERK	7902	17-DEC-80	800	
20						
7499	ALLEN	SALESMAN	7698	20-FEB-81	1600	300
30						
7521	WARD	SALESMAN	7698	22-FEB-81	1250	500
30						

```
        7566 JONES       MANAGER         7839 02-APR-81        2975
          20

        7654 MARTIN      SALESMAN        7698 28-SEP-81        1250          1400
          30

        7698 BLAKE       MANAGER         7839 01-MAY-81        2850
          30

        7782 CLARK       MANAGER         7839 09-JUN-81        2450

     EMPNO ENAME         JOB              MGR HIREDATE           SAL    COMM
---------- ---------- ---------- ---------- --------- ---------- ----------
    DEPTNO HAIR_COLOR
---------- ----------------
          10

        7788 SCOTT       ANALYST         7566 09-DEC-82        3000
          20

        7839 KING        PRESIDENT            17-NOV-81        5000
          10

        7844 TURNER      SALESMAN        7698 08-SEP-81        1500             0
          30

        7876 ADAMS       CLERK           7788 12-JAN-83        1100
          20

        7900 JAMES       CLERK           7698 03-DEC-81         950
          30

        7902 FORD        ANALYST         7566 03-DEC-81        3000
          20

     EMPNO ENAME         JOB              MGR HIREDATE           SAL    COMM
---------- ---------- ---------- ---------- --------- ---------- ----------
    DEPTNO HAIR_COLOR
---------- ----------------

        7934 MILLER      CLERK           7782 23-JAN-82        1300
          10

14 rows selected.
```

Woah! What happened to our query output? It's wrapped around and hard to read! This is because in the SQL*Plus session above, there is only space for 80 characters of data per line, and SQL*Plus automatically repeats column headings for every "page" of output. When we selected all the columns from the EMP table, there were more than 80 characters of data per line and therefore each record wrapped to a new line. In the result set above, you can see the EMPNO column is right on top of the DEPTNO column on the far left-hand side of the window for each record. You can also see that the column headings were repeated halfway through the results because, in this SQL*Plus session, the query returned more than a single page of output. Once we started the second page, SQL*Plus repeated the headers for us.

There are three options when one encounters this particular issue in SQL*Plus:

❑ Live with it. Most people understand how to read multi-line result sets because they occur frequently in SQL*Plus. The repeating column headings could be helpful, especially if you have multi-line result sets and a large number of columns.

❑ Query a smaller number of columns. Instead of looking at all the data in the table, try to boil it down to only the data you need to see.

❑ Format your results. Using SQL*Plus, you can modify the way it outputs data to the screen and therefore can still select all your columns and have an easy-to-read result set all at the same time. You can also modify SQL*Plus's page size so that column headings are repeated for whatever row count you want. You could have headings repeated every 10, 100, 10000 rows, or not repeated at all!

*If your query results differ from those shown above, it may be that a **profile** has been created to set up the SQL*Plus environment for you. A profile is basically a file called* login.sql *(personal profiles) or* glogin.sql *(site profile) that runs every time you successfully log in to the database using SQL*Plus. We will talk more about profiles in Chapter 9.*

Formatting Your Results

SQL*Plus is equipped with a number of commands for formatting result sets, and in this section we're going to investigate some of these commands, and how to use them.

COLUMN

In SQL*Plus, when you perform a query the data is returned in rows and columns. For each column in the result set of your query, SQL*Plus allows you to specify display attributes using the COLUMN command.

For instance, if you are selecting the SAL column from the EMP table, you might want to format the data to look like a dollar figure rather than just a series of numbers strung together. You could use the following COLUMN command to achieve this:

```
SQL> connect scott/tiger
Connected.
SQL> select ename, sal
  2    from emp
  3   where ename like 'A%'
  4  /

ENAME             SAL
---------- ----------
ALLEN            1600
ADAMS            1100

SQL> column sal format $9,999.99
SQL> select ename, sal
  2    from emp
  3   where ename like 'A%'
```

```
    4  /

ENAME            SAL
---------- ----------
ALLEN        $1,600.00
ADAMS        $1,100.00
```

The text string $9,999.99 is a format mask that tells Oracle to replace the 9s with the numeric value of the column you are selecting. So, in our output the number 1600, when the format mask $9,999.99 is applied, equals $1,600.00. For alphanumeric data (values consisting of characters, letters, symbols, etc.), you can specify the width of the column to be used as follows:

```
SQL> describe user_objects
 Name                                      Null?    Type
 ----------------------------------------- -------- ---------------------------
 OBJECT_NAME                                        VARCHAR2(128)
 SUBOBJECT_NAME                                     VARCHAR2(30)
 OBJECT_ID                                          NUMBER
 DATA_OBJECT_ID                                     NUMBER
 OBJECT_TYPE                                        VARCHAR2(18)
 CREATED                                            DATE
 LAST_DDL_TIME                                      DATE
 TIMESTAMP                                          VARCHAR2(19)
 STATUS                                             VARCHAR2(7)
 TEMPORARY                                          VARCHAR2(1)
 GENERATED                                          VARCHAR2(1)
 SECONDARY                                          VARCHAR2(1)

SQL> select object_type, object_name
  2    from user_objects
  3    order by object_type, object_name
  4  /

OBJECT_TYPE
------------------
OBJECT_NAME
---------------------------------------------------------------------------
INDEX
PK_DEPT

INDEX
PK_EMP

TABLE
BONUS

TABLE
DEPT

TABLE
EMP
```

```
TABLE
SALGRADE


6 rows selected.
```

Note that USER_OBJECTS *is another data dictionary view that shows information about those database objects that the current user owns.*

In this query, the OBJECT_NAME column takes up an entire line when it is displayed, since the width of the OBJECT_NAME column is 128 characters. Although the data does not take up that much space, SQL*Plus is not aware of that and formats the columns returned according to the length of the column definition in the database. We can override this using the COLUMN command in SQL*Plus, as follows:

```
SQL> column object_name format a30
```

The "a" in "a30" stands for alphanumeric. This is used for character-based columns. 30 is the width of the column. Now that the OBJECT_NAME column is defined, we need to rerun the query. You can rerun queries or PL/SQL code in SQL*Plus using the RUN command or by using the / character:

```
SQL> -- we could use RUN, or
SQL> /

OBJECT_TYPE          OBJECT_NAME
-------------------- ------------------------------
INDEX                PK_DEPT
INDEX                PK_EMP
TABLE                BONUS
TABLE                DEPT
TABLE                EMP
TABLE                SALGRADE

6 rows selected.
```

In our formatted results, we see the OBJECT_NAME column has been constrained to 30 characters and now each row fits on a single line. For this particular query this works just fine, because none of the values of the OBJECT_NAME column exceed 30 characters. If one of the values did exceed 30 characters, however, it would wrap onto the next line.

PAUSE

Queries can return zero rows or many millions of rows, depending on your SQL (the actual number of rows you can retrieve is virtually limitless). When SQL*Plus outputs the data, it is typically very fast and not all that easy to keep up with. For queries or reports that contain more data than your screen can see at one time, you need to have a buffer in your window to store the data that has scrolled off the screen, and you need to get used to scrolling up and down to view the results of your queries.

This is where the PAUSE command comes in. Using the following statement will tell SQL*Plus to stop spooling output to the screen after each page.

```
SQL> set pause on
```

Now, when you execute a query that is longer than a page in size, the output will stop until you hit the *Enter* key. Once you hit the *Enter* key, another page of output will be spooled to your display.

One warning to keep in mind regarding the PAUSE command is that when you submit your query, Oracle will pause once before the first page is displayed. This means you will execute the query and it will seem as if Oracle is not doing anything. Hitting the *Enter* key will prompt SQL*Plus to begin spooling data to the screen, and you will see your first page. To turn pause off, use the following command:

```
SQL> set pause off
```

This prompts a logical question, "how big is a page"? That takes us to the next SQL*Plus setting, PAGESIZE.

PAGESIZE

When executing queries, SQL*Plus first outputs the column headers for the data you are selecting, and then the data is spooled under the appropriate column heading. SQL*Plus will spool out a number of rows corresponding to the SQL*Plus PAGESIZE setting before it will spool the column headers again. Although the default PAGESIZE is 14, you can modify this as we see now.

Try It Out – Setting Your Pagesize

Let's alter our PAGESIZE setting to see the effects it has on our query output. We'll set the PAGESIZE to 10, and then select the ROWNUM and OBJECT_NAME columns from the ALL_OBJECTS view of the data dictionary.

```
SQL> set pagesize 10
SQL> select rownum, object_name
  2    from all_objects
  3   where rownum < 20
  4  /

    ROWNUM OBJECT_NAME
---------- ------------------------------
         1 /1001a851_ConstantDefImpl
         2 /1005bd30_LnkdConstant
         3 /10076b23_OraCustomDatumClosur
         4 /10297c91_SAXAttrList
         5 /10322588_HandlerRegistryHelpe
         6 /103a2e73_DefaultEditorKitEndP
         7 /1048734f_DefaultFolder

    ROWNUM OBJECT_NAME
---------- ------------------------------
         8 /104b85c5_LogFileOutputStream
         9 /10501902_BasicFileChooserUINe
        10 /105072e7_HttpSessionBindingEv
        11 /106faabc_BasicTreeUIKeyHandle
        12 /1079c94d_NumberConstantData
```

```
    13 /107a9fdd_AttributeDefHolder
    14 /10804ae7_Constants

    ROWNUM OBJECT_NAME
---------- ------------------------------
    15 /108343f6_MultiColorChooserUI
    16 /10845320_TypeMapImpl
    17 /108549fd_SessionReference
    18 /10948dc3_PermissionImpl
    19 /1095ce9b_MultiComboBoxUI

19 rows selected.
```

How it works

In this example, you can see that selecting 19 records using a PAGESIZE of 10 produced 3 pages of output. At first this might seem wrong, because 19 records divided by 10 should be two pages. However, upon further investigation, a "page" does not comprise the records in the output. Instead, a "page" is made up of any output SQL*Plus spools to the screen. Therefore, the first "page" is 10 rows of screen real estate:

```
                                                        1
    ROWNUM OBJECT_NAME                                   2
---------- ------------------------------                3
     1 /1001a851_ConstantDefImpl                         4
     2 /1005bd30_LnkdConstant                            5
     3 /10076b23_OraCustomDatumClosur                    6
     4 /10297c91_SAXAttrList                             7
     5 /10322588_HandlerRegistryHelpe                    8
     6 /103a2e73_DefaultEditorKitEndP                    9
     7 /1048734f_DefaultFolder                           10
```

The second page is 10 rows of screen real estate as well:

```
                                                        1
    ROWNUM OBJECT_NAME                                   2
---------- ------------------------------                3
     8 /104b85c5_LogFileOutputStream                     4
     9 /10501902_BasicFileChooserUINe                    5
    10 /105072e7_HttpSessionBindingEv                    6
    11 /106faabc_BasicTreeUIKeyHandle                    7
    12 /1079c94d_NumberConstantData                      8
    13 /107a9fdd_AttributeDefHolder                      9
    14 /10804ae7_Constants                               10
```

This makes perfect sense for those users who set their PAGESIZE to the number of lines on their SQL*Plus display; the blank lines, column headings, separator between the column headings, and the data and rows of data are all displayed on a screen correctly.

LINESIZE

Using LINESIZE, you can alter the default LINESIZE that SQL*Plus establishes for you (80). When SQL*Plus spools out as many characters as it thinks your LINESIZE should be, it wraps the output to the next line. If your window is particularly wide, then you can use a wider LINESIZE, avoiding the wrap.

```
SQL> show linesize
linesize 80
SQL> set linesize 120
```

It is helpful to use a LINESIZE setting that matches (or is less than) the width of the SQL*Plus window. That way, you don't miss data because it is printed out beyond the far right-hand side of the window.

FEEDBACK

FEEDBACK tells SQL*Plus to output a line at the end of your queries indicating the number of records that were returned in the query. There is a FEEDBACK setting that indicates the number of records that must be returned in the query results for SQL*Plus to show the message. By default, FEEDBACK is ON and the number of rows that must be returned for it to operate is 6 or more. For example, if we query the EMP table we can see the default FEEDBACK settings in action:

```
SQL> set pagesize 1000
SQL> show feedback
FEEDBACK ON for 6 or more rows
SQL> select empno, ename, job
  2    from emp
  3    where rownum < 7
  4  /

     EMPNO ENAME      JOB
---------- ---------- ---------
      7369 SMITH      CLERK
      7499 ALLEN      SALESMAN
      7521 WARD       SALESMAN
      7566 JONES      MANAGER
      7654 MARTIN     SALESMAN
      7698 BLAKE      MANAGER

6 rows selected.
```

We can turn FEEDBACK off using the following command:

```
SQL> set feedback off
SQL> select empno, ename, job
  2    from emp
  3    where rownum < 7
  4  /

     EMPNO ENAME      JOB
---------- ---------- ---------
      7369 SMITH      CLERK
      7499 ALLEN      SALESMAN
      7521 WARD       SALESMAN
      7566 JONES      MANAGER
      7654 MARTIN     SALESMAN
      7698 BLAKE      MANAGER
```

This is also configurable by providing an integer value to the FEEDBACK setting indicating the minimum number of records that must be returned in a query before this output is enabled. By setting an integer for the FEEDBACK setting, FEEDBACK is automatically turned back on.

```
SQL> set feedback 3
SQL> select empno, ename, job
  2    from emp
```

```
    3   where rownum < 3
    4   /

    EMPNO ENAME       JOB
---------- ---------- ---------
      7369 SMITH      CLERK
      7499 ALLEN      SALESMAN

SQL> select empno, ename, job
  2     from emp
  3   where rownum < 4
  4   /

    EMPNO ENAME       JOB
---------- ---------- ---------
      7369 SMITH      CLERK
      7499 ALLEN      SALESMAN
      7521 WARD       SALESMAN

3 rows selected.
```

NUMFORMAT

One issue that may arise is the format used by SQL*Plus when you query a number value from the database. The default value for NUMFORMAT is 10, meaning SQL*Plus will try to fit all the number data in 10 spaces of output. If you know you are dealing with numbers greater than 10 characters (such as large numbers with many digits to the right of the decimal point), you might try setting NUMFORMAT to a larger value. Let's take a look at how to set these formats in SQL*Plus.

> *For now, don't worry about learning how to create tables and insert data since this information will be explained in the next chapter.*

The first thing we do is create a simple table, and insert three relatively long values into it:

```
SQL> create table t( my_column number );

Table created.

SQL> insert into t values ( 1234567890 );

1 row created.

SQL> insert into t values ( 12345678901 );

1 row created.

SQL> insert into t values ( 12345678901234567890 );

1 row created.
```

Now when we query the values from the table, SQL*Plus tries to fit the results in 10 character widths:

```
SQL> select *
  2    from t;

MY_COLUMN
----------
1234567890
1.2346E+10
1.2346E+19

3 rows selected.
```

If we know that we will be dealing with numbers greater than 10 digits, we can use an alternative NUMFORMAT for those queries:

```
SQL> set numformat 99999999999999999999.99999999999999
SQL> /

                         MY_COLUMN
------------------------------------
        1234567890.00000000000000
       12345678901.00000000000000
 12345678901234567890.00000000000000

3 rows selected.
```

To reset NUMFORMAT to its default value, set it to two contiguous double quotes:

```
SQL> set numformat ""
SQL> /

MY_COLUMN
----------
1234567890
1.2346E+10
1.2346E+19
```

LONG

By default, this value is 80. If you try to query a table or view that has a LONG column, only the first 80 characters of that particular column would be displayed. By making the LONG column longer, more data from the column can be displayed.

Earlier in this chapter, we queried a data dictionary view named USER_TABLES. Let's look at the definition for this view. It just so happens that another view in the data dictionary contains the definitions for all those views defined in the database that a user can see. This view is called ALL_VIEWS.

```
SQL> select text
  2    from all_views
  3   where view_name = 'USER_TABLES';
```

```
TEXT
--------------------------------------------------------------------------
select o.name, decode(bitand(t.property, 4194400), 0, ts.name, null),
       dec
```

If we didn't know better, we might think the USER_TABLES view was broken! Since we now know, however, that this is happening because SQL*Plus will only show us 80 columns of LONG columns (TEXT is a LONG column), we can adjust our SQL*Plus settings to accommodate:

```
SQL> set pagesize 1000
SQL> set long 10000
SQL> /
```

Your output will now be more complete!

Wrapping Up SQL*Plus

For now, our tour of SQL*Plus comes to an end. The information you've received thus far is meant to give you the skills you need to get SQL*Plus started and use it to interact with the database. Later in the book, we are going to look in more depth at SQL*Plus, and how you can use it for advanced reporting, installation scripts, and more.

Let's move on to take a closer look at SQL itself.

What Is SQL?

First of all, let's get something straight. Although "Structured Query Language" implies you are asking questions of the database, the term in itself is somewhat of a misnomer, since you also use SQL to create and remove database objects, insert, update, and delete data in the database, and perform various administrative tasks in support of day-to-day operations.

SQL is not Oracle proprietary technology; it is the standard language for relational database management systems. It was created by IBM back in the 1970s, and has since been adopted by the ANSI/ISO standards body for refinement and continued development. The ANSI (American National Standards Institute) defines various levels of compliance for the standards they publish. SQL is no different. At the time of this writing, there are four levels in the SQL standard, known as the SQL-92 ANSI standard:

1. Entry level. Most vendors build their SQL engines to comply with level 1. This level is not much more than the last ANSI SQL standard, SQL-89. Oracle was ANSI SQL-92 certified in 1993 with Oracle 7.

2. Transitional. As far as feature requirements go, the transitional level is approximately "halfway" from entry level to intermediate.

3. Intermediate. Intermediate SQL-92 compliance requires a number of new features in the database beyond that of entry or transitional compliance. Features include, but are not limited to the following:

- Dynamic SQL
- Cascade delete for referential integrity
- DATE and TIME data types
- Domains
- Variable length character strings
- A CASE expression
- CAST functions between data types

4. Full. This is the highest and final level of ANSI SQL-92 compliance. It adds more features to the intermediate standard, including but not limited to the following:

- Connection management
- A BIT string data type
- Deferrable integrity constraints
- Derived tables in the FROM clause
- Sub-queries in CHECK clause
- Temporary Tables

Although Oracle is entry-level SQL-92 ANSI compliant, Oracle also provides additional SQL statements that are not ANSI standard, but are nevertheless useful and powerful. We are not going to differentiate between those things that are ANSI standard and those that are Oracle specific. You do need to keep in mind, however, that SQL written for Oracle may not always work on other databases and vice versa. Most of the database providers on the market today have some level of compliance to ANSI SQL-92, but they all provide their own proprietary SQL constructs to provide more functionality for their users. Just consider this as another way RDBMS vendors differentiate themselves.

The first thing to understand is that there are various categories of SQL. The following list represents the different types of SQL you will use when working with Oracle:

- Data Manipulation Language (**DML)**
- Data Definition Language (**DDL**)
- Transaction control statements
- Session control statements
- System control statements

Later in this chapter, we are going to look in more detail at the first class of SQL statements, DML. We will discuss the other categories of SQL throughout the book.

Why Is SQL Important?

SQL isn't just a feature in a relational database. Quite simply, it enables you to interact with the database in order to create objects, insert data into tables, retrieve data from the database, and much, much more.

In order to start understanding SQL let's begin by looking at relational tables and how to use them.

What's in a Table?

Tables are objects used for storing data in relational databases; they contain both rows and columns. You can visualize a table as looking like a spreadsheet. A horizontal line is a row; a vertical line is a column.

Columns are used for storing an attribute of data for a particular row of data in the table. Each column in a table has a column name and a data type. Some data types have a length and others a scale and a precision. For instance, the VARCHAR2 data type has a length indicating how many bytes the column can hold. A VARCHAR2 column that could be 10 bytes would be written as VARCHAR2(10). A NUMBER data type, on the other hand, has a precision indicating how many digits can be in the column for a single row, and a scale indicating the number of those digits that may be to the right-hand side of the decimal place. NUMBER columns for a monetary value, for example, might be written as NUMBER(11,2). This would allow eleven digits total, with two digits to the right of the decimal place for fractional units of money.

Rows contain values for the columns defined in the table definition, and make up the contents of the table.

The following diagram is an example of the DEPARTMENTS table from the SCOTT schema that shows us rows and columns:

	Column 1	Column 2	Column 3
	DEPTNO	DNAME	LOCATION
Row 1	10	Accounting	New York
Row 2	20	Research	Dallas
Row 3	30	Sales	Chicago
Row 4	40	Operations	Boston

In this table, the column names are: DEPTNO, DNAME, and LOCATION, while the four rows consist of 10 Accounting New York, 20 Research Dallas, 30 Sales Chicago and 40 Operations Boston.

To learn more about the table definition you can use the DESCRIBE command as follows:

```
DESCRIBE <TABLE_NAME>
```

The DESCRIBE command runs a report on the Oracle's data dictionary to show three basic pieces of information about the table's columns:

❏ NAME. This is the column name.

❏ NULL? This specifies whether or not a column may have a NULL value. We'll discuss NULL values in more detail later in this chapter.

❏ TYPE. This is the data type and length (or scale and precision) for the column. We will talk in much greater depth about data types in the next chapter.

Try It Out – Describing a Table

Let's try out the DESCRIBE command. Start up SQL*Plus, connect as the SCOTT user and use the following command to learn more about the DEPT table's columns:

```
$ sqlplus scott/tiger

SQL*Plus: Release 9.0.1.0.0 - Production on Mon Oct 15 12:10:44 2001

(c) Copyright 2001 Oracle Corporation.  All rights reserved.


Connected to:
Oracle 9i Enterprise Edition Release 9.0.1.0.0 - Production
With the Partitioning option
JServer Release 9.0.1.0.0 - Production

SQL> describe dept
 Name                                      Null?    Type
 ----------------------------------------- -------- --------------------------
 DEPTNO                                    NOT NULL NUMBER(2)
 DNAME                                              VARCHAR2(14)
 LOC                                               VARCHAR2(13)
```

Now that we know how the columns are laid out in a table, the data makes more sense. Each attribute of a row either has data that conforms to the column definition or a NULL value. This depends on whether or not the column definition allows NULL values.

```
SQL> select *
  2    from dept
  3   /

    DEPTNO DNAME          LOC
---------- -------------- -------------
        10 ACCOUNTING     NEW YORK
        20 RESEARCH       DALLAS
        30 SALES          CHICAGO
        40 OPERATIONS     BOSTON

4 rows selected.
```

When we query all the data from the DEPT table, we can see there are four rows of data in the table. Each of the DEPTNO values are numbers, and have no more than 2 digits each. Each of the DNAME and LOC values are character data no longer than 14 or 13 characters, respectively.

Data Manipulation Language

Now that we have taken a general look at tables, we'll look a little deeper at using them by considering **Data Manipulation Language** (DML). DML is identified as all those SQL statements that query data from the database, or manipulate (hence the name) data that is contained somewhere in the database.

Queries

SELECT statements, or queries, are used to ask the database for information. As you will see, the number of questions you can ask of the database is virtually unlimited. In SQL, statements are broken down into a number of sections, or clauses. The clauses of a SELECT statement are:

- ❏ WITH
- ❏ SELECT
- ❏ FROM
- ❏ WHERE
- ❏ GROUP BY
- ❏ HAVING
- ❏ ORDER BY

The SELECT clause identifies those columns you want to be shown, and the FROM clause tells Oracle what data source to use to find those columns. As an example, consider the following simple query:

```
SQL> select job_id, job_title
  2     from jobs
SQL> /
```

As you can see, we are simply asking for the job ID and the job title for all the jobs in the JOBS table. There is a SELECT clause:

```
select job_id, job_title
```

...and a FROM clause:

```
from jobs
```

These two clauses are the only two required in a query issued to Oracle. If we try to remove the FROM clause, we get the following error:

```
SQL> select job_id, job_title
  2   /

select job_id, job_title
                        *
ERROR at line 1:
ORA-00923: FROM keyword not found where expected
```

If you try to remove the SELECT clause, Oracle has no idea what you are trying to do as FROM is not a valid first word in a SQL statement:

```
SQL> from jobs

SP2-0042: unknown command "from jobs" - rest of line ignored.
```

You can write a query to ask for all the columns in a table by using the asterisk (*) to denote "all the columns in the table". So the following query would result in all the columns in the table being returned:

```
SQL> select *
  2   from jobs;
```

You'll notice, in our query above, we write the SELECT clause on one line, and the FROM clause on another. You should also note that whitespace in SQL is ignored for the most part, and that carriage returns only make a difference if you enter more than one simultaneously (two carriage returns in SQL*Plus brings you back to a new SQL*Plus command prompt). Indentation doesn't really matter, but it helps readability of your SQL. We could submit the query above as follows and it would work in exactly the same way:

```
SQL> select * from jobs;
```

We would strongly encourage you to come up with a standard way of writing your SQL and to stick to it.

Now that you have seen a couple of queries, let's try it out using the familiar SCOTT schema we used to connect to the database earlier in the chapter.

Try It Out – Write a query

1. Let's write a query that lists the DEPTNOs and the DNAMEs in the DEPT table. First of all let's get the table definition by submitting the following in SQL*Plus:

```
SQL> desc dept
 Name                                      Null?    Type
 ----------------------------------------- -------- ----------------------------
 DEPTNO                                    NOT NULL NUMBER(2)
 DNAME                                              VARCHAR2(14)
 LOC                                               VARCHAR2(13)
```

2. Given the column names we are interested in and the name of the table, your query should now look something like the following:

```
SQL> select deptno, dname
  2    from dept;

   DEPTNO DNAME
---------- --------------
       10 ACCOUNTING
       20 RESEARCH
       30 SALES
       40 OPERATIONS
```

The WHERE clause

When you ask for information, such as "What is all the employee data in my EMP table?" Oracle takes you literally. It is going to tell you what *all* the data is. However, if you only want to see some of this data, such as the data for one employee, then you can use a WHERE clause. The WHERE clause is found after the FROM clause in the query, as follows:

```
select <columns>
  from <data source>
 where <conditional_expression>;
```

The <conditional_expression> consists of one or more conditions that evaluate to a Boolean value (namely TRUE or FALSE). Within these conditions, there are a variety of operators that can be used to compare values, some of which are listed below:

❑   A = B. Evaluates to TRUE if the value of A equals the value of B.

❑   A > B. Evaluates to TRUE if the value of A is greater than the value of B.

❑   A < B. Evaluates to TRUE if the value of A is less than the value of B.

❑   A != B; A <> B. Evaluates to TRUE if the value of A does not equal the value of B.

❑   BETWEEN A AND B. Evaluates to TRUE if the value is greater than or equal to A and less than or equal to B.

❑   A LIKE B. LIKE is a comparison using pattern matching. In this particular condition, if the value of A contains a pattern that matches the value of B, this condition evaluates to TRUE. Wildcards can be used in LIKE expressions. Oracle SQL wildcards are '%' for 0, 1, or many characters, and '_' for any single character.

❑   A NOT <conditional_expression>. NOT is an operator that allows us to test to ensure an expression is not true. For example, A NOT B, or A NOT LIKE 'B%'.

This is not an exhaustive list, but should provide a sufficient grounding to get you started. An example of operator use follows, where we write a query to determine all those employees whose ENAME begins with 'A':

```
SQL> select empno, ename
  2    from emp
  3   where ename like 'A%';

    EMPNO ENAME
---------- ----------
     7499 ALLEN
     7876 ADAMS
```

The "%" character is a wildcard, so the question above evaluates to "Tell me the EMPNO and ENAME for all those employees whose ENAME starts with capital A and is followed by 0, 1, or many characters". Notice the A character in the WHERE clause is the first character in the expression, so the query asks for all the employees whose last names have A as their first character.

Binary operators

The WHERE clause can be made up of many expressions that will be evaluated against the rows you are selecting. There are two binary operators you can use to link these expressions together, **AND** and **OR**. The AND operator returns TRUE if the expression on the left-hand side of the AND operator and on the right-hand side of the AND operator evaluate to TRUE. In the following query, we want to see all those employees who are in the sales department (DEPTNO = 30) that have a commission greater than 0 (COMM > 0):

```
SQL> select empno, ename, sal, comm
  2    from emp
  3   where deptno = 30
  4     and comm > 0
  5  /

    EMPNO ENAME             SAL       COMM
---------- ---------- ---------- ----------
     7499 ALLEN            1600        300
     7521 WARD             1250        500
     7654 MARTIN           1250       1400
```

The OR operator returns TRUE if either the expression on the left-hand side of the OR operator is TRUE, or the expression on the right-hand side of the OR operator evaluates to TRUE. In the following query, we select all those employees who have either exceptional salaries **or** exceptional commissions:

```
SQL> select empno, ename, deptno, sal, comm
  2    from emp
  3   where sal >= 3000
  4      or comm >= 500
  5  /

    EMPNO ENAME          DEPTNO        SAL       COMM
---------- ---------- ---------- ---------- ----------
     7521 WARD               30       1250        500
     7654 MARTIN             30       1250       1400
     7788 SCOTT              20       3000
     7839 KING               10       5000
     7902 FORD               20       3000
```

We can see from the first two rows in the result set, that WARD' and MARTIN's SAL is not greater than 3000. Their COMM, however, is greater than or equal to 500. SCOTT, KING, and FORD were included in the query results because their SALs were greater than 3000. It didn't matter that their COMM values were smaller than 500, because their SALs satisfied one of the WHERE conditions.

Operator and Condition Precedence

When putting conditions and operators together in an expression, Oracle has a precedence by which it determines the order of evaluation. Oracle evaluates higher precedence operators and conditions before it evaluates lower precedence operators and conditions. Operators or conditions with the same level of precedence are evaluated from left to right. The following bullet points list operators, in their order of precedence from highest to lowest:

- ❏   +, -. Identity, negation

- ❏   *, /. Multiplication, division

- ❏   +, -, ||. Addition, subtraction, concatenation

The condition precedence meanwhile is as follows:

- ❏   =, !=, <, >, <=, >=. Comparison conditions

- ❏   IS [NOT] NULL, LIKE, [NOT] BETWEEN, [NOT] IN, EXISTS. Comparison conditions

- ❏   NOT. Negation

- ❏   AND. Conjunction

- ❏   OR. Disjunction

Joining Tables Using the WHERE Clause

WHERE clauses can be used to join tables in a multi-table SELECT statement. In the FROM clause, we can specify more than one table or view, and we can use a table join to put the tables and/or views together. In the next example, we will get a list of all the last names and job titles for those employees whose salary is greater than 10000:

```
SQL> select jobs.job_title, employees.last_name, salary
  2    from jobs, employees
  3   where jobs.job_id = employees.job_id
  4     and employees.salary > 10000
  5  /

JOB_TITLE                              LAST_NAME                      SALARY
------------------------------------   ----------------------------   ----------
President                              King                            24000
Administration Vice President          Kochhar                         17000
Administration Vice President          De Haan                         17000
Finance Manager                        Greenberg                       12000
Purchasing Manager                     Raphaely                        11000
Sales Manager                          Russell                         14000
Sales Manager                          Partners                        13500
```

Sales Manager	Errazuriz	12000
Sales Manager	Cambrault	11000
Sales Manager	Zlotkey	10500
Sales Representative	Vishney	10500
Sales Representative	Ozer	11500
Sales Representative	Abel	11000
Marketing Manager	Hartstein	13000
Accounting Manager	Higgins	12000

Here you can see we performed a query that asked for information from both the JOBS table and the EMPLOYEES table. To get the job title from the job table, we ask Oracle the question "What are the job titles for all those employees whose salary is greater than 10000?" In order to tell Oracle how to answer the question, we must join the tables using the JOB_ID column from both tables. In the EMPLOYEES table, each employee record contains a JOB_ID that refers to the JOB_ID column in the JOBS table.

Understanding NULLs

NULL is a term used to describe something that is undefined. A NULL column means there is no value assigned to the column.

In Oracle, when performing conditional operations such as IF COL_A = <Some Value>, the possible return values are TRUE, FALSE, and UNKNOWN. If you ask whether a column equals 50 for instance, and the column is NULL, there is no way of telling whether the column is 50 or not. If the column is NULL, it is unknown, so it *could be* 50, but it *might not be* 50.

Let's look at some examples of evaluating NULL values in our queries using the SCOTT schema's DEPT table. First, we'll insert a single record into the table with a NULL column, LOC (location):

```
SQL> connect scott/tiger
Connected.
SQL> insert into dept ( deptno, dname, loc )
  2   values ( 50, 'IT', NULL )
  3   /

1 row created.

SQL> select *
  2     from dept
  3   /

    DEPTNO DNAME          LOC
---------- -------------- -------------
        10 ACCOUNTING     NEW YORK
        20 RESEARCH       DALLAS
        30 SALES          CHICAGO
        40 OPERATIONS     BOSTON
        50 IT

5 rows selected.
```

Querying the table after inserting a row shows us the new row in the DEPT table. Next, let's try to select those rows from the table where the LOC equals NULL and those rows from the table where the LOC does not equal NULL:

```
SQL> select *
  2     from dept
  3   where loc = NULL
  4  /

no rows selected
```

The result of this query shows us that NULL does not equal NULL. No rows were selected in this query since the answer is always UNKNOWN. Even the row we just inserted, where the LOC column is NULL, does not satisfy the WHERE condition. NULL does not equal NULL, ever. It is always UNKNOWN.

Fortunately, Oracle provides two SQL operators for testing whether a value is NULL or not. These operators are known as IS NULL and IS NOT NULL. If we use these operators we get more informative results:

```
SQL> select *
  2     from dept
  3   where loc IS NULL
  4  /

    DEPTNO DNAME          LOC
---------- -------------- --------------
        50 IT

1 row selected.

SQL> select *
  2     from dept
  3   where loc IS NOT NULL
  4  /

    DEPTNO DNAME          LOC
---------- -------------- --------------
        10 ACCOUNTING     NEW YORK
        20 RESEARCH       DALLAS
        30 SALES          CHICAGO
        40 OPERATIONS     BOSTON

4 rows selected.
```

Now we can see that one row in the table has a NULL LOC column, while four rows in the table have LOC columns that are not NULL.

ORDER Your Results

Relational databases, including Oracle, do not guarantee any sort order for your queries, unless you explicitly use an ORDER BY clause. ORDER BY lets you determine how you want to sort the answer to your question. Let's write a couple of SELECT statements with different ORDER BY clauses to see how the results differ:

Instead of continuing to use the SCOTT user, we'll connect to the HR user to perform these code samples. For more information about installing these schemas in your database, refer to Appendix D.

```
SQL> connect hr/hr
Connected.
SQL> select last_name, salary
  2    from employees
  3    where salary > 12000
  4    order by salary
  5  /

LAST_NAME                    SALARY
------------------------ ----------
Hartstein                     13000
Partners                      13500
Russell                       14000
Kochhar                       17000
De Haan                       17000
King                          24000

6 rows selected.
```

As you can see, we sorted by salary in ascending order. Ascending is the default order, and can be explicitly specified using the keyword ASC. To sort by salary in descending order, we would execute the following:

```
SQL> select last_name, salary
  2    from employees
  3    where salary > 12000
  4    order by salary desc
  5  /
```

Try It Out – Sorting By Multiple Columns

In the following query, we will sort by JOB_ID first and SALARY second. This gives us a breakdown of who's making the most money by job title:

```
SQL> select last_name, job_id, salary
  2    from employees
  3    where salary > 12000
  4    order by job_id, salary
  5  /

LAST_NAME                JOB_ID        SALARY
------------------------ ---------- ----------
King                     AD_PRES        24000
Kochhar                  AD_VP          17000
De Haan                  AD_VP          17000
Hartstein                MK_MAN         13000
Partners                 SA_MAN         13500
Russell                  SA_MAN         14000

6 rows selected.
```

How It Works

Using a multi-column sort order, in this case, we specify that records are sorted first by the employee's JOB_ID, and subsequently by the employee's SALARY. By default, values are sorted *ascending* and so smaller salaries should be listed first in the query results above higher salaries. This holds true only for a situation where more than one employee has the same JOB_ID. For instance, if we sorted by SALARY first, Kochar would be listed above King. Since we sorted by JOB_ID first, however, King is above Kochar. Since Partners and Russell have the same JOB_ID, Oracle sorted those two rows according to the SALARY column.

There are two further points to bear in mind, regarding ORDER BY clauses:

❑ The column you are ordering by does not have to appear in your SELECT clause. This can be helpful when you don't necessarily want to display the data you are using to order your results.

❑ You can order your queries by referring to the numeric column position in your SELECT clause.

> Although this is *possible*, it is not recommended. People who use positional ordering in their queries will sometimes forget to modify each of the numbers in the **ORDER BY** clause when they add columns to the **SELECT** clause. This will cause the sort order to be based on the wrong columns, seemingly breaking the query.

GROUP BY and HAVING

The GROUP BY clause is used for grouping sets of records in the result set of a query for the purpose of aggregating data, or displaying a single row of summary information for the entire group.

In the following query, we want to analyze SALARY information by JOB_ID by selecting those columns from HR's EMPLOYEES table:

```
SQL> select job_id, salary
  2     from employees
  3     order by job_id
  4  /

JOB_ID          SALARY
----------  ----------
AC_ACCOUNT        8300
AC_MGR           12000
AD_ASST           4400
AD_PRES          24000
AD_VP            17000
AD_VP            17000
FI_ACCOUNT        9000
FI_ACCOUNT        7800
FI_ACCOUNT        8200
FI_ACCOUNT        7700
FI_ACCOUNT        6900
...
```

```
ST_MAN            8000
ST_MAN            8200
ST_MAN            7900
ST_MAN            6500
ST_MAN            5800

107 rows selected.
```

Note that not all the rows have been shown here

As you can see, for each JOB_ID there are many SALARY values. This is a great example of where the GROUP BY clause comes in handy. In the following query, we use a few SQL functions to compute the average salary (AVG), the sum of all the salaries (SUM), the maximum salary (MAX), and the count of the rows per group:

Don't worry about the syntax for the SQL functions (AVG, SUM, MAX, etc.), we will look at these in Appendix A.

```
SQL> select job_id, avg(salary), sum(salary), max(salary), count(*)
  2     from employees
  3     group by job_id
  4  /

JOB_ID      AVG(SALARY) SUM(SALARY) MAX(SALARY)   COUNT(*)
---------- ------------ ------------ ----------- ----------
AC_ACCOUNT         8300         8300        8300          1
AC_MGR            12000        12000       12000          1
AD_ASST            4400         4400        4400          1
AD_PRES           24000        24000       24000          1
AD_VP             17000        34000       17000          2
FI_ACCOUNT         7920        39600        9000          5
FI_MGR            12000        12000       12000          1
HR_REP             6500         6500        6500          1
IT_PROG            5760        28800        9000          5
MK_MAN            13000        13000       13000          1
MK_REP             6000         6000        6000          1
PR_REP            10000        10000       10000          1
PU_CLERK           2780        13900        3100          5
PU_MAN            11000        11000       11000          1
SA_MAN            12200        61000       14000          5
SA_REP             8350       250500       11500         30
SH_CLERK           3215        64300        4200         20
ST_CLERK           2785        55700        3600         20
ST_MAN             7280        36400        8200          5

19 rows selected.
```

A quick query on the EMPLOYEES table for the salaries of all the Stock Managers (JOB_ID = ST_MAN) validates our GROUP BY query above:

```
SQL> select salary
  2    from employees
  3    where job_id = 'ST_MAN'
  4  /

    SALARY
----------
      8000
      8200
      7900
      6500
      5800

5 row selected.
```

Perform some quick arithmetic, and we can see that the SALARY of all employees with JOB_ID = 'ST_MAN' equals 36400; and if we divide that value by the number of employees with that JOB_ID, we get the answer 7280.

Alongside the GROUP BY clause, there is an additional clause provided to allow you to filter the groups of rows returned from your GROUP BY query. This HAVING clause is for queries using GROUP BY clauses only, and always contains an aggregate SQL function, such as AVG, SUM, MAX, etc.

To demonstrate this, we'll look at two queries using GROUP BY, one with no HAVING clause, and the other with a HAVING clause.

First, let's select the average salary of employees by JOB_ID.

```
SQL> select job_id, avg(salary) avg_salary
  2    from employees
  3    group by job_id
  4    order by avg(salary) desc
  5  /

JOB_ID      AVG_SALARY
----------  ----------
AD_PRES          24000
AD_VP            17000
MK_MAN           13000
SA_MAN           12200
AC_MGR           12000
FI_MGR           12000
PU_MAN           11000
PR_REP           10000
SA_REP            8350
AC_ACCOUNT        8300
FI_ACCOUNT        7920
ST_MAN            7280
HR_REP            6500
MK_REP            6000
IT_PROG           5760
```

```
        AD_ASST          4400
        SH_CLERK         3215
        ST_CLERK         2785
        PU_CLERK         2780

    19 rows selected.
```

Now we want to filter this list, to see all those JOB_ID's whose employees make an average salary greater than or equal to 10000.

```
SQL> select job_id, avg(salary) avg_salary
  2    from employees
  3    group by job_id
  4    having avg(salary) >= 10000
  5    order by avg(salary) desc
  6  /

JOB_ID     AVG_SALARY
---------- ----------
AD_PRES         24000
AD_VP           17000
MK_MAN          13000
SA_MAN          12200
AC_MGR          12000
FI_MGR          12000
PU_MAN          11000
PR_REP          10000

8 rows selected.
```

As you can see, by using the HAVING clause we were able to filter out the job titles whose average SALARY was greater than or equal to 10000.

> Don't confuse the **HAVING** clause with the **WHERE** clause. **WHERE** clause constraints are evaluated on the data before it is grouped, whereas **HAVING** clause constraints are evaluated on the results of the data after it has been grouped together.

Joins

While the majority of the queries demonstrated so far have concentrated on using one table in the FROM clause, it is commonplace to want to query data from more than one table. For instance, if we wanted to know what department a particular employee worked in, the only information we could get from the EMPLOYEES table is the DEPARTMENT_ID of the department. It's more than likely we'd rather know the *name* of the department that employee works in. In order to get this information, we have to look in the DEPARTMENTS table at the DEPARTMENT_NAME column. One of the rows in that table has the same DEPARTMENT_ID as the employee's DEPARTMENT_ID value, and that's the way we match up an EMPLOYEES record with a DEPARTMENTS record.

In order for us to do this, the parent table (in this example, the DEPARTMENTS table) must have a **primary key**. The primary key is a column (or columns) in a table that uniquely identify each row in a table. In the EMPLOYEES table, the primary key is the EMPLOYEE_ID. In the DEPARTMENTS table, it's DEPARTMENT_ID.

Tables are related to each other by what is known as a **foreign key**. A foreign key is a column or set of columns in a row that refer to a primary key of another table. The DEPARTMENT_ID column in the EMPLOYEES table refers to the DEPARTMENT_ID column in the DEPARTMENTS table.

We will talk more about keys in the next chapter.

In order for us to query information from more than one table and have the results make sense, we need to tell Oracle how to filter the records based on the related columns. If Oracle does not know how to join the tables, your query will result in a **Cartesian product**.

A Cartesian product is when each record of one table is joined to every record of another table. To illustrate this, let's query the EMPLOYEES table to find out which employees work in the Accounting and Marketing departments (DEPARTMENT_IDs 20 and 110):

```
SQL> select employee_id, last_name
  2    from employees
  3   where department_id in (20, 110);

EMPLOYEE_ID LAST_NAME
----------- -------------------------
        201 Hartstein
        202 Fay
        205 Higgins
        206 Gietz

4 rows selected.
```

If we wanted to query data out of the EMPLOYEES and DEPARTMENTS table at the same time, we can do so by providing a comma-separated list of tables in the FROM clause, and fully qualified column names in the SELECT clause:

```
SQL> select employees.employee_id, employees.last_name,
  2         departments.department_name
  3    from employees, departments
  4   where employees.department_id in (20, 110)
  5     and departments.department_id in (20, 110)
  6  /

EMPLOYEE_ID LAST_NAME                 DEPARTMENT_NAME
----------- ------------------------- ----------------------------
        201 Hartstein                 Marketing
        202 Fay                       Marketing
        205 Higgins                   Marketing
        206 Gietz                     Marketing
```

```
     201 Hartstein                 Accounting
     202 Fay                       Accounting
     205 Higgins                   Accounting
     206 Gietz                     Accounting

 8 rows selected.
```

If you inspect the query results, you will see each employee is listed twice, once for each department that matched the WHERE clause. This is a Cartesian product. We did not tell Oracle how to map a row in EMPLOYEES to a row in the DEPARTMENTS table, and so it mapped each row in EMPLOYEES to *every* row in the DEPARTMENTS table.

In order to avoid this situation we can provide a join condition (by altering the WHERE clause), in order to tell Oracle how to join the tables.

```
SQL> select employees.employee_id, employees.last_name,
  2          departments.department_name
  3    from employees, departments
  4   where employees.department_id in (20, 110)
  5     and departments.department_id = employees.department_id
  6  /

EMPLOYEE_ID LAST_NAME                         DEPARTMENT_NAME
----------- ------------------------------    -----------------------------------
        201 Hartstein                         Marketing
        202 Fay                               Marketing
        205 Higgins                           Accounting
        206 Gietz                             Accounting

4 rows selected.
```

In the original query (with the Cartesian product), we told Oracle to give us the rows from the DEPARTMENTS table where the DEPARTMENT_ID is either 20 or 110. In this query, we tell Oracle to give us the DEPARTMENTS record(s) where the DEPARTMENT_ID equals the DEPARTMENT_ID from the EMPLOYEES table.

> It is important to note that in the above query the columns being selected are fully qualified using dot notation in the form TABLE.COLUMN within the SELECT clause. We comma delimit the tables from which we are querying in the FROM clause, and we join the tables using an expression in the WHERE clause.

Table Aliases

Table aliases (formerly known as correlation names) are "short names" for each table in your FROM clause meant to uniquely identify the data source, but to act as an abbreviation. The above query could be rewritten as follows:

```
SQL> select e.employee_id, e.last_name, d.department_name
  2    from employees e, departments d
  3   where d.department_name in ('Accounting','Marketing')
  4     and e.department_id = d.department_id
  5  /
```

This achieves the same results with much less SQL code. In the code sample above we use 'E' to stand for EMPLOYEES. We use 'D' to stand for DEPARTMENTS.

Qualifying column names is only mandatory for column names that are duplicated in each table. If we do not qualify column names in our query, then Oracle is unable to perform the query, as the following example illustrates:

```
SQL> select e.employee_id, e.last_name, department_name
  2    from employees e, departments
  3   where department_name in ('Accounting','Marketing')
  4     and e.department_id = department_id
  5  /
    and e.department_id = department_id
                         *
ERROR at line 4:
ORA-00918: column ambiguously defined
```

Oracle is unable to determine which table the unqualified DEPARTMENT_ID column reference in line 4 refers to, and raises an error.

Column Aliases

Columns in a query can also be assigned to an alias. This is accomplished by specifying the alias of the column name after the column is designated in the SELECT clause. The alias is optionally enclosed in double quote marks. You can also alias a column by using the (optional) keyword AS (see below).

By default, column names in the SELECT clause are listed in the query results in upper case as a heading to the columns. Placing double quotes around the column alias ensures case sensitivity of the column alias, and allows you to specify spaces and special characters in the alias name.

```
SQL> select employee_id "Emp #", last_name Last,
  2         department_name AS "Department"
  3    from employees e, departments d
  4   where d.department_id = e.department_id
  5     and d.department_id = 30
  6  /

    Emp # LAST                      Department
---------- ------------------------ ---------------------------
      114 Raphaely                  Purchasing
      115 Khoo                      Purchasing
      116 Baida                     Purchasing
      117 Tobias                    Purchasing
```

```
        118 Himuro              Purchasing
        119 Colmenares          Purchasing

6 rows selected.
```

In the result set you can see the relevant column headings reflect the alias names instead of the originals. When you alias columns, the column headings take on the alias names. Also, aliases that are inside quotation marks are treated differently. You can use any string of characters inside quotation marks, and those characters will become the column heading in the result set. In a normal alias, however, the alias name must be a valid Oracle identifier.

ANSI Joins in Oracle 9i

Up until Oracle 9*i*, joining tables in the WHERE clause (as we have been doing up until now) was the only way to perform joins in your queries. Now however, it is possible to use new joining syntax to carry this out in the FROM clause. The different types of joins you can perform are as follows:

- ❏ NATURAL
- ❏ INNER
- ❏ OUTER
    - ❏ LEFT
    - ❏ RIGHT
    - ❏ FULL

Natural Joins

When we join two tables with a natural join, Oracle joins all those columns from the first table to any column in the second table with the same name. In natural joins, you do not explicitly name columns to use to perform the join, since it is done for you.

```
SQL> select employee_id, last_name, department_name
  2    from employees natural join departments
  3   where department_name = 'Purchasing'
  4  /

EMPLOYEE_ID LAST_NAME                     DEPARTMENT_NAME
----------- ------------------------      -----------------------------
        119 Colmenares                    Purchasing
        118 Himuro                        Purchasing
        117 Tobias                        Purchasing
        116 Baida                         Purchasing
        115 Khoo                          Purchasing

5 rows selected.
```

Natural joins are an example of a feature that's good in theory but bad in practice. The join columns must have the same name in each table. This forces designers to name related columns in tables that will be joined with the same names simply to join the tables. You cannot have other columns in the tables with the same name unless you plan on Oracle using them to join the tables together. For example, if the EMPLOYEES table and the DEPARTMENTS table both had an ADDRESS column, Oracle would try to join the two tables using both the DEPARTMENT_ID and ADDRESS columns.

Also, it is illegal to use table aliases in natural joins, therefore there is no way of annotating which table columns are actually being retrieved from.

Inner Joins

Inner joins use join conditions in the FROM clause just like natural joins, but you must specify the columns from each table to join on:

```
SQL> select e.employee_id, e.last_name, d.department_name
  2     from employees e inner join departments d
  3        on e.department_id = d.department_id
  4    where e.job_id = 'SA_MAN'
  5  /

EMPLOYEE_ID LAST_NAME               DEPARTMENT_NAME
----------- ----------------------- ------------------------------
        145 Russell                 Sales
        146 Partners                Sales
        147 Errazuriz               Sales
        148 Cambrault               Sales
        149 Zlotkey                 Sales

5 rows selected.
```

When you perform an inner join, only rows that satisfy the join condition are returned. In the query above, if there were an employee in the EMPLOYEES table that had no DEPARTMENT_ID, that employee's record would not show up in the query results.

```
SQL> insert into employees
  2   (employee_id, last_name, email, hire_date, job_id, department_id)
  3  values
  4  (99999, 'Doe', 'john@doe.com', '01-JAN-2002', 'SA_MAN', null);

1 row created.

SQL>
SQL> select e.employee_id, e.last_name, d.department_name
  2     from employees e inner join departments d
  3        on e.department_id = d.department_id
  4    where e.job_id = 'SA_MAN'
  5  /

EMPLOYEE_ID LAST_NAME               DEPARTMENT_NAME
----------- ----------------------- ------------------------------
        145 Russell                 Sales
```

```
        146 Partners                 Sales
        147 Errazuriz                Sales
        148 Cambrault                Sales
        149 Zlotkey                  Sales

5 rows selected.
```

Don't worry about the syntax for inserting records, we'll get into that later in the chapter.

Even though we inserted another employee into the EMPLOYEES table with a JOB_ID equal to SA_MAN, the row was still not returned. You'll notice Mr. Doe has no DEPARTMENT_ID. When Oracle does the inner join, it looks to see if there is a corresponding row in the DEPARTMENTS table with no DEPARTMENT_ID. If it found a row, the row would be included in the results. Since Oracle found no department row without a DEPARTMENT_ID, it was excluded.

Outer Joins

An outer join simply extends the results of an inner join. The results of an outer join will be all those rows that satisfy the join condition, along with rows from one table that do not have corresponding rows in the other table to satisfy the join condition.

In our sample above, we showed how after we inserted an employee with no DEPARTMENT_ID, that employee was not included in the results of an inner join on the DEPARTMENT_ID column. With an outer join, on the other hand, this employee *would* be included in the query results:

```
SQL> select e.employee_id, e.last_name, d.department_name
  2    from employees e left outer join departments d
  3      on e.department_id = d.department_id
  4   where e.job_id = 'SA_MAN'
  5  /

EMPLOYEE_ID LAST_NAME                    DEPARTMENT_NAME
----------- -------------------------    -------------------------------
        145 Russell                      Sales
        146 Partners                     Sales
        147 Errazuriz                    Sales
        148 Cambrault                    Sales
        149 Zlotkey                      Sales
      99999 Doe

6 rows selected.
```

In line 2 above, we see the syntax for performing an outer join is:

```
from employees e left outer join departments d
```

The term left refers to which table will return all the rows (provided they satisfy the WHERE constraints), regardless of whether there is a corresponding row in the right table. In our query above, we performed the outer join on the EMPLOYEES table because we wanted to make sure we included employees who did not have a corresponding row in the DEPARTMENTS table.

63

We can also perform **right outer joins**. This simply means we want to return all the rows from the table on the right of the join condition instead of the table on the left. For instance, if we were to query the tables for all those employees and departments that were at a particular location, we may want to include the departments that don't have employees:

```
SQL> select e.employee_id, e.last_name, d.department_name
  2    from employees e right outer join departments d
  3      on e.department_id = d.department_id
  4   where d.location_id = 1700
  5   order by d.department_name, e.last_name
  6  /

EMPLOYEE_ID LAST_NAME                   DEPARTMENT_NAME
----------- --------------------------- -------------------------------
        206 Gietz                       Accounting
        205 Higgins                     Accounting
        200 Whalen                      Administration
                                        Benefits
                                        Construction
                                        Contracting
                                        Control And Credit
                                        Corporate Tax
        102 De Haan                     Executive
        100 King                        Executive
        101 Kochhar                     Executive
        110 Chen                        Finance
        109 Faviet                      Finance
        108 Greenberg                   Finance
        113 Popp                        Finance
        111 Sciarra                     Finance
        112 Urman                       Finance
                                        Government Sales
                                        IT Helpdesk
                                        IT Support
                                        Manufacturing
                                        NOC
                                        Operations
                                        Payroll
        116 Baida                       Purchasing
        119 Colmenares                  Purchasing
        118 Himuro                      Purchasing
        115 Khoo                        Purchasing
        114 Raphaely                    Purchasing
        117 Tobias                      Purchasing
                                        Recruiting
                                        Retail Sales
                                        Shareholder Services
                                        Treasury

34 rows selected.
```

In the right outer join, we see there are in fact departments with no employees, which we wouldn't have seen in either an inner join or left outer join.

The last type of outer join is the **full outer join**. A full outer join is like doing a left outer join AND a right outer join at the same time. In the example queries we have been using, a full outer join would return all those rows that satisfied the join condition (EMPLOYEES.DEPARTMENT_ID = DEPARTMENTS.DEPARTMENT_ID), any employees that did not have matching department rows, and any departments that did not have any matching employees rows. Full outer joins are expensive because, under the covers, Oracle actually performs a left outer join of the entire query, then a right outer join of the entire query, puts the results together and eliminates the duplicate records.

Prior to Oracle 9i, outer joins were indicated by placing a plus sign surrounded by parenthesis (+) next to the table that is not being outer joined. This is due to the way Oracle accomplishes outer joins. When it joins the table being outer joined to the other table and determines there are no matching rows to satisfy the join condition, Oracle makes up a row to temporarily satisfy the join condition so the outer joined table's rows will be included in the query results. Although the *concept* of a left or right outer join existed before Oracle 9i's new ANSI-compliant syntax, it was implemented with this special character as follows:

```
SQL> select e.employee_id, e.last_name, d.department_name
  2    from employees e, departments d
  3   where e.department_id = d.department_id(+)
  4     and e.job_id = 'SA_MAN'
  5  /
```

In line 3 you can see the D.DEPARTMENT_ID column has the (+) characters next to it to indicate the EMPLOYEES table is being outer joined.

Self Joins

In some tables you create, you may have what is known as a self-referencing foreign key. This means one column is a foreign key to the primary key of the same table. A perfect example of this is the MANAGER_ID column in the HR schema's EMPLOYEES table. The MANAGER_ID column in one row is the EMPLOYEE_ID of another row. For example:

```
SQL> select employee_id, last_name, job_id, manager_id
  2    from employees
  3   order by employee_id
  4  /

EMPLOYEE_ID LAST_NAME                JOB_ID     MANAGER_ID
----------- ------------------------ ---------- ----------
        100 King                     AD_PRES
        101 Kochhar                  AD_VP             100
        102 De Haan                  AD_VP             100
        103 Hunold                   IT_PROG           102
        104 Ernst                    IT_PROG           103
...
        205 Higgins                  AC_MGR            101
        206 Gietz                    AC_ACCOUNT        205

107 rows selected.
```

In this query, we have simply selected the first ten rows of the EMPLOYEES table to show you how the MANAGER_ID column relates to the EMPLOYEE_ID column. From the query results above, we can start to see how employees report to each other:

- ❏ King (100) manages Kochar (101) and De Haan (102)
- ❏ Kochar (101) manages Higgins (205)
- ❏ De Haan (102) manages Hunold (103)
- ❏ Hunold (103) manages Ernst (104)
- ❏ Higgins (205) manages Gietz (206)

Using a self join, you can look at an employee and that employee's manager information on the same row in a query to verify our findings in the list above.

In order to write a self join you simply specify the source table twice in the FROM clause, and you must alias the table name to resolve the ambiguity. As an example:

```
SQL> select e1.last_name "Employee",
  2           e2.last_name "Reports To"
  3    from employees e1 left outer join employees e2
  4      on e1.manager_id = e2.employee_id
  5    order by e1.employee_id
  6  /

Employee                        Reports To
------------------------------  ------------------------------
King
Kochhar                         King
De Haan                         King
Hunold                          De Haan
Ernst                           Hunold
...
Higgins                         Kochhar
Gietz                           Higgins

107 rows selected.
```

In our example we simply specified the same table twice in the FROM clause, and used a WHERE clause expression to join the two tables on the EMPLOYEE_ID and MANAGER_ID columns. By aliasing the tables in the FROM clause, Oracle views the two tables as separate data sources, and retrieves the data accordingly.

Set Operators

Oracle provides the ability to combine two or more SQL queries into a single statement, through the use of four set operators, UNION, UNION ALL, INTERSECT, and MINUS. We will look at examples of each of these in due course.

A query that utilizes a set operator is known as a **compound query**. Oracle provides some guidelines to be followed when writing compound queries:

- ❏ In each of the individual queries that make up a compound query, the number of values and the data types of the SELECT list must match.

❑ You cannot specify an ORDER BY clause in any of the individual queries included in the compound query.

❑ You cannot use set operators on large object data types, such as BLOBs, or LONGs. These data types are covered in the next chapter.

❑ You cannot use collections, such as nested tables or varrays, in a set operator SELECT list. (We will discuss these further in Chapter 3).

In the sample queries below, we use two queries on the same table to help demonstrate the differences between these set operators.

UNION

A UNION statement adds all those rows from the first query to all the rows in the second query, eliminate any duplicates, and return the results. In the following example, we can see the first query selects the EMPLOYEE_ID and LAST_NAME for all the employees whose LAST_NAME column begins with either A or B. The second query selects all the EMPLOYEE_ID and LAST_NAME for all the employees whose LAST_NAME column begins with either a B or a C.

Obviously, that means employees whose LAST_NAME column begins with a B are being selected from both the first and second queries. With a UNION statement, however, duplicate rows are filtered out of the result set:

```
SQL> connect hr/hr
Connected.
SQL> select employee_id, last_name
  2    from employees
  3   where last_name like 'A%'
  4      or last_name like 'B%'
  5  union
  6  select employee_id, last_name
  7    from employees
  8   where last_name like 'B%'
  9      or last_name like 'C%'
 10  /

EMPLOYEE_ID LAST_NAME
----------- -------------------------
        174 Abel
        166 Ande
        130 Atkinson
        105 Austin
        204 Baer
        116 Baida
        167 Banda
        172 Bates
        192 Bell
        151 Bernstein
        129 Bissot
        169 Bloom
        185 Bull
```

```
        187 Cabrio
        148 Cambrault
        154 Cambrault
        110 Chen
        188 Chung
        119 Colmenares

19 rows selected.
```

UNION ALL

UNION ALL statements work much the same way as a standard UNION statement, except the duplicate rows are not filtered from the list. The same query as above will yield the following in this case:

```
SQL> select employee_id, last_name
  2      from employees
  3    where last_name like 'A%'
  4        or last_name like 'B%'
  5  union all
  6  select employee_id, last_name
  7      from employees
  8    where last_name like 'B%'
  9        or last_name like 'C%'
 10  /

EMPLOYEE_ID LAST_NAME
----------- ------------------------
        174 Abel
        166 Ande
        130 Atkinson
        105 Austin
        204 Baer
        204 Baer
        116 Baida
        116 Baida
        167 Banda
        167 Banda
        172 Bates
        172 Bates
        192 Bell
        192 Bell
        151 Bernstein
        151 Bernstein
        129 Bissot
        129 Bissot
        169 Bloom
        169 Bloom
        185 Bull
        185 Bull
        187 Cabrio
        148 Cambrault
        154 Cambrault
```

```
            110  Chen
            188  Chung
            119  Colmenares

   28 rows selected.
```

INTERSECT

INTERSECT is a set operator that takes two queries, puts the values together, and returns the distinct records that exist in both result sets. None of those rows that are exclusively returned either in the first query, or the second query, are included in the result set.

Using the same queries we have been using in our previous set operators, we can expect to retrieve all the employees where the LAST_NAME starts with a B in an INTERSECT set. This is because all the rows that are returned in *only* the first query or *only* the second query are filtered:

```
SQL> select employee_id, last_name
  2     from employees
  3    where last_name like 'A%'
  4       or last_name like 'B%'
  5  intersect
  6  select employee_id, last_name
  7     from employees
  8    where last_name like 'B%'
  9       or last_name like 'C%'
 10  /

EMPLOYEE_ID LAST_NAME
----------- -------------------------
        116  Baida
        129  Bissot
        151  Bernstein
        167  Banda
        169  Bloom
        172  Bates
        185  Bull
        192  Bell
        204  Baer

 9 rows selected.
```

MINUS

The MINUS set operator returns all those records that are returned from the first query, but not the second. The first query returns employees whose LAST_NAME starts with A and B, and the second query returns employees whose LAST_NAME starts with B or C. Therefore, the MINUS set operator using those two queries should expect to return all those employees whose LAST_NAME begins with an A.

```
SQL> select employee_id, last_name
  2     from employees
  3    where last_name like 'A%'
  4       or last_name like 'B%'
```

```
   5  minus
   6  select employee_id, last_name
   7    from employees
   8   where last_name like 'B%'
   9      or last_name like 'C%'
  10  /

EMPLOYEE_ID LAST_NAME
----------- ------------------------
        105 Austin
        130 Atkinson
        166 Ande
        174 Abel

4 rows selected
```

Other DML Statements

Aside from queries, DML also comprises of SQL statements used to insert, update, and delete records in your tables. Each statement is different, so we'll look at each in turn.

INSERT Statements

INSERT statements, as you may have already guessed, put new records inside tables. There are many, many concepts in Oracle related to inserting records, but for now let's just concentrate on a simple insert statement into a table. We'll use the JOBS table, from the HR schema, to demonstrate this functionality. The JOBS table consists of four columns, namely JOB_ID, JOB_TITLE, MIN_SALARY, and MAX_SALARY. We'll begin by writing an insert using all the columns:

```
SQL> insert into jobs (job_id, job_title, min_salary, max_salary)
  2  values ('IT_DBA', 'Database Administrator', 4000.00, 10000.00)
  3  /

1 row created.
```

Note that this INSERT could also be written as:

```
SQL> insert into jobs
  2  values ('IT_DBA', 'Database Administrator', 4000.00, 10000.00)
  3  /

1 row created.
```

As you can see from these two statements, the INSERT clause optionally contains a list of the columns you are inserting data into, in order to associate the values provided in your VALUES clause with the columns in the INSERT clause.

> **Explicitly listing the columns you are inserting into is the recommended method, since it avoids the problem of ambiguous columns, or, even worse, insertion of data in the wrong columns.**

The only columns that are absolutely necessary in this case are the JOB_ID and JOB_TITLE columns, since they have a NOT NULL constraint associated. As a result, we can use the following INSERT statement to create a record that has no MAX_SALARY value:

```
SQL> insert into jobs (job_id, job_title, min_salary)
  2  values ('IT_AUTHOR', 'Technical Author', 5000.00)
  3  /

1 row created.
```

In this case, you can see we have created a job that has a MIN_SALARY of 5000, but there is no MAX_SALARY. (This way, Technical Authors do not have a salary cap!) Performing the following query shows our new records in the table:

```
SQL> select job_id, job_title
  2    from jobs
  3  /

JOB_ID      JOB_TITLE
----------  ----------------------------------
AD_PRES     President
AD_VP       Administration Vice President
...
HR_REP      Human Resources Representative
PR_REP      Public Relations Representative
IT_AUTHOR   Technical Author
IT_DBA      Database Administrator

21 rows selected.
```

Note that not all the rows returned are shown here.

UPDATE Statements

Changing records is accomplished using the UPDATE statement. Let's assume, for example, we would like to give all the Programmers a 15% raise, because they are doing such a great job writing Oracle databases applications. You do this by telling Oracle the table you want to update, how you want to update it, and providing a WHERE clause to filter the records that will be updated, as follows:

```
SQL> -- first list the programmers' existing salaries
SQL> select job_id, last_name, salary
  2    from employees
  3   where job_id in ('IT_PROG', 'ST_CLERK')
  4   order by job_id, last_name
```

71

```
    5  /

JOB_ID      LAST_NAME                           SALARY
----------  --------------------------------  ----------
IT_PROG     Austin                              4800
IT_PROG     Ernst                               6000
IT_PROG     Hunold                              9000
IT_PROG     Lorentz                             4200
IT_PROG     Pataballa                           4800
ST_CLERK    Atkinson                            2800
ST_CLERK    Bissot                              3300
ST_CLERK    Davies                              3100
ST_CLERK    Gee                                 2400
ST_CLERK    Ladwig                              3600
ST_CLERK    Landry                              2400
ST_CLERK    Mallin                              3300
ST_CLERK    Markle                              2200
ST_CLERK    Marlow                              2500
ST_CLERK    Matos                               2600
ST_CLERK    Mikkilineni                         2700
ST_CLERK    Nayer                               3200
ST_CLERK    Olson                               2100
ST_CLERK    Patel                               2500
ST_CLERK    Philtanker                          2200
ST_CLERK    Rajs                                3500
ST_CLERK    Rogers                              2900
ST_CLERK    Seo                                 2700
ST_CLERK    Stiles                              3200
ST_CLERK    Vargas                              2500

25 rows selected.

SQL> -- now we'll update the IT_PROG employees, NOT the ST_CLERKs
SQL> update employees
  2      set salary = salary * 1.15
  3    where job_id = 'IT_PROG'
  4  /

5 rows updated.

SQL> select job_id, last_name, salary
  2      from employees
  3    where job_id in ('IT_PROG', 'ST_CLERK')
  4    order by job_id, last_name
  5  /

JOB_ID      LAST_NAME                           SALARY
----------  --------------------------------  ----------
IT_PROG     Austin                              5520
IT_PROG     Ernst                               6900
IT_PROG     Hunold                             10350
IT_PROG     Lorentz                             4830
IT_PROG     Pataballa                           5520
```

ST_CLERK	Atkinson	2800
ST_CLERK	Bissot	3300
ST_CLERK	Davies	3100
ST_CLERK	Gee	2400
ST_CLERK	Ladwig	3600
ST_CLERK	Landry	2400
ST_CLERK	Mallin	3300
ST_CLERK	Markle	2200
ST_CLERK	Marlow	2500
ST_CLERK	Matos	2600
ST_CLERK	Mikkilineni	2700
ST_CLERK	Nayer	3200
ST_CLERK	Olson	2100
ST_CLERK	Patel	2500
ST_CLERK	Philtanker	2200
ST_CLERK	Rajs	3500
ST_CLERK	Rogers	2900
ST_CLERK	Seo	2700
ST_CLERK	Stiles	3200
ST_CLERK	Vargas	2500

```
25 rows selected.
```

In the second query, you can see all those records that were of JOB_ID IT_PROG were updated, whereas the ST_CLERK employees were not. This is due to line three of the UPDATE statement that indicated which records to update. This is an important task to perform when you do updates to your database. Most of the time, we are content to know that the changes we asked the database to perform have been completed. It is equally important to ensure that the update did not change anything it should not have.

DELETE Statements

Putting data *into* the database is great, but as soon as you provide the ability to insert a record into the database, users will demand the functionality to remove records, as well. Removing records from the database is performed using the DELETE statement.

As with the UPDATE statement, you are going to specify the table you want to remove records from, and an expression to filter the records that are actually being removed. If you do not provide such an expression, then the DELETE statement will remove all the records in your table.

As a quick example, let's begin by inserting a couple of bogus records into the EMPLOYEES table:

```
SQL> insert into employees(
  2    employee_id, first_name, last_name, email,
  3    hire_date, job_id, salary)
  4  values(
  5    9695, 'Thomas', 'Kyte', 'tkyte@somecompany.com',
  6    SYSDATE-3650, 'FI_MGR', 20001)
  7  /
```

73

```
1 row created.

SQL> insert into employees(
  2      employee_id, first_name, last_name, email,
  3      hire_date, job_id, salary, manager_id)
  4  values(
  5      9696, 'Sean', 'Dillon', 'sdillon@somecompany .com',
  6      SYSDATE, 'IT_AUTHOR', 20000, 9695)
  7  /

1 row created.

SQL> insert into employees(
  2      employee_id, first_name, last_name, email,
  3      hire_date, job_id, salary, manager_id)
  4  values(
  5      9697, 'Chris', 'Beck', 'clbeck@somecompany .com',
  6      SYSDATE, 'IT_AUTHOR', 20000, 9695)
  7  /

1 row created.

SQL> insert into employees(
  2      employee_id, first_name, last_name, email,
  3      hire_date, job_id, salary, manager_id)
  4  values(
  5      9698, 'Mark', 'Piermarini', 'mbpierma@somecompany.com',
  6      SYSDATE, 'IT_PROG', 20000, 9695)
  7  /

1 row created.

SQL> insert into employees(
  2      employee_id, first_name, last_name, email,
  3      hire_date, job_id, salary, manager_id)
  4  values(
  5      9699, 'Fred', 'Velasquez', 'wvelasqu@somecompany.com',
  6      SYSDATE, 'IT_DBA', 20000, 9695)
  7  /

1 row created.
```

This produces the following records:

```
SQL> select employee_id, last_name, job_id
  2      from employees
  3  where employee_id = 9695
  4      or manager_id = 9695
  5  order by employee_id
  6  /

EMPLOYEE_ID LAST_NAME                      JOB_ID
----------- ------------------------       ----------
       9695 Kyte                           MGR
```

```
        9696 Dillon                      IT_AUTHOR
        9697 Beck                        IT_AUTHOR
        9698 Piermarini                  IT_PROG
        9699 Velasquez                   IT_DBA
```

Now we can selectively delete them as we wish. If we decide there should be no more authors in the company, then we can carry out the following:

```
SQL> delete
  2     from employees
  3    where job_id = 'IT_AUTHOR'
  4   /

2 rows deleted.
```

A quick query shows us that there are no longer authors reporting to that manager:

```
SQL> select employee_id, last_name, job_id
  2     from employees
  3    where employee_id = 9695
  4       or manager_id = 9695
  5    order by employee_id
  6   /

EMPLOYEE_ID LAST_NAME                    JOB_ID
----------- ------------------------     ----------
       9695 Kyte                         MGR
       9698 Piermarini                   IT_PROG
       9699 Velasquez                    IT_DBA
```

> Note that **DELETE** statements are not restricted to one condition. You can pass as many conditions as you like in the **WHERE** clause of a **DELETE** statement.

COMMIT and ROLLBACK

In Oracle, changes you make to your data (through INSERT, UPDATE, and DELETE for instance) are not permanent until you tell Oracle to make them so. This is accomplished using a SQL statement known as COMMIT.

Changes you make to data during your session are not visible by other users until they are committed to the database. This is due to the way Oracle manages transactions in the database. A **transaction** is a series of SQL statements executed by a user during a database session that are treated as one logical unit of work. In Oracle, either an entire transaction succeeds or an entire transaction fails. As a result, not only do COMMITs save changes to the database, but they also end the current transaction and begin a new one.

When you are modifying data in the database, you may find at some point that you need to undo the changes you have made, for one reason or another. In order to undo all the changes you have made to the database in the current transaction, you can use the ROLLBACK statement. Oracle maintains all the data necessary to modify the database so it looks exactly like it did before you began your transaction. ROLLBACKs also serve to end the current transaction and begin a new one.

Transactions, commits, and rollbacks are discussed in much more detail in Chapter 12.

Try It Out – Committing Changes

In order to show how COMMITS work, we will use two SQL*Plus sessions.

1. Start up a SQL*Plus window, connect to the database as the HR user and insert some data into the DEPARTMENTS and EMPLOYEES tables as follows:

```
SQL> connect hr/hr
Connected.
SQL> insert into departments
  2    ( department_id, department_name )
  3  values
  4    ( 1234, 'Data Center Operations' );

1 row created.

SQL> insert into employees
  2    ( employee_id, last_name, email, hire_date, job_id, department_id )
  3  values
  4    ( 123451, 'Lawson', 'lawson@somegroovycompany.com', '01-JAN-2002',
  5      'IT_PROG', 1234 );

1 row created.

SQL> insert into employees
  2    ( employee_id, last_name, email, hire_date, job_id, department_id )
  3  values
  4    ( 123452, 'Wells', 'wells@somegroovycompany.com', '01-JAN-2002',
  5      'IT_PROG', 1234 );

1 row created.

SQL> insert into employees
  2    ( employee_id, last_name, email, hire_date, job_id, department_id )
  3  values
  4    ( 123453, 'Bliss', 'bliss@somegroovycompany.com', '01-JAN-2002',
  5      'IT_PROG', 1234 );

1 row created.
```

2. If we now write the following query, we should see the data we have just inserted:

```
SQL> select d.department_name, e.last_name
  2    from departments d inner join employees e
  3      on d.department_id = e.department_id
  4    where d.department_id = 1234
  5  /

DEPARTMENT_NAME                 LAST_NAME
------------------------------  -------------------------
Data Center Operations          Lawson
Data Center Operations          Wells
Data Center Operations          Bliss
```

3. Now, open a *different* SQL*Plus window (leave the first session open), and connect to the database using the *same* user account (HR). Let's run the same query on the DEPARTMENTS and EMPLOYEES tables:

```
SQL> connect hr/hr
Connected.
SQL> select d.department_name, e.last_name
  2    from departments d inner join employees e
  3      on d.department_id = e.department_id
  4    where d.department_id = 1234
  5  /

no rows selected
```

4. Here we see that the rows inserted in our first session are not visible, since we did not commit them. Let's make the changes permanent and end our transaction using a COMMIT statement in our first session:

```
SQL> commit;

Commit complete.
```

5. Now if we run the query again in the second session, it will be successful:

```
SQL> select d.department_name, e.last_name
  2    from departments d inner join employees e
  3      on d.department_id = e.department_id
  4    where d.department_id = 1234
  5  /

DEPARTMENT_NAME                 LAST_NAME
------------------------------  -------------------------
Data Center Operations          Lawson
Data Center Operations          Wells
Data Center Operations          Bliss
```

How It Works

Prior to committing the transaction in our first session, we were unable to see the changes made to the DEPARTMENTS and EMPLOYEES tables in the second session. Once we finished the transaction by issuing a COMMIT statement in our first session, then we were able to see the data immediately in our second session.

Rollback

Rolling transactions back is very similar, and can be demonstrated very easily using a single session in the database. Let's begin by deleting some of the rows out of the EMPLOYEES table:

```
SQL> delete
  2     from employees
  3     where department_id = 1234;

3 rows deleted.
```

Now the rows have been deleted. If we look for the employee named Lawson who was assigned to DEPARTMENT_ID 1234, we can see that row was one of the three deleted:

```
SQL> select employee_id, last_name, email
  2     from employees
  3     where last_name = 'Lawson'
  4  /

no rows selected
```

Now let's issue a ROLLBACK. Performing the same query now yields a result for Lawson:

```
SQL> rollback;

Rollback complete.

SQL> select employee_id, last_name, email
  2     from employees
  3     where last_name = 'Lawson'
  4  /

EMPLOYEE_ID LAST_NAME                      EMAIL
----------- ------------------------------ --------------------------
     123451 Lawson                         lawson@somegroovycompany.com
```

Summary

In this chapter, you have received an introduction to the use of SQL*Plus to talk to the Oracle database. We also outlined the differences between SQL, PL/SQL, and SQL*Plus. Although you haven't learned any PL/SQL code yet, you should now be able to tell it apart from SQL and the SQL*Plus tool. We discussed how to start up SQL*Plus in command-line mode and in GUI mode, and we briefly looked into connecting to databases over the network using Oracle Net Services.

We discussed using DML to select, insert, update, and delete from the database. We looked at the various parts of a SELECT statement, how to order our query results, and how to filter out rows in our queries. We covered NULL values and what to expect when you encounter them in expressions, conditions and operations of your SQL. We also considered how to use JOINS in order to extend the scope of our queries, to allow for querying data in multiple tables.

Finally, we looked at committing and rolling back our transactions using COMMIT and ROLLBACK. This overview illustrates not only how to save the changes you made to your database, but also how to recover from adverse changes you may make to your database by using the ROLLBACK statement.

The SQL language is constantly changing, and you will find that the more you learn, the more there is to discover! This chapter only represents our first step into the language of SQL. Each of the topics discussed in this introductory chapter will be elaborated upon in other areas of the book. In the next chapter, for instance, we will be learning how to use the Data Definition Language (DDL) to create and manage objects such as users and tables.

Creating and Managing Users and Tables

In order to store and manage data in Oracle efficiently you need to understand the tools at your disposal. You are going to use the database to store your data. This data will be held in tables, and these tables are owned by user accounts. In other words, you need to learn both how to create (and manage) user accounts, and how to create tables to store your data.

To this end we will cover the following in this chapter:

- ❏ Data Definition Language (DDL). This is the language used to create database objects such as user, tables, constraints, and so on. We will briefly discuss how DDL works and how it differs from standard DML.

- ❏ How to create our own user accounts. We will learn the syntax used in creating, altering, and dropping user accounts. We will also take a look at how to modify user accounts once you've created them.

- ❏ The different data types available for use in Oracle tables.

- ❏ How to create tables from scratch, or copy tables that already exist.

- ❏ How to create constraints on tables.

- ❏ How to obtain information about objects in your database by using the data dictionary.

Data Definition Language

DDL is generally used in creating and administering the database. It uses SQL to create objects, configure database security, manipulate statistics, and much, much more.

In the previous chapter, we introduced COMMIT and ROLLBACK. By issuing the COMMIT statement after performing inserts, updates, and deletes in your tables, the modifications are made permanent in your database. The ROLLBACK statement, on the other hand, causes the changes (since your last COMMIT or ROLLBACK) to be lost.

When you submit a DDL statement to the database, an implicit COMMIT statement is generated before and after it is executed (even if the DDL fails). This is because DDL cannot be rolled back, which in turn means that any uncommitted changes made prior to the DDL statement submission can't be rolled back either.

After the DDL has completed (since it can't be rolled back), Oracle calls another implicit COMMIT in order to begin a new transaction for you. To illustrate this, if we submitted the following pseudo code:

```
insert into some_table values (...);
insert into some_table values (...);
insert into some_table values (...);

create table another_table( column1 data type, column2 data type );

insert into another_table values(...);
insert into another_table values(...);
insert into another_table values(...);
```

then in the background, Oracle will do the following for us:

```
insert into some_table values (...);
insert into some_table values (...);
insert into some_table values (...);

commit;
create table another_table( column1 data type, column2 data type );
commit;

insert into another_table values(...);
insert into another_table values(...);
insert into another_table values(...);
```

If the next statement we submitted was a ROLLBACK, the first three records inserted into the SOME_TABLE table would still be there. The three records inserted into ANOTHER_TABLE would be lost.

There are many SQL reserved words used in DDL, but we will focus here simply on the three most frequently used standard statements, namely CREATE, ALTER, and DROP, which allow you to create, alter and drop database objects.

Valid Oracle Identifiers

Although there are no rules about how appropriate a name is for objects in the database, you should strive to choose meaningful names. Six months after your system is in production, you will typically have to dig back into your database schema to fix a bug or tune part of the application. Using good naming conventions from the beginning will help you remember what objects you are looking at, what they're for, and why they exist.

Aside from simply using common sense and meaningful names for your objects, there are rules Oracle enforces for naming objects. For a name to be considered a **valid Oracle identifier** it must adhere to the following rules:

- ❏ It cannot be a reserved word

- ❏ It must be between 1 and 30 characters. The exceptions to this are database names (8 characters max) and database links (128 characters max)

- ❏ It must begin with an alphabetical character from your database character set

- ❏ It can only contain alphabetical characters from your database character set, along with the following characters: # $ _ (In addition, database link names can contain at signs '@' and periods '.')

- ❏ It cannot contain (single or double) quotation marks

> **Another way to name a column (or almost any Oracle database object, for that matter) is to surround the name with double quotes. Double quotes lets you use any characters you want for a name. Even Oracle reserved words such as SELECT, TABLE, DELETE, etc. can be used for objects if they are within double quotes.**

Some valid Oracle identifiers include:

- ❏ EMP

- ❏ DEPT

- ❏ MY_COLUMN_NAME

- ❏ SomeColumn

- ❏ "3D TABLE"

- ❏ "TRUNCATE"

- ❏ " "

Whereas the following list of identifiers are invalid:

- ❏ %EMP (cannot contain % character)

- ❏ SELECT (Oracle reserved word)

- ❏ THIS_NAME_IS_LONGER_THAN_30_CHARACTERS

- ❏ 1STCOLUMN (cannot begin with a number)

- ❏ SEAN'S_TABLE (cannot contain quotes)

Tablespaces

Before we begin looking into creating user accounts and tables in our database, we first need to understand that, in Oracle, databases are divided into separate units of storage known as **tablespaces**. These tablespaces are where tables, indexes and other database objects that consume disk space are stored. For instance, in older Oracle (prior to 9*i*) database installations, there is a tablespace named USERS used to store user SCOTT's data. In Oracle 9*i*, the EXAMPLE tablespace is used to store the sample schemas' data. Tablespaces are discussed in more detail in Chapter 5.

Users

To work with Oracle you'll want to create your own user accounts for your data. It is important that you do so, since you should avoid using either the SYS and SYSTEM accounts supplied by Oracle, or the sample user accounts, such as SCOTT and HR, which we used in the previous chapter. The former are administrative accounts, while the latter are demonstration accounts, which should be used with their own database objects only.

Creating Users

One of the things you will need throughout this chapter and the rest of the book is an account with sufficient privileges to take full advantage of all the features we discuss. We will create this user account here (giving it the name ORACLE_ADMIN) and grant it the DBA role by using the following DDL:

```
SQL> connect system/manager
Connected.
SQL> create user oracle_admin
  2   identified by oracle_admin
  3   /

User created.

SQL> grant create session, dba
  2   to oracle_admin;

Grant succeeded.
```

Let's break this down and see what is going on. To create the user account we need to connect to the database as the user SYSTEM, and issue the CREATE statement:

```
SQL> connect system/manager
Connected.
SQL> create user oracle_admin
  2   identified by oracle_admin
```

The user created here is named ORACLE_ADMIN, and we use the clause IDENTIFIED BY <identifier> to indicate the password for the user account (in this case it is also ORACLE_ADMIN). It also sets up default and temporary tablespaces for the account, as we'll look at later in this chapter. Next, we'll grant this user account the appropriate privileges to connect to the database.

```
SQL> grant create session, dba
  2   to oracle_admin;

Grant succeeded.
```

CREATE_SESSION is a system privilege that gives the user the ability to connect to the database. DBA is a role that has over 120 system privileges, and so will allow you to do just about anything in the database that needs to be done.

> The **DBA** role gives a user account full control of the database. Although this kind of power is absolutely necessary when administering a database, it is also very dangerous in the hands of the wrong user. Be very careful when granting this role to users. Remember, it is very easy to make a mistake that can corrupt your database to the point where the only way to fix it is to restore from backups!

For more information about privileges, roles and security with user accounts, see Chapter 13.

There are many other clauses in the CREATE USER statement that can be used to modify properties of the user account. Most attributes have default values and so do not need to be explicitly assigned unless they don't suit your requirements.

Some of the options available when creating a USER are as follows:

❑ DEFAULT TABLESPACE. Unless otherwise specified, objects created by a user will be stored in their user's **default** tablespace. If not specified explicitly, this defaults to SYSTEM.

❑ TEMPORARY TABLESPACE. Temporary segments, such as space needed for sorts in queries, are allocated in a user's temporary tablespace. Up until Oracle 9*i*, this defaulted to the SYSTEM tablespace. In Oracle 9*i*, the default temporary tablespace is TEMP.

❑ QUOTA. Users are given quotas on the tablespaces in which they store data. This is the maximum amount of space the user can allocate in a tablespace.

❑ PASSWORD EXPIRE. Using this clause will mean that the user has to change their password on the first occasion that they log in.

Altering Users

When administering Oracle databases, there will be a variety of reasons for you to modify user accounts. Some of the more common ones are listed here:

❑ Resetting a user password

❑ Locking and unlocking accounts

❑ Modifying the user's default or temporary tablespace

❑ Modifying tablespace quotas

We will take a look in this section at how we can do this.

Resetting Passwords

While only administrative accounts can reset passwords for other user accounts, any user has the ability to change their own password. So, for example, if we create a user account named HR_AUDIT:

```
SQL> create user hr_audit
  2  identified by hr_audit
  3  /
```

```
User created.
SQL> grant create session, resource
  2  to hr_audit
  3  /

Grant succeeded.
```

Then we can use the ALTER USER command, in conjunction with an IDENTIFIED BY clause to change the password for user HR_AUDIT from HR_AUDIT to ORACLE.

```
SQL> connect hr_audit/hr_audit
Connected.
SQL> alter user hr_audit
  2  identified by oracle;

User altered.
```

Locking and Unlocking Accounts

In Oracle, user accounts can be locked so that they cannot be used. In Oracle 9*i*, a number of user accounts are created by default during the installation of a database, and these user accounts have default passwords. This was identified as a security risk, so the Oracle developers responded by locking all these accounts.

If, for example, we try to connect to the OE account (OE is one of the sample schemas, alongside SCOTT and HR, which we'll see more of in the next chapter), we will receive the following message:

```
SQL> connect oe/oe
ERROR:
ORA-28000: the account is locked


Warning: You are no longer connected to ORACLE.
```

To lock and unlock accounts we use the using the following syntax:

```
ALTER USER <username> ACCOUNT [LOCK|UNLOCK];
```

Since we need to be able to use the OE account we'll now unlock it. To do this we connect to the database using either the account ORACLE_ADMIN we created earlier, or another privileged user account, and issue the following:

```
SQL> connect oracle_admin/oracle_admin
Connected.
SQL> alter user oe account unlock;

User altered.

SQL> connect oe/oe
Connected.
```

As you can see, the OE account is now unlocked and we can use it to connect to the database.

Modifying Tablespace Settings

If we consider the HR_AUDIT account that we altered the password of in the previous section, we know that by default it will use the tablespaces SYSTEM and TEMP (for any temporary data). This is not to be recommended, so we need to take a look at how we can change these default settings.

Let's now take a look at what tablespaces exist in our database by connecting as user ORACLE_ADMIN and querying the DBA_TABLESPACES view.

Views are simply stored queries, which we will look in detail at in Chapter 14. Don't worry about the syntax here; it is the resulting list of tablespaces which we are interested in.

```
SQL> select tablespace_name, contents
  2    from dba_tablespaces
  3    order by tablespace_name
  4  /

TABLESPACE_NAME                     CONTENTS
----------------------------------  ---------
CWMLITE                             PERMANENT
DRSYS                               PERMANENT
EXAMPLE                             PERMANENT
INDX                                PERMANENT
P1                                  PERMANENT
P2                                  PERMANENT
P3                                  PERMANENT
P4                                  PERMANENT
SYSTEM                              PERMANENT
TEMP                                TEMPORARY
TOOLS                               PERMANENT
UNDOTBS                             UNDO
USERS                               PERMANENT

13 rows selected.
```

As we can see, there is a USERS tablespace, which we can use instead of the SYSTEM tablespace. Let's modify the HR_AUDIT account we created earlier to use USERS as the default tablespace:

```
SQL> alter user hr_audit
  2    default tablespace users
  3    temporary tablespace temp;

User altered.
```

This sets the default tablespace to USERS, and the temporary tablespace to TEMP.

Modifying Tablespace Quotas

Now that we have the user HR_AUDIT, we should be able to create many different types of objects. However, although HR_AUDIT has been granted the ability to create objects, it has not been granted the privilege to take up space in the USERS tablespace (the tablespace we assigned to the user in the previous example). If we try to create a table, for example, we will receive the following error message:

87

```
SQL> create table retired_employees(
  2      employee_id number,
  3      last_name   varchar2(30)
  4  )
  5  /
create table retired_employees(
*
ERROR at line 1:
ORA-01950: no privileges on tablespace 'USERS'
```

Don't worry about the CREATE TABLE syntax for now, since we'll discuss it in greater detail later in the chapter.

In order to create a table, the HR_AUDIT user account must be granted a QUOTA in the USERS tablespace. While we are granting this quota, we'll also grant some space in the TEMP tablespace, and revoke any access to the SYSTEM tablespace. We can do this using a single ALTER USER statement:

```
SQL> connect oracle_dba/oracle_dba
Connected.
SQL> alter user hr_audit
  2  quota unlimited on users
  3  quota 10M on temp
  4  quota 0M on system
  5  /

User altered.
```

The syntax here is fairly straightforward. UNLIMITED is a keyword indicating that the user can store data in the USERS tablespace until it is entirely full. We set the upper limit of storage space in the TEMP tablespace to be 10M (10 Megabytes) and 0M in the SYSTEM tablespace.

Dropping Users

To delete user accounts we simply use the DROP USER command. There is an optional keyword CASCADE, which if used at the end of the DROP USER command, lets Oracle know that all the user's objects (tables, views, and procedural code for example) should be dropped before the user is removed from the database. Not only will this ensure that Oracle drops all the user's objects, but it will also drop any constraints in other user's schemas that refer to the dropped user's tables, and invalidate any objects owned by other users that reference the dropped user's objects.

Note that Oracle does not drop roles created by the user.

Try it Out – Creating and Dropping Users

1. First, we will connect to the database using our ORACLE_ADMIN account, and create a new user named DROPME, with the password DOOMED. We will set the default tablespace to be the USERS tablespace with an UNLIMITED quota. We will then grant DROPME the privilege to create tables:

```
SQL> connect oracle_admin/oracle_admin
Connected.
SQL> create user dropme
  2  identified by doomed
  3  default tablespace users
  4  temporary tablespace temp
  5  quota unlimited on users
  6  /

User created.

SQL> grant create session, create table
  2  to dropme
  3  /

Grant succeeded.
```

2. Now connect to the database as the DROPME user and create a simple table as follows:

```
SQL> connect dropme/doomed
Connected.

SQL> create table employees_backup (
  2      employee_id number,
  3      last_name    varchar2(30),
  4      email        varchar2(100)
  5  )
  6  /

Table created.
```

3. Now we'll use our ORACLE_ADMIN account (which has the DROP USER privilege) to drop the user DROPME:

```
SQL> connect oracle_admin/oracle_admin
Connected.
SQL> drop user dropme;
drop user dropme
*
ERROR at line 1:
ORA-01922: CASCADE must be specified to drop 'DROPME'
```

4. The problem here is that the DROPME user owns a table. To get around this we use the CASCADE keyword as follows:

89

```
SQL> drop user dropme cascade;

User dropped.
```

How It Works

In the first step we create the user account DROPME, using syntax which we have already seen. We also grant the CREATE TABLE privilege to DROPME by issuing the command:

```
SQL> grant create session, create table
  2  to dropme
```

In the second step we create a table as user DROPME. We'll look at this syntax in more detail in the next section.

When we then try and drop the user DROPME, we get an error message:

```
SQL> drop user dropme;
drop user dropme
*
ERROR at line 1:
ORA-01922: CASCADE must be specified to drop 'DROPME'
```

The problem here is that DROPME owns the table EMPLOYEES_BACKUP, which we created in step 2. To get around this we need to use the CASCADE clause:

```
SQL> drop user dropme cascade;

User dropped.
```

Oracle Data Types

Having learned how to create, alter, and drop user accounts in our database, let's now look at creating tables in our database. The first thing we need to do is to look at the basic data types available to us in Oracle. What we look at here is not an exhaustive listing, and you will see some of the more advanced data types (such as user-defined types and collections of values) in later chapters.

Number Types

Number types are used for storing numeric data such as integers, floating point values, and real numbers. There are various number types we need to consider here. NUMBER data types in Oracle have a **precision** and a **scale**. The precision is the total number of digits in the number, and can be anything between one and thirty-eight digits. The scale ranges from -84 to 127, and describes the number of digits to the right of the decimal point in any given number.

When creating a table you declare a NUMBER column, using the following syntax:

```
<column_name> NUMBER ( precision [ , scale ] )
```

The following are some examples of NUMBER column declarations:

❑ NUMBER. A number with no precision or scale is NUMBER(38). This is the maximum size for a number column.

❑ NUMBER(9,2). This is a number that is nine digits long, which allows two digits to the right hand side of the decimal point. Valid numbers include 1, 123456, 1234567.89, but not 12345678 (eight digits to left of decimal, only seven possible).

❑ NUMBER(3). This is an integer with 3 digits of precision.

❑ NUMBER(4,10). Describes a very small number (such as .0000001234). When the scale is greater than the precision, there must be (scale – precision) zeros before a number is found. For instance, a number of .000001 would be too large for this data type declaration.

Character Types

Character types are used to declare columns containing alphanumeric data. We'll take a look at the different character types available to us, and then discuss some of the rules governing how they relate to one another.

CHAR

The CHAR data type is used for storing **fixed-length** character strings. Once a CHAR column is defined, it will always be the length you specified in the size of the declaration. Assigning values of shorter length to the column will cause SQL to pad the remaining length with spaces. For instance:

```
SQL> create table authorized_blends(
  2      bean_name char(50)
  3  );

Table created.

SQL> insert into authorized_blends values( 'Papua New Guinea' );

1 row created.

SQL> insert into authorized_blends values( 'Ethiopia' );

1 row created.

SQL> insert into authorized_blends values( 'Sumatra' );

1 row created.

SQL> select bean_name, length( bean_name )
  2      from authorized_blends
  3  /

BEAN_NAME                                          LENGTH(BEAN_NAME)
-------------------------------------------------- -----------------
```

91

```
Papua New Guinea                                              50
Ethiopia                                                     50
Sumatra                                                      50
```

Here we create a table called `AUTHORIZED_BLENDS` and insert three values into a column named `BEAN_NAME`. Even though we inserted three different types of coffee, with three different lengths, when we select the `LENGTH` of the column we find that every row is the same length. This is because each row has been padded out to 50 characters in length. As a result, instead of storing `Sumatra` (7 characters) we store `Sumatra`

(50 characters).

`CHAR` columns have a default size of 1 byte, and a maximum size of 2000 bytes. `CHAR` columns are created using the following syntax:

```
<column_name> CHAR [ (size) ]     <--- prior to Oracle 9i
<column_name> CHAR [ (size [CHAR | BYTE])] <--- Oracle 9i and beyond
```

We will discuss the difference between these two `CHAR` data type declarations in the section entitled Length Semantics opposite.

NCHAR

`NCHAR` data types store fixed-length character data much the same way as the `CHAR` data type does, above. The difference between the two involves the way in which `NCHAR` data is stored in the database.

Prior to Oracle 9*i*, `NCHAR` data types were used to store data in the database's national character set. This character set enabled developers and administrators to extend the standard database character set, in order to store data in languages and character sets other than English. If the database's national character set was a fixed width character set (where all the characters are of a certain, known width), then the `NCHAR` size specified was the number of bytes the column could contain. If the national character set was a variable length, the column's size was specified in characters, determining the number of characters that could be contained in the column.

In Oracle 9*i*, the `NCHAR` data type has been changed to be a Unicode-only data type. Since Unicode character sets are variable length, the size of `NCHAR` columns in Oracle 9*i* always specifies the number of characters that can be stored, rather than the number of bytes of data that can be consumed by the column. The maximum size of an `NCHAR` column is 2000 bytes.

VARCHAR2

The `VARCHAR2` data type is much the same as the `CHAR` type, the difference between the two being that declarations of type `VARCHAR2` are of variable length, not fixed. When columns are declared of `VARCHAR2` type, they will only be as long as the value that is assigned. Inserting values with a length less than that prescribed by the column definition will *not* cause values to be padded with spaces, and therefore `VARCHAR2`s are used in place of `CHAR` data types on almost all occasions.

When declaring a variable of type `VARCHAR2`, you must specify its size. This is not optional. `VARCHAR2` columns have a maximum size of 4000 bytes. Use the following syntax to create `VARCHAR2` columns:

```
<column_name> VARCHAR2 (size)         <--- prior to Oracle 9i
<column_name> VARCHAR2 (size [CHAR | BYTE] ) <--- Oracle 9i and beyond
```

We will discuss the difference between these two CHAR data type declarations in the section entitled Length Semantics, below.

NVARCHAR2

NVARCHAR2 columns store variable-length character-based data and work in much the same way as the VARCHAR2 data type. The key difference between them is the way in which NVARCHAR data is stored in the database.

As we said before, prior to Oracle 9*i*, NVARCHAR data types were used to store data in the database's national character set. If the database's national character set was a fixed width character set, the NVARCHAR size specified was the number of bytes the column could contain. If the national character set was a variable length, the column's size was specified in characters, which specified the number of characters that could be contained in the column.

In Oracle 9*i*, the NVARCHAR data type can be one of two Unicode data types AL16UTF16 or UTF8. Since Unicode character sets are variable length, the size of NVARCHAR columns in Oracle 9*i* always specifies the number of characters than can be stored, not the number of bytes of data that can be consumed by the column.

Length Semantics

Another important point to note here is that Oracle does not automatically take into account multibyte character sets. Therefore, if you declare a variable or constant of CHAR data type, and you are using a multibyte character set in your database, you may encounter a numeric value error, string too large error because you are trying to put too much data in your column. This is because characters in a multibyte character set take up more than one byte, and the column will only hold the number of bytes used in the data type declaration.

Prior to Oracle 9*i*, the only way to prevent this was to use the largest amount of data that you could find in one character of a multibyte character set, and multiply this by the length you wanted to allow in your column. For a column of CHAR(20), this would mean you would declare a CHAR(120), since some characters are represented with as many as 6 bytes in UTF8) This is extremely problematic, however, because anybody inserting data into the column might believe they have been afforded space for 120 characters instead of twenty.

To avoid this problem in Oracle 9*i*, the words BYTE or CHAR can be appended to the size of the column to tell Oracle how to interpret the number. BYTE is the same as the default data type declaration. A size of (20 BYTE) means 'store twenty bytes of data in this column'. We have seen however, that a user may not be able to store 20 characters in this column. Instead, the size can be (20 CHAR) which means 'store 20 characters of data in this database's current character set for this column'. In our previous example we could have issued the following:

```
SQL> create table authorized_blends(
  2    bean_name char(50 char)
  3  );

Table created.
```

> Note that Oracle recommends against using these type conventions in your column's data type declarations. Instead, you and/or your team should decide on whether to use **BYTE** or **CHAR** length semantics for all of your **CHAR** and **VARCHAR2** columns. Once this has been decided, the database parameter **NLS_LENGTH_SEMANTICS** should be set with the appropriate value. You should consult a database administrator to get this done.

RAW

The RAW data type is similar to VARCHAR2, though RAW columns are used to store variable length binary data instead of character data. The maximum length of a RAW column is 2000 bytes. RAWs are declared using a size in the same way CHAR and VARCHAR2 columns are, but there is no consideration for BYTE or CHAR. This is because RAW columns do not store character data, and therefore the size is always the number of bytes that can be contained in the column.

LONG and LONG RAW

LONG and LONG RAW are provided for backwards compatibility with Oracle 7.x and should not be used in Oracle 8 or higher databases. Oracle offers the LOB data types, introduced in Oracle 8, as an alternative.

The LONG data type is used for storing large amounts of variable-length character data in a single column. LONG columns can be up to 2 gigabytes in size. In Oracle 8, this was replaced by the data type CLOB or NCLOB.

LONG RAW data types are just like the name describes... a RAW data type that can be much larger than 2000 bytes. When declaring LONG RAW columns, the size is not specified. Instead, LONG RAW columns can contain up to 2 gigabytes of binary data or bytes. In Oracle 8, administrators are advised to use the BLOB or BFILE data type.

Large Objects

Large Objects, or LOBs, were introduced in Oracle 8. They provide a more flexible storage mechanism for large amounts of data, both binary and character-based than the previous LONG RAW data type afforded. In particular:

- ❑ LOBs have a number of options when it comes to storing the physical data in the database. You can store the LOB inline, which means in the same physical block(s) as the rest of the data in the column's table. You can also store the LOB out-of-line, which means in a different area on disk. This option is useful when the database reads data from the table since, if the LOB column is not one of those needing to be queried, it is not included in the read. Finally, you can store the LOB outside of the database in a file known as a BFILE.

- ❑ LOBs can be used in Oracle object types. For developers using object types to encapsulate functionality and provide an object-oriented interface to their data and functionality, this is extremely important.

- ❑ LOBs support piecewise access to data. This means you have random access to data in a LOB, instead of having to update the entire column every time it needs to be modified (which can cause a large amount of unnecessary I/O).

❑ Each type of LOB can store 4 gigabytes of data.

❑ Functionality for working with LOBs is provided in the Oracle-supplied PL/SQL package DBMS_LOB. You can find more about DBMS_LOB in Appendix B.

LOB Types

There are a few different types of LOBs:

❑ **Binary Large Objects** (BLOBs). BLOBs are used to store binary data. A typical BLOB might contain images, audio files, video, etc.

❑ **Character Large Objects** (CLOBs). CLOBs are used for storing large amounts of character data. CLOBs are commonly used in place of the VARCHAR2 column to store text in applications when the data could be greater than 4,000 characters (the upper limit of a VARCHAR2 column).

❑ **National Character Large Objects** (NCLOBs). As with NCHAR and NVARCHAR data types, NCLOBs store data in the national character set of the database.

❑ **Binary Files** (BFILEs). BFILE columns contain pointers to large binary files stored on the file system of the database server. Oracle offers built-in functionality to enable users to read from BFILEs.

LOB Locators

A LOB Locator is the object that is physically stored in a table's record when the LOB is stored out-of-line or in a BFILE. It is basically a pointer to the real LOB that tells Oracle how to retrieve it at need. This avoids Oracle having to wade through hundreds of records with LOBs stored in the table's blocks, when performing a full table scan. With a LOB locator stored in the table instead of the actual data, Oracle reads the table's blocks and the LOB locator's impact is minimal.

DATES and TIMES

Data types related to a point in time, such as 12:00 am January 1st 1990 or May 18th 1971 are referred to as **datetimes**. Periods of time, such as two hours or one month, are commonly referred to as **intervals**. Oracle provides the following classes of these data types:

❑ DATE

❑ TIMESTAMP *

❑ TIMESTAMP WITH TIME ZONE *

❑ TIMESTAMP WITH LOCAL TIME ZONE *

❑ INTERVAL YEAR TO MONTH *

❑ INTERVAL DAY TO SECOND *

*Those marked with an * are available in Oracle 9i only*

Oracle provides quite a bit of native functionality (such as time zone resolution and date interval arithmetic).

Each of the datetime and interval data types is broken down into individual fields. The following table outlines valid values for each of these fields, which should help explain the use of particular data types:

Datetime field	Datetime values	Interval values
YEAR	-4712 to 9999 (but not zero)	Any positive or negative integer
MONTH	1 to 12	0 to 11
DAY	1 to 31	Any positive or negative integer
HOUR	0 to 23	0 to 23
MINUTE	0 to 59	0 to 59
SECOND	0 to 59.999999999	0 to 59.999999999
TIMEZONE HOUR	-12 to 13	
TIMEZONE MINUTE	0 to 59	

DATE

The DATE data type stores date and time information, and remains the only date-related data type in Oracle 8*i* and below. There are a variety of ways to create a date value in Oracle. In Oracle 8*i*, the functions TO_DATE and SYSDATE create date values. TO_DATE takes a string literal and converts it to a date value. SYSDATE creates a date value representing the point in time that the SYSDATE function was called (on the host server). As an example of using these functions, consider the following:

```
SQL> connect hr_audit/hr_audit
Connected.
SQL> create table company_events (
  2     event_name    varchar2( 100 ),
  3     event_date    date )
  4  /

Table created.

SQL> insert into company_events ( event_name, event_date )
  2  values ( 'Oracle Open World', TO_DATE( '2-DEC-2001', 'DD-MON-YYYY' ) )
  3  /

1 row created.

SQL> insert into company_events ( event_name, event_date )
  2  values ( 'Created DATE Sample code', SYSDATE )
  3  /

1 row created.

SQL> column event_name format a40
SQL> select *
  2     from company_events
  3  /
```

```
EVENT_NAME                                  EVENT_DAT
------------------------------------------  ---------
Oracle Open World                           02-DEC-01
Created DATE Sample code                     11-OCT-01
```

Here we create a table called COMPANY_EVENTS with two columns, EVENT_NAME and EVENT_DATE. We then insert data into these columns:

```
SQL> insert into company_events ( event_name, event_date )
  2  values ( 'Oracle Open World', TO_DATE( '2-DEC-2001', 'DD-MON-YYYY' ) )
  3  /

1 row created.

SQL> insert into company_events ( event_name, event_date )
  2  values ( 'Created DATE Sample code', SYSDATE )
  3  /

1 row created.
```

In the first INSERT we use the TO_DATE function to format the entry 2-DEC-2001 as 02-DEC-2001. In the second insert we use the SYSDATE function to return the time at which we carried out the modifications to the COMPANY_EVENTS table. A SELECT for all rows in the table shows us that this formatting was successful.

The format mask in the TO_DATE function is optional. The only proviso here is that the literal date value must be in the correct format for the database in order for the function to succeed. The default date formats are as follows:

❑ Oracle 9*i*: DD-MON-RR

❑ Oracle 8.0 and up: DD-MON-RR

❑ Oracle 7.3 and earlier: DD-MON-YY

The RR in the preceding date formats was designed to avoid some of the problems associated with the Year 2000 problem. When a 2 digit year number is passed to Oracle in this format, it will return a year in the next century if the year is less than 50 and the last 2 digits of the current year are greater than or equal to 50 or return a year in the preceding century if the year is greater than or equal to 50 and the last 2 digits of the current year are less than 50.

Using the administrative account ORACLE_ADMIN, we can determine the default date format of our database using the SHOW PARAMETERS SQL*Plus command, as follows:

```
SQL> connect oracle_admin/oracle_admin
Connected.
SQL> show parameters nls_date_format

NAME                                 TYPE        VALUE
------------------------------------ ----------- ----------------------------
nls_date_format                      string
```

In the case where there is no value for NLS_DATE_FORMAT, this means it is undefined in the initialization parameter file for the database, and the default setting will be used as outlined in the bulleted list above.

When dealing with date formats in Oracle tools running on a Windows client, you need to remember that Oracle usually sets the NLS_LANG setting in the registry of the client machine. If a client tool sets the NLS_LANG setting, then all NLS_* parameters on the server machine are ignored. This means the NLS_DATE_FORMAT reported in SQL*Plus will not be used by the client tool, and calling the TO_DATE function, without explicitly using a date format string, will fail.

We should also note in passing that in Oracle 9*i* you can specify a date value using a date literal with the DATE keyword. This is accomplished using the following syntax:

```
SQL> insert into company_events ( event_name, event_date )
  2  values ( 'Created an Oracle 9i DATE value', DATE '2001-10-11' )
  3  /

1 row created.

SQL> select *
  2    from company_events
  3  /

EVENT_NAME                               EVENT_DAT
---------------------------------------- ---------
Oracle Open World                        02-DEC-01
Created DATE Sample code                  19-JAN-02
Inserted ANOTHER DATE Sample              19-JAN-02
Created an Oracle 9i DATE value           11-OCT-01
```

However, using the DATE method for creating date values limits you to the day, month and year fields (you can't specify other values, there are no hours, minutes, or seconds). The literal date string must be in the YYYY-MM-DD format.

TIMESTAMP

TIMESTAMP is one of the new data types offered in Oracle 9*i*. While similar to DATE, you can specify a precision for the SECONDS field in a TIMESTAMP column (the DATE data type can only store whole seconds). Use the following syntax when declaring columns of TIMESTAMP type:

```
<column_name> TIMESTAMP [ SECONDS_PRECISION ]
```

As an example of this, let's create a table called OTHER_COMPANY_EVENTS that has a DATE column (named EVENT_DATE) and a TIMESTAMP column (named EVENT_TIMESTAMP).

```
SQL> connect oracle_admin/oracle_admin
Connected.

SQL> create table other_company_events (
  2    event_name          varchar2( 100 ),
  3    event_date          date,
```

```
     4     event_timestamp timestamp )
     5  /
Table created.

SQL> insert into other_company_events
     2    ( event_name, event_date, event_timestamp )
     3  values
     4    ( 'Created COMPANY_EVENTS table', sysdate, sysdate )
     5  /

1 row created.
```

Having created the table, and inserted some values into it, let's query the two columns and compare the results:

```
SQL> column event_name      format a28
SQL> column event_date      format a18
SQL> column event_timestamp format a28
SQL> select event_name,
     2          to_char(event_date, 'DD-MON-YY HH24:MI:SS') event_date,
     3          event_timestamp
     4    from other_company_events
     5  /

EVENT_NAME                   EVENT_DATE          EVENT_TIMESTAMP
---------------------------- ------------------- ----------------------------
Created COMPANY_EVENTS table 11-OCT-01 13:31:09  11-OCT-01 01.31.09.000000 PM
```

In this example, we inserted SYSDATE into both columns, EVENT_DATE and EVENT_TIMESTAMP. When we select the data from the table, we can see the TIMESTAMP column has six digits of precision for the SECONDS field, whereas the DATE column does not store fractional seconds.

> *The reason we stored six digits of precision for the seconds field is because six is the default precision of a TIMESTAMP column. Valid values for the SECONDS precision are from zero to nine.*

TIMESTAMP WITH TIME ZONE

TIMESTAMP WITH TIME ZONE data types are an extension of the TIMESTAMP data type. When assigning a value to a TIMESTAMP WITH TIME ZONE column, you specify the value for the TIMESTAMP along with an offset that represents the number of hours and minutes between the local time and the Universal Time Coordinated, or **UTC** (formerly known as Greenwich Mean Time, GMT). Use the following syntax when declaring a column of type TIMESTAMP WITH TIME ZONE:

```
<column_name> TIMESTAMP [ SECONDS_PRECISION ] WITH TIME ZONE
```

Time zone programming is greatly simplified with this data type. When evaluating two variables of this type, the difference in time zones is automatically managed by Oracle.

In the following example, we have a system that manages conference call schedules. Since the conference calls happen all around the world, we need an efficient way for determining when the calls are happening according to our local time. Currently, there are three calls scheduled for December 01:

❑   Sales Strategy Call in Washington D.C. at 3:00pm

❑   Product Features in San Francisco at 4:00pm

❑   Football Highlights in London at 8:00pm (at the pub)

Try It Out – Using TIMESTAMP WITH TIME ZONE

1.   We begin by creating a table named CONFERENCE_CALLS, and insert the relevant information regarding our three calls:

```
SQL> create table conference_calls (
  2     title   varchar2(100),
  3     phone   varchar2(20),
  4     place   varchar2(100),
  5     starts  timestamp with time zone )
  6  /

Table created.

SQL> insert into conference_calls (title, phone, place, starts)
  2   values ('Sales Strategy', '212.123.4567', 'Washington',
  3          TIMESTAMP '2001-12-01 15:00:00.000000 EST')
  4  /

1 row created.

SQL> insert into conference_calls (title, phone, place, starts)
  2   values ('Product Features', '650.123.4567', 'San Francisco',
  3          TIMESTAMP '2001-12-01 17:00:00.000000 PST')
  4  /

1 row created.

SQL> insert into conference_calls (title, phone, place, starts)
  2   values ('Football Highlights', '44 1234 5678', 'London',
  3          TIMESTAMP '2001-12-01 20:00:00.000000 GMT')
  4  /

1 row created.
```

2.   Let's assume that we live in Columbus Ohio. We determine what time zone we are in by issuing the following query:

```
SQL> select dbtimezone from dual;

DBTIME
------
-05:00
```

3.   Now we issue a query which asks for all the calls which start at 15:00 (or 3:00pm) Columbus Ohio time:

```
SQL> select title, phone
  2    from conference_calls
  3    where starts = TIMESTAMP '2001-12-01 15:00:00.000000 -5:00'
  4  /

TITLE                    PHONE
------------------------  --------------------
Sales Strategy           212.123.4567
Football Highlights      44 1234 5678
```

How It Works

To determine which time zone we are in we use the built-in SQL function DBTIMEZONE:

```
SQL> select dbtimezone from dual;
```

For the person who lives in Columbus Ohio the time zone is -05:00. To find out the call we need to be on, we issue the following query which asks for all the calls taking place at 15:00 (or 3:00pm) Columbus Ohio time:

```
SQL> select title, phone
  2    from conference_calls
  3    where starts = TIMESTAMP '2001-12-01 15:00:00.000000 -5:00'
```

TIMESTAMP WITH LOCAL TIME ZONE

TIMESTAMP WITH LOCAL TIME ZONE is much the same as a TIMESTAMP WITH TIME ZONE, though in the case of the former the time zone data is stored in the column according to your session time zone. The following syntax is used to declare a column of type TIMESTAMP WITH LOCAL TIME ZONE:

```
<column_name> TIMESTAMP [ SECONDS_PRECISION ] WITH LOCAL TIME ZONE
```

Using the same values we inserted in the last example, let's create a new table using a TIMESTAMP WITH TIME ZONE STARTS column.

```
SQL> create table local_conference_calls (
  2    title    varchar2(100),
  3    phone    varchar2(20),
  4    place    varchar2(100),
  5    starts   timestamp with local time zone )
  6  /

Table created.

SQL> insert into local_conference_calls (title, phone, place, starts)
  2  values ('Sales Strategy', '212.123.4567', 'New York',
  3          TIMESTAMP '2001-12-01 15:00:00.000000 EST')
  4  /

1 row created.

SQL> insert into local_conference_calls (title, phone, place, starts)
```

```
   2  values ('Product Features', '650.123.4567', 'San Francisco',
   3          TIMESTAMP '2001-12-01 17:00:00.000000 PST')
   4  /

1 row created.

SQL> insert into local_conference_calls (title, phone, place, starts)
   2  values ('Football Highlights', '44 1234 5678', 'London',
   3          TIMESTAMP '2001-12-01 20:00:00.000000 GMT')
   4  /

1 row created.
```

Then we'll set the time zone for our session using the ALTER SESSION SQL statement. This tells Oracle we are operating from a time zone that might be different from the database's time zone. After this, we can query the CONFERENCE_CALLS table to find out what time each of the calls start, according to our session's time zone rather than the time zones of where the calls are being conducted:

```
SQL> alter session set time_zone = '-05:00'
   2  /

Session altered.

SQL> column title format a25
SQL> column starts format a30
SQL> select title, starts
   2    from local_conference_calls
   3  /

TITLE                      STARTS
-------------------------  ------------------------------
Sales Strategy             01-DEC-01 03.00.00.000000 PM
Product Features           01-DEC-01 08.00.00.000000 PM
Football Highlights        01-DEC-01 03.00.00.000000 PM
```

Now let's assume we're going to fly to London to be on site for the football highlights conference call. If we still needed to attend the product features conference call, we could set our session to London's time zone and submit the same query to find out when we need to be on the phone according to London's time:

```
SQL> alter session set time_zone = 'GMT'
   2  /

Session altered.

SQL> select title, starts
   2    from local_conference_calls
   3  /

TITLE                      STARTS
-------------------------  ------------------------------
Sales Strategy             01-DEC-01 08.00.00.000000 PM
Product Features           02-DEC-01 01.00.00.000000 AM
Football Highlights        01-DEC-01 08.00.00.000000 PM
```

> Note that in Oracle 8*i*, this time zone translation would have to be done programmatically. In Oracle 9*i*, this is all handled for us behind the scenes.

INTERVAL YEAR TO MONTH

Interval types shed a whole new light on date-related data types. An interval is a measurement of time that can be used in your SQL processing to manipulate datetime or other interval values.

The first kind of interval is INTERVAL YEAR TO MONTH, which is used for storing time periods of months or years. In order to declare a column of this type, use the following syntax:

```
INTERVAL YEAR [ ( YEAR_PRECISION ) ] TO MONTH
```

The YEAR_PRECISION value specifies the number of digits that may be contained in the YEAR field of the interval value. Valid values are from 0 to 9, and the default is 2.

INTERVAL DAY TO SECOND

INTERVAL DAY TO SECOND is the other interval data type in Oracle 9*i*, used for storing days, hours, minutes, and seconds. Use the following syntax for declaring a column of type INTERVAL DAY TO SECOND:

```
INTERVAL DAY [ ( DAY_PRECISION ) ] TO SECOND [ ( SECONDS_PRECISION ) ]
```

The DAY_PRECISION and SECONDS_PRECISION values specify the number of digits that may be contained in the DAY and SECOND fields, respectively. Valid values are from 0 to 9, and the defaults are 2 digits for days and 6 digits for seconds.

In the following example, we are storing the amount of time our employees spend on breaks throughout the day. Whenever a user starts a break, they record the start time. When their break ends, they record the end time. Instead of storing the start time and the end time, we will store the amount of time that was taken in the break. In order to do this, we first create a table to record the information:

```
SQL> create table employee_breaks(
  2     employee_id  number,
  3     break_reason varchar2(100),
  4     break_time   interval day(1) to second(2) );

Table created.
```

Now we'll populate it with some sample data for the types of breaks one might take throughout a work day:

```
SQL> insert into employee_breaks ( employee_id, break_reason, break_time )
  2  values ( 100, 'COFFEE BREAK',
  3          TIMESTAMP '2001-09-03 12:47:00.000000' -
```

103

```
     4                TIMESTAMP '2001-09-03 13:13:00.000000' );

SQL> insert into employee_breaks ( employee_id, break_reason, break_time )
  2  values ( 100, 'BIO BREAK',
  3                TIMESTAMP '2001-09-03 13:35:00.000000' -
  4                TIMESTAMP '2001-09-03 13:39:00.000000' );

SQL> insert into employee_breaks ( employee_id, break_reason, break_time )
  2  values ( 100, 'PUB BREAK',
  3                TIMESTAMP '2001-09-03 16:30:00.000000' -
  4                TIMESTAMP '2001-09-03 17:00:00.000000' );

SQL> insert into employee_breaks ( employee_id, break_reason, break_time )
  2  values ( 100, 'FOOTBALL SCORE UPDATE',
  3                TIMESTAMP '2001-09-03 17:00:00.000000' -
  4                TIMESTAMP '2001-09-03 17:30:00.000000' );

1 row created.
```

Now that we have some sample data in the table, let's run a query to find out what values were stored in our INTERVAL DAY TO SECOND column:

```
SQL> column break_reason format a30
SQL> column break_time format a30
SQL> select employee_id, break_reason, break_time
  2      from employee_breaks;

EMPLOYEE_ID BREAK_REASON                   BREAK_TIME
----------- ------------------------------ ------------------------------
        100 COFFEE BREAK                   -0 00:26:00.00
        100 BIO BREAK                      -0 00:04:00.00
        100 PUB BREAK                      -0 00:30:00.00
        100 FOOTBALL SCORE UPDATE          -0 00:30:00.00
```

In the query results, we can see that employee 100 took a total of 0 days, 0 hours, 26 minutes, and 0 seconds on coffee breaks. Not only that, but they also took 4 minutes for bio breaks, and 60 minutes on pub and football score breaks.

ANSI Data Types

Oracle supports industry standard ANSI data types, as well as IBM DB/2 and SQL/DS data types. This is useful for a number of reasons:

❑ Some database design tools export ANSI-compliant SQL, which can be used by a number of different types of database.

❑ SQL scripts used on other databases can be used in Oracle without needing to be converted to Oracle syntax.

When columns are created using ANSI, IBM DB/2, or SQL/DS data types, these data types are implicitly converted into an appropriate Oracle built-in data type. This is illustrated in the following example (don't worry about the particular data types for now, we'll explain those later in this section):

```
SQL> create table foo (
  2    a    integer,
  3    b    dec( 9, 2 ),
  4    c    character varying( 30 ),
  5    d    national char( 3 )
  6  )
  7  /

Table created.

SQL> describe foo
 Name                           Null?    Type
 ------------------------------ -------- ------------------------
 A                                       NUMBER(38)     <--- was INTEGER
 B                                       NUMBER(9,2)    <--- was DEC
 C                                       VARCHAR2(30)   <--- was CHARACTER VARYING
 D                                       NCHAR(3)       <--- was NATIONAL CHAR
```

So in this example we can see that INTEGERs are converted to NUMBER(38), DEC(9,2) is converted to NUMBER(9,2), and so on. The following chart lists the ANSI, DB/2 and SQL/DS data types that Oracle supports, and the Oracle data type that is used for each:

Numeric Data Type Conversion Chart

Alternative SQL Data type	Oracle Equivalent Data type
NUMERIC (PRECISION, SCALE)	NUMBER (PRECISION, SCALE)
DECIMAL (PRECISION, SCALE)	NUMBER (PRECISION, SCALE)
INTEGER	NUMBER (38)
INT	NUMBER (38)
SMALLINT	NUMBER (38)
FLOAT(b)	NUMBER
DOUBLE PRECISION	NUMBER
REAL	NUMBER

Character Data Type Conversion Chart

Alternative SQL Data type	Oracle Equivalent Data type
CHARACTER (size)	CHAR (size)
CHAR (size)	CHAR (size)
CHARACTER VARYING (size)	VARCHAR (size)
CHAR VARYING (size)	VARCHAR (size)
NATIONAL CHARACTER (size)	NCHAR (size)

Table continued on following page

Alternative SQL Data type	Oracle Equivalent Data type
NATIONAL CHAR (size)	NCHAR (size)
NCHAR (size)	NCHAR (size)
NATIONAL CHARACTER VARYING (size)	NVARCHAR2 (size)
NATIONAL CHAR VARYING (size)	NVARCHAR2 (size)
NCHAR VARYING (size)	NVARCHAR2 (size)

Creating Tables

In order to store and manage data in Oracle, understanding how to maintain tables is paramount. We have already seen some simple CREATE TABLE statements in this chapter to help us understand how to use various data types. Let's take a deeper look at the CREATE TABLE statement and how we can create more useful tables to manage our data.

First of all, for simplicity, we are going to concentrate on heap-organized tables. Oracle has quite a few different types of tables that are used for different reasons. You will see more about other table types, and more complex table properties in Chapter 7.

The syntax for the CREATE TABLE statement is long and complex. Instead of trying to show all the options for the statement here, we will concentrate on some of the most common options for creating tables.

The simplest and most common method for creating tables uses the following syntax:

```
CREATE TABLE [SCHEMA.]<table_name> (
   <column_name> <data type> [DEFAULT <expression>] [<constraint>]
[,<column_name> <data type> [DEFAULT <expression>] [<constraint>]]
[,...]
);
```

Let's break this down further:

- ❑ SCHEMA. This is the schema name, or user name, that the table will belong to.
- ❑ TABLE_NAME. This is the name of the table to be created.
- ❑ COLUMN_NAME. This is the name of the column to be created in this table. Column names must be unique within a single table, but can be the same within different tables.
- ❑ DATA TYPE. As explained earlier in the chapter, each column has its own data type. When a data type is designated for a column, it must have a length and/or precision and scale, depending on which data type is being specified.
- ❑ DEFAULT <expression>. For each column, you may define a default value in the event of no value being given with the column insert statement. <expression> can be a static value or almost any SQL function. For more information about SQL Functions see Appendix A.

❑ CONSTRAINT. You may optionally define constraints on each column you create. These are rules that must be satisfied for the value in the column to be valid. You will learn more about constraints later in this chapter.

As you can see, although this is a very basic explanation of the syntax for the CREATE TABLE statement, it is still somewhat complex. In summary, a simple CREATE TABLE statement consists of two things: the table name and the column list. There can only be one table name, but there can be one or more columns as long as each name is unique for a single table. (Note that the table name and each column name must be a valid Oracle identifier as we discussed earlier.)

Let's illustrate this by creating an EMPLOYEE_HISTORY table, which stores information such as the number of times an employee has worked for the company, the employee's salary history, a reason for the termination, total time of employment with the company across tenures.

Try It Out – Creating an Employee History Table

1. To create the table we issue the following:

```
SQL> create table employee_history
  2  ( employee_id       number(6) not null,
  3    salary            number(8,2),
  4    hire_date         date default sysdate,
  5    termination_date date,
  6    termination_desc varchar2(4000),
  7    constraint emphistory_pk
  8       primary key (employee_id, hire_date)
  9  )
 10  /

Table created.
```

2. Now that our table is created, we can use the SQL*Plus DESCRIBE command to see a description of the table:

```
SQL> describe employee_history
 Name                                      Null?    Type
 ----------------------------------------- -------- ----------------------------
 EMPLOYEE_ID                               NOT NULL NUMBER(6)
 SALARY                                             NUMBER(8,2)
 HIRE_DATE                                 NOT NULL DATE
 TERMINATION_DATE                                   DATE
 TERMINATION_DESC                                   VARCHAR2(4000)
```

How It Works

To better understand the CREATE TABLE statement, we'll break it down a piece at a time and explain exactly what's happening. The first line of the statement specifies the name of the table.

```
SQL> create table employee_history
```

Line 2 creates a column named `EMPLOYEE_ID` of `NUMBER(6)` type. The words `NOT NULL` instruct Oracle to create a constraint on the column which means that it MUST have a value in order for a row to be inserted into this table.

```
2  ( employee_id     number(6) not null,
```

The next line creates the `SALARY` column, which is of `NUMBER(8,2)` type. This means that the maximum salary for any employee in this company is $999,999.99.

```
3    salary          number(8,2),
```

The next two lines create the `HIRE_DATE` and `TERMINATION_DATE` columns, both of which are of `DATE` types. We used the `DATE` type for these columns instead of the `TIMESTAMP` type because there is no reason to store fractional seconds or time zone information. In the `HIRE_DATE` column, we default the value of the column to `SYSDATE`. In other words, if no value is provided for this column in an insert statement then the `SYSDATE` function will be executed and the return value will be placed in the column.

```
4    hire_date       date default sysdate,
5    termination_date date,
```

Line 6 creates the `TERMINATION_DESC` column, which is of `VARCHAR2(4000)` type.

```
6    termination_desc varchar2(4000),
```

The last couple of lines in the `CREATE TABLE` statement define another constraint, namely the **primary key** of the table. The primary key is the column(s) in the table that uniquely identify each row from one another.

```
7    constraint emphistory_pk
8       primary key (employee_id, hire_date)
9  )
10 /
```

There are many more properties which you can specify when using the `CREATE TABLE` statement. We will see more of these in Chapter 7.

Constraints

In Oracle, there are a number of declarative integrity constraints available for ensuring your data is valid and works with the rest of your database. Typically, these are rules that apply to the data such as whether there must be a value for a column, what the valid values are, whether or not the value must be unique amongst the rest of the rows in the table, and so on.

Declarative integrity is the enforcement of rules for columns of a table. Oracle allows you to create and store rules along with the table definition, ensuring that they are enforced for all rows being stored in the table (and as close to the data as possible) .

Referential integrity is a large part of what makes Oracle a relational database. Values in one row refer to records in another row, most commonly in a different table. Basically, a row in table A 'relates' to a row in table B. These rules are a part of the table definition, and when rows are inserted, updated, or deleted, the rules are checked.

In this section, we'll take a look at the different types of constraints and how to manage them in your database. Those constraints we are going to discuss can be created either using the CREATE TABLE command, or after the table is created as a part of an ALTER TABLE command.

Note that there is more detailed information regarding the modification of tables and columns in Chapter 7.

Constraint Syntax

The following syntax provides a generic template for creating constraints on individual columns in the CREATE TABLE statement:

```
CREATE TABLE [SCHEMA.]<table_name> (
  <column_name> <data type> [DEFAULT <expression>] [<constraint>]
[,<column_name> <data type> [DEFAULT <expression>] [<constraint>]]
[,...]
);
```

Constraints can also be added to tables by using the ALTER TABLE statement as follows:

```
ALTER TABLE [SCHEMA.]<table_name>
ADD [CONSTRAINT [<name>]]
    <constraint definition>
);
```

In both the CREATE and ALTER TABLE statements, the [<CONSTRAINT>] syntax looks like this:

```
[CONSTRAINT [<name>]] <constraint definition>
```

Many of the reserved words in the constraint syntax are optional. For instance, the reserved word CONSTRAINT is optional. If you use the reserved word CONSTRAINT, you have the option of naming the constraint. If you do not name the constraint, Oracle will assign a system-generated name to the constraint for you.

<constraint definition> varies depending on the type of constraint you are creating. You will learn how to write the appropriate syntax for each of the constraint types in the sections below.

Primary Keys

The primary key of a table ensures that there are no duplicate rows in a single table. Although you can create a table without primary keys, it is generally regarded as poor practice and should be avoided. Amongst all the rows in a table, the primary key column or collection of columns must be unique and may not be NULL. Primary keys in Oracle can be made up of one or many columns for a single table (a primary key can consist of up to 32 columns).

In the following example, we are going to show what happens when we have a table with no primary key. We will then add a primary key constraint to the table and show how this affects the same operations we carried out previously.

Try It Out – No Primary Key

1. We are going to use the DEPT table that belongs to the SCOTT schema in order to create a table in our HR_AUDIT schema. In order to do this, we need to grant SELECT privilege on the DEPT privilege to HR_AUDIT on the DEPT table. We use the following GRANT statement to accomplish this:

```
SQL> connect scott/tiger
Connected.
SQL> grant select on dept to hr_audit;

Grant succeeded.
```

2. Now we will create a table called ANOTHER_DEPT in the HR_AUDIT schema using a CREATE TABLE AS SELECT statement:

```
SQL> connect hr_audit/hr_audit
Connected.
SQL> create table another_dept
  2  as select *
  3       from scott.dept;

Table created.
```

3. We take a quick check to see that this was successful, by querying for all records in the ANOTHER_DEPT table:

```
SQL> select *
  2    from another_dept;
  3  /

    DEPTNO DNAME          LOC
---------- -------------- --------------
        10 ACCOUNTING     NEW YORK
        20 RESEARCH       DALLAS
        30 SALES          CHICAGO
        40 OPERATIONS     BOSTON

4 rows selected.
```

4. To see whether any constraints have been copied across let's attempt to insert an identical row to one of those already in the table:

```
SQL> insert into another_dept
  2  values (40, 'OPERATIONS', 'BOSTON');

1 row created.
```

5. A quick look at the ANOTHER_DEPT data now reveals that we have duplicate rows for operations in Boston:

```
SQL> select *
  2   from another_dept;

    DEPTNO DNAME          LOC
---------- -------------- --------------
        10 ACCOUNTING     NEW YORK
        20 RESEARCH       DALLAS
        30 SALES          CHICAGO
        40 OPERATIONS     BOSTON
        40 OPERATIONS     BOSTON

5 rows selected.
```

6. To confirm that no constraints exist in the table, let's try adding a row without a DEPTNO or DNAME:

```
SQL> insert into another_dept (loc)
  2   values ('RESTON')
  3   /

1 row created.

SQL> select * from another_dept;

    DEPTNO DNAME          LOC
---------- -------------- --------------
        10 ACCOUNTING     NEW YORK
        20 RESEARCH       DALLAS
        30 SALES          CHICAGO
        40 OPERATIONS     BOSTON
        40 OPERATIONS     BOSTON
                          RESTON

6 rows selected.
```

How It Works

In order to create the table ANOTHER_DEPT we issued the command:

```
SQL> create table another_dept
  2   as select *
  3       from scott.dept;

Table created.
```

This allowed us to create the table by copying all the data from the DEPT table in the SCOTT schema. We then tested whether any constraints were copied across from the DEPT table, by attempting to insert a row identical to an existing one in the ANOTHER_DEPT table:

```
SQL> insert into another_dept
  2   values (40, 'OPERATIONS', 'BOSTON');

1 row created.
```

This is successful, indicating that no constraints currently exist on the ANOTHER_DEPT table. We verify that this is true by inserting a row without a DEPTNO or DNAME. As you can see, at no stage has Oracle reported any problem with our data. However, if we attempt these inserts on a table with a primary key in place, we will see how Oracle manages this type of violation.

Try It Out – With a Primary Key

1. We begin by dropping the ANOTHER_DEPT table and recreating:

```
SQL> drop table another_dept;

Table dropped.

SQL> create table another_dept
  2  as select *
  3        from scott.dept;

Table created.
```

2. Now we create a primary key for the table using the ALTER TABLE statement:

```
SQL> alter table another_dept
  2  add constraint another_dept_pk
  3  primary key( deptno );

Table altered.
```

3. Now, we try to perform the same inserts we used in the last example, to see if the primary key constraint is enforced:

```
SQL> insert into another_dept
  2  values( 40, 'OPERATIONS', 'BOSTON' );
insert into another_dept values( 40, 'OPERATIONS', 'BOSTON' )
*
ERROR at line 1:
ORA-00001: unique constraint (HR_AUDIT.ANOTHER_DEPT_PK) violated

SQL> insert into another_dept (loc)
  2  values( 'RESTON' );
insert into another_dept (loc)
*
ERROR at line 1:
ORA-01400: cannot insert NULL into ("HR_AUDIT"."ANOTHER_DEPT"."DEPTNO")
```

How It Works

We began by recreating the ANOTHER_DEPT table, using the same syntax as in our previous example. We then defined a primary key constraint by issuing:

```
SQL> alter table another_dept
  2    add constraint another_dept_pk
  3    primary key( deptno );

Table altered.
```

In line one of the ALTER TABLE statement, we indicate the table we want to modify. Line two tells Oracle we are adding a constraint to the table named ANOTHER_DEPT_PK. Finally in line 3, we indicate that we are creating a primary key constraint on the DEPTNO column.

Some guidelines to keep in mind when defining primary keys in your tables are as follows:

❑   There may only be one primary key on any given table.

❑   No two rows in a table can have the same primary key.

❑   Primary key columns cannot be NULL.

Foreign Keys

Tables can be related in Oracle through the use of what are known as **foreign key** constraints. A constraint is placed on a column or set of columns in one table (the **child** table). As a part of the constraint definition, the child table's column(s) are defined as referencing a matching column or set of columns in another table (the **parent** table). If a row is inserted into the child table with a non-NULL value in the foreign key column(s), there must be a row in the parent table that has the same value in the referenced column(s). If there is no corresponding row in the parent table, the insert will fail. This establishes a parent-child relationship between the tables, and is the basis for referential integrity in the database.

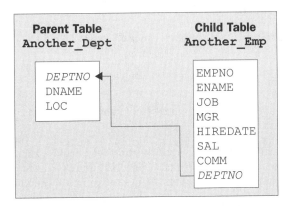

In the diagram above, we see an example of a foreign key relationship. Here we have a table named ANOTHER_EMP with a DEPTNO column. In the ANOTHER_EMP table, if there is a value in the DEPTNO column, there must be a row in the ANOTHER_DEPT table with a corresponding value in the DEPTNO column.

Let's build these tables in the HR_AUDIT schema. To create the ANOTHER_EMP table, we'll use the EMP table in the SCOTT schema:

```
SQL> connect scott/tiger
SQL> grant select on emp to hr_audit;

Grant succeeded.

SQL>connect hr_audit/hr_audit

SQL> create table another_emp as
  2    select *
  3      from scott.emp
  4  /

Table created.
```

Now that the table is created, we need to define the foreign key. This is accomplished using the ALTER TABLE statement, in a similar manner as we created the primary key in the previous section:

```
SQL> alter table another_emp
  2    add constraint another_dept_fk
  3    foreign key (deptno) references another_dept (deptno)
  4  /

Table altered.
```

In line three, we see a little difference from the primary key clause we used earlier. When defining a foreign key, we first identify the column in the child table that the constraint is defined upon, and then we define the table and column that the child table's foreign key column references. In this case, the DEPTNO column in ANOTHER_EMP references the DEPTNO column in ANOTHER_DEPT.

If we try to insert a row into the ANOTHER_EMP with a DEPTNO value that does not exist in the ANOTHER_DEPT table, the insert will fail:

```
SQL> insert into another_emp (empno, ename, deptno, job)
  2    values (8000, 'DILLON', 50, 'TECHGUY')
  3  /
insert into another_emp (empno, ename, deptno)
*
ERROR at line 1:
ORA-02291: integrity constraint (SCOTT.FK_ANOTHER_DEPT) violated - parent key
not found
```

These two tables are a perfect example of a parent-child relationship. Employees belong to departments. In order for an employee to have a department value, that department must exist in the ANOTHER_DEPT table. There are some guidelines to keep in mind when using foreign key constraints:

- ❑ The columns being referenced in the parent table must be a unique key or a primary key (see below for more information about unique keys).

- ❑ Foreign keys can be made up of more than one column. These are known as composite foreign keys. Composite foreign keys have child table columns to match the number of parent table columns.

- ❑ When inserting records into a child table, foreign key columns can have NULL values inserted, regardless of whether the parent table has NULL values in the corresponding column or not. This can cause great confusion and can be avoided by using a NOT NULL constraint on the child table columns.

❑ Foreign keys can be self-referential constraints, meaning they can point back to the same table. An example of this is in the SCOTT schema, in the EMP table. The MGR column is a foreign key to the EMPNO column in the same table.

Unique Constraints

Unique constraints ensure that each row in a table will have a unique value for a given column or set of columns, provided that value is not NULL. As with foreign key constraints, there are some guidelines to follow when using unique constraints:

❑ There may be multiple rows in a table with NULL values in a column that has an associated unique constraint. Since NULL values do not equal another NULL value, rows with NULLs in unique constraint columns are said to be unique.

❑ Unique constraints may be created with multiple columns. These are known as composite unique keys.

❑ Unique keys can be made up of up to 32 columns.

❑ When a unique key constraint is defined, Oracle creates a unique index under the covers to enforce uniqueness. If a unique index already exists for the columns defined in the unique key, Oracle uses the existing index.

You can read more about indexes in Chapter 8.

As an example of a unique constraint, we'll create one for the ANOTHER_EMP table. We'll add a column to the table called SSN, and then add a unique constraint to the table for this column:

```
SQL> alter table another_emp
  2  add (
  3    ssn varchar2( 9 )
  4  );

Table altered.

SQL> alter table another_emp
  2  add constraint another_emp_ssn_uk
  3  unique( ssn );

Table altered.
```

Now if we try to insert the same value in this column for more than one row, we see that the unique key constraint causes an error:

```
SQL> update another_emp set ssn='123456789';
update another_emp set ssn='123456789'
       *
ERROR at line 1:
ORA-00001: unique constraint (HR_AUDIT.ANOTHER_EMP_SSN_UK) violated
```

CHECK Constraints

CHECK constraints are conditions that are evaluated for every row in the table. If the condition evaluates to FALSE for any record in the table at the point when the constraint is created, then its creation will fail.

In the following example, we'll create a CHECK constraint. CHECK constraints can be created as a part of the CREATE TABLE command, or after the table is created as a part of the ALTER TABLE command. To create the CHECK constraint, we'll add a column to the ANOTHER_EMP table named GENDER. The constraint we'll use is that the values must be either MALE or FEMALE.

```
SQL> alter table another_emp
  2    add (
  3      gender   varchar(10));

Table altered.

SQL> alter table another_emp
  2    add constraint ck_gender
  3    check (gender in ('MALE', 'FEMALE'));

Table altered.
```

In order to make the records in the table conform to the constraint, we'll update the GENDER column in each of the rows with either MALE or FEMALE, depending on whether the EMPNO is odd or even. To do this, we use the MOD function, which returns the modulus of two numbers.

```
SQL> update another_emp
  2      set gender = 'MALE'
  3    where mod(empno,2) = 0
  4  /

10 rows updated.

SQL> update another_emp
  2      set gender = 'FEMALE'
  3    where mod(empno,2) = 1
  4  /

4 rows updated.

SQL> select ename, job, gender
  2      from another_emp
  3    order by gender, ename
  4  /

ENAME        JOB         GENDER
----------   ---------   ----------
ALLEN        SALESMAN    FEMALE
KING         PRESIDENT   FEMALE
SMITH        CLERK       FEMALE
WARD         SALESMAN    FEMALE
ADAMS        CLERK       MALE
BLAKE        MANAGER     MALE
CLARK        MANAGER     MALE
FORD         ANALYST     MALE
```

```
JAMES       CLERK       MALE
JONES       MANAGER     MALE
MARTIN      SALESMAN    MALE
MILLER      CLERK       MALE
SCOTT       ANALYST     MALE
TURNER      SALESMAN    MALE

14 rows selected.
```

Now that all of the rows have valid values that conform to the CHECK constraint on the GENDER column, we'll try to insert a record that does not:

```
SQL> insert into another_emp (empno, ename, gender)
  2  values (8001, 'PAT', 'UNKNOWN')
  3  /
insert into another_emp (empno, ename, gender)
*
ERROR at line 1:
ORA-02290: check constraint (SCOTT.CK_GENDER) violated
```

As you can see, since Pat's gender is UNKNOWN, it failed the check constraint. This row cannot be inserted into the ANOTHER_EMP table.

CREATE TABLE AS SELECT

As we saw in a previous example, it is possible to create tables by querying another table and allowing the result set of the query to be materialized into a normal table using the CREATE TABLE <table_name> AS SELECT statement. The ANOTHER_EMP and ANOTHER_DEPT tables in this chapter were both created using the EMP and DEPT tables from the SCOTT schema.

In the next example, we will create a table with no rows, effectively duplicating a table structure without inserting any rows into the table.

Try it Out – Duplicating a Table Structure

1. We'll use the EMPLOYEES table again, and make a copy of the table with a query that returns no rows. In order to accomplish this, use the following syntax:

```
SQL> create table emp_copy as
  2  select *
  3    from scott.emp
  4   where 1 = 0
  5  /

Table created.

SQL> select *
  2    from emp_copy
  3  /

no rows selected
```

How It Works

When we issue the CREATE TABLE command, we tell Oracle to create the table by copying the columns from user SCOTT's EMP table. Once the table is created, Oracle populates the new table with any rows that are returned from the SELECT statement. We used a WHERE clause (WHERE 1=0) in order to ensure that no rows were returned from the query. Since this expression always equals FALSE no rows will be returned.

> Note that when using the CREATE TABLE ... AS SELECT syntax to create tables, supporting objects (such as constraints, indexes, and triggers) are not created as a result of the operation.

The Data Dictionary

Every Oracle database has a data dictionary, and anybody who administers Oracle databases or builds applications using Oracle has heard of (and used) it. The data dictionary is a catalog of your entire Oracle database. As you create users, tables, constraints, and other database objects, Oracle automatically maintains a catalog of the items stored in the database. You can use this catalog to answer some of the following:

❑ What are the names and properties of all the tables I own?

❑ What are the names and attributes of all the tables I have privileges to see?

❑ Retrieve the source code for some stored procedural code I created.

❑ Show me all the data files that store data for a particular tablespace.

❑ List all those objects that are dependent on some other object.

❑ List all the columns and column attributes for a particular table.

❑ And *many, many* more.

As a simple example of a data dictionary view, we will look at USER_TABLES, one of the views available to all database users. The USER_TABLES view shows information about all those tables that the current user owns (you can find more information on this view in Appendix C). If we use the SQL*Plus DESCRIBE command on the USER_TABLES view, we will see all those attributes that make up a table in the database:

```
SQL> describe user_tables
 Name                                      Null?    Type
 ----------------------------------------- -------- ----------------------------
 TABLE_NAME                                NOT NULL VARCHAR2(30)
 TABLESPACE_NAME                                    VARCHAR2(30)
 CLUSTER_NAME                                       VARCHAR2(30)
 IOT_NAME                                           VARCHAR2(30)
 PCT_FREE                                           NUMBER
 PCT_USED                                           NUMBER
 INI_TRANS                                          NUMBER
```

MAX_TRANS	NUMBER
INITIAL_EXTENT	NUMBER
NEXT_EXTENT	NUMBER
MIN_EXTENTS	NUMBER
MAX_EXTENTS	NUMBER
PCT_INCREASE	NUMBER
FREELISTS	NUMBER
FREELIST_GROUPS	NUMBER
LOGGING	VARCHAR2(3)
BACKED_UP	VARCHAR2(1)
NUM_ROWS	NUMBER
BLOCKS	NUMBER
EMPTY_BLOCKS	NUMBER
AVG_SPACE	NUMBER
CHAIN_CNT	NUMBER
AVG_ROW_LEN	NUMBER
AVG_SPACE_FREELIST_BLOCKS	NUMBER
NUM_FREELIST_BLOCKS	NUMBER
DEGREE	VARCHAR2(10)
INSTANCES	VARCHAR2(10)
CACHE	VARCHAR2(5)
TABLE_LOCK	VARCHAR2(8)
SAMPLE_SIZE	NUMBER
LAST_ANALYZED	DATE
PARTITIONED	VARCHAR2(3)
IOT_TYPE	VARCHAR2(12)
TEMPORARY	VARCHAR2(1)
SECONDARY	VARCHAR2(1)
NESTED	VARCHAR2(3)
BUFFER_POOL	VARCHAR2(7)
ROW_MOVEMENT	VARCHAR2(8)
GLOBAL_STATS	VARCHAR2(3)
USER_STATS	VARCHAR2(3)
DURATION	VARCHAR2(15)
SKIP_CORRUPT	VARCHAR2(8)
MONITORING	VARCHAR2(3)
CLUSTER_OWNER	VARCHAR2(30)
DEPENDENCIES	VARCHAR2(8)

Talk about a great deal of data about tables! Most of the columns we see in the view are relevant to every table you own, while others are only relevant for a particular table. In this chapter, we have only explored a fraction of the options available for creating tables. The USER_TABLES view hints at the wealth of options available for creating and managing tables, which you will learn more about in Chapter 7.

Instead of using every column available in the data dictionary views, we can use particular columns to satisfy our questions. For instance, let's say we're interested in knowing which tables we own and the tablespaces in which they exist. We can write a simple query to answer this question as follows:

```
SQL> connect hr_audit/hr_audit
Connected.
SQL> select table_name, tablespace_name
  2    from user_tables
  3    order by table_name
```

```
    4  /

TABLE_NAME                        TABLESPACE_NAME
------------------------------    ------------------------------
ANOTHER_DEPT                      USERS
ANOTHER_EMP                       USERS
AUTHORIZED_BLENDS                 USERS
COMPANY_EVENTS                    USERS
EMPLOYEE_BREAKS                   USERS
EMPLOYEE_HISTORY                  USERS
OTHER_COMPANY_EVENTS              USERS

7 rows selected.
```

If we want further information about the tables we own, we can use a number of other views available from the data dictionary:

❏　USER_TAB_COLUMNS – This view provides data about not only those columns that exist in tables, but in views and clusters that belong to the current user as well.

❏　USER_TAB_MODIFICATIONS – This table contains all those modifications that were made to tables owned by the current user since the last time the table was **analyzed** by the Oracle optimizer (we'll see more details on this in Chapter 6).

❏　USER_TAB_PRIVS – This table holds all the grants that have been made for tables where the current user either owns the table, has granted access to the table to another user, or has received a grant on the table from another user.

❏　USER_TABLES. This view, as we have already seen, contains meta data about tables owned by the user.

From this short list of views, it is easy to see that the data dictionary contains vast amounts of information regarding the contents of your Oracle database. Bear in mind that we have only talked about views on tables here. There are many other views available with a great deal of information regarding objects such as constraints, database links, indexes, and many more.

Data Dictionary Scope

The USER_TABLES view will only ever show us information about tables the current user owns. A database administrator account (such as ORACLE_DBA), on the other hand, can use the DBA_TABLES view to see table data for all users in the database. Let's try this by connecting as ORACLE_ADMIN, and issuing the following:

```
SQL> connect oracle_admin/oracle_admin
SQL> select owner, table_name, tablespace_name
  2      from dba_tables
  3    where owner in ('SCOTT', 'HR')
  4    order by owner, tablespace_name, table_name
  5    /

OWNER     TABLE_NAME                     TABLESPACE_NAME
```

```
--------  -------------------------------  -------------------
HR        DEPARTMENTS                      EXAMPLE
HR        EMPLOYEES                        EXAMPLE
HR        JOBS                             EXAMPLE
HR        JOB_HISTORY                      EXAMPLE
HR        LOCATIONS                        EXAMPLE
HR        REGIONS                          EXAMPLE
HR        COUNTRIES
SCOTT     BONUS                            SYSTEM
SCOTT     DEPT                             SYSTEM
SCOTT     EMP                              SYSTEM
SCOTT     SALGRADE                         SYSTEM

11 rows selected.
```

This illustrates the fact that views have different scope. What we mean by this is that the USER_TABLES view is available to any user, so they can see information about the tables within their own user account. However, without higher-level privileges such as we gave the ORACLE_ADMIN account, a user can't use the DBA_TABLES view to see what tables are owned by other users.

We'll see more about granting privileges to users in Chapter 13 on Security.

One further view on tables is the ALL_TABLES view, which includes information not only about those tables you own, but also those tables that you have been granted privileges on. A good example of this is the HR_AUDIT user we created in this chapter. This user was granted privileges on some of SCOTT's tables, and the ALL_TABLES view reflects this:

```
SQL> select owner, table_name
  2    from all_tables
  3    order by owner, table_name
  4  /

OWNER                            TABLE_NAME
-------------------------------  -------------------------------
HR                               DEPARTMENTS
HR                               EMPLOYEES
HR_AUDIT                         ANOTHER_DEPT
HR_AUDIT                         ANOTHER_EMP
HR_AUDIT                         AUTHORIZED_BLENDS
HR_AUDIT                         COMPANY_EVENTS
HR_AUDIT                         EMPLOYEE_BREAKS
HR_AUDIT                         EMPLOYEE_HISTORY
HR_AUDIT                         OTHER_COMPANY_EVENTS
LBACSYS                          LBAC_AUDIT_ACTIONS
MDSYS                            CS_SRS
MDSYS                            OGIS_SPATIAL_REFERENCE_SYSTEMS
MDSYS                            SDO_ANGLE_UNITS
MDSYS                            SDO_AREA_UNITS
MDSYS                            SDO_DATUMS
MDSYS                            SDO_DIST_UNITS
MDSYS                            SDO_ELLIPSOIDS
MDSYS                            SDO_PROJECTIONS
```

MDSYS	USER_CS_SRS
MDSYS	USER_TRANSFORM_MAP
OE	WAREHOUSES
SCOTT	DEPT
SCOTT	EMP
MDSYS	CS_SRS
MDSYS	OGIS_SPATIAL_REFERENCE_SYSTEMS
MDSYS	SDO_ANGLE_UNITS
MDSYS	SDO_AREA_UNITS
MDSYS	SDO_DATUMS
MDSYS	SDO_DIST_UNITS
MDSYS	SDO_ELLIPSOIDS
MDSYS	SDO_PROJECTIONS
MDSYS	USER_CS_SRS
MDSYS	USER_TRANSFORM_MAP
OLAPSYS	OS_CHILD_INSTANCES
OLAPSYS	OS_OSA_PRIVILEGES
SYS	AUDIT_ACTIONS
SYS	DUAL
SYS	ODCI_SECOBJ$
SYS	ODCI_WARNINGS$
SYS	PLAN_TABLE
SYS	PSTUBTBL
SYS	STMT_AUDIT_OPTION_MAP
SYS	SYSTEM_PRIVILEGE_MAP
SYS	TABLE_PRIVILEGE_MAP
SYSTEM	DEF$_TEMP$LOB
SYSTEM	HELP
WKSYS	WK$CHARSET
WKSYS	WK$CRAWLER_CONFIG_DEFAULT
WKSYS	WK$LANG
WKSYS	WK$MIMETYPES

Now there is an unexpected result! Who would have thought HR_AUDIT had access to all those tables? Did all these users grant privileges on these tables to the HR_AUDIT user explicitly? Well, the answer to that is no. These tables are included in the ALL_TABLES view because privileges on these tables have been granted to the PUBLIC role. If we remember early in the chapter when we created users, we talked briefly about roles. The DBA role is what enabled the ORACLE_DBA user account to perform all the administrative commands. The PUBLIC role is a role granted to every user in the database by default. All the tables in the ALL_TABLES view above, except for those owned by HR_AUDIT and SCOTT, are granted to PUBLIC. For more information about privileges and security see Chapter 13.

Oracle's data dictionary uses a convenient naming standard to provide a form of scope for the various views it contains. DBA_ indicates any object (of the type indicated in the view name) in the database. USER_ provides detailed information about all those objects (of the type indicated in the view name) the current user owns. The ALL_ views list all the objects that the currently logged-in user has access to view.

The second half of the view name lists the objects that are described in the view. ALL_**TABLES** or DBA_**DATA_FILES** relate to tables and data files, respectively. In this manner, when you look at the name of a data dictionary view it is very easy to get a good understanding of the type of data contained within the view.

We didn't get terribly deep in this chapter discussing all the views available in the data dictionary or how we can use them to get interesting information about our database. In Appendix C, you will find a much more detailed listing of the available views, what kind of data they contain, and why you would use them. Additionally, in Chapter 19 we'll look at a variety of helpful scripts that use the power of the data dictionary to help us with our day-to-day operations on the database.

Summary

In this chapter we began by discussing DDL, the language used to create and manage objects in our database. We learned how our sessions behave when we issue DDL statements to the database in the middle of inserts, updates, and deletes. We then moved on to take a look at the CREATE, ALTER, and DROP statements. We saw how to create users, some of the common reasons for altering users in the database, and how to drop users.

We then took a look at the various data types available for use in our tables, and moved on to consider how to use them in creating tables. We saw how to duplicate a table structure using the CREATE TABLE AS SELECT syntax, and how to build constraints on tables to define primary keys, foreign keys, unique indexes, and check constraints.

We ended the chapter by taking an introductory glance at the data dictionary, Oracle's catalog of meta data, which provides all the information we could ever ask for about our database.

This, and the previous chapter, provides you with a firm foundation to begin your journey through the rest of this book. Understanding how to manage users and tables is a skill that is absolutely necessary for administrators and developers alike, and we'll revisit these topics later in the book.

The New 9*i* Sample Schemas

Throughout the first three chapters of this book, we have seen the use of database schemas such as SCOTT and HR. If you don't already know, these database schemas are prepackaged by Oracle with the database. For many years now, Oracle instructors, administrators, programmers, and users have been using the trusty SCOTT schema for simple queries, updates, and deletes in order to learn, test, and/or tune their databases. These schemas are what we call **sample schemas**. Sample schemas are collections of database objects such as tables, views, and indexes, which come prepopulated with data representative of a small or medium-sized company.

With the newest version of the Oracle database Oracle 9*i*, comes a whole new set of sample schemas, which aim to expand on what the SCOTT schema can offer users. These schemas all form a part of the same virtual company, and each of them has its own business focus. There is, for example, a separate schema for the human resources department, the order entry department, and the shipping department. In the course of this chapter we'll discuss what's included with each schema and how each exploits a unique area of Oracle technology, but before we get ahead of ourselves, let's back up a step and take a more detailed look at SCOTT. After all, it has earned its place in Oracle, and every good Oracle user should know their way around EMP and DEPT.

The SCOTT Schema

The SCOTT schema was produced to provide a few example tables along with data that could be used to demonstrate some of the features of the database. It's a fairly simple schema, as indicated by the following Data Structure Diagram:

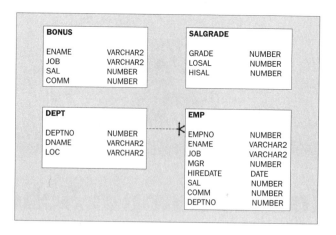

For more information regarding installation of the SCOTT schema, please refer to Appendix D.

Why SCOTT, you ask? SCOTT/TIGER was the original username/password combination for the Oracle database back in the days of Oracle version 1, 2, and 3. SCOTT was named after one of the founding programmers of Oracle Corporation, Bruce Scott. TIGER, of course, was the name of Bruce's cat.

Over the past 25 years, Oracle demonstrations around the world have revolved around this oversimplified version of a company's Human Resources department. As a result, not only will you find references to the SCOTT schema in this book, but also in many other Oracle books, as well as on the USENET newsgroups, IRC channels and instructor-led training. The frequency of its use reflects the fact that the SCOTT schema is well known and people can relate to it. When you talk to an experienced Oracle user, they can usually name many of the employees from the SCOTT.EMP table!

That being said, the Oracle database has progressed to a point where the database features showcased in the SCOTT schema are generally considered a staple of most other relational databases. If we want to truly show off the capabilities of the Oracle database, we are going to have to step up our samples considerably! With that in mind, let's move on to discuss the new sample schemas introduced in Oracle 9*i*.

The Oracle 9*i* Sample Schemas

Oracle introduces a whole new genre of sample schema in the 9*i* release of its flagship product, the database. Instead of trying to pack every feature, option, and technology available in the Oracle line-up in one schema, the samples have been broken out into many schemas. Although it may seem like overkill to some, by creating a variety of sample schemas the user has the option of using the one most appropriate to what they are doing.

Oracle technology can be utilized in a wide variety of environments. High-speed online transaction processing and data warehousing have been the typical "opposite ends of the rainbow" when it comes to providing case scenarios for technology solutions. Although you could use one schema to show how to do online transaction processing and data warehousing in the same tables, you would never implement a practical solution that way. What we typically find in today's industry is either a variety of schemas in a single database instance, or a number of distributed databases on a network to solve different real world computing requirements. The new Oracle 9*i* sample schemas model this scenario admirably.

The Oracle 9*i* sample schemas attempt to model a real-world sales organization, with a suite of typical business departments. These different departments come with different information technology needs, and each sample schema uses different Oracle technologies to solve their respective problems. In addition, each schema is designed to target a particular technical audience. For example, a beginner would most likely want to start by using the Human Resources schema, whereas a data warehousing database administrator would more likely choose the Sales History schema to get familiar with.

Let's now take a look at the business domain of each schema, and what kinds of Oracle technology we can expect to find. The schemas are as follows:

- ❑ HR – Human Resources. The human resources department basically manages employees, departments, jobs, and facilities. This schema was developed for beginners, and introduces both basic subjects and simple database objects. You can think of HR as a new and improved version of the SCOTT schema, with a large number of allies (in the form of the other schemas) to complement its capabilities.

- ❑ OE – Order Entry. Order Entry is responsible for tracking all the sales transactions the company and the product inventory. This schema, along with the Online Catalog subschemas, are more advanced than the Human Resources schema, but also remain focused on standard Oracle technology (you will see how the other schemas pick functional and technical areas to focus on such as multimedia content or data warehousing). This schema will exploit more complex features and functionality of the Oracle database. You will find INSTEAD-OF triggers, object-relational technology, columns of XMLType, and more in the OE schema.

- ❑ PM – Product Media. Product media stores multimedia content about the company's product line in the database for publishing on the web and in print. PM utilizes **Oracle Intermedia**, and is designed with a multimedia focus for publishing audio, video, and visual data. In addition, PM makes heavy use of LOB column types.

- ❑ QS – Queued Shipping. The shipping department is responsible for tracking product shipments from the company to the customer, and uses six schemas to accomplish its job. QS, QS_ES, QS_WS, QS_OS, QS_CB, and QS_CS make up the collection of Queued Shipping schemas. Each of the schemas makes up a separate department in the company which plays a role in the shipping of products, while the QS schema as a whole makes heavy use of Oracle's **Advanced Queuing** functionality.

- ❑ SH – Sales History. Sales history provides historical data about sales the company has seen, in order to provide a firm foundation for decision making in the future. The Sales History schema is for data warehousing concepts.

Many of the features available in the new 9i schemas use optional technologies, which may or may not be installed in your database. Some of the more advanced features used in these schemas will not be covered in this book. For more information regarding options and features in your particular database, see Appendix E.

A Deeper Look At Each Schema

Now that you have an understanding of what each schema is for, let's dig in a little and get a deeper knowledge of the schemas' inner workings.

Human Resources

The Human Resources schema, or HR schema, enables management of departments, employees, job, and salary information. The following diagram details the data structure diagram for the HR schema.

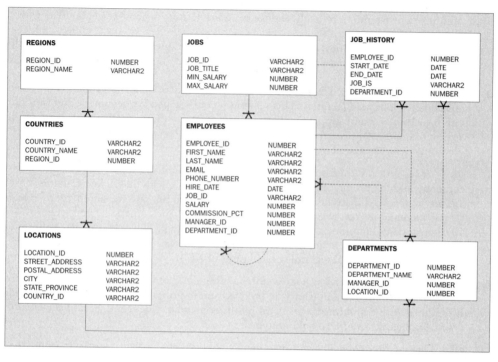

If you compare this diagram to the SCOTT/TIGER data structure diagram, you can see that there is far more detailed information being tracked in the Human Resources schema. For each employee, HR stores a unique employee number, first and last names, e-mail address, phone number, hire date, job, salary, commission, manager's employee number and department number. The DEPARTMENTS table describes each department by using a unique department id, a department name, a manager, and a location. This location includes both a country and a region, with separate tables describing these two details. HR also tracks employees' job history through the JOB_HISTORY table, which details when employees change jobs or departments.

In addition to simply storing this information, there are indexes and triggers that enforce business rules about the data:

❏ The EMPLOYEE_ID column is the primary key. This means that each employee must have a unique employee ID.

❏ NOT NULL constraints exist on the LAST_NAME, EMAIL, HIRE_DATE, and JOB_ID columns. This means a value must be provided when the record is inserted or updated.

❏ The SECURE_DML trigger defined on the table ensures that changes are only made during the hours of 08:00am and 6:00pm, Monday through Friday. Violating this rule causes an error to be raised and the change will fail.

- ❑ The UPDATE_JOB_HISTORY trigger defined on the table ensures that after any update of the JOB_ID or DEPARTMENT_ID column, a record is inserted into the JOB_HISTORY table recording the change.

- ❑ If a value is provided for the DEPARTMENT_ID, that DEPARTMENT_ID must exist in the DEPARTMENTS table.

- ❑ If a value is provided for the JOB_ID, that JOB_ID must exist in the JOBS table.

- ❑ If a value is provided for the MANAGER_ID, that same value must exist in the EMPLOYEE_ID column in a different row in the EMPLOYEES table. This value indicates that the employee has a manager. Therefore, the manager must have a row in the table as well. This is known as a **self Join**.

These are the primary business rules defined for the EMPLOYEES table. The majority of the tables across all of the sample schemas have been constructed in this manner, with constraints, indexes, and triggers.

You can find more information regarding indexes, views, and triggers, in Chapters 8, 14, and 15 respectively.

Although we will not go into this level of detail on the remaining tables in the sample schemas, you should be aware that for each of the tables this layer of business rules exists. In this way if you run into any problems when trying to perform INSERT, UPDATE, or DELETE operations on the tables, you understand what is going on behind the scenes.

In addition to the standard information mentioned above, employees and departments are optionally assigned a **Distinguished Name** or DN. These DN's are used by **Lightweight Directory Access Protocol** (**LDAP**) servers, in order to uniquely identify an entry in its database.

*Note that Oracle released an industry standard LDAP server product named **Oracle Internet Directory (OID)**, which is available separately from the Oracle 9i database.*

By adding a DN column to the EMPLOYEES table and the DEPARTMENTS table, the HR schema can be integrated with Oracle's LDAP server.

> **Note that this is an optional feature of the HR schema, since you can utilize the schema without using an LDAP server.**

You will also notice that the DN column is not in the HR data structure diagram. If it were, then the employees and departments would put their DN column in the EMPLOYEES and DEPARTMENTS tables, respectively.

The Human Resources schema can be utilized as a fully functional employee information system. At Oracle, we have an application called People that is a web-based employee directory. This application allows web browsers on the Oracle intranet to search for Oracle employees using a simple text expression. The data you can expect to find is information about each employee (such as you might find in the EMPLOYEES table), an organizational hierarchy (using MANAGER_ID to link back to the EMPLOYEES table, and the DEPARTMENTS tables), and a work address (LOCATIONS table).

A slightly modified version of the PEOPLE *application is discussed in great detail in Case Study 2.*

As simple as it might sound, the People system is arguably one of the most widely used applications on our intranet. It receives well over 250,000 hits per day. Armed with only the data in the Human Resources schema, one could write a very powerful, very popular web-based employee directory.

Order Entry

The Order Entry schema, or OE schema, is for managing customers, sales orders, and product inventories from the various channels in which the company does business.

The following diagram details the data structure diagram for the OE schema. As we learned earlier, there is more complexity to the Order Entry schema in comparison to the Human Resources schema.

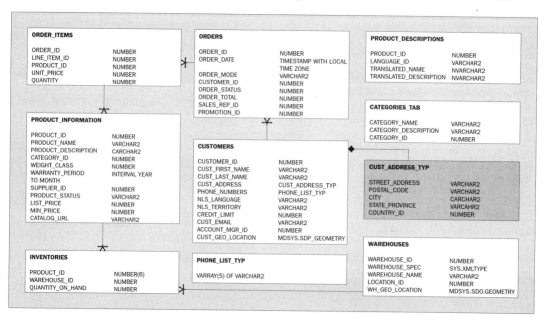

Customer data can be stored in OE. Not only can we record a customer's name, address, and a collection of their phone numbers, but we can also track their language preferences and territory. In addition we can record whether a given customer has a credit limit, an account manager, and/or a geographic location.

After customers, the next predominant piece of information being managed by the OE schema concerns products. This company has various categories of products to offer their customers. A simple SELECT statement from the categories_tab table will produce an overview of the product set:

```
SQL> column category_name format a20
SQL> column category_description format a100 word_wrapped
SQL> set linesize 78
SQL> column category_name format a20
```

```
SQL> column category_description format a50 word_wrapped
SQL> select category_name, category_description
  2    from categories_tab
  3    order by category_name
  4  /


CATEGORY_NAME          CATEGORY_DESCRIPTION
--------------------   --------------------------------------------------
hardware               computer hardware and peripherals
hardware1              monitors
hardware2              printers
hardware3              harddisks
hardware4              memory components/upgrades
hardware5              processors, sound and video cards, network cards,
                       motherboards

hardware6              keyboards, mouses, mouse pads
hardware7              other peripherals (CD-ROM, DVD, tape cartridge
                       drives, ...)

hardware8              miscellaneous hardware (cables, screws, power
                       supplies ...)

office equipment       office furniture and supplies
office1                capitalizable assets (desks, chairs, phones ...)
office2                office supplies for daily use (pencils, erasers,
                       staples, ...)

office3                manuals, other books
office4                miscellaneous office supplies
online catalog         catalog of computer hardware, software, and office
                       equipment

software               computer software
software1              spreadsheet software
software2              word processing software
software3              database software
software4              operating systems
software5              software development tools (including languages)
software6              miscellaneous software

22 rows selected.
```

Products are tracked using two tables, PRODUCT_DESCRIPTIONS and PRODUCT_INFORMATION. These two tables join together to provide a great deal of information about the company's product line. Oracle even provides the ability to have product descriptions stored for all the various languages Oracle supports. The standard product ID, name, and description columns are present. The category ID referred to in the query above can be found in the PRODUCT_INFORMATION table. You will also find the weight class data in this table to help in determining shipping requirements. There is a product status attribute for each product that indicates status values obsolete, orderable, planned, or under development. The warranty period for each product is also maintained. See the Order Entry data structure diagram for more information.

Two other tables of note here are the ORDERS and ORDER_ITEMS tables. When company representatives take orders for products, they can record all the information they need regarding that order in these two tables. The date the order was taken, the mode the order was taken in (online, direct), the customer who made the order, the status of the order, which sales representative received the order, and the total cost are tracked in the ORDERS table. The ORDER_ITEMS table tracks each of the line items on the order, recording information such as the line item ID, the product ID, the price of the item and the quantity ordered.

Finally, the OE schema tracks product inventory. We store the quantity of a given product in any given warehouse. There are multiple warehouses throughout the company, so we use location identifiers to point us to geographical regions. There is also an Oracle Spatial column in the WAREHOUSES table that provides us with a key into Oracle Spatial technology.

Oracle Spatial is technology in the database for supporting location and geographical data.

In the OE schema, there are two database object types that deserve mention in passing:

- ❑ CUST_ADDRESS_TYP. This is an object type used in the CUSTOMERS table. It contains a number of attributes (see the data structure diagram, above) that relate to the customer's address.

- ❑ PHONE_LIST_TYP. This is a VARRAY of VARCHAR2(25)s. This varray is stored as a single column in the CUSTOMERS table, and is used to store up to five phone numbers.

What we have not discussed is the inter-schema dependency of the OE schema on the HR schema. OE shares the tables owned by HR in order to leverage information like account managers, sales representatives, etc. When the OE schema is being created, a number of metonyms are created for the Human Resources tables, and the HR schema grants appropriate privileges to the OE schema.

The ONLINE CATALOG subschema represents the object-relational components of the OE schema. When the ONLINE CATALOG subschema is installed, a number of database objects are created to provide an object-oriented interface to the Order Entry data. The CATEGORIES_TAB above, for instance, is an object table, rather than a standard relational table. ONLINE CATALOG also defines quite a few object views built upon the Order Entry data. This demonstrates Oracle's ability to build an object model on top of an existing relational data model. You will read more about objects in Chapter 19.

The OE schema is a good example of what an office supply or a computer retail store might use to manage their entire ordering process. Using the data in the Order Entry tables, a sales organization would be perfectly equipped to provide accurate product information to potential customers, take sales orders, quantify order revenue, store customer information, give accurate inventory information for customers ordering products in different geographical locations, and more. As you learn more about the other sample schemas, we will see how the Order Entry functionality is integrated with other departments of our virtual company to round out the company's IT infrastructure.

Product Media

The Product Media schema, or PM schema, is for managing multimedia data that describes the company's products. Online media such as video, audio, and images are stored in the database along with print media data types. This is one of our specialized schemas, as it focuses on multimedia content and the functionality provided by **Oracle Intermedia**.

Oracle Intermedia is the component of the Oracle database that supports multimedia content types.

In addition to Intermedia data storage, the PM schema also heavily relies on the use of LOB column types for storing data.

The Product Media schema is a perfect example of a real-world business requirement being solved in Oracle 9*i* with the use of Oracle technology, namely Oracle Intermedia. For instance, our fictitious company might store multimedia data and/or print media. Therefore, there are examples in the Product Media schema to do such things as:

❑ Storing thumbnails and full-size images for web publishing in Oracle

❑ Storing audio clips in Oracle

❑ Storing video in Oracle

❑ Performing processing on image types for conversion to web-compliant image types

By employing Oracle Intermedia, these tasks are made relatively easy where they were once rather difficult to accomplish.

There are two tables in the Product Media Schema, ONLINE_MEDIA and PRINT_MEDIA. Both of these tables reference the PRODUCT_INFORMATION table belonging to Order Entry. The following diagram shows the Product Media schema, along with the references to the Order Entry table, PRODUCT_INFORMATION.

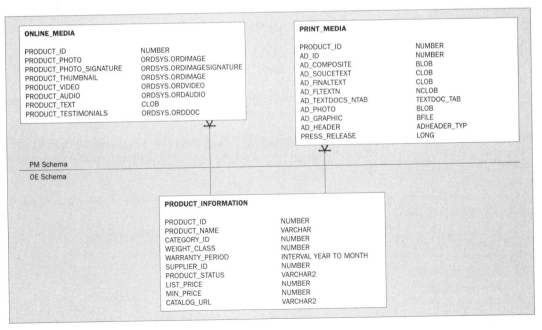

The PRINT_MEDIA table has an object type (adheader_typ) and a nested table of objects (TEXTDOC_TAB) stored in each record of the table. This shows how objects and collections of objects can be stored along with relational columns in the same table to model more complex data. ONLINE_MEDIA is another example of a table that contains object types and scalar datatypes in the same table. Each of the ORDSYS.ORD___ columns is an Intermedia object type. These Intermedia object types store not only the binary data such as an image, audio, or video; but also a variety of meta data about that multimedia type. Not only do object types in Oracle have many types of attributes, but they also have "methods", or procedures and functions that are a part of the object definition itself. The attributes and methods are made available to you in your applications. We'll take a look at one of the object types, ORDSYS.ORDIMAGE, and get a feel for the type of functionality available.

To display all of the attributes of the ORDSYS.ORDIMAGE type, as well as each of the methods of this object, we can use the following syntax in the SQL*Plus window:

```
SQL> desc ordsys.ordimage
 Name                                    Null?    Type
 --------------------------------------- -------- ---------------------------
 SOURCE                                           ORDSOURCE
 HEIGHT                                           NUMBER(38)
 WIDTH                                            NUMBER(38)
 CONTENTLENGTH                                    NUMBER(38)
 FILEFORMAT                                       VARCHAR2(4000)
 CONTENTFORMAT                                    VARCHAR2(4000)
 COMPRESSIONFORMAT                                VARCHAR2(4000)
 MIMETYPE                                         VARCHAR2(4000)
```

> **Note that we will look in more detail at SQL*Plus in more detail in Chapter 9**

The first attribute, SOURCE, is of ORDSOURCE type. This is yet another Intermedia object type that contains data such as the BLOB (the actual image data), the type of data stored in the BLOB, the location of the data stored in the BLOB, and when the BLOB was last updated (this is only a few of the attributes in that object type). ORDSOURCE also comes with its own methods as well.

Other attributes in the ORDSYS.ORDIMAGE object type help to describe the image object. Height, width, size, MIMEtype, and other columns give you easy access to important information for the objects stored in your database.

As was mentioned earlier, objects also have methods. Here is a listing of some of the methods available in the ORDSYS.ORDIMAGE object type:

```
 METHOD
 ------
 MEMBER PROCEDURE COPY
 Argument Name                   Type                        In/Out Default?
 ------------------------------- --------------------------- ------ --------
 DEST                            ORDIMAGE
```

```
METHOD
------
  MEMBER FUNCTION GETHEIGHT RETURNS NUMBER

METHOD
------
  MEMBER FUNCTION GETWIDTH RETURNS NUMBER

METHOD
------
  MEMBER FUNCTION GETCONTENTLENGTH RETURNS NUMBER

METHOD
------
  MEMBER FUNCTION GETCONTENT RETURNS BLOB
```

These are only a few of the many member methods available in the `ORDSYS.ORDIMAGE` *object type. These were chosen because they are fairly self explanatory and show some of the functionality available with the object type.*

As you can see, the object types of Oracle Intermedia offer a great deal of functionality for managing the multimedia content in your database. A key point to take away from this short explanation of object types, however, is not how robust Intermedia is, but rather how flexible and powerful the Oracle object model is. As we mentioned earlier, objects are discussed in much greater detail in Chapter 16.

Queued Shipping

Our virtual company wants to use a messaging system to facilitate self-service ordering by customers online. When a customer initiates an order, the system needs to create the order, bill the customer, and ensure the order is shipped through the appropriate region according to the customer's location.

In the future, the company may choose to use this messaging system to provide a business-to-business interface for suppliers or business partners, and so will use industry standard mechanisms for message data. XML has become the standard for exchanging data, and the Oracle database can take full advantage of XML data.

A customer makes their order and the system queues an order that will be processed by the ORDER ENTRY department. Once the order is processed by order entry, the appropriate shipping department receives a message indicating the order is ready to be shipped. In addition to the regional shipping centers being notified, the billing center and customer service are made aware of the order being processed. Once the appropriate shipping center has the order message, it can either ship the order or place the order in back order status. This change in the order's status is also made available to customer service. This not only allows the customer service department to see what the order status is, but this information can also be made available to the customer. Once the order is shipped, the customer billing department is notified and the customer is billed appropriately. The billing information is sent to customer service, and the order is complete.

The QS_CS schema has one table, named ORDER_STATUS_TABLE, for storing order status. This is the only table created (besides the queue tables which are created through the Advanced Queue APIs) in the entire Queued Shipping schema install. Instead of showing a data structure diagram with one table, let's instead look at a flow of the messages in the queue system created for Queued Shipping schemas.

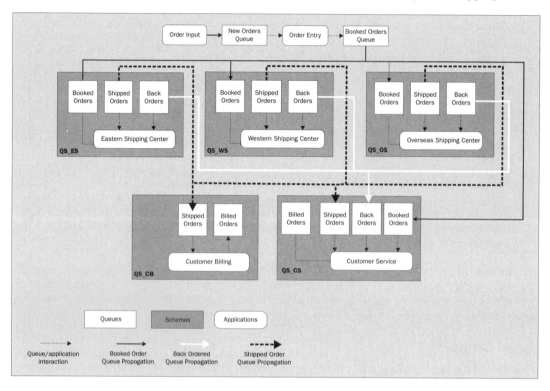

With this flow diagram we can see how messages are transferred from department to department to facilitate a clean, intuitive order – shipping – billing cycle.

Everything starts with order entry at the top of the diagram. The Order Input process generates orders that are fed into the New Orders Queue. This queue is processed by the Order Entry application, and the orders are placed in the Booked Orders Queue. Orders in the Booked Orders Queue are sent to the appropriate shipping center (East, West, or Overseas) as well as Customer Service.

At this point, the shipping center gets the order fulfilled and shipped to the customer, and the Customer Service department is aware of the status of the order. At the appropriate shipping center, the Shipping Center application is responsible for either shipping the order, or putting the order in back order status. Back ordered products are eventually shipped once products are on hand, and the order is placed in the shipped orders queue.

Once the order is shipped, the Customer Service and Customer Billing departments are notified via the shipped orders queue, and the customer is billed. The billed order is placed on the Billed Orders queue, which notifies customer service and the order is then complete.

Now you can see how all the pieces come together in the ordering cycle. Providing product information on the Web, having sales representatives presenting products to potential customers, and sending catalogs to interested parties will get a retail organization nowhere unless they have a way to get the orders fulfilled. With the Queued Shipping schemas, the order cycle is made efficient, informative, and easy to understand.

By providing a working example of a somewhat complex messaging implementation in the sample schemas, Oracle has given its users an easy-to-use tutorial on Advanced Queues. Using the Queued Shipping schemas, users with no experience in wielding Oracle's Advanced Queue technology will find the learning curve much less steep.

Sales History

In today's business environment, companies have found that all the sales information in the world is worthless unless people making decisions can accurately generate reports on that information in a meaningful and timely manner. **Decision support** is a term used to describe the use of information technology in the decision-making process.

The Sales History schema is designed to demonstrate how a typical decision support system would work. The purpose of this type of schema is to provide reports that show the results of sales efforts for our virtual company. In the Sales History schema, a good amount of sample data is loaded into the tables during the schema installation. This gives us a repository of sales data to use when creating the various reports the schema will provide. In a production decision support system, data is loaded into the schema's tables on a regular basis, usually in a batch manner so as not to interfere with the querying and reporting processes that the system is designed for.

The Sales History schema is an example of a traditional data warehouse. The tables are arranged in a **star schema** design, where there is one large SALES table in the center, and a number of small lookup, or dimension tables around the outside of the SALES table. The SALES table typically has a large amount of data (all the sales facts) whereas the dimension tables, compared to the SALES table, are relatively small.

The following data structure diagram shows the Sales History schema:

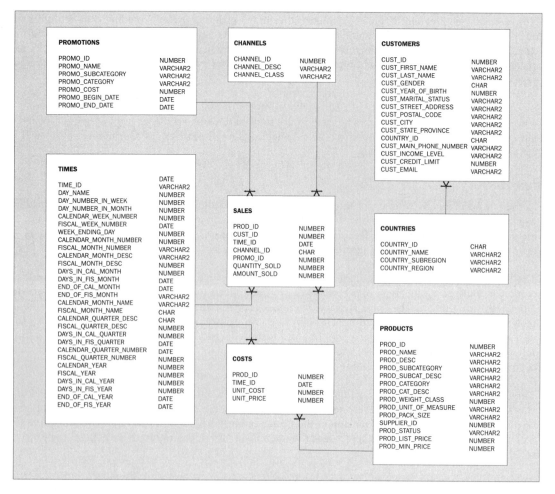

Here you can see the SALES table having a number of foreign keys to the dimension tables located around the outside of the diagram. This allows us to efficiently store lookup data for the records in the SALES table.

Now that we have taken a look into the business drivers behind the new sample schemas in Oracle 9*i*, let's dig into the technology side a little deeper.

A Gradual Approach To Learning

The manner in which the schemas are targeted for different audiences encourages new Oracle users to learn the technology via a structured approach. For instance, a beginner would start with Human Resources. This could familiarize him with relational concepts, querying data, database manipulation language, database definition language, and some of the more basic concepts.

Once our new Oracle user is comfortable with the Human Resources schema, they can move on to the Order Entry schema. In this new schema, he will encounter object types, XML support, Oracle Spatial, and other more advanced features of the database.

Next, the user can look into speciality areas provided by the remaining schemas. A multimedia expert might decide to drill into the Product Media schema. The user who is designing a publish-and-subscribe message-based system would find the Queued Shipping schema very helpful in getting them started with Oracle Advanced Queues. Data warehousing enthusiasts would do best to investigate and learn the Sales History schema.

Finding Out More About the Sample Schemas

Now that we have an overview of the new Oracle 9i sample schemas, what they are all for, and what they all contain in terms of database objects, we're ready to start using them. In order to understand how to do this, and how to get information from the schemas, it's important that you understand how to get definitions of schema objects directly out of the database.

Database Object Descriptions

In this section we'll take a look in the database to find objects that belong to our sample schemas, and then use SQL queries to extract definitions of those objects directly from the database. What this section does not do, is to list every table, view, type, and procedure definition for each of our twelve sample schemas. This is partially because there are over four hundred objects that belong to the sample schemas, but mainly because you will learn far more about these schemas and the Oracle Data Dictionary by using it to find information as you need it.

> **All the scripts required for the following Try It Out sections are available from the code download for this book at http://www.apress.com/.**

Try It Out – Getting a Database List

The first query we will write will give us all the objects, categorized by object type, for a particular schema. Save the following script to a file named `dbls.sql`, on your local hard drive. If you place it in your working directory, you will not have to specify the path name when we call the file from SQL*Plus:

```
column object_name format a30
column tablespace_name format a30
column object_type format a12
column status format a1
break on object_type skip 1

select object_type, object_name,
       decode(status,'INVALID','*','') status,
       tablespace_name
  from user_objects a, user_segments b
```

```
   where a.object_name = b.segment_name (+)
     and a.object_type = b.segment_type (+)
  order by object_type, object_name
 /
column status format a10
```

Connect to the database as the schema you would like to understand further, and execute the script we just saved:

```
SQL> connect hr/hr
Connected.
SQL> @dbls

OBJECT_TYPE  OBJECT_NAME                      S TABLESPACE_NAME
------------ -------------------------------- - -----------------------------
INDEX        COUNTRY_C_ID_PK                    EXAMPLE
             DEPT_ID_PK                         EXAMPLE
             DEPT_LOCATION_IX                   EXAMPLE
             EMP_DEPARTMENT_IX                  EXAMPLE
             EMP_EMAIL_UK                       EXAMPLE
             EMP_EMP_ID_PK                      EXAMPLE
             EMP_JOB_IX                         EXAMPLE
             EMP_MANAGER_IX                     EXAMPLE
             EMP_NAME_IX                        EXAMPLE
             JHIST_DEPARTMENT_IX                EXAMPLE
             JHIST_EMPLOYEE_IX                  EXAMPLE
             JHIST_EMP_ID_ST_DATE_PK          EXAMPLE
             JHIST_JOB_IX                       EXAMPLE
             JOB_ID_PK                          EXAMPLE
             LOC_CITY_IX                        EXAMPLE
             LOC_COUNTRY_IX                     EXAMPLE
             LOC_ID_PK                          EXAMPLE
             LOC_STATE_PROVINCE_IX              EXAMPLE
             REG_ID_PK                          EXAMPLE

PROCEDURE    ADD_JOB_HISTORY
             SECURE_DML

SEQUENCE     DEPARTMENTS_SEQ
             EMPLOYEES_SEQ
             LOCATIONS_SEQ

TABLE        COUNTRIES
             DEPARTMENTS                        EXAMPLE
             EMPLOYEES                          EXAMPLE
             JOBS                               EXAMPLE
             JOB_HISTORY                        EXAMPLE
             LOCATIONS                          EXAMPLE
             REGIONS                            EXAMPLE

TRIGGER      SECURE_EMPLOYEES
             UPDATE_JOB_HISTORY
```

```
VIEW            EMP_DETAILS_VIEW

34 rows selected.
```

How It Works

What we have accomplished in this example is the execution of a SQL script (saved on our computer) in the SQL*Plus tool. By saving the script in a file, we eliminate the need to rekey it into SQL*Plus every time we want to see this information. It's like storing instructions for SQL*Plus to give us a list of our database objects. When we used the command @dbls.sql, SQL*Plus knew it should open the dbls.sql file and run it for us. Using this methodology, you can save SQL commands you commonly run on your hard drive for convenience.

The dbls.sql script is a custom script that we use on our development team to get a list of those database objects owned by the current user. The list categorizes the objects by object type (INDEX. PROCEDURE, SEQUENCE, TABLE, TRIGGER, VIEW, etc.) and shows helpful information for each object. For example, objects that consume space and that are stored in tablespaces, such as tables and indexes, list the tablespace name in which they are stored. For objects that can be "invalidated", there is a column entitled S (for "Status") that will show us if an object is invalid. Those columns will contain an asterisk if the object is invalid.

Try It Out – Table Details

Now that we know all the objects that belong to the current user, let's look a little closer at one of the tables listed. Save the following script to your filesystem, and name it desc.sql:

```
set verify off
set linesize 72
set pagesize 9999
set feedback off
variable owner varchar2(30)
variable tname varchar2(30)
begin
  :owner := USER;
  :tname := upper('&1');
end;
/
Prompt Datatypes for Table &1
column data_type format a20
column column_name heading "Column Name"
column data_type   heading "Data|Type"
column data_length heading "Data|Length"
column nullable    heading "Nullable"
select column_name,
       data_type,
       substr(
       decode( data_type, 'NUMBER',
              decode( data_precision, NULL, NULL,
                '('||data_precision||','||data_scale||')' ),
          data_length),
```

```
                   1,11) data_length,
          decode( nullable, 'Y', 'null', 'not null' ) nullable
from all_tab_columns
where owner = :owner
  and table_name = :tname
order by column_id
/
prompt
prompt
Prompt Indexes on &1
column index_name heading "Index|Name"
column Uniqueness heading "Is|Unique" format a6
column columns format a32 word_wrapped

select substr(a.index_name,1,30) index_name,
     decode(a.uniqueness,'UNIQUE','Yes','No') uniqueness,
max(decode( b.column_position,  1, substr(b.column_name,1,30),
NULL )) ||
max(decode( b.column_position,  2, ', '||
substr(b.column_name,1,30), NULL )) ||
max(decode( b.column_position,  3, ', '||
substr(b.column_name,1,30), NULL )) ||
max(decode( b.column_position,  4, ', '||
substr(b.column_name,1,30), NULL )) ||
max(decode( b.column_position,  5, ', '||
substr(b.column_name,1,30), NULL )) ||
max(decode( b.column_position,  6, ', '||
substr(b.column_name,1,30), NULL )) ||
max(decode( b.column_position,  7, ', '||
substr(b.column_name,1,30), NULL )) ||
max(decode( b.column_position,  8, ', '||
substr(b.column_name,1,30), NULL )) ||
max(decode( b.column_position,  9, ', '||
substr(b.column_name,1,30), NULL )) ||
max(decode( b.column_position, 10, ', '||
substr(b.column_name,1,30), NULL )) ||
max(decode( b.column_position, 11, ', '||
substr(b.column_name,1,30), NULL )) ||
max(decode( b.column_position, 12, ', '||
substr(b.column_name,1,30), NULL )) ||
max(decode( b.column_position, 13, ', '||
substr(b.column_name,1,30), NULL )) ||
max(decode( b.column_position, 14, ', '||
substr(b.column_name,1,30), NULL )) ||
max(decode( b.column_position, 15, ', '||
substr(b.column_name,1,30), NULL )) ||
max(decode( b.column_position, 16, ', '||
substr(b.column_name,1,30), NULL )) columns
from all_indexes a, all_ind_columns b
where a.owner = :owner
and a.table_name = :tname
and b.table_name = a.table_name
and b.table_owner = a.owner
```

```
and a.index_name = b.index_name
group by substr(a.index_name,1,30), a.uniqueness
/
prompt
prompt
prompt Triggers on &1
set long 5000
select trigger_name, trigger_type,
     triggering_event, trigger_body
from user_triggers where table_name = :tname
/
```

The desc.sql report is used to find the columns, indexes, and triggers for a given table by passing the table name on the SQL*Plus command line, as follows:

```
SQL> @desc.sql EMPLOYEES
Datatypes for Table EMPLOYEES

                         Data            Data
Column Name              Type            Length    Nullable
--------------------     --------------- --------  --------
EMPLOYEE_ID              NUMBER          (6,0)     not null
FIRST_NAME               VARCHAR2        20        null
LAST_NAME                VARCHAR2        25        not null
EMAIL                    VARCHAR2        25        not null
PHONE_NUMBER             VARCHAR2        20        null
HIRE_DATE                DATE            7         not null
JOB_ID                   VARCHAR2        10        not null
SALARY                   NUMBER          (8,2)     null
COMMISSION_PCT           NUMBER          (2,2)     null
MANAGER_ID               NUMBER          (6,0)     null
DEPARTMENT_ID            NUMBER          (4,0)     null


Indexes on EMPLOYEES

Index                Is
Name                 Unique Indexed Columns
-------------------- ------ ------------------------------------
EMP_DEPARTMENT_IX    No     DEPARTMENT_ID
EMP_EMAIL_UK         Yes    EMAIL
EMP_EMP_ID_PK        Yes    EMPLOYEE_ID
EMP_JOB_IX           No     JOB_ID
EMP_MANAGER_IX       No     MANAGER_ID
EMP_NAME_IX          No     LAST_NAME, FIRST_NAME


Triggers on EMPLOYEES

Trigger              Is                   Triggering
Name                 Unique               Event
-------------------- -------------------- -------------------------------
TRIGGER_BODY
-----------------------------------------------------------------------
SECURE_EMPLOYEES     BEFORE STATEMENT     INSERT OR UPDATE OR DELETE
BEGIN
```

```
    secure_dml;
END secure_employees;

UPDATE_JOB_HISTORY    AFTER EACH ROW         UPDATE
BEGIN
  add_job_history(:old.employee_id, :old.hire_date, sysdate,
                   :old.job_id, :old.department_id);
END;
```

How It Works

Although SQL*Plus does offer a DESCRIBE command, as we saw in Chapter 2, the desc.sql script may be more appropriate if you are looking for more information about the table than the basic column names, data types, and "nullability".

This custom describe command (the desc.sql script) is more verbose because it performs detailed queries on the data dictionary for the table name passed to the script. First, the script queries the ALL_TAB_COLUMNS view for detailed information about the columns in the table. Next, we query the ALL_INDEXES and ALL_IND_COLUMNS views for detailed information about the indexes defined for the table. Finally, we query USER_TRIGGERS to show triggers created for the table.

Try It Out – View Details

The next object type we will investigate is views. A view is a custom representation of data that is queried from existing tables (or other views) in your database. Basically, a view is a stored query in the database that you can use just like you would use a table (in most cases). We will discuss views in much more detail in Chapter 14.

In order to get a report describing a view in the database, use the following script to create a file named descview.sql, or download it from the web site:

```
set verify off
set linesize 72
set pagesize 9999
set feedback off
variable owner varchar2(30)
variable vname varchar2(30)
begin
  :owner := USER;
  :vname := upper('&1');
end;
/
Prompt Datatypes for View &1
column data_type format a20
column column_name heading "Column Name"
column data_type    heading "Data|Type"
column data_length heading "Data|Length"
column nullable    heading "Nullable"
select column_name,
       data_type,
       substr(
```

```
        decode( data_type, 'NUMBER',
                decode( data_precision, NULL, NULL,
                  '('||data_precision||','||data_scale||')' ),
            data_length),
                1,11) data_length,
        decode( nullable, 'Y', 'null', 'not null' ) nullable
from all_tab_columns
where owner = :owner
  and table_name = :vname
order by column_id
/
prompt
prompt
prompt Triggers for View &1
set long 5000
select trigger_name, trigger_type,
     triggering_event, trigger_body
from user_triggers where table_name = :vname
/
prompt
prompt
prompt View Definiton for View &1
set long 5000
select text
from user_views where view_name = :vname
/
```

Although views and tables are relatively close in definition, we need to use a different query for views than we do for tables. The desc.sql script we used earlier to view table details will not work for view information because desc.sql queries views in the data dictionary that only show table data. descview.sql queries data dictionary views that show data regarding views.

In this example, we'll use the OC_ORDERS view that belongs to the OE schema:

```
SQL> connect oe/oe
Connected.
SQL> @descview.sql OC_ORDERS

Datatypes for View OC_ORDERS

                          Data              Data
Column Name               Type              Length    Nullable
------------------------  ----------------  --------  --------
ORDER_ID                  NUMBER            (12,0)    null
ORDER_MODE                VARCHAR2          8         null
CUSTOMER_REF              CUSTOMER_TYP      76        null
ORDER_STATUS              NUMBER            (2,0)     null
ORDER_TOTAL               NUMBER            (8,2)     null
SALES_REP_ID              NUMBER            (6,0)     null
ORDER_ITEM_LIST           ORDER_ITEM_LIST   36        null
                          _TYP
```

```
Triggers on OC_ORDERS

Trigger               Is                    Triggering
Name                  Unique                Event
-------------------   --------------------  ------------------------------
TRIGGER_BODY
------------------------------------------------------------------------------
ORDERS_TRG            INSTEAD OF            INSERT
begin
    insert into orders (order_id, order_mode, order_total,
                        sales_rep_id, order_status)
             values (:NEW.order_id, :NEW.order_mode,
                     :NEW.order_total, :NEW.sales_rep_id,
                     :NEW.order_status);
end;


ORDERS_ITEMS_TRG     INSTEAD OF            INSERT
declare
    prod  product_information_typ;
begin
    select DEREF(:NEW.product_ref) into prod from dual;
    insert into order_items values (prod.product_id, :NEW.order_id,
                                    :NEW.line_item_id, :NEW.unit_price,
                                    :NEW.quantity);
end;


View Definition for View OC_ORDERS

TEXT
------------------------------------------------------------------------------
select o.order_id, o.order_mode,make_ref(oc_customers,o.customer_id),
       o.order_status,o.order_total,o.sales_rep_id,
       cast(multiset(select l.order_id,l.line_item_id,l.unit_price,l.quantity,
                     make_ref(oc_product_information,l.product_id)
                 from order_items l
                 where o.order_id = l.order_id)
           as order_item_list_typ)
    from orders o
```

How It Works

Just like the previous scripts, descview.sql is a stored script that we run from SQL*Plus. There are primarily three types of data generated from this script. First, the data types of the view are displayed. Next, any triggers that are defined on the view are displayed. (Even though views don't store rows themselves, you can define a trigger on a view to store data in the underlying relational tables that make up the view's contents.) Finally, the SQL statement that was used to define the view is displayed in the last section.

Try It Out – Stored Procedure Details

Finally, we will take a look at the stored procedural code for one of our schemas. For procedural code, the database listing report you saw at the beginning of this section was useful in showing you what the status is for each object owned by the current user. For instance, if some change in the database invalidated a procedure, function, package, or package body, you would see that indicator in the status (titled S in the output) column of the dbls.sql report. If you are actually employing the procedure, function, or package in your code, however, you need a more in-depth understanding of the procedural code you are using. In this case we use the SQL*Plus DESCRIBE command to see more details about procedural code. Let's use the QS_ADM schema and describe the QS_APPLICATIONS package:

```
SQL> connect qs_adm/qs_adm
Connected.
SQL> desc QS_APPLICATIONS
PROCEDURE BILLING_APP
PROCEDURE GET_SHIP_NOTIFICATION
Argument Name                  Type                    In/Out Default?
------------------------------ ----------------------- ------ --------
ORDERID                        NUMBER                  IN
STATUS                         NUMBER                  OUT
TRACKING_ID                    VARCHAR2                OUT
PROCEDURE NEW_ORDER_DRIVER
Argument Name                  Type                    In/Out Default?
------------------------------ ----------------------- ------ --------
QS_OSTART                      NUMBER                  IN
QS_OSTOP                       NUMBER                  IN
PROCEDURE NEW_ORDER_ENQ
Argument Name                  Type                    In/Out Default?
------------------------------ ----------------------- ------ --------
SIMPLEORDER                    SIMPLEORDER_TYP         IN
CUSTOMER                       CUSTOMER_TYP            IN
ITEMS                          ORDERITEMLIST_VARTYP    IN
PROCEDURE QS_MOVE_ORDERS
PROCEDURE SHIPPING_APP
Argument Name                  Type                    In/Out Default?
------------------------------ ----------------------- ------ --------
CONSUMER                       VARCHAR2                IN
```

By design, the DESCRIBE SQL*Plus command will show you the arguments and data types of a procedure or function. PL/SQL (which we will discuss further in Chapter 10) is meant to implement a black-box style of development, so the exposed procedures and functions are in the package specification. The information you receive by using the DESCRIBE command includes those procedures and/or functions that are in the specification.

For more information about packages, procedures, and functions see Chapter 11.

Now that we have seen a number of scripts to help us learn more about the sample schemas, let's look at another way Oracle provides to document a schema's tables and columns.

Self Documenting Schemas

Oracle provides a way for table owners to store plain-text comments about their table or columns in the database. During the installation of the sample schemas, each schema has a script that creates these comments for their respective tables and columns. This is accomplished using the SQL command CREATE COMMENT.

> *You can find more information about installing the Oracle 9i Sample Schemas in Appendix D.*

For example, the Human Resources schema uses a script named hr_comnt.sql to define its table and column comments. Here's an example of some of the CREATE COMMENT commands in that file:

```
COMMENT ON TABLE jobs
IS 'jobs table with job titles and salary ranges. Contains 19 rows.
References with employees and job_history table.';

COMMENT ON COLUMN jobs.job_id
IS 'Primary key of jobs table.';

COMMENT ON COLUMN jobs.job_title
IS 'A not null column that shows job title, e.g. AD_VP, FI_ACCOUNTANT';

COMMENT ON COLUMN jobs.min_salary
IS 'Minimum salary for a job title.';

COMMENT ON COLUMN jobs.max_salary
IS 'Maximum salary for a job title';
```

Once the comments for the schemas are created, you need to be able to easily view them. To do this, save the following script to a file named comments.sql:

```
set linesize 78
set verify off
variable tname varchar2(200)
begin
  :tname := upper('&1');
end;
/

column comments format a75 heading "Comments" word_wrapped
prompt Table comments for table &1
select comments
  from user_tab_comments
 where table_name = :tname
/

column column_name format a20 heading "Column Name" word_wrapped
column comments format a55 heading "Comments" word_wrapped
prompt
prompt
prompt Column comments for table &1
```

```
select column_name, comments
  from user_col_comments
 where table_name = :tname
 order by column_name
/
```

This script queries the data dictionary views USER_TAB_COMMENTS and USER_COL_COMMENTS in order to display all those comments for a particular table. Using the script on the JOBS table, you can see all the comments created by the Human Resources installation script:

```
SQL> connect hr/hr
Connected.
SQL> @comments JOBS

PL/SQL procedure successfully completed.

Table comments for table JOBS

Comments
----------------------------------------------------------------------
jobs table with job titles and salary ranges. Contains 19 rows.
References with employees and job_history table.




Column comments for table JOBS

Column Name          Comments
-------------------- -------------------------------------------------
JOB_ID               Primary key of jobs table.
JOB_TITLE            A not null column that shows job title, e.g. AD_VP,
                     FI_ACCOUNTANT

MAX_SALARY           Maximum salary for a job title
MIN_SALARY           Minimum salary for a job title.
```

Using the comments.sql script, you and your development team can easily add plain-text comments to the tables and columns in your applications. This provides a database-maintained way of finding out exactly what those tables and columns are for, without having to access a source code control system or some external repository of information. It is good practice to use this script on tables belonging to the Oracle 9i sample schemas, since it will give you better insight as to what these tables are for and how you can use them to learn more about Oracle and demonstrate Oracle technology to others.

Summary

In this chapter, we have looked at Oracle's sample schemas, why they were built and what they are for. We reviewed the SCOTT schema, discussed its history and why it was necessary to come up with new schemas for the database. We then took a look at these new schemas and the rationale behind creating them, and briefly considered what each schema is used for. In this chapter, we have really only skimmed the surface of the functionality showcased with the new Oracle 9i sample schemas. In doing this, we have tried to illustrate how the new schemas in Oracle 9i can be used by both novice and more experienced users, to broaden their abilities in areas they may not have yet ventured into.

At the time of writing, the Oracle 9i database is at version 9.0.1. As new versions of the database are released there are likely to be changes to these schemas, in order to show off any new functionality and options available. Hopefully this chapter has shown you that these schemas are a good place to look for useful samples of technology being implemented as new releases are published.

Architecture

In this chapter, we are going to introduce you to the architectural underpinnings of the Oracle database. Most people who have read about Oracle will have heard about its three core competencies, namely:

❏ **Scalability** – The ability of the Oracle system to take on an increased workload, and scale its system resource usage accordingly. This means that a given system can deal as effectively with 10,000 users, each running five simultaneous sessions, as it can with 10.

❏ **Reliability** – No matter what operating system crashes, power outages, or system failures occur, Oracle can be configured so as to ensure 100% integrity in retrieval of your data and transactions.

❏ **Manageability** – Database administrators have the ability to finely tune how Oracle uses memory, how often Oracle writes data to disk and how the database allocates operating system processes for users connecting to the database.

To make best use of these capabilities, we need to consider how Oracle is put together. There are a number of terms to grasp, many of which are interlinked, but hopefully as we work through this chapter you'll be able to begin to piece together an understanding of the fuller picture. To that end during the course of this chapter we'll be discussing:

❏ Why it is important to understand the architecture

❏ Connections between user processes and the database using Oracle Net Services

❏ Server Processes

❏ Files

❏ Memory Areas

❏ Background Processes

Why Learn the Architecture?

Oracle's architecture is made up of many moving parts. It reminds me of a car that can run really, really fast if the engine is built and tuned properly, or can handle rough terrain as long as the driver has modified the structure to accommodate the harsh environment. An application's functionality, and the manner in which users use that application, will dictate how a database performs based on the way it has been configured. Oracle can be the fastest Formula One racecar on the track or the most durable Humvee on the side of the mountain; it's all in how you tell it to operate.

To this end, Oracle provides a highly 'deployable' solution. What this means is that many of the details of the operating system are abstracted from application developers and database administrators alike. Applications can be written once and deployed on just about any server operating system available. So, for example, you might build your application on a database running on your development server which is a dual processor Windows 2000 server. Once the application has been built and debugged, you could deploy it, with no code changes, to a quad processor Sun Solaris machine running on Solaris hardware in a matter of minutes (depending on the size of the application and data!). At some later date, your IT department might decide to migrate all of your company's hardware investments to Linux. No matter what the reason for this type of hardware change, Oracle will run in a similar fashion on any of these platforms. You can simply export any and all schemas from the original database and import them into the target database. No changes are necessary on the client machine unless you need to change the network configuration to point to the new server(s). The server application will not need to be modified at all, provided you have built your application inside the database.

That being said, I would like to offer a word of warning. Nobody administers an Oracle database in a production environment without having either a system administrator a phone call away, or an intimate understanding of the operating system the database is running on. When you install the database you need to create user accounts and groups at the operating system level to utilize the Oracle software. You need to place files on the file system and your database could take up the lion's share of the best file storage solution. In order to configure the memory areas of the database you need to understand what other processes will run on the server, so as to be able to determine how much real memory the database will have access to, as well as how much memory will be unavailable (having been allocated to other processes on the same server).

By understanding how Oracle's architecture works, you get an appreciation of why these things are so important, and how they impact the operation of your database and therefore your application. Throughout this chapter, we'll walk through the many components of Oracle's underlying architecture. We'll discuss how each of these components works autonomously as well as how they work together. Let's begin by looking at what happens when we first try and connect to an Oracle instance.

Making Connections

In this section we will discuss the three areas of Oracle architecture that work together to give us the ability to connect to a database instance. They are:

❑   User Processes

❑   The Oracle Listener

❑   The Oracle Net Client

User Processes

A **user process** can be thought of as some piece of software (such as a client tool) attempting to connect to the database. The user process communicates with the database using **Oracle Net Services,** which is a suite of components providing network connectivity over a variety of network wire-level protocols. Oracle Net shields application developers and database administrators from the complexity of configuring different network protocols on different hardware platforms. Instead of having to edit the registry on a Windows 2000 server, or the configuration files in /etc on a Linux server, Oracle uses a few simple configuration files (in a single location in the Oracle installation area) to manage Oracle Net. Oracle provides (and encourages the use of) tools such as Oracle Net Manager and Oracle Net Configuration Assistant to configure your Oracle Net Services configuration.

Since the same files are used on every platform, it is easy enough to learn the syntax for them on the operating system you are most comfortable with, and then use that knowledge to configure the files on any server.

The Oracle Listener

The **listener** is a process that normally runs on the Oracle database server and is responsible for 'listening' for connection requests from client applications. The client is responsible for sending along a **service name** to the listener in the initial connection request. This service name is an identifier used to uniquely identify the database instance to which the client is attempting to connect.

Note that, while we will concentrate our discussion here on database services, Oracle listeners are capable of listening for other services besides database instances such as HTTP servers and IIOP servers.

The listener accepts the request, determines whether the request is valid or not, and routes the connection to the appropriate **service handler**. A service handler is some process that the client request is attempting to connect with. In the case of a database service, the two types of service handlers are dedicated server processes or shared server processes. We will discuss dedicated and shared servers a little later in this chapter. Once the connection is routed to the appropriate service handler, the listener's responsibilities have been fulfilled and it awaits additional connection requests.

Up to (and including) Oracle version 8.0, listeners had to be configured statically. This means the listener configuration files had to include the information about the database the listener wanted to connect to. Oracle 8*i* and Oracle 9*i* databases can configure their services dynamically with the listener. **Dynamic registration** (otherwise known as **service registration**) is done through the Oracle background process called the **process monitor**, or **PMON** (we'll come back to PMON later in the chapter). Dynamic registration means the database tells the listener (either a local listener, on the same server as the database or a remote listener) what services are available in the server.

Even if you have not explicitly set up a static listener configuration in your listener configuration files, and your database does not use dynamic registration, the listener uses default values when it is started. The standard listener uses the following assumptions:

❑ **Network protocol:** TCP/IP

❑ **Hostname:** The host the listener is running on

❑ **Port:** 1521

Listener Configuration

If you wish to configure your listener manually, the configuration information can be found in the listener.ora file normally located in $ORACLE_HOME/network/admin on Unix, and %ORACLE_HOME%\network\admin on Windows. On both platforms, an environment variable called TNS_ADMIN can be created that points to the directory where the Oracle Net Services files are located. This is convenient for administrators who want to place their configuration files somewhere other than the default location.

An example of a listener.ora file (on a Linux server) is as follows:

```
LISTENER =
  (ADDRESS_LIST=
    (ADDRESS=(PROTOCOL=tcp)(HOST=slaphappy.us.oracle.com)(PORT=1521))
  )

SID_LIST_LISTENER=
  (SID_LIST=
    (SID_DESC=
      (GLOBAL_DBNAME=slapdb.us.oracle.com)
      (SID_NAME=slapdb)
      (ORACLE_HOME=/u01/app/oracle/Oracle 9i)
    )
  )

SAVE_CONFIG_ON_STOP_LISTENER = ON
LOG_FILE_LISTENER = lsnr.log
LOG_DIRECTORY_LISTENER = /u01/app/oracle/Oracle 9i/network/log
TRACE_FILE_LISTENER = lsnr
TRACE_DIRECTORY_LISTENER = /u01/app/oracle/Oracle 9i/network/log
TRACE_LEVEL_LISTENER = OFF
```

The first entry, LISTENER, is a named listener process that will listen on port 1521, on slaphappy.us.oracle.com, using the TCP/IP protocol. LISTENER is the default name for the Oracle listener when you install the database, but it is possible to create multiple listeners with different names listening on different ports.

The SID_LIST_LISTENER identifies the services available to clients connecting to LISTENER. The SID part stands for **System Identifier**. In the configuration above, SLAPDB is the global database name and US.ORACLE.COM the global database domain that was assigned to the database during installation. SLAPDB is the instance name assigned to the database during installation, and ORACLE_HOME is the directory where the Oracle database is installed.

While a listener is running, it is possible to modify its configuration using a utility Oracle provides called lsnrctl (the utility name can vary from version to version). This is a line-mode application that offers a number of helpful operations such as STOP, START, RELOAD, STATUS, SHOW (parameters), SET (parameters) and others. In the listener configuration file above, SAVE_CONFIG_ON_STOP_LISTENER is a setting that tells Oracle Net Services whether changes to the listener's settings will be written to the listener.ora file or not.

LOG_FILE_LISTENER and LOG_DIRECTORY_LISTENER identify the location of log files for the listener. Events such as long waits for connections, connectivity problems, unexpected denials, or unexpected listener shutdowns will log useful information in the log file. The trace file, identified by the settings TRACE_FILE_LISTENER and TRACE_DIRECTORY_LISTENER, will provide additional details about the operation of Oracle Net components.

Tracing is performed to varying degrees of verbosity. In the configuration above, the TRACE_LEVEL_LISTENER is set to OFF. This means no trace information will be recorded in the trace files, no matter what goes wrong with the listener. Valid settings for TRACE_LEVEL_LISTENER are as follows:

- ❑ OFF. No trace information is generated at all.

- ❑ USER. Trace information is recorded to provide details about errors caused by user connections.

- ❑ ADMIN. The listener traces at a level that would show an administrator any problems with the installation and/or configuration of the listener.

- ❑ SUPPORT. This trace level is used when you call Oracle Service Support (OSS). The information generated in trace files for SUPPORT levels can be sent to OSS for analysis and troubleshooting of problems you may be encountering.

Oracle Net Client

When you use an Oracle client tool such as SQL*Plus, Oracle Enterprise Manager or Oracle Net Manager, the tool understands how to talk to the Oracle database by using the Oracle Net Services client adapter. This allows you to run the client tool from any workstation, provided the tool supports its operating system (Oracle is quickly moving the majority of its management tools over to Java, so operating system support is not generally an issue).

The Oracle client tools, just like the server, must be configured to talk to a database somewhere on the network. For the listener, this file was called listener.ora, while in the case of the client it is called tnsnames.ora. tns stands for **t**ransparent **n**etworking **s**ubstrat, while names simply refers to the 'names' of databases contained in the configuration file. Inside a tnsnames.ora file is a list of **connection descriptors** that can be used by Oracle's tools to connect to a database. A connection descriptor is an entry in the file that specifies information such as the hostname of the server, the protocol used to communicate with the server and the port to use to talk to the listener. An example of a tnsnames.ora file is as follows:

```
SLAPDB.US.ORACLE.COM =
  (DESCRIPTION =
    (ADDRESS_LIST =
      (ADDRESS = (PROTOCOL = TCP)
                 (HOST = slaphappy.us.oracle.com)
                 (PORT = 1521)
      )
    )
    (CONNECT_DATA =
      (SERVICE_NAME = slapdb.us.oracle.com)
    )
  )
```

This style of connecting an Oracle Net client to an Oracle Net listener is known as **localized management**. This means each computer on the network that wants to connect to an Oracle database maintains the connection descriptors in a local configuration file.

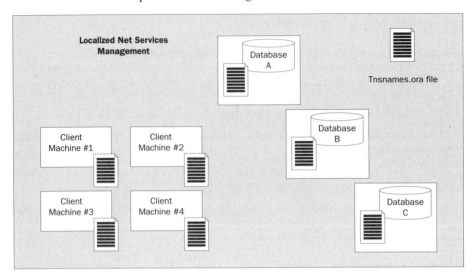

In the diagram above, we see in localized net services management there is a `tnsnames.ora` file on every machine that is capable of connecting to a database. On each of the client machines, you see a `tnsnames.ora` file. Each database server also has a `tnsnames.ora` file. To make things even more confusing, if you have a client or server with more than one Oracle product installed, you may very well have more than one.

So let's say a user on Client Machine #1 wants to connect to Database A. They would start up their database application (SQL*Plus, for instance) using a connect string such as `scott/tiger@slapdb.us.oracle.com`. SQL*Plus would then read the local `tnsnames.ora` file to find an entry corresponding to `slapdb.us.oracle.com`. Using our sample `tnsnames.ora` file above, it would then attempt to contact a database listener on `slaphappy.us.oracle.com`, running on port 1521, with a request to connect the SCOTT user, using the password `tiger`, to the database service named `slapdb.us.oracle.com`.

Although using localized management is convenient for adding, configuring, and removing services, it is problematic when service information (such as a database's server, listener port, service name, etc.) changes. Every `tnsnames.ora` file that refers to that service must be updated. For every client and server machine that has an entry for that service, an administrator or savvy database user must either use an Oracle Net Services utility or manually change the configuration file.

To resolve the administrative nightmare that is localized net services management, Oracle supports **centralized management** of Oracle Net configuration details. This means all the computers on the network point to some central repository that tells the client where to find the database. Up until Oracle 8*i*, the only central repository of services was an **Oracle Names server**. Oracle 8*i* introduced the ability for Oracle Net clients to access an LDAP-compliant **directory server** (named Oracle Internet Directory) for finding services. We won't be talking about these methods of connecting to Oracle, but configuration instructions can be found in the *Oracle 9i Net Services Administrator's Guide* available from http://download-uk.oracle.com/otndoc/Oracle 9i/901_doc/network.901/a90155/toc.htm.

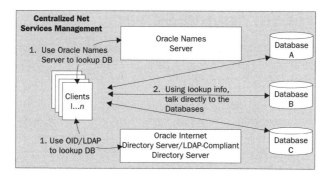

In centralized management, client machines and database servers are configured to look at a central resource for their connection data. In the diagram above, the clients would have entries in their local configurations that point to either an Oracle Names Server or an LDAP-compliant directory server for their connection data. When a user wanted to connect to the database service slapdb.us.oracle.com as the user SCOTT, the tool would take a different path to get its connection details. SQL*Plus (as an example of a database application) would first read the local configuration and find out it should use a names server (or a directory server) for its connection details. It would find out how to connect to the names server from the local configuration and then make a request across the network to the names server for the database connection information for the slapdb.us.oracle.com service. Now the only time changes have to be made to client configurations is when the connection to the names server or directory server changes. Changes to database services, hostnames, ports, service names and other connection details are made centrally and clients get the new connection information the next time they try to connect.

The nice thing about Oracle's Net Services is that it's not an all-or-nothing proposition. You could easily use a central names server or directory server for your corporate applications. Other databases or services that you connect to using net services can be specified in a local tnsnames.ora file. You can then configure database applications on your machine to first check the local configuration in your tnsnames.ora file for connection data, and if the service name is not found there, the tool will make the request to the names or directory server.

An entire book could easily be devoted to Oracle's Net Services and all that they encompass. The purpose of this section of the chapter is to give you a high-level understanding of how Oracle's networking substrat works, and some of the options afforded to you when working with Oracle across a network.

Server Processes

Once Oracle Net Services accepts the user process's connection request it routes the user process to a **server process**. Once this has happened, the server process is responsible for marshaling requests and responses between the user process and the Oracle instance. Whenever a user process submits a query, the server process is responsible for executing the query, reading data from disk into the buffer cache, retrieving the results of the query and then returning the answer to the user process. Even if the response happens to be an error of some kind, the server process will deliver the error information to the user process for appropriate handling. Depending on the server architecture, the connection between the user and server process is maintained so subsequent requests are managed without having to re-establish a connection. There are two different architectures available in Oracle for connecting user processes with server processes, which we mentioned earlier, namely dedicated server and shared server. We'll now take a closer look at them.

Dedicated Server vs. Shared Server

In **dedicated server** mode, as the name suggests, each user process that connects to the database is given its own dedicated server process. This is the way the Oracle database is configured when you install it, and generally the way most database administrators run their databases.

Whereas a dedicated server has a one-to-one mapping of user processes to server processes, a shared server uses a many-to-one relationship. Each server process is responsible for serving many user processes.

> *Prior to Oracle 9i, shared server was called **Multi-Threaded Server (MTS)**. Developers who are familiar with setting up MTS on their database will find most of the concepts have stayed the same, but there are new names for all of the MTS_ related database parameters. The old settings have been maintained for Oracle 8i backward compatibility.*

In shared server mode there is an additional component called the **dispatcher** that is responsible for routing user processes to server processes. When a user process requests a connection to a shared server, Oracle Net Services routes the session request to the dispatcher, not to a server process. The dispatcher then sends the request into a request queue, where the first i\(idle) shared server picks it up. The result generated is placed into a response queue, which in turn is monitored by the dispatcher, and returned to the client.

> **Note that to the user process, there is no difference between working with one mode or the other. The difference between them comes simply from how the process uses memory areas, as we shall see later in this chapter.**

Although configuring a shared server mode is slightly more difficult and some consideration must be given to the clients connecting to the server processes, there are a number of reasons why you would want to use it:

- ❑ It uses a smaller number of server processes (on UNIX-based systems) or threads (on Windows NT/2000-based systems). This is because the user processes share them. With dedicated server, 1000 users connecting to the database over the network would require 1000 server processes (on Unix) or server threads (on Windows) to be started up on the database machine. In a shared server, this number could be greatly reduced because one server process might serve 5, 10, or even 50 user processes (depending of course, on your application).

- ❑ It reduces memory consumption. As you will see later when we discuss memory areas, each server process is allocated its own **Program Global Area (PGA)**. Since we are running a much smaller number of server processes, the need to allocate the greater number of PGAs is eliminated.

- ❑ When it is mandatory. For the **Enterprise Java Beans (EJB)** container in the Oracle database, you must use the **Internet Inter-Orb Protocol (IIOP)** to connect to beans running inside this container. Currently, this must be configured using a shared server.

Using a shared server is not a difficult thing; it's just a different thing. When you have user populations in the thousands you should give serious consideration to employing a shared server.

Files

Now that we have seen the process underlying connection to the database, we'll take a look at the file system that Oracle utilizes. The data dictionary, your application data, parameters to be used for database startup, transaction logs, files for managing the physical structure of the database, and many other types of files are utilized by the processes of the Oracle database in its day-to-day operations. Let's begin by taking a look at the parameter files.

Parameter files

Parameter files are used to configure the database when the instance is started. When creating a database, you use an initialization file (a form of parameter file commonly referred to as a `pfile` or an `init.ora` file) to specify values for a variety of settings to be used in the database. These settings include things such as the name of the database instance (the SID), the locations of key files for your database, and the size of the key memory areas for your instance. There are many, many other parameters specified in this initialization file. The name of this file is typically `init<SID>.ora`. For example, if the database's instance name is `SLAPDB`, then its initialization file is `initslapdb.ora`. The contents of this file are very straightforward. You will find a parameter and its value separated by an equals sign on each line. As an example, this is an excerpt from an `init.ora` file on a Linux server:

```
############################################
# Diagnostics and Statistics
############################################
background_dump_dest=/u01/app/oracle/Oracle 9i/admin/slapdb/bdump
core_dump_dest=/u01/app/oracle/Oracle 9i/admin/slapdb/cdump
timed_statistics=TRUE
user_dump_dest=/u01/app/oracle/Oracle 9i/admin/slapdb/udump


############################################
# Distributed, Replication and Snapshot
############################################
distributed_transactions=0
db_domain=us.oracle.com
remote_login_passwordfile=EXCLUSIVE


############################################
# File Configuration
############################################
control_files=("/u01/app/oracle/Oracle 9i/oradata/slapdb/control01.ctl",
"/u01/app/oracle/Oracle 9i/oradata/slapdb/control02.ctl", "/u01/app/oracle/Oracle
9i/oradata/slapdb/control03.ctl")
...
```

After the database is created, the initialization file is only used during instance startup. When the instance starts up, it reads this file to establish the settings we discussed previously, along with a great many other database parameters available to administrators to set in the file. Almost every parameter has a default value, and therefore the initialization files will vary in size depending on how the database is configured to meet specific needs.

A comprehensive list of the database parameters can be found online in the "Oracle 9i Database Reference" (part of the official Oracle documentation available from http://otn.oracle.com/docs/content.html) in the "Initialization Parameters" section (for Oracle 9i Release 1 (9.0.1) this is available from http://download-uk.oracle.com/otndoc/Oracle9i/901_doc/server.901/a90190/ch1.htm)

Parameter files are used for a number of reasons. Obviously, there are default settings that you will want to modify to accommodate your database needs. The number of cursors that can be open in the database, the number of processes the database can manage at any one time, and the default language or character set of the database are settings you will alter depending on the needs of the applications and users accessing the database. Other parameters, on the other hand, can be used to tune the instance. Memory parameters such as the size of the shared pool, the default block size for the database, and the number of blocks in the buffer cache are prime examples of these types of parameters. We will be taking a closer look at these memory parameters later in this chapter.

> **Before you modify settings in this file, make sure you fully understand not only the parameter you are changing, but also the impact it will have on your database once the change is activated. If parameters are not set properly your database will run inefficiently, and might not even run at all!**

Those parameters that can only be updated by shutting down the database are known as **static initialization parameters**. There are however a number of parameters that can be updated within the current database instance, and they are known as **dynamic initialization parameters**. Such dynamic parameters can be updated using one of two SQL statements:

- ❑ ALTER SYSTEM – this command has a global impact, and affects all sessions currently active on the database.

- ❑ ALTER SESSION – this command will only modify the parameter for the length of the current session.

As an example of modifying server parameters, let's look at changing a couple of parameters at the system level in our database. First, we'll look at the values for OPEN_CURSORS and UTL_FILE_DIR. We would most likely want to modify OPEN_CURSORS on a system-wide basis because any cursor opened by a user counts against the OPEN_CURSORS count. The same goes for UTL_FILE_DIR. If any user in the database wants to use the UTL_FILE database-supplied package to read or write to/from files on the host file system, the server parameter UTL_FILE_DIR must be configured properly. Let's find some values for these parameters and then try to modify them using ALTER SYSTEM:

```
SQL> show parameters open_cursors

NAME                         TYPE                VALUE
------------------------------------ ---------------- ------------------

open_cursors                 integer             300

SQL> show parameters utl_file_dir
```

```
NAME                     TYPE              VALUE
----------------------------------------------------

utl_file_dir             string/tmp
```

Let's assume we want to modify our OPEN_CURSORS parameter to be 500 instead of 300, and our UTL_FILE_DIR to be /home/sdillon instead of /tmp. Here we see that OPEN_CURSORS is a dynamic initialization parameter (because we can perform it without shutting down the database), whereas UTL_FILE_DIR is static (because it is rejected whilst the database is running):

```
SQL> alter system set open_cursors = 500
  2  /

System altered.

SQL> alter system set utl_file_dir = '/home/sdillon'
  2  /
alter system set utl_file_dir = '/home/sdillon'
                       *
ERROR at line 1:
ORA-02095: specified initialization parameter cannot be modified
```

Changes made to parameters in a running instance are lost once the database is shut down and restarted. In order for the changes to persist across an instance shutdown and startup, the initialization file must be modified or, in the case of Oracle 9i, you must use **server parameter files**.

Server Parameter Files

Server parameter files are a new type of parameter file offered in Oracle 9i for managing database parameters and values. Server parameter files are an alternative to static text initialization files (init<SID>.ora). These binary files can be thought of as a repository for parameters and values that *can* persist across an instance shutdown and startup. When changes are made to database parameters using the ALTER SYSTEM SQL statement, the user executing the statement has the option of making the change in the server parameter file, memory, or both. If a change is made to a server parameter file, the change will be persistent and manual modifications to a static initialization file are unnecessary. The ALTER SYSTEM SQL statement has three different options for specifying the 'scope' of a change:

❑   SPFILE. When you specify the scope of SPFILE, parameters that can be modified while an instance is online will take effect immediately. A restart is not necessary. For parameters that cannot be changed while an instance is running, the change will be made in the server parameter file only, and will take effect only after the instance has been restarted.

❑   MEMORY. This is the default behavior and represents the only functionality that was available prior to Oracle 9i. ALTER SYSTEM statements that specify SCOPE = MEMORY will take place immediately and no change to the server parameter file will be made. Once the instance restarts, these changes to database parameters are lost. For ALTER SYSTEM statements using SCOPE = MEMORY, database parameters that cannot be changed until the database is restarted will return an error, since the change can only take place when the instance is restarted (as we saw in the example above).

❏ BOTH. This option for the scope of an ALTER SYSTEM command is the previous two scopes combined. The only parameters that can be specified in this command are those that can change while an instance is running. Once the change is made, all sessions will immediately be affected by the change and the server parameter file is updated so the change will be reflected even after the instance has been restarted.

There are three views in the data dictionary you can use to investigate your database parameters (for more on using views, see Chapter 14). These are V$PARAMETER, V$SYSTEM_PARAMETER, and V$SPPARAMETER. Querying these views will return the following characteristics of the database parameters as they relate to your session, the system, and the server parameter files.

❏ V$PARAMETER. What the database parameters are for your current session.

❏ V$PARAMETER2. The same as V$PARAMETER, but listed parameters appear as two different rows instead of one comma-delimited row (as in V$PARAMETER).

❏ V$SYSTEM_PARAMETER. What the database parameters are for the entire system. New sessions get their parameter values from this view.

❏ V$SYSTEM_PARAMETER2. This is just like V$PARAMETER2, where list parameters appear as two different rows instead of one comma-delimited row.

❏ V$SPPARAMETER. This view contains the contents of the stored parameter file.

Control Files

Control files are binary files that are used by the Oracle server during startup to identify the physical files and structure of the database. They provide a directory of the necessary files required whenever a new instance is created. Oracle will also update the control file during normal database operations so that it is ready for the next time.

When you create a control file, it is recommended that you create more than one copy and, if possible, place these copies on different physical devices. In this way, if one device crashes, you will have a good copy of the control file to be used to start up and recover the database. Without the control files, recovering an Oracle database becomes very complicated.

Data Files

Data files are where your data resides. These files are of critical importance to the stability and integrity of your data. Without these files, you have no data and therefore you have no database.

To understand how data is stored in the database, we need to look at the logical storage constructs that exist within Oracle, and illustrate how Oracle's logical storage eventually maps to physical storage.

Tablespaces

Tablespaces are the largest logical storage structure you will deal with in Oracle. Everything you create in the database is stored in a tablespace. Every Oracle database is preconfigured with a SYSTEM tablespace, which stores the data dictionary and system-managed information. Users and applications normally use their own tablespaces to store data. Data written into temporary tables, blocks written to disk for large sort operations, and many other types of temporary data are written into a tablespace.

Users have a default tablespace and a temporary tablespace. A **default tablespace** is the tablespace where a user's objects are stored by default. When you create a table, you can optionally tell Oracle which tablespace to store the table's data in. If you don't specify a tablespace, Oracle will store the table's data in your default tablespace. A user's **temporary tablespace** is where temporary data is written. When you do queries that cause blocks to be paginated to disk (because there is not enough room to process the entire query in memory) the data is paginated to your temporary tablespace. When you write data into temporary tables this data is written to your temporary tablespace.

Segments

A segment is the stored representation of database objects you create. Every table you create has a logical segment stored in a tablespace. Segments are created for any object you create that requires space consumption on disk. There are three types of segment:

❑   **Data segments** are where normal application data, such as tables, indexes, clusters, and table partitions, are stored.

❑   **Temporary segments** are those within temporary tablespaces, used to store items such as temporary tables, and SQL operations that cause paginated memory.

❑   **Rollback segments** are used for managing UNDO data in our database and for providing a **read-consistent view** of the database for transactions.

Rollback Segments, Oracle's Undo Mechanism

When you modify data in the database, the changes are not permanent until you commit your data to it. You can change every row in a one-million-row table, and decide later to roll back the change, meaning nobody will ever know that you tried to change the records. When we roll back a transaction, therefore, any changes we have made since our last COMMIT statement have to be taken back. This is where rollback segments earn their paycheck.

A rollback segment is responsible for storing the necessary information to roll back changes you make to the database. It records copies of the data as it existed before a transaction modified it. When you roll back your transaction, the information contained in the rollback segments are used to 'undo' the changes you have made to the database.

Once a transaction has been committed, the UNDO data is left in the rollback segments to provide a read-consistent view for queries that began before the commit. This works great in theory but sometimes fails due to improperly sized rollback segments. Committed UNDO data in the rollback segments only lasts as long as it takes Oracle to write new UNDO data to the segment. If your rollback segments are too small, new UNDO data will overwrite UNDO data that might be necessary in ongoing long queries. When the ongoing query tries to reconstruct a read-consistent view of the data, and the committed UNDO data has been overwritten by new UNDO data, Oracle returns the error:

```
ORA-01555 snapshot-too-old.
```

With **Automatic Undo Management** in Oracle 9*i*, there have been significant steps towards resolving this issue.

Automatic Undo Management

Automatic Undo Management is a new concept in Oracle 9*i* that alleviates the need to create, manage, resize or specify rollback segments for transactions. In Oracle 8*i* and earlier releases of the database, administrators had to manually create tablespaces to store their rollback segments. Rollback segments had to be sized appropriately depending on the types of transactions users were performing and the amount of time it took for users to complete queries. Sizing rollback segments involved knowledge, experience, and a bit of luck in most cases.

In Oracle 9*i*, administrators can create UNDO **tablespaces** to manage all the rollback data necessary for the instance. There is no need to size individual rollback segments in this mode of operation, as the database will automatically manage all the transactions' UNDO data in this tablespace for you.

Using automatic undo offers a new feature previously not available with manual rollback segment mode called UNDO **Retention**. UNDO_RETENTION is a new init.ora parameter that specifies the number of seconds that rollback data should be left available after a transaction has committed. This is a way to ensure long-running queries in a system will run successfully without encountering the ORA-01555 snapshot too old error. As we learned earlier in this chapter, this error occurs because committed data is overwritten in the rollback segments with new rollback data. By retaining data in the rollback segment for a longer period of time, long running queries and serialized transactions are that much less likely to produce it.

Another new concept related to UNDO data management is UNDO **Quota**. In Oracle, a feature called **Resource Manager** allows you to restrict the consumption of various resources from users. Some examples of resources you can restrict are query times, CPU utilization for processes, and temporary space utilization. With Resource Manager, you define groups of users called **consumer groups**, and assign these groups an UNDO_QUOTA. This prevents users from running ill-behaved transactions that consume more than their share of UNDO space in the UNDO tablespace.

You aren't forced to use this style of undo management; it's simply a (**strongly recommended**) option. There is a new init.ora parameter called UNDO_MODE in Oracle 9i that allows you to specify the undo mode you wish to use in your database:

❑   #undo_management = auto

❑   #undo_management = manual

❑   #undo_tablespace = UNDOTBS

You can read more about committing and rolling back transactions in the next chapter and also in Chapter 12, Transactions and Concurrency.

Extents

Now that we have learned about tablespaces and various types of segments, we'll look at **extents**. Segments are made up of one or more extents. An extent is a collection of logically contiguous data blocks used to store data for the segment.

When a database object is created (one that requires space consumption, anyway), it also creates one or more extents to store its data. The number of extents and the size of the extents being created are specified in the storage clause for the object being created. For instance, you might create a table using the following SQL statement:

```
SQL> create table my_hash_table (
  2     name          varchar2(30),
  3     value    varchar2(4000) )
  4  tablespace users
  5  storage (
  6     initial       1M
  7     next          512K
  8     pctincrease   0
  9     minextents    2
 10     maxextents    unlimited )
 11  /

Table created.
```

In Oracle 9i, the default extent management style for tablespaces is locally managed, not dictionary managed (there is more on these concepts later). That means INITIAL, NEXT, PCTINCREASE, and MAXEXTENTS are completely unnecessary in the statement above.

Here we are creating a table MY_HASH_TABLE to be stored in the USERS tablespace. The storage clause indicates four parameters to help Oracle understand how the table should be created:

❑ INITIAL. This is the size of the first extent created for this object. In this case, we are making a one MB extent.

❑ NEXT. This is the extent size for subsequent extents. The second extent allocated for this table (and every one thereafter) will be 512 KB.

❑ MINEXTENTS. This is the number of extents to be allocated right away. When the Table created message is returned, 2 extents have been created to store rows for the MY_HASH_TABLE table.

❑ MAXEXTENTS. This is the maximum number of extents that can be made for this table. This can be a number value or UNLIMITED. For my particular table, I chose to use an unlimited number of extents.

Once we have written over (1 MB + 512 KB) 1.5 MB of data to this table, Oracle will have to extend the segment by allocating another extent. This extent might not be contiguous to the other extents (in fact it could even be in a different file), but will be in the same tablespace (USERS) as the other extents for the object. Once that extent has filled up and Oracle needs to put more data in the table, another extent will be allocated.

In Oracle 8, locally managed tablespaces were introduced that made this form of extent management obsolete. As far as extent management goes, locally managed tablespaces handle this in one of two ways. Either every extent is the same size, or Oracle manages the size of the extents that are allocated for the segment. Either way, the extent management is completely handled for you. Specifying storage clause attributes at the object level is considered poor practice and unnecessary in the more recent versions.

Data Blocks

Data blocks represent the finest level of logical data storage in the database. At the lowest level, an extent is made up of a collection of contiguous data blocks. Extents make up segments, segments make up tablespaces, and tablespaces make up the database. There is some confusion about the relationship between Oracle's data blocks and the operating system's data blocks. To clear this up, even though the operating system might use a 1/2k block size, Oracle can use a variety of block sizes that are completely unrelated to them.

In Oracle 8*i* and previous releases of the database, the block size had to be the same for every tablespace in the database. In general, block sizes are 2 KB, 4 KB, 8 KB, 16 KB, or 32 KB. Normally, they are 2, 4, or 8 KB. In Oracle 9*i*, however, databases are allowed to specify a data block size for each tablespace. In designing your database, different block sizes can be used for different types of data and/or different types of data access.

These are the parts of a data block and the type of information held in each one:

❑ **Block header**. Information such as the type of data (segment type) and the physical location of the block is stored in the header.

❑ **Table directory**. Data from more than one table can be stored in a single block. The table directory tells Oracle which tables are stored in the block.

❑ **Row directory**. This tells Oracle the physical location of each row within the block.

❑ **Free space**. When a block is first allocated, it only has free space and there is no row data. As rows are inserted, the free space gets smaller and smaller until the block is completely full of rows (depending on the storage parameters for the segment).

❑ **Row data**. This is where the actual rows are stored within the block.

These are the logical and physical structures of data files in the Oracle database. As you get more familiar with Oracle, you will find that having a deeper and more detailed understanding of these structures, how they work, how to size them, and how they affect the performance of your applications will become critical in your success as an Oracle administrator. Database developers don't have to be as savvy when it comes to the physical and logical storage of these structures; however, the information included in this section is something every Oracle developer should have a thorough understanding of.

Pre-allocated Files

When you create a data file for a tablespace using the CREATE TABLESPACE or the ALTER TABLESPACE SQL commands, you will normally tell Oracle how big to make the data file in the SIZE clause of the SQL statement. For example:

```
SQL> create tablespace MY_APPLICATION_TABLESPACE
  2  datafile '/u01/app/oracle/Oracle 9i/oradata/slapdb/myapp.dbf' size 20M
  3  autoextend on next 10M maxsize 1000M
  4  extent management local uniform size 1M
  5  /

Tablespace created.
```

In this case, the SIZE 20M clause tells Oracle to make a 20 MB file for this tablespace. The file is created at the same time as the tablespace, and the 20 MB are pre-allocated so Oracle can write to the file without worrying about running out of space. Even though you may not have a single block of data stored in the tablespace yet, the file system still shows a 20 MB file as this listing from my filesystem on UNIX shows:

```
$ cd /u01/app/oracle/Oracle 9i/oradata/slapdb/
$ ls -l myapp.dbf
-rw-r-----    1 oracle    dba        20979712 Dec  7 10:00 myapp.dbf
```

When using Oracle Managed Files or if the data file already exists (such as when you are reusing an existing data file) you don't have to specify the size of the file. We'll talk more about Oracle Managed Files later in this chapter.

Redo Log Files

Where your database files store the most current representation of data in the tables, indexes and other structures of the database, your redo log files record all the changes that have taken place in your database. They are your transaction logs. These files are of critical importance, as they are used for instance recovery in the case of some media failure, power outage or other crash that causes your database to shut down or somehow get corrupted unexpectedly. Without these files, the only recovery you could hope to perform is to restore your last complete backup. We we'll see more about redo log files when we discuss the log writer later in this chapter.

Temporary Files

Temporary files in Oracle are handled a little differently from standard data files. These files do contain data, but only for temporary operations such as sorting data that doesn't fit in the **Program Global Area** (PGA) or for data that is inserted into temporary tables or indexes. The data is only stored temporarily, and is dropped from the database completely once the session that created it is done with it.

Each user in the database has a temporary tablespace assigned to their account. When a user needs to write data to a temporary tablespace as with large SORT BY or GROUP BY operations in SELECT statements, or when inserting data into temporary tables, this temporary tablespace is used. Temporary tablespaces should *always* be created using a temporary file instead of a standard data file. The syntax for this is as follows:

```
SQL> create temporary tablespace temp_tblspace
  2  tempfile '/u01/app/oracle/Oracle 9i/oradata/slapdb/temp_tblspace.dbf'
  3  size 10M
  4  extent management local
  5  uniform size 512K
  6  /

Tablespace created.
```

Dictionary Managed Temporary Tablespaces

When creating temporary tablespaces, you need to determine whether you will use locally managed or dictionary managed tablespaces. The preferred mechanism in Oracle 8*i* and Oracle 9*i* is locally managed tablespaces. The syntax we used above would create a locally managed tablespace because of the clauses we used in the CREATE TABLESPACE statement. In order to create a dictionary managed temporary tablespace with the same structure as our TEMP_TBLSPACE tablespace above, use the following syntax:

```
SQL> create tablespace temp_tblspace_dm
  2  datafile '/u01/app/oracle/Oracle 9i/oradata/slapdb/temp_tblspace_dm.dbf'
  3  size 10M
  4  default storage(
  5    initial     1M
  6    next        512K
  7    minextents  1
  8    pctincrease 0)
  9  extent management dictionary
 10  temporary
 11  /

Tablespace created.
```

There are quite a few differences in this statement, when compared to the CREATE TABLESPACE statement used for a locally managed tablespace:

Dictionary Managed Temporary Tablespace	Locally Managed Temporary Tablespace
CREATE TABLESPACE	CREATE TEMPORARY TABLESPACE
DATAFILE	TEMPFILE
EXTENT MANAGEMENT DICTIONARY	EXTENT MANAGEMENT LOCAL
DEFAULT STORAGE clause	AUTOEXTEND clause
TEMPORARY at the end of the statement	TEMPORARY as a part of CREATE TEMPORARY TABLESPACE

'Temporary' Standard Tablespaces

A common mistake people tend to make is to create a tablespace that will be used as the temporary tablespace for user accounts, but the tablespace is not a *temporary* tablespace, it is a normal tablespace (using a datafile rather than a tempfile). The following code is an example of this:

```
SQL> create tablespace temp_tblspace2
  2  datafile '/u01/app/oracle/Oracle 9i/oradata/slapdb/tempspace2.dbf'
  3  size 10M
  4  extent management local
  5  uniform size 64K
  6  /

Tablespace created.
```

170

Although assigning a user's temporary tablespace to a normal tablespace (in other words, *not* a temporary tablespace) works fine, it can cause extra work for your database administrator. Standard tablespaces should be backed up as part of normal backup and recovery procedures and our example just added an additional, unnecessary one to the list. You should avoid doing this if possible.

Oracle Managed Files

In Oracle 8*i*, the files you have learned about are managed largely through the operating system's standard file I/O interface. For example, when you create a database you specify the directory and filename for files such as the system tablespace, redo log files, control files, and parameter files. This assumes that you know the target file system the database will be installed upon. This also assumes you know the directory structure of the target database host or at least the directory tree where all these files will reside.

In tablespace operations, when you create a new tablespace you must give Oracle the fully qualified filename that will be the data file containing the tablespace's segments. When you extend a tablespace manually by adding a data file, you must indicate the new data file name. A problem that plagued Oracle for years (before Oracle 9*i*) arises when you drop a tablespace from the database. The data file for the tablespace is left on the file system, along with all the space consumption that goes with it. If the tablespace was 500 MB, there is now a useless 500 MB file on the file system. The file must be removed manually. If a new tablespace is created, you can use the CREATE TABLESPACE <TABLESPACE_NAME> <SIZE> REUSE command to tell Oracle to reuse the file for the new tablespace. This will resize the file to the size specified in the CREATE TABLESPACE command.

Managing the physical files is a tedious, time-consuming problematic process. Imagine if a database administrator were to drop a large tablespace and delete the wrong file from the file system! If you want to create a 'scratch' database, or a small test/development database, managing the files, for this database is nothing but unnecessary overhead. If you write a reusable SQL script to create a test database, you have to know the target platform because you have to tell Oracle which files to use. These are just a few of the issues Oracle 8*i* databases (and all previous releases) have to deal with regarding file management.

In Oracle 9*i*, however, Oracle introduces **Oracle Managed Files**. When an administrator uses Oracle Managed Files for their database, manual file management is eliminated for the following types of database objects:

❏   Tablespaces

❏   Control files

❏   Online redo log files

Using Oracle Managed Files does not preclude an administrator using the old style of file management *as well*. You can still specify explicit filenames for your tablespaces, redo log files and control files. A hybrid approach can be used for databases that have upgraded to Oracle 9*i* from Oracle 8*i*, for instance.

Enabling Oracle Managed Files is simple. In your parameter file, you can set a parameter named DB_CREATE_FILE_DEST to the default directory Oracle should use for data files, temp files, online redo log files and control files. Since Oracle recommends you mirror control files and online redo log files on multiple devices, you can set multiple parameters named with a sequential number in the format DB_CREATE_ONLINE_LOG_DEST_*n*. Your parameters might look like the following on a Windows 2000 database server:

171

```
db_create_file_dest = 'D:\Oracle\groovylap\oradata'
db_create_online_log_dest_1 = 'D:\Oracle\groovylap\oradata'
db_create_online_log_dest_2 = 'E:\Oracle\groovylap\oradata'
db_create_online_log_dest_3 = 'F:\Oracle\groovylap\oradata'
```

When online redo log files or control files are created by the database, they are placed in these destination directories according to the sequence number at the end of the parameter name. The first file would be created in D:\Oracle\groovylap\oradata, the second in E:\Oracle\groovylap\oradata and so on. One file will be created for each DB_CREATE_ONLINE_LOG_DEST_n parameter you have specified in your parameter file. If you haven't specified any extra parameters, Oracle will use the DB_CREATE_FILE_DEST parameter. Note that if this parameter is not set, Oracle will be unable to use Oracle Managed Files.

Memory Areas

There are a number of memory areas that participate in the well-orchestrated symphony that is the Oracle database. Oracle's server processes and many background processes are responsible for writing, updating, reading, and removing data from these memory areas. Different memory areas have different purposes in the architecture, and it is important to know what each memory area is used for in order to understand the flow of data and processes during the database's operations. This section will teach you about the three major memory areas in the Oracle instance:

- ❑ **System Global Area** (**SGA**). This is the instance's shared memory area for all the users to access. Data blocks, transaction logs, data dictionary information, and so on, are stored in the SGA.

- ❑ **Program Global Area** (**PGA**). This is a class of memory that is not shared; it is dedicated to a particular server process and is accessed only by that process.

- ❑ **User Global Area** (**UGA**). This memory area stores session states for the user processes we discussed earlier in the chapter. The UGA is a part of the SGA or the PGA, depending on whether your database is configured in a dedicated or shared server mode. It stores data for a user's session.

In this section we'll take a more focused look at how different memory areas interact with the files of the database, and how shared server and dedicated server change the way the memory is configured.

System Global Area (SGA)

As indicated above, the SGA is a shared memory area and is the hub of the database operations. It contains pieces of data such as cached data blocks (stored in memory for use by users' sessions), SQL statements (and their execution plans) that have been executed against the database, and program units such as procedures, functions and triggers that are executed (and thus, shared) by many users. This data is stored in a shared memory area for fast access by the large number of processes that run in an Oracle instance. All users connected to the database use the data stored in the SGA. Since the data is shared, the System Global Area is sometimes referred to as the **Shared Global Area**.

As disk space is pre-allocated when tablespaces are created, the SGA is also pre-allocated from the operating system's memory when the instance is started. If there is not enough memory in the server to fit the entire SGA, portions of the SGA will be paged to disk. This leads to undue poor performance because Oracle assumes the SGA is in real memory. When the host operating system is not able to accommodate the real memory requirements, Oracle is forced to 'virtualize' the unavailable memory by using temporary space in data files.

> **This unexpected I/O contention and constant paging of memory is not how Oracle is meant to be used in a production environment, and should be avoided at all costs.**

There are a few different areas within the SGA we will review. Each area within the SGA is used to store some piece of data that is shared amongst users, and by breaking the data up into different areas we can tune our database by sizing and configuring these areas according to the needs of our applications.

Block Buffer Cache

The **block buffer cache**, otherwise known as the **database buffer cache** or simply **buffer cache**, is used to store copies of data blocks that have been read into memory. These data blocks are put there by server processes executing either a SQL statement that needs to read those data blocks to answer a query submitted by a user process, or an update of data blocks according to a user process's instructions. The data blocks are stored in the buffer cache so that when server processes need to read or write to them, Oracle can avoid performing unnecessary disk I/O thus enhancing read/write performance of the database.

As server processes read data blocks into the buffer cache, the buffer cache uses internal mechanisms for tracking which blocks should be written to disk and which blocks should be timed out of the buffer cache due to lack of use. In Oracle 8i and Oracle 9i, this is accomplished by maintaining a count (known as the **touch count**) of the number of times a particular block is accessed. As a block is read, its touch count is incremented. This way when Oracle needs to flush blocks from the buffer cache to make room for new blocks being read into memory by server processes, it just finds the blocks with the smallest touch counts and flushes them from the buffer.

> *In Oracle 8.0, there is no concept of a touch count. The mechanism used to maintain this data is known as a **Least Recently Used** list, or LRU. All the blocks in the buffer cache are listed in the LRU, and as the blocks are accessed they are moved toward the most-recently-used end of the list, or the tail. All the other blocks are moved toward the least-recently-used end, or the head. As a block is read into the buffer cache it is inserted into the tail of the LRU. If a block isn't accessed, it eventually ends up 'sliding' to the head of the LRU. When a server needs to make room for new blocks being read into the buffer cache, the blocks listed at the head of the LRU will be flushed from memory because they are the blocks that have been accessed the least.*

The other mechanism used in the buffer cache to maintain information about data blocks is called the **Write List** (or **Dirty List**). This list is responsible for identifying those blocks within the buffer cache that have been modified by a server process. The data blocks on this list need to be flushed to disk before they are purged from memory. When a user updates a record in the database, Oracle gets the data block containing that record into the buffer cache (if it's not already there) and modifies the block in memory. Once it has been modified it is placed on the write list to make sure the next time the database writer is invoked to flush dirty buffers to disk, this modified data block is included in the write.

173

Buffer Caches for Block Sizes

In Oracle 9*i*, tablespaces may have different block sizes. This is helpful because different types of data and different types of application will benefit from using different block sizes. Because there are different block sizes, there are different buffer caches for each block size.

The database parameter that defines the default block size for the entire database is db_block_size. For the default buffer cache (default meaning the buffer cache for blocks of the database's default block size), the database parameter is db_cache_size. For each of the other block sizes in the database, there are corresponding db_*nk*_cache_size parameters (that is, db_2k_cache_size, db_4k_cache_size, etc.). It should be noted that you cannot have a db_*nk*_cache_size parameter defined for the default database block size. A typical init.ora file might read as follows for the buffer cache parameters:

```
db_block_size=8192
db_cache_size=20971520
db_2k_cache_size=20971520
db_4k_cache_size=20971520
# The following would be illegal because 8k is the default block size
# db_8k_cache_size=20971520
```

Redo Log Buffer

The **redo log buffer**, otherwise known as the **redo buffer**, stores data that is targeted for the online redo log files. These files are our transaction logs, recording all committed transactions that occur in the database for the purpose of instance recovery. The redo log buffer acts in a similar fashion to the buffer cache in this regard, with transaction data being temporarily cached in the redo log buffer. This temporary storage of data to memory and periodic write to disk is a performance mechanism. It simply speeds up the virtual I/O speed of writing our transaction data to disk.

Due to the high frequency of disk writes the log buffer is relatively small in relation to other memory areas in the SGA, such as the buffer cache, the shared pool, and the large pool. The default size of the redo log buffer is either 500K or 128K x CPU_COUNT, whichever is greater (CPU_COUNT being the number of CPUs in your host operating system available to Oracle). It makes no sense whatsoever to have a redo log buffer of 500 MB since the log writer flushes the buffer to disk as soon as it contains 1 MB of data.

The initialization parameter LOG_BUFFER specifies the size, in bytes, of the redo log buffer. The default setting for the redo log buffer is four times the maximum size of a block on the host operating system.

Shared pool

The **shared pool** is used to store information in memory for use by other sessions. Such information includes SQL statements, PL/SQL code, control structures (such as locks to table rows or memory areas), and data dictionary information. This information is shared and accessible by all users, being stored as a part of the SGA. The shared pool is broken into many separate areas, but two are of particular interest to us here:

❑ **The library cache**. Stores SQL execution plans and cached PL/SQL code.

❑ **The dictionary cache**. Stores data dictionary information.

174

The library cache is used to store SQL statements and PL/SQL code issued against the database. A lot of work must be done to answer a SQL statement, and the shared pool is provided to store the results of this work so, if the same statement is encountered later, it can avoid doing the same work again. We'll see more details on the processing of queries in Chapter 6, *Processing SQL*.

The data dictionary in Oracle is used heavily in almost every single thing you do in the database. Even if you are not submitting queries directly against the data dictionary, Oracle uses tables and views behind the scenes to provide results to queries, perform DML operations on tables and execute DDL statements. For this reason, Oracle has a special space in the shared pool known as the **dictionary cache** for storing this data dictionary information.

The shared pool uses a modified **Least Recently Used (LRU)** algorithm that is much the same as the block buffer cache in Oracle 8.0. As space is needed in the shared pool for new entries, items in the shared pool that have not been used will be released from memory to make room. As SQL statements are reused or PL/SQL code is executed, it is moved to the most-recently-used end of the LRU. Blocks in the shared pool are release from the least-recently-used end of the LRU to make room for new entries in the shared pool.

The database parameter SHARED_POOL_SIZE is used to size the shared pool. This value is specified in bytes.

Large Pool

The **large pool** is an optional memory space that can be configured by the database administrator for a different class of memory storage. The reason this area is called the *large pool* is not because its overall size should be any larger than any other memory area in the SGA; it is because it stores cached data in chunks larger than 4K, the size of the chunks in the shared pool.

The way Oracle allocates and frees data in this pool is significantly different from the other memory areas we have discussed. There is no touch count or least-recently-used list to manage the large pool. Chunks of memory in the large pool are allocated and maintained until they are no longer needed, and then they are released.

Not only is the large pool different because of the typical size of data it stores, but also because of the types of data it stores:

❑   Session memory for shared server processes

❑   Backup and restore operations

❑   Parallel execution message buffers

When the database is configured in shared server mode, server processes store their session-specific data in the large pool instead of the shared pool. Once the session logs out, we know the memory will never be used again and therefore the large pool will free the memory to be used by other sessions. In backup and restore operations, the memory used for recovering or backing up the database should not be contending for space in the shared pool or buffer cache. These types of operation will allocate the necessary area to perform their work and once it is complete the memory will be freed.

Program Global Area (PGA)

The PGA is an area of memory used to store private data for an individual server process. Unlike the single SGA, which is a shared memory area accessible by all the server processes, the database writer, the log writer, and many other background processes, there is one PGA for each server process. PGAs are accessible only by their own server process.

There is a memory area called the **User Global Area (UGA)**, which stores a session's state. The location of the UGA is dependent on whether the server is operating in shared server or dedicated server mode. In dedicated server mode, the UGA is allocated in the PGA and is only accessible by the server process. In shared server mode, however, the UGA is allocated in the large pool, and is accessible by any server process. That is because different server processes will handle a user process's requests. In this case, if the UGA (the user's session state) were stored in a server process's PGA, subsequent requests served by other server processes would not be able to access the data.

This means if your server is running in shared server mode, you need to size your large pool appropriately. The large pool needs to be big enough to hold everything the large pool normally stores, but also session state for every user that can be connected to your database concurrently. The danger that exists when running in shared server mode is that a session that consumes too much memory can cause memory problems for the rest of the sessions in the database. In order to prevent runaway sessions, you can set the PRIVATE_SGA database parameter to the amount of memory a user can allocate.

> **This further emphasizes the fact that databases that are to run in shared server mode need to be configured for it; you can't just switch any application or database from dedicated mode to server mode and expect everything to work fine.**

Background Processes

The following processes run as a part of the database regardless of whether users are connected to it or not. Each process has its own area of responsibility and in most cases, if the process crashes, the database will also crash.

Process Monitor (PMON)

The PMON has two main responsibilities:

❑ Monitoring server processes to ensure broken or failed processes are destroyed and their resources are freed.

Consider using a server process that updates a large number of rows in a table. Each row the process updates is locked until the transaction is either committed or rolled back. If the server process were to die for any reason, then the database would be under the impression that those rows are all locked and would wait for them to be released before allowing other users to update them. PMON takes care of that situation. In the case of shared server processes, PMON also restarts the server process so that Oracle can continue to service inbound user process requests.

❑ Registering the database's services with the Oracle listener on the host operating system.

The global database name, the SID, and any other services supported in the database are registered with the listener.

> **Note that PMON wakes up from time to time to perform these operations, rather than just running continuously.**

System Monitor (SMON)

Oracle's SMON has a number of responsibilities. While we can't cover all of these here, some of the most important are as follows:

❑ In the event of a failed instance, it is SMON that is responsible for carrying out crash recovery, on restarting the system. This includes tasks such as rolling back uncommitted transactions and applying redo log entries (from the archived redo log files) to the database for transactions that were not yet written to the data files when the instance crashed.

❑ SMON will clean up temporary segments that were allocated but not freed. In dictionary managed tablespaces, the time taken to clear up temporary segments can be extreme if there are a large number of extents. This can cause performance problems during database startup because SMON will try to clean up temporary segments at this time.

For example, consider a case where Oracle must shut down the database with the ABORT option. When this happens, the temporary segments are not freed. When the database starts back up, SMON is responsible for freeing those temporary segments. For dictionary managed tablespaces, Oracle must perform recursive SQL behind the scenes in order to free up temporary segments. In locally managed tablespaces, this isn't necessary.

❑ SMON will also perform extent coalescing in dictionary managed tablespaces. That is to say that if there is more than one free extent situated contiguously in a tablespace, SMON can combine them into a single extent so that requests for larger extents on disk can be satisfied. Whenever Oracle has to allocate a new extent, it tries to find a free extent large enough. If it does not find a free extent on the first pass, it will coalesce all the adjacent free extents in the tablespace, and then look again. Only after this has been done will Oracle allocate a new extent in a tablespace. This can become a considerable waste of time, because there may be many free extents in the tablespace that can be coalesced, meaning all this work must be done before Oracle finishes writing the data into the new extent. If all the contiguous free extents have been coalesced for you, this process will go quickly.

For this to work, in the case of dictionary-managed tablespaces, the PCTINCREASE storage parameter for the tablespace must be greater than zero.

> **Note that it is possible to coalesce contiguous free extents in your database manually, simply by using the ALTER TABLESPACE <TABLESPACE_NAME> COALESCE SQL statement.**

Database Writer (DBWn)

The database buffer cache, as we discussed earlier, contains data that has been used by users. Data blocks are read from disk into the buffer cache where they are read from, and modified by, the various server processes. When it is time for these blocks in the buffer cache to be written back to disk, the database writer is responsible for performing these data writes.

In Oracle, there are many times when operations are queued up for execution at some later time. This is called a **deferred operation** and can be beneficial to performance the long run, because operations can be performed in bulk rather than one at a time. The **database writer** is a perfect example of this notion. Server processes read the data blocks they need from data files into memory if they are not already there. This operation happens immediately. Those blocks can be modified in memory by the server processes as the user process tells the server process to do so. This process happens immediately. The writing of those blocks back to disk, however, is performed in a deferred fashion. This is because the server process may come back and use the same data blocks again. If they are flushed to disk immediately, that means Oracle would have to read them into memory again, which could be a severe waste of time. Another server process may want to read these data blocks, or modify them, once it is able to acquire the appropriate locks on the block(s). Again, if these blocks had to be read from, and written back to, the data files every time a server process wanted to use them, the performance would be miserable. This is why the writes are deferred until such time as Oracle needs to write the blocks back to disk.

For example, if a user needs to see all the data in the EMPLOYEE table, his server process reads the data blocks containing the EMPLOYEE table data from disk into the block buffer cache. When the read is complete, those blocks stay in memory for a period of time, either for use by the same or some other server process. If another user comes along and needs to update the EMPLOYEE table, the blocks are in memory and can be modified in place without having to reread them from disk before the modification can be completed. The data is still not written to disk simply because it was modified in memory; it stays in the buffer cache until Oracle decides it's time to do a database write. When Oracle needs to write these blocks from memory to the database, they are all written at the same time.

Without understanding Oracle's architecture, you might think that when you execute a COMMIT statement, your changes to the data are written to disk to be saved. This is, after all, the way that most applications work, and it makes sense to think that Oracle might do the same thing. Commits, however, have no bearing whatsoever on when the database writer performs a write. The database writer performs writes of blocks from memory to disk for one of two different reasons:

1. There isn't enough room in the buffer cache for blocks being read from disk by server processes. In this case, dirty (modified) buffers are written to disk to accommodate the new blocks.

2. Oracle needs to perform a **checkpoint**.

A checkpoint is an event that takes place in the database that causes database writer to flush blocks from the buffer pool to disk. Don't get the false impression that a checkpoint is the only way to 'save' your data. In the log writer section below, we'll learn more about Oracle's fast commit mechanism and how it ensures our data is 'saved' and there's more on checkpoints later in the chapter too.

For most systems, one database writer is enough and this is what Oracle recommends for single processor systems. Oracle does allow for up to 10 database writers (DBW0 through DBW9), however. Applications that perform frequent inserts, updates, or deletes to data can benefit from having more than one database writer configured.

Log Writer (LGWR)

The LGWR is responsible for recording all the database's committed transactions in the online redo log files. This process writes all the data from the redo log buffer into the active online redo log file. The log writer executes this write in four different situations:

❑   A commit from a transaction

❑   The redo log buffer becomes one-third full

❑   The amount of data in the redo log buffer hits 1 MB.

❑   Every three seconds

Although the transaction commit has been written to the online redo log file, the changes may not yet be written to the data files. In other words it is the commit record within the redo log file that determines whether a transaction has been committed, rather than any writing to the data files. This process is known as a **fast commit** – the entry is written to the redo log file, while the write to the data files is carried out at a later point.

During periods of high activity, the log writer will also perform what is called a **grouped commit**. This happens when the log writer is in the process of flushing the redo log buffer to disk and one or more transactions are committed before the log writer is able to complete the I/O. Each user process is queued while the current write is completed, before all the outstanding writes are carried out simultaneously by the log writer.

When you start up your instance, you must have at least two redo log files online at all times. Oracle writes to the first file from the beginning of the file in a serial fashion until it has completely filled the file with redo log entries. Once the file is full, it performs what is called a **log switch** and begins writing to the next file. Each time Oracle stops writing to a log file and begins writing to a new one, it performs a log switch. Oracle uses a circular pattern to write to these files, returning to the first file only after all other redo log files have been filled completely.

At the time the log writer performs the log switch, it causes a checkpoint to occur. This tells the database writer to write the dirty buffers from the buffer cache to the data files. This is important because the log writer is going to start writing transactions to another one of the redo log files. The log file that is about to be overwritten may contain redo entries that correspond to buffer cache entries that have not yet been written to disk. If the log writer, in reusing this redo log file, overwrites these redo log entries before their corresponding buffer cache entries are flushed to the data files, there is no way to recover the transactions in the case of an instance failure. If Oracle crashes, the buffer cache (and all other memory areas for that matter) is lost. If the log writer does not tell the database writer to flush these dirty buffers to disk before it overwrites the transactions in the redo log files, there is no way to recover them. They aren't in memory, and they aren't in the redo log! So, to prevent this scenario, the LGWR triggers a checkpoint before it overwrites any outstanding transactions in a redo log file.

> **Note that this checkpoint may well cause a temporary 'hang' in the database, since it will suspend processing until the checkpoint is complete.**

Archiver (ARCn)

Whereas an instance failure can be recovered by the transaction logs in the online redo log files, a media failure cannot. If a disk encounters an unrecoverable crash, the only way to recover the database is from a backup. Typically, backups are performed on a monthly, weekly, even daily basis. Redo log files, however, are not intended to hold a day's worth of transactions. Therefore, we need to save the transactions before they are overwritten.

This is where the **archiver** process comes in. Most production databases operate in ARCHIVELOG mode. This mode allows all redo log files to be archived, rather than being reused without copies being made (NOARCHIVELOG mode). The archiver does its work as your database moves along, effectively performing backups in a 'hot' or 'online' fashion. There is no need to shut down the database in order to run archiver because it works while changes are logged to the database. Oracle fills up a redo log file, and then performs a log switch to stop writing in one redo log file and begin writing in another.

At the point of a log switch, the archiver process will write the transaction data from the redo logs to some offline storage such as a tape or network file system, before the log writer continues to write over existing redo log files. The archiver process makes it possible to maintain every change that has ever been made to a database.

Now, when our disk drive fails, we have a perfect recovery solution. We use the latest backup we have for any files that were on that disk. Then we roll forward all the transactions that took place in the archived redo logs and the online redo logs, fully recovering our database.

Checkpoint (CKPT)

The CKPT process is responsible for updating all the control files and data file headers with the latest checkpoint information. This operation is known as a checkpoint. The database writer will flush its buffers to disk periodically, which triggers checkpoints. As we mentioned above, log switches also cause checkpoints to fire. Checkpoint information is used during database recovery. As SMON is recovering the database, it determines which checkpoint was recorded last in the data files. Every entry in the online redo log files *after* the last recorded checkpoint in the data file headers and control files must be reapplied to the data files.

A checkpoint can be set manually using the ALTER SYSTEM CHECKPOINT command, though there is normally no need for you to use this. If you wanted to shutdown the database quickly, this process manually advances the checkpoint. This happens in the shutdown anyway, but it can make the shutdown appear to be faster, since you have already checkpointed the data.

Your database is going to fire a checkpoint every time the redo log switch occurs. This is the minimum checkpoint frequency you can specify in your database. You can increase the frequency of checkpoint events by modifying init.ora parameters such as LOG_CHECKPOINT_INTERVAL and LOG_CHECKPOINT_TIMEOUT. LOG_CHECKPOINT_INTERVAL tells Oracle how many physical operating system blocks can be written to the redo log file after an incremental checkpoint before a checkpoint is triggered. LOG_CHECKPOINT_TIMEOUT specifies the number of seconds that can pass between an incremental checkpoint and the last write to the redo log. The default for this setting on Oracle 9i Standard Edition is 900 seconds (15 minutes), and the default setting on Oracle 9i Enterprise Edition is 1800 seconds (30 minutes). In order to verify your checkpoints are firing at a desired frequency, you can use the database parameter LOG_CHECKPOINTS_TO_ALERT=true. This will add a log entry to the database's alert log every time a checkpoint occurs.

Job Queue Coordinator, Job Processes (CJQ0 & Jnnn)

Oracle provides functionality in Oracle for scheduling processes, or **jobs**, to be run in the background of the database. These jobs are scheduled to be run on a particular date and time, and can be given a time interval for subsequent execution. For example, you can tell the database to create a summary table for you each evening at 12:00am. In this way, the summary information is available for reporting the next day without having to wait for Oracle to run the query in real time. Additional functionality in the database affords you the ability to modify and remove jobs that have been submitted to the database.

In Appendix B, *Supplied Packages*, we talk about the PL/SQL package DBMS_JOB and how to use this functionality to schedule your own processes to run in the job system.

Up until Oracle 9i, there were a fixed number (36) of job processes (known then as SNP0 through SNP9, and SNPA through SNPZ). These job processes were responsible for executing job queue processes. New in Oracle 9i, job processes are created and managed by a process known as the **Job Queue Coordinator**, confusingly abbreviated to CJQ. Whereas in Oracle 8i, the number of job processes executing at any given time could never be more than 36, in Oracle 9i the CJQ can start up to 1000 job queue processes (J000 through J999).

The data dictionary view called DBA_JOBS is available to review jobs that are running in the database. There are views for USER_JOBS and ALL_JOBS as well.

Recoverer (RECO)

In Oracle, it is possible to make a single transaction that updates data in more than one database. Such a transaction is described as a distributed transaction, since it is carried out on distributed databases (in other words databases other than the one you are currently working in). This is effective for many types of systems that must stay in sync with each other. Typically, the database that the client is logged into initially acts as a coordinator, asking the other databases whether they are prepared to commit (for example to a data update). If all the databases send back an affirmative response then the coordinator sends a message to make the commit permanent on all these databases. If any of the databases send back a negative answer, because they are not prepared for the commit, then the entire transaction is rolled back. This process is known as a two-phase commit, and is the means by which the atomicity of the distributed databases is maintained. If an update occurs on one system, the same update must occur on the other system.

In a stand-alone Oracle instance, the PMON is responsible for periodically waking up to determine if any server processes have failed and left any transaction data that must be cleaned up in the instance. For distributed transactions, this job is left up to the **recoverer** process. If there is an error at the point where the remote databases have sent back their 'prepared state' as YES, but before the coordinator has told them to commit, then the transaction becomes an **in-doubt distributed transaction** and, as a result, the responsibility of the recoverer process. The recoverer will attempt to contact the coordinator and determine the status of the transaction; connection attempts will continue, at given time intervals, until successful. The time between connection attempts grows exponentially with each connection failure. The recoverer will commit (or roll back) the transaction once the coordinator has been contacted.

> **Note that if the failure occurs prior to the 'prepared state' messages being sent, or after the coordinator has issued an order to commit or rollback, there is no doubt about the outcome of the transaction.**

Overview of the Architecture

There has been an architectural diagram used for years and years to provide a high-level view of Oracle's composition. The diagram has been changed slightly over time to accommodate new features and components of the database, but remains pretty close to its original. Now that we have discussed the files, processes, memory areas, and network architecture this diagram can serve us well as a bird's-eye view of the Oracle architecture and help to fix the concepts and lessons you have learned here about it.

In the following diagram, you will find almost every component of the Oracle architecture represented. At the center of the picture is the SGA containing the various memory pools (large pool, redo log buffer, database buffer cache, shared pool and Java pool). Surrounding the SGA are the background processes that interact with the SGA for the many reasons discussed throughout the chapter. We also see the server processes (S*nnn*) below the SGA that act as a go-between for the database buffer cache, the database files and the user processes. At the bottom left-hand side we see the archiver process (ARCn) which works in conjunction with the SGA and the log writer to store data offline in the archive logs. At the top of the diagram, we see the recoverer process that is communicating with the SGA and other databases to resolve failures in distributed transactions.

Another thing to point out in this diagram are the methods of communication between the processes, memory areas, files, and distributed databases. Although arrows between components certainly mean there is some form of communication going on, this diagram uses different arrows to represent the different types of communication that take place in the system. We find network communication happening between the recoverer process and distributed databases because Oracle Net Services are used for this communication. Process-to-memory communication is used when processes must read or write to and from the SGA. Finally, I/O is also represented in its own way to show where processes are writing or reading from the different types of files involved in the Oracle database.

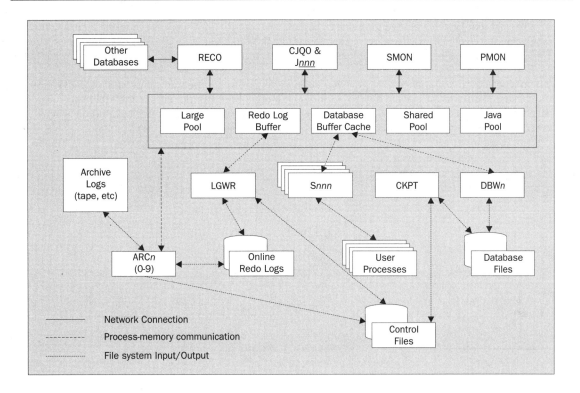

Summary

Oracle's architecture is yet another part of the database you could spend months learning and mastering. In this chapter, we have discussed all the fundamental concepts of the database architecture to give you a better understanding of how things work in the database as well as in the operating system and across the network.

We talked about the individual processes involved in Oracle's process architecture. User processes talk to server processes either directly using dedicated server, or by using a dispatcher with shared server. We discussed how the server processes read data from disk into the buffer cache of the database, to be used to virtually speed up the I/O of the database. Each of the background processes were reviewed, giving you an understanding of the moving parts involved in storing, modifying, and retrieving data in the database.

There are many different types of file in the database, each with a particular purpose in life. Data files, temporary files, control files, parameter files, and redo log files all serve to store your database's data dictionary, application data, hardware structure, initialization parameters, and transaction logs. Oracle uses a logical structure to store your data in tablespaces, segments, extents, and finally data blocks at the most granular level.

We learned that Oracle's shared global area is used to make file I/O seem much faster than it actually is. Oracle stores data blocks read from disk in the block buffer cache, stores SQL statements executed by server processes in the shared pool, and maintains a running log of all changes in the redo log buffer.

The purpose of this chapter was to give you an overview of what's 'behind the scenes' of the Oracle database. In order to master the database, understanding all the components of the architecture is mandatory. Understanding these concepts gives you a foundation of knowledge to build on when creating Oracle applications and administering production databases.

Processing Statements in Oracle

In this chapter, we will explore what happens when Oracle executes the statements that you submit to it. We'll investigate the complex actions that take place in order to execute both a simple statement such as SELECT * FROM EMP, and a more complex UPDATE statement. We'll see what database processes (as described in Chapter 5) are involved, what memory structures are used and the general procedure Oracle goes through to execute each and every statement you submit.

Classes of SQL Statements

Before we get into how Oracle executes statements, we'll want to make a distinction between various types of statement. For the purpose of our discussion here, there are three statement types:

- ❑ **DDL**: Data Definition Language statements. These are statements such as CREATE, TRUNCATE, and ALTER, which are used to create structures in the database, set permissions and so on. They are the means by which you maintain the Oracle data dictionary.

- ❑ **DML**: Data Manipulation Language statements. These are statements that modify or access information including INSERT, UPDATE, and DELETE.

- ❑ **Queries**: These are your standard SELECT statements. Queries are those statements that return data and do not modify it, and are a subset of DML statements that we'll treat separately.

It is important to note that most DML statements include a query statement, as we have defined them here. As an example, let's consider the following statement:

```
Update emp set ename = 'KINGSLEY' where ename = 'KING';
```

This is definitely a DML statement as we defined above, since it involves modification of the table EMP (setting a new ENAME) via:

```
Update emp set ename = 'KINGSLEY'
```

However, it also contains a query statement in the form of the WHERE clause:

```
where ename = 'KING'
```

Therefore, when we discuss DML, everything that held true for queries will hold true for it as well. DML just does more work than a simple SELECT would.

In the following sections, we'll discuss how statements are executed by Oracle, and the steps that it undertakes to process each and every SQL statement. Then, we'll look at how the steps are accomplished, what processes are involved, and what happens to the data.

How Statements Are Executed

Queries and DML are very similar in terms of the stages of execution Oracle will undertake to carry them out. It is only when we look at the outcome of these two statement types that we see the real difference. While a SELECT statement produces a result set (in other words a set of rows), a DML statement modifies the values in a result set but does not return this result set.

In comparison to both query and DML statements, DDL is more like an internal command to Oracle. It's not a generalized query against some tables, but rather a directive to do something. For example if you issue:

```
Create table t ( x int primary key, y date );
```

that will cause Oracle to do many things like checking to see that you have the CREATE TABLE privilege, allocating space for the table, creating an entry in the data dictionary, and so on. It is very different from what will happen later when we SELECT * FROM T. It is interesting to note however that a CREATE TABLE statement may include a SELECT in it. We can issue:

```
Create table t as select * from scott.emp;
```

So, much as DML may contain a query, so may DDL. When DDL contains a query, the query portion is processed like any other query would be.

Let's look at the four steps Oracle will go through to execute these statements, namely:

❑   Parsing

❑   Optimization

❑   Row source generation

❑   Statement execution

In the case of DDL, only the first and last steps really apply in general, since it will parse the statement and then execute it. It makes no sense to 'optimize' a CREATE statement (there is only one way to create something) and there is no generic plan that needs to be created (the steps to create a table are well known and coded directly into Oracle). It should be noted that if the CREATE statement includes a query, the query is processed as any other query would be – with all of the above steps taking place.

Parsing

This is the first step in the processing of any statement in Oracle. **Parsing** is the act of breaking the submitted statement down into its component parts, determining what type of statement it is (query, DML, or DDL), and performing various checks on it.

The parsing process performs three main functions:

❑ **Syntax Checking**. Is the statement a valid one? Does it make sense given the SQL grammar documented in the SQL Reference Manual? Does it follow all of the rules for SQL?

❑ **Semantic Analysis**. Is the statement valid in light of the objects in the database, do the tables and columns referenced exist? Do you have access to the objects and are the proper privileges in place? Are there ambiguities in the statement – for example if there are two tables T1 and T2 and both have a column X, the query SELECT X FROM T1, T2 WHERE ... is ambiguous as we don't know which table to get X from.

❑ **Checking the shared pool**. Has the statement already been processed by another session?

The differences between the syntax and semantic checks are hard to see since, if either fails, Oracle simply returns the statement with an error code and message, rather than specifying a message such as 'failed the syntax check'. So for example, this statement fails with a syntax error:

```
SQL> select from where 2;
select from where 2
            *
ERROR at line 1:
ORA-00936: missing expression
```

While the following statement fails with a semantic error (since the statement would have succeeded if the table NOT_A_TABLE existed and we had permission to access it):

```
SQL> select * from not_a_table;
select * from not_a_table
              *
ERROR at line 1:
ORA-00942: table or view does not exist
```

To recap then, if the statement *could* have executed given the proper objects and privileges, you have a **semantic error**; if the statement could not execute under any circumstances, then you have a **syntax error**.

The next step in the parsing operation is to see if the statement we are currently parsing has already been processed by some other session. If it has, then we may be in luck since it could already be stored in the shared pool. If this is the case then we can perform a **soft parse**, in other words avoid optimization and query plan generation, and get straight to the execution phase. This significantly shortens the process by which we get our query going. If, on the other hand, we must parse, optimize, and generate the plan for the query, then we are performing what is known as a **hard parse**. This distinction is very important. When developing our applications we want a very high percentage of our queries to be soft parsed, in order to be able to skip the optimize/generate phases, since these phases are very CPU intensive. If we have to hard parse a large percentage of our queries, then our system will function much more slowly.

Before we consider how to maximize our use of soft parsed queries, let's quickly revisit the shared pool that we first saw in Chapter 5, to discuss how the reuse of parsed queries is accomplished.

How Oracle Uses the Shared Pool

As we have seen, once Oracle has parsed the query and it passes the syntax and semantic checks, it will look in the shared pool component of the SGA to see if that exact same query has already been processed by another session. To do this, when Oracle receives a statement from us, it will **hash** it. Hashing is the act of taking the original SQL text, sending it through a function, and getting a number back. We can actually see this value if we have access to some V$ tables. V$ tables are known as **dynamic performance tables** in Oracle and are where the server stores many interesting bits of information for us.

In Chapter 18, we'll see more examples and uses for these V$ tables. For now, the V$SQL view will be used to show us what is in the shared pool, SQL wise.

Access to the V$ tables is gained by:

❑ *having the SELECT_CATALOG_ROLE granted to your account*

❑ *having another role (such as DBA) that has the SELECT_CATALOG_ROLE*

If you don't have access to the V$ tables and the V$SQL view, then you won't be able to do all of this Try It Out, but it should be easy enough to follow what's going on.

Try It Out – Observing Different Hash Values

1. To start with, we'll execute two queries that look, to all intents and purposes, the same to you and me:

```
SQL> select * from dual;

D
-
X

SQL> select * from DUAL;

D
-
X
```

However, to Oracle they are distinctly different; Oracle has stored two different instances of this query in the shared pool.

2. We can see this by querying the dynamic performance view V$SQL which will show us the hash value for each of the two queries we just ran:

```
SQL> select sql_text, hash_value from v$sql
  2  where upper(sql_text) = 'SELECT * FROM DUAL';


SQL_TEXT                HASH_VALUE
-------------------- ----------
select * from DUAL   1708540716
select * from dual   4035109885
select sql_text, hash_value from v$sql
where upper(sql_text) = 'SELECT * FROM DUAL';
```

As far as you and I are concerned our original two queries appear the same, since the only difference between them is that we capitalized DUAL in one query but not the other. However, to Oracle they appear to be very different, since each query has had a different hash value assigned to it.

Normally we wouldn't need to actually see the hash values, because they are for Oracle's internal use. Once they have been generated, Oracle will search the shared pool for all statements that have the same hash value. It will then compare the SQL_TEXT it finds to the SQL you submitted to make sure that the text in the shared pool is exactly the same. This comparison step is important, since one of the properties of a hash function is that two different strings can in fact hash to the same number.

> **Hashing is not a unique mapping of a string to a number.**

Once Oracle verifies your statement is identical to the statement in the shared pool, it must also verify that they mean the same thing semantically. This is confusing at first, as the above SELECT * FROM DUAL example shows. However, it is important, since a query that is submitted by one user does not have to access the same set of tables as another user. For example take the simple query:

```
Select * from emp;
```

If user SCOTT executes that, then clearly it should really be processed as:

```
select * from SCOTT.emp;
```

However, if some other user submits that exactly the same SELECT * FROM EMP, can we simply reuse the existing query plan that Oracle already has already made? The answer is, it depends. If the EMP table referred to in this identical query is the same SCOTT.EMP table, then yes. If the EMP table referred to is some *other* database object, then the answer is no. You see, there can be many EMP objects in the database, so a simple SELECT * FROM EMP submitted by different users might be a different query altogether. The point to take away from this is that there may be many different query plans in the shared pool for what appear to be identical queries, since each query actually accesses different objects. They all look the same to you and me, but to Oracle they don't and must be treated differently. Consider the confusion if SELECT * FROM EMP always accessed SCOTT.EMP just because SCOTT ran it first.

193

To summarize where we are at this point in the parsing process, Oracle has:

❑   Parsed the query

❑   Checked the syntax

❑   Verified the semantics

❑   Computed the hash value

❑   Found a match

❑   Verified there is a query exactly the same as ours (it references the same objects)

There is one last check it will make before it will return from the parse step and report that a soft parse has been done. That last step is to verify that the queries were parsed in the same **environment**. The environment is considered to be all of the session settings that can affect query plan generation such as the SORT_AREA_SIZE or OPTIMIZER_MODE. The SORT_AREA_SIZE tells Oracle how much memory it is allowed for sorting data without using the disk to store temporary results. A larger SORT_AREA_SIZE may generate a different optimized query plan than a small setting. Oracle might opt to choose a plan that sorts the data rather than one that uses an index to read the data, for example. The OPTIMIZER_MODE tells Oracle what optimizer to actually use; we'll cover this in more detail below in the *Optimizer* section.

So, if we were to continue with the SELECT * FROM DUAL example we tried out earlier, and execute the following code:

```
SQL> alter session set OPTIMIZER_MODE = first_rows;
Session altered.

SQL> select * from dual;

D
-
X

SQL> select sql_text, hash_value, parsing_user_id
  2    from v$sql
  3   where upper(sql_text) = 'SELECT * FROM DUAL'
  4  /

SQL_TEXT                HASH_VALUE PARSING_USER_ID
--------------------    ---------- ---------------
select * from DUAL      1708540716             103
select * from dual      4035109885             103
select * from dual      4035109885             103
```

we find that there are now 3 queries that look alike, two of which appear to be identical same text, same objects, even executed by the same USER as shown by the PARSING_USER_ID. The difference between these two queries however is that the first one was parsed with the default optimizer mode (CHOOSE) whereas the one we have just carried out was parsed in FIRST_ROWS mode. If we had just reused the existing plan generated under CHOOSE mode, we would have the wrong plan for FIRST_ROWS. Hence, Oracle created a new query plan with these different session settings in mind and cached it in the shared pool for others to use. If we extend our query against V$SQL just a little – adding the OPTIMIZER_MODE column, this subtle difference will become clear:

```
SQL> select sql_text, hash_value, parsing_user_id, optimizer_mode
  2    from v$sql
  3    where upper(sql_text) = 'SELECT * FROM DUAL'
  4  /

SQL_TEXT                HASH_VALUE PARSING_USER_ID OPTIMIZER_
----------------------- ---------- --------------- ----------
select * from DUAL      1708540716             103 CHOOSE
select * from dual      4035109885             103 CHOOSE
select * from dual      4035109885             103 FIRST_ROWS
```

Now we can clearly see that they have the same text and the same hash, but they are different nonetheless due to the optimizer mode used to optimize each query.

In Chapter 18, Tuning Tools, we'll take a look at how you can ensure that your queries make the best use of the shared pool to avoid hard parsing and the increased load it places on the database.

Finally at this point, when Oracle has done all of this work and found a match, it can return from the parse process and report that a soft parse has been done. We don't see this report because it is used internally by Oracle to indicate that it can now finish the parse process. If no match is found, a hard parse will be required.

Optimization

OK, once we've got past the initial parse phase of the statement execution, we'll end up at the optimizer when doing a hard parse. As we saw above, we can skip this step when reusing SQL but every distinct query/DML statement will go through optimization at least once.

The job of the optimizer is quite simple on the face of it, since its goal is to find the *best* way to execute your query to get the answer as fast as possible. While its job description is very simple, what it has to do is quite complex. There could be literally thousands of ways to execute any single query and it must find the best one. In order to determine which query plan is the most appropriate, Oracle uses one of two optimizers:

❑ The **Rule Based Optimizer** (RBO) – this optimizes queries based on a static set of rules that dictate the preferred method of executing a query. The rules are coded directly into the Oracle database kernel. The RBO will generate only one query plan – the one the rules tell it to generate.

❑ The **Cost Based Optimizer** (CBO) – this optimizes queries based on statistics collected about the actual data being accessed. It will use information such as the number of rows, the size of the data set, and many other pieces of information when deciding on the optimum plan. The CBO will generate many (perhaps thousands) of possible query plans, alternative approaches to solving your query, and assign a numeric cost to each query plan. The query plan with the lowest cost will be used.

Before we can understand how Oracle decides which optimizer to use, we need to look at one system/session parameter in some detail. That parameter is the OPTIMIZER_MODE. Above, we used this to show that Oracle will consider queries to be different if the OPTIMIZER_MODE is set differently. Here we will define the OPTIMIZER_MODE and the values it may assume. The OPTIMIZER_MODE is a system setting that a DBA can set in a database's initialization file. By default it has a value of CHOOSE that allows Oracle to pick the optimizer it would like to use (we'll look at the rules used to make that choice shortly). The DBA may decide to override the default and set this to parameter to:

❑ RULE: specifies Oracle should use the RBO if possible.

❑ FIRST_ROWS: Oracle will use the CBO and generate a query plan that attempts to get the first rows of the query back as fast as possible.

❑ ALL_ROWS: Oracle will use the CBO and generate a query plan that attempts to get the last rows of the query (and therefore, all of the rows) back as fast as possible.

This parameter may be overridden at the session level as we have seen above via the ALTER SESSION command. This is useful for applications where the developers wish to specify the optimizer they would like to use and for testing.

Now, on to how Oracle picks which optimizer to use and when. Oracle will utilize the CBO whenever any of the following are true:

❑ Statistics exist for at least one of the objects referenced by the query and the OPTIMIZER_MODE system or session parameter is not set to RULE.

❑ Your OPTIMIZER_MODE system/session parameter is set to some value other than RULE or CHOOSE.

❑ Your query accesses an object that requires the CBO such as a partitioned table or an index organized table. If terms such as index organized or partitioned don't mean anything to you so far then don't worry, we'll be covering them in the next chapter.

❑ Your query contains any valid hint other than the RULE hint. Hints are a method of telling Oracle how you would like the query to be optimized, such as using a certain index. See Chapter 18 for more details.

❑ You use certain SQL constructs that are only understood by the CBO, such as performing a JOIN in a CONNECT BY query (CONNECT BY queries are covered in detail in Chapter 17, *Advanced Querying*).

It is recommended that all applications use the CBO these days. The RBO, used with Oracle since the very first releases, is considered the legacy approach to query optimization and many new features are simply not available with it. For example, the RBO cannot be used if you want to use:

❑ Partitioned tables

❑ Bitmapped Indexes

❑ Index Organized Tables

❑ Fine Grained Auditing with rules

- ❑ Parallel Query Operations
- ❑ Function-based indexes

Note that this list is not exhaustive, and gets larger with each release. In this chapter, we will consider the CBO the optimizer of choice and will not be discussing the RBO in any detail.

If you would like to learn more about the RBO optimizer and how it works, the Oracle 9i Database Performance Guide and Reference (available from http://download-uk.oracle.com/otndoc/Oracle9i/901_doc/server.901/a87503/toc.htm for Release 9.0.1) details exactly how it works and what rules it will apply to develop a query plan.

The CBO isn't as straightforward to understand as the RBO. The RBO, by definition, follows a set of rules and so is very predictable. The CBO uses statistics to determine what plan to use for a query. When the statistics change, the query plan may change as well. This is in stark contrast to the RBO where, once a query has a plan, that same plan will be generated each and every time that query is submitted (since the same rules will apply). With the CBO, different statistics will result in different plans.

In order to appreciate and visualize what this means, we can use a small example. In SQL*Plus we will copy the EMP and DEPT tables from the SCOTT schema and add primary/foreign keys to these tables. We'll then compare the plans of the RBO and CBO using a tool embedded in the SQL*Plus product called AUTOTRACE (we'll take a more in-depth look at AUTOTRACE in Chapter 18). To start the example, we will execute the following SQL.

Try It Out – Comparing Optimizers

1. Make sure you are logged on to your database as a user other than SCOTT and then copy the SCOTT.EMP and SCOTT.DEPT tables with the CREATE TABLE command:

```
SQL> create table emp
  2  as
  3  select * from scott.emp;
Table created.

SQL> create table dept
  2  as
  3  select * from scott.dept;
Table created.
```

2. Now we are ready to add the primary keys to our EMP and DEPT tables:

```
SQL> alter table emp
  2  add constraint emp_pk primary key(empno);
Table altered.

SQL> alter table dept
  2  add constraint dept_pk primary key(deptno);
Table altered.
```

3. And a foreign key from EMP to DEPT:

```
SQL> alter table emp
  2   add constraint emp_fk_dept
  3      foreign key (deptno) references dept;
Table altered.
```

4. Next, we'll enable the AUTOTRACE facility from within SQL*Plus (if you find yourself unable to do this, see Chapter 18 for information on setting up the tool). The specific AUTOTRACE command we are using will show us the optimized query plan Oracle would use to execute our query (it doesn't actually execute the query):

```
SQL> set autotrace traceonly explain
```

5. Now we've enabled AUTOTRACE, we'll run a query against our tables:

```
SQL> select *
  2    from emp, dept
  3   where emp.deptno = dept.deptno;

Execution Plan
----------------------------------------------------------
   0      SELECT STATEMENT Optimizer=CHOOSE
   1    0   NESTED LOOPS
   2    1     TABLE ACCESS (FULL) OF 'EMP'
   3    1     TABLE ACCESS (BY INDEX ROWID) OF 'DEPT'
   4    3       INDEX (UNIQUE SCAN) OF 'DEPT_PK' (UNIQUE)
```

We are currently using the RBO in this case since we have not gathered any statistics (these are newly created tables); we are not accessing any special objects that require the CBO and our optimizer goal is set to CHOOSE. We can also tell that we are using the RBO from our output. (We'll be able to compare this to output from the CBO a little later.) Here the RBO optimizer has chosen a plan that will FULL SCAN the EMP table. For each row it finds in the EMP table, it will take the DEPTNO field and go to the DEPT_PK index to find the DEPT record that matches this DEPTNO, in order to perform the join.

If we simply analyze the existing tables (which are in fact very small right now), we'll discover that using the CBO we get a very different plan.

6. ANALYZE is a command typically used by the DBA to gather statistics regarding our tables and indexes – it needs to be run so that the CBO has some statistics to act on. Let's do it now:

```
SQL> analyze table emp compute statistics;
Table analyzed.

SQL> analyze table dept compute statistics;
Table analyzed.
```

7. Now that that our tables have been analyzed, we'll rerun our query and see what query plan Oracle would use this time around:

```
SQL> select *
  2    from emp, dept
  3    where emp.deptno = dept.deptno;
```

```
Execution Plan
----------------------------------------------------------
   0      SELECT STATEMENT Optimizer=CHOOSE (Cost=3 Card=14 Bytes=700)
   1    0   HASH JOIN (Cost=3 Card=14 Bytes=700)
   2    1     TABLE ACCESS (FULL) OF 'DEPT' (Cost=1 Card=4 Bytes=72)
   3    1     TABLE ACCESS (FULL) OF 'EMP' (Cost=1 Card=14 Bytes=448)
```

Here, the CBO has decided to FULL SCAN both tables (read the entire tables) and HASH JOIN them. This is primarily because it understands:

❑ We want to access every row in both tables ultimately.

❑ The tables are small.

❑ Accessing every row via an index (as before) in small tables is slower than full scanning them.

How It Works

The CBO took into account the size of the objects when deciding upon a plan. One of the interesting things to note in the AUTOTRACE outputs from the RBO and the CBO is that the CBO plans contain more information. In the plans generated by the CBO we see things such as:

❑ COST – the numeric value assigned to this step of the query plan. This is an internal number used by the CBO when comparing the relative costs of many alternative plans available for the same query, in order to find the one with the lowest overall cost.

❑ CARD – the cardinality of the step, in other words the estimated number of rows that will be generated by this step. For example, we can see the TABLE ACCESS (FULL) of DEPT is estimated to return 4 records, which is accurate since the DEPT table has only 4 records in it.

❑ BYTES – the size in bytes of the data generated by this step in the plan. This is the average rowsize for the underlying set of columns multiplied by the estimated number of rows.

You'll note that we did not see this information when using the RBO, and hence this is one way to see which optimizer is being used.

If we 'trick' the CBO into thinking these tables are much larger than they really are, then we can see the difference size and the current statistics make.

Try It Out – Comparing Optimizers 2

In order to accomplish this we will utilize a supplied database package called DBMS_STATS (supplied packages are the subject of Appendix B, although this one is not discussed specifically). Using this package we can set arbitrary statistics on tables (something you might perhaps want to do for testing, to see what the generated plans will be under various circumstances).

1. Here, we use DBMS_STATS to trick the CBO into thinking that the EMP table has 10 million records and the DEPT table one million (don't worry about the code, you'll learn all about PL/SQL later in the book):

199

```
SQL> begin
  2     dbms_stats.set_table_stats
  3     ( user, 'EMP', numrows => 10000000, numblks => 1000000 );
  4     dbms_stats.set_table_stats
  5     ( user, 'DEPT', numrows => 1000000, numblks => 100000 );
  6  end;
  7  /

PL/SQL procedure successfully completed.
```

2. Now we'll execute exactly the same query as before, to see the effect of our new statistics:

```
SQL> select *
  2     from emp, dept
  3     where emp.deptno = dept.deptno;

Execution Plan
----------------------------------------------------------
   0      SELECT STATEMENT Optimizer=CHOOSE
               (Cost=406930 Card=2500000000000 Bytes=125000000000000)
   1    0   MERGE JOIN
               (Cost=406930 Card=2500000000000 Bytes=125000000000000)
   2    1     TABLE ACCESS (BY INDEX ROWID) OF 'DEPT'
               (Cost=2 Card=1000000 Bytes=18000000)
   3    2       INDEX (FULL SCAN) OF 'DEPT_PK' (UNIQUE)
               (Cost=1 Card=1000000)
   4    1     SORT (JOIN)
               (Cost=406928 Card=10000000 Bytes=320000000)
   5    4       TABLE ACCESS (FULL) OF 'EMP'
               (Cost=151774 Card=10000000 Bytes=320000000)
```

You can see that the optimizer chooses a very different plan than before. Rather than hashing these apparently very large tables, it will instead MERGE them together. For the smaller DEPT table, it will use the index to sort the data, and since there isn't an index on the DEPTNO column in the EMP table, sort the entire EMP table by DEPTNO in order to merge the results together.

3. If we force the use of the RBO by setting the OPTIMIZER_MODE parameter to RULE (even though we have these statistics), we can see that its behavior is entirely predicable:

```
SQL> alter session set OPTIMIZER_MODE = RULE;
Session altered.

SQL> select *
  2     from emp, dept
  3     where emp.deptno = dept.deptno;

Execution Plan
----------------------------------------------------------
   0      SELECT STATEMENT Optimizer=RULE
   1    0   NESTED LOOPS
   2    1     TABLE ACCESS (FULL) OF 'EMP'
   3    1     TABLE ACCESS (BY INDEX ROWID) OF 'DEPT'
   4    3       INDEX (UNIQUE SCAN) OF 'DEPT_PK' (UNIQUE)
```

Regardless of the amount of data in the underlying tables, the RBO will always
generate the exact same plan over and over, if it is given the same set of database
objects (tables and indexes).

Row Source Generator

The row source generator is simply the piece of software within Oracle that receives the output from the
optimizer and formats it into the actual execution plan. For example, right before this section we see a
query plan as printed by the AUTOTRACE facility within SQL*Plus. That tree structured plan was the
output of the row source generator; the optimizer developed the plan and the row source generator
turned it into a data structure that the rest of the Oracle system can use.

Execution Engine

The **execution engine** is the process that takes the output of the row source generator and uses it to
produce a result set or modify tables. For example, using the last AUTOTRACE plan from above, the
execution engine would read the entire EMP table. It would then read each row performing an INDEX
UNIQUE SCAN, a step where Oracle will look in a UNIQUE index to find a value, on the DEPT_PK index.
It uses the value it returns to find the ROWID (address of a row containing the file, block, and slot on that
block where that row can be found) of that specific DEPTNO. It would then access the DEPT table by that
ROWID.

The execution engine is the workhorse of the entire process since it's what actually executes the
generated query plan. It performs the I/O to read data, sorts data, joins data, and stores results in
temporary space when needed and so on.

Statement Execution Summary

In this section on statement execution, we have seen the 4 stages that statements you submit to Oracle
will pass through in order to be processed. The following is a flowchart summarizing this processing:

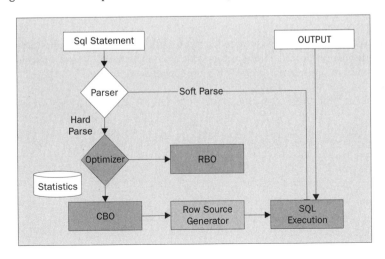

When a SQL statement is submitted to Oracle, the parser will determine if it needs to be hard parsed or soft parsed.

If the statement is soft parsed, we can go straight to the SQL execution step and get our output.

If the statement must be hard parsed, we send it to the optimizer, which will either use the RBO or CBO to process the query. Once the optimizer has generated what it believes to be the optimal plan, it will forward the plan to the row source generator.

The row source generator will convert the optimizer output into a format the rest of the Oracle system can process, namely an iterative plan that can be stored in the shared pool and executed. This plan is then used by the SQL engine to process the query and generate the answer (that is, the output).

A Query from Start To Finish

Now it is time for us to look at how Oracle processes a query from start to finish. We'll look at two very simple, but different, queries in order to demonstrate some of the ways in which Oracle accomplishes the processing of a query. Our examples focus on a common question asked by developers, namely, "How many rows of data will come back from my query?" The answer is simply that in general Oracle doesn't know, until you actually fetch the last row of data, how many rows will be returned. We can guess (the AUTOTRACE facility above showed us that 'guess') but it is nothing more than that. In order to understand this better, we'll take a look at a query that can start returning rows long before it ever gets near the last row, as well as a query that must wait until many (or all) rows have been processed before returning a single record.

For this discussion, we'll use the two queries:

```
Select * from one_million_row_table;
```

and

```
Select * from one_million_row_table order by c1;
```

Here, ONE_MILLION_ROW_TABLE is a table we put a million rows in (we won't actually do that, we are just using it as a discussion point). There are no indexes on this table, it is not sorted in any way, and so our ORDER BY clause in the second query will have lots of work to do.

The first query SELECT * FROM ONE_MILLION_ROW_TABLE will have a very simple plan, consisting of one step:

```
TABLE ACCESS (FULL) OF ONE_MILLION_ROW_TABLE
```

What this means is that Oracle will go to the database and read each and every block of the table either from disk or from the buffer cache. Under normal circumstances (no parallel query, no table partitioning, etc.), the table will be read from its first extent to its last, in order. The nice thing is that we will start getting data back from this query *immediately*. As fast as Oracle can read the information, our client application will receive the rows. This is one of the reasons why we cannot determine how many rows a query will return before we actually get the last row – even Oracle does not know how many rows will be returned. When Oracle starts processing this query, all it knows is what extents the table is made up of; it doesn't know exactly how many rows are in these extents (it can guess based on the statistics but it doesn't know). We do not wait until the last row has been processed to get the first row here, hence we won't know until we are done exactly what the row count is.

The second query on the other hand will be a little different. It will go through two steps in most circumstances. There will be a TABLE ACCESS (FULL) OF ONE_MILLION_ROW_TABLE step, which will feed its results into a SORT (ORDER BY) step (to order the database by column C1). Here, we will wait for quite a while to get the first row since we must read, process, and SORT all one million rows before we can do so. So this time, rather than getting the first row right away, we'll wait until every row has been processed, with the results most likely stored in some temporary segments in our database (depending on our SORT_AREA_SIZE system/session parameter). As we fetch our results, they will come from this temporary space.

So, in summary, Oracle will attempt to return answers to us as soon as it can, given the constraints of the query. In the above example, if there was an index on C1, and C1 was defined as NOT NULL, Oracle may have used that index to read the table via the index (without sorting it). This would give us the first rows very fast in response to our query. However, it would be slower to get the last row via this process as reading one million rows from an index can be quite slow (a FULL SCAN and SORT would in all likelihood be more efficient). So, it will depend on the optimizer used (the RBO will pretty much always pick an index if one is available) and the optimizer goal. For example, the CBO running in its default mode of CHOOSE or running with the mode of ALL_ROWS would full scan and sort whereas the CBO running in FIRST_ROWS optimization mode would most likely use the index.

DML from Start To Finish

Now we will take a look at how DML statements that modify the database are processed. We'll look at how REDO and UNDO are generated, and how they fit into DML transactions and their recovery. We'll show what would happen in the case of a particular transaction, shown below, to build on the more general discussion in the last chapter and reinforce your understanding of this complex topic. It is important for developers as well as DBAs to have a good working knowledge of what really happens when an update takes place. You need to understand the ramifications of your actions.

As an example, we will investigate what might happen with a transaction like this:

```
Insert into t (x,y) values (1,1);
Update t set x = x+1 where x = 1;
Delete from t where x = 2;
```

We will follow this transaction down different paths. What happens if the system fails after the update, what happens if we succeed and commit, and what happens if we roll back.

The initial insert into T will generate both REDO and UNDO. The UNDO data generated will be enough information to make the INSERT 'go away' if we need it to, in response to a ROLLBACK statement or to a failure. The REDO data generated will be enough information to make the insert 'happen again', if we need to do it again due to a system failure. The UNDO data may comprise many pieces of information. There may be indexes on the columns X and Y for example, and their changes must be undone upon a rollback as well. As we learned in the last chapter, UNDO data is stored in a rollback segment or, in Oracle 9i, in an UNDO tablespace. An important concept to understand is that UNDO is protected by the REDO entries just like any other piece of data. In other words, UNDO data is treated just like table data or index data and changes to rollback segments are logged. We will see this a little later in this chapter when we discuss what would happen if the system crashed during our DML activity. Also, when UNDO data is created, it is cached in the buffer cache just like any other piece of data would be. So, after we have executed the INSERT statement above (not having got to the UPDATE or DELETE as yet) we'll have a situation like the one shown in the following diagram:

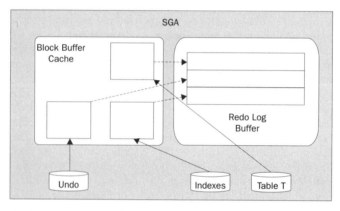

There are some cached, modified UNDO (rollback) blocks, index blocks, and table data blocks, all of which are in the block buffer cache. Each of these modified blocks is protected by entries in the redo log buffer. All of this information is cached right now.

Let's now consider a scenario where there is a system crash at this stage. Although the SGA is wiped out, we don't actually need anything that was in there, so it will be as if this transaction never happened when we restart. None of the blocks with changes got flushed, and none of the REDO information got flushed.

In another scenario, the buffer cache might be filled right up. In this case, the DBWR must make room and flush the blocks we just modified. To do this the DBWR will start by asking LGWR to flush the REDO blocks that protect the database blocks first.

> **Before DBWR can write any of the blocks that are changed to disk, LGWR must flush the REDO information related to these blocks.**

This makes sense, because if we flush the modified blocks for table T, and do not flush the REDO for the associated UNDO blocks, and the system then failed, we would have a modified table T block with no UNDO information associated with it. We need to flush the redo log buffers before writing these blocks out so that we can *redo* all of these changes to get the SGA back into the state it is in right now, to allow a rollback to take place.

So, at this point, we have the situation depicted above. We have generated some modified table and index blocks. These have created some new rollback segment blocks, and all three types of blocks have generated REDO to protect them. It is very likely that at some point during our processing, the redo log buffer will be flushed (Oracle flushes this buffer on a recurring basis), and some of our changes from the block buffer cache may go to disk as well. In that case the picture becomes:

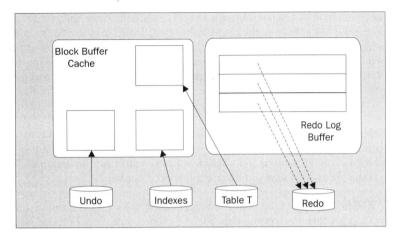

Next, we do the UPDATE. Much the same takes place. This time, the amount of UNDO will be larger and we have the following picture:

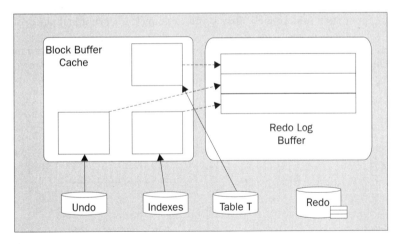

We have more new UNDO blocks added to the cache. We have modified database table and index blocks so that we can UNDO the UPDATE if necessary. We have also generated more redo log buffer entries. Some of our redo log entries generated so far have been flushed to disk and some of them remain in the cache.

If our system were to crash right now and then started up again, Oracle would read the redo logs, and find some redo log entries for our transaction (since we flushed them). Given the state we left the system in, with the REDO entries for the insert in the redo log files, and the REDO for the update still in the buffer, Oracle would 'roll forward' the INSERT only (it is as if the UPDATE never occurred). We would end up with a picture much like the first with some undo blocks (to undo the INSERT), modified table blocks (right after the INSERT), and modified index blocks (right after the INSERT). Now Oracle will discover that our transaction never committed and will roll it back since the system is doing crash recovery and, of course, our session is no longer connected. It will take the UNDO it just rolled forward in the buffer cache, and apply it to the data and index blocks, making them look as they did before the INSERT took place. Now everything is back the way it was. The blocks that are on disk may, or may not, reflect the INSERT (it depends if our blocks got flushed or not before the crash). If they do, the INSERT has been, in effect, undone and when the blocks are flushed from the buffer cache, the data file will reflect that. If they do not reflect the insert then so be it, they will be overwritten later anyway.

This scenario covers the rudiments of a crash recovery. The system performs this as a two-step process. First it rolls forward, bringing the system right to the point of failure, and then it proceeds to roll back everything that had not yet committed. This action will resynchronize the data files. It replays the work that was in progress, and undoes anything that had not yet completed.

If instead of the system crashing at this point, the application rolls back the transaction, Oracle will find the UNDO information for this transaction, either in the cached undo blocks (most likely), or on disk if they have been flushed (likely for very large transactions only). It will apply the UNDO information to the data and index blocks in the buffer cache, or if they are no longer in the cache, request and read them from disk into the cache to have the UNDO applied to them. These blocks will later be flushed to the data files in their original form. This scenario is one that is played out much more often than system crashes, with an application initiating a rollback and undoing the work it just performed.

Now, onto the DELETE. Much the same happens here. UNDO is generated, blocks are modified, and REDO is sent over to the redo log buffer. In fact, it is so identical to the UPDATE that we are going to go right onto the COMMIT. Here, Oracle will flush the redo log buffer to disk and the picture will look like this:

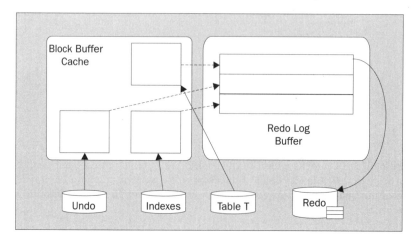

Some of the modified blocks are in the buffer cache and maybe some of them have been flushed to disk. All of the REDO information necessary to replay this transaction is safely on disk and the changes are now permanent. If we were to read the data directly from the data files, we probably would see the blocks as they existed *before* the transaction took place, as DBWR most likely has not yet written them. That is OK, the redo log files can be used to restore those blocks in the event of a failure. The UNDO information will hang around until the rollback segment wraps around and reuses those blocks. We need that UNDO to provide for consistent reads of the affected objects that began before our transaction took place.

DDL Processing

Lastly, we'll take a look at how Oracle processes DDL. DDL is how you get to modify the Oracle data dictionary. In order to create a table, you don't write an INSERT INTO USER_TABLES statement, but instead issue a CREATE TABLE statement. Under the covers, Oracle does a lot of SQL for you (known as **recursive SQL**, since it is SQL done as a side effect of other SQL). It is this recursive SQL that actually modifies the Oracle data dictionary tables for us, via inserts/updates and deletes.

Therefore, DDL is really processed much like any other query or DML statement but with one crucial difference. Carrying out a DDL action will cause a COMMIT to be issued *before* the DDL is executed and either a COMMIT or ROLLBACK will happen immediately afterwards. That is, DDL is executed like this pseudo code:

```
Commit;
DDL-Statement;
If ( Error ) then
    Rollback;
Else
    Commit;
End if;
```

This is important for you to note since that COMMIT will commit any outstanding work you have in process – that is, if you execute:

```
Insert into some_table values ( 'Before' );
Create table T ( x int );
Insert into some_table values ( 'After' );
Rollback;
```

only the insert of the After row will be rolled back, since your first INSERT was committed before Oracle even attempted the CREATE TABLE statement. Even if the CREATE TABLE itself fails, the Before insert will have been committed.

Summary

In this chapter we have covered all of the steps Oracle takes in the processing of our SQL statements. We started with a discussion of the different classes of statements we might submit, namely queries (SELECT statements), DML statements (queries, INSERT, UPDATE and DELETE), and finally DDL statements, those statements that create or alter objects in the database.

We covered in detail how Oracle will parse a query, both syntactically and semantically, to verify it is correct. We saw how this will result in either a soft parse or a hard parse, with a soft parse being preferable whenever possible. In the event of a hard parse, we covered the additional steps that are needed to process the statement, namely optimization and row source generation.

We covered the Oracle optimizer and its two modes RULE and COST. We learned that all applications developed today should be making use of the CBO, as many existing and most all new features added to Oracle are available only with this optimizer mode. In this section we laid out the conditions that cause Oracle to choose between the optimizers and how you can see which it is using with AUTOTRACE in SQL*Plus, a topic we'll revisit in Chapter 18.

We closed this chapter with an overview of how SELECT statements in general, and DML statements specifically, are processed by Oracle. In the DML processing section, we took an in-depth look at how Oracle uses REDO and UNDO together to provide for protection from failures and how our inserts, updates, and deletes interact with this information.

Tables

Tables are basic structures that store data in rows and columns. However, just as Oracle has added features to the database as a whole, so it has enhanced the concept of tables over time to accommodate more complex application requirements. In this chapter, we are going to look at:

- ❑ The most commonly used types of tables available in Oracle, and why you might use each type.
- ❑ Table properties you will encounter in Oracle that affect the way the table operates.
- ❑ How to ALTER, DROP, and TRUNCATE tables.

An Introduction To Tables in Oracle

In Oracle, storing data has never been easier or more efficient. In addition to all the enhancements that have been made to the SQL optimizer, the database kernel, the database administration configuration options, and so on, Oracle has released new types of tables to accommodate a wider variety of data storage, data access, and performance requirements.

For all types of table, Oracle allows developers and administrators to specify various table attributes that determine things such as:

- ❑ Which tablespace contains the table
- ❑ How Oracle physically stores the table on disk
- ❑ How Oracle maps the table's data to memory when it is read from disk
- ❑ How Oracle handles logging for certain operations on the table

There are also attributes unique to each of the various types of table. As we take a look at each in turn, we will talk about these attributes, and how they affect the operation of your tables. More important than the individual attributes, however, is that you understand the various types of tables, and why you might choose one over the other. In your applications, a normal relational table will get the job done. One of the other types of tables, however, might get it done much faster, using less disk space and less processor resource along the way.

The new table types can also save you time when developing or administering solutions. As you read about the different types of table available, you will find that they were made to satisfy requirements other than those of a standard table with heap storage. These requirements were usually satisfied by developers and/or administrators working around the problem by solving them some other way, but these workarounds are no longer necessary because Oracle's new table types take care of these problems.

Types of Tables

In this section, we will learn about the most commonly used table types, how to create them and why we would use them.

Heap Tables

The most basic type of table is a **heap table**. The term *heap* refers to the manner in which the data is randomly stored on disk. Basically, Oracle writes rows to blocks on disk with no regard to where other rows are stored. When rows are inserted into a heap table, the database writes the data into the first segment with sufficient free space. As rows are updated and deleted, space is made available for new inserts.

To illustrate heap tables we will model the training and education department of a company which deals primarily with the information technology industry.

Try It Out – Creating Heap-Organized Tables

1. The first table we'll create is called SUBJECTS, representing the categories of classes that will be taught in the training department.

```
SQL> create table subjects (
  2     subject_id     number not null,
  3     subject_name   varchar2(30) not null,
  4     description    varchar2(4000)
  5  )
  6  tablespace users
  7  /

Table created.
```

As you can see we have created three columns named SUBJECT_ID, SUBJECT_NAME, and DESCRIPTION. These columns have the data types NUMBER, VARCHAR2(30), and VARCHAR2(4000) respectively. Note the use of the NOT NULL clause, to ensure that both subject_id and subject_name have values.

2. Now the SUBJECTS table is created, we will make the SUBJECT_ID column the primary key of the table using an ALTER TABLE command:

```
SQL> alter table subjects
  2     add constraint pk_subjects
  3     primary key (subject_id)
```

```
  4  /
```

Table altered.

3. Having created the SUBJECTS table we can move on to creating a child table called COURSES, which will store courses taught in the subject areas within the SUBJECTS table.

```
SQL> create table courses (
  2      course_id    number not null,
  3      course_name  varchar2(60) not null,
  4      subject_id   number not null,
  5      duration     number(2),
  6      skill_lvl    varchar2(12) not null
  7  )
  8  tablespace users
  9  /
```

Table created.

In this case we have created the columns COURSE_ID (data type NUMBER), SUBJECT_ID (data type NUMBER), COURSE_NAME (data type VARCHAR2(60)), DURATION (data type NUMBER(2)), and SKILL_LVL (data type VARCHAR2(12)).

4. Now we need to define a number of constraints in order to enforce business rules defined in our Education Department. First of all we want the COURSE_ID column of the COURSES table to be the primary key. The coding for this is as follows:

```
SQL> alter table courses
  2      add constraint pk_courses
  3      primary key (course_id)
  4  /
```

Table altered.

Secondly, we want the foreign key (SUBJECT_ID) column for COURSES to reference the SUBJECTS table:

```
SQL> alter table courses
  2      add constraint fk_course_subj
  3      foreign key (subject_id) references subjects (subject_id)
  4  /
```

Table altered.

Finally we want to implement a check constraint on the SKILL_LVL column to ensure that the only possible values for the rows in this column are BEGINNER, INTERMEDIATE, or ADVANCED:

```
SQL> alter table courses
  2      add constraint ck_level check(
  3      skill_lvl in ('BEGINNER', 'INTERMEDIATE', 'ADVANCED')
```

```
    4  )
    5  /

Table altered.
```

How It Works

This gives you an example of creating two heap-organized tables related to each other. We used the `TABLESPACE` clause to ensure that the tables were placed in the right tablespace, and used constraints to help enforce some business rules related to the data that will reside in the tables.

External Tables

New in Oracle9*i* **external tables** are read-only tables stored on a filesystem outside of the database. Prior to Oracle9*i*, the only way to use data stored in flat files on the operating system was to load it into the database via the SQL*Loader utility, or by manually creating a heap-organized table using `INSERT` statements corresponding to the data in the flat file.

> *We won't be discussing the SQL*Loader utility any further here, but you can read more about it at* http://technet.oracle.com.

Suppose we use Microsoft Excel to manage a list of teachers and phone numbers for our training department. Prior to Oracle9*i*, if we wished to continue to use Excel to manage the list of names, but wanted to make the data available to our Oracle database, we would have had to load the data into the database using SQL*Loader. However, as soon as Excel updates the file, the original work performed by SQL*Loader is wasted. Not only does the load have to be performed again, but the database also has either to remove all the original records before inserting the modified data, or account for updates to existing records, deleted records, and new records. Basically, this is a large amount of unnecessary work.

With external tables, instead of copying the data into the database, and being forced to keep it up-to-date, we can simply leave the data in the flat file and allow the database to read it in place. In this way, the external application can update the data as it sees fit, and SQL*Loader never has to be invoked to perform data loads.

Try It Out – Creating and Using External Tables

In the example to follow, we'll create a sample external table based on a text file (`teacher.csv`) containing comma-separated values. Excel can use these files, so it saves us from having to write custom code to tell Oracle how to read an Excel spreadsheet.

> *You can find the* `teacher.csv` *file in the code download for this book at* www.apress.com

1. In order to create an external table, Oracle needs to know where on the operating system the file is located. This is accomplished using a **directory object**, which is a database object that acts as an alias for directories on the server's file system. To create a directory that points to the location of our data file you need the `CREATE ANY DIRECTORY` privilege, which means either using a DBA account or granting this permission to the user account you are using for your examples:

```
SQL> create directory ext_data_files
  2     as 'D:\ORACLE\ORA90\EXTERNAL'
  3  /

Directory created.
```

In this case we create a directory named `ext_data_files`, and point to the `D:\ORACLE\ORA90\EXTERNAL` directory on the server. You will need to amend this pathway to wherever you have located the `teacher.csv` file.

2. Now we are ready to create the table definition for the external table. You should note here, that the table data itself is not stored inside the database. The only information Oracle stores is the meta data about the external table. The database is responsible for retrieving the data from the external data source at the time a query on the external table is submitted:

```
SQL> create table teachers_ext (
  2     first_name      varchar2(15),
  3     last_name       varchar2(15),
  4     phone_number    varchar2(12)
  5  )
  6  organization external (
  7     type oracle_loader
  8     default directory ext_data_files
  9     access parameters (
 10       fields terminated by ',' )
 11     location ('teacher.csv')
 12  )
 13  reject limit unlimited
 14  /

Table created.
```

3. Now that the table is created, we can perform a SQL query on it, asking for information from the Oracle database about the file stored on the operating system:

```
SQL> select first_name ||' '|| last_name "Name", phone_number "Phone"
  2     from teachers_ext
  3     order by last_name
  4  /

Name                           Phone
------------------------------ ------------------------------
Robert Balfe                   123-0106
Richard Clauser                123-0100
Mark Freeman                   123-0107
Brian Gilbert                  123-0109
Shane Hogeland                 123-0101
Lance Horner                   123-0103
David Jaffe                    123-0108
Carl Meyers                    123-0102
```

```
Robert Slagle                123-0104
John Thompson                123-0105
Robert Weyant                123-0110

11 rows selected.
```

The `11 rows selected` message indicates that Oracle found eleven records in the external table. If you open up the data file, you will see that it does indeed have eleven records. You will also notice that the file was not changed or modified in any way, Oracle simply read the file in place according to the definition of the external table `TEACHERS_EXT`, and made the data available to the database.

How It Works

The `CREATE TABLE` statement is a bit more complex than for a standard heap-organized table, so we'll step through the entire DDL statement.

The first five lines are much the same as any other `CREATE TABLE` statement:

```
SQL> create table teachers_ext (
  2    first_name      varchar2(15),
  3    last_name       varchar2(15),
  4    phone_number    varchar2(12)
  5  )
```

Having mapped the contents of the data file to columns in the table, we then indicate that the table being created is an external table by using the `ORGANIZATION EXTERNAL` clause:

```
  6  organization external (
  7    type oracle_loader
```

In the next section of the `CREATE TABLE` statement, the `DEFAULT_DIRECTORY` and `LOCATION` attributes are used to specify where the external file is located on the file system of the operating system:

```
  8    default directory ext_data_files
  9    access parameters (
 10      fields terminated by ',' )
 11    location ('teacher.csv')
 12  )
```

We will discuss ACCESS PARAMETERS later in this section.

The final clause in the `CREATE TABLE` statement is the `REJECT LIMIT` clause:

```
 13  reject limit unlimited
 14  /
```

This clause tells Oracle how many errors the database will allow during the conversion of the source data to the column data types mapped in the table definition. If you perform a query and Oracle encounters more than this number of conversion errors, the query fails. The default value for REJECT LIMIT is zero. UNLIMITED is a keyword that indicates that conversion errors are ignored and the query will never fail. At worst, if every record in the external data file fails due to a conversion error, querying this table would simply return no rows.

This example has provided a basic example of creating and querying an external table. The next few sections explain in more detail various aspects of external tables.

TYPE (or Access Driver Type)

An external table's **access driver** is the utility used to transform data from its native format into the format presented to the server. In other words the table creator/owner can use the access driver to modify source file(s) so that they are readable by the database.

Oracle comes with the default access driver ORACLE_LOADER, though you should note that access drivers can be built to support other external table types.

DEFAULT DIRECTORY

When you create an external table, you are really only storing meta data inside the database. The data itself is stored outside the database. When defining the external table, you define a default directory telling Oracle where the files for the external table are located on the file system.

In the above example we created a directory object to be used in our CREATE TABLE statement. While the SYSTEM user is the only user (by default) that has the permissions to create such objects, it is possible to grant READ and/or WRITE permissions to other users on the directory objects created. Taking the default directory that we have already created, EXT_DATA_FILES, we can grant permissions as follows:

```
SQL> grant all on directory ext_data_files to scott
  2  /

Grant succeeded.
```

This would give SCOTT the ability to create external tables and use the EXT_DATA_FILES directory object in the table definition.

BADFILE and NOBADFILE

When your external table is being read, the database may encounter a data type conversion error, and be unable to convert the source data into the column definitions for the external table in the database. Data values which aren't converted will be written to a BADFILE, if you use the following syntax in your CREATE TABLE statement:

```
SQL> create table teachers_ext (
  2    first_name      varchar2(15),
  3    last_name       varchar2(15),
  4    phone_number    varchar2(12)
```

```
 5  )
 6  organization external (
 7    type oracle_loader
 8    default directory ext_data_files
 9    access parameters (
10      records delimited by newlines
11      badfile ext_data_files:'teacher.bad'
12      fields terminated by ',' )
13    location ('teacher.csv')
14  )
15  reject limit unlimited
16  /
```

If we consider our previous example, then if there were a record in the external data file that looked like this:

```
    .        .
    .        .
    .        .
David,Jaffe,123-0108
Brian,Gilbert, 123-0109
Robert,Weyant, 123-0110
Ravi,Ananthapadmanabha, 123-0111
```

Oracle would not be able to read it. This is because Ananthapadmanabha is 17 characters long and the column definition for the LAST_NAME is 15 characters. Querying the table would return all the records that could be converted successfully. The records that could not be read (in this case, Ravi Ananthapadmanabha) are sent to the BADFILE, which would then look like this:

```
Ravi,Ananthapadmanabha,123-0111
```

If a BADFILE is specified in the CREATE TABLE statement, then one will be created for you, with a filename format of TABLENAME_PROCESSID.bad. PROCESSID refers to the operating system process id of the access driver. If you wanted to specify a BADFILE yourself and wanted to use the process id, you could do so with the substitution variable %p (as in mybadfile_%p).

To reiterate, Oracle writes to the BADFILE records that fail to be converted into the table's definition of a row. In the previous example, Ravi's last name was too long, so the entire row was logged in the BADFILE and it was not returned in the query. If we had a table definition and one of the columns was NUMBER, any row in the data file without a valid NUMBER in that column would fail and be logged in the BADFILE.

> **This file will be overwritten for every query that is executed against the table where there are failed records. This means at any time we look at the file, we will see the rows that were in the data file that failed the conversion the last time a user actually queried the table.**

BADFILEs are helpful because they give the table owner one file to examine to find records that have failed. For administrators who are using external tables in their applications, using a BADFILE is important in helping fix either the source data or the table definition to ensure all the data in the source can be read by Oracle.

If there is no reason to fix the data, or these types of conversion errors do not matter, then the NOBADFILE clause can be used when creating the table. This will cause Oracle to disregard data type conversion errors completely, and erroneous records will simply be ignored. NOBADFILE is specified in the CREATE TABLE command as follows:

```
SQL> create table teachers_ext (
  2     first_name      varchar2(15),
  3     last_name       varchar2(15),
  4     phone_number    varchar2(12)
  5  )
  6  organization external (
  7     type oracle_loader
  8     default directory ext_data_files
  9     access parameters (
 10        nobadfile
 11        fields terminated by ',' )
 12     location ('teacher.csv')
 13  )
 14  reject limit unlimited
 15  /
```

If neither BADFILE nor NOBADFILE is specified in the CREATE TABLE statement, Oracle will create a BADFILE by default, using the table name and a .BAD extension in the directory where the data file is located.

LOGFILE and NOLOGFILE

LOGFILEs are used to write error messages encountered when Oracle attempts to access the data file. This is very useful when setting up new external tables because errors in external tables will occur most commonly when the table is first created. If the operating system is limiting Oracle from reading the file, or if the source data file does not exist for instance, these errors will be recorded in the log file.

NOLOGFILE is used when the errors encountered while accessing the external data source should be ignored. If this clause is specified, Oracle will not write the errors to any log file at all.

If the CREATE TABLE statement does not specify LOGFILE or NOLOGFILE, Oracle will create a LOGFILE by default. The name of the LOGFILE will be <table name>.LOG

In summary, external tables are a great alternative to manual loading of external data files into the database. In the first release of Oracle9i, external tables are read-only, and are only useful for querying the data. Oracle provides no native way to update or delete records in these tables yet. Additionally, Oracle cannot create indexes on external tables. This can be somewhat limiting, depending on the needs of your table.

The lack of indexing capabilities means external tables will always be full scanned by Oracle in SELECT statements. If you need to index an external table, you might opt to create a standard table (or index-organized table, as discussed below) based on the contents of the external table. Your standard table could then be indexed. You could use Oracle's internal job- scheduling mechanism, DBMS_JOB, to manage the refreshes between the external table and the standard table (you can read more about DBMS_JOB in Appendix D).

Index-Organized Tables

An **index-organized table** (or **IOT**) is a table structure stored like an index to assist query performance. Index-organized tables offer this great query performance at the cost of insert and update performance. Imagine picking up a Webster's Dictionary and looking up the meaning of some word. When you search for a word in the dictionary, you open the book to the approximate location of the word. You know where the word will be found based on its alphabetical order, and so search forward or backward based on where you opened the book. This is a real-life example of a B-Tree index in action. This is also a perfect example of an index-organized table.

Let's take a look at an example of creating an index-organized table:

```
SQL> create table states (
  2     state_id          varchar2(2),
  3     state_name        varchar2(20),
  4     constraint states_pk
  5       primary key (state_id)
  6  )
  7  organization index
  8  /

Table created.
```

In this example, we have a simple lookup table that consists of two columns, STATE_ID and STATE_NAME. The table is most commonly accessed by looking up the STATE_NAME, based upon the STATE_ID column. The clause at the end of the statement, ORGANIZATION INDEX, tells Oracle that the table is index-organized.

In an index-organized table, the data is written to disk as if it were one large B-Tree index sorted on the primary key column(s) of the table. This typically results in better read performance for queries against IOTs when accessed using the table's primary key column(s). The same query on a standard heap table requires an indexed read, firstly to read the index blocks and determine where on disk the data blocks are. Once this is done, Oracle must then fetch the relevant data blocks into memory. This is approximately twice as many block reads as would have to be performed by an IOT, where all the data is stored in the index itself, and there is no need to go after any additional data blocks.

Having said that, IOTs are much more difficult to maintain than heap-organized tables. When rows are written into a heap table, Oracle simply uses the first available space in the table's extent to write the data. For an IOT, however, when a row is inserted it must organize the data in its 'place'. Since an IOT is organized like an index, Oracle writes the data to the appropriate data block according to the primary key of the new row being inserted. The rows that are currently stored in the block can be moved to accommodate the new block being written.

SQL-based access to index-organized tables in your application is no different from that to a heap-organized table. You still SELECT, INSERT, UPDATE, and DELETE from index-organized tables in the same way you would any other table. When you submit a query on a heap-organized table, Oracle may use an index to access the table. This depends on a variety of factors, such as (but not limited to):

❑ The optimizer being used (cost-based or rule-based)

❑ The columns specified in the WHERE clause of the query

❑ Whether or not any indexes are created on the table that correspond to the columns in the WHERE clause of the query

If Oracle decides to use an index, it is because the estimated cost (the resources necessary to perform the query) will be smaller than if it performed a full table scan. If Oracle decides to use an index, it first consults the index to determine which data blocks it needs to read before carrying out those reads to retrieve the actual data. As an example, let's observe how Oracle performs an indexed read, based on the number of rows in the table. First, we'll create a small table:

```
sdillon@SLAPDB.US.ORACLE.COM> create table t as
  2    select *
  3      from all_objects
  4     where rownum < 51
  5  /

Table created.
```

The table has been created with 50 rows, so let's create an index on the OBJECT_ID column:

```
sdillon@SLAPDB.US.ORACLE.COM> create index t_idx
  2  on t( object_id )
  3  /

Index created.
```

Now we'll analyze the table to help the Oracle SQL optimizer determine whether it should use an indexed read or a full table scan when we query it:

```
sdillon@SLAPDB.US.ORACLE.COM> analyze table t compute statistics
  2  /

Table analyzed.
```

We can now use the SQL*Plus AUTOTRACE facility to look at how Oracle is querying the data:

```
sdillon@SLAPDB.US.ORACLE.COM> set autotrace on
sdillon@SLAPDB.US.ORACLE.COM> select *
  2    from t
  3   where object_id = 10
  4  /
```

```
no rows selected


Execution Plan
----------------------------------------------------------
   0      SELECT STATEMENT Optimizer=CHOOSE (Cost=1 Card=1 Bytes=88)
   1    0   TABLE ACCESS (FULL) OF 'T' (Cost=1 Card=1 Bytes=88)

Statistics
----------------------------------------------------------
        0  recursive calls
        6  db block gets
        3  consistent gets
        0  physical reads
        0  redo size
      918  bytes sent via SQL*Net to client
      372  bytes received via SQL*Net from client
        1  SQL*Net roundtrips to/from client
        0  sorts (memory)
        0  sorts (disk)
        0  rows processed

sdillon@SLAPDB.US.ORACLE.COM> set autotrace off
```

When we perform a query based on the column in the index, you might think Oracle would choose to do an indexed read. However, to perform an indexed read on this table, we would require reading at least one index block and one table data block. In this case, a full scan of the table requires fewer reads.

Let's now add more records to table t:

```
sdillon@SLAPDB.US.ORACLE.COM> drop table t
  2  /

Table dropped.

sdillon@SLAPDB.US.ORACLE.COM> create table t as
  2     select *
  3       from all_objects
  4      where rownum < 10001
  5  /

Table created.

sdillon@SLAPDB.US.ORACLE.COM> create index t_idx
  2  on t( object_id )
  3  /

Index created.

sdillon@SLAPDB.US.ORACLE.COM> analyze table t compute statistics
  2  /
```

```
Table analyzed.

sdillon@SLAPDB.US.ORACLE.COM> set autotrace traceonly
sdillon@SLAPDB.US.ORACLE.COM> select *
  2    from t
  3    where object_id = 10
  4  /

no rows selected


Execution Plan
----------------------------------------------------------
    0      SELECT STATEMENT Optimizer=CHOOSE (Cost=2 Card=1 Bytes=84)
    1    0   TABLE ACCESS (BY INDEX ROWID) OF 'T' (Cost=2 Card=1 Bytes=84)
    2    1     INDEX (RANGE SCAN) OF 'T_IDX' (NON-UNIQUE) (Cost=1 Card=1)

Statistics
----------------------------------------------------------
          0  recursive calls
          0  db block gets
          2  consistent gets
          0  physical reads
          0  redo size
        918  bytes sent via SQL*Net to client
        372  bytes received via SQL*Net from client
          1  SQL*Net roundtrips to/from client
          0  sorts (memory)
          0  sorts (disk)
          0  rows processed
```

Now, since there are so many rows, you can see from the results of our AUTOTRACE command, that Oracle chooses to perform an indexed read instead of a full table scan.

In the case of tables that are almost always accessed via a particular index (with infrequent updates or inserts), performance can be improved by using index-organized tables instead of heap-organized tables. This is because Oracle does not have to determine whether or not it should use an index as an access path to the table. In addition, Oracle's storage requirements are minimized since there is no need to store both the index data and table data.

There are three further properties of index-organized tables which we will take a look at now.

COMPRESS and NOCOMPRESS

Compression is actually an option for all indexing, not only IOTs, and refers to the manner in which the data in the index is physically stored in the data block. The value specified in the COMPRESS attribute (an integer) directly corresponds to the number of columns in the primary key of the index-organized table that should *not* be stored multiple times. The leading columns will be stored once, and subsequent entries will only store the remaining columns that differ from the first. In the following example we create two index-organized tables, one with compression and one without, to illustrate this point:

223

```
SQL> connect hr/hr
Connected.
SQL> create table locations_iot (
  2      region_id, country_id, location_id,
  3      primary key ( region_id, country_id, location_id )
  4  )
  5  organization index
  6  nocompress
  7  as select c.region_id, l.country_id, l.location_id
  8      from locations l, countries c
  9      where l.country_id = c.country_id
 10  /

Table created.

SQL> create table locations_iot_c (
  2      region_id, country_id, location_id,
  3      primary key ( region_id, country_id, location_id )
  4  )
  5  organization index
  6  compress 2
  7  as select c.region_id, l.country_id, l.location_id
  8      from locations l, countries c
  9      where l.country_id = c.country_id
 10  /

Table created.
```

Both tables were created with the same data using almost identical CREATE TABLE statements. The only difference is on line 7 of each statement, in the COMPRESS/NOCOMPRESS property. The following tables depict how the data is stored in the data blocks on the disk.

The first table depicts the LOCATIONS_IOT table with NOCOMPRESS set as the compression property:

1, CH, 2900	1, CH, 3000	1, DE, 2700	1, IT, 1000	1, IT, 1100
1, NL, 3100	1, UK, 2400	1, UK, 2500	1, UK, 2600	2, BR, 2800
2, CA, 1800	2, CA, 1900	2, MX, 3200	2, US, 1400	2, US, 1500
2, US, 1600	2, US, 1700	3, AU, 2200	3, CN, 2000	3, IN, 2100
3, JP, 1200	3, JP, 1300	3, SG, 2300		

Similarly, in the case of the LOCATIONS_IOT_C table with COMPRESS 2 set as the compression property:

1, CH, 2900	3000	1, DE, 2700	1, IT, 1000	1100
1, NL, 3100	1, UK, 2400	2500	2600	2, BR, 2800
2, CA, 1800	1900	2, MX, 3200	2, US, 1400	1500
1600	1700	3, AU, 2200	3, CN, 2000	3, IN, 2100
3, JP, 1200	3, JP, 1300	3, SG, 2300		

In the `LOCATIONS_IOT` table, each block entry has all three values because there is no compression in the table. In the `LOCATIONS_IOT_C` table, however, there are block entries smaller than the rest. For instance, the first block entry is `1, CH, 2900`. The second entry is `3000`. This is because the two leading columns in the second entry are the same as the first, and need not be repeated. The same compression is realized for `REGION_ID/COUNTRY_ID` combinations:

- ❑ `1, CH`
- ❑ `1, IT`
- ❑ `1, UK`
- ❑ `2, CA`
- ❑ `2, US`

This results in a smaller amount of data stored in the block.

OVERFLOW

Normally, indexes represent one key column (or at most a small number of columns) within a table. In general, large columns, such as large `VARCHAR2` columns or `LOB`s, are not stored in indexes and so B-Tree indexes are small, tightly clustered blocks. In index-organized tables, however, the size of each row can be very large, reducing some of the performance gains realized by organizing the data as an index. `OVERFLOW` is a mechanism provided for such tables, which allows the most common data queried to be in the base index blocks, and the less common (or larger data columns) to be stored in another segment, called the **overflow segment**. Two options are available for specifying how data will be stored in or migrated to the overflow segment, `INCLUDING` and `PCTTHRESHOLD`.

INCLUDING

When the `INCLUDING` clause is used, the administrator specifies a column in the table that will divide the columns into those columns stored in the table's normal data segment (including the primary key columns), and those columns (including the one listed) that are stored in the overflow segment.

Using the `LOCATIONS_IOT` table above, we will create an index-organized table that includes all the columns of the `HR` schema's `LOCATIONS` table. The key columns will be stored in the table's data segment, and all the other columns will be stored in the overflow segment:

```
SQL> create table locations_inc (
  2    region_id, country_id, location_id, street_address,
  3    postal_code, city, state_province,
  4    primary key ( region_id, country_id, location_id )
  5  )
  6  organization index
  7  nocompress
  8  overflow
  9  including street_address
 10  as select c.region_id, l.country_id, l.location_id, l.street_address,
 11             l.postal_code, l.city, l.state_province
 12       from locations l, countries c
 13      where l.country_id = c.country_id
 14  /

Table created.
```

In this example, the table named `LOCATIONS_INC` is created as an index-organized table. The rows that will populate the table are being extracted from the `LOCATIONS` and `COUNTRIES` tables (as seen in the `AS SELECT` clause of the `CREATE TABLE` statement). The `LOCATIONS_INC` table will be stored in two different segments, the primary segment containing `REGION_ID`, `COUNTRY_ID`, and `LOCATION_ID`. The second segment, known as the overflow segment, contains the `STREET_ADDRESS`, `POSTAL_CODE`, `CITY`, and `STATE_PROVINCE` columns.

PCTTHRESHOLD

All the data for a row must fit within the percentage of the block size identified by the `PCTTHRESHOLD` value. Any row larger than that size will be broken up into two storage locations:

- ❑ Key columns are stored in the table's segment
- ❑ All other columns are stored in the overflow segment

`PCTTHRESHOLD` is effective when you have data that is variable in length, and there is no way of telling whether the size of a row will be small or large from row to row. By storing large amounts of data in the overflow segment, read performance is improved for queries that access the key columns, since these columns are stored in the primary table segment. These queries can avoid accessing the larger overflow segment.

In summary, one of the nicest features about using index-organized tables is that you don't have to change your code to use them. An index-organized table is the same as any other table as far as SQL is concerned, so if you find a table in your application that is used mostly for reads, and is queried mostly on (a) primary key column(s), you can recreate the table as an index-organized table and reap the benefits. We have noted some of the drawbacks to their use however, and it is only by trying them out and testing them in your applications that you will learn when they will prove useful to you.

Temporary Tables

Oracle's **temporary tables** are tables whose data exists for the life of a transaction or a session. Data is inserted into the temporary table after the transaction or session begins, and dropped once the transaction or session is complete. In this way developers have access to a temporary storage area for the lifetime of any application logic (such as stored PL/SQL code) that they wish to execute.

> **Note that temporary tables are completely different to heap tables. Inserting data into a heap table, only to remove it once the transaction ends, is incredibly inefficient.**

Oracle's temporary tables work somewhat differently from most other relational database vendors' temporary tables, since you do not need to create a temporary table on every occasion that you want to use temporary storage. Instead, as a part of your application development, you create a temporary table *once* and *only once*, just as you would create normal application tables. In this way, every time a temporary table is used in your application to store rows, the overhead of recreating the table first is not incurred. As a result, you can assign the table name in development just as you do for any other table, with a similar naming convention.

Temporary tables, in contrast to heap tables, do not need to maintain locks on records they contain, since other users will never be able to see those records. Equally, they have no need to maintain other than a minimal amount of redo information since, in the event of a database failure, the user does not expect to continue the application logic halfway through a transaction or session.

Space for temporary tables is not allocated until a user actually inserts data into the table, in contrast to heap tables, which allocate an extent once the CREATE TABLE statement is executed. Not only that, but the space that is allocated for storing the user's data comes from their temporary tablespace, rather than a tablespace that contends with permanent objects' data storage.

Although the data storage mechanisms for temporary tables differ greatly from those for standard heap tables, the two table types do have some similarities:

❏   You can truncate session-specific temporary tables. (The TRUNCATE TABLE command is explained later in this chapter).

❏   You can create indexes on temporary tables.

❏   You can create views on temporary tables.

❏   You can create triggers on temporary tables (triggers could be used to assist in enforcing referential integrity, as you cannot create foreign keys on temporary tables).

Temporary tables should always be used in applications where data is required to be stored temporarily. The following list of behavior attributes shows the ways in which Oracle treats temporary tables so as to improve the performance of such applications:

❏   Redo logs are not created for temporary tables.

❏   A data segment is not allocated until the first INSERT statement is issued against the temporary table.

❏   The TRUNCATE TABLE command only truncates the data in the table for the session that issues the command. Data for other sessions using the table is not affected.

❏   Indexes on temporary tables are treated the same way as temporary tables are treated, with regard to transaction and session scope.

❏   DML locks are not acquired on temporary tables, since no two sessions or transactions can operate against the same rows.

Try It Out – Creating Temporary Tables

In this section, we will create two temporary tables, one for transactions and one for sessions. This will show the difference in the two temporary table types, and give you an understanding of how to create them yourself.

1.   First, we create the two tables (note that the term GLOBAL in GLOBAL TEMPORARY TABLE is standard; there is no other kind of temporary table):

```
SQL> create global temporary table session_tab
  2     on commit preserve rows
  3     as select *
  4            from employees
  5  /

Table created.

SQL> select count(*)
  2     from session_tab
  3  /

  COUNT(*)
----------
       107

SQL> create global temporary table transaction_tab
  2     on commit delete rows
  3     as select *
  4            from employees
  5            where 1 = 0
  6  /

Table created.

SQL> insert into transaction_tab
  2     select *
  3     from employees
  4  /

107 rows created.

SQL> select count(*)
  2     from transaction_tab
  3  /

  COUNT(*)
----------
       107
```

2. Now let's issue a COMMIT statement and see what effect this has:

```
SQL> commit;

Commit complete.

SQL> select count(*)
  2     from session_tab;

  COUNT(*)
----------
```

```
        107

SQL> select count(*)
  2      from transaction_tab;

COUNT(*)
----------
        0
```

As you can see, the records in SESSION_TAB were preserved through the COMMIT, while the records in TRANSACTION_TAB were deleted.

3. Next, we will disconnect from the session and reconnect to the same user to see how restarting the session will affect the tables:

```
SQL> disconnect
Disconnected from Oracle9i Enterprise Edition Release 9.0.1.1.1 - Production
With the Partitioning option
JServer Release 9.0.1.1.1 - Production
SQL> connect hr/hr
Connected.
SQL> select count(*)
  2      from session_tab;

COUNT(*)
----------
        0

SQL> select count(*)
  2      from transaction_tab;

COUNT(*)
----------
        0
```

How It Works

In each of the CREATE GLOBAL TEMPORARY TABLE statements we declare whether the temporary table is transaction- or session-specific. In the case of SESSION_TAB we issued the following:

```
SQL> create global temporary table session_tab
  2      on commit preserve rows
```

The ON COMMIT PRESERVE ROWS clause specifies that for each commit, all rows should remain in the table as is. Since a session may span many transactions, and the records in the temporary table can remain in the table across transactions, PRESERVE ROWS specifies a session-specific temporary table. In contrast to this, in the case of TRANSACTION_TAB we issued:

```
SQL> create global temporary table transaction_tab
  2      on commit delete rows
```

The ON COMMIT DELETE ROWS specifies that for each commit, all rows in the temporary table are dropped. Since commits delimit transactions, DELETE ROWS specifies a transaction-specific temporary table.

You'll also notice that when we created the TRANSACTION_TAB table, we used the clause:

```
WHERE clause of 1 = 0
```

This is so as to avoid any rows inserted into the table in the CREATE statement being deleted following execution of the CREATE GLOBAL TEMPORARY TABLE statement. As a rule, a COMMIT statement is issued behind the scenes before and after a DDL statement is executed. After we create the TRANSACTION_TAB table, we insert records into the table using an INSERT INTO SELECT statement.

We verify that we have 107 records in each table by issuing the SELECT COUNT(*) statement.

Once a COMMIT or ROLLBACK is issued, the transaction has ended. When we reissue the SELECT COUNT(*) queries, we see that the records in SESSION_TAB remain unaffected, while the records in TRANSACTION_TAB have been removed. It is only when we disconnect from the database, and end our session that we see the records removed from the SESSION_TAB table. Reconnecting to the database and issuing a further SELECT COUNT(*) statement verifies that both the TRANSACTION_TAB and the SESSION_TAB tables are now empty.

Other Table Types

There are three other table types, which we need to mention in passing, though further details on these falls outside of the scope of this book.

❑   Partitioned tables are created by splitting very large tables into smaller pieces (partitions). A partitioned table is really just one table as far as applications are concerned, but may aid administrators, since they can work on individual partitions, rather than the entire table.

❑   **Clustered tables**, or **clusters** as they are commonly known, are two or more tables that are stored together physically. The tables are stored in the same data blocks rather than data blocks of their own since it is assumed that the tables will *almost* always be queried together (using some form of join in a SQL statement). This can help to reduce the number of disk reads required in querying, since all the required rows are stored together on common data blocks.

❑   **Hash clustered** tables are similar to clustered tables in that two or more tables are stored together physically on disk. The difference between the two is the method Oracle uses to store and retrieve the rows. In the case of clusters, rows are retrieved using key values that are stored in a separate index, while in the case of hash clusters, Oracle uses a **hash function** to determine the location of the data block that stores the row(s) being retrieved.

You can read more about these three table types at www.oracle.com.

Table Properties

When using Oracle to manage an application's data, the properties of the tables will dictate how the tables are created, how they are stored on disk, and ultimately, how the application will perform once the tables are populated and are in use. In this section, we will discuss various table attributes that are used in the CREATE TABLE and ALTER TABLE commands to specify the way a table behaves in an application.

The TABLESPACE Clause

In Chapter 5, we learned that tablespaces are logical objects that store database objects. When a table is created, it must be placed in a tablespace. This provides a 'bucket' for the data of the table to be stored and is accomplished by using the TABLESPACE clause within CREATE TABLE and ALTER TABLE commands. Note however, that the TABLESPACE clause is optional. Tables created without explicitly specifying the TABLESPACE clause are placed in the default tablespace of the user account creating the table. Let's illustrate this by connecting to the database as user SCOTT and using the USER_USERS view to determine the default tablespace name:

```
SQL> connect scott/tiger
Connected.
SQL> select default_tablespace
  2    from user_users
  3  /

DEFAULT_TABLESPACE
-------------------------------
SYSTEM
```

We can see that the DEFAULT_TABLESPACE for the SCOTT schema is SYSTEM. If we now create a table FOO without specifying a TABLESPACE, then we can query the USER_TABLES view to determine the TABLESPACE_NAME for the table as follows:

```
SQL> create table foo (
  2    a int )
  3  /

Table created.

SQL> select table_name, tablespace_name
  2    from user_tables
  3  where table_name = 'FOO'
  4  /

TABLE_NAME                      TABLESPACE_NAME
------------------------------  ------------------------------
FOO                             SYSTEM
```

The result here shows that the DEFAULT_TABLESPACE is indeed SYSTEM. To specify a tablespace we need to drop the table FOO, and recreate it using the following coding:

```
SQL> drop table foo
  2  /

Table dropped.

SQL> create table foo (
  2      a int )
  3  tablespace users
  4  /

Table created.

SQL> select table_name, tablespace_name
  2      from user_tables
  3    where table_name = 'FOO'
  4  /

TABLE_NAME                      TABLESPACE_NAME
------------------------------  ------------------------------
FOO                             USERS
```

Now we see that we have created table FOO in the USERS tablespace.

Note that if there is no USERS tablespace, then you will receive the error message:

```
ORA-00959: tablespace 'USERS' does not exist.
```

You can use the following query (within an administrative account such as DBA) to find another suitable tablespace name:

```
select tablespace_name
  from dba_tablespaces
 order by tablespace_name;
```

If you return the error message:

```
ORA-01950: no privileges on tablespace 'USERS'.
```

this means the SCOTT user does not have privileges to store data in the USERS tablespace. You can rectify this by issuing the following ALTER USER statement (again from an administrative account):

```
alter user SCOTT quota unlimited on users;
```

> **Note that you can specify the user's default tablespace when creating users in Oracle. This particular clause is optional and if omitted, the value will default to SYSTEM.**

This is commonly overlooked and users often end up with all their objects in the SYSTEM tablespace. Placing all of one's objects in the SYSTEM tablespace can be likened to putting all your files in the C:\ directory on Windows, or in the root directory (/) on a UNIX machine. This causes a variety of problems, including:

❑ Database cluttering. Since all objects are in a single tablespace, manageability of your data becomes very difficult.

❑ Performance issues incurred from having to read an application's table data off (potentially) the same device as the SYSTEM tablespace. (Tablespaces may be spread across disks/devices, but it's not the default setup.)

❑ Space contention. The SYSTEM tablespace is where Oracle stores its own data (such as the data dictionary) needed to operate the instance. Contending for space in this will impair system performance.

Identifying and Eliminating SYSTEM Invaders

Before setting TABLESPACE clauses for CREATE TABLE statements, you should check the user accounts in your database to ensure none of them have the SYSTEM tablespace set as their default tablespace. In the following query, we'll look for all those schemas in our database that violate this rule:

```
SQL> connect system/manager
Connected.
SQL> select username, default_tablespace, temporary_tablespace
  2     from dba_users
  3   where default_tablespace = 'SYSTEM'
  4      or temporary_tablespace = 'SYSTEM'
  5  /

USERNAME                           DEFAULT_TABLESPACE TEMPORARY_TABLESPACE
---------------------------------- ------------------ --------------------
SYS                                SYSTEM             TEMP
SYSTEM                             SYSTEM             TEMP
DBSNMP                             SYSTEM             TEMP
OSE$HTTP$ADMIN                     SYSTEM             TEMP
AURORA$ORB$UNAUTHENTICATED         SYSTEM             TEMP
AURORA$JIS$UTILITY$                SYSTEM             TEMP
SCOTT                              SYSTEM             TEMP
OUTLN                              SYSTEM             TEMP
ORDSYS                             SYSTEM             TEMP
ORDPLUGINS                         SYSTEM             TEMP
MDSYS                              SYSTEM             TEMP
LBACSYS                            SYSTEM             TEMP

12 rows selected.
```

As you can see we have quite a few user accounts with a default tablespace of SYSTEM. Since we are only worried about user SCOTT in this case, we'll modify SCOTT's default tablespace so that new tables will be written somewhere besides the SYSTEM tablespace:

```
SQL> alter user scott
  2    default tablespace users
  3  /

User altered.

SQL> select default_tablespace, temporary_tablespace
  2    from dba_users
  3    where username = 'SCOTT'
  4  /

DEFAULT_TABLESPACE              TEMPORARY_TABLESPACE
------------------------------  ------------------------------
USERS                           TEMP
```

If user SCOTT now creates a table without explicitly specifying the TABLESPACE clause, the table data will be stored in the USERS tablespace by default:

```
SQL> connect scott/tiger
Connected.
SQL> create table t(
  2    a int
  3  )
  4  /

Table created.

SQL> select table_name, tablespace_name
  2    from user_tables
  3    where table_name = 'T'
  4  /

TABLE_NAME                      TABLESPACE_NAME
------------------------------  ------------------------------
T                               USERS

1 row selected.
```

> **Don't change the default or temporary tablespace properties for the SYS or SYSTEM schemas. These are internal accounts created and managed by the database.**

LOGGING and NOLOGGING

LOGGING and NOLOGGING are optional parameters that can be issued along with a CREATE TABLE statement. The term *logging* refers to the Oracle **redo log**, which records all changes made to the data in the database. In the event of a failure that prevents data being transferred from the memory to the database's data files, those changes can be retrieved from the redo log. This helps to prevent data loss, increasing reliability.

When NOLOGGING is specified in a CREATE TABLE statement, the table is known as a **nologging table**. Operations that happen against this table can potentially cause less logging in the database. For many people, this implies that if a table is created using the NOLOGGING clause, operations performed on the table (such as INSERTs, UPDATEs, DELETEs, and so on) will generate *no* redo log. Unfortunately, this is not the way LOGGING and NOLOGGING work.

When a nologging table is created, the redo log generation is suppressed, but only for particular operations. During these operations, the details of what data is being changed are disregarded. However it is not true to say that no redo log is created, since the internal structure of the database (the data dictionary, in particular) is changing, and those changes *are* recorded. This causes a lot of confusion for administrators who expect no redo log activity when their tables are created with NOLOGGING specified. Aside from the actions listed below, redo log activity for changes in the table behaves as normal. The actions that can take advantage of the NOLOGGING clause are as follows:

❑ CREATE TABLE AS SELECT

❑ SQL*LOADER direct path load

❑ Direct path insert (via the /*+ APPEND */ hint)

> *We have seen how to use the CREATE TABLE AS SELECT statement, but the other two actions here are beyond the scope of our discussion, and are included for the sake of completeness.*

Do not be confused about the purpose of the LOGGING and NOLOGGING clauses. Normal operations of tables will be recorded in the redo log for recovery in case the instance fails. There is only one way to avoid this, namely by using global temporary tables, as we discussed earlier.

The STORAGE Clauses

Effectively managing space consumption in the database, directly impacts the ability of the database to grow and store data. When you create objects in Oracle (tables and indexes, for example), you specify how the object consumes space on disk. This is done with the storage clause of the object. If a tablespace is created without a storage clause, the storage attributes get default values (see below for specifics). When other objects are created, they inherit the storage attributes of the tablespace. So, for example, if a tablespace has MIN_EXTENTS 5, then any table created will also get MIN_EXTENTS 5 (subsequent changes to the tablespace's storage clause will *not* affect the table's storage attributes).

When an object that consumes storage is created, it is stored in logical objects called extents, which we introduced in Chapter 5. As objects grow, they consume more and more extents.

Prior to Oracle8*i*, extents and space allocation in general was managed in the data dictionary. Whenever Oracle had to create a new extent, low-level queries of the data dictionary tables had to be performed to find the next available extent in the target tablespace. The data dictionary then had to be updated with the new extent information once it had been allocated. The target tablespace was known as a **dictionary-managed** tablespace. This could lead to performance issues if large numbers of extents were being allocated at the same time, since Oracle can only allocate one extent at a time in the data dictionary.

When specifying a storage clause of a CREATE TABLE command you can use the following parameters:

❏   INITIAL – this will be the size of the first extent created. When a table is created, with a known amount of data, the administrator can set the INITIAL parameter to a size which accommodates all of the data for the table. This would fit all the data into a single extent, eliminating the chances for fragmentation or a cumbersome number of extents for the table.

❏   NEXT – After the first extent in a table is full, the NEXT parameter will tell Oracle how much space to allocate for subsequent extents. NEXT can be thought of as a parameter used for maintenance. When working with tables in dictionary-managed tablespaces, administrators would fit all the data for a table into the INITIAL extent. NEXT would typically be set to an adequate size to allow for growth of that table.

❏   PCTINCREASE – For administrators that were unsure of the amount of growth required for an object, the PCTINCREASE parameter provided a 'growing' next extent size. Each time an extent was allocated, the NEXT size would increase by the PCTINCREASE percentage. However, this means that your extent size will grow *each* time another extent is allocated, and it is recommended that PCTINCREASE should be set to 0 in all cases.

❏   MINEXTENTS – When creating a table in a dictionary-managed tablespace, the administrator can tell Oracle to allocate more than one extent at the time the table is created. In a table with INITIAL and NEXT sizes set to 1 MB, and PCTINCREASE set to 0, a MINEXTENTS parameter of 5 would mean the table would allocate five 1 MB extents upon creation (5 MB of space).

❏   MAXEXTENTS – This parameter specifies the upper boundary for the number of extents that may be allocated for a table. In a table with INITIAL and NEXT sizes set to 1 MB, and PCTINCREASE set to 0, a MAXEXTENTS parameter of 10 would mean the table could not grow beyond 10 MB in size (unless an administrator changed the MAXEXTENTS attribute of the table).

In Oracle 8*i*, Oracle introduced **locally managed** tablespaces and made the INITIAL, NEXT, PCTINCREASE, MINEXTENTS, and MAXEXTENTS storage attributes pretty much obsolete. These types of tablespace offered administrators the option of having Oracle manage the extents, rather than manually configuring and administering their tables' storage. The tasks involved in local extent management were reduced to determining whether you wanted uniform extent sizes or the database to 'auto-allocate' extents. As a result, all the previously mentioned storage attributes can be put away in the 'we-probably-won't-ever-need-this-again' bucket.

Locally managed tablespaces do not use the data dictionary for extent management. Free space is managed in a bitmap, stored in the tablespace itself, that acts as a map of the tablespace. When an extent has to be allocated, the tablespace uses the bitmap to find the first space big enough for the new extent. There is no SQL issued against the data dictionary at all, which prevents the potential extent management bottleneck seen in dictionary-managed tablespaces.

Prior to Oracle9*i*, all tablespaces were created as dictionary-managed by default. In Oracle9*i*, all tablespaces created (except SYSTEM), are locally managed using auto-allocated extents. This is not to say that you don't have the option of using dictionary-managed tablespaces. You would, for example, need to use a dictionary-managed tablespace if you wanted to use different extent sizes for each of the objects stored inside the tablespace.

Storage Summary

Locally-managed tablespaces remove much of the burden of extent allocation and size maintenance from the database administrator. There are few reasons why you would need to use dictionary managed tablespaces in Oracle 9*i*. In general it is better to use uniform extent sizes instead of auto-allocation of extents, since uniform extent sizes allow any free extent in the database to be used for any other segment in the tablespace.

If you need to utilize storage attributes for your tablespaces you should always specify them, rather than using the default values. This ensures that you give thought to the types of objects that will be stored in the tablespace and how much space they will consume. Never specify storage attributes at the object level (tables, indexes, etc), but instead, allow them to inherit their storage clause from the tablespace. More information can be found about tablespaces, extents and segments in Chapter 5.

CACHE and NOCACHE

When performing full table scans in Oracle, the data blocks read into the buffer cache are stored at the least recently used end of the **Least Recently Used** list (**LRU**). This means that these blocks will be aged out of the buffer cache as soon as a 'normal' query is performed, and data must be read into the buffer cache.

When creating tables, the CACHE clause can override this behavior. When a full table scan is performed on a table that was created using the CACHE clause, the data blocks are read into the buffer cache and placed at the most recently used end of the LRU.

CACHE should be specified for tables such as small lookup tables and tables that will not use indexes for one reason or another. Non-indexed reads typically cause full table scans and data blocks read by full table scans are quickly aged out of the SGA. If your table will be accessed quite frequently, the CACHE clause will help to minimize physical reads of the data blocks.

NOCACHE is the default value when creating tables. Tables created without explicitly specifying the CACHE clause are effectively a NOCACHE table. Data blocks read from such tables are aged out of the SGA normally. For more information about this process, see Chapter 5.

ALTER TABLE

Using tables in the Oracle database is not hard to do, but creating the perfect table on the first try is next to impossible. After tables are created and begin to be used, requirements or issues are likely to occur that were not planned for. So, Oracle has made a very verbose ALTER TABLE statement available for changing all manner of table attributes.

There are many types of modifications that can be made to tables, and discussing every detail and nuance is well beyond the scope of this chapter. Instead, this section will cover some of the most commonly used ALTER TABLE commands, and how to employ them effectively. They are:

❑   Add, modify, or drop columns in the table

❑   Renaming tables

❑ Moving tables to new tablespaces

❑ Changing the storage attributes of a table

❑ Changing table properties, such as LOGGING and NOLOGGING or CACHE and NOCACHE

Altering Columns in Tables

During the development and maintenance phases of a project, tables are changed to accommodate new data storage requirements and various modifications in functionality. Performance-wise, dropping a table and recreating it is out of the question, so Oracle offers the ability to add new columns, modify existing columns, and altogether remove columns from existing tables without impacting any other data in the table.

In the following example, we'll create a table and use the ALTER TABLE command to make changes to the table's columns. We begin by creating the table PEOPLE, and inserting some values:

```
SQL> create table people(
  2      employee_id      number(9),
  3      first_name       varchar2(15),
  4      last_name        varchar2(20),
  5      email            varchar2(25),
  6      constraint pk_people primary key (employee_id)
  7  )
  8  /

Table created.

SQL> insert into people
  2  values (1, 'Tom', 'Kyte', 'tkyte@us.oracle.com');

1 row created.

SQL> insert into people
  2  values (2, 'Sean', 'Dillon', 'sdillon@us.oracle.com');

1 row created.

SQL> insert into people
  2  values (3, 'Christopher', 'Beck', 'clbeck@us.oracle.com');

1 row created.

SQL> commit;

Commit complete.
```

To verify that our record insertion was successful, let's query the PEOPLE table as follows:

```
SQL> select *
  2      from people
  3  /
```

```
EMPLOYEE_ID FIRST_NAME      LAST_NAME            EMAIL
----------- --------------- -------------------- -------------------------
          1 Tom             Kyte                 tkyte@us.oracle.com
          2 Sean            Dillon               sdillon@us.oracle.com
          3 Christopher     Beck                 clbeck@us.oracle.com
```

As you can see our table is now populated with data. The first thing we can do is add a PHONE_NUMBER column by issuing the following:

```
SQL> alter table people
  2   add (
  3     phone_number     varchar2(10)
  4   )
  5  /

Table altered.

SQL> select *
  2     from people;

EMPLOYEE_ID FIRST_NAME   LAST_NAME EMAIL                     PHONE_NUMBER
----------- ------------ --------- ------------------------- -------------
          1 Tom          Kyte      tkyte@us.oracle.com
          2 Sean         Dillon    sdillon@us.oracle.com
          3 Christopher  Beck      clbeck@us.oracle.com
```

As you can see, since we added a new column to the table but did not modify any existing rows, none of the rows in the database contain data for the new column.

NOT NULL Column Constraints

You can only specify NOT NULL as a constraint for a column if the table contains no records. This is because Oracle attempts to validate all the rows in the table once the NOT NULL constraint is applied to the column. If there are existing records then these will fail the validation, and, since the constraint cannot be added, neither can the column. There is a work-around to this problem, however. We begin by adding the desired column to the table (in this case SSN):

```
SQL> alter table people
  2   add (
  3     ssn         number(9)
  4   )
  5  /

Table altered.
```

Now we update every existing record with a value for the SSN column:

```
SQL> update people
  2      set ssn = 123456789
  3    where employee_id = 1;

1 row updated.

SQL> update people
  2      set ssn = 234567890
  3    where employee_id = 2;

1 row updated.

SQL> update people
  2      set ssn = 345678901
  3    where employee_id = 3;

1 row updated.
```

At this point we modify the existing column so that it will not accept NULLs:

```
SQL> alter table people
  2  modify (
  3    ssn number(9) not null
  4  )
  5  /

Table altered.

SQL> desc people
 Name                                      Null?    Type
 ----------------------------------------- -------- -------------------------

 EMPLOYEE_ID                               NOT NULL NUMBER(9)
 FIRST_NAME                                         VARCHAR2(15)
 LAST_NAME                                          VARCHAR2(20)
 EMAIL                                              VARCHAR2(25)
 PHONE_NUMBER                                       VARCHAR2(10)
 SSN                                       NOT NULL NUMBER(9)
```

As you can see our NOT NULL constraint has now been successfully applied to the SSN column.

It is worth noting here that if you modify your table columns by constraining the data type, for example by shortening a data type's length, then Oracle may reject the change if data already exists in the column that would violate the column's data type following the change.

Dropping Columns and Marking Columns Unused

Not only can you modify columns that exist in your tables, you can also drop them entirely. Prior to Oracle 8*i* any unused column in the table either had to be carried as added overhead, or a new table recreated without the unwanted column using the CREATE TABLE AS SELECT statement. In Oracle 8*i* and above however, it is possible to drop a column by simply issuing the statement:

```
ALTER TABLE <table name> DROP COLUMN
```

This operation rewrites the table to disk and leaves out the old column data, and is a way of 'reclaiming' the space that was once used for the unwanted column.

For larger tables, there is another operation you can use to avoid having to perform an entire rewrite on the table:

```
ALTER TABLE <table name> SET UNUSED COLUMN <column name>
```

This differs from the ALTER TABLE <table name> DROP COLUMN command since the table is not rewritten, and nor is the space reclaimed. The column is simply ignored by Oracle after the statement is executed. This introduces a loss of data storage for this extent since that data cannot be overwritten until the column is dropped completely. If it is necessary to reclaim this lost storage space, then the table needs to be reorganized (and the column dropped).

In both the DROP COLUMN and SET UNUSED COLUMN variations of ALTER TABLE, you can drop or mark more than one column at a time. To illustrate this, we'll log in as user SCOTT and use tables from the HR schema. We'll begin by granting the necessary privileges on the tables owned by HR to SCOTT:

```
SQL> connect hr/hr
Connected.
SQL> grant select on departments to scott;

Grant succeeded.

SQL> grant select on locations to scott;

Grant succeeded.

SQL> grant select on countries to scott;

Grant succeeded.

SQL> grant select on regions to scott;

Grant succeeded.
```

Now we can create our DEPARTMENTS table, and then carry out a SELECT statement to verify that we have included the information we want in our table:

```
SQL> connect scott/tiger
Connected.
SQL> create table departments as
  2     select d.department_id, d.department_name, d.manager_id,
  3            d.location_id, c.country_name, r.region_name
  4       from hr.departments d, hr.locations l, hr.countries c, hr.regions r
  5      where d.location_id = l.location_id
  6        and l.country_id = c.country_id
  7        and c.region_id = r.region_id
```

```
   8   /

Table created.

SQL> select department_name, country_name, region_name
  2    from departments
  3    order by 3, 2, 1
  4    /

DEPARTMENT_NAME             COUNTRY_NAME                    REGION_NAME
-------------------------   ------------------------------  ---------------
Marketing                   Canada                          Americas
Accounting                  United States of America        Americas
Administration              United States of America        Americas
        .                          .                                .
        .                          .                                .
        .                          .                                .
Public Relations            Germany                         Europe
Human Resources             United Kingdom                  Europe
Sales                       United Kingdom                  Europe

27 rows selected.
```

After creating our table, however, we have now realized that we don't need to maintain the
COUNTRY_NAME or REGION_NAME columns in the DEPARTMENTS table, since those values are available
in other tables. With this in mind, we need to drop the columns. We can do this by dropping one
column at a time:

```
SQL> alter table departments
  2    drop column country_name
  3    /

Table altered.


SQL> alter table departments
  2    drop column region_name
  3    /

Table altered.
```

Or indeed, we can drop both columns in the same statement:

```
SQL> -- First we'll add the old columns back!
SQL> alter table departments
  2    add(
  3      country_name   varchar2(40),
  4      region_name    varchar2(15)
  5    )
  6    /

Table altered.

SQL> alter table departments
  2    drop (
```

```
   3     country_name, region_name )
   4   /

Table altered.
```

In the case of large tables you may not be able to afford to rewrite them (particularly if they are in constant use). Instead of dropping columns, you can set them to be UNUSED, until a later time when you can drop them altogether. We can accomplish this in the case of the DEPARTMENTS table as follows:

```
SQL> alter table departments
  2   add(
  3     country_name   varchar2(40),
  4     region_name    varchar2(15)
  5   )
  6   /

Table altered.

SQL> alter table departments
  2   set unused (
  3     country_name, region_name )
  4   /

Table altered.
```

Here, we have added the COUNTRY_NAME and REGION_NAME columns back into the DEPARTMENTS table, and then marked both columns as UNUSED. To determine how many unused columns we have in our tables we can use the USER_UNUSED_COL_TABS data dictionary view as follows:

```
SQL> select *
  2   from user_unused_col_tabs;

TABLE_NAME                            COUNT
------------------------------- ----------
DEPARTMENTS                               2
```

At a point when this table does not need to be online 24/7 or when you have planned maintenance time, you could remove the columns from the database and reclaim the storage space by issuing the command we saw earlier:

```
ALTER TABLE departments DROP UNUSED COLUMNS
```

Note that if you used the following coding to insert records into the DEPARTMENTS table:

```
insert into departments( department_id, department_name, manager_id,
                         location_id, country_name, region_name )
values ( l_department_id, l_department_name, l_manager_id, l_location_id,
         l_country_name, l_region_name );
```

this code will break if the COUNTRY_NAME or REGION_NAME columns are dropped (or marked unusable).

243

Renaming Tables

Changing the name of a table is a relatively easy task to perform. The `ALTER TABLE` command is as follows:

```
SQL> alter table people
  2  rename to employees
  3  /

Table altered.
```

> **Renaming tables is very easy, but the impact can be very dramatic. Caution should be exercised when the name of a table needs to be modified. While Oracle automatically updates foreign keys, constraint definitions, and table relationships in the data dictionary, it does not update stored code modules in the database, stored reports or queries, or client applications. Any of these later objects (such as a client application) that use a table, which is then renamed, will fail.**

Moving Tables To New Tablespaces or Storage

The manner in which tables are stored on, and read from, disk affects overall database performance. Typically, the entire database is built with the underlying table storage architecture predesigned. Tables belong in a certain place depending on how the database will access them, where other database objects live, and the physical architecture of the storage media. A table's storage attributes are designated in view of the type of table being created and how it will be used in the application.

There are many reasons why an administrator might want to change the storage attributes of a table, such as:

❑ The table is in an inappropriate tablespace

❑ The manner in which the table is being used by the application changes

❑ The data being stored in the table changes (in other words, new columns are added, or changes to existing columns made)

The `ALTER TABLE <table name> MOVE` statement is used for this purpose. To illustrate this, let's look at our database and see if there are any tables in the `SYSTEM` tablespace:

```
SQL> connect scott/tiger
Connected.
SQL> select tablespace_name, table_name
  2    from user_tables
  3   where table_name in ('EMP', 'DEPT', 'BONUS', 'SALGRADE')
  4   order by 1, 2
  5  /
```

TABLESPACE_NAME	TABLE_NAME
SYSTEM	BONUS
SYSTEM	DEPT
SYSTEM	EMP
SYSTEM	SALGRADE

Since, as we explained earlier, it is generally poor practice to keep tables in this tablespace, we want to move these tables to another tablespace. In order to see that the data actually moves from one segment to another, we will look at the data dictionary view USER_SEGMENTS before and after we perform the ALTER TABLE statement:

```
SQL> select segment_name, tablespace_name
  2    from user_segments
  3   where segment_name = 'EMP'
  4  /

SEGMENT_NA       TABLESPACE_NAME
---------------- ------------------------------
EMP              SYSTEM

SQL> alter table emp move
  2  tablespace users
  3  /

Table altered.

SQL> select segment_name, tablespace_name
  2    from user_segments
  3   where segment_name = 'EMP'
  4  /

SEGMENT_NA       TABLESPACE_NAME
---------------- ------------------------------
EMP              USERS
```

When we moved the table from the SYSTEM tablespace to the USERS tablespace, the segment was migrated from one tablespace to another. Since the segment is actually a chunk of data stored in a data file, and the USERS tablespace is in a different data file to the SYSTEM tablespace, the data was physically moved to another data file as well.

Changing Miscellaneous Table Properties

Sometimes, when tables are created, it is impossible to know all the requirements that will be placed on them during the life cycle of the applications they support. We try to build tables with as much foresight as possible, but from time to time we realize we can get better performance or incur less resource cost by changing a table's attributes. We discussed the table attributes earlier in the chapter.

For instance, if an application has a table that is being full scanned frequently, and this is the desired behavior, the table would benefit by having its data blocks cached in the buffer cache memory area. If the blocks are quickly aged out of memory due to other queries being executed, this table's data will be read into memory, aged out of memory, and read into memory over and over again. Instead, we could set the CACHE attribute on the table to tell Oracle to put the data blocks at the 'most recently used' end of the 'least recently used' list, thereby forcing Oracle to keep the blocks in memory (for a longer amount of time, at least). This is accomplished using the ALTER TABLE command:

```
alter table <table name> [cache|nocache] ;
```

The same methodology can be used for the LOGGING and NOLOGGING properties of a table:

```
alter table <table name> [logging|nologging] ;
```

For more information about caching data blocks in memory see Chapter 5.

ALTER TABLE Wrap Up

This chapter has covered some of the most common types of changes you will make to your tables. It certainly does not encompass the full spectrum of changes Oracle makes available to its users. Almost every attribute of a table can be modified. Also, for each of the different types of tables we discussed earlier in the chapter, attributes that pertain only to those table types can be changed as well. Full documentation on the ALTER TABLE command can be found in the Oracle *SQL Reference*.

DROP TABLE

Another task you will perform when maintaining your database is dropping tables. From time to time, it is necessary to remove a table from the database completely, or you may be dropping tables that were created for a particular task and are no longer needed.

The syntax for the DROP TABLE command is as follows:

```
DROP TABLE <TABLE_NAME> [ CASCADE CONSTRAINTS ];
```

In the following example, we create and populate the table DROP_ME, before dropping it:

```
SQL> create table drop_me (
  2    a    int,
  3    b    int
  4  )
  5  /

Table created.

SQL> insert into drop_me
  2  values ( 1, 1 );
```

```
1 row created.

SQL> insert into drop_me
  2  values ( 1, 2 );

1 row created.

SQL> insert into drop_me
  2  values ( 2, 1 );

1 row created.

SQL> drop table drop_me;

Table dropped.
```

There is a fundamental difference between removing all the data from a table, and dropping the table from the database. Even if you delete all the records from the table using the DELETE command, the table will still exist and be available after all the records have been removed. When you drop the table, however, the table is gone and the only way to insert records into it would be to create a new table with the same table properties.

CASCADE CONSTRAINTS

There is only one optional parameter to the DROP TABLE command, and this is called CASCADE CONSTRAINTS. This is used for tables, which have foreign keys that reference the table being dropped. If CASCADE CONSTRAINTS is *not* specified, and an administrator attempts to drop a table that has records in a child table, the operation will fail and the user will be issued with an error. By specifying CASCADE CONSTRAINTS, all child table foreign keys are dropped.

To illustrate this, we begin by creating a table named GENDER_TAB, and inserting some records into it:

```
SQL> create table gender_tab (
  2     gender_id  char(1),
  3     gender_nm  varchar2(6),
  4     constraint gender_pk primary key ( gender_id ),
  5     constraint gender_id_ck check ( gender_id in ( 'M', 'F' ) )
  6  )
  7  /

Table created.

SQL> insert into gender_tab
  2  values ( 'F', 'Female' );

1 row created.

SQL> insert into gender_tab
  2  values ( 'M', 'Male' );

1 row created.
```

Now we make a table (PEOPLE) that references the GENDER_TAB table using a foreign key:

```
SQL> create table people (
  2      first_name          varchar2(20),
  3      last_name           varchar2(25),
  4      gender              char(1)
  5  )
  6  /

Table created.

SQL> alter table people
  2      add constraint people_gender_fk
  3      foreign key ( gender )
  4      references gender_tab
  5  /

Table altered.

SQL> insert into people
  2      values ( 'Sean', 'Dillon', 'M' );

1 row created.

SQL> insert into people
  2      values ( 'Christopher', 'Beck', 'M' );

1 row created.

SQL> insert into people
  2      values ( 'Nicole', 'Ellis', 'F' );

1 row created.
```

Now that the tables are created, we realize that there is no need for the GENDER_TAB table, and would like to drop it. However, if we use the DROP TABLE command, we see the following:

```
SQL> drop table gender_tab;
drop table gender_tab
           *
ERROR at line 1:
ORA-02449: unique/primary keys in table referenced by foreign keys
```

This error indicates we tried to drop a table that is referenced by a foreign key in some other table. Since we just created these tables, we know it is the PEOPLE table.

At this point we have a choice. We can either drop the constraint explicitly, or we can drop the table using the CASCADE CONSTRAINTS clause on the DROP TABLE command. If we use the latter, then Oracle will drop all the constraints for us:

```
SQL> drop table gender_tab
  2      cascade constraints
  3  /

Table dropped.
```

TRUNCATE TABLE

TRUNCATE TABLE is a DDL statement used for removing all the data in a table without removing the table itself. Any indexes that exist for this table are also truncated. TRUNCATE TABLE can be used for heap-organized tables, index-organized tables, and temporary tables. Use the following syntax to perform a TRUNCATE TABLE command:

```
TRUNCATE TABLE [ SCHEMA. ] <table name> [ DROP STORAGE | REUSE STORAGE ]
```

TRUNCATE TABLE is a fast way of removing every record from a table, and is also more efficient than using a DELETE statement because it does not generate any rollback data.

There are some important points to note when using TRUNCATE TABLE though:

❑ You must have the DROP TABLE privilege in order to execute the TRUNCATE TABLE command

❑ All child foreign keys must be disabled before the TRUNCATE TABLE can be issued. If any tables reference the table being truncated, the statement will fail. (Self-referencing foreign keys do not have to be disabled.)

❑ ON DELETE triggers do not fire during a TRUNCATE TABLE operation.

❑ Since TRUNCATE TABLE is a DDL statement, it commits before and after it executes, and cannot be rolled back.

DROP STORAGE or REUSE STORAGE

During the lifetime of a table, extents are allocated to store the rows of data that populate the table. A table might only allocate the number of extents indicated by the MINEXTENTS storage attribute of the table, or it could allocate hundreds of extents depending on the number of rows that were inserted in the table, the size of each row, and the capacity of the extents. When the TRUNCATE TABLE statement is issued, the administrator must determine whether he wants either to give these extents back to the tablespace for consumption by other objects, or keep the extents for use by the table.

DROP STORAGE

DROP STORAGE is the default behavior for TRUNCATE TABLE. When DROP STORAGE is used, the table's original storage properties are restored. This means only the original extent(s) for the table (MINEXTENTS) is maintained for new rows in the table, and all additional extents are freed for use by other objects in the tablespace. If the table will not return to its original size, or it will take a long time for the table to grow back to its original size, DROP STORAGE should be used. This ensures that there isn't a large chunk of storage space in the tablespace unavailable to other objects for either a long period of time, or worse, forever.

249

REUSE STORAGE

If the REUSE STORAGE clause is used, all the extents that have been allocated for this table's storage are left alone, and will remain available for use by the table as new rows are inserted into the table. For rapidly growing tables, where the TRUNCATE statement is used to quickly drop the rows in order to clean the table for new rows being inserted, REUSE STORAGE should be used. This relieves Oracle from having to continually allocate new extents for this table.

Truncating Temporary Tables

When truncating temporary tables, only the rows inserted into the table during the user's session are removed. This is a great way for resetting a session-specific temporary table when a process needs to empty and repopulate the table before the session ends. It doesn't make any sense to use TRUNCATE TABLE on a transaction-specific temporary table, as a COMMIT would be more efficient. In a transaction-specific temporary table, a COMMIT statement removes the rows from the table anyway, and the space will not be reused.

Summary

This chapter has considered not only the different types of table available to you, but also some of their important attributes, as well as how to alter the properties and attributes of tables within the database.

In discussing index-organized, external, and temporary table types, we have illustrated how the properties of the tables you create can be tailored to your specific needs, in order to aid the performance. Gaining experience in using these various table types will greatly enhance the efficiency of your database.

Having looked at the different table types, we then considered how to set some of their properties, in order to suit your needs. We have only been able to give you a flavor here of the many properties that you can modify in creating and maintaining tables, but armed with this knowledge you will now be able to extend the capabilities of the tables in your database.

Indexes

The appropriate use of indexes can turn an otherwise sluggish and recalcitrant application into a highly responsive and productive business tool. Unfortunately, the converse is also true. Scattering inappropriate indexes around an application without careful thought is perfectly capable of turning it into a lumbering behemoth that's not much use to anyone. Working out whether an index is appropriate, and how best to create it if it is, is something of an acquired skill – which this chapter will help you to acquire. We're first going to look at what goes on inside Oracle when you opt to create a simple one, and then use that information to see how the additional index features available in recent Oracle releases can best be harnessed. During the course of the chapter we'll look at:

- ❏ What are indexes
- ❏ Indexes in Oracle
- ❏ Knowing the value and the cost of indexes
- ❏ Indexing multiple columns, key compression, skip scanning, and reverse key indexes
- ❏ Some myths of indexing
- ❏ Function-based indexes
- ❏ Bitmap and Bitmap Join indexes

Indexes At Work

When you are in a hurry to find some information from this book about a particular aspect of Oracle, there are two approaches. You can flick through pages more or less sequentially, and hope to stumble across the right topic. Or, if you've any sense, you'll turn to the back of the book and use the index that has been thoughtfully provided by the publisher. The index won't actually tell you anything about the topic itself, of course, but it will give you a subject heading and a reference to the page where full details about that topic can be found in the body of the book.

Using the index to locate a particular bit of information in this way will usually be much quicker than flicking through the pages sequentially. For a start, the index *only* contains the topic headings, with practically all the juicy details for each topic stripped away. Searching through tens of topics is very quick therefore, since you're scanning through one or two keywords for each one, not entire paragraphs. What's more, the topics will be listed *alphabetically*, whereas within the body of the book itself, the order in which topics appear will depend on what order the Author had in mind. Knowing that the information is in a sorted order means that, if you are searching for the 'Constraints' topic, you can dip into the index around the letter C, scan a few entries, and rapidly find your page reference. There is, in other words, no need to wade through all the A and B entries first. What's more, given that the index is in a sorted order, having found the entry for 'Constraints', once you see that the next entry is for the subject of (let us say) 'Crash Recovery', it's obvious that there can be no other references to the subject of constraints elsewhere in the index (and hence we can stop searching it).

An index, therefore, allows us to perform fast, targeted, and intelligent retrieval of the pointers to where the full information we are actually after is located. By contrast, the full scan through the book requires us to read entire paragraphs and pages of text, and if we are lucky enough to stumble across a particular subject of interest, there is no guarantee that the same subject will not be dealt with later on in the book. In other words, we really need to continue reading until the book's very end to be sure that we retrieve all possible information about it. That's going to be a random and rather slow process, relatively speaking.

If time were of the essence, which of these two possible information retrieval methods would you choose?

Indexes in Oracle

Oddly enough, Oracle is no different! The 'real' information we seek when attempting to produce a report or perform a piece of DML is, of course, composed of fields making up rows, stored in a table. But the same principles apply.

Rows stored in a regular table are stored in no particular order, thereby satisfying a central tenet of relational database theory. When they are first inserted, the user has no control over the physical location where Oracle chooses to place them. That means retrieving *particular* rows from a table would require Oracle to scan, sequentially, through all possible rows until it happens to stumble across the right ones. Even if Oracle gets lucky and finds a row that matches the search criteria very early on, it can't afford to stop scanning until it reaches the logical end of the table. Just because it has found a match for the row, doesn't mean that this is the *only* match.

Such a scan for information is known as a **full table scan**. Full table scans require us to load and read all the blocks of a table below what is known as the **high water mark**, which is the name given to the logical end of a table. For a large table, that might mean reading hundreds of blocks to retrieve a single row, which is clearly not an efficient way to retrieve individual rows.

However, if Oracle knows that there is an index on a part (or parts) of a table, then the search does not have to be this sequential, or indeed inefficient. A simple example might help explain Oracle's approach in such cases.

Consider the following table:

EMPNO	NAME	DEPT	SAL	Etc...
70	Bob	10	450	...
10	Frank	10	550	...
30	Ed	30	575	...
20	Adam	20	345	...
40	David	10	550	...
60	Graham	30	625	...
50	Charles	20	330	...
...	...	...	...	...

Here we see employees stored in a table in no particular order. Suppose we wish to locate the salary details for Frank. Without an index, we must scan all 7 rows, and then keep going, because although we find a Frank in the second row, there is no guarantee that this is the only Frank in the table. Only when we reach the high water mark of the table can we stop searching, since that tells us there are no more rows to come.

At this point, we can issue the following piece of SQL, however:

```
Create index emp_name_idx
On emp(name);
```

This creates an index (carefully named as EMP_NAME_IDX so that we know, just by looking at its name, that it is an index built on the NAME column of the EMP table), which means that Oracle undertakes a full scan of the table once more, retrieving the name field from each record, and sorting them into ascending alphabetical order. This sort takes place in memory in the first instance, but swaps down to a temporary tablespace, if that proves insufficient to hold the entire sort. Oracle also associates each name retrieved with the rowid of the row it came from. (The rowid is the physical address of a row in a table, telling us what object it came from, what file it's found on, and the specific block within that file). At the end of the process, we have a new index segment that looks like this:

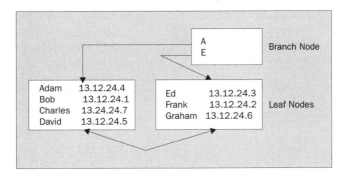

We've simplified this diagram for the sake of clarity, and determined an arbitrary rule regarding this index, namely that no block can contain more than 4 entries. In real life, you'd obviously fit far more entries than that in a block, but the principle is sound. Blocks can only accommodate a finite number of entries.

This index is a **B-Tree Index**, where the data we are interested in are located within what are termed **Leaf Nodes**, at the base of the index. If there is more than one leaf node in an index, Oracle constructs **Branch Nodes** to point to them. Within each leaf node, we see the **key data** upon which the index is built, and the **rowid** of the parent row in the original table.

> *Incidentally, the 'B' in 'B-Tree' doesn't stand, as often thought, for 'binary', but rather for 'balanced'. Balanced in this sense means that Oracle guarantees that you'll never have to travel through more levels of the index on one side than on the other before arriving at a leaf node entry. The structure is maintained by Oracle in such as way as to ensure that, no matter where an index entry resides, it takes the same amount of I/O to retrieve it.*

Finally, note that leaf nodes link to each other in both directions. A search for a number of rows involving scans through a number of leaf nodes, doesn't need to keep visiting the top of the index structure. Having finished with one leaf node, it can move directly to the next.

A search for Frank using this index means that we must first visit the branch node. We'll discover from this node that the entry for Frank must be in the second leaf node (because its value is greater than 'E'). We therefore have to perform a second block read to read that second leaf node, whereupon we can start scanning its contents. This scan is much faster than scanning through entire rows in the main table, since only one field (the one that was included in the index definition) is present. When we encounter Frank as the second entry in the leaf node, we cannot actually stop the scan (because there may be other Franks). However, as soon as we encounter an entry which is 'not Frank', we know (because of the sorted order) that there can't be any other Franks elsewhere in the index. So, having located the only Frank in town, we read his rowid and can perform one final block read (in this case, from File 12, block 24) to retrieve his salary details from the actual table.

To sum up here then, we have three block reads to get to the relevant table data (one for the branch node, one for the leaf node, and one for the relevant block from the table). Compare that with the potentially dozens of reads required to perform a full scan on a large table, and you can see that index retrieval of data is generally going to be much faster.

Try It Out – Building and Using an Index

1. We'll begin by making sure that SCOTT can create a usefully large table, and can assess the costs involved from selecting from it:

```
SQL> connect system/manager
Connected.
SQL> grant dba to scott;

Grant succeeded.

SQL> connect scott/tiger
Connected.
```

```
SQL> @?\rdbms\admin\utlxplan

Table created.
```

2. Now we're connected as SCOTT, let's copy one of the data dictionary views into a table of our own. DBA_OBJECTS is a good one to use, because it's so large. We'll restrict the possible owners in this example to minimize the difference you might experience if you're working with different versions of the database:

```
SQL> create table indextest as select * from dba_objects
  2  where owner in ('OUTLN','PUBLIC','SCOTT','SYS','SYSTEM');

Table created.
```

3. If we're going to be able to assess the costs of select statements, we need to calculate statistics on our new table. Given the large number of rows in our new table, it would also be a good idea to make sure that SQL*Plus only displays the costs of our queries, not the (endless pages of) results!

```
SQL> analyze table indextest compute statistics;

Table analyzed.

SQL> set autotrace trace explain
```

4. Now we can start selecting. Let's try and retrieve just one row from our table:

```
SQL> select owner, object_name from indextest
  2  where object_name = 'DBA_INDEXES';

Execution Plan
----------------------------------------------------------
   0      SELECT STATEMENT Optimizer=CHOOSE (Cost=10 Card=1 Bytes=20)
   1    0   TABLE ACCESS (FULL) OF 'INDEXTEST' (Cost=10 Card=1 Bytes=2
          0)
```

5. We'll now create an index on the OBJECT_NAME column, and see what difference that makes to the costs of our query:

```
SQL> create index indxtest_objname_idx
  2  on indextest (object_name);

Index created.

SQL> select owner, object_name from indextest
  2  where object_name = 'DBA_INDEXES';

Execution Plan
----------------------------------------------------------
   0      SELECT STATEMENT Optimizer=CHOOSE (Cost=2 Card=1 Bytes=20)
```

```
      1    0    TABLE ACCESS (BY INDEX ROWID) OF 'INDEXTEST' (Cost=2 Card=
                1 Bytes=20)

      2    1       INDEX (RANGE SCAN) OF 'INDXTEST_OBJNAME_IDX' (NON-UNIQUE
                ) (Cost=1 Card=1)
```

How It Works

The first time we selected a single row from the table, no index was available for use, and the optimizer was forced to scan the entire table. That shows up in the execution plan as the line:

```
TABLE ACCESS (FULL) OF 'INDEXTEST' (Cost=10 Card=1 Bytes=20)
```

The cost there is a relative cost, so the absolute number it shows is not particularly meaningful. It's simply an indication of the amount of CPU and I/O work Oracle has to do to resolve the query. The key point is what happens to that cost when we do the exact same query once more, but this time with an index available to help things out:

```
TABLE ACCESS (BY INDEX ROWID) OF 'INDEXTEST' (Cost=2 Card=
            1 Bytes=20)

      2    1       INDEX (RANGE SCAN) OF 'INDXTEST_OBJNAME_IDX' (NON-UNIQUE
                ) (Cost=1 Card=1)
```

This time, the cost is assessed as '2', which is 5 times smaller than before. The execution plan also reveals that we scan the index first, in order to pick up the ROWID of the entire row as stored in the table, and then visit the table itself. Notice that the table access this time is by ROWID, rather than FULL. In other words, having visited the index, we now know the rowid of the record we are after, and can jump straight to the correct place within the table.

When Is an Index Useful?

So far, we've made the advantages of indexes over full table scans sound so overwhelming that there's probably a perfectly legitimate question lurking on the tip of your tongue. If indexes are that good, why not index every column on every table and have done with it?

There are two points to bear in mind when answering that one. First, Oracle does its best to make full table scans as cheap and as efficient as it can make them. Whenever the optimizer decides to perform a full table scan, it reads table blocks in batches, not one at a time. This is known as a multi-block read, and it means that a scan of a table that consists of, say, 50 blocks can actually be carried out with a mere handful of read passes on the hard disk, rather than 50 individual reads. The precise number of blocks that Oracle can read in one pass depends very much on the hardware and operating system it is running on, and on the block size of the database you're dealing with. Typically, you'll find that disks can read 64K or 128K of data in a single read, which means that if you have an 8K block database, then 8 or 16 blocks can be read at a time. Our 50 block table might therefore be read in just 7 or 4 passes.

Since our index requires 3 reads, and the full table scan just 4, the index is marginally more useful. However, if the table were only (say) 25 blocks big, then a full scan could be accomplished in, perhaps, just two multi-block reads. At this point the index is actually slowing down the retrieval of data!

This brings us to the second point to consider when deciding whether or not an index is going to be useful. Given Oracle's ability to read several blocks in one pass, it sets the threshold for when it will even think about using an index (if present) fairly high. If your query is thought by Oracle to be selecting from around 2 to 5% or more of the total number of records, it will tend to perform a full table scan regardless of whether an index is available or not.

The reasoning behind that from Oracle's point of view is that an index entry points to an individual table block, and these are read one at a time. So if you use an index that ends up pointing you to lots of blocks, you are signing up for lots of individual block reads. That's lots of I/O, and lots of I/O means poor performance. Why not, therefore, simply bite the bullet and do a full scan of the table blocks in the first place, since full scans use multi-block reads, and thus minimize the I/O involved.

Both of these factors mean, therefore, that good indexes are selective indexes, referencing just a few percent of the total number of records.

Try It Out – Discovering When an Index Is Useful

1. We'll first switch AUTOTRACE off in our SQL*Plus session, so as to discover some basic information about the INDEXTEST table we created earlier:

```
SQL> set autotrace off
SQL> select owner, count(*) from indextest
  2  group by owner;

OWNER                              COUNT(*)
-------------------------------- ----------
OUTLN                                     7
PUBLIC                                 1391
SCOTT                                     4
SYS                                    3439
SYSTEM                                  356
```

2. We'll create a new index on the OWNER column of our table:

```
SQL> create index indxtest_owner_idx
  2  on indextest (owner);

Index created.
```

3. We'll now switch AUTOTRACE back on so that we can see whether the optimizer finds our new index useful for resolving the next few queries:

```
SQL> set autotrace trace explain
SQL> select owner, object_name from indextest
  2  where owner='SYS';
```

259

```
Execution Plan
-----------------------------------------------------------
   0       SELECT STATEMENT Optimizer=CHOOSE (Cost=10 Card=1039 Bytes=2
           0780)

   1    0    TABLE ACCESS (FULL) OF 'INDEXTEST' (Cost=10 Card=1039 Byte
           s=20780)
```

```
SQL> select owner, object_name from indextest
  2  where owner='SCOTT';

Execution Plan
-----------------------------------------------------------
   0       SELECT STATEMENT Optimizer=CHOOSE (Cost=10 Card=1039 Bytes=2
           0780)

   1    0    TABLE ACCESS (FULL) OF 'INDEXTEST' (Cost=10 Card=1039 Byte
           s=20780)
```

4. Having failed to get our index used so far, we'll try the following:

```
SQL> analyze table indextest compute statistics for columns owner;

Table analyzed.

SQL> select owner, object_name from indextest
  2  where owner='SYS';

Execution Plan
-----------------------------------------------------------
   0       SELECT STATEMENT Optimizer=CHOOSE (Cost=10 Card=3439 Bytes=6
           8780)

   1    0    TABLE ACCESS (FULL) OF 'INDEXTEST' (Cost=10 Card=3439 Byte
           s=68780)
```

```
SQL> select owner, object_name from indextest
  2  where owner='SCOTT';

Execution Plan
-----------------------------------------------------------
   0       SELECT STATEMENT Optimizer=CHOOSE (Cost=2 Card=4 Bytes=80)
   1    0    TABLE ACCESS (BY INDEX ROWID) OF 'INDEXTEST' (Cost=2 Card=
           4 Bytes=80)

   2    1      INDEX (RANGE SCAN) OF 'INDXTEST_OWNER_IDX' (NON-UNIQUE)
           (Cost=1 Card=4)
```

How It Works

Our first query showed us the number of objects owned by each owner. The exact numbers you get when you try this will vary, depending on what version of the database you are working with, but we're only interested in their relative size anyway, not their absolute values. We got results looking like this:

```
OUTLN                           7
PUBLIC                       1391
SCOTT                           4
SYS                          3439
SYSTEM                        356
```

Now, you might think from this that an index on the OWNER column would be used if we were selecting from SCOTT's objects (he only has 4 out of over 5,000, which is much less than 1% of the total number of records). Equally, you might think that we'd use a full table scan in selecting from SYS's objects, since these represent well over half the total number of records, after all. In fact, having created the appropriate index, we discovered that the optimizer refuses to use it, no matter which user we select from.

This is because, perhaps unfortunately, you need to think like the optimizer when considering selectivity. As far as the optimizer is concerned we've got just 5 possible owners, and so (based on the sort of statistics we computed for the table earlier), whichever one we select from, we appear to the optimizer to be asking for 20% of the available records. As you can see, 20% is not selective enough to persuade the optimizer to use the available index.

To get the optimizer to realize that, although there are only 5 possible owners, one of them relates to a huge number of rows and one of them only to a few, we can create a **histogram** on the OWNER column. That's what the command:

```
SQL> analyze table indextest compute statistics for columns owner;
```

did for us. Histograms are (if you remember your high school math!) a tool to reveal frequency distributions, and when the optimizer can use one for the owner in our table, it discovers that most records are owned by SYS, while only a few are owned by SCOTT. It's this new knowledge about the skewed nature of our data that allows it to be more intelligent about whether it should use the index on that column or not, which is what we see in the second set of queries we performed. Suddenly, whether we are selecting for SYS's or SCOTT's records *does* make a difference as to whether the index is used or not.

The Cost of Indexes

Our index made finding Frank's salary details efficient and the above discussion showed that a highly selective index is always likely to make retrieving data out of a table much more efficient than a full table scan. But that is about where the good news ends, since we've rather forgotten that data also has to be put *into* a table. The insertion of a new row into a table must now also insert a corresponding entry into the *index* on that table. That's two inserts, not just one, which means that inserts slow down in the presence of indexes.

What's more, it's not just inserts that are affected, since updates and deletes have to keep the index up-to-date, too. Hence the general rule that indexes slow down DML (yet another good reason for not splattering unnecessary indexes all over the place).

How Inserting Rows Affects the Index

Let us imagine that we have added another 15 rows into the table. Our index on the NAME column of that table might therefore end up looking like this:

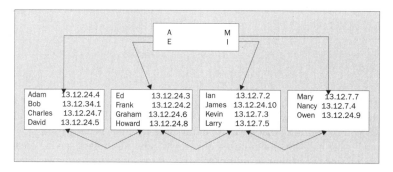

Again, we see that the index is highly packed (the maximum permissible 4 entries per block is true for 3 of our 4 leaf nodes), and thus nicely efficient. But that is only true because we have cunningly arranged to employ people in ascending alphabetical order of name! What happens if (as is likely to happen in real life) we employ someone called Bill?

Well, the entry in the base table is not a problem: Bill's new record will be housed in whatever table block happens to have some free space (the precise location of his record in the table is irrelevant). It should be obvious, however, that if the index is to retain any meaning or function, there is only one possible place to insert the index entry for Bill, namely in block 1. The problem here is that block 1 is already full of its permitted 4 records.

Clearly, we have to somehow arrange for room to be made so that Bill's index entry can be slotted into an appropriate place. What therefore happens is this. We split that first leaf node, and redistribute its existing entries so that there is room for the new entry. On average, and as a general rule, Oracle puts 50% of the entries into one half of the split, and 50% into the other. Note that the exact split very much depends on the nature of the data, is up to Oracle to decide, and that we have no control over it at all. In our case, we might see our index looking like this:

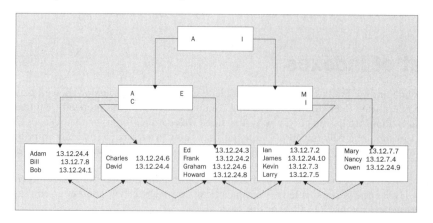

Notice how the 'Adam-Bob-Charles-David' block has been split. 'Adam-Bob' are now in one block, and 'Charles-David' in another. That means there's room in the first block to fit in the new entry for Bill.

But that split meant that the branch block had more than its permitted 4 entries, so we've actually also had to acquire another branch block, and redistribute its entries around so that two branch nodes are referencing all the leaf nodes. With two possible branch nodes, we have to create a new singleton branch node right at the top of the tree, to point to the other branches. Singleton branch nodes are known as the **Root Node** of the index.

That means our index now has three levels, not two as before. We say that the **height** of the index is 3. When the height of an index increases, additional I/O is required to get to the leaf nodes. Our earlier search for Frank required 3 block reads (1 branch node, 1 leaf node, 1 table block). That same search now requires 4 reads (1 root node, 1 branch node, 1 leaf node, 1 table block). Additional I/O means slower performance.

Block splits, therefore, occur when data arrives at the table which requires new entries in the index to be slotted in between existing entries. Such an insert to a table necessitates considerable reshuffling of the index structure, and may induce cascading reshuffles 'upwards' in the tree hierarchy, thereby increasing the index's height, and thus reducing performance. It should be said, however, that Oracle's automatic re-balancing of indexes subject to ongoing DML is efficient enough to mean that heights more than 3 are pretty unusual. As a result, the height of an index is not where the major cost of insert activity in the presence of an index arises. Rather, it's the reshuffling activities themselves, and the acquisition of extra blocks (potentially, extra *extents* if we've already used up all the blocks in the existing extents), which cause our insert to take longer to complete than it otherwise would.

There's also the issue of disk space. You'll notice, for example, that whereas before our leaf nodes were all efficiently packed with their permitted 4 entries, there are now two which are under-filled. One is only 75% packed, and the 'Charles-David' node is only 50% packed. Instead of densely packed leaf nodes, we have nodes littered with pockets of empty space. Rather like a soufflé, therefore, indexes on tables subject to lots of inserts will, over time, have a tendency to become full of fresh air, and this 'airiness' of an index is where the main costs of inserts are found. Airy indexes make inefficient use of the disk space they consume.

Now, it is true that the space that occurs in leaf nodes as a result of block splits will be eventually re-used, *if* you make further inserts that can use it. In our case, for example, if we were now to insert a record for an employee called Daniel, then this can use some of the 50% empty space that's currently available in the 'Charles-David' node. Until, and unless, those new (and appropriately positioned) entries are made, though, the space created by a block split is simply wasted space. With the days of the multi-gigabyte hard disk well and truly upon us, this might seem a trivial issue, until you consider that sometimes Oracle needs to scan along the base of the index to resolve a query. An index that comprises mostly empty leaf nodes is going to require more I/O to scan it fully than one that is nicely compacted. That translates into slower performance for such queries.

Is there anything we can do to prevent block splits? Well, we can certainly try. The PCTFREE attribute can be (and ought to be) specified when creating the index. Setting PCTFREE when the index is first created causes leaf nodes to be filled only part way before being considered closed to further entries. This ensures that there is some free space in every leaf node in which a new insert (made after the initial index creation), which happens to want to slot in between existing ones, can be accommodated.

Having this empty space already available in the index does nothing very much for the efficiency with which we're using our disk space, of course, and it immediately means that a scan of the index takes longer than if we'd set PCTFREE to zero. However, it does mean that an insert which might otherwise need to induce a block split before it can be slotted into the index, should be able to find some suitable space without particular effort. Such an insert should therefore proceed more quickly than one that has to split blocks. As is often the case, we're effectively required to trade space for speed, and in this particular case, speed of the insert against speed of any possible index scans.

Unfortunately, there are no guarantees. If you set PCTFREE to, say, 10% (which happens to be the default, just as it is for tables), then everything is fine. That is until you fill up that 10% with a swathe of new inserts. At this point, the leaf node is as full as it can be, so any further single insert into that node will *still* have to cause a block split.

In summary: indexes that are created on tables subject to lots of new inserts will experience gradual degradation of their storage and performance efficiency, if those inserts need to be housed amongst existing index entries. This gradual deterioration of performance can be reversed (by rebuilding the index on a regular basis), but that's a high maintenance option, and one that itself impacts upon database performance and availability. We can try to pre-empt the need to rebuild an index by wasting space in its leaf nodes, using the PCTFREE setting of the create index statement. However, this doesn't guarantee that block splits and degradation won't occur eventually, and it does mean that the index is composed of large amounts of fresh air before we even start.

Try It Out – Indexes and Inserts

1. If you've carried out the earlier 'Try-It-Outs', your INDEXTEST table will have been modified since it was first created. To ensure that we're working on a level playing field, we'll recreate it and the index from scratch here. This time we'll be careful to make sure that we fill all the leaf nodes up as fully as possible:

```
SQL> set autotrace off
SQL> drop table indextest;

Table dropped.

SQL> create table indextest as select * from dba_objects
  2  where owner in ('OUTLN','PUBLIC','SCOTT','SYS','SYSTEM');

Table created.

SQL> create index indxtest_objname_idx
  2  on indextest (object_name)
  3  pctfree 0;

Index created.

SQL> analyze table indextest compute statistics;

Table analyzed.
```

2. Before we proceed to destabilize our index, let's see how big it is at the moment:

```
SQL> analyze index indxtest_objname_idx validate structure;

Index analyzed.

SQL> select name, height, lf_blks, pct_used
  2  from index_stats;

NAME                               HEIGHT    LF_BLKS   PCT_USED
------------------------------  ----------  ---------- ----------
INDXTEST_OBJNAME_IDX                    2         18         93
```

3. Now we'll insert a new record into the underlying table that has to be placed into the first available leaf node (even though it's 100% full!):

```
SQL> insert into indextest (owner, object_name)
  2  values ('AAAAAAAAAA','AAAAAAAAAAAAAAAAAAAA');

1 row created.

SQL> commit;

Commit complete.
```

4. Now let's see what that's done to our index. To do this, we recompute our statistics to see the results of the change:

```
SQL> analyze index indxtest_objname_idx validate structure;

Index analyzed.

SQL> select name, height, lf_blks, pct_used
  2  from index_stats;

NAME                               HEIGHT    LF_BLKS   PCT_USED
------------------------------  ----------  ---------- ----------
INDXTEST_OBJNAME_IDX                    2         19         88
```

5. Finally, we'll add in a new record to the underlying table that can be housed at the end of the index, and see what effect this has on our index statistics:

```
SQL> insert into indextest (owner, object_name)
  2  values ('ZZZZZ','_ZZZZZZZZZZ');

1 row created.

SQL> commit;

Commit complete.

SQL> analyze index indxtest_objname_idx validate structure;
```

```
Index analyzed.

SQL> select name, height, lf_blks, pct_used
  2  from index_stats;

NAME                              HEIGHT      LF_BLKS    PCT_USED
------------------------------- ---------- ---------- ----------
INDXTEST_OBJNAME_IDX                   2           19          88
```

6. Now we'll repeat the above steps, only this time we'll recreate the index first with some empty space reserved in each of the leaf nodes by setting a more appropriate PCTFREE value:

```
SQL> alter index indxtest_objname_idx rebuild pctfree 10;

Index altered.

SQL> analyze index indxtest_objname_idx validate structure;

Index analyzed.

SQL> select name, height, lf_blks, pct_used
  2  from index_stats;

NAME                              HEIGHT      LF_BLKS    PCT_USED
------------------------------- ---------- ---------- ----------
INDXTEST_OBJNAME_IDX                   2           20          84
```

7. Let's now re-analyze the statistics for the same inserts as before:

```
SQL> insert into indextest (owner, object_name)
  2  values ('AAAAAAAAAA','AAAAAAAAAAAAAAAAAAAAAA');

1 row created.

SQL> commit;

Commit complete.

SQL> analyze index indxtest_objname_idx validate structure;

Index analyzed.

SQL> select name, height, lf_blks, pct_used
  2  from index_stats;

NAME                              HEIGHT      LF_BLKS    PCT_USED
------------------------------- ---------- ---------- ----------
INDXTEST_OBJNAME_IDX                   2           20          84
```

```
SQL> insert into indextest (owner, object_name)
  2  values ('ZZZZZ','_ZZZZZZZZZZ');              (Note the underscore here!)

1 row created.

SQL> commit;

Commit complete.

SQL> analyze index indxtest_objname_idx validate structure;

Index analyzed.

SQL> select name, height, lf_blks, pct_used
  2  from index_stats;

NAME                                HEIGHT    LF_BLKS    PCT_USED
--------------------------------- ---------- ---------- ----------
INDXTEST_OBJNAME_IDX                  2          20         84
```

How It Works

The first time we did the inserts, the leaf rows were as full as they could possibly be. So when our first insert was made into the table, we had to make room with a block split to allow the index entry to be housed at the beginning of the index. We can see that this happened by comparing the two numbers, LF_BLKS (leaf blocks) and PCT_USED:

Before the insert, the INDEX_STATS view read like this:

```
NAME                                HEIGHT    LF_BLKS    PCT_USED
--------------------------------- ---------- ---------- ----------
INDXTEST_OBJNAME_IDX                  2          18         93
```

That is, we had 18 leaf nodes, and the index was 93% used. Given that we'd said all leaf nodes should be filled 100%, you might wonder why the index itself only reports a 93% usage rate. That's simply because the last leaf node is not fully used, since there simply aren't enough rows in the table to fill the last node, so it's sitting there with some unfilled space available.

After the insert, the same report showed:

```
NAME                                HEIGHT    LF_BLKS    PCT_USED
--------------------------------- ---------- ---------- ----------
INDXTEST_OBJNAME_IDX                  2          19         88
```

So we've obviously acquired a new leaf node (because the first block had to split into two to make room for the new entry). What's more, the PCT_USED has dropped significantly, since neither the original node that's been split, nor the new one that received some of the old one's entries, are completely full. There's now some empty space at the beginning of the index, not just at the end.

267

The second insert we performed did not change the index statistics at all, however. That's because an object name that starts with an underscore character needs to be inserted at the very end of the index, and as we already know, the last leaf node was not completely full to begin with. This meant that there was already some vacant space into which the new record could be slotted, and there was no need for block splits. As a result there were no new blocks, and no deterioration in the PCT_USED figure. (Actually, if the report went to enough decimal places of precision, you'd have seen a tiny *increase* in the degree of usage, because previously empty space is now being used to house the new entry.)

Having then rebuilt the index with a PCTFREE of 10, the INDEX_STATS view showed us this:

```
NAME                               HEIGHT     LF_BLKS    PCT_USED
-----------------------------   ----------  ----------  ----------
INDXTEST_OBJNAME_IDX                    2          20          84
```

So, despite being freshly rebuilt, the index is already occupying two more blocks than the index initially required, because 10% of every node is currently lying empty. Once again, you might have expected the PCT_USED column to show us a value of 90, instead of 84, but that would only have been the case if there were exactly the right number of rows to fill the last leaf node to the 90% mark.

Before we begin, then, the index is full of more 'fresh air' than before. But the good news is that neither of our subsequent inserts make the slightest difference to what the INDEX_STATS view reports. That's because there's enough room in the first of our leaf nodes to accommodate our first insert without the need for a block split. Of course, if we inserted enough new records with object names starting 'AAAA...', then we'd eventually fill up the first node to the brim, and the next similar insert would have to induce a block split.

As an exercise which we'll leave to you, see how many such records you have to insert before the block split happens! It's that sort of calculation you need to have in mind when determining whether a PCTFREE of 10 is sufficient for your proposed indexes.

How Updating and Deleting Rows Affects the Index

What about updates and deletes? Do they have the same sort of space consequences as inserts?

Imagine that Bob, having just recently been promoted to the Executive Floor, decides that he wishes henceforth to be known as Robert. There is no problem updating the table to reflect the change using:

```
alter table emp set name='Robert' where name='Bob'.
```

But what if we made a similar change to the index? Well, our first leaf node would end up looking like this:

Hopefully it's obvious that it is entirely unacceptable for an 'R' entry to be sitting in what is clearly the 'A-B' leaf node.

So updates to a table *cannot* result in updates to the index, because leaf node entries would end up being mislocated. Instead, we have to mark the original leaf entry as being dead, and *insert* an entirely new entry in a locationally-appropriate leaf node. That new insertion might, of course, end up inducing a block split if it needed to make room for itself. In our simple example, we're lucky. We end up with this:

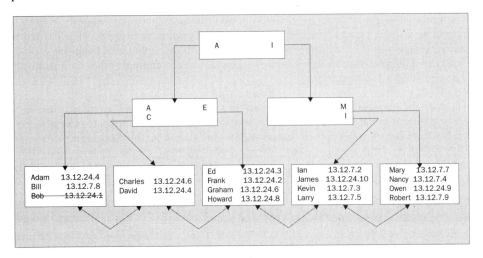

So, in this case, we managed to avoid a block split, since there was room to accommodate a new entry for 'Robert' in the fifth leaf node. However, our first leaf node now only has 50% effective entries, though 75% of the space has been used, since one of the entries has been marked as a deleted leaf row. You might wonder why we simply mark entries for deletion in this way, instead of *actually* deleting them. It's simply because performing an actual delete would take more time. We're seeking to minimize the impact on DML performance, not aggravate it.

The deletion of rows from the base table is handled in a similar way. The index entry for the row being deleted is merely marked for deletion, but the space it occupies in the leaf node is not released.

Both updates and deletes on the base table therefore further add to our index woes, because we are left with dead entries taking up space within the leaf nodes. Of course, other DML that we perform on the table can make use of the space currently occupied by our dead entries. For example, if we were to insert a new record for someone called Brian or Barry, then their index entries can both be slotted into our first leaf node. One of them will reuse the space formerly occupied by Bob's old entry. Until such inserts are made, however, it remains the case that our index is once again full of pockets of fresh air, and taking up more space than a nicely compacted and tidied-up version would do. Extra space means extra I/O to read it all, and that means that any query that requires Oracle to scan through the index will perform more poorly than it otherwise would do.

I should perhaps mention that Oracle does actually go to the trouble of removing dead entries when every single entry in the leaf node is dead. Until that happens, the block is considered still to be positionally significant. For example, if we delete not just Bob's record, but also Bill's, that still leaves 'Adam' as a valid entry within that first node. As a result, that node can only accept new entries which make sense for that node. 'Bruce' would find a home there, as would 'Adriana', but even though most of the node is (effectively) empty space, a 'William' entry would not be able to be housed there. However, if we were to mark *every* entry in that node as deleted, then clearly the block has no positional significance at all. Once we clear out all the dead entries, a 'William' entry could use it perfectly well.

You'll also find that deleted entries are cleared out on other occasions. For example, if fresh insert activity is taking place within a block that contains deleted entries (some of which are being re-used by that activity), Oracle will take the opportunity to clear out all deleted entries from that block. That's just Oracle's way of attempting to slip index housekeeping actions in amongst other data management work, and not re-visit blocks unnecessarily.

This is all quite different from tables, where space in a block is available for reuse by any new insert, whatever its data values happen to be, once the block has been cleared down to whatever the PCTUSED for that table has been set to. What we've said earlier about an index block needing to be cleared down completely before it can be used by a new entry for, say, 'William' implies instead that PCTUSED for an index is implicitly zero – (and can never be set to anything other than zero). Attempting to specify your own PCTUSED at the time of index creation will produce an error.

Try it Out – Updating and Deleting with Indexes

1. As before, we'll recreate the INDEXTEST table, to ensure that we're starting with a clean slate. Then we'll recalculate statistics on our OBJECT_NAME index, and perform a simple update to see the effect:

```
SQL> drop table indextest;

Table dropped.

SQL> create table indextest as select * from dba_objects
  2  where owner in ('OUTLN','PUBLIC','SCOTT','SYS','SYSTEM');

Table created.

SQL> create index indxtest_objname_idx
  2  on indextest (object_name) pctfree 10;

Index created.

SQL> analyze index indxtest_objname_idx validate structure;

Index analyzed.

SQL> select name, height, lf_rows, del_lf_rows, pct_used
  2  from index_stats;

NAME                                   HEIGHT    LF_ROWS DEL_LF_ROWS   PCT_USED
------------------------------ ---------- ---------- ----------- ----------
```

```
INDXTEST_OBJNAME_IDX                      2      5197          0          84

SQL> update indextest set object_name='DBA_INDEXES2' where
object_name='DBA_INDEXES';

2 rows updated.

SQL> commit;

Commit complete.

SQL> analyze index indxtest_objname_idx validate structure;

Index analyzed.

SQL> select name, height, lf_rows, del_lf_rows, pct_used
  2  from index_stats;

NAME                             HEIGHT    LF_ROWS DEL_LF_ROWS   PCT_USED
------------------------------ ---------- ---------- ----------- ----------
INDXTEST_OBJNAME_IDX                  2      5199          2          84
```

2. Now we'll perform a delete (again calculating fresh statistics to see the effects):

```
SQL> delete from indextest where object_name like 'ALL_T%';

36 rows deleted.

SQL> commit;

Commit complete

SQL> analyze index indxtest_objname_idx validate structure;

Index analyzed.

SQL> select name, height, lf_rows, del_lf_rows, pct_used
  2  from index_stats;

NAME                             HEIGHT    LF_ROWS DEL_LF_ROWS   PCT_USED
------------------------------ ---------- ---------- ----------- ----------
INDXTEST_OBJNAME_IDX                  2      5199         38          84
```

3. Now we'll perform a fresh insert into the table, and see what result that has for the index:

```
SQL> insert into indextest (owner, object_name)
  2  values ('ZZZZ','ZZZ_INSERT');

1 row created.

SQL> commit;
```

```
Commit complete.

SQL> analyze index indxtest_objname_idx validate structure;

Index analyzed.

SQL> select name, height, lf_rows, del_lf_rows, pct_used
  2  from index_stats;

NAME                                 HEIGHT     LF_ROWS DEL_LF_ROWS   PCT_USED
------------------------------ ---------- ---------- ----------- ----------
INDXTEST_OBJNAME_IDX                      2        5200          38         84
```

And one final insert or two to see if things can be made to change:

```
SQL> insert into indextest (owner, object_name)
  2  values ('ZZZZ','ALL_TESTINSERT');

1 row created.

SQL> commit;

Commit complete.

SQL> analyze index indxtest_objname_idx validate structure;

Index analyzed.

SQL> select name, height, lf_rows, del_lf_rows, pct_used
  2  from index_stats;

NAME                                 HEIGHT     LF_ROWS DEL_LF_ROWS   PCT_USED
------------------------------ ---------- ---------- ----------- ----------
INDXTEST_OBJNAME_IDX                      2        5165           2         84

SQL> insert into indextest (owner, object_name)
  2  values ('ZZZZ','DBA_INDEX');

1 row created.

SQL> commit;

Commit complete.

SQL> analyze index indxtest_objname_idx validate structure;

Index analyzed.

SQL> select name, height, lf_rows, del_lf_rows, pct_used
  2  from index_stats;

NAME                                 HEIGHT     LF_ROWS DEL_LF_ROWS   PCT_USED
------------------------------ ---------- ---------- ----------- ----------
INDXTEST_OBJNAME_IDX                      2        5164           0         84
```

How It Works

Our first SELECT on the INDEX_STATS table produces the result:

NAME	HEIGHT	LF_ROWS	DEL_LF_ROWS	PCT_USED
INDXTEST_OBJNAME_IDX	2	5197	0	84

This tells us that we started out with 5197 rows, none of which were marked as deleted leaf rows (the DEL_LF_ROWS column contains 0).

Our first piece of DML was a simple update of the object DBA_INDEXES to DBA_INDEXES2. That happened to update 2 rows.

```
SQL> update indextest set object_name='DBA_INDEXES2' where
object_name='DBA_INDEXES';

2 rows updated.
```

The INDEX_STATS view then reported that there were 5199 rows, with 2 of them marked as deleted leaf rows.

NAME	HEIGHT	LF_ROWS	DEL_LF_ROWS	PCT_USED
INDXTEST_OBJNAME_IDX	2	5199	2	84

Note here that your result may differ, but the absolute numbers are not important.

Here is the proof that updates cause new entries to be inserted into the index with the new values, and the pre-existing entries merely to be marked for deletion, not directly updated *in situ*. By performing an update, we've therefore actually acquired two *extra* rows in the table, and the two originals have been marked as dead entries.

Our next piece of DML was a delete of all the rows from the table starting with the letters DBA_T.

```
SQL> delete from indextest where object_name like 'ALL_T%';
```

There happened to be 36 rows in the table matching this criterion, as shown in our freshly calculated statistics:

NAME	HEIGHT	LF_ROWS	DEL_LF_ROWS	PCT_USED
INDXTEST_OBJNAME_IDX	2	5199	38	84

Notice that the total number of leaf rows in the index hasn't changed at all. This demonstrates that deletes from a table don't actually delete the corresponding entries out of the index. The number of d*eleted* leaf rows, on the other hand, has shot up to 38, with 36 of them marked as dead entries, together with the two resulting from our earlier update.

273

So far, then, we have 38 'slots' within the index which don't actually have a purpose, but are sitting within the physical body of the index (and so taking up space within it).

Our next set of inserts attempted to see if we could somehow reclaim this space. To start with, we inserted a new row into the table for an object whose name began with 'ZZZ'.

```
insert into indextest (owner, object_name)
  values ('ZZZZ','ZZZ_INSERT');
```

The INDEX_STATS report produced after that insert showed us that there were *still* 38 deleted leaf rows present in the index. Clearly, that insert reused not a jot of the space generated by our earlier DML activity. Quite simply, such a new record needed to be housed towards the end of the index, whereas our previous update of OBJECT_NAME generated some dead entries in the middle of the index, and the delete of a batch of ALL_T records generated some dead entries near the front of the index. Your fresh inserts have to be able to fit into the slots made freeable by the earlier DML if they are to reclaim them, and this particular one didn't fit the bill.

Finally, therefore, we performed a couple of inserts that were deliberately designed to fit into the space made reuseable by our earlier deletes and updates. In neither case did we insert records which exactly matched the ones previously updated or deleted. You can be fairly certain that no object called ALL_TESTINSERT existed beforehand when we deleted everything that started with ALL_T; likewise we previously got rid of an entry for DBA_INDEXES, not one called DBA_INDEX. There is no need to match the names exactly. The point is that the new object names were sufficiently close to the old entries' names that they could be fitted into the space previously used by them.

The surprise might be that our first insert, of a single new ALL_TESTINSERT object, caused all 36 slots previously marked as deleted leaf rows by our earlier bulk delete to be cleared out of the index:

NAME	HEIGHT	LF_ROWS	DEL_LF_ROWS	PCT_USED
INDXTEST_OBJNAME_IDX	2	5165	2	84

By indicating that we wanted to reuse *one* of the old ALL_T slots, Oracle took the opportunity to tidy up the entire block. Hence, all 36 deleted entries were cleaned out, reducing the total number of leaf rows within the index, and taking our count of deleted leaf rows down to 2. The new single entry for DBA_INDEX was able to fit into the block occupied by the two deleted entries for DBA_INDEXES, and so both entries were cleaned out, leaving the index entirely free of deleted leaf entries.

This is actually a bit of a free gift from Oracle. In both cases, our new inserts could only physically occupy one of the multiple slots made vacant by the tidying-up process, so both the affected leaf nodes now have rather more free space in them than they started with, given the PCTFREE setting we used. Subsequent insert activity on either node is therefore less likely to need to induce a block split than might be the case for inserts on the other nodes. Given that the cleanout process takes place whilst the node is resident in memory (specifically, as it occupies a buffer in the Data Buffer Cache), all that's involved is some CPU cycles. So Oracle is trading some current CPU cycles (which tend to be plentiful) against some (potential) future disk I/O. Gifts don't get much freer than that!

However, the usual warning still applies. This efficient reclaiming of space only happened because our new inserts were able to make use of the space. Our first insert wasn't able to, because it was positionally inappropriate for it to do so, and if subsequent inserts had been of the same nature, or few and far between, then the deleted entries would have still been clogging up our index.

DML and Indexes

Hopefully the above discussion has made it clear that indexes on tables subject to any significant degree of DML activity are potentially problematical. At any given moment, such an index, if it could be inspected, might contain large pockets of empty space as a result of both block splits induced by previous inserts, and large numbers of entries that are effectively dead as a result of updates or deletions. Now all is not lost, because if we continue to perform further DML, we may well be able to make use of the space, or replace the dead entries with new, live ones. But whether we do so or not depends entirely on what sort of DML continues to be performed on the table, and how much of it there is.

Instead of waiting for further DML to make efficient use of the space created by prior DML, you (or, more usually, the DBA!) can choose to rebuild the index. At this point all dead entries are removed, and all blocks nicely re-compacted (effectively reversing the effect of block splits). However, index rebuilds are fairly expensive options (even with the new 8i and 9i 'online rebuild' feature in place), requiring plenty of free disk space, a degree of table locking which might not be convenient, and large amounts of I/O which affects everybody trying to make concurrent use of the database. It's also true that the second a rebuild is complete, the entire process of block splitting and creating dead entries starts all over again, so it's always going to be an uphill struggle.

For the developer wondering whether to index particular columns of a table subject to DML, it is therefore important to weigh up the costs of indexing (space usage, space wastage, additional I/O, slower DML because both table and index segments require maintenance) against the possible benefits (faster retrieval of data where selectivity is reasonably high). In weighing up such factors, you should also consider whether it might not be preferable to create indexes as and when they are needed, and get rid of them when the need passes. Imagine an accounting application that needs to produce month-end reports, for example. No doubt there are several indexes that could be created in order to speed those reports up. However, since they are only generated at the end of the month, is it sensible to be slowing down everyday DML activity for the remaining 30 days of the month by having such indexes permanently in existence? You should always see if there are opportunities within an application for dynamically creating indexes as they are needed, rather than having them permanently slowing DML down.

Concatenation

At this point, you ought to be getting the impression that indexes are not necessarily a particularly good idea! They have high costs, which are frequently forgotten or ignored by developers, and creating indexes with wild abandon is a distinctly bad idea. For that reason, it's a good idea to always strive to minimize the number of indexes that need to be created on a table.

One of the principal tools at your disposal to achieve that particular goal is to use **concatenated B-Tree** indexes. These are indexes that are built on a group of columns, rather than a single column.

As a simple (though admittedly rather unrealistic) example of concatenation, we could issue this command:

```
create index emp_name_no_idx
on emp(name, empno)
pctfree 25;
```

Our leaf nodes would then look like this:

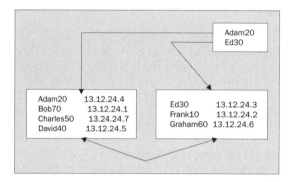

When you see the index structured in this way, it is rapidly apparent that a search for the employee with an EMPNO of 30 is *not* going to be able to make effective use of the index at all. The employee numbers are scattered all through the index, in no particular order, because the NAME field is the one that takes priority in the sort. In other words, *the order of fields* in a concatenated index is extremely significant, and makes a huge difference as to how the Oracle optimizer subsequently decides to make use (or not) of the index.

In the case of this example, a search for a particular employee number may actually make use of the index. We'd have to scan the entire index, but that is still likely to be quicker than having to scan the entire table. If the index was a concatenation of several large columns, which together represented a relatively large proportion of the entire rowlength, the chances of the optimizer choosing to wade through the index are pretty slim.

> *Oracle 9i is cleverer than this, since it has the ability to 'skip scan' through an index, rather than scan the whole thing from start to finish. We'll look at this a little later on.*

Exactly the same information as before could have been included in the index, but in a different order:

```
create index emp_name_no_idx
on emp(empno, name)
pctfree 25;
```

Such an index *would* now allow very fast retrieval of the relevant record by employee number. However, if for example you suddenly ask to see all employees called Graham, then you are back to square one.

When you choose to concatenate indexes, therefore, you need to bear in mind the *usual* way in which the data will be retrieved, and where you want the speed advantages of index lookup to apply. To this end, bear in mind that an old Oracle myth still abounds that the leading column of a concatenated index should be the most selective (in our case, that would be the NAME field). That's not been true since around Oracle 5, and should be ignored as bad advice. The usual determinant should be what the predicates of my queries are most often going to be.

Key Compression of B-Tree Indexes

Key compression was a feature new to Oracle 8*i*, and works as follows. Imagine a table containing details of parks and public spaces, the landscape features on each site to which work needs to be done, and the details of the jobs themselves.

For example:

```
Britten Park, Rose Bed 1, Prune
Britten Park, Rose Bed 1, Mulch
Britten Park, Rose Bed 1, Spray
Britten Park, Shrub Bed 1, Mulch
Britten Park, Shrub Bed 1, Weed
Britten Park, Shrub Bed 1, Hoe
```

...and so on. With a traditional B-Tree index, the leaf node would contain entries such as this:

```
BRITPK, RB1, PRUNE
BRITPK, RB1, MULCH
BRITPK, RB1, SPRAY
BRITPK, SB1, MULCH
```

However, if we create the index using the new compression feature, we would issue the following command:

```
create index landscp_job_idx
on landscp(site,feature,job)
compression 2;
```

...and the leaf node entries are then constructed rather differently. The first 2 columns (due to the COMPRESSION 2 clause) are lifted into a special "prefix" area of the node, and the remaining column is then left as the main leaf node entry, as follows:

```
Prefix 0: BRITPK, RB1 3
Prefix 1: BRITPK, SB1 3


PRUNE 0
MULCH 0
SPRAY 0
MULCH 1
WEED 1
HOE 1
```

As you can see the non-selective data is listed once in the prefix area of the node, with a reference to the number of entries linked to each prefix (it happens in this case to be 3 entries per prefix). Then, within the 'body' of the leaf node, each entry is linked back to its parent prefix.

The crucial advantage here is that the repetitive (in other words, the non-selective, seldom changing) key values are stored only once in the leaf node (in the prefix area), rather than once per entry. Potentially large amounts of space are thus saved, and you can pack in far more leaf entries than before. In some cases, it's possible to practically halve the size of the index compared with its non-compressed cousin.

Smaller indexes mean firstly that the optimizer is more likely to want to make use of them, even without hints in your code; and secondly that the I/O needed to read the index when it *is* read is reduced, so index read performance is itself increased. (The CPU usage goes up somewhat as the server has to uncompress the index in memory to make use of it, but, assuming your CPU is not being thrashed to death in the first place, the decision as to whether to trade CPU for disk I/O is a no-brainer - CPU wins every time.) Since key compression can therefore lead directly to significant performance improvements, you should at least *think* about compression (if only to rule it out after due analysis) every time you feel the need to create a B-Tree index.

In this regard, you should be aware that compression doesn't have to be used purely for concatenated indexes. *Wherever* you have a non-unique index (even on a single field) on data with relatively low selectivity, it's worth at least investigating its benefits. Using our earlier EMP table example, if we had 53 employees called Frank, compression would have helped on the single column index on NAME, since it would have resulted in one prefix for Frank, and 53 references to the various rowids in the main table.

For unique indexes, however, single-column compression would be meaningless: the entire index would be constructed in the prefix area, with nothing left for the bulk of the leaf node at all! Therefore, compression for unique indexes is only sensible when it is a concatenated index, and one (or more) of the key fields is, on its own, of fairly low selectivity. The rule is then that the degree of compression for such indexes must be one less than the number of columns being indexed.

Skip-scanning of Indexes

Skip scanning of indexes is a new feature introduced with Oracle 9*i*. Its arrival means that you need to worry slightly less than before about the order of fields in a concatenated index, since the Optimizer will make an intelligent scan of the index even where your query is selecting a field that is not the leading column of the index.

Suppose we have a concatenated index on two fields LANGUAGE and COUNTRY. Note that there are fewer languages than possible countries (English, for example, is spoken in dozens of countries). Therefore, the index has been created with the least-selective column as its leading key. We might have the following sort of index, therefore:

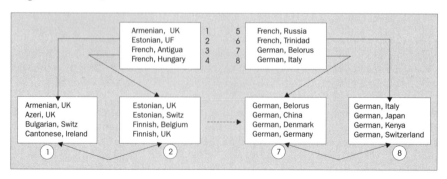

We haven't shown the entire index structure here, but instead have focused on the first and last couple of leaf nodes, and their respective branch nodes. We've numbered them too, which will hopefully help as you read the next few paragraphs!

Let's consider what we would need to look at in the index if we issued a statement such as:

```
select * from table where Country='Switzerland'
```

In all earlier versions of Oracle, you'd be signing up (as we discussed before) for, at the very best, a full scan of the *index*. It's probable that the Optimizer might just opt for a full *table* scan instead, since the query predicate is on the non-leading column of the index. However, in 9*i* the Optimizer is a bit smarter. It can deduce whether a leaf node *might* contain the entry we are searching for by intelligently using the information provided by the branch blocks, and remembering what it has encountered in previous leaf nodes.

For example, we know from the branch nodes that the first leaf node starts with 'Armenian, UK', and the second with 'Estonian, UK'. Can Switzerland appear in that node? Of course it can, since between 'Armenian' and 'Estonian' there are a host of possibilities, any one of which might include Switzerland ('Bulgarian, Switzerland' is one that springs to mind, but 'Danish, Switzerland' is a possibility too). We must therefore scan the first leaf node as it might contain an entry for Switzerland.

Again, the branch node entries tell us that leaf node 2 must be less that 'French, Antigua', because that's what the third node is known to start with. Since we already know that it starts with 'Estonian, UK', could Switzerland be in this node? Yes, because 'Finnish, Switzerland' could make an appearance. Therefore, node 2 must be read.

In the same manner, leaf node 3 is known to start with 'French, Antigua', but be less than 'French, Hungary'. It is therefore logically obvious that Switzerland cannot possibly be in this leaf node, and we needn't read it at all. Likewise, node 4 can also be skipped in its entirety, since its entries are known to lie between 'French, Hungary' and 'French, Russia' , which leaves no room for an entry for Switzerland.

Node 5, however, could contain an entry for Switzerland, entered between 'French, Russia' and 'French, Trinidad'. So we must read node 5. However, as we scan the entries for node 5, the moment we encounter an entry for 'French, T<*something*>', we can stop scanning for anything else. Having hit the "T" entries without encountering Switzerland, it's obvious that Switzerland can't be in the node.

Node 6 must be read, because the branch nodes tell us it contains entries between 'French, Trinidad' and 'German, Belorus', and it might therefore contain an entry for, say, 'Gaelic, Switzerland'. You might think that unlikely, but it's logically possible, so we must read the leaf node to check.

Node 7 can be skipped completely. Between 'German, Belorus' and 'German, Italy' there cannot be an entry for Switzerland. We must finally read Node 8, because after 'German, Italy', there is plenty of scope for 'German, Switzerland', 'Hungarian, Switzerland' or even 'Uzbeki, Switzerland'!

The net result of this is that, of the 8-node index, we had to read 5 of its blocks on disk (nodes 1, 2, 5, 6, and 8), but three of them were skipped entirely (nodes 3, 4, and 7). That's getting on for half the I/O associated with this sort of index (accessed in earlier Oracle versions). What's more, of the 5 blocks we were forced to read from disk, 1 of them (node 5) only had to be scanned until we came across an entry which logically precluded the existence of an entry that we were interested in.

279

This mechanism comes about simply because the Optimizer in Oracle 9*i* is able to make logical deductions about what can be in a leaf node by being aware of what the branch node implies can be in there. There's no special configuration or setup required to make it happen. It results, however, in concatenated indexes being usable, even when their leading key is not supplied as a query predicate. This allows us to miss logically inappropriate bits of it out of the search, which improves our performance, in comparison to the alternative of a full index scan.

What this boils down to is that in Oracle 9*i* we don't need to be as concerned with the order of columns in a concatenated index as we were in previous versions. This doesn't mean that we can completely ignore it however. The example we have looked at works because the leading column of the index was the *least* selective column. Had the more selective COUNTRY column been the leading key, then many fewer nodes would have been skipped in performing a query for the language 'French', for example.

The conclusion to be drawn from this discussion about concatenation, compression, and skip scanning of B-Tree indexes is, therefore, that concatenation has great benefits in reducing the use of unnecessary single-key indexes, but that the ordering of the columns makes a difference. Other things being equal, the leading columns of the index should be the ones that most usually correspond with what the application supplies as its query predicates. However, within the bounds of that general advice, you should think of making the least selective columns the leading columns of the index. Doing so gives you the opportunity to compress the index, and, in 9*i*, you get improved scanning of the index even when the query predicate is for a non-leading column.

> *In the following example we'll show results obtained with Oracle 8i. We'll show you the results obtained in Oracle 9i when we discuss the results in the 'How It Works' section.*

Try it Out – Concatenation, Compression, and Skip-scanning of Indexes

1. We'll start by making sure that our test table is freshly created, and free from any modifications arising from previous examples.

```
SQL> drop table indextest;

Table dropped.

SQL> create table indextest as select * from dba_objects
  2  where owner in ('OUTLN','PUBLIC','SCOTT','SYS','SYSTEM');

Table created.
```

2. We first need to find out something about the contents of our test table (remember that your results *will* vary, depending on what version and edition of the database you're running):

```
SQL> select distinct owner from indextest group by owner;

OWNER
------------------------------
OUTLN
PUBLIC
SCOTT
```

```
SYS
SYSTEM

SQL> select count(object_name) from indextest order by object_name;

COUNT(OBJECT_NAME)
------------------
             23876
```

3. Now let's create a concatenated index and see how (and whether) the optimizer makes use of it. From an earlier Try It Out, you may remember that getting the optimizer to use an index on the OWNER column at all is practically impossible because of the low cardinality of the data, so we'll calculate a histogram on that column to help it along a bit:

```
SQL> create index indxtest_owner_object_name_idx on indextest(owner, object_name);

Index created.

SQL> set autotrace trace explain;

SQL> analyze table indextest compute statistics;

Table analyzed.

SQL> analyze table indextest compute statistics for columns owner;

Table analyzed.

SQL> select owner, object_type from indextest
  2  where owner='SCOTT';

Execution Plan
----------------------------------------------------------
   0      SELECT STATEMENT Optimizer=CHOOSE (Cost=3 Card=15 Bytes=210)
   1    0   TABLE ACCESS (BY INDEX ROWID) OF 'INDEXTEST' (Cost=3 Card=
          15 Bytes=210)

   2    1     INDEX (RANGE SCAN) OF 'INDXTEST_OWNER_OBJECT_NAME_IDX' (
          NON-UNIQUE) (Cost=2 Card=15)




SQL> select owner, object_type from indextest
  2  where object_name = 'DBA_INDEXES';

Execution Plan
----------------------------------------------------------
   0      SELECT STATEMENT Optimizer=CHOOSE (Cost=50 Card=2 Bytes=78)
   1    0   TABLE ACCESS (FULL) OF 'INDEXTEST' (Cost=50 Card=2 Bytes=7
          8)
```

4. Now let's recreate the index, this time with the order of the columns reversed, and see if that has any effect on our queries:

```
SQL> drop index INDXTEST_OWNER_OBJECT_NAME_IDX;

Index dropped.

SQL> create index indxtest_objectname_owner_idx on indextest(object_name, owner);

Index created.

SQL> select owner, object_type from indextest
  2  where owner='SCOTT';

Execution Plan
----------------------------------------------------------
   0      SELECT STATEMENT Optimizer=CHOOSE (Cost=50 Card=15 Bytes=210
          )

   1    0   TABLE ACCESS (FULL) OF 'INDEXTEST' (Cost=50 Card=15 Bytes=
          210)


SQL> select owner, object_type from indextest
  2  where object_name = 'DBA_INDEXES';

Execution Plan
----------------------------------------------------------
   0      SELECT STATEMENT Optimizer=CHOOSE (Cost=3 Card=2 Bytes=78)
   1    0   TABLE ACCESS (BY INDEX ROWID) OF 'INDEXTEST' (Cost=3 Card=
          2 Bytes=78)

   2    1     INDEX (RANGE SCAN) OF 'INDXTEST_OBJECTNAME_OWNER_IDX' (N
          ON-UNIQUE) (Cost=2 Card=2)
```

5. This time, we'll see what happens when we compress the index, in each of its flavors. We'll first get the physical size of our current index, so that we have something to compare it with once we've compressed it:

```
SQL> set autotrace off
SQL> analyze index indxtest_objectname_owner_idx validate structure;

Index analyzed.

SQL> select name, lf_blks, pct_used from index_stats;

NAME                              LF_BLKS    PCT_USED
------------------------------- ---------- ----------
INDXTEST_OBJECTNAME_OWNER_IDX        139          89
```

```
SQL> alter index INDXTEST_OBJECTNAME_OWNER_IDX rebuild compress 1;

Index altered.

SQL> analyze index indxtest_objectname_owner_idx validate structure;

Index analyzed.

SQL> select name, lf_blks, pct_used from index_stats;

NAME                               LF_BLKS    PCT_USED
----------------------------    ----------  ----------
INDXTEST_OBJECTNAME_OWNER_IDX          112          44
```

6. Now we'll see if the new degree of compression affects the use of the indexes by the optimizer:

```
SQL> set autotrace trace explain
SQL> select owner, object_type from indextest
  2  where owner='SCOTT';

Execution Plan
----------------------------------------------------------
   0      SELECT STATEMENT Optimizer=CHOOSE (Cost=50 Card=15 Bytes=210
          )

   1    0   TABLE ACCESS (FULL) OF 'INDEXTEST' (Cost=50 Card=15 Bytes=
          210)




SQL> select owner, object_type from indextest
  2  where object_name = 'DBA_INDEXES';

Execution Plan
----------------------------------------------------------
   0      SELECT STATEMENT Optimizer=CHOOSE (Cost=4 Card=2 Bytes=78)
   1    0   TABLE ACCESS (BY INDEX ROWID) OF 'INDEXTEST' (Cost=4 Card=
          2 Bytes=78)

   2    1     INDEX (RANGE SCAN) OF 'INDXTEST_OBJECTNAME_OWNER_IDX' (N
          ON-UNIQUE) (Cost=2 Card=2)
```

7. Finding that the index with OBJECT_NAME as its leading column doesn't compress particularly well, nor helps our queries very much, let's drop the index, and recreate it with OWNER as its leading column. Again, we'll compress it, and check its vital statistics before we attempt to use it in a query:

```
SQL> drop index INDXTEST_OBJECTNAME_OWNER_IDX;

Index dropped.

SQL> create index INDXTEST_OWNER_OBJECTNAME_IDX on indextest(owner,object_name)
compress 1;

Index created.

SQL> set autotrace off
SQL> select name, lf_blks, pct_used from index_stats;

no rows selected

SQL> analyze index INDXTEST_OWNER_OBJECTNAME_IDX validate structure;

Index analyzed.

SQL> select name, lf_blks, pct_used from index_stats;

NAME                                  LF_BLKS    PCT_USED
------------------------------------- ---------- ----------
INDXTEST_OWNER_OBJECTNAME_IDX             121         89

SQL> set autotrace trace explain
SQL> select owner, object_type from indextest
  2  where owner='SCOTT';

Execution Plan
----------------------------------------------------------
   0      SELECT STATEMENT Optimizer=CHOOSE (Cost=3 Card=15 Bytes=210)
   1    0   TABLE ACCESS (BY INDEX ROWID) OF 'INDEXTEST' (Cost=3 Card=
          15 Bytes=210)

   2    1     INDEX (RANGE SCAN) OF 'INDXTEST_OWNER_OBJECTNAME_IDX' (N
          ON-UNIQUE) (Cost=2 Card=15)




SQL> select owner, object_type from indextest
  2  where object_name = 'DBA_INDEXES';

Execution Plan
----------------------------------------------------------
   0      SELECT STATEMENT Optimizer=CHOOSE (Cost=50 Card=2 Bytes=78)
   1    0   TABLE ACCESS (FULL) OF 'INDEXTEST' (Cost=50 Card=2 Bytes=7
          8)
```

How it Works

From the queries we ran in step 2, we know that there are many thousands of different object names, but only 5 possible owners. Put another way, OBJECT_NAME is a high cardinality column, while OWNER is a rather low cardinality column.

In step 3, we created a two-column concatenated index, with OWNER as its leading key. We then tried two queries, the first using OWNER in its WHERE clause, the second using OBJECT_NAME. In other words, the first query supplied the leading key of the index (in its WHERE clause), and the second one didn't. The results were as expected:

```
SQL> select owner, object_type from indextest
  2  where owner='SCOTT';

Execution Plan
----------------------------------------------------------
    0      SELECT STATEMENT Optimizer=CHOOSE (Cost=3 Card=15 Bytes=210)
    1    0   TABLE ACCESS (BY INDEX ROWID) OF 'INDEXTEST' (Cost=3 Card=
           15 Bytes=210)

    2    1     INDEX (RANGE SCAN) OF 'INDXTEST_OWNER_OBJECT_NAME_IDX' (
           NON-UNIQUE) (Cost=2 Card=15)
```

When we supply the leading key of the index as our selection criterion, the index is used. We get a range scan of the index, and the whole query is resolved with a cost of 3.

However, when we supply the secondary key as our selection criterion, the index is not used at all (remember that this is 8*i* we're talking about so far). The optimizer has decided that scanning through the entire index to retrieve the secondary key, (and then using that as the pointer to the table), is too expensive, and instead opts to scan the entire table to start with, at a total cost of 50 (that's getting on for 17 times more expensive than before).

```
SQL> select owner, object_type from indextest
  2  where object_name = 'DBA_INDEXES';

Execution Plan
----------------------------------------------------------
    0      SELECT STATEMENT Optimizer=CHOOSE (Cost=50 Card=2 Bytes=78)
    1    0   TABLE ACCESS (FULL) OF 'INDEXTEST' (Cost=50 Card=2 Bytes=7
           8)
```

Running this second query in Oracle 9*i* will result in drastically different results. The execution plan we'll now see is as follows:

```
SQL> select owner, object_type from indextest
  2  where object_name = 'DBA_INDEXES';

Execution Plan
----------------------------------------------------------
    0      SELECT STATEMENT Optimizer=CHOOSE (Cost=7 Card=1 Bytes=26)
    1    0   TABLE ACCESS (BY INDEX ROWID) OF 'INDEXTEST' (Cost=7 Card=
           1 Bytes=26)

    2    1     INDEX (SKIP SCAN) OF 'INDXTEST_OWNER_OBJECT_NAME_IDX' (N
           ON-UNIQUE) (Cost=6 Card=1)
```

You'll notice the magic words SKIP SCAN in our results, which means that Oracle is now able to make good use of a non-leading key in an index.

To complete the story of concatenation, in step 4 we recreated our index with the keys swapped in order. Now we use OBJECT_NAME (high cardinality) as the leading key, and OWNER (low cardinality) as the secondary key. Exactly the same queries as before were then submitted, and the results were neatly reversed. In Oracle 8*i*, the query for OWNER = SCOTT (the secondary key) required a full table scan, and the query for OBJECT_NAME = DBA_INDEXES (the leading key) used the index. The costs of the two queries were also neatly reversed.

If you're wondering what happens in 9*i*, it's a good question! In fact, in the case of the query for OWNER = SCOTT, 9*i* does *not* use skip scanning. What you actually get is this:

```
SQL> select owner, object_type from indextest
  2  where owner='SCOTT';

Execution Plan
----------------------------------------------------------
   0      SELECT STATEMENT Optimizer=CHOOSE (Cost=10 Card=11 Bytes=121
          )

   1    0   TABLE ACCESS (FULL) OF 'INDEXTEST' (Cost=10 Card=11 Bytes=
          121)
```

The 9*i* optimizer feels that not enough of the index is going to be skipped to make a skip scan worthwhile. As you may recall from a previous example, user SCOTT owns around 4 objects, while user SYS owns several thousand, which maybe helps to explain Oracle's decision. SCOTT has so few index entries that to find them buried amongst all the others would be like the proverbial search for a needle in a haystack. It doesn't help, either, that SCOTT, SYSTEM and SYS all have similar names that are close to each other in the index, since this reduces the scope for skipping.

We can see here that the optimizer can use concatenated indexes whatever the order of concatenation, provided that what you then supply as your WHERE predicates most often matches the leading key. However, we also see that in Oracle 9*i*, we can use the index (because of skip scanning) in situations where 8*i* wouldn't, provided that the low cardinality column is the leading key in the index, and not a subsidiary key.

In Steps 5 and 6, we experimented with compression of indexes. Our first attempt was to compress the index when OBJECT_NAME (high cardinality) was the leading key. The results were pretty poor. The number of leaf nodes was reduced from 139 to 122, but the utilization plummeted from a reasonable 89% to a paltry 44%. Did compression help our queries? No! The search for SCOTT's objects yielded the same table scan as before, while the search for DBA_INDEXES used the index. This is exactly what you might have expected.

What you may have missed, though, is that the cost of using the index in its compressed state, in comparison to its uncompressed state in Step 4, actually went *up*! Compare the execution plan before compression:

```
Execution Plan
-----------------------------------------------------------
   0      SELECT STATEMENT Optimizer=CHOOSE (Cost=3 Card=2 Bytes=78)
   1    0   TABLE ACCESS (BY INDEX ROWID) OF 'INDEXTEST' (Cost=3 Card=
          2 Bytes=78)

   2    1     INDEX (RANGE SCAN) OF 'INDXTEST_OBJECTNAME_OWNER_IDX' (N
          ON-UNIQUE) (Cost=2 Card=2)
```

with the one following compression:

```
Execution Plan
-----------------------------------------------------------
   0      SELECT STATEMENT Optimizer=CHOOSE (Cost=4 Card=2 Bytes=78)
   1    0   TABLE ACCESS (BY INDEX ROWID) OF 'INDEXTEST' (Cost=4 Card=
          2 Bytes=78)

   2    1     INDEX (RANGE SCAN) OF 'INDXTEST_OBJECTNAME_OWNER_IDX' (N
          ON-UNIQUE) (Cost=2 Card=2)
```

The cost change in this example is not exactly huge (3 to 4), but that it has gone up at all should remind you that compression is most useful when it's the *low* cardinality column that's the leading key. We saw the truth of this statement in step 7. Once OWNER was the leading key, the physical structure of the compressed index compared rather favorably to the uncompressed version:

```
NAME                              LF_BLKS    PCT_USED
-----------------------------   ----------  ----------
INDXTEST_OWNER_OBJECTNAME_IDX       121         89
```

The number of leaf nodes hasn't decreased much from the earlier example of compression, but the PCT_USED remains respectably high. Although in this particular case the existence of compression wasn't enough to persuade the optimizer to use the index in new ways, the select for SCOTT's objects showed a cost of 3, indicating that compression hasn't actually degraded our performance in this instance.

Indexes and Constraints

It is a (sometimes unfortunate) fact of Oracle life that declaring certain constraints when creating (or modifying) a table, implicitly causes Oracle to create indexes on the constrained columns. The chief culprits are unique and primary key constraints. Consider the following coding:

```
create table inventory(
partno number(4) constraint invent_partno_pk primary key,
partdesc varchar2(35) constraint invent_partdesc_uq unique);
```

This will cause two indexes to be created for this table, one on each column, whether you like it or not. The name of those indexes will be the same as the name of the constraints, which is a good reason for always naming your constraints properly. If you don't, then Oracle will name them with highly non-intuitive names such as SYS_C00013.

As an aside here, the name SYS_C00013 indicates that it is a SYStem generated name, relating to 'C'onstraints, sequentially numbered by Oracle itself.

The difficulty with the automatic generation of indexes for such constraints is that you might not get quite what you wanted. In particular, and by default, Oracle will create *unique* indexes to enforce such constraints. That might not seem so surprising, since the essence of primary key and unique constraints is, surely, their uniqueness. While this is true, it has also been possible since Oracle version 8 to enforce such constraints with *non-unique* indexes, and there are some very good reasons why this can be the preferred option.

The trouble really arises when we consider what happens to the index used to enforce a constraint when the constraint is (for whatever reason) disabled. The rule is that, if the constraint is enforced with a unique index, then on disabling the constraint, the index will be summarily dropped, without a word of warning. If, however, it's enforced with a non-unique index, the index is retained, *whatever* you do to the constraint itself.

This might not seem a particular problem, until you consider that re-enabling a constraint would cause any required indexes that had previously been dropped to be recreated from scratch. As we suggested earlier, creating indexes is an expensive process, because it involves a lot of I/O and some fairly significant table locks that will prevent any DML taking place on the table for the duration of the initial build.

Fortunately, it *is* possible to take control of constraints so that they are enforced with non-unique indexes that don't just vanish. The trick is to make use of the idea of **deferrable** constraints, which were introduced in Oracle 8.0. To do that, we'd rewrite our previous CREATE TABLE statement like this:

```
create table inventory(
partno number(4) constraint partno_pk primary key deferrable initially immediate,
partdesc varchar2(35) constraint partdesc_uq unique deferrable initially
immediate);
```

A deferred constraint is one that is not actually checked until a transaction attempts to commit. Until that moment, therefore, Oracle must allow DML to take place that could violate every constraint ever devised for a table. You might perform a bulk load of, say, 10,000 rows all of which violate the primary key, but we must nevertheless allow those records to reside in the table until you come to commit the inserts (at which point, the rows will be rejected, and reversed out of the table, thereby ensuring that the constraint is only *temporarily* violated). If the *table* must permit violating records to reside within it, we can't have a unique index lurking in the background, because its awareness of its *own* uniqueness being violated would cause it to want to reject the records as they are inserted. In other words, deferred primary key and unique constraints *must* be enforced with non-unique indexes.

Having said that, you'll notice that the syntax we used above was as follows:

```
...primary key deferrable initially immediate;
```

The constraint here is not even *actually* deferred. What we're saying here is that, one day, we might *want* to defer it. The constraint is thus deferr*able*, though right now we want it to be enforced as an **immediate** constraint (that is, checked and enforced as each new row is entered into the table). That is still enough to cause Oracle to use non-unique indexes to enforce the constraint. This is because if the day came when we wanted to actually defer the constraint, and it had previously been enforced with a unique index, then Oracle would have to drop the original index and recreate a brand-new, non-unique one from scratch. That would be an extremely expensive procedure.

Incidentally, you might be concerned that there is some price to pay for having a primary key or unique constraint enforced with non-unique indexes. Surely Oracle would have to scan more of the index to check for uniqueness when fresh DML is performed? Actually, there's no performance impact whatsoever, for the simple reason that the optimizer is smart enough to know that if the column is declared to be unique (or primary key) at the table level, then the *contents* of the index must itself be unique. After all, even a deferred constraint gets checked eventually (at commit time), so it's ultimately just as impossible to get non-unique rows into the table (and hence the index), as it would be if the index were genuinely unique. As a result, the optimizer treats the index as unique for the purposes of selecting data from that column, and performance is just as good as if the thing had been declared unique in the first place.

One final consideration arises when you start declaring primary key or unique constraints. Since you're going to have indexes created for you anyway, you need to consider whether there is any opportunity to combine them with others that you could create on different columns. The point here is that if an index capable of being used to enforce the constraint *already* exists when the constraint is actually declared for the table, then Oracle will *not* create another index (which would take up extra space, and require an expensive build process), but will simply use the existing index.

The only rule to bear in mind when contemplating such a venture is that your own index must have the constrained column as its leading key. As an example, let us say we create the following table:

```
create table inventory(
partno number(4),
partdesc varchar2(35),
price number(8,2),
warehouse varchar2(15));
```

Clearly, the PARTNO column should be the primary key for this table (as before). However our application happens to make us search for parts by the location in which they are stored, meaning that an index on the WAREHOUSE column would be useful. To save ourselves the bother of creating two separate indexes we can issue this command:

```
Create index invent_part_loc_idx
On inventory (partno, warehouse)
Pctfree 10
Tablespace idx01;
```

We can then add a constraint to the table like this:

```
Alter table inventory add (
Constraint invent_partno_pk primary key (partno)
Using index invent_part_loc_idx);
```

At this point, Oracle will check that it can use the pre-existing index, and do so if it's satisfied that it can. Now, bearing in mind what was said earlier about queries wanting to use the non-leading key of a concatenated index, this might or might not produce acceptable performance. You'd have to check carefully whether searches by WAREHOUSE become painfully slow. But, particularly with 9*i*'s new skip scanning abilities, it's perfectly possible that it might be a trade-off worth making.

To this end, be aware that 9*i* also has a rather nice feature which means that you can achieve this same end-result without having to create the indexes and the constraints in two separate steps. In 9*i* you can include a complete CREATE INDEX clause as part of the CREATE TABLE statement, which will achieve exactly the same result as before:

```
Create table inventory (
partno number(4) constraint invent_partno_pk primary key
using index (
    create index invent_part_loc_idx
    on inventory (partno, warehouse)
    pctfree 10
    tablespace indx01),
partdesc varchar2(35),
price number(8,2),
warehouse varchar2(15));
```

Foreign Key Constraints

Oracle does *not* create indexes automatically on columns on which a foreign key constraint is declared. Unfortunately, the lack of an index on a foreign key column can pose potentially awful locking issues for an application.

If the parent table's primary key is ever updated or deleted from then, in the absence of an index on the child table's foreign key, the *entire* child table is subject to a lock which prohibits all further DML on the table until the parent table's transaction is committed or rolled back. If an index is present, however, then the locking activity caused by the parent table transaction takes a different sort of lock on the index entry itself, and leaves the child table unlocked. DML on those child rows, whose parent is affected by the transaction, is still not possible, but all other rows can be modified without a problem.

Clearly, having a large table suddenly locked from all DML activity is not exactly what a busy OLTP application is likely to find acceptable. You therefore need to consider building indexes on any foreign key that is declared, in order to stop the problem arising.

In Oracle 9*i*, the situation has improved somewhat. An update to the parent table still takes a lock on the entire child table in the absence of an index. However, that lock is almost immediately released after it is taken, rather than when the transaction completes with a commit or rollback. Unfortunately, the problem has not gone away entirely, because that child lock still needs to be acquired, and if there are any transactions outstanding in the child table before the parent update starts, it cannot be acquired. At this point, the parent transaction queues for the lock, meaning that all further child table transactions queue up behind it. In other words, you still get a failure to perform DML on the child table, and so consideration as to whether to build indexes on the child table's foreign key is still needed.

You should approach this problem with some care. Having a child table locked for the duration of an update is not exactly pleasant, but neither is having a bunch of indexes on foreign keys particularly good for DML performance (bearing in mind that every index slows down DML). The first thing to consider is whether the parent table is *ever* going to have its primary key modified, or records deleted. If such parent table transactions are never going to take place, the need for the index on the child foreign key doesn't arise. If you do decide to index the child table though, you should definitely consider compressing it. Almost by definition, it won't be a unique index, and therefore, despite being a single-column index, it can make good use of the 8*i* compression feature.

As with primary key and unique constraints, you should also consider creating concatenated indexes to deal with this table locking issue. Provided that the foreign key column is the leading key of an index, there is absolutely nothing to stop you including additional columns in the same index. By doing so, you'll be creating a single, concatenated index instead of multiple separate ones, thus cutting down a bit on disk space, and saving yourself the additional I/O that would be needed to build multiple indexes. The usual worries over queries on the non-leading column needing to scan the index (or, in 9*i*, having to skip scan it) apply however. Again it is a matter of careful testing and thoughtfully weighing up the costs and benefits.

Reverse Key Indexes

Indexes on column, which are also primary keys, have another major performance problem associated with them. Quite frequently, you will want the primary key of a table to be an auto-incrementing sequence number, populated by a trigger when the other row data is inserted. That is indeed what has happened with the EMPNO field of our earlier EMP table:

EMPNO	NAME	DEPT	SAL	Etc...
70	Bob	10	450	...
10	Frank	10	550	...
30	Ed	30	575	...
20	Adam	20	345	...
40	David	10	550	...
60	Graham	30	625	...
50	Charles	20	330	...
...	...	...	...	...

The EMPNO column is, therefore, what is somewhat laboriously known as a **monotonically incrementing sequence number,** and indexes on such fields have an unfortunate habit of crippling multi-user applications.

To see why, think what a normal B-Tree index would look like:

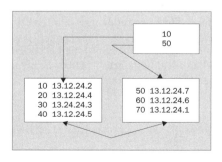

Notice that the index is well compacted, with each leaf node being filled with its maximum permitted number of entries (the 4-entry limit we arbitrarily imposed earlier). Now, as we employ new people and perform fresh inserts on the table, it should be evident that we are in absolutely no danger of ever needing to revisit an earlier leaf node. The next employee will get an EMPNO of 80, the one after that 90, and so on. We will never, however, get a new employee with an EMPNO of 25. That is, of course, the whole point of a monotonically incrementing sequence number (it only ever goes *up*).

This is good in one respect, since it means that we are never going to experience a block split amongst the leaf nodes, because no new entries will ever have to slot in amongst existing ones. Therefore, remembering that for indexes the PCTFREE setting is designed to prevent block splits, it should be apparent that there is absolutely no point in setting PCTFREE to anything other than 0. That means that an index on a monotonically incrementing sequence number can make full use of its leaf nodes, packing in data very tightly, and will always be a very efficient user of space.

However, there is a price to pay for this efficiency. Every new index entry will always take place on the last (right-most) leaf node. As the existing nodes fill up with entries, we'll have to acquire additional leaf nodes, and it will always be the freshly acquired leaf node that gets all the insert activity directed at it. Deletes can cause similar problems. Typically, the tables such indexes are built on are subject to periodic bulk deletes of the earliest entries (imagine an orders system, for example, where you index on date, and regularly clear out all orders generated more than 12 months ago). That translates into extensive contention for the first (left-most) leaf nodes within the index.

This means that if 100 users simultaneously insert (or delete) a new record into the table, they will all be fighting for access to the same leaf node. That is of particular concern where the application is running in a Parallel Server environment, but it can also arise where a single instance is being run on a multi-processor box. The contention for the last leaf node for indexes on monotonically incrementing sequence numbers is potentially horrendous, and can result in massive waits for access to the node. This directly manifests itself in extremely poor response times for users attempting to perform a simple bit of DML.

So, we might devise a general rule that you should *never* index a monotonically incrementing sequence number, because doing so risks awful performance problems. Unfortunately, you probably don't have a choice in the matter. Sequence numbers are usually used as the primary key of a table and, as we've already seen, every primary key *requires* an index to be created, and Oracle will create one itself if you don't do the deed first.

What we need is some sort of mechanism that would scatter our inserts randomly across the base of the index. This capability was introduced in Oracle 8.0 with the **Reverse Key** Index. The principle of the reverse key index is simple enough. In structure and format, it's just an ordinary B-Tree index. However, if you enter a new record in the table with a sequence number of, say, 7891, we index it as 1987. If you enter sequence number 7892, we index it as 2987. 7901 gets indexed as 1097, and so on.

Note that, while the three sequence numbers just mentioned are incremental (in ascending order), the index entries are not. Translated into leaf node activity, that means that inserts on the index are taking place in all possible leaf nodes, not just the last one. The contention issue thus disappears.

At what cost though? Well, you are now scattering your new inserts back and forth across the base of the index. That means you are inserting new leaf node entries amongst existing entries, which means that block splits are a possibility once again, with all their implied performance degradation and space issues. To prevent that, of course, you can set PCTFREE to a non-zero value when you first create the index, and immediately introduce an element of wasted space before you even begin populating the thing! Reverse key indexes are, as a result, going to be bigger and emptier than a non-reversed equivalent, which may well translate into more I/O to retrieve a given index entry. Before opting for reversing, therefore, you need to be fairly sure that the contention issue (manifesting itself as 'buffer busy waits' on the leaf node) is serious enough so that the cure isn't worse than the disease.

What is potentially much worse though, from an application developer's point of view, is that it is now no longer possible to use the index for performing range scans of values. In an ordinary index, the following command would be easy to perform:

```
select for employees with employee numbers between 5600 and 6120
```

All those numbers would be housed next to each other in some part of the index, and we could easily locate the first one, before continuing to scan incrementally until reaching the last. In a reversed index, those same entries are all over the place. 5601 is at the beginning of the index (1065), but 5609 is somewhere near the end (9065), and 5611 is back at the beginning again (1165). If the index is used by the optimizer at all, it will be fully scanned from one end to the other. However, there's a fair chance that it won't be used at all.

That is perhaps not as disastrous as it sounds, since it is highly unlikely that you would ever *want* to select a range of employees by their employee numbers. In the case of an orders system, it would be unusual to receive a complaint regarding all orders with numbers between 7823 and 8109. The majority of complaints will concern a single order number, which means that the lack of range scanning ability in the index is irrelevant.

Reverse key indexes therefore need to be thought about carefully before plunging in. The space and block split issues are significant, and introduce performance degradation problems of their own. The contention issue you are trying to cure needs to be bad enough to warrant this treatment. Your application may also have a real need for range scans that a reverse key would simply prohibit. Life's not easy weighing such pro's and con's!

If you choose to use a reverse key index, creating them is simply a matter of including the one word reverse at the end of what the normal index syntax would be. In the case of our EMP table example, for instance, we might have issued the following command:

```
create index emp_empno_pk
on emp(empno) reverse;
```

Incidentally, and in case it isn't obvious, the reversal of the key is totally transparent to the users! When faced with a complaint regarding order number 23894, the user does not have to indulge in some mental gymnastics before submitting a query for order 49832. The user queries the data in the normal way, leaving the reversing to the optimizer.

Function-based Indexes

One of the most common problems people have with Oracle is that it is sensitive to case. If, in our `EMP` table, we store people's names as Fred and Bob, then a search for FRED, BOB, fred, or bob will turn up no rows. If you're uncertain how users have entered data, this can be a significant problem.

Of course, there's long been a way around the problem. You'd issue your select statements along these lines:

```
Select name, salary, dept
From emp
Where upper(name)='BOB';
```

That way, it doesn't matter what permutation of case the users came up with when they entered the data, if there's a Bob in the table somewhere, this query will find it.

Unfortunately, with such a query you are asking for a selection of records based on a value that is not actually stored in the table. And if it's not in the table, it certainly won't be in the index. So, even if there is an index on the `NAME` column, Oracle will be forced to perform a full table scan and compute the `UPPER` function for each row encountered.

Prior to Oracle 8*i* if you wanted index access to the upper case version of the employee's name, then you were more or less forced to add a new column to the table, update it so that it stored a forced uppercase version of the name, and then index it in the usual manner. This is cumbersome at best, and violates every relational principle devised, since there would now be a dependency established between the 'real' `NAME` column and the column with the upper case version of the name. Update the one, and you have to remember to update the other. Fail to do so, and your data are no longer consistent.

Fortunately that all changed with Oracle 8*i*, since you now have the option of creating what is known as a **function-based** index on the `NAME` column directly. It's just a regular B-Tree index (and hence the syntax used to create one is broadly the same as for a regular index), but based upon a function applied to the table data, not directly on the table data itself.

In our case, the following command would be sufficient:

```
create index upper_name_idx
on emp(upper(name));
```

Now, when we issue our query, we are likely to be able to make use of this index to tell us which rows should be selected. This should mean that our query is faster than if we perform a full table scan. We should note here that the `WHERE` predicate of our query does not need to be computed for each record as we go, since the index is actually storing the pre-computed value. In addition to this, as our table data is updated, the index is updated for us automatically (remembering that 'updates' to the index take the form of marking the original entry for deletion and inserting a new value elsewhere).

Technically, Oracle pulls off this bit of handiwork by creating a hidden column in the table itself, with a name such as `SYS_NC0001$`, and gives that column a default value of whatever the function is that you used to create the index. You can see this column by performing a query against the `OBJ$` table of the data dictionary, using a subselect on the `DBA_TABLES` view to specify which table it is that you're interested in:

```
select * from sys.col$ where obj#=
(select object_id from dba_objects where object_name='EMP' and owner='SCOTT');
```

The range of functions that you can use when building a function-based index is as broad as your imagination allows. You can use many of the built-in Oracle functions (such as LTRIM, RTRIM, LEN, UPPER and so on), provided that they return a single answer for a single row. This rules out functions such as SUM, MAX, and AVG. If you attempt to use any of these then you'll return a group function not allowed error.

In addition to the internal Oracle functions, you can also use any functions you've created yourself, written in PL/SQL, Java, or C. However, it is important to bear in mind that it is possible for the function you have created to become invalidated, at which point all function-based indexes based on that function also get invalidated and marked as disabled. Users will suddenly notice that reports, which used to take seconds to complete, suddenly start taking many minutes to finish (because they've reverted to doing full table scans) . What's rather worse is that any DML which would ordinarily update the now-disabled index, starts returning an ORA-30554 function based index name is disabled error message.

There are a number of other points to bear in mind if you wish to use function-based indexes. First, you won't even be able to create them unless you have been granted the QUERY REWRITE system privilege. Second, if you want to create such indexes on tables in other schemas, then you require the GLOBAL QUERY REWRITE privilege. Third, even if you manage to create the right index, the optimizer won't actually be able to use them unless the QUERY_REWRITE_ENABLED init.ora parameter is set to be TRUE.

Note that this last parameter can be switched on dynamically by using the command:

```
alter session set query_rewrite_enabled=true
```

Having set up all these privileges, you will also need to set the init.ora parameter QUERY_REWRITE_INTEGRITY to be TRUSTED. This is actually rather unfortunate, because that parameter also determines how the database uses materialized views. This means that there's a potential conflict between what the application demands from the point of view of function-based indexes, and what it requires for effective use of its materialized views.

You'll see more about materialized views in Chapter 14.

When you are creating your own functions to be used with function-based indexes, you must declare them to be **deterministic**. That means you have to solemnly declare that the function is invariable (that is, returns the same result) given the same set of inputs. That rules out, for example, developing a function that contains a call to SYSDATE, since every time the function is called, the SYSDATE will have changed, even though the inputs to the function (derived from the invariant table data) haven't. Note that it's entirely up to you to check this (Oracle will not check this for you), and you can expect some pretty weird and spectacularly incorrect results if you get it wrong!

The basic syntax for a function looks like this:

```
create or replace function blah (
        Parameters defined here
return number [or char etc] deterministic
as
begin
        Function code goes here
end;
/
```

Functions are covered in more detail in Chapter 11.

The optimizer is pretty smart in working out whether it is possible to use a function-based index to resolve a query. The WHERE predicate supplied by the query does *not* have to be identical to the one used to create the index.

For example, consider the situation where you issue this command:

```
create index maths_idx
on emp(sal+empno+sqrt(sal));
```

The index created here is useable even if the query is for `where sqrt(sal)+sal+empno=456`. In other words, it is aware of the mathematical ideas of commutative operations, and can see that the index can resolve the query, regardless of the order in which the various pieces of the function are supplied during the query.

It can't work wonders, though. Try a query such as `where sqrt(sal)+sal=456-empno` and it will be stuck. You're getting dangerously close to wanting the optimizer to be able to solve simultaneous equations there!

Index-only Scans

There is one particular class of queries where it can be tricky to persuade the optimizer to use a function-based index at all. These queries will return an answer that could theoretically be obtained entirely from the index itself, by performing an index-only scan.

For example, if we created the following function-based index:

```
Create index emp_funct_comm_idx
On emp (sqrt(comm.));
```

then you might expect that the following query could be answered by looking at the index alone, without referencing the table at all:

```
select sqrt(comm.) from emp order by sqrt(comm.);
```

After all, there's not a thing in the select statement that can't be found within the index in its own right.

Unfortunately, that's not what happens in practice. The trouble is that the query is (apparently) asking to see the square root of the commission for every employee (it's admittedly an odd request!), yet there's no guarantee that the index contains an entry for every employee. If some employees have a NULL commission in the table, for example, then they don't get included in the index (NULLs are never included in indexes).

Knowing whether a column is nullable or not, therefore, is important for the optimizer to work out whether it can resolve the query entirely within the index, or whether it must revert to performing a full table scan. If you were able to place a NOT NULL constraint on the commission column, that would give the optimizer the assurance it needs that all rows are referenced in the index, and it would then, sure enough, choose to use the index. Unfortunately, the optimizer in 8*i* was not quite smart enough to deduce that if the *table* was Not Null for a particular column, an index on that column must reference every row. In other words the presence or absence of a NOT NULL constraint made no difference to whether it would use the function-based index or not.

Fortunately, that's been fixed in Oracle 9*i*, and the optimizer *is* now able to deduce when a function is able to return a result for every row in the table. Accordingly, 9*i* is rather more likely to use an available function-based index than 8*i* ever was.

Try it Out – Function-based Indexes

1. We'll begin by recreating the INDEXTEST table, and setting QUERY_REWRITE_ENABLED=TRUE, so that we can use a function-based index. We'll begin by creating a regular B-Tree index on the OBJECT_NAME column, and see whether we can use that for case-insensitive searches:

```
SQL> alter session set QUERY_REWRITE_ENABLED=TRUE;

Session altered.

SQL> set autotrace trace explain
SQL> drop table indextest;

Table dropped.

SQL> create table indextest as select * from dba_objects
  2  where owner in ('OUTLN','PUBLIC','SCOTT','SYS','SYSTEM');

Table created.

SQL> analyze table indextest compute statistics;

Table analyzed.

SQL> create index indxtst_objname_idx on indextest(object_name);

Index created.

SQL> select object_name, owner from indextest
```

```
  2  where upper(object_name) ='DBA_INDEXES';

Execution Plan
----------------------------------------------------------
   0      SELECT STATEMENT Optimizer=CHOOSE (Cost=50 Card=239 Bytes=71
          70)

   1   0    TABLE ACCESS (FULL) OF 'INDEXTEST' (Cost=50 Card=239 Bytes
          =7170)
```

2. With a regular B-tree index on the OBJECT_NAME column, it is clear that we are out of luck after all. Let's get rid of that index, and replace it with a function-based one:

```
SQL> drop index indxtst_objname_idx;

Index dropped.

SQL> create index indxtst_objname_fidx on indextest(upper(object_name));

Index created.

SQL> select object_name,owner from indextest
  2  where upper(object_name) ='DBA_INDEXES';

Execution Plan
----------------------------------------------------------
   0      SELECT STATEMENT Optimizer=CHOOSE (Cost=2 Card=239 Bytes=717
          0)

   1   0    TABLE ACCESS (BY INDEX ROWID) OF 'INDEXTEST' (Cost=2 Card=
          239 Bytes=7170)

   2   1      INDEX (RANGE SCAN) OF 'INDXTST_OBJNAME_FIDX' (NON-UNIQUE
          ) (Cost=1 Card=239)
```

3. Now we'll see if we can persuade the optimizer to resolve a query purely within the index. That's easy enough to do in theory, as long as we don't select any columns which aren't actually *in* the index!

```
SQL> select upper(object_name) from indextest;

Execution Plan
----------------------------------------------------------
   0      SELECT STATEMENT Optimizer=CHOOSE (Cost=50 Card=23876 Bytes=
          596900)

   1   0    TABLE ACCESS (FULL) OF 'INDEXTEST' (Cost=50 Card=23876 Byt
          es=596900)
```

4. Finally, we'll try to see if altering the table definition itself can help make the index useable. Results will vary depending on what version of the database you're using, but in 8*i* you should see:

```
SQL> alter table indextest modify object_name NOT NULL;

Table altered.

SQL> select upper(object_name) from indextest;

Execution Plan
----------------------------------------------------------
   0      SELECT STATEMENT Optimizer=CHOOSE (Cost=50 Card=23876 Bytes=
          596900)

   1    0   TABLE ACCESS (FULL) OF 'INDEXTEST' (Cost=50 Card=23876 Byt
            es=596900)
```

5. And here's exactly the same thing, but done in $9i$:

```
SQL> alter table indextest modify object_name NOT NULL;

Table altered.

SQL> select upper(object_name) from indextest;

Execution Plan
----------------------------------------------------------
   0      SELECT STATEMENT Optimizer=CHOOSE (Cost=4 Card=5204 Bytes=78
          060)

   1    0   INDEX (FAST FULL SCAN) OF 'INDXTST_OBJNAME_FIDX' (NON-UNIQ
            UE) (Cost=4 Card=5204 Bytes=78060)
```

How It Works

Creating a regular B-Tree index on the OBJECT_NAME column was of no use whatsoever to the optimizer in resolving a query that asked for a match on UPPER(OBJECT_NAME). It had no choice but to perform a full table scan. Creating a function-based index, however, allowed the optimizer to perform a range scan on the index to retrieve the results. Notice the comparative costs in the two cases; with a normal B-Tree index, the cost was 50, but with the function-based index in place, that dropped to a mere 2.

The next test we did was to see whether we could persuade the index to perform an index-only scan within the function-based index alone. The problem here is potential table records with a NULL value for the OBJECT_NAME column. NULL entries are not included within non-unique indexes, whether regular B-Tree or function-based. So if the query seems to imply that it wants to see entries with NULL values, the optimizer can't use the index, since any NULL values will not be included in the index.

The query we submitted in step 3 fell directly into this trap, because we had no WHERE clause attached to it. This implied that we wanted a return of all rows, which meant the index couldn't be used. Note that this was true for both $8i$ and $9i$.

In step 4, however, we see a subtle difference between $8i$ and $9i$ in this respect. We modified the table itself so that the OBJECT_NAME column was now declared to be NOT NULL:

```
alter table indextest modify object_name NOT NULL;
```

As we can see from the resulting query plan, this makes no difference. The query will still be answered by using a full table scan. However in the case of 9i, the optimizer realizes that if the table column is NOT NULL, then the index references all table rows, and now opts to perform a fast scan within the index to resolve the query.

> *If the index was concatenated, incidentally, **all** of the indexed columns would need to be declared NOT NULL before an index-only scan could be used in this way.*

What you should have learned from this is that, under most circumstances, function-based queries are an excellent performance-booster for queries on function-modified data (though remember to beware of invalidation of your own user-defined functions, since that brings all DML activity on the table to a grinding halt). We have also seen that in Oracle 9i it is much easier to avoid the potential pitfalls of queries which don't explicitly exclude nullable rows, than it was in 8i.

Bitmap Indexes

Let's consider the following table:

ID	MANAGER	DEPT	GENDER	Etc...
70	QS	10	M	...
10	RW	10	M	...
60	RW	30	F	...
20	QS	20	F	...
40	QS	10	M	...
30	RW	30	M	...
50	RW	20	F	...
...	...	...	...	...

Let's now think about what a regular B-Tree index would look like if it were created on, let's say, the GENDER column. Pretty stupid is the short answer, as you can see:

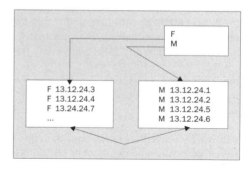

We have one branch block containing two possible values, and then a whole bunch of 'F' ('Female') leaf nodes, followed by a further bunch of 'M' ('Male') nodes. It's not exactly a highly selective index! Any selection for the column at all is likely to return around half the total number of rows. At this point you'll recall that Oracle is unlikely even to touch an index when the query is selecting for more than about 2 to 5% of the rows. An index like this, then, would be consuming space and slowing down DML activity for no reason whatsoever and is completely useless.

Data with very few distinct values like this is said to have a low **cardinality**. (Cardinality can be defined as 'the propensity to have different values'). The cardinality of gender is two, as is the cardinality of the MANAGER column in the table shown above. The DEPARTMENT column has a cardinality of three. The cardinality of the ID column, however, being a monotonically incrementing sequence number, is potentially equal to the number of rows in the table (every value is different from every other value).

The point here, then, is that low cardinality and B-Tree indexes are not a good mix (unless you are using low cardinality columns in concatenated, compressed B-Tree indexes, of course – see above).

Does this mean we are forever doomed to perform full table scans when selecting low cardinality columns? Fortunately not, since we can use **Bitmap Indexes** for such columns.

To create such an index, you use similar syntax as is the case for a regular index:

```
create bitmap index emp_mgr_bmp
on emp(manager);
```

Once issued, this command causes a DML lock to be placed on the entire table for the duration of our complete table scan (no DML activity at all is permitted for the duration of this scan). As we scan the table, we construct a 'truth table' for each value encountered in the MANAGER column. In our case, we discover two possible managers, and the truth table would look like this:

QS	RW
1	0
0	1
0	1
1	0
1	0
0	1
0	1

This truth table is then actually stored in a classic B-Tree format, with each leaf node being used to store the entire bitmap for one of the values discovered (if the bitmap doesn't fit within a single node, we just go ahead and acquire additional nodes in which to house the excess). In our case, the index would look like this:

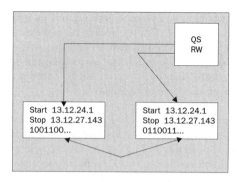

Notice that the 1s and 0s are pretty meaningless as pointers to rows in themselves, but that the inclusion in the key of a start and stop rowid allows us to deduce the physical address for a row in the table given the *relative* position of the various 1s and 0s.

If we repeat this process for the remaining two columns in our table, and build bitmap indexes for the DEPARTMENT and GENDER columns, we'd produce the following truth tables:

10	20	30	F	M
1	0	0	0	1
1	0	0	0	1
0	0	1	1	0
0	1	0	1	0
1	0	0	0	1
0	0	1	0	1
0	1	0	1	0

With all three indexes in place we are now in a position to swiftly answer (via the indexes), a query to show which females, managed by RW, work in department 30.

The optimizer, confronted with such a query, retrieves the FEMALE bitmap from the GENDER bitmap index, the RW bitmap from the MANAGER bitmap index, and the 30 bitmap from the DEPARTMENT bitmap index. It will then proceed to perform a Boolean AND operation on them:

F	0	0	1	1	0	0	1
RW	0	1	1	0	0	1	1
30	0	0	1	0	0	1	0
AND	0	0	1	0	0	0	0

Clearly, the only record that possesses all three attributes (and hence satisfies our query) is the third one. Since the indexes have already told us the start and stop rowid of the table rows, it is relatively easy to deduce the physical address of the one row that satisfies all the supplied criteria, and retrieve it from the table.

In this simple example, we see how the retrieval of three bitmap leaf nodes (that is, three I/Os) allows us to process seven different records for three different conditions in just one Boolean operation.

What's more, the operation wouldn't get any harder (or involve any more I/O) if the query had been for 'females managed by RW *or* in department 30'. We'd still retrieve the same three bitmaps, and just perform a Boolean "OR" operation in comparing the last two. That is in stark contrast to how B-Tree indexes work. A search for 'Frank *or* Mary', for example, would have to navigate down one side of the index to get the entry for Frank, jump back to the root node, and navigate down the other side to get Mary's entry, which clearly requires additional I/O. Bitmap indexes are therefore much more efficient for OR tests than regular B-Tree indexes.

To summarize then, bitmap indexes are compact objects (because storing a string of bits representing even several million rows is not going take up a lot of space) created on low cardinality columns; they make testing many rows for multiple conditions very fast, since they can perform "OR" operations as efficiently as AND operations.

Note that bitmap indexes only exist in the Enterprise Edition of Oracle. Of more significance however, is that their compactness means that a single leaf node contains entries referring to potentially hundreds of rows. If such a node ever needed to be locked for the purposes of making changes to it (such as would be needed if a new row were to be inserted into the underlying table) then any *other* transaction needing to make changes to the same set of index entries would have to wait until the original transaction finishes (commits or rolls back). Concurrent DML activity on the underlying table is therefore difficult to achieve when there's a bitmap index on that table. Since OLTP applications are forever doing concurrent DML, this all boils down to a simple rule: bitmap indexes and OLTP systems shouldn't be seen anywhere near each other.

On the other hand in the case of data warehouses bitmap indexes are ideal, since the amount of data is huge, the need to query for multiple low cardinality attributes is high, and concurrent DML is practically non-existent.

Let's be clear that it is the *concurrency* of the DML activity on a table that is the issue here, not the mere fact of DML activity in itself. In fact, since they were first introduced as a feature of version 7, Oracle has progressively made improvements to the way bitmap indexes get updated as the result of DML on the underlying table. Changes that need to be made to a bitmap index, as a result of a transaction, are only performed at the end of the statement, and are handled as a single, mammoth update to the entire bitmap. That sort of asynchronous approach is completely different from the synchronous updates that are made to B-Tree indexes (where the index maintenance takes place as each table row is modified). Despite that, though, it remains the case that even non-concurrent DML and bitmap indexes don't live particularly happily together. The implementation of the asynchronous update to the index means that they tend to fragment significantly as DML is performed.

Two final points about bitmap indexes need to be made. First, we've mentioned that they are only useful for low cardinality data, but low cardinality should not be thought of in absolute terms. It has been known, for example, for bitmap indexes to be built on Zip (or Post) Code data. In this case the cardinality is absolutely high (in the order of thousands, at least), but relatively low compared with the millions of possible households. It's the *relatively* low cardinality that makes bitmap indexes useful.

Secondly, placing a single bitmap index on a table is pretty pointless. Bitmap indexes derive their usefulness from being combined with many other bitmap indexes, since it's only when we start performing Boolean ANDs and ORs that they start producing results for us. In other words, only when many columns are indexed with them can you make any productive use of them. Ordinarily, and as we hope was made clear earlier, having multiple indexes all over a table would be a performance nightmare. But since bitmap indexes shouldn't get within a mile of a table subject to heavy DML in the first place, this is not going to be a concern.

Bitmap Join Indexes

Oracle 9*i* introduced a new feature whereby it is possible to create a bitmap index on a table, based on some value actually contained within a completely different table. Such an index, while structurally just another bitmap index, is known as a **bitmap join index**.

To see how they work, consider the two tables below:

SALES

ORDNO	CUSTCODE	VALUE
101	A	103.40
102	A	123.90
103	B	9832.90
104	D	546.75
105	C	798.34

CUSTOMERS

CUSTCODE	NAME	LOCATION
A	Acme Inc	New York
B	Bretts plc	London
C	Coals Pty	Sydney
D	D'Allain	Paris

Now suppose that you wish to know the total value of sales in New York. Sales values are available from the SALES table, but the location New York is only available from the CUSTOMERS table. That means you're going to have to query both tables, and join them via the CUSTCODE column that's common to both. You're likely to end up having to scan the entire CUSTOMERS table when you perform such a join, because the LOCATION column that you need is probably not indexed. Even if it *were* to be indexed, the cardinality of locations compared with the total number of customers is probably going to be low enough to persuade the optimizer that it's not worth using this index anyway. If your CUSTOMERS table contains a mere 4 rows, then a full scan of the table is nothing to worry about; if it contains thousands of rows, you're in trouble.

The new bitmap join index feature of 9*i*, however, allows us to create an index on the SALES table, based on the LOCATION column of the CUSTOMERS table. We'd issue the following command:

```
create bitmap index cust_location_bmj
on sales(customers.location)
from sales, customers
where sales.custcode=customers.custcode;
```

The resulting bitmap index would look like this:

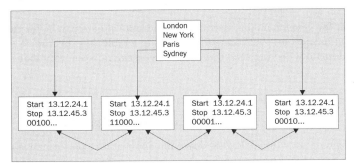

If we now issue our query like this:

```
select sum(sales.value)
from sales, customers
where sales.custcode=customers.custcode
and customers.location='New York';
```

...then the optimizer can resolve the query by retrieving the NEW YORK bitmap from the index. That bitmap reads '11000...', which tells us that it is the first two rows in the SALES table that relate to sales in New York. We can now retrieve these records in the usual manner by selecting from the SALES table.

Note that the query hasn't touched the CUSTOMERS table at all. It has simply made use of a bitmap index (which is likely to be small and compact, and so quick to read) which stores an *implied* value not actually held in the main table. In that sense, a bitmap join index is rather like a function-based index, since both are indexes on a 'virtual' value not actually stored in the table.

When you start to consider that a bitmap join index can be based on more than 2 tables, the advantages can be huge. Queries such as: "find the records in table A that satisfy criterion 1 in table B *and* criterion 2 in table C" can be performed without the need to touch tables B or C (or D, E, and so on!). For tables with multiple foreign keys, referencing large dimension tables, where queries frequently make reference to non-key attributes in those dimension tables, the performance improvements, when bitmap join indexes are built appropriately, will be significant.

On the other hand, you need to remember that bitmap indexes and DML of any sort don't sit too comfortably together, so this is strictly a data warehouse solution. In addition to this, with a bitmap join index in place, only one of the tables involved can be updated at any time. In other words, if another user is updating the SALES table, I will not be able to update the CUSTOMERS table until they've committed or rolled back. My transaction will simply be queued.

There's also one significant restriction, namely that a row in the main table cannot simultaneously appear to be TRUE (that is, identified with a '1') in more than one bitmap. In terms of our SALES and CUSTOMERS tables, in other words, we couldn't have two customers with the code "A", one in New York and one in Paris. The only way to ensure that this sort of duplication is avoided is to create a constraint, which declares the CUSTCODE column unique (or, rather more likely, the primary key of the CUSTOMERS table, which amounts to the same thing in practice). If you attempt to create a bitmap join index where such a constraint has *not* been created on the dimension table, you'll get an ORA-25954: missing primary key or unique constraint on dimension error message.

305

Summary

It's a common error for developers just starting out (and unfortunately even for those who have been around a bit) to slap indexes on everything that moves in a table, 'just in case' they might one day be used for a query. Hopefully, having read this chapter, you can now see why that's a poor way to develop applications, since:

❑ Every index you create slows down DML

❑ Every index you create consumes space and other database resources

❑ Indexes degrade over time, slowing down the application's performance as they do so

❑ To restore an index's efficiency, the administrator must rebuild them fairly frequently, and rebuilds themselves are expensive operations that impact upon performance and data availability

❑ If the optimizer thinks the index is unhelpful in resolving a query, it won't be used: and then you've consumed space, database resources, and slowed down application performance for no reason at all

Yet in the right circumstances, a carefully crafted index can speed up data retrieval enormously. To recap here:

❑ A good index will be built on columns which are frequently used as predicates for queries or table joins

❑ A B-Tree index will be thought useful by the optimizer if it is fairly selective (remember the 2-5% rule), or if the query can be answered by referencing the index alone

❑ If concatenated, the order of the columns should be considered carefully, with the order largely being determined by the nature of the queries that will be making use of it

❑ Every index should at least be considered for compression

❑ Function-based indexes can bring great performance and programming gains, but beware the user-defined function that gets invalidated, and the potential trouble with `Nulls` not being excluded from the requested result set

❑ Reverse keys can be productive, in case where 'buffer busy waits' on the index are really bad

❑ Effective use of bitmap indexes requires lots of them, and little or no DML

In short, there's more to indexes than meets the eye. You need to consider the design of your application carefully, in order to determine which would be good indexes to have. In making this decision you need to consider the different types of indexes that we have discussed, and whether you are able to take advantage of features such as compression, reversing, and skip-scanning. Above all else, you have to weigh their maintenance costs against their reporting and querying benefits.

Mastering SQL*Plus

As graphical user interface (GUI) operating systems such as Windows, Mac, and various flavors of UNIX using the X Windowing System have become more popular, so many database administrators, developers, and users alike have looked to Oracle to provide GUIs for the database, rather than the traditional command-line tools.

SQL*Plus, the tool that we are about to discuss in greater detail, is a command-line tool. There is no graphical user interface – no charts, no right-mouse clicks. Although Oracle might claim to have a GUI SQL*Plus tool on the Windows platform (as we saw in Chapter 2), it's no more than a command-line tool you can invoke without using a DOS window. Though the lack of a true GUI makes SQL*Plus appear old-fashioned to many users, it is a very useful tool, as we shall see throughout this chapter. While using a command-line tool may appear more labor intensive, it does mean that you must have a rigorous understanding of the tasks you wish to perform. This can only help in eliminating errors. Since GUI tools are still executing the SQL behind the scenes, there are times when they are unable to take advantage of the latest, greatest, or most intricate features offered in SQL, since the tool simply won't understand how to specify these options.

One further advantage of command-line versus GUI tool administration relates to stored scripts. Most people who use GUI tools to create a table, for instance, will simply use a 'Create Table Wizard' to define their columns, referential integrity, storage options, and so on. People using a command line will typically write a script to create the table. This script will be saved on their file system, and might even be stored in some source control system. What's nice about the script approach is that you can document your design decisions, such as why you have used a particular data type, within the script. You might store different versions of the same script to illustrate how your table has progressed over time. These options aren't typically built into GUI tools.

The primary difference between the GUI SQL*Plus, and the command-line SQL*Plus, is a menu to help set up your environment and configure the tool. This will become more important as you learn to personalize the tool for your use.

This brief discussion should help to illustrate the usefulness of the command-line mode of SQL*Plus, while showing you that it is useful for you to learn how to accomplish tasks in both the command-line and GUI modes. In this way if you find that writing the SQL out in command-line mode is tedious and long winded, you can switch to work with a GUI tool to speed things along.

In this chapter, we will look at:

- ❏ The advanced startup options available in SQL*Plus, including site and user profiles
- ❏ How to customize your SQL*Plus scripts and output
- ❏ The SQL*Plus HELP command
- ❏ The SQL*Plus buffer

Advanced Startup Options

Let's begin here by taking a look at the startup options available with the command-line SQL*Plus tool. If you open up a command window and enter the command `sqlplus`, you will see an explanation of all the options at your disposal when starting the tool:

```
$ sqlplus -

SQL*Plus: Release 9.0.1.0.0 - Production

Usage: SQLPLUS [ [<option>] [<logon>] [<start>] ]
where <option> ::= -H | -V | [ [-M <o>] [-R <n>] [-S] ]
      <logon>  ::= <username>[/<password>][@<connect_string>] | / | /NOLOG
      <start>  ::= @<filename>[.<ext>] [<parameter> ...]
        "-H" displays the SQL*Plus version banner and usage syntax
        "-V" displays the SQL*Plus version banner
        "-M <o>" uses HTML markup options <o>
        "-R <n>" uses restricted mode <n>
        "-S" uses silent mode
```

As you can see, there are a lot of options available. Let's take a quick look at each of them in turn:

- ❏ `-` or `-H`: Using the dash (or `-H`) as a startup option will tell SQL*Plus to output the version banner and the usage information.

- ❏ `-V`: This tells SQL*Plus to output the version banner, so you know what version of SQL*Plus you are running.

- ❏ `-M <o>`: This is for markup. When using SQL*Plus, you can ask the tool to output data in HTML markup instead of normal text. For some people, this may be an easy way to produce HTML tagged data from SQL*Plus.

- ❏ `-R <n>`: R stands for `RESTRICT`. By using this option, you can disable certain SQL*Plus commands for interacting with the operating system. There are three levels, getting more and more restrictive as the number increases. The restrictions disable the following commands:

  - ❏ Level 1: `EDIT`, `HOST`, and `!`
  - ❏ Level 2: `EDIT`, `HOST`, `!`, `SAVE`, `SPOOL`, `STORE`
  - ❏ Level 3: `EDIT`, `GET`, `HOST`, `!`, `SAVE`, `SPOOL`, `START`, `@`, `@@`, `STORE`

To illustrate these restrictions let's begin by opening up a SQL*Plus session and issuing the dir command:

```
$ sqlplus sdillon/sdillon

SQL*Plus: Release 9.0.1.0.0 - Production on Sun Jul 15 16:09:54 2001

(c) Copyright 2001 Oracle Corporation.  All rights reserved.

Connected to:
Oracle 8i Enterprise Edition Release 9.0.1.1.0 - Production
With the Partitioning option
JServer Release 9.0.1.0.0 - Production

SQL> host dir
total 4
-rw-r--r--    1 sdillon   dba            76 Jun 24 10:36 afiedt.buf

SQL> exit
Disconnected from Oracle 8i Enterprise Edition Release 9.0.1.1.0 - Production
With the Partitioning option
JServer Release 9.0.1.0.0 - Production
```

As you can see, since we did not specify any restrictive options, we were able to interact with the operating system at will. If however we open up another session and issue the following:

```
$ sqlplus -R 3 sdillon/sdillon

SQL*Plus: Release 9.0.1.0.0 - Production on Sun Jul 15 16:10:11 2001
(c) Copyright 2001 Oracle Corporation.  All rights reserved.

Connected to:
Oracle 8i Enterprise Edition Release 9.0.1.1.0 - Production
With the Partitioning option
JServer Release 9.0.1.0.0 - Production

SQL> host dir
SP2-0738: Restricted command "host" not available
```

We specify here a restriction level of 3 which, as the most restrictive level, means that we are unable to run the host dir command. (We'll discuss the HOST command later in this chapter.)

❑   -S: SILENT mode. This disables prompts and SQL*Plus-related information from being echoed to the screen. This is effective when running SQL*Plus from other commands, as you will see later in the chapter.

LOGON

If you need reminding of how to start up the SQL*Plus tool and connect to either a local or remote database, look back to Chapter 2. We will simply note here that Oracle also supports a form of **single-sign on** using operating system (OS) authentication. In other words, you log into the operating system, but pass no credentials to the database through SQL*Plus. With OS authentication, Oracle knows how to figure out what database user your operating system account maps to, and assumes that if you have been authenticated by the OS you have permission to use the database account as well.

311

> **Your database administrator can assist you in configuring OS authentication.**

If you start up SQL*Plus and do not specify a logon method, you will be prompted for a username and password. Note that the password is not echoed to the screen:

```
$ sqlplus

SQL*Plus: Release 9.0.1.0.0 - Production on Sun Jul 15 15:57:45 2001
(c) Copyright 2001 Oracle Corporation.  All rights reserved.

Enter user-name: sdillon
Enter password:

Connected to:
Oracle 9i Enterprise Edition Release 9.0.1.1.0 - Production
With the Partitioning option
JServer Release 9.0.1.0.0 - Production

SQL>
```

Setting Up Profiles

One of the most important, yet most commonly overlooked features of SQL*Plus, is **profiles**. A profile is simply a SQL file that contains SQL*Plus settings, SQL queries and/or PL/SQL blocks. It allows you to set up the SQL*Plus environment to meet your needs. For those of you familiar with UNIX, SQL*Plus profiles are like .profile for setting up your shell. There are two types of profiles, Site and User.

Site Profiles

A **site profile** is a SQL*Plus script created by the database administrator, which establishes default settings for users utilizing SQL*Plus on a database server.

This is done by creating a file named glogin.sql on the machine where SQL*Plus is executing. The file is located in the following location:

❏ Unix: $ORACLE_HOME/sqlplus/admin/glogin.sql

❏ Windows: %ORACLE_HOME%/sqlplus/admin/glogin.sql

SQL*Plus searches for the site profile when it starts up. If it finds the file in the location specified above, it runs the script just like it would any other script. This means that any user using SQL*Plus on a database server will have the environment settings and SQL*Plus commands from the site profile executed every time the tool is invoked. These are not mandatory settings, and can be overridden by the user. These should be thought of as settings that would be useful for users, not as settings imposing limitations or restrictions on the users.

An example of a `glogin.sql` site profile is as follows:

```
--
-- Copyright (c) Oracle Corporation 1988, 2000.  All Rights Reserved.
--
-- NAME
--   glogin.sql
--
-- DESCRIPTION
--   SQL*Plus global login startup file.
--
--   Add any sqlplus commands here that are to be executed when a user
--   starts SQL*Plus on your system
--
-- USAGE
--   This script is automatically run when SQL*Plus starts
--

-- For backward compatibility
SET PAGESIZE 14
SET SQLPLUSCOMPATIBILITY 8.1.7

-- Used by Trusted Oracle
COLUMN ROWLABEL FORMAT A15

-- Used for the SHOW ERRORS command
COLUMN LINE/COL FORMAT A8
COLUMN ERROR    FORMAT A65  WORD_WRAPPED

-- Used for the SHOW SGA command
COLUMN name_col_plus_show_sga FORMAT a24

-- Defaults for SHOW PARAMETERS
COLUMN name_col_plus_show_param FORMAT a36 HEADING NAME
COLUMN value_col_plus_show_param FORMAT a30 HEADING VALUE

-- Defaults for SET AUTOTRACE EXPLAIN report
COLUMN id_plus_exp FORMAT 990 HEADING i
COLUMN parent_id_plus_exp FORMAT 990 HEADING p
COLUMN plan_plus_exp FORMAT a60
COLUMN object_node_plus_exp FORMAT a8
COLUMN other_tag_plus_exp FORMAT a29
COLUMN other_plus_exp FORMAT a44
```

Keep in mind that, since these files are located on the server, SQL*Plus clients from other computers will not execute this script. Only SQL*Plus clients executing from the same machine as the `glogin.sql` file will use the global site profile.

User Profiles

The user profile is a personalized profile file, just like the site profile, but can be individualized for each user. Whenever SQL*Plus is started, the tool looks for a file called `login.sql`, which is the user profile. By default, SQL*Plus first looks in the current working directory for this file. If there is no `login.sql` in this directory, SQL*Plus looks in each directory in the SQLPATH environment variable, in order. As soon as SQL*Plus finds a file named `login.sql`, the file is executed and the search ends. If there is no file, then SQL*Plus just doesn't execute the file.

For more information about the SQLPATH *environment variable, see Chapter 19.*

Changes made to the SQL*Plus environment every time the tool is invoked should be considered for inclusion in the user profile. An example of a `login.sql` file is as follows:

```
set echo off
set describe depth all
define _editor=vi

set serveroutput on size 1000000

column object_name format a30
column segment_name format a30
column file_name format a40
column name format a30
column file_name format a30
column what format a30 word_wrapped
column tablespace_name format a30 word_wrapped
column default_tablespace format a30 word_wrapped
column temporary_tablespace format a30 word_wrapped

set trimspool on
set long 5000
set linesize 100
set pagesize 9999

column global_name new_value gname
set termout off
select lower(user) || '@' || global_name global_name
  from global_name;
set termout on
set sqlprompt '&gname> '
```

START

The START command gives the user the ability to run a script from a file or a Uniform Resource Identifier (URI). The syntax for the START option is as follows:

```
@ {uri | filename[.ext] } [arg...]
@@ filename [.ext] [arg...]
sta[rt] {uri | filename[.ext]} [arg...]
```

We should note here that the definition of Uniform Resource Identifiers, as issued by the Worldwide Web Consortium is as follows:

'Uniform Resource Identifiers (URIs) are short strings that identify resources in the web: documents, images, downloadable files, services, electronic mailboxes, and other resources. They make resources available under a variety of naming schemes and access methods such as HTTP, FTP, and Internet mail addressable in the same simple way.'

More information can be found regarding the naming and addressing of URIs and URLs on the W3C web site at http://www.w3.org/Addresssing/.

In short, URIs offer SQL*Plus the ability to run scripts that are stored on the web at a remote location. In SQL*Plus version 9.0.1, the HTTP, FTP, and GOPHER protocols are supported in URIs.

> **Note that this support is currently only available on Windows platforms.**

This feature means that you can put all of your most commonly used SQL scripts on a web server, and if you need them at somebody else's machine you can just call them from SQL*Plus. As an example, here is what you might do in a SQL*Plus session to find all those invalid objects in somebody's schema:

```
SQL> @http://slaphappy.us.oracle.com/sqlpath/invalid.sql

OBJECT_TYPE          OBJECT_NAME                      STATUS
-------------------- -------------------------------- ----------
FUNCTION             CONCAT_LIST                      INVALID

PACKAGE BODY         MANAGE_EMPS                      INVALID
                     MY_PKG                           INVALID
                     XMLTEST                          INVALID

VIEW                 EMP_VIEW                         INVALID
```

What we have done here is to connect to SLAPHAPPY.US.ORACLE.COM and opened up a file called invalid.sql.

Stored files can contain queries, or routines for executing common administrative tasks in the database stored somewhere on your file system. SQL*Plus can be invoked and passed a file to be run instantly, without having to manually write the script out. Alternatively developers can run reports using shell scripts that invoke SQL*Plus, and pass a SQL script to the tool so that the data will be spooled to the console for review. We'll talk more about running scripts later in the chapter, but let's look at a couple of examples of using the START syntax when invoking the SQL*Plus tool.

We can use SQL*Plus to investigate a table to find out the names, data types, lengths, and precisions of all the columns in the database. To do this we carry out the following steps:

- ❑ Start up SQL*Plus
- ❑ Authenticate ourselves to the database (starting up and authenticating can be done in a single step, as shown below)
- ❑ Enter the DESCRIBE (DESC) command
- ❑ Check the results
- ❑ Exit the tool

As a quick example, in this case we connect to the database as user SDILLON (password SDILLON), use the DESC command to look at the columns in the EMP table, and then exit the SQL*Plus session:

```
$ sqlplus sdillon/sdillon

SQL*Plus: Release 9.0.1.0.0 - Production on Mon Jul 16 20:51:47 2001
(c) Copyright 2001 Oracle Corporation.  All rights reserved.

Connected to:
Oracle 8i Enterprise Edition Release 9.0.1.1.0 - Production
With the Partitioning option
JServer Release 9.0.1.0.0 - Production

SQL> desc emp
 Name                                      Null?    Type
 ----------------------------------------- -------- ----------------------------
 EMPNO                                     NOT NULL NUMBER(4)
 ENAME                                              VARCHAR2(10)
 JOB                                                VARCHAR2(9)
 MGR                                                NUMBER(4)
 HIREDATE                                           DATE
 SAL                                                NUMBER(7,2)
 COMM                                               NUMBER(7,2)
 DEPTNO                                             NUMBER(2)

SQL> exit
Disconnected from Oracle 8i Enterprise Edition Release 9.0.1.1.0 - Production
With the Partitioning option
JServer Release 9.0.1.0.0 - Production
```

This isn't difficult, but it definitely falls in the 'tedious' category. Instead, let's write a shell script that does all the repetitive tasks for us, leaving us to only input information that is absolutely necessary. Save the following script to a file named `desc.sql`:

```
describe &1
exit
```

*In this script we execute the DESCRIBE command on &1. The & character is used in SQL*Plus to denote variables, and in this case &1 denotes the first parameter passed into the script from the command line. We could use the same methodology for multiple command-line parameters by using &2, &3 and so on.*

To be able to execute this script on the Windows platform, save the following to a file named `desc.cmd`:

```
sqlplus -S %1 @desc.sql %2
```

In the case of UNIX, save the following shell script to a file named `desc`:

```
sqlplus -S $1 @desc.sql $2
```

Note that UNIX users will also need to make the `desc` file executable, by issuing the command `chmod u+x desc`.

In this `desc` file we use the `-S` option, so that SQL*Plus banners and tool output is suppressed. The first parameter we pass in to `desc.sql` includes the username and password. The reason we only use one parameter for both of these values is to allow for cases where users are connecting to a remote database and wish to call the script as follows:

```
desc scott/tiger@somedatabase emp
```

The second parameter passed is the table that we want to describe.

We can invoke `desc` from the command prompt as follows:

```
$ desc scott/tiger emp
 Name                                      Null?    Type
 ----------------------------------------- -------- ----------------------------
 EMPNO                                     NOT NULL NUMBER(4)
 ENAME                                              VARCHAR2(10)
 JOB                                                VARCHAR2(9)
 MGR                                                NUMBER(4)
 HIREDATE                                           DATE
 SAL                                                NUMBER(7,2)
 COMM                                               NUMBER(7,2)
 DEPTNO                                             NUMBER(2)

$
```

And as you can see we successfully return the same results as in our first example.

Try It Out – Invoking SQL*Plus

1. Let's begin by writing the SQL script that we'll include in our shell script. Save the following script as `versions.sql`:

```
select banner
  from v$version
/
exit
```

2. Now we write the shell script and save it as `versions.cmd` (`versions` on UNIX):

```
sqlplus -S sdillon/sdillon @versions.sql
```

You'll have to provide your own username and password here in place of `sdillon/sdillon`.

3. We can now invoke the script from the command line as follows:

```
$ versions

BANNER
----------------------------------------------------------------
Oracle 9i Enterprise Edition Release 9.0.1.0.0 - Production
PL/SQL Release 9.0.1.0.0 - Production
CORE    9.0.1.0.0       Production
TNS for Solaris: Version 9.0.1.0.0 - Production
NLSRTL Version 9.0.1.0.0 - Production
```

How It Works

This is very similar to the previous example we looked at. In this case, the `versions` script calls SQL*Plus, connects to the database, uses the `-S` option to suppress SQL*Plus messages, and then calls the SQL script. The SQL script outputs version information for the various database components in the Oracle database. The major difference between this example and the previous one is that, in this case, we provide the username and password in the script, rather than relying on the user to enter that information on the command line.

The GUI SQL*Plus Startup Options

Even though the GUI SQL*Plus tool starts from an icon in Windows, the startup options are exactly the same as for the tool's command-line version. The only difference is that, in the GUI mode of SQL*Plus, there is a menu available for performing common tasks such as retrieving files into the SQL*Plus buffer, saving scripts to the file system, invoking a custom text editor, and so on. Many of the commands you commonly use from the command prompt in the command-line mode of SQL*Plus are mapped to menu items in the GUI. For example, in the command-line version, in order to set the width of a line in your query results you would use the command:

```
SET LINESIZE n
```

Whereas in the GUI, you would simply use the Options | Environment menu to open the Environment dialog where you can set all the SQL*Plus environment settings.

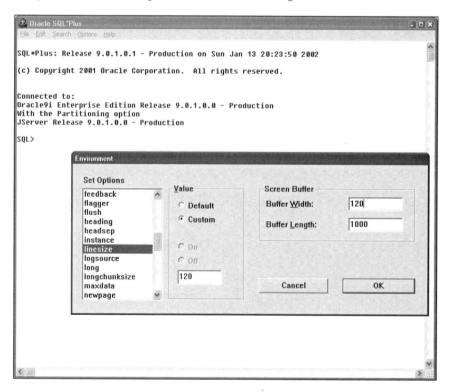

Earlier in the chapter, we discussed starting up SQL*Plus in restricted mode. If we start up the GUI SQL*Plus tool with the -R option, you will find that the menu items are restricted as well. Let's demonstrate this functionality by carrying out the following.

❑ Open a DOS window and type the command sqlplusw to open up SQL*Plus.

❑ Now connect to a database using the SCOTT user account.

❑ Run the SQL script we created earlier in the chapter, desc.sql, using the following command:

```
@desc.sql emp
```

If you didn't connect as SCOTT, you may have to use a different table name.

Now do the same thing except, in the first step, open SQL*Plus by typing sqlplusw -R 3. When you now run the SQL script, you should receive the following error:

```
SP2-0738: Restricted command "@ (START)" not available
```

This means, of course, that SQL*Plus was started in restricted mode and cannot run the START command.

The bottom line is that the two modes of SQL*Plus are equivalent when it comes to startup options. If you prefer to use GUI tools with menu options, your choice will most likely be the GUI version of SQL*Plus. As you learn how to make these calls from the command line, however, you might just rethink your position. Let's now look at using the tool in your day-to-day operations.

Using SQL*Plus Day-to-Day

Let's take a look at the features SQL*Plus offers to support you in your day-to-day interaction with the database. We are going to discuss how to customize the tool's output, and how to ask the tool for help. Not only that, but we'll also consider how to work with the all-powerful SQL*Plus buffer, and wrap up with some useful scripts that you can use in SQL*Plus to learn more about your Oracle database.

SQL*Plus Commands: A Primer

In SQL*Plus, there are commands available to the user that allow you to customize the behavior of the tool. Oracle has dedicated a large portion of its SQL*Plus documentation to explaining the intricate details of each command available in the tool. We won't regurgitate all of this here. Instead, we will simply review some of the most frequently used commands and how they can be used.

COLUMN

The basic COLUMN command was introduced in Chapter 2; so in this chapter we'll take a look at some of the other options available using this command.

Column Headings

By default, headings of columns in query results are the names of the column selected out of the database. When you use an expression to create a column in your query, the expression itself is used for the heading. Consider the following example:

```
SQL> connect scott/tiger
Connected.
SQL> select ename, sal, sal * 1.1
  2     from emp
  3  /

ENAME            SAL    SAL*1.1
---------- ---------- ----------
SMITH            800        880
ALLEN           1600       1760
WARD            1250       1375
...
```

Here we connect as user SCOTT, and query the EMP table. Notice that the heading of the second column in our output is SAL*1.1. In other words, SQL*Plus took the expression we used to create the output and used this as the column name. We can alias the column name in the query (in order to change the heading), by issuing the following:

```
SQL> select ename, sal, sal * 1.1 raise
  2     from emp
  3  /

ENAME            SAL      RAISE
---------- ---------- ----------
SMITH            800        880
...
```

As you can see our output now names the column RAISE. If we want to expand these column headings to make them more understandable to someone not familiar with the EMP table, we can use the COLUMN command as follows:

```
SQL> column ename    heading "Employee"
SQL> column sal      heading "Salary"
SQL> column raise    heading "Raise"
SQL> select ename, sal, sal * 1.1 raise
  2     from emp
  3  /

Employee     Salary      Raise
---------- ---------- ----------
SMITH            800        880
...
```

You should note here that column headings for character data types are truncated to the length of the database column. In other words, if our heading happened to be longer than the data type, the name will be cut off:

```
SQL> column ename   heading "Employee Name"
SQL> /

Employee N     Salary     Raise
---------- ---------- ----------
SMITH             800        880
```

To ensure that your column heading will be displayed in full you can format the column to be at least the width of the heading as follows:

```
SQL> column ename format a13 heading "Employee Name"
SQL> /

Employee Name     Salary     Raise
------------- --------- ---------
SMITH            800.00    880.00
```

As a reminder here the a represents the data type alphanumeric and 13 is the length of the string.

Number Formatting

There are a variety of options in the COLUMN command to configure formatting numeric columns. In the following table, we list the most commonly used characters in number column format masks, and how they affect the output of the number data in your query results:

Character	Example	Explanation
9	9999	Each character in the format mask represents a place holder for digits returned in the query results.
0	999.00	Each zero represents a digit that will consume a digit in the query results. This is commonly used for leading or trailing zeros.
$	$9999	This prefixes the number with a dollar sign.
S	S9999	Displays the sign type for the number. Useful for positive and negative numbers in query results.
PR	9999PR	Displays negative numbers in angle brackets.
D or .	99D99, 99.99	Places a decimal point in the place where the D or . is.
,	9,999	Places a comma in the place where the , is.

Table continued on following page

Character	Example	Explanation
RN or rn	RN	Displays roman numerals, in upper-or lowercase depending on the case of the format mask.
DATE	date	Assumes the number in a Julian date, and displays the resulting value in MM/DD/YY format.

Miscellaneous Column Options

The COLUMN command has a number of further optional commands which we'll list here for completeness:

- ❏ CLEAR. This clears the column settings for a particular column.
- ❏ CLEAR COLUMNS. This resets the column settings for all columns.
- ❏ JUSTIFY { LEFT | CENTER | RIGHT }. Using justify will cause the column heading to be justified according to the orientation you pass (left, center or right).
- ❏ NEW_VALUE <VARIABLE>. This assigns the value of the column to a variable identified by the name passed to the command.
- ❏ PRINT | NOPRINT. This controls whether or not the column and its heading are displayed in the query output.
- ❏ ON | OFF. This controls whether or not SQL*Plus uses the column attributes specified by the COLUMN command.

DESCRIBE

The DESCRIBE command returns descriptions of the objects stored in your database. For tables, views, and synonyms that point to tables (or views), DESCRIBE lists the columns and attributes for each column. DESCRIBE also outputs the specification of procedures, functions, and packages.

The syntax for the DESCRIBE command is:

```
DESC[RIBE] {[schema.]object[@connect_identifier]}
```

We have used the DESCRIBE command on several occasions in previous chapters, but we'll provide a quick reminder here. If you connect to the database as user SCOTT then you can run the DESCRIBE command in one of two ways:

```
SQL> describe emp
 Name                                      Null?    Type
 ---------------------------------------- -------- ----------------------
 EMPNO                                     NOT NULL NUMBER(4)
 ENAME                                              VARCHAR2(10)
 JOB                                               VARCHAR2(9)
 MGR                                                NUMBER(4)
 HIREDATE                                           DATE
 SAL                                                NUMBER(7,2)
```

```
    COMM                                        NUMBER(7,2)
    DEPTNO                                      NUMBER(2)

SQL> desc dept
    Name                              Null?    Type
    --------------------------------- -------- ---------------------------
    DEPTNO                            NOT NULL NUMBER(2)
    DNAME                                      VARCHAR2(14)
    LOC                                        VARCHAR2(13)
```

The DESCRIBE function can also be used to describe units of PL/SQL in the database. Procedures, functions, and packages are all capable of being described through SQL*Plus, and this is helpful when writing PL/SQL code that uses other program units.

In the following code sample, we use DESCRIBE on DBMS_OUTPUT, the database package used for sending output to the screen in SQL*Plus:

```
SQL> describe dbms_output
PROCEDURE DISABLE
PROCEDURE ENABLE
 Argument Name                     Type                    In/Out Default?
 --------------------------------- ----------------------- ------ --------
 BUFFER_SIZE                       NUMBER(38)              IN     DEFAULT
PROCEDURE GET_LINE
 Argument Name                     Type                    In/Out Default?
 --------------------------------- ----------------------- ------ --------
 LINE                              VARCHAR2                OUT
 STATUS                            NUMBER(38)              OUT
PROCEDURE GET_LINES
 Argument Name                     Type                    In/Out Default?
 --------------------------------- ----------------------- ------ --------
 LINES                             TABLE OF VARCHAR2(255)  OUT
 NUMLINES                          NUMBER(38)              IN/OUT
PROCEDURE NEW_LINE
PROCEDURE PUT
 Argument Name                     Type                    In/Out Default?
 --------------------------------- ----------------------- ------ --------
 A                                 VARCHAR2                IN
PROCEDURE PUT
 Argument Name                     Type                    In/Out Default?
 --------------------------------- ----------------------- ------ --------
 A                                 NUMBER                  IN
PROCEDURE PUT_LINE
 Argument Name                     Type                    In/Out Default?
 --------------------------------- ----------------------- ------ --------
 A                                 VARCHAR2                IN
PROCEDURE PUT_LINE
 Argument Name                     Type                    In/Out Default?
 --------------------------------- ----------------------- ------ --------
 A                                 NUMBER                  IN
```

This not only works on Oracle's supplied PL/SQL, but also on program units you write yourself.

We can also use the DESCRIBE command to view details of object types used in tables. We will see more on this inChapter 16.

323

PROMPT

The PROMPT command outputs a line of data to the screen. This is very helpful when trying to communicate information to a user in a stored script. For instance, if you were to write a query and want to provide a plain text description of the data the user is about to see, you might use the PROMPT command to do so. Store the following script in a file named usernames.sql:

```
prompt
prompt This is a list of users and their default
prompt tablespaces

select username, default_tablespace
  from dba_users
/
```

Now run the file in SQL*Plus using the START or @ command.

You must run this as a user who has access to the DBA_USERS view.

```
SQL> @usernames.sql

This is a list of users and their default
tablespaces

USERNAME                         DEFAULT_TABLESPACE
------------------------------   ------------------------------
SYS                              SYSTEM
SYSTEM                           SYSTEM
DBSNMP                           SYSTEM
  .                                .
  .                                .
  .                                .
WKSYS                            DRSYS
ORDPLUGINS                       SYSTEM
ORDSYS                           SYSTEM

29 rows selected.
```

ACCEPT

The ACCEPT command is used when interacting with a user running a script which inputs data to be assigned to a variable. ACCEPT allows the author to specify the variable data type, a format for the data being input, and a default value in the case where the user executing the script specifies no value. HIDE can also be used to hide the value being entered into SQL*Plus, which is helpful when specifying data such as passwords. The syntax for the ACCEPT command is as follows:

```
ACC[EPT] variable [NUM[BER] | CHAR | DATE] [FOR[MAT] format]
    [DEF[AULT] default] [PROMPT text | NOPR[OMPT]] [HIDE]
```

Data type, format, default, PROMPT, and HIDE are all optional settings when writing the ACCEPT command. If a data type and/or format is specified, however, SQL*Plus will only accept a valid value according to the data type and/or format mask. This reassures the author of the script that the data being provided will work in the context of the variable used. Consider the following script:

```
prompt C R E A T E   N E W   E M P L O Y E E   R E C O R D
prompt
prompt Enter the employee's information:
prompt
accept l_ename char format a10 prompt 'Last name: '
accept l_empno number format '9999' prompt 'Employee #: '
accept l_sal number format '99999.99' prompt 'Salary [1000]: ' default '1000.00'
accept l_comm number format '99999.99' prompt 'Commission % [0]: ' default '0'
accept l_hired date format 'mm/dd/yyyy' prompt 'Hire date (mm/dd/yyyy): '

prompt List of available jobs:
select distinct job
  from emp
 order by job
/
accept l_job char format a9 prompt 'Job: '

prompt List of managers and employee numbers:
select empno, ename
  from emp
 order by ename
/
accept l_mgr number format '9999' prompt 'Manager''s Employee #: '

prompt List of department numbers and names:
select deptno, dname
  from dept
 order by deptno
/
accept l_dept number format '99' prompt 'Department #: '

insert into emp (empno, ename, job, mgr, hiredate, sal, comm, deptno)
values (&l_empno, '&l_ename', '&l_job', &l_mgr,
        to_date('&l_hired','mm/dd/yyyy'), &l_sal, &l_comm, &l_dept)
/
```

This script is used for accepting all the data necessary to insert a record in the EMP table. If you execute the script, you will see how the ACCEPT command works. If you enter data that is invalid (in other words, characters in a number field or an invalid date format), SQL*Plus will let you know by displaying an error code and message:

```
SQL> @new_emp.sql
C R E A T E   N E W   E M P L O Y E E   R E C O R D

Enter the employee's information:

Last name: Ellison
Employee #: 1
```

325

```
Salary [1000]: 0
Commission % [0]: 99
Hire date (mm/dd/yyyy): 05-MAY-1973
SP2-0685: The date "05-MAY-1973" is invalid or format mismatched "mm/dd/yyyy"
Hire date (mm/dd/yyyy):
```

During the execution of the new_emp.sql script, we entered an invalid date format string. SQL*Plus immediately recognized the error, output error text indicating the problem, and then asked for the hire date value again.

SHOW

The SHOW command is helpful when trying to find out more information about a number of different things, including:

❏   SQL*Plus environment settings

❏   Errors in PL/SQL code or database objects being compiled by Oracle

❏   init.ora parameters

SQL*Plus Environment Settings

When using SQL*Plus, the SQL*Plus commands are used to configure the environment. For instance, you can use the SPOOL command to send all output to a file as well as the screen. SQL*Plus does not have a status bar or any other type of visual indicator that this is happening, however. This can be good or bad, depending on how you look at it. There is no need to clutter your screen real estate with every setting in SQL*Plus, but equally those settings need to be accessible. Using the SHOW command, you can quickly and easily see how the SQL*Plus environment is currently set up. Consider the case where you may or may not be spooling data to a file. In order to quickly see how SPOOL is configured we can use the following command:

```
SQL> show spool
```

This will return one of two results:

```
spool OFF
```

or

```
spool ON
```

This begs the question, what are *all* of the SQL*Plus environment settings available for the SHOW command? This question is easily answered using the SHOW ALL command:

```
SQL> show all
appinfo is OFF and set to "SQL*Plus"
arraysize 15
autocommit OFF
autoprint OFF
```

```
autorecovery OFF
autotrace OFF
blockterminator "." (hex 2e)
    .
    .
    .
timing OFF
trimout ON
trimspool ON
ttitle OFF and is the first few characters of the next SELECT statement
underline "-" (hex 2d)
USER is "SCOTT"
verify ON
wrap : lines will be wrapped
```

Errors in Compiling PL/SQL or Database Objects

When using SQL*Plus to write PL/SQL, or to create certain database objects, SQL*Plus will not display any detailed error messages by default. They must be asked for explicitly using the SHOW ERRORS command.

The SHOW ERRORS command can be applied to the following object types:

- ❑ Procedures

- ❑ Functions

- ❑ Packages

- ❑ Package Bodies

- ❑ Triggers

- ❑ Views

- ❑ Types

- ❑ Type Bodies

- ❑ Dimensions

- ❑ Java Source

- ❑ Java Classes

The following code illustrates compiling a PL/SQL procedure that fails:

```
SQL> create or replace procedure show_emp( p_empno in number )
  2  is
  3  begin
  4    for c1 in (select *
  5                 from emp
  6                where empno = p_empno) loop
  7      dbms_output.put_line('Name: ' || c1.ename);
  8      dbms_output.put_line('Job: ' || c1.job);
  9      dbms_output.put_line('Salary: ' || c1.sal);
 10      dbms_output.put_line('Commission: ' || c1.comm);
 11    end;
 12  end show_emp;
 13  /

Warning: Procedure created with compilation errors.
```

Compiling this code into Oracle results in a compilation error. The error message is not very informative however, and would benefit greatly from the use of the SHOW ERRORS command. The default behavior of SHOW ERRORS is to show the errors for the most recently compiled object in the currently executing SQL*Plus session. Therefore, if you execute the SHOW ERRORS command before attempting to compile any other code into Oracle, the errors for PROCEDURE SHOW_EMP will be displayed:

```
SQL> show errors
Errors for PROCEDURE SHOW_EMP:

LINE/COL ERROR
-------- -----------------------------------------------------------------
11/6     PLS-00103: Encountered the symbol ";" when expecting one of the
         following:
         loop
         The symbol "loop" was substituted for ";" to continue.
```

If the procedural code is in a script with other statements, however, there are two ways in which you can see the errors when SQL*Plus displays the none-too-helpful error message:

```
Warning: Procedure created with compilation errors
```

❑ You can place the SHOW ERRORS message after each CREATE statement.

❑ You can wait until the entire script executes, and use the SHOW ERRORS PROCEDURE SHOW_EMP syntax to see the errors for particular objects that may have failed in your script.

Including the SHOW ERRORS command after each statement is easiest. If there are no errors SQL*Plus simply outputs the following text.

```
SQL> create or replace procedure show_emp( p_empno in number )
  2  is
  3  begin
  4    for c1 in (select *
  5                  from emp
  6                 where empno = p_empno) loop
  7      dbms_output.put_line('Name: ' || c1.ename);
  8      dbms_output.put_line('Job: ' || c1.job);
  9      dbms_output.put_line('Salary: ' || c1.sal);
 10      dbms_output.put_line('Commission: ' || c1.comm);
 11    end loop;  -- changed from end; to end loop; to fix error
 12  end show_emp;
 13  /

Procedure created.

SQL> show errors
No errors.
```

init.ora Parameters

Database administrators in Oracle need to have quick access to the init.ora parameters for their databases. Using SQL*Plus, it is easy to quickly see the values of the current init.ora parameters in the database. Simply use the SHOW PARAMETERS command, as follows:

Note that in this example you must be connected as a user who has SELECT privilege on the dictionary view V_$PARAMETER.

```
SQL> show parameters block

NAME                                 TYPE        VALUE
------------------------------------ ----------- --------------------------
db_block_buffers                     integer     0
db_block_checking                    boolean     FALSE
db_block_checksum                    boolean     TRUE
db_block_size                        integer     8192
db_file_multiblock_read_count        integer     8
```

By using the SHOW PARAMETERS BLOCK command, SQL*Plus performs a query behind the scenes and displays the results on the screen:

```
SQL> -- show parameters db_ is like running the following query:
SQL> select name name_col_plus_show_param,
  2         decode(type,1,'boolean',2,'string',
  3                      3,'integer',4,'file',
  4                      6,'big integer','unknown') type,
  5         value value_col_plus_show_param
  6    from v$parameter
  7   where upper(name) like upper('%block%')
  8   order by name_col_plus_show_param,rownum
  9  /

NAME                                 TYPE        VALUE
------------------------------------ ----------- --------------------------
db_block_buffers                     integer     0
db_block_checking                    boolean     FALSE
db_block_checksum                    boolean     TRUE
db_block_size                        integer     8192
db_file_multiblock_read_count        integer     8

6 rows selected.
```

VARIABLE

Using the VARIABLE command creates a bind variable which can be used in PL/SQL code during your SQL*Plus session. Bind variables can be one of many types, including:

❏ NUMBER

❏ CHAR

❏ CHAR(n[CHAR|BYTE])

❏ NCHAR

❏ NCHAR(n)

❏ VARCHAR2(n[CHAR|BYTE])

- ❏ NVARCHAR2(n)

- ❏ CLOB

- ❏ NCLOB

- ❏ REFCURSOR

> **Note that DATE is specifically excluded from this list.**

Bind variables provide an effective way to store state across SQL statements and PL/SQL blocks in an ongoing SQL*Plus session. Variables declared within the scope of a PL/SQL block live only for the duration of that PL/SQL block's execution. Therefore, local PL/SQL variables assigned in one PL/SQL block cannot be referenced in another PL/SQL block. (There is more about this in the next chapter.) Bind variables offer a solution to this.

Here is a quick example of using bind variables in a SQL*Plus session. Consider the following script named `deptemps.sql`:

```
connect hr/hr

set define '&'
set verify off

column department_name format a30 heading "Department Names"

select department_name
  from departments
 order by 1
/

variable did number
accept dname prompt 'Enter the department name to report on: '

begin
  select department_id into :did
    from departments
   where upper(department_name) like upper('%&dname%')
     and rownum = 1;
end;
/

column department_id   format 99999 heading "Id"
column department_name format a15   heading "Name" word_wrapped
column manager_name    format a15   heading "Manager"
column location        format a20   heading "Location"

ttitle left 'Department Information' skip 2

select d.department_id, d.department_name,
       e.last_name manager_name,
       l.city || ' ' || l.state_province location
  from departments d, employees e, locations l
 where d.department_id = :did
   and d.location_id = l.location_id(+)
```

```
      and d.manager_id = e.employee_id(+)
/

clear break
ttitle off

column job_title     format a20 heading "Job"
column first_name    format a12 heading "First Name"
column last_name     format a12 heading "Last Name"
column phone_number  format a20 heading "Phone Number"
break on job_title
ttitle left 'Department Employees' skip 2;

select j.job_title, e.first_name, e.last_name, e.phone_number
  from employees e, jobs j
 where e.department_id = :did
   and e.job_id = j.job_id
/

ttitle off
```

Executing this script allows us to report departmental information and an employee list for the department specified. The bind variable DID stores the name of the department we wish to look at, and is then used in a query in order to return the departmental information and employee list we require. In SQL*Plus, the execution of the script looks like this:

```
SQL> @deptemps

Department Names
-------------------------------
Accounting
Administration
Benefits
Construction
Contracting
Control And Credit
Corporate Tax
Executive
Finance
Government Sales
Human Resources
IT
IT Helpdesk
IT Support
Manufacturing
Marketing
NOC
Operations
Payroll
Public Relations
Purchasing
Recruiting
Retail Sales
Sales
Shareholder Services
Shipping
Treasury

27 rows selected.
```

```
Enter the department name to report on: Finance

PL/SQL procedure successfully completed.

Department Information

    Id Name            Manager          Location
------ --------------- ---------------- --------------------
   100 Finance         Greenberg        Seattle Washington


no rows selected


Department Employees

Job                     First Name    Last Name     Phone Number
--------------------    -----------   ------------  --------------------
Finance Manager         Nancy         Greenberg     515.124.4569
Accountant              Luis          Popp          515.124.4567
                        Jose Manuel   Urman         515.124.4469
                        Ismael        Sciarra       515.124.4369
                        John          Chen          515.124.4269
                        Daniel        Faviet        515.124.4169


6 rows selected.
```

In this case we chose to look at the FINANCE department. Note that there is no error checking in this script, so entering invalid department names will result in an error.

This is only a brief overview of the most commonly used SQL*Plus commands. There are many other commands available for your use, and in the next section we are going to learn how to use SQL*Plus to find out more about them.

Built-In SQL*Plus HELP

Ultimately, SQL*Plus commands are only helpful if you know how to use them. There are a lot of them, and each command has a number of options. It can be difficult, if not impossible, to remember every option of every command. Help is at hand, however. SQL*Plus has a built-in Help system that will put all the information you need to know about the SQL*Plus commands at your immediate disposal.

Built-in HELP

The command HELP in SQL*Plus is your friend. Try typing the following command at the SQL prompt:

```
SQL> help index

Enter Help [topic] for help.

 @              COPY         PAUSE        SHUTDOWN
 @@             DEFINE       PRINT        SPOOL
 /              DEL          PROMPT       SQLPLUS
 ACCEPT         DESCRIBE     QUIT         START
```

```
APPEND        DISCONNECT   RECOVER               STARTUP
ARCHIVE LOG   EDIT         REMARK                STORE
ATTRIBUTE     EXECUTE      REPFOOTER             TIMING
BREAK         EXIT         REPHEADER             TTITLE
BTITLE        GET          RESERVED WORDS (SQL)  UNDEFINE
CHANGE        HELP         RESERVED WORDS (PL/SQL) VARIABLE
CLEAR         HOST         RUN                   WHENEVER OSERROR
COLUMN        INPUT        SAVE                  WHENEVER SQLERROR
COMPUTE       LIST         SET
CONNECT       PASSWORD     SHOW
```

If you receive the error:

```
SQL> help index
SP2-0171: HELP not accessible.
```

This means the Help system is not installed in your database. To rectify this read the section below entitled *Installing HELP*.

The HELP index is the list of words available for use in the Help system. Simply type help [topic] to review the notes for that particular word:

```
SQL> help column

COLUMN
------

Specifies display attributes for a given column, such as:
     - column heading text
     - column heading alignment
     - NUMBER data format
     - column data wrapping

Also lists the current display attributes for a single column
or all columns.

COL[UMN] [{column | expr} [option...] ]

where option is one of the following clauses:
     ALI[AS] alias
     CLE[AR]
     ENTMAP {ON|OFF}
     FOLD_A[FTER]
     FOLD_B[EFORE]
     FOR[MAT] format
     HEA[DING] text
     JUS[TIFY] {L[EFT] | C[ENTER] | C[ENTRE] | R[IGHT]}
     LIKE {expr | alias}
     NEWL[INE]
     NEW_V[ALUE] variable
     NOPRI[NT] | PRI[NT]
     NUL[L] text
     OLD_V[ALUE] variable
     ON|OFF
     WRA[PPED] | WOR[D_WRAPPED] | TRU[NCATED]
```

The SQL*Plus Help system typically displays the same attributes about each command. Here is what you can expect to see:

❑ The title of the command

❑ A text description of the command

❑ Any shortcuts for the command (for example, COL instead of COLUMN)

❑ All the mandatory and optional arguments that may be passed to the command

Installing HELP

Help is offered by the SQL*Plus tool, but it relies on the connected database being configured for the Help system. By default, it is installed on the database.

You see, SQL*Plus Help is nothing more than a table called HELP owned by SYSTEM. When you issue a HELP command at the SQL prompt, SQL*Plus issues a query to the database behind the scenes and displays the results to you in the tool. For instance, if you issue HELP INDEX, it is the equivalent of SQL*Plus issuing the following query:

```
select *
  from system.help
 where topic = upper('index');
```

If the database does not have the HELP table installed in the SYSTEM schema, when SQL*Plus issues the query and gets an error indicating the table does not exist, the tool in turn gives you the error:

```
SP2-0171: HELP not accessible
```

If your database does not have HELP installed, it is trivial to set it up. Go to the ORACLE_HOME\sqlplus\admin\help directory. In this directory, you will find all the files you need to set up SQL*Plus help. Connect to your database, and run the following command:

```
> sqlplus system/<system_password> @hlpbld.sql helpus.sql
```

The hlpbld.sql file creates the HELP table and executes a script to load the Help text into the table. The script it calls is the first parameter passed to it, in this case the helpus.sql filename. The US in this case stands for the language used in the help text. For other language distributions this file may be different.

This command creates the HELP table, and inserts all the records necessary for the default HELP topics. If you have a database administrator who manages the database, ask them to install the SQL*Plus Help system.

Entering a New HELP Topic

Since the data that makes up the Help system is stored in a table, you can modify the records in the table and change the results of your HELP commands. In Oracle 9i, a number of the SQL*Plus commands from previous versions are now obsolete. These obsolete commands (and their alternatives) are listed in the SQL*Plus Help entries, and explained further in *Appendix F* of the *SQL*Plus Users Guide and Reference* (from Oracle version 8.1.5 onwards).

In this example we will take the detailed explanation given in the *SQL*Plus Users Guide and Reference* and enter this data into our SQL*Plus Help index. This will aid users who require SQL*Plus Help in order to help configure their SQL*Plus environment.

Try It Out – Customizing SQL*Plus Help

1. Connect to your Oracle database as the SYSTEM user and execute the following SQL statements:

```
delete
  from help
 where topic = 'OBSOLETE'
/

insert into help values ('OBSOLETE', 1, NULL);
insert into help values ('OBSOLETE', 2, ' OBSOLETE');
insert into help values ('OBSOLETE', 3, ' --------');
insert into help values ('OBSOLETE', 4, NULL);
insert into help values ('OBSOLETE', 5, ' As new releases of SQL*Plus are
released, commands change and ');
insert into help values ('OBSOLETE', 6, ' sometimes made OBSOLETE. This table
provides a list of obsolete');
insert into help values ('OBSOLETE', 7, ' commands and alternative commands.');
insert into help values ('OBSOLETE', 8, NULL);
insert into help values ('OBSOLETE', 9, ' For explanations of alternative
commands, please reference ');
insert into help values ('OBSOLETE',10, ' Appendix F of the SQL*Plus Users Guide
and Reference.');
insert into help values ('OBSOLETE',11, NULL);
insert into help values ('OBSOLETE',12, ' BTITLE(old form)      BTITLE');
insert into help values ('OBSOLETE',13, ' COLUMN DEFAULT        COLUMN CLEAR');
insert into help values ('OBSOLETE',14, ' DOCUMENT              REMARK');
insert into help values ('OBSOLETE',15, ' NEWPAGE               SET NEWPAGE');
insert into help values ('OBSOLETE',16, ' SET BUFFER            EDIT');
insert into help values ('OBSOLETE',17, ' SET CLOSECURSOR       none');
insert into help values ('OBSOLETE',18, ' SET DOCUMENT          none');
insert into help values ('OBSOLETE',19, ' SET MAXDATA           none');
insert into help values ('OBSOLETE',20, ' SET SCAN              SET DEFINE');
insert into help values ('OBSOLETE',21, ' SET SPACE             SET COLSEP');
insert into help values ('OBSOLETE',22, ' SET TRUNCATE          SET WRAP');
insert into help values ('OBSOLETE',23, ' SHOW LABEL            none');
insert into help values ('OBSOLETE',24, ' TTITLE(old form)      TTITLE');
insert into help values ('OBSOLETE',25, NULL);
```

2. Now you can run the following HELP command:

```
SQL> help obsolete

OBSOLETE
--------

As new releases of SQL*Plus are released, commands change and
sometimes made OBSOLETE. This table provides a list of obsolete
commands and alternative commands.

For explanations of alternative commands, please reference
Appendix F of the SQL*Plus Users Guide and Reference.
```

```
     BTITLE(old form)      BTITLE
     COLUMN DEFAULT        COLUMN CLEAR
     DOCUMENT              REMARK
     NEWPAGE               SET NEWPAGE
     SET BUFFER            EDIT
     SET CLOSECURSOR       none
     SET DOCUMENT          none
     SET MAXDATA           none
     SET SCAN              SET DEFINE
     SET SPACE             SET COLSEP
     SET TRUNCATE          SET WRAP
     SHOW LABEL            none
     TTITLE(old form)      TTITLE
```

How It Works

We begin by deleting the existing records in the HELP table, and then repopulate it with the values we want to include in the HELP listing. Now, when we look for help on OBSOLETE, we get the list of obsolete commands, prefaced with a pointer to further information on these topics.

Working with the SQL*Plus Buffer

SQL*Plus stores your recently run command(s) in what is known as a **buffer**, or a **stored memory area**. By storing these commands in the buffer, the user is able to recall, edit, and run the last SQL statement that they entered.

There are two ways to modify a command stored in the buffer. You can pass the contents of the buffer to an editor, such as Notepad or vi, or you can use the SQL*Plus default editor. These certainly are not exclusive; you can edit an entire script in Notepad, save the script, and subsequently use SQL*Plus commands to modify pieces of your buffer as well. It's just handy to know you are not restricted to one or the other. First, we'll discuss modifying the contents of the buffer outside of SQL*Plus, using an editor of your choice.

Setting Your Editor

To utilize either vi or Notepad as your editor in the SQL*Plus tool, you use the DEFINE command as follows:

```
SQL> define _editor=vi
SQL> -- or perhaps --
SQL> define _editor=notepad
```

Note that you can include the DEFINE _EDITOR setting within your user profile, as you will see if you look back to the login.sql file shown in the *User Profiles* section above. This avoids manually setting it on each occasion that you start up SQL*Plus. Once this is set, you can use the EDIT command to modify the most recent SQL statement or PL/SQL block entered into SQL*Plus. Using the EDIT command with no contents in the buffer results in the following error:

```
SQL> clear buffer -- this command clears the contents of the SQL*Plus buffer
buffer cleared
SQL> edit
SP2-0107: Nothing to save error.
```

Ordinarily, when you invoke the EDIT command, SQL*Plus takes the last SQL statement or PL/SQL block entered into SQL*Plus and writes it to a file in your current working directory named afiedt.buf.

> *Note that some operating systems have different SQL*Plus edit file names. These can be changed using the SET EDITFILE command.*

The contents of the file can be modified appropriately. At the time the editing tool is exited, the contents of the buffer file are automatically read back into the SQL*Plus buffer, and can be run using the / character or RUN command.

Don't be confused by the difference between the SQL*Plus buffer and the edit file. The buffer is a place in memory that you can modify using SQL*Plus commands. The edit file (afiedt.buf) is only used when you invoke the EDIT command.

There are a few SQL*Plus commands that are helpful when using an external editor:

❑   ED[IT] [filename[.ext]] – The EDIT command, as discussed above, is used for invoking an application and passing the contents of the SQL*Plus buffer to it. By omitting the filename parameter, the contents of the afiedt.buf file will be passed to the editor.

❑   SAV[E] filename[.ext] [CREATE|REPLACE|APPEND] – The SAVE command is used for saving the contents of the SQL*Plus buffer to a file. filename indicates the name of the file that will store the contents. There is one optional parameter which specifies the context of the SAVE command.

  ❑   CREATE – Used to make a new file. This will fail if the file already exists. This is useful when you only want to save the file if the filename does not already exist.

  ❑   REPLACE – Used to either create a new file filename, or overwrite the file filename if it already exists. This is useful when the file already exists but you don't mind overwriting it.

  ❑   APPEND – This option is used when the contents of the SQL*Plus buffer should be added to the end of filename. This is useful when saving SQL statements or PL/SQL blocks to a file, but the contents of the file should be kept.

Editing with SQL*Plus

It is not always necessary to use an external editor to edit the commands in the SQL*Plus buffer. In the case of simple changes, you might choose to use the SQL*Plus tool and its built-in editing commands to modify the contents of the buffer. Here is a brief description of the commands available:

❑   L[IST] [terms] – This command lists the contents of the SQL*Plus buffer. The line marked with an asterisk (*) is the **current** line in the SQL*Plus buffer. You can optionally pass **terms** to indicate the part of the SQL*Plus buffer you'd like to list. Omitting the terms from the LIST command results in all lines being displayed. Terms are as follows:

  ❑   n – Passing a single line number will show you that line only.

  ❑   * – Using the asterisk character lists the current line.

- ❑   LAST – Passing the word LAST lists the last line in the buffer.

- ❑   n n2 – Passing two line numbers, separated by a space, will show the range between the two lines, inclusive. In this case, n and/or n2 can be replaced with the asterisk (*) and the reserved word LAST. This effectively shows ranges using the current line of the buffer and/or the last line of the buffer.

- ❑   A[PPEND] text – Append is used when you wish to add text to the end of a line in the SQL*Plus buffer. The text will be added to the current line.

- ❑   C[HANGE] separator OLD [separator NEW] – The CHANGE command is a very flexible way to perform expression substitution. Simply specify the text to be modified as the OLD parameter, and the text to replace it as the NEW parameter. The separator character can be any non-alphanumeric character (such as ., , , *, ^, !, and so on). Just be careful that the value used is not a part of the substitution values OLD or NEW. Additionally, the NEW value and its separator character can be omitted, which basically means substitute the old value with nothing, or delete it.

- ❑   DEL[ETE] [terms] – Use the DELETE command to remove lines from your SQL statement. You can pass terms to the DELETE command as we discussed for the LIST command, above.

- ❑   I[NPUT] text – The INPUT command is used to input lines into the SQL*Plus buffer *after* the current line. The contents of the new line will be the text passed to the INPUT command.

Try It Out – Using the SQL*Plus Editor

1. The first thing we'll do here is enter an invalid query into SQL*Plus:

```
SQL> select department_id, department_name
  2      from departmens;
   from departmens
         *
ERROR at line 2:
ORA-00942: table or view does not exist.
```

2. Now, using the LIST command, we'll examine the statement to find the error. Executing LIST with no parameters shows all the contents of the SQL*Plus buffer:

```
SQL> list
  1  select department_id, department_name
  2*    from departmens
```

SQL*Plus outputs the contents of the buffer, and on line two you can see an asterisk after the line number 2. This tells us that line 2 is the current line. Using CHANGE or INPUT commands at this point will affect this line.

3. We can see that the table name DEPARTMENS is misspelt. We will now use the CHANGE command to fix the mistake.

```
SQL> change.mens.ments
  2*   from departments
```

As you can see SQL*Plus will output the results of your change commands as soon as you execute them.

4. Now let's add a WHERE clause and an ORDER BY clause to our statement using the INPUT command:

```
SQL> list
  1  select department_id, department_name
  2*   from departments

SQL> input  where department_id between 10 and 40
SQL> list
  1  select department_id, department_name
  2    from departments
  3* where department_id between 10 and 40
SQL> input  order by 2
SQL> list
  1  select department_id, department_name
  2    from departments
  3  where department_id between 10 and 40
  4* order by 2
```

5. Finally, using the SQL*Plus execution character, /, you can execute the contents of the SQL*Plus buffer:

```
SQL> /

DEPARTMENT_ID DEPARTMENT_NAME
------------- ---------------------------
           10 Administration
           40 Human Resources
           20 Marketing
           30 Purchasing
```

Scripts

Instead of writing commonly used SQL statements and PL/SQL blocks each time you use them, you can save them in files known as **scripts**. These scripts are specifically designed for performing a wide variety of tasks *over and over again*. Using stored copies of queries, you save a great deal of time by not having to retype those statements next time they are to be run. Not only that, but you also help to prevent things such as syntax errors or mathematical errors in cases where you are using arithmetic on data in the database.

In this section, we are going to take a look at best practices for storing commonly executed SQL and PL/SQL in scripts, to help you save time and realize a great increase in productivity when using SQL*Plus.

START, @, @@

We have seen previously how to call a script by using the START or @ command. To recap here the START and @ command basically work in the same way. You pass a filename as the first parameter, and any parameters expected by the script you are running can be passed in (and after) position 2 of the command line arguments.

When calling a script, you must qualify the directory name if the file is not in your current working directory. For example:

```
SQL> @C:\oracle\sqlstuff\fudual.sql 10, 'Beginning Oracle 9i Programming, from
Wrox Press'
```

In this case the values 10 and Beginning Oracle 9i Programming, from Wrox Press were passed to the file fudual.sql as command line parameters. The file fudual.sql is located in the C:\oracle\sqlstuff directory.

Note however that you can use absolute or relative path naming.

This presents a problem, however. One nice feature of using scripts in SQL*Plus is that the statements in the file are read directly into the tool. This means that you can mix SQL*Plus commands, SQL, and PL/SQL, (as well as running other scripts) in the same script. This becomes increasingly difficult when putting together complex scripts, such as installation scripts that must execute many other files. With what we have learned thus far, we have a problem if we need to run scripts that are in directories other than the current working directory. Consider the following two files:

The first is called depts.sql:

```
accept did prompt 'Enter Department Id: ' default 10

select *
  from departments
 where department_id = &did
/

@emps.sql &did
```

The second is called emps.sql:

```
select first_name, last_name, job_id
  from employees
 where department_id = &1
/
```

Now, if these two scripts are in the current working directory, calling depts.sql from SQL*Plus will result in the proper results:

```
SQL> @depts
Enter Department Id: 100

DEPARTMENT_ID DEPARTMENT_NAME                       MANAGER_ID LOCATION_ID
------------- ------------------------------------- ---------- -----------
          100 Finance                                      108        1700
```

```
FIRST_NAME              LAST_NAME                    JOB_ID
--------------------    -------------------------    ----------
Nancy                   Greenberg                    FI_MGR
Daniel                  Faviet                       FI_ACCOUNT
John                    Chen                         FI_ACCOUNT
Ismael                  Sciarra                      FI_ACCOUNT
Jose Manuel             Urman                        FI_ACCOUNT
Luis                    Popp                         FI_ACCOUNT

6 rows selected.
```

In this case the scripts are stored in a common directory on the file system. What we'd prefer to do however is place them in appropriate directories, depending on the purpose of the script. Let's move these two scripts into the C:\oracle\samples directory. That's where we'll keep all custom queries and scripts to operate against the HR schema and SCOTT schema objects.

After we have moved the files, trying to run the script will result in an error:

```
SQL> @c:\oracle\samples\depts.sql
Enter Department Id: 10

DEPARTMENT_ID DEPARTMENT_NAME                      MANAGER_ID LOCATION_ID
------------- ------------------------------------ ---------- -----------
           10 Administration                              200        1700

SP2-0310: unable to open file "emps.sql"
```

This is because on line 8 of depts.sql, the script instructs SQL*Plus to execute the emps.sql file in the current working directory. Since we are currently in the c:\oracle\working directory, it does not see the emps.sql file that we moved into the c:\oracle\samples directory. This is where the @@ command comes in useful.

When you call scripts that subsequently call other scripts, you can use the @@ command to tell SQL*Plus to look for files relative to the file it is currently running. So if we issue the following command:

```
SQL> @@c:\oracle\samples\depts.sql
```

SQL*Plus looks in the c:\oracle\samples directory for the depts.sql. When it encounters line 8, the @emps.sql command, it now looks for that file in the same directory.

HOST Commands

In SQL*Plus, you can execute a command on the operating system from within the tool. This is helpful in a variety of situations, so let's take a look at some examples of how to use HOST commands.

Using the HOST (or ! on Unix, and $ on VMS) command with no parameters will result in SQL*Plus placing you in the operating system shell. On Windows 2000, using HOST places you in a DOS shell:

```
SQL> host
Microsoft Windows 2000 [Version 5.00.2195]
(C) Copyright 1985-2000 Microsoft Corp.

C:\Oracle\samples>
```

Passing an argument to the HOST command will pass the argument on to the operating system for execution, and you will remain in SQL*Plus. For example:

```
SQL> host dir
 Volume in drive C has no label.
 Volume Serial Number is 94D4-9EC3

 Directory of C:\Oracle\samples

08/12/2001  07:03p    <DIR>          .
08/12/2001  07:03p    <DIR>          ..
08/12/2001  11:55a                30 afiedt.buf
08/12/2001  03:03p               134 depts.sql
08/12/2001  03:04p                86 emps.sql
08/12/2001  02:31p                64 fmdual.sql
               4 File(s)           314 bytes
               2 Dir(s)  2,302,210,048 bytes free
```

Summary

In this chapter, we have reviewed SQL*Plus and what it has to offer as a database access tool. SQL*Plus is not the prettiest tool to look at, and has no options for generating graphs or charts, but it does offer a high degree of efficiency when writing SQL statements, editing SQL and PL/SQL, and performing database administration tasks such as starting up and shutting down the database.

This chapter has focussed primarily on what useful commands exist within SQL*Plus to aid you in automating repetitive tasks (using scripts), and customizing the output from your interaction with the database. We have seen that there are a wide range of commands available within SQL*Plus, and that the HELP utility is invaluable in providing a reminder of what they are.

©2000 by Lauren Ruth Wiener (http://www.verbing.cor

PL/SQL

This chapter is an introduction to the **programmatic language of the database, PL/SQL**. We've already learned how to interact with the database using SQL, but it leaves something to be desired when building enterprise applications. PL/SQL is a natural procedural extension to SQL in Oracle, and you will find that the tight integration between them makes coding PL/SQL-based applications both intuitive and powerful. Most programming languages that interact with a database must establish a form of connection, giving the programmer a clear sense of separation between the language and the database. In PL/SQL, this doesn't happen. You can include SQL statements in your code any time you need to do so, without ever having to establish a connection to the database, because PL/SQL is executed within the Oracle itself.

In this chapter, we'll look at the basics of PL/SQL programming. In particular:

- ❑ What it means to develop anonymous (or unnamed) PL/SQL blocks
- ❑ How to declare variables and constants in your PL/SQL
- ❑ The differences between SQL and PL/SQL data types
- ❑ How to use cursors to integrate SQL with PL/SQL in your code
- ❑ How to use built-in functionality to perform commonly executed routines
- ❑ Which loop constructs and conditional statements to use in your code to manipulate the process flow of your PL/SQL code
- ❑ How to trap and handle potential errors in your code

An Overview

PL/SQL is a structured programming language loosely based on another programming language, Ada. As we already mentioned, SQL statements alone won't let you build an application; you need to use some other language like C or Java that connects to the database to do the application's work. PL/SQL is an Oracle-exclusive product, written and enhanced by Oracle Corporation as new releases of the database are introduced to the industry.

PL/SQL will not run in any database other than Oracle. Generally, you write PL/SQL code and store it in the form of procedures, functions, packages (all covered in the next chapter) or triggers (covered in Chapter 15). These are stored in the database and reused by any users of the database that have the appropriate privileges. In Chapter 5, we talked about pooling SQL statements in the shared pool for reuse by many users. PL/SQL is no different, as it is stored once in the shared pool for access by many users.

PL/SQL is case insensitive, so although you will see mixed case in our examples throughout the chapter you should select a coding standard that suits you and your development team. In my routines, I use l_ and g_ as prefixes in my local and global variable/constant names, respectively. Almost all my code is in lowercase, although many people like to use uppercase for Oracle reserved words to help code readability. Whatever works best for you and your team will prevail, just make sure everybody agrees on one standard to ensure the best use of the shared pool.

Now that we've talked about it, let's start writing some PL/SQL!

> *Reminder: all the code for the examples in this chapter is available for you to download from http://www.apress.com/.*

Block-Based Development

PL/SQL code is built in a modular fashion, using **blocks**. They are the building blocks for larger programs and applications. Each one is a logical grouping of variables, executable code, and error-handling code.

Let's take a look at a sample block, and then break it down into its three sections:

```
SQL> set serveroutput on
SQL> declare
  2    l_text varchar2(100);
  3  begin
  4    l_text := 'Hello, World!';
  5    dbms_output.put_line(l_text);
  6  exception
  7    when others then
  8      dbms_output.put_line('We encountered an exception!');
  9      raise;
 10  end;
 11  /
Hello, World!

PL/SQL procedure successfully completed.
```

The first section in this block is called the **declaration**. The declaration is the portion of the block where all **variables** and **constants** are defined. A variable is defined by the user, to hold a specified value of a particular data type. This value can be changed as necessary by the routine when it runs. A constant holds a value but it cannot be changed, either by the definer or the system during compilation. We'll look more closely at both later in the chapter.

The declaration block in our code sample above was made up of the following two lines:

```
SQL> declare
  2    l_text varchar2(100);
```

DECLARE is a not only a reserved word in Oracle, but also marks the beginning of a new block. For a list of reserved words in SQL and PL/SQL, you can use this command in SQL*Plus:

```
SQL> help reserved words
```

We see in line 2 that we are defining a variable named L_TEXT of type VARCHAR2, and a length of 100.

BEGIN is the next reserved word we find, and it denotes the beginning of the **executable section** in our block. This is where the work is typically performed. This is *not* to say code logic cannot be performed in the other sections of a block, because it can be performed in any of them. Most of the time the work is carried out between the BEGIN and EXCEPTION, or END reserved words, however.

The executable section of our block looks like this:

```
  3  begin
  4    l_text := 'Hello, World!';
  5    dbms_output.put_line(l_text);
```

Lines 4 and 5 assign the value Hello, World! to the variable L_TEXT and uses PUT_LINE procedure of the DBMS_OUTPUT PL/SQL package to display the contents of the variable to the standard output (in the case of SQL*Plus, the output spools out directly to the screen).

> *You can read more about procedures and packages in Chapter 11. More on Oracle-supplied packages such as DBMS_OUTPUT can be found in Appendix B.*

The last section is the **exception block**, also commonly known as the **error-handling section,** of the PL/SQL block. As the name suggests, this is where we are going to check for and handle errors we might run across in the declarative or executable sections of our block. If errors are encountered, Oracle will stop processing those sections of the block and 'jump to' this exception block. This is a form of fallback mechanism. It's a way for you to proactively trap errors that might occur in your code.

```
  6  exception
  7    when others then
  8      dbms_output.put_line('We encountered an exception!');
  9      raise;
```

Later in this chapter, you will learn more about exceptions and how to handle them. For now, it is enough to understand that an exception is the method through which PL/SQL informs us of errors.

And finally, the end of the block is denoted by the END keyword. When this keyword is encountered, PL/SQL knows it can 'forget about' local variable declarations and this block's processing is complete.

Now you know what one is, it's about time you wrote a block for yourself.

Try It Out – The PL/SQL Block

Type the following code (which will print some output to your screen) into SQL*Plus:

```
set serveroutput on
declare
  l_number number := 1;
begin
  l_number := 1 + 1;
  dbms_output.put_line( '1 + 1 = ' || to_char( l_number ) || '!' );
exception
  when others then
    dbms_output.put_line( 'We encountered an exception!' );
end;
/
```

The execute character / at the end of your block tells SQL*Plus to pass the block of code you have just entered to the database when you hit the *enter* key after it. The / character is the default **block terminator** in SQL*Plus. When SQL*Plus encounters the block terminator, it takes the contents of the buffer (in this case, our PL/SQL block) and passes them to the PL\SQL engine in Oracle.

The output from our block is:

```
1 + 1 = 2!

PL/SQL procedure successfully completed.
```

How It Works

The first thing of interest in our block is the declaration section where we have declared a variable (L-NUMBER) of type NUMBER. We then enter the executable portion of the block where we assign a value to our variable, and send some data to DBMS_OUTPUT.PUT_LINE.

In our call to DBMS_OUTPUT.PUT_LINE, we send the value:

```
'1 + 1 = ' || to_char( l_number ) || '!'
```

The first portion of this string literal is 1 + 1 = , and then we see two pipe characters (|) side by side. (||). Next, we pass variable L_NUMBER to the function TO_CHAR(), and lastly there are two more pipe characters with ! at the end of the line.

Two pipe characters side by side is Oracle's **concatenate operator**. TO_CHAR() is an Oracle built-in function that turns a numeric data type into a character data type. So, armed with this information, we see this takes the character literal '1 + 1 =', concatenated with the character representation of variable L_NUMBER, concatenated with character literal !, and ends up with '1 + 1 = 2!' returned to the screen. For more information on supplied SQL functions like TO_CHAR(), see Appendix A.

Block Nesting

In addition to the standard PL/SQL block, you can also create blocks that contain additional blocks, or sub-blocks. A block can contain another block in the executable and exception sections. In the sample below, you'll see comments indicating the beginning and end of the first and second blocks (a comment is anything after -- on a line). For instance:

```
SQL> set serveroutput on
SQL> declare                        -- begin first block
  2     l_text varchar2(20);
  3  begin
  4     l_text := 'First Block';
  5     dbms_output.put_line(l_text);
  6     declare                      -- begin second block
  7        l_more_text varchar2(20);
  8     begin
  9        l_more_text := 'Second Block';
 10        dbms_output.put_line(l_more_text);
 11     end;                         -- end second block
 12  end;                            -- end first block
 13  /
First Block
Second Block

PL/SQL procedure successfully completed.
```

Block nesting is useful for quite a few reasons and, as you become more proficient with PL/SQL, you'll see why it is not only useful but mandatory. Nesting blocks inside one another will become more important for us once we start learning about variable scope and exception handling later in the chapter.

Declarations

As we have seen, you can declare variables and constants to use throughout your PL/SQL code. You may choose to assign values to variables; constants must be **initialized**, that is, have a value assigned when they are declared. These variables and constants can then be used throughout a particular PL/SQL code block, or block nested within it.

Variables and Constants

Each of your variables and constants must be defined in the declaration section of a block. For each variable you must specify the name and a data type, so that you can specify values in the executable section:

```
SQL> declare
  2     l_number_variable number;
  3  begin
  4     l_number_variable := 50;
  5  end;
```

```
 6  /

PL/SQL procedure successfully completed.
```

Optionally, you can assign a value to the variable on the same line of code in the declaration section (known as **initializing** the variable). We could do this by combining lines 2 and 4 from the previous example:

```
SQL> declare
  2    l_number_variable number := 50;
  3  begin
  4    -- NULL; means do nothing. The executable section
  5    -- needs at least one line of code to be valid.
  6    null;
  7  end;
  8  /

PL/SQL procedure successfully completed.
```

Constants are declared in much the same way as variables, but there are a couple of differences to be aware of. As the name suggests, constants cannot be changed. In order to assign a value, you must initialize the constant at the time of declaration, and you must specify the reserved word CONSTANT to the left of the data type. For instance:

```
SQL> declare
  2    l_number_constant  constant number := 50;
  3  begin
  4    null;
  5  end;
  6  /

PL/SQL procedure successfully completed.
```

If we try to declare a constant without initializing it in the declare block, we will receive an error:

```
SQL> declare
  2    l_number_constant constant number;
  3  begin
  4    null;
  5  end;
  6  /
  l_number_constant  constant number;
  *
l_number_constant  constant number;
*
ERROR at line 2:
ORA-06550: line 2, column 1:
PLS-00322: declaration of a constant 'L_NUMBER_CONSTANT' must contain an
initialization assignment
ORA-06550: line 2, column 20:
PL/SQL: Item ignored
```

This error is officially known as an exception, but it is a different type of exception from those we can specify ourselves in exception blocks. This exception is caught during the compilation of the block, and cannot be recovered from. An exception section in this block would not catch the error (see the later section on *Exceptions Raised in Declarations* for more on this).

If we try to assign a value to our constant in the executable portion of our block we will raise a different exception:

```
SQL> declare
  2     l_number_constant constant number := 50;
  3  begin
  4     l_number_constant := 51;
  5  end;
  6  /
l_number_constant := 51;
*
ERROR at line 4:
ORA-06550: line 4, column 1:
PLS-00363: expression 'L_NUMBER_CONSTANT' cannot be used as an assignment
target
ORA-06550: line 4, column 1:
PL/SQL: Statement ignored
```

Understanding the error messages you might cause as a result of mistakes in your code is useful. As you come to recognize the exceptions you are seeing, you will find them easier to fix. In this case, perhaps you need to make the constant a variable so the value can change in the executable portion of your block.

Assigning Values To Variables and Constants

There are numerous ways to assign values to variables (in the declarative and executable sections of blocks) and constants (in the declarative section). The first, and most common, is to use the PL/SQL **assignment operator** : =. The syntax for using this is typically as follows:

```
variable datatype := expression;   -- in the declarative section of a block
variable := expression;            -- in the executable section of a block
```

You may also use the reserved word DEFAULT, as an alternative, when initializing a variable or constant in the declarative section of a block, for example:

```
variable datatype default expression;
```

In general, using DEFAULT is a more readable way of saying "the normal value for this variable should be some value". Although using DEFAULT on a constant declaration works, it may seem somewhat misleading, giving the impression that the value can be overridden or changed. Since this is not the case, I always use the assignment operator for constant initialization.

Here's an example of using the DEFAULT keyword to assign a value to a variable:

```
SQL> declare
  2      l_days_in_week    constant number := 7;
  3      l_weeks_in_month number default 4;
  4  begin
  5      l_weeks_in_month := 5;
  6  end;
  7  /

PL/SQL procedure successfully completed.
```

So in this case, the standard value of days in a week would be 7, but the number of weeks in a month varies. With a variable, if I don't initialize it in the declare section of the block, it is implicitly assigned to NULL (we'll look at what this means a little later in the chapter).

In addition to the reserved word DEFAULT, you may also choose to use the NOT NULL operator on your variables. Using NOT NULL means a value may change, but it can never be assigned to NULL. Attempting to assign a variable declared with the NOT NULL attribute to NULL, will result in an exception being thrown:

```
SQL> declare
  2      l_number number not null := 1;
  3      l_another_number number;
  4  begin
  5      l_number := 2;
  6      l_number := l_another_number;
  7  end;
  8  /
declare
*
ERROR at line 1:
ORA-06502: PL/SQL: numeric or value error
ORA-06512: at line 6
```

On line 2, we declare a variable named L_NUMBER with the NOT NULL attribute. We assign a value of 1 in the declaration, to prevent the automatic assignment of the value NULL, which would cause our PL/SQL to fail. In line 3, we specify another variable, L_ANOTHER_NUMBER, but do not give it a value, thereby automatically assigning it the value NULL. In line 5 we show assigning L_NUMBER to other values is perfectly valid. In line 6, however, we attempt to assign L_NUMBER to whatever the value of L_ANOTHER_NUMBER is. This fails because L_ANOTHER_NUMBER is NULL, as we can see in the error message it produces.

Visibility and Scope

When declaring variables and constants, there are rules governing the scope and visibility of your declarations. **Scope** is the block(s) in which you can reference an identifier, such as the name of a variable. An identifier is **visible** only in those areas of your blocks where you can reference it with an unqualified name (that is, without prefixing the identifier with the name of the block it is defined in).

In single blocks, identifiers defined in the declaration section are in scope and visible throughout.

In nested blocks, identifiers defined in the parent block are in scope and visible throughout both the parent block itself and in any nested (or child) blocks. Identifiers defined in the declaration of the child block are only in scope and visible within the child block itself. The following example illustrates this:

```
SQL> declare
  2    l_parent_number number;
  3  begin
  4    -- l_parent_number is visible and in scope
  5    l_parent_number := 1;
  6
  7    declare
  8      l_child_number number := 2;
  9    begin
 10      -- l_child_number is visible and in scope
 11      dbms_output.put_line('parent + child = ' ||
 12                           to_char(l_parent_number + l_child_number));
 13    end;
 14
 15    -- l_child_number is now not visible nor in scope:
 16    l_child_number := 2;
 17  end;
 18  /
  child_number := 2;
  *
ERROR at line 16:
ORA-06550: line 16, column 3:
PLS-00201: identifier 'CHILD_NUMBER' must be declared
ORA-06550: line 16, column 3:
PL/SQL: Statement ignored
```

Here we declare a variable, L_PARENT_NUMBER, in the parent block. This is then in scope and visible throughout the executable section of the parent block. It is also visible inside the executable block of the child block, because that child block is within the scope of the parent block. We can see this because we are able to use the value of L_PARENT_NUMBER on line 12, within the child block. We then declare a variable in the declaration section of the child block, L_CHILD_NUMBER, which is only in the scope of that block, and therefore not visible in the parent block. Again we use this successfully on line 12 but we are unsuccessful when we attempt to use it on line 16, within the parent block.

There is also an important limitation on visibility when dealing with nested blocks. You might reasonably think that by declaring a variable in the declarative section of a block, no matter the order in which the declarations are placed, we can reference that variable any place in the declarative section of the same block. This will not work, however, if you try to reference a variable before you declare it because PL/SQL requires an identifier be declared before we use it in our code. Here's an example to show what happens when we try it:

```
SQL> declare
  2    l_number number := l_another_number;
  3    l_another_number number := 10;
  4  begin
  5    null;
```

```
 6  end;
 7  /
 l_number number := l_another_number;
                    *
ERROR at line 2:
ORA-06550: line 2, column 22:
PLS-00320: the declaration of the type of this expression is incomplete or
malformed
ORA-06550: line 2, column 12:
PL/SQL: Item ignored
```

Visibility is very important when it comes to referencing identifiers in your code. The PL/SQL interpreter/compiler has no idea there is a variable L_ANOTHER_NUMBER in the code block above, until it is declared. Therefore, line 2 is invalid and will not compile. An easy solution would be to reverse the position of the two variable declarations in order to provide visibility of L_ANOTHER_NUMBER to L_NUMBER.

Defining the Indefinable: NULL Explained

In Oracle, NULL is a reserved word meaning *missing, unknown, or inapplicable value*. Basically, it is something that is undefined. In many of the examples you have read thus far, we have used NULL without ever explicitly assigning anything to NULL. This is because NULL is normally assigned to variables that are not assigned a value when they are declared. In the following code sample, all four variable declarations produce exactly the same result: a VARCHAR2 variable which evaluates to a NULL value:

```
SQL> declare
 2     l_value1 varchar2(100);
 3     l_value2 varchar2(100) := '';
 4     l_value3 varchar2(100) := null;
 5     l_value4 varchar2(100) default null;
 6  begin
 7     null;
 8  end;
 9  /

PL/SQL procedure successfully completed.
```

Not all variables are assigned to NULL when they are declared, however. CHAR variables assigned to ' ' are not assigned to NULL. This is also true in PL/SQL records or when declaring instances of PL/SQL tables. We will look into these constructs later, but for now just know variables that are not initialized are assigned to be NULL most of the time.

Not only can we define variables to the value of NULL, but we can also use the reserved word NULL in the executable portion of any PL/SQL block to act as a **stub**, or **placeholder** for something to be coded at a later time, as we saw earlier. Some programmers refer to this as a **NO-OP** (no operation). This is effective when you have no executable code to execute in your PL/SQL block, as not defining any executable code in your PL/SQL block will cause a compiler error to occur:

```
SQL> declare
  2     l_text varchar2(100);
  3  begin
  4  end;
  5  /
end;
*
ERROR at line 4:
ORA-06550: line 4, column 1:
PLS-00103: Encountered the symbol "END" when expecting one of the following:
begin case declare exit for goto if loop mod null pragma
raise return select update while with <an identifier>
<a double-quoted delimited-identifier> <a bind variable> <<
close current delete fetch lock insert open rollback
savepoint set sql execute commit forall merge
<a single-quoted SQL string> pipe
```

By specifying NULL as a stub in your executable section, you can "stub" the block to be used at a later time. This will become more useful when you are writing stored procedural code such as procedures, functions and packages and you need to temporarily "stub" your code, with the intent to come back later to fill it in.

Finally, we should note that NULL values in PL/SQL are evaluated in exactly the same way as they are in SQL (we discussed this in Chapter 2, in the *Understanding NULLs* section). A variable assigned NULL does not equal another variable assigned NULL. A variable assigned a NULL value is not different from another variable assigned NULL.

Using %TYPE and %ROWTYPE

A way for you to declare a variable without having to specify a particular data type is using %TYPE and %ROWTYPE. These two attributes allow us to specify a variable and have that variable's data type be defined by a table/view column or a PL/SQL package variable.

%TYPE and %ROWTYPE are used for different reasons. %TYPE is used when you are declaring an individual variable, *not* a record (don't worry, records are explained in detail later). %ROWTYPE is used when you are declaring a record variable that will represent an entire row of a table, view or cursor (again, cursors are explained later). For instance:

```
SQL> connect hr/hr

SQL> describe departments
 Name                                      Null?    Type
 ----------------------------------------- -------- ----------------------------
 DEPARTMENT_ID                             NOT NULL number(4)
 DEPARTMENT_NAME                           NOT NULL varchar2(30)
 MANAGER_ID                                         number(6)
 LOCATION_ID                                        number(4)
```

```
SQL> declare
  2     l_dept          departments%rowtype;
  3     l_another_dept departments.department_name%type;
  4  begin
  5     l_dept.department_id := 1000;
  6     l_dept.department_name := 'Graphic Art';
  7
  8     insert into departments(
  9       department_id, department_name)
 10     values(
 11       l_dept.department_id, l_dept.department_name);
 12     l_dept.department_id := 1001;
 13     l_another_dept := 'Web Design/User Interface';
 14
 15     insert into departments(
 16       department_id, department_name)
 17     values(
 18       l_dept.department_id, l_another_dept);
 19
 20     dbms_output.put_line('The departments created were ' ||
 21       l_dept.department_name || ' and ' || l_another_dept);
 22  end;
 23  /

PL/SQL procedure successfully completed.
```

Using %TYPE and %ROWTYPE is helpful for two key reasons. First, as you can see, you do not need to know the data type at the time of declaration. Additionally, if the data type of the variable you are referencing changes, your %TYPE or %ROWTYPE variable changes at run-time without you having to rewrite your variable declaration.

This gives you a working knowledge of using %TYPE and %ROWTYPE. They become increasingly important when you start writing procedures, functions, and packages, and as such, you will see more of the %TYPE and %ROWTYPE attributes in the next chapter.

PL/SQL Data Types

PL/SQL can use the same data types as SQL, with some differences in boundaries. SQL data types in general have been discussed earlier in the book, so there's no need to go over them again here. Instead, I'd like to outline the differences between SQL and PL/SQL data types that you should be aware of. There are also a few PL/SQL specific data types and we'll take a look at those too.

Character Data Types

First a table comparing the SQL ranges and the PL/SQL ranges for character-related data types:

Data type	SQL boundaries	PL/SQL boundaries	Other information
CHAR	1 .. 2000	1 .. 32767	
LONG	1 .. 2GB	1 .. 32760	
LONG RAW	1 .. 2GB	1 .. 32760	
RAW	1 .. 2000	1 .. 32767	
VARCHAR2	1 .. 4000	1 .. 32767	Also known as VARCHAR and STRING (*).
NCHAR	1 .. 2000 (bytes)	1 .. 32767/3 (UTF8) or 1 .. 32767/2 (AL16UTF16)	In Oracle 9*i*, the two database National languages are either UTF8 or AL16UTF16.
NVARCHAR2	1 .. 4000 (bytes)	1 .. 32767/3 (UTF8) or 1 .. 32767/2 (AL16UTF16)	In Oracle 9*i*, the two database National languages are either UTF8 or AL16UTF16.

* – Even though the two VARCHAR2 subtypes (VARCHAR, STRING) can be used interchangeably with VARCHAR2, Oracle recommends using VARCHAR2 because at some point in the future VARCHAR might become a separate data type with a different implementation.

Numeric Data Types

As for numeric-related data types in PL/SQL, there are two to cover that we did not discuss earlier in the book (most notably in Chapter 3). These are PLS_INTEGER and BINARY_INTEGER.

PLS_INTEGER

PLS_INTEGER is a data type created for use in PL/SQL only. You cannot store PLS_INTEGERs in database columns. PLS_INTEGERs are signed integers between $-2^31 ... 2^31$. This gives us a maximum range of -2147483648 ... 2147483648. PLS_INTEGERs have a smaller range than NUMBER variables, and therefore take up less memory. Additionally, PLS_INTEGERs use CPU arithmetic and are therefore faster than NUMBERS and BINARY_INTEGERs, which use database library APIs to perform arithmetic.

BINARY_INTEGER

BINARY_INTEGERs are similar to PLS_INTEGERs in than they require less memory than NUMBER variables but are generally slower than PLS_INTEGERs. BINARY_INTEGERs are the base data type for the following subtypes:

Subtype	Definition
NATURAL	Variables that are non-negative numbers.
NATURALN	NATURAL variables that may not be NULL.
POSITIVE	Variables that are non-negative numbers greater than zero.
POSITIVEN	POSITIVE variables that may not be NULL.
SIGNTYPE	Variables of this type may be -1, 0, or 1. They are useful in programming tri-state logic in your PL/SQL applications.

BOOLEAN

There is a BOOLEAN data type available in PL/SQL that is unavailable in SQL as a database column. BOOLEAN variables may be TRUE, FALSE, or NULL, and can be used as a single parameter to conditional statements. For an example of this data type in action, see *Try It Out - ITE Function* in Chapter 11.

PL/SQL Collections

It is necessary to provide a mechanism for declaring collections of objects in one form or another in most programming languages. The same is true in PL/SQL, which has a variety of collection types for this purpose. They are:

❑ **Records**. These store one-to-many scalar attributes in a single collection called a record.

❑ **PL/SQL Tables**. These are 'tables' used in your PL/SQL code that live only for the life of your application. They are very similar to arrays in other languages, and cannot be stored in database tables.

❑ **VARRAYs**. This is a collection that can be stored in a table column. varrays are fixed-size collections usually used for storing small collections.

❑ **NESTED TABLES**. This is another collection that can be stored in a table column. A NESTED TABLE is variable in size, and is therefore appropriate when you don't know how big the collection will be or you know it will contain a large amount of data.

Let's take a look at each of them in turn.

Records

In PL/SQL, you can declare a record type to be used as a related set of variables. These collections of variables are called **records**. Inside a record you will store one-to-many scalar attributes, in much the same way you would create a table. When using records in your PL/SQL, you first need to define the structure of the record, and then you can make variables of that record type. This differs from the way we normally define variables because most scalar types or %TYPE/%ROWTYPE types are already defined for us. Once you have declared variables of the record type, you can assign values to the individual attributes of the record variable. To define a record type, use the following syntax:

```
TYPE <record_name> IS RECORD(
   field_declaration {, field_declaration, field_declaration }
);
```

The area `field_declaration` above refers to a declaration of a field in your record. This means every time you declare a variable of your record type, it will have one of these fields. The field declaration is much the same as any other variable declaration. You can define your fields to be any PL/SQL type except `REF CURSOR` (more on these later). In general, a field declaration is much the same as a standard variable declaration in the declarative portion of a PL/SQL block. For example:

```
SQL> Set serverout on
SQL> declare
  2     type location_record_type is record (
  3        street_address         varchar2(40),
  4        postal_code            varchar2(12),
  5        city                   varchar2(30),
  6        state_province         varchar2(25),
  7        country_id             char(2) not null := 'US'
  8     );
  9
 10     l_my_loc location_record_type;
 11  begin
 12     l_my_loc.street_address := '1 Oracle Way';
 13     l_my_loc.postal_code := '20190';
 14     l_my_loc.city := 'Reston';
 15     l_my_loc.state_province := 'VA';
 16     dbms_output.put_line( 'MY LOCATION IS:' );
 17     dbms_output.put_line( l_my_loc.street_address );
 18     dbms_output.put( l_my_loc.city||', '||l_my_loc.state_province );
 19     dbms_output.put_line( '  '||l_my_loc.postal_code );
 20     dbms_output.put_line( l_my_loc.country_id );
 21  end;
 22  /
MY LOCATION IS:
1 Oracle Way
Reston, VA  20190
US

PL/SQL procedure successfully completed.
```

Assigning, manipulating, and referencing a field within your record is very similar to the way you work with a standard variable. As you may have noticed on lines `12` through `20` above, you must prefix the field name with the name of your record variable.

You can also assign a record variable to another record variable, provided they are of the same base record type. You cannot assign a record variable to another record variable if the base record type is not the same, regardless of whether the fields inside the record are the same or not. In the following code, we will illustrate this concept:

```
SQL> declare
  2     type emp_rec_t is record(
  3        empno          number,
```

```
4      name           varchar2(60),
5      job            varchar2(60),
6      sal            number(9,2),
7      location       varchar2(255)
8    );
9
10   type mgr_rec_t is record(
11     empno          number,
12     name           varchar2(60),
13     job            varchar2(60),
14     sal            number(9,2),
15     location       varchar2(255)
16   );
17
18   empty_emp emp_rec_t;
19   empty_mgr mgr_rec_t;
20
21   l_sean      emp_rec_t;
22   l_chris     emp_rec_t;
23   l_tom       mgr_rec_t;
24 begin
25   l_sean.empno       := 100;
26   l_sean.name        := 'Sean Dillon';
27   l_sean.job := 'Technologist';
28   l_sean.sal := 99.99;
29   l_sean.location := '2d Floor, OSI Building';
30
31   l_chris         := l_sean;
32   l_chris.empno := 101;
33   l_chris.name    := 'Christopher Beck';
34
35   l_tom           := l_chris;
36   l_tom.empno := 5;
37   l_tom.name    := 'Tom Kyte';
38   l_tom.job     := 'Technologist';
39 end;
40 /
  l_tom           := l_chris;
                  *
ERROR at line 35:
ORA-06550: line 35, column 16:
PLS-00382: expression is of wrong type
ORA-06550: line 35, column 3:
PL/SQL: Statement ignored
```

On line 31 you see we were able to effectively copy all the values from the L_SEAN record variable to the L_CHRIS record variable. This is useful because a few of the attributes of the record are the same, and this minimizes the number of assignments we need to perform. Attempting to do the same thing on line 35, however, fails. This is because the TOM record and the CHRIS record are two different base record types (MGR_REC_T and EMP_REC_T, respectively). Therefore, the assignment fails on line 35, indicating the expression is of the wrong type.

PL/SQL Tables

PL/SQL tables, or **index-by tables** as they are sometimes known, are non-persistent tables that can be used in PL/SQL routines to emulate an array. You define a type of PL/SQL table, and then declare variables of that type. You can then add records to your PL/SQL table and reference them in much the same way you would reference an element in an array. These tables are one-dimensional arrays, and should not be confused with full-blown Oracle tables.

PL/SQL tables are initially sparse, which means you declare a table variable of the table type, and it has no elements so it takes up no space. When you declare a value in the table, you must provide an integer that then acts as a psuedo-primary key for the PL/SQL table. Let's look at an example, using the HR schema:

```
SQL> set serverout on
SQL> declare
  2     type my_text_table_type is table of varchar2(200)
  3       index by binary_integer;
  4
  5     type my_emp_table_type is table of employees%rowtype
  6       index by binary_integer;
  7
  8     l_text_table my_text_table_type;
  9     l_emp_table  my_emp_table_type;
 10  begin
 11     l_text_table(1) := 'Some varchar2 value';
 12     l_text_table(2) := 'Another varchar2 value';
 13
 14     l_emp_table(10).employee_id := 10;
 15     l_emp_table(10).first_name  := 'Sean';
 16     l_emp_table(10).last_name   := 'Dillon';
 17     l_emp_table(10).email       := 'sdillon@somecorp.com';
 18     l_emp_table(10).hire_date   := to_date('01-NOV-1996');
 19     l_emp_table(10).job_id      := 'ST_CLERK';
 20
 21     l_emp_table(20).employee_id := 20;
 22     l_emp_table(20).first_name  := 'Chris';
 23     l_emp_table(20).last_name   := 'Beck';
 24     l_emp_table(20).email       := 'clbeck@somecorp.com';
 25     l_emp_table(20).hire_date   := to_date('01-JAN-1996');
 26     l_emp_table(20).job_id      := 'SH_CLERK';
 27
 28     dbms_output.put     ('We have ' ||l_text_table.count|| ' varchar2''s ');
 29     dbms_output.put_line('and ' ||l_emp_table.count|| ' employees.');
 30     dbms_output.put_line('-');
 31     dbms_output.put_line('vc2(1)='||l_text_table(1));
 32     dbms_output.put_line('vc2(2)='||l_text_table(2));
 33     dbms_output.put_line('-');
 34     dbms_output.put_line('l_emp_table(10)='||l_emp_table(10).first_name);
 35     dbms_output.put_line('l_emp_table(20)='||l_emp_table(20).first_name);
 36
 37  end;
 38  /
```

```
We have 2 varchar2's and 2 employees.
-
vc2(1) = Some varchar2 value
vc2(2) = Another varchar2 value

-
l_emp_table(10) = Sean
l_emp_table(20) = Chris


PL/SQL procedure successfully completed.
```

In this relatively simple example there are a number of PL/SQL table concepts introduced. Let's take a closer look at what we have done here, and explain each of the sections.

Defining PL/SQL Tables

First of all, there are the PL/SQL table type declarations:

```
2    type my_text_table_type is table of varchar2(200)
3       index by binary_integer;
4
5    type my_emp_table_type is table of employees%rowtype
6       index by binary_integer;
7
8    l_text_table my_text_table_type;
9    l_emp_table  my_emp_table_type;
```

In the first five lines, we declare two different PL/SQL table types. The first table type, MY_TEXT_TABLE_TYPE, is a simple PL/SQL table with one column, a VARCHAR2(200). The second table, MY_EMP_TABLE_TYPE, is a PL/SQL table using the %ROWTYPE definition of the EMPLOYEES table. Lines 8 and 9 declare variables defined as our PL/SQL table types.

Assigning Values To PL/SQL Tables

In these 14 lines of code, we assigned values to our PL/SQL tables:

```
11    l_text_table(1) := 'Some varchar2 value';
12    l_text_table(2) := 'Another varchar2 value';
13
14    l_emp_table(10).employee_id := 10;
15    l_emp_table(10).first_name  := 'Sean';
16    l_emp_table(10).last_name   := 'Dillon';
17    l_emp_table(10).email       := 'sdillon@somecorp.com';
18    l_emp_table(10).hire_date   := to_date('01-NOV-1996');
19    l_emp_table(10).job_id      := 'ST_CLERK';
20
21    l_emp_table(20).employee_id := 20;
22    l_emp_table(20).first_name  := 'Chris';
23    l_emp_table(20).last_name   := 'Beck';
24    l_emp_table(20).email       := 'clbeck@somecorp.com';
25    l_emp_table(20).hire_date   := to_date('01-JAN-1996');
26    l_emp_table(20).job_id      := 'SH_CLERK';
```

Here, we are only declaring two records in each of our PL/SQL table variables. In lines 11 and 12 you can see we reference the record of the PL/SQL table with an index operator. The index operator is the value inside the parenthesis next to the variable name. This indicates to the PL/SQL parser that we are talking about the record in that table uniquely identified by that value. The index operator must be a valid BINARY_INTEGER, as indicated in the PL/SQL table type definition in lines 2 through 6.

Now that you have seen an example of assigning values to PL/SQL tables, let's take a look at a graphical representation of them. L_TEXT_TABLE is simply a table of our indexes and VARCHAR2(200)s:

INDEX	VARCHAR2(200)
1	SOME VARCHAR2 VALUE
2	ANOTHER VARCHAR2 VALUE

The index of this table could have been other numbers; we just used 1 and 2 because there is no reason to use other numbers. Another example of a PL/SQL table of VARCHAR2(200)s might have employee names in the VARCHAR2(200) column, and the employee's ID for the index. The only requirements of the index column for a table is that it is a BINARY_INTEGER, and it is unique.

The second table is a little more complex. We are defining a table that is the %ROWTYPE of the EMPLOYEES table. If we use the DESCRIBE command on the EMPLOYEES table, we can see that there are eleven columns making up our PL/SQL table variable's columns.

```
SQL> desc employees
 Name                                      Null?    Type
 ----------------------------------------- -------- ----------------------------
 EMPLOYEE_ID                               NOT NULL NUMBER(6)
 FIRST_NAME                                         VARCHAR2(20)
 LAST_NAME                                 NOT NULL VARCHAR2(25)
 EMAIL                                     NOT NULL VARCHAR2(25)
 PHONE_NUMBER                                        VARCHAR2(20)
 HIRE_DATE                                 NOT NULL DATE
 JOB_ID                                    NOT NULL VARCHAR2(10)
 SALARY                                             NUMBER(8,2)
 COMMISSION_PCT                                     NUMBER(2,2)
 MANAGER_ID                                         NUMBER(6)
 DEPARTMENT_ID                                      NUMBER(4)
```

In our code sample, however, we only assign values to six of the columns, so L_EMP_TABLE looks like this:

INDEX	EMPLOYEE_ID	FIRST_NAME	LAST_NAME	EMAIL
10	10	SEAN	DILLON	SDILLON@SOMECORP.COM
20	20	CHRIS	BECK	CLBECK@SOMECORP.COM

INDEX	PHONE_NUMBER	HIRE_DATE	JOB_ID	SALARY
10	NULL	01-Nov-1996	ST_CLERK	NULL
20	NULL	01-Jan-1996	SH_CLERK	NULL

INDEX	COMMISSION_PCT	MANAGER_ID	DEPARTMENT_ID
10	NULL	NULL	NULL
20	NULL	NULL	NULL

Due to printing limitations, the table cannot be shown complete, but is instead displayed split into three, with the INDEX column repeated for clarity.

The columns that have not been defined are still a part of each record in our PL/SQL table, they are simply unassigned, or NULL.

Referencing Values in PL/SQL Tables

In the next 8 lines of code, we referenced the values of our PL/SQL tables and sent those values to the output buffer:

```
28    dbms_output.put    ('We have ' ||l_text_table.count|| ' varchar2''s ');
29    dbms_output.put_line('and ' ||l_emp_table.count|| ' employees.');
30    dbms_output.put_line('-');
```

In lines 28 and 29, we see the PL/SQL tables collection method COUNT. The COUNT method can be used to return the number of records in a PL/SQL table. We will talk more about table attributes a little later in the chapter. In lines 31, 32, 34, and 35 you can see we are accessing records of the PL/SQL tables by using the appropriate index operator. There is a key difference between accessing values of MY_VC2_TABLE and MY_EMP_TABLE: MY_VC2_TABLE is a single-column table, which means we do not have a column name to refer to, and referencing the values in a single-column table can be accomplished by simply referring the variable name with an index operator:

```
31    dbms_output.put_line('vc2(1) = ' ||l_text_table(1));
32    dbms_output.put_line('vc2(2) = ' ||l_text_table(2));
33    dbms_output.put_line('-');
```

In the multiple-column PL/SQL table, you must use dot notation to access values by their column name. In lines 34 and 35, we are referring to the FIRST_NAME column of each record:

```
34    dbms_output.put_line('l_emp_table(10)='||l_emp_table(10).first_name);
35    dbms_output.put_line('l_emp_table(20)='||l_emp_table(20).first_name);
```

Deleting Records From a PL/SQL Table

There are a couple of techniques I use to delete the records from my PL/SQL tables. Let's walk through an example to present them.

Try It Out – Deleting PL/SQL Table Records

1. First, we declare a PL/SQL table type with two variables of type VARCHAR2. The first variable will be used for our operations; the second will remain empty (you'll see why later in the code).

```
SQL> declare
  2     type my_text_table_type is table of varchar2(200)
  3       index by binary_integer;
  4
  5     l_text_table      my_text_table_type;
  6     l_empty_table     my_text_table_type;
```

2. Now our type and variables are declared, let's create a few entries in our table and use the COUNT method to display the number of entries in the table.

```
  8  begin
  9     l_text_table(10) := 'A value';
 10     l_text_table(20) := 'Another value';
 11     l_text_table(30) := 'Yet another value';
 12
 13     dbms_output.put_line('We start with ' || l_text_table.count ||
 14                          ' varchar2s ');
 15     dbms_output.put_line('-');
 16
```

3. Next, using the DELETE method, we will pass an index to be deleted from the table. The binary integer 20 we pass into this function, indicates we are removing the entry with a corresponding index of 20, not the 20th entry. So after this is complete, the entry ANOTHER VALUE is gone:

```
 17     l_text_table.DELETE(20);
 18     dbms_output.put      ('After using the DELETE operator on the second ');
 19     dbms_output.put      ('record (ie, DELETE(20), we have
                             '||l_text_table.count);
 20     dbms_output.put_line(' varchar2s ');
 21     dbms_output.put_line('-');
 22
```

4. The next few lines we'll use the DELETE method with no index parameter at all. This is used to remove all entries from the table:

```
 23     l_text_table.DELETE;
 24     dbms_output.put      ('After using the DELETE operator, we have ');
 25     dbms_output.put_line(l_text_table.count || ' varchar2s ');
 26     dbms_output.put_line('-');
 27
```

5. Lastly, we will add a couple of new rows to the table to exercise one more method of deleting rows from a PL/SQL table variable:

```
28      l_text_table(15) := 'some text';
29      l_text_table(25) := 'some more text';
30      dbms_output.put      ('After some assignments, we end up with ');
31      dbms_output.put_line(l_text_table.count || ' varchar2s ');
32      dbms_output.put_line('-');
33
```

Once we have a couple of more rows in the table, we assign the NULL table variable L_EMPTY_TABLE to the L_TEXT_TABLE variable. In the end, this has the same effect as the DELETE method; the table variable is assigned to a NULL table and therefore it no longer has entries. Once we've assigned the NULL table to our L_TEXT_TABLE variable, we check the count once again.

```
34      l_text_table := l_empty_table;
35      dbms_output.put  ('Once we assign our populated table to an empty ');
36      dbms_output.put_line('table, we end up with ' || l_text_table.count);
37      dbms_output.put_line(' varchar2s ');
38   end;
39   /
We start with 3 varchar2s
-
After using the DELETE operator on the second record (ie, DELETE(2), we have 2
varchar2s
-
After using the DELETE operator, we have 0 varchar2s
-
After some assignments, we end up with 2 varchar2s
-
Once we assign our populated table to an empty table, we end up with 0
varchar2s

PL/SQL procedure successfully completed.
```

How It Works

In this example, we use two methods to clear a PL/SQL table of all its records. The first way, shown on line 17, is to use the DELETE operator. Using DELETE causes all the records in the PL/SQL operator to be deleted. The second way, shown on line 34, assigns the PL/SQL table records to an uninitialized variable, L_EMPTY_TABLE, which is an empty variable of the same type that we defined earlier. This has the same effect.

FIRST, NEXT and LAST

We've already discussed the COUNT collection method used on a PL/SQL table variable to return the number of entries in the table. In this section, we'll look at a few more of these collection methods and how we can use them in our PL/SQL code to help us when working with table variables:

❑   **FIRST** is used to return the 'first', or smallest index of a PL/SQL table. When working with these tables, you do not always know what the indexes are, so directly referencing the first entry in a PL/SQL table could very well be impossible without this function.

❑   **LAST** is much the same as FIRST, except it returns the 'last', or largest index.

❑ **NEXT** is used to find the next index of a PL/SQL table variable. When you call NEXT, you pass in an existing index and the method returns the next largest index. If you pass in the last index of the table, NEXT returns NULL.

In the following code sample, we'll create a simple PL/SQL table using a CURSOR FOR LOOP. The loop is responsible for executing a query and looping through the result set, one record at a time (we will look more closely at CURSOR FOR LOOPs a little later in the chapter). We will use a column from the query as the index for our PL/SQL table variable so we will not know at run-time what the indexes are. Once the PL/SQL table is built, we will loop through it to get the index and the values stored in the table using FIRST and NEXT:

```
SQL> connect scott/tiger
Connected.
SQL> set serveroutput on
SQL> declare
  2      type my_text_table_type is table of varchar2(200)
  3        index by binary_integer;
  4
  5      l_text_table      my_text_table_type;
  6      l_index           number;
  7  begin
  8      for emp_rec in (select * from emp) loop
  9          l_text_table(emp_rec.empno) := emp_rec.ename;
 10      end loop;
 11
 12      l_index := l_text_table.first;
 13      loop
 14        exit when l_index is null;
 15        dbms_output.put_line(l_index ||':'|| l_text_table(l_index));
 16        l_index := l_text_table.next(l_index);
 17      end loop;
 18  end;
 19  /
7369:SMITH
7499:ALLEN
7521:WARD
7566:JONES
7654:MARTIN
7698:BLAKE
7782:CLARK
7788:SCOTT
7839:KING
7844:TURNER
7876:ADAMS
7900:JAMES
7902:FORD
7934:MILLER

PL/SQL procedure successfully completed.
```

Using FIRST and NEXT, we were still able to retrieve every record of the PL/SQL table without knowing any of the actual index values. Using DBMS_OUTPUT, we spooled the index (which is, in fact, the employee's EMPNO) and the value of the PL/SQL table (the employee's ENAME) to SQL*Plus.

When Oracle introduced object-technology to the database in Oracle 8, one of the highlighted features was object collections that could be stored in database tables (Chapter 16 takes a much more thorough look at Oracle object technology). The two object collections were the **VARRAY** and the **NESTED TABLE**. The first object collection we will discuss is the VARRAY.

VARRAYS

VARRAYs are PL/SQL collections that can be stored in columns of your tables. When you create a VARRAY, you must provide a maximum size for it. Once you start adding elements to a VARRAY, it consumes space. These collections are dense objects, which means there is no way to delete an individual element contained in one. To reference VARRAY elements we use standard subscript syntax with the VARRAY variable name.

Let's step through an example demonstrating all of the above:

Try It Out – Creating and Using VARRAYs

1. First we connect as the user SCOTT and then we make a simple object type that will become the data type for values we store in the VARRAY.

```
SQL> connect scott/tiger
SQL> create type employee_type as object (
  2      employee_id         number,
  3      first_name          varchar2(30),
  4      last_name           varchar2(30)
  5  );
  6  /

Type created.
```

2. Next, we declare the VARRAY type that we will use for our variable.

```
SQL> create type employee_list_type as varray(50) of employee_type
  2  /

Type created.
```

3. Now, we'll create a table that will store the collection. The EMPLOYEES column will store the EMPLOYEE_LIST_TYPE, which is the VARRAY.

```
SQL> create table departments (
  2      department_id    number,
  3      department_name  varchar2(30),
  4      manager          employee_type,
  5      employees        employee_list_type )
  6  /

Table created.
```

4. Now that all the types and structures are in place, we can add a couple of rows to the table. Keep in mind, when we add one row to the DEPARTMENTS table, we can add zero, one, or many rows to the EMPLOYEES varray:

```
SQL> insert into departments ( department_id,
  2                            department_name,
  3                            manager,
  4                            employees )
  5  values ( 10,
  6           'Accounting',
  7           employee_type( 1, 'Danielle', 'Steeger' ),
  8           employee_list_type(
  9             employee_type( 2, 'Madison', 'Sis' ),
 10             employee_type( 3, 'Robert', 'Cabove' ),
 11             employee_type( 4, 'Michelle', 'Sechrist' ))
 12  )
 13  /

1 row created.

SQL> insert into departments ( department_id,
  2                            department_name,
  3                            manager,
  4                            employees )
  5  values ( 20,
  6           'Research',
  7           employee_type( 11, 'Ricky', 'Lil' ),
  8           employee_list_type(
  9             employee_type( 12, 'Ricky', 'Ricardo' ),
 10             employee_type( 13, 'Lucy', 'Ricardo' ),
 11             employee_type( 14, 'Fred', 'Mertz' ),
 12             employee_type( 15, 'Ethel', 'Mertz' ))
 13  )
 14  /

1 row created.
```

5. Here we see how to do inserts into the table using standard INSERT SQL statements along with an **inline varray** or **inline object constructor**. An inline object constructor is when, whenever you create an object, you also create an instance of that object using a default method provided. The name of the method is the same as the object name, and the arguments to the method are the attributes of the objects. In first the INSERT statement above, we inserted an EMPLOYEE_TYPE object into the MANAGER column using the constructor method syntax.

We also used an object constructor for the EMPLOYEE_LIST_TYPE varray on lines 8 through 12. Each element of the EMPLOYEE_LIST_TYPE varray is an EMPLOYEE_TYPE, so each element uses the EMPLOYEE_TYPE default object constructor to create an instance of an EMPLOYEE_TYPE. We'll look in more detail at constructors in Chapter 16.

6. The table is now populated with a VARRAY, so we can use a variety of types of queries to get data in its VARRAY column. Here is a simple query of the EMPLOYEES and DEPARTMENT_NAME columns from the DEPARTMENTS table:

```
SQL> column department_name format a13
SQL> column employees format a63 word_wrapped
SQL> select department_name, employees
  2    from departments
  3  /


DEPARTMENT_NA EMPLOYEES(EMPLOYEE_ID, FIRST_NAME, LAST_NAME)
------------- ------------------------------------------------------------
Accounting    EMPLOYEE_LIST_TYPE(EMPLOYEE_TYPE(2, 'Madison', 'Sis'),
              EMPLOYEE_TYPE(3, 'Robert', 'Cabove'), EMPLOYEE_TYPE(4,
              'Michelle', 'Sechrist'))

Research      EMPLOYEE_LIST_TYPE(EMPLOYEE_TYPE(12, 'Ricky', 'Ricardo'),
              EMPLOYEE_TYPE(13, 'Lucy', 'Ricardo'), EMPLOYEE_TYPE(14, 'Fred',
              'Mertz'), EMPLOYEE_TYPE(15, 'Ethel', 'Mertz'))

2 rows selected.
```

Here we see we query the EMPLOYEES varray column out of the table as a single entity.

NESTED TABLEs

The last type of collection we are going to explore is the NESTED TABLE. These are very similar to index-by tables. The most significant difference is the fact that a nested table can be stored in a database column whereas index-by tables cannot. Using a nested table is much like having an array of records in your database column. Up to Oracle 9i, it was impossible to have a nested table within a table, but now you can. This gives database developers the ability to model a multidimensional array within a single database column.

Nested tables are much the same as VARRAYs, with a few notable exceptions:

❑ NESTED TABLEs are sparse whereas VARRAYs are dense. You can delete individual elements of a nested table but not of a VARRAY.

❑ NESTED TABLEs do not have an upper boundary (outside of the normal upper bounds of a database table), whereas VARRAYs are fixed-size.

❑ NESTED TABLEs are stored in a system-generated table, whereas VARRAYs are stored in a tablespace, either inline (4K or less) or out-of-line.

Let's take a look at an example of using NESTED TABLEs in our database. We'll make an ORDERS table that resembles the OE schema's ORDERS table. We'll use a NESTED TABLE in ORDERS to store the line items for each order. Then we'll populate the table with all the orders from the OE schema's ORDERS table.

Try It Out - Orders

1. First we need to create the ORDER_ITEM_TYPE. This will store each of the line items for our ORDERS table. When the object is created, we create the ORDER_ITEM_LIST_TYPE, which is a table of ORDER_ITEM_TYPE:

Please note: you must be logged in as a user that can see the OE schema's objects, but is not the OE user itself.

```
SQL> connect oracle_admin/oracle_admin
Connected.
SQL> create type order_item_type as object (
  2     line_item_id      number(3),
  3     product_id        number(6),
  4     unit_price        number(8,2),
  5     quantity  number(4)
  6  )
  7  /

Type created.

SQL> create type order_item_list_type as table of order_item_type
  2  /

Type created.
```

2. Next, we will create our own ORDERS table:

```
SQL> create table orders(
  2     order_id  number(12) not null,
  3     order_date        timestamp(6) with local time zone,
  4     customer_id       number(6),
  5     order_items       order_item_list_type )
  6     nested table order_items store as order_items_tab
  7  /

Table created.
```

3. Now that we have the table created, let's migrate the OE.ORDERS table to the ORDERS table we just created. We begin by declaring a variable and then using a CURSOR FOR LOOP to select the data in the OE.ORDERS table:

You will learn about CURSOR FOR LOOPS in more detail in the Cursors section, overleaf.

```
SQL> declare
  2     l_lineitems orders.order_items%type;
  3  begin
  4     l_lineitems := order_item_list_type();
  5     for ord in (select *
  6                   from oe.orders
  7                  order by order_date) loop
  8
```

The first time we enter this loop the variable will be empty, but the next time we go into it there will most likely be elements that we need to remove, so we need to add the following line to remove them:

```
 9        l_lineitems.delete;
```

Now we'll use another CURSOR FOR LOOP to select the order items from OE.ORDERS where the ORDER_ID is the same as the ORDER_ID in our own ORDERS table.

```
10        for items in (select *
11                        from oe.order_items
12                        where order_id = ord.order_id
13                        order by line_item_id) loop
```

Next we use the EXTEND collection method. This makes a new element in the collection. Once L-LINEITEMS is extended, we can assign a new ORDER_ITEM_TYPE type element to it. Notice we also use the COUNT collection method to ensure we are assigning the new ORDER_ITEM_TYPE object to the element we just created with the EXTEND method:

```
14        l_lineitems.extend;
15        l_lineitems(l_lineitems.count) :=
16          order_item_type( items.line_item_id, items.product_id,
17                             items.unit_price, items.quantity );
18        end loop;
19
```

Now we have all the order information we need to add a record to our ORDERS table:

```
20        insert into orders (order_id, order_date, customer_id, order_items)
21        values (ord.order_id, ord.order_date, ord.customer_id,l_lineitems);
22     end loop;
23   end;
24 /
```

```
PL/SQL procedure successfully completed.
```

Collections are a core component of the PL/SQL language. VARRAYs and NESTED TABLEs were added in Oracle 8.0 to support object technology in the database and the ability to store collections. When you are deciding what type of collection to use, give serious consideration to PL/SQL tables. If you do not have to store the collection in a column, there are advantages to using them instead of NESTED TABLEs or VARRAYs. For example, PL/SQL tables can have negative subscripts; NESTED TABLEs and VARRAYs cannot. To add another element to a NESTED TABLE or VARRAY, you must use the collection method EXTEND. This is unnecessary in index-by tables.

Cursors

Oracle extended the SQL language with PL/SQL to provide a programming language inside the database. There are a multitude of reasons why PL/SQL was a great idea for the database, but suffice it to say in the end, PL/SQL is a language for getting work done close to the data. PL/SQL has a large number of features for integrating SQL into your stored procedural logic.

This is where **cursors** make their debut. A cursor is a type of pointer built into PL/SQL for querying the database, retrieving a set of records (that we refer to as a **result set**), and allowing a developer to access the result set a row at a time. This lets programmers accomplish tasks that require procedural code to be performed on each record in a result set individually. Cursors give us programmatic access to our data.

Two of the most common cursor types used in Oracle are explicit cursors and implicit cursors. An **explicit cursor** is one where you, as a PL/SQL programmer, *explicitly* code the PL/SQL routines necessary to manage your cursor. The entire life of the cursor is under your control, and therefore you have a detailed level of control over how PL/SQL access records in the result set. You define the cursor, open the cursor, fetch data out of the cursor, and close the cursor with appropriate PL/SQL code. **Implicit cursors**, on the other hand, can be used in your PL/SQL without providing any explicit code to process the cursor itself. You still have a result set of records to work with, using implicit cursors, but you have to do no explicit coding to manage the cursor's life cycle.

Explicit Cursors

The first type of cursor we will learn about is the explicit cursor. Explicit cursors have a standard operating procedure. First, you must declare your cursor using the following syntax:

```
CURSOR cursor_name [(parameter [, parameter]...)]
    [RETURN return_type] IS some select statement;
```

Cursors have a life cycle all of their own. When you want to use a cursor in your PL/SQL code, you will do the following:

- ❑ **Open the cursor.** This parses the query identified by the cursor, binds any inputs and makes it so you can call fetch successfully. Rows are not actually retrieved from the database until the next step.

- ❑ **Fetch from the cursor.** This executes the query and finds those rows that should be returned based on the cursor's query. Fetching from the cursor retrieves rows from the database. Typically, you will define local variables to act as buffer(s) for the data fetched from the cursor. You will fetch a record into your buffer, and then process that particular record.

- ❑ **Close the cursor**. This completes the cursor processing and makes it so you cannot fetch any more rows from the cursor. Once a cursor is closed, you can re-open the cursor for further processing, possibly using a different parameter value to produce a new result set.

Explicit Cursor Options

As a part of the syntax for declaring an explicit cursor, you may optionally specify parameters and a return type. Parameters let you pass in values to the cursor when you open it, allowing you to specify constraints on your queries at run-time, rather than having to hard-code those constraints at compile time. We'll look at an example of passing parameters to a cursor in the next code sample.

Return types on cursors simply let the developer using the cursor know what to expect in the result set. Unless you write a cursor query yourself, you might not know what columns will be returned when you try to use it. Not knowing the columns in the cursor is likely to mean that you will not be able to employ it because you have no idea what data will be returned. A return type must be a single entity, such as a TABLE%ROWTYPE or a PL/SQL type of some kind. We'll see an example of using a return type in the REF CURSOR example, later on.

Let's take a look at a PL/SQL block using an explicit cursor to find data about employees from a particular department:

```
SQL> connect hr/hr
SQL> set serveroutput on
SQL> declare
  2     cursor emp_cur (p_deptid in number)
  3     is select *
  4         from employees
  5         where department_id = p_deptid;
  6
  7     l_emp employees%rowtype;
  8  begin
  9     dbms_output.put_line('Getting employees for department 30');
 10     open emp_cur(30);
 11     loop
 12       fetch emp_cur into l_emp;
 13       exit when emp_cur%notfound;
 14       dbms_output.put('Employee id ' || l_emp.employee_id || ' is ');
 15       dbms_output.put_line(l_emp.first_name || ' ' || l_emp.last_name);
 16     end loop;
 17     close emp_cur;
 18
 19     dbms_output.put_line('Getting employees for department 90');
 20     open emp_cur(90);
 21     loop
 22       fetch emp_cur into l_emp;
 23       exit when emp_cur%notfound;
 24       dbms_output.put('Employee id ' || l_emp.employee_id || ' is ');
 25       dbms_output.put_line(l_emp.first_name || ' ' || l_emp.last_name);
 26     end loop;
 27     close emp_cur;
 28  end;
 29  /
Getting employees for department 30
Employee id 114 is Den Raphaely
Employee id 115 is Alexander Khoo
Employee id 116 is Shelli Baida
Employee id 117 is Sigal Tobias
Employee id 118 is Guy Himuro
Employee id 119 is Karen Colmenares
Getting employees for department 90
Employee id 100 is Steven King
Employee id 101 is Neena Kochhar
Employee id 102 is Lex De Haan

PL/SQL procedure successfully completed.
```

In this example, you can see we define a cursor that selects a number of records from the EMPLOYEES table when passed a DEPARTMENT_ID as a parameter on opening. We then declare a variable L_EMP of EMPLOYEES%ROWTYPE that will act as a buffer for the records fetched from our cursor, once it is opened.

On line 10, we open the cursor and pass the DEPARTMENT_ID 30. This executes the query and identifies the record(s) that will make up the result set. We loop over the cursor, fetching one record per loop into the L_EMP variable. As soon as the fetch returns no records, the EMP_CUR%NOTFOUND condition will evaluate to TRUE and the EXIT WHEN condition on line 13 will cause the loop to end. An important point to notice in this particular line of code, is that the SELECT clause in the query for the cursor matches the buffer you are fetching into. Once we have opened and fetched the cursor into our local variable, we can view any data that was retrieved by the cursor. In lines 14 and 15, we simply send the EMPLOYEE_ID, FIRST_NAME, and LAST_NAME to the DBMS_OUTPUT buffer for display. On line 17, we close the EMP_CUR cursor, and on lines 20 through 27, we follow the same steps for a different DEPARTMENT_ID, 90. This shows us that we can reopen a cursor that has already been opened, provided it is closed first.

A **PL/SQL loop** is a **control structure** that lets you execute a block of PL/SQL statements a multitude of times. This is perfect for a scenario in which you have to perform some processing for each record in the result set, but the exact number of records in the result set is uncertain at the time you write the routine. We will take a deeper look at loops later in the chapter in the *Control Statements* section, but for now it is important to understand that loops let us execute a series of PL/SQL statements one time for each record returned in our cursor.

Implicit Cursors

An implicit cursor is one that is created as a result of some operation in your PL/SQL code wherein you do not explicitly create a cursor variable, yet Oracle provides a result set for use in your PL/SQL. We will examine two different kinds of implicit cursors here; an Oracle predefined implicit cursor named **SQL**, assigned when you use data manipulation language (DML) in your PL/SQL, and **CURSOR FOR LOOP**s. Let's look at each in turn.

The name SQL may be somewhat confusing, but the following code sample shows UPDATE statements against our DEPARTMENTS table to demonstrate the usefulness of the implicit cursor it denotes:

```
SQL> declare
  2   begin
  3     update departments
  4        set department_name = department_name
  5      where 1 = 2;
  6
  7     dbms_output.put ('An update with a WHERE clause 1 = 2 effects ');
  8     dbms_output.put_line(sql%rowcount || ' records.');
  9
 10     update departments
 11        set department_name = department_name;
 12
 13     dbms_output.put('No WHERE clause in an update effects ');
 14     dbms_output.put_line(sql%rowcount || ' records.');
 15   end;
 16   /
An update with a WHERE clause 1 = 2 effects 0 records.
No WHERE clause in an update effects 29 records.

PL/SQL procedure successfully completed.
```

The other form of implicit cursor is referred to as a CURSOR FOR LOOP. CURSOR FOR LOOPs are for when you use the FOR LOOP statement along with a query that will be used to produce your result set. The loop implicitly processes the result set by executing a set of PL/SQL statements inside it for every record returned. In the following code sample, we can see a CURSOR FOR LOOP in action:

```
SQL> connect hr/hr
SQL> set serveroutput on
SQL> declare
  2  begin
  3    for my_dept_rec in (select department_id, department_name
  4                               from departments
  5                               order by 1)
  6    loop
  7      dbms_output.put('Department #' || my_dept_rec.department_id);
  8      dbms_output.put_line(' is named ' || my_dept_rec.department_name);
  9    end loop;
 10  end;
 11  /
Department #10 is named Administration
Department #20 is named Marketing
Department #30 is named Purchasing
     .                        .
     .                        .
     .                        .
Department #250 is named Retail Sales
Department #260 is named Recruiting
Department #270 is named Payroll

PL/SQL procedure successfully completed.
```

Cursor Attributes

Cursor attributes return meta data about the execution of a SQL statement. For instance, we might want to know how many records are in the result set, whether or not a cursor is open or closed and whether or not records were found the last time we tried to fetch a row from the result set. To access this meta data, you use an operator on the name of your cursor that tells Oracle which SQL statement the meta data should be returned for. There are four cursor attributes to cover:

Attribute	Definition
%FOUND	Indicates that there were records found when the PL/SQL code last fetched from the cursor's result set.
%NOTFOUND	The opposite of the %FOUND operator. %NOTFOUND indicates the last time the PL/SQL code fetched from the cursor, there were no records left in the result set.
%ROWCOUNT	Returns the count of the records that have been fetched from the cursor at the current point in time.
%ISOPEN	Returns TRUE when the cursor has been opened, but not closed. This operator is effective when your code conditionally opens and closes cursors based on some logic.

The following example shows an explicit cursor that selects data from the HR EMPLOYEES table. We'll use each of the attributes we just defined to allow us to modify the behavior of the cursor, depending on what's happening:

```
SQL> declare
  2    cursor emps
  3    is select *
  4         from employees
  5         where rownum < 6
  6         order by 1;
  7
  8    emp employees%rowtype;
  9    row number := 1;
 10  begin
 11    open emps;
 12    fetch emps into emp;
 13
 14    loop
 15      if emps%FOUND then
 16        dbms_output.put_line('Looping over record ' ||row|| ' of ' ||
 17                             emps%ROWCOUNT);
 18        fetch emps into emp;
 19        row := row + 1;
 20      elsif emps%NOTFOUND then
 21        exit; -- EXIT statement exits the LOOP, not the IF stmt
 22      end if;
 23    end loop;
 24
 25    if emps%ISOPEN then
 26      close emps;
 27    end if;
 28  end;
 29  /
Looping over record 1 of 1
Looping over record 2 of 2
Looping over record 3 of 3
Looping over record 4 of 4
Looping over record 5 of 5

PL/SQL procedure successfully completed.
```

Now we've seen some simple implicit and explicit cursors, let's try out a more complex example that compares them.

Try It Out – Implicit and Explicit Cursors

We'll use the data in the HR EMPLOYEES table again. This time we'll analyze employee salaries. First, we will take a look at each job and find out what the minimum, maximum, and average salaries are for each job. Then we will take a look at each employee in a particular job title and find out what they make individually:

```
SQL> declare
  2    cursor programmers
  3    is select e.first_name || ' ' || e.last_name name,
  4           e.salary
```

```
 5           from employees e, jobs j
 6         where e.job_id = j.job_id
 7           and j.job_title = 'Programmer'
 8         order by salary;
 9
10    name        varchar2(200);
11    salary      number(9,2);
12 begin
13    for c1 in (select j.job_title, j.min_salary, j.max_salary,
14                      avg(e.salary) avg_salary
15                 from employees e, jobs j
16                where e.job_id = j.job_id
17                group by j.job_title, j.min_salary, j.max_salary
18                order by j.job_title) loop
19      dbms_output.put_line(c1.job_title||'s, average $'||c1.avg_salary);
20    end loop;
21
22    open programmers;
23    fetch programmers into name, salary;
24    dbms_output.put_line(chr(13) || chr(13));
25    dbms_output.put_line('PROGRAMMERS');
26    dbms_output.put_line('------------------------');
27    while programmers%FOUND loop
28      dbms_output.put_line(name || ' makes $' || salary);
29      fetch programmers into name, salary;
30    end loop;
31    close programmers;
32 end;
33 /
```

```
Accountants, average $7920
Accounting Managers, average $12000
Administration Assistants, average $4400
Administration Vice Presidents, average $17000
Finance Managers, average $12000
Human Resources Representatives, average $6500
Marketing Managers, average $13000
Marketing Representatives, average $6000
Presidents, average $24000
Programmers, average $5760
Public Accountants, average $8300
Public Relations Representatives, average $10000
Purchasing Clerks, average $2780
Purchasing Managers, average $11000
Sales Managers, average $12200
Sales Representatives, average $8350
Shipping Clerks, average $3215
Stock Clerks, average $2785
Stock Managers, average $7280

PROGRAMMERS
------------------------
Diana Lorentz makes $4200
David Austin makes $4800
```

```
Valli Pataballa makes $4800
Bruce Ernst makes $6000
Alexander Hunold makes $9000

PL/SQL procedure successfully completed.
```

How It Works

This particular demonstration shows up the efficiency of CURSOR FOR LOOPS, and illustrates my general preference toward using implicit cursors rather than explicit cursors. You should try to minimize the use of explicit cursors simply due to the additional cursor control code you must explicitly write in order to manage the SQL integration. Implicit cursors are much easier to use; there is less code to manage (the cursor declaration, open, fetch, and close are all handled for you) and they are faster as well! PL/SQL has less code to interpret at run-time.

For instance, the following lines of code were necessary to make the explicit cursor work:

```
2     cursor programmers
3     is select e.first_name || ' ' || e.last_name name,
4              e.salary
5        from employees e, jobs j
6       where e.job_id = j.job_id
7         and j.job_title = 'Programmer'
8       order by salary;
9
10    name      varchar2(200);
11    salary    number(9,2);
  .         .
  .         .
  .         .
22    open programmers;
23    fetch programmers into name, salary;
  .         .
  .         .
  .         .
27    while programmers%FOUND loop
28      dbms_output.put_line(name || ' makes $' || salary);
29      fetch programmers into name, salary;
30    end loop;
31    close programmers;
```

There are sixteen lines of code in all. That isn't all that bad, considering the power and functionality gained through a cursor. However, let's take a look at the implicit cursor to find out how many lines of code were necessary:

```
13    for c1 in (select j.job_title, j.min_salary, j.max_salary,
14                      avg(e.salary) avg_salary
15                 from employees e, jobs j
16                where e.job_id = j.job_id
17                group by j.job_title, j.min_salary, j.max_salary
18                order by j.job_title) loop
19      dbms_output.put_line(c1.job_title||'s, average $'||c1.avg_salary);
20    end loop;
```

Not only is it just 8 lines of code, but more importantly, look at the simplicity of using the implicit cursor. There is no need to declare *any* variables: neither a cursor variable nor a single variable to hold data fetched from the cursor. Additionally, as we said before, there is no need to supply the commands to control the cursor. You don't need to handle closing cursors in the exception block, either.

Implicit and explicit cursors don't handle every case, however. There will be cases in your PL/SQL code where you need to build a SQL query in a cursor dynamically. You may have no way of knowing what the query is going to be at the time you write your code. In these cases, you would use a dynamic cursor, or a REF CURSOR.

REF CURSORS and Cursor Variables

Explicit and implicit cursors are **static** by definition. When you use them, the query is defined at the time the cursor is created. There are many cases, however, when the query you need to use for a cursor is unknown until run-time, in which case you need to open a cursor for a query, and process the result set appropriately. Oracle uses REF CURSORs and cursor variables to satisfy this requirement.

There are two types of REF CURSORs to understand:

❑ **Strongly-typed (restrictive)** REF CURSORs

❑ **Weakly-typed (non-restrictive)** REF CURSORs

Strong REF CURSORs require you to declare the return type that will comprise the result set of the query you use. A weak REF CURSOR is defined with no return type, and can be used to retrieve any result set.

To declare a REF CURSOR, use the following syntax:

```
TYPE ref_cursor_name IS REF CURSOR [RETURN return_type];
```

So to demonstrate declaring the two types of REF CURSORs we have discussed:

```
SQL> declare
  2     type refcur_t is ref cursor;
  3
  4     type emp_refcur_t is ref cursor
  5       return employees%rowtype;
  6  begin
  7     null;
  8  end;
  9  /

PL/SQL procedure successfully completed.
```

Once we have our REF CURSOR defined, we must declare a **cursor variable**. A cursor variable is simply a variable of some REF CURSOR type.

In the next example, we will define a custom record type, and then use it to declare our REF CURSOR return type. This is a strong REF CURSOR because the result set type is known at declaration time.

Try It Out – A Strong REF CURSOR

1. First we'll declare a custom record type with employee information and job titles:

```
SQL> declare
  2    type emp_job_rec is record(
  3      employee_id      number,
  4      employee_name    varchar2(56),
  5      job_title        varchar2(35)
  6    );
  9
```

2. Next, we declare a REF CURSOR with the custom record as the REF CURSOR return type:

```
 10    type emp_job_refcur_type is ref cursor
 11      return emp_job_rec;
 12
```

3. Now we declare a cursor variable:

```
 13    emp_refcur emp_job_refcur_type;
 14
```

4. And lastly in our declaration section, we declare a variable of the record type to hold fetched records:

```
 15    emp_job      emp_job_rec;
 16  begin
```

5. Now we need to open EMP_REFCUR using a query that matches our custom record type:

```
 17    open emp_refcur for
 18      select e.employee_id,
 19             e.first_name || ' ' || e.last_name "employee_name",
 20             j.job_title
 21        from employees e, jobs j
 22       where e.job_id = j.job_id
 23         and rownum < 11
 24       order by 1;
 25
```

6. Finally standard cursor operations fetch the result set into a buffer, and display the contents of the buffer using DBMS_OUTPUT. In this example, we use a WHILE loop instead of a FOR loop to show different styles.

```
 26    fetch emp_refcur into emp_job;
 27    while emp_refcur%FOUND loop
 28      dbms_output.put(emp_job.employee_name || '''s job is ');
 29      dbms_output.put_line(emp_job.job_title);
```

```
30      fetch emp_refcur into emp_job;
31    end loop;
32  end;
33  /
Steven King's job is President
Neena Kochhar's job is Administration Vice President
Lex De Haan's job is Administration Vice President
Alexander Hunold's job is Programmer
Bruce Ernst's job is Programmer
David Austin's job is Programmer
Valli Pataballa's job is Programmer
Diana Lorentz's job is Programmer
Nancy Greenberg's job is Finance Manager
Daniel Faviet's job is Accountant

PL/SQL procedure successfully completed.
```

You can now see that we have taken each employee's first name and last name, and concatenated them together to form a single name that constitutes the EMPLOYEE_NAME field in the EMP_JOB_REC custom record type.

Weak REF CURSORs are interesting because you are not required to supply a result set definition when you declare the REF CURSOR itself. In the next example, we will use the SQL*Plus ACCEPT and PROMPT functions to ask the user what information they'd like to see. Based on the user's response, the script will output different data.

Try It Out – A Weak REF CURSOR

For this example, put the following code into a file named refex.sql or download it from the web site.

1. First we get SQL*Plus into the right modes, and tell it what we would like it to prompt the user with:

```
set echo off
set serveroutput on
set verify off
set define '&'

prompt
prompt 'What table would you like to see?'
accept tab prompt '(L)ocations, (D)epartments, or (E)mployees : '
prompt
```

2. Then we declare our weak REF CURSOR:

```
declare
  type refcur_t is ref cursor;
  refcur refcur_t;

  type sample_rec_type is record (
```

```
    id           number,
    description varchar2(200));
  sample sample_rec_type;
```

3. Now we capture the first character of the user's selection:

```
    selection varchar2(1) := upper(substr('&tab',1,1));
begin
```

4. Now we need to output a small amount of data from the selected table, based on the user's input:

```
  if selection = 'L' then
    open refcur for
      select location_id, street_address || ' ' || city
        from locations
        where rownum < 11
        order by 1;
    dbms_output.put_line('Sample LOCATION data:');

  elsif selection = 'D' then
    open refcur for
      select department_id, department_name
        from departments
        where rownum < 11
        order by 1;
    dbms_output.put_line('Sample DEPARTMENT data:');

  elsif selection = 'E' then
    open refcur for
      select employee_id, first_name || ' ' || last_name
        from employees
        where rownum < 11
        order by 1;
    dbms_output.put_line('Sample EMPLOYEE data:');

  else
```

5. Next we need to cater for a confused user and tell them what to enter if they didn't get it right the first time.

```
    dbms_output.put_line('Please enter ''L'', ''D'', or ''E''.');
    return;
  end if;

  dbms_output.put_line('--------------------');
```

6. Then we fetch a record from our REF CURSOR into our local variable:

```
fetch refcur into sample;
```

7. Finally, we'll output the result set of our cursor variable:

```
  while refcur%FOUND loop
    dbms_output.put_line('#' || sample.id || ' is ' || sample.description);
    fetch refcur into sample;
  end loop;
  close refcur;
end;
/
```

8. Once you have the file created, execute it from SQL*Plus and enter the letter *L, D,* or *E* to get your results, as follows:

```
SQL> @refex

'What table would you like to see?'
(L)ocations, (D)epartments, or (E)mployees : L

Sample LOCATION data:
--------------------
#1000 is 1297 Via Cola di Rie Roma
#1100 is 93091 Calle della Testa Venice
#1200 is 2017 Shinjuku-ku Tokyo
#1300 is 9450 Kamiya-cho Hiroshima
#1400 is 2014 Jabberwocky Rd Southlake
#1500 is 2011 Interiors Blvd South San Francisco
#1600 is 2007 Zagora St South Brunswick
#1700 is 2004 Charade Rd Seattle
#1800 is 147 Spadina Ave Toronto
#1900 is 6092 Boxwood St Whitehorse

PL/SQL procedure successfully completed.
```

As you can see, weak REF CURSORs provide some flexibility when you are unsure what kind of query you will be making to the database.

Singleton SELECTs

There have been 'Singleton SELECTs' since PL/SQL came around. They are code constructs that allow developers to select a value (or a list of values) into a variable (or a list of variables). By adding a simple INTO clause into a standard SELECT statement within the PL/SQL code, a single row queried from a table or some data source can be assigned to a variable (or a list of variables):

```
SQL> connect scott/scott
SQL> set serverout on
SQL> declare
```

```
  2     l_empno   emp.empno%type;
  3     l_ename   emp.ename%type;
  4   begin
  5     select empno, ename
  6       into l_empno, l_ename
  7       from emp
  8      where rownum = 1;
  9     dbms_output.put_line(l_empno||':'||l_ename);
 10   end;
 11   /
7369:SMITH

PL/SQL procedure successfully completed.
```

This is a very basic and easy construct, you write a query and include an INTO clause that catches the values that are returned from Oracle in the result set. You need to be careful, however, as the result set must have one and only one row. If the query returns no rows, you will receive a NO_DATA_FOUND exception. If the query returns more than one row, you will receive a TOO_MANY_ROWS exception. You must have a corresponding variable for each value in the SELECT statement. You can also use variables that represent entire row types (using %ROWTYPE).

Due to the errors that may be encountered, people are using singleton SELECTs less and less these days, preferring to use implicit cursors instead. There is no need to declare local variables to hold values selected in an implicit cursor and there is no need to do the exception handling for the cases where the query returns more or less than one row.

Control Statements

Oracle provides a number of **process control statements** to assist in your development efforts. Control statements are conditional statements and loop constructs to help us build the code that gets executed in your PL/SQL. There are a variety of different types of conditional statements and looping constructs, in order to help make your code efficient and readable.

In this chapter, up to this section, there have been quite a few examples of conditional statements and loop constructs in our sample code. In order to write code that actually performs some work, it is difficult not to use them. SQL on its own has no concept of flow or controlling statements. This is where PL/SQL starts to show real value.

Conditionals

Conditions are expressions that evaluate to a Boolean value; true, false, or NULL. If a condition evaluates to true, that condition's code will be processed. Conversely, code contained in conditions that evaluate to false will be ignored. When a condition evaluates to NULL, it is neither true nor false. In conditional statements this can become a point of confusion but if you review the section in Chapter 3, on *Understanding* NULLs, you can refresh your memory and avoid this confusion.

IF...THEN...ELSE Statements

One of the most common conditional statements found in PL/SQL is the IF...THEN...ELSE statement. The name IF...THEN...ELSE is really a misnomer because there is a lot more to it than these three words. Let's look at some examples of how we might construct some different IF...THEN...ELSE statements.

1.
```
IF expression1 THEN
    plsql_statement1;
END IF;
```

2.
```
IF expression1 THEN
    plsql_statement1;
ELSE
    plsql_statement2;
END IF;
```

3.
```
IF expression1 THEN
    plsql_statement1;
ELSIF expression2 THEN
    plsql_statement2;
ELSIF expression3 THEN
    plsql_statement3;
    . . .
ELSE
    plsql_statement3;
END IF;
```

In statement 1, if EXPRESSION1 evaluates to True, PLSQL_STATEMENT1 is executed, and programmatic control is passed to the end of the END IF clause. No other expressions are evaluated in an IF...THEN...ELSE statement once an expression evaluates to True.

If the first expression to the right of the IF statement does not evaluate to True, the next statement to be evaluated would be the first ELSE clause, as we see in statement 2.

In statement 3, we see the addition of ELSIF expressions, which are evaluated in order until one evaluates to True. If all the ELSIF expressions evaluate to False, PL/SQL looks for an ELSE clause. ELSE is the *catch-all* statement. If all the expressions are False, and there is an ELSE statement, the PL/SQL statements in the ELSE block will be executed. If there is no ELSE clause, control is simply passed beyond the END IF clause and the conditional statement executes no code other than that necessary to determine if conditions were met.

Let's have a go at an example where we use statements of this type.

Try It Out – The IF...THEN... ELSE Example

We'll use the method we saw earlier of setting SQL*Plus so that it asks the user for input, then we'll use IF...THEN...ELSE to evaluate it.

1. Write the following code into a file named if_then_else.sql (or download it from the web site) and run it in SQL*Plus:

```
set echo off
set define '&'
set verify off
set serveroutput on size 10000

prompt
accept NUM prompt 'Enter a single digit number : '
prompt

declare
  l_num number := &NUM;
begin
  if l_num = 1 then
    dbms_output.put_line('You selected one');
  elsif l_num = 2 then
    dbms_output.put_line('You selected two');
  elsif l_num = 3 then
    dbms_output.put_line('You selected three');
  elsif l_num = 4 then
    dbms_output.put_line('You selected four');
  elsif l_num = 5 then
    dbms_output.put_line('You selected five');
  elsif l_num = 6 then
    dbms_output.put_line('You selected six');
  elsif l_num = 7 then
    dbms_output.put_line('You selected seven');
  elsif l_num = 8 then
    dbms_output.put_line('You selected eight');
  elsif l_num = 9 then
    dbms_output.put_line('You selected nine');
  elsif l_num = 0 then
    dbms_output.put_line('You selected zero');
  else
    dbms_output.put_line('You selected more than one digit...');
  end if;
end;
/
```

2. Now we can run it and see what happens:

```
SQL> @if_then_else

Enter a single digit number : 2

You selected two

PL/SQL procedure successfully completed.

SQL> @if_then_else

Enter a single digit number : 9
```

```
You selected nine

PL/SQL procedure successfully completed.

SQL> @if_then_else

Enter a single digit number : 32

You selected more than one digit...

PL/SQL procedure successfully completed.
```

As you can see, the user receives an appropriate response that depends on the number they type in.

CASE Statements

Before Oracle 9*i*, the only conditional statement available was IF...THEN...ELSE. Although that works great, it is cumbersome to write ELSIF clauses for all the possibilities of a potential expression. Instead, developers wanted to use CASE statements that use a WHEN condition to evaluate expressions, so they have been added in the latest version of the database. CASE statements are quicker to code.

There are two forms of the PL/SQL CASE statement. The first form takes a value which is then compared to each WHEN clause:

```
CASE value
  WHEN expression1 THEN
    plsql_statement1;
  [WHEN expression2 THEN
    plsql_statement2;]
     . . .
  [ELSE
    plsql_statement3;]
END CASE;
```

The second form does not take a value on the CASE line, but rather it evaluates each expression in the WHEN clause to find the first expression that evaluates to True:

```
CASE
  WHEN condition1 THEN
    plsql_statement1;
  [WHEN condition2 THEN
    plsql_statement2;]
     . . .
  [ELSE
    plsql_statement3;]
END CASE;
```

IF...THEN...ELSE statements that have many ELSIF clauses should be rewritten as CASE statements in Oracle 9*i*. If we take the example we tried out earlier, and alter it to use a CASE statement instead, we can demonstrate this.

Try It Out – The CASE Example

You can either modify your `if_then_else.sql` script from earlier and save it as `case.sql`, or create it from scratch by copying or downloading the code below:

```
set echo off
set define '&'
set verify off
set serveroutput on size 10000

prompt
accept NUM prompt 'Enter a single digit number : '
prompt

declare
  l_num number := &NUM;
begin
  case l_num
    when 1 then dbms_output.put_line('You selected one');
    when 2 then dbms_output.put_line('You selected two');
    when 3 then dbms_output.put_line('You selected three');
    when 4 then dbms_output.put_line('You selected four');
    when 5 then dbms_output.put_line('You selected five');
    when 6 then dbms_output.put_line('You selected six');
    when 7 then dbms_output.put_line('You selected seven');
    when 8 then dbms_output.put_line('You selected eight');
    when 9 then dbms_output.put_line('You selected nine');
    when 0 then dbms_output.put_line('You selected zero');
    else dbms_output.put_line('You selected more than one digit...');
  end case;
end;
/
```

This script executes and responds in exactly the same way as `if_then_else.sql` earlier.

How It Works

This is a simple enough process to explain. The CASE statement takes the value passed on the CASE line and begins comparing it to the values passed to each WHEN condition in the CASE statement. The first match that is found is executed, and then the CASE statement ends.

In CASE statements, if there are no WHEN clauses that evaluate to the selected value, process control will be passed to the ELSE clause. As a developer, you have the option of providing an ELSE clause yourself, or letting PL/SQL choose one for you. It just so happens that PL/SQL has an interesting ELSE clause it provides in cases where you do not choose to provide one yourself:

```
ELSE raise CASE_NOT_FOUND;
```

We can show this with a slight modification to our example above. If we comment out the ELSE clause:

```
--else dbms_output.put_line('You selected more than one digit...');
```

we can run `case.sql` again, inputting a multi-digit number to see what happens:

```
SQL> @case

Enter a single digit number : 99

declare
*
ERROR at line 1:
ORA-06592: CASE not found while executing CASE statement
ORA-06512: at line 4
```

As you can see, our CASE statement begins on line 4 and this is the line that receives the exception CASE_NOT_FOUND. In my opinion, this is a rather bold way to handle the situation. I'd much rather deal with this myself, by adding necessary error handling code.

Loops

A loop, as you have already seen, is a program control construct we use to iterate over a series of PL/SQL statements and execute them between 0 and an infinite number of times (an infinite number of times being commonly referred to as an **infinite loop**). There are three basic types of loop statements used in PL/SQL: unconstrained, FOR, and WHILE. Let's examine each of them in turn.

Unconstrained Loops

The most basic loop is referred to as an **unconstrained loop**. Unconstrained referring to the fact that without an EXIT statement, the loop will run forever. The command you issue to PL/SQL to stop executing a loop statement is EXIT. Additionally, EXIT WHEN can be used if you want to perform an evaluation to determine whether or not you want to break out of your loop. We'll show examples of both in the following code:

```
SQL> declare
  2      l_loops number := 0;
  3  begin
  4      dbms_output.put_line('Before my loop');
  5
  6      loop
  7        if l_loops > 4 then
  8          exit;
  9        end if;
 10        dbms_output.put_line('Looped ' || l_loops || ' times');
 11        l_loops := l_loops + 1;
 12      end loop;
 13
 14      dbms_output.put_line('After my loop');
 15  end;
 16  /
Before my loop
Looped 0 times
Looped 1 times
Looped 2 times
```

```
Looped 3 times
Looped 4 times
After my loop

PL/SQL procedure successfully completed.
```

It is quite common to break out of a loop based on an evaluation so, in this case, it would be better to use an EXIT WHEN statement instead of explicitly coding an IF...THEN...ELSE statement. Lines 7 through 9 above can become a single line, like this:

```
SQL> declare
  2    l_loops number := 0;
  3  begin
  4    dbms_output.put_line('Before my loop');
  5
  6    loop
  7      exit when l_loops > 4;
  8      dbms_output.put_line('Looped ' || l_loops || ' times');
  9      l_loops := l_loops + 1;
 10    end loop;
 11
 12    dbms_output.put_line('After my loop');
 13  end;
 14  /
Before my loop
Looped 0 times
Looped 1 times
Looped 2 times
Looped 3 times
Looped 4 times
After my loop

PL/SQL procedure successfully completed.
```

FOR Loops

In many situations, the number of times you will loop is determined by some numeric evaluation. The loop statement itself is changed slightly, like this:

```
SQL> declare
  2    l_names dbms_sql.varchar2_table;
  3  begin
  4    l_names(1) := 'Whitney';
  5    l_names(2) := 'Jordan';
  6    l_names(3) := 'Cameron';
  7
  8    for idx in 1 ... l_names.COUNT loop
  9      dbms_output.put_line('Name (' || idx || ') is ' || l_names(idx));
 10    end loop;
 11  end;
 12  /
Name (1) is Whitney
Name (2) is Jordan
```

```
Name (3) is Cameron

PL/SQL procedure successfully completed.
```

The first point to note about the FOR loop is that the number of loop iterations is evaluated once and only once. In the above code sample, if we were to add records to the names variable inside the loop, it would still only pass over the loop three times.

Next, the FOR loop provides a loop counter you can use in your PL/SQL statements inside the loop. The loop counter must count from the value on the left of the loop value range to the value on the right of the loop value range, inclusive, in steps of one. So in the example above the code will loop three times for the values 1, 2, and 3.

In our code sample above, we can use the loop counter IDX to represent which loop iteration we are on. In line 9, we concatenate an IDX to our string in order to identify which record of the L_NAMES PL/SQL table we are showing. In addition to being a loop counter, we can also use IDX as an index to our PL/SQL table. This loop counter is a local variable whose scope is the duration of the loop processing. We can't use the loop counter until it is created in the FOR LOOP when the statement executes, nor after the END LOOP statement is encountered and the loop ends.

You can also use FOR loops in reverse order, by using the keyword REVERSE in your definition. We could reverse the order of the names in the last example by changing line 8 to read:

```
8    for idx in REVERSE 1 .. l_names.COUNT loop
```

WHILE Loops

The last type of loop we will discuss is the WHILE loop. This loop is much the same as an unconditional loop, but you specify the EXIT clause in the loop definition. For example, our original unconditional loop with an EXIT WHEN statement could be rewritten like this:

```
SQL> declare
  2      loops number := 0;
  3  begin
  4      dbms_output.put_line('Before my loop');
  5
  6      while loops < 5 loop
  7          dbms_output.put_line('Looped ' || loops || ' times');
  8          loops := loops + 1;
  9      end loop;
 10
 11      dbms_output.put_line('After my loop');
 12  end;
 13  /
Before my loop
Looped 0 times
Looped 1 times
Looped 2 times
```

```
Looped 3 times
Looped 4 times
After my loop

PL/SQL procedure successfully completed.
```

In this case, the WHILE evaluation is performed on each iteration of the loop, but there is no need to add an explicit EXIT or EXIT WHEN statement to finish the process. There is a significant difference between FOR and WHILE loops to take note of. A FOR loop will always execute the code inside the loop statement at least once. A WHILE loop might never execute the contents of the loop statement. This is one way to help differentiate which type of loop you might use in your PL/SQL routines, depending on what you need the code to do.

Control Statements Summary

FOR loops are more efficient than using a conditional IF...THEN...ELSE loop, or an EXIT WHEN statement, when the number of times you need to loop is predetermined or will not change throughout the life of the loop statements. We could have written the code sample above with an unconditional loop using an EXIT clause inside an IF...THEN...ELSE statement, or with an EXIT WHEN command. However, the IF...THEN...ELSE statement would be evaluated on every iteration of the loop, as would the EXIT statement. In the following example, we will use a loop with a large number of iterations to show the difference in execution speeds (we'll set the timer in SQL*Plus so we can see how long each takes).

```
SQL> set timing on
SQL> declare
  2    some_string varchar2(255);
  3  begin
  4    for idx in 1 .. 100000 loop
  5      some_string := rpad('*',254,'*');
  6    end loop;
  7  end;
  8  /

PL/SQL procedure successfully completed.

Elapsed: 00:00:01.15
```

Compare this to an unconditional loop using an EXIT WHEN statement:

```
SQL> set timing on
SQL> declare
  2    l_idx           pls_integer := 0;
  3    l_some_string varchar2(255);
  4  begin
  5    loop
  6      l_idx := l_idx + 1;
  7      exit when l_idx = 100000;
  8      l_some_string := rpad('*',254,'*');
  9    end loop;
 10  end;
```

```
  11  /

PL/SQL procedure successfully completed.

Elapsed: 00:00:01.70
```

In this case, we only see a difference of .55 seconds, which might seem insignificant. However, these are very simple examples, and we are only executing each block once. In my office, we run an intranet application that receives over 100,000 hits daily. If each hit were to *only* run these two blocks of code, simply changing the type of loop would save you 55,000 seconds of processing time.

This does not mean unconditional loops perform slowly, nor does it mean FOR loops are unusually fast. It simply means that different loops are appropriate for different situations.

Error Handling

Last, but certainly not least important, is our section on **PL/SQL error handling**. As with any other programming language, writing software that is expected to handle user input and process variable data is prone to error conditions. I like to say there are a lot of moving parts. With so many moving parts in your code, you need an effective and efficient mechanism for trapping and handling issues that will cause your code to fail. For PL/SQL, error handling is managed with the use of **exceptions**.

An exception is an **error condition** that occurs during the execution of some PL/SQL code in the Oracle database. At any point in time, while the PL/SQL engine is executing some block of code, an error may be encountered and the corresponding exception for that error will be **raised**. When an exception is raised, PL/SQL passes programmatic control to the **exception handler** portion of the block. The exception handler is where you write code to handle various problems your code may encounter during its execution.

If you have no exception handler in your block, the exception is **propagated**, or sent to the caller of the block. For instance, if you code a PL/SQL block with no exception handlers, any code causing an exception to be raised will be sent to SQL*Plus. SQL*Plus's way of dealing with this is by spooling the exception information to the screen.

In order to use exceptions effectively in your PL/SQL, there are a number of concepts you need to understand. Let's just drill right into the fundamentals.

Exception Section

As we mentioned at the beginning of the chapter, you can optionally include an exception section in each PL/SQL block you develop. This type of section begins with the keyword EXCEPTION, and is the last section of a PL/SQL block. Each exception section can be further broken down into individual **exception handlers**.

The exception handler is much like an evaluation you might find in an IF...THEN...ELSE statement or a CASE statement. The syntax is as follows:

```
exception
  when <EXCEPTION_EXPRESSION> then
    <plsql_statements>
[ when <EXCEPTION_EXPRESSION> then
    <plsql_statements>        ]
[   . . .                     ]
```

where each EXCEPTION_EXPRESSION can be one of the following:

- ❑ one predefined exception (or some combination of Oracle-predefined exception separated by Boolean logic operators).

- ❑ a user-defined exception.

- ❑ A PRAGMA EXCEPTION_INIT exception.

The PLSQL_STATEMENTS you find after the THEN clause is the code you utilize to handle the error condition appropriately.

Let's look at each of the three types of exception expression in turn, and the PL/SQL statements you are able to use with them to produce your desired result.

Predefined Exceptions

Oracle provides a large list of predefined exceptions for you to use in your PL/SQL to check for common conditions that cause your code to fail. They are defined in Oracle's core PL/SQL libraries and are identified by names that you can use in your PL/SQL exception handlers.

Let's look at a common example of some PL/SQL code encountering an exception. Assume you have a PL/SQL block of code that inserts a record into a table. The table has a primary key that uniquely identifies a record, and therefore if you attempt to insert a row into the table with a duplicate primary key, the insert will fail. If we use the HR schema, and try to insert a record into the DEPARTMENTS table where the primary key already exists, the insert will fail:

```
SQL> declare
  2     l_dept departments%rowtype;
  3  begin
  4     l_dept.department_id := 100;
  5     l_dept.department_name := 'Tech Dudes';
  6     insert into departments ( department_id, department_name )
  7     values( l_dept.department_id, l_dept.department_name );
  8  end;
  9  /
declare
*
ERROR at line 1:
ORA-00001: unique constraint (HR.DEPT_ID_PK) violated
ORA-06512: at line 6
```

Our code fails and SQL*Plus reports that we violated a unique constraint named HR.DEPT_ID_PK at line 6. HR.DEPT_ID_PK is the primary key constraint created for the DEPARTMENTS table. If you try to insert two records into the same table using the exact same primary key values, this is the exception that will be raised. Oracle calls it a DUP_VAL_ON_INDEX exception. If we know that the exception is, we can easily trap it in an exception handler in our block and deal with it more constructively:

```
SQL> set serverout on
SQL> declare
  2      l_dept departments%rowtype;
  3  begin
  4      l_dept.department_id := 100;
  5      l_dept.department_name := 'Tech Dudes';
  6      insert into departments ( department_id, department_name )
  7      values( l_dept.department_id, l_dept.department_name );
  8  exception
  9      when DUP_VAL_ON_INDEX then
 10          dbms_output.put_line('We encountered the DUP_VAL_ON_INDEX exception.');
 11          dbms_output.put_line('This is where we''d write out own handler code.');
 12  end;
 13  /
We encountered the DUP_VAL_ON_INDEX exception.
This is where we'd write out own handler code.
```

As you can see, we tried to insert a new record with an existing primary key into the DEPARTMENTS table again, and raised the same exception. On line 9, our block trapped the exception and outputted a couple of lines of text.

Here are some of the other predefined exceptions you might find useful to use in the same way as we did above:

❑ CURSOR_ALREADY_OPEN – This exception is raised when you try to execute an OPEN statement on a cursor that has already been opened. Either check to see if the cursor is open in your code using the %ISOPEN cursor attribute or close the cursor before calling OPEN.

❑ DUP_VAL_ON_INDEX – When inserting records into a table, if there is a column with a unique index, this exception will be raised if the unique index is violated.

❑ INVALID_NUMBER – During an implicit conversion of a character string into a number variable, the character string does not equal a valid number (in other words, '1' = 1, and '2' = 2, but three does not represent 3).

❑ NO_DATA_FOUND – As you have seen, NO_DATA_FOUND is when you try to populate a variable with the results of a SELECT INTO statement that returns no records. Additionally, referencing records of a PL/SQL table that does not exist will also throw NO DATA FOUND.

❑ TOO_MANY_ROWS – Using a SELECT INTO statement that returns more than one record will throw a TOO_MANY_ROWS exception because there is nowhere to store the returned records.

There are quite a few other Oracle predefined exceptions, which can be found in Chapter 7 of the Oracle PL/SQL User's Guide and Reference, Handling PL/SQL Errors. You can view this online at http://download-uk.oracle.com/otndoc/Oracle9i/901_doc/appdev.901/a89856/07_errs.htm.

User-Defined Exceptions

In addition to the Oracle-predefined exceptions, you can also define your own exceptions to be used in your code. This allows you to define custom error handling code in the same manner as the PL/SQL engine handles errors. This is simply good programming practice, and makes for intuitive, manageable code.

Try It Out – What Temperature is Your Porridge?

Let's produce some PL/SQL that will use user-defined exceptions to tell a user whether their porridge is too hot, too cold, or just right.

1. Put the following code in a file and save it as `temps.sql`, or download it from the web site:

```
set echo off
set verify off
set define '&'

prompt 'How hot is your bowl of porridge (numerically in degrees F)?:'
accept temp default '100'

declare
  porridge_too_hot   exception;
  porridge_too_cold  exception;
begin
  case
    when '&temp' < 90.00 then raise porridge_too_cold;
    when '&temp' > 140.00 then raise porridge_too_hot;
    else null;
  end case;

  dbms_output.put_line('The porridge temperature is just right');

exception
  when VALUE_ERROR then
    dbms_output.put_line('Please enter a numeric temperature (like 100)');

  when porridge_too_hot then
    dbms_output.put_line('The porridge is way too hot...');

  when porridge_too_cold then
    dbms_output.put_line('The porridge is way too cold...');
end;
/
```

2. Now let's run the script a few times with various inputs to see how it reacts:

```
SQL> @temps
'How hot is your bowl of porridge (numerically in degrees F)?:'
120
The porridge temperature is just right
```

```
PL/SQL procedure successfully completed.

SQL> @temps
'How hot is your bowl of porridge (numerically in degrees F)?:'
50
The porridge is way too cold...

PL/SQL procedure successfully completed.

SQL> @temps
'How hot is your bowl of porridge (numerically in degrees F)?:'
999999
The porridge is way too hot...

PL/SQL procedure successfully completed.

SQL> @temps
'How hot is your bowl of porridge (numerically in degrees F)?:'
ONE HUNDRED AND TWENTY
Please enter a numeric temperature (like 100)

PL/SQL procedure successfully completed.
```

As you can see, once we create our own user-defined exceptions, they work exactly the same way as Oracle's predefined ones.

How It Works

You can see that we prompt the user for a numeric value, which we will check to see if it is valid. In this case, the number the user enters represents the temperature of a bowl of porridge, and we are trying to figure out whether it is too hot or too cold to eat.

Let's take a look at the example and investigate what we've done. In the declaration section, we define our user-defined exceptions:

```
declare
  porridge_too_hot  exception;
  porridge_too_cold exception;
```

In the executable section, we use a CASE statement to check the value that was accepted by SQL*Plus, and we raise an exception when an error condition is encountered (for the purposes of this example, when the temperature is less than 90.00 or greater than 140.00):

```
case
  when '&temp' < 90.00 then raise porridge_too_cold;
  when '&temp' > 140.00 then raise porridge_too_hot;
  else null;
end case;

dbms_output.put_line('The porridge temperature is just right');
```

If the replacement variable is found to be between 90 and 140, we send a message to `dbms_output.put_line` indicating that the porridge temperature is in our valid range. If the replacement variable is not within our valid range, the appropriate exception is raised and programmatic control is passed to the exception handler.

In the EXCEPTION section of the block you see three different exceptions being accounted for:

❑ VALUE_ERROR

❑ PORRIDGE_TOO_HOT

❑ PORRIDGE_TOO_COLD

VALUE_ERROR is an Oracle predefined exception that will be thrown if the user enters something other than a valid numeric value when prompted for the porridge temperature. This is because Oracle raises a VALUE_ERROR exception when PL/SQL tries to convert a string literal containing invalid numeric characters to a number. The other two exceptions are the ones we define ourselves:

```
when porridge_too_hot then
    dbms_output.put_line('The porridge is way too hot...');

  when porridge_too_cold then
    dbms_output.put_line('The porridge is way too cold...');
 end;
```

They can be raised by name in exactly the same way as the predefined ones.

PRAGMA EXCEPTION_INIT

Pragmas are a way to tell the compiler to do something. They are a holdover from the Ada language. A pragma can be thought of as a pseudo-instruction. `Pragma EXCEPTION_INIT` is a way for a PL/SQL developer to associate a user-defined exception with an Oracle error condition. For instance, if you were to write a block of PL/SQL that encountered some error in Oracle that did not throw a predefined Oracle exception, but was an error nonetheless, you would get a not-so-friendly error stack indicating your problem. Here's an example of just that type of error:

```
SQL> connect hr/hr
Connected.
SQL> set define '&'
SQL> set verify off
SQL> declare
  2    l_update_text varchar2(100) :=
  3      'update &table_name
  4          set &updated_column_name = '':a''
  5        where &key_column_name = :a';
  6  begin
  7    execute immediate l_update_text using '&update_column_value',
&key_column_value;
  8  end;
```

```
   9  /
Enter value for table_name: employees
Enter value for updated_column_name: first_name
Enter value for key_column_name: employee_number
Enter value for update_column_value: Sean
Enter value for key_column_value: 1000
declare
*
ERROR at line 1:
ORA-00904: invalid column name
ORA-06512: at line 7
```

You'll notice that we have used a statement called EXECUTE IMMEDIATE. This is **Dynamic SQL**, and will be covered in more detail in Appendix B, in the DBMS_SQL section. For now, it's enough to know that you can pass a statement to EXECUTE IMMEDIATE and it will be evaluated at run-time, not at compile time. This is handy for situations when you don't know what kind of DML statements you are going to have to put together. In the example, this is exactly what we are showing. We have written a generic script that will update one column in a table based on a one-column key. The script will use the SQL*Plus replacement character (set define '&') to prompt the user for the appropriate values to use in the SQL statement. Given the SQL statement in the L_UPDATE_TEXT variable and the inputs we entered above, we would have produced the following SQL:

```
update employees
   set first_name = :a
 where employee_number = :b;
```

:A *and* :B *are bind variables and will be replaced with* Sean *and* 1000, *respectively. For more information on bind variable usage see Chapter 18.*

The SQL statement is invalid. Even though we have a table named EMPLOYEES with a column named FIRST_NAME, the key column we are using is EMPLOYEE_NUMBER. If we were to attempt this update without the EXECUTE IMMEDIATE in our PL/SQL, the routine wouldn't even compile because the statement would have been checked for validity at compile time and would have failed. Since the entire premise around our UPDATE above is that it is dynamic, and we don't know what the statement will be at compile time, we must accommodate bad input values such as a wrong column name or non-existent table.

Using PRAGMA EXCEPTION_INIT, we can do just that. We can create a user-defined exception called INVALID_COLUMN_NAME and tell the compiler to associate it with the error we received above. Then we can catch and handle this exception in our code as follows (Note: the dynamic update statement has changed slightly on lines 6 through 8):

```
SQL> set define '&'
SQL> set verify off
SQL> set serveroutput on
SQL> declare
  2     invalid_column_name exception;
  3     pragma exception_init(invalid_column_name, -904);
  4
```

```
 5    l_update_text varchar2(100) :=
 6       'update &&table_name
 7          set &&updated_column_name = '':a''
 8        where &&key_column_name = :a';
 9  begin
10    execute immediate l_update_text
11      using '&update_column_value', &key_column_value;
12  exception
13    when INVALID_COLUMN_NAME then
14      dbms_output.put('ERROR! You entered an invalid column name ');
15      dbms_output.put('(&updated_column_name or &key_column_name). Please ');
16      dbms_output.put_line('check your table definition and try again');
17  end;
18  /
Enter value for table_name: employees
Enter value for updated_column_name: first_name
Enter value for key_column_name: employee_number
Enter value for update_column_value: Sean
Enter value for key_column_value: 1000
ERROR! You entered an invalid column name (first_name or employee_number). Please
check your table definition and try again

PL/SQL procedure successfully completed.
```

In our code above, you can see we trapped the exception that was thrown in our previous example by declaring an exception (INVALID_COLUMN_NAME). We used PRAGMA EXCEPTION_INIT to associate it with the exception code we received in the first block we ran (-904), and handled the exception when it was thrown.

> *The exception code can be found by looking in the error stack you receive and finding the ORA-##### error. The ##### will be the numeric code you need to use.*

Oracle's predefined exceptions, such as NO_DATA_FOUND, VALUE_ERROR, or DUP_VAL_ON_INDEX, are all Pragma EXCEPTION_INIT calls in the package STANDARD. So in effect, Oracle has simply used Pragma EXCEPTION_INIT to set up some of the most common errors PL/SQL developers typically run into.

Exception Propagation

Exception propagation is PL/SQL's way of ensuring errors are either handled, or the user running the application is notified of the error condition. For nested PL/SQL blocks, an exception thrown in a nested block, which is not handled in the exception block of the nested PL/SQL block, will be propagated to the parent block for handling. This exception propagation will continue until an appropriate exception handler catches the exception, or the executable code stops processing and the error is passed back to the host environment running the PL/SQL.

Try it Out – Exception Propagation

1. Code the following PL/SQL into a file in your working directory (`excprop.sql`) and run the file in SQL*Plus:

```
SQL> begin
   2    begin
   3      begin
   4        begin
   5          begin
   6            declare
   7              fname employees.first_name%type;
   8            begin
   9              select first_name
  10                into fname
  11                from employees
  12                where 1=2;
  13            exception
  14              when NO_DATA_FOUND then
  15                dbms_output.put_line('block #6');
  16            end;
  17          exception
  18            when NO_DATA_FOUND then
  19              dbms_output.put_line('block #5');
  20          end;
  21        exception
  22          when NO_DATA_FOUND then
  23            dbms_output.put_line('block #4');
  24        end;
  25      exception
  26        when NO_DATA_FOUND then
  27          dbms_output.put_line('block #3');
  28      end;
  29    exception
  30      when NO_DATA_FOUND then
  31        dbms_output.put_line('block #2');
  32    end;
  33  exception
  34    when NO_DATA_FOUND then
  35      dbms_output.put_line('block #1');
  36  end;
  37  /
```

2. Now that you have the file created, we'll run it in SQL*Plus:

```
SQL> set serverout on
SQL> set echo off
SQL> connect hr/hr
Connected.
SQL> @excprop.sql
block #6

PL/SQL procedure successfully completed.
```

How It Works

In our code, we have nested PL/SQL blocks five layers deep. In the innermost block, we execute a SELECT INTO statement with a WHERE clause that will never resolve to True. When performing SELECT INTO statements, this particular condition raises a NO_DATA_FOUND exception. It just so happens that the block containing the SELECT INTO statement has an exception handler for the NO_DATA_FOUND exception, therefore line 9 raises NO_DATA_FOUND, line 14 catches the exception, and line 15 executes sending the message block #6 to the output buffer. Since the exception was successfully handled in the innermost block, no other exceptions are raised, and the PL/SQL blocks all complete successfully.

Let's try something, however. Let's remove the NO_DATA_FOUND exception handler from our innermost PL/SQL block to see what happens. We'll comment out lines 13 to 15 and re-execute the block. Try to determine, without looking ahead, what message will be sent to the output buffer:

```
13  --        exception
14  --          when NO_DATA_FOUND then
15  --            dbms_output.put_line('block #6');
```

If you guessed that the output will be block #5, you were right! Since there is no exception handler in our innermost block, the exception is then propagated, or handed off, to the parent block. Therefore line 18 will catch the NO_DATA_FOUND exception, and line 19 will send its message to the output buffer.

Now, let's take another example, but this time with a user-defined exception, CHILD_ERROR:

```
SQL> declare
  2    CHILD_ERROR exception;
  3  begin
  4    raise CHILD_ERROR;
  5  end;
  6  /
declare
*
ERROR at line 1:
ORA-06510: PL/SQL: unhandled user-defined exception
ORA-06512: at line 4
```

This isn't a difficult problem to solve. All we need to do is create an appropriate exception handler. If we don't do that though, the generic ORA-06510: PL/SQL: unhandled user-defined exception becomes a serious problem if we then use this routine in stored procedures, functions, or packages, where other users might encounter it. Those users are not likely to be able to access or edit the code themselves and, without doing so, there is no way to know what the error condition is.

I recommend strict coding standards for when you start using user-defined exceptions because you do not want to cause another developer the problem of not being able to understand the errors they are receiving with *your* code. Whenever you define a user-defined exception, write the exception handler immediately. This prevents you from not handling your own exceptions and propagating a very frustrating problem onto somebody else's list of 'things to figure out'.

User-Defined Exceptions Scope and Visibility

Scope and visibility rules apply to user-defined exceptions the same way they apply to variables and constants. An exception declared in a parent block is visible in the nested block, but not the other way around. Declaring an exception in a nested block will not provide visibility once programmatic control has left the nested block into the parent block. If an unhandled user-defined exception is propagated from its defining block, there is no way to catch the exception unless you use the catch-all exception, OTHERS. For instance:

```
SQL> begin
  2     declare      --start of nested block
  3       NESTED_EXCEPTION exception;
  4     begin
  5       raise NESTED_EXCEPTION;
  6     end;          --end of nested block
  7   exception
  8     when NESTED_EXCEPTION then
  9       dbms_output.put_line('NESTED_EXCEPTION caught!');
 10   end;
 11   /
    when NESTED_EXCEPTION then
         *
ERROR at line 8:
ORA-06550: line 8, column 8:
PLS-00201: identifier 'NESTED_EXCEPTION' must be declared
ORA-06550: line 0, column 0:
PL/SQL: Compilation unit analysis terminated
```

As you can see, the parent block's exception section is not visible to the nested block's exception declarations. This does not imply that a parent block should declare all the exceptions that would be used within a nested block's code. More appropriately, a nested block should be responsible for handling any exceptions that are raised in its own executable section. There are three ways to overcome the problem we just saw:

❑ by declaring exceptions in the parent block, which may make total sense in some situations, and no sense whatsoever in others.

❑ by ensuring any user-defined exception has a corresponding exception handler that resolves the exception's error conditions in the block in which the exception is defined. This is most likely the best way, as a user-defined exception can never be propagated beyond its definition block.

❑ by using the WHEN OTHERS THEN clause. This means that if the exception has not been explicitly named in the exception section, the WHEN OTHERS THEN clause will catch the rest of the exceptions. This exception handler acts like a 'catch-all' handler for any exceptions thrown that are not explicitly handled, including Oracle-predefined exceptions.

Let's look at an example using nested blocks and user-defined exceptions where we add a WHEN OTHERS THEN clause to the end of the parent block:

```
SQL> set serverout on
SQL> declare
  2       PARENT_ERROR exception;
```

```
 3      begin
 4        declare
 5          CHILD_ERROR exception;
 6        begin
 7          raise CHILD_ERROR;
 8        exception
 9          when CHILD_ERROR then
10            dbms_output.put_line('nested block exception handler');
11            raise;
12        end;
13      exception
14        when PARENT_ERROR then
15          dbms_output.put_line('parent block exception handler');
16
17        when OTHERS then
18          dbms_output.put_line('Caught the OTHERS exception');
19          raise;
20
21      end;
22      /
nested block exception handler
Caught the OTHERS exception
declare
*
ERROR at line 1:
ORA-06510: PL/SQL: unhandled user-defined exception
ORA-06512: at line 19
```

As you can see, we declare a user-defined exception at line 2 named PARENT_ERROR. We then declare an exception named CHILD_ERROR in our nested block. We raise the CHILD_ERROR exception on line 8, and catch it at line 10. This all works just fine. We raise the PARENT_ERROR exception on line 12, but it is not caught at line 14.

This is because the exception raised was the user-defined exception declared on line 6, not line 2. Line 14 in our code sample is looking for the PARENT_ERROR exception defined on line 2, which was never raised.

As you can see, even though the exception propagated to the parent block in line 12 is a user-defined block that has lost all its visibility, the WHEN OTHERS exception handler in line 17 still caught the exception and subsequently raised the error.

> WHEN OTHERS THEN exception handlers must be declared last in the exception section of your
> PL/SQL block. Violating this rule results in a PL/SQL exception that reminds you of this.

One other thing to notice about our use of the WHEN OTHERS exception handler is that the last line is a RAISE statement. Using the WHEN OTHERS exception handler in PL/SQL is somewhat lazy to begin with, so you should try to handle any exceptions that could be raised in your code explicitly, rather than relying on a 'catch-all' handler. This makes you understand your code that much better, and also ensures errors don't go unhandled during the run-time of your code. There are so many times when people use this clause only to find out later that an issue was being caught in this exception handler and then being ignored because the RAISE statement was not used. A WHEN OTHERS exception handler without a RAISE statement should be treated like a bug in your code.

Exceptions Raised in Declarations

An exception thrown in the declaration section of a nested block will not be caught in the exception section of that block. These exceptions are thrown and can only be caught by a parent block's exception handler. In a PL/SQL routine that is a single block, the exception will be thrown but its exception block will not handle it. Here's an example where we throw an exception in the declaration section by declaring a numeric variable and assigning a character value to it:

```
SQL> declare
  2     l_number number default 'MY NUMBER';
  3  begin
  4     null;
  5  exception
  6     when OTHERS then
  7        dbms_output.put_line('Exception caught');
  8        raise;
  9  end;
 10  /
declare
*
ERROR at line 1:
ORA-06502: PL/SQL: numeric or value error: character to number conversion error
ORA-06512: at line 2
```

There are two ways to handle this situation. First, if you need to catch the exception in the same block, don't make your variable assignment until the executable section. I'm not suggesting you avoid using DEFAULT values for variables, but if you absolutely need to catch an exception in the same block you could code the above statement like this (notice the "Exception caught" message after the PL/SQL block):

```
SQL> declare
  2     l_number number;
  3  begin
  4     l_number := 'MY NUMBER';
  5  exception
  6     when OTHERS then
  7        dbms_output.put_line('Exception caught');
  8        raise;
  9  end;
 10  /
Exception caught
declare
*
ERROR at line 1:
ORA-06502: PL/SQL: numeric or value error: character to number conversion error
ORA-06512: at line 8
```

In nested blocks we would handle these types of exception in the parent block's exception handler, as we said. Since the nested block is a part of the parent block's execution, it makes sense that the error handling routine would go into the parent block's exception handler:

```
SQL> begin
  2     declare
  3        l_number number default 'MY NUMBER';
  4     begin
  5        null;
```

```
  6    exception
  7      when OTHERS then
  8        dbms_output.put_line('Exception caught in inner block');
  9    end;
 10  exception
 11    when others then
 12      dbms_output.put_line('Exception caught in outer block');
 13      raise;
 14  end;
 15  /
Exception caught in outer block
begin
*
ERROR at line 1:
ORA-06502: PL/SQL: numeric or value error: character to number conversion error
ORA-06512: at line 13
```

In these simple examples, we are blatantly declaring a numeric variable and assigning a character value to it to throw the error. In your code you probably won't do something as ridiculous as this, but you might be assigning to a variable values that are unknown at compile time. If you are expecting input from a user in a SQL*Plus script, or perhaps you are calculating a value based on a variable in a parent block, the values you don't know at compile time will break your code at run-time. Now that you understand the behavior of errors raised in the declaration section of your PL/SQL blocks, you can proactively instrument your code to ensure you handle these types of problem before they occur.

SQLCODE and SQLERRM

There are two new 'variables' available for use within your exception handler. These are SQLCODE and SQLERRM. SQLCODE is the error code used to identify the error you received. SQLERRM is a plain-text message used to identify what the error is. These two variables can be used in any exception handler, but become very important when used in conjunction with WHEN OTHERS. Since any thrown exception will be caught in the WHEN OTHERS exception handler, using SQLCODE and SQLERRM provides a 'self-describing' error mechanism. For example:

```
SQL> connect scott/tiger
Connected.
SQL> set serverout on
SQL> declare
  2    l_emp emp%rowtype;
  3  begin
  4    select *
  5      into l_emp
  6      from emp;
  7    dbms_output.put_line('EMPNO: ' || l_emp.empno);
  8    dbms_output.put_line('ENAME: ' || l_emp.ename);
  9  exception
 10    when others then
 11      dbms_output.put('Exception encountered! (');
 12      dbms_output.put_line(sqlcode || '): ' || sqlerrm);
 13      raise;
 14  end;
 15  /
Exception encountered! (-1422): ORA-01422: exact fetch returns more than requested
number of rows
declare
```

```
*
ERROR at line 1:
ORA-01422: exact fetch returns more than requested number of rows
ORA-06512: at line 13
```

You can see we caught an exception in our WHEN OTHERS handler with a SQLCODE of 1422 and a SQLERRM of exact fetch returns more than requested number of rows. In lines 4 through 6 in our code block, we select a record from the EMP table into L_EMP. The problem with this is we can only store one row in the variable, and there are fourteen records in the table. We tried to fetch one row when there was more than one record returned in the query. To fix this, we could either use a WHERE clause in the query to uniquely identify a row, or we could use a cursor instead of a local variable.

Summary

In this chapter, we have explored programming PL/SQL in the Oracle database in terms of introductory concepts. We have taken a look at block-based programming, and how PL/SQL logically divides a block of code into areas of responsibility such as variable and constant declaration, execution code, and error-handling code. We took a look at how data types in PL/SQL are different from data types in SQL. We learned how to declare data types based on the table owner's columns using the appropriate syntax, TABLE.COLUMN%TYPE.

Cursors allow us to introduce SQL queries to our PL/SQL code, effectively integrating the programmatic constructs with the data stored in the database. There is a wide variety of built-in functionality to help manipulate our date, character, and number variables. Along the way, we also delved into PL/SQL programming constructs such as conditional logic, loop statements, and error-handling code.

There are manuals upon manuals in the Oracle documentation set that explain every nuance of PL/SQL programming there is to know. When put into context, this chapter is, most definitely, a small peek at the gargantuan beast that is the PL/SQL language. It is similar to a beginner's swimming lesson. You now know how to stay afloat in the water, and can get from one side of the pool to the other. You have made the first strokes towards writing effective PL/SQL code in your database. As you proceed through the book, we are going to teach you the backstroke (procedures and functions), the breaststroke (triggers), and the almighty butterfly (packages). Now that you have the foundations, let's dig into the fun stuff!

Procedures, Functions, and Packages

In the chapter on PL/SQL, you saw how powerful and useful this programming language could be. I'm sure any developers reading it also noticed that it was a little limiting though. All there seemed to be were anonymous (unnamed), self-contained blocks of code that can be run from the SQL*Plus prompt. Well that is not the case at all. Developers can name their PL/SQL blocks, parameterize them, store them in the database and reference or run them from any database client or facility such as SQL*Plus, Pro*C, or even JDBC.

These named PL/SQL programs are called **stored procedures** and **functions**. Collections of these are known as **packages**. In this chapter we will explain the benefits of using procedures, functions and packages, as well as the differences between these three similar constructs and when to use each of them. In this way you will learn how to develop and write your own.

Advantages and Benefits

Let's begin by exploring the advantages of using stored procedures, functions, and packages over anonymous PL/SQL blocks:

❑ **Extensibility**. Using procedures and functions gives the developer the ability to add functionality. Writing your own routines gives you the flexibility to extend the database's core abilities. This does not mean that you will change how Oracle works (that would be bad), but it does let you create additional procedures and functions that you can use and share with others.

❑ **Modularity**. Any good developer knows that it is important to write modular code. You should always try to define the individual processes in your application by developing small, manageable procedures that can fit together to produce more complex applications. Small, discrete procedures are easier to modify than more complex ones and can be shared more effectively.

❏ **Reusability**. Since these routines can be named and saved in the database, any number of applications can execute them (as long as they have the appropriate privilege to do so). This ability to reuse code is essential in the development process. Consider a procedure that logs activity, something that you would want to do throughout your code. Instead of writing the logging logic over and over again, you can simply create a LOG_MESSAGE() procedure and then call it whenever appropriate. A single copy of the procedure is important for performance too. Once a procedure is read into memory, subsequent calls can read it directly from there, without having to repeat the process.

❏ **Maintainability**. To continue with the example in the section above, consider what would happen if the table where the log messages were being stored, changed. Having a single place where you need to make that change makes your code much more maintainable. Otherwise you would have to go through all the code in the entire application and make multiple changes. This just wastes time and is prone to further mistakes.

❏ **Abstraction and Data Hiding**. Let's assume that you are calling a procedure called GIVE_EMPLOYEE_RAISE() that you did not write. You supply it with some information and expect it to work, in other words you expect the employee to get their raise. It is a black box to you as a user. The implementation of how that happens is not important, since all you need to know is what it's supposed to do. All the complication and complexity of the process is hidden to the caller.

❏ **Security**. Just as views can be used as a security mechanism, so can procedures. You can set up your application so that the only means of accessing its data is through the procedures and functions that you supply. This not only makes the data more secure, but also ensures that it is correct. As the developer, you can be assured that the data has not been altered, except through your **Application Program Interfaces** (**APIs**).

Now we've seen the benefits, let's get down to the practicalities, beginning with stored procedures.

Please note: the code for all the examples in this chapter is available to download from the Apress web site at http://www.apress.com/.

Procedures

A **stored procedure** is essentially a named PL/SQL block that can be parameterized, stored in the database, and then invoked (or called) by another application or PL/SQL routine. Let's dive right in and create the world's simplest procedure:

```
SQL> create procedure my_proc as
  2  begin
  3    null;
  4  end my_proc;
  5  /

Procedure created.
```

That's it. You can call and execute it and it will run. It won't do anything because the body of the stored procedure is one command, NULL which will do nothing, but it is a valid stored procedure.

> Notice when creating a stored procedure, you need to put a **/** by itself on the last line of the procedure to tell SQL*Plus to process the lines you previously typed or loaded in.

Syntax

Now let's look at the syntax for creating a stored procedure:

```
 1 [CREATE [OR REPLACE]]
 2 PROCEDURE procedure_name[(parameter[, parameter]...)]
 3 [AUTHID {DEFINER | CURRENT_USER}] {IS | AS}
 4 [PRAGMA AUTONOMOUS_TRANSACTION;]
 5 [local declarations]
 6 BEGIN
 7   executable statements
 8 [EXCEPTION
 9 exception handlers]
10 END [name];
```

Most of this syntax is very similar to an anonymous PL/SQL block. There are small differences between the BEGIN-EXCEPTION-END blocks, since in the case of stored procedures the outermost block can end with an optional END PROCEDURE_NAME; (as defined in line 10), and there is no DECLARE keyword in a procedure. The declaration section is anything that comes prior to the BEGIN keyword (see line 5). Other than that, all the differences deal with the naming and behavior of the block of code.

CREATE OR REPLACE

The syntax may look a little confusing, so let's break it down and go over it one piece at a time. The first line [CREATE [OR REPLACE]] is needed if this is a **stand-alone** procedure, in other words one that is not defined within a package. The optional OR REPLACE phrase is needed when you are trying to create, or more correctly, recreate a stored procedure with a name already existing in your schema. Just as with database views, the OR REPLACE option allows the developer to modify the object, but retain all the privileges granted to it, even if the replaced version performs a completely different task.

Let's edit our initial example, so as to do what every first computer program must do, and print 'Hello World'.

```
SQL> create procedure my_proc as
  2  begin
  3    dbms_output.put_line ( 'Hello World' );
  4  end my_proc;
  5  /

create procedure my_proc as
                  *
ERROR at line 1:
ORA-00955: name is already used by an existing object
```

413

An error! We had previously created a stored procedure with the name MY_PROC, so we need to use the CREATE OR REPLACE command to overwrite the older version with this new version.

Note that it is not possible to use the syntax REPLACE PROCEDURE MY_PROC, since this will throw a syntax error. You must use CREATE OR REPLACE in order to overwrite existing versions of any given procedure.

> **You will get the same error if you attempt to create a stored procedure with a name that any other object in your schema has. It does not matter if the object is a table, view, index, sequence, whatever. Every object in your schema must be uniquely named.**

If we use the correct syntax, we can modify our procedure like this:

```
SQL> create or replace procedure my_proc as
  2  begin
  3    dbms_output.put_line( 'Hello World' );
  4  end my_proc;
  5  /

Procedure created.
```

Executing a Stored Procedure

Now that we have this stored procedure, we want to see it in action, and make sure it does what we expect it to. To execute your procedure, you simply call it from within a PL/SQL anonymous block:

```
SQL> set serverout on
SQL> begin
  2    my_proc;
  3  end;
  4  /
Hello World

PL/SQL procedure successfully completed.
```

First we issued the SQL*Plus command, SET SERVEROUT ON, to tell SQL*Plus that we wanted it to display the output from the Oracle supplied package DBMS_OUTPUT (there's more on this package in Appendix B). Then we created a BEGIN-END anonymous PL/SQL block in order to call MY_PROC.

> **Every stored procedure can be called in this manner.**

Alternatively, there is a shortcut that makes calling procedures a little bit easier. You can use the EXECUTE command, or EXEC for short, from within SQL*Plus:

```
SQL> execute my_proc;
Hello World

PL/SQL procedure successfully completed.
```

*Calling EXECUTE <PROCEDURE_NAME> is identical to calling the procedure in an anonymous PL/SQL block. It's a convenience function of SQL*Plus and not a PL/SQL command.*

Security

Since a stored procedure is stored in the database, it is a database object. And just like any other object, access to it can be controlled through privileges. Where tables and views have privileges such as SELECT, INSERT, UPDATE, and DELETE, procedures have the privilege EXECUTE. Granting EXECUTE on a procedure to a user or role gives that entity the ability to run it; granting it to the role PUBLIC makes it available to all.

Try It Out – Access To Procedures

1. Let's begin by creating three database users, CHRIS, SEAN, and MARK. You'll need to connect with an account with the DBA role to do this, such as the ORACLE_ADMIN user we created in Chapter 3, or SYSTEM.

```
SQL> connect oracle_admin/oracle_admin
Connected.
SQL> create user chris identified by chris;

User created.

SQL> grant connect, resource to chris;

Grant succeeded.

SQL> create user sean identified by sean;

User created.

SQL> grant connect, resource to sean;

Grant succeeded.

SQL> create user mark identified by mark;

User created.

SQL> grant connect, resource to mark;

Grant succeeded.
```

2. Now let's create a procedure as user MARK. This is a very simple procedure. It performs no work but will help us demonstrate access privileges:

```
SQL> connect mark/mark
Connected.
SQL> create procedure marks_procedure as
  2  begin
```

```
    3    null;
    4    end;
    5    /

Procedure created.
```

3. Now let's attempt to execute this procedure as user CHRIS:

```
SQL> connect chris/chris
Connected.
SQL> execute mark.marks_procedure

BEGIN mark.marks_procedure; END;

    *
ERROR at line 1:
ORA-06550: line 1, column 7:
PLS-00201: identifier 'MARK.MARKS_PROCEDURE' must be declared
ORA-06550: line 1, column 7:
PL/SQL: Statement ignored
```

CHRIS is unable to access and execute MARK's procedure. By default, as with other objects, only the owner has access to their procedures initially. To allow access to their procedures they must explicitly grant access to others.

> **Be careful when you get this error. Check that it is indeed a privilege error and not a typo.**

4. Let's go back and grant CHRIS EXECUTE privilege on the procedure:

```
SQL> connect mark/mark
Connected.
SQL> grant execute on marks_procedure to chris;

Grant succeeded.

SQL> connect chris/chris
Connected.
SQL> execute mark.marks_procedure;

PL/SQL procedure successfully completed.
```

Once CHRIS has been granted EXECUTE, he can access and execute MARK's procedure.

Notice that CHRIS needed to preface the procedure name with the owner, MARK. Again, accessing a stored procedure is just like accessing any other database object. If you do not own it, or do not have a synonym for it, you must access it with the OWNER.OBJECT naming convention.

5. Now let's attempt to execute the procedure as user SEAN.

```
SQL> connect sean/sean
Connected.
SQL> execute mark.marks_procedure

BEGIN mark.marks_procedure; END;

      *
ERROR at line 1:
ORA-06550: line 1, column 7:
PLS-00201: identifier 'MARK.MARKS_PROCEDURE' must be declared
ORA-06550: line 1, column 7:
PL/SQL: Statement ignored
```

Although CHRIS can execute the procedure, SEAN has no privilege to do so.

6. Now let's connect as user MARK and GRANT EXECUTE to PUBLIC and then see if SEAN can execute MARK's procedure once we've done it:

```
SQL> connect mark/mark
Connected.
SQL> grant execute on marks_procedure to public;

Grant succeeded.

SQL> connect sean/sean
Connected.
SQL> execute mark.marks_procedure

PL/SQL procedure successfully completed.
```

> Note that granting **EXECUTE** to **PUBLIC** for a procedure makes it accessible to every database user. Although **SEAN** has not been given direct access, he inherited the **EXECUTE** privilege via the **PUBLIC** role.

Parameters

Procedures can be **parameterized**. This means that a caller of a procedure can pass in values for it to use. Parameters can be of any valid PL/SQL type and they come in three modes: IN, OUT, and IN OUT.

❑ IN parameters are passed in by the caller and can only be read by the procedure. That is to say that they are read-only values, and can't be changed by the procedure. This is the most commonly used mode of parameter behavior and is the default where no parameter mode indicator is given. IN parameters can also have default values so the caller does not need to supply a value for them.

417

❑   OUT parameters can be written to by the procedure. These are useful when the procedure needs to pass back multiple pieces of information to the caller. OUT parameters cannot be defaulted, and a variable, not a constant or expression, must be passed to OUT parameters.

❑   IN OUT parameters, as the name suggests, have the properties of both IN and OUT parameters. Procedures can both read and write their values.

Procedures can have any combination of the three types of parameters and they can be defined in any order in the parameter list. Let's look at a few examples.

IN Parameters

We'll connect as our user CHRIS and create a simple procedure INSERT_INTO_T(). This takes in one parameter P_PARM and, as the procedure name suggests, inserts its value into the table T:

```
SQL> connect chris/chris
Connected.

SQL> create table t(
  2    n number
  3  )
  4  /

Table created.

SQL> create or replace
  2  procedure insert_into_t( p_parm in number ) is
  3  begin
  4    insert into t values ( p_parm );
  5  end insert_into_t;
  6  /

Procedure created.
```

Let's try to execute our new procedure and see what happens:

```
SQL> select * from t;

no rows selected

SQL> exec insert_into_t( p_parm => 100 );

PL/SQL procedure successfully completed.

SQL> select * from t;

         N
----------
       100
```

Don't worry at this point about the notation we used to pass the parameter,
(P_PARM => 100), since we will be discussing this in detail in the next section.

As you can see, table T was empty initially. After a call to our procedure, T now contains one row. That row's value is the value we passed into the procedure, proving that the procedure executed the INSERT statement within its body.

Let's change the procedure to take in a second parameter, which we will also insert into table T:

```
SQL> create or replace
  2  procedure insert_into_t(
  3    p_parm1 in number,
  4    p_parm2 in number ) is
  5  begin
  6    insert into t values ( p_parm1 );
  7    insert into t values ( p_parm2 );
  8  end insert_into_t;
  9  /

Procedure created.
```

Execution will be just the same as before, except that this time, we'll need to supply two values:

```
SQL> exec insert_into_t( p_parm1 => 101, p_parm2 => 102 );

PL/SQL procedure successfully completed.

SQL> select * from t;

         N
----------
       100
       101
       102
```

Now we'll change the procedure again, and alter the table T to include information about which parameter inserted which value:

```
SQL> drop table t
  2  /

Table dropped.

SQL> create table t(
  2    n number,
  3    parm varchar2(20)
  4  )
  5  /

Table created.

SQL> create or replace
  2  procedure insert_into_t(
```

```
3    p_parm1 in number,
4    p_parm2 in number ) is
5  begin
6    insert into t values ( p_parm1, 'p_parm1' );
7    insert into t values ( p_parm2, 'p_parm2' );
8  end insert_into_t;
9  /

Procedure created.
```

Again, we execute in the same way, with two values, but this time the name of the parameter that inserted each value is stored in the PARM column:

```
SQL> exec insert_into_t( p_parm1 => 200, p_parm2 => 201 );

PL/SQL procedure successfully completed.

SQL> select * from t;

        N PARM
---------- --------------------
      200 p_parm1
      201 p_parm2
```

Parameter Passing

There are three ways in which we can pass parameters:

❑ Using Named Notation

❑ Using Positional Notation

❑ Using Mixed Notation

We'll take a look at each of them in turn here.

Named Notation

In the examples above, we explicitly named each parameter. This is known as **Named Notation**. It takes the form of:

```
PROCEDURE_NAME( PARM_NAME => VALUE [, PARM_NAME => VALUE] )
```

Calls are formed to the procedure by naming each formal parameter, following with =>, which is made up of an equals sign (=) and a greater than sign (>), and closed by the expression. In the example above, you could read the call:

```
SQL> exec insert_into_t( p_parm1 => 200, p_parm => 201 );
```

as "INSERT_INTO_T, P_PARM1 gets the value 200, and P_PARM gets the value 201". The => or arrow indicates what parameter is assigned which expression. That way we explicitly tell the PL/SQL procedure which value gets assigned to which parameter. Using Named Notation makes reading, reviewing, and debugging code much easier, especially if the parameters are named well. It allows you to see exactly which values are being passed to which parameters. The order in which you pass them is not important as long as you supply all the required parameters. Let's look at an example with three parameters and see what happens when we call the procedure with the parameters out of order:

```
SQL> create or replace
  2  procedure three_parms(
  3    p_p1 number,
  4    p_p2 number,
  5    p_p3 number ) as
  6  begin
  7    dbms_output.put_line( 'p_p1 = ' || p_p1 );
  8    dbms_output.put_line( 'p_p2 = ' || p_p2 );
  9    dbms_output.put_line( 'p_p3 = ' || p_p3 );
 10  end three_parms;
 11  /

Procedure created.

SQL> set serverout on
SQL> exec three_parms( p_p1 => 12, p_p3 => 3, p_p2 => 68 );
p_p1 = 12
p_p2 = 68
p_p3 = 3

PL/SQL procedure successfully completed.
```

Notice that we passed the parameters to the procedure in the order P_P1, P_P3, P_P2, even though the procedure has them defined in the order P_P1, P_P2, P_P3. As long as we name our parameters, order is not important.

Positional Notation

Named Notation can be very long-winded. Consider a procedure with 10 or more parameters. That is a lot of typing to call a routine. A shorter notation that most developers use is known as **Positional Notation** parameter passing. This is where you pass the parameters based on the order of how they are defined in the procedure. If we call the procedure with the values in the exact same order as above, but this time do not explicitly name the parameters, we get a different result:

```
SQL> exec three_parms( 12, 3, 68 );
p_p1 = 12
p_p2 = 3
p_p3 = 68

PL/SQL procedure successfully completed.
```

Parameters P_P2 and P_P3 have changed values. This is where problems can arise. If you do not know the order in which the parameters are defined, you can get very unpredictable results.

> **Be careful if you use this Positional Notation when calling procedures.**

There are advantages to using Positional notation however, notably that you do not need to know the names of the parameters in order to reference them and, as we said, it's quicker to do.

Mixed Notation

You can mix both Named and Positional Notation parameter passing. This is known as **Mixed Notation** parameter passing. The procedure above could also be called this way:

```
SQL> exec three_parms( 12, 3, p_p3 => 68 );
p_p1 = 12
p_p2 = 3
p_p3 = 68


PL/SQL procedure successfully completed.
```

Here I started out using positional notation for the first two parameters, then switched to named notation. If there were fourth and fifth parameters, I would have to keep with the named notation. Once you start named notation, you must use it for the rest of the parameter list. In this example it was not necessary to use named notation at all. I supplied all the parameters with values so it was not required that I name any of them. In the next section, we'll see examples where Mixed Notation makes life easier.

Default Values

Up to now, we have always supplied a value for each and every parameter that a procedure defines, but we don't have to if the procedure has a default value. The procedure author can define a default value for any IN parameter.

> **Please note: OUT and IN OUT parameters cannot be defaulted.**

Let's look at an example:

```
SQL> create or replace
  2  procedure default_values(
  3    p_parm1 varchar2,
  4    p_parm2 varchar2 default 'Chris',
  5    p_parm3 varchar2 default 'Sean' ) as
  6  begin
  7    dbms_output.put_line( p_parm1 );
  8    dbms_output.put_line( p_parm2 );
  9    dbms_output.put_line( p_parm3 );
 10  end default_values;
 11  /

Procedure created.

SQL> set serverout on
```

```
SQL> exec default_values( 'Tom', p_parm3 => 'Joel' );
Tom
Chris
Joel

PL/SQL procedure successfully completed.
```

Notice, that we supplied only two values to the DEFAULT_VALUES() procedure. Since P_PARM2 has a default value of Chris, we did not need to supply a value. P_PARM3 also had a default value but we overrode it with the value Joel. This shows how it is sometimes useful to use Mixed Notation when passing parameters.

Default values are useful when the inputs to your routine do not change very often. Consider a procedure that creates a new employee. This procedure may take in FIRST_NAME, LAST_NAME, HIRE_DATE, SALARY, and EMPLOYEE_TYPE. The first four parameters will be different for every employee usually, but EMPLOYEE_TYPE may be defaulted to FT for full time.

```
procedure hire_employee(
    first_name varchar2,
    last_name varchar2,
    hire_date date,
    salary number,
    employee_type varchar2 default 'FT' )
```

Only in the case where you are hiring a part-time employee, would the caller need to override that default value.

Default values are provided for convenience only. You can just as easily supply a value for the defaulted parameter and the procedure will use that value for processing.

Adding Parameters

As a good rule of thumb, if you ever need to add a parameter to your live stored procedure, always add it as the last parameter. This way any routine currently calling your procedure using Positional Notation will continue to work as long as the parameter you add is defaulted. If you add the parameter anywhere but as the last parameter in the procedure's definition, you could cause every routine calling your procedure to either throw an error, or get unwanted or unexpected results.

Common Errors

When calling a procedure, you might make mistakes in your parameter passing. The most common ones are:

- ❑ Supplying a named parameter not defined in the procedure
- ❑ Not supplying enough parameters
- ❑ Supplying too many parameters
- ❑ Supplying a parameter with an invalid data type

Any of these mistakes will produce the following error message:

```
SQL> exec default_values( p_parm4 => 'Tom' );
BEGIN default_values( p_parm4 => 'Tom' ); END;

      *
ERROR at line 1:
ORA-06550: line 1, column 7:
PLS-00306: wrong number or types of arguments in call to 'DEFAULT_VALUES'
ORA-06550: line 1, column 7:
PL/SQL: Statement ignored
```

In the above example, we attempted to call the DEFAULT_VALUES() procedure and supply it with a parameter name not defined for the procedure. The following error was raised:

```
PLS-00306: wrong number or types of arguments in call to 'DEFAULT_VALUES'
```

This same error will be encountered if too few, or too many parameters are supplied to a procedure.

The fourth error on our list may also generate a conversion error message. Calling our THREE_PARMS() procedure with VARCHAR2 values instead of NUMBERS causes the following:

```
SQL> exec three_parms( 'Chris', 'Sean', 'Tom' );
BEGIN three_parms( 'Chris', 'Sean', 'Tom' ); END;

*
ERROR at line 1:
ORA-06502: PL/SQL: numeric or value error: character to number conversion error
ORA-06512: at line 1
```

Knowing the error messages generated by certain types of mistakes will help you quickly diagnose a problem and fix it.

OUT Parameters

Up to now our example procedures have only taken in values and processed them. We have not seen any mechanism to return values from the routine to the caller. OUT parameters allow us to do that. Using the SCOTT.EMP table we can write a lookup procedure that will return the ENAME and SAL of the employee whose EMPNO we supply:

```
SQL> connect scott/tiger
SQL> create or replace
  2  procedure emp_lookup(
  3    p_empno in      number,
  4    o_ename     out emp.ename%type,
  5    o_sal       out emp.sal%type ) as
  6  begin
  7    select ename, sal
  8      into o_ename, o_sal
```

```
 9        from emp
10      where empno = p_empno;
11   exception
12     when NO_DATA_FOUND then
13        o_ename := 'NULL';
14        o_sal := -1;
15   end emp_lookup;
16   /

Procedure created.
```

Executing this stored procedure from SQL*Plus is a bit trickier than using the shortcut EXECUTE. We must either write our own anonymous PL/SQL block that declares two local variables or use the SQL*Plus VARIABLE command to bind in the values. Why? Well, since this procedure returns values via its OUT parameters, we need to supply it with the variables to return values into.

Here is how we would call our EMP_LOOKUP procedure using the VARIABLE command in SQL*Plus. First we define two variables:

```
SQL> variable name varchar2(10);
SQL> variable sal number;
```

so that we can execute the procedure:

```
SQL> exec emp_lookup( '7782', :name, :sal );

PL/SQL procedure successfully completed.
```

To see the results we can use the PRINT command in SQL*Plus:

```
SQL> print name

NAME
------------------------------
CLARK

SQL> print sal

       SAL
----------
      2450
```

Or we can just project the values and select them from DUAL:

```
SQL> select :name, :sal
  2     from dual
  3  /

:NAME                               :SAL
------------------------------ ----------
CLARK                               2450
```

425

Calling the same procedure from an anonymous PL/SQL block might look like this:

```
SQL> set serverout on
SQL> declare
  2     l_ename emp.ename%type;
  3     l_sal emp.sal%type;
  4  begin
  5     emp_lookup( 7782, l_ename, l_sal );
  6     dbms_output.put_line( 'Ename = ' || l_ename );
  7     dbms_output.put_line( 'Sal = ' || l_sal );
  8  end;
  9  /
Ename = CLARK
Sal = 2450

PL/SQL procedure successfully completed.
```

Before we move on, let's note a couple of features of the examples we've just looked at:

❑   Firstly, the procedure itself defined its OUT parameters with types of TABLE.COLUMN%TYPE. This is a good practice to use when you know the variable you are defining will hold a database column value. It ensures that the variable is of the correct type and size. If the underlying database column is altered, you will not have to modify your code to account for the change, it will automatically handle it.

❑   Second, in the anonymous PL/SQL block, notice that the variables passed in as the OUT parameters are defined to be the same types as the parameters in the EMP_LOOKUP procedure. This is important, since if you pass in different types, it may compile but it will generate run-time type conversion errors. Always make sure the types match.

Common Errors

Procedures with OUT parameters must be supplied with variables, otherwise they do not have a place to write values back to. If you attempt to execute this type of procedure with a constant or expression, you will get the following error:

```
SQL> create or replace
  2  procedure out_parms( p_parm out number ) as
  3  begin
  4     null;
  5  end out_parms;
  6  /

Procedure created.

SQL> exec out_parms( 123 );
BEGIN out_parms( 123 ); END;

                *

ERROR at line 1:
ORA-06550: line 1, column 18:
PLS-00363: expression '123' cannot be used as an assignment target
ORA-06550: line 1, column 7:
PL/SQL: Statement ignored
```

Even though the procedure does not explicitly attempt to set the parameter's value, it implicitly does so when it returns to the calling procedure or block. It quite clearly states that the expression 123 cannot be used as an assignment target.

IN OUT Parameters

As the name implies, IN OUT parameters can be used to pass values in, and return values from, a stored procedure. They are useful when you need to pass an INPUT variable to a procedure that may be modified by the procedure itself.

A good example of the type of procedure where you would need this functionality is a swap routine:

```
SQL> create or replace
  2  procedure swap(
  3    p_parm1 in out number,
  4    p_parm2 in out number ) as
  5    l_temp number;
  6  begin
  8    l_temp := p_parm1;
  9    p_parm1 := p_parm2;
 10    p_parm2 := l_temp;
 11  end swap;
 12  /

Procedure created.
```

The SWAP procedure needs both to read the parameter values and change them, so it's necessary to define them as IN OUT parameters. We can run this by writing an anonymous block to execute it:

```
SQL> set serverout on
SQL> declare
  2    l_num1 number := 100;
  3    l_num2 number := 101;
  4  begin
  5    swap( l_num1, l_num2 );
  6    dbms_output.put_line( 'l_num1 = ' || l_num1 );
  7    dbms_output.put_line( 'l_num2 = ' || l_num2 );
  8  end;
  9  /

l_num1 = 101
l_num2 = 100

PL/SQL procedure successfully completed.
```

Notice that the local variables, L_NUM and L_NUM2, were initialized to 100 and 101 respectively and after the call to SWAP, their values were switched.

These IN OUT parameters are the best of both worlds, or so it may seem. You can pass values in and get values out using them. This can be very useful, but also dangerous. Imagine if every procedure you invoked could alter your local parameters. You would have no control over your data and it would make it extremely difficult to maintain and debug if a problem arose. And just like with OUT parameters, you must supply variables and not constants or expressions to every IN OUT parameter or you will receive the same expression X cannot be used as an assignment target error. In summary, you should only use IN OUT parameters when necessary.

NOCOPY

When you are passing large data structures around as parameters, it can often be useful to use the NOCOPY hint.

Consider a procedure that has both an IN parameter and an IN OUT parameter. The IN parameter is **passed by reference**. That means a read-only pointer is passed to the actual memory location of the variable.

> *Note that pointers are small amounts of data to pass around. It does not matter how big the actual value in the parameter is because all that gets passed is a pointer to the location.*

Conversely, the OUT parameter is **passed by value**. That means its value is copied into the parameter and upon successful completion of the procedure, the new value is copied back into the variable initially passed. This can cause severe overhead in procedure processing if the data is quite large, such as a PL/SQL table.

NOCOPY allows you to hint to the compiler to pass both OUT and IN OUT parameters by reference as if they were IN parameters. In this case, however, the reference would be updateable, not read-only as it would be with an IN parameter. This saves on the amount of data that needs to be passed to and from the procedure. But NOCOPY is a hint not a directive, so the compiler can ignore it. Even so it usually succeeds and benefits PL/SQL programs that pass large amounts of data via OUT and IN OUT parameters.

There is a side effect of using the NOCOPY hint. There can be unexpected return results. Consider a procedure with an OUT parameter. In the normal execution of this procedure, the value of the parameter is copied to the formal parameter. Processing then commences. If the procedure exits with an unhandled exception, no values are copied back to the parameters passed and it seems that any changes made to the formal parameters prior to the exception were rolled back. This is not the case when OUT and IN OUT parameters are passed by reference.

Since both the variable passed and the parameter point to the same memory location, any changes made to the parameter are immediately made to the variable passed as well. If the procedure exits with an unhandled exception, the value of the variable is not rolled back and its value is undefined. This can be avoided by having a default WHEN...OTHERS...THEN exception handler in every procedure that has a NOCOPY parameter. In the exception block you would need to assign those parameters some known value.

Parameter Order

There is no restriction on the order of defining parameters. IN, OUT, and IN OUT parameters with or without default values, can be mixed and matched however the developer sees fit. One convention is to put the required parameters, those without default values, first in the list, followed by the OUT parameters, then the IN OUT and lastly, the IN parameters with default values. Defining them in this order makes it more likely that the caller will be able to use Positional Notation when executing your procedure. Consider the following:

```
procedure get_balance( p_date            in     date default sysdate,
                        p_value           out    number,
                        p_name            in     varchar2 default user,
                        p_account_number  in     number )
```

The only required parameters are P_VALUE and P_ACCOUNT_NUMBER. Since they are the second and fourth parameters, to call this procedure, you either need to call it with Named Notation or pass all four parameters, even if you want to use the default. Ideally you would want the procedure defined as follows:

```
procedure get_balance( p_account_number in     number
                        p_value          out    number,
                        p_date           in     date default sysdate,
                        p_name           in     varchar2 default user )
```

Now you can call it with Positional Notation, supplying only the first two parameters and accepting the defaults for the latter two.

This ordering is not a requirement, but just good development technique when defining procedures.

Local Declarations

Just like anonymous PL/SQL blocks, procedures can have local variables defined. These definitions happen right after the optional parameter list. In an anonymous PL/SQL block, it was prefaced with the DECLARE reserve word. That is not necessary in a procedure declaration since we start it with the CREATE OR REPLACE syntax.

If you took notice of our last example, SWAP(), you would have seen that we used a local variable, L_TEMP.

```
SQL> create or replace
  2  procedure swap(
  3    p_parm1 in out number,
  4    p_parm2 in out number ) as
  5    --
  6    l_temp number;
  7  begin
```

It is defined immediately after the AS and before the BEGIN. It can then be accessed anywhere in the confines of the procedure itself. Once the procedure ends, any local variables go out of scope, meaning they are no longer accessible.

Besides local variables, many other things can be defined in the local declaration section. You can define records, types, arrays, and even other procedures. You might be asking yourself, why would you ever define a procedure within another procedure? Good question! You could argue that you could just create a second procedure and have the first call it, and you would be correct. That is a viable option, but if that helper procedure is specific to just the original, we could also argue that it makes more sense to keep them together. It is a matter of preference.

The alternative, and more widely used, means of accomplishing this nesting of procedures is to use packages. We'll see examples of this later on.

AUTHID

The AUTHID directive of a procedure tells Oracle whose permissions this procedure runs with. By default, a stored procedure runs as the caller, but with the privileges of its definer. The CURRENT_SCHEMA of the procedure will be that of its definer, meaning that all objects referenced in the procedure will be de-referenced as the definer of the procedure. This is known as running with **definer's rights** and is important to understand. It is the basis of how security with procedures can be used. You can explicitly define a procedure to have definer rights by adding the AUTHID directive:

```
create or replace
procedure foo AUTHID DEFINER as
begin
   null;
end foo;
```

This is not required though since this is the default behavior. Consider our user MARK. He has a table on which he has revoked all privileges from everyone, making it impossible for any normal user (except himself) to access it. Now MARK writes a procedure that inserts a supplied value into the table along with who inserted the row. He grants EXECUTE on this procedure to PUBLIC. Although no user has privilege to insert directly into the table besides MARK, anyone using MARK's procedure can insert a row since it will run with the privilege of MARK. All objects referenced in the procedure will be de-referenced as if MARK was accessing them. If an object is referenced in the procedure, access will be granted or denied as if MARK was doing it himself. The CURRENT_SCHEMA is MARK but the SESSION_USER is whoever is executing it.

Let's implement the scenario above and use the previously created database accounts, CHRIS and MARK.

Try It Out – AUTHID DEFINER

1. We begin by connecting to the database as user MARK and creating a NUMBERS table.

```
SQL> connect mark/mark
Connected.

SQL> create table numbers(
  2    n number,
  3    username varchar2(30) )
  4  /

Table created.
```

2. Now we create a procedure called INSERT_NUMBERS, which allows insertions of values into the NUMBERS table:

```
SQL> create or replace
  2  procedure insert_numbers( p_num number ) authid definer as
  3  begin
  4    insert into numbers values ( p_num, user );
  5  end insert_numbers;
  6  /

Procedure created.
```

3. Now we grant EXECUTE on the procedure to PUBLIC.

```
SQL> grant execute on insert_numbers to public;

Grant succeeded.
```

4. Now we connect as user CHRIS, and attempt an insert into the NUMBERS table:

```
SQL> connect chris/chris
Connected.

SQL> insert into mark.numbers values ( 12345, 'SEAN' );
insert into mark.numbers values ( 12345, 'SEAN' )
                  *
ERROR at line 1:
ORA-00942: table or view does not exist
```

Notice here, that since MARK has not granted INSERT on the table NUMBERS to CHRIS, he is unable to INSERT into the table directly. Notice too that CHRIS was trying to spoof the table by inserting SEAN's name as the inserter of the row.

5. Let's now execute the INSERT_NUMBERS procedure as CHRIS and review the table's contents (that only MARK can access):

```
SQL> exec mark.insert_numbers( 12345 );

PL/SQL procedure successfully completed.

SQL> connect mark/mark
Connected.

SQL> select * from numbers;

         N USERNAME
---------- ------------------------------
     12345 CHRIS

1 row selected.
```

How It Works

Now using a stored procedure owned by MARK, the executor of the procedure has the privileges of the owner. This means that user CHRIS can perform an INSERT into MARK's NUMBERS table, even though he has no privileges in the table itself. You will notice in the procedure, the table NUMBERS is referenced but not qualified with the owner. CHRIS was successful in executing it even though he does not have a table named NUMBERS in his schema or a synonym pointing to MARK's NUMBERS table. Since the procedure was created with definer rights, when executed, it will de-reference all objects as if the executor was the definer. So when CHRIS references the table NUMBERS within that procedure, he finds MARK's table even though he cannot reference it outside the scope of that procedure.

This is very important for security, since it gives the procedure author and application developer greater control on how the data is accessed. If all access to base tables is limited, and the only access to the data is via stored procedures, then the developer will be able to guarantee the integrity of the data. If an error does arise, then they will know that it has to be in the API that was developed.

Alternately, you can define a procedure to run with the privileges of the caller. This is known as using **invoker rights** and is accomplished by defining your procedure with the AUTHID of CURRENT_USER:

```
create or replace
procedure foo AUTHID CURRENT_USER as
begin
  null;
end foo;
```

This has the opposite effect to definer rights. The privileges of the caller and not the definer are affected. You would use this option when you want to defer privilege checking to run-time, as opposed to compile time. You can, with an AUTHID CURRENT_USER procedure, successfully compile a call when you have no privileges to the objects it accesses. This allows the developer to develop code that he may ultimately not have access to. If a user attempts to execute that procedure and does not have privileges on the objects it accesses, a run-time error will occur.

Let's alter our last example to be AUTHID CURRENT_USER and view the effects.

Try It Out – AUTHID CURRENT_USER

We will use the exactly the same procedure as in the previous example, only changing the AUTHID clause.

1. We begin by recreating the INSERT_NUMBERS procedure as user MARK.

```
SQL> connect mark/mark
Connected.

SQL> create or replace
  2  procedure insert_numbers( p_num number ) authid current_user as
  3  begin
  4    insert into numbers values ( p_num, user );
  5  end insert_numbers;
  6  /

Procedure created.
```

Notice, the only line that changed is line 2, where we have now made it AUTHID CURRENT_USER.

2. Now let's attempt to execute the procedure as user CHRIS:

```
SQL> connect chris/chris
Connected.

SQL> exec mark.insert_numbers( 12345 );
BEGIN mark.insert_numbers( 12345 ); END;

*
ERROR at line 1:
ORA-00942: table or view does not exist
ORA-06512: at "MARK.INSERT_NUMBERS", line 3
ORA-06512: at line 1
```

How It Works

Attempting to execute the procedure MARK.INSERT_NUMBERS() yielded a very different outcome from the last time. Since the procedure was defined as AUTHID CURRENT_USER, when executed, objects within the procedure will be de-referenced as the CURRENT_USER. In this case, when CHRIS executes the procedure and references the table NUMBERS, it is looking for a NUMBERS table within his CURRENT_SCHEMA. No such object is available so ORA-00942 - table or view does not exist makes perfect sense.

PRAGMA AUTONOMOUS_TRANSACTION

In Chapter 12 we will discuss what a transaction is, as well as what it means to COMMIT or ROLLBACK, and the effects that this has on the work previously done. At a high level, any work performed within your transaction will be 'saved' to the database when a COMMIT is issued. Conversely, any work performed within your transaction when a ROLLBACK is issued, will be reversed, returning the data to how it was before the transaction began.

Procedures can do work like inserting and updating. We have seen this in earlier examples, with procedures that INSERT into tables. These procedures can be within larger transactions. If a COMMIT is issued in one of our procedures, any prior work will be committed. This is not always a good thing. Consider a routine that logs to a database table. We do not want to lose any of the logging information, so we COMMIT after every insert. But the logging is just a small part of a much larger process. If that process encounters an error, it might want to roll back any work previously performed. If the logging routine committed any work, that would be impossible to do.

Oracle, as of version 8*i*, supports the concept of a transaction within a transaction. This subtransaction is allowed to perform its own work and commit or roll back independently of the parent transaction. Using this method the developer is able to write logging routines, or other such procedures, that must always succeed regardless of whether the parent transaction is committed or rolled back.

To accomplish this, you need to include the PRAGMA AUTONOMOUS_TRANSACTION directive when defining your stored procedure.

```
create or replace
procedure log_message( p_message varchar2 ) as
pragma autonomous_transaction;
begin
  insert into log_table values ( p_message );
  commit;
end log_message;
```

This simple example is quite powerful. You can call this procedure anywhere within your transaction and you are guaranteed that the LOG_TABLE will have the rows you inserted (provided of course, that P_MESSAGE is not larger than the column in LOG_TABLE), regardless of whether the parent transaction commits or rolls back.

Try It Out – Logging with Autonomous Transactions

Let's see autonomous transactions work. We'll take the log procedure above and call it from an anonymous block that inserts rows into a second table, and then rolls back.

1. Let's begin by creating the LOG_TABLE and TEMP_TABLE tables as the user CHRIS.

```
SQL> create table log_table(
  2    username varchar2(30),
  3    date_time timestamp,
  4    message varchar2(4000) );

Table created.

SQL> create table temp_table(
  2    n number );

Table created.
```

For this example, we have chosen to create a log table with not only a MESSAGE column, but also USERNAME and DATE_TIME columns, in order to capture who logged the message and when. The TEMP_TABLE table is just a second table to do work against.

2. Now we create the LOG_MESSAGE() procedure.

```
SQL> create or replace
  2  procedure log_message( p_message varchar2 ) as
  3  pragma autonomous_transaction;
  4  begin
  5    insert into log_table( username, date_time, message )
  6    values ( user, current_date, p_message );
  7    commit;
  8  end log_message;
  9  /

Procedure created.
```

Note that CURRENT_DATE is a function new to Oracle 9i. To compile this procedure in Oracle 8i you would need to use the SYSDATE function instead.

This is our AUTONOMOUS_TRANSACTION procedure. Notice the PRAGMA in line 3. This procedure inserts into the log table and then commits.

3. After inspecting both the LOG_TABLE and TEMP_TABLE tables, we will execute an anonymous PL/SQL block to INSERT into the TEMP_TABLE and call LOG_MESSAGE() before performing a ROLLBACK:

```
SQL> select * from temp_table;

no rows selected

SQL> select * from log_table;

no rows selected

SQL> begin
  2     log_message( 'About to insert into temp_table' );
  3     insert into temp_table( n )
  4     values( 12345 );
  5     log_message( 'rolling back insert into temp_table' );
  6     rollback;
  7  end;
  8  /

PL/SQL procedure successfully completed.
```

We call LOG_MESSAGE() prior to inserting and rolling back. Remember though, that the LOG_MESSAGE() procedure performs a COMMIT. In reviewing the code above and following the logic, you might think that the insert that happened at line 3 would be committed by the COMMIT in the procedure LOG_MESSAGE() which was called at line 5. The ROLLBACK at line 6 should do nothing, but inspecting the tables shows that this is not so:

```
SQL> select * from temp_table;

no rows selected

SQL> select * from log_table;

USERNAME DATE_TIME                       MESSAGE
-------- ------------------------------  ------------------------------------
CHRIS    27-NOV-01 03.31.19.000000 PM    About to insert into temp_table
CHRIS    27-NOV-01 03.31.19.000000 PM    rolling back insert into temp_table

2 rows selected.
```

There are no rows in TEMP_TABLE and yet both rows inserted into LOG_TABLE are there. The outer transaction, the PL/SQL block, was rolled back while the subtransactions, or autonomous transactions, were committed.

Autonomous transactions are very useful for operations such as logging, or other types of work where that work needs to be committed, yet not interfere with the caller's transaction.

Functions

Functions, like procedures, are named PL/SQL blocks stored in the database. The same rules are followed for creating them. Security on them and parameter passing is also identical. The main distinguishing characteristic of a function is that it *must* return a value. This value can be a simple data type, like a NUMBER or a VARCHAR2, or a complex one like a PL/SQL array or an object.

Syntax

The syntax for creating a function looks a little more complicated than that of a procedure. There are a number of attributes such as PIPELINED shown in the syntax for completeness, but will not discuss them further in this chapter.

```
 1 [CREATE [OR REPLACE]]
 2 FUNCTION function_name[( parameter[, parameter]...)] RETURN datatype}
 3 [AUTHID {DEFINER | CURRENT_USER}]
 4 [PARALLEL_ENABLE[{[CLUSTER parameter BY ( column_name [,
   column_name]...])|[ORDER parameter BY ( column_name [,
   column_name]...])[(PARTITION parameter BY{[ {RANGE|HASH} ( column_name
   [,column_name]...)]|ANY})]]
 5 [DETERMINISTIC] {IS | AS}
 6 [PIPELINED [USING implementation_type]]
 7 [AGGREGATE [UPDATE VALUE] {WITH EXTERNAL CONTEXT] USING
   implementation_type]
 8 [PRAGMA AUTONOMOUS_TRANSACTION;]
 9 [ local declarations]
10 BEGIN
11 executable statements
12 [EXCEPTION
13 exception handlers]
14 END [name];
```

Return Values

One of the big differences between the syntax for defining stored procedures and functions can be seen in line 2 of the syntax the mandatory RETURN data type clause. This is the type of value that the function will return. From within your function, at any point in the body, you simply code a RETURN <expression>; where the expression evaluates to the RETURN data type of the function itself. Let's look at an example:

```
SQL> create or replace
  2  function first_function return varchar2 as
  3  begin
  4    return 'Hello World';
```

```
   5   end first_function;
   6   /

Function created.
```

Here the function `FIRST_FUNCTION()` will return the string `Hello World` when executed.

> **Note that when calling a function you must always capture the return value!**

To capture the return value, you assign the call to a local variable, as illustrated below:

```
SQL> set serverout on
SQL> declare
   2    l_str varchar2(100) := null;
   3  begin
   4    l_str := first_function;
   5    dbms_output.put_line( l_str );
   6  end;
   7  /
Hello World

PL/SQL procedure successfully completed.
```

In the example above you can see that the local variable `L_STR` was initially assigned the value of `NULL` in the declaration of the block, then assigned the value of the function call to `FIRST_FUNCTION()`.

Functions can be used as `IN` parameters to other procedures and functions as well. They will be evaluated first and their values passed into the procedure called. Here's an example:

```
SQL> create or replace
   2  procedure show_it( p_text varchar2 ) as
   3  begin
   4    dbms_output.put_line( p_text );
   5  end show_it;
   6  /

Procedure created.

SQL> exec show_it( first_function );
Hello World

PL/SQL procedure successfully completed.
```

We passed the return value of the function into our procedure. We assigned the `IN` parameter `P_TEXT` the value of the return value of the function.

The `?:` operator in the programming languages C and Java is a very handy function, the syntax for which is as follows:

437

```
boolean expression ? true_value : false_value
```

This says that if the Boolean expression is TRUE return the TRUE_VALUE value, otherwise return the FALSE_VALUE value. It is a shortcut for:

```
if  expression then
  return true_value;
else
  return false_value;
end if;
```

It allows you to conditionally return one of two supplied values depending on the Boolean expression supplied. No operator like that exists for PL/SQL. Let's write a function that provides the same functionality in PL/SQL, hence the name ITE, short for IF-THEN-ELSE.

Try It Out – ITE Function

1. Let's begin by defining the function specification that we require.

We know we need a function, and that it should take in three parameters, a BOOLEAN, and two VARCHAR2s. We also know that it should return a VARCHAR2. Our coding so far will look as follows:

```
SQL> create or replace
  2  function ite(
  3    p_expression boolean,
  4    p_true varchar2,
  5    p_false varchar2 ) return varchar2 as
```

2. Now we can fill in the body of the function, ensuring that every exit point is covered with a return VARCHAR2 expression statement. If we don't cover every exit point then the function will not work properly, so we need to check the P_EXPRESSION value. If it is True then we return the P_TRUE value, otherwise we should return the P_FALSE value:

```
  6  begin
  7    if p_expression then
  8      return p_true;
  9    end if;
 10    return p_false;
 11  end ite;
 12  /

Function created.
```

3. Next we'll need to test our coding to see if it does what we want it to do:

```
SQL> exec dbms_output.put_line( ite( 1=2, 'Equal', 'Not Equal' ) );
Not Equal
```

```
PL/SQL procedure successfully completed.

SQL> exec dbms_output.put_line( ite( 2>3, 'True', 'False' ) );
False

PL/SQL procedure successfully completed.
```

How It Works

There it is. At first it might look a little strange passing 1=2 or 2>3 as parameters but remember that the P_EXPRESSION parameter is a BOOLEAN and so requires a value of TRUE or FALSE. Oracle will resolve all the parameters prior to calling the function itself. It evaluates 1=2 as FALSE and passes that value along.

This function can save a lot of typing. Consider the case of a procedure into which you wish to pass either value1 or value2. One way of doing this is to check the condition first, by setting a local variable to the appropriate value, but then you have an extra local variable to clutter up your code, as illustrated by the following:

```
if condition then
  l_var := value1;
else
  l_var := value2;
end if;
my_proc( l_var );
```

Alternatively, you can call the procedure conditionally with value1 or value2, but this then leaves you with two calls to the procedure, which will result in a performance hit:

```
if condition then
  my_proc( value1 );
else
  my_proc( value2 );
end if;
```

As a final possibility, we can use the handy utility function, in this case ITE(), and get the code down to one line:

```
my_proc( ite( condition, value1, value2 ) );
```

It may look a bit strange at first, but it is a time saver when developing.

Deterministic

A function is said to be **deterministic** if for a given input, it will always return exactly the same result. The UPPER() built-in function is deterministic. If you give it the input SaMaNtHa, it will always return SAMANTHA. You cannot create a function as deterministic if it will not return the same values each time. To hint a function DETERMINISTIC, all you need to do is the following:

```
SQL> create or replace
  2   function total_compensation(
  3     p_salary number,
  4     p_commission number ) return number
  5   deterministic as
  6   begin
  7     return nvl(p_salary,0) + nvl(p_commission,0);
  8 end total_compensation;
  9 /

Function created.
```

We know that given any two numbers as inputs, the output will always be the sum of them.

The purpose of hinting a function DETERMINISTIC is to help out the optimizer. The optimizer can choose to use the previous result from a deterministic function when the same inputs are supplied, since it should produce the same result. For intensive function processing, this can save many CPU cycles. Also, you must use a deterministic function for a function-based index (these are explained in Chapter 8, *Indexes*).

Common Errors

Here are some common mistakes you might make while developing functions:

❑ Forgetting to capture the return value.

❑ Trying to define a function that does not return a value.

❑ Defining a function without a return data type.

Knowing what these errors look like will help you to avoid them and quickly fix them when they do arise, so let's look at examples of each.

In PL/SQL, functions always return a value and the caller must accept that value, otherwise you will get an error:

```
SQL> exec first_function
BEGIN first_function; END;

      *
ERROR at line 1:
ORA-06550: line 1, column 7:
PLS-00221: 'FIRST_FUNCTION' is not a procedure or is undefined
ORA-06550: line 1, column 7:
PL/SQL: Statement ignored
```

In the above example, Oracle attempts to execute FIRST_FUNCTION() as a procedure since it is called as if it is one. As the FIRST_FUNCTION() we created earlier was a function, not a procedure, it cannot be executed in this way. No procedure exists with that name so the execution fails.

Just as we have to always accept the return value of a function, a function must always supply one. Oracle will allow you to create a function without a RETURN <EXPRESSION> statement:

```
SQL> create or replace
  2    function bad_function return number as
  3    begin
  4      null;
  5    end bad_function;
  6    /

Function created.
```

but if you attempt to execute it, an error will be returned as shown below:

```
SQL> exec show_it( bad_function );
BEGIN show_it( bad_function ); END;

*
ERROR at line 1:
ORA-06503: PL/SQL: Function returned without value
ORA-06512: at "CHRIS.BAD_FUNCTION", line 3
ORA-06512: at line 1
```

PL/SQL is expecting a value back from the function BAD_FUNCTION() but none is returned so an error is raised. This is something you need to be aware of when coding functions.

> **Every exit point needs a RETURN <EXPRESSION> statement.**

So, for example, in the case of a function with an exception handler, you need to remember to return something from the exception handler as well.

Another common mistake when defining a function is failing to define a return data type:

```
SQL> create or replace
  2    function no_return_type as
  3    begin
  4      return null;
  5    end no_return_type;
  6    /

Warning: Function created with compilation errors.

SQL> show errors
Errors for FUNCTION NO_RETURN_TYPE:

LINE/COL ERROR
-------- -----------------------------------------------------------------
1/25     PLS-00103: Encountered the symbol "AS" when expecting one of the
         following:
         ( return compress compiled wrapped
```

441

The error `PLS-00103` happens here because the definition of the PL/SQL function is incorrect. There is no return type defined for this function.

Packages

Packages are constructs that allow you to logically group procedures, functions, object types, and items into a single database object.

Packages usually consist of two pieces, the specification and the body. The **specification** is the public interface to the package. The **body**, when present, contains the implementation of the specification along with any private routines, data, and variables.

Syntax

As was the case with functions, we will show the full syntax for defining packages, but will not discuss its every feature here. For more information please refer to the Oracle documentation *PL/SQL Users Guide And Reference*, available from
http://download-uk.oracle.com/otndoc/Oracle 9i/901_doc/appdev.901/a89856/toc.htm.

```
CREATE [OR REPLACE] PACKAGE package_name
  [AUTHID {CURRENT_USER | DEFINER}]
  {IS | AS}
  [PRAGMA SERIALLY_REUSABLE;]
  [collection_type_definition ...]
  [record_type_definition ...]
  [subtype_definition ...]
  [collection_declaration ...]
  [constant_declaration ...]
  [exception_declaration ...]
  [object_declaration ...]
  [record_declaration ...]
  [variable_declaration ...]
  [cursor_spec ...]
  [function_spec ...]
  [procedure_spec ...]
  [call_spec ...]
  [PRAGMA RESTRICT_REFERENCES(assertions) ...]
END [package_name];

[CREATE [OR REPLACE] PACKAGE BODY package_name {IS | AS}
  [PRAGMA SERIALLY_REUSABLE;]
  [collection_type_definition ...]
  [record_type_definition ...]
  [subtype_definition ...]
  [collection_declaration ...]
  [constant_declaration ...]
  [exception_declaration ...]
  [object_declaration ...]
```

```
      [record_declaration ...]
      [variable_declaration ...]
      [cursor_body ...]
      [function_spec ...]
      [procedure_spec ...]
      [call_spec ...]
[BEGIN
   sequence_of_statements]
END [package_name];]
```

Specification

The package specification (or spec) is the interface to your package. Everything defined in it is accessible to the caller, and can be referenced by anyone with EXECUTE privilege for the package. Procedures defined within the spec can be executed, variables can be referenced, and types can be accessed. These are the public features of the package.

In the following example we will define a package called EMPLOYEE_PKG with two procedures, PRINT_ENAME() and PRINT_SAL():

```
SQL> create or replace
  2  package employee_pkg as
  3    procedure print_ename( p_empno number );
  4    procedure print_sal( p_empno number );
  5  end employee_pkg;
  6  /

Package created.
```

Notice that we did not supply any code for the procedures, but simply defined their names and inputs instead. The local declarations and BEGIN-END block has been excluded. That is because the spec just exposes what is available, not how it is implemented.

The execution of packaged procedures is very similar to that of stand-alone procedures. The only difference is that you need to reference the PACKAGE_NAME.PROCEDURE_NAME when invoking it. Attempting to execute either of these procedures right now will result in an error.

```
SQL> execute employee_pkg.print_ename( 1234 );
BEGIN employee_pkg.print_ename( 1234 ); END;

*
ERROR at line 1:
ORA-04068: existing state of packages has been discarded
ORA-04067: not executed, package body "SCOTT.EMPLOYEE_PKG" does not exist
ORA-06508: PL/SQL: could not find program unit being called
ORA-06512: at line 1
```

So here we find that the package body does not exist. There is no implementation for these procedures and no code; only the interface currently exists. We need to write the code behind these routines, which is done in the package body.

Body

The package body is where you actually do the coding of your subroutines, implementing the interface defined in the spec. Every procedure and function exposed in the spec must be implemented in the body:

```
SQL> create or replace
  2  package body employee_pkg as
  3
  4     procedure print_ename( p_empno number ) is
  5        l_ename emp.ename%type;
  6     begin
  7       select ename
  8         into l_ename
  9         from emp
 10        where empno = p_empno;
 11       dbms_output.put_line( l_ename );
 12     exception
 13       when NO_DATA_FOUND then
 14         dbms_output.put_line( 'Invalid employee number' );
 15     end print_ename;
```

In the first procedure, PRINT_ENAME(), we define a local variable of the type EMP.ENAME%TYPE and we select the ENAME from the table EMP into that variable, where the EMPNO is equal to the parameter P_EMPNO passed in. If a matching row is found, the value is printed. If no row is found an exception of NO_DATA_FOUND will be thrown. We catch it in the exception handler and print an appropriate message.

The second procedure, PRINT_SAL(), works in exactly the same way except that we select out the SAL value from the EMP table:

```
 16
 17     procedure print_sal( p_empno number ) is
 18        l_sal emp.sal%type;
 19     begin
 20       select sal
 21         into l_sal
 22         from emp
 23        where empno = p_empno;
 24       dbms_output.put_line( l_sal );
 25     exception
 26       when NO_DATA_FOUND then
 27         dbms_output.put_line( 'Invalid employee number' );
 28     end print_sal;
 29
 30  end employee_pkg;
 31  /

Package body created.
```

Now when we execute either procedure, we will get results:

```
SQL> set serverout on
SQL> execute employee_pkg.print_ename( 1234 );
Invalid employee number

PL/SQL procedure successfully completed.

SQL> execute employee_pkg.print_ename( 7782 );
CLARK

PL/SQL procedure successfully completed.

SQL> execute employee_pkg.print_sal( 7782 );
2450

PL/SQL procedure successfully completed.
```

Along with the implementation of the procedures defined in the spec, you can also define procedure, that are private to the package itself. Packages cannot contain other packages though. The **private procedures and functions** can be referenced by any other routine defined in the package, but nothing outside of the package has access. They are useful when many of your procedures and functions share some common functionality, but that functionality is exclusive to the package itself. A procedure LOG_MESSAGE() is a good example of this. Our package needs to be able to log its messages, but we do not want to allow others to do so. So we could define the LOG_MESSAGES() procedure in the body, to ensure that only other procedures and functions within the package could access it.

Another private function that we might want to consider for our package is a generic employee lookup. If you look at the code above, the two procedures do almost the exact same thing. Repeating code like that is not good programming practice. We could move the common functionality into a private procedure or function, thereby ensuring that we only have to modify the code in one place if the lookup logic changes.

Try It Out – Private Procedures and Functions

Let's implement the two suggestions above, as the SCOTT user. We are going to want to:

❑ Write a private function LOG_MESSAGES()

❑ Move common functionality from public procedures into a private function

If you haven't already created the EMPLOYEE_PKG specification in the Specification section above, you'll need to do that first.

1. Let's begin by creating or redefining the package body.

```
SQL> create or replace
  2   package body employee_pkg as
  3
```

2. Now we can write the LOG_MESSAGE() procedure:

```
 4    procedure log_message( p_message varchar2 ) is
 5    pragma autonomous_transaction;
 6    begin
 7      insert into log_table( username, date_time, message )
 8      values ( user, current_date, p_message );
 9      commit;
10    end log_message;
11
```

Remember that the CURRENT_DATE function is only available to Oracle 9i users. Oracle 8i users will have to use SYS_DATE instead.

This is exactly the same LOG_MESSAGE() procedure we saw in the above example using AUTONOMOUS_TRANSACTIONS. Notice that we can still use that directive in the package as well. The only change to it is that we do not begin with the CREATE or CREATE OR REPLACE because we were defining it in the package body.

3. We now write a function that returns a row from the EMP table.

```
12    function get_emp_record( p_empno number ) return emp%rowtype is
13       l_emp_record emp%rowtype;
14    begin
15       log_message( 'Looking for record where EMPNO = ' || p_empno );
16       select *
17         into l_emp_record
18         from emp
19        where empno = p_empno;
20       return l_emp_record;
21    exception
22       when NO_DATA_FOUND then
23          return null;
24    end get_emp_record;
25
```

This function first logs the fact that it is looking for a record. Then it tries to find a matching record in the EMP table. If it finds one it returns it, otherwise the exception handler catches the NO_DATA_FOUND error and returns NULL. This function will be used by either public procedure to look up data.

4. Next we write a procedure that prints a line to the screen and logs that you have printed it:

Note: This procedure uses the CASE structure, which is an Oracle 9i feature. It can be rewritten to use an IF-THEN-ELSE if you are using an older version of Oracle.

```
26    procedure print_data( p_emp_record emp%rowtype,
27                          p_column varchar2 ) is
28       l_value varchar2(4000);
29    begin
```

```
30        if p_emp_record.empno is null then
31           log_message( 'No Data Found.' );
32           dbms_output.put_line( 'No Data Found.' );
33        else
34           case p_column
35              when 'ENAME' then
36                 l_value := p_emp_record.ename;
37              when 'SAL' then
38                 l_value := nvl(p_emp_record.sal,0);
39              else
40                 l_value := 'Invalid Column';
41           end case;
42           log_message( 'About to print ' || p_column || ' = ' || l_value );
43           dbms_output.put_line( p_column || ' = ' || l_value );
44        end if;
45     end print_data;
46
```

The PRINT_DATA() procedure does the work of printing out the requested data. It first determines if a record was found by checking to see if the EMPNO is NULL. Since the EMPNO is the primary key, it cannot be NULL if a record was found. If a record has been located, it determines what data to print and then, using the Oracle supplied package DBMS_OUTPUT, prints it to the screen.

5. Now we reimplement the public procedures and finish the package.

```
48   procedure print_ename( p_empno number ) is
49   begin
50      print_data( get_emp_record( p_empno ), 'ENAME' );
51   end print_ename;
52
53   procedure print_sal( p_empno number ) is
54   begin
55      print_data( get_emp_record( p_empno ), 'SAL' );
56   end print_sal;
57
58   end employee_pkg;
59   /
```

```
Package body created.
```

Notice that the public procedure has now been rewritten in one line. The PRINT_DATA() procedure takes in as its parameters, an EMP%ROWTYPE and a VARCHAR2 for the column name. It just so happens that the GET_EMP_RECORD() function will return an EMP%ROWTYPE, so we can use the call to that function as the first parameter to PRINT_DATA().

6. Let's test the package to see if it works as we are expecting:

```
SQL> exec employee_pkg.print_ename( 7781 );
No Data Found.

PL/SQL procedure successfully completed.
```

```
SQL> exec employee_pkg.print_ename( 7782 );
ENAME = CLARK

PL/SQL procedure successfully completed.

SQL> select * from log_table;

USERNAME DATE_TIME                       MESSAGE
-------- ------------------------------- -----------------------------------------
SCOTT    30-NOV-01 08.07.12.000000 PM Looking for record where EMPNO = 7782
SCOTT    30-NOV-01 08.07.12.000000 PM About to print ENAME = CLARK
SCOTT    30-NOV-01 08.07.06.000000 PM Looking for record where EMPNO = 7781
SCOTT    30-NOV-01 08.07.06.000000 PM No Data Found.
```

Now we can grant the EXECUTE privilege on our package to the appropriate users and roles and they will be able to use it, although they can only see the procedures in the spec. All the complicated code, and how it actually works, is hidden in the package body. The body is a black box to the caller. Users are not aware that the logging is happening. All they will know is that the data will be printed correctly.

Package Variables and Other Declarations

You can define package level variables, known as **global variables**. These variables can be defined in either the package spec or the package body. Those defined in the spec can be referenced just as the procedures and functions in the spec can, and are known as **public variables**. These values can be read and altered by anyone with EXECUTE privilege on the package. Defining package level variables in the body makes the variables accessible only to the procedures implemented in the body, and these are known as **private variables**.

Package level variables differ from local variables of procedures and functions since they maintain their state throughout the life of your database session. That means that we can set a global variable with one call, do some other work, then come back and recall its value while procedures are executed and then go away again. Once a package has been referenced in a session, it is said to have been **instantiated**. And once instantiated, all package level variables, both private and public, will maintain state for the life of that database session, or until the package is recompiled.

Try It Out – Package Variables

1. First we'll make a package (VARIABLES) with one public and one private package level variable, and procedures to set and print the private value. There is no need to write routines for the public package variable since we can set, and read, that value directly.

```
SQL> create or replace
  2  package variables as
  3    g_public_number number := null;
  4    procedure set_private_number( p_num number );
  5    procedure print_private_number;
  6  end variables;
```

```
   7  /

Package created.

SQL> create or replace
  2  package body variables as
  3      g_private_number number := null;
  4
  5      procedure set_private_number( p_num number ) is
  6      begin
  7        g_private_number := p_num;
  8      end set_private_number;
  9
 10      procedure print_private_number is
 11      begin
 12        dbms_output.put_line( nvl(to_char(g_private_number),'null' ) );
 13      end print_private_number;
 14
 15  end variables;
 16  /

Package body created.
```

2. Now we can directly access the public package variable, and indeed reinitialize it:

```
SQL> exec dbms_output.put_line( nvl( to_char(variables.g_public_number), 'null' )
);
null

PL/SQL procedure successfully completed.

SQL> exec variables.g_public_number := 123;

PL/SQL procedure successfully completed.

SQL> exec dbms_output.put_line( nvl( to_char(variables.g_public_number), 'null' )
);
123

PL/SQL procedure successfully completed.
```

Notice how it maintains its value from one call to the next. Initially it was NULL. We then set it to 123, while the next call to the package still had its value as 123.

3. Attempting to access the private package variable produces an error message:

```
SQL> exec variables.g_private_number := 456;
BEGIN variables.g_private_number := 456; END;

                  *

ERROR at line 1:
```

```
ORA-06550: line 1, column 17:
PLS-00302: component 'G_PRIVATE_NUMBER' must be declared
ORA-06550: line 1, column 7:
PL/SQL: Statement ignored
```

The variable G_PRIVATE_NUMBER is not defined in the spec but the body. Anything not defined in the spec can only be referenced by the package itself. This is how packages hide data.

4. Accessing the private package variable through the public procedure works just fine:

```
SQL> exec variables.set_private_number( 456 );

PL/SQL procedure successfully completed.

SQL> exec variables.print_private_number;
456

PL/SQL procedure successfully completed.
```

Notice again, its value is maintained across calls to the package.

5. However, if we reconnect, or get a new session, the package's state is reset and the values that were set are lost:

```
SQL> connect scott/tiger
Connected.

SQL> set serverout on
SQL> exec dbms_output.put_line( nvl( to_char(variables.g_public_number), 'null' )
);
null

PL/SQL procedure successfully completed.

SQL> exec variables.print_private_number;
null

PL/SQL procedure successfully completed.
```

The package state is unique in each database session. If both CHRIS and SEAN set the public package variable in SCOTT's package, each of them has their own copy of that package's data. The code is shared across sessions, but the data is unique. That way one session cannot alter or affect the data in another concurrently running session.

Package variables can be a nice way to store some session data and share data with other procedures within your session. Remember though, that a second call into a package does not reset its values. You can get yourself into real trouble if you use global package variables, private and public, and don't remember to reset their values manually, if you are expecting them to have their defaults for every call into the package.

Instantiation Block

A package can have a block of code that will run once, on the first occasion that a session accesses any element of the package. This could be a call to a procedure defined in the spec, or simply reading the value of a public package variable. The first access is known as the **package instantiation**, since at that point the package will execute the instantiation code. It is only called once and it is done automatically. You do not have control over whether or not it is called, since if the block exists, it will be executed. The code is listed in an unnamed block defined at the package body level, and can perform any legal PL/SQL commands. You can use this block to log when the package was first accessed, and initialize your package level variables within it. We could change the example above to have it initialize the two package variables.

```
SQL> create or replace
  2  package body variables as
  3    g_private_number number := null;
  4
  5    procedure set_private_number( p_num number ) is
  6    begin
  7      g_private_number := p_num;
  8    end set_private_number;
  9
 10    procedure print_private_number is
 11    begin
 12      dbms_output.put_line( nvl(to_char(g_private_number),'null' ) );
 13    end print_private_number;
 14
 15  begin
 16
 17    select count(*)
 18      into g_public_number
 19      from emp;
 20
 21    g_private_number := dbms_random.random;
 22
 23  end variables;
 24  /

Package body created.
```

Note that this code will only compile on Oracle 9i, since the DBMS_RANDOM package is only available to Oracle 9i users.

Lines 15 through 22 are the instantiation block. This code will execute upon the first reference to the package. We could have initialized G_PRIVATE_NUMBER in its declaration since it is PL/SQL. Note that there is no way, other than using the instantiation code, to initially set the G_PUBLIC_NUMBER's value to the result of a query.

```
SQL> exec variables.print_private_number;
574963488

PL/SQL procedure successfully completed.

SQL> exec dbms_output.put_line( nvl( to_char(variables.g_public_number), 'null' )
);
14

PL/SQL procedure successfully completed.
```

Both variables have values, even though we did not explicitly set them. They were initialized by the instantiation code to be the random numbers it supplied.

Overloading

Overloading is where two or more procedures and functions, defined within a single package, share the same name. Stand-alone procedures and functions must be uniquely named but packaged procedures and functions can share the same name if, *and only if,* their signatures differ. This means that within a package you can define two procedures with the same name as long as their parameter lists differ in number, order, or types of parameters. It is not good enough for them to just differ in parameter name, input/output mode, or return type.

As an illustration of this, the following two statements are invalid, since both procedures contain only one varchar2 parameter:

```
procedure foo( p_parm1 varchar2 );
procedure foo( p_parm2 varchar2 );
```

The next declaration is invalid because the only difference between the parameters is the mode:

```
procedure foo( p_parm1 in varchar2 );
procedure foo( p_parm1 out varchar2 );
```

The following declarations are valid because the parameter types are different:

```
procedure foo( p_parm1 varchar2 );
procedure foo( p_parm1 number );
```

```
procedure foo( p_parm1 number, p_parm2 varchar2 );
procedure foo( p_parm1 varchar2, p_parm2 varchar2 );
```

```
procedure foo;
procedure foo( p_parm1 number );
function foo return number;
function foo( p_parm1 number ) return varchar2;
```

Note that it is not possible to overload subprograms if they only differ in the data type of their parameters or return types, and the data types are in the same family.

As an illustration of this, the following two statements are invalid, because NUMBER and REAL are in the same family of data types:

```
procedure foo( p_parm1 number );
procedure foo( p_parm2 real );
```

Overloading is important for making coding easier. You have probably already used overloaded functions and not even realized it. Consider the built-in Oracle function TO_CHAR().

```
SQL> select to_char( sysdate, 'HH24:MI:SS' ) "DATE" from dual;

DATE
--------
09:47:22

SQL> select to_char( 111, '099.99' ) "NUMBER" from dual;

NUMBER
-------
 111.00
```

You can pass in either a DATE or a NUMBER and it still works.

Try It Out – Overload SWAP()

Back in the discussion of IN OUT parameters, we wrote a procedure named SWAP().

```
SQL> create or replace
  2  procedure swap(
  3    p_parm1 in out number,
  4    p_parm2 in out number ) as
  5  --
  6    l_temp number;
  7  begin
  8    l_temp := p_parm1;
  9    p_parm1 := p_parm2;
 10    p_parm2 := l_temp;
 11  end swap;
 12  /

Procedure created.
```

It's a great procedure if all you ever need to do is swap numbers. Let's package this procedure and overload it to also swap VARCHAR2 and dates as well.

1. First of all, we'll create the spec:

```
SQL> create or replace
  2  package utilities as
  3    procedure swap( p_parm1 in out number,
  4                    p_parm2 in out number );
  5    procedure swap( p_parm1 in out varchar2,
  6                    p_parm2 in out varchar2 );
  7    procedure swap( p_parm1 in out date,
  8                    p_parm2 in out date );
  9  end utilities;
 10  /

Package created.
```

This is valid because it follows the rules for overloading (since the parameters differ in type).

2. Now we need to write the SWAP procedure for numbers:

```
SQL> create or replace
  2  package body utilities as
  3
  4    procedure swap( p_parm1 in out number,
  5                    p_parm2 in out number ) is
  6      l_temp number;
  7    begin
  8      dbms_output.put_line( 'Swapping number' );
  9      l_temp := p_parm1;
 10      p_parm1 := p_parm2;
 11      p_parm2 := l_temp;
 12    end swap;
 13
```

We added a call to DBMS_OUTPUT.PUT_LINE on line 8 so we can get feedback as to when this procedure is invoked. This is just a simple swap algorithm. We assign the first parameter to a temporary holding variable, then assign the first parameter the value of the second parameter. Lastly, we assign the second parameter the value of the temporary variable, which was set to the value of the first parameter. The parameters have now swapped values.

3. Now we write the other swap procedures we require. With a simple change to the initial SWAP() procedure, we can easily code the remaining two:

```
 14    procedure swap( p_parm1 in out varchar2,
 15                    p_parm2 in out varchar2 ) is
 16      l_temp varchar2(32767);
 17    begin
 18      dbms_output.put_line( 'Swapping varchar2' );
 19      l_temp := p_parm1;
 20      p_parm1 := p_parm2;
 21      p_parm2 := l_temp;
 22    end swap;
 23
 24    procedure swap( p_parm1 in out date,
```

```
25                         p_parm2 in out date ) is
26        l_temp date;
27     begin
28        dbms_output.put_line( 'Swapping date' );
29        l_temp := p_parm1;
30        p_parm1 := p_parm2;
31        p_parm2 := l_temp;
32     end swap;
33
34   end utilities;
35   /

Package body created.
```

4. Now we can test what we've written to see it in action:

```
SQL> set serverout on

SQL> declare
  2     l_num1 number := 1;
  3     l_num2 number := 2;
  4     l_date1 date := sysdate;
  5     l_date2 date := sysdate + 1;
  6  begin
  7     utilities.swap( l_num1, l_num2 );
  8     dbms_output.put_line( 'l_num1 = ' || l_num1 );
  9     dbms_output.put_line( 'l_num2 = ' || l_num2 );
 10     utilities.swap( l_date1, l_date2 );
 11     dbms_output.put_line( 'l_date1 = ' || l_date1 );
 12     dbms_output.put_line( 'l_date2 = ' || l_date2 );
 13  end;
 14  /
Swapping number
l_num1 = 2
l_num2 = 1
Swapping date
l_date1 = 02-DEC-01
l_date2 = 01-DEC-01

PL/SQL procedure successfully completed.
```

On lines 7 and 10 we made what appears to be a call to the same procedure, but in fact it is a completely different procedure as proven by the output. Oracle resolved the calls based on the data types passed in.

Dependencies

Just like other objects in the database, procedures have dependencies and, in turn, are depended upon. Tables with foreign keys are dependent on the tables they reference, views are dependent on their underlying tables, and procedures are dependent on the database objects (such as tables, views, and even other stored procedures) they reference.

When you successfully compile a procedure into the database, it is said to be **valid**. You can query the data dictionary view USER_OBJECTS to verify this:

```
SQL> select object_name, status
  2    from user_objects
  3    where object_type = 'PROCEDURE';

OBJECT_NAME          STATUS
-------------------- -------
LOG_MESSAGE          VALID

1 row selected.
```

If a change is made to a referenced object, your procedure becomes **invalid**, even if that change does not directly affect your procedure.

Try It Out – Dependencies in Action

Here we are going to see what happens when an object that a stored procedure relies on is altered.

1. Let's begin by creating a table named BAR and a stored procedure that is dependent on it.

```
SQL> create table bar( n number );

Table created.

SQL> create or replace procedure foo as
  2    l_n bar.n%type;
  3  begin
  4    null;
  5  end foo;
  6  /

Procedure created.
```

The procedure is dependent on the table BAR because FOO() declares a local variable whose type is that of the column N.

2. Now we can review the status of the procedure, by executing the following:

```
SQL> select object_name, status
  2    from user_objects
  3    where object_type = 'PROCEDURE';

OBJECT_NAME          STATUS
-------------------- -------
FOO                  VALID
LOG_MESSAGE          VALID

2 rows selected.
```

This is just what we expected. The procedure FOO() compiled successfully so its status is VALID.

You may well see other procedures listed in your output from USER_OBJECTS, if you created them earlier.

3. Let's now see what happens when we alter the table BAR by adding a column:

```
SQL> alter table bar add c char(1);

Table altered.
```

Here we have made a small change to the table BAR, but did not alter the column N. This would suggest that our procedure FOO() is still VALID since nothing it is dependent on is INVALID, and the column it references has not changed.

4. Let's now take another look at the status of the procedure:

```
SQL> select object_name, status
  2     from user_objects
  3     where object_type = 'PROCEDURE';

OBJECT_NAME          STATUS
-------------------- -------
FOO                  INVALID
LOG_MESSAGE          VALID

2 rows selected.
```

Here we see that the procedure FOO() is now INVALID, illustrating what we said earlier in our discussion, namely that *any* change to a referenced object will invalidate your procedure. It does not matter if the change directly affects it or not. That fact that the object was altered invalidates all procedures that reference it.

5. Now let's see what happens when we attempt to execute the procedure:

```
SQL> exec foo

PL/SQL procedure successfully completed.

SQL> select object_name, status
  2     from user_objects
  3     where object_type = 'PROCEDURE';

OBJECT_NAME          STATUS
-------------------- -------
FOO                  VALID
LOG_MESSAGE          VALID

2 rows selected.
```

Now we see that the procedure FOO() is VALID and it executed successfully. When an INVALID procedure is invoked, Oracle will attempt to recompile it before executing it. If it is successful in its recompilation, it executes the procedure and no one even knows that the recompilation even happened.

This is not just a nice feature, but also a required one. Imagine if my procedure called SEAN's procedure, which in turn called a procedure owned by MARK and that the procedure owned by MARK referenced a table in JOEL's schema. If JOEL then added a column to his table, then all three of the stored procedures would be marked INVALID by Oracle. It would be nearly impossible if it were up to each individual procedure owner to keep their procedures constantly VALID. As you can see, a small change can easily cascade throughout your database, affecting and invalidating many, many objects.

You might be thinking it would make sense if, upon a change to the table, the dependent procedures were immediately recompiled. This is not really a good idea. If the altered table were referenced directly or indirectly by most of the objects in the database, then the overhead of recompiling them all would be too great. Even if the recompile was attempted, and an error encountered, the table owner may not have access to the offending procedure to rectify the error. So if the change did truly break a procedure, should the change to the table be rolled back? Or should the procedure owner modify their code to account for the change? The latter makes much more sense. In general, referencing objects should not dictate what changes can be made to the referenced object. Rather, the referenced object should be mindful of what the change could possibly do to any object referencing it, but should not be constrained from make changes that may affect referencing objects.

Advantages of Packages

Besides logically grouping functionality and hiding data, packages have a big advantage over stand-alone procedures and functions in terms of dependencies. We have seen that packages are usually made up of a spec and a body. All access to a package is made via the public procedures and functions defined in the spec only. Since nothing can access the body directly, it makes sense that nothing is dependent on the body. That means we can change the body as much as we want and not invalidate any other objects that reference the spec. This is a great advantage packages have over stand-alone procedures and functions. Although we have seen that Oracle will attempt to recompile INVALID code when it is invoked, it takes time and the caller (your application) pays the price of the recompile.

Imagine if you were working on some low- level code in you application and every time you recompiled your code, the entire application became invalid. Your database would burn a great many cycles just to recompile so you can execute. That is just a waste of time, for you, your CPU, and Oracle. Packages shield us from this problem.

Try It Out – Changing a Package

1. We'll create a packaged procedure SHIELD.FOO() which is dependent on the table BAR (so create that now if you haven't already done so). If we alter the table, it should be marked INVALID:

```
SQL> create or replace
  2  package shield as
  3    procedure foo;
  4  end shield;
```

```
    5  /

Package created.

SQL> create or replace
   2   package body shield as
   3     procedure foo is
   4       l_n bar.n%type;
   5     begin
   6       null;
   7     end foo;
   8   end;
   9   /

Package body created.
```

2. Now let's alter the table to include a new column and see what effect this has:

```
SQL> alter table bar add d date;

SQL> select object_type, status
   2    from user_objects
   3    where object_name = 'SHIELD'
   4  /

OBJECT_TYPE          STATUS
-------------------- -------
PACKAGE              VALID
PACKAGE BODY         INVALID
```

At this point we can see clearly that only the package body is INVALID. The spec and anything that references it is still VALID. Using packages has enabled us to make changes and not invalidate a possibly large number of procedures and functions in the database.

In general, package specifications do not change often, but the implementations of them do. Any time you find a bug in your code, or the underlying tables you reference change, or you chose a faster algorithm to process your data, you'll want to change the implementation. Recompiling the package body will have no effect on the spec and any objects dependent on the spec. For this reason alone, there is almost never a reason to use a stand-alone procedure and, if you do, then the possible side effects can drastically hurt performance. Using packages results in good use of the shared pool and buffer pool, and consequently less CPU time, than the equivalent stack of stand-alone procedures that would need processing.

Data Dictionary

Procedures are stored objects in the database. Oracle stores information about every object in the data dictionary. We can query everything about a procedure using the appropriate data dictionary views.

You can read more about the Data Dictionary in Appendix C.

List All Your Stored Procedures

Using the following query, you can list every procedure, function, and package in your schema.

```
SQL> select object_name, object_type
  2    from user_objects
  3   where object_type in ( 'PROCEDURE', 'FUNCTION',
  4                          'PACKAGE', 'PACKAGE BODY' );

OBJECT_NAME                    OBJECT_TYPE
------------------------------ ------------------
BAD_FUNCTION                   FUNCTION
FIRST_FUNCTION                 FUNCTION
FOO                            PROCEDURE
LOG_MESSAGE                    PROCEDURE
SHIELD                         PACKAGE
SHIELD                         PACKAGE BODY
SHOW_IT                        PROCEDURE

7 rows selected.
```

This shows that, in the current schema, there are 2 functions, 3 procedures and a package spec and body.

Retrieve Your Code from the Database

Not only can we find out what procedures are in a given schema, we can also retrieve the code that makes up the procedure. The dictionary view USER_SOURCE will give us that information:

```
SQL> desc user_source
 Name                                      Null?    Type
 ----------------------------------------- -------- ----------------------------
 NAME                                               VARCHAR2(30)
 TYPE                                               VARCHAR2(12)
 LINE                                               NUMBER
 TEXT                                               VARCHAR2(4000)

SQL> select text
  2    from user_source
  3   where name = 'LOG_MESSAGE'
  4     and type = 'PROCEDURE'
  5   order by line;

TEXT
--------------------------------------------------------------------------------
procedure log_message( p_message varchar2 ) as
pragma autonomous_transaction;
begin
   insert into log_table( username, date_time, message )
   values ( user, current_date, p_message );
```

```
    commit;
end log_message;

7 rows selected.
```

Every line of code for every procedure, function, and package is stored in the data dictionary. If you are ever unsure of what version of your procedure is running, you can select the current version from the database and modify it. When we need to make a change to a stored procedure and do not know where the file containing the source is, we can just select the current working copy from the database and make the changes to that. That way we are assured that our changes are to the most recent copy. You should never have to worry about losing source code since it is stored in your database, and your DBA should be regularly backing up the databases (they are aren't they?!).

It's also useful sometimes to use the SQL*Plus DESCRIBE, or DESC, command to describe packages:

```
SQL> desc employee_pkg
PROCEDURE PRINT_ENAME
 Argument Name                  Type                     In/Out Default?
 ------------------------------ ------------------------ ------ --------
 P_EMPNO                        NUMBER                   IN
PROCEDURE PRINT_SAL
 Argument Name                  Type                     In/Out Default?
 ------------------------------ ------------------------ ------ --------
 P_EMPNO                        NUMBER                   IN
```

Here we see SQL*Plus reporting that the package EMPLOYEE_PKG has two procedures and each one has one input parameter named P_EMPNO of type NUMBER. Neither parameter has a default.

Wrap Utility

Since PL/SQL is stored in plain text in the database, Oracle has a facility to encrypt (or **wrap**) your PL/SQL, where it will change your PL/SQL into a version of code that only the database can interpret. This way you can protect your intellectual property by making it impossible for anyone to know how your code works.

The WRAP utility is located in $ORACLE_HOME/bin, and the syntax for WRAP is:

```
wrap -iname=<input_file_name> [-oname=<output_file_name>]
```

By default, WRAP assumes that your input file's extension will be .sql. That means the following are equivalent:

```
C:\sql> wrap iname=file
C:\sql> wrap iname=file.sql
```

By default, if no output file name is supplied, WRAP will generate a file with the same name as the input file but with a .plb extension.

Let's say we want to wrap the implementation of the UTILITIES package we wrote above, and have saved the code for the package body into a file called utilities.sql on the local file system. To wrap the code, all we need to do is issue the following from the command prompt:

```
C:\sql>wrap iname=utilities.sql

PL/SQL Wrapper: Release 9.0.1.0.0- Production on Sat Dec 01 14:07:37 2001

Copyright (c) Oracle Corporation 1993, 2001.  All Rights Reserved.

Processing utilities.sql to utilities.plb
```

Examining the newly created utilities.plb file you will see something that looks like this:

```
create or replace
package body utilities wrapped
0
abcd
abcd
abcd
abcd
abcd
abcd
abcd
abcd
abcd
abcd
abcd
abcd
abcd
abcd
abcd
3
b
9000000
1
4
0
10
2 :e:
1PACKAGE:
1BODY:
1UTILITIES:
1SWAP:
1P_PARM1:
1OUT:
1NUMBER:
1P_PARM2:
...
```

Not very readable by humans, but Oracle can understand that just fine. You can now compile this file into the database just as if it were normal PL/SQL. The only difference is that when the code is now queried out of the dictionary, this wrapped code is what will be returned. Your business logic is now safe.

> **The downside is that you must maintain a copy of the source file outside the database, since wrapping code is a one-way process. Once wrapped, it cannot be unwrapped. Be warned!**

It is good practice if you are going to wrap your packages, to only wrap the package body. Leave the spec in clear text, since you will not be exposing anything about how the package works to its users. This will also benefit the users since they will be able to view your spec and see the interfaces defined.

Summary

Oracle's programming language, PL/SQL, is a robust and powerful language. It contains most of the constructs found in other programming languages like C and Java. With the inclusion of procedures, functions, and packages, you have all the tools you need to write fully-fledged applications completely stored within the database. Your application and your data can co-exist and both benefit from the robust and secure environment that is Oracle.

Procedures, functions, and packages allow us to write reusable code that can either be accessed within a schema or shared database wide. Oracle's security helps us to manage access to these program units by treating them as any other database objects. As you become more skilled in writing PL/SQL and stored procedures, you will see the benefit of storing your application and your data together.

Transactions and Concurrency

In this chapter we will explore two concepts that truly set a database management system apart from a file system. If you compare a file system to a database, you'll discover many similarities between the two. We can create files in a file system, in the same way as we'll create tables in a database. These files can be located in different directories, just as we have schemas or owners in the database. We can write data to these files, just as we insert rows into tables. However, two features that set the database apart from the file system in a dramatic fashion are transaction management and concurrency control.

In discussing these two features we will look at the following in this chapter:

- ❏ What a transaction in Oracle is

- ❏ How to control transactions in Oracle

- ❏ How Oracle implements concurrency controls in the database, allowing many users to access and modify the same data tables simultaneously.

What Is a Transaction?

Before we go any further, we need to have an understanding of exactly what a transaction is in the database. It is really a quite simple concept, and there are many real-life analogies that you encounter every day such as:

- ❏ Shopping at a store. You take something off the shelf, put it into your shopping cart or basket, and then pay for it.

- ❏ Transferring funds from your savings account to your checking account at an ATM.

- ❏ Going to work, getting your paycheck.

Let's consider the second example in the above list. In transferring funds, we update the savings account record by taking away some amount of money, and also update the checking account record by adding that same amount. Completion of this transfer requires both of these events to occur (in order). You would not want the update to the savings account record to happen without a corresponding update to the checking account. Equally, while you would be quite happy if the update to the checking account to add some money happened, but the update to the savings account to take away money did not, the bank itself would be quite upset! We can talk about the transaction here, as the atomic action of updating *both* the checking and savings account records. In other words, either both updates must happen, or neither update can be allowed.

This is precisely the role that transactions play in the database. They allow you to group a set of statements together and either execute all of them (and have their changes saved), or have none of the work any of them have performed saved. In other words it's an all or nothing proposition with transactions.

> *We should note in passing here that these groups of statements are also known as logical units of work in database speak. A transaction is, as a result, sometimes referred to as a logical unit of work.*

Without transactions in the database, the very simple act of transferring funds, which in this example would require two SQL statements, would be a very dangerous activity. If the system failed after one update and before the other, then either you or the bank would be out of pocket. Not only that, but there would be no easy way to trace this missing money; it would simply "vanish". This is what transactions are designed to prevent, since they ensure that we can execute a sequence of data manipulation language (DML) statements and have the work performed by each, either saved as a whole or undone as a whole.

Transaction Control Statements

One important concept in Oracle is that there is no 'begin transaction' statement. You do not *begin* a transaction explicitly. A transaction implicitly begins with the first statement that modifies data, or in some way requires a transaction. Issuing either a COMMIT or ROLL BACK statement explicitly ends transactions.

As discussed above, transactions are atomic, that is to say that either every statement succeeds or none of the statements will succeed. There are a number of transaction control statements available that allow us to control this behavior, some of which we will look at here:

- ❑ COMMIT
- ❑ ROLL BACK
- ❑ SAVEPOINT
- ❑ ROLL BACK TO <SAVEPOINT>
- ❑ SET TRANSACTION
- ❑ SET CONSTRAINT(S)

Now we'll take a look at each command in more depth.

COMMIT Processing

In its simplest form, you would just issue the SQL command COMMIT. A commit ends your transaction and makes permanent (durable) any changes you have performed. As a developer, you should always explicitly terminate your transactions with a COMMIT or ROLL BACK, otherwise the tool/environment you are using will pick one or the other for you. If you exit your SQL*Plus session without committing or rolling back for example, SQL*Plus will assume you wish to commit your work, and will do so for you. Whether you wanted that committed or not isn't relevant. If you exit a Pro*C program on the other hand, a ROLL BACK will take place.

> To avoid any such ambiguity always explicitly **COMMIT** or **ROLL BACK** your work.

A commit is a very fast operation, regardless of the transaction size. One might think that the bigger a transaction is (in other words, the more data it affects), the longer a commit will take. This is not true. The response time of a commit is generally 'flat' regardless of the transaction size. This is because a commit does not really have too much work to do, but what it does do is vital.

If you understand this, then you will avoid what many developers do, which is to artificially constrain the size of their transactions, committing every so many rows, instead of committing when a logical unit of work has been performed. They do this in the mistaken belief that they are lessening the load on the system resources; in fact they are increasing them. If a commit of 1 row takes X units of time, and the commit of one thousand rows takes the same X units of time, then performing work in a manner that does one thousand 1 row commits will necessarily take an additional 1,000*X units of time to perform. By only committing when you have to (when the transaction is complete), you will not only increase performance but also reduce contention for shared resources (the log files, locks that protect shared data structures in the SGA, and the like).

So, why is a commit's response time fairly flat, regardless of the transaction size? Well, it is because before we even go to commit in the database, we have already done the really hard work. We've already modified the data in the database, we've already done 99.9% of the work.

When we commit, there are three tasks left for us to perform:

❑ Generation of a **SCN (System Change Number)** for our transaction. This is Oracle's internal clock, how it tells *database time*. This SCN is not a clock in the traditional sense since it does not advance over time. Instead, it advances whenever a transaction is committed, and is used internally by Oracle to order transactions.

❑ Writing all of our *remaining* buffered redo log entries to disk and recording the SCN in the online redo log files as well. This is performed by the LGWR (a database background process we saw in Chapter 5). This step is actually the 'commit' and what makes the transaction durable as discussed above. If this step occurs, we have committed.

❑ Release of all locks held by our session (and every user who was waiting on locks we held).

As you can see, there is very little to do in order to process a commit. The lengthiest operation is, and always will be, the activity performed by LGWR, as this is physical disk Input/Output (IO). The amount of time spent by LGWR here will be limited by the fact that it has already been flushing the contents of the redo log buffer on a regular basis. LGWR will not buffer all of the work you do in one go, rather it will incrementally flush the contents of the redo log buffer in the background as we are going along, much like your disk caching software running on your PC does. This is to avoid having a commit wait for a very long time in order to flush all of your redo at once. LGWR carries out flushing:

❑   every 3 seconds

❑   when the log buffer in the SGA is 1/3 full or contains 1Mb or more buffered data

❑   upon any transaction commit

So, even if we have a long running transaction, much of the buffered redo log it generates will have been flushed to disk prior to committing.

You can find more details on this in Chapter 5.

ROLL BACK Processing

A roll back allows us to undo our work. We might need a roll back in the event of an error in our application, or simply because the end user running our program decided not to save the changes they made. Without being able to roll back upon an error or user command, we would not be able to support transactions in the database.

In its simplest form you would just issue ROLL BACK. A roll back ends your transaction and undoes any changes you have outstanding. It does this by reading information you stored in the roll back segments or UNDO tablespace, and restoring the database blocks to the state they were in prior to your transaction beginning.

Unlike a commit, the time to roll back a transaction is a function of the amount of data modified. This is to be expected, since a roll back has to physically undo the work we've done. As with a commit there is a series of operations that must be performed. In a similar way to a COMMIT, the database will do a lot of work for us prior to a ROLL BACK. When we roll back we have the remaining tasks to carry out:

❑   Undo all of the changes made. This is accomplished by reading UNDO data we generated and in effect reversing our operation. If we inserted a row then a roll back will delete it. If we updated a row, a roll back will update it back. If we deleted a row, a roll back will re-insert it again.

❑   Release all locks held by our session (and every user who was waiting on rows we had locked).

The point here is that you don't want to roll back unless you have to. It is expensive to perform, since you spent a lot of time doing the work and you'll spend a lot of time undoing the work. Rolling back should be the exception rather than the rule in your code. Don't do work unless you are fairly sure you are going to want to commit it.

Further details on the REDO mechanism can be found in Chapter 5.

SAVEPOINT and ROLL BACK TO SAVEPOINT

A SAVEPOINT allows you to create a marked point within a transaction. You may have multiple savepoints in a single transaction. When used with a ROLL BACK TO <SAVEPOINT NAME>, it allows you to selectively roll back a group of statements within a larger transaction.

You may roll back your transaction to that marked point without rolling back any of the work that preceded it. So, you could issue two UPDATE statements, and then issue a SAVEPOINT. After the SAVEPOINT you could issue two DELETE statements, and upon hitting an error of some sort, you can roll back to the named SAVEPOINT. This will undo the DELETE statements, but will not undo the previous two UPDATE statements. It should be noted that this ROLL BACK TO <SAVEPOINT NAME> simply undoes a bit of the work you've done. Your transaction won't end until you issue a COMMIT or ROLL BACK.

Savepoints are a useful transaction feature, since they allow you to divide a single large transaction into a series of smaller parts. While all of the statements executed are still part of the larger transaction, you can group certain statements together and roll them back as if they were a single statement. Any other prior statements in the transaction are unaffected.

These are most useful in application programs where you would like the work done by a particular subroutine or function to either entirely succeed or entirely fail. For example, suppose you are developing an application in Java using JDBC. You have a series of functions, each of which performs a couple of DML SQL statements (inserts/updates and deletes) in order to accomplish its job. What you would like to do is ensure that each function works as an atomic statement, just as a stored procedure does. To accomplish this, you would start the function with a SQL statement such as:

```
Savepoint function_name;
```

where function_name is the name of your function. If you encountered an error during the course of your processing, you would simply issue:

```
Roll back to function_name;
```

This statement would roll back all of the work done *since* the savepoint was issued, but nothing before that. It would not end your transaction, but would just undo the work you had performed since the savepoint call. This coding will allow the caller of your function to understand that if your function is successful then all of their changes will be made. Equally, if they return an error from the function then *none* of their changes will have been made. This coding practice is to be strongly encouraged in order to develop modular pieces of reusable code that work well with other such modules, and can be assembled together into a larger transaction.

SET TRANSACTION

This statement allows you to set various attributes of your transaction, such as its isolation level (see below for a list of isolation levels), whether it is read-only or read-write, and also to use a specific roll back segment.

The SET TRANSACTION statement must be the first statement issued in a transaction. That is to say that it must be issued prior to any INSERT, UPDATE, or DELETE statements, or indeed any other statement that begins a transaction. The scope of SET TRANSACTION is the current transaction only. As soon as you commit or roll back, the effects of the SET TRANSACTION statement are complete as well.

469

The SET TRANSACTION statement allows you to:

❑ Specify the isolation level of your transaction

❑ Specify a specific roll back segment to use for your transaction

❑ Name your transaction

We will only discuss the first of these here. The reason for this is that in Oracle 9*i*, the use of ROLL BACK segments is optional, and even when roll back segments were mandatory, it was rare to have to use this command. The naming of transactions is very simple and its usefulness is only realized with distributed transactions which are beyond the scope of this book. You can refer to the *Oracle SQL Reference* guide for a discussion of these two options.

The important SET TRANSACTION statements we will be using here are:

❑ SET TRANSACTION READ ONLY

❑ SET TRANSACTION READ WRITE

❑ SET TRANSACTION ISOLATION LEVEL SERIALIZABLE

❑ SET TRANSACTION ISOLATION LEVEL READ COMMITTED

> It is important to note that each of these **SET TRANSACTION** statements is in fact mutually exclusive. If you choose to make your transaction **READ ONLY** for example, you cannot also choose for it to be **READ WRITE**, **SERIALIZABLE**, or **READ COMMITTED**. You must **COMMIT** or **ROLL BACK** before setting your transaction attribute again.

READ ONLY

The command SET TRANSACTION READ ONLY will do two things. First and most obvious, it will ensure that you cannot perform DML operations that modify data such as INSERT, UPDATE, or DELETE. If you try to do so, you will receive an error, as shown below:

```
SQL> set transaction read only;
Transaction set.

SQL> update emp set ename = lower(ename);
update emp set ename = lower(ename)
          *
ERROR at line 1:
ORA-01456: may not perform insert/delete/update operation inside a READ ONLY
transaction
```

That is clear enough. The other side effect of a READ ONLY transaction is a little subtler. By setting our transaction to READ ONLY we have in effect frozen our view of the database to that point in time. What I mean by this is that, regardless of what other sessions do in the database, the database will appear to us as it looked at the point in time when we issued the SET TRANSACTION statement. Why would this be useful? Let's consider that it is one o'clock in the afternoon on a busy day. You need to run a report. This report will execute perhaps many dozens of queries, pulling data in from many sources. All of the data is related and, in order for it to make sense, it must all be consistent. In other words you need each of the queries to see the database 'as of one o'clock'. If each query sees the database at a different point in time, then the end results in our report will be meaningless.

To ensure that your data is consistent you could lock each and every table you need to query for the report and prevent anyone from updating them. In this way you could run the report safely in isolation. (We will see more about locking later in this chapter). This rather draconian approach has the drawback that at one o'clock on a busy day *all* processing except for your report must cease. This is unacceptable. As an alternative approach you can use the SET TRANSACTION READ ONLY statement to freeze your view of the database at one o'clock. This allows you to have the best of both worlds. While it appears to you as if the report is the only thing executing in the database, in actual fact the database is still processing all of the other user transactions.

More details on how this is physically implemented can be found in the Multi-Versioning section later in this chapter.

Try It Out – Frozen Views

1. To run this example, you'll need to open up three sessions in SQL*Plus (in other words three separate SQL*Plus windows). You'll also need to create a table, by issuing the following command:

```
create table t as select object_id from all_objects where rownum <= 2000;
```

2. The following table shows what commands to execute in each session in order to observe the difference between a READ ONLY and a READ WRITE transaction:

Time	Session 1	Session 2	Session 3	Comments
T1	Set transaction read only;			
T2	Select count(*) from t;	Select count(*) from t		Both sessions will see 2000 rows
T3			Delete from t where rownum <= 500;	Delete 500 rows from T but do not commit

Table continued on following page

Time	Session 1	Session 2	Session 3	Comments
T4	Select count(*) from t;	Select count(*) from t;		Both sessions will still see 2000 rows due to multi-versioning (see later section on concurrency control for details)
T5			Commit;	Make the 500 deleted rows permanently deleted
T6	Select count(*) from t;	Select count(*) from t;		Session 1 will *still* see 2,000 rows. Session 2 will now see 1,500 rows! Session 1 will continue to see 2,000 rows in table T until it commits or rolls back
T7			Insert into t select * from t;	Doubles the size of T to 3,000 records.
T8			Commit;	Makes the changes visible
T9	Select count(*) from t;	Select count(*) from t;		Session 1 continues to see 2,000 rows. Session 2 now sees all 3,000 rows.
T10	Commit;			
T11	Select count(*) from t;			Session 1 now sees 3,000 rows as well.

READ WRITE

The second command, SET TRANSACTION READ WRITE, is infrequently used since it is in fact the default. It is rarely, if ever, necessary to issue this command and it is included here simply for the sake of completeness.

ISOLATION LEVEL SERIALIZABLE

SET TRANSACTION ISOLATION LEVEL SERIALIZABLE, is in some ways very similar to READ ONLY. Once you issue this statement, the database will appear 'frozen' in time for you, regardless of the changes taking place. You are completely isolated from the effects of other transactions just as we saw in the case of a READ ONLY transaction. You can see changes you make, but not any other changes that have taken place. The major difference here is that you can perform any DML statement you need in a serializable transaction.

We'll look further into serializable transactions in the section on Isolation below.

ISOLATION LEVEL READ COMMITTED

This command, much like setting the transaction as READ WRITE, is of limited use as it is the default mode of operation in Oracle when setting the isolation level. The one time it is useful is if you have used an ALTER SESSION command earlier in your session to change the default isolation level for your session's transactions from READ COMMITTED to SERIALIZABLE. Issuing the ISOLATION LEVEL READ COMMITTED command would reset the default.

SET CONSTRAINTS

In Oracle, constraints may be validated either immediately upon execution of a DML statement, or deferred until transaction commit time. The SET CONSTRAINT statement allows you to set the enforcement mode of deferrable constraints in your transaction. Individual constraints can be deferred using:

```
set constraint constraint_name deferred
```

Or you can set all constraints that can be deferred to be so using:

```
set constraints all deferred
```

You can change their enforcement mode back to immediate by using the keyword IMMEDIATE instead of DEFERRED in these commands. To see this command in action, we'll use a small example:

```
SQL> drop table t;
Table dropped.

SQL> create table t
  2  ( x int,
  3    constraint x_greater_than_zero check ( x > 0 )
  4              deferrable initially immediate
  5  )
  6  /
Table created.
```

Here we create a table T, with a column X that only accepts values where "x > 0" is not false. This constraint is allowed to be deferred, (since in line 4 we set it as DEFERRABLE) and its initial state will be IMMEDIATE, meaning it will be checked for each statement. Let's see if the constraint works:

```
SQL> insert into t values ( -1 );
insert into t values ( -1 )
*
ERROR at line 1:
ORA-02290: check constraint (SCOTT.X_GREATER_THAN_ZERO) violated
```

Sure enough, we cannot insert the value −1 into X. Now we use the SET CONSTRAINT command to defer the verification of this constraint as follows:

```
SQL> set constraint x_greater_than_zero deferred;
Constraint set.
```

473

Now it will appear that we can in fact insert −1

```
SQL> insert into t values ( -1 );
1 row created.
```

However, we'll never be able to commit that statement in the database:

```
SQL> commit;
commit
*
ERROR at line 1:
ORA-02091: transaction rolled back
ORA-02290: check constraint (SCOTT.X_GREATER_THAN_ZERO) violated
```

There are two ways to use this command, either by specifying a set of constraint names or by using the keyword ALL. So for example, to defer the constraint X_GREATER_THAN_ZERO we issued:

```
set constraint x_greater_than_zero deferred;
```

We could just as easily have issued the following:

```
Set constraints all deferred;
```

The difference here is that the second version, with ALL, would have affected all deferrable constraints in our session, not just the one we were interested in. It is recommended that if you know the name of the constraint you are interested in deferring, you use it explicitly rather than deferring all constraints. Some applications might not be expecting the constraints to be deferred and may behave inappropriately. Also, it is a good idea to use:

```
Set constraint <constraint_name> immediate;
```

or

```
Set constraints all immediate;
```

in order to explicitly validate your constraints. We could, for example, issue the following in our above example:

```
SQL> set constraint x_greater_than_zero deferred;
Constraint set.

SQL> insert into t values ( -1 );
1 row created.

SQL> set constraint x_greater_than_zero immediate;
set constraint x_greater_than_zero immediate
*
ERROR at line 1:
ORA-02290: check constraint (SCOTT.X_GREATER_THAN_ZERO) violated
```

This will allow you to gracefully recover from an error, instead of having the entire transaction rolled back by the database! If you remember, when we used COMMIT to validate the constraints, Oracle returned the following error message:

```
SQL> commit;
commit
*
ERROR at line 1:
ORA-02091: transaction rolled back
ORA-02290: check constraint (SCOTT.X_GREATER_THAN_ZERO) violated
```

Oracle rolled back our transaction (as highlighted in bold). By using the SET CONSTRAINT <constraint_name> IMMEDIATE command, we were able to find that we had violated some constraint, while our transaction remained in effect. The constraint is still in the deferred mode, it could not be made immediate, but we have the opportunity to either fix the data and then try again, *or* roll back. It's up to us, not decided for us.

Now that we have an understanding of what a transaction is, and what transaction control statements we have at our disposal, it's time to go a little deeper into the database concepts behind transactions.

ACID Properties of Transactions

ACID is an acronym that stands for:

❑ **Atomicity** – A transaction either totally happens, or none of it happens

❑ **Consistency** – A transaction takes the database from one consistent state to the next

❑ **Isolation** – The effects of a transaction may not be visible to other transactions in the system until that transaction has been committed

❑ **Durability** – Once the transaction is committed, it is permanent

These four features describe the rules of a transaction. A transaction is atomic in nature, it either happens or it doesn't. Part of a transaction will never be made permanent while another part fails. A transaction provides for data consistency in the database; when a transaction is committed, all of the information is assured to be logically consistent with all business rules defined in the database. A transaction is isolated from outside effects and likewise does not affect others until it is committed. Lastly, and perhaps most importantly, a transaction is durable. Once committed, its changes are permanent.

Atomicity

In Oracle transactions are atomic. In other words, either all of the work is committed or none of the work is committed. To supplement the ATM example, which we considered in our introduction to transactions, we will look at another short example here.

Let's begin by creating a test table T. To do this we need to drop the table of the same name that we created earlier.

```
SQL> drop table t;
Table dropped.

SQL> create table t ( x number(1) );
Table created.
```

Now we'll modify this table by issuing two INSERT commands:

```
SQL> insert into t values ( 1 );
1 row created.

SQL> insert into t values ( 2 );
1 row created.
```

At this point in time, since we are done submitting statements to the database in this transaction, either both rows will be saved or neither row will be saved.

> **We will never find a case where the first row is made permanent and the second row is not (and vice-versa).**

If we want to undo this work, we roll back, and check what this achieves by selecting all records from table T:

```
SQL> roll back;
Roll back complete.

SQL> select * from t;
no rows selected
```

On the other hand, if we perform the two statements and commit them:

```
SQL> insert into t values ( 1 );
1 row created.

SQL> insert into t values ( 2 );
1 row created.

SQL> commit;
Commit complete.

SQL> select * from t;

         X
----------
         1
         2
```

they are made permanent. If the database crashes right now, those rows will be in there when it restarts. These changes are now durable (permanent), and the only way to remove these rows is to physically delete them.

This atomic property of transactions is extended to individual statements within the database as well. That is, each statement either entirely succeeds or entirely fails. A single statement will never leave just part of its job done. Note here that stored procedures are also treated as atomic statements by Oracle. That is to say that either they happen, or they don't.

You can read more about stored procedures by looking back to Chapter 11.

Consistency

This is a very important feature of transactions, since any transaction takes the database from one logically consistent state to another logically consistent state. That is to say that, before the transaction begins, all of the data in the database satisfies all of the business rules (constraints) that you have put in place in the database. Similarly, at the time you commit the transaction the database will satisfy all of the business rules you have in place.

In between those two points however, the database may be logically inconsistent, as far as our transaction's view of the data is concerned. As we'll see in the *Isolation* section below however, the rest of the users in the database are isolated from your changes. We can see this temporary **logical inconsistency** by considering a slightly more sophisticated example. We'll introduce a database trigger (t_trigger), which simply prints out the changes we make to our table (row by row) as they happen. The table and trigger we'll use are as follows:

```
SQL> drop table t;
Table dropped.

SQL> create table t
  2  ( x int,
  3    constraint t_pk primary key(x)
  4  )
  5  /
Table created.

SQL> create trigger t_trigger
  2  AFTER update on T for each row
  3  begin
  4      dbms_output.put_line( 'Updated x=' || :old.x ||
  5                          ' to x=' || :new.x );
  6  end;
  7  /
Trigger created.
```

You can find more details on triggers in Chapter 15.

Having created our table, we now have a business rule in place in the form of the primary key constraint. No row in table T may have a value for X that is the same as the value for X in some other row in the table.

Now, we'll insert a couple of rows into T to work on:

```
SQL> insert into t values ( 1 );
1 row created.

SQL> insert into t values ( 2 );
1 row created.
```

That concludes the setup for this example. Now we will attempt to update table T and set every row to the number 2. This will of course fail due to the primary key constraint. (Note that we use SET SERVEROUTPUT ON in order to be able to see the output from our trigger):

```
SQL> set serveroutput on
SQL> begin
  2          update t set x = 2;
  3   end;
  4   /
Updated x=1 to x=2
Updated x=2 to x=2
begin
*
ERROR at line 1:
ORA-00001: unique constraint (OPS$TKYTE.T_PK) violated
ORA-06512: at line 2
```

The interesting thing to note here is that both rows in the table (momentarily) had the same value for X (the number 2)! We can see this because both rows were updated (as highlighted in bold). It was only *after* the INSERT completed all of its work that it failed in this case. It was only then that Oracle realized that the entire set of work performed by this insert would result in a logically inconsistent set of data. At this point it undid all the work performed and reported the error.

Now, if we issue a successful statement such as the following:

```
SQL> begin
  2          update t set x = x+1;
  3   end;
  4   /
Updated x=1 to x=2
Updated x=2 to x=3

PL/SQL procedure successfully completed.

SQL> commit;
Commit complete.
```

We can see that for a brief moment in time, following our update of the row with a value of 1, but prior to our update of the second row, both rows again had the value of 2. The constraint was not validated at that point in time (it could not be, else we could not perform many operations in the database), but rather *after* the entire set of work was performed by the statement. After all rows were modified, the database was deemed logically consistent (it satisfied all of our business rules) and the statement succeeded.

That demonstrates statement level consistency in the database. Now, how about transaction level consistency? We can see this at work by using **deferrable constraints**, those that are validated when you commit, rather than statement by statement. These are useful for performing certain complex operations, where logical inconsistency from statement to statement is removed by the time all the statements in the transaction have been executed. A prime example of this is in the implementation of UPDATE CASCADE logic, which you use in updating the primary key of a table that has child tables reliant on this primary key. If consistency is validated statement by statement, you could not update the parent table's primary key. If you updated the parent first, it would fail since it would leave orphaned children. If you updated the child first, that would fail since the parent record would not be found. Using deferrable constraints we can solve this chicken and egg problem and update the tables in any order we desire.

> Note that in practice you should avoid updating a primary key if at all possible.

Let's follow through an example in order to see this at work.

Try It Out – Transaction Level Consistency

1. We'll create two tables PARENT and CHILD. The CHILD table will have a foreign key to the PARENT table and this foreign key will be defined as deferrable.

```
SQL> create table parent( pk int,
  2                        constraint parent_pk primary key(pk) );
Table created.

SQL> create table child ( fk,
  2                        constraint child_fk foreign key(fk)
  3                        references parent deferrable );
Table created.
```

2. Now let's populate these tables with some data:

```
SQL> insert into parent values( 1 );
1 row created.

SQL> insert into child values( 1 );
1 row created.

SQL> commit;
Commit complete.
```

3. Now, we'll try to update the PARENT table and change its primary key value:

```
SQL> update parent set pk = 2;
update parent set pk = 2
       *
ERROR at line 1:
ORA-02292: integrity constraint (SCOTT.CHILD_FK) violated - child record found
```

479

This update fails since it would orphan a child record. We created the constraint DEFERRABLE but it is not yet operating in deferred mode (deferrable constraints operate in immediate mode, and so are checked at the statement level). We'll find of course that an update of the CHILD table fails for the same reason:

```
SQL> update child set fk = 2;
update child set fk = 2
       *
ERROR at line 1:
ORA-02291: integrity constraint (SCOTT.CHILD_FK) violated - parent key not found
```

4. To get around this, we'll simply tell Oracle we would like the constraint CHILD_FK to be deferred, meaning that we don't want it to be checked at the statement level:

```
SQL> set constraints child_fk deferred;
Constraint set.
```

5. Now we can update the PARENT table without error:

```
SQL> update parent set pk=2;
1 row updated.

SQL> select * from parent;

        PK
----------
         2

SQL> select * from child;

        FK
----------
         1
```

As you can see our database is logically inconsistent right now (again, only we can see this. Other sessions in our system do not see this apparent inconsistency). If we were to try and commit right now, we would find:

```
SQL> commit;
commit
*
ERROR at line 1:
ORA-02091: transaction rolled back
ORA-02292: integrity constraint (SCOTT.CHILD_FK) violated - child record found
```

The database ensured that, at the time the transaction ended, all of the data complied with the business rules. In this case, it discovered that the data was not consistent and rolled back our transaction. All the work we performed was *undone* since it violated our business rules.

6. Let's try that again, and see how we can ask Oracle to verify the logical consistency of our data without rolling us back. We'll start by setting the constraint DEFERRED again and then updating the parent table again to redo what Oracle just undid:

```
SQL> set constraints child_fk deferred;
Constraint set.

SQL> update parent set pk=2;
1 row updated.
```

We can see that our data is now inconsistent with our constraint:

```
SQL> select * from parent;

        PK
----------
         2

SQL> select * from child;

        FK
----------
         1
```

7. Let's now set the CHILD_FK constraints to IMMEDIATE. This will cause Oracle to validate the consistency of our business rules straight away:

```
SQL> set constraints child_fk immediate;
set constraints child_fk immediate
*
ERROR at line 1:
ORA-02291: integrity constraint (SCOTT.CHILD_FK) violated - parent key not found
```

Here, the act of setting the constraint back into immediate mode caused Oracle to find an error. This time however, instead of rolling back all of our outstanding work, it simply failed the SET CONSTRAINTS statement (our parent record update is still outstanding).

8. Now we can update the CHILD record, check the constraints again and commit:

```
SQL> update child set fk = 2;
1 row updated.

SQL> set constraints child_fk immediate;
Constraint set.

SQL> commit;
Commit complete.
```

481

This will result in consistent data that satisfies our constraint:

```
SQL> select * from parent;

        PK
----------
         2

SQL> select * from child;

        FK
----------
         2
```

That completes our look at statement and transaction level consistency within Oracle.

The important points to remember are:

❑ Statements may cause the data to become temporarily inconsistent in the database. This condition will be detected at the appropriate time and will not be allowed to persist beyond a statement or transaction

❑ You can control when Oracle will verify that the data is logically consistent, either statement by statement, by some arbitrary grouping of statements, or at the transaction level.

❑ You will never be able to commit information that violates the business rules you have programmed into the database, it is one of the basic tenets of the RDBMS itself.

Isolation

Isolation is the capability of the database to permit concurrent modifications and reads of data within it. Isolation is used not only to protect other transactions from your transaction, but also to protect *your* transaction from other transactions as well! While others are protected from seeing your changes, you are protected from their changes too. What do we mean by this? Well, let's consider a case where I update a row in a table (without committing) and you are allowed to read that row's values including my (uncommitted) changes. This would result in you making a bad decision based on information that is wrong, incomplete, or was never saved (I might have rolled back the changes that you read). It is very important for the database to prevent this from occurring.

This topic is of such importance that ANSI (American National Standards Institute) has even included the definition of isolation and formal definitions of various levels of isolation in the SQL standard itself. The ANSI/ISO SQL92 standard defines four levels of transaction isolation with different possible outcomes for the same transaction mixes. That is, the same work performed in the same fashion with the same inputs, may result in different answers given your isolation level. These isolation levels are defined in terms of three 'reads' that are permitted (or illegal) at a given level. These are:

❑ **Dirty read** – The meaning of this is as bad as it sounds. You are permitted to read uncommitted 'dirty' data. This is the effect you would achieve by just opening an OS file someone else is writing to, and reading whatever data happened to be there. Data integrity is compromised, foreign keys violated, unique constraints ignored.

❑ **Non-repeatable read** – This simply means that if you read a row at time T1, and attempt to re-read that row at time T2, the row may have changed. It may have been deleted or updated, for example.

❑ **Phantom read** – This means that if you executed a query at time T1, and re-execute it at time T2, additional rows may have been added to the database, which affect your results. This differs from the non-repeatable read in that in this case, data you already read has not been changed but rather that *more* data satisfies your query criteria than before.

SQL92 takes these three 'reads' and creates four isolation levels based on their existence, or otherwise. They are:

Isolation Level	Dirty Read	Non-Repeatable Read	Phantom Read
Read Uncommitted	Permitted	Permitted	Permitted
Read Committed	Forbidden	Permitted	Permitted
Repeatable Read	Forbidden	Forbidden	Permitted
Serializable	Forbidden	Forbidden	Forbidden

Oracle supports two of the above isolation levels (read committed and serializable) exactly as they are defined. Oracle also defines an isolation level, named READ_ONLY, which is not part of the ANSI standard. A read-only transaction has the capabilities of both a repeatable read and a serializable transaction. Note however that updates by a read-only transaction are not permitted (other sessions may update data, but not the read-only transaction).

In the section above on Transaction Control Statements, we saw the SET TRANSACTION commands we can use to set our isolation level for our transactions.

Durability

Durability is one of the most important features offered by the database. It ensures that once a transaction is committed its changes are permanent. They won't 'go away' due to some system failure or mistakes. The database, via its **online redo logs** (also referred to as transaction logs and covered in Chapter 5), ensures that everything needed to restore your data, in the event of a system failure or crash, is in place.

A detailed discussion of the mechanics of data protection is beyond the scope of this book (the *Oracle Server Concepts Manual* does go into the mechanics of this). What we'll present here is simply an overview of what takes place.

When we modify data in the database via SQL INSERT, UPDATE, and DELETE statements, Oracle generates two pieces of important information – UNDO and REDO. As their names imply, UNDO is used to undo or roll back a transaction's work while REDO is used to redo the work. The purpose of UNDO is clear, since it is like the revert or undo function in a word processor. The purpose of REDO is less clear at first. Why would we want to 'redo' a transaction? The answer is for durability purposes. In other words, to ensure that in the event of some system failure, we can recover (REDO) our transaction.

In order to understand why a separate REDO is necessary to accomplish this, we'll need to understand exactly what happens when we modify data. Let's consider a very simple statement:

```
Update t set x = x+1 where x = 2;
```

When this executes, Oracle will find the database block (or blocks) that contain values where X equals two and bring them into the buffer cache if necessary (they may already be there). It will then modify these cached blocks and change the value of 2 to 3 as directed. When it does this, it also generated some UNDO information into the roll back segments or UNDO tablespace (depending on how your DBA configured your database). This UNDO information contains instructions on how to find these blocks again (their block addresses) and what to do to them to put them back (change the 3 back into a 2). This UNDO information is stored in the buffer cache as well. At the same time as the database updated the block and generated this UNDO information, it also generated REDO entries. These REDO entries contain the instructions as how to find these blocks again and *redo* the work we just did (change the 2 into a 3). This REDO information is stored in the Log Buffer located in the SGA (see Chapter 5 for details on the SGA).

Now we decide to COMMIT this transaction, to make the changes permanent. Before we do this, all or most of our changes are stored solely in memory. The database blocks from the data files are in the buffer cache, our UNDO information is in the buffer cache and our REDO information is in the log buffer, all of which are contained in the SGA. If the system crashed right now these changes would of course be lost forever. So, before Oracle returns SUCCESS for the COMMIT, it will flush the contents of the log buffer to the REDO log files. Once Oracle is sure the REDO information is safely stored on disk (and it is a common practice to have many copies of the REDO logs so the information typically exists on many disks, not just one), it can consider the transaction committed and returns success. Now, if the system fails, we have sufficient information recorded in the redo logs to 'replay' that transaction all over again. This is a key component to making the changes *durable*.

Concurrency Control

One of the key challenges in developing multi-user, database-driven applications is to maximize concurrent access (multiple users accessing data simultaneously), but at the same time, to ensure that each user is able to read and modify the data in a consistent fashion. The **locking** and **concurrency** controls that allow this to happen are key features of any database, and Oracle excels in providing them.

In this section we're going to take a look at how Oracle locks data, and the implications of this model for writing multi-user applications.

Locking

Let's start with a basic definition. A **lock** is a mechanism used to regulate concurrent access to a shared resource. Note how we used the term 'shared resource', not 'database row' or 'database table'. It is true that Oracle locks table data at the row level, but it uses locks at many different levels to provide concurrent access to various resources. For example, while a stored procedure is executing, the procedure itself is locked in a mode that allows others to execute it, but will not permit another user to alter it in any way. Locks are used in the database to permit concurrent access to these shared resources while at the same time providing data integrity and consistency.

Most of the times, locks are totally transparent to us as developers. When we update a row, we do not have to lock it, since Oracle does it for us. There are times when explicit locks are necessary, but most of the time, locking is managed automatically.

In a single-user database, locks are not necessary. There is, by definition, only one user modifying the information. However, when multiple users are accessing and modifying data or data structures, it is crucial to have a mechanism in place to prevent concurrent modifications to the same piece of information. This is what locking is all about.

What we'll do in this section is look at some of the pitfalls associated with the fact that there are locks in the database and how to avoid them. This is not to say locks are evil. Far from it, since without them we could not perform concurrent operations. Locks are something you must understand however, in order to build high-performing, scalable applications, and to be able to pinpoint problem areas in your applications.

Deadlocks

We'll start out with a simple definition of what a deadlock is. In short, a deadlock is a standstill situation, when two sessions have gotten into a situation that causes each of them to wait for the other. Deadlocks occur when two people hold a resource that both want.

Oracle handles deadlocks very simply. When a deadlock is detected (and they are detected immediately), Oracle will choose one of the sessions as a "victim". That session will get an error informing it that the resource it attempted to access is locked by another session (which in turn is blocked waiting for something the victim has locked). At this point, the victim has to make a choice whether to try something else, complete its transaction and commit, or roll back and try again later. Regardless of what the victim decides, the other waiting session will continue only when the victim completes its transaction by committing or rolling back.

A deadlock is a very easy situation to demonstrate. In this example, we'll have two tables, A and B in our database, and each will have a single row in it.

Try It Out – Causing a Deadlock

1. We create the two tables we need as follows:

```
SQL> create table a as select 1 x from dual;
Table created.

SQL> create table b as select 1 x from dual;
Table created.
```

2. Now, all we need to do is open a SQL*PLUS session and update table A.

```
SQL> update a set x = x+1;
1 row updated.
```

3. Next, we'll open another SQL*Plus session in another window, while keeping our first session going. In this session, we'll update table B as follows:

485

```
SQL> update b set x = x+1;
1 row updated.
```

4. Now, we'll attempt to update table A in this same session (the one we just modified table B in).

```
SQL> update a set x = x+1;
```

We will immediately become blocked (the SQL prompt will not come back). The first session has this row locked already. This is not a deadlock; this is just blocking. We have not yet deadlocked since there is a chance that the first session will commit or roll back, and the second session will simply continue at that point.

5. Now, we will go back to our first session, and update table B, which will cause a deadlock. One of the two sessions will be chosen as a 'victim', and will have its statement rolled back. They will receive an error such as:

```
update a set x = x+1
        *
ERROR at line 1:
ORA-00060: deadlock detected while waiting for resource
```

(In my test, the second session, the one that was blocked, received the error message.) The other session will remain blocked. Oracle will not roll back the entire transaction; only one of the statements that causes the deadlock is rolled back. The above session still has the row in table B locked, and the other session is patiently waiting for the row to become available. The session that received the deadlock message must decide how it wants to deal with it. It can commit the outstanding work, it could roll it back, or it could continue down an alternative path and commit later. As soon as this session does commit or roll back, the other blocked session will continue as if nothing ever happened.

Oracle considers deadlocks so unusual, that it creates a trace file on the server every time one does occur.

Chapter 18 has more information regarding how to locate the trace file for your session.

The contents of the trace file will have something along the lines of:

```
*** 2001-02-23 14:03:35.041
*** SESSION ID:(8.82) 2001-02-23 14:03:35.001
DEADLOCK DETECTED
Current SQL statement for this session:
update a set x = x+1
The following deadlock is not an ORACLE error. It is a
deadlock due to user error in the design of an application
or from issuing incorrect ad-hoc SQL. The following...
```

It will also contain other transaction-related information that will help you track down how the deadlock came about. Obviously, Oracle considers deadlocks an error on its behalf. Unlike many other RDBMSs, deadlocks are so rare in Oracle they can be considered virtually non-existent. You must typically come up with artificial conditions to get one.

Lock Escalation

Locks may be held at many levels. You might have a lock on a row, or indeed a lock on a table. Some databases (though not Oracle) lock data at the block level. In some databases, locks are a scarce resource and having many locks can negatively impact the performance of the system. In these databases, you may find that your 100 row-level locks are converted into a single table-level lock, in order to conserve these resources. This process, known as **lock escalation** involves the system decreasing the **granularity** of your locks. In other words, you had them at the row level and now have a single lock at some higher level. You are now using one lock to lock everything you had before (and typically more than you before as well).

> **Oracle will never escalate a lock.**

Lock escalation is not a desirable attribute of a database. The fact that a database supports escalating locks implies there is some inherent overhead in its locking mechanism, that there is significant work performed to manage hundreds of locks. In Oracle the overhead to have one lock or a million locks is the same – none.

Oracle practices **lock conversion** or **promotion** (both terms are synonymous, though Oracle typically refers to it as conversion). It will take a lock at the lowest level possible (the least restrictive lock possible) and will convert that lock to a more restrictive level. For example, if you select a row from a table with the FOR UPDATE clause, two locks will be applied. One lock is placed on the row you selected. This lock is termed exclusive, since it will prevent anyone else from locking that specific row. The other lock is placed on the table itself, and is termed a ROW SHARE TABLE lock. This will prevent other sessions from getting an exclusive lock on the table (in order to alter the structure of the table, for example). All other statements are permitted. We can even have another session come in and make the table read-only using LOCK TABLE x IN SHARE MODE. As soon as I update that row however, Oracle will convert my ROW SHARE TABLE lock into a ROW EXCLUSIVE TABLE lock. This conversion happens transparently. This lock is slightly more restrictive then the row share table lock was. For example, before we did the update, another session could have locked the table in share mode, preventing modifications. Once we update, that other session cannot be allowed to prevent modifications, as there is one taking place already. Since Oracle transparently promoted the lock, all this happens naturally.

A detailed discussion of every lock type and the rules of promotion is beyond the scope of this book. You can find more details in the *Oracle Server Concepts Manual*.

Lost Updates

Blocking is what happens when one session holds a lock on a resource that another session is requesting. The requesting session will be blocked until the holding session gives up the locked resource. However, in almost every case, blocking is avoidable. In this section, we will look at what blocking is, how it happens and techniques to avoid it.

The primary cause of blocking is an update applied to data you do not already have locked. This seems obvious, since if you haven't updated it, of course you don't have it locked.

Blocking is most frequently observed in an interactive application. The application has read some data out of the database, and is allowing the user to modify the data on screen. When the user hits a Submit button, the changes are applied to the database via updates. Later the user might hit a Commit or Save button to make the changes permanent. Here is where the blocking comes in. If some other user reads out the same data, and they hit Submit before our first user does, then they have locked the data. The first user hits Save and gets blocked. The solution to this is *not* to blindly commit after every update. The problem here is that you are suffering from a data integrity issue in the first place. The second session would blindly overwrite the first session's data, as soon as the first session commits.

This particular problem is so frequently observed that it even has a name. It is commonly referred to as the **lost update**. This is a database issue that crops up time and time again when a GUI programmer, with little or no database training, is given the task of writing a database application. They get a working knowledge of SELECT, INSERT, UPDATE, and DELETE statements, and then set about writing the application. Consider, for example, an employee update screen, which allows a user to change an address, work number, and so on. The application itself is very simple, with a small search screen to generate a list of employees, and the ability to drill down into the details of each employee. It should be a piece of cake. So, we write the application with no locking on our part, just simple selects and updates.

Our end user (USER1) now opens our application and navigates to the details screen, changes an address on the screen, hits Save, and receives confirmation that the update was successful. Fine, except that when USER1 checks the record the next day, the old address is still listed. How could that have happened? Unfortunately it can happen all too easily. In this case another end user (USER2) had queried the same record about 5 minutes before but had then left his desk, with the old data still displayed on his screen. USER1 came along, queried the data on his terminal, performed his update, received confirmation, and even re-queried to see the change for himself. However, USER2 then returned from his meeting, updated the work telephone number field and hit Save, blissfully unaware of the fact that he had just overwritten USER1's changes to the address field with the old data! The developer, finding it easier to update all columns instead of figuring out exactly which columns changed, just resets the address back to the old value.

Notice that, for this to happen, USER1 and USER2 didn't even need to be working on the record at the exact same time. All it needed was for them to be working on the record at *about* the same time. You would not believe how many times this happens in the real world. When it does, it completely destroys people's confidence in the application, especially since it seems so random, so sporadic, and is totally irreproducible in a controlled environment (leading the developer to believe it must be a user error). Many tools, such as Oracle Forms, transparently protect you from this behavior by ensuring the record is unchanged from when you queried it (and locked) before you make any changes to it. Sadly many others (such as a handwritten VB or Java program) do not. What the tools that protect you do behind the scenes, or what the developer must implement, is to use one of two types of locking (detailed below).

Pessimistic Locking

Pessimistic locking sounds bad but, trust me, it isn't. In pessimistic locking, you are saying "I believe there is a high probability of someone changing the same data I am reading (and will eventually update), therefore, before I waste time changing any data, I will lock the row in the database, preventing other sessions from updating it". You are being pessimistic, since you believe there is a good chance that if you change the values of a row, someone else will have done that at about the same time. You would like to prevent this from happening. So, what we do before we change the copy of the data we selected out (and before the UPDATE statement is ever executed), is lock it.

In order to do this, you would issue a query similar to the following:

```
Select *
  From Table
 Where column1 = :old_column1
   And column2 = :old.column2
   And …..
   And primary_key = :old.primary_key
FOR UPDATE NOWAIT;
```

where `:old.column1`, `:old.column2`, and so on are the original values the application selected out of the database. What the application does is to take these values of the row and go back to the database. It then queries that exact same row again, while locking it at the same time. Since all tables have a primary key (and the select here will retrieve at most one record since it includes the primary key) and primary keys should be immutable (we never update them) we'll get one of three outcomes from this statement:

❑   We will get our row back and this row will be locked from updates by others (but not from reads). For example, USER1 queries the record and the application automatically locks that row. Nobody else can now update that row until it is 'released'.

❑   We will get an ORA-00054 Resource Busy error. Someone else already has that row locked, and we must wait for it. For example, USER2 queries the record, gets the data on his screen, but later finds that he cannot update it. He must wait for USER1 to finish with it.

❑   We will get zero rows back since someone has already changed the row. The data on our screen is stale. The application needs to requery and lock the data, before allowing the end user to modify any of the data to avoid the lost update. For example, when USER2 gets the Resource Busy message, he leaves his desk. When he comes back and tries again, USER1 has updated the phone field and committed the changes. The application now recognizes that the underlying data has changed so requeries the data and lets USER2 look at that data before allowing him to make any modifications.

This is called **pessimistic locking** since we lock the row before we attempt to update. We are not optimistic that the row would remain unchanged otherwise (hence the name pessimistic). The flow of activities in your application would be:

❑   Query the data without locking:

```
SQL> SELECT EMPNO, ENAME, SAL FROM EMP WHERE DEPTNO = 10;

    EMPNO ENAME           SAL
---------- ---------- ----------
      7782 CLARK          2450
      7839 KING           5000
      7934 MILLER         1300
```

❑   Allow the end user to 'look' at the data. Eventually, they pick a row they would like to update. Let's say in this case, they choose to update MILLER's row. Our application will at that point in time (before they make any changes, even on screen) issue (with the values 7934, MILLER, and 1300 for the bind variables):

```
SQL> SELECT EMPNO, ENAME, SAL
  2    FROM EMP
  3   WHERE EMPNO = :EMPNO
  4     AND ENAME = :ENAME
  5     AND SAL = :SAL
  6     FOR UPDATE NOWAIT
  7  /

     EMPNO ENAME            SAL
---------- ---------- ----------
      7934 MILLER          1300
```

This locks that row for us, and ensures that data has not been changed by anyone between the time we initially read it from the database and the time we decided to update it. If that query returned NO DATA we then know someone else must have modified the data and our application must requery that row before allowing the end user to modify it. If that query returns ORA-00054 Resource Busy that means another session has that row locked and we must wait until later to do our update.

❑ Assuming we locked the row, eventually our application will issue some update, and commit the changes:

```
SQL> UPDATE EMP
  2    SET ENAME = :ENAME, SAL = :SAL
  3   WHERE EMPNO = :EMPNO;
1 row updated.

scott@TKYTE816> commit;
Commit complete.
```

We have now very safely changed that row. It is not possible for us to overwrite someone else's changes, since we verified the data did not change between the time we initially read it out and when we locked it. We will not block in the database – since we locked the data in a non-blocking fashion prior to updating it.

In Oracle pessimistic locking works very well. It gives the user the confidence that the data they are modifying on the screen is currently 'owned' by them. You could have the application release the lock if the user walks away and doesn't actually use the record for some period of time, or use Resource Profiles in the database to time out idle sessions. This will avoid the issue of the person locking a row and going home for the night.

Optimistic Locking

The second method, referred to as **optimistic locking**, keeps both the old and new values in the application. On updating the data, we use an update that will set the columns to their new values, while at the same time verifying that the row in the database has the *same* values it did when we read it out. An update that does that looks like this:

```
Update table
   Set column1 = :new_column1, column2 = :new_column2, ….
 Where column1 = :old_column1
   And column2 = :old_column2
```

Note that we not only set the columns to the new values, we also verify that each column we are updating has the same value it did when we read it out in the first place. This is accomplished in the WHERE clause.

Here, we are optimistically hoping that the data doesn't get changed. In this case, if our UPDATE updates one row then we got lucky, since the data didn't change between the time we read it out and the time we got around to submitting the update. If we update *zero* rows, then we lose, since someone else changed the data and now we must figure out what we want to do in order to avoid the lost update. Should we make the end user rekey the transaction, after querying up the new values for the row (potentially frustrating them no end, as there is a chance the row will change yet again)? Should we try to merge the values of the two updates, performing update conflict resolution based on business rules (lots of code)? And so on.

In order to take a quick look at how this works, we'll use two SQL*Plus sessions against the SCOTT DEPT table. In this example, we'll use optimistic locking and see what happens when we get to update the row, and what happens when we don't (since someone else already updated the row).

We start by logging in as the user SCOTT and opening up two SQL*Plus sessions, which we'll consider as two separate users (USER1 and USER2). The following SELECT statement is then issued by both users:

```
SQL> select * from dept where deptno = 10;

    DEPTNO DNAME          LOC
---------- -------------- -------------
        10 ACCOUNTING     NEW YORK
```

Both users will see this result on their screen. Now, USER1 decides to change the LOC from NEW YORK to BOSTON. At the same time, USER2 decides to change the LOC from NEW YORK to ALBANY. Both users now make their respective changes within their own session (Note that they haven't really done the update in the database yet). Their user interface will have saved the values of the row as it existed when they read it out of the database.

Now, they are ready to save their changes. Assuming that USER1 does the update first, they might submit this to the database:

```
SQL> update dept
  2     set loc = 'BOSTON'
  3   where deptno = 10
  4     and dname = 'ACCOUNTING'
  5     and loc = 'NEW YORK';
1 row updated.

SQL> commit;
Commit complete.
```

Note: in a real application, you would use bind variables, not character string literals as we have here.

As we can see they've successfully updated one row and committed the transaction. Now, USER2 executes the following:

491

```
SQL> update dept
  2      set loc = 'ALBANY'
  3    where deptno = 10
  4      and dname = 'ACCOUNTING'
  5      and loc = 'NEW YORK';

0 rows updated.
```

Here zero rows are updated, since a record with DEPTNO=10 and LOC=NEW YORK no longer exists. We optimistically thought it would, but it doesn't, since USER1 updated the record.

Pessimistic vs. Optimistic

In the case of pessimistic locking you verify that the row the user wishes to modify hasn't changed and lock it *before* they make any changes. In the case of optimistic locking you wait until the time of the update before checking whether or not the row has changed. Pessimistic locking allows you to assure the user that their update will not block *and* that it will proceed without conflict when they do update the data in the database. In the case of optimistic locking however, you will have to inform your end user that their transaction cannot proceed, if the data has been changed at any point up until they wish to perform an update. At this point they must requery the data and do it over (else a lost update will occur).

In other words, the big advantage of pessimistic locking is that the end user will find out that their changes will not go through *before* they expend any time making a modification. In the case of optimistic locking, the end user will spend some amount of time making the change only to be told at update time "sorry, the data was changed by someone else, try again".

While locking the row before making any changes means that other users will be locked out from that row, if you do not do this, then those other users will just be disappointed when they go to update the row anyway. The fact is that, ultimately, only one user will be able to update the row. Since locking the row in Oracle does not prevent reads of that record, any normal activity is not prevented from taking place. On the other hand the locking of that row will prevent others from even attempting to update that row.

Multi-versioning and Read Consistency

Oracle operates a multi-version read consistent concurrency model. Essentially, this is the mechanism by which Oracle provides for:

❑ **Read-consistent queries**: Queries that produce consistent (that is, correct) results with respect to a point in time.

❑ **Non-blocking queries**: Queries are never blocked by writers of data.

These are two very important concepts in the Oracle database. The term **multi-versioning** basically comes from the fact that Oracle is able to simultaneously maintain multiple versions of the data in the database. If you understand how multi-versioning works, you will always understand the answers you get from the database. Before we explore in a little more detail how Oracle does this, here is a simple demonstration of multi-versioning in Oracle:

```
SQL> drop table t;
Table dropped.

SQL> create table t as select * from all_users;
Table created.

SQL> set serveroutput on
SQL> declare
  2          cursor c1 is select username from t;
  3          l_username  varchar2(30);
  4  begin
  5          open c1;
  6
  7          delete from t;
  8          commit;
  9
 10          loop
 11                  fetch c1 into l_username;
 12                  exit when c1%notfound;
 13                  dbms_output.put_line( l_username );
 14          end loop;
 15          close c1;
 16  end;
 17  /
SYS
SYSTEM
OUTLN
DBSNMP
...
```

In this example, we created a test table, T, and loaded it with some data from the ALL_USERS table. We opened a cursor on that table (but didn't fetch any data from it).

> **Bear in mind that Oracle does not 'answer' the query. It doesn't copy the data anywhere when you open a cursor (imagine how long it would take to open a cursor on a one billion row table if it did). The cursor opens instantly and it answers the query as it goes along. In other words, it just reads data from the table as you fetch from it, one row at a time.**

In the same session (or another session – the results would be the same), we then proceeded to delete all data from that table. We even went as far as to commit work on that delete. The rows are gone, or so we'd think. In fact, they are retrievable via the cursor. The fact is that the result set returned to us by the OPEN command was pre-ordained at the point in time that we opened it. We have no way of knowing what the answer will be until we fetch the data, but the result is immutable from our cursor's perspective. It is not that Oracle copied all of the data above to some other location when we opened the cursor; it was actually the delete that preserved our data for us by placing it into an UNDO tablespace or roll back segment.

493

This is what multi-versioning and read consistency are all about. Getting the correct, consistent answer in a scalable, highly concurrent fashion. In Oracle, using multi-versioning, you get an answer that is consistent with respect to the point in time that the query began execution.

Let's consider a further example. Suppose you have a table called ACCOUNTS, with three columns named ACCOUNT_ID, ACCOUNT_TYPE, and BALANCE. It can be created as follows:

```
Create table accounts
( account_id   number,
  account_type varchar2(20),
  balance      number
);
```

Your job is to report the sum of BALANCE accurately and quickly upon demand. You will report the time of day and the total of all account balances. This sounds easy, and the query you need to perform is simply:

```
Select current_timestamp, sum(balance) total_balance from accounts;
```

> Note that CURRENT_TIMESTAMP is a built-in column in Oracle 9i that returns the current date and time. You will need to use SYSDATE in earlier versions of Oracle.

However, the problem is somewhat complicated by the fact that while we are doing this many hundreds or even thousands of transactions will be applied to this database table. People will transfer money from their savings to checking accounts, they'll be making withdrawals, deposits, and so on (we are a very busy bank perhaps). So, as we are running this query the data is changing in the database. We've already seen how we could use a READ ONLY or SERIALIZABLE transaction to solve this problem. In this particular case though, we don't even need to do that, since we have but one SQL query and Oracle processes *all* statements in a read-consistent fashion. What we are more interested in right now is how this actually takes place.

Let's say that the ACCOUNTS table looks like this:

ACCOUNT_ID	ACCOUNT_TYPE	BALANCE
1234	Savings	100
5678	Checking	4321
2542	Savings	6232
7653	Savings	234
... <hundreds of thousands of rows>		
1234	Checking	100

Our query will process, row by row, each of the rows in this table when summing up the BALANCE column. At the same time, the owner of ACCOUNT_ID 1234 is going to transfer $50 from their savings account to their checking account to pay some bills. Let's walk through what happens as these two events take place. In this case our story will have two endings, with one to demonstrate what happens when a query detects locked data, and the other to demonstrate what happens when it detects data that has changed and that it should not see:

Time	Event	Comments
T1	We begin the query in Session 1	It will start reading the table. This will take a couple of minutes, as the ACCOUNTS table is very large. This query has already read the "first row" for the savings account for ACCOUNT_ID 1234 but hasn't gotten to the checking account row yet.
T2	The owner of account 1234 starts a transaction at an ATM	
T3	The owner of account 1234 selects TRANSFER FUNDS and chooses to move $50 from their checking to savings account	The data in the database is updated so the checking account now has $50 and the savings account has $150. The work is *not* yet committed (but UNDO information is stored).
T4	Our query finally gets to the checking account row for ACCOUNT_ID 1234.	What should happen here? In most every other popular database, the answer would be "the query will wait of course". In Oracle it will not.
T5	Detecting that the data is locked by the work performed at T3, our query retrieves the UNDO information (the 'before' image of the data) and uses the image of the data that was current as of time T1	Oracle reads around the lock, it does not wait. Our query will read $100 for the checking account.
T6	Our report is done	
T7	The ATM commits and completes	

The interesting part of this is what occurs at time T5 in the above timeline. Oracle reads around the locked data, never stopping the processing of our query (giving us non-blocking reads), and getting the accurate answer as of time T1.

So, having seen what happens when Oracle detects locked data, let's look at what happens if the data is not locked. We'll pick up our story at time T4 again:

T4	The ATM session commits, finishes the transfer	The funds are moved. Other sessions will now have the ability to see $150 in savings and $50 in checking for ACCOUNT_ID 1234
T5	Our query finally gets to the checking account row for ACCOUNT_ID 1234	It is not locked anymore, no one is updating it
T6	Detecting that the data was modified *after* time T1, our query retrieves the UNDO information and uses the image of the data that was current as of time T1	Our query will again read $100 for the checking account.
T7	Our report is done	

The interesting thing to note here is that even though the data was committed, we did not read it. Instead, we read the data as it existed when our query began. If we did read it as it was modified then you would report out a balance sum that was $50 less than existed in the bank *ever*. You would in effect be reporting a number that never existed. No money left the bank, none came in; we just moved some from one row to another. Now, while $50 might not keep you up at night worrying, just remember that there were hundreds of thousands of rows and thousands of transactions. The number you report could be so far off from reality as to be meaningless. In Oracle you need not worry about that issue. It cannot happen, since the data will always be read consistent.

Summary

In this chapter we began by looking at what a transaction consists of, and then learnt about the ACID properties supplied by the database that provide for Atomic, Consistent, Isolated, and Durable transactions. We learned about the transaction control statements we have at our disposal and how and when to use them.

When looking at concurrency control, we discussed two major and complex topics in the form of locking and multi-versioning read consistency. We also learned about locking in the database and more importantly the major locking issues surrounding deadlocks and blocking. We learned what a deadlock is and saw how we can diagnose one with the trace files, as well as avoid blocking waits in the database altogether. We saw two different schemes that may be used to avoid blocking in the database: pessimistic and optimistic locking of data, and summarized the pros and cons of each. We then learnt that multi-versioning and read consistency provide us with non-blocking reads (our queries never stop) and consistent, accurate answers. This is a crucial point. Multi-versioning gives us accurate results with no loss of concurrency in the database.

Security

Up until this point, we have learned about the large variety of database objects you can create in an Oracle database, as well as how to exploit them in an application. However, if we have no way of making our database objects and applications secure, then their usefulness will be severely limited. If, for example, we developed an application to manage Human Resource information, which allowed any individual to either view all employee salaries, or, even worse, update any employee's salary, it is doubtful that it would prove popular! In any basic database application, there is usually some subset of information available to the public, some information only available to the author, and a full set of information that is exclusively available to a group of privileged individuals.

To this end, the Oracle database provides a rich security infrastructure we can exploit in our applications, and in this chapter we will look at the following topics:

- ❑ What is database security
- ❑ Database users and schemas
- ❑ System Privileges
- ❑ Object Privileges
- ❑ Role-based Security
- ❑ PL/SQL and Roles
- ❑ Fine-grained access control
- ❑ Application Contexts
- ❑ Data Security

Overview of Database Security

Security is a widely used term, especially in the age of Internet applications, where it can refer to many different technologies. Within the scope of web applications, you typically hear the term 'security' in terms of the system encrypting the data transmitted to and from your web browser. You may also think of security as synonymous with authentication, that is, challenging and end-user to supply their username and password so we can validate who they say they are. However, in this chapter, we're going to focus on security only at the database level. You should note that database security is just one component of any effective overall security design and implementation. True security involves the database, the client, and the database server, as well as every major component in between, including application servers, transaction servers, and network hardware. It is important to have a clear understanding of how to implement security properly within an Oracle database application. In this way our database-centric systems, such as a human resources application, an employee address book application, or even a web-based mail application, are capable of excluding non-authorized users from accessing the information they maintain.

Users and Schemas

There's no better place to start talking about security than at the most primitive units, namely a database **user** and a database **schema**. People often use the terms 'user' and 'schema' interchangeably, but they are distinct. A database schema is defined as a collection of database objects, while the name of that schema is the name of the user who owns or controls this collection of database objects. All database objects, such as tables, views, indexes, triggers, Java stored procedures, PL/SQL packages, functions, etc, are owned by a user in an Oracle database. Even the data dictionary of Oracle, the system catalog, is a part of the schema named SYS.

> Note that there can be a user in an Oracle database who does not own any database objects (and hence is not a schema), but there can be no such thing as an unnamed schema or collection of database objects.

A traditional interpretation of a user is really nothing more than a name and password combination that uniquely identifies a set of credentials. Anyone who accesses the Oracle database using a combination of name and password is accessing it as a specific user. Your ATM card and PIN are analogous to a database username and password. Although the bank issues the ATM card and PIN to you, there is no guarantee when the ATM card is used along with the PIN (password) that it's truly you. The bank just has a record of someone with your credentials having accessed their system. In a similar fashion, using a simple database use name and password does not guarantee that the user of this information was the original recipient of it.

Creating a database user was introduced in Chapter 2, but we will review it here for the sake of completeness. All you need do is connect to an Oracle database as someone who has been granted the ability to create users, and specify the new user's name and password. In the same statement, you can optionally specify the default tablespace and the temporary tablespace associated with the new user.

Remember that a tablespace is a logical object used to store database objects.

1. Let's try and create a new user called GEORGE by logging on to Oracle as user SCOTT, and typing in the following code (highlighted in bold):

```
SQL> connect scott/tiger
Connected.
SQL> create user george identified by jetson;
create user george identified by jetson
                                  *
ERROR at line 1:
ORA-01031: insufficient privileges
```

As you should see, the user SCOTT has not been granted the ability to create new users.

2. If we now connect as user SYSTEM however, we should prove more successful:

```
SQL> connect system/manager
Connected.
SQL> create user george identified by jetson;

User created.
```

In this case the user SYSTEM has been granted the ability to create new users. By including the IDENTIFIED BY clause in the CREATE USER statement, we are specifying the password that is associated with database user GEORGE. Note that we could have specified IDENTIFIED EXTERNALLY, indicating that this is a database user account, which will be validated externally (usually by the operating system that the client uses). Alternatively we could have used the clause IDENTIFIED GLOBALLY, meaning that the credentials for the user would be maintained in some form of enterprise directory service, typically an LDAP (Lightweight Directory Access Protocol) server, such as the Oracle Internet Directory.

Note that the statement containing the user's identifier and password is sent to the Oracle database via some medium (typically an Oracle Net Services connection). Unless this is an encrypted network channel, anyone snooping on this network connection could easily capture the user's identifier and password.

System Privileges

In the Oracle database, there are two classes of privileges:

❑ **Object-level** privileges are those granted from a user to access or manipulate database objects. For example, a database user who wishes to insert a row into the SCOTT.EMP table must have been granted a specific privilege to do this.

❑ **System** privileges, rather than controlling access to specific database objects, are used either to permit access to various features, or permit certain tasks within an Oracle database. It is these privileges that we will focus on in this section.

Oracle 9*i* has over 100 distinct system privileges, and each one of these should be granted sparingly, to those individuals who will maintain and manage your Oracle databases. To look at the set of distinct system privileges available in your Oracle database, you can issue a query against the database view DBA_SYS_PRIVS.

Note that the number of Oracle system privileges has evolved with each release of the database, so if you are not running a 9i instance the list in your database will not match those of the example below.

Try It Out – Viewing System Privileges

1. If you type in the code highlighted in bold below, you should see results similar to those shown:

```
SQL> connect system/manager
Connected.
SQL> desc dba_sys_privs;
 Name                                    Null?    Type
 --------------------------------------- -------- --------------
 GRANTEE                                 NOT NULL VARCHAR2(30)
 PRIVILEGE                               NOT NULL VARCHAR2(40)
 ADMIN_OPTION                                     VARCHAR2(3)

SQL> select distinct privilege
  2     from dba_sys_privs
  3     order by privilege;

PRIVILEGE
----------------------------------------
ADMINISTER DATABASE TRIGGER
ADMINISTER RESOURCE MANAGER
ADMINISTER SECURITY
ALTER ANY CLUSTER
ALTER ANY DIMENSION
ALTER ANY INDEX
ALTER ANY INDEXTYPE
ALTER ANY LIBRARY
ALTER ANY OUTLINE
ALTER ANY PROCEDURE
ALTER ANY ROLE

...
127 rows selected.
```

In the example above (in a 9*i* database), 127 different system privileges were granted to various users. Your total count may be different, as this query only locates those rows where the privilege has been granted, not simply if the privilege exists.

The basic syntax to grant a system privilege is as follows:

```
GRANT system_privilege TO username [WITH ADMIN OPTION];
```

> To grant a database user a specific system privilege, and also give them the ability
> to grant this same privilege to other users, include **WITH ADMIN OPTION** in your
> **GRANT** statement.

Likewise, the basic syntax to remove a system privilege from a database user is as follows:

```
REVOKE system_privilege FROM username;
```

Note that the database user revoking system privileges does not need to be the same user who issued the original grant of the system privilege. Any database user with ADMIN OPTION for the system privilege can revoke that system privilege from any other user.

> Great care should be taken when granting any system privileges to users, let alone
> system privileges with **ADMIN OPTION**.

Before any user can connect to an Oracle database, they need to be given permission to do so by being granted the CREATE SESSION privilege.

Try It Out – Connecting To an Oracle Database

1. Let's try and connect to the database as user GEORGE:

```
SQL> connect george/jetson;
ERROR:
ORA-01045: user GEORGE lacks CREATE SESSION privilege; logon denied


Warning: You are no longer connected to ORACLE.
```

As you can see user GEORGE has not been granted the CREATE SESSION privilege. We need to connect as user SYSTEM and grant this privilege:

```
SQL> connect system/manager
Connected.
SQL> grant create session to george;

Grant succeeded.
```

2. Now if we try and connect as user GEORGE we should be successful:

```
SQL> connect george/jetson
Connected.
```

Now that user GEORGE can connect to this particular database, he should be able to move happily along and start creating his database objects. Note however, that despite being able to connect to the database, he will still remain restricted in the tasks that he can perform, unless he has been granted sufficient permissions by the DBA.

Try It Out – Creating a Table

1. Let's try creating a table as user GEORGE:

```
SQL> create table mytable( id number );
create table mytable( id number )
 *
ERROR at line 1:
ORA-01031: insufficient privileges
```

As you can see user GEORGE has insufficient privileges to do this.

2. To grant the CREATE TABLE privilege to user GEORGE we need to connect as user SYSTEM and type in the following:

```
SQL> connect system/manager
Connected.
SQL> grant create table to george;

Grant succeeded.
```

3. Now we reconnect as user GEORGE and attempt to create a table once again:

```
SQL> connect george/jetson;
Connected.
SQL> create table mytable( id number );
create table mytable( id number )
 *
ERROR at line 1:
ORA-01950: no privileges on tablespace 'SYSTEM'
```

How It Works

So why can't GEORGE create a table, even though he has been granted the CREATE TABLE privilege? Firstly, to create database objects in an Oracle database, you need privilege on a tablespace.

If you need a reminder about tablespaces then look back to Chapter 5.

It's obvious from the example above that GEORGE does not have privilege to create his table in the SYSTEM tablespace. What is more important to note however, is that when a user is created and is not assigned a tablespace, the SYSTEM tablespace is used by default. In this case, since no tablespace was specified in the CREATE TABLE statement, GEORGE has attempted to create the table in the SYSTEM tablespace.

> Since the data dictionary for the entire Oracle database is maintained in the SYSTEM tablespace, permitting objects to be stored in the SYSTEM tablespace is a sure way to create contention and slow down the whole operation of your entire database.

It's always prudent to restrict non-DBA users in your database to a specific tablespace and with a specific space quota on their assigned tablespace. Not doing so will eventually result in a call, usually around 4:00 AM, telling you that your production system has been halted because of lack of disk space or space in a tablespace.

Try It Out – Creating a Table As User GEORGE

1. To enable user GEORGE to create a table, we need to alter his privileges by connecting as user SYSTEM:

```
SQL> connect system/manager
Connected.
SQL> alter user george
  2   default tablespace users
  3   temporary tablespace temp
  4   quota 10M on users
  5   quota 5M on temp;

User altered.
```

Here we have changed the default tablespace for user GEORGE to USERS and set the default temporary tablespace to TEMP. Additionally, we use the QUOTA keyword to grant him 10 MB of space in the USERS tablespace and 5 MB in the TEMP tablespace.

2. Now when we connect as user GEORGE the CREATE TABLE statement should be successful:

```
SQL> connect george/jetson
Connected.
SQL> create table mytable( id number );

Table created.
```

The CONNECT and RESOURCE roles

Later in this chapter, we will thoroughly review Oracle database roles. For the time being it is sufficient to understand that database roles are simply nothing more than a user-defined named group of privileges (and even other roles). In a given Oracle database instance there are a number of roles already defined, including CONNECT, RESOURCE, and EXP_FULL_DATABASE. Although the mere existence of these roles does not expose any security hole in Oracle (as the roles first need to be granted to a user), it is important to know something of what these roles can accomplish.

A common mistake made when creating users is to immediately grant them CONNECT and RESOURCE system-level roles. When you do this, you're actually granting thirteen distinct system-level privileges. The CONNECT role itself, for example, beyond including the CREATE SESSION system privilege, also includes CREATE TABLE, CREATE SYNONYM, and six other system privileges. But the most significant reason why you would not want to haphazardly grant these roles is for tablespace permissions (in other words, where a user is permitted to create and store their database objects). Grantees of the RESOURCE role automatically receive the UNLIMITED TABLESPACE system privilege as well, even though this system privilege is not truly a part of the RESOURCE role. The UNLIMITED TABLESPACE system privilege lets a user consume an unlimited amount of space in **any** tablespace, including the SYSTEM tablespace. It is a good idea to revoke the UNLIMITED TABLESPACE privilege from any user granted the RESOURCE role.

In general, if you are attempting to create a secure system using an Oracle database, you should never have need to use any of the predefined database roles. A security-conscious administrator will want to create and manage their own set of distinct database roles, providing nothing more than the absolute minimum number of privileges for users to access and manipulate the Oracle database.

The Oracle 9i SQL Reference manual contains an exhaustive list and explanation of all of the system privileges.

Object Privileges

Whereas system privileges control access to various system-level facilities in an Oracle database, object privileges are used to control access to specific database objects. These privileges can be granted by any database user, in allowing access to the objects contained in their schema (or another schema if the grant was given with WITH GRANT OPTION specified). Whereas system privileges are granted with the ability to grant the privilege to others using WITH ADMIN OPTION, objects privileges are granted with the ability to grant the privilege to others using WITH GRANT OPTION. A database user always has all privileges to the objects they own (in other words the objects contained in their schema). In general, system privileges are used to permit or constrain execution of DDL (Database Definition Language) statements, while object privileges are used to permit or prevent execution of DML (Database Manipulation Language) statements.

In contrast to the plethora of distinct Oracle system privileges, the list of object privileges is shorter and easily understandable. The most frequently utilized object privileges are as follows:

❏ SELECT applies to tables, views, and sequences. This privilege allows a user to issue a query against a table or view, or select a value from a sequence.

❏ INSERT, UPDATE, and DELETE all apply to tables and views. These privileges enable a user to insert new rows, delete existing rows, or update existing rows in a table or view.

❏ EXECUTE applies to PL/SQL procedures, function, and packages, and other executable elements (such as Java classes). The EXECUTE privilege enables an end user to directly execute a procedure, function, or Java class. Note that not only does this give an end user the ability to execute but also to compile the procedure, function, or package.

❏ INDEX and REFERENCES apply only to tables. The INDEX privilege is required to create an INDEX on a table that is in a different schema than that of a user. In the same fashion, REFERENCES is required when the user wishes to create a foreign key constraint to a table in another schema.

❑ ALTER applies only to tables and sequences. ALTER is required to modify the definition of a table or sequence.

Object privileges are granted in a similar manner to system privileges:

```
GRANT object_privilege ON object_name TO username [WITH GRANT OPTION];
```

To grant a database user a specific object privilege, and also give him the ability to grant this same privilege to other users, include WITH GRANT OPTION in your GRANT statement.

In the same fashion, the basic syntax to remove an object privilege from a database user is as follows:

```
REVOKE object_privilege ON object_name FROM username;
```

When attempting to perform a DML operation against a database object for which you have not been granted any privilege, the most common error encountered is either:

ORA-00942: table or view does not exist

Or:

ORA-04043: object <object_name> does not exist.

Once you have been granted at least one object privilege on a database object, and you attempt to perform an operation for which privilege has not been granted, the most frequently encountered error message is:

ORA-01031: insufficient privileges.

> Note that for all practical purposes, if a database user has not been granted any privilege on a database object, the object appears not to exist.

Try It Out – Granting Object Privileges

1. If you haven't already, then connect to your database as user GEORGE. Now grant user SCOTT the SELECT privilege on the MYTABLE table by typing the following statement:

```
SQL> grant select on mytable to scott;

Grant succeeded.
```

You should see the Grant succeeded message as shown.

2. Now connect as user SCOTT and test whether you can carry out a SELECT by typing in the following statement:

```
SQL> connect scott/tiger
Connected.
SQL> select count(*) from george.mytable;

  COUNT(*)
----------
         0
```

Again you should see the same message as shown above.

3. Now, as user SCOTT, attempt to grant privileges on this table to user SYSTEM:

```
SQL> grant select on george.mytable to system;
grant select on george.mytable to system
                       *
ERROR at line 1:
ORA-01031: insufficient privileges
```

4. We need to grant the SELECT privilege on table MYTABLE to user SCOTT, so let's do that now:

```
SQL> connect george/jetson
Connected.
SQL> grant select on mytable to scott with grant option;

Grant succeeded.
```

5. Finally, let's re-attempt the grant of privileges to user SYSTEM by user SCOTT:

```
SQL> connect scott/tiger
Connected.
SQL> grant select on george.mytable to system;

Grant succeeded.
```

As you can see on this occasion we receive a more positive execution message.

How It Works

In the first part of the Try Out we grant SELECT privilege to user SCOTT, who is then able to carry out a SELECT statement on the table GEORGE.MYTABLE. However when user SCOTT attempts to grant SELECT privilege to user SYSTEM, permission is denied. To get around this, user GEORGE grants user SCOTT the SELECT privilege on MYTABLE, while specifying the WITH GRANT OPTION clause. This gives user SCOTT sufficient privileges to carry out the SELECT privilege grant to user SYSTEM he originally planned.

In the example above, note that user SCOTT had to fully qualify the reference to the table MYTABLE contained in the GEORGE schema. If the schema name GEORGE was not prefixed to the table reference, the Oracle database would interpret this as either a reference to a table contained in the current schema (that is, in the SCOTT schema) or a reference to a table via a synonym.

In summary, we see that we can not only grant permission to select from a table in a different schema, but we can also give the grantee (the user receiving the grant) the ability to give that same grant to other users (by specifying WITH GRANT OPTION in our GRANT statement).

Try It Out – Examining Table Privileges

To examine the table privileges in an existing Oracle database, you can query the database views USER_TAB_PRIVS, ALL_TAB_PRIVS, or DBA_TAB_PRIVS.

1. Let's query the USER_TAB_PRIVS view:

```
SQL> connect george/jetson
Connected.

SQL> desc user_tab_privs;
 Name                                      Null?    Type
 ----------------------------------------- -------- ------------
 GRANTEE                                   NOT NULL VARCHAR2(30)
 OWNER                                     NOT NULL VARCHAR2(30)
 TABLE_NAME                                NOT NULL VARCHAR2(30)
 GRANTOR                                   NOT NULL VARCHAR2(30)
 PRIVILEGE                                 NOT NULL VARCHAR2(40)
 GRANTABLE                                          VARCHAR2(3)

SQL> column grantee format a10
SQL> column owner format a10
SQL> column table_name format a10
SQL> column grantor format a10
SQL> column privilege format a10
SQL> column grantable format a4
SQL> select * from user_tab_privs;

GRANTEE    OWNER      TABLE_NAME GRANTOR    PRIVILEGE  GRAN
---------- ---------- ---------- ---------- ---------- ----
SYSTEM     GEORGE     MYTABLE    SCOTT      SELECT     NO
SCOTT      GEORGE     MYTABLE    GEORGE     SELECT     YES
```

How It Works

Interpreting the results of our query against the view USER_TAB_PRIVS, we see that SELECT privilege on the table GEORGE.MYTABLE was granted from SCOTT to SYSTEM, and this was not a grantable privilege (that is, SYSTEM was not given permission to make further SELECT grants on this table). The first row of this output shows our very first grant, where GEORGE granted SELECT privilege on the table GEORGE.MYTABLE to SCOTT, and this was a grantable privilege.

Revoking Object Privileges

> **Only the creator of a grant can revoke the privileges granted by them to another database user.**

User GEORGE can revoke the SELECT privilege on table GEORGE.MYTABLE granted to user SCOTT as follows:

```
SQL> revoke select on mytable from scott;

Revoke succeeded.
```

However, if user GEORGE then attempts to revoke the SELECT privilege on GEORGE.MYTABLE granted to user SYSTEM he will fail with the following error message:

```
SQL> revoke select on mytable from system;
revoke select on mytable from system
*
ERROR at line 1:
ORA-01927: cannot REVOKE privileges you did not grant
```

So even though database user GEORGE owns the table on which a privilege has been granted, since GEORGE did not grant this privilege, he cannot revoke it.

The ALL PRIVILEGES Shortcut

The ALL or ALL PRIVILEGES shortcut exists to provide an easy mechanism to grant all object privileges available for a database object. ALL is not a database privilege itself; it is nothing more than a shortcut to grant a group of object privileges. If user GEORGE carries out the following GRANT statement:

```
SQL> grant all on mytable to scott;

Grant succeeded.
```

then when taking a look at the USER_TAB_PRIVS view he will see the following:

```
SQL> select * from user_tab_privs;

GRANTEE     OWNER       TABLE_NAME  GRANTOR     PRIVILEGE   GRAN
----------  ----------  ----------  ----------  ----------  ----
SCOTT       GEORGE      MYTABLE     GEORGE      DELETE      NO
SCOTT       GEORGE      MYTABLE     GEORGE      INDEX       NO
SCOTT       GEORGE      MYTABLE     GEORGE      INSERT      NO
SCOTT       GEORGE      MYTABLE     GEORGE      SELECT      NO
SCOTT       GEORGE      MYTABLE     GEORGE      UPDATE      NO
SCOTT       GEORGE      MYTABLE     GEORGE      REFERENCES  NO
SCOTT       GEORGE      MYTABLE     GEORGE      ALTER       NO

7 rows selected.
```

The example clearly shows how the grant of ALL on GEORGE.MYTABLE to SCOTT actually results in seven distinct object privileges being granted. Note that once these privileges are granted, they can still be selectively revoked. For example:

```
SQL> revoke alter on mytable from scott;

Revoke succeeded.
```

The INSERT, UPDATE and REFERENCES privileges

The object privileges INSERT, UPDATE, and REFERENCES can be granted, not only on all columns, but also on specific columns in a table or view. While you have already seen the use of both INSERT and UPDATE, the object privilege REFERENCES gives a user the ability to create a foreign key constraint on a table, even if that user does not have any other object privilege on the table. As we'll see in the next chapter, you can implement a form of application security through database views, providing access to a table via a view for only specific columns. However, some application security requirements exist where a user can have access to view all of the columns in a table or view, but only have permission to update or insert a subset of them.

To illustrate this, let's begin by connecting to our database as user GEORGE, and creating a table named SPROCKETS:

```
SQL> create table sprockets (
  2       id number,
  3       description varchar2(200),
  4       quantity    number )
  5  /

Table created.
```

GEORGE now grants UPDATE privilege to user SCOTT, but only on the ID and DESCRIPTION columns:

```
SQL> grant update (id, description)
  2       on sprockets
  3       to scott;

Grant succeeded.
```

Now, if user GEORGE carries out an INSERT on the SPROCKETS table it will be successful:

```
SQL> insert into sprockets (id, description, quantity)
  2  values( 1, 'Titanium', 25 );

1 row created.

SQL> commit;

Commit complete.
```

However, if we now connect to the database as user SCOTT, and attempt to UPDATE the QUANTITY column in the table GEORGE.SPROCKETS an error message will be generated:

```
SQL> connect scott/tiger
Connected.

SQL> update george.sprockets
  2     set quantity = 3;
update george.sprockets
               *
ERROR at line 1:
ORA-01031: insufficient privileges
```

If, on the other hand, user SCOTT carries out an UPDATE of the DESCRIPTION column in the GEORGE.SPROCKETS table then it will be successful:

```
SQL> update george.sprockets
  2     set description = 'Nickel Cadmium';

1 row updated.
```

Database Roles

Database applications are often composed of tens, hundreds, and sometimes thousands of different database objects. A database administrator would quickly become overwhelmed if they had to ensure that explicit object privileges are granted to (or revoked from) every user of the application. Given a company with a large employee population and a typical amount of turnover, simply keeping on top of database object privileges for a single application would become a full-time position.

In addition, as people advance through different positions within a company, their privileges on certain database objects need to change. A receptionist would certainly have less access to private information in an employee HR database than a Director. Likewise, a Director may only be permitted to see certain information about employees within his organization, whereas a Vice President would most likely have access to more detailed information. It would be nice if, somehow, this could be accommodated by the Oracle database.

Database **roles** are simply a named collection of privileges, which significantly reduce the burden of privilege maintenance for users. Roles can be a named collection of either object or system privileges (or both). The database administrator simply needs to create distinct database roles, which reflect the security privileges of the organization and application, and grant these roles to users (rather than granting discrete privileges).

While roles are often named after job functions, there is no requirement to do this. As an example, in the case of a Human Resources application, you may have four different roles defined as EMPLOYEE, MANAGER, HR_ADMIN, and CEO. These four roles will be assigned to employees in the company, so as to match their job function. But, since roles are used primarily for organization and ease-of-administration, there's nothing preventing the administrator from creating roles ROLE1 through ROLE4 instead. However, as the same holds true for database object naming, it is prudent to name objects and roles with meaningful names.

The basic syntax to create a database role is:

```
CREATE ROLE role;
```

A further option allows you to create a more secure password-protected role, such that when any user attempts to enable a role for their session, they are first required to specify a password. The only caveat is that Oracle provides the ability to specify 'default roles' for users, which are roles that are automatically enabled at logon. Password-protected roles can be specified as default roles, and a user will never be prompted for a password.

Once a role is created, it may seem to be similar in function to an actual database user. That is, granting privileges to a role is almost identical to the GRANT statement for a user, as revocation of privileges from database roles is to the REVOKE statement.

> **Just as with database privileges being granted to users, a database user cannot grant a privilege to a role unless the privileges were granted to them with either WITH ADMIN OPTION or WITH GRANT OPTION.**

Try It Out – Creating database Roles

1. Connect as user GEORGE, and create a new database role named ASSEMBLY_LINE, by typing the following:

```
SQL> connect george/jetson
Connected.
SQL> create role assembly_line;

Role created.
```

2. Now let's revoke all privileges on the SPROCKETS table from user SCOTT:

```
SQL> revoke all on sprockets from scott;

Revoke succeeded.
```

3. Now we grant SELECT, INSERT, and UPDATE privileges on the GEORGE.SPROCKETS table to the database role ASSEMBLY_LINE:

```
SQL> grant select, insert, update on sprockets to assembly_line;

Grant succeeded.
```

4. If we now look at the database view for privileges, we can see that the role ASSEMBLY_LINE appears in the GRANTEE column:

```
SQL> column grantee format a15
SQL> column owner format a10
SQL> column table_name format a10
SQL> column grantor format a10
SQL> column privilege format a10
SQL> column grantable format a4
SQL> select * from user_tab_privs;

GRANTEE          OWNER       TABLE_NAME GRANTOR     PRIVILEGE   GRAN
---------------  ----------  ---------- ----------  ----------  ----
ASSEMBLY_LINE    GEORGE      SPROCKETS  GEORGE      SELECT      NO
ASSEMBLY_LINE    GEORGE      SPROCKETS  GEORGE      UPDATE      NO
ASSEMBLY_LINE    GEORGE      SPROCKETS  GEORGE      INSERT      NO
```

An alternative view of the same reporting information gleaned from the USER_TAB_PRIVS view, but restricted to just database roles, can be gathered from the database view ROLE_TAB_PRIVS:

```
SQL> desc role_tab_privs;
 Name                                      Null?    Type
 ----------------------------------------- -------- -------------
 ROLE                                      NOT NULL VARCHAR2(30)
 OWNER                                     NOT NULL VARCHAR2(30)
 TABLE_NAME                                NOT NULL VARCHAR2(30)
 COLUMN_NAME                                        VARCHAR2(30)
 PRIVILEGE                                 NOT NULL VARCHAR2(40)
 GRANTABLE                                          VARCHAR2(3)

SQL> column role format a15
SQL> column privilege format a10
SQL> column column_name format a10
SQL> select * from role_tab_privs;

ROLE             OWNER       TABLE_NAME COLUMN_NAM PRIVILEGE   GRAN
---------------  ----------  ---------- ---------- ----------  ----
ASSEMBLY_LINE    GEORGE      SPROCKETS             INSERT      NO
ASSEMBLY_LINE    GEORGE      SPROCKETS             SELECT      NO
ASSEMBLY_LINE    GEORGE      SPROCKETS             UPDATE      NO
```

Properties of Roles

Roles can be granted other roles, and those roles in turn may be assigned other roles. An administrator could create a basic role called HR, grant certain privileges to this role, then define two additional roles, HR_ADMIN and HR_MANAGER, composed not only of the HR role but also other distinct object (and possibly system) privileges.

Once a role has been defined, it can be granted to a user (or another role) using the following basic syntax:

```
GRANT role_name TO user [WITH ADMIN OPTION]
GRANT role_name TO role_name [WITH ADMIN OPTION]
```

Changes made to database roles are effective immediately; there is no need to terminate all user sessions and have them log in again for the changed privileges to take effect. As a result, it's always a good idea to start by creating roles and assign them to users, even when the entire application or database security model is not complete. In this way, privileges can be easily granted to (or revoked from) the database roles and immediately take effect.

As an example of this, let's consider the case where user GEORGE grants the role ASSEMBLY_LINE to user SCOTT:

```
SQL> grant assembly_line to scott;

Grant succeeded.
```

Now, if user SCOTT attempts to DELETE from the table GEORGE.SPROCKETS, an error message is generated:

```
SQL> connect scott/tiger
Connected.
SQL> delete from george.sprockets;
delete from george.sprockets
             *
ERROR at line 1:
ORA-01031: insufficient privileges
```

This error message is generated because the DELETE privilege on this table was not granted on this role. However, the INSERT privilege was granted to the ASSEMBLY_LINE role, so user SCOTT can carry out the following successfully:

```
SQL> insert into george.sprockets values( 3, 'Chromium', 100 );

1 row created.

SQL> commit;

Commit complete.
```

Enabling and Disabling Database Roles

Database roles can be either **enabled** or **disabled** for a database user's session. Unless an administrator has removed all default roles for a database user, all roles granted to a user are enabled for a database session. You can quickly view what roles are enabled for the current database session by querying the database view SESSION_ROLES.

To enable database roles for the current database session, you must issue the SET ROLE statement. A list of database roles can be specified in one SET ROLE statement. Any role not specified in this list will then become disabled in the current database session. Using the SET ROLE ALL command enables all roles assigned to a user in the current database session.

Try It Out – Enabling Roles

1. Connect to your database as user SYSTEM, alter the user SCOTT so that there is no default role, and then examine the roles granted to SCOTT:

```
SQL> connect system/manager
Connected.
SQL> alter user scott default role none;

User altered.

SQL> alter user scott default role connect, resource;

User altered.

SQL> desc dba_role_privs;
 Name                                      Null?    Type
 ----------------------------------------- -------- ------------
 GRANTEE                                             VARCHAR2(30)
 GRANTED_ROLE                              NOT NULL VARCHAR2(30)
 ADMIN_OPTION                                        VARCHAR2(3)
 DEFAULT_ROLE                                        VARCHAR2(3)

SQL> select granted_role, admin_option, default_role
  2     from dba_role_privs
  3     where grantee = 'SCOTT';

GRANTED_ROLE                  ADM DEF
----------------------------- --- ---
CONNECT                       NO  YES
RESOURCE                      NO  YES
```

> Note that for the purposes of this example, we actually use the roles CONNECT and RESOURCE. In practice, as we highlighted earlier, you should use these roles with extreme caution.

2. Now connect as user SCOTT and look at the SESSION_ROLES view:

```
SQL> connect scott/tiger
Connected.
SQL> select * from session_roles;

ROLE
---------------
CONNECT
RESOURCE
```

3. Now let's attempt an INSERT into the table GEORGE.SPROCKETS:

```
SQL> insert into george.sprockets values( 4, 'Cobalt', 100 );
insert into george.sprockets values( 4, 'Cobalt', 100 )
                *
ERROR at line 1:
ORA-00942: table or view does not exist
```

4. An error occurs because the ASSEMBLY_LINE role is no longer available by default, and the SESSION_ROLE view only has permission enabled for the CONNECT and RESOURCE privileges. To enable ASSEMBLY_LINE, we type in the following command (and view the role again to check that we were successful):

```
SQL> set role assembly_line;

Role set.

SQL> select * from session_roles;

ROLE
---------------
ASSEMBLY_LINE
```

5. Now we can use the ALL keyword in order to expand the privileges granted to SESSION_ROLES:

```
SQL> set role all;

Role set.

SQL> select * from session_roles;

ROLE
---------------
CONNECT
RESOURCE
ASSEMBLY_LINE
```

6. If user SCOTT now attempts an INSERT into table GEORGE.SPROCKETS, it will be successful:

```
SQL> insert into george.sprockets values( 4, 'Cobalt', 100 );

1 row created.
```

Password Protecting Database Roles

An additional level of security can be gained by password protecting a database role. Any non-default role that is password protected needs to include the role password when being enabled. Use of a password-protected role is often convenient when you wish to temporarily suspend access to a collection of database objects without have to revoke privileges. If you apply a password to an existing role, and this role is not a part of your user's default roles, access to certain objects or privileges is suspended until they are provided the role password.

The only caveat is that users can have a password protected role enabled without ever specifying the role password. All roles that are part of the default roles are enabled at database session creation time, regardless of whether the role is password protected or not.

Try It Out – Password Protection

1. Let's connect to our Oracle database as user GEORGE and alter the ASSEMBLY_LINE role so that it is password protected:

```
SQL> connect george/jetson
Connected.

SQL> alter role assembly_line identified by robot;

Role altered.
```

2. Now connect as user SCOTT and attempt to carry out an INSERT into the GEORGE.SPROCKETS table:

```
SQL> connect scott/tiger
Connected.
SQL> insert into george.sprockets values( 5, 'Carbon', 60 );
insert into george.sprockets values( 5, 'Carbon', 60 )
                  *
ERROR at line 1:
ORA-00942: table or view does not exist
```

3. User SCOTT needs to provide the password for the ASSEMBLY_LINE role, and is then able to carry out the INSERT successfully:

```
SQL> set role assembly_line identified by robot;

Role set.

SQL> insert into george.sprockets values( 5, 'Carbon', 60 );

1 row created.
```

How It Works

In our example, the role ASSEMBLY_LINE is altered to become a password-protected role. Then, the database user SCOTT, who has already been granted this role, fails to insert a record into the SPROCKETS table. The insert is successful once the correct password is given for the role.

PL/SQL and Database Roles

Up until now, the primary focus of this chapter has been overall database security and database object security. At this point we will turn our attention to application security as it relates to PL/SQL and the Oracle database.

By default, PL/SQL functions, procedures, and packages execute with the namespace and privileges of the 'definer' of the object.

> **It is important to note that these compiled objects execute with the privileges granted directly to the defining user and not with privileges granted via object privileges from a database role.**

This has confused developers, who may test certain DML statements in SQL*Plus as a particular database user, then find the same statements within a PL/SQL procedure do not compile. The majority of the time, this is due to object privileges being granted via a role and not directly to the defining user.

If, for example user SCOTT connects to the database, with the ASSEMBLY_LINE role enabled by default, then he will have the following privileges:

```
SQL> connect scott/tiger
Connected.
SQL> select * from session_roles;

ROLE
------------------------------
CONNECT
RESOURCE
ASSEMBLY_LINE
```

To test this, user SCOTT attempts an INSERT into the GEORGE.SPROCKETS table, which is successful:

```
SQL> insert into george.sprockets values( 6, 'Aluminum', 10 );

1 row created.

SQL> rollback;

Rollback complete.
```

We use the ROLLBACK *command to undo this* INSERT.

Now, however, user SCOTT wishes to attempt exactly the same insert statement through the use of a database procedure named ADD_SPROCKET:

```
SQL> create or replace procedure add_sprocket
  2  as
  3  begin
  4  insert into george.sprockets values( 6, 'Aluminum', 10 );
  5  end;
  6  /

Warning: Procedure created with compilation errors.
```

```
SQL> show errors
Errors for PROCEDURE ADD_SPROCKET:

LINE/COL ERROR
-------- -------------------------------------------------------
4/1      PLS-00201: identifier 'SPROCKETS' must be declared
4/1      PL/SQL: SQL Statement ignored
```

This procedure fails to execute, since privileges on the SPROCKETS table have been granted via a
database role and not directly to SCOTT. This means that the SPROCKETS table is not located in the
namespace for SCOTT. To remedy this situation, all that needs to happen is for the database user
GEORGE to directly grant INSERT privilege on this table to SCOTT (rather than relying upon the
database role).

```
SQL> connect george/jetson
Connected.
SQL> grant insert on sprockets to scott;

Grant succeeded.
```

Now when user SCOTT attempts to create the ADD_SPROCKET procedure he is successful:

```
SQL> connect scott/tiger
Connected.
SQL> create or replace procedure add_sprocket
  2  as
  3  begin
  4  insert into george.sprockets values( 6, 'Aluminum', 10 );
  5  end;
  6  /

Procedure created.
```

A quick sanity test when developing DML statements for your application (and simulating from
SQL*Plus how they will execute inside a PL/SQL procedure), is to issue SET ROLE NONE to disable all
roles, and then issue your desired statement(s). So, for example, if we revisit our previous example, we
connect as user GEORGE, and revoke the INSERT privilege previously granted to user SCOTT:

```
SQL> connect george/jetson
Connected.
SQL> revoke insert on sprockets from scott;

Revoke succeeded.
```

We now reconnect as user SCOTT and issue the SET ROLE NONE statement, disabling all roles:

```
SQL> connect scott/tiger
Connected.
SQL> set role none;

Role set.
```

Now when an INSERT is attempted it fails (since all database roles are disabled):

```
SQL> insert into george.sprockets values( 6, 'Aluminum', 10 );
insert into george.sprockets values( 6, 'Aluminum', 10 )
                    *
ERROR at line 1:
ORA-00942: table or view does not exist
```

The classic application development security methodology is to **not** grant direct privileges on tables and views to database users. Rather, access to the underlying tables and views is provided exclusively through a PL/SQL procedure, function, or package, while privileges to execute these compiled objects are provided via database roles. The greatest benefit of this approach is that no end user can directly manipulate an application's tables and views except through the methods that you expose. Building security directly into your application, rather than in the database, implies that the security implementation is only valid for your application. However, if you only provide the ability to modify your application's tables and views via PL/SQL procedures, functions, and packages, then your database object security will be maintained for all applications (SQL*Plus, Active Server Pages, other PL/SQL, or even Java) that access your Oracle database.

By default, PL/SQL is executed with the rights of the definer, that is, as the database user that contains the PL/SQL program unit in their schema. A PL/SQL procedure contained in the SCOTT schema will be executed with the privileges of database user SCOTT, regardless of who invoked it. As long as the database user invoking it is given execute permission on the PL/SQL object, it will execute as the defined owner. The only exception to this rule is when a PL/SQL object is defined to execute with the privileges of the user invoking it rather than the defined user. Since Oracle 8*i*, you have the ability to define whether a PL/SQL subprogram executes with the rights of the definer or with the rights of the user invoking it. We will explore this advanced topic shortly.

Try It Out – Definer's Rights

To demonstrate definer's rights, we will use the database view USER_OBJECTS. This view, which is a part of every Oracle database, is used to provide a view of all objects owned by the current user.

1. We begin by connecting as user SYSTEM and granting CREATE PROCEDURE privilege to user GEORGE:

```
SQL> connect system/manager
Connected.
SQL> grant create procedure to george;

Grant succeeded.
```

2. Now we connect as user GEORGE and create a procedure called SHOW_OBJECTS (which displays the names of all database objects):

```
SQL> connect george/jetson
Connected.
SQL> create procedure show_objects
  2  as
  3  begin
  4      for c1 in (select object_name, object_type
  5                   from user_objects
  6                   order by object_name ) loop
  7          dbms_output.put_line('Name: ' || c1.object_name || ' Type: ' ||
                                                        c1.object_type );
  8      end loop;
  9  end;
 10  /

Procedure created.
```

3. Executing SHOW_OBJECTS gives us the following results:

```
SQL> set serveroutput on
SQL> exec show_objects;
Name: MYTABLE Type: TABLE
Name: SHOW_OBJECTS Type: PROCEDURE
Name: SPROCKETS Type: TABLE

PL/SQL procedure successfully completed.
```

4. We can issue the same query directly from within SQL*Plus which will give us the same results:

```
SQL> column object_name format a20
SQL> column object_type format a20
SQL> select object_name, object_type
  2    from user_objects
  3    order by object_name
  4  /

OBJECT_NAME          OBJECT_TYPE
-------------------- --------------------
MYTABLE              TABLE
SHOW_OBJECTS         PROCEDURE
SPROCKETS            TABLE

3 rows selected.
```

How It Works

In the example, we granted the CREATE PROCEDURE privilege to database user GEORGE, and then created a simple procedure to loop through all rows of the USER_OBJECTS view and display the names and types of each database object. Issuing the same query directly from SQL*Plus, proves that the results of the database procedure are correct.

Let's now look carefully at the results of this procedure when executed by user SCOTT.

```
SQL> connect scott/tiger
Connected.
SQL> set serveroutput on;
SQL> exec george.show_objects;
Name: MYTABLE Type: TABLE
Name: SHOW_OBJECTS Type: PROCEDURE
Name: SPROCKETS Type: TABLE

PL/SQL procedure successfully completed.
```

As you can see the SHOW_OBJECTS procedure gives us three objects, MYTABLE, SHOW_OBJECTS, and SPROCKETS, as we saw in the above example. However, if we then carry out a SELECT statement from within SQL*Plus we get a different list of objects:

```
SQL> select object_name, object_type
  2    from user_objects
  3    order by object_name
  4  /

OBJECT_NAME            OBJECT_TYPE
--------------------   --------------------
ADD_SPROCKET           PROCEDURE
BONUS                  TABLE
DEPT                   TABLE
EMP                    TABLE
PK_DEPT                INDEX
PK_EMP                 INDEX
SALGRADE               TABLE

7 rows selected.
```

So, why the difference in results? Well, since GEORGE defined the stored procedure SHOW_OBJECTS, when database user SCOTT runs the procedure the list of results returned is identical to that obtained when it was executed as database user GEORGE. In other words the procedure is executed as the database user who has defined the stored procedure (namely GEORGE). It is only when user SCOTT runs a SELECT against the USER_OBJECTS view from SQL*Plus that he sees all the objects within the SCOTT namespace.

Enabling Invoker's Rights

One of the new features introduced in Oracle 8*i*, is the ability to designate PL/SQL at compile time to execute as the database user *invoking* the PL/SQL procedure or function, rather than the database user that has defined it.

Enabling invoker's rights for PL/SQL is especially simple. The basic syntax in PL/SQL is:

```
CREATE [OR REPLACE] { FUNCTION | PACKAGE | PROCEDURE } object_name
[AUTHID {CURRENT_USER |  DEFINER}] AS…
```

In creating such PL/SQL statements, if the AUTHID clause is omitted, then the PL/SQL subprogram will execute with the definer's namespace and privileges by default. Changing the AUTHID clause to CURRENT_USER will result in the PL/SQL subprogram executing with the namespace and privileges of the database user invoking it.

Although PL/SQL executed as the defining database user will always be the norm, there are circumstances where PL/SQL executing as the invoking user is preferred. The best example of such circumstances is in accessing any of the database object views provided by the Oracle data dictionary, as we showed in the previous example.

Try It Out – Invoker's Rights

1. Let's connect to the database as user GEORGE and recreate the SHOW_OBJECTS procedure:

```
SQL> connect george/jetson
Connected.
SQL> create or replace procedure show_objects
  2    authid current_user as
  3    begin
  4        for c1 in (select object_name, object_type
  5                        from user_objects
  6                        order by object_name ) loop
  7            dbms_output.put_line('Name: ' || c1.object_name || ' Type: ' ||
c1.object_type );
  8            end loop;
  9    end;
 10  /

Procedure created.
```

2. Executing SHOW_OBJECTS gives us the results we saw earlier:

```
SQL> set serveroutput on
SQL> exec show_objects
Name: MYTABLE Type: TABLE
Name: SHOW_OBJECTS Type: PROCEDURE
Name: SPROCKETS Type: TABLE

PL/SQL procedure successfully completed.
```

3. Now let's connect as user SCOTT and view the results of SHOW_OBJECTS:

```
SQL> connect scott/tiger
Connected.

SQL> set serveroutput on
SQL> exec george.show_objects;
Name: ADD_SPROCKET Type: PROCEDURE
Name: BONUS Type: TABLE
Name: DEPT Type: TABLE
Name: EMP Type: TABLE
```

```
Name: PK_DEPT Type: INDEX
Name: PK_EMP Type: INDEX
Name: SALGRADE Type: TABLE

PL/SQL procedure successfully completed.
```

How It Works

In this case we recreate the procedure SHOW_OBJECTS, but insert an AUTHID clause:

```
SQL> create or replace procedure show_objects
  2  authid current_user as
```

This clause indicates that the procedure should execute as the database user invoking it, so when we run SHOW_OBJECTS as user SCOTT we now see the results we would expect.

Fine-Grained Access Control

In this section of the chapter we focus on application security implemented using a feature introduced in Oracle 8*i* called **Fine-Grained Access Control**. This feature lives under many monikers, including FGAC, DBMS_RLS, row-level security, and (occasionally) striping.

> **Note that striping is not really an accurate term to use, since this has to do with how data is laid out across an array of physical disks.**

Everything in this chapter up until now has focused on the end-user population being physical database users. With the proliferation of web applications built with a variety of technologies, end-developers need a way to provide security mechanisms to their application when the end-user may be a non-database "lightweight" user.

> *Fine-grained access control can be used with database users, but database authentication is not a prerequisite.*

So what is fine-grained access control? It is a feature of the Oracle database, managed by the database, which is used to develop a robust security policy. This security policy is enforced at all times, regardless of the access mechanism to the database. In the previous section, we saw how it was beneficial to **avoid** providing direct access to manipulate tables in your application. Rather, it is more secure to provide a PL/SQL subprogram that manipulates the tables directly, with the end user invoking this subprogram. This security is in place regardless of the end client application. With fine-grained access control, the security policy is applied directly to the tables or views of an application. So even if your end users wish to run reports directly against application tables or views using their favorite report-writing tool, you now have a method of permitting this action while still enforcing security.

In simple terms, fine-grained access control is implemented via a security policy, which is applied to a table. This policy defines, at run-time, an additional predicate to be appended to a query when performing a DML operation against the table. A policy can be used for multiple types of DML statements, or you can choose to use a distinct policy for each type of DML statement.

The steps to create and apply a policy are:

1. Create a function with input parameters and an output type as required by Oracle security policies. The body of this function should return a predicate that will restrict the results based upon your requirements.

2. Determine which DML statements (SELECT, INSERT, UPDATE, and DELETE) you want your policy to apply to.

3. Using the supplied PL/SQL package DBMS_RLS, add the policy using the ADD_POLICY procedure, referencing the function you created in step 1. Ensure that the database user SYS has granted your user EXECUTE privilege on DBMS_RLS.

The function defined in step 1 can be designed to restrict rows based upon an infinite number of variables such as who the current database user is, the time of day, data in other tables associated with the user, the machine they're accessing your application from, and so on. It's an incredibly flexible method for implementing security in the database.

Let's assume the developer George Jetson has a requirement to provide user SCOTT with query access to his SPROCKETS table. But for whatever reason, user SCOTT is only permitted to see those sprockets that have an ID less than 4. This would be implemented using the following:

```
SQL> connect sys/change_on_install
Connected.
SQL> grant execute on dbms_rls to george;

Grant succeeded.

SQL> connect george/jetson
Connected.

SQL> create or replace function security_fn1(
  2      p_obj_schema in varchar2,
  3      p_obj_name   in varchar2 )
  4  return varchar2 is
  5  begin
  6      if user = 'SCOTT' then
  7          return 'id < 4';
  8      else
  9          return '';
 10      end if;
 11  end;
 12  /

Function created.
```

While the argument names within the policy function do not need to be the same as the ones above, the function should always take two input arguments of type VARCHAR2 and return a variable type of VARCHAR2. In addition, it should be noted that the first parameter will always be interpreted as the object schema, and the second parameter as the object name. This function will determine who the database user accessing the table is, and if it is user SCOTT, will return additional constraints to be applied to the query. Although the arguments P_OBJ_SCHEMA and P_OBJ_NAME are not utilized in our security function at run-time, Oracle will pass these arguments the schema name and table name for which the policy is being applied. This enables the application developer to create a generic security function and have it included in a policy against a variety of tables, with the behavior being determined by the context in which it is used.

Using the function created previously, the user GEORGE now adds a security policy to the SPROCKETS table:

```
SQL> begin
  2      dbms_rls.add_policy(
  3          object_schema    => 'GEORGE',
  4          object_name      => 'SPROCKETS',
  5          policy_name      => 'POLICY1',
  6          function_schema  => 'GEORGE',
  7          policy_function  => 'SECURITY_FN1',
  8          statement_types  => 'SELECT',
  9          update_check     => FALSE );
 10  end;
 11  /

PL/SQL procedure successfully completed.
```

Note that not only can the tables or view (as well as the security functions) belong to a different schema, but the policy can also be applied to specific types of DML statements. In this case, the policy was defined so as to only apply to the SELECT statement.

Now, to see that this policy is in effect, we begin by carrying out a SELECT statement on the ID column of the SPROCKETS table as user GEORGE:

```
SQL> select id
  2      from sprockets
  3      order by id;

        ID
----------
         1
         3
         4
         5

4 rows selected.
```

As you can see all 4 rows in the table are returned. If user GEORGE now grants the SELECT privilege to user SYSTEM then user SYSTEM also returns all 4 rows:

```
SQL> grant select on sprockets to system;

Grant succeeded.

SQL> connect system/manager
Connected.
SQL> select id
  2     from george.sprockets
  3     order by id;

        ID
----------
         1
         3
         4
         5

4 rows selected.
```

However, if user SCOTT now connects and carries out the same SELECT statement, he only sees two results:

```
SQL> connect scott/tiger
Connected.
SQL> select id
  2     from george.sprockets
  3     order by id;

        ID
----------
         1
         3

2 rows selected.
```

Here we can see that our policy is truly in effect. When querying as the user GEORGE or SYSTEM, we are able to view all rows in the underlying SPROCKETS table. Our database policy was active, but since the security function determined that the connected user in both cases was not SCOTT, it returned an empty predicate to attach to the current query, allowing all results to be returned. However, when the user SCOTT attempted to query this same table, the policy's security function now returned the additional clause ID < 4, and limited the actual rows seen by SCOTT.

At this point, you may be asking yourself why we couldn't just accomplish this requirement using a database view. The answer, of course, is that we could have done exactly that. However, let's say that the user GEORGE still has the requirement that user SCOTT can only see those sprockets with an ID less than 4, but can only insert rows into the SPROCKETS table with an ID greater than 10. This would be very difficult to achieve using database views but becomes rather trivial to implement using security policies. User GEORGE can simply create a further security function named SECURITY_FN2:

```
SQL> connect george/jetson
Connected.
SQL> create or replace function security_fn2(
  2        p_obj_schema in varchar2,
  3        p_obj_name   in varchar2 )
  4  return varchar2 is
  5  begin
  6      if user = 'SCOTT' then
  7          return 'id > 10';
  8      else
  9          return '';
 10      end if;
 11  end;
 12  /

Function created.
```

The function is very similar to the previous one created, though in this case if user SCOTT is returned then only ID values greater than 10 can be returned. Now GEORGE adds the security policy:

```
SQL> begin
  2      dbms_rls.add_policy(
  3          object_schema   => 'GEORGE',
  4          object_name     => 'SPROCKETS',
  5          policy_name     => 'POLICY2',
  6          function_schema => 'GEORGE',
  7          policy_function => 'SECURITY_FN2',
  8          statement_types => 'INSERT',
  9          update_check    => TRUE );
 10  end;
 11  /

PL/SQL procedure successfully completed.
```

This time, in the call to add the security policy, we specified UPDATE_CHECK with a value of TRUE. This optional argument, only applicable to INSERT and UPDATE statements, ensures that the policy is verified after the actual DML statement. In essence, this ensures that data cannot be modified in, or inserted into, a table if it would violate the security policy.

Now let's see what happens when user SCOTT attempts an INSERT:

```
SQL> connect scott/tiger
Connected.
SQL> insert into george.sprockets values( 9, 'Tungsten', 60 );
insert into george.sprockets values( 9, 'Tungsten', 60 )
                *
ERROR at line 1:
ORA-28115: policy with check option violation
```

As expected, the security policy prevented the user SCOTT from inserting data that would have violated the policy (namely an ID value lower than 10). However, the following INSERT, which is within the bounds of the security policy, is permitted:

```
SQL> insert into george.sprockets values( 11, 'Tungsten', 60 );

1 row created.

SQL> rollback;

Rollback complete.
```

Application Contexts

The power of fine-grained access control can be further enhanced through the use of **application contexts** (another feature introduced with Oracle 8*i*). As we'll see shortly, application contexts can be used in any environment, removing the need to somehow tie application security to an actual database username. In a Web environment, the identity of a user can be determined from something other than a database username (such as a cookie). Application contexts enable you to exploit and use this information. In this way fine-grained access control is even more applicable to a wide range of applications, from client-server security to OLTP web applications.

An application context is nothing more than a named construct that has a value associated with it. This means that different users can be accessing application contexts of the same name but with values distinct to their session. The most important facet of application contexts is that they are tightly bound to a PL/SQL procedure, and it is only this procedure that can be used to actually set the value of an attribute of the context. This is extremely important from a security standpoint. As an application may use security policies to restrict or permit access to information, the policy may actually employ information derived from data in another table, or information maintained in PL/SQL global variables. Spoofing, or modification, of this information can be minimized if the security policy uses an application context, whose value can only be set in a single PL/SQL procedure.

Try It Out – Application Contexts

1. Let's begin by connecting as user SYSTEM, and granting CREATE privilege to user GEORGE:

```
SQL> connect system/manager
Connected.
SQL> grant create any context to george;

Grant succeeded.
```

2. Now we connect as user GEORGE and create a procedure named SET_JETSON_CONTEXT:

```
SQL> connect george/jetson
Connected.
SQL> create or replace procedure set_jetson_context
  2  as
  3      l_context_name varchar2(255) := 'Jetson_Context';
  4  begin
```

```
 5        if substr(user,1,1) = 'S' then
 6            dbms_session.set_context( l_context_name, 'Can_View', 'YES' );
 7            if user = 'SYSTEM' then
 8                dbms_session.set_context( l_context_name, 'Max_ID', '100');
 9            else
10                dbms_session.set_context( l_context_name, 'Max_ID', '10');
11            end if;
12        else
13            dbms_session.set_context( l_context_name, 'Can_View', 'NO' );
14        end if;
15 end;
16 /
```

Procedure created.

3. To bind this procedure to a specific context, GEORGE issues:

```
SQL> create context jetson_context using set_jetson_context;
```

Context created.

4. To set the values of the application context GEORGE then issues:

```
SQL> exec set_jetson_context;
```

PL/SQL procedure successfully completed.

5. To examine the values of this context we query from DUAL using the built-in SYS_CONTEXT function, which will take as arguments the context namespace and the parameter name:

```
SQL> select sys_context('Jetson_Context', 'Can_View') from dual;

SYS_CONTEXT('JETSON_CONTEXT','CAN_VIEW')
-----------------------------------------------------------------------
NO

1 row selected.

SQL> select sys_context('Jetson_Context', 'Max_ID') from dual;

SYS_CONTEXT('JETSON_CONTEXT','MAX_ID')
-----------------------------------------------------------------------


1 row selected.
```

6. In order to verify that the application context is working correctly, we grant an execute privilege to user SCOTT:

```
SQL> grant execute on set_jetson_context to scott;

Grant succeeded.
```

7. Now user SCOTT can execute the SET_JETSON_CONTEXT procedure successfully:

```
SQL> connect scott/tiger
Connected.
SQL> exec george.set_jetson_context;

PL/SQL procedure successfully completed.
```

8. A query on DUAL reveals that the application context is working successfully:

```
SQL> select sys_context('Jetson_Context', 'Can_View') from dual;

SYS_CONTEXT('JETSON_CONTEXT','CAN_VIEW')
------------------------------------------------------------------
YES

1 row selected.

SQL> select sys_context('Jetson_Context', 'Max_ID') from dual;

SYS_CONTEXT('JETSON_CONTEXT','MAX_ID')
------------------------------------------------------------------
10

1 row selected.
```

How It Works

User GEORGE creates a procedure to manipulate the application context named JETSON_CONTEXT. This is a construct that will be used to maintain several name value pairs. This procedure first examines the database username, verifying whether the first letter of the username begins with S or not. If it does, then an application context value named CAN_VIEW is given a value of YES:

```
create or replace procedure set_jetson_context
  2   as
  3       l_context_name varchar2(255) := 'Jetson_Context';
  4   begin
  5       if substr(user,1,1) = 'S' then
  6           dbms_session.set_context( l_context_name, 'Can_View', 'YES' );
```

If the database username does begin with S and is equal to SYSTEM, another application context value called MAX_ID is given a value of 100; otherwise it's given a value of 10:

```
 7              if user = 'SYSTEM' then
 8                  dbms_session.set_context( l_context_name, 'Max_ID', '100');
 9              else
10                  dbms_session.set_context( l_context_name, 'Max_ID', '10');
11              end if;
```

If the database username doesn't begin with an S then CAN_VIEW is given the value NO:

```
12      else
13          dbms_session.set_context( l_context_name, 'Can_View', 'NO' );
14      end if;
15  end;
```

GEORGE then issues the statement:

```
SQL> create context jetson_context using set_jetson_context;
```

At this point, no other procedure, package, or code could modify the name-value pairs of application JETSON_CONTEXT outside of the PL/SQL procedure SET_JETSON_CONTEXT. Even the database owner of the context itself, GEORGE, cannot programmatically override the security associated with this context, short of replacing the definition of the context altogether. If GEORGE attempts to override the security an error message is generated as shown below:

```
SQL> exec dbms_session.set_context('Jetson_Context', 'Can_View', 'YES');
BEGIN dbms_session.set_context('Jetson_Context', 'Can_View', 'YES'); END;

*
ERROR at line 1:
ORA-01031: insufficient privileges
ORA-06512: at "SYS.DBMS_SESSION", line 58
ORA-06512: at line 1
```

at the point when GEORGE issues:

```
SQL> exec set_jetson_context;
```

The values of the application context have been set, based upon the database user (in other words GEORGE) executing this procedure. To examine the values of this context, GEORGE issues a query from DUAL:

```
SQL> select sys_context('Jetson_Context', 'Can_View') from dual;

SYS_CONTEXT('JETSON_CONTEXT','CAN_VIEW')
-----------------------------------------------------------------------
NO

1 row selected.
```

533

```
SQL> select sys_context('Jetson_Context', 'Max_ID') from dual;

SYS_CONTEXT('JETSON_CONTEXT','MAX_ID')
-----------------------------------------------------------------------


1 row selected.
```

As expected, the value of parameter CAN_VIEW is NO, and the value of MAX_ID, which was never set, is NULL.

Now, once user GEORGE has granted him the appropriate privilege, user SCOTT can execute the SET_JETSON_CONTEXT procedure:

```
SQL> grant execute on set_jetson_context to scott;

Grant succeeded.

SQL> connect scott/tiger
Connected.

SQL> exec george.set_jetson_context;

PL/SQL procedure successfully completed.
```

We should note in passing here, however, that if user SCOTT had attempted the following, an error message would have been generated:

```
SQL> exec set_jetson_context;
BEGIN set_jetson_context; END;


     *

ERROR at line 1:
ORA-06550: line 1, column 7:
PLS-00201: identifier 'SET_JETSON_CONTEXT' must be declared
ORA-06550: line 1, column 7:
PL/SQL: Statement ignored
```

Finally, we query DUAL to get the values of CAN_VIEW and MAX_ID:

```
SQL> select sys_context('Jetson_Context', 'Can_View') from dual;

SYS_CONTEXT('JETSON_CONTEXT','CAN_VIEW')
-----------------------------------------------------------------------
YES

1 row selected.

SQL> select sys_context('Jetson_Context', 'Max_ID') from dual;
```

```
SYS_CONTEXT('JETSON_CONTEXT','MAX_ID')
----------------------------------------------------------------
10

1 row selected.
```

Connecting as user SCOTT, you can see that the values for the parameters of the application context are appropriately set, based upon the logic that was originally defined in the SET_JETSON_CONTEXT procedure.

At this point, it should be clearer how application contexts and fine-grained access control are a perfect match for one another. Whereas the example procedure used to set the application context was based upon the value of the database username, this could really be based upon any value available in your environment. A perfect example where application contexts and fine-grained access control can be employed is in web applications, and in particular, reading the value of a browser's cookie. The values of an application context could be set after reading the value of an encrypted cookie. The security policies would then return the predicates based upon the values of the parameters within the application context. All of a sudden, we have security enforced by the database for a user population that is not in the database!

Data Security

Up until this point, we have looked at the different methods and techniques to secure objects (and control privileges) within an Oracle database. However, it is also possible to natively encrypt or protect data contained within the database, using facilities introduced in Oracle 8i 8.1.6 (and refined in subsequent releases). The PL/SQL package DBMS_OBFUSCATION_TOOLKIT gives application developers the ability to selectively encrypt (or *obfuscate*) application data maintained in the Oracle database.

Let's consider as an example a situation where you need to maintain user passwords in an Oracle table. You can choose to do this a number of ways. Firstly, you can choose to store the data unencrypted in plain text. The drawback of this method is that anyone who (intentionally or otherwise) gains access to this password table, all of a sudden has access to every user password for your application.

Alternatively you can encrypt the data, using either your own encryption algorithms, or one provided by Oracle in the DBMS_OBFUSCATION_TOOLKIT package. In this way your application could easily encrypt and decrypt the data, using the unencrypted form only when necessary. However, anyone who knows the encryption key, including administrators and application developers, will be able to easily decode the data.

A third way that user passwords can be stored securely is via a **hash** (or **message digest**) of the data. Secure hash functions can typically be classified as 'one-way functions'. That is to say that the function generates a distinct value from its input. It is not computationally feasible to determine the input value given the result of the function. This process is very similar to the way in which the Oracle database computes and stores database user passwords in the database. That is to say that Oracle applies a one-way function to the user password and generates a value. At authentication time, the one-way function is applied to the user-entered password, and the result of the function is compared with the stored value of the function. In this way, Oracle never decrypts a user's password, since only the computed values are used in the comparison. The Oracle database provides facilities to compute industry-standard MD5 message digests using the DBMS_OBFUSCATION_TOOLKIT package. We'll see more about this a little later.

DES (**Data Encryption Standard**) is an internationally accepted standard for secure data encryption, while **triple DES** is a recent refinement of the original DES algorithm. The DBMS_OBFUSCATION_TOOLKIT contains PL/SQL procedures and functions to perform both DES encryption/decryption, and (as of Oracle 8*i* 8.1.7) procedures and functions for triple DES encryption/decryption.

The methods for DES encryption and decryption are actually quite simple to use. While in Oracle 9*i*, there are over 25 different procedures and functions in the PL/SQL package DBMS_OBFUSCATION_TOOLKIT, we will focus on just a few in this chapter.

DES3ENCRYPT and DES3DECRYPT

The DES3ENCRYPT and DES3DECRYPT procedures take three arguments, namely:

❑ INPUT STRING – the input string to be either encrypted or decrypted. Note that the input string must be a multiple of 8 bytes.

❑ KEY STRING – the string to be used as the key during encryption. The key string must be 128 bits if WHICH=0, and 192 bits if WHICH=1.

❑ WHICH – the mode argument that controls whether two keys or three keys are used during encryption. TwoKeyMode is specified with an argument value of 0, while ThreeKeyMode is specified with an argument value of 1. TwoKeyMode is the default.

The result of the DES3ENCRYPT function is the encrypted string, and the result of the DES3DECRYPT function is the decrypted string.

For convenience, we can easily construct a function MY_ENCRYPT, which automatically pads our INPUT STRING and KEY STRING values to the required length, before executing the DES3ENCRYPT function. It will look like this:

```
SQL> create or replace function my_encrypt(
  2       p_input_string in varchar2,
  3       p_key_string   in varchar2 )
  4  return varchar2
  5  is
  6       l_encrypted_value varchar2(4000);
  7       l_input_string    varchar2(4000);
  8       l_key_string      varchar2(4000);
  9  begin
 10       --
 11       -- Pad the input string to a multiple of 8 bytes (required)
 12       --
 13       l_input_string := rpad( p_input_string,
 14                        (trunc(length( p_input_string) / 8) + 1) * 8, chr(0));
 15       --
 16       -- Pad the key string to 16 bytes (required)
 17       --
 18       l_key_string    := rpad( p_key_string, 16 , chr(0));
 19       l_encrypted_value := dbms_obfuscation_toolkit.des3encrypt(
 20                            input_string => l_input_string,
```

```
21                                           key_string   => l_key_string );
22      return l_encrypted_value;
23  end;
24  /

Function created.
```

In the same fashion, we can create a function MY_DECRYPT to perform the decryption, padding the input string and key values to the appropriate lengths.

```
create or replace function my_decrypt(
    p_input_string in varchar2,
    p_key_string   in varchar2 )
return varchar2
is
    l_decrypted_value varchar2(4000);
    l_input_string    varchar2(4000);
    l_key_string      varchar2(4000);
begin
    --
    -- Pad the input string to a multiple of 8 bytes (required)
    --
    l_input_string := rpad( p_input_string,
                      (trunc(length( p_input_string) / 8) + 1) * 8, chr(0));
    --
    -- Pad the key string to 16 bytes (required)
    --
    l_key_string   := rpad( p_key_string, 16 , chr(0));
    l_decrypted_value := dbms_obfuscation_toolkit.des3decrypt(
                             input_string => l_input_string,
                             key_string   => l_key_string );
    return l_decrypted_value;
end;
/

Function created.
```

With these two functions in place, we are can now easily (and securely) encrypt and decrypt an arbitrary data value (keeping in mind that our functions, as written, permit only a 4000 byte value). Let's look at an example of using the MY_ENCRYPT encryption function:

```
SQL> select my_encrypt('MyData', 'thekey') from dual;

MY_ENCRYPT('MYDATA','THEKEY')
-----------------------------------------------------
•î?@ •••
```

We return what appears to be a raw binary value. To make this raw output more readable, we can convert it into a hexadecimal string representing the byte values, using the Oracle SQL function RAWTOHEX:

```
SQL> select rawtohex(my_encrypt('MyData', 'thekey')) from dual;

RAWTOHEX(MY_ENCRYPT('MYDATA','THEKEY'))
----------------------------------------------------------------
128C3F40EAB51FF2
```

As we can see using triple DES encryption of the data value MyData, in combination with the key thekey, results in an encrypted binary value, with a hex representation of 128C3F40EAB51FF2.

At this point, anyone who has the correct key should be able to take this same encrypted value and decrypt it into our original string. Let's see whether our MY_DECRYPT function is successful:

```
SQL> select my_decrypt( utl_raw.cast_to_varchar2(hextoraw('128C3F40EAB51FF2')),
'thekey')
  2    from dual
  3  /

MY_DECRYPT(UTL_RAW.CAST_TO_VARCHAR2(HEXTORAW('128C3F40EAB51FF2')),'THEKEY')
--------------------------------------------------------------------------------
MyData   ~••q¶u([
```

> *You'll notice in this example that not only did we successfully decrypt our original value, but it also appears that we retrieved some additional 'garbage' with it. This is due to the padding of NULL characters to our original data value.*

Dealing with binary values in SQL*Plus is never fun, so we had to exploit a few functions here. Remember that the MY_DECRYPT function took as its first argument a VARCHAR2 variable. Since our encrypted value was truly a binary value, and we had it represented as a series of bytes in hexadecimal format, we first had to convert it back to a raw value, which was accomplished using the Oracle SQL function HEXTORAW. Once we had this value in raw form, we then needed to cast (or convert) this raw value to a VARCHAR2 representation for our function, which was done via the Oracle-supplied CAST_TO_VARCHAR2 function in the UTL_RAW package.

> *Within a normal program where you never really need to see the encrypted value in a readable format, these steps would not be necessary.*

Although it is enormously convenient to perform DES3 encryption directly in the database, care must be taken when using these procedures. Since there is a key associated with this algorithm, theoretically anyone who has access to the key has the ability to decrypt the data. The security of this encrypted data is only as secure as your key. As a result, it is always prudent to limit the methods and people who can ever access the key used to encrypt your data. In addition, there is a performance penalty to pay for performing these encryption and decryption routines. The stronger the encryption, the more time it will take and the more server resources will be consumed to perform these operations. The DES encryption procedures and functions supplied by Oracle can be of huge benefit when implementing a secure application, but they should be used selectively.

Message Digests

Oracle provides PL/SQL procedures and functions to compute the message digest of data within the DBMS_OBFUSCATION_TOOLKIT package. A message digest should not be perceived as 'encryption', since it is nothing more than a computed value uniquely computed for any given message. MD5 is an industry standard implementation of a message digest, and is provided by Oracle in this toolkit. In Oracle 8*i* 8.1.7 and later, Oracle has provided methods to quickly compute the MD5 message digest of data.

The specifications of the relevant procedures and functions are as follows:

```
PROCEDURE MD5
 Argument Name                  Type                     In/Out Default?
 ------------------------------ ------------------------ ------ --------
 INPUT                          RAW                      IN
 CHECKSUM                       RAW(16)                  OUT

FUNCTION MD5 RETURNS RAW(16)
 Argument Name                  Type                     In/Out Default?
 ------------------------------ ------------------------ ------ --------
 INPUT                          RAW                      IN

PROCEDURE MD5
 Argument Name                  Type                     In/Out Default?
 ------------------------------ ------------------------ ------ --------
 INPUT_STRING                   VARCHAR2                 IN
 CHECKSUM_STRING                VARCHAR2(16)             OUT

FUNCTION MD5 RETURNS VARCHAR2(16)
 Argument Name                  Type                     In/Out Default?
 ------------------------------ ------------------------ ------ --------
 INPUT_STRING                   VARCHAR2                 IN
```

Rather than just providing a simple checksum computation, one of the distinguishing features of MD5 is that it will produce not only unique values for every type of 'message', but also produce dramatically different values.

Let's now look at a simple example:

```
SQL> set serveroutput on
  1  declare
  2      l_md varchar2(16);
  3  begin
  4      l_md := dbms_obfuscation_toolkit.md5(
  5          input_string => '911' );
  6      dbms_output.put_line( 'MD5 of 911: ' ||
  7          utl_raw.cast_to_raw( l_md ));
  8      --
  9      l_md := dbms_obfuscation_toolkit.md5(
 10          input_string => '411' );
 11      dbms_output.put_line( 'MD5 of 411: ' ||
```

```
  12              utl_raw.cast_to_raw( l_md ));
  13  end;
  14  /
MD5 of 911: B56A18E0EACDF51AA2A5306B0F533204
MD5 of 411: 17D63B1625C816C22647A73E1482372B

PL/SQL procedure successfully completed.
```

As our example demonstrates, even though the input message varies by only one byte (911 and 411), the resultant message digest is *dramatically* different. This type of algorithm thwarts would-be attackers who would otherwise examine similar input messages and attempt to compute (or guess at) the correct message digest. It is important to note that the input data value is not stored in the message digest, that is, it is not encrypted. It is computationally unfeasible to author a procedure which could compute the input value given the message digest.

MD5 message digest computation is ideal for the computation and storage of secure data in an application, especially for user credentials. With MD5, you are virtually guaranteed a unique message digest for every distinct input value. As a result you could store the message digests of user passwords in a table in your database, When the user then enters their password for your application, you can compute the message digest of the credentials they entered, and compare this with the stored value in the database. If the message digests match, then you can be certain that the password entered by the user is equal to their original password. Note that this is done without ever knowing (or having to decrypt) the original password.

Summary

Database security is a critical element of any application and must be well understood, not only by database administrators but also by application developers. In this chapter, we have covered a broad spectrum of topics related to security. Oracle's functionality offers organizations security policies with varying levels of sophistication, ranging from the creation and management of database users, through database roles and all the way up to flexible fine-grained access control.

An important rule to remember is that any user, whether administrator, developer, or end user, should be given the *minimum* set of privileges and access necessary to get their job done. Compromise this rule, and you implicitly comprise the security of your data and application.

Views

A view is a tailored presentation of the data stored in the database. In layman's terms, a view is a stored query. It can be used just as if it was a table but the key distinction is that a view does not store data – it is simply a stored query definition. However, the data is accessible through the view just as if you were accessing a normal table. You can select from it, join to it, and in some cases, you can INSERT, UPDATE, and DELETE from it. As such, a view can be considered a **virtual table**. There are four types of views in Oracle:

❑   Relational Views

❑   Inline Views

❑   Object Views

❑   Materialized View

These four types of views give the data modeler and application developer many tools for enforcing security, enhancing performance, and making querying easier. Inline views enable the application developer to define views on the fly. Object views are an object-relational feature of Oracle that allow the developer and modeler to build an object layer on top of the relational data so that they can model real-world entities using objects and take advantage of object-oriented functionality. Materialized views allow the developer to precalculate view results and store those values, enabling faster response times for your queries. In a nutshell, a view can be used to:

❑   Enforce security

❑   Enhance performance

❑   Hide complexity

❑   Provide abstraction

❑   Customize presentation of data

Let's take a look at each of these view types, how to create them and how we might use them successfully in our development environments.

Relational Views

A relational view is basically a stored query, the output of which can be treated as if it were a table. It is a stored object based on relational data. As discussed in the introduction, you can think of a view as a virtual table. You can query a view just as if you were querying a table and you can use views in just about every place you can use tables. However, the data retrieved from the relational view is still stored in the base tables, not in the view. Thus, a view takes up very little storage of its own – just the view definition itself is stored in the data dictionary. Relational views can be built on physical database tables (**base tables**), upon other views, or upon a combination of the two. They have the same restrictions as tables with regard to the maximum permissible number of columns in that they can have up to 1000 columns. You can also INSERT into, UPDATE, and DELETE from views just as if they were tables, although with some restrictions on these operations (which we will discuss in more detail later).

Creating A View

The full syntax for creating a view can get a bit complicated since it covers a myriad of options, most of which we do not need to go into here. If you are interested in seeing the full syntax, we refer you to the Oracle documentation at http://technet.oracle.com/doc/server.815/a67779/toc.htm. To create a simple relational view, we would use the following DDL command:

```
CREATE [OR REPLACE] VIEW <VIEW_NAME> as <QUERY>;
```

For example, if we wanted to create a view called MY_VIEW, based on a table called MY_TABLE and comprising the columns C1 and C2, we would issue the following command:

```
create view MY_VIEW as
select c1, c2
from MY_TABLE;
```

This is a very simple single table view. However, views can be very complex. We can join tables and views together. We can apply functions to the columns so that they display something different than the raw data. The query that makes up the view can have a GROUP BY, ORDER BY, and/or HAVING clauses. They can be made up of a UNION of two queries. Just about any query can be made into a view.

Just like any other action a user performs in the database, creating a view requires the appropriate privileges:

❑   We need the privilege to select from each and every base table (and view) referenced in our view. Remember, a relational view is nothing more than a stored query. If you are unable to successfully issue a query, you will be unable to define that query as a view.

❑   We need to have had the system privileges CREATE VIEW or CREATE ANY VIEW granted directly, or via a role, if we are to be able to create relational views by issuing the CREATE VIEW command.

We will discuss the security of views in more detail a little later on in the chapter (see also Chapter 13).

Connect to the database as SYS, SYSTEM, or another privileged user (such as the ORACLE_ADMIN user we showed you how to create in Chapter 3), and execute the following command to give a user the ability to create views:

```
SQL> grant create view to <username>;
```

So, if we have the appropriate privilege to access the underlying objects referenced in the view, and the privilege to create a view in the database, then we are ready to go. So let's take a look at an example that demonstrates how to create a view and how this allows us to customize the presentation of data and to enforce security.

Try It Out – Creating a Relational View

We are going to create a view that is based on the EMPLOYEES table in the HR schema of the Oracle 9*i* sample schemas, so let's first take a quick look at our base table:

```
SQL> desc employees
 Name                                      Null?    Type
 ----------------------------------------- -------- ------------
 EMPLOYEE_ID                               NOT NULL NUMBER(6)
 FIRST_NAME                                         VARCHAR2(20)
 LAST_NAME                                 NOT NULL VARCHAR2(25)
 E-MAIL                                    NOT NULL VARCHAR2(25)
 PHONE_NUMBER                                       VARCHAR2(20)
 HIRE_DATE                                 NOT NULL DATE
 JOB_ID                                    NOT NULL VARCHAR2(10)
 SALARY                                             NUMBER(8,2)
 COMMISSION_PCT                                     NUMBER(2,2)
 MANAGER_ID                                         NUMBER(6)
 DEPARTMENT_ID                                      NUMBER(4)
```

We want everybody to have access to the name, e-mail address and phone number of every employee in the company. However, if we simply grant everybody access to the EMPLOYEES table, where this information is stored, then each employee's salary will also be exposed. Not a good idea! Therefore, we are going to build a relational view, called COMPANY_PHONE_BOOK, which only contains the appropriate fields. Each employee can then be granted access to our view, rather than the base table.

1. Create the view as follows:

```
SQL> connect hr/hr
Connected.

SQL> create view company_phone_book as
  2      select last_name || ', ' || first_name name,
  3             phone_number,
  4             e-mail
  5      from employees;

View created.
```

2. We can now describe the view and select data from it just as though it were a table:

```
SQL> desc company_phone_book
 Name                                        Null?    Type
 ------------------------------------------- -------- -------------------------

 NAME                                                 VARCHAR2(47)
 PHONE_NUMBER                                         VARCHAR2(20)
 E-MAIL                                      NOT NULL VARCHAR2(25)

SQL> select *
  2     from company_phone_book
  3     order by name;

NAME                          PHONE_NUMBER          E-MAIL
----------------------------- --------------------- -------------------------
Abel, Ellen                   011.44.1644.429267    EABEL
Ande, Sundar                  011.44.1346.629268    SANDE
Atkinson, Mozhe               650.124.6234          MATKINSO
    .          .                     .                  .
    .          .                     .                  .
    .          .                     .                  .
Weiss, Matthew                650.123.1234          MWEISS
Whalen, Jennifer              515.123.4444          JWHALEN
Zlotkey, Eleni                011.44.1344.429018    EZLOTKEY

107 rows selected.
```

How It Works

Creating the view is a straightforward process. We simply use the CREATE VIEW <view_name>AS command:

```
create view company_phone_book as
```

We then simply select the field that will comprise our view. The first thing to note is that views allow us to customize or tailor how the data is presented. This gives the data modeler full control over what the application developer, and ultimately the end user, can see. We created a new column called NAME by concatenating the LAST_NAME and FIRST_NAME columns, separated by a comma. This is called a **virtual column**. When we DESCRIBE the COMPANY_PHONE_BOOK view, we see this new column name along with its data type and size:

```
SQL> desc company_phone_book
 Name                                        Null?    Type
 ------------------------------------------- -------- -------------------------

 NAME                                                 VARCHAR2(47)
```

The database tells us that the NAME column is a VARCHAR2(47). The database calculated this size by adding together the length of the FIRST_NAME column, 20, the LAST_NAME column, 25, and the extra two characters (a comma and a space). This newly created column can be treated just as if it was a real database column. We can SELECT it, apply functions to it (SUBSTR(), INSTR(), and so on – see Appendix A for details on these functions), and apply ORDER BY and GROUP BY clauses to it.

Second, note that we only made certain columns available through this view, thus demonstrating how we can use views as a security mechanism. Although employees' e-mail and phone numbers may be public, I'm pretty sure that salaries and commissions are usually not. If we restrict access to the base table and only allow access through our views, we can control not only *how*, but *which*, rows and columns can be viewed. Rest assured however, that all the values are still there – they are just not accessible using this view. You can learn more about restricting access to base tables, views, and other database objects in Chapter 13.

As a final point, remember that the user does not know, or generally need to know, the "inner workings" of our view. The users get the information they need and do not need to know where it comes from. They see the employee's name in the <last_name>, <first_name> format and do not need to know how that field is constructed. This complexity is hidden. However, information regarding the definition of view is available should we require it.

Retrieving View Definitions

All view definitions are stored in the database in the data dictionary. We can query the appropriate views within the data dictionary to retrieve the view definition, in other words the query that makes up the view.

Let's say we were interested in how our phone book view is constructed. The data dictionary provides a view called USER_VIEWS through which we can obtain details on every view that we have created in our own schema. Let's look at the USER_VIEWS view and see how we can get the definition of our view from it:

```
SQL> desc user_views
 Name                                        Null?    Type
 ------------------------------------------- -------- --------------
 VIEW_NAME                                   NOT NULL VARCHAR2(30)
 TEXT_LENGTH                                          NUMBER
 TEXT                                                 LONG
 TYPE_TEXT_LENGTH                                     NUMBER
 TYPE_TEXT                                            VARCHAR2(4000)
 OID_TEXT_LENGTH                                      NUMBER
 OID_TEXT                                             VARCHAR2(4000)
 VIEW_TYPE_OWNER                                      VARCHAR2(30)
 VIEW_TYPE                                            VARCHAR2(30)
 SUPERVIEW_NAME                                       VARCHAR2(30)
```

You can find more information about the Data Dictionary in Appendix C.

We'll explain a little later on what most of these columns tell us, but for now, we are just interested in the TEXT of the view. This is the column where the database contains the actual query that defines the view:

```
SQL> select text
  2    from user_views
  3    where view_name = 'COMPANY_PHONE_BOOK';

TEXT
-----------------------------------------------------------------------------
select last_name || ', ' || first_name name,
phone_number,
e-mail
from employees

SQL>
```

Thus we get the full view definition and we can see the table on which the view is based and the manner in which it was constructed.

Changing the View Definition

Your phone book is popular but you receive feedback to the effect that it would be very useful to include each employee's company ID. How do we add columns (or change existing columns) in our COMPANY_PHONE_BOOK view? Try the following:

```
SQL> create view company_phone_book as
  2    select employee_id emp_id,
  3           last_name || ', ' || first_name name,
  4           phone_number,
  5           e-mail
  6      from employees;
create view company_phone_book as
             *
ERROR at line 1:
ORA-00955: name is already used by an existing object
```

We got an ORA-00955 error, stating that an existing object already uses that name. Well, that makes sense since we do already have a view, named COMPANY_PHONE_BOOK. There are a number of possible solutions to this problem. We could simply assign a different name to our new view, but we really want it to be called COMPANY_PHONE_BOOK since that is the name with which the user is familiar. An alternative would be to drop the existing view using the command (see the section on *Dropping Views*, below)

We would then be free to create a new view with that same name. This would work *but* when you drop a view, all associated grants are also dropped. When you issue a new CREATE VIEW command you will get a new view on which no privileges are granted. Imagine if you had granted users and roles the privilege to select from your view – you will now have to go through the whole process again. With this in mind, the best option is to use the CREATE OR REPLACE command:

```
SQL> create or replace view company_phone_book as
  2    select employee_id emp_id,
  3           last_name || ', ' || first_name name,
  4           phone_number,
```

```
   5              e-mail
   6         from employees;

View created.

SQL> desc company_phone_book
 Name                                            Null?     Type
 ----------------------------------------------- --------- ------------------------

 EMP_ID                                          NOT NULL  NUMBER(6)
 NAME                                                      VARCHAR2(47)
 PHONE_NUMBER                                              VARCHAR2(20)
 E-MAIL                                          NOT NULL  VARCHAR2(25)
```

Not only does this mean that we get the job done in a single step, but also the CREATE OR REPLACE VIEW command enables us to change the view definition without losing any access privileges previously granted.

Dropping Views

If you want to get rid of a view that you no longer use, it is quite easy. You can just issue the DROP VIEW command:

```
SQL> drop view company_phone_book;

View dropped.

SQL> desc company_phone_book
ERROR:
ORA-04043: object company_phone_book does not exist
```

Since we will be using this view later on in the chapter, it makes sense to recreate it:

```
SQL> create or replace view company_phone_book as
  2     select employee_id emp_id,
  3            last_name || ', ' || first_name name,
  4            phone_number,
  5            e-mail
  6        from employees;

View created.
```

Notice that even though the view did not exist, the CREATE OR REPLACE command worked. As the name suggests, if the object does not exist, it will be created. If the view does exist, then it will be replaced. Remember, any privileges previously granted on our view will have been lost when we issued the DROP VIEW command.

Constraints in Views

Not only do views allow us to restrict which columns we can see, they can also be used to constrain which rows are returned. Let's say we wanted to create a view that showed only the people hired in the year 2000. We could use the following:

```
SQL> create view emps_hired_in_2000 as
  2    select *
  3      from employees
  4      where to_char( hire_date, 'YYYY' ) = '2000';

View created.

SQL> select count(*)
  2    from emps_hired_in_2000;

  COUNT(*)
----------
        11
```

Let's take this further and consider a view in which we want to get a count of how many people were hired each year. The view would look something like this:

```
SQL> create view yearly_hire_totals as
  2    select to_char( hire_date, 'YYYY' ) year,
  3           count(*) total
  4      from employees
  5      group by to_char( hire_date, 'YYYY' )
  6      order by to_char( hire_date, 'YYYY' );

View created.

SQL> select *
  2    from yearly_hire_totals;

YEAR     TOTAL
----  ----------
1987         2
1989         1
1990         1
1991         1
1993         1
1994         7
1995         4
1996        10
1997        28
1998        23
1999        18
2000        11

12 rows selected.
```

There are three things to note about this view. First, it would be cumbersome to maintain a table that answered this question with a SELECT * query. We would need to put triggers on the base table EMPLOYEES, and when any INSERT, UPDATE, or DELETE activity occurred, we would need to update this table, causing the database to do extra work. In some cases, that might be more desirable, but not in our case. We have a small dataset and use this view infrequently, but we update our EMPLOYEES table constantly.

Second, by including the ORDER BY clause in the view definition, we have established a default order of data presentation for our view. There is no order in a table. There is no guarantee that a SELECT * FROM T will always bring the data back in the same order. There is no first-in, first-out rule as some people believe. By allowing us to use an ORDER BY clause in a view (this was a new feature in 8*i*), it gives the view author yet even more control over how the view is displayed.

Thirdly, the view hides the complexity of the query. The application developer does not need to know how the view is constructed. They merely need to know that if they SELECT from it, they will get the results required. The view author did all the hard work of building the constraints.

Try It Out – Constraints and Security

This method of constraining rows in a view can be used for display purposes, as in the example above, but it can also be used as a security mechanism. Consider a view that constrains the rows returned based on who you are. A view like this would return a different result depending on who you were logged in as. Let's try and make one.

Using the EMPLOYEES table in the HR schema, we notice that there is a column called E-MAIL. For our purposes, let's assume that the value stored in that column is not only the user's e-mail address but also their database login ID.

1. With the above assumption in mind, create the MY_REPORTS view:

```
SQL>  connect hr/hr
 Connected.

SQL> create or replace
  2  view my_reports as
  3  select last_name, first_name
  4    from employees
  5   where manager_id = ( select employee_id
  6                          from employees
  7                         where e-mail = user )
  8   order by last_name
  9  /

View created.
```

2. Grant the privilege to SELECT from this view to the PUBLIC role:

```
SQL> grant select on my_reports to public;

Grant succeeded.
```

3. Since the user `HR` is not an employee, selecting from the view should yield no rows.

```
SQL> show user
USER is "HR"
SQL> select *
  2    from my_reports
  3  /

no rows selected
```

4. Let's now create a user `SKING`, who is a manager at the company and who has `SKING` as their e-mail address (and hence database login). First we need to connect as a privileged user to create the `SKING` account. We'll use our `ORACLE_ADMIN` user here, but it could also be `SYS` or `SYSTEM`:

```
SQL> connect oracle_admin/oracle_admin
Connected.
```

5. We now create the `SKING` account and grant the appropriate privileges:

```
SQL> create user sking identified by sking;

User created.

SQL> grant connect, resource to sking;

Grant succeeded.
```

6. Now connect as `SKING` and select from the `MY_REPORTS` view:

```
SQL> connect sking/sking
Connected.

SQL> select *
  2    from hr.my_reports
  3  /

LAST_NAME                   FIRST_NAME
------------------------    --------------------
Kochhar                     Neena
De Haan                     Lex
Raphaely                    Den
Weiss                       Matthew
Fripp                       Adam
Kaufling                    Payam
Vollman                     Shanta
Mourgos                     Kevin
Russell                     John
Partners                    Karen
Errazuriz                   Alberto
```

```
Cambrault              Gerald
Zlotkey                Eleni
Hartstein              Michael

14 rows selected.
```

This time the view returns data; the list of employees that have SKING as their manager. Notice that the view is stored in the HR schema, so we have to reference that schema when we are connected as SKING.

How It Works

The key to this view is in lines 5-7:

```
5    where manager_id = ( select employee_id
6                           from employees
7                          where e-mail = user )
```

We use the USER value (in this case SKING) to determine who is logged in. We then use the currently logged in user's EMPLOYEE_ID to constrain the rows returned to only those employees who have a MANAGER_ID matching the EMPLOYEE_ID.

Every employee can select from this view and every employee will only see his/her direct reports. There is no way to spoof this view and have it return employees who do not report to you unless you log in as a different user but then the security of that account has been compromised, not the view's security.

Join Views

All of the views that we have examined so far have been based on a single table. However, as stated earlier, views can be expressed by just about any query including those that join tables. Looking in the HR schema, you should find a predefined view called EMP_DETAILS_VIEW. Let's take a closer look at it:

```
SQL> desc emp_details_view
 Name                                             Null?    Type
 ------------------------------------------------ -------- ------------
 EMPLOYEE_ID                                      NOT NULL NUMBER(6)
 JOB_ID                                           NOT NULL VARCHAR2(10)
 MANAGER_ID                                                NUMBER(6)
 DEPARTMENT_ID                                             NUMBER(4)
 LOCATION_ID                                               NUMBER(4)
 COUNTRY_ID                                                CHAR(2)
 FIRST_NAME                                                VARCHAR2(20)
 LAST_NAME                                        NOT NULL VARCHAR2(25)
 SALARY                                                    NUMBER(8,2)
 COMMISSION_PCT                                            NUMBER(2,2)
 DEPARTMENT_NAME                                  NOT NULL VARCHAR2(30)
 JOB_TITLE                                        NOT NULL VARCHAR2(35)
 CITY                                             NOT NULL VARCHAR2(30)
 STATE_PROVINCE                                            VARCHAR2(25)
 COUNTRY_NAME                                              VARCHAR2(40)
 REGION_NAME                                               VARCHAR2(25)
```

EMP_DETAILS_VIEW has all the columns that appear in the EMPLOYEES table, but there are extra columns that do not appear in this table. The view author has joined the EMPLOYEES table with other tables to get the extra data. As a result, we can use this view just as is, selecting from it and applying our own predicates, just as if it were a base table. All the complex join conditions are hidden from us as well as any additional constraints applied and any transformations (SUBSTR(), CONCAT(), TO_CHAR(), and so on) to the selected columns.

We are interested in how this view was constructed so let's retrieve the view definition from the USER_VIEWS view:

```
SQL> set long 5000

SQL> select text
  2    from user_views
  3    where view_name = 'EMP_DETAILS_VIEW';

TEXT
-------------------------------------------------------------------------------
SELECT
    e.employee_id,
    e.job_id,
    e.manager_id,
    e.department_id,
    d.location_id,
    l.country_id,
    e.first_name,
    e.last_name,
    e.salary,
    e.commission_pct,
    d.department_name,
    j.job_title,
    l.city,
    l.state_province,
    c.country_name,
    r.region_name
FROM
    employees e,
    departments d,
    jobs j,
    locations l,
    countries c,
    regions r
WHERE e.department_id = d.department_id
    AND d.location_id = l.location_id
    AND l.country_id = c.country_id
    AND c.region_id = r.region_id
    AND j.job_id = e.job_id
WITH READ ONLY
```

Notice that the EMP_DETAILS_VIEW joins six tables. This is what is known as a **join view**. Simply put, a join view is a view based on more than one base table or view. If you had to type out this query every time you wanted these details, it would quite cumbersome! It is much easier and cleaner to select from the view and have all the complexities of the joins taken care of for you.

Notice the last line of the view: WITH READ ONLY. That is a **subquery restriction clause**. It tells the database that this view is read-only. No INSERT, UPDATE, or DELETE commands may be performed through this view. This gives the view author more control over how this view will be used. It is just like granting only SELECT privileges on a table, but with the added assurance that the other grants, INSERT, UPDATE, and DELETE cannot be obtained either by accident or subversively. This protects our data's integrity from malicious users and poorly written applications. It is another benefit of using views.

Validating Views

When we create a view, Oracle will verify that the query is valid. Later on, certain changes made to the base tables may cause the view to become invalid. For example:

❑ Changing a column name or dropping it completely from the base table or view

❑ Dropping the base table or view on which our view is based

❑ Changing the base table or view such that it becomes invalid will in turn cause our view to become invalid

To remedy such situations, we can either recompile our view with the ALTER VIEW <VIEW_NAME> COMPILE command, recreate our view with the CREATE OR REPLACE VIEW command, or fix the base table or view upon which our view is based.

Try It Out – Invalidating and Re-validating Views

We'll demonstrate a simple example whereby changes we make to a base table will invalidate a view that we have created. We'll then look at how to validate our view based on the new base table.

1. Let's first start off with a simple base table:

```
SQL> connect scott/tiger

SQL> create table t(
  2    id number,
  3    data varchar2(200) );

Table created.
```

2. Next, we can create a view on our base table, T, which just renames the columns:

```
SQL> create view view_t as
  2    select id view_id, data view_data
  3      from t;

View created.
```

3. Now populate the base table with some data and retrieve it using the view:

```
SQL> insert into t
  2  values ( 1, 'ACB' );

1 row created.

SQL> select *
  2     from view_t;

   VIEW_ID VIEW_DATA
---------- --------------------
         1 ACB
```

4. At a later date, we have to update our base table, T, to accommodate new storage requirements. The column DATA now has a different size and there is a new column DATA2, for storing CLOBs:

```
SQL> Alter table t
  2  modify
  3  (
  4   id number,
  5   data varchar2(255)
  6  );

Table altered.

SQL> Alter table t
  2  ADD
  3  (
  4   data2 varchar2(100)
  5  );

Table altered.
SQL> desc t
 Name                                      Null?    Type
 ----------------------------------------- -------- -------------

 ID                                                 NUMBER
 DATA                                               VARCHAR2(255)
 DATA2                                              CLOB
```

This is all fine but unfortunately our view, VIEW_T, is now invalid. When we made the changes to the base table Oracle flagged the view as INVALID in the data dictionary:

```
SQL> select object_name, status
  2     from user_objects
  3     where object_name = 'VIEW_T';

OBJECT_NAME                     STATUS
------------------------------- ----------
VIEW_T                          INVALID
```

5. We need to revalidate it. With Oracle, this is simplicity itself. We can simply select from the view as if nothing had happened:

```
SQL> select *
  2     from view_t;

   VIEW_ID VIEW_DATA
---------- --------------------
         1 ACB
```

When we issued the SELECT, Oracle automatically recompiled it. If you inspect USER_OBJECTS again, you'll see that our view is now valid. Alternatively, we could have also manually recompiled the view as follows:

```
SQL> alter view view_t compile;

View altered.
```

6. If we were now to actually drop the base table our view would again become invalid:

```
SQL> drop table t;

Table dropped.

SQL> select *
  2     from view_t;
 from view_t
      *
ERROR at line 2:
ORA-04063: view "HR.VIEW_T" has errors
```

The FORCE Option

We can use the FORCE option to make Oracle accept our view definition, regardless of whether or not it is valid. This actually allows us to create a view that is invalid! For example:

```
SQL> create view invalid_view as
  2     select *
  3        from table_that_does_not_exist;
   from table_that_does_not_exist
        *
ERROR at line 3:
ORA-00942: table or view does not exist


SQL> create force view invalid_view as
  2     select *
  3        from table_that_does_not_exist;

Warning: View created with compilation errors.
```

Oracle noted that the view had errors but did allow us to create it. But why would we want to do that? Well, consider a situation where the base tables were being created by data modeler A and the views were being created by data modeler B. Using the FORCE option, B would be able to compile all his views into the database, without being dependent on A. Or more likely, say we want to create a view on a table for which we currently do not have SELECT privileges, because it is defined in another schema. This feature allows us to create the view, and then when we are granted SELECT access, we are all set to go.

Updating and Deleting Through a View

Updating data through a view can be tricky. Whether or not we can update a view depends on how the view is constructed. If the view is like our COMPANY_PHONE_BOOK view, then most of the columns are updateable by default. We can ask the data dictionary which columns are and which columns are not updateable, using the USER_UPDATABLE_COLUMNS view:

```
SQL> desc user_updatable_columns
 Name                                              Null?    Type
 ------------------------------------------------- -------- ------------
 OWNER                                             NOT NULL VARCHAR2(30)
 TABLE_NAME                                        NOT NULL VARCHAR2(30)
 COLUMN_NAME                                       NOT NULL VARCHAR2(30)
 UPDATABLE                                                  VARCHAR2(3)
 INSERTABLE                                                 VARCHAR2(3)
 DELETABLE                                                  VARCHAR2(3)
```

The columns are fairly simple and straightforward. Each of the columns UPDATABLE, INSERTABLE, and DELETABLE will contain either a YES or NO value. If we look at our phone book view we will see the following:

```
SQL> select *
  2    from user_updatable_columns
  3   where table_name = 'COMPANY_PHONE_BOOK';

OWNER  TABLE_NAME          COLUMN_NAME   UPD INS DEL
------ ------------------- ------------- --- --- ---
HR     COMPANY_PHONE_BOOK  EMP_ID        YES YES YES
HR     COMPANY_PHONE_BOOK  NAME          NO  NO  NO
HR     COMPANY_PHONE_BOOK  PHONE_NUMBER  YES YES YES
HR     COMPANY_PHONE_BOOK  E-MAIL            YES YES YES
```

Just as you probably expected, all the view columns based directly on base table columns, with no changes, are fully updateable directly through this view, with nothing extra for the view author to do. The NAME column is not updateable because is it the result of joining two columns, FIRST_NAME and LAST_NAME. We cannot update virtual columns directly because the database does not know how to apply our changes:

```
SQL> update company_phone_book
  2    set e-mail = 'CLBECK'
  3   where emp_id = 100;
```

```
1 row updated.

SQL> update company_phone_book
  2     set name = 'Beck, Christopher'
  3   where emp_id = 100;
  set name = 'Beck, Christopher'
      *
ERROR at line 2:
ORA-01733: virtual column not allowed here
```

The USER_UPDATABLE_COLUMNS view does not lie! The NAME column is not updateable. However, what if we really do want to be able to update the NAME field through the view – after all, it would seem like fairly standard functionality for our view to provide. In order to do this, we need to make use of a special type of database **trigger**.

Updating a View Using an INSTEAD OF Trigger

A trigger is a precompiled program that is stored in the database and is invoked automatically in response to a specified event occurring on the table that the trigger 'protects'.

Full details on triggers will be given in Chapter 15.

When an INSTEAD OF trigger is fired, Oracle will perform the action defined in the trigger instead of (hence the name) the statement that triggered it. Let's create an INSTEAD OF trigger for our view so that we can update the name field:

```
SQL> create trigger update_name_company_phone_book
  2  INSTEAD OF
  3  update
  4  on company_phone_book
  5  begin
  6    update employees
  7       set employee_id = :new.emp_id,
  8           first_name = substr( :new.name, instr( :new.name, ',' )+2 ),
  9           last_name = substr( :new.name, 1, instr( :new.name, ',' )-1 ),
 10           phone_number = :new.phone_number,
 11           e-mail = :new.e-mail
 12     where employee_id = :old.emp_id;
 13* end;

Trigger created.
```

Now, our INSTEAD OF trigger handles the updating of the base table's columns properly:

```
SQL> select *
  2    from company_phone_book
  3   where emp_id = 100;

   EMP_ID NAME                 PHONE_NUMBER        E-MAIL
```

```
          100 King, Steven         515.123.4567        CLBECK

SQL> update company_phone_book
  2      set name = 'Beck, Christopher'
  3    where emp_id = 100;

1 row updated.

SQL> select *
  2      from company_phone_book
  3    where emp_id = 100;

    EMP_ID NAME                     PHONE_NUMBER         E-MAIL
---------- -------------------- -------------------- ------------------------
       100 Beck, Christopher    515.123.4567         CLBECK
```

It works just fine, and it works the same way for join views. In fact, INSTEAD OF triggers are often a necessity for updating views based on multiple tables, and can be very complex in many cases.

The WITH CHECK OPTION Constraint

Often, the author of a view will use the WITH CHECK OPTION constraint. With this constraint enabled, Oracle will only allow inserts and updates through the view if the data being inserted or updated can be selected using the view. Let's take a look at an example. First we create a view using this constraint. This view allows a user to view only those employees with DEPARTMENT_ID equal to 10:

```
SQL> create view department_10 as
  2      select *
  3        from employees
  4      where department_id = 10
  5      with check option;

View created.
```

We can select from the view and see that, in fact, only one employee is in department 10:

```
SQL> select employee_id, first_name, last_name
  2      from department_10;

EMPLOYEE_ID FIRST_NAME           LAST_NAME
----------- -------------------- ------------------------
        200 Jennifer             Whalen
```

According to the USER_UPDATABLE_COLUMNS view, all the columns are updateable:

```
SQL> select *
  2      from user_updatable_columns
  3    where table_name = 'DEPARTMENT_10';
```

```
OWNER    TABLE_NAME       COLUMN_NAME      UPD INS DEL
-------  ---------------  ---------------  --- --- ---
HR       DEPARTMENT_10    EMPLOYEE_ID      YES YES YES
HR       DEPARTMENT_10    FIRST_NAME       YES YES YES
HR       DEPARTMENT_10    LAST_NAME        YES YES YES
HR       DEPARTMENT_10    E-MAIL               YES YES YES
HR       DEPARTMENT_10    PHONE_NUMBER     YES YES YES
HR       DEPARTMENT_10    HIRE_DATE        YES YES YES
HR       DEPARTMENT_10    JOB_ID           YES YES YES
HR       DEPARTMENT_10    SALARY               YES YES YES
HR       DEPARTMENT_10    COMMISSION_PCT   YES YES YES
HR       DEPARTMENT_10    MANAGER_ID       YES YES YES
HR       DEPARTMENT_10    DEPARTMENT_ID    YES YES YES

11 rows selected.
```

Now let's try and move Jennifer Whalen to department 20:

```
SQL> update department_10
  2 set department_id = 20
  3 where employee_id = 200;
update department_10
       *
ERROR at line 1:
ORA-01402: view WITH CHECK OPTION where-clause violation
```

The WITH CHECK OPTION has prevented us from modifying data that is not accessible through the view. In essence, the update command is attempting to modify data associated with department 20. However, the whole point of the view was to restrict our access to only those employees in department 10. It would work in the same way if we attempted to insert a new employee into any department other than department 10. It would fail. The WITH CHECK OPTION ensures both data security and data integrity by forbidding users from affecting data they do not have access to.

Views and Performance

Remember, relational views are just queries, and as a result must be parsed and executed when you SELECT from them. Their efficiency is dependent upon well-structured queries as well as good use of both reused SQL (thereby avoiding hard parsing, as we discussed in Chapter 6) and indexes. This is important to bear in mind when you wish to join an existing view to a table. Problems arise when Oracle is unable to simply merge the additional table into the view's query for the purposes of execution. This means that it must materialize the view (physically generate the entire result set for the view and then join that to the additional table), which may well reduce performance in comparison to the original view. It all depends on the question being asked.

Whenever possible, Oracle will attempt to merge your query with the view to form a single query. If we issue the following query against our view DEPARTMENT_10:

```
SQL> select employee_id, last_name, first_name, salary
  2     from department_10
  3   where manager_id = 101;
```

EMPLOYEE_ID	LAST_NAME	FIRST_NAME	SALARY
200	Whalen	Jennifer	4400

Oracle will transform that query into:

```
select employee_id, last_name, first_name, salary
  from employees
 where department_id = 10
   and manager_id = 101;
```

Oracle will do this so that it can take advantage of any indexes on the base tables. So, it is important to know the structure of the views and the base tables if you are writing optimized SQL. This rewriting of your query is completely transparent to the user and the application though. It happens as part of Oracle's SQL optimizer. There is nothing that the view author needs to do in order to allow Oracle to use the indexes, other than write well-formed and well thought out SQL.

Inline Views

Since version 7.1 (documented in version 7.2), Oracle has supported the feature of **inline views**. Inline views are not schema objects. An inline view is essentially a query that is embedded in a parent query and can be used anywhere that a `table_name` can be used. An inline view may appear in the FROM clause of a SELECT statement, as well as in INSERT INTO, UPDATE, and even DELETE FROM statements. An inline view is transitory – it only exists for the lifetime of the parent query, but it gives the developer the ability to use the results of the view in any part of the whole query. The best thing to do is to demonstrate this with an example.

Try It Out – Creating an Inline View

Here, our inline view will be a SELECT query that is embedded directly into the FROM clause of a parent SELECT query. We'll give the inline view an alias and use that name to refer to the view from the parent query.

In this example, the budgeting department is preparing a report that gives a breakdown on the number of people employed in each department. The percentage distribution may be used to calculate the stationery budget for each department. We can achieve this as follows:

```
SQL> select department_name, count(*),
  2         to_char( (count(*)/total_emp.cnt)*100, '90.99' ) || '%' pct
  3    from departments,
  4         employees,
  5         ( select count(*) cnt
  6             from employees ) total_emp
  7   where departments.department_id = employees.department_id
  8   group by department_name, total_emp.cnt
  9  /
```

```
DEPARTMENT_NAME          COUNT(*) PCT
-------------------- ---------- -------
Accounting                    2   1.87%
Administration                1   0.93%
Executive                     3   2.80%
Finance                       6   5.61%
Human Resources               1   0.93%
IT                            5   4.67%
Marketing                     2   1.87%
Public Relations              1   0.93%
Purchasing                    6   5.61%
Sales                        34  31.78%
Shipping                     45  42.06%

11 rows selected.
```

Our query lists the departments, the number of employees in each department and the percentage of the workforce that this number represents.

How It Works

In order to calculate the percentage of the workforce employed by each department, we need two pieces of information. Firstly, a count of the total number of employees, which we can obtain as follows:

```
select count(*) from employees;
```

Secondly, we need a count of the number of employees in each department:

```
select department_name, count(*)
from departments, employees,
where departments.department_id = employees.department_id
group by department_name
```

We create an inline view that calculates the total number of employees. We give the inline view a correlation name, or **alias**, of TOTAL_EMP so that we can refer to the calculated value and use it elsewhere in the query:

```
5          ( select count(*) cnt
6              from employees ) total_emp
```

We embed our inline view in the FROM clause of a parent query that calculates the number of employees in each department. With this value, we use TOTAL_EMP.CNT as the denominator to calculate the percentage of employees in each department:

```
SQL> select department_name, count(*),
  2          to_char ( (count(*)/total_emp.cnt)*100, '90.99' ) || '%' pct
  3      from departments,
  4          employees,
  5          ( select count(*) cnt
  6              from employees ) total_emp
```

Thus we obtain our answer with a single query. An alternative solution would be to create the TOTAL_EMP view as an actual schema object (a normal relational view) and then issue a query joining that view with the DEPARTMENTS and EMPLOYEES tables. There may be occasions where this approach would be beneficial (perhaps if the inline view were a complex query). However, if the view is specific to the needs of this one query then it would be cumbersome to create a relational view for just this one query. It's much easier and cleaner in this case to use an inline view. If you find yourself using the same inline view over and over again, then it would make sense to create a relational view instead.

Analytical functions are another option for solving questions like the one above. See Chapter 17 for more information.

Let's take a look at a second example of a situation where inline views are very useful.

Try It Out – Top 5

1. Say we want to answer the following question: 'Who were the first five employees hired by the company?' Well, it is easy enough to get an employee listing in order of hire date:

```
SQL> select last_name, hire_date
  2    from employees
  3    order by hire_date;

LAST_NAME                     HIRE_DATE
------------------------- ---------
King                          17-JUN-87
Whalen                        17-SEP-87
Kochhar                       21-SEP-89
Hunold                        03-JAN-90
Ernst                         21-MAY-91
    .                             .
    .                             .
    .                             .
Ande                          24-MAR-00
Banda                         21-APR-00
Kumar                         21-APR-00

107 rows selected.
```

2. So if we want a query that returns just the first five employees hired, I'm sure you are thinking that we can just use the ROWNUM pseudo-column to restrict the number of rows returned to five. Let's give it a try:

```
SQL> select last_name, hire_date
  2    from employees
  3    where rownum < 6
  4    order by hire_date;

LAST_NAME                     HIRE_DATE
------------------------- ---------
King                          17-JUN-87
Kochhar                       21-SEP-89
Hunold                        03-JAN-90
Ernst                         21-MAY-91
De Haan                       13-JAN-93
```

Almost the correct answer, but if you look at the results above, you will see that Whalen is missing and De Haan should not be listed. Now, if you run this exact same query on your 9*i* database, you might well get different results. Sounds like Oracle has a bug, doesn't it? Actually, it is working just fine. To understand why, you have to understand how Oracle applies the row number to the result. The ROWNUM pseudo-column returns a number that simply reflects the order in which the rows are selected from the underlying tables. The first row selected will have a ROWNUM value of 1, and so on. However, that row number is assigned to each selected row *before* the ORDER BY clause is applied.

3. In order to get the right answer, we need to force the ordering to occur before the ROWNUM is assigned. Sounds like a perfect place to use an inline view:

```
SQL> select last_name, hire_date
  2    from ( select last_name, hire_date
  3             from employees
  4             order by hire_date )
  5   where rownum <= 5;

LAST_NAME                 HIRE_DATE
------------------------- ---------
King                      17-JUN-87
Whalen                    17-SEP-87
Kochhar                   21-SEP-89
Hunold                    03-JAN-90
Ernst                     21-MAY-91
```

The inline view orders the EMPLOYEES table by the HIRE_DATE. Then, using that ordered result set, we apply the ROWNUM constraint and get the first five people hired.

There is one caveat to mention. In our example above, if there were two employees hired on 21-MAY-91 and the HIRE_DATE column only had precision to the day (in other words, no time component) then Oracle would randomly give you back just one of those two employees. It is not a bug with Oracle; it is a problem with the question that we asked. As long as you realize this and understand what Oracle will do in such cases, then you will be fine. We will see how to overcome this issue using analytic functions in Chapter 17.

Object Views

Oracle is an object-relational database. Not only can you store data in relational table, but you can also store it in objects. With Oracle 8, Oracle introduced the concept of object types and object-oriented technology to its traditional relational database. Back in 1997, when Oracle 8 was announced, Java was becoming the language of the internet; CORBA, RMI, and DCOM were fighting the distributed object war; and object databases were gaining ground on Oracle, which did not support object-oriented functionality in its database product. With Oracle 8, Oracle merged the two concepts to allow a developer to create an object type, create an object of that type, and store that object instance in a database table.

Oracle's object-relational technology is, as the name suggests, an object "layer" built on top of the relational structures. Underneath the object layer, the data is stored in relational tables but Oracle allows us to encapsulate this data in an **object type** – basically a user-defined, composite data type that allows the developer to accurately model real-world entities. So, instead of thinking of selecting data from the appropriate columns of an EMPLOYEES table, for information on a particular employee, we can instead think of selecting an individual customer, modeled by an object stored in the database. In addition we can start to take advantage of special object-oriented features associated with these object types – but we will discuss that in more detail in Chapter 16. So, for example, we can define a CUSTOMER object type, in the following manner:

```
CREATE TYPE Customer is OBJECT (
    name        VARCHAR2(30),
    e-mail      VARCHAR2(20) );
```

Now we have our object type, we can store it in an object table for customer objects:

```
CREATE TABLE Customer_Table OF Customer;
```

However, what if you already have your application built, you only used relational tables in your schema, and now you would like to take advantage of the object-relational features of Oracle without having to redesign your schema and rebuild your application? Well there is a solution: **object views**.

We can create object views based on our object types and we can then query and modify our data through these views just as normal. Let's see it in action.

Try It Out – Creating an Object View

1. In this example, we shall create a new object type in the database and then create an object view based on that type. In order to create a new type, the user must have the CREATE TYPE privilege granted to them:

```
SQL> create type employee_type is object(
  2          employee_id number,
  3          name varchar2(47),
  4          e-mail varchar2(25),
  5          phone_number varchar2(20)
  6  );
  7  /
Type created.

SQL> create view ov_company_phone_book
  2      of employee_type
  3      with object oid ( employee_id ) as
  4        select e.employee_id,
  5              e.last_name || ', ' || e.first_name,
  6              e.e-mail,
  7              e.phone_number
  8         from employees e
  9  /

View created.
```

2. Let's take a look at our new object view:

```
SQL> desc ov_company_phone_book
 Name                                       Null?    Type
 ------------------------------------------ -------- -------------------------

 EMPLOYEE_ID                                         NUMBER
 NAME                                                VARCHAR2(47)
 E-MAIL                                              VARCHAR2(25)
 PHONE_NUMBER                                        VARCHAR2(20)
```

How It Works

We created a type, EMPLOYEE_TYPE, and then created an object view, OV_COMPANY_PHONE_BOOK, based on that type. The two key lines of the CREATE VIEW syntax, which are different from anything you've seen with relational views, are as follows:

```
2     of employee_type
```

This tells us that our view will return objects of type EMPLOYEE_TYPE. On the next line we have:

```
3     with object oid ( employee_id ) as
```

This line specifies an object identifier for our object view. You can consider it to be similar to the primary key of the object type within the view and we specify EMPLOYEE_ID since that is the primary key field in the underlying data, so it will be a unique value for each "row" in the object view. If we do not supply a WITH OBJECT OID clause, Oracle will use the object identifier from the original table or object view on which our object view is based. Once we have defined an OID, we can make use of an Oracle built-in data type called a REF that will allow us to refer to our object and perform actions on it (see Chapter 16 for full details on the REF data type).

The rules for updating object views are the same as those for relational views. If Oracle can determine what and how to update the data, it will. Otherwise, the developer will need to supply an INSTEAD OF trigger, just as we did in the relational examples earlier.

As you will recall from our relational examples, Oracle stores all view definitions in its data dictionary, accessible through the USER_VIEWS view. Earlier, we concentrated on the text field, which shows us the query that defines the view. We noted then that there are many more columns in the USER_VIEWS table and some of these columns have meaning for object views. Let's take a look:

```
SQL> select VIEW_TYPE_OWNER, VIEW_TYPE, OID_TEXT
  2    from user_views
  3   where view_name = 'OV_COMPANY_PHONE_BOOK'
  4  /

VIEW_TYPE_OWNER    VIEW_TYPE          OID_TEXT
-----------------  ---------------    -----------
HR                 EMPLOYEE_TYPE      employee_id
```

Since the columns VIEW_TYPE_OWNER, VIEW_TYPE, and OID_TEXT have values, we know from this view definition that this view must be an object view. This tells us the view named OV_COMPANY_PHONE_BOOK will return a type of HR.EMPLOYEE_TYPE and that the REF for this view is employee_id. This information, plus the actual text of the view, stored in the USER_VIEWS view, is enough to recreate the CREATE VIEW command.

Benefits of Object Views

I'm sure you are asking yourself, 'Why would I want to create this view as an object view when we already have a COMPANY_PHONE_BOOK view?' There are a few reasons why you might want to do this.

The first and most obvious reason is that you just want to learn about object views. You can create this view and try out different things with no impact on your existing application, unless of course you begin to update through this view, which might cause unwanted changes in your application. And once you become comfortable with object views, you can slowly migrate your relational data model over to an object-relational model without having to change the underlying storage of the data.

Secondly, object views can often lead to better performance. This is because the relational data is packaged up by Oracle into objects and these objects are sent over the network as a single unit. If an object contains data from multiple relational tables, you could possibly save many network round trips retrieving all the data. Consider a department object that contains a VARRAY of employee objects (see Chapter 10). With a single call, you will get the department data, as well as all of the employees' data that belongs to that department, in a single object.

Thirdly, using object views could let you retrieve your data into a client-side cache. Then, your 3GL application could make use of the data natively, once it was mapped into the programming languages' native structures. For example, you could fetch data from an object view into a C program's cache, and then reference that object just as if it was a C structure. When changes are made you can use the OCI (Oracle Call Interface for C) API to push the object's value back to the database server. Oracle will then perform the update through the object view. It will either natively update the underlying data, or if you have set it up so, run the INSTEAD OF trigger on the object view.

Materialized Views

The last type of view that we will discuss is the **materialized view**. Readers familiar with previous versions of Oracle might know these objects by their old name, the **snapshot**. Since Oracle 8*i*, they have been renamed to materialized views while being enhanced to support query rewrite, refresh on commit, and other features that we will explore in a moment. These views are used for a variety of tasks and in a variety of environments, from data warehouses to distributed and mobile computing.

Basically, a materialized view is the result of a query stored in the database. Unlike a relational view, whose results are determined at run-time, the results of a materialized view are precomputed and stored. Since the results are stored, materialized views take up space, but do not let that deter you from using them. They can dramatically enhance the performance of your application when you are querying very large amounts of data. In this respect you can compare them to indexes, which also take up space but which we all use to increase performance.

Using materialized views properly can make for much faster query results. Consider a data warehouse application where there are millions upon millions of records and you ask questions about the sums and averages of that data. If every time you issued a query, Oracle had to derive that information, it might have to full scan the table, meaning that it would have to visit each and every row of the table to add up the sum or calculate the average. This could take a long time. With materialized views, you have Oracle precompute the aggregate results and store them in a special summary table. The next time you issue the query, the result will be retrieved from that summary table.

Materialized views are an advanced feature so we will only scratch the surface of this topic here. However, this section will give you a good feel for the power of this feature. For a more in-depth analysis, see Tom Kyte's Expert One-on-One Oracle (Apress, 1590592433).

Let's look at how to create and use one in a data warehouse scenario. First, we need to create a large table on which to base our materialized view. Let's use a table with the structure of the ORDERS table in the OE schema in Oracle 9*i*. That table looks like this:

```
SQL> desc orders
 Name                            Null?    Type
 ------------------------------- -------- ----------------------------

 ORDER_ID                        NOT NULL NUMBER(12)
 ORDER_DATE                      NOT NULL TIMESTAMP(6) WITH LOCAL TIME ZONE
 ORDER_MODE                               VARCHAR2(8)
 CUSTOMER_ID                     NOT NULL NUMBER(6)
 ORDER_STATUS                             NUMBER(2)
 ORDER_TOTAL                              NUMBER(8,2)
 SALES_REP_ID                             NUMBER(6)
 PROMOTION_ID                             NUMBER(6)

SQL> select count(*)
  2    from orders;

  COUNT(*)
----------
       105
```

There are not that many rows in this table so let's make a new ORDERS table with many more rows:

```
SQL> create table my_orders as
  2    select *
  3      from orders;

Table created.

SQL> insert into my_orders
  2    select *
  3      from my_orders;

105 rows created.
```

```
SQL> /

210 rows created.

SQL> /

420 rows created.

SQL> /

840 rows created.

SQL> /

1680 rows created.

SQL> /

3360 rows created.

SQL> /

6720 rows created.

SQL> /

13440 rows created.

SQL> /

26880 rows created.

SQL> /

53760 rows created.

SQL> select count(*)
  2     from my_orders;

  COUNT(*)
----------
    107520
```

OK, now we have a reasonably large table and we want to run some summary queries on the data. We want to ask the question, 'How many orders has each customer made?' This is a pretty straightforward question, but the database has to do a lot of work to answer it:

In order to see the performance statistics in our examples, you will need to configure the AUTOTRACE facility and create and grant the PLUSTRACE role. This process is described in Chapter 18. So, you can either skip forward and set this up or simply examine the data given here, since it is really the concepts that are important rather than the actual figures.

```
SQL> set autotrace on
SQL> set timing on
SQL> select customer_id,
  2         count(*) total_orders
  3     from my_orders
  4     group by customer_id
  5   /

CUSTOMER_ID TOTAL_ORDERS
----------- ------------
        101         4096
        102         4096
        103         4096
          .            .
          .            .
          .            .
        168         1024
        169         1024
        170         1024

47 rows selected.

Elapsed: 00:00:00.01

Execution Plan
----------------------------------------------------------
   0      SELECT STATEMENT Optimizer=CHOOSE
   1    0   SORT (GROUP BY)
   2    1     TABLE ACCESS (FULL) OF 'MY_ORDERS'

Statistics
----------------------------------------------------------
          0  recursive calls
          5  db block gets
       1294  consistent gets
        465  physical reads
          0  redo size
       3391  bytes sent via SQL*Net to client
       1066  bytes received via SQL*Net from client
          7  SQL*Net roundtrips to/from client
          2  sorts (memory)
          0  sorts (disk)
         47  rows processed
```

It took 1294 consistent gets to calculate the result, and we only have 107,000 records. That is high. Imagine a real data warehouse with millions and millions of records. That query could take some time to satisfy. Enter materialized views. With this feature, we can precompute or materialize the answer and select it much more easily. Even better, once we have created our materialized view, Oracle will maintain it as we add more data. Let's make one for the query above. The materialized view owner will need the database privilege CREATE MATERIALIZED VIEW granted to them (or to a role to which he or she has access). Also, they will need the QUERY REWRITE privilege and this must be granted directly (not via a role).

Try It Out – Creating a Materialized View

Here is the code to create our materialized view, MY_ORDERS_MV:

```
SQL> set timing off
SQL> create materialized view my_orders_mv
  2    build immediate
  3  refresh on commit
  4   enable query rewrite
  5  as
  6    select customer_id,
  7           count(*) total_orders
  8      from my_orders
  9     group by customer_id
 10  /

Materialized view created.

SQL> set timing on
SQL> select *
  2    from my_orders_mv;

CUSTOMER_ID TOTAL_ORDERS
----------- ------------
        101         4096
        102         4096
        103         4096
          .            .
          .            .
          .            .
        168         1024
        169         1024
        170         1024

47 rows selected.

Elapsed: 00:00:00.01

Execution Plan
----------------------------------------------------------
   0      SELECT STATEMENT Optimizer=CHOOSE
   1    0   TABLE ACCESS (FULL) OF 'MY_ORDERS_MV'

Statistics
----------------------------------------------------------
          0  recursive calls
          6  db block gets
          7  consistent gets
          0  physical reads
          0  redo size
       3393  bytes sent via SQL*Net to client
       1004  bytes received via SQL*Net from client
          7  SQL*Net roundtrips to/from client
          1  sorts (memory)
          0  sorts (disk)
         47  rows processed
```

From 1294 consistent gets to just 12 – that is not a bad saving. There is no real change in the timing – 107,000 rows may seem like a lot, but to Oracle it really isn't very many (it's a powerful database!). However, if there were millions of rows then you really would see a performance enhancement from using the view.

How It Works

What we did first was to turn the timing off, since we switched it on for the previous example. Next, we created the MY_ORDERS_MV materialized view. The options specified in the compilation will be explored in a moment but, for the time being, all you need to know is that this materialized view basically consists of the following query:

```
6    select customer_id,
7           count(*) total_orders
8      from my_orders
9     group by customer_id
```

Then, we set the timing back on and selected the contents of the materialized view to demonstrate the speed increase.

Immediate Population

Perhaps you're thinking that we could simply have built our own summary table, based on the above query. Well sure, but notice some of the options that were included in the CREATE MATERIALIZED VIEW statement:

```
2    build immediate
```

This tells Oracle to populate the materialized view right now. An alternative option is **build deferred**, which will populate the view later. Why would you ever want to do that? Well, imagine we know that it is a very system-intensive act to populate our materialized view. We do not want to tax the system at peak usage times but we do want to continue to develop using our new materialized view. We create the materialized view now so that other database objects can reference it and be compiled properly. However, we defer the population to a time when we know the database and the system will be idle. It is very similar to creating a table and leaving it empty. We can select from it, reference it in procedures and functions, and build views against it even though it is empty. Then, we load the data later, when the system is idle.

Auto Population

The following line is where the power of the materialized view really starts to become apparent:

```
3    refresh on commit
```

This tells Oracle to keep this materialized view up to date when the base table changes and the work is committed. Let's see that in action:

```
SQL> set timing off
SQL> select count(*)
  2      from my_orders_mv;

  COUNT(*)
----------
        47

SQL> insert into my_orders (
  2      order_date,
  3      customer_id,
  4      order_total )
  5  values (
  6      sysdate,
  7      123456,
  8      '100.00' );

1 row created.

SQL> commit;

Commit complete.

SQL> select count(*)
  2      from my_orders_mv;

  COUNT(*)
----------
        48
```

As you can see, our materialized view initially had 47 rows in it, representing the 47 distinct customers. We inserted a new row into the base table, MY_ORDERS, with a CUSTOMER_ID that we knew did not already exist, and Oracle automatically updated our materialized view. If we were going maintain our own simple summary in this manner, we would have to build INSERT, UPDATE, and DELETE triggers on the base table. Just think of all the extra code that you would have to write, test, and maintain (not to mention the high probability of producing serialization and deadlocks). With materialized views, Oracle will do it all for you.

Now there is a trade-off here. Since the materialized view will be rebuilt whenever changes to the base table are committed, the commit will take more time than usual (if you have millions of rows, then the commit time will be very much longer). However, if you are only inserting occasionally but querying all the time, the extra time spent on the commit will be negligible compared to the amount of time saved for the many queries. In general though, use of materialized views in this fashion is actually best suited to read-intensive systems. It can have adverse effects in OLTP systems because the process of keeping the materialized view in sync on every commit could put undue overhead on the system and decrease concurrency on certain operations. Consider that our view has 47 rows. Updating a row in the view, in order to keep the view in sync with the base table, will involve locking one of those 47 rows. So we can have a maximum of 47 people committing changes at any one time. As such, in OLTP systems it is common to refresh the views during off-peak times (by specifying REFRESH ON DEMAND).

Query Rewrite

Let's say that once you have deployed your application, you realize that it would benefit from a materialized view, but you cannot change the application. Well you don't need to change the queries in your application to make it use a materialized view. That is what the following line is all about:

```
4    enable query rewrite
```

If the conditions are right, this option allows Oracle to automatically rewrite our query to use the materialized view. Let's see this in action. Remember the initial query against the base table MY_ORDERS:

```
SQL> set autotrace on
SQL> set timing on
SQL> select customer_id,
  2         count(*) total_orders
  3   from my_orders
  4   group by customer_id;

CUSTOMER_ID TOTAL_ORDERS
----------- ------------
        101         4096
        102         4096
        103         4096
          .            .
          .            .
          .            .
        168         1024
        169         1024
        170         1024
     123456            1

48 rows selected.

Elapsed: 00:00:01.23

Execution Plan
----------------------------------------------------------
   0      SELECT STATEMENT Optimizer=CHOOSE (Cost=529 Card=47 Bytes=141)
   1    0   SORT (GROUP BY) (Cost=529 Card=47 Bytes=141)
   2    1     TABLE ACCESS (FULL) OF 'MY_ORDERS' (Cost=311 Card=107520
Bytes=322560)
```

Using the AUTOTRACE facility, we can see that we do a full table scan on MY_ORDERS. This is a pretty costly procedure if we are doing it over and over again. If we enable QUERY REWRITE then Oracle will determine that our query can be satisfied by the materialized view MY_ORDERS_MV and use that instead. It will still have to full scan it, but there are only 48 rows, not 100,000.

```
SQL> alter session set query_rewrite_enabled=true;

Session altered.

SQL> select customer_id,
  2         count(*) total_orders
```

575

```
  3    from my_orders
  4    group by customer_id;

CUSTOMER_ID TOTAL_ORDERS
----------- ------------
        101         4096
        102         4096
        103         4096
          .            .
          .            .
          .            .
        168         1024
        169         1024
        170         1024
     123456            1

48 rows selected.

Elapsed: 00:00:00.57

Execution Plan
----------------------------------------------------------
   0      SELECT STATEMENT Optimizer=CHOOSE (Cost=1 Card=41 Bytes=1066)
   1    0   TABLE ACCESS (FULL) OF 'MY_ORDERS_MV' (Cost=1 Card=41 Bytes=1066)
```

You can see that, even though we queried against the MY_ORDERS table, Oracle used the
MY_ORDERS_MV materialized view to answer our question. Also, the query does not need to match the
materialized view query exactly in order for Oracle to use the view to answer it:

```
SQL> set autotrace off
SQL> select count(*)
  2    from my_orders;

  COUNT(*)
----------
    107520

Elapsed: 00:00:00.57

Execution Plan
----------------------------------------------------------
   0      SELECT STATEMENT Optimizer=CHOOSE (Cost=1 Card=1 Bytes=13)
   1    0   SORT (AGGREGATE)
   2    1     TABLE ACCESS (FULL) OF 'MY_ORDERS_MV' (Cost=1 Card=41 Bytes=533)
```

Oracle still used the materialized view instead of the base table because it determined that it could
answer the question with MY_ORDER_MV.

We hope this clearly demonstrates how your existing application can take advantage of this feature. All
you need to do is identify where a materialized view might help increase performance, create it, and
your applications will just start using it under the covers.

It is recommended that you always allow Oracle to rewrite your queries instead of selecting directly
from the materialized view because then you have the ability to modify and enhance the materialized
view, without requiring the applications to change. If the materialized view is removed, the application
would still run. It would be slower, but it would still run.

Summary

In this chapter we discussed views. We saw that there are many different objects in Oracle that are called views and they each behave a little differently and serve a different purpose. Relational views help the view author hide the complexities of querying the data and can also be used to hide both columns and rows. Inline views are a convenient way for developers to take advantage of views without needing to create them ahead of time. Object views give the developers the ability to package up relational data into a single object. Materialized views increase the performance of queries by pre-computing summary data and using it whenever it can to satisfy queries against the base tables. Armed with the knowledge of these objects and their proper usage, an application developer and data modeler can greatly increase performance and simplify the development process.

Triggers

Triggers are blocks of code that execute, or fire, automatically when certain events happen. Although triggers are very much like other procedures in the database, the user cannot call them directly. Oracle handles the execution of the appropriate trigger or triggers when the event requires it. The user is given no indication that Oracle is executing triggers, unless of course the trigger causes an error that the developer has not handled properly. In that case the event that caused the trigger to fire will fail.

Triggers are used to enhance the default functionality of Oracle in order to provide a highly customizable database. Some of the functions that a trigger can perform are:

- ❑ Allow/restrict modification to a table
- ❑ Automatically generate derived columns
- ❑ Enforce data integrity
- ❑ Provide auditing and logging
- ❑ Prevent an invalid transaction
- ❑ Enable complex business logic

Triggers are useful in that they execute irrespective of the user performing the action. It is true that you can code a trigger that only does something if user A, B, or C is the user who caused the trigger to fire, but the trigger will fire for everyone who performs that action. There is no way to circumvent a trigger. This is necessary if you are to rely on triggers to enforce your business logic. Consider an EMPLOYEE table that is used by both the Human Resources and Payroll applications. A trigger could be placed on that table to ensure that the data inserted into it was properly formatted. Otherwise it would be up to each application to maintain that logic, and any changes would need to be made in both places. With triggers, this business logic is stored in the database in one place and all users are guaranteed to use it.

Triggers can be written in PL/SQL or Java and stored in the database, or they can be written in C, as a database callout. In this chapter we will explore triggers written in PL/SQL. We will learn when and when not to use them. We will learn about the different types of trigger and how to create each of them. By the end of this chapter, you should have a clear understanding of what triggers are and why you should use them.

Getting Started

Here is an example of a trigger that I have created on the EMPLOYEES table in the sample HR schema in my Oracle 9*i* database:

```
SQL> create trigger biufer_employees_department_id
  2    before insert or update
  3        of department_id
  4        on employees
  5    referencing old as old_value
  6                new as new_value
  7    for each row
  8      when ( new_value.department_id <> 80 )
  9  begin
 10    :new_value.commission_pct := 0;
 11  end;
 12  /

Trigger created.
```

There is quite a lot going on in this trigger so let's break it down into its pieces. We'll start with the different parts of the trigger.

Parts of a Trigger

When you define a trigger, there are four main parts:

❏   Trigger Name

❏   Triggering Statement

❏   Trigger Restriction

❏   Triggered Action

Trigger Name

The **trigger name** is just that; the name of the trigger. Every object in the database has a name and this object is no different. From the example above, you can see that my trigger is named BIUFER_EMPLOYEES_DEPARTMENT_ID:

```
SQL> create trigger biufer_employees_department_id
```

This name probably seems a little strange. It is a naming convention that I try and use. You can name your triggers anything you want as long as it is unique within the set of triggers that you own and follows the naming rules for all objects in an Oracle database. I try and put as much information into the name of the trigger, so that when I query the data dictionary to see which triggers are present, I get an indication of what kind of triggers they are. My naming convention is as follows:

- ❑ BIUFER – Stands for **b**efore **i**nsert or **u**pdate **f**or **e**ach **r**ow. This tells me what kind of trigger it is, and when it fires. If this were an **a**fter **d**elete **f**or **e**ach **r**ow trigger, then my trigger's name would start with ADFER_.

- ❑ EMPLOYEES – Stands for the EMPLOYEES table. This tells me which table this trigger is on.

- ❑ DEPARTMENT_ID – Stands for the column DEPARTMENT_ID. This indicates to me that the trigger is contingent on that column's values. Since it is not necessary for a trigger to be dependent on a column, you might not use this part of the naming convention.

Everyone has their own way of naming objects. I would suggest that you use this one or something similar to help you when you look back at your application in six months or a year from now and try to determine which triggers do what.

Triggering Statement

The **triggering statement** is the event that will cause Oracle to execute the trigger. This event can be one or more of the following:

- ❑ Data Manipulation Language statements (INSERT, UPDATE, or DELETE) on tables and some views

- ❑ Data Definition Language statements (CREATE, ALTER, or DROP) on any schema objects

- ❑ Startup and shutdown of the database

- ❑ System errors

- ❑ Various system actions

In our example trigger above, lines 2 through 7 form the triggering statement:

```
2     before insert or update
3         of department_id
4         on employees
5     referencing old as old_value
6                 new as new_value
7     for each row
```

This says that the event, which will cause this trigger to be implicitly fired by Oracle, occurs whenever there is:

- ❑ An INSERT into the EMPLOYEES table, regardless of whether department_id is specified or not

- ❑ An UPDATE to the DEPARTMENT_ID column of the EMPLOYEES table

That does not mean that the body of the trigger will be executed, it just means that Oracle will consider doing it, based on the trigger restriction.

Trigger Restriction

Even though the event causing a trigger to fire has occurred, this does not necessarily mean that Oracle will execute it. Oracle will first determine if there are any restrictions on the trigger, as the WHEN clause is not mandatory, and then evaluate any restriction before executing the trigger. In our example above, the restriction is:

```
8      when ( new_value.department_id <> 80 )
```

This says that if the new value of the column department_id is not equal to 80, the trigger should be executed. Any Boolean expression can be used in the WHEN clause. You can access full BEFORE and AFTER images of the row in DML triggers. On an update we have access to what the row was before the update, OLD_VALUE, and what the row will be after the insert is complete, NEW_VALUE.

Triggered Action

The **triggered action** is the body of the trigger. Oracle will execute this block when the following two things occur:

- ❑ The correct statement is issued

- ❑ The trigger restriction, if present, evaluates to true

In our example the triggered action is:

```
 9  begin
10     :new_value.commission_pct := 0;
11  end;
```

This is pretty straightforward. It says set the new value of the column commission_pct to be 0.

Think about that for a second though. You issue an INSERT to the table EMPLOYEES and you set the DEPARTMENT_ID = 60 and the COMMISSION_PCT = 25, along with the other required fields. Then you go and select the row you just created and the commission_pct is zero! That could be confusing since Oracle does not tell you that it has changed your input values, it just does it. Let's see that in action:

```
SQL> insert into employees(
  2    employee_id, last_name, first_name, hire_date, job_id,
  3    email, department_id, salary, commission_pct )
  4  values (
  5    12345, 'Beck', 'Christopher', '20-MAY-1995', 'TECH',
  6*   'clbeck@us.oracle.com', 60, 10000, .25 );

1 row created.

SQL> select commission_pct
  2    from employees
  3    where employee_id = 12345;

COMMISSION_PCT
```

```
              --------------
                         0

   1 row selected.
```

There you go: we set the COMMISSION_PCT to 25 and inserted it, but the trigger fired because DEPARTMENT_ID was not equal to 80 and it changed our COMMISSION_PCT value to 0. We could update the commission_pct but as long as the trigger is enabled and the DEPARTMENT_ID is not equal to 80, Oracle will fire the trigger and override the value we input or updated. This is a great way to enforce business rules in your applications or to support derived values or complex default values that are not easily defaulted using the DEFAULT clause of the CREATE TABLE command.

Types of Triggers

Oracle has different types of triggers to enable the developer to accomplish a variety of tasks. These trigger types include:

- ❏ Statement triggers
- ❏ Row triggers
- ❏ INSTEAD OF triggers
- ❏ System event triggers
- ❏ User event triggers

Let's take a look at each trigger type in turn, see how they work, and investigate how we can use them effectively.

Statement Triggers

Statement triggers are triggers on a particular statement or statements that act on a table or in some cases, a view. Statement triggers can be attached to INSERT, UPDATE, or DELETE statements, or any combination of those statements, so you can have a single trigger on INSERT or UPDATE of a table, or a trigger on the INSERT and DELETE of a table. You can even have multiple INSERT statement triggers on a single table. It does not matter what combination you have, each statement trigger fires just once for that given statement. It does not matter how many rows an UPDATE statement affects, an UPDATE statement trigger will just be called once. If there are multiple UPDATE statement triggers on a table, then each of them will be called once but just one time each and in no particular order. Be careful to keep that fact in mind when coding your triggers.

> If there are two of the same type of trigger on a particular table, there are no guarantees to the order in which they will fire.

Creating a Statement Trigger

You might want to create an INSERT, UPDATE,or DELETE statement trigger on a table that does a security check to verify that the user attempting the operation has the appropriate privileges according to the business rules of your application. A simple trigger of this type might look like the following:

```
SQL> create table foo( a number );

Table created.

SQL> create trigger biud_foo
  2     before insert or update or delete
  3         on foo
  4  begin
  5    if user not in ( 'CLBECK', 'SDILLON' ) then
  6      raise_application_error( -20001,
  7          'You do not have access to modify this table.' );
  8    end if;
  9  end;
 10  /

Trigger created.
```

What this trigger does is raise an error if the user attempting to modify the table FOO is neither CLBECK nor SDILLON. Of course you could have just granted INSERT, UPDATE, and DELETE exclusively to those two users, but that does not stop users with the database privilege UPDATE ANY TABLE from modifying the table. This demonstrates the usefulness of this approach. Also, the former approach would not stop those who gain privileges to the table FOO surreptitiously. This trigger ensures that only the users CLBECK and SDILLON can modify FOO. Even privileged users like SYS and SYSTEM will not be able to modify our FOO table while our trigger is active.

Determining Errors During Creation

If you attempt to create a trigger and you get a syntax error, you will see the following warning:

```
SQL> create trigger bi_foo
  2     before insert
  3         on foo
  4  begin
  5    null  -- missing ";"
  6  end;
  7  /

Warning: Trigger created with compilation errors.
```

This tells us that the trigger had a syntax error. Issuing a SHOW ERRORS from SQL*PLUS will do just that – show us the errors:

```
SQL> show errors
Errors for TRIGGER BI_FOO:
```

```
LINE/COL ERROR
-------- ----------------------------------------------------------------
3/1      PLS-00103: Encountered the symbol "END" when expecting one of the
         following:
         ;
         The symbol ";" was substituted for "END" to continue.
```

The SHOW ERRORS command works in the same way for creating triggers as it does for creating stored procedures, functions, and packages.

Try It Out – Logging When Table Is Modified

Let's create a trigger that logs when a table is modified. We know that we need to use a statement trigger, but we also need a table to apply the trigger to, and a table to log the changes. Let's use a copy of the EMPLOYEES table found in the HR schema and create a log table called EMPLOYEES_LOG.

1. The first thing to do is to create a copy of the EMPLOYEES table and call it EMPLOYEE_COPY:

```
SQL> create table employees_copy as
  2    select *
  3      from hr.employees;

Table created.
```

2. Next, we create a table to log to. We'll name this EMPLOYEES_LOG:

```
SQL> create table employees_log(
  2    who varchar2(30),
  3    when date );

Table created.
```

3. Now we can create the trigger on the EMPLOYEES_COPY table, which will populate the EMPLOYEES_LOG table in a statement trigger:

```
SQL> create trigger biud_employees_copy
  2    before insert or update or delete
  3      on employees_copy
  4  begin
  5    insert into employees_log(
  6      who, when )
  7    values(
  8      user, sysdate );
  9  end;
 10  /

Trigger created.
```

4. We can test this trigger by giving everyone in the company a 10 percent raise:

```
SQL> update employees_copy
  2      set salary = salary * 1.1;

107 rows updated.

SQL> select *
  2      from employees_log;

WHO                                WHEN
-----------------------------      ---------
OPS$CLBECK                         15-JUL-01
```

5. The output above shows that the user OPS$CLBECK modified the EMPLOYEES_COPY table on 15th July 2001, demonstrating that the trigger works fine.

How about making everyone in department 10 redundant:

```
SQL> delete from employees_copy
  2      where department_id = 10;

1 row deleted.

SQL> select *
  2      from employees_log;

WHO                                WHEN
-----------------------------      ---------
OPS$CLBECK                         15-JUL-01
OPS$CLBECK                         15-JUL-01
```

How It Works

Creating the two tables used in this example is a fairly simple and self-explanatory task so we will skip straight to discussing the mechanics of the statement trigger we created and used on the EMPLOYEES_COPY table. It is a simple enough example and on lines 2 and 3,

```
  2      before insert or update or delete
  3          on employees_copy
```

it says that this trigger will fire before INSERTs, UPDATEs, and DELETEs on the EMPLOYEES_COPY table. Then in the trigger body, we insert the user executing the statement using the USER built-in function and put the date in by using the SYSDATE() built-in function. To test the trigger, we update the triggering table and then select from the log table, observing that there was in fact a row inserted in EMPLOYEES_LOG.

In the second test, we again modify the triggering table and check the log table. We see that there are now two rows in our log table. If the INSERT, UPDATE, or DELETE fails, no record will be inserted into the EMPLOYEE_LOG table. The same goes for a ROLLBACK. The action that the trigger performs is part of the transaction – if the transaction rolls back, the work performed by the trigger also rolls back.

This is really good, but our log table seems to be lacking a few things. For example, we have no idea what modifications took place, only that something happened. It looks like we are going to have to modify our trigger to capture some more information. We will do this as the chapter unfolds.

Cascading Triggers

Something to be mindful of is the concept of **cascading triggers**. This means that the actions of your trigger cause another trigger to fire and so on. Consider that you have three tables, A, B, and C. On table A there is an INSERT trigger that inserts a row into table B. And on table B there is a trigger that inserts a row into table C. This is an example of cascading triggers. This is completely valid; just be aware that this situation may exist when you are developing your application because it could have performance implications or even unintended effects.

Modifying Triggers

We can update or change our triggers by using the CREATE OR REPLACE command. This allows us to change the trigger body, the restriction clause, and so on. You are basically redefining the entire trigger. You could CREATE OR REPLACE a trigger named A so that it changed from an INSERT trigger on table FOO to an UPDATE trigger on table BAR if you chose to. If you are using our naming convention detailed earlier though, then you would not want to. I bring this point up to illustrate two issues:

❏   The name of the trigger has no bearing on what kind of trigger it is

❏   The CREATE OR REPLACE command does just that, it creates or replaces the trigger

So far, all we have used is the CREATE statement. If you attempt a CREATE trigger command and the trigger already exists, you'll get the following error.

```
SQL> create trigger biud_employees_copy
  2     before insert or update or delete
  3         on employees_copy
  4  begin
  5    null;
  6  end;
  7  /
create trigger biud_employees_copy
              *
ERROR at line 1:
ORA-04081: trigger 'BIUD_EMPLOYEES_COPY' already exists
```

Since we have already created a trigger called BIUD_EMPLOYEES_COPY in the previous example, the CREATE statement fails. We need to issue a CREATE OR REPLACE instead:

```
SQL> create or replace trigger biud_employees_copy
  2     before insert or update or delete
  3         on employees_copy
  4  begin
  5    null;
  6  end;
  7  /

Trigger created.
```

So now we have recreated our trigger, but we recreated it with a NULL body, rendering it functionless. That's OK though, because we are going to modify it again to help us solve some of the issues we had with the trigger's first incarnation.

To remove a trigger from the database altogether, just issue DROP TRIGGER <TRIGGER_NAME>.

Determining Which Statement Is Active

We may want to know which statement has caused the trigger to fire. That would be easy if we created our trigger on just one type of statement. In our example above, we could have created three triggers; one on each statement type. Then we would know exactly which statement caused it to fire. That seems like the hard way to do it though, and I'm all about making things easy for others and myself.

In an executing trigger, you can ask Oracle which statement caused the trigger to fire. All you need to do is reference the INSERTING, UPDATING, or DELETING **conditional predicate**. If the value is true, that type of statement initiated your trigger.

```
begin
  if inserting then
    -- An INSERT statement causes me to fire
  elsif updating then
    -- An UPDATE statement causes me to fire
  elsif deleting then
    -- An DELETE statement causes me to fire
  end if;
end;
```

You can also use conditional predicates to test if a certain column is being updated in an UPDATE trigger. In our example above, if the table FOO had a column COL1 and COL2 in it, and we only wanted to run some code if either column was being updated then you could do something like the following:

```
if UPDATING( 'COL1' ) or UPDATING( 'COL2' )then
  -- do something
end if;
```

This gives the trigger author even more control over what code in the trigger is executed.

As you have seen, Oracle allows you to create a trigger on multiple events and, by using conditional predicates, create just a single trigger to handle all your actions. I would not necessarily suggest that you do this in all cases. It can get really confusing when you go back to edit your trigger and it is handling many different tasks. In our case though, we are just logging and so it is better to combine the actions in one single purpose-trigger for multiple statements.

One last thing to know about the conditional predicates INSERTING, UPDATING, and DELETING is that they can only be referenced in the trigger body. If your trigger calls a PL/SQL routine, that routine is not able to refer to those predicates. If it tries, it will result in an error.

Now that we know we can determine the statement type, let's change our example so we can log what statement caused the trigger to fire.

Try It Out – Capturing the Statement Type

1. We will also need to modify the EMPLOYEES_LOG table so we can store more data, so let's do that first, adding an ACTION column:

```
SQL> alter table employees_log
  2    add ( action varchar2(20) );

Table altered.

SQL> desc employees_log
 Name                                      Null?    Type
 ----------------------------------------- -------- ----------------------------
 WHO                                                VARCHAR2(30)
 WHEN                                               DATE
 ACTION                                             VARCHAR2(20)
```

2. Next we modify the existing BIUD_EMPLOYEES_COPY trigger so that it logs the statement type:

```
SQL> create or replace trigger biud_employees_copy
  2    before insert or update or delete
  3        on employees_copy
  4  declare
  5    l_action employees_log.action%type;
  6  begin
  7    if INSERTING then
  8      l_action := 'Insert';
  9    elsif UPDATING then
 10      l_action := 'Update';
 11    elsif DELETING then
 12      l_action := 'Delete';
 13    else
 14      raise_application_error( -20001,
 15         'You should never ever get this error.' );
 16    end if;
 17
 18    insert into employees_log(
 19      who, action, when )
 20    values(
 21      user, l_action, sysdate );
 22  end;
 23  /

Trigger created.
```

3. Let's try out the new trigger by hiring a new employee:

```
SQL> insert into employees_copy(
  2    employee_id,
  3    last_name,
```

```
   4      email,
   5      hire_date,
   6      job_id )
   7  values
   8      ( 12345,
   9        'Beck',
  10        'clbeck@us.oracle.com',
  11        sysdate,
  12        'TECH' );

1 row created.

SQL> select *
  2      from employees_log;

WHO                            WHEN       ACTION
----------------------------   ---------  --------------------
OPS$CLBECK                     15-JUL-01
OPS$CLBECK                     15-JUL-01
OPS$CLBECK                     15-JUL-01  Insert
```

4. Now give them a salary of $500,000.00:

```
SQL> update employees_copy
  2      set salary = 500000.00
  3  where employee_id = 12345;

1 row updated.

SQL> select *
  2      from employees_log;

WHO                            WHEN       ACTION
----------------------------   ---------  --------------------
OPS$CLBECK                     15-JUL-01
OPS$CLBECK                     15-JUL-01
OPS$CLBECK                     15-JUL-01  Insert
OPS$CLBECK                     15-JUL-01  Update
```

How It Works

The first thing that we do is to alter the EMPLOYEES_LOG table. See Chapter 7 for more information on this.

Next we modify our original trigger so it can determine which statement caused its execution, and then set a local variable in the trigger to that statement name using an IF...THEN...ELSE PL/SQL programming construct. In lines 7-16, we check the conditional predicates INSERTING, UPDATING, and DELETING and set the appropriate value. Then from line 18, we log our modification to the EMPLOYEES_LOG table.

After that, we insert a new record in the EMPLOYEES_COPY table and then check the log. This time, we see that not only was there a third record, but it indicates that an INSERT caused it.

Finally, we perform an UPDATE on the EMPLOYEES_COPY table, giving the new employee a salary, and again check the log and we see that yes another record has been created and that an UPDATE was what caused it to be logged.

We have seen how we can create triggers, modify them, and even determine which statement caused it to fire. Now we would like to know what actually changed when the update occurred and how many rows were affected. That is going to be a bit more challenging and we are going to have to learn a few more concepts first.

BEFORE and AFTER

From our examples above, you can see that statement triggers can fire BEFORE the statement is executed, making it a great way to enhance security, enable business rules, and log actions. But can we create an AFTER statement trigger? The answer, no surprises, is yes. They follow all the same rules as the BEFORE statement, but are executed by Oracle after the statement completes instead of prior to the execution of the statement.

We could have just as easily used an AFTER statement trigger in our logging examples above. In fact, it would probably be better to log in an AFTER statement trigger. If the insert fails for any reason, nothing gets logged. If we log first, then insert, and the insert fails, the database needs to roll back that log insert.

Similarly, we would not want to do a security check in an AFTER statement trigger. If we did, Oracle would perform the action, then execute the trigger, then possibly roll back the changes, if the security check fails. This is just causing the database unnecessary work. So keep that in mind when determining when to have your trigger fire.

Row Triggers

Not only can we create triggers that fire for each INSERT or UPDATE or DELETE statement on a table, but we can also define triggers that will fire for each row affected. These are knows as **row triggers**. They are defined like statement triggers, but with two exceptions.

- ❑ Firstly, they include the FOR EACH ROW clause in the triggering statement of the trigger definition and can include the optional REFERENCING clause as we have seen in the first example in this chapter.

- ❑ The second major difference is, you can reference the values of the rows being affected and, in a BEFORE...FOR EACH ROW trigger, even set them within the trigger body. This gives the trigger author the ability to default certain values like the primary key or to completely override the values coming in and set their own values, like we saw in the first example in this chapter.

Another use of row triggers is formatting data on the way into the table. In the example below we assign a default value to a column, but we could have just as easily applied an INITCAP(), a SUBSTR(), an UPPER() or LOWER(), or even a hand-written function, to a :NEW_VALUE column value to format the data, ensuring its integrity. This makes it easier to select the data or to create constraints in our queries. If we are guaranteed that the data is in a certain format, we can create predicates in our WHERE clauses much more simply.

591

For example, we can apply an UPPER() function to a :NEW_VALUE column value in a FOR EACH ROW trigger. When we use that column in a WHERE clause, we can be assured that its values will all be uppercase. That way we can write:

```
where col1 = upper( 'some_value' )
```

instead of:

```
where upper( col1 ) = upper( 'some_value' )
```

This will also allow us to use a standard index on COL1 if such an index exists. Otherwise we would be required to create a function-based index. See Chapter 8 for more information on indexes.

Defining a FOR EACH ROW Trigger

Let's take a look at our initial example with one minor change. Instead of putting the trigger on the EMPLOYEES table, we will put it on our EMPLOYEES_COPY table:

```
SQL> create trigger biufer_employees_department_id
  2     before insert or update
  3        of department_id
  4        on employees_copy
  5        referencing old as old_value
  6                    new as new_value
  7        for each row
  8     when ( new_value.department_id <> 80 )
  9  begin
 10     :new_value.commission_pct := 0;
 11  end;
 12  /

Trigger created.
```

Line 7 has the clause FOR EACH ROW, defining this trigger as a row trigger. This tells Oracle to attempt to execute this trigger for every row affected by an INSERT or UPDATE.

Correlation Names and the REFERENCING Clause

In row triggers, you can access the values of the affected row. This is accomplished by applying a **correlation name** to the column's names. By referencing the column with the appropriate correlation name, you can get the Before statement values and the After statement values. The default correlation name for the Before image is :OLD and I am sure you can guess that the After image's correlation name is :NEW.

- ❏ In an INSERT trigger, only the :NEW values are available. Since the row did not previously exist, there cannot be an :OLD, or Before image.

- ❏ Conversely, there is no :NEW or After image in a DELETE trigger. We are not changing the row, so there are no new values to reference.

- ❏ UPDATE triggers have both beFore and After images, :OLD and :NEW values of each column.

When you define your trigger, you are able to change the correlation names using the REFERENCING clause. In the example above, I renamed the before statement correlation name to OLD_VALUE and the after statement correlation name to NEW_VALUE. The renaming is not usually necessary and is rarely done. Oracle gives you this ability to allow you to avoid confusion between similarly named objects. Assume that you had a table named NEW and you want to create a BEFORE INSERT trigger to default one of the columns. You can use the REFERENCING clause to rename the NEW correlation name to something else and in our example above we did just that. Notice how the NEW_VALUE correlation name is used in place of the default one, NEW. Also, if you just do not like using NEW and OLD you can change them. I would suggest that you not change them if you can avoid it.

Let's try and create a row trigger on a table that populates the primary key with a sequence value. This is a very common use of a FOR EACH ROW trigger:

Try It Out – Assigning a Sequence Number To the Primary Key

1. First of all we create a table and a sequence. The table we will create is named FOO, so if this already exists, then drop it using the following command:

```
SQL> drop table foo;

Table dropped.
```

2. Now can create a fresh FOO table and a sequence to go with it:

```
SQL> create table foo(
  2    id number primary key,
  3    data varchar2(100) );

Table created.

SQL> create sequence foo_seq;

Sequence created.
```

3. The next step is to create the row trigger to populate the primary key:

```
SQL> create trigger bifer_foo_id_pk
  2    before insert
  3       on foo
  4      for each row
  5  begin
  6    select foo_seq.nextval
  7      into :new.id
  8      from dual;
  9  end;
 10  /

Trigger created.
```

4. Now we can test it out:

```
SQL> insert into foo ( data )
  2  values ( 'Christopher' );

1 row created.

SQL> insert into foo ( id, data )
  2  values ( 5, 'Sean' );

1 row created.

SQL> select *
  2     from foo;

       ID DATA
---------- --------------------
        1 Christopher
        2 Sean
```

Using this trigger, we can ensure that the ID value will be populated from the sequence. If we relied on the application to issue the INSERT INTO FOO VALUES (FOO_SEQ.NEXTVAL, 'BLAH'), data could become corrupt if applications chose to insert some other value for ID.

How It Works

The first couple of steps are straightforward. We simply create the database objects ready for our example. The real work begins when we create the BIFER_FOO_ID_PK trigger. Let's break this down and discuss it in detail:

```
SQL> create trigger bifer_foo_id_pk
```

Here we are naming our trigger. As I said earlier, the name does not matter as long as it follows Oracle naming standards, but it is good practice to name it something descriptive. You can tell from my trigger's name that it is a **b**efore **i**nsert **f**or **e**ach **r**ow trigger on the FOO table and that it has something to do with the ID column and the primary key.

The next three lines define what kind of trigger it is, when it will fire and to which table it is attached:

```
2     before insert
3         on foo
4         for each row
```

The rest is the body of the trigger. This is the work to be performed:

```
5  begin
6     select foo_seq.nextval
7         into :new.id
8         from dual;
9  end;
```

Notice that I referenced the :NEW.ID value and selected the FOO_SEQ.NEXTVAL directly into it. Using this technique allows us to default the ID column regardless of whether or not a value is even supplied for it.

In testing this example, we did not supply a value for ID in the first INSERT. When we selected it from the table though, ID had a value. In the second INSERT, we supplied 5 for the value of ID, but when selected, its value was 2. The row trigger we've written either supplies a value for the missing value or overrides the value we supplied. So as you can see, row triggers are a great way to ensure the data that gets into your tables is exactly the data they are designed to hold and not incorrect data that an application may attempt to insert. This helps us ensure data integrity.

Recall that in our first two *Try It Out* sections, we were logging the actions on the EMPLOYEES_COPY table. We were able to determine who was performing the action and what actions were performed, but not what rows were affected, or how many. Using a combination of BEFORE and AFTER statement triggers and row triggers, we can answer those questions. Let's see how.

This is going to be a pretty large example. It will encompass all the things we have learnt up to this point. What we want to do is log not only what changes occurred to the SALARY column, but also what they were and how many rows were affected. OK, let's get started.

Try It Out – Row Counts and Logging Column Changes

1. First, alter the EMPLOYEES_LOG table, increasing the size of the ACTION column:

```
SQL> alter table employees_log modify action varchar2(2000);

Table altered.
```

2. Next, we create a package specification (see Chapter 11, *Procedures, Functions, and Packages,* for more information on packages) called STATE_PACKAGE. In this specification, we will put a global variable called ROWS_CHANGED that we can access from our triggers. This will be a counter for the number of row affected for a given statement. It will allow us to keep state from one row trigger execution to the next one. We need to do this because individual row trigger executions, even for the same statement, cannot keep state from one execution to another. If an UPDATE statement affects 5 rows, and there is an UPDATE FOR EACH ROW trigger on the table, it will fire 5 times. Those five triggers cannot share data directly with each other.

```
SQL> create package state_package as
  2     rows_changed number;
  3  end state_package;
  4  /

Package created.
```

3. Now we modify the BEFORE statement trigger BIUD_EMPLOYEES_COPY to initialize the global package variable to zero:

```
SQL> create or replace trigger biud_employees_copy
  2     before insert or update or delete
  3         on employees_copy
  4  begin
  5     state_package.rows_changed := 0;
```

595

```
    6   end;
    7   /

Trigger created.
```

4. Here, we create a row trigger called BIUDFER_EMPLOYEES_COPY to increment the global
package variable for each row affected, and to log changes to the SALARY column:

```
SQL> create trigger biudfer_employees_copy
    2     before insert or update or delete
    3         on employees_copy
    4         for each row
    5   declare
    6     l_action employees_log.action%type;
    7   begin
    8
    9     if INSERTING then
   10       l_action := 'Insert';
   11     elsif UPDATING then
   12       l_action := 'Update';
   13     elsif DELETING then
   14       l_action := 'Delete';
   15     else
   16       raise_application_error( -20001,
   17           'You should never ever get this error.' );
   18     end if;
   19
   20     state_package.rows_changed := state_package.rows_changed + 1;
   21
   22     if UPDATING( 'SALARY' ) then
   23       l_action := l_action || ' - ' ||
   24                   'Salary for employee_id ' || :old.employee_id ||
   25                   ' changed from ' || :old.salary ||
   26                   ' to ' || :new.salary;
   27     end if;
   28
   29     insert into employees_log(
   30       who, action, when )
   31     values(
   32       user, l_action, sysdate );
   33
   34   end;
   35   /

Trigger created.
```

5. In this next section, we create an AFTER statement trigger named AIUD_EMPLOYEES_COPY to
log the total number of rows affected by accessing the global package variable:

```
SQL> create trigger aiud_employees_copy
    2     after insert or update or delete
    3         on employees_copy
    4   declare
```

```
 5      l_action employees_log.action%type;
 6    begin
 7      if INSERTING then
 8        l_action := state_package.rows_changed || ' were ' || 'inserted';
 9      elsif UPDATING then
10        l_action := state_package.rows_changed || ' were ' || 'updated';
11      elsif DELETING then
12        l_action := state_package.rows_changed || ' were ' || 'deleted';
13      else
14        raise_application_error( -20001,
15            'You should never ever get this error.' );
16      end if;
17
18      insert into employees_log(
19        who, action, when )
20      values(
21        user, l_action, sysdate );
22
23    end;
24    /

Trigger created.
```

6. We can test out our work so far by giving a 5 percent pay rise to every employee in the department with an ID of 20:

```
SQL> update employees_copy
  2      set salary = salary * 1.05
  3    where department_id = 20;

2 rows updated.

SQL> select *
  2      from employees_log;

WHO         WHEN       ACTION
----------  ---------  ------------------------------------------------------------
OPS$CLBECK  15-JUL-01
OPS$CLBECK  15-JUL-01
OPS$CLBECK  15-JUL-01  Insert
OPS$CLBECK  15-JUL-01  Update
OPS$CLBECK  18-JUL-01  Update - Salary for employee_id 201 changed from 13000
                       to 13650

OPS$CLBECK  18-JUL-01  Update - Salary for employee_id 202 changed from 6000
                       to 6300

OPS$CLBECK  18-JUL-01  2 were updated

7 rows selected.
```

How It Works

Wow, that's a pretty big example. At first it might look a little overwhelming. We are using both `BEFORE` and `AFTER` statement-level triggers and a row-level trigger. Plus we are using a package variable. If you take it piece by piece though, it is pretty easy to understand.

The first step is to modify the `EMPLOYEES_LOG` table to make the `ACTION` column larger because we were going to store more than just the statement type.

Next, we create a package with a globally available variable. We need this because we need a place to store a value that will be available from one row trigger execution to another. We cannot create a local variable in the trigger because we know that once we leave a `BEGIN...END` block of code, any variables declared in that block are no longer available or in scope. A package, once instantiated, is available for the life of our connection. Its state, in globally defined variables, remain, available across blocks of code executions, trigger executions, and even `COMMIT`s and `ROLLBACK`s. This makes it the perfect place to store our `ROW_CHANGED` counter.

Then, we modified our original `BEFORE` statement trigger to just initialize the global package variable to 0. As I just explained, the package state remains across statement executions, so to get an accurate count of the rows affected, we need to set `ROWS_CHANGED` back to zero before every action on the `EMPLOYEES_COPY` table.

After this, we create the large row trigger `BIUD_EMPLOYEES_COPY`. Much of the work here, we've seen before in earlier examples. Since we are now interested in the number of rows affected, we need to do this work in the row trigger. First we determine the type of statement we are executing:

```
 7    if INSERTING then
 8      l_action := state_package.rows_changed || ' were ' || 'inserted';
 9    elsif UPDATING then
10      l_action := state_package.rows_changed || ' were ' || 'updated';
11    elsif DELETING then
12      l_action := state_package.rows_changed || ' were ' || 'deleted';
13    else
14      raise_application_error( -20001,
15          'You should never ever get this error.' );
16    end if;
```

Then we increment the global package variable by one:

```
20    state_package.rows_changed := state_package.rows_changed + 1;
```

Next, if we are updating the `SALARY` column, we append to the action how we are changing the `SALARY` column:

```
22    if UPDATING( 'SALARY' ) then
23      l_action := l_action || ' - ' ||
24                  'Salary for employee_id ' || :old.employee_id ||
25                  ' changed from ' || :old.salary ||
26                  ' to ' || :new.salary;
27    end if;
```

And lastly, we log the change:

```
29      insert into employees_log(
30        who, action, when )
31      values(
32        user, l_action, sysdate );
```

Following this, we wrote the AFTER statement trigger, AUID_EMPLOYEES_COPY. This trigger is fired after all the rows have been changed. Our row trigger BIUDFER_EMPLOYEES_COPY will have fired once for every row affected, incrementing the global package variable ROWS_CHANGED once per row. That variable's value must equal the number of row affected by the issuing statement, so we log that.

Finally, we test all this out. We update all employees in department 20, giving them a 5 percent pay rise. Then we query the EMPLOYEES_LOG table and see if all this actually worked. What we see is that there are three new records from the last example. (Notice the date change. That's because these two examples were written and tested on different days.)

```
OPS$CLBECK 18-JUL-01 Update - Salary for employee_id 202 changed from 6000
                     to 6300

OPS$CLBECK 18-JUL-01 2 were updated
```

The new records show that we updated two employees. Our triggers logged the old and new values, and then gave us a count of the number of rows affected. So, it all seemed to work just like we wanted. The one thing missing in this example is a record of the actual statement that caused these two rows to be updated. The *Event Attribute Functions* section later in the chapter will show how we can determine this.

One thing I would like to point out here is that triggers are not free. What I mean is that processing triggers takes *time*. How much time? Well, that depends on how complex your triggers are. Consider the example we have just seen. We issued a single update statement, which affected two rows. Behind the scenes, four triggers are fired, and three additional INSERTs are performed. This causes more processing on the database, more rollback to be generated, and all this processing takes time. Just be aware of this when using triggers. The flip side of this is having to code this logic everywhere an update would occur, which is likewise bad.

> *Overhead is something that can be avoided – hence most of the time functionality like this isn't overhead, it's the price of your requirement. Whether you did this in the client code or the trigger – there would be a performance price.*

INSTEAD OF Triggers

Unlike statement and row triggers, which are executed either before or after executing the statement that caused the trigger to fire, INSTEAD OF triggers are triggers that Oracle will execute in place of the actual issuing statement. That might sound like a really bad idea at first.

But consider a user issuing an INSERT against a view. There is an INSTEAD OF insert trigger on the view. Instead of performing the INSERT, Oracle runs your trigger. Your trigger can then perform any action it was coded to perform. It could insert your data into the base table or another table altogether. It could log the fact that you tried to insert this data. It could delete rows from a completely unrelated table. It depends on what you coded the trigger to do.

Why Do We Have Them?

So why does Oracle allow this? What good could come out of allowing the developer and/or the data modeler to override the default functionality of the database? Believe it or not, there are plenty of reasons why you would want to do it. Consider a join view, a view based on multiple tables and/or views. If issue an INSERT against that view, Oracle may not be able to figure out how to perform it because the column you are inserting into is both the primary key of one of the tables and a foreign key in the other table. Or the column you selected in the view is a column based on a function like SUBSTR() or a CONCAT() of two or more columns. It would be impossible for Oracle to know how to insert those values correctly. Since you wrote the view, you know how the INSERT should work so Oracle gives you the ability to teach it.

If you have already read Chapter 14, *Views*, you have probably seen an INSTEAD OF trigger. And the code to create one should make much more sense now. Let's look at the example that we used in the chapter on views.

Defining an INSTEAD OF Trigger

As a recap, here is the code to create the COMPANY_PHONE_BOOK view:

```
SQL> create or replace view company_phone_book as
  2     select employee_id emp_id,
  3            last_name || ', ' || first_name name,
  4            phone_number,
  5            email
  6       from hr.employees;

View created.
```

And now we can create our trigger, UPDATE_NAME_COMPANY_PHONE_BOOK:

```
SQL> create trigger update_name_company_phone_book
  2     instead of
  3       update
  4           on company_phone_book
  5   begin
  6     update employees
  7        set employee_id = :new.emp_id,
  8            first_name = substr( :new.name, instr( :new.name, ',' )+2 ),
  9            last_name = substr( :new.name, 1, instr( :new.name, ',' )-1 ),
 10            phone_number = :new.phone_number,
 11            email = :new.email
 12      where employee_id = :old.emp_id;
 13   end;
 14   /

Trigger created.
```

Most of the trigger's definition is exactly the same as the definition of the statement and row triggers, except with one addition. On line 2 you can see the key words:

```
     2    instead of
```

This tells Oracle that this is an INSTEAD OF trigger. Combined with lines 3 and 4, you can see that this trigger is an INSTEAD OF UPDATE trigger on the COMPANY_PHONE_BOOK view.

Notice in the trigger body that there is an UPDATE to the table EMPLOYEES. If you remember from Chapter 14, the COMPANY_PHONE_BOOK view was a view built on the EMPLOYEES table. So, if we attempt to update this view, we are really updating the base table. And since the view had a column that was the result of a function, we needed to teach Oracle how to update the base table correctly.

Another place INSTEAD OF triggers are used is with modifying object views, nested tables, and other views that use DISTINCT, GROUP BY, CONNECT BY, START WITH, and group functions like COUNT() and SUM().

One thing to remember is that there are no BEFORE and AFTER INSTEAD OF triggers. INSTEAD OF triggers are always the same as After row-level triggers. They will fire once per affected row and you can not modify their :NEW values.

Let's see an INSTEAD OF trigger in action, by creating a DEPARTMENT_VIEW that selects department information and all the employees in that department in a single row. We can accomplish this by creating two types and a view with a nested table. Then, we will need to create an INSTEAD OF trigger to allow us to insert data into our new view. To make things easier, I am going to create this on copies of the EMPLOYEES and DEPARTMENTS tables in the HR sample schema of Oracle 9*i*.

Try It Out – Inserting Into a Complex View

1. First of all, we need to create the copies of the HR tables:

```
SQL> create table employees_copy2 as
  2    select *
  3      from hr.employees;

Table created.

SQL> create table departments_copy2 as
  2    select *
  3      from hr.departments;

Table created.
```

2. Now create the types that we need to use, one object type and one table type. We will use these to cast the rows from the EMPLOYEES table in the nested table view.

Note that you need CREATE TYPE privileges here – something that the HR user doesn't have set by default.

```
SQL> create type employee_type as object(
  2    last_name varchar2(25),
  3    email varchar2(25),
  4    hire_date date,
```

```
  5     job_id varchar2(10) )
  6  /

Type created.

SQL> create type employees_list as
  2     table of employee_type
  3  /

Type created.
```

3. Here, we create the complex view:

```
SQL> create view dept_emp_view as
  2     select d.department_id,
  3            d.department_name,
  4            cast( multiset( select e.last_name,
  5                                   e.email,
  6                                   e.hire_date,
  7                                   e.job_id
  8                            from employees_copy2 e
  9                            where e.department_id = d.department_id )
 10                 as employees_list ) emps
 11     from departments_copy2 d
 12  /

View created.
```

4. And now the INSTEAD OF trigger:

```
SQL> create trigger io_bifer_dept_emp_view
  2     instead of
  3       insert
  4         on dept_emp_view
  5         for each row
  6  begin
  7    insert into departments_copy2(
  8      department_id, department_name )
  9    values(
 10      :new.department_id, :new.department_name );
 11
 12    for i in 1 .. :new.emps.count loop
 13      insert into employees_copy2(
 14        last_name, email,
 15        hire_date, job_id,
 16        department_id )
 17      values(
 18        :new.emps(i).last_name, :new.emps(i).email,
 19        :new.emps(i).hire_date, :new.emps(i).job_id,
 20        :new.department_id );
 21    end loop;
```

```
22  end;
23  /
```

Trigger created.

5. Now to test the code that we have just written:

```
SQL> insert into dept_emp_view(
  2    department_id, department_name, emps )
  3  values(
  4    '1000', 'Tech Writing', employees_list(
  5      employee_type('Beck', 'clbeck@us.oracle.com',
  6                    '01-JAN-90', 'TECH'),
  7      employee_type('Dillon', 'sdillon@us.oracle.com',
  8                    '01-JAN-90', 'TECH')));

1 row created.

SQL> select *
  2    from dept_emp_view
  3   where department_id = 1000;

DEPARTMENT_ID DEPARTMENT_NAME EMPS(LAST_NAME, EMAIL, HIRE_DATE, JOB_ID)
------------- --------------- -------------------------------------------------
         1000 Graphic Art     EMPLOYEES_LIST(EMPLOYEE_TYPE('Beck', 'clbeck@u
                              s.oracle.com', '01-JAN-90', 'TECH'), EMPLOYEE_
                              TYPE('Dillon', 'sdillon@us.oracle.com', '01-JA
                              N-90', 'TECH'))

         1000 Tech Writing    EMPLOYEES_LIST(EMPLOYEE_TYPE('Beck', 'clbeck@u
                              s.oracle.com', '01-JAN-90', 'TECH'), EMPLOYEE_
                              TYPE('Dillon', 'sdillon@us.oracle.com', '01-JA
                              N-90', 'TECH'))
```

How It Works

The first couple of steps are just setting up the environment that we need to test. We create the tables, types, and the view that we would use.

You can read more about creating these objects in their respective chapters, Chapter 7, Tables, and Chapter 14, Views.

Then we create the INSTEAD OF trigger. You will notice that what this trigger is doing is breaking up our insert to the DEPT_EMP_VIEW view, and performing inserts into the correct base tables. First, we insert into the DEPARTMENTS_COPY2 table:

```
  6  begin
  7    insert into departments_copy2(
  8      department_id, department_name )
  9    values(
 10      :new.department_id, :new.department_name );
```

603

Note how we reference the inserted values with the :NEW correlation name. Next, we have to loop over all the EMPLOYEE_TYPE objects in the EMPLOYEES_LIST object:

```
12    for i in 1 .. :new.emps.count loop
13      insert into employees_copy2(
14        last_name, email,
15        hire_date, job_id,
16        department_id )
17      values(
18        :new.emps(i).last_name, :new.emps(i).email,
19        :new.emps(i).hire_date, :new.emps(i).job_id,
20        :new.department_id );
21    end loop;
```

and insert into the EMPLOYEES_COPY2 table one row for each EMPLOYEE_TYPE object we encountered.

Lastly, we test it by inserting a single row into the DEPT_EMP_VIEW. That insert triggers our IO_BIFER_DEPT_EMP_VIEW trigger to fire, which in turn inserts our data into the base tables EMPLOYEES_COPY2 and DEPARTMENTS_COPY2. If we query the base table we should see those rows:

```
SQL> select department_name
  2    from departments_copy2
  3    where department_id = 1000;


DEPARTMENT_NAME
---------------
Graphic Art
Tech Writing

SQL> select last_name, email
  2    from employees_copy2
  3    where department_id = 1000;

LAST_NAME                EMAIL
------------------------ -------------------------
Beck                     clbeck@us.oracle.com
Dillon                   sdillon@us.oracle.com
```

INSTEAD OF triggers are invaluable when you need to create and modify data through join views and complex views.

System Event Triggers

Oracle also allows developers to create a trigger on certain system events. These events are:

❑   Database startup

❑   Database shutdown

❑   Server errors

These events are instance-wide. They are not associated with certain tables or rows like the triggers we have seen earlier. Let's look at a simple example:

```
SQL> create trigger ad_startup
  2     after STARTUP
  3        on DATABASE
  4  begin
  5    -- do some stuff here
  6  end;
```

The creation of these triggers is similar to the other triggers, but the triggering action and the object it is associated with is different. In the example above, we have an AFTER STARTUP trigger so it must be associated with the database. The same goes for the BEFORE SHUTDOWN trigger. SERVERERROR triggers can either be associated with the database or with a particular schema, thus giving you more control over when these triggers will fire.

User Event Triggers

User event triggers, also know as **client triggers**, are triggers that can be associated with actions or events other than INSERT, UPDATE, and DELETE, namely user logon/logoff, DDL, and DML actions. These events include both BEFORE and AFTER triggers on the following statements and commands:

- ❑ CREATE
- ❑ ALTER
- ❑ DROP
- ❑ ANALYZE
- ❑ ASSOCIATE STATISTICS
- ❑ DISASSOCIATE STATISTICS
- ❑ AUDIT
- ❑ NOAUDIT
- ❑ COMMENT
- ❑ GRANT
- ❑ REVOKE
- ❑ RENAME
- ❑ TRUNCATE

The following event just has a BEFORE trigger:

- ❑ LOGOFF

And these just have AFTER triggers:

- ❑ SUSPEND

Try It Out – Log Dropped Objects

1. Let's log every object that the user SCOTT drops. First we need a table to store the information in.

```
SQL> connect scott/tiger
Connected.

SQL> create table dropped_objects(
  2     object_name varchar2(30),
  3     object_type varchar2(30),
  4     dropped_on date );

Table created.
```

2. Next, we create the BEFORE DROP trigger.

```
SQL> create or replace
  2  trigger log_drop_trigger
  3    before drop
  4    on scott.schema
  5  begin
  6    insert into dropped_objects
  7    values ( ora_dict_obj_name,
  8              ora_dict_obj_type,
  9              sysdate );
 10  end;
 11  /

Trigger created.
```

3. Now we create and drop a few objects.

```
SQL> create table drop_me(
  2    x number )
  3  /

Table created.

SQL> create view drop_me_view
  2  as select * from drop_me;

View created.

SQL> drop view drop_me_view
  2  /

View dropped.

SQL> drop table drop_me
  2  /

Table dropped.
```

4. Now we query the table and see the results:

```
SQL> select *
  2     from dropped_objects
  3  /

OBJECT_NAME                     OBJECT_TYPE                     DROPPED_O
------------------------------- ------------------------------- ---------
DROP_ME_VIEW                    VIEW                            16-JAN-02
DROP_ME                         TABLE                           16-JAN-02
```

Check out the *Event Attribute Functions* section for a complete listing of all the functions that are available to your user event triggers, to supply information about the events that caused them to be triggered.

Enabling and Disabling Triggers

So far, we have seen how we can CREATE, CREATE OR REPLACE, and DROP triggers. We have not seen how we can ALTER one though. If you think about it, what would you want to alter? If you want to change the trigger body, you could just REPLACE it. If you no longer wanted it to fire, then you could DROP it. What if you wanted to temporarily disable it? Could you? Of course you can. You would issue the following command:

```
SQL> alter trigger <TRIGGER_NAME> disable;
```

This sets the status of the trigger to DISABLED. This means that the trigger still exists, the database knows about it, but it will not fire. It is just as if there was no trigger there at all. There are reasons why you would want to do this. For example, you have a BEFORE INSERT FOR EACH ROW trigger that performs data formatting. It might INITCAP() the first and last names, format the phone number, UPPER() a title, and so on. All these are great reasons to have such a trigger, but we are going to be loading a large amount of data, millions of rows in fact, and we already are assured that the data is properly formatted. There is no reason for the database to have to fire a trigger that, in reality, will do work which will take time, but accomplish nothing. In this case, we could disable the trigger, load our data, and then re-enable it with the following:

```
SQL> alter trigger <TRIGGER_NAME> enable;
```

Let's give this a try for ourselves and see it in action.

Try It Out – Disable a Trigger

1. First, we will create a new table:

```
SQL> create table all_upper_data(
  2     data varchar2(255) );

Table created.
```

2. Then we create a BEFORE INSERT FOR EACH ROW trigger that UPPER()s that data column:

```
SQL> create trigger bifer_all_upper_data
  2    before insert
  3        on all_upper_data
  4      for each row
  5  begin
  6    :new.data := upper( :new.data );
  7  end;
  8  /

Trigger created.
```

3. Now let's insert a row and verify that the trigger did indeed fire:

```
SQL> insert into all_upper_data( data )
  2  values ( 'chris' );

1 row created.

SQL> select *
  2    from all_upper_data;

DATA
--------------------
CHRIS
```

4. Let's disable the trigger, insert another row and see what the data now looks like:

```
SQL> alter trigger bifer_all_upper_data disable;

Trigger altered.

SQL> insert into all_upper_data( data )
  2  values ( 'sean' );

1 row created.

SQL> select *
  2    from all_upper_data;

DATA
--------------------
CHRIS
sean
```

5. We'll re-enable the trigger and insert one more row:

```
SQL> alter trigger bifer_all_upper_data enable;

Trigger altered.

SQL> insert into all_upper_data( data )
```

```
  2   values ( 'mark' );

1 row created.

SQL> select *
  2      from all_upper_data;

DATA
--------------------
CHRIS
sean
MARK
```

How It Works

This was a pretty easy demonstration, but I just want to point out a few things. We know for a fact that the trigger BIFER_ALL_UPPER_DATA is working properly from the results of our first insert. We inserted CHRIS and when it was selected we got CHRIS. After we disabled the trigger, when we inserted the value SEAN, we see that it was not uppercased, proving that the trigger was not executed.

Then, in the final step, we re-enabled the trigger and inserted a third row. Again, you can see that the enabled trigger modified the value mark, changing it to MARK. Notice though, that the data inserted while the trigger was not active is still in lowercase. This is important to realize. Enabling a disabled trigger will not cause the trigger to fire for rows and statements that it would have fired for if it had been enabled when the statement was issued. What this means is that triggers do not work on the existing data in a table, only on the new and currently modified data. If you disable a trigger, just remember to enable it, otherwise any new data will not be processed and you could wind up with corrupt data.

Transactions and Triggers

Triggers are written in PL/SQL, so anything that you can do in PL/SQL, you can do in a trigger. Well anything besides COMMIT or ROLLBACK the current transaction that is. Imagine if your trigger was allowed to COMMIT your transaction. Yikes! Issuing an INSERT into a table would cause your transaction to COMMIT and you would have *no* control over that. Any constraints on the table would not have been validated when the trigger fired, so we would not yet know if the data that the trigger wanted to COMMIT was valid. This is why Oracle does not allow COMMITs and ROLLBACKs in triggers. Since DDL statements do an implicit COMMIT, they too are not allowed in triggers.

Well I say this, but there are ways around this behavior. Sort of. If your trigger calls a procedure that you wrote, and that procedure is defined to be an autonomous transaction, then within that procedure you must COMMIT and ROLLBACK but it does not affect the current transaction that caused the trigger to fire initially. Consider our logging trigger. Only statements that COMMIT show up in our log table. If we moved the INSERT INTO log table statement into a procedure that was defined as an autonomous transaction, and committed in that procedure, we would have to log not only everything that actually happened to the table, but also everything that was attempted. It might be interesting to see which transactions were rolled back or failed.

609

Getting Trigger Information from the Data Dictionary

In the HR sample schema in the Oracle 9*i* database there is an INSERT or UPDATE or DELETE statement trigger named SECURE_EMPLOYEES on the EMPLOYEES table. This trigger ensures that changes to the table only occur on weekdays and between the hours of 8AM and 6PM. I found this out when I was trying to test some examples for this book over a weekend and the database denied my INSERT and UPDATE requests against the EMPLOYEES table. I did not even know that the trigger was there until then:

```
SQL> update employees set salary = salary * 1.1;
update employees set salary = salary * 1.1
       *
ERROR at line 1:
ORA-20205: You may only make changes during normal office hours
ORA-06512: at "HR.SECURE_DML", line 6
ORA-06512: at "HR.SECURE_EMPLOYEES", line 2
ORA-04088: error during execution of trigger 'HR.SECURE_EMPLOYEES'
```

Once I was greeted with the friendly error message, I wanted to know exactly what the trigger was doing. Since I know that Oracle stores all its information in its data dictionary, I know that I can query everything about the triggers on my table. The data dictionary view I used was USER_TRIGGERS.

```
SQL> desc user_triggers
 Name                                      Null?    Type
 ---------------------------------------- -------- -----------------------
 TRIGGER_NAME                                       VARCHAR2(30)
 TRIGGER_TYPE                                       VARCHAR2(16)
 TRIGGERING_EVENT                                   VARCHAR2(227)
 TABLE_OWNER                                        VARCHAR2(30)
 BASE_OBJECT_TYPE                                   VARCHAR2(16)
 TABLE_NAME                                         VARCHAR2(30)
 COLUMN_NAME                                        VARCHAR2(4000)
 REFERENCING_NAMES                                  VARCHAR2(128)
 WHEN_CLAUSE                                        VARCHAR2(4000)
 STATUS                                             VARCHAR2(8)
 DESCRIPTION                                        VARCHAR2(4000)
 ACTION_TYPE                                        VARCHAR2(11)
 TRIGGER_BODY                                       LONG
```

Looks like everything that I want to know about this trigger is in this view. All I need to do is select it. Let's start by getting all the triggers on HR's EMPLOYEES table:

```
SQL> select trigger_name
  2    from user_triggers
  3   where table_name = 'EMPLOYEES'
  4     and table_owner = 'HR';

TRIGGER_NAME
------------------------------
SECURE_EMPLOYEES
UPDATE_JOB_HISTORY
```

We see there are two triggers on the EMPLOYEES table. From the error message above, we know that the trigger that caused our UPDATE to fail is called SECURE_EMPLOYEES. With the trigger's name, I can get the body of the trigger, the code that is actually run when this trigger is fired. I can also determine when the trigger will fire along with what will cause it to fire:

```
SQL> select trigger_type, triggering_event, when_clause, trigger_body
  2    from user_triggers
  3    where trigger_name = 'SECURE_EMPLOYEES';

TRIGGER_TYPE     TRIGGERING_EVENT   WHEN_CLAUSE TRIGGER_BODY
---------------- ------------------ ----------- ----------------------
BEFORE STATEMENT INSERT OR UPDATE               BEGIN
                 OR DELETE                        secure_dml;
                                                END secure_employees;
```

The trigger in question is a BEFORE STATEMENT trigger, and it will fire for every INSERT or UPDATE or DELETE. The TRIGGER_BODY appears to run a PL/SQL procedure called SECURE_DML(). With a little more querying of the data dictionary (see Chapter 11, *Procedures, Functions, and Packages*), I found the code of the procedure:

```
PROCEDURE secure_dml
IS
BEGIN
   IF TO_CHAR (SYSDATE, 'HH24:MI') NOT BETWEEN '08:00' AND '18:00'
        OR TO_CHAR (SYSDATE, 'DY') IN ('SAT', 'SUN') THEN
        RAISE_APPLICATION_ERROR (-20205,
               'You may only make changes during normal office hours');
   END IF;
END secure_dml;
```

What this code basically does is raise an error if the current time is not between 8AM and 6PM or if it is Saturday or Sunday. That's right in line with our error message:

```
ORA-20205: You may only make changes during normal office hours.
```

You can use this method for retrieving any, and all, information about triggers. You can check the STATUS column to see if the trigger is enabled or disabled. You can query the REFERENCING_NAME column to determine if the trigger author overrode the default :NEW and :OLD values. All the information is right there in that view.

Event Attribute Functions

You can retrieve certain attributes about the event that caused the trigger to execute. Calling the appropriate function in the body of the trigger can access these attributes. Many of these functions were introduced in Oracle 8*i* (8.1.6), whereas in earlier versions of Oracle, some of these functions were accessible via the SYS package. Now Oracle 9*i* has created these public synonyms, all beginning with ORA_, for your convenience. Below is a list of the functions and a brief explanation of what they return:

Function	Description
ORA_CLIENT_IP_ADDRESS()	Returns the IP address of the client in the LOGON event.
ORA_DATABASE_NAME()	Returns the database name.
ORA_DES_ENCRYPTED_PASSWORD()	Returns the encrypted password of the user being created or altered.
ORA_DICT_OBJ_NAME()	Returns the name of the object which was referenced. For an INSERT statement, it would be the table/view being inserted into.
ORA_DICT_OBJ_NAME_LIST(NAME_LIST OUT ORA_NAME_LIST_T)	Returns the number of objects modified by the event along with the names of those objects via the OUT parameter.
ORA_DICT_OBJ_OWNER()	Returns the object owner of the referenced object.
ORA_DICT_OBJ_OWNER_LIST(NAME_LIST OUT ORA_NAME_LIST_T)	Returns the number of owners whose objects were modified by the event, along with their names via the OUT parameters.
ORA_DICT_OBJ_TYPE()	Returns the object type of the object modified by the event.
ORA_GRANTEE(USER_LIST OUT ORA_NAME_LIST_T)	Returns the number of grantees of a GRANT event and the names of those users via the OUT parameter.
ORA_INSTANCE_NUM()	Returns the number of the current instance.
ORA_IS_ALTER_COLUMN(COLUMN_NAME VARCHAR2)	A Boolean function returning whether or not the given column was altered.
ORA_IS_CREATING_NESTED_TABLE()	A Boolean function returning whether or not the event created a nested table.
ORA_IS_DROP_COLUMN(COLUMN_NAME VARCHAR2)	A Boolean function returning true if the given column was dropped; otherwise false.
ORA_IS_SERVERERROR(ERROR_NUMBER NUMBER)	Returns true if the supplied error number is on the error stack.
ORA_LOGIN_USER()	Returns the login user name.
ORA_PARTITION_POS()	Returns the character position within the SQL text where you would find the PARTITION clause.
ORA_PRIVILEGES(PRIVILEGE_LIST OUT ORA_NAME_LIST_T)	Returns the number of privileges granted or revoked by the event, along with the names of those privileges via the OUT parameter.

Function	Description
`ORA_REVOKEE (` `USER_LIST OUT ORA_NAME_LIST_T)`	Returns the number of users affected by the `REVOKE` event along with a list of the users via the `OUT` parameter.
`ORA_SERVER_ERROR (` `POSITION BINARY_INTEGER)`	Returns the error number at the supplied position of the error stack. 1 is the top of the stack.
`ORA_SERVER_ERROR_DEPTH ()`	Returns the depth of the error stack.
`ORA_SERVER_ERROR_MSG (` `POSITION BINARY_INTEGER)`	Returns the error text at the supplied position of the error stack. 1 denotes the top of the stack.
`ORA_SERVER_ERROR_NUM_PARAMS (` `POSITION BINARY_INTEGER)`	Given the error stack position, it returns the number of values substituted into the error message.

`ORA_SERVER_ERROR_PARAM (`
`POSITION BINARY_INTEGER,`
`PARAM BINARY_INTEGER)`
	Returns the actual text that was substituted for the `%s` in the error message given the position in the stack and the positional number of the parameter. 1 for position means the top of the stack.

`ORA_SQL_TXT (` `SQL_TEXT OUT ORA_NAME_LIST_T)`	Returns the SQL text of the event in the `OUT` parameter along with returning the number of elements that the SQL text has been broken into to be stored in the `OUT` parameter.
`ORA_SYSEVENT ()`	Returns the system event that fired the trigger.
`ORA_WITH_GRANT_OPTION ()`	Boolean function returning `true` if the privileges granted were `WITH GRANT OPTION`.

`ORA_SPACE_ERROR_INFO (`
`ERROR_TYPE OUT VARCHAR2,`
`OBJECT_TYPE OUT VARCHAR2,`
`OBJECT_OWNER OUT VARCHAR2,`
`TABLE_SPACE_NAME OUT VARCHAR2,`
`OBJECT_NAME OUT VARCHAR2,`
`SUB_OBJECT_NAME OUT VARCHAR2)`
	A Boolean function returning `true` if the error is related to a space issue. It will also return information regarding the statement via the `OUT` parameters.

In earlier *Try It Out* sections, we created triggers and packages to log when rows were inserted, updated, and deleted. We also captured who was issuing the statements and even the number of rows affected. Until now though, we did not have any way to know what the actual statement was. Now we can use the functions above.

Try It Out – Log the Actual Statement That Caused the Trigger To Fire

1. We will modify our AFTER statement trigger to also log the statement, adding the event attribute function `ora_sql_txt()` to capture the SQL text and then log it:

```
SQL> create or replace trigger aiud_employees_copy
  2    after insert or update or delete
  3      on employees_copy
  4  declare
  5    l_action employees_log.action%type;
  6    l_sql_text ora_name_list_t;
  7  begin
  8    if INSERTING then
  9      l_action := state_package.rows_changed || ' were ' || 'inserted';
 10    elsif UPDATING then
 11      l_action := state_package.rows_changed || ' were ' || 'updated';
 12    elsif DELETING then
 13      l_action := state_package.rows_changed || ' were ' || 'deleted';
 14    else
 15      raise_application_error( -20001,
 16          'You should never ever get this error.' );
 17    end if;
 18
 19    insert into employees_log(
 20      who, action, when )
 21    values(
 22      user, l_action, sysdate );
 23
 24    l_action := 'The statement that causes the change was:' || chr(10);
 25
 26    for i in 1 .. ora_sql_txt( l_sql_text ) loop
 27      l_action := l_action || l_sql_text(i);
 28    end loop;
 29
 30    insert into employees_log(
 31      who, action, when )
 32    values(
 33      user, l_action, sysdate );
 34
 35  end;
 36  /

Trigger created.
```

2. Now to test it, give every employee in the department with ID 20 another 5 percent raise, and look at the results in the EMPLOYEES_LOG table:

```
SQL> update employees_copy
  2    set salary = salary * 1.05
  3  where department_id = 20;

2 rows updated.

SQL> select *
  2    from employees_log;

WHO        WHEN      ACTION
```

```
---------- --------- ------------------------------------------------------
OPS$CLBECK 15-JUL-01
OPS$CLBECK 15-JUL-01
OPS$CLBECK 15-JUL-01 Insert
OPS$CLBECK 15-JUL-01 Update
OPS$CLBECK 18-JUL-01 Update - Salary for employee_id 201 changed from 13000
                     to 13650

OPS$CLBECK 18-JUL-01 Update - Salary for employee_id 202 changed from 6000
                     to 6300

OPS$CLBECK 18-JUL-01 2 were updated
OPS$CLBECK 30-JUL-01 Update - Salary for employee_id 201 changed from 13650
                     to 14332.5

OPS$CLBECK 30-JUL-01 Update - Salary for employee_id 202 changed from 6300
                     to 6615

OPS$CLBECK 30-JUL-01 2 were updated
OPS$CLBECK 30-JUL-01 The statement that causes the change was:
                     update employees_copy
                         set salary = salary * 1.05
                     where department_id = 20

11 rows selected.
```

How It Works

Notice there are now four new records dated 30-JUL-01. The first three look just like those dated 18-JUL-01. The last record is the new one. You can see that we captured and logged the UPDATE statement. Firstly, on line 6 we had to declare a local variable to receive the SQL text:

```
6     l_sql_text ora_name_list_t;
```

And in lines 24 through 33 we fetched the text into the local variable, looped over that array variable, building up the SQL text that was chopped into pieces, and then logged it in our EMPLOYEES_LOG table:

```
24    l_action := 'The statement that causes the change was:' || chr(10);
25
26    for i in 1 .. ora_sql_txt( l_sql_text ) loop
27      l_action := l_action || l_sql_text(i);
28    end loop;
29
30    insert into employees_log(
31      who, action, when )
32    values(
33      user, l_action, sysdate );
```

Some of these functions do not make sense in every situation. Calling ORA_REVOKEE() in an INSERT trigger is meaningless. It is useful in the user trigger on REVOKE. Make sure you use the appropriate functions in the appropriate triggers.

Summary

Triggers serve a multitude of purposes:

- ❏ They are a great way to control how data is entered and maintained in your tables, enabling the data modeler to ensure that the data entered is formatted properly

- ❏ They allow us to tie our business rules directly to our data and prevent users circumventing these rules

- ❏ They can be used as a security feature. They can be coded to ensure that only certain users can modify your data

- ❏ They can help us log what is actually happening to our data and when it happened, when something happens to any object in the database or just certain schemas

- ❏ They can be used to teach Oracle how to handle complex user-defined data types

And since the triggers are in the database and are attached to the objects or events themselves, Oracle manages their execution. We are assured that no matter what client application accesses our data, they will be executed.

Objects

Beginning with Oracle 8, the database has had the ability not only to deal with simple predefined data types such as NUMBER, DATE, and VARCHAR2, but also with data types created by the developer. These new data types allow the developer to model their application using object-oriented concepts but still take advantage of the relational world. Oracle refers to it as the **object-relational** model.

Note that while the object-relational model uses object-oriented concepts, it is not a pure object-oriented database. When object-oriented languages such as Java and C++ were becoming popular, object-oriented databases started springing up in the market place to provide well-integrated persistent storage mechanisms for these languages. Instead of Oracle creating a new database that was purely object-oriented data storage, they decided to build an object model into their existing relational database. This allowed Oracle to support the new object-oriented programmer's requirements, while maintaining the features its users had come to know such as security, reliability, manageability, and performance.

The first release of Oracle's object functionality was not quite what object-oriented programmers needed. Oracle 8's object implementation was missing some key object-oriented features such as inheritance and polymorphism (we'll discuss these a little later). At this time, Oracle's primary focus was on providing an object model that would allow developers to do the following:

❑   Model real-world objects and applications using objects inside the database.

❑   Instantiate, modify, and store object instances in object tables in the database.

❑   Create an object model on top of existing relational tables using object views.

It succeeded in its goals and then some. Not only did Oracle create an object-relational model that accomplished the goals above, but it also implemented this object model using its own functionality inside the database.

With Oracle 9*i*, there have been numerous advances in the object-relational model. There are features such as inheritance, polymorphism, and type evolution. New polymorphic data types have been added to the database to help facilitate the new object-relational model's capabilities. A variety of SQL functions have also been added to work with them. In short, Oracle 9*i* has revolutionized the object-relational model's capabilities.

In this chapter, we will cover:

❑ What object types are and how they are implemented in Oracle.

❑ How to create, modify, and drop object types.

❑ What type evolution is, and why it is so important to Oracle's object-relational model.

❑ What object tables are, and how to use them.

❑ New features in Oracle 9i such as inheritance and polymorphism.

This is only a sample of the topics we will cover throughout the chapter. Objects are increasingly important in the database and, having learned the lessons here, you will be able to use them effectively. Now that we know the history behind Oracle's object-relational model and some of what we can expect in the pages to come, let's get to it.

Please note, the code for all the examples in this chapter is available from the Apress web site (http://www.apress.com/) in the download for this book.

Object-Oriented Concepts

An **object** is a programmer's model of a real-world entity. It contains data specific to the entity being modeled and functions or **methods** to access and manipulate that data. A PERSON object would contain information about a person such as NAME, SEX, DATE_OF_BIRTH, and MARITAL_STATUS. It might also contain methods like CHANGE_NAME() and CHANGE_MARITAL_STATUS(), so if a woman gets married and decides to take her husband's last name, the object can be updated to reflect the changes. This is known as **encapsulation**. The attributes and the methods to manipulate those objects are all part of the same object.

In the object-oriented world, objects can inherit the attributes and functionality of other objects. If they inherit from only a single object, that is known as **single inheritance**, while if they can inherit from two or more objects directly is known as **multiple inheritance**. Objects can inherit from objects, which themselves have inherited from other objects. So, object A can inherit from object B that inherited from object C. Object A will have all the methods and attributes of both B and C even though it does not inherit from C directly. This is known as an **object hierarchy**. In Oracle 8, inheritance could be simulated, but it was not true inheritance. Oracle 9i supports a true single hierarchy inheritance model.

You cannot have an object-oriented discussion without hearing the term **polymorphism**, indeed, you've already heard it several times in this one. Polymorphism is the ability to appear in many forms. In the OO world, objects that can be treated like different object types are said to be polymorphic. For example, an object of type EMPLOYEE may have been modeled to inherit from a PERSON type. Any object of type EMPLOYEE can also be treated like a PERSON. This ability to take on the characteristics of different object types is polymorphism. This feature, although not supported in Oracle 8, is now supported in Oracle 9i.

What Is an Object Type?

In Oracle, object types are user-defined data types. These newly defined data types can comprise simple data types, collections, or any other previously defined object types. You can also associate functions or methods with an object type to implement its behaviors. An example might look like this:

```
create type person_type as object(
  name varchar2(100),
  sex char(1),
  date_of_dirth date,
  marital_status char(1),
  member procedure change_name( p_name varchar2 ) );
```

Object types themselves are just the definition of what the object will look like and how it will behave. We have to instantiate or create an instance of that object type in order to use it. Think of it this way – the data type DATE is useless by itself, but a variable, or instance, of a DATE is useful.

It is important to remember that the object-relational features available in Oracle 8 upwards don't alter the fact that Oracle is a relational database. Under the covers, all object instances (of our object types) are still stored in relational tables. Oracle manages the mappings and storage of these object instances for you. You, as the developer, can work with these real-world entities as a single unit. In other words, you can select the object instance BOOK and not have to know that a BOOK comprises the object instances AUTHOR, PUBLISHER, EDITOR, CHAPTER,and PAGE.

Oracle object types give us the ability to communicate more easily with applications written in Java and C++, which use objects. We can model Oracle object types to match objects used in these applications and then use an appropriate programming interface to store (or **persist**) instances of the objects in relational or object tables. Retrieving the instances is also easy and convenient. A single request for an object type may, in fact, pull information from many relational tables. Oracle will marshal the data into an object and return it in a single network round trip.

Using object types allows you to mix both relational and object-oriented concepts in the same application. Older applications that did not use object types can still take advantage of these new features by using object views, and can still reference the object types of other applications using SQL. It is not necessary to choose one implementation over the other.

Objects vs. Collections

Many people confuse object types with collection types and use the terms interchangeably, but that is a mistake. While both are user defined data types, *collections* consist solely of the data types VARRAY and NESTED TABLE. These data types facilitate the storage of data within a table. Both NESTED TABLE and VARRAY can be defined as a column of a table, giving you the ability to store an entire subtable or NESTED TABLE as a single column in one row of a relational table.

VARRAYs are fixed-size, ordered arrays. Elements within a VARRAY are accessed via an index of the array corresponding to their positions within it. The elements of a VARRAY must all be of the same type. The element type can be any simple data type or user-defined object type.

621

NESTED TABLEs are an unordered set of elements of the same data type. The elements, like those of VARRAYs, must be of the same type and can be any simple data type or user-defined object type.

VARRAYs and NESTED TABLEs are explored in much greater detail in Chapter 10, PL/SQL.

Having considered a definition of object types, as distinct from collections, let's get into how we create and use them practically.

Using Object Types

Just like a PL/SQL package, an object type has a **specification** and an optional **body**. The specification, or spec, defines the public interface to the object type. The body is the implementation of the object type. That is where you write the code behind the methods defined in the spec.

The syntax for the spec is as follows.

```
CREATE [OR REPLACE] TYPE type_name
[AUTHID {CURRENT_USER | DEFINER}]
{ {IS | AS} OBJECT | UNDER supertype_name }
(
   attribute_name datatype[, attribute_name datatype]...
   [{MAP | ORDER} MEMBER function_spec,]
   [{FINAL| NOT FINAL} MEMBER function_spec,]
   [{INSTANTIABLE| NOT INSTANTIABLE} MEMBER function_spec,]
   [{MEMBER | STATIC} {subprogram_spec | call_spec}
     [, {MEMBER | STATIC} {subprogram_spec | call_spec}]...]
)
   [{FINAL| NOT FINAL}]
   [ {INSTANTIABLE| NOT INSTANTIABLE}];
```

The object type's optional body is defined by using the following syntax:

```
[CREATE [OR REPLACE]
TYPE BODY type_name {IS | AS}
   { {MAP | ORDER} MEMBER function_body;
     | {MEMBER | STATIC} {subprogram_body | call_spec};}
   [{MEMBER | STATIC} {subprogram_body | call_spec};]...
END;]
```

We will learn what this all means and how to use it as we go along.

Creating an Object Type

Let's start off by creating a very simple object type:

```
SQL> create or replace
  2  type person as object(
  3    first_name varchar2(100),
```

```
    4    last_name varchar2(100) )
    5  /

Type created.
```

Here we created an object type called PERSON. It has two attributes, FIRST_NAME and LAST_NAME. They are both of data type VARCHAR2(100).

Attribute names must be unique to the object type itself and can be of any Oracle data type (including user-defined types) except the following:

- ❑ LONG and LONG RAW

- ❑ NCHAR, NCLOB, and NVARCHAR2

- ❑ ROWID and UROWID

- ❑ PL/SQL specific types, including BINARY_INTEGER, BOOLEAN, PLS_INTEGER, RECORD, REF CURSOR, %TYPE, and %ROWTYPE

- ❑ Any type defined within a PL/SQL package

Oracle object types must be defined with at least one attribute and can have a maximum of 1000. Methods (discussed later) are optional, as you can see from the example above which omits them.

We can DESCRIBE an object type within SQL*Plus just as we can DESCRIBE tables, views, and procedures:

```
SQL> desc person
 Name                                        Null?    Type
 ------------------------------------------- -------- ------------------------
 FIRST_NAME                                           VARCHAR2(100)
 LAST_NAME                                            VARCHAR2(100)
```

Now that we have created an object, let's see how we can use it.

Constructor Method

The following, very simple, example shows the basics of using an object type:

```
SQL> set serverout on

SQL> declare
  2      l_person person;
  3  begin
  4      l_person := person( 'Christopher', 'Beck' );
  5      dbms_output.put_line( l_person.first_name );
  6  end;
  7  /
Christopher

PL/SQL procedure successfully completed.
```

In line 2 we declare a local variable of type PERSON. At that point the object instance does not exist. Its value is NULL. There is no way to access any of the object's attributes until we create an instance of it at line 4, by instantiating the local variable L_PERSON as an object of type PERSON.

This is accomplished by invoking the CONSTRUCTOR method of the PERSON object type. The CONSTRUCTOR method is responsible for creating a new instance of an object and returning it to the caller. The object type definer does not have to define the CONSTRUCTOR method because every object has an implicit, system-defined CONSTRUCTOR. As in Java, the CONSTRUCTOR has the same name as the object type. Every CONSTRUCTOR 's method takes all the attributes of the object type as its parameters. These parameters are not defaulted so you must supply a value for each one of them, even if the value you supply is NULL.

If you attempt to instantiate an object type with the wrong number of parameters, you will receive the following error:

```
SQL> declare
  2     l_person person;
  3  begin
  4     l_person := person( 'Sean' );
  5     dbms_output.put_line( l_person.first_name );
  6  end;
  7  /

   l_person := person( 'Sean' );
                 *
ERROR at line 4:
ORA-06550: line 4, column 15:
PLS-00306: wrong number or types of arguments in call to 'PERSON'
ORA-06550: line 4, column 3:
PL/SQL: Statement ignored
```

Here we attempted to create a PERSON object while supplying only a FIRST_NAME. Again, you must supply a value for every attribute. In the *Methods* section, later in the chapter, we'll see a technique for defining our own CONSTRUCTORs that can take in fewer parameters.

Object Types in Tables

Our object type can now be used as a column in a relational database table. It is then known as a **column object**.

```
SQL> create table person_table(
  2     name person,
  3     age number )
  4  /

Table created.
```

This is our first exposure to mixing the relational world and the object-oriented world. Note that we can still DESCRIBE the table as if it were a normal relational table:

```
SQL> set describe depth all
SQL> desc person_table
 Name                                          Null?     Type
 --------------------------------------------- --------  ----------------------
 NAME                                                    PERSON
    FIRST_NAME                                           VARCHAR2(100)
    LAST_NAME                                            VARCHAR2(100)
 AGE                                                     NUMBER
```

Since the NAME column is of our user-defined object type, we need to create an instance of a PERSON prior to insertion. Notice I use the SQL*Plus command SET DESCRIBE DEPTH ALL. This was done so that not only would the DESCRIBE list the columns in the table, but it would also traverse the object types and describe them as well. If I had left DESCRIBE at its default of DEPTH 1, the result would have been:

```
SQL> set describe depth 1
SQL> desc person_table
 Name                                          Null?     Type
 --------------------------------------------- --------  ----------------------
 NAME                                                    PERSON
 AGE                                                     NUMBER
```

The column NAME is shown as type PERSON but the PERSON type is not expanded.

To add data to our table, we can create an instance of the object type inline, and then use it to insert values:

```
SQL> declare
  2     l_person person;
  3  begin
  4     l_person := person( 'Christopher', 'Beck' );
  5     insert into person_table
  6     values ( l_person, 33 );
  7  end;
  8  /

PL/SQL procedure successfully completed.
```

We can also convert strings into a PERSON object using the CONSTRUCTOR method, in order to insert values into the table:

```
SQL> insert into person_table
  2  values ( person( 'Sean', 'Dillon' ), 30 );

1 row created.
```

You can consider this in terms of a string, such as DEC 3, 1968, which you want to store in a date column. If your NLS_DATE_FORMAT was DD-MON-YY, you would need to apply the TO_DATE() function to that string in order to convert it into a DATE. In the same way here, you have two strings, Sean and Dillon, which you need to convert into a PERSON object using the CONSTRUCTOR method.

We can select the information from the table just as if there were no object types within the table:

```
SQL> select *
  2     from person_table
  3  /

NAME(FIRST_NAME, LAST_NAME)
-----------------------------------------------------------------------------
       AGE
----------
PERSON('Christopher', 'Beck')
        33

PERSON('Sean', 'Dillon')
        30
```

The output is a bit strange looking at first but it makes sense. There are two columns in the PERSON_TABLE table, a NAME column and an AGE column. The NAME column is of type PERSON, as indicated by the column heading in the SQL*Plus output, which shows the NAME column to consist of the attributes FIRST_NAME and LAST_NAME. The individual rows indicate that the type of the NAME column is PERSON and show the values of each attribute of that type.

If you want to access the individual attributes of the object type you need to alias the table and reference it as follows:

```
SQL> select p.name.first_name
  2     from person_table p
  3  /

NAME.FIRST_NAME
-----------------------------------------------------------------------------
Christopher
Sean
```

> **Note that Oracle requires you to use table aliases when specifying object attributes in your queries, in order to avoid name resolution problems.**

The only time that the alias is optional is when you are referencing a top-level object. In our case we could access NAME directly, but not the individual attributes of NAME. If we attempt to access the individual attributes, then we receive the following error:

```
SQL> select name.last_name
  2     from person_table
  3  /
select name.last_name
            *
ERROR at line 1:
ORA-00904: invalid column name
```

At this point we have seen not only how to create objects, but also how to store data in them, and retrieve data from them. However we have only created objects with simple data types.

Try It Out – Objects Within Objects

Let's see if we can now expand on our original PERSON object (if you haven't created it yet, you'll need to do that), by creating an EMPLOYEE object type which contains a PERSON object type along with an EMPNO and a HIREDATE. This simulates inheritance but is known as **composition**.

```
SQL> create or replace
  2    type employee as object(
  3      name person,
  4      empno number,
  5      hiredate date )
  6  /

Type created.
```

As you can see, once you create an object type you can use it just like any other data type. It is just a bit trickier when you want a new instance of one, since you need to instantiate not only the object, but also any object within that object.

> Note that you can pass **NULL** in for any of the attributes, even other object types.

To create a new instance of an EMPLOYEE object type you need to do the following:

```
SQL> declare
  2    l_emp employee;
  3  begin
  4    l_emp := employee( person( 'Tom', 'Kyte' ), 12345, '01-JAN-01' );
  5    dbms_output.put_line( 'Empno: ' || l_emp.empno );
  6    dbms_output.put_line( 'First Name: ' || l_emp.name.first_name );
  7  end;
  8  /
Empno: 12345
First Name: Tom

PL/SQL procedure successfully completed.
```

Notice how we had to call the PERSON CONSTRUCTOR as a parameter of the EMPLOYEE CONSTRUCTOR. This is because we needed to supply an instance of a PERSON, since the EMPLOYEE object type has a PERSON object type within it. We could have created the PERSON object first and then supplied that value to the EMPLOYEE CONSTRUCTOR, but we managed to accomplish this in one step.

> Note that when we wanted to access attributes in the inner object **PERSON**, we were required to use the dot-notation to access the attributes correctly.

The EMPLOYEE object type can be included as a column in a table just as the PERSON object type was. It does not matter that the EMPLOYEE object has embedded objects of its own, since *all* objects are treated the same. The difference is in the instantiation and accessing of attributes.

Modifying and Deleting Types

Prior to Oracle 9*i*, once you created an object type and then another object or table that depended upon it, you were unable to modify your initial object type (by adding an attribute, or removing a member function for example). The only way to accomplish any modifications was to break all dependencies on that object, which entailed dropping all objects that referenced it, or dropping the table (or the column within the table) that referenced it. This presented major issues for developers who stored objects in tables, because in order to update that object type, the data would have to be unloaded to a staging table, the table dropped, the object recreated, the table rebuilt, and the staging data reloaded into the new object. This was more than impractical; it was unusable. You basically had to get your object data model correct on the first try or spend a lot of time destroying and recreating objects and tables just because you want to add a new attribute to a low-level object type.

In our example above with PERSON and EMPLOYEE, if we wanted to add an AGE attribute to the PERSON object, we would have been unable to just alter the PERSON object. We would first have had to drop the EMPLOYEE type and any other object (table, PL/SQL unit, etc.) that referenced the PERSON object, alter the PERSON object, and finally recreate all the objects that we had just dropped.

New in 9*i*, we have the ability to alter object types with other objects dependent on them, without dropping those that depend on them first. This is known as **type evolution**.

Type Evolution

All views, program units, index types, and operators that are dependent upon an object type are marked INVALID when that object type evolves. The next time they are referenced, they will be recompiled and validated. If that is successful, access is allowed and processing continues. If unsuccessful, then an appropriate error is raised and the developer can address it. An example of when a developer intervention is required is if a new attribute is added to an object type. Every reference to the object type's CONSTRUCTOR is now invalid. Remember, an object type's CONSTRUCTOR takes in as its parameters every attribute within the object type's specification. Any program unit that instantiates that object type needs to be modified to handle the new CONSTRUCTOR definition.

If a table (or other object) is dependent upon a type you wish to evolve, changes have to be made to those objects as well. Both the definition of the object type and the physical storage characteristics required to handle adding, dropping, or altering attributes will change. This involves physically changing every instance of that object type located in every row and every table to reflect the changes. This can take a considerable length of time if there are many instances of that object within your database. The developer has the ability to either defer the evolution of the individual instances of the object type and perform the evolution manually later, or allow the evolution to happen piecemeal as the instance itself is accessed.

INVALIDATE

When altering a table, the developer has two options, INVALIDATE or CASCADE. If they choose the INVALIDATE option, every object which references the object type being altered will be marked INVALID. The syntax for this is as follows:

```
[[INVALIDATE] |
[CASCADE [[NOT] INCLUDING TABLE DATA] [[FORCE] <exceptions-clause>]
```

Let's consider the PERSON_TABLE that we previously created:

```
SQL> desc person_table
 Name                                      Null?    Type
 ----------------------------------------- -------- ----------------------
 NAME                                               PERSON
    FIRST_NAME                                      VARCHAR2(100)
    LAST_NAME                                       VARCHAR2(100)
 AGE                                               NUMBER
```

We can see that it is dependent upon the PERSON object type. Let's alter the PERSON object type and add a new attribute, SSN:

```
SQL> alter type person add attribute ssn varchar2(11) INVALIDATE;

Type altered.

SQL> desc person
 Name                                      Null?    Type
 ----------------------------------------- -------- ----------------------
 FIRST_NAME                                         VARCHAR2(100)
 LAST_NAME                                          VARCHAR2(100)
 SSN                                                VARCHAR2(11)
```

Note: you may encounter an error when trying to DESCRIBE the object after altering it. This is due to a bug in the current version of Oracle, which will be fixed in later versions. To see the DESCRIBE information in this case; you need to alter the object, disconnect from Oracle and connect again. Once you have reconnected, and set the DESCRIBE depth to ALL, you will be able to see the output as shown.

We use the INVALIDATE option to cause Oracle to mark all dependent database objects INVALID. Now when we attempt to DESCRIBE the PERSON_TABLE, we get the following error.

```
SQL> desc person_table
ERROR:
ORA-24372: invalid object for describe
```

The PERSON_TABLE table is invalid along with any other database object that depended upon the PERSON object type. We, as the developers, must now go and manually validate these database objects before they can be used again.

> The **INVALIDATE** option should only be used if you are sure that no problems will be encountered in evolving dependent database objects. This option allows the **ALTER** command for an object type to occur regardless of its effects on other database objects.

For the PERSON_TABLE table to become useful again, we now need to alter the table to validate it:

```
SQL> alter table person_table upgrade including data;

Table altered.

SQL> desc person_table
 Name                                      Null?    Type
 ----------------------------------------- -------- ------------------------
 NAME                                               PERSON
    FIRST_NAME                                       VARCHAR2(100)
    LAST_NAME                                        VARCHAR2(100)
    SSN                                              VARCHAR2(11)
 AGE                                                NUMBER
```

Here we gave the option UPGRADE INCLUDING DATA. This physically altered every instance of the PERSON object in the table and set the SSN to NULL:

```
SQL> select *
  2    from person_table
  3  /

NAME(FIRST_NAME, LAST_NAME, SSN)
--------------------------------------------------------------------------------
       AGE
----------
PERSON('Christopher', 'Beck', NULL)
        33

PERSON('Sean', 'Dillon', NULL)
        30
```

We could also have supplied the UPGRADE NOT INCLUDING DATA option. This option alters the definition (or meta data) of the table but leaves the instances of the object type unchanged. The table would then be valid even though the objects stored in it were the older version of the object type. They would be converted as necessary when accessed via DML statements. Any of SELECT, INSERT, UPDATE, or DELETE will cause the object instance at that time to evolve to the new version. Any newly created rows would contain instances of the new version of the PERSON object type.

CASCADE

A safer option is CASCADE. The CASCADE option will validate that the changes proposed in the ALTER TYPE statement will not cause errors with respect to the dependent objects. If errors are detected, the ALTER statement fails. You still have the ability to defer evolution of the existing object type instances, by using the NOT INCLUDING TABLE DATA option.

In the previous example we had to manually validate the PERSON_TABLE table. Let's evolve the PERSON object again, but use the CASCADE option and let the database validate the dependent objects for us:

```
SQL> alter type person
  2  add attribute dob date
  3  cascade not including table data
  4  /

Type altered.

SQL> desc person
 Name                                           Null?    Type
 ---------------------------------------------- -------- -----------------------
 FIRST_NAME                                              VARCHAR2(100)
 LAST_NAME                                               VARCHAR2(100)
 SSN                                                     VARCHAR2(11)
 DOB                                                     DATE
```

Note: you may encounter an error when trying to DESCRIBE the object after altering it, as with the previous example of altering an object type. You can work around it in exactly the same way.

Here, we have added another attribute (DOB) to the PERSON object, and used the CASCADE option so that all dependent database objects will be validated at this time. The NOT INCLUDING TABLE DATA tells Oracle not to migrate existing PERSON instances to the new version, but to defer that until the instance is actually accessed via a DML statement. We can DESCRIBE the PERSON_TABLE and see that the changes have cascaded to it.

```
SQL> desc person_table
 Name                                           Null?    Type
 ---------------------------------------------- -------- -----------------------
 NAME                                                    PERSON
    FIRST_NAME                                           VARCHAR2(100)
    LAST_NAME                                            VARCHAR2(100)
    SSN                                                  VARCHAR2(11)
    DOB                                                  DATE
 AGE                                                     NUMBER
```

Although the table is valid, the data within the table is not. The instances of PERSON have not yet evolved to the new version and will not do so until you UPGRADE the table manually, or access the individual instances of PERSON. The later case is as easy as selecting them as follows:

```
SQL> select *
  2      from person_table
  3  /

NAME(FIRST_NAME, LAST_NAME, SSN, DOB)
------------------------------------------------------------------------------
       AGE
----------
PERSON('Christopher', 'Beck', NULL, NULL)
       33

PERSON('Sean', 'Dillon', NULL, NULL)
       30
```

As you can see the select statement caused the instances to migrate and the new attribute, DOB, to be defaulted to NULL.

The FORCE option, to be used in conjunction with CASCADE, allows you to ignore errors and proceed with the ALTER statement just like the INVALIDATE option does, but with two distinctions:

❑   FORCE can *only* be used in conjunction with CASCADE, which will attempt to validate all dependent database objects. This is in direct contrast to the INVALIDATE option, which just alters the object type leaving the validation to be performed manually by the developer.

❑   INVALIDATE provides no feedback as to what database objects were affected, while CASCADE – FORCE will log any errors it had in evolving object types to the specified exceptions table. This exceptions table must already have been created using DBMS_UTILITY.CREATE_ALTER_TYPE_ERROR_TABLE so we won't look at using it here.

Type evolution makes many of the pains of developing with (and changing) object types go away by automating the migration process.

Dropping Types

To drop a type you need to use the DROP TYPE <TYPE_NAME> command.

If we wanted to drop the object types we have created so far, this is how we would do it:

```
SQL> drop type employee;

Type dropped.

SQL> drop table person_table;

Table dropped.

SQL> drop type person;

Type dropped.
```

The EMPLOYEE type includes a PERSON type in its definition. It is said to be dependent on the PERSON type. You cannot drop a type if another type or table depends on it. In this case, PERSON_TABLE also depends on a PERSON type, so we had to drop it before PERSON too. When both of its dependent objects had been dropped, we could drop PERSON too.

If we had dropped the PERSON object type first, we would have seen the following error:

```
SQL> drop type person;
drop type person
*
ERROR at line 1:
ORA-02303: cannot drop or replace a type with type or table dependents
```

Methods

Methods are procedures and functions associated with object types. These methods are defined within the object itself. Method names must be different from any of the attributes defined within the object, but follow the same overloading rules as packaged procedures (see Chapter 11, *Procedures, Functions, and Packages,* for these rules).

Methods are defined in the type specification and the method implementation is defined in the type body.

There are three types of methods, MEMBER, STATIC, and CONSTRUCTOR. You have already seen CONSTRUCTOR methods. They are created by Oracle and are used to create an instance of the particular object. The difference between the MEMBER and STATIC methods is the context from which they can be called.

STATIC methods are only called on the object type itself. They are used to set up any data that is not instance specific. MEMBER methods are called on the *instance* of an object. This is the one place where you use the object type and not an instance of the type to perform some action.

To execute a STATIC method within the PERSON type, you would call it like this.

```
person.static_method();
```

Notice that we use the *object type* and not an instance of the object.

Let's recreate our EMPLOYEE object to include a MEMBER method:

```
SQL> create or replace
  2  type employee as object(
  3    name person,
  4    empno number,
  5    hiredate date,
  6    sal number,
  7    commission number,
  8    member function total_compensation return number,
  9    static function new( p_empno number,
 10                         p_person person ) return employee )
 11  /

Type created.
```

Just as we define attributes in the spec, we also define methods. We see that our object type includes a PERSON object type, a MEMBER method called TOTAL_COMPENSATION(), and a STATIC method called NEW(). The NEW() method returns an EMPLOYEE type. This will be our alternative CONSTRUCTOR.

If we DESCRIBE the EMPLOYEE object we see the following:

```
SQL> set describe depth all
SQL> desc employee
 Name                              Null?    Type
```

```
------------------------------------------- -------- ---------------------------
  NAME                                               PERSON
    FIRST_NAME                                       VARCHAR2(100)
    LAST_NAME                                        VARCHAR2(100)
    SSN                                              VARCHAR2(11)
    DOB                                              DATE
  EMPNO                                              NUMBER
  HIREDATE                                           DATE
  SAL                                                NUMBER
  COMMISSION                                         NUMBER


METHOD
------
  MEMBER FUNCTION TOTAL_COMPENSATION RETURNS NUMBER


METHOD
------
  STATIC FUNCTION NEW RETURNS EMPLOYEE
  Argument Name                    Type                    In/Out Default?
  ----------------------------- ------------------------ ------ --------
  P_EMPNO                          NUMBER                  IN
  P_PERSON                         PERSON                  IN
```

We now need to implement the TOTAL_COMPENSATION() and NEW() methods in the type body:

```
SQL> create or replace
  2  type body employee as
  3    member function total_compensation return number is
  4    begin
  5      return nvl( self.sal, 0 ) +
  6              nvl( self.commission, 0 );
  7    end;
  8    static function new( p_empno number,
  9                        p_person person ) return employee is
 10    begin
 11      return employee( p_person, p_empno, sysdate, 10000, null );
 12    end;
 13  end;
 14  /

Type body created.
```

Here the MEMBER method returns the sum of the SAL and COMMISSION attributes. It wraps each in a call to NVL() to ensure that we are not attempting to replace NULL with zero.

You will have noticed several references to SELF.<attribute_name>. SELF is a built-in parameter that every MEMBER method accepts as its first parameter. You can explicitly define it like this:

```
member function total_compensation( self in out employee ) return
number
```

Or you can implicitly reference it as we did earlier. In MEMBER procedures, if SELF is defined in the parameter list, it defaults to a mode of IN OUT. MEMBER functions where no SELF is defined in the parameter list, default to IN mode. Defining the SELF parameter explicitly has the side effect of making the function uncallable from within a SQL statement (you can't call functions with IN OUT parameters in SQL). This might be what you want. Consider a MEMBER function called GIVE_RAISE() which takes in a percentage increase and returns the new salary. Calling this from SQL over and over again will keep increasing the employee's salary (which may not be a bad thing if you are the employee). TOTAL_COMPENSATION() on the other hand just displays information. There is no reason why you shouldn't be able to call this function from SQL, and in fact you would probably want to. Also, no other parameter or local variable may be called SELF and SELF must be of the same data type as the object type.

When no modifier is applied to attributes, SELF is implied. Lines 5 and 6 opposite could have also been written omitting the SELF modifier as follows:

```
5        return nvl( sal, 0 ) +
6               nvl( commission, 0 );
```

Try It Out – Using Member Methods

Now that we have this type with a MEMBER method and a STATIC method, let's put them to use by creating an instance of the EMPLOYEE object type using our CONSTRUCTOR, NEW(). Then we'll display the salary using the method TOTAL_COMPENSATION(). Finally, we'll change the COMMISSION of the instance and display the total compensation again:

```
SQL> set serverout on
SQL> declare
  2    l_employee employee;
  3  begin
  4    l_employee := employee.new( 12345,
  5                                person( 'Joel', 'Kallman',
  6                                        '123-45-6789', '01-JAN-01' ) );
  7    dbms_output.put_line( l_employee.total_compensation() );
  8    l_employee.commission := 250;
  9    dbms_output.put_line( l_employee.total_compensation() );
 10  end;
 11  /
10000
10250

PL/SQL procedure successfully completed.
```

In this example we created a local variable of type EMPLOYEE at line 2. At line 4 we instantiate the EMPLOYEE object by calling the STATIC method NEW(). Notice how we referenced NEW():

```
4    l_employee := employee.new( 12345,
```

We referenced it through the type itself, EMPLOYEE, and not an instance of the type, L_EMPLOYEE. That is what differentiates STATIC method functions from MEMBER method functions.

Also, our CONSTRUCTOR NEW() only took in two parameters, but our EMPLOYEE object has 5 attributes. We did not supply HIREDATE, SALARY, and COMMISSION directly for the creation of an instance of EMPLOYEE. They were hard-coded into the NEW() STATIC method. The NEW() method calls the default CONSTRUCTOR for the object type, supplies all the necessary values and returns a fully instantiated instance of an object. We have used this technique to 'default' attributes of the object. For objects that have many attributes, where most of them can be derived or defaulted, using this technique is a must.

Line 7 is where we make our first call to the method TOTAL_COMPENSATION(). Notice how it is qualified with the EMPLOYEE instance we created. Using a normal PL/SQL function, we would have had to pass in the instance of the object type as a parameter, but in the case of MEMBER methods, they are associated with the instance and are referenced through the instance itself.

At line 8 we modify the COMMISSION attribute. Then at line 9 we display the total compensation again, and we can see from the output that the commission was indeed added to the total compensation in the second call at line 9.

MEMBER methods are used to manipulate and access data within the object. In the example above, it would have been possible to have a MEMBER procedure called UPDATE_COMMISSION() and have that method modify the COMMISSION attribute rather than access it directly. It is up to the developer since either way is valid.

Map

Variables, or instances, of data types such as NUMBER, VARCHAR2, and DATE, have an order to them, which allow them to be compared to one another or sorted. Object type instances have no predefined order. To allow Oracle to compare and sort like objects, you can supply an optional MAP method.

The MAP method accepts as its parameter the SELF built-in parameter. It returns a scalar value, which can be used to compare and order the object type. An object type can only have one MAP method defined.

If we attempt to compare two EMPLOYEE objects, we get the following error:

```
SQL> declare
  2     l_employee1 employee;
  3     l_employee2 employee;
  4  begin
  5     l_employee1 := employee.new( 12345, null );
  6     l_employee2 := employee.new( 67890, null );
  7     if l_employee1 = l_employee2 then
  8        dbms_output.put_line( 'They are equal' );
  9     end if;
 10  end;
 11  /

    if l_employee1 = l_employee2 then
                   *
ERROR at line 7:
ORA-06550: line 7, column 18:
PLS-00526: A MAP or ORDER function is required for comparing objects in PL/SQL.
```

In our EMPLOYEE example, there is no definitive way to order them. We could order them by DOB, HIREDATE, SSN, or indeed a combination of these. The MAP method returns some value to order the object by. Let's add a MAP method to the EMPLOYEE object type:

```
SQL> create or replace
  2  type employee as object(
  3    name person,
  4    empno number,
  5    hiredate date,
  6    sal number,
  7    commission number,
  8    map member function convert return number )
  9  /

Type created.


SQL> create or replace
  2  type body employee as
  3    map member function convert return number is
  4    begin
  5      return self.empno;
  6    end;
  7  end;
  8  /

Type body created.
```

Having defined the MAP method CONVERT(), we can now compare EMPLOYEE object types and order them numerically in queries based on the EMPNO attribute:

```
SQL> declare
  2     l_employee1 employee;
  3     l_employee2 employee;
  4  begin
  5     l_employee1 := employee( null, 12345, '01-JAN-01', 100, 100 );
  6     l_employee2 := employee( null, 67890, '01-JAN-01', 100, 100 );
  7     if l_employee1 > l_employee2 then
  8       dbms_output.put_line( 'Employee 1 is greater' );
  9     end if;
 10     if l_employee1 < l_employee2 then
 11       dbms_output.put_line( 'Employee 2 is greater' );
 12     end if;
 13     if l_employee1 = l_employee2 then
 14       dbms_output.put_line( 'Employees are equal' );
 15     end if;
 16  end;
 17  /
Employee 2 is greater

PL/SQL procedure successfully completed.
```

Here we create two instances of an EMPLOYEE object, each having a different EMPNO. When we attempt to compare them at lines 7, 10, and 13, Oracle executes the MAP method for each of them and compares the scalar values returned. Since we created the object type EMPLOYEES, it is up to us to determine if, and how, the two instances relate to one another. In this example we chose to relate them by EMPNO.

Order

An object type can alternatively contain a single ORDER method. The ORDER method will simply compare one object's value to another. This optional method must be a function. It takes as its parameters, SELF and another parameter of the same type as the object itself. This function must return a numerical value. If a positive value is returned, then SELF is greater than the object passed in. If a negative value is returned, SELF is less than the object passed in. If zero is returned, the objects are equal.

Let's reimplement our EMPLOYEE object with an ORDER method instead of a MAP method:

```
SQL> create or replace
  2  type employee as object(
  3    name person,
  4    empno number,
  5    hiredate date,
  6    sal number,
  7    commission number,
  8    order member function match ( p_employee employee ) return integer )
  9  /

Type created.


SQL> create or replace
  2  type body employee as
  3    order member function match ( p_employee employee ) return integer is
  4    begin
  5      if self.empno > p_employee.empno then
  6        return 1;
  7      elsif self.empno < p_employee.empno then
  8        return -1;
  9      else
 10        return 0;
 11      end if;
 12    end;
 13 end;
 14 /

Type body created.
```

Now we can execute exactly the same code as we did in the MAP method section to compare two employee objects in terms of their employee numbers, and we should get identical results.

Either method, MAP or ORDER, is equally capable of comparing objects to each other in both SQL and PL/SQL. If neither method is defined, comparisons of object types are restricted to SQL and then only to comparison for equality. Equality in that case is determined by comparing each and every attribute in the two object type instances.

MAP methods are more efficient when sorting or merging large numbers of objects. A single call is all that is required to map the objects into scalar values and then order the entire set. With ORDER methods, since you can only compare two elements at a time, you must call the ORDER method over and over again to compare a large dataset. Hash joins (a process Oracle uses to join tables) require the use of a MAP method when working with object types since such joins are based on the object types' value.

Inheritance

So far all our examples using object types have used either a single object (PERSON) or an object that included another object (EMPLOYEE included a PERSON object). We could access any of the PERSON attributes through the EMPLOYEE object, but we knew we were doing it. It required special syntax and dot-notation constructs to correctly access the attributes in the object type included within our other object type. In the EMPLOYEE object type, if we wanted to reference the FIRST_NAME, we had to go through the EMPLOYEE object and down into the PERSON object. It would look something like this:

```
l_employee.name.first_name := 'CAMERON';
```

That EXTRA.NAME level of direction was cumbersome. Imagine if the PERSON object also included an object type and that one included another object type and so on. The number of .<NAMES> would quickly grow and become quite unmanageable. True object-oriented programmers would scoff at this implementation.

This methodology has been replaced in Oracle 9*i* with the ability to subtype an object type and, as a result, to support true inheritance from the supertype with full polymorphism. What that means is that Oracle's object model is now a true object-oriented implementation. Let's take a closer look at these new features.

Creating a Subtype

A **subtype** is an object type that inherits the attributes and methods from the parent or **supertype**. The subtype has a subset of the values of the supertype. For example, you might have a supertype called SHAPE and subtypes named CIRCLE, SQUARE, and TRIANGLE, which inherit from the SHAPE supertype.

Sometimes you will hear the relationship between a supertype and subtype called the IS-A relationship.

A subtype is a supertype. A SQUARE is a SHAPE. The reverse is not true. A supertype is not a subtype. A SHAPE is not a SQUARE.

In our running example, the EMPLOYEE object can be considered a subtype of PERSON. An EMPLOYEE is a PERSON. But our implementation lacked both inheritance and polymorphism. Let's re-implement these objects using inheritance.

Let's start out by creating a new object type called NEW_PERSON:

```
SQL> create or replace
  2    type new_person as object (
  3      first_name varchar2(100),
  4      last_name varchar2(100),
  5      dob date,
  6      phone varchar2(100),
  7      member function get_last_name return varchar2,
  8      member function get_phone_number return varchar2 )
  9    not final
 10    /

Type created.
```

The syntax is the same as before except for line 9. The option NOT FINAL was added here, which tells Oracle that this object type can be subtyped (in other words that other object types can inherit from it). By default all object types are FINAL and no subtyping is permitted. You must explicitly define your object to be NOT FINAL (or alter an object already created using the ALTER TYPE DDL command) in order to subtype an object type. Besides the NOT FINAL option, there is nothing that we have not already seen. The PERSON has 4 attributes, FIRST_NAME, LAST_NAME, DOB, and PHONE and two MEMBER functions, GET_PHONE_NUMBER() and GET_LAST_NAME().

The type body implements the MEMBER methods:

```
SQL> create or replace
  2    type body new_person as
  3      member function get_last_name return varchar2 is
  4      begin
  5        return self.last_name;
  6      end;
  7      member function get_phone_number return varchar2 is
  8      begin
  9        return self.phone;
 10      end;
 11    end;
 12    /

Type body created.
```

Creating and accessing this NOT FINAL type is no different from accessing a FINAL type. All the same rules apply.

Now we are ready to subtype NEW_PERSON and create a NEW_EMPLOYEE object type.

```
SQL> create or replace
  2    type new_employee under new_person (
  3      empno number,
  4      hiredate date,
  5      work_phone varchar2(100),
```

```
     6      overriding member function get_phone_number return varchar2,
     7      member function get_home_phone_number return varchar2 )
     8  not final
     9  /

  Type created.
```

There is a lot going on here so let's look at it closely:

Line 2 has the UNDER <OBJECT_TYPE> keyword. This tells Oracle that this new object will be a subtype of <OBJECT_TYPE>, in this case NEW_PERSON. Since NEW_PERSON was defined as NOT FINAL, this is legal syntax. One thing that you might have noticed is missing from this definition is an attribute of the NEW_PERSON object type. We do not need to include it. We defined this type as being UNDER NEW_PERSON. In doing that, we inherited all its attributes and methods.

At line 6, we use the OVERRIDING keyword to describe the MEMBER method GET_PHONE_NUMBER(). We need to do this because in the supertype NEW_PERSON object type, there is also a MEMBER method called GET_PHONE_NUMBER() with the same inputs and outputs. This new version of the MEMBER method **shadows** or **overrides** the supertype's version of it. If the new MEMBER method followed the rules of overloading functions and procedures, it would not be necessary to include the OVERRIDING keyword. We will see more on this a little later on.

At line 8 we again define this class as NOT FINAL in case we chose to subtype the EMPLOYEE object type.

Now let's implement the NEW_EMPLOYEE type body:

```
  SQL> create or replace
     2  type body new_employee as
     3     overriding member function get_phone_number return varchar2 is
     4     begin
     5       return self.work_phone;
     6     end;
     7     member function get_home_phone_number return varchar2 is
     8     begin
     9       return self.phone;
    10     end;
    11  end;
    12  /

  Type body created.
```

The NEW_EMPLOYEE object type body is very simple. We just need to implement the MEMBER methods that were defined in the spec. The OVERRIDING MEMBER method GET_PHONE_NUMBER() returns the WORK_PHONE and not PHONE. That makes sense, since if we refer to a NEW_EMPLOYEE and want their phone number, we will certainly want their work phone and not the home phone.

When we DESCRIBE this type we see the following:

```
SQL> desc new_employee
new_employee extends SCOTT.NEW_PERSON
new_employee is NOT FINAL
Name                                         Null?    Type
----------------------------------------    --------  ------------------------
 FIRST_NAME                                            VARCHAR2(100)
 LAST_NAME                                             VARCHAR2(100)
 DOB                                                   DATE
 PHONE                                                 VARCHAR2(100)
 EMPNO                                                 NUMBER
 HIREDATE                                              DATE
 WORK_PHONE                                            VARCHAR2(100)

METHOD
------
 MEMBER FUNCTION GET_LAST_NAME RETURNS VARCHAR2

METHOD
------
 MEMBER FUNCTION GET_PHONE_NUMBER RETURNS VARCHAR2

METHOD
------
 MEMBER FUNCTION GET_HOME_PHONE_NUMBER RETURNS VARCHAR2
```

This description tells us a lot. The first two lines tell us that the NEW_EMPLOYEE type extends the NEW_PERSON type and that it is NOT FINAL. (Remember, NOT FINAL means that the type can be subtyped). The next few lines list the attributes of the object type. Notice that there is no distinction made as to where the attributes were initially defined. We know that FIRST_NAME was defined in the NEW_PERSON object type and EMPNO was defined in the NEW_EMPLOYEE object type but there is no indication of that here. There is no need to know that. As far as we are concerned, all these attributes are available to the NEW_EMPLOYEE object type.

The last few lines describe the methods available to the object type. Again, there is no indication of which type the methods were defined in, or that they are overriding another supertype's method. The implementation is not important to the user of this object.

Manipulating Supertypes and Subtypes

We will start out with creating a table that has a column of type NEW_PERSON:

```
SQL> create table new_person_table( p new_person );

Table created.
```

Now let's populate this table with some data:

```
SQL> insert into new_person_table values
  2  ( new_person( null, 'Kyte', null, '703.555.5555' ) )
  3  /

1 row created.
```

```
SQL> insert into new_person_table values
  2  ( new_employee( null, 'Beck', null, '703.555.1111', 1234, null,
'703.555.2222' ) )
  3  /

1 row created.

SQL> insert into new_person_table values
  2  ( new_employee( null, 'Dillon', null, '703.555.3333', 5678, null,
'703.555.4444' ) )
  3  /

1 row created.
```

Notice, the first row we inserted was a NEW_PERSON type, since we called the NEW_PERSON CONSTRUCTOR method. No problems here since column P in the NEW_PERSON_TABLE is a NEW_PERSON object type.

The next two rows we inserted were NEW_EMPLOYEE object types. Even though the NEW_PERSON_TABLE has a column of type NEW_PERSON, we are still able to store NEW_EMPLOYEE object types. That is because the NEW_EMPLOYEE object type is a subtype of NEW_PERSON. Any subtype can be stored within an object that is its supertype. Since column P is of type NEW_PERSON, and NEW_EMPLOYEE is a subtype of NEW_PERSON, the insertion succeeds. This is polymorphism at work, the ability of the supertype to be substituted for any of its subtypes.

While this is pretty nifty, it is also confusing. We now have a table that has different types in the same column. Luckily, Oracle supplies some built-in functions to determine and manage this. We'll see some of them in a little while, but first let's examine our NEW_PERSON_TABLE table:

```
SQL> select *
  2    from new_person_table;

P(FIRST_NAME, LAST_NAME, DOB, PHONE)
-----------------------------------------------------------------------
PERSON(NULL, 'Kyte', NULL, '703.555.5555')
EMPLOYEE(NULL, 'Beck', NULL, '703.555.1111', 1234, NULL, '703.555.2222')
EMPLOYEE(NULL, 'Dillon', NULL, '703.555.3333', 5678, NULL, '703.555.4444')
```

Here we can actually see that there are in fact NEW_EMPLOYEE and NEW_PERSON objects in our table. We can select the values just as we did previously:

```
SQL> select x.p.last_name
  2    from new_person_table x
  3  /

P.LAST_NAME

-----------------------------------------------------------------------
Kyte
Beck
Dillon
```

We are still required to alias the table, just as we were when we created the EMPLOYEE type containing a PERSON object type, at the beginning of the chapter. In this query, we select out the LAST_NAME. Since both NEW_PERSON and NEW_EMPLOYEE have a LAST_NAME attribute, this is a valid SQL statement. That is not true for the EMPNO. Only the rows that are of type NEW_EMPLOYEE have an EMPNO attribute. Selecting the EMPNO from the NEW_PERSON_TABLE table will cause an error:

```
SQL> select x.p.empno
  2    from new_person_table p
  3  /
select x.p.empno
              *
ERROR at line 1:
ORA-00904: invalid column name
```

We can use combinations of TREAT() and IS OF to avoid this error, and we'll look at this next.

TREAT

The TREAT() function allow us to treat a supertype as if it were a subtype. This gives us the ability to select EMPNO from a NEW_PERSON object. Since there is no such value, NULL will be returned:

```
SQL> select treat( x.p as new_employee ).empno empno,
  2            x.p.last_name last_name
  3    from new_person_table x
  4  /

     EMPNO LAST_NAME
---------- ----------
           Kyte
      1234 Beck
      5678 Dillon
```

We see that the first column tells Oracle to treat the column returned as an EMPLOYEE object type. This allows us to select the EMPNO from what in reality is a PERSON, which has no attribute EMPNO.

IS OF

The IS OF predicate can test an object type to determine what kind of object it is. Since we are interested in only those rows in PERSON_TABLE that are actually EMPLOYEE object types, we can constrain what rows we return by using this predicate as follows:

```
SQL> select treat( x.p as new_employee ).empno empno,
  2            x.p.last_name last_name
  3    from new_person_table x
  4   where p is of ( new_employee )
  5  /

     EMPNO LAST_NAME
---------- ----------
      1234 Beck
      5678 Dillon
```

Note that we must still use the TREAT() function when referencing the EMPNO attribute since the column P we are selecting is a NEW_PERSON object type. We must cast or treat it as if it were the subtype, in order to reference the subtype's attribute EMPNO. The use of IS OF constrained the rows returned to those of type NEW_EMPLOYEE.

Overriding Methods

In our example we defined a MEMBER method as OVERRIDING. This was because we wanted to define a MEMBER function in the subtype with exactly the same signature as a MEMBER function in the supertype. Defining it as OVERRIDING allowed us to accomplish that. Let's see what is happening here:

```
SQL> select x.p.get_last_name() last_name,
  2         x.p.phone phone,
  3         treat( x.p as new_employee ).work_phone work_phone,
  4         x.p.get_phone_number() "GET_PHONE_NUMBER()",
  5         treat( x.p as new_employee ).get_phone_number()
                                     treat_as_new_employee
  6    from new_person_table x
  7  /

LAST_NAME  PHONE        WORK_PHONE    GET_PHONE_NUMBER() TREAT_AS_EMPLOYEE
---------- ------------ ------------- ------------------ -----------------
Kyte       703.555.5555               703.555.5555
Beck       703.555.1111 703.555.2222  703.555.2222       703.555.2222
Dillon     703.555.3333 703.555.4444  703.555.4444       703.555.4444
```

The first column we select is the GET_LAST_NAME() method, that was defined in the PERSON object type and inherited by the NEW_EMPLOYEE object type. The same version of the method is invoked regardless of what kind of object it really is.

The second column we select is the attribute PHONE. Again, it was defined in the NEW_PERSON object type and inherited by the NEW_EMPLOYEE object type. It exists in both types so it is safe to select.

The third column selected is the WORK_PHONE. Since the NEW_PERSON object type does not have that attribute, we must use the TREAT() function to cast the supertype as a subtype. No value actually exists for WORK_PHONE when the object is of type NEW_PERSON, so NULL is returned.

The fourth column selected is where things begin to get interesting. The MEMBER function GET_PHONE_NUMBER() was initially defined in the NEW_PERSON object, but was then redefined in the NEW_EMPLOYEE object with the keyword OVERRIDING. This means that the method exists in both object types, but that different code is executed depending on which type of object invokes it. Notice those objects that are NEW_EMPLOYEE object types return the WORK_PHONE attribute while the PERSON object type returns the PHONE attribute.

To further demonstrate this point, we select as our fifth column the GET_PHONE_NUMBER() again, but this time, we treat the column as if it were from NEW_ EMPLOYEE. This will force all the objects to execute the version of GET_PHONE_NUMBER() which was defined in the NEW_EMPLOYEE object type. That version of the method does not exist for the NEW_PERSON objects so NULL is returned.

This was a large example with a lot going on. The take-home message here is that the methods and attributes you access depend on the object's actual type and/or the subtype it is being cast into.

FINAL / NOT FINAL

At this point we have seen how objects types can be FINAL and NOT FINAL. MEMBER methods can also be defined with the same attributes. By default, MEMBER functions are defined as NOT FINAL. That means that we can override them in a subtype, as we did in our NEW_PERSON/NEW_EMPLOYEE example. If the method GET_PHONE_NUMBER() had been defined as FINAL in the NEW_PERSON object type, we would not have been allowed to override it in the subtype NEW_EMPLOYEE. We would have received an error as shown below:

```
SQL> create or replace
  2  type super_type as object(
  3    n number,
  4    final member procedure cannot_override
  5  )
  6  not final
  7  /

Type created.

SQL> create or replace
  2  type sub_type
  3  under super_type(
  4    overriding member procedure cannot_override
  5  )
  6  /

Warning: Type created with compilation errors.

SQL> show error
Errors for TYPE SUB_TYPE:

LINE/COL ERROR
-------- -------------------------------------------------------------------
0/0      PL/SQL: Compilation unit analysis terminated
3/21     PLS-00637: FINAL method cannot be overriden or hidden
```

The error message says it all. In the type SUPER_TYPE, we define a FINAL MEMBER method. That means that we cannot override it. The object type SUB_TYPE attempts to do just that and receives the appropriate error message.

The same holds true for any attempt to subtype a FINAL object type. By default, object types are FINAL. If you attempt to subtype a FINAL type, you will get this error:

```
SQL> create or replace
  2  type super_type as object(
  3    n number
  4  )
  5  final
  6  /
```

```
    Type created.

    SQL> create or replace
      2  type sub_type
      3  under super_type(
      4    v varchar2(200)
      5  )
      6  /

    Warning: Type created with compilation errors.

    SQL> show error
    Errors for TYPE SUB_TYPE:

    LINE/COL ERROR
    -------- ---------------------------------------------------------------
    1/1      PLS-00590: attempting to create a subtype UNDER a FINAL type
```

INSTANTIABLE / NOT INSTANTIABLE

Object types and MEMBER methods can be defined as NOT INSTANTIABLE. If you define an object type as NOT INSTANTIABLE, you cannot create an instance of this type. There is neither a default nor user-defined CONSTRUCTOR. MEMBER methods defined as NOT INSTANTIABLE, while not implemented by the supertype, must be overridden and implemented by the subtype.

The availability of NOT INSTANTIABLE object types might not sound like a very useful feature. If you cannot create instances of an object type, what good is it? Well, it can be extremely useful if you subtype it. It provides you with two key features, consistency and interoperability. You get consistency, because all the subtypes will inherit the attributes and methods of the supertype. Furthermore, NOT INSTANTIABLE MEMBER methods must be implemented by each subtype, ensuring all subtypes have a distinct implementation of a common method. Interoperability is achieved through the fact that all the subtype instances can be stored in a table with a column of the supertype. You also get that with normal supertype/subtype objects, but in this case the supertype cannot be instantiated. Its purpose is to provide a blueprint that all the subtypes are required to follow. If you are familiar with the programming language Java, the NOT INSTANTIABLE object type is like an Abstract Class.

Consider a NOT INSTANTIABLE object type, SHAPE, that contains a NOT INSTANTIABLE MEMBER method called CALCULATE_AREA() and an attribute NUMBER_OF_SIDES. By itself, it's not very useful. We do not know what kind of shape it is and we don't have any information to calculate the area. It makes no sense to have an instance of a SHAPE object. Declaring it to be NOT INSTANTIABLE ensures that an instance of it cannot exist. If you subtype it with an object type called SQUARE and add an attribute SIDE, you now have a useful object type. We are required to implement the CALCUALTE_AREA() method for SQUARE. We can subtype SHAPE again, this time with an object type called CIRCLE. The CIRCLE object type contains the attribute DIAMETER. Again we must implement the CALCUALTE_AREA() method, but it will be a completely different implementation from SQUARE. Every subtype of SHAPE must follow this blueprint and implement CALCULATE_AREA(). It forces a uniform structure for all shape types. We could have just created SQUARE and CIRCLE without subtyping SHAPE but then we would have lost the ability to store all the shapes in one column in the database. We would also lose the control over enforcing that shapes must define a method called CALCUALTE_AREA().

Let's define an object type, SHAPE:

```
SQL> create or replace
  2  type shape as object(
  3    number_of_sides number,
  4    not instantiable member function calculate_area return number
  5  )
  6  not instantiable not final
  7  /

Type created.
```

But if we attempt to instantiate an object of that type, we get an error:

```
SQL> declare
  2      l_shape shape;
  3  begin
  4      l_shape := shape( 2 );
  5  end;
  6  /
  l_shape := shape( 2 );
              *
ERROR at line 4:
ORA-06550: line 4, column 14:
PLS-00713: attempting to instantiate a type that is NOT INSTANTIABLE
ORA-06550: line 4, column 3:
PL/SQL: Statement ignored
```

The error occurred at line 4, when we attempted to create a new instance of a SHAPE type. Defining it as NOT INSTANTIABLE guarantees that no instances of SHAPE can exist. Let's put what we have just learned to use:

Try It Out – The Company Example

In our company, there are two types of employees; consultants and sales reps. They share some common attributes but they are compensated very differently. The sales rep gets a salary and commission while the consultant is paid on a flat hourly rate. Both types of employees can take vacation. We are going to model these two employee types using a common supertype.

Let's create another NOT INSTANTIABLE object type, but this time we'll subtype it as well. Let's make and abstract an EMPLOYEE type which has the attributes NAME, EMPNO, HIREDATE, and VACATION_USED. It should also have three methods – a FINAL method called VACATION() which will record vacation taken for an EMPLOYEE, a NOT INSTANTIABLE method called GIVE_RAISE() whose function is obvious, and another NOT INSTATIABLE method called YEARLY_COMPENSATION() to calculate and print out the yearly salary for an employee.

1. First we need to drop the PERSON_TABLE and the EMPLOYEE object type we created earlier. We want to start with a clean slate. If you did not create these objects, then you can skip this step.

```
SQL> drop table person_table;

Table dropped.

SQL> drop type employee;

Type dropped.
```

2. Now, let's define the EMPLOYEE object:

```
SQL> create or replace
  2   type employee as object(
  3     name varchar2(100),
  4     empno number,
  5     hiredate date,
  6     vacation_used number,
  7     final member procedure vacation( p_days number ),
  8     not instantiable member procedure give_raise( p_increase number ),
  9     not instantiable member function yearly_compensation return number
 10   )
 11   not instantiable
 12   not final
 13   /

Type created.
```

Notice that at line 12 we define the object type as NOT FINAL. We want to be able to subtype this object type so we need to specify it this way. The methods are defined as either NOT INSTANTIABLE or FINAL and the object type itself is NOT INSTANTIABLE at line 11.

3. Implementing this object type is easy. We only need to supply the functionality for the method VACATION():

```
SQL> create or replace
  2   type body employee as
  3     final member procedure vacation( p_days number ) is
  4     begin
  5       if p_days + self.vacation_used <= 10 then
  6         self.vacation_used := self.vacation_used + p_days;
  7       else
  8         raise_application_error(
  9           -20001,
 10           'You are ' || to_char(p_days + self.vacation_used - 10) ||
 11           ' days over your vacation limit.' );
 12       end if;
 13     end;
 14   end;
 15   /

Type body created.
```

All we do in this routine is check and see if the number of vacation days previously taken, VACATION_USED, and the number currently being taken, P_DAYS, is greater than 10. If it is, we raise an error. If it is not greater, we add to VACATION_USED the number of days of vacation currently being taken.

4. The EMPLOYEE type declaration is complete. Now we need to subtype EMPLOYEE. First lets define a CONSULTANT object type:

```
SQL> create or replace
  2  type consultant
  3  under employee(
  4    hourly_rate number,
  5    overriding member procedure give_raise( p_increase number ),
  6    overriding member function yearly_compensation return number
  7  )
  8  /

Type created.
```

The CONSULTANT object type subtypes EMPLOYEE. It adds one extra attribute, HOURLY_RATE. Because EMPLOYEE had NOT INSTANTIABLE methods declared, any subtype is required to implement them by OVERRIDING them. Since the method VACATION() was FINAL, nothing can be done to it.

5. The implementations of the methods for the CONSULTANT object type are pretty straightforward:

```
SQL> create or replace
  2  type body consultant as
  3    overriding member procedure give_raise( p_increase number ) is
  4    begin
  5      self.hourly_rate := self.hourly_rate + p_increase;
  6    end;
  7    overriding member function yearly_compensation return number is
  8    begin
  9      return self.hourly_rate * 40 * 52;
 10    end;
 11  end;
 12  /

Type body created.
```

The GIVE_RAISE() method increase the attribute HOURLY_RATE by P_INCREASE, the amount passed in. The YEARLY_COMPENSATION() method calculates how much money this instance of a CONSULTANT makes and returns it. The calculation is based on the HOURLY_RATE multiplied by 40 hours a week multiplied by 5 weeks a year.

6. Now that we have completed the CONSULTANT object type definition, let's define the SALES_REP:

```
SQL> create or replace
  2  type sales_rep
  3  under employee(
  4    salary number,
  5    commission number,
  6    overriding member procedure give_raise( p_increase number ),
  7    member procedure give_commission( p_increase number ),
  8    overriding member function yearly_compensation return number
  9  )
 10  /

Type created.
```

The SALES_REP object type also subtypes EMPLOYEE, inheriting all of its attributes and methods. It adds two additional attributes, SALARY and COMMISSON, as well as one additional MEMBER method, GIVE_COMMISSION(). It too must override the NOT INSTANTIABLE method in the supertype.

7. That gives us a total of three methods that we must now implement in the body:

```
SQL> create or replace
  2  type body sales_rep as
  3    overriding member procedure give_raise( p_increase number ) is
  4    begin
  5      self.salary := self.salary + (self.salary * (p_increase/100));
  6    end;
  7    member procedure give_commission( p_increase number ) is
  8    begin
  9      self.commission := self.commission + p_increase;
 10    end;
 11    overriding member function yearly_compensation return number is
 12    begin
 13      return self.salary + self.commission;
 14    end;
 15  end;
 16  /

Type body created.
```

Again, these implementations are very simple. GIVE_RAISE() increases the SALARY attribute by the percentage passed in. GIVE_COMMISSION() increases the COMMISSION attribute. The YEARLY_COMPENSATION() method returns a SALES_REP, yearly compensation which is calculated as the total of SALARY and COMMISSION.

We now have two subtypes, CONSULTANT and SALES_REP, under the EMPLOYEE object type.

8. We'll need a table to store instances of these objects:

```
SQL> create table employees( e employee )
  2  /

Table created.
```

9. Let's now create a simple anonymous block and take our new object types for a test run. Since both SALES_REP and CONSULTANT are subtypes of EMPLOYEE, we can store either in a column of type EMPLOYEE. First we declare two local variables, one of each subtype we just finished defining:

```
SQL> set serverout on
SQL> declare
  2     l_consultant consultant;
  3     l_sales_rep sales_rep;
```

These objects are useless until we instantiate them. Lines 5 and 6 accomplish that:

```
  4  begin
  5     l_consultant := consultant( 'Derrick', 12345, sysdate, 0, 19.50 );
  6     l_sales_rep := sales_rep( 'Julie', 67890, sysdate, 0, 50000, 0 );
  7
```

Next we call the GIVE_RAISE() method for each instance. We give the CONSULTANT a $4.75 hourly increase, while we give the sales rep a 3% salary increase and a commission of $100 by invoking GIVE_COMMISSION() at line 10.

```
  8     l_consultant.give_raise( 4.75 );
  9     l_sales_rep.give_raise( 3 );
 10     l_sales_rep.give_commission( 100 );
 11
```

We persist our object in the EMPLOYEES table. Remember L_SALES_REP and L_CONSULTANT are of different types, but because they are both share common supertype EMPLOYEE, they can both be stored in a column of EMPLOYEE.

```
 12     insert into employees values ( l_sales_rep );
 13     insert into employees values ( l_consultant );
 14
```

Here we are looping over all the records in the EMPLOYEES table and select two values from each object instance that we find. We select the result from the method YEARLY_COMPENSATION() and the attribute NAME. Remember, when selecting object instances from a table like this, Oracle requires you to alias the table. We used the alias EMPS at line 17 to do that. We prefaced each element that we selected with that alias. At line 19, we displayed the information we retrieved using DBMS_OUTPUT.PUT_LINE().

```
 15     for c in ( select emps.e.yearly_compensation() yc,
 16                       emps.e.name name
 17                from employees emps )
 18     loop
 19        dbms_output.put_line( c.name || ' makes ' || to_char(c.yc) || ' a
                                                            year.' );
 20     end loop;
 21
```

The last thing we do is have the SALES_REP instance take some vacation. First we take 5 days and then 7 more days. Notice that we attempt to take 12 days total of vacation, but we are only allowed to take at most 10.

```
22    l_sales_rep.vacation( 5 );
23    l_sales_rep.vacation( 7 );
23  end;
24  /
```

10. Here are the results:

```
Julie makes 51600 a year.
Derrick makes 50440 a year.

declare
*
ERROR at line 1:
ORA-20001: You are 2 day(s) over your vacation limit.
ORA-06512: at "SCOTT.EMPLOYEE", line 8
ORA-06512: at line 23
```

The first two lines are delivered by the DBMS_PUT_PUT.PUT_LINE() at line 19. The sales rep Julie started out making $50,000/year and no commission. She was given a 3% raise and $100 commission. If we do the math we can see that $51600 is correct. The consultant Derrick's initial hourly rate was $19.50 but we increased it by $4.75. He works 40 hours a weeks and is paid 52 weeks a year. Again, doing the math shows that $50440 is the correct figure.

Those numbers match with what our test produced, so everything worked just as we had expected. But what about the vacation request made to the L_SALES_REP instance? Remember we submitted 12 days when the max is 10.

We got an error telling us that we are 2 day over the vacation limit. If you recall, we attempted to take 12 days total (lines 22 and 23). The error message is correct.

Object Tables

Object tables are tables in which every row represents an object. They are similar to tables created with only one column, consisting of an object type. Accessing and manipulating the data is a little different. We'll see this difference later on.

Consider the following object definition:

```
SQL> create or replace
  2  type address as object(
  3    id number,
  4    street varchar2(100),
  5    state varchar2(2),
```

```
     6     zipcode varchar(11)
     7  )
     8  /

Type created.
```

This is just a simple object type definition. The ADDRESS object type has 4 attributes and no MEMBER methods. Using this type we can create an object table:

```
SQL> create table address_table of address
  2  /

Table created.
```

If we DESCRIBE it, it appears to be a simple relational table:

```
SQL> desc address_table
 Name                                      Null?    Type
 ----------------------------------------- -------- --------------------------
 ID                                                 NUMBER
 STREET                                             VARCHAR2(100)
 STATE                                              VARCHAR2(2)
 ZIPCODE                                            VARCHAR2(11)
```

In fact we can insert values into this object table just as we would into a relational table. Oracle will take the inputs in the VALUES clause of the INSERT statement and call the default CONSTRUCTOR for the base object. In this case, it will call the CONSTRUCTOR of the ADDRESS object type and insert the values into our ADDRESS_TABLE object table:

```
SQL> insert into address_table
  2  values ( 1, '1910 Oracle Way', 'VA', '21090' )
  3  /

1 row created.
```

We can also insert the object itself: In the following INSERT statement we call the default CONSTRUCTOR of the ADDRESS type and insert the object directly into the table:

```
SQL> insert into address_table
  2  values ( address( 2, '123 Main Street', 'NJ', '07728' ) )
  3  /

1 row created.
```

When we select the data from this table, it appears to be a relational table:

```
SQL> select *
  2    from address_table
  3  /

        ID STREET               ST ZIPCODE
---------- -------------------- -- -----------
         1 1910 Oracle Way      VA 21090
         2 123 Main Street      NJ 07728
```

> Note that if we want to retrieve the data as an object, we need to use the
> VALUE ( ) function.

VALUE()

The VALUE ( ) function takes the table alias of our object table in as a parameter, and returns the object instance from the appropriate row or rows, depending on the constraints applied in the query:

```
SQL> select value(a)
  2      from address_table a
  3  /

VALUE(A)(ID, STREET, STATE, ZIPCODE)
----------------------------------------------------------------------
ADDRESS(1, '1910 Oracle Way', 'VA', '21090')
ADDRESS(2, '123 Main Street', 'NJ', '07728')
```

Now that we have this object table of addresses, we can build pointers or REFs to the individual rows.

REF Data Type

REF data types are to objects what foreign keys are to relational data. REFs provide a means of associating an object instance with one or more rows. Working with our object table ADDRESS_TABLE, we can create an EMPLOYEE_LOCATION table:

```
SQL> create table employee_location(
  2      empno number,
  3      loc_ref ref address scope is address_table )
  4  /

Table created.
```

The syntax on line 3 might look a little strange so let's take a closer look at it. We are declaring a column with the name LOC_REF. Its type is a REF to an ADDRESS object type. That means a pointer to an ADDRESS instance is stored in the column. We also **scope** the REF. That means that we have restricted the location of the object instances that the REF points to. In our case, the LOC_REF can only point to instances of ADDRESS object that are in the object table, ADDRESS_TABLE.

This method of using REFs allows us to have many EMPLOYEEs reference the same ADDRESS instance. That is good relational modeling. If we need to make a change to an ADDRESS, we need only make it in one place, namely the ADDRESS_TABLE. The alternative would be to have an instance of ADDRESS associated with every EMPLOYEE. That might make sense if it were the home address, but many employees share a common work address so only one copy of that ADDRESS instance should exist.

Let's continue on and populate the EMPLOYEE_LOCATON table. We need to make REFs to the ADDRESS_TABLE, by using the REF ( ) function.

REF()

The REF () function creates a REF object data type pointing to an instance of an object in an object table. It accepts a table alias of the object table as its parameter, and returns a REF to the appropriate row or rows.

Let's add some data to the EMPLOYEE_LOCATION table:

```
SQL> insert into employee_location
  2    select 12345, ref(a)
  3      from address_table a
  4     where id = 1
  5  /

1 row created.

SQL> insert into employee_location
  2    select 67890, ref(a)
  3      from address_table a
  4     where id = 2
  5  /

1 row created.

SQL> insert into employee_location
  2    select 24680, ref(a)
  3      from address_table a
  4     where id = 1
  5  /

1 row created.
```

We've now populated the table with three rows. Each INSERT statement we used is populated with a SELECT from the ADDRESS_TABLE. We did that so that we could get the REF to the appropriate instance in that table. We also selected a constant value for EMPNO.

Now when we SELECT from the EMPLOYEE_LOCATION table we see the following:

```
SQL> select *
  2    from employee_location
  3  /

     EMPNO
----------
LOC_REF
--------------------------------------------------------------------------
     12345
0000220208913837B2C058445AB1526587FEF6AA605E508149D7F845F29BEE248CB4622039

     67890
0000220208BF6E9E75821241EE8732BB8708F6F6635E508149D7F845F29BEE248CB4622039

     24680
0000220208913837B2C058445AB1526587FEF6AA605E508149D7F845F29BEE248CB4622039
```

The LOC_REF value is a pointer to instances of the ADDRESS object type. To view the actual instance itself, you need to dereference the REF.

DEREF()

REF data types can be **dereferenced** so that the instance to which they point to can be viewed. The DEREF() function does this for us. It takes a REF data type in as its parameter, and returns the object instance corresponding to the REF.

If we now select the DEREF() of our REFs, the result is much more readable:

```
SQL> select empno,
  2         deref(loc_ref)
  3    from employee_location
  4  /

     EMPNO
----------
DEREF(LOC_REF)(ID, STREET, STATE, ZIPCODE)
--------------------------------------------------------------------------------
     12345
ADDRESS(1, '1910 Oracle Way', 'VA', '21090')

     67890
ADDRESS(2, '123 Main Street', 'NJ', '07728')

     24680
ADDRESS(1, '1910 Oracle Way', 'VA', '21090')
```

Dangling REFs

We initially said that REFs were like foreign keys, and that is true, but there is a caveat. The object instance that a REF points to can be deleted without consideration of what may reference it. This is the opposite of how a foreign key works, because a foreign key requires that the parent row it references must exist. REFs do not have such a restriction. If a referenced object instance is deleted, any REFs that were pointing to it are said to be **dangling**. That is, they are pointing to an instance that no longer exists. This cannot happen in a foreign key relationship in a relational table.

Let's see what actually happens if we delete one of the ADDRESS instances in the object table ADDRESS_TABLE:

```
SQL> delete from address_table
  2  where id = 1
  3  /

1 row deleted.
```

What effect has this had on the EMPLOYEE_LOCATION table?

```
SQL> select *
  2    from employee_location
  3  /
```

```
        EMPNO
----------
LOC_REF
---------------------------------------------------------------------
        12345
0000220208913837B2C058445AB1526587FEF6AA605E508149D7F845F29BEE248CB4622039

        67890
0000220208BF6E9E75821241EE8732BB8708F6F6635E508149D7F845F29BEE248CB4622039

        24680
0000220208913837B2C058445AB1526587FEF6AA605E508149D7F845F29BEE248CB4622039
```

There are still three rows and the REFs seem fine, but actually two of them are dangling, since they are pointing to an instance of an ADDRESS object that no longer exists. If we attempt to DEREF() these REFs we see:

```
SQL> select empno,
  2          deref(loc_ref)
  3     from employee_location
  4  /

        EMPNO
----------
DEREF(LOC_REF)(ID, STREET, STATE, ZIPCODE)
---------------------------------------------------------------------
        12345

        67890
ADDRESS(2, '123 Main Street', 'NJ', '07728')

        24680
```

The dangling REFs return NULL when we attempt to de-reference them. We can easily determine which (if any) REFs in our tables are dangling by using the IS DANGLING predicate.

IS DANGLING

The IS DANGLING predicate is used to determine if the instance corresponding to a REF is still valid. It is used in a similar fashion to the IS NULL predicate:

```
SQL> select empno
  2     from employee_location
  3   where loc_ref is dangling
  4  /

        EMPNO
----------
        12345
        24680
```

Here we select the EMPNO column from the EMPLOYEE_LOCATION table, where the LOC_REF is found to be dangling.

To clean up dangling REFs, you can update the REFs to Null:

```
SQL> update employee_location
  2     set loc_ref = null
  3   where loc_ref is dangling;

2 rows updated.
```

Summary

We have just completed a whirlwind tour of Oracle's object-relational features. We learned a fair amount of what there is to know about creating and managing objects in the database. Some of the lessons we learned in this chapter are:

- ❏ How to create and manage objects. We learned how to create objects that contain attributes and methods to model real-world entities. These objects can be persisted in relational tables and/or object tables.

- ❏ The differences between objects and collections. One of the most common misconceptions developers have about the Oracle object-relational model is that collections are the same as objects. We took a look at the difference between these two, distinct concepts.

- ❏ We learned the limitations of Oracle 8. Oracle 8 is unable to perform inheritance, so we looked at some best practices for implementing a pseudo inheritance model using objects that include other objects.

- ❏ We explored the new features of Oracle 9i. In Oracle 9i, a variety of new object-relational features were added to the database, including inheritance, polymorphism, and type evolution. We explored a number of these new features to understand better how Oracle's object-relational model meets the needs of object-oriented designers and programmers.

Whereas a relational database supporting object-oriented data storage was once thought impossible, Oracle 9i has made it a reality. This chapter has given you the skills necessary to employ an object-relational model in your own databases and applications.

©2000 by Lauren Ruth Wiener (http://www.verbing.com)

Advanced Querying

In this chapter we'll explore some of the more advanced options for querying in SQL. Much of what we will show you is not standard SQL, but powerful extensions to it that Oracle allows you to perform. Many answers that would normally only be returned using programming constructs, can instead be returned via a single query. This will save you both development and processing time.

The topics we'll be discussing are:

- ❑ Hierarchical Queries – These queries return hierarchical results, such as employees who report to a particular manager.

- ❑ Aggregate Functions – These extend functions such as COUNT(), in order to work on groups of rows, rather than a single row.

- ❑ Pipelined Functions – These allow you to treat a PL/SQL function you write as if it were a database table and select from it.

- ❑ SQL writing SQL – Queries that write SQL for you.

- ❑ Analytic Functions – These perform a wide range of tasks such as finding the top N records in a group of lists.

- ❑ MERGE – A function that allows us to perform either an insert or an update in a single statement.

All of the examples in this chapter can be run on an Oracle 9*i* instance as the sample user SCOTT.

Hierarchical Queries

Hierarchical queries, or CONNECT BY queries as they are sometimes referred to, are an Oracle-specific feature. This class of query allows you to select data and have it returned to you in a hierarchical order. Consider the classic example of an employee table, which contains a column indicating who the employee's manager is. Since managers are employees, they will also be entered in the employee's table. You now have a self-referencing table. Generating a hierarchical listing of the company using basic SQL isn't possible, since you need to look at more than one row of the table at a time.

To solve this problem you could write a recursive PL/SQL routine to figure it out. Something like this would answer the question:

```
SQL> create or replace
  2  procedure company_listing (
  3    p_start_with varchar2,
  4    p_level number default 0 ) as
  5  begin
  6    dbms_output.put_line( lpad( ' ', p_level*2, ' ' ) || p_start_with );
  7    for c in ( select *
  8                  from emp
  9                 where mgr in ( select empno
 10                                  from emp
 11                                 where ename = p_start_with )
 12                 order by ename )
 13    loop
 14      company_listing( c.ename, p_level+1 );
 15    end loop;
 16  end company_listing;
 17  /
Procedure created.
```

This procedure is a recursive routine that prints out the hierarchy of employees. It starts out at line 6 by printing the current employee passed in. Then at line 7 it creates a list of employees that report to that employee and loops over each one calling itself recursively. You can execute it as follows:

```
SQL> set serveroutput on format wrapped

SQL>  exec company_listing( 'KING' );
KING
  BLAKE
    ALLEN
    JAMES
    MARTIN
    TURNER
    WARD
  CLARK
    MILLER
  JONES
    FORD
      SMITH
    SCOTT
      ADAMS

PL/SQL procedure successfully completed.
```

Notice that we use SET SERVEROUT ON FORMAT WRAPPED to make sure that SQL*Plus does not strip off the leading spaces that we have printed in the routine. We execute our procedure using the EXEC command of SQL*Plus.

Although this works, it's expensive in terms of both development and processing. We had to write a recursive stored procedure and are restricted as to what column the `start with` predicate is applied to (in this case ENAME). If we wanted to change it so we could supply the EMPNO instead, we would have to write another stored procedure or make this one much more complex (at far higher development cost).

It would be much easier if we could write a single query to answer this question. It is possible to achieve this using some of the extensions to the SELECT statement that Oracle provides, as we'll take a look at now.

Basics

The procedure above can be replaced with the following query:

```
SQL>  select lpad( ' ', (level-1)*2, ' ' ) || ename ename
  2      from emp
  3      start with ename = 'KING'
  4   connect by mgr = prior empno
  5   /

ENAME
-------------------------------------------------------------------------------
KING
  JONES
    SCOTT
      ADAMS
    FORD
      SMITH
  BLAKE
    ALLEN
    WARD
    MARTIN
    TURNER
    JAMES
  CLARK
    MILLER

14 rows selected.
```

It's that easy. Only four lines as against 15 for the procedure (and it's infinitely more flexible). This query can just as easily be issued from a Java as a C program, since the work of building the hierarchy is done on the server rather than the client. This makes it much easier to execute than the COMPANY_LISTING procedure above, which requires the developer to fetch the results from the DBMS_OUTPUT buffer and then display them.

Let's now look in more detail at these 4 lines.

Start With

The START WITH hierarchical clause of a SELECT statement indicates to Oracle the row with which the hierarchy should begin, and is declared as follows:

```
START WITH <condition>
```

In the example above, we used the employee name (ENAME) KING.

```
3      start with ename = 'KING'
```

The start with condition can be anything which is valid in the WHERE clause. It can contain multiple conditions:

```
start with ename = 'JONES' or ename = 'SCOTT'
```

It can even contain a subquery.

```
Start with deptno in ( select deptno
                         from dept
                        where dname in ('SALES', 'SUPPORT' ) )
```

Any row that matches the START WITH criteria will be made a root node of the result set. This can cause confusion in your results, if your START WITH criteria result in rows that appear in each other's trees. In the code fragment above, we suggested that you could use ename = 'JONES' or ename = 'SCOTT' and you can. However, SCOTT is a child of JONES, so using this criterion will cause the SCOTT tree to be generated twice (once because it is a child of JONES and once because it is the root).

```
SQL>  select lpad( ' ', (level-1)*2, ' ' ) || ename ename
  2       from emp
  3      start with ename = 'JONES' or ename = 'SCOTT'
  4    connect by prior empno = mgr
  5    /

ENAME
------------------------------------------------------------------
SCOTT
  ADAMS
JONES
  SCOTT
    ADAMS
  FORD
    SMITH

7 rows selected.
```

> **You need to be aware of this so as to avoid inadvertently generating multiple copies of the same result set.**

In our initial example, starting with ename = 'KING' will generate the entire company listing. However, as soon as KING retires as CEO our application will fail. We need a more generic START WITH clause to get the entire listing in all cases. Best practice here is to model your hierarchy data such that the top (root) nodes all share a common parent. This can either be some imaginary employee who is really a placeholder for the top of the tree, or indeed no parent at all. In the case of the EMP table KING's MGR is NULL (in other words the root node has no parent), and knowing this allows us to write the query generically.

```
SQL> select nvl( to_char(mgr), 'NULL' ) mgr
  2    from emp
  3    where ename = 'KING';

MGR
----------------------------------------
NULL

SQL>  select lpad( ' ', (level-1)*2, ' ' ) || ename ename
  2      from emp
  3      start with mgr is null
  4    connect by mgr = prior empno;

ENAME
--------------------------------------------------------------------------
KING
  JONES
    SCOTT
      ADAMS
    FORD
      SMITH
  BLAKE
    ALLEN
    WARD
    MARTIN
    TURNER
    JAMES
  CLARK
    MILLER

14 rows selected.
```

Now when KING leaves the company, you will not need to rewrite your query since the new CEO will be inserted into the EMP table with no MGR.

Connect By Prior

The CONNECT BY clause tells Oracle how to relate one row to another. It defines the parent-child (hierarchical) relationship between the rows. This class of query is one of the rare cases in which Oracle looks at two different rows from the same table and compares them without having that table in the FROM clause multiple times. You distinguish the current row from the alternative row by using the keyword PRIOR. The PRIOR refers to the parent row. In our example above we used:

```
  4    connect by mgr = prior empno;
```

That says, *'find me the row or rows in which the* EMPNO *of the last row we looked at is now currently the* MGR'. This takes a little time to get a firm grasp of. It can be confusing at first. However, if you put the PRIOR on the wrong side of the equals sign you'll know right away, since instead of walking down the tree, you will walk up it:

```
SQL>  select lpad( ' ', (level-1)*2, ' ' ) || ename ename
  2       from emp
  3      start with ename = 'SMITH'
  4   connect by empno = prior mgr;

ENAME
-----------------------------------------------------------------------------
SMITH
  FORD
    JONES
      KING
```

Notice in this query, SMITH is the root node and his manager is listed below him. That's because putting the PRIOR clause where we did asked a completely different question. This time we asked, *'Give me all the row or rows in which the last-row-we-examined value of* MGR *is the* EMPNO *of the current row'*. Placing the PRIOR on the other side of the equals sign is not an error as you can see, it just depends on what question you are trying to answer.

The PRIOR keyword can also be used in the SELECT clause to refer to columns from the previous row.

```
SQL>  select lpad( ' ', (level-1)*2, ' ' ) || ename ename, prior ename manager
  2       from emp
  3      start with mgr is null
  4   connect by prior empno = mgr;

ENAME                   MANAGER
--------------------    ----------
KING
  JONES                 KING
    SCOTT               JONES
      ADAMS             SCOTT
    FORD                JONES
      SMITH             FORD
  BLAKE                 KING
    ALLEN               BLAKE
    WARD                BLAKE
    MARTIN              BLAKE
    TURNER              BLAKE
    JAMES               BLAKE
  CLARK                 KING
    MILLER              CLARK

14 rows selected.
```

Here we selected out the ENAME and the manager's ENAME at the same time. Those values do not exist in the same row and we did not join the table to itself. In other words we accessed two different rows of data at the same time.

Level

The last thing to explain about the initial example is LEVEL. LEVEL is a pseudo-column available in every query executed in Oracle. It is a numeric value indicating what *level* in the tree you are. In non-hierarchical queries, level is useless since every row is at the same level. Its value will always be 0:

```
SQL> select ename, level
  2    from emp;

ENAME                     LEVEL
-------------------- ----------
SMITH                         0
ALLEN                         0
WARD                          0
JONES                         0
MARTIN                        0
BLAKE                         0
CLARK                         0
SCOTT                         0
KING                          0
TURNER                        0
ADAMS                         0
JAMES                         0
FORD                          0
MILLER                        0

14 rows selected.
```

In hierarchical queries, the LEVEL value indicates the level in the tree starting with the root node as level 1:

```
SQL>  select lpad( ' ', (level-1)*2, ' ' ) || ename ename, level
  2      from emp
  3      start with mgr is null
  4    connect by prior empno = mgr;

ENAME                     LEVEL
-------------------- ----------
KING                          1
  JONES                       2
    SCOTT                     3
      ADAMS                   4
    FORD                      3
      SMITH                   4
  BLAKE                       2
    ALLEN                     3
    WARD                      3
    MARTIN                    3
    TURNER                    3
    JAMES                     3
  CLARK                       2
    MILLER                    3

14 rows selected.
```

You can see as you move further down the tree that the level is increased by 1 each time.

LEVEL is useful for a couple of things. Firstly, you can use it as we did in our initial query to aid in formatting the information:

```
SQL>  select lpad( ' ', (level-1)*2, ' ' ) || ename ename
```

We use the function LPAD() to prepend blank spaces to the ENAME in order to show on the screen the level in the tree where the ENAME resides. The pseudo-column LEVEL determines the number of blanks that are added.

Secondly we can use it when answering the question, *'Show me a list of my first and second level reports'*:

```
SQL>  select lpad( ' ', (level-1)*2, ' ' ) || ename ename
  2     from emp
  3     start with mgr is null
  4   connect by prior empno = mgr and level <= 3;

ENAME
--------------------
KING
  JONES
    SCOTT
    FORD
  BLAKE
    ALLEN
    WARD
    MARTIN
    TURNER
    JAMES
  CLARK
    MILLER

12 rows selected.
```

SCOTT's and FORD's reports do not show up since they are at LEVEL 4. LEVEL can be used like any other column in a table. Just remember that its value indicates the level in the tree.

Notice that we put the LEVEL <= 3 in the CONNECT BY clause and not in the WHERE clause. While it will work in either clause, it is more efficient to process it in the CONNECT BY clause. This is because Oracle applies the CONNECT BY clause prior to building the hierarchy, while it would apply the WHERE clause after the entire tree was build. In other words, in our example we only ask Oracle to build a tree where the LEVEL <= 3. All rows with a higher LEVEL are not processed. If we had instead used WHERE LEVEL <= 3, Oracle would have built the entire tree, then removed all the nodes beyond LEVEL 3. This requires much more processing time.

Order Siblings By

In the examples above, there is order to the result set, but it's hierarchical. What if we wanted to order the results so that each manager is listed alphabetically? If we used a conventional ORDER BY clause applied to the entire result set then Oracle would order the result set hierarchically and *then* apply the ORDER BY clause, disturbing the original hierarchical order:

```
SQL>  select lpad( ' ', (level-1)*2, ' ' ) || ename ename
  2      from emp
  3      start with mgr is null
  4    connect by prior empno = mgr
  5      order by ename;

ENAME
--------------------------------
      ADAMS
    ALLEN
  BLAKE
  CLARK
      FORD
      JAMES
  JONES
KING
    MARTIN
    MILLER
    SCOTT
      SMITH
    TURNER
    WARD

14 rows selected.
```

We can see that the data is indeed ordered alphabetically but the hierarchical order is lost. We have no idea who reports to who. All we know is what level each is on. To avoid this we can use the ORDER SIBLINGS BY clause, which is new in Oracle 9i. This allows us to order each subtree independently of the rest of the result set.

```
SQL>  select lpad( ' ', (level-1)*2, ' ' ) || ename ename
  2      from emp
  3      start with mgr is null
  4    connect by prior empno = mgr
  5      order siblings by ename;

ENAME
--------------------
KING
  BLAKE
    ALLEN
    JAMES
    MARTIN
    TURNER
    WARD
  CLARK
    MILLER
  JONES
    FORD
      SMITH
    SCOTT
      ADAMS

14 rows selected.
```

Notice that all three of KING's direct subordinates (BLAKE, CLARK, and JONES) are alphabetically ordered and that each subtree is also alphabetically ordered.

SYS_CONNECT_BY_PATH()

Also new in Oracle 9*i* is the built-in function SYS_CONNECT_BY_PATH(). When running a hierarchical query, we can use this function to return the entire path, from root to end node. In the case of MILLER in our examples, his path would be KING-CLARK-MILLER. The syntax for the SYS_CONNECT_BY_PATH() function is:

```
SYS_CONNECT_BY_PATH( <column>, <separator character> )
```

Let's see it in action:

```
SQL>  select lpad( ' ', (level-1)*2, ' ' ) || ename ename,
  2           sys_connect_by_path( ename, '-' ) path
  3       from emp
  4     start with mgr is null
  5   connect by prior empno = mgr
  6  /

ENAME                  PATH
-------------------    -----------------------------------------
KING                   -KING
  JONES                -KING-JONES
    SCOTT              -KING-JONES-SCOTT
      ADAMS            -KING-JONES-SCOTT-ADAMS
    FORD               -KING-JONES-FORD
      SMITH            -KING-JONES-FORD-SMITH
  BLAKE                -KING-BLAKE
    ALLEN              -KING-BLAKE-ALLEN
    WARD               -KING-BLAKE-WARD
    MARTIN             -KING-BLAKE-MARTIN
    TURNER             -KING-BLAKE-TURNER
    JAMES              -KING-BLAKE-JAMES
  CLARK                -KING-CLARK
    MILLER             -KING-CLARK-MILLER

14 rows selected.
```

In older releases of Oracle, it was possible to get the same results but you would be required to write a recursive PL/SQL function to achieve it.

Joins

In previous versions of Oracle, hierarchical queries had to be based on a single table. It was invalid syntax to specify multiple tables in the FROM clause of the query. We can see this if we attempt the following query from within an Oracle 8*i* database in the SCOTT schema:

```
scott@ORA8I.WORLD> select lpad( ' ', (level-1)*2, ' ' ) || emp.ename ename,
  2          dept.dname
  3      from emp, dept
  4     where emp.deptno = dept.deptno
  5     start with mgr is null
  6   connect by mgr = prior empno
  7  /
 select lpad( ' ', (level-1)*2, ' ' ) || emp.ename ename,
 *
ERROR at line 1:
ORA-01437: cannot have join with CONNECT BY
```

To get around this, we'd have to modify the query as follows:

```
scott@ORA8I.WORLD> SQL> select e.ename,
  2          dname
  3      from dept,
  4          ( select h.*,
  5                   rownum r
  6             from ( select lpad( ' ', (level-1)*2, ' ' ) ||
  7                           emp.ename ename,
  8                           deptno
  9                      from emp
 10                    start with mgr is null
 11                  connect by mgr = prior empno ) h
 12            ) e
 13     where e.deptno = dept.deptno
 14     order by r15  /

ENAME                 DNAME
--------------------  --------------
KING                  ACCOUNTING
  JONES               RESEARCH
    SCOTT             RESEARCH
      ADAMS           RESEARCH
    FORD              RESEARCH
      SMITH           RESEARCH
  BLAKE               SALES
    ALLEN             SALES
    WARD              SALES
    MARTIN            SALES
    TURNER            SALES
    JAMES             SALES
  CLARK               ACCOUNTING
    MILLER            ACCOUNTING

14 rows selected.
```

That works just fine but it's awkward to code. However, in Oracle 9*i*, you can have a join condition directly in the hierarchical query:

```
scott@ORA9I.WORLD> select lpad( ' ', (level-1)*2, ' ' ) || emp.ename ename,
  2         dname
  3    from emp, dept
  4    where emp.deptno = dept.deptno
  5    start with mgr is null
6 connect by mgr = prior empno
  7 /

ENAME                           DNAME
------------------------------  --------------
KING                            ACCOUNTING
  CLARK                         ACCOUNTING
    MILLER                      ACCOUNTING
  JONES                         RESEARCH
    FORD                        RESEARCH
      SMITH                     RESEARCH
    SCOTT                       RESEARCH
      ADAMS                     RESEARCH
  BLAKE                         SALES
    ALLEN                       SALES
    MARTIN                      SALES
    JAMES                       SALES
    TURNER                      SALES
    WARD                        SALES

14 rows selected.
```

User-Defined Aggregate Functions

Oracle enables developers to write their own functions to add custom functionality to those available within the database. For example, you may want to create a function that strips vowels out of a string, or one which sums the digits of a string that has been passed in. Let's create a table with two columns ID (of data type NUMBER) and DS (of data type INTERVAL DAY TO SECOND):

```
SQL> create table interval_table(
  2      id number,
  3      ds interval day(5) to second )
  4  /

Table created.
```

The INTERVAL DAY TO SECOND data type is new to Oracle 9i (as we saw in Chapter 3) and stores a period of time in days, hours, minutes, and seconds.

Now we can populate this table with some data:

```
SQL> insert into interval_table
  2  select decode( mod(rownum,2),1,1,2),
  3         numtodsinterval ( rownum, 'hour' )
  4    from all_objects
  5   where rownum < 11
```

```
    6  /

10 rows created.
```

Here we used the new Oracle 9*i* function, NUMTODSINTERVAL() to create INTERVAL DAY TO SECOND values. Now, when we query the INTERVAL_TABLE table we see 10 INTERVAL DAY TO SECOND values ranging from 1 hour to 10 hours.

```
SQL> select *
  2     from interval_table
  3  /

        ID DS
---------- -------------------------------
         1 +00000 01:00:00.000000
         2 +00000 02:00:00.000000
         1 +00000 03:00:00.000000
         2 +00000 04:00:00.000000
         1 +00000 05:00:00.000000
         2 +00000 06:00:00.000000
         1 +00000 07:00:00.000000
         2 +00000 08:00:00.000000
         1 +00000 09:00:00.000000
         2 +00000 10:00:00.000000

10 rows selected.
```

Suppose we want to sum the intervals to get a total. You might think that using the SUM() function would do it. However, if we try this we see that SUM() does not support the INTERVAL data type:

```
SQL> select sum( ds )
  2     from interval_table
  3  /
select sum( ds )
            *
ERROR at line 1:
ORA-00932: inconsistent datatypes
```

In Oracle 9*i*, you have the ability to implement your own aggregate functions. They will work just as any built-in aggregate function does, and can even be implemented as analytic functions (we'll look further at analytic functions later in this chapter), or applied to ranges of data. These functions are implemented using an object type, which we discussed in the previous chapter.

This object type must implement a specific interface or API. Oracle requires that the object have the following four methods defined within it:

❑   Static function ODCIAggregateInitialize(sctx IN OUT <impltype>). This method initializes any local variables within the object.

❑   Member function ODCIAggregateIterate(self IN OUT <impltype>, val <inputdatatype>). This method performs the work of the aggregate.

673

❏ Member function ODCIAggregateTerminate(self IN OUT <impltype>, ReturnValue <return_type>, Flags IN number). This method will return the aggregated value.

❏ Member function ODCIAggregateMerge(self IN OUT <impltype>, Ctx2 IN <impltype>). This function takes the two aggregation contexts as input, merges them, and returns the single, merged instance of the aggregation context.

There are two other member functions that can be supplied:

❏ Member ODCIAggregateDelete(self IN OUT <impltype>,Val IN <inputdatatype>). This will remove the current element from the aggregation. You need to supply this if you are using your aggregate function as an analytic function with ranges (windows) of data.

❏ Member ODCIAggregateWrapContext(self IN OUT <impltype>). This function is invoked if the aggregate function has been declared to have external context and is transmitting partial aggregates from slave processes. You need this when the aggregate function is implemented as an external function.

Note that all the methods start with ODCI, which stands for Oracle Data Cartridge Interface. IMPLTYPE is the type of the object itself, RETURN_TYPE is the data type that the aggregate function will return, and INPUTDATATYPE is the data type that is passed into the aggregate function.

Let's build our own aggregate function that sums interval data types. First we need to define the object interface (or specification).

```
SQL> create or replace
  2  type day_to_second_sum_type as object
  3  (
  4
  5    total interval day to second,
  6
  7    static function
  8      ODCIAggregateInitialize( sctx in out day_to_second_sum_type )
  9      return number,
 10
 11    member function
 12      ODCIAggregateIterate( self in out day_to_second_sum_type ,
 13                            value in interval day to second )
 14      return number,
 15
 16    member function
 17      ODCIAggregateTerminate( self in day_to_second_sum_type,
 18                              returnValue out interval day to second,
 19                              flags in number)
 20       return number,
 21
 22    member function
 23      ODCIAggregateMerge( self in out day_to_second_sum_type,
 24                          ctx2 in day_to_second_sum_type)
 25      return number
 26  );
 27  /

Type created. .
```

The only extra information that we included here, aside from the required clauses, is the local variable TOTAL. We need that in order to maintain a running total of the intervals. Implementation of the type body is pretty straightforward.

We start off by implementing the ODCIAggregateInitialize function. This creates an instance of the DAY_TO_SECOND_SUM_TYPE and defaults the TOTAL local variable to 0:

```
SQL> create or replace
  2  type body day_to_second_sum_type as
  3
  4    static function
  5      ODCIAggregateInitialize ( sctx in out day_to_second_sum_type )
  6      return number is
  7    begin
  8      sctx := day_to_second_sum_type( numtodsinterval( 0, 'SECOND' ) );
  9      return ODCIConst.Success;
 10    end;
```

Next we code the ODCIAggregateIterate function. This is where we add up all the intervals passed into the aggregate function for each group of rows:

```
 11
 12    member function
 13      ODCIAggregateIterate( self in out day_to_second_sum_type,
 14                            value in interval day to second )
 15      return number is
 16    begin
 17      self.total := self.total + value;
 18      return ODCIConst.Success;
 19    end;
 20
```

Then we implement the ODCIAggregateTerminate function. This function's purpose is to return the aggregated value via the out parameter RETURNVALUE:

```
 21    member function
 22      ODCIAggregateTerminate( self in day_to_second_sum_type,
 23                              returnValue out interval day to second,
 24                              flags in number)
 25      return number is
 26    begin
 27      returnValue := self.total;
 28      return ODCIConst.Success;
 29    end;
 30
```

Lastly, we code the ODCIAggregateMerge function. Here we write the code to combine two aggregates passed in. If Oracle needs to merge aggregates during execution of the user-defined aggregate, then it will call this method to do so.

```
31    member function
32      ODCIAggregateMerge( self in out day_to_second_sum_type,
33                         ctx2 in day_to_second_sum_type )
34      return number is
35    begin
36      self.total := self.total + ctx2.total;
37      return ODCIConst.Success;
38    end;
39
40  end;
41  /

Type body created.
```

The last step for writing our aggregate function is to write the function itself:

```
SQL> create or replace
  2  function ds_sum(input interval day to second )
  3  return interval day to second
  4  parallel_enable aggregate
  5  using day_to_second_sum_type;
  6  /

Function created.
```

We have created a function DS_SUM() which takes in an INTERVAL DAY TO SECOND data type and returns the same type. We have defined it as an aggregate function on lines 4 and 5:

```
  4  parallel_enable aggregate
  5  using day_to_second_sum_type;
```

Now all we need to do is use it just as we would the SUM() function:

```
SQL> select ds_sum( ds )
  2    from interval_table
  3  /

DS_SUM(DS)
---------------------------------------------------------------------
+000000002 07:00:00.000000000
```

We get the correct result of 2 days and 7 hours. Not only that, but we can also group by the ID column:

```
SQL> select id, ds_sum( ds ) ds
  2    from interval_table
  3    group by id
  4  /

        ID DS
---------- ----------------------------
         1 +000000001 01:00:00.000000000
         2 +000000001 06:00:00.000000000
```

This seems like a lot of work for such a simple request, but it's really not. After you create one or two of these aggregate functions, you'll realize that it's quite easy and that the timesavings, in terms of development and maintenance, are well worth it. You can find more about user-defined aggregate functions in the Oracle documentation *Oracle 9i Data Cartridge Developer's Guide*.

Table and Pipelined Functions

Table functions and **pipelined functions** give us the ability to create a collection of rows, and return this collection as if it were rows in a table. In this way we can select from any collection as if it were a virtual table.

Table Function

Table functions can be used in the FROM clause of your query and are treated just like relational tables. They will return either a NESTED TABLE type or VARRAY type. They are accessed in the FROM clause by using the key word TABLE.

A simple example of using this could be a **virtual table** function. We'll make a function that will return a table with as many rows as you need. This is useful when building a list of numbers. For example, we might need to populate a list with values 1 through 10 in order to allow a user to select a ranking. Let's look first at how we might have had to achieve this before Oracle 9*i*:

```
SQL> select rownum
  2    from all_objects
  3   where rownum < 11
  4  /

    ROWNUM
----------
         1
         2
         3
         4
         5
         6
         7
         8
         9
        10

10 rows selected.
```

That works just fine as long as the table you project against has enough rows to satisfy your range. If we wanted just the numbers 6 through 10 we could use the same technique but, instead of selecting rownum, we could select rownum+5.

```
select rownum+5
  from all_objects
 where rownum < 6
```

677

Every time that we needed a range, a new query had to be written to generate this.

In Oracle 9*i* we can use a table function to greatly simplify our work here. We start out by creating a data type, VIRTUAL_TABLE_TYPE, which will be the return type of our table function. Table functions always return a collection and in our case, it will return a collection of type NUMBER:

```
SQL> create type virtual_table_type as table of number
  2  /

Type created.
```

Then we can go on to create the VIRTUAL_TABLE table function using our new data type:

```
SQL> create or replace
  2  function virtual_table( p_start number,
  3                          p_end number ) return virtual_table_type as
```

Here we define our function. It takes in two parameters, P_START and P_END, which define the end points of the range of numbers that the function generates. It returns the VIRTURAL_TABLE_TYPE we previously created.

```
  4    l_vt_type virtual_table_type := virtual_table_type();
```

Now we define a local variable of the return type. We will populate this local variable and return it.

```
  5  begin
  6    for i in p_start .. p_end loop
  7      l_vt_type.extend();
  8      dbms_output.put_line( 'adding ' || i || ' to collection...' );
  9      l_vt_type(l_vt_type.count) := i;
 10    end loop;
```

Here we loop through our range and populate the local variable with those values.

```
 11    dbms_output.put_line( 'done...' );
 12    return l_vt_type;
 13  end virtual_table;
 14  /

Function created.
```

All that is left to do is return the local variable to the caller. We now have a function that can generate any contiguous range of BINARY_INTEGER types.

We added the DBMS_OUTPUT.PUT_LINE() calls to demonstrate the interaction between SQL and PL/SQL. If we select from this function we see that the entire data set needs to be in memory before the query can be realized (and processing in the anonymous block can continue):

678

```
SQL> set serveroutput on
SQL> begin
  2     for x in ( select *
  3                     from table( virtual_table( -2, 2) ) )
  4     loop
  5       dbms_output.put_line( 'printing from anonymous block ' ||
  6                             x.column_value );
  7     end loop;
  8  end;
  9  /
adding -2 to collection...
adding -1 to collection...
adding 0 to collection...
adding 1 to collection...
adding 2 to collection...
done...
printing from anonymous block -2
printing from anonymous block -1
printing from anonymous block 0
printing from anonymous block 1
printing from anonymous block 2

PL/SQL procedure successfully completed.
```

Notice here that we reference X.COLUMN_VALUE in the DBMS_OUTPUT.PUT_LINE() call. COLUMN_VALUE is the default column name when you select from a TABLE OF <SCALAR_DATA_TYPE>. In our example, we select from a function that returns a VIRTUAL_TABLE_TYPE we defined as TABLE OF NUMBER.

You should also note that we see all the messages from the VIRTUAL_TABLE() function before we see even one of the anonymous PL/SQL messages. Remember on line 8 of the VIRTUAL_TABLE() function, we used DBMS_OUTPUT.PUT_LINE() to display a message that we were adding "X to the collection". The fact that we see all of those messages grouped together and displayed, before any of the messages that are generated in the anonymous block, demonstrates that the table function completed prior to the processing of the anonymous PL/SQL block's loop.

In this case, the processing is not intensive but it could have been. It is not optimal to wait until the table function completes before processing can continue. It would be much better if we could iteratively return rows from the function as the calling routine needed them, and we'll look at how to do this now.

Pipelined Function

New in Oracle 9i is the ability to stream data from a function one row at a time. We can use table functions and **pipeline** them, so that they return a row as soon as it is available. Let's take our VIRTUAL_TABLE function and modify it to make it pipelined:

```
SQL> create or replace
  2  function virtual_table( p_start number,
  3                          p_end number ) return virtual_table_type
  4  pipelined as
```

```
 5   begin
 6     for i in p_start .. p_end loop
 7       dbms_output.put_line( 'returning row ' || i );
 8       pipe row(i);
 9     end loop;
10     dbms_output.put_line( 'done...' );
11     return;
12   end virtual_table;
13   /
```

```
Function created.
```

There are a few things to notice about the rewritten function. First, on line 4, notice the PIPELINED keyword. This tells Oracle that this function will return its results one row at a time. On line 8 we see the command PIPE ROW(data). This is where the function pushes the rows of data back to the caller. Notice though, it does not return the return type of the function, but rather the base type of the collection of the return type. In this example the return type is defined as a VIRTUAL_TABLE_TYPE but we are piping NUMBERs back to the caller. That is because the VIRTUAL_TABLE_TYPE was previously defined as a table of numbers:

```
SQL> create type virtual_table_type as table of number
  2   /
```

This may cause some people confusion since we are used to returning the data type defined in the function specification from a function. Not only that, but the RETURN on line 11 is an empty return (though functions usually return their data type).

Now if we run this pipelined function we will see a slightly different result:

```
SQL> set serveroutput on
SQL> begin
  2     for x in ( select *
  3                    from table( virtual_table( -2, 2 ) ) )
  4     loop
  5       dbms_output.put_line( 'printing from anonymous block ' ||
  6                                 x.column_value);
  7     end loop;
  8   end;
  9   /
returning row -2
printing from anonymous block -2
returning row -1
printing from anonymous block -1
returning row 0
printing from anonymous block 0
returning row 1
printing from anonymous block 1
returning row 2
printing from anonymous block 2
done...

PL/SQL procedure successfully completed.
```

This time the output messages from the table function and the anonymous block are interwoven, proving that the function returned the rows one at a time as the caller requested them. This could bring dramatic performance increases when your pipelined functions are process intensive. The processing will now be spread across each row processed, not completely finished prior to the first row being returned. Not only that, but the entire data set need not be stored in memory prior to consumption or processing of the first row by the caller.

In the above example, we have been passing in scalar values into the table functions. We could also pass in a CURSOR as the input if we wanted to. So far we have also only passed out scalar values. Let's extend our example in order to return a user-defined type. We are going to write a simple pivot function. It expects a cursor that selects two columns, the 'key' to pivot on and the data to display for each key. This function will assume the data is sorted by the key value. The query that we expect to be passed in should look something like:

```
select KEY, DATA
  from T
 order by KEY
```

The first thing we need to create is an ELEMENTTYPE type that will hold all the values associated with the key:

```
SQL> create or replace
  2    type elementType as table of varchar2(100)
  3  /

Type created.
```

This is just a simple table of VARCHAR2. Now we want an object to represent the row we will return. It will contain the key value and the associated elements:

```
SQL> create or replace
  2    type rowType as object(
  3      key number,
  4      data elementType )
  5  /

Type created.
```

Notice that the data element is of the type ELEMENTTYPE, which is the user-defined type that we have just created. Lastly, we need an object that is a collection of ROWTYPE:

```
SQL> create or replace
  2    type resultType as table of rowType
  3  /

Type created.
```

Remember, a pipelined table function is defined as returning a collection of the 'row', but pipes back individual rows. Our function is defined as returning resultType but pipes rowType. In this function we loop over the CURSOR passed in and populate ROWTYPE objects and then pipe them back to the caller when the KEY value changes. Let's take a look at it one piece at a time.

```
SQL> create or replace
  2  function pivot( p_cursor in sys_refcursor )
  3  return resultType pipelined as
  4    l_key    varchar2(4000);
  5    l_data   varchar2(4000);
  6    l_last   varchar2(4000);
  7    l_row    rowType;
```

We define our function called PIVOT, which takes in as its only parameter, a SYS_REFCURSOR. The function will return a resultType but notice on line 3 we define it as being PIPELINED. This tells Oracle that this function will return data a row at a time. Lines 4-7 are declarations of local variables that we use.

```
  8  begin
  9    loop
 10      fetch p_cursor into l_key, l_data;
 11      exit when p_cursor%notfound;
 12
```

Here we enter a loop and will fetch a row at a time from P_CURSOR, while storing the results in the local variables L_KEY and L_DATA. When all rows have been selected from the cursor, we exit the loop.

We now determine if the key we are pivoting on has changed.

```
 13      if ( l_last is null or l_key <> l_last ) then
 14        if ( l_row is not null ) then
 15          pipe row( l_row );
 16        end if;
 17
```

If it has, and if we have a row L_ROW to return to the caller, we need to pipe back to them.

```
 18        l_row := rowType( l_key, elementType( l_data ) );
 19        l_last := l_key;
```

We need to now create a new instance of a ROWTYPE to start collecting the next group of data.

```
 20      else
 21        l_row.data.extend();
 22        l_row.data( l_row.data.count ) := l_data;
 23      end if;
```

If the key value has not changed from the last row we retrieved from P_CURSOR, then we need to extend the collection data in L_ROW and populate it with the data that we fetched out of P_CURSOR.

```
 24      end loop;
 25      if ( l_row is not null ) then
 26        pipe row( l_row );
 27      end if;
```

Outside the loop we pipe back the last L_ROW we were building.

```
 28      close p_cursor;
 29      return;
 30    end;
 31    /

Function created.
```

There are two key things to note here (aside from the fact that we defined the function as PIPELINED). On lines 15 and 26 we issue the command PIPE ROW(). This is where we are returning data to the caller. Although the function is defined as returning a resultType, we are piping back ROWTYPEs. Then at line 29 we call return, but return nothing. In a standard function, calling a return and not supplying any expression would result in an error.

To use our function we can call it like this:

```
SQL> select *
  2    from table( pivot( cursor( select deptno, ename
  3                                from emp
  4                                order by deptno ) ) )
  5    /

KEY DATA
---- -------------------------------------------------------------
 10 ELEMENTTYPE('CLARK', 'KING', 'MILLER')
 20 ELEMENTTYPE('SMITH', 'ADAMS', 'FORD', 'SCOTT', 'JONES')
 30 ELEMENTTYPE('ALLEN', 'BLAKE', 'MARTIN', 'JAMES', 'TURNER', 'WARD')
```

The FROM clause in line 2 might look complicated but really it's not. It just builds upon what you have already learned. Looking at it from inside out, we see a query first. This query is then cast as a CURSOR and that CURSOR is passed into the table function PIVOT. The results from the PIVOT function are then cast as a TABLE and its values are displayed just as any rows from a relational table are displayed.

We have taken the EMP table and flattened it into three rows, one row for each DEPTNO. Included in each row is a list of the ENAMEs assigned to that department. Although each department has a different number of employees, the fact that we used the ELEMENTTYPE to hold them allows us to expand to have as many employees as we need. We could have accomplished this by creating an object view on the EMP and DEPT tables but we would then be locked into getting back just this pivot. Instead of this, we can just as easily build a list of SALs by DEPTNO using this same PIVOT function. All we need to do is change the CURSOR:

```
SQL> select *
  2    from table( pivot( cursor( select deptno, sal
  3                                from emp
  4    order by deptno ) ) )
```

```
  5   /

      KEY DATA
      ----  -----------------------------------------------------------------
       10  ELEMENTTYPE('2450', '5000', '1300')
       20  ELEMENTTYPE('800', '1100', '3000', '3000', '2975')
       30  ELEMENTTYPE('1600', '2850', '1250', '950', '1500', '1250')
```

Using table functions gives us the ability to create very dynamic and very flexible data sources to select from. If we write them as pipelined functions, we do not incur the overhead of executing the entire function before we can process the first row returned. The applications for table and pipeline functions are numerous. We have shown just a few examples of how to use them but there are many more. You can, for instance, use them to load data from an external table directly into the database with a single command. We could write a pipelined function which accepted a CURSOR of SELECT * FROM EXTERNAL TABLE. The pipelined function could transform the data, formatting it properly, and then pipe the data back out. The rows returned could then be inserted into a database table. The statement to perform that might look like:

```
insert into database_table
select *
   from table( pipeline_function( select *
                                     from external_table ) );
```

This avoids the three step alternative, which is to load the raw data into a table, run a PL/SQL routine to process and format it, and then load the data into the proper table.

Using Queries To Write SQL with SQL

What do we mean by this? Well let's say that we wanted to create public synonyms for every table in our schema. While we could do this by simply writing a CREATE SYNONYM statement for each table, this would be liable to induce typing errors, and is repetitious. What we can do instead is to create a file called create_tab_syns.sql as follows:

```
set heading off
set feedback off
set echo off

spool tabsyns.sql

select 'create public synonym ' || table_name ||
       ' for ' || table_name || ';'
   from user_tables;

spool off

set echo on
set heading on
set feedback on
```

To run the file we go to a SQL*Plus prompt and simply type the following:

```
SQL> @create_tab_syns
```

It's not very exciting but it did do something. Let's view the file called `tabsyns.sql` and we should see our CREATE SYNONYM statements.

```
SQL> edit tabsyns.sql

create public synonym BONUS for BONUS;
create public synonym DEPT for DEPT;
create public synonym EMP for EMP;
create public synonym SALGRADE for SALGRADE;
```

There are countless uses for this technique. DBAs, for example, can use this technique to change the default tablespace for all the users. All they need do is modify the query in our `create_tab_syns.sql` file to read as follows:

```
select 'alter user ' || username ||
       ' default tablespace users_default;'
  from dba_users
 where username not in ( 'SYS', 'SYSTEM' );
```

Or the DBA can lock out all the users from the database:

```
select 'alter user ' || username ||
       ' account lock;'
  from dba_users
 where username not in ( 'SYS', 'SYSTEM' );
```

Any mass SQL statements that you need to run are prime candidates for this technique, providing that they can be answered by use of the data dictionary. Note that an understanding of the data dictionary is essential to using this technique successfully. You can consult Appendix C for a listing of the most commonly used dictionary views.

Alternately, you can bypass the file generation altogether and just use the following PL/SQL:

```
SQL> create or replace
  2  procedure run_it( p_cursor sys_refcursor ) as
  3    l_command varchar2(32767);
  4  begin
  5    loop
  6      fetch p_cursor into l_command;
  7      exit when p_cursor%notfound;
  8      execute immediate l_command;
  9    end loop;
 10  end run_it;
 11  /

Procedure created.
```

This procedure takes in as it parameter a SYS_REFCURSOR. On line 6 it fetches a row at a time into the local variable L_COMMAND. Then on line 8, we use the EXECUTE IMMEDIATE command to execute the statements.

Either of these methods will work and which of them you use is simply a matter of preference.

Analytic Functions

Oracle supplies a class of functions known as analytic functions. These functions are very powerful and allow you to answer questions in a single query that in the past would have required writing either procedural code, or inefficient SQL queries. These functions are defined using the following syntax:

```
function_name( parameter, parameter, … )
over ( <partition-clause> <order-by-clause> <windowing-clause> )
```

This breaks down as follows:

❑ Function_name – This is the name of the analytic function that we are invoking.

❑ Parameter – These are the inputs to the function.

❑ Over – Keyword indicating that this function is an analytic function. The aggregate function SUM() if combined with OVER, is processed as an analytic function. The clause following OVER is the slice of data the analytic function will be performed on.

❑ Partition-clause – This optional clause, when present, segments the result set into groups. The analytic function is then performed on each individual group.

❑ Order-by-clause – This will order the individual groups of data, though this is not required by all of the analytic functions. Some analytic functions like LAG() and LEAD(), which deal with previous and next values in a group, require this clause. If you are using windows, then you need to include this clause.

❑ Windowing-clause – This allows you to build a window within the group that the function will work against. Windows can be either ranges of data values (range window) or an offset from the current row (row windows).

There is a lot to digest here. We'll now take a look at analytic functions to return results such as:

❑ Running totals

❑ Next and Previous values

❑ Rankings

❑ Top N-Queries

❑ First and last values

After seeing these examples, you should have a better understanding of both what analytic function can do and how they do it.

Calculating Running Totals

The aggregate function SUM() could calculate the sum of the values for a result set, or for individual groups, if a GROUP BY clause was used. However, what it can't do is to keep a running total of the sum of the current row and all previous rows. To accomplish this we need to use the analytic version of SUM().

Connected as the user SCOTT we can run the following.

```
SQL> select ename,
  2         sal,
  3         sum(sal) over ( order by ename
  4                         range between
  5                         unbounded preceding and
  6                         current row ) running_total
  7    from emp
  8   order by ename
  9  /

ENAME             SAL RUNNING_TOTAL
---------- ---------- -------------
ADAMS            1100          1100
ALLEN            1600          2700
BLAKE            2850          5550
CLARK            2450          8000
FORD             3000         11000
JAMES             950         11950
JONES            2975         14925
KING             5000         19925
MARTIN           1250         21175
MILLER           1300         22475
SCOTT            3000         25475
SMITH             800         26275
TURNER           1500         27775
WARD             1250         29025

14 rows selected.
```

Let's examine exactly what is happening here.

```
  3         sum(sal) over ( order by ename
  4                         range between
  5                         unbounded preceding and
  6                         current row ) running_total
```

In line 3 we call the analytic function SUM(), giving (SAL) as the input parameter of the function. The OVER keyword is required to indicate that the function is an analytic one, while the ORDER BY ENAME clause specifies the order of our window (range of data). It is important because we want a running total. RANGE BETWEEN UNBOUNDED PRECEDING AND CURRENT ROW is the windowing clause. This defines the range we should use when applying the function as between UNBOUNDED PRECEDING (in other words all previous rows), and the CURRENT ROW. This allows us to generate a running total of SAL values, since we will sum for every row that we have seen so far. Since we ordered our window by ENAME, we need to ensure that the results come out in the same order by including line 8, ORDER BY ENAME.

The concepts and definitions explained in the introduction to this section should make more sense now. We see how we can define and use analytic functions, how to define a window and how to order it. The only thing missing in this example was the partition-clause. We can add one now, in order to calculate a running total by department (DNAME).

```
SQL> break on dname skip 1

SQL> select dname,
  2         ename,
  3         sal,
  4         sum(sal) over ( partition by dname
  5                         order by dname, ename
  6                         range between
  7                         unbounded preceding and
  8                         current row ) dept_running_total
  9    from emp, dept
 10   where emp.deptno = dept.deptno
 11   order by dname, ename
 12  /

DNAME           ENAME          SAL  DEPT_RUNNING_TOTAL
--------------- ----------  -------- -------------------
ACCOUNTING      CLARK         2450               2450
                KING          5000               7450
                MILLER        1300               8750

RESEARCH        ADAMS         1100               1100
                FORD          3000               4100
                JONES         2975               7075
                SCOTT         3000              10075
                SMITH          800              10875

SALES           ALLEN         1600               1600
                BLAKE         2850               4450
                JAMES          950               5400
                MARTIN        1250               6650
                TURNER        1500               8150
                WARD          1250               9400

14 rows selected.
```

This example builds on what we saw in the first example, by adding a partition-clause to the analytic function at line 4. This clause breaks up our result set into groups based on the DNAME. Notice how we have the running total for each individual group. When a new group starts, the sum is reset and starts anew.

Note that to obtain the DNAME, we were required to join the tables EMP and DEPT. This shows that there is no restriction on joining tables when using analytic functions.

We also changed the order-by-clause to ORDER BY DNAME, ENAME, since we are partitioning by DNAME. This ensures that our window is correct. If we had just ordered by DNAME, then we would receive the total sum of the group for every row. We used the BREAK ON DNAME SKIP 1 statement at the beginning of the code block to insert a blank line between each DNAME result set.

At this point we're going to let you in on a little secret. We have made these first two examples a little harder than they needed to be. The windowing-clause RANGE BETWEEN UNBOUNDED PRECEDING AND CURRENT ROW is actually the default window when using an order-by-clause. In other words it could be omitted and you would get identical results. We included it here, simply in order to demonstrate what was actually going on.

We should also note here that we are not constrained to use only one analytic function per query. We can combine these two examples and get the running total for both the department and the entire data set in the same query, as follows.

```
SQL> break on dname skip 1

SQL> select dname,
  2         ename,
  3         sal,
  4         sum(sal) over ( partition by dname
  5                         order by dname, ename ) dept_running_total,
  6         sum(sal) over ( order by dname, ename ) running_total
  7    from emp, dept
  8   where emp.deptno = dept.deptno
  9   order by dname, ename
 10  /
```

DNAME	ENAME	SAL	DEPT_RUNNING_TOTAL	RUNNING_TOTAL
ACCOUNTING	CLARK	2450	2450	2450
	KING	5000	7450	7450
	MILLER	1300	8750	8750
RESEARCH	ADAMS	1100	1100	9850
	FORD	3000	4100	12850
	JONES	2975	7075	15825
	SCOTT	3000	10075	18825
	SMITH	800	10875	19625
SALES	ALLEN	1600	1600	21225
	BLAKE	2850	4450	24075
	JAMES	950	5400	25025
	MARTIN	1250	6650	26275
	TURNER	1500	8150	27775
	WARD	1250	9400	29025

```
14 rows selected.
```

Here we can see the results from both analytic functions in one query. The fact that they are executed independently of one another is evident by the fact that their groups overlap. The DEPT_RUNNING_TOTAL has three groups, one for each DNAME. At the start of a new group, the sum resets. On the other hand, the RUNNING_TOTAL column only has one group (remember, there is no partition-clause in that analytic function call). Its sum calculation spans the three groups of the other.

689

> **A query can contain any number of analytic functions, each with its own partition-clause and groups.**

You should also notice the omission of the windowing-clauses in each of the analytic functions. Since the default behavior is the behavior that we want, we do not need to include it. If we wanted to change the range, then it would be required.

Next and Previous Values

The `LAG()` and `LEAD()` functions allow you to query a group of values, in order to retrieve the `Nth` values from either in front of, or behind, your current row's values. Let's look at an example of this by connecting to the database as the user `SCOTT` and issuing the following:

```
SQL> select ename,
  2         sal,
  3         lead( ename, 1, 'N/A' ) over ( order by sal ) next_ename,
  4         lead( sal, 1, null ) over ( order by sal ) next_sal,
  5         lead( ename, 2, 'N/A' ) over ( order by sal ) next_ename,
  6         lead( sal, 2, null ) over ( order by sal ) next_sal
  7    from emp
  8   order by sal
  9  /

ENAME             SAL NEXT_ENAME   NEXT_SAL NEXT_ENAME   NEXT_SAL
---------- ---------- ---------- ---------- ---------- ----------
SMITH             800 JAMES            950 ADAMS            1100
JAMES             950 ADAMS           1100 WARD             1250
ADAMS            1100 WARD            1250 MARTIN           1250
WARD             1250 MARTIN          1250 MILLER           1300
MARTIN           1250 MILLER          1300 TURNER           1500
MILLER           1300 TURNER          1500 ALLEN            1600
TURNER           1500 ALLEN           1600 CLARK            2450
ALLEN            1600 CLARK           2450 BLAKE            2850
CLARK            2450 BLAKE           2850 JONES            2975
BLAKE            2850 JONES           2975 SCOTT            3000
JONES            2975 SCOTT           3000 FORD             3000
SCOTT            3000 FORD            3000 KING             5000
FORD             3000 KING            5000 N/A
KING             5000 N/A                  N/A

14 rows selected.
```

Here we used the `LEAD()` function to look ahead at the next two rows ordered by `SAL`. This function takes in three parameters. The first is the expression it will return. The second is how many rows ahead to look and the third is the default value it will return if the row ahead does not exist. In this example for instance, `FORD` only has one person making more money than himself (`KING`), so his `LEAD()` of 2 is `NULL`. Likewise `KING` is the highest paid employee so both `LEAD()` statements result in a `NULL` value.

LAG() works in exactly the same way as LEAD() except that it looks back N rows (instead of forwards):

```
SQL> select ename,
  2         sal,
  3         lag( ename, 1, 'N/A' ) over ( order by sal ) prev_ename,
  4         lag( sal, 1, null ) over ( order by sal ) prev_sal
  5    from emp
  6   order by sal
  7  /

ENAME             SAL PREV_ENAME   PREV_SAL
---------- ---------- ---------- ----------
SMITH             800 N/A
JAMES             950 SMITH             800
ADAMS            1100 JAMES             950
WARD             1250 ADAMS            1100
MARTIN           1250 WARD             1250
MILLER           1300 MARTIN           1250
TURNER           1500 MILLER           1300
ALLEN            1600 TURNER           1500
CLARK            2450 ALLEN            1600
BLAKE            2850 CLARK            2450
JONES            2975 BLAKE            2850
SCOTT            3000 JONES            2975
FORD             3000 SCOTT            3000
KING             5000 FORD             3000

14 rows selected.
```

Here we see that no employee earns less than SMITH, since there is no prior row to retrieve, while JAMES earns more than SMITH (SMITH lags one behind JAMES). Not only that, but ADAMS earns more than JAMES, since JAMES lags behind ADAMS.

However, in practice you really only ever need to use one of the functions. This is because supplying a negative row value to LEAD() causes it to look back to previous rows. For example a LAG() of 1 is the same as a LEAD() of −1, while a LAG() of −1 is equivalent to a LEAD() of 1.

These functions can also be used with the PARTITION BY clause to produce grouped results. For example, we can get the next salary within each department using the following query:

```
SQL> break on dname skip 1

SQL> select deptno,
  2         ename,
  3         sal,
  4         lead( ename, 1, 'N/A' ) over ( partition by deptno
  5                                        order by sal ) next_ename,
  6         lead( sal, 1, null ) over ( partition by deptno
  7                                     order by sal ) next_sal
  8    from emp
  9  /
```

```
     DEPTNO ENAME             SAL NEXT_ENAME    NEXT_SAL
---------- ----------  ---------- ----------  ----------
        10 MILLER            1300 CLARK             2450
        10 CLARK            2450 KING             5000
        10 KING             5000 N/A

        20 SMITH             800 ADAMS            1100
        20 ADAMS            1100 JONES            2975
        20 JONES            2975 SCOTT            3000
        20 SCOTT            3000 FORD             3000
        20 FORD             3000 N/A

        30 JAMES             950 WARD             1250
        30 WARD             1250 MARTIN           1250
        30 MARTIN           1250 TURNER           1500
        30 TURNER           1500 ALLEN            1600
        30 ALLEN            1600 BLAKE            2850
        30 BLAKE            2850 N/A

14 rows selected.
```

Let's consider a further example, in the form of a web application wizard-like interface, where we need to know the next and previous pages. This information is stored in a table (PAGES) in the database, so that we can add or remove pages in the wizard process and not have to recode the application. Each Page id is stored with a sequence number indicating its order in the process, as follows:

```
SQL> create table pages(
  2      page_id number,
  3      seq     number )
  4  /

Table created.

SQL> insert into pages values ( 1, 10 );

1 row created.

SQL> insert into pages values ( 2, 20 );

1 row created.

SQL> insert into pages values ( 3, 30 );

1 row created.

SQL> insert into pages values ( 4, 40 );

1 row created.

SQL> commit;

Commit complete.
```

We used the sequence values 10, 20, 30, etc., here, simply so that if we wanted to insert a new page in between pages 1 and 2, we can insert a new row with sequence number 15 (you could use any numbering convention you preferred in its place).

Having created the table, let's get the previous and next PAGE_ID values for page 3:

```
SQL>  select lag( page_id, 1, null )
  2              over ( order by seq ) prev,
  3          page_id,
  4          lead( page_id, 1, null )
  5              over ( order by seq ) next
  6    from pages
  7    where page_id = 3
  8    /

      PREV    PAGE_ID        NEXT
---------- ---------- ----------
                    3
```

So why did we not get the expected values of 2 and 4? The problem here is that the WHERE clause is being applied before the analytic functions. Since the constraint pag_id = 3 restricts the data set to a single row, the analytic functions cannot now see ahead or back because those rows have been filtered out. We need to find a way to apply the analytic functions first and then apply the WHERE constraint. We can accomplish that by pushing the query into an inline view as follows:

```
SQL>  select *
  2    from ( select lag( page_id, 1, null )
  3                  over ( order by seq ) prev,
  4              page_id,
  5              lead( page_id, 1, null )
  6                  over ( order by seq ) next
  7           from pages )
  8    where page_id = 3
SQL>  /

      PREV    PAGE_ID        NEXT
---------- ---------- ----------
         2          3          4
```

I'm sure you might be saying that we could have determined the next and previous pages using +/- 1 from the current PAGE_ID (since their sequence numbers are in numerical order). In this example that is true. But what if we had inserted PAGE_ID 5 in between pages 2 and 3? We'll use a sequence value of 25 for page 5 to illustrate how easily we can achieve this here:

```
SQL>  insert into pages values ( 5, 25 );

1 row created.

SQL>  commit;
```

```
Commit complete.

SQL> select *
  2    from ( select lag( page_id, 1, null )
  3                     over ( order by seq ) prev,
  4                  page_id,
  5                  lead( page_id, 1, null )
  6                     over ( order by seq ) next
  7              from pages )
  8    where page_id = 3
  9  /

      PREV    PAGE_ID       NEXT
---------- ---------- ----------
         5          3          4
```

Here LAG() and LEAD() were able to look at previous and next rows within an ordered group. In this case the group is the entire result set and the column SEQ orders it. Without using these analytic functions, you would either have to write a PL/SQL function or a series of inefficient queries to determine the same answer.

Ranking and Top-N

Let's say we wanted to find the top 10 employees within the company in terms of length of service. We can easily get the employees in order by HIREDATE and assign each one a ranking as follows:

```
SQL> select rownum, x.*
  2    from ( select ename,
  3                  hiredate
  4             from emp
  5            order by hiredate ) x
  6  /

    ROWNUM ENAME      HIREDATE
---------- ---------- ---------
         1 SMITH      17-DEC-80
         2 ALLEN      20-FEB-81
         3 WARD       22-FEB-81
         4 JONES      02-APR-81
         5 BLAKE      01-MAY-81
         6 CLARK      09-JUN-81
         7 TURNER     08-SEP-81
         8 MARTIN     28-SEP-81
         9 KING       17-NOV-81
        10 JAMES      03-DEC-81
        11 FORD       03-DEC-81
        12 MILLER     23-JAN-82
        13 SCOTT      19-APR-87
        14 ADAMS      23-MAY-87

14 rows selected.
```

We accomplished this by using an inline view to select out the relevant data, and then in the outer query, applying the pseudo-column ROWNUM:

```
SQL> select rownum, x.*
  2    from ( select ename,
  3                      hiredate
  4              from emp
  5              order by hiredate ) x
  6  /
```

Since ROWNUM is applied to the row before the Order By clause is processed we needed to use this inline view. If we had simply selected the ROWNUM and then ordered the same query, then we'd see results that look something like:

```
SQL> select rownum, ename, hiredate
  2    from emp
  3    order by hiredate
  4  /

    ROWNUM ENAME                HIREDATE
--------- -------------------- ---------
        1 SMITH                17-DEC-80
        2 ALLEN                20-FEB-81
        3 WARD                 22-FEB-81
        4 JONES                02-APR-81
        6 BLAKE                01-MAY-81
        7 CLARK                09-JUN-81
       10 TURNER               08-SEP-81
        5 MARTIN               28-SEP-81
        9 KING                 17-NOV-81
       12 JAMES                03-DEC-81
       13 FORD                 03-DEC-81
       14 MILLER               23-JAN-82
        8 SCOTT                19-APR-87
       11 ADAMS                23-MAY-87

14 rows selected.
```

As you can see the results are in the proper order but the ROWNUM is out of whack, since the database grabbed the 14 rows in no particular order, assigned each a ROWNUM, then ordered the result set. We used the trick of using an inline view so that the database first ordered the results and *then* assigned each of them a ROWNUM.

Getting back to the example, if we had applied a constraint of where rownum < 11 we would have gotten the first 10 rows. But there is a problem with this. Look at records 10 and 11. Both JAMES and FORD were hired on the same day but JAMES was given a higher rank in our query because the database found his record first. In other words we need to clarify what our original requirement was. Do we want to show the top 10 longest serving employees? Or do we simply want to return 10 employees with long service? If we had asked the second question then our answer above would be valid. We just need to realize that there may be more records returned than just those that satisfy the criteria. If we want to return all the employees with the top 10 lengths of service, then we can use either RANK() or DENSE_RANK(). RANK() will leave gaps in the ranking if multiple records have the same rank, while DENSE_RANK() won't. In other words, in our example above RANK() will number the next row after JAMES and FORD 12 (since there are two records ranked 10), while DENSE_RANK() will simply number it 11.

To illustrate this difference we'll build the same group for each function in the following example. Since there is no partition-clause the group is the entire data set, and we order the group by HIREDATE.

```
SQL> select rank() over ( order by hiredate ) "RANK",
  2         dense_rank() over ( order by hiredate ) "DENSE_RANK",
  3         ename,
  4         hiredate
  5    from emp
  6   order by hiredate
  7  /

      RANK DENSE_RANK ENAME      HIREDATE
---------- ---------- ---------- ---------
         1          1 SMITH      17-DEC-80
         2          2 ALLEN      20-FEB-81
         3          3 WARD       22-FEB-81
         4          4 JONES      02-APR-81
         5          5 BLAKE      01-MAY-81
         6          6 CLARK      09-JUN-81
         7          7 TURNER     08-SEP-81
         8          8 MARTIN     28-SEP-81
         9          9 KING       17-NOV-81
        10         10 JAMES      03-DEC-81
        10         10 FORD       03-DEC-81
        12         11 MILLER     23-JAN-82
        13         12 SCOTT      19-APR-87
        14         13 ADAMS      23-MAY-87

14 rows selected.
```

Now both JAMES and FORD are given a rank of 10. The RANK() function assigns the 12th record a rank of 12 while DENSE_RANK() assigns it 11. This difference is important to note. If we had wanted the top 11, we would get different results depending upon which function we used. RANK() would return the employees with length of service ranking 11 and less, while DENSE_RANK() would return all those employees with the top N lengths of service.

We can apply a partition-clause to either of these functions. Let's determine the RANK of the employees by the HIREDATE for each year. We need to partition by year as follows:

```
SQL> select rank() over ( partition by to_char(hiredate,'yy')
  2                      order by hiredate ) "RANK",
  3         ename,
  4         hiredate
  5    from emp
  6   order by hiredate
  7  /

      RANK ENAME                HIREDATE
--------- -------------------- ---------
         1 SMITH                17-DEC-80
         1 ALLEN                20-FEB-81
         2 WARD                 22-FEB-81
         3 JONES                02-APR-81
         4 BLAKE                01-MAY-81
```

```
          5  CLARK              09-JUN-81
          6  TURNER             08-SEP-81
          7  MARTIN             28-SEP-81
          8  KING               17-NOV-81
          9  JAMES              03-DEC-81
          9  FORD               03-DEC-81
          1  MILLER             23-JAN-82
          1  SCOTT              19-APR-87
          2  ADAMS              23-MAY-87

   14 rows selected.
```

Now we have four groups, one for each of the distinct years that employees were hired (1980, 1981, 1982 and 1987). Notice here that we partitioned not by a column, but by the result of the function `TO_CHAR()`. We used `TO_CHAR()` to return the year from the `HIREDATE` and instructed the `RANK()` function to group on that. This is not unique to the `RANK()` function. You can create partitions like this for any of the analytic functions that accept a partition-clause.

First and Last Values

The `FIRST_VALUE()` and `LAST_VALUE()` functions, as the names imply, return the first and last values in a data group. As an example of using `FIRST_VALUE()` we'll write a query which returns the difference in salaries between employees within a given department:

```
SQL> clear breaks
breaks cleared

SQL> break on deptno skip 1

SQL> select ename,
  2          deptno,
  3          sal,
  4          sal - first_value( sal ) over ( partition by deptno
  5                                          order by sal ) diff
  6     from emp
  7     order by deptno, sal
  8  /

ENAME            DEPTNO         SAL        DIFF
----------     ----------  ----------  ----------
MILLER               10        1300           0
CLARK                          2450        1150
KING                           5000        3700

SMITH                20         800           0
ADAMS                          1100         300
JONES                          2975        2175
SCOTT                          3000        2200
FORD                           3000        2200
```

```
JAMES            30         950          0
WARD                       1250        300
MARTIN                     1250        300
TURNER                     1500        550
ALLEN                      1600        650
BLAKE                      2850       1900

14 rows selected.
```

In this query, at line 4, we select the FIRST_VALUE() of SAL by DEPTNO and subtract it from the current row's SAL to calculate the DIFF column for our report. The syntax for FIRST_VALUE() is just like the other analytic functions we have already seen. And as you might have guessed, the LAST_VALUE() function can be used in the same way. We could build a report that returns how much less money each employee makes in comparison to the highest paid person within a given department.

There are many more analytic functions than we have been able to explore here. A complete reference can be found in the Oracle *SQL Reference* documentation.

MERGE

New in Oracle 9*i* is the SQL statement MERGE, which gives you the ability to select the rows from a table A and either insert or update rows into a table B based on some criterion. In writing an application against a database, it's a common requirement to code the following logic at some point:

```
get some data
if row already exists then
  update existing row
else
  insert new row.
end if;
```

It would be nice if we could either update or insert with just a single command. In Oracle 9*i* you can use the MERGE command to accomplish just that. Consider the following tables, first TABLE_A:

```
SQL> create table table_a(
  2    id number )
  3  /

Table created.

SQL> insert into table_a
  2    select rownum
  3      from all_tables
  4    where rownum < 7
  5  /

6 rows created.
```

```
SQL> select *
  2     from table_a
  3  /

        ID
----------
         1
         2
         3
         4
         5
         6

6 rows selected.
```

and now TABLE_B:

```
SQL> create table table_b(
  2     id number,
  3     status varchar2(255) )
  4  /

Table created.

SQL> insert into table_b values( 1, 'NEW' );

1 row created.

SQL> insert into table_b values( 3, 'NEW' );

1 row created.

SQL> insert into table_b values( 5, 'NEW' );

1 row created.

SQL> select *
  2     from table_b
  3  /

        ID STATUS
---------- --------------------
         1 NEW
         3 NEW
         5 NEW
```

Now we want to ensure that all existing ID values in TABLE_A are also in TABLE_B. If the ID is currently in TABLE_B then its status will be set to OLD. Otherwise a new record will be inserted and its STATUS will be set to NEW. In PL/SQL this might look like this:

```
  1  declare
  2    l_cnt number;
  3  begin
  4    for c in ( select id from table_a ) loop
  5      select count(*)
```

```
 6          into l_cnt
 7          from table_b
 8        where id = c.id;
 9      if l_cnt > 0 then
10          update table_b
11             set status = 'OLD'
12           where id = c.id;
13      else
14          insert into table_b
15          values ( c.id, 'NEW' );
16      end if;
17    end loop;
18  end;
```

If you were using Java or C you would need to code it specifically for that language. Not only that, but you would also have two network round trips to the server, one for the SELECT and another for either the INSERT or UPDATE. The MERGE statement is more efficient because it allows you to do all the logic in a single SQL command. It only requires one round trip to the server, and is the same command regardless of the language issuing it.

The syntax for MERGE consists of five clauses:

❑ MERGE INTO – defines the table/view that will be merged

❑ USING – defines the source of the data to be updated or inserted

❑ ON – defines the condition on which the statement will either insert or update. If the condition is TRUE, you perform the update clause; if FALSE the insert clause

❑ WHEN MATCHED THEN UPDATE – defines the column(s) to be updated

❑ WHEN NOT MATCHED THEN INSERT – defines the column(s) to be inserted into

Let's use it to implement our logic:

```
SQL> merge into table_b b
  2  using ( select *
  3              from table_a ) a
  4    on ( a.id = b.id )
  5  when matched then
  6      update set status = 'OLD'
  7  when not matched then
  8      insert values ( a.id, 'NEW' )
  9  /

6 rows merged.

SQL> select *
  2     from table_b
  3  /

        ID STATUS
```

```
---------- --------------------
         1  OLD
         3  OLD
         5  OLD
         6  NEW
         4  NEW
         2  NEW

6 rows selected.
```

The MERGE statement can also be used to carry out the operation, *'Insert the row into the table if the row does not already exist, otherwise update the row with new values.'* This is similar to the previous example, though in this case we simply want to insert (or update) a record in our table, rather than selecting this record from another table first. Let's begin by creating the table MY_DATA:

```
SQL> create table my_data(
  2     id number,
  3     data varchar2(100) )
  4  /

Table created.
```

Now we populate the table with some data:

```
SQL> insert into my_data
  2     select rownum, to_char( to_date( rownum, 'J' ), 'JSP' )
  3       from all_objects
  4      where rownum < 6
  5  /

5 rows created.
```

Our table now looks like this:

```
SQL> select *
  2     from my_data
  3  /

        ID DATA
---------- --------------------
         1 ONE
         2 TWO
         3 THREE
         4 FOUR
         5 FIVE

5 rows selected.
```

To spell out the row number in the DATA column we use a little trick with the TO_DATE() and TO_CHAR() functions. First, the inner TO_DATE(rownum, 'J') converts the ROWNUM into a DATE using the format mask of J, a Julian day. Then we convert that DATE back into a VARCHAR2 with the outer TO_CHAR(<date>, 'JSP') using the format mask JSP. This mask converts the date to a Julian day (J), while using the SP (spell) modifier to instruct TO_CHAR() to spell out the result.

We now add another row to the table:

```
SQL> insert into my_data values ( 6, 'SIC' );

1 row created.
```

The insert worked but now we need to modify that row and change SIC to SIX. The problem is that we cannot be sure if another application has deleted our row. We need to check to see if the row still exists and if it does, then lock it and update it. If the row no longer exists, we will insert a new one. Here's how we would achieve this in PL/SQL:

```
SQL> declare
  2     l_row my_data%rowtype;
  3  begin
  4     select *
  5       into l_row
  6       from my_data
  7      where id = 6
  8        for update;
  9
 10     update my_data
 11        set data = 'SIX'
 12      where id = 6;
 13
 14     commit;
 15  exception
 16     when NO_DATA_FOUND then
 17        insert into my_data
 18        values ( 6, 'SIX' );
 19  end;
 20  /

PL/SQL procedure successfully completed.
```

However we can use the MERGE statement to perform this logic in a single statement. On this occasion we'll correct value 7 (since we used 6 in the example above):

```
SQL> insert into my_data values( 7, 'SEVRN' );

1 row created.

SQL> select *
  2    from my_data
  3  /
```

```
        ID DATA
---------- --------------------
         1 ONE
         2 TWO
         3 THREE
         4 FOUR
         5 FIVE
         6 SIX
         7 SEVRN

7 rows selected.
```

Having realized our mistake, we can use the MERGE statement to rectify it:

```
SQL> merge into my_data
  2  using ( select 7 x
  3               from dual )
  4    on ( id = x )
  5  when matched then
  6      update set data = to_char(to_date(7, 'J'), 'JSP' )
  7  when not matched then
  8      insert values ( 7, to_char(to_date(7, 'J'), 'JSP' )
  9  /

1 row merged.

SQL> select *
  2     from my_data
  3  /

        ID DATA
---------- --------------------
         1 ONE
         2 TWO
         3 THREE
         4 FOUR
         5 FIVE
         6 SIX
         7 SEVEN

7 rows selected.
```

In the USING clause, we projected the constant 7 onto the DUAL table. We did this in order to create a row with the ID value that we wished to merge. MERGE will insert a row if you project a value onto DUAL that does not meet the constraint in the ON clause. Using DUAL tricks MERGE into thinking that the data is coming from another table, and ensures that when we project the row, we only get one copy of it back.

Summary

In this chapter we have shown you just a few of the advanced features of SQL. This is by no means a complete list, but should help you understand that SQL is much more than the basic SELECT FROM queries that most people think of. We have seen a number of ways in which you can enhance your queries. We began by looking at hierarchical queries, and how we can return groups of results such as line management chains. We then went on to consider aggregate functions, as well as table and pipelined functions. These functions allow us to easily extend our basic SQL and avoid large amounts of PL/SQL coding for returning complex results. We finished off by looking at analytic functions, and seeing how we can use them to return results such as the previous and next rows in a collection, or the top-N results in a group. The bottom line is that SQL can be very powerful when its full range of features are exploited.

Tuning Tools

By this stage in the book you have learned about the underlying architecture of the Oracle database, as well as how you go about creating and manipulating your own data within it. You might well have begun to create your own queries, and thought about applications where you might be able to use them. In Chapter 6, we looked at how Oracle helps you optimize your queries through the use of the Rule- and Cost-based optimizers. However, the optimizers can only suggest execution plans (in the case of the Cost-based optimizer on the basis of its own statistics), rather than optimize their actual execution. This is where tuning comes into play.

What do we mean by tuning? Well, sadly for many developers, we mean tuning after the fact. The application is already live and performing really slowly. At this point we need to figure out how to make it run faster, and quickly, because there are a large number of irate users! This is a very difficult task, since tuning after the fact requires the investigative skills of a detective, in unraveling a mystery, as well as a fine mix of both technical skills and people skills (no one ever wants to have the finger pointed at them). There is no hard and fast roadmap to follow in after-the-fact tuning.

So how can we avoid this difficult task? The answer is to tune *as* you develop. System tuning should be a design time activity, something you build into the entire system, in order to try and avoid performance problems when your application finally goes live. Tuning a system after the fact is really a case of recoding and re-architecting, *not* tuning!

So, what facilities do we have as a developer, as we consider performance when developing our applications? In this chapter, we will explore three tools/commands, all of which can be of use to every Oracle developer:

❏   EXPLAIN PLAN – a SQL command that will tell you how Oracle would process a given query, and show you the plan Oracle would use

❏   AUTOTRACE – a SQL*Plus facility to show you either how Oracle will perform the query, or how it performed the query, along with statistics regarding the processed query

❏   TKPROF – a command-line tool that will tell you what SQL your application executed and how that SQL performed

These are tools you should be using day to day, in order to be able to identify potential performance issues as you develop.

> **Do not consider tuning as a post-deployment activity, since this will only make the task of sorting out your application's performance more difficult.**

An Approach To Tuning

At this point you may be wondering how on earth you can begin to think about tuning your applications. After all, we've just told you that there is no road map for after-the-fact tuning! Even in tuning during development, we will encounter different problems in the case of different applications. While experience is a great asset, it is not something we can teach you here. What *we* can do however is to consider some best practices, which will help in ensuring that your applications run as efficiently as possible.

So what constitutes a best overall approach to tuning? We can summarize this with the following stages:

❑ **Tuning is a constant thing** – It is part of the application from conception to deployment and beyond. There is no beginning or end!

❑ **Experiment** – Don't be afraid to try out different designs, different data models and different features, not only on paper, but also in development. Oracle provides literally thousands of features, many of which do similar things slightly differently. An approach that is successful in one set of conditions might not be so successful given different constraints. Try and discover what the real world performance is, since there is no single 'best solution'. Sometimes partitioning data will increase performance, sometimes not. Sometimes interMedia Text can speed up your searches, sometimes not. Sometimes a hash cluster is the best thing in the world, sometimes not. Remember that there are neither 'evil' features, which should be avoided at all costs, nor 'good' features that solve all problems.

❑ **Benchmark in isolation** – If you cannot get your application to run fast in single user mode, it will only run slower in real life. Record these benchmarks, in order to be able to compare them to past and future tests. In this way it will be a lot easier for you to notice the module that used to take 1 second to run, and now takes 1 minute. Automating these benchmarks by writing scripts makes running them on a recurring basis very easy.

❑ **Benchmark to scale** – Once you've got your application running fast in single user mode, you need to see what happens when you have multiple users. To do this, you need to use quantities of data and simulated users, which are as representative as possible of the real situation when the application goes live. It isn't possible to simply multiply a single user scenario into a 10 user one, or a 10 user scenario into a 100 user one. If you really need to support X users with Y volume of data on day 1, you need to ensure that you have tested that. Either that or be prepared to not go live on that day. Again, recording these benchmarks will allow you to compare current results to history, and quickly discover the implementation that causes performance to nosedive. Not only that, but if you find that your application proves popular and has to be redesigned to support (X+1000) users and (Y+1000) data, then you'll have the statistics on increased throughput to show your manager (rather than a piece of guesswork) when you need to justify the purchase of new hardware (or software).

❑ **Program defensively** – Instrument your code and leave it instrumented in production. Instrumentation is the practice of having a way to trace your application from the "outside". TKPROF with SQL_TRACE (covered in detail below) is an instrumentation tool. The simple DEBUG package described in Case Study 1 is a tool you can use to instrument your PL/SQL applications, allowing them to create a custom trace file with messages you design. The Oracle database is heavily instrumented so that when something goes seriously wrong, a trace file is generated with the necessary debugging information. This trace file will allow the diagnosis and correction of the vast majority of errors. You need this capability in your application as well. The only way to make things go faster is to understand where they are going slow. If you just point at a process and say 'it is going slow', you'll have a hard time tuning it. If the process is heavily instrumented and has the ability to log itself on demand, you'll be able to figure out where things are going slow.

❑ **Have identified performance metrics from day 1** – If your goal is to simply 'go as fast as you can' when you are benchmarking then you will be doing so for the rest of your life! Everything can always go a little faster, but each application will be subject to constraints, even if it is simply a case of what hardware it is run on. You need to know what your constraints are, and develop them accordingly. Metrics are the only way to be able to set meaningful performance targets when benchmarking.

Benchmarking

As a quick example to illustrate the difference between benchmarking in isolation, and to scale, consider the following sequence of statements. This piece of code will read the first record from a table T and lock it using the FOR UPDATE clause in the SELECT statement. It will then 'process' this record in some fashion (what the process does isn't really relevant here: it just does some work). After successfully processing this record it will then delete it and commit:

```
Declare
   L_rec t%rowtype;
Begin
   Select *  into l_rec from T where rownum = 1 FOR UPDATE;
   Process( l_rec );
   Delete from t where t.pk = l_rec.pk;
   Commit;
End;
```

In isolation this piece of code works fine, processing the first record in a table very quickly. You might time this in isolation and decide that you are capable of performing 5 transactions per second (TPS). You might be tempted to extrapolate this figure, and think that if you run 10 of these processes then you'll be able to do 50 TPS. The problem is that you will still only do 5 TPS (if that) with 10 processes, since they will all serialize. In other words, they will all try and lock the first record, in order to carry out the rest of the commands, and only one of them can do this at any one time.

> **Getting something to run fast in isolation is great; getting it to run fast with many users is another thing altogether.**

709

Bind Variables

As we saw in Chapter 6, if Oracle is unable to find your SQL statement in the shared pool, then it has to go through the arduous process of parsing the query fully, optimizing the plan, and so on. This is not only CPU intensive, but also tends to lock portions of the SGA for relatively long periods. The larger the number of user processes parsing queries, the longer the wait for the latch on the library cache and the greater the likelihood of the system grinding to a halt.

Clearly the reuse of queries from the shared pool, and minimization of the need for hard parses, is of great importance in optimizing our applications. However, we should note here that whitespace, formatting, and comments will all affect how statements are considered. Each query in the following list, for example, is considered to be different by Oracle:

```
Select * from dual;

SELECT *
  FROM dual;

SELECT * FROM DUAL D;

Select * /* get all of the columns */ from dual /* our table */;
```

So, one thing to keep in mind as you are generating your applications is that you want to consistently use the exact same query text everywhere you can. Using stored procedures and hiding the SQL in a function or procedure is an excellent approach, since everyone will call the function or procedure and using the exact same syntax. Using functions, procedures, or methods (whatever your language calls them) in your own application language is another excellent approach. Instead of putting the same query into two different pieces of code, where the chance for introducing differences in the text of the query exists, you can code the query once and put it into a reusable function. This is not only a good overall coding practice, but will also make better use of the shared pool in Oracle.

Quite often our queries will only differ in terms of the changing nature of a WHERE clause. To avoid the need for a hard parse in this case we need to use **bind variables**. A bind variable is a way to pass inputs and get outputs from SQL. It is a placeholder you put into a query that tells Oracle "I will supply you a value for this later, just generate a plan for now and when I actually execute the statement, I'll supply the actual value you should use". The following shows an example of a query without bind variables and one with bind variables:

```
Select * from emp where ename = 'KING';
Select * from emp where ename = :bv;
```

The second query uses bind variables and, since it is more generic, can be reused more readily. That single query can be used to find *any* employee in the database whereas the first query can only find KING.

As a quick example of why bind variables are so important, we'll try a little performance test. We'll use some advanced dynamic SQL features of PL/SQL in order to demonstrate this.

> **Note that if you want to run this more than once then you will need access to a DBA privileged command, in order to flush the shared pool.**

We will begin by emptying the shared pool of all cached query plans (we don't want to find any hits when we test). Then we'll run a series of queries that do not use bind variables followed by the exact same query using bind variables. We'll finish by comparing the time each took to do its thing. In order to get the timings down to the 1/100th of a second, we'll be using a supplied Oracle utility DBMS_UTILITY.GET_TIME. To begin, we'll flush the shared pool and use the SET SERVEROUTPUT command to ensure that the output from DBMS_OUTPUT will be displayed by SQL*Plus:

```
SQL> alter system flush shared_pool;
System altered.
SQL> set serveroutput on
```

Now we are ready to run the test code. We'll begin by declaring two local variables. L_START will be used to record our start time at the beginning of a loop. L_CNT will be used as a temporary variable only:

```
SQL> declare
  2      l_start number;
  3      l_cnt   number;
  4  begin
```

Now we are ready to try an example where we do not use bind variables. Here we will save the start time and then utilize EXECUTE IMMEDIATE to execute the query SELECT * FROM DUAL WHERE DUMMY = 'i' (i = 1 to 100). Once we've looped 100 times we'll print out the elapsed time in hundredths of seconds:

```
  5      l_start := dbms_utility.get_time;
  6
  7      for i in 1 .. 100
  8      loop
  9          execute immediate
 10          'select count(*) from dual
 11            where dummy = ''' || to_char(i) || ''''
 12          INTO l_cnt;
 13      end loop;
 14
 15      dbms_output.put_line( 'No Binds ' ||
 16              (dbms_utility.get_time-l_start) || ' hsecs' );
 17
```

Now, we'll again loop 100 times, performing the same timings and queries, but this time we'll execute the exact same query each and every time. Instead of putting in the literal 1, 2, 3, ... 100 in the query text, we'll supply a value for the bind variable (:X) with each query. This is accomplished by inserting the clause USING to_char(i); in the EXECUTE IMMEDIATE statement:

```
18
19        l_start := dbms_utility.get_time;
20
21        for i in 1 .. 100
22        loop
23            execute immediate
24            'select count(*) from dual where dummy = :x'
25            INTO l_cnt
26            USING to_char(i);
27        end loop;
28
29        dbms_output.put_line( 'Binding ' ||
30                   (dbms_utility.get_time-l_start) || ' hsecs' );
31    end;
32    /
No Binds 16 hsecs
Binding 4 hsecs

PL/SQL procedure successfully completed.
```

The comparison of the speed of execution of the two loops tells us that if we hard code the values in executing simple queries like:

```
Select * from dual where dummy = '1';
Select * from dual where dummy = '2';
...
```

then it will take 4 times longer than executing the following statement for the same number of times:

```
Select * from dual where dummy = :x;
```

This really only tells half of the story. We have seen increased parse times as a direct result of not reusing statements. What we did not see is that if we had two people doing this at the same time then it would get even worse. The point here is that the shared pool is a large shared memory structure, and only one session at a time can modify its contents. If everyone generates unique queries by not using bind variables then *everyone* will need to modify the shared pool, everyone will need to lock it momentarily, modify it and unlock it. Even though this happens fast, it happens one user at a time, resulting in queues forming, as other users wait for this resource. With two users you'll go slower than with one; add another user doing the same thing and you'll wait even longer. By the time you have 10s, 100s, or 1000s of users then the waits become enormously long. (That is, if you can even get into the 100s or 1000s since the system may be so taxed at that point optimizing statements that it appears to be at a standstill).

So, the two points to take away from this section are:

❑   Attempt to isolate your SQL. Don't code the same query in more than one location, since this will reduce the chance of having different case, different whitespace, and so on.

❑   Use bind variables everywhere you can from the very beginning. Every language out there supports the use of bind variables in SQL, so make sure you do it. The importance of this cannot be overstated.

Am I Using Bind Variables?

So, having told you to use bind variables whenever possible, the natural follow-up question is 'how can I tell if I am?' To help you with this, we can take a look at a script which points out statements that look like they could be made identical if they used bind variables. In order to show you how this script works, we'll artificially fill up the shared pool with 'bad' SQL that doesn't use bind variables. We'll start by creating a table to test with:

```
SQL> create table t ( x int );
Table created.
```

To populate the table we'll dynamically execute a series of INSERT statements that, if we typed them into SQL*Plus, would look like this:

```
Insert into t values ( 1 );
Insert into t values ( 2 );
...
insert into t values ( 100 );
```

To automate this we use EXECUTE IMMEDIATE and run an anonymous PL/SQL block to generate the 100 insert statements:

```
SQL> begin
  2      for i in 1 .. 100
  3      loop
  4          execute immediate 'insert into t values ( ' || i || ')';
  5      end loop;
  6  end;
  7  /

PL/SQL procedure successfully completed.
```

Now, we're ready for the script. It starts by creating a function (REMOVE_CONSTANTS) that removes constants from strings. It will take SQL statements such as these:

```
Insert into t values ( 'hello', 55 );
Insert into t values ( 'world', 66 );
```

And turn them into statements of this kind:

```
Insert into t values ( '#', @);
```

In other words any string that appears in a SQL statement, from 'Hello' to 'World' will be turned into #, to ensure that all strings look the same. Likewise, we'll convert any numbers, such as 55 and 66 in our above example, into @ so that all numbers will look the same. In this way all statements that could look the same if they used bind variables will be clearly visible to us. For example, both of the above unique inserts will become the same insert statement after substitution. The function to do this transformation for us begins by turning character string constants like 'Hello' into #:

```
SQL> create or replace
  2  function remove_constants( p_query in varchar2 )
  3  return varchar2
  4  as
  5      l_query long;
  6      l_char  varchar2(1);
  7      l_in_quotes boolean default FALSE;
  8  begin
  9      for i in 1 .. length( p_query )
 10      loop
 11          l_char := substr(p_query,i,1);
 12          if ( l_char = '''' and l_in_quotes )
 13          then
 14              l_in_quotes := FALSE;
 15          elsif ( l_char = '''' and NOT l_in_quotes )
 16          then
 17              l_in_quotes := TRUE;
 18              l_query := l_query || '''#';
 19          end if;
 20          if ( NOT l_in_quotes ) then
 21              l_query := l_query || l_char;
 22          end if;
 23      end loop;
```

It then turns all numbers in the string into @:

```
 24      l_query := translate( l_query, '0123456789', '@@@@@@@@@@' );
```

Then, it will replace all sequences of @s with a single @ and all extra spaces with a single space.

```
 25      for i in 0 .. 8 loop
 26          l_query := replace( l_query, lpad('@',10-i,'@'), '@' );
 27          l_query := replace( l_query, lpad(' ',10-i,' '), ' ' );
 28      end loop;
```

It does this by issuing the equivalent of:

```
L_query := replace( l_query, '@@@@@@@@@@', '@' ); -- replace 10 @'s with one
L_query := replace( l_query, '          ', ' ' ); -- replace 10 spaces

L_query := replace( l_query, '@@@@@@@@@', '@' ); -- replace 9 @'s with one
L_query := replace( l_query '         ', ' ' ); -- replace 9 spaces with one
...
l_query := replace( l_query, '@@', '@' ); -- replace 2 @'s with one
l_query := replace( l_query, '  ', ' ' ); -- replace 2 spaces with one
```

For example, the number 1234567 which is turned into @@@@@@@ will become a single @.

Lastly, we'll return the UPPER of the query with the constants removed.

```
 29       return upper (l_query);
 30  end;
 31  /
Function created.
```

This will ensure that the queries:

```
Select * from emp where empno = 1234;
Select * from EMP where EMPNO = 5678;
```

will both become:

```
SELECT * FROM EMP WHERE EMPNO = @;
```

showing that they could both use the same shared SQL plan.

Now we'll take a look at the main body of the script. We'll make a copy of the V$SQLAREA table, since this view is expensive to query and we only want to query it once. V$SQLAREA is a dynamic performance view maintained by Oracle that shows us what unique SQL statements are currently in the shared pool. We copy it into the temporary table so that we can work on its contents efficiently:

```
SQL> create global temporary table sql_area_tmp
  2  on commit preserve rows
  3  as
  4  select sql_text, sql_text sql_text_wo_constants
  5    from v$sqlarea
  6   where 1=0
  7  /
Table created.

SQL> insert into sql_area_tmp (sql_text)
  2  select sql_text from v$sqlarea
  3  /
436 rows created.
```

Now, we go through and update each and every row in that table to compute the transformed SQL_TEXT, removing the constants:

```
SQL> update sql_area_tmp
  2      set sql_text_wo_constants = remove_constants(sql_text)
  3  /
436 rows updated.
```

And now we are ready to find the 'bad' SQL:

```
SQL> select sql_text_wo_constants, count(*)
  2      from sql_area_tmp
  3   group by sql_text_wo_constants
  4  having count(*) > 10
```

```
   5    order by 2
   6  /

SQL_TEXT_WO_CONSTANTS                  COUNT(*)
------------------------------------  ----------
INSERT INTO T VALUES ( @)                  100
```

The result obtained here, shows that there are 100 INSERT statements in my shared pool that differ by only one numeric field in the values clause. This would *most likely* indicate that someone forgot to use bind variables. Note however, that there are some legitimate cases where you might have a reasonable number of copies of SQL statements in the shared pool. For example, there might be 5 tables named T in the database, meaning that we need 5 statements, since the query plans are all different.

EXPLAIN PLAN

EXPLAIN PLAN is a SQL command that you can use to see the optimized query plan Oracle would use for your query. We can see this plan without actually executing the query. This is very useful when you have a statement, such as an UPDATE, which you don't want to perform over and over when testing, but wish to tune nonetheless. It is also useful when you are trying different query syntax or hints and would like to see if the query plan being generated is the one you are hoping for.

Before we can use the EXPLAIN PLAN command, we need a PLAN_TABLE table. This is a normal database table that has a specific set of columns in it, which the EXPLAIN PLAN command will populate with rows that represent our query plan. To create this table, you simply execute the supplied script found in $ORACLE_HOME/rdbms/admin/utlxplan.sql, if you are running on Unix, or %ORACLE_HOME%\rdbms\admin\utlxplan.sql if you are running on Windows:

```
SQL> @%ORACLE_HOME%\rdbms\admin\utlxplan.sql
Table created.
```

Once that table is created, we can begin generating plans into it. The syntax for the EXPLAIN PLAN command is simply:

```
EXPLAIN PLAN
    SET STATEMENT_ID = <some name>
    FOR <sql-statement>
```

where you will supply some name for the query (to identify its rows in the PLAN_TABLE table) and some SQL query to generate a query plan for. A very quick example would be:

```
SQL> EXPLAIN PLAN
  2       SET STATEMENT_ID = 'example' FOR
  3    SELECT ename,dname
  4      FROM emp  inner join dept
  5        ON ( emp.deptno = dept.deptno )
  6  /
Explained.
```

Here our query will retrieve details regarding the ENAME and DNAME columns, joining data from both the EMP and DEPT tables using the DEPTNO column.

Now, the plan has been generated and is stored in the PLAN_TABLE table. If you did a simple SELECT * from this table, you would see all of the data (but it would not make a great deal of sense). Instead, we will use the supplied script UTLXPLS.SQL to review this information:

```
SQL>   @%ORACLE_HOME%\rdbms\admin\utlxpls.sql

Plan Table
-------------------------------------------------------------------------------
| Operation              |  Name  |Rows | Bytes|  Cost  | Pstart| Pstop |
-------------------------------------------------------------------------------
| SELECT STATEMENT       |        |  14 |  252 |     3  |       |  ...  |
| HASH JOIN              |        |  14 |  252 |     3  |       |  ...  |
|   TABLE ACCESS FULL    |DEPT    |   4 |   44 |     1  |       |       |
|   TABLE ACCESS FULL    |EMP     |  14 |   98 |     1  |       |       |
-------------------------------------------------------------------------------

7 rows selected.
```

This query retrieves the *last* query plan we ran EXPLAIN_PLAN on (using a timestamp that is included in the PLAN_TABLE table) and presents us with a nice listing of what the query will do at run-time. The columns we observe here are:

❑ **Operation** – what the optimizer is doing at this step. For example, you'll see operations such as INDEX RANGE SCAN indicating an index is being used, and TABLE ACCESS FULL for full scans.

❑ **Name** – the name of the object being accessed when applicable. This will typically be a table name or index name.

❑ **Rows** – the estimated number of rows that will result from executing this step of the query plan. This will be populated only when using the Cost-based optimizer.

❑ **Bytes** – the estimated number of bytes of data that will result from executing this step of the query plan. This will be populated only when using the Cost-based optimizer.

❑ **Cost** – the relative cost of executing this step of the query plan. Used internally by the Cost-based optimizer when choosing from a set of possible execution plans.

❑ **Pstart** – only visible when using partitioned tables and partition elimination. This will show the starting partition in the query plan. Partitions before this one in the table will not be accessed by that step of the query plan.

❑ **Pstop** – only visible when using partitioned tables and partition elimination. This will show the ending partition in the query plan. Partitions after this one in the table will not be accessed by that step of the query plan.

Here, in this example, we can see that Oracle will FULL SCAN the EMP table, and estimates that it will find 14 rows there, occupying 98 bytes. Similarly, when it performs a FULL SCAN of the DEPT table, it is expecting to find 4 rows and use 44 bytes of storage. When it joins the two tables together, it expects the resulting set to be 14 rows in size. Since we have our tables analyzed, EXPLAIN PLAN is able to show us this information.

717

> Note that the presence of the rows, bytes, and cost information indicates that we are using the Cost based optimizer. More details on optimizers can be found in Chapter 6.

Let's now take a look at what we'd see if we used the Rule based Optimizer instead:

```
SQL> alter session set optimizer_goal = rule;
Session altered.

SQL> EXPLAIN PLAN
  2    SET STATEMENT_ID = 'example' FOR
  3    SELECT ename,dname
  4    FROM emp  inner join dept
  5    ON ( emp.deptno = dept.deptno )
  6    /
Explained.

SQL>  @%ORACLE_HOME%\rdbms\admin\utlxpls.sql

Plan Table
---------------------------------------------------------------------------
| Operation                    | Name    | Rows | Bytes| Cost  | Pstart| Pstop |
---------------------------------------------------------------------------
| SELECT STATEMENT             |         |      |      |       |       |       |
|  NESTED LOOPS                |         |      |      |       |       |       |
|   TABLE ACCESS FULL          |EMP      |      |      |       |       |       |
|   TABLE ACCESS BY INDEX RO   |DEPT     |      |      |       |       |       |
|    INDEX UNIQUE SCAN         |PK_DEPT  |      |      |       |       |       |
---------------------------------------------------------------------------

8 rows selected.
```

As you can see the query plan is significantly different, given the exact same data and database.

> Note that this information does not tell us which query is better, since we cannot tell how much work they would do. In order to see that work, we'll need to actually execute the queries, see how they perform, and analyze the results. That is the purpose of the next two tools AUTOTRACE and TKPROF.

AUTOTRACE

AUTOTRACE is a SQL*Plus facility that may be enabled in your database. To get this up and running you need to have administration rights to the system and perform the following steps:

❑ Log into SQL*Plus as SYSDBA

❑ Run the script @%ORACLE_HOME%/sqlplus/admin/plustrace

❑ Grant PLUSTRACE to PUBLIC (or to specific users/roles)

For example:

```
C:\>sqlplus "sys/manager as sysdba"

SQL*Plus: Release 8.1.6.0.0 - Production on Sat Jan 12 13:40:13 2002
  (c) Copyright 1999 Oracle Corporation.  All rights reserved.
Connected to:
Oracle 8i Enterprise Edition Release 8.1.6.0.0 - Production
With the Partitioning option
JServer Release 8.1.6.0.0 - Production

SQL> @%ORACLE_HOME%/sqlplus/admin/plustrace

SQL> drop role plustrace;
Role dropped.

SQL> create role plustrace;
Role created.

SQL> grant select on v_$sesstat to plustrace;
Grant succeeded.

SQL> grant select on v_$statname to plustrace;
Grant succeeded.

SQL> grant select on v_$session to plustrace;
Grant succeeded.

SQL> grant plustrace to dba with admin option;
Grant succeeded.

SQL> set echo off
SQL> grant plustrace to public;
Grant succeeded.
```

The PLUSTRACE role that is created simply provides access to some important V$ tables used in performance testing, namely:

❑   v$sesstat: table of statistics by session

❑   v$statname: a mapping of a statistic number (ID) to name

❑   v$session: a table that can be used to find our session identifier, to identify our rows in the v$sesstat table

Once the PLUSTRACE role is installed and granted to you, you need to ensure that the PLAN_TABLE table is installed in your schema (as documented above in the *Explain Plan* section), before you are ready to use AUTOTRACE. Using AUTOTRACE is very easy, since all we need to do is enter SET AUTOTRACE ON and SQL*Plus does the rest for us. So, for example, to run AUTOTRACE on our previous query we simply execute:

```
SQL> set autotrace on

SQL> SELECT ename,dname
  2    FROM emp  inner join dept
  3      ON ( emp.deptno = dept.deptno )
  4  /

ENAME      DNAME
---------- --------------
SMITH      RESEARCH
ALLEN      SALES
WARD       SALES
JONES      RESEARCH
MARTIN     SALES
BLAKE      SALES
CLARK      ACCOUNTING
SCOTT      RESEARCH
KING       ACCOUNTING
TURNER     SALES
ADAMS      RESEARCH
JAMES      SALES
FORD       RESEARCH
MILLER     ACCOUNTING

14 rows selected.

Execution Plan
----------------------------------------------------------
   0      SELECT STATEMENT Optimizer=CHOOSE (Cost=3 Card=14 Bytes=252)
   1    0   HASH JOIN (Cost=3 Card=14 Bytes=252)
   2    1     TABLE ACCESS (FULL) OF 'DEPT' (Cost=1 Card=4 Bytes=44)
   3    1     TABLE ACCESS (FULL) OF 'EMP' (Cost=1 Card=14 Bytes=98)

Statistics
----------------------------------------------------------
        0  recursive calls
        4  db block gets
        3  consistent gets
        0  physical reads
        0  redo size
     1132  bytes sent via SQL*Net to client
      503  bytes received via SQL*Net from client
        2  SQL*Net roundtrips to/from client
        0  sorts (memory)
        0  sorts (disk)
       14  rows processed
```

When we ran the query we got to see the results, followed by the EXPLAIN PLAN output showing the query plan used to actually execute the query, along with some very important system statistics.

The output of EXPLAIN PLAN looks very similar to the results we observed in the preceding section on EXPLAIN PLAN, but is formatted a little differently. (In fact, if you compare this EXPLAIN PLAN output to the preceding section, you'll find the data contained therein is identical.) That is because the AUTOTRACE feature simply automates the call to the EXPLAIN PLAN command for us.

The next section of the AUTOTRACE output is information about the run-time work actually performed by our query. Here we can see many important pieces of information such as how many logical I/Os and physical I/Os our query performed, how many sorts, the number of rows processed and so on. The following table shows what each piece of information is, what it means and how to interpret it, given our results above:

Statistic	Meaning	Interpretation
Recursive calls	This is the number of recursive SQL statements Oracle performed in order to process our query. This recursive SQL might have been performed in order to hard parse our query, allocate additional space in a table to allow for an insert to succeed, or indeed have been triggered by some DML operation.	We observed 0 recursive calls for our query. From this we can infer that all of the information necessary to parse our query was found in the dictionary or library cache in the SGA. Oracle did not need to execute any SQL to retrieve additional information to process our query.
Db block gets	These are blocks read in **current** mode (in other words as they exist now) from the database. Normally, blocks are read in **consistent** mode, in other words, as they existed when the query began (as explained in Chapter 5). In the case of SELECT statements, most blocks will not be read in current mode, while in the case of INSERT, UPDATE, and DELETE statements, many blocks will be read in current mode. This is because Oracle needs to see the current state of the block before it can modify it.	We observed 4 db block gets. These block gets were performed in order to read the segment header for each of the tables involved. When Oracle performs a full table scan, it will read the segment header in current mode in order to determine how to physically read the table. In other words Oracle needs to determine where the extents of the table are on the disk. In version 9*i*, Oracle typically reads this segment header data twice while processing the query (for a total of 4 since we have 2 tables). In version 8*i*, you may observe this number being higher (4 per table). This is unavoidable when performing a full table scan (try SELECT * FROM DUAL, and you'll get similar results).
Consistent gets	These are blocks read in consistent mode (as explained in Chapter 5). In the case of queries, most blocks are read in consistent mode, while for DML operations that modify the data, the "query" portion of the statement will read blocks in consistent mode, and the "write" portion of the query will modify the blocks in current mode	We observed 3 consistent gets, showing that we read three blocks in consistent read mode.

Table continued on following page

Statistic	Meaning	Interpretation
Physical reads	This is a count of the number of physical blocks we had to read in order to process our query.	We observed 0 physical I/Os, indicating that all of the data we needed was cached in memory. This is the best case scenario! You can calculate your cache hit ratio for your query using the formula: $100 * \{1 - [(\text{physical-reads})/(\text{db block gets+consistent gets})]\}$ In our case, our cache hit was 100%. If we'd have had 1 physical read, our cache hit would have been: $100* [1-(1/7)] = 85\%$
Redo size	The amount of redo generated by our statement. You will typically observe redo on statements that modify the database such as an UPDATE.	We observed 0 bytes of redo generated for our SELECT statement. (While it is possible for a SELECT to generate REDO activity in some circumstances, in most cases you would expect 0 bytes of redo log to be generated for them.)
Bytes sent via SQL*Net to client	This is the size in bytes of the data sent from the server to the client.	We observed 1,132 bytes of data sent from the server to the client (SQL*Plus). This data represents our result set.
Bytes received via SQL*Net from client	This is the size in bytes of the data sent from the client to the server.	We observed 503 bytes of data sent from the client to the server. This data represents our requests to the server including the query we executed and requests for the result set (our 'fetches').
SQL*Net roundtrips to/from client	This is the number of roundtrips from the client to the server; how many calls we made.	We observed 2 roundtrips. In this case one roundtrip was for the parsing of the query and the other for the retrieval of the data. SQL*Plus by default retrieves 15 rows at a time and as a result, since we retrieved 14 rows, it could do the entire fetch in one call.
Sorts (memory)	The number of sorts Oracle performed in memory.	We observed 0 sorts. This is to be expected in our case, as we did not require any data to be sorted.

Statistic	Meaning	Interpretation
Sorts (disk)	The number of sorts Oracle performed that were too large to fit into memory.	We observed 0 of these sorts as well.
Rows processed	The number of rows Oracle returned from this query.	We observed 14 rows (which matches with our result set).

Now that AUTOTRACE is turned on in our session, every SELECT, INSERT, UPDATE, or DELETE we execute will produce this information. Typically, you want to trace one or two statements and then turn off AUTOTRACE. Disabling AUTOTRACE is as easy as:

```
SQL> set autotrace off
```

AUTOTRACE is typically used to compare the work performed by a query under different circumstances, or to compare the performance of various equivalent queries (similar queries written in different ways). Let's revisit the EXPLAIN PLAN example above, and see what happens to our query if we execute it using the Rule-based optimizer.

Here we'll use a variation of AUTOTRACE, one that executes the entire query but suppresses the display of the data (useful when the result set is potentially large and you are only interested in the performance metrics):

```
SQL> set autotrace traceonly
SQL> alter session set optimizer_goal=rule;
Session altered.

SQL> SELECT ename,dname
  2    FROM emp  inner join dept
  3      ON ( emp.deptno = dept.deptno )
  4  /
14 rows selected.

Execution Plan
----------------------------------------------------------
   0      SELECT STATEMENT Optimizer=RULE
   1    0   NESTED LOOPS
   2    1     TABLE ACCESS (FULL) OF 'EMP'
   3    1     TABLE ACCESS (BY INDEX ROWID) OF 'DEPT'
   4    3       INDEX (UNIQUE SCAN) OF 'PK_DEPT' (UNIQUE)

Statistics
----------------------------------------------------------
        0   recursive calls
        2   db block gets
       30   consistent gets
        0   physical reads
        0   redo size
     1132   bytes sent via SQL*Net to client
```

```
  503  bytes received via SQL*Net from client
    2  SQL*Net roundtrips to/from client
    0  sorts (memory)
    0  sorts (disk)
   14  rows processed
```

Notice how we enabled AUTOTRACE using the TRACEONLY option. This tells SQL*Plus to parse the query and fetch all of the data but not to print the data on the screen. Consequently it will simply show us the query plan and the run-time statistics.

Now, we can compare the run-time characteristics of the plan generated by the Cost-based optimizer and the Rule-based one. Most of the statistics are the same with the glaring exception of db block gets and consistent reads. While the Cost-based optimizer performed a total of 7 combined block gets and consistent reads, the Rule-based optimizer performed a total of 32 combined block gets and consistent reads. In this case, one can deduce that the Cost- based optimizer, with its query plan that avoids the indexes on such small tables, developed the superior plan. The Rule-based optimizer, since it does not take the statistics associated with the tables into consideration, chose the wrong (less optimal) query plan in this case.

Before we move on to the next tool for performance tuning, TKPROF, we'll summarize all of the ways AUTOTRACE can be enabled in SQL*Plus and explain what each does:

Command	What it does
SET AUTOTRACE ON	The simplest form of AUTOTRACE. This enables the AUTOTRACE facility and will cause SQL*Plus to display the results of the SQL statement (its output), as well as the EXPLAIN PLAN for the statement, and the session statistics.
SET AUTOTRACE TRACEONLY	This enables the AUTOTRACE facility but causes SQL*Plus to suppress the display of the output. This is useful when you do not need to see the query results (the result set) but only wish to review the run-time performance statistics and query plans used.
SET AUTOTRACE ON EXPLAIN	Same as SET AUTOTRACE ON but suppresses the statistics report. This shows the query result set and the EXPLAIN PLAN.
SET AUTOTRACE ON STATISTICS	Same as SET AUTOTRACE ON but suppresses the EXPLAIN PLAN report. This shows the query result set and the performance statistics.

Command	What it does
SET AUTOTRACE TRACEONLY EXPLAIN	This only shows the EXPLAIN PLAN for a SQL statement and suppresses both the result set display and the statistics. If the SQL statement is a SELECT statement then SQL*Plus will not fetch any of the data. Therefore, this can be used very efficiently to see the EXPLAIN PLAN of a long running query without actually running the query. In short, this command is a very easy way to automate the generation of a query plan without using the EXPLAIN PLAN command and querying the PLAN_TABLE table yourself.
SET AUTOTRACE TRACEONLY STATISTICS	This is the same as SET AUTOTRACE TRACEONLY but suppresses the EXPLAIN PLAN report. This shows only the run-time statistics (db block gets, consistent gets, etc.) for the SQL statement.

AUTOTRACE is one of the easiest performance tools to use as it is readily available via SQL*Plus and SQL*Plus does most all of the work for you. If it is not enabled in your database, ask your DBA or Administrator to set it up right away since you'll be able to make immediate use of it in your day-to-day development.

Trace Files and TIMED_STATISTICS

Looking at query plans, and returning some statistics on such plans is all well and good, but how do we determine where the performance issue in a system lies? Given that, on many occasions, you will be tuning a system that you did not write, knowing where to look is difficult. The SQL_TRACE and TIMED_STATISTICS settings, as well as the TKPROF tool are a great place to start.

In a nutshell, SQL_TRACE enables the logging of all the SQL your application performs, performance statistics on the execution of that SQL, and the query plans your SQL actually used. TIMED_STATISTICS is a parameter that enables the server to tell us how long each step takes. TKPROF is a simple program used to format the raw trace file into something more readable. What we will do in this section is show you how to use SQL_TRACE and TKPROF, and to explain the meaning of what is included in the files used by these facilities. We will not so much describe how you might take a particular query and tune it, as show how to use these tools to find the queries to tune.

> For more information on tuning individual queries we recommend either 'Oracle 8i Designing and Tuning for Performance', or 'Oracle 9i Database Performance Guide and Reference'.

The parameter TIMED_STATISTICS controls whether Oracle will collect timing information for various activities in the database. It has two settings, TRUE and FALSE. This feature is so useful that it is advisable to leave it on (in other words set to TRUE) even when not tuning, since its performance impact on a database is negligible in general. It may be set at either the SYSTEM or the SESSION level and may be 'globally' set in the initialization file for the database. If you put it in the init.ora file for your instance, you will simply add:

```
timed_statistics=true
```

In this way the next time you restart the database it will be enabled.

Alternatively, to enable it for your session you may issue:

```
SQL> alter session set timed_statistics=true;
Session altered.
```

or you can turn it on for the entire system by issuing:

```
SQL> alter system set timed_statistics=true;
System altered.
```

Setting Up Tracing

SQL_TRACE may also be enabled at the system or session level. It generates so much output, and is such a performance impact, that you will almost always selectively enable it. Rarely, if ever, will you want to enable it for the system in the init.ora file. SQL_TRACE has two settings, TRUE and FALSE, and if set to TRUE will generate trace files to the directory specified in the init.ora parameter file. In the case of a dedicated server connection this is USER_DUMP_DEST, while in the case of a shared server connection (MTS connection prior to Oracle 9i) it is BACKGROUND_DUMP_DEST.

> **Note however, that attempting to use SQL_TRACE with a shared server connection is not to be recommended, since the output from your session's queries will be written to various trace files as your session migrates from shared server to shared server. Under shared server, interpreting SQL_TRACE results is nearly impossible.**

Another important init.ora parameter is MAX_DUMP_FILE_SIZE. This limits the maximum size of a trace file Oracle will generate. If you discover that your trace files are truncated, you will need to increase this setting. It may be changed via an ALTER system or session command. MAX_DUMP_FILE_SIZE may be specified in one of three ways:

❑ A numerical value for MAX_DUMP_FILE_SIZE specifies the maximum size in operating system blocks.

❑ A number followed by a K or M suffix specifying the file size in kilobytes or megabytes.

❑ The string UNLIMITED. This means that there is no upper limit on trace file size, allowing dump files to be as large as the operating system permits.

So, for example, you can set the limit of your maximum dump file to 20 megabytes via the following command:

```
SQL> alter session set max_dump_file_size = '20m';
Session altered.
```

> Note that **UNLIMITED** is a far too easy way to completely fill up a file system in this manner; a setting of 50-100Mb should be more than sufficient.

So, what are the various ways to enable SQL_TRACE? There are quite a few, but the more common ones are:

❑ ALTER SESSION SET SQL_TRACE=TRUE|FALSE – Executing this SQL will enable the default mode of SQL_TRACE in the current session. This is most useful in an interactive environment (such as SQL*Plus), or embedded in an application so that the application may turn SQL_TRACE on and off at will. Adding a facility to your application that allows SQL_TRACE to be turned on and off easily (such as a command line switch or menu select) is to be encouraged, since it allows you to easily turn on SQL_TRACE when a performance problem is detected.

❑ SYS.DBMS_SYSTEM.SET_SQL_TRACE_IN_SESSION – This packaged procedure allows us to set SQL_TRACE on and off for any existing session in the database. All we need to do is identify the SID and SERIAL# for the session, both of which are available in the dynamic performance view V$SESSION (as we saw earlier).

❑ ALTER SESSION SET EVENTS – We can set an event to enable tracing with more information than is normally available via the ALTER SESSION SET SQL_TRACE=TRUE statement. The SET EVENTS approach is not documented or supported by Oracle Corporation, however a search on Google for alter session set events 10046 will reveal many web sites that document this feature. Using this event we can not only get everything that SQL_TRACE tells us, but can also see the values of bind variables used by our SQL (very useful!) as well as the wait events (what slowed us down) for our SQL.

The ALTER SESSION SET SQL_TRACE and SYS.DBMS_SYSTEM methods of setting SQL_TRACE on are so straightforward as to be self-explanatory. The EVENT method however, is a little more obscure. It uses an internal (and undocumented) event facility within Oracle. In short, the command you would use will look like this:

```
alter session set events '10046 trace name context forever, level <n>';
alter session set events '10046 trace name context off';
```

where N is one of the following values:

❑ N = 1 – enables the standard SQL_TRACE facility. (This is no different than setting SQL_TRACE=true)

❑ N = 4 – enables standard SQL_TRACE but also captures bind variable values in the trace file

❑ N = 8 – enables standard SQL_TRACE but also captures wait events at the query level into the trace file. As a quick reminder here wait events are things that stop our query from processing momentarily, such as completion of I/O (disk read/write)

❑ N = 12 – enables standard SQL_TRACE and includes both bind variables and waits

So, now we know how to turn SQL_TRACE on, the question becomes how can we best make use of it? As stated previously, it would be useful to have a switch of some sort built-in to all of your developed applications, which you can use to tell the application to enable SQL_TRACE. This allows easy capture of SQL_TRACE information for a single session. Many Oracle tools already allow you to do this. For example, if you use Oracle forms, you can execute:

```
C:\> ifrun60 module=myform userid=scott/tiger statistics=YES
```

statistics=YES is a flag to forms to tell it to issue ALTER SESSION SET SQL_TRACE=TRUE.

If you have a single user with a performance issue, then SQL_TRACE allows you to avoid sitting with the user and getting them to try and recall the steps that they took, in order to reproduce the slowdown. Instead, you can simply ask them to run with SQL_TRACE enabled, and when they reproduce the performance problem, you'll have the trace file information available to help figure out where the problem lies. If you trace with bind variables and wait events, you'll have more than enough information to figure out what is going wrong.

What about the case of an application that wasn't SQL_TRACE enabled, or an application provided by a third party? In the case of a client-server application, once the relevant session is logged into the database, you can query v$SESSION in order to determine the session's SID and Serial#. A call to SYS.DBMS_SYSTEM.SET_SQL_TRACE_IN_SESSION can now enable tracing of that single session. Web-based applications (where sessions are short, and come and go frequently) are trickier, since we need to trace a 'user' rather than a session. To 'see' the user whenever they are in the database, we can use the LOGON DDL trigger. For example:

```
create or replace trigger logon_trigger
after logon on database
begin
  if ( user = 'SOME NAME' ) then
    execute immediate
    'ALTER SESSION SET SQL_TRACE=TRUE';
  end if;
end;
/
```

This will enable tracing any time a user with SOME NAME logs into the database. Now the application does not have to participate in the setting of SQL_TRACE, since we'll do this ourselves.

Using and Interpreting TKPROF Output

TKPROF is nothing more than a simple command-line tool to format a raw trace file into something we can read easily. It is an excellent utility that, arguably, is not used enough.

What we'll do in this section is to run a query with tracing enabled. We'll take a detailed look at the `TKPROF` report and learn what we need to look for in these reports. So, we'll begin by verifying that timed statistics is enabled (it is almost useless to execute `SQL_TRACE` without it) and then enable `SQL_TRACE`:

```
SQL> show parameter timed_statistics;

NAME                                 TYPE        VALUE
------------------------------------ ----------- -------------------------
timed_statistics                     boolean     TRUE

SQL> alter session set sql_trace=true;
Session altered.
```

Then we run the query we want to look at. This query simply generates a count of objects owned by each user in the database:

```
SQL> select owner, count(*)
  2  from all_objects
  3  group by owner;

OWNER                            COUNT(*)
------------------------------ ----------
AURORA$JIS$UTILITY$                    71
CTXSYS                                227
DEMO                                   14
HR                                     34
...
SYS                                 14977
SYSTEM                                339
```

Lastly, we run a query to get the trace file name. This is done by retrieving the necessary information from the Oracle-supplied V$ tables. In this case `C.VALUE` is the directory into which Oracle will create trace files and `A.SPID` is the unique session identifier Oracle will use when generating the filename. On Windows, the trace file is to be found in:

```
SQL> select c.value || '\ORA' || to_char(a.spid,'fm00000') || '.trc'
  2     from v$process a, v$session b, v$parameter c
  3   where a.addr = b.paddr
  4     and b.audsid = userenv('sessionid')
  5     and c.name = 'user_dump_dest'
  6  /

C.VALUE||'\ORA'||TO_CHAR(A.SPID,'FM00000')||'.TRC'
-----------------------------------------------------------------------
C:\Oracle 9i\admin\ORCL\udump\ORA01476.trc
```

To find the trace file on a UNIX instance, you'd need to execute the following:

```
SQL> select c.value || '/' || d.instance_name || '_ora_' ||
                               to_char(a.spid,'fm99999') || '.trc'
  2    from v$process a, v$session b, v$parameter c, v$instance d
  3    where a.addr = b.paddr
  4      and b.audsid = userenv('sessionid')
  5      and c.name = 'user_dump_dest'
  6  /


C.VALUE||'/'||D.INSTANCE_NAME||'_ORA_'||TO_CHAR(A.SPID,'FM99999')||'.TRC'
------------------------------------------------------------------------
/export/home/Oracle 9i/admin/ora9i/udump/ora9i_ora_1213.trc
```

> **It is important to note that trace files will always be generated on the database server, not the client machine that accessed the database.**

This makes sense once you figure out that it is your dedicated server (running on the database machine) process that creates this file. One issue with trace files is that you may be unable to read these files unless you are in the administrative group for ORACLE (for example, the DBA group in UNIX). If not, you should ensure that your DBA edits the init.ora file of your test and development machines as follows:

```
_trace_files_public = true
```

After the server is restarted, this will allow all users to read trace files on the server. You should *not* use this setting on a production machine as these files can contain sensitive information.

> *Notice that this init.ora parameter is undocumented and unsupported by Oracle Corporation. However, as we highlighted earlier a quick search on Google will generate references to this parameter.*

Now that we know where our trace file is, we can format it using the TKPROF command-line utility. In its simplest form we will just execute:

```
C:\Oracle 9i\admin\ORCL\udump>tkprof ORA01476.TRC report.txt

TKPROF: Release 9.0.1.0.0 - Production on Sat Dec 8 13:17:31 2001

(c) Copyright 2001 Oracle Corporation. All rights reserved.
```

As you can see, all we need do is supply the names of the input (ORA01476.TRC) and output (report.txt) files, and we can then edit the report.txt file to find (among many other queries) the query we executed. Any other queries you see in there that you did not execute are recursive SQL.

> *For a reminder about recursive SQL code please look back to Chapter 6.*

Looking at our query we see:

```
select owner, count(*)
from all_objects
group by owner

call     count      cpu    elapsed   disk      query    current       rows
-------  ------  --------  ---------  ------  ---------  ---------  ----------
Parse        1     0.00      0.00        0          0          0           0
Execute      1     0.00      0.00        0          0          0           0
Fetch        3     2.76      2.86        0     170874          3          29
-------  ------  --------  ---------  ------  ---------  ---------  ----------
total        5     2.76      2.86        0     170874          3          29

Misses in library cache during parse: 0
Optimizer goal: CHOOSE
Parsing user id: 99

Rows     Row Source Operation
-------  -------------------------------------------------------
     29  SORT GROUP BY
  31205   FILTER
  31569    TABLE ACCESS BY INDEX ROWID OBJ$
  31633     NESTED LOOPS
     63      TABLE ACCESS FULL USER$
  31569      INDEX RANGE SCAN (object id 37)
      0  FIXED TABLE FULL X$KZSPR
      1  FIXED TABLE FULL X$KZSPR
      0  FIXED TABLE FULL X$KZSPR
      0  FIXED TABLE FULL X$KZSPR
      1  FIXED TABLE FULL X$KZSPR
      1  FIXED TABLE FULL X$KZSPR
      1  FIXED TABLE FULL X$KZSPR
      1  FIXED TABLE FULL X$KZSPR
      1  FIXED TABLE FULL X$KZSPR
      1  FIXED TABLE FULL X$KZSPR
      1  FIXED TABLE FULL X$KZSPR
      1  FIXED TABLE FULL X$KZSPR
      1  FIXED TABLE FULL X$KZSPR
      1  FIXED TABLE FULL X$KZSPR
  14522  TABLE ACCESS BY INDEX ROWID OBJAUTH$
  81237   NESTED LOOPS
  63826    FIXED TABLE FULL X$KZSRO
  14524    INDEX RANGE SCAN (object id 109)
    850   TABLE ACCESS BY INDEX ROWID IND$
    919    INDEX UNIQUE SCAN (object id 39)
```

TKPROF is showing us a lot of information here. We'll take it piece by piece:

```
select owner, count(*)
from all_objects
group by owner
```

First we see the original query as the server received it. (In this case, it is exactly as we'd typed it in.) Next comes the overall execution report for this query:

```
call       count       cpu    elapsed   disk      query    current        rows
-------   ------   -------   --------   ------   --------   --------   ---------
Parse          1      0.00      0.00         0          0          0           0
Execute        1      0.00      0.00         0          0          0           0
Fetch          3      2.76      2.86         0     170874          3          29
-------   ------   -------   --------   ------   --------   --------   ---------
total          5      2.76      2.86         0     170874          3          29
```

Here we see the three main phases of the query:

❑ The PARSE phase where Oracle finds the query in the shared pool (soft parse) or creates a new plan for the query (hard parse).

❑ The EXECUTE phase. This is the work done by Oracle upon the OPEN or EXECUTE of the query. For a SELECT, this will generally be 'empty' whereas for an UPDATE, this will be where all of the work is done.

❑ Then, there is the FETCH phase. For a SELECT, this will be where most of the work is done and visible, but a statement like an UPDATE will show no work (you don't 'fetch' from an update).

The column headings in this section have the following meanings:

❑ CALL – Will be one of PARSE, EXECUTE, FETCH, or TOTAL. Simply denotes which phase of query processing we are looking at.

❑ COUNT – How many times the event occurred. This can be a very important number. We will take a look at how to interpret the values opposite.

❑ CPU – In CPU seconds, how much time was spent on this phase of the query execution. This is only filled in if TIMED_STATISTICS was enabled. These timings are in hundredths of seconds, so a value of 0.0 here indicates the operation took less than $1/100^{th}$ of a second.

❑ ELAPSED – How long this phase of query execution took as measured by the wall clock. This is only filled in if TIMED_STATISTICS is enabled.

❑ DISK – How many physical I/Os to the disk our query performed.

❑ QUERY – How many blocks we processed in 'consistent read' mode. This will include counts of blocks read from the rollback segment in order to roll back a block.

❑ CURRENT – How many blocks were read in 'current' mode. Current mode blocks are retrieved as they exist right now, not in a consistent read fashion. Normally, blocks retrieved for a query are gotten as they existed when the query began. Current mode blocks are gotten as they exist right now, not from a previous point in time. During a SELECT, we might see current mode retrievals due to reading the data dictionary to find the extent information for a table to do a full scan (we need the 'current' information on that, not the consistent read). During a modification, we will access the blocks in current mode in order to write to them.

❑ ROWS – How many rows were affected by that phase of processing. A SELECT will show them in the FETCH phase. An UPDATE would show how many rows were updated in the EXECUTE phase.

The important threads or facts to look for, in this section of the report, are as follows:

A high (near 100%) parse count to execute count ratio when the execute count is greater than one. Here you take the number of times you parsed this statement and divide by the number of times you executed it. If this ratio is 1 then you parsed this query each and every time you executed it and that needs to be corrected. We would like this ratio to approach zero. Ideally, the parse count would be one and the execute count would be higher than one. If we see a high parse count, this implies we are performing many soft parses of this query. If you recall from Chapter 6, this can drastically reduce your scalability and will impact your run-time performance even in a single user session. You should ensure that you parse a query once per session and execute it over and over; you never want to have to parse your SQL for each execution.

Execute count of one for all or nearly all SQL. If you have a TKPROF report in which all SQL statements are executed one time only, you are probably not using bind variables. In a real application trace, we would expect very little 'unique' SQL; the same SQL should be executed more than once. Too much unique SQL typically implies you are not using bind variables correctly.

A large disparity between CPU time and elapsed time. This would indicate that you spent a lot of time waiting for something. If you see that you took one CPU second to execute but it required ten seconds by the wall clock, it means you spent 90 percent of your run-time waiting for a resource. We'll see later on in this section how we can determine the cause of the wait. This wait could be for any number of reasons. For example, an update that was blocked by another session would have a very large elapsed time versus CPU time. A SQL query that performs lots of physical disk I/O might have lots of wait time for I/O to complete.

A large CPU or elapsed time number. These are your queries that represent the 'lowest hanging fruit'. If you can make them go faster, your program will go faster. Many times, there is one monster query gumming up the works; fix this and the application works just fine.

A high (FETCH COUNT)/(rows fetched). Here we take the number of FETCH calls (three in our example) and the rows fetched count (29 in our example). If this number is near one, and the rows fetched count is greater than one, our application is not performing bulk fetches.

Note that every language/API has the ability to bulk fetch (fetch many rows at a time in a single call).

If you do not utilize the ability to bulk fetch, you will spend much more time performing round trips from the client to the server than you should. This excessive switching back and forth, in addition to generating a very 'chatty' network situation, is much slower than fetching many rows in one call. How you direct your application to bulk fetch is 'language/API'-dependent. For example, in Pro*C you would precompile with prefetch=NN, in Java/JDBC you would call the setRowPreFetch method, and in PL/SQL you would use the BULK COLLECT directive in a FETCH INTO. The above example shows that SQL*Plus (the client we used) called fetch three times in order to retrieve twenty nine rows. This shows that SQL*Plus used an array size of at least ten rows.

An excessively high disk count. This is harder to evaluate as a rule of thumb, however if the disk count = query + current mode block count, then all blocks were read from disk. We would hope that if the same query were executed again, some of the blocks would be found in the SGA. You should consider a high disk count value to be a red flag, and something to investigate. You might have to do some SGA resizing or work on the query to develop one that requires fewer block reads.

An excessively high query or current count. This indicates that your query does a lot of work. Whether this is an issue or not is subjective. Some queries just hit a lot of data, as our example above does. However a query that is executed frequently should have relatively small counts. If you add query and current mode blocks from the total line and divide that by the count column from the execute line, you would expect a small number.

Now, onto the next part of the report:

```
Misses in library cache during parse: 0
Optimizer goal: CHOOSE
Parsing user id: 99
```

The `misses in library cache` with zero misses is telling us that the query we executed was found in the shared pool, since we did not generate a miss on the library cache during this parse (and as a result performed a soft parse of the query). The very first time a query is executed, we would expect this count to be one. If almost every query you execute has a one for this value, it would indicate you are not reusing SQL (and that you need to fix it).

The second line, the optimizer goal, informs us of the optimizer mode that was in place during the execution of this query. In this case, we used the default setting of CHOOSE meaning Oracle will choose to use either the Cost-based or Rule-based optimizer based on the existence of statistics on the referenced tables.

Lastly, the USERID used to parse the query is presented. This can be resolved into a USERNAME via:

```
SQL> select * from all_users where user_id = 99;

USERNAME                        USER_ID CREATED
------------------------------ --------- ---------
SCOTT                                99 10-MAR-01
```

In this case the result shows us that the user SCOTT ran it. The last section of the TKPROF report for this query is the query plan. The query plan that appears by default is shown below:

```
Rows     Row Source Operation
-------  ---------------------------------------------------
     29  SORT GROUP BY
  31205   FILTER
  31569    TABLE ACCESS BY INDEX ROWID OBJ$
  31633     NESTED LOOPS
     63      TABLE ACCESS FULL USER$
  31569      INDEX RANGE SCAN (object id 37)
      0  FIXED TABLE FULL X$KZSPR
      1  FIXED TABLE FULL X$KZSPR
      0  FIXED TABLE FULL X$KZSPR
      0  FIXED TABLE FULL X$KZSPR
      1  FIXED TABLE FULL X$KZSPR
      1  FIXED TABLE FULL X$KZSPR
      1  FIXED TABLE FULL X$KZSPR
      1  FIXED TABLE FULL X$KZSPR
```

```
       1     FIXED TABLE FULL X$KZSPR
       1     FIXED TABLE FULL X$KZSPR
       1     FIXED TABLE FULL X$KZSPR
       1     FIXED TABLE FULL X$KZSPR
       1     FIXED TABLE FULL X$KZSPR
       1     FIXED TABLE FULL X$KZSPR
   14522     TABLE ACCESS BY INDEX ROWID OBJAUTH$
   81237       NESTED LOOPS
   63826         FIXED TABLE FULL X$KZSRO
   14524         INDEX RANGE SCAN (object id 109)
     850       TABLE ACCESS BY INDEX ROWID IND$
     919         INDEX UNIQUE SCAN (object id 39)
```

This is the actual query plan that was used by Oracle at run-time. The interesting thing about this plan is that the rows that flow through each step of the plan are visible. We can see for example that 14,522 rows were fetched from OBJAUTH$. These counts are the row counts of the rows flowing out of that step of the execution plan.

> Note that in Oracle 8.0 and before, this count was the count of rows inspected by that phase of the execution plan (the number of rows flowing into this step). For example, if 50,000 rows were considered in **OBJAUTH$**, but a **WHERE** clause was used to exclude them, then a TKPROF report from Oracle 8.0 would have reported 50,000 instead.

Using this sort of information you can see what steps you might want to avoid in a query, and restructure the query in order to come up with a more efficient plan.

You'll notice that there are a mixture of object names (for example, TABLE ACCESS BY INDEX ROWID IND$) and object IDs (for example, INDEX UNIQUE SCAN (object id 39)). This is because the raw trace file does not record all of the object names, only the object IDs for some objects. TKPROF will not connect to the database to turn the object IDs into object names by default. We can easily turn this object ID into an object name via the query:

```
SQL> select owner, object_type, object_name
  2  from all_objects
  3  where object_id = 39;

OWNER                            OBJECT_TYPE          OBJECT_NAME
-------------------------------  -------------------  ---------------
SYS                              INDEX                I_IND1
```

So in this case the index I_IND1 corresponds to the object_id 39, and is owned by user SYS. Alternatively, we could use the EXPLAIN= parameter with TKPROF as follows:

```
C:\oracle\ADMIN\tkyte816\udump>tkprof ora01124.trc x.txt explain=scott/tiger
```

but in this case, we would probably receive:

```
error during parse of EXPLAIN PLAN statement
ORA-01039: insufficient privileges on underlying objects of the view
```

In other words, we don't have permission to access the base table. However, if we use the SYS account (or any other account with suitable privileges) then we would be able to generate the EXPLAIN PLAN for this query.

A word of caution about the use of the EXPLAIN= syntax. While this will help you to see the EXPLAIN PLAN query, this may differ considerably from the actual query used at run time. For this reason the only plan that can be trusted is the plan saved in the trace file itself.

TKPROF has many command-line options and if you just type TKPROF on the command line, you'll get to see them all:

```
C:\Oracle 9i\admin\ORCL\udump>tkprof
Usage: tkprof tracefile outputfile [explain= ] [table= ]
              [print= ] [insert= ] [sys= ] [sort= ]
  table=schema.tablename   Use 'schema.tablename' with 'explain=' option.
  explain=user/password    Connect to ORACLE and issue EXPLAIN PLAIN.
  print=integer     List only the first 'integer' SQL statements.
  aggregate=yes|no
  insert=filename   List SQL statements and data inside INSERT statements.
  sys=no            TKPROF does not list SQL statements run as user SYS.
  record=filename   Record non-recursive statements found in the trace file.
  waits=yes|no      Record summary for any wait events found in the trace file.
  sort=option       Set of zero or more of the following sort options:
    prscnt  number of times parse was called
    prscpu  cpu time parsing
    prsela  elapsed time parsing
    prsdsk  number of disk reads during parse
    prsqry  number of buffers for consistent read during parse
    prscu   number of buffers for current read during parse
    prsmis  number of misses in library cache during parse
    execnt  number of execute was called
    execpu  cpu time spent executing
    exeela  elapsed time executing
    exedsk  number of disk reads during execute
    exeqry  number of buffers for consistent read during execute
    execu   number of buffers for current read during execute
    exerow  number of rows processed during execute
    exemis  number of library cache misses during execute
    fchcnt  number of times fetch was called
    fchcpu  cpu time spent fetching
    fchela  elapsed time fetching
    fchdsk  number of disk reads during fetch
    fchqry  number of buffers for consistent read during fetch
    fchcu   number of buffers for current read during fetch
    fchrow  number of rows fetched
    userid  userid of user that parsed the cursor
```

One of the most useful options is the `sort=` option. Not only does it allow you to sort by the various CPU and elapsed time metrics to get the 'worst' queries to pop up to the top of the trace file, but you can also use this to find the queries that do too much I/O. For most of the time, it will be sufficient to use `tkprof tracefilename reportfilename` and nothing else. This shows us the SQL more or less in the order it was executed at run-time. You can then use tools such as `grep` in UNIX or `find` in Windows to extract all of the 'total' lines so as to know what queries to zoom in on. For example:

```
C:\Oracle 9i\admin\ORCL\udump>find "total" report.txt

---------- REPORT.TXT
total       1      0.00      0.00      0          0          0          0
total       5      2.76      2.86      0     170874          3         29
total       6      2.76      2.86      0     170874          3         29
total       0      0.00      0.00      0          0          0          0
```

This shows us that we need to edit `report.txt` and search for `2.86` if we want to speed up this process, since it is the *longest* elapsed time in the entire TKPROF report. Fixing this query will have the biggest payback in making our application execute more quickly. There are other statements in there but this is the most immediately important one we need to focus on if we want this to go faster.

TKPROF and Waits

In the previous section we mentioned that a large disparity between CPU time and elapsed time indicated that you spent a lot of time waiting for some process to be completed. In this section we'll see how to find out what it was that we were waiting for.

When we explored the ways in which SQL_TRACE may be enabled, we saw there was a way to enable it via an EVENT. This event allowed us to capture bind variable values, or wait events, or both, in the trace file. With Oracle 9i we can use TKPROF to see these wait events as well, whereas in Oracle 8i (and previous versions), you need to read the raw trace file to see them.

In order to see how this works, we are going to set up an artificial wait condition. We'll need to use two sessions for this (two SQL*Plus windows). In the first session, logged in as SCOTT, we execute:

```
SQL> select empno from emp where ename = 'KING' for update;

    EMPNO
----------
     7839
```

That locked KING's record in that session. Now, leaving that session open and active, we'll start a second session in another SQL*Plus window.

> **Be sure to leave the first session running while you start this second session (also as user SCOTT) otherwise this example won't work!**

737

We begin this second session by turning on SQL_TRACE with the level set sufficiently high so as to capture the wait events in the trace file:

```
SQL> alter session set events '10046 trace name context forever, level 12';
Session altered.

SQL> update emp set sal = sal*1.1 where empno = 7839;
```

This UPDATE will be blocked, since the row is locked by another (our first) session. At this point, we go back to the first session that has the row locked and issue a COMMIT. That immediately unlocks our second session and allows it to execute. Now, we can exit SQL*Plus and upon running TKPROF on our trace file, we'll see something like this:

```
update emp set sal = sal*1.1
where
 empno = 7839


call       count      cpu    elapsed  disk     query     current       rows
-------    ------   -------- ---------- -----  ----------  ----------   ----------
Parse          1     0.06      0.12      0          0           0             0
Execute        1     0.02     20.46      1          2           3             1
Fetch          0     0.00      0.00      0          0           0             0
-------    ------   -------- ---------- -----  ----------  ----------   ----------
total          2     0.08     20.58      1          2           3             1

Misses in library cache during parse: 1
Optimizer goal: CHOOSE
Parsing user id: 54

Rows       Row Source Operation
-------    ---------------------------------------------------------
      1    UPDATE EMP
      1     INDEX UNIQUE SCAN (object id 31384)


Elapsed times include waiting on following events:
  Event waited on                               Times   Max. Wait   Total Waited
  ----------------------------------------      Waited  ----------   ------------
  db file sequential read                          1       0.02          0.02
  enqueue                                          7       3.08         20.37
  SQL*Net message to client                        1       0.00          0.00
  SQL*Net message from client                      1       0.00          0.00
```

Here, we see a very large disparity between the CPU time (0.02 CPU seconds) and the Elapsed time of 20.46 seconds. We obviously waited a long time for something here and TKPROF is telling us exactly what it is, namely **enqueue**. An enqueue is a lock in Oracle terms, and we were waiting for a lock to be released (in other words waiting for some other transaction to give up some resource). What's more we can see that we waited 7 times for it and the maximum length of time that we waited for was 3 seconds. Overall we waited almost 21 seconds before this lock was released and we could proceed.

If you are still using Oracle 8i or previous versions, then TKPROF will not print out this information. Instead, you must manually edit the trace file and look at it.

Summary

In this chapter we took a fairly in-depth look at what facilities are available to us when we attempt to discover where in our applications the performance problems lie. If you understand, not only how to trace your application, through the use of SQL_TRACE and the TKPROF tool, but also how to interpret the results, you'll be halfway done with the tuning of your application. The other half is left to you, in figuring out why your query needs to access a million block buffers, or why it is waiting five minutes on enqueue waits.

We have highlighted the fact that tuning, when done after-the-fact, is one of the hardest things to do, whereas tuning as part of the development process is much easier to perform.

If you make performance part of the application from day one, you will find tuning to be a science, rather than some form of 'black art'. Anyone can do it if it is part of the process. In order to achieve this goal, you will need to do things such as set metrics that applications can be tested against, and develop your code so that you have the ability to diagnose where slowdowns are occurring. Finding where the problem lies is the biggest battle we have in tuning, so use of any commands or tools that can aid the search is vital in maintaining efficient applications.

And just in case you missed it above, bind variables are important. Soft parsing is the way forward in maintaining application performance. It is just too easy to do it the right way in this case, so don't make the mistake of not using them.

A SQL Toolkit

If you haven't realized it yet, you will soon come to recognize the value of having a repository of scripts to perform common tasks and execute useful reports in the database. Without a set of scripts at your disposal, you are constantly rewriting common SQL statements and wasting valuable time that could be spent doing other things, such as tuning your database or writing that application enhancement your users have been asking for.

In developing such script repositories, or toolkits as they can be described, there are two points to bear in mind:

- ❑ You should have a SQL toolkit that contains a variety of scripts for performing your most common tasks.

- ❑ Having a SQL toolkit does not relieve you of having to understand how to write useful queries for new requirements and new situations. Even though you might have a huge repository of SQL scripts, their effectiveness is only as good as your ability to modify them to meet your needs.

In this chapter, we are going to take a look at the SQL toolkit we use as a foundation for our application and database development needs. As applications take shape, and as a database begins developing operational patterns and performance behavior, these scripts will be modified or augmented with other, more useful queries. The point here is to provide you with a baseline in developing your own toolkits. For those of you who are novices with SQL, this chapter should also help to show you some real-world uses of complex SQL, utilizing some of Oracle's more intricate functions to get useful information from our databases.

The following is a list of all the scripts found in this chapter along with a brief description of each.

- ❑ LOGIN. This is your user profile, and runs every time you log in to SQL*Plus. Commands used every time you run SQL*Plus go here.

- ❑ CONNECT. Enables you to connect as a user and rerun your user profile.

- ❑ BIGDATE. Changes all date formats to long form instead of short.

- ❑ FLAT. Creates a comma-delimited list of values from a table.

❑ PRINT_TABLE. This is a procedure that outputs the results of a SQL query in a more readable fashion. Especially useful with long select lists.

❑ COMPBODY. Compiles all invalid package bodies.

❑ COMPPROC. Compiles all invalid PL/SQL procedures.

❑ COMPTRIG. Compiles all invalid PL/SQL triggers.

❑ COMPVIEW. Compiles all invalid views.

❑ COMPILE_SCHEMA. Compiles all invalid objects.

❑ GETOBJECT. Generates the SQL required to recreate any object supported by DBMS_METADATA in Oracle 9*i*.

❑ GETCODE. Gets a code listing for a stored PL/SQL object (procedure, function, package).

❑ GETALLCODE. Generates code files for all the procedures, functions, and packages in the current schema.

❑ GETVIEW. Generates the SQL required to recreate a view.

❑ GETALLVIEWS. Same as GETVIEW, but for ALL views in the current user's schema.

❑ INVALID. Shows all the invalid objects in the current user's schema.

❑ CREATECTL. Creates a SQL*Loader control file.

❑ DBLS. Lists all the objects you own, the tablespaces that hold their data, status, etc.

❑ DBLSL. Same as DBLS.SQL but accepts a search string as an argument.

❑ FREE. Runs a report showing space utilization of tablespaces in the database.

❑ INDEX. Lists indexes and all the indexed columns for the tables in this schema.

❑ SHOWSQL. This script provides a list of all the current database sessions along with an overview of the current activity in the database (queries running, procedural code running, etc.).

❑ SHOWSPACE. Shows information about space in the database (free blocks, total blocks, total bytes, unused blocks & bytes, etc).

> **Please note: all of these scripts are available from http://www.apress.com/ in the code download for the book.**

SQLPATH

Before you get started, it might help for you to identify a directory on your file system where you will store all the scripts we'll look at here. When you are operating in SQL*Plus, you don't want to have to type in a fully qualified path and filename each time you want to run one of these scripts. What you can do therefore is to define an environment variable called SQLPATH and store all your scripts there. SQL*Plus, when it attempts to execute a file (following your use of the START or @ syntax), looks first in the current directory and then in the directory known as SQLPATH.

In UNIX, the syntax for setting this environment variable will depend on your shell. In `bash`, it is as follows (`$ORACLE_HOME/sqlstuff` is the directory where all my scripts reside):

```
export SQLPATH=/u01/app/oracle/Oracle 9i/sqlstuff
```

In the C shell, it is as follows:

```
setenv SQLPATH /u01/app/oracle/Oracle 9i/sqlstuff
```

On Windows there are two possible methods, using either the GUI or a DOS prompt. To use the Windows GUI tool for setting up environment variables:

- ❑ Right-mouse click on **My Computer**, click on **Properties**
- ❑ Click on the **Advanced** tab
- ❑ Click on the **Environment Variables** button
- ❑ Click the **New** button
- ❑ Type `SQLPATH` in the **Variable name** field and also type the name of your chosen directory in the **Variable value** field

Alternatively, in your DOS session, you can simply type:

```
SET SQLPATH=C:\<your directory here>
```

`SQLPATH` will then be established for the lifetime of that DOS session. Once you close the tool, the environment variable is forgotten.

Once your `SQLPATH` is established, save all your files in the directory it relates to. This will let you call them from SQL*Plus without specifying a directory name.

Scripts

Without further ado let's now take a detailed look at each of the scripts listed above. One thing to point out before we begin is that many of these scripts create temporary files in your working directory, or in a temporary directory somewhere on your file system (such as `/tmp` or `c:\temp`). Some people feel that this is a poor way of doing things since:

- ❑ You may not have write privileges in the directory you are working in, which means that the file cannot be created and the script will fail.
- ❑ If more than one person is logged into a multi-user operating system, and two people run scripts that use the same file concurrently, you could run into problems.
- ❑ The script might attempt to write the file, fail because the file is not writeable, and then execute the existing temp file after it fails. The temp file could be a malicious script of some kind.

These issues should be kept constantly in mind when you are using these scripts with your database. If you are working in your own directories, and understand the file security for the operating system you are working on, you can protect yourself from these problems.

LOGIN

The `login.sql` file is a SQL script used for your **user profile**. Your user profile contains a number of SQL*Plus settings to customize the SQL*Plus environment to your needs (you can find more information on user profiles if you look back to Chapter 9). For instance, if you use a text editor (such as vi) to edit your SQL scripts, then every time you start up SQL*Plus you have to type the command `define _editor=vi` (or whatever your editor happens to be) to let SQL*Plus know to call vi whenever you try to edit a file. Instead of this repeated typing you can just drop the command in your `login.sql` file.

In order for the `login.sql` file to run, it needs to be in the current working directory or in your `SQLPATH`. There is also a global `login.sql` file named `glogin.sql` that runs every time SQL*Plus starts. Where `login.sql` is typically a login file for an individual user, `glogin.sql` is the global login file used for any user that logs into SQL*Plus. On Unix, this file is located in the `$ORACLE_HOME/sqlplus/admin` directory. On Windows platforms, it can be found in the `%ORACLE_HOME%\sqlplus\admin` folder.

As you can tell from this description a `login.sql` script is useful to any SQL*Plus users.

Script

This is an example of a `login.sql` file. You can place any valid SQL*Plus command in your `login.sql` file you wish.

```
set echo off
set serveroutput on size 1000000
define _editor=vi

column object_name format a30
column segment_name format a30
column file_name format a40
column name format a30
column file_name format a30
column what format a30 word_wrapped

set trimspool on
set long 5000
set linesize 100
set pagesize 9999

column global_name new_value gname
set termout off
select lower(user) || '@' || global_name global_name
   from global_name;
set termout on
set sqlprompt '&gname> '

column TABLESPACE_NAME format a30 word_wrapped
column DEFAULT_TABLESPACE format a30 word_wrapped
column TEMPORARY_TABLESPACE format a30 word_wrapped
```

CONNECT

When you use a SQL prompt that contains or includes your current user name, SQL*Plus doesn't automatically use the CONNECT command to change this username. The connect.sql script will rerun the LOGIN.SQL command, resetting your SQL*Plus prompt according to your username.

Again this will prove useful to anybody who uses SQL*Plus.

Script

```
connect &1
@@login.sql
```

On Windows platforms, you will need to replace connect &1 with connect %1.

Example

```
scott@SLAPDB.US.ORACLE.COM> connect sdillon/sdillon
Connected.
scott@SLAPDB.US.ORACLE.COM> -- we are connected as sdillon now
scott@SLAPDB.US.ORACLE.COM> @connect sdillon/sdillon
Connected.
sdillon@SLAPDB.US.ORACLE.COM>
```

In the first line above we use the standard CONNECT command as user SDILLON, but the username in the SQL prompt (SCOTT) was not changed. In the third line we ran the connect.sql script, and the SQL prompt was reset by login.sql to show the current username.

BIGDATE

When querying date information in a database, the information returned is going to be in the default date format of the database, as identified by the init.ora parameter NLS_DATE_FORMAT. The default format is DD-MON-YY. In the bigdate.sql script, we modify this format for our session to make the date format DD-MON-YYYY HH24:MI:SS. This allows us to see the hour, minute, and second fields of the date column we are querying.

This script will prove useful to anybody who is querying dates from the database. Programmers can also choose to use this syntax in their applications where the default date format is not informative enough and an entire session will benefit from using a different date format.

Script

```
alter session set nls_date_format = 'dd-MON-yyyy hh24:mi:ss';
```

Example

```
scott@SLAPDB.US.ORACLE.COM> select ename, hiredate
  2     from emp
  3     where rownum < 4
  4  /
```

```
ENAME        HIREDATE
----------   ---------
SMITH        17-DEC-80
ALLEN        20-FEB-81
WARD         22-FEB-81


scott@SLAPDB.US.ORACLE.COM> @bigdate

Session altered.

scott@SLAPDB.US.ORACLE.COM> select ename, hiredate
  2      from emp
  3    where rownum < 4
  4  /

ENAME        HIREDATE
----------   --------------------
SMITH        17-dec-1980 00:00:00
ALLEN        20-feb-1981 00:00:00
WARD         22-feb-1981 00:00:00
```

> Note that changing the default **NLS_DATE_FORMAT** parameter may well affect other scripts or stored PL/SQL in your applications that rely on the default date format.

You can also write a SHORTDATE.SQL script. In the SHORTDATE.SQL script you would use an ALTER SESSION command such as:

```
alter session set nls_data_format = 'DD-MON-YYYY';
```

This would let you switch back and forth between the date formats in your session, and reset the default NLS_DATE_FORMAT parameter once you were done, by using it as a "big date".

FLAT

The flat.sql script is useful when you need to export data from a table. This table creates a comma-delimited list of values representing the rows from the table. Any Oracle user who needs to export data for use by some other program, such as Microsoft Excel, could use this script to export data from Oracle.

Script

```
set wrap off
set linesize 100
set feedback off
set pagesize 0
set verify off
set termout off
```

```
spool _flat&1..sql
prompt select
select lower (column_name)||'||chr(44)||'
  from user_tab_columns
 where table_name = upper('&1')
   and column_id != (select max(column_id)
                       from user_tab_columns
                      where table_name = upper('&1'))
/
select lower(column_name)
  from user_tab_columns
 where table_name = upper('&1')
   and column_id = (select max(column_id)
                      from user_tab_columns
                     where table_name = upper('&1'))
/
prompt from &1
prompt /
spool off
set termout on
set verify on
@_flat&1..sql
host rm _flat&1..sql
```

Note here that Windows users should change the final line here so as to read:

```
host del _flat&1..sql
```

Example

First, let's look at a very basic sample of this script, by exporting the SCOTT.EMP table:

```
sdillon@SLAPDB.US.ORACLE.COM> connect scott/tiger
scott@SLAPDB.US.ORACLE.COM> @flat.sql emp
7369,SMITH,CLERK,7902,17-DEC-80,800,,20
7499,ALLEN,SALESMAN,7698,20-FEB-81,1600,300,30
7521,WARD,SALESMAN,7698,22-FEB-81,1250,500,30
7566,JONES,MANAGER,7839,02-APR-81,2975,,20
7654,MARTIN,SALESMAN,7698,28-SEP-81,1250,1400,30
7698,BLAKE,MANAGER,7839,01-MAY-81,2850,,30
7782,CLARK,MANAGER,7839,09-JUN-81,2450,,10
7788,SCOTT,ANALYST,7566,09-DEC-82,3000,,20
7839,KING,PRESIDENT,,17-NOV-81,5000,,10
7844,TURNER,SALESMAN,7698,08-SEP-81,1500,0,30
7876,ADAMS,CLERK,7788,12-JAN-83,1100,,20
7900,JAMES,CLERK,7698,03-DEC-81,950,,30
7902,FORD,ANALYST,7566,03-DEC-81,3000,,20
7934,MILLER,CLERK,7782,23-JAN-82,1300,,10
```

What's nice about this particular script is you can change it to fit your needs. For instance, let's say we want to write a shell script (in Unix) or a command file (in Windows) to produce our export file from our favorite Unix shell or DOS. This is easily accomplished by calling SQL*Plus in silent mode and redirecting your output to a file. You'll need to modify the flat.sql script and add the following line to the end:

```
exit
```

You can now create the following `flat.cmd` file, or `flat` shell script to call SQL*Plus, login to the database, execute the script and redirect the output to a file:

```
sqlplus -S $1/$2 @flat.sql $3 > $3.csv
```

Once the `flat.sql` script has been modified, and the `flat` (or `flat.cmd`) file is created, you can test your scripts as follows:

```
$ flat hr hr departments

(sdillon@slaphappy)(toolkit)(11/11/01)(1033)
$ cat departments.csv
10,Administration,200,1700
20,Marketing,201,1800
30,Purchasing,114,1700
40,Human Resources,203,2400
50,Shipping,121,1500
60,IT,103,1400
70,Public Relations,204,2700
80,Sales,145,2500
. . .
250,Retail Sales,,1700
260,Recruiting,,1700
270,Payroll,,1700
```

PRINT_TABLE

Have you ever used SQL*Plus to query a table, and the result set is wrapped over six lines? If there are a large number of columns in your query, you may want to use PRINT_TABLE.SQL to help format the return data, especially if you are only returning a small number of rows. This script accepts a SQL statement and displays the result set one column and value per line. For queries that display a large number of columns, readability is improved tenfold.

If you need to query the database and the results are wrapped over multiple lines, you need this script. Administrators and programmers alike will find great utility in this script, as the command-line SQL*Plus tool doesn't lend itself to displaying result sets that are wider than the screen allows.

Script

The following script is for people using Oracle 8.1.5 and above. The AUTHID CURRENT_USER clause makes this procedure an **invoker's rights** procedure, meaning the procedure executes as the person calling it, not the person who created it. This particular feature was not introduced until Oracle 8.1.5. For people with databases of a lower version, keep reading and you'll find a script that you can use.

```
create or replace procedure print_table( p_query in varchar2 )
AUTHID CURRENT_USER
is
   l_theCursor    integer default dbms_sql.open_cursor;
   l_columnValue  varchar2(4000);
```

```
   l_status           integer;
   l_descTbl          dbms_sql.desc_tab;
   l_colCnt           number;
begin
   execute immediate 'alter session set nls_date_format=
                     ''dd-mon-yyyy hh24:mi:ss'' ';

   dbms_sql.parse( l_theCursor, p_query, dbms_sql.native );
   dbms_sql.describe_columns( l_theCursor, l_colCnt, l_descTbl );

   for i in 1 .. l_colCnt loop
     dbms_sql.define_column(
     l_theCursor, i, l_columnValue, 4000 );
   end loop;

   l_status := dbms_sql.execute(l_theCursor);

     execute immediate
       'alter session set nls_date_format=''dd-MON-rr'' ';
     raise;  while ( dbms_sql.fetch_rows(l_theCursor) > 0 ) loop
     for i in 1 .. l_colCnt loop
       dbms_sql.column_value( l_theCursor, i, l_columnValue );
       dbms_output.put_line( rpad( l_descTbl(i).col_name, 30 )
                             || ': ' || l_columnValue );
     end loop;
     dbms_output.put_line( '-----------------' );
   end loop;
   execute immediate
     'alter session set nls_date_format=''dd-MON-rr'' ';
exception
   when others then
     execute immediate
       'alter session set nls_date_format=''dd-MON-rr'' ';
     raise;
end;
/
```

For users using Oracle 8.0.4 through Oracle 8.1.4, the following alternative script can be used:

```
set verify off
declare
   l_thecursor        integer default dbms_sql.open_cursor;
   l_columnvalue      varchar2(4000);
   l_status           integer;
   l_desctbl          dbms_sql.desc_tab;
   l_colcnt           number;

   procedure execute_immediate( p_sql in varchar2 )
   is
   begin
       dbms_sql.parse(l_thecursor,p_sql,dbms_sql.native);
       l_status := dbms_sql.execute(l_thecursor);
   end;

   procedure p ( p_str in varchar2 )
   is
```

```
          l_str   long := p_str;
   begin
      loop
          exit when l_str is null;
          dbms_output.put_line( substr( l_str, 1, 250 ) );
          l_str := substr( l_str, 251 );
      end loop;
   end;
begin
   execute_immediate( 'alter session set nls_date_format=
                      ''dd-mon-yyyy hh24:mi:ss'' ' );

   dbms_sql.parse( l_theCursor, replace( '&1', '"', '''' ),
                   dbms_sql.native );
   dbms_sql.describe_columns( l_theCursor, l_colCnt, l_descTbl );

   for i in 1 .. l_colCnt loop
     dbms_sql.define_column(
     l_theCursor, i, l_columnValue, 4000 );
   end loop;

   l_status := dbms_sql.execute(l_theCursor);

   while ( dbms_sql.fetch_rows(l_theCursor) > 0 ) loop
     for i in 1 .. l_colCnt loop
       dbms_sql.column_value( l_theCursor, i, l_columnValue );
       p( rpad( l_descTbl(i).col_name, 30 ) || ': ' || l_columnValue );
     end loop;
     dbms_output.put_line( '-----------------' );
   end loop;
   execute_immediate( 'alter session set nls_date_format=
                      ''dd-MON-yy'' ' );
exception
   when others then
     execute_immediate( 'alter session set nls_date_format=
                        ''dd-MON-yy'' ' );
   raise;
end;
/
set verify on
```

Try It Out – Using PRINT_TABLE

1. Now let's show how we can use PRINT_TABLE to display the results of a rather "wide" result set. We'll perform a standard query using SQL*Plus on the DBA_TABLESPACES view:

```
sdillon@SLAPDB.US.ORACLE.COM> select *
  2    from dba_tablespaces
  3   where tablespace_name = 'USERS'
  4  /

TABLESPACE_NAME                 BLOCK_SIZE INITIAL_EXTENT NEXT_EXTENT MIN_EXTENTS
MAX_EXTENTS
------------------------------- ---------- -------------- ----------- ----------- -
----------
```

PCT_INCREASE	MIN_EXTLEN	STATUS	CONTENTS	LOGGING	EXTENT_MAN	ALLOCATIO	PLU
SEGMEN							
------------	----------	---------	---------	---------	----------	---------	--- ---
---							
USERS			8192		65536		1
2147483645							
	65536	ONLINE	PERMANENT	LOGGING	LOCAL	SYSTEM	NO
MANUAL							

2. The results are complete, but not very readable. Using PRINT_TABLE, we can fix this. Simply pass the query to the PRINT_TABLE procedure as follows and see how much easier the result set is to read:

```
sdillon@SLAPDB.US.ORACLE.COM> exec print_table('select * from dba_tablespaces
where tablespace_name = ''USERS''')
TABLESPACE_NAME              : USERS
BLOCK_SIZE                   : 8192
INITIAL_EXTENT              : 65536
NEXT_EXTENT                 :
MIN_EXTENTS                 : 1
MAX_EXTENTS                 : 2147483645
PCT_INCREASE                :
MIN_EXTLEN                  : 65536
STATUS                      : ONLINE
CONTENTS                    : PERMANENT
LOGGING                     : LOGGING
EXTENT_MANAGEMENT           : LOCAL
ALLOCATION_TYPE             : SYSTEM
PLUGGED_IN                  : NO
SEGMENT_SPACE_MANAGEMENT    : MANUAL
-------------------

PL/SQL procedure successfully completed.
```

One thing to note about PRINT_TABLE, if you haven't already noticed it in our examples above, is that you must double your quotation marks in queries passed to PRINT_TABLE. The query is read as a VARCHAR2 variable, and therefore the quotation marks must be matched properly.

COMP Scripts

As an Oracle developer, you will find yourself modifying package specifications, tables, and other database objects that will cause Oracle stored procedural code to become 'invalid'. In PL/SQL, when an object that a stored PL/SQL module is dependent upon changes, it must be recompiled. Oracle typically does this automatically the first time the code is invoked, but you might want to manually recompile the code for a variety of reasons:

❑ **Performance**. Don't make your users wait for all your procedural code to be recompiled when they are using the application.

❑ **Testing**. Find out where the errors are, where a dependent object will not work based on changes that have been made.

❑ **Convenience**. Instead of manually writing ALTER <OBJECT_TYPE> ... COMPILE commands, the COMP*.SQL family of scripts will compile all the invalid procedures in one script.

Each script is responsible for querying the data dictionary (USER_OBJECTS, to be exact) to find all those PL/SQL objects (of a particular class) that are invalid, and it tries to recompile each of them in turn. Once the recompile is complete, the script queries the data dictionary again to execute the SHOW ERRORS command for any objects that were not compiled successfully.

Database developers who work heavily with PL/SQL procedural objects (packages, procedures, functions, triggers, etc.) are prime candidates for using these scripts. Database administrators that are managing the stored procedure code in the database will also benefit from this script.

COMPBODY

This script recompiles the package bodies that have been invalidated.

Script

```
set pause off
set heading off
set feedback off
set linesize 80
spool xxtmpxx.sql
select 'alter package "' || object_name || '" compile body;'
  from user_objects
 where object_type = 'PACKAGE BODY'
   and status = 'INVALID'
/
spool off
set heading on
set feedback on
@xxtmpxx.sql
select 'show errors package body ' || object_name
  from user_objects
 where object_type = 'PACKAGE BODY'
   and status = 'INVALID'
/
host rm xxtmpxx.sql
```

On Windows platforms, we need to replace host rm xxtmpxx.sql with host del xxtmpxx.sql. Be sure to make this change in each of the following scripts if you are using a Windows platform. Note that we remove the temporary file after we are done using it on each occasion we run a script.

Try It Out

1. First, let's create a copy of the SCOTT.EMP table (this assumes you are using a user other than SCOTT that has privilege to SELECT from SCOTT's EMP table):

```
sdillon@SLAPDB.US.ORACLE.COM> create table emp as
  2  select * from scott.emp
  3  /

Table created.
```

2. Now we'll create a PL/SQL package to add a record to the table we just created. In the database, using the EMP table in the package body below creates a dependency between this package body and the EMP table we just created.

```
sdillon@SLAPDB.US.ORACLE.COM> create or replace package manage_emps as
  2     procedure add_emp(p_ename varchar2, p_empno number, p_mgr     number,
  3                       p_sal    number,  p_comm  number, p_deptno number);
  4   end manage_emps;
  5   /

Package created.

sdillon@SLAPDB.US.ORACLE.COM> create or replace package body manage_emps as
  2     procedure add_emp(p_ename varchar2, p_empno number, p_mgr     number,
  3                       p_sal    number,  p_comm  number, p_deptno number)
  4     is
  5     begin
  6        insert into emp (empno, ename, mgr, sal, comm, deptno)
  7        values (p_empno, p_ename, p_mgr, p_sal, p_comm, p_deptno);
  8     end add_emp;
  9   end manage_emps;
 10   /

Package body created.
```

3. We can use the package to add a row to the table as follows:

```
sdillon@SLAPDB.US.ORACLE.COM> begin
  2     manage_emps.add_emp('CAMERON','805',null,3000,null,10);
  3   end;
  4   /

PL/SQL procedure successfully completed.
```

4. Now we will add a few columns to the EMP table.

```
sdillon@SLAPDB.US.ORACLE.COM> alter table emp
  2   add(
  3     address varchar2(30),
  4     city    varchar2(30),
  5     state   varchar2(2)
  6   )
  7   /

Table altered.

sdillon@SLAPDB.US.ORACLE.COM> select *
  2     from user_objects
  3   where status = 'INVALID'
  4   /
```

```
OBJECT_NAME                       SUBOBJECT_NAME                      OBJECT_ID
------------------------------    ------------------------------    ----------
DATA_OBJECT_ID OBJECT_TYPE        CREATED    LAST_DDL_ TIMESTAMP
-------------- ---------------    ---------  --------- -------------------
STATUS  T G S
-------  - - -
MANAGE_EMPS                                                             35034
               PACKAGE BODY       11-NOV-01 11-NOV-01 2001-11-11:12:53:28
INVALID N N N
1 row selected.
```

5. We execute the `compbody.sql` script, and the invalid package body is recompiled for us:

```
sdillon@SLAPDB.US.ORACLE.COM> @compbody

alter package "MANAGE_EMPS" compile body;

Package body altered.

no rows selected
```

How It Works

In the code example above, we created a sample table to work with, and a package that inserted records into the table. We then modified the table and when we queried the USER_OBJECTS view, saw that the MANAGE_EMPS package body we created was INVALID. We used the COMPBODY script to recompile it.

If you look at the ADD_EMP procedure in the MANAGE_EMPS package, you will see not only why it was invalidated, but also why it recompiled successfully without code modifications. Since this procedure performs an insert into the EMP table it is *dependent* upon this table. When the EMP table was modified, Oracle invalidated any objects that depended on the table. The recompile was a success because the modification to the table did not break the procedure. If, when we altered the table, we had dropped a column that was referenced in the procedure, we would have received an error when we ran the COMPBODY.SQL script.

In many cases, it is not necessary to manually recompile your packages (or any of your stored PL/SQL for that matter). If you execute an invalid package, procedure, or function, Oracle will automatically recompile it for you. If the recompilation works successfully, the status will be updated to 'VALID' and the code will be executed. The COMPBODY.SQL script is most useful when making changes to database objects, since it allows you to assess the impact of the changes on all of your stored PL/SQL code.

The remaining scripts in the COMP*.SQL family are very similar to `compbody.sql`, and so will not include examples.

COMPPROC

This script recompiles the PL/SQL procedures that have been invalidated.

```
set heading off
set feedback off
set linesize 80
spool xxtmpxx.sql
```

```
select 'alter procedure "' || object_name || '" compile;'
  from user_objects
 where object_type = 'PROCEDURE'
   and status = 'INVALID'
/
spool off
set heading on
set feedback on
@xxtmpxx.sql
select 'show errors procedure ' || object_name
  from user_objects
 where object_type = 'PROCEDURE'
   and status = 'INVALID'
/
host rm xxtmpxx.sql
```

COMPTRIG

`comptrig.sql` recompiles all triggers that have been invalidated.

```
set heading off
set feedback off
set linesize 80
spool xxtmpxx.sql
select 'alter TRIGGER "' || object_name || '" compile;'
  from user_objects
 where object_type = 'TRIGGER'
   and status = 'INVALID'
/
spool off
set heading on
set feedback on
@xxtmpxx.sql
select 'show errors trigger ' || object_name
  from user_objects
 where object_type = 'TRIGGER'
   and status = 'INVALID'
/
host rm xxtmpxx.sql
```

COMPVIEW

`compview.sql` recompiles all views that have been invalidated.

```
set heading off
set feedback off
set linesize 80
spool xxtmpxx.sql
select 'alter view "' || object_name || '" compile;'
  from user_objects
 where object_type = 'VIEW'
   and status = 'INVALID'
/
spool off
set heading on
set feedback on
@xxtmpxx.sql
```

```
select 'show errors view ' || object_name
  from user_objects
 where object_type = 'VIEW'
   and status = 'INVALID'
/
host rm xxtmpxx.sql
```

COMPILE_SCHEMA

Many people believe that PL/SQL objects need to be compiled in a certain order for the compilation to be successful, since compiling one procedure can invalidate a dependent PL/SQL object. However, the bottom line is that all the objects, no matter what the dependency order, will be compiled as long as we try to compile them each at least once. The order we compile them in doesn't matter.

In *'Expert One on One Oracle'* (Apress, ISBN 1590592433) you can find an explanation of how to do this as an administrative account that compiles all those objects in other users' schemas. We have modified this script here, so that you can execute the procedure as any user, and only those objects in the invoking user's schema will be recompiled.

Try it Out – Make the COMPILE_SCHEMA Functionality

1. First, we will make a session-based temporary table to hold the names of each object we have compiled at least once for our session.

```
set verify off
set define &
column u new_val uname
select user u from dual;

drop table compile_schema_tmp
/

create global temporary table compile_schema_tmp (
  object_name    varchar2(30),
  object_type    varchar2(30),
  constraint compile_schema_tmp_pk
  primary key( object_name, object_type )
)
on commit preserve rows
/

grant all on compile_schema_tmp to public
/
```

2. We then write a procedure that retrieves the next object to compile from the schema's PL/SQL objects:

```
create or replace procedure get_next_object_to_compile(
  p_cmd out varchar2,
  p_obj out varchar2,
  p_typ out varchar2 )
```

756

```
is
begin
  select 'alter ' || a.object_type || ' ' ||
         user || '.' || object_name || ' ' ||
         decode( object_type, 'PACKAGE BODY', ' compile body',
                 ' compile' ), object_name, object_type
    into p_cmd, p_obj, p_typ
    from dba_objects a
   where owner = USER
     and status = 'INVALID'
     and object_type <> 'UNDEFINED'
     and not exists( select null
                       from &uname..compile_schema_tmp b
                      where a.object_name = b.object_name
                        and a.object_type = b.object_type )
     and rownum = 1;

  insert into compile_schema_tmp ( object_name, object_type )
  values ( p_obj, p_typ );
end get_next_object_to_compile;
/
```

3. Now that we have a procedure that will retrieve the command to compile each invalid object in our schema, let's write a procedure to use it. The procedure we will write is called COMPILE_SCHEMA, and will be responsible for getting all the objects that need to be compiled, compiling them, and notifying the caller whether the operation was successful or not.

```
create or replace procedure compile_schema
  authid current_user
is
  l_cmd varchar2(512);
  l_obj user_objects.object_name%type;
  l_typ user_objects.object_type%type;
begin
  delete from &uname..compile_schema_tmp;
  loop
    get_next_object_to_compile( l_cmd, l_obj, l_typ );
    dbms_output.put_line( l_cmd );
    begin
      execute immediate l_cmd;
      dbms_output.put_line( 'Successful' );
    exception
      when others then
        dbms_output.put_line( sqlerrm );
    end;
    dbms_output.put_line( chr(9) );
  end loop;
exception -- get_next_object_to_compile raises this when done
  when no_data_found then
    dbms_output.put_line('all done now');
    null;
```

```
end compile_schema;
/
show errors

grant execute on compile_schema to public
/
```

4. Now that COMPILE_SCHEMA is set up, let's use it. You can create the procedure as any user
you want to, provided that they have the necessary privileges to create a temporary table and
procedures. Put the scripts above in a file called compile_schema.sql, and run it from an
account in your database:

```
scott@SLAPDB.US.ORACLE.COM> @connect sdillon/sdillon
Connected.
sdillon@SLAPDB.US.ORACLE.COM> grant select on dba_objects to scott;
Grant succeeded.
sdillon@SLAPDB.US.ORACLE.COM> @connect scott/tiger
Connected.
scott@SLAPDB.US.ORACLE.COM> @compile_schema
U
--------------------------------
SCOTT

Table created.


Grant succeeded.


Procedure created.


Procedure created.

No errors.

Grant succeeded.
```

How It Works

In step 1 we use a SQL*Plus COLUMN (named UNAME) to store the name of the owner of the table
COMPILE_SCHEMA_TMP to use in the procedure we need to create. The temporary table created uses
the ON COMMIT PRESERVE ROWS command since the rows in the table will have to stay in place while
we run DDL statements. As DDL statements cause an implicit commit before and after they execute, a
transaction-based temporary table would not work because as soon as we issued the first ALTER
<OBJECT_TYPE> COMPILE statement, the rows would be removed and we'd have no history of what
was already compiled. Since every user in the database will use this temporary table, we grant privileges
for the table to PUBLIC.

The procedure created in step 2 queries the DBA_OBJECTS view for any invalid object that is not in the COMPILE_SCHEMA_TMP table above (or undefined). (Note that the user that owns this procedure will have to have SELECT privilege on DBA_OBJECTS). Once it finds an invalid object, it inserts a new entry for the object into the COMPILE_SCHEMA_TMP table to record the fact that this object has been selected. The values are "passed" back to the caller of this procedure through OUT parameters. Note that the procedure uses invoker's rights, meaning that the database will execute a procedure using your own privilege set. Typically in Oracle, when you execute another user's procedure, the database uses definer's rights, and executes the procedure using the other user's set of privileges.

The procedure created in step 3 is relatively straightforward. We declare a few variables to store the compile command, the object name, and the object type. We then delete all the records from the COMPILE_SCHEMA_TMP table so each time we execute the COMPILE_SCHEMA procedure, we know the table to hold the names and types of our compiled objects is empty before we begin. The code enters a loop and calls the GET_NEXT_OBJECT_TO_COMPILE procedure to retrieve the command, the object name, and the object type. The code then executes the command (via the EXECUTE IMMEDIATE L_CMD line) and prints out the "Successful" message if the compile works. If any exceptions are encountered then an error message will be displayed instead. Once GET_NEXT_OBJECT_TO_COMPILE has no more invalid objects to return, it will throw a NO_DATA_FOUND exception. This is how we break out of the loop and is expected, so we handle the NO_DATA_FOUND exception at the bottom of the COMPILE_SCHEMA procedure and simply use the NULL; command. Then we grant the execute command on COMPILE_SCHEMA to PUBLIC so that any user can execute it.

GET Scripts

The purpose of the get*.sql series of scripts, is to extract DDL from the database and save it in a file on your file system. In Oracle 9*i*, the DBMS_METADATA supplied package manages the majority of this functionality for you in the getobject.sql script. The DBMS_METADATA script supports many object types including functions, indexes, packages, procedures, and tables.

For those of you interested in more information about DBMS_METADATA *and the database types listed here, see the Supplied PL/SQL Packages and Types Reference in the Oracle documentation.*

For non-Oracle 9*i* users we are including reverse engineering scripts for generating many of the above-listed database types into files without the use of the DBMS_METADATA package. Oracle 9*i* users need only use getobject.sql and skip the other scripts in this section.

GETOBJECT

This script is the only one you will need if you are running Oracle 9*i*. It uses the DBMS_METADATA PL/SQL-supplied package to extract DDL scripts, and is capable of exporting any of the object types listed above. The script will create a file using the object type and the object name (in other words emp_table.sql for the EMP table, or test_procedure.sql for a PL/SQL procedure named TEST).

Let's take a look at the script and see some examples of using it.

Script

```
set serveroutput on size 100000
set echo off
set verify off
```

```
set feedback off
set termout off
set lines 100
spool &2._&1..sql
declare
  l_clob clob;
  l_amt  pls_integer := 255;
  l_idx  pls_integer := 1;
  l_next pls_integer := 0;
begin
  if ('&1') is null or ('&2') is null then
    dbms_output.put_line('prompt Object name or object type is null');
  end if;

  select dbms_metadata.get_ddl(upper('&1'),upper('&2'))
    into l_clob
    from dual;

  loop
    l_next := dbms_lob.instr(l_clob,chr(10),l_idx);
    exit when l_next = 0;
    dbms_output.put_line(dbms_lob.substr(l_clob,l_next-l_idx,l_idx));
    l_idx := l_next + 1;
  end loop;
  dbms_output.put_line('/');
end;
/
spool off
set termout on
prompt Wrote &2._&1..sql
set feedback on
```

Example

In this example, we get the EMP table DDL for the SCOTT schema, and use a simple CREATE INDEX statement to index the ENAME column in the EMP table. When we use the getobject.sql script on the index we create, we see our simple syntax for creating the index pales in comparison to the DDL produced from the getobject.sql script. This is because Oracle produces the full DDL, not the shorthand version we are normally accustomed to writing.

```
sdillon@SLAPDB.US.ORACLE.COM> @connect scott/tiger
Connected.
scott@SLAPDB.US.ORACLE.COM> @getobject table emp
Wrote emp_table.sql
scott@SLAPDB.US.ORACLE.COM> host cat emp_table.sql
CREATE TABLE "SCOTT"."EMP"
(      "EMPNO" NUMBER(4,0) NOT NULL ENABLE,
       "ENAME" VARCHAR2(10),
       "JOB" VARCHAR2(9),
       "MGR" NUMBER(4,0),
       "HIREDATE" DATE,
       "SAL" NUMBER(7,2),
       "COMM" NUMBER(7,2),
       "DEPTNO" NUMBER(2,0)
```

```
) PCTFREE 10 PCTUSED 40 INITRANS 1 MAXTRANS 255 LOGGING
STORAGE(INITIAL 65536 NEXT 1048576 MINEXTENTS 1 MAXEXTENTS 2147483645 PCTINCREASE
0
FREELISTS 1 FREELIST GROUPS 1 BUFFER_POOL DEFAULT) TABLESPACE "USERS"
/

scott@SLAPDB.US.ORACLE.COM> create index emp_ename_idx
  2  on emp( ename )
  3  /

Index created.

scott@SLAPDB.US.ORACLE.COM> @getobject index emp_ename_idx
Wrote emp_ename_idx_index.sql
scott@SLAPDB.US.ORACLE.COM> host cat emp_ename_idx_index.sql
CREATE INDEX "SCOTT"."EMP_ENAME_IDX" ON "SCOTT"."EMP" ("ENAME")
PCTFREE 10 INITRANS 2 MAXTRANS 255
STORAGE(INITIAL 65536 NEXT 1048576 MINEXTENTS 1 MAXEXTENTS 2147483645 PCTINCREASE
0
FREELISTS 1 FREELIST GROUPS 1 BUFFER_POOL DEFAULT) TABLESPACE "USERS"
/
```

For those of you on Windows platforms, you'll need to replace the SQL*Plus command:

```
host cat emp_ename_idx_index.sql
```

with

```
host type emp_ename_idx_index.sql
```

GETCODE

For Oracle users who haven't yet upgraded to Oracle 9*i*, getcode.sql is a nice alternative to the DBMS_METADATA wrapper, getobject.sql.

Script

Copy the following script to a file named getcode.sql.

```
set feedback off
set heading off
set termout off
set linesize 1000
set trimspool on
set verify off
spool &1..sql
prompt set define off
select decode( type||'-'||to_char(line,'fm99999'),
               'PACKAGE BODY-1', '/'||chr(10),
               null) ||
       decode(line,1,'create or replace ', '' ) ||
       text text
```

```
     from user_source
  where name = upper('&1')
  order by type, line;
prompt /
prompt set define on
spool off
set feedback on
set heading on
set termout on
set linesize 100
```

Example

As an example, we'll use the HR schema from the Oracle 9*i* Sample Schemas.

```
sdillon@SLAPDB.US.ORACLE.COM> connect HR/HR
Connected.
hr@SLAPDB.US.ORACLE.COM> @getcode secure_dml
hr@SLAPDB.US.ORACLE.COM> host cat secure_dml.sql
set define off

create or replace PROCEDURE secure_dml
IS
BEGIN
  IF TO_CHAR (SYSDATE, 'HH24:MI') NOT BETWEEN '08:00' AND '18:00'
        OR TO_CHAR (SYSDATE, 'DY') IN ('SAT', 'SUN') THEN
  RAISE_APPLICATION_ERROR (-20205,
    'You may only make changes during normal office hours');
  END IF;
END secure_dml;
/
set define on
```

On Windows platforms, you'll need to replace host cat secure_dml.sql with host type secure_dml.sql.

GETALLCODE

This script is used for calling getcode.sql on all procedures, functions, and packages that belong to the current user. Each object's DDL is written to its own file. A master install file is also created entitled getallcode_INSTALL.sql, which can be invoked to run each of the individual DDL files created for each of the procedures, functions, and packages.

Script

```
set termout off
set heading off
set feedback off
set linesize 50
spool xtmpx.sql
select '@getcode ' || object_name
from user_objects
where object_type in ( 'PROCEDURE', 'FUNCTION', 'PACKAGE' )
/
```

```
spool off
@xtmpx.sql
set termout off
set heading off
set feedback okk
spool getallcode_INSTALL.sql
select '@' || object_name
from user_objects
where object_type in ( 'PROCEDURE', 'FUNCTION', 'PACKAGE' )
/
spool off
set heading on
set feedback on
set linesize 130
set termout on
host cat xtmpx.sql
```

Example

Now let's try using this script. We'll connect to the database as the HR/HR user. If you're not using the Oracle 9*i* Sample Schemas, make sure you have PL/SQL objects in your schema. You can check this by running the following query:

```
sdillon@SLAPDB.US.ORACLE.COM> @connect hr/hr
Connected.
hr@SLAPDB.US.ORACLE.COM> select object_name, object_type
  2      from user_objects
  3    where object_type in ( 'PROCEDURE', 'FUNCTION', 'PACKAGE' )
  4   /

OBJECT_NAME                         OBJECT_TYPE
------------------------------      ------------------
ADD_JOB_HISTORY                     PROCEDURE
AUDIT_PKG                           PACKAGE
SECURE_DML                          PROCEDURE
SHOW_SPACE                          PROCEDURE

4 rows selected.
```

If you are using a schema that does not have PL/SQL code, getallcode.sql will appear to do nothing. When you are using a database schema with PL/SQL code, run the getallcode.sql script:

```
hr@SLAPDB.US.ORACLE.COM>@getallcode
@getcode ADD_JOB_HISTORY
@getcode AUDIT_PKG
@getcode SECURE_DML
@getcode SHOW_SPACE
```

As you can see, this script spools out the names of each of the PL/SQL objects it generates for you. Once the script is done, you can check the current directory and see that each of the objects have been extracted from the database into their own files. Next, we'll take a look at the install file that was created for us. It is named getallcode_INSTALL.sql (NOTE: Windows users should change host cat getallcode_INSTALL.sql to host type getallcode_INSTALL.sql):

```
hr@SLAPDB.US.ORACLE.COM> host cat getallcode_INSTALL.sql
@ADD_JOB_HISTORY
@AUDIT_PKG
@SECURE_DML
@SHOW_SPACE
```

Running this file will instruct SQL*Plus to read each of the files that were created in the first half of the getallcode.sql script. On Windows you should change host cat getallcode_INSTALL.sql to host type getallcode_INSTALL.sql.

GETVIEW

getview.sql retrieves the DDL necessary to recreate a view and saves it to a file on the file system.

Script

```
set heading off
set feedback off
set linesize 1000
set long 5000
set trimspool on
set verify off
set termout off
set embedded on

column column_name format a1000
column text format a1000

spool &1..sql
prompt create or replace view &1 (
select decode(column_id,1,'',',') || column_name   column_name
  from user_tab_columns
 where table_name = upper('&1')
 order by column_id
/
prompt ) as
select text
  from user_views
 where view_name = upper('&1')
/
prompt /
spool off

set termout on
set heading on
set feedback on
set verify on
```

Example

```
sdillon@SLAPDB.US.ORACLE.COM> @connect hr/hr
Connected.
hr@SLAPDB.US.ORACLE.COM> select view_name
  2     from user_views
  3    order by 1
  4   /
```

```
EMP_DETAILS_VIEW

1 row selected.

hr@SLAPDB.US.ORACLE.COM> @getview emp_details_view
hr@SLAPDB.US.ORACLE.COM> !cat emp_details_view.sql
create or replace view emp_details_view (
EMPLOYEE_ID
,JOB_ID
,MANAGER_ID
,DEPARTMENT_ID
,LOCATION_ID
,COUNTRY_ID
,FIRST_NAME
,LAST_NAME
,SALARY
,COMMISSION_PCT
,DEPARTMENT_NAME
,JOB_TITLE
,CITY
,STATE_PROVINCE
,COUNTRY_NAME
,REGION_NAME
) as
SELECT
  e.employee_id,
  e.job_id,
  e.manager_id,
  e.department_id,
  d.location_id,
  l.country_id,
  e.first_name,
  e.last_name,
  e.salary,
  e.commission_pct,
  d.department_name,
  j.job_title,
  l.city,
  l.state_province,
  c.country_name,
  r.region_name
FROM
  employees e,
  departments d,
  jobs j,
  locations l,
  countries c,
  regions r
WHERE e.department_id = d.department_id
  AND d.location_id = l.location_id
  AND l.country_id = c.country_id
  AND c.region_id = r.region_id
  AND j.job_id = e.job_id
WITH READ ONLY

 /
```

GETALLVIEWS

This script is used for calling `getview.sql` on all the views that belong to the current user. Each view's DDL is written to its own file. A master install file is also created entitled `getallviews_INSTALL.sql`, which can be invoked to run each of the individual DDL files that were created for each of the views.

Script

```
set heading off
set feedback off
set linesize 1000
set trimspool on
set verify off
set termout off
set embedded on
spool xtmp.sql
select '@getaview ' || view_name
from user_views
/
spool off
spool getallviews_INSTALL.sql
select '@' || view_name
from user_views
/
spool off
set termout on
set heading on
set feedback on
set verify on
@xtmp.sql
```

Example

```
hr@SLAPDB.US.ORACLE.COM> @connect hr/hr
hr@SLAPDB.US.ORACLE.COM> @getallviews.sql
hr@SLAPDB.US.ORACLE.COM> host dir
EMP_DETAILS_VIEW.sql   getallviews_INSTALL.sql   xtmp.sql

hr@SLAPDB.US.ORACLE.COM> host cat getallviews_INSTALL.sql
@EMP_DETAILS_VIEW
```

INVALID

This script shows all those objects that have a status of INVALID in the current user's schema. Oracle programmers will use this procedure when they are creating and altering objects in the database. Administrators, who are performing installations, or updates to packages or products in the database, can also use this to quickly find any objects that have been invalidated as a result of their operations.

Script

```
break on object_type skip 1
column status format a10
select object_type, object_name, status
```

766

```
   from user_objects
  where status = 'INVALID'
  order by object_type, object_name
 /
```

CREATECTL

This script is used to create a SQL*Loader control script file for a table passed as an argument to the script from SQL*Plus. Typical SQL*Loader control files follow a particular pattern, and instead of continuously writing control files over and over again, we can spool the contents of the most common control file to a file (appropriately named `<table_name>.ctl`).

The control file created with this script matches the output format from the FLAT.SQL script above. Using these two scripts together would allow you to extract a table of data into a text file, and produce a control file to load that table data into another schema or database.

Don't be misled, however; this script is not **only** for data files exported using the FLAT.SQL script. You can use CREATECTL.SQL to produce control files for a variety of data files. You should review the contents of the control file this script creates, and modify it depending on factors such as how the data in your `data file` looks, how your fields are terminated, and which columns you want to be populated.

Users of the SQL*Loader tool will be able to use this script in their data-loading/control file authoring efforts.

Script

Let's walk through this a piece at a time to explain what is happening throughout the script. In the first part of the section, we turn off the SQL*Plus options VERIFY, FEEDBACK, and HEADING so the file that is spooled from SQL*Plus will not include any of this meta data. We set the LINESIZE to 120 because we know, based on the SQL query below, that no line will be greater than 100 characters in length. We set the PAGESIZE to 0 because this is an unlimited page size.

```
set verify off
set feedback off
set heading off
set linesize 120
set pagesize 0
```

We use three SQL*Plus COLUMN commands to format columns that will be selected in the body of the script. The NOPRINT clause tells SQL*Plus to suppress any output that is selected from columns named either OC2 or OC2. The FORMAT A80 option tells SQL*Plus to use a column 80 characters wide to display data queried from a column named DATA. If more than 80 characters are selected, the overflow will run over into the next line.

```
column oc1 noprint
column oc2 noprint
column data format a80
```

Next, we open a spool file using the table name. The & character is used to define a variable in SQL*Plus. &1 indicates the first parameter passed in to the script. Therefore, &2 would be the second argument to the script, &3 would be the third, and so on. For CREATECTL.SQL, we only use one argument to the script, the table name. Once the SQL*Plus formatting options are established and the column options are set up, we open a spool file using the command SPOOL &1..ctl, where &1 will be replaced with the first argument to the script. One would think if we passed EMPLOYEES as the argument, the result would be EMPLOYEES..ctl. It's not though. When definition characters (&) are followed by a period (.) it acts as a delimiter between the variable name and the next character. If it didn't, SQL*Plus might erroneously think that the variable name was &1..ctl instead of just &1. So the result is actually EMPLOYEES.ctl.

```
spool &1..ctl
```

Now we actually begin the queries. You'll see there are three queries stuck together using UNION statements. The first query is responsible for writing the header data of the SQL*Loader control file. This is just the static text that is selected in the top query. Of the three columns being queried in the top query, only the data column will be included in the result set. This is because of the NOPRINT options on the OC1 and OC2 columns at the top of this script. These two columns are included in the query to guarantee a sort order in the results of the union. The first column is a 1; the second column is a 0.

The second query selects all the columns from the USER_TAB_COLUMNS view that belong to the table passed in as the argument to the script. The DECODE statement ensures that the first column is not preceded by a comma (as it's the first command and should not have a comma in front of it). We use two columns in this query that will not be displayed as well. The first column is a 2, the second column is the COLUMN_ID of the USER_TAB_COLUMNS view. This guarantees that the set of rows from this query will be included after the first query's rows (remember the first column in the first query was a 1, this one is 2), and the rows in this query will be ordered by the COLUMN_ID (the second column).

The third query simply selects a closing parenthesis to wrap up the control file. The first column in this query is a 3, the second column is a 0. The net result is that we end up with three result sets in this query, which are then combined through the use of a UNION command to form one continuous stream of data. The results are sorted based on the first two columns (OC1 and OC2 in all three queries) of each query.

```
select 1 oc1, 0 oc2,
    'LOAD DATA ' || chr(10) ||
    'INFILE ''&1..dat'' ' || chr(10) ||
    'INTO TABLE &1 ' || chr(10) ||
    'FIELDS TERMINATED BY "," (' data
from dual
union
select 2 oc1, column_id oc2, decode( column_id, 1, '', ', ' ) ||
    '"' || column_name || '"'
from user_tab_columns
where table_name = upper( '&1' )
union
select 3 oc1, 0 oc2, ')'
from dual
order by 1, 2
/
spool off
set feedback on
set heading on
```

Try It Out

1. Using the HR schema, we'll create a SQL*Loader control file for the EMPLOYEES table like this:

```
hr@SLAPDB.US.ORACLE.COM> connect hr/hr
Connected.
hr@SLAPDB.US.ORACLE.COM> @createctl employees
```

2. The result of the first query in the union is:

```
LOAD DATA
INFILE 'employees.dat'
INTO TABLE employees
FIELDS TERMINATED BY "," (
```

3. The result of the second query of the union is:

```
"EMPLOYEE_ID"
, "FIRST_NAME"
, "LAST_NAME"
, "E-MAIL"
, "PHONE_NUMBER"
, "HIRE_DATE"
, "JOB_ID"
, "SALARY"
, "COMMISSION_PCT"
, "MANAGER_ID"
, "DEPARTMENT_ID"
```

4. Finally, here is the result of the third and final query of the union.

```
)
```

When we put them all together, we get a SQL*Loader control file that is formatted properly to load the results of our flat.sql script.

DBLS

DBLS, or "database list", was named after the ls command in Unix, which lists files and directories in the current working directory. This script runs a report that returns the following columns:

- ❑ **Object type**. The types that can be reported on through dbls.sql include: Function, Index, LOB, Package, Package Body, Procedure, Table, Trigger, and View

- ❑ **Object name**. The unique identifier assigned to each object to make it unique

- ❑ **Object status**. This will be either nothing or an asterisk (*). The asterisk indicates that the object is in an invalid state

❑ **Tablespace name.** For those objects that require physical storage in the database, the tablespace that contains the object is listed in this column

Developers will usually use this script more than database administrators. DBAs might alter this script slightly to report similar data such as which tables exist in which tablespaces, for example.

Script

```
column object_name format a30
column tablespace_name format a30
column object_type format a20
column status format a1

break on object_type skip 1

select object_type, object_name,
       decode( status, 'INVALID', '*', '' ) status,
       decode( object_type,
               'TABLE',
               (select tablespace_name
                  from user_tables
                 where table_name = object_name),
               'TABLE PARTITION',
               (select tablespace_name
                  from user_tab_partitions
                 where partition_name = subobject_name),
               'INDEX',
               (select tablespace_name
                  from user_indexes
                 where index_name = object_name),
               'INDEX PARTITION',
               (select tablespace_name
                  from user_ind_partitions
                 where partition_name = subobject_name),
               'LOB',
               (select tablespace_name
                  from user_segments
                 where segment_name = object_name),
               null ) tablespace_name
  from user_objects a
 order by object_type, object_name
/
column status format a10
```

Try It Out

1. In this example, we will look at the default SCOTT schema and the objects that are created by default for SCOTT. To do this you'll need to reset your SCOTT user, by running the installation scripts located at $ORACLE_HOME/sqlplus/demo/demobld.sql on Unix, and at %ORACLE_HOME%\sqlplus\demo\demobld.sql on Windows platforms. Running the DBLS script gives the following:

```
hr@SLAPDB.US.ORACLE.COM> connect scott/tiger
Connected.
scott@SLAPDB.US.ORACLE.COM> @dbls

OBJECT_TYPE   OBJECT_NAME                       S TABLESPACE_NAME
------------  --------------------------------  - ----------------------------
TABLE         BONUS                               USERS
              DEPT                                USERS
              DUMMY                               USERS
              EMP                                 USERS
              SALGRADE                            USERS
```

How It Works

Running `dbls.sql` shows us that there are five tables for the user. In the results obtained here the third column has a header of S representing the status of the object in the result. In this column we use an asterisk to show that an object is invalid and a blank entry if it is valid. If this doesn't suit then you could modify the script to print out the entire word `"INVALID"` and the column heading to be STATUS. You can accomplish this by replacing the second query column in the script above...

```
decode( status, 'INVALID', '*', '' ) status,
```

with...

```
decode( status, 'INVALID', 'INVALID', '' ) status,
```

DBLSL

`DBLSL.SQL` lists information about all the objects the current user owns that match the first argument passed on the command line. The columns returned from `DBLSL.SQL`, and the potential audience, are the same as for `DBLS.SQL`.

Script

```
column object_name format a30
column tablespace_name format a30
column object_type format a20
column status format a1

break on object_type skip 1

select object_type, object_name,
       decode( status, 'INVALID', '*', '' ) status,
       decode( object_type,
               'TABLE',
               (select tablespace_name
                  from user_tables
                 where table_name = object_name),
               'TABLE PARTITION',
               (select tablespace_name
```

```
                    from user_tab_partitions
                   where partition_name = subobject_name),
                'INDEX',
                (select tablespace_name
                   from user_indexes
                  where index_name = object_name),
                'INDEX PARTITION',
                (select tablespace_name
                   from user_ind_partitions
                  where partition_name = subobject_name),
                'LOB',
                (select tablespace_name
                   from user_segments
                  where segment_name = object_name),
                null ) tablespace_name
   from user_objects a
  where object_name like upper('%&1.%')
  order by object_type, object_name
/
column status format a10
```

Example

In this example, we simply call the `dbls1.sql` script twice, passing it two different arguments, `DEPT` and `EMP`. When the script queries `USER_OBJECTS` for all those objects whose object name is 'like' the search string, those values are displayed in the result set.

```
scott@SLAPDB.US.ORACLE.COM> @dbls1 emp

OBJECT_TYPE          OBJECT_NAME                          S TABLESPACE_NAME
-------------------- ---------------------------------- - ---------------------INDEX
EMP_ENAME_IDX                    USERS

TABLE                EMP                                  USERS

VIEW                 EMP_DEPTS


scott@SLAPDB.US.ORACLE.COM> @dbls1 dept

OBJECT_TYPE          OBJECT_NAME                          S TABLESPACE_NAME
-------------------- ---------------------------------- - ---------------------TABLE
DEPT                             USERS

VIEW                 EMP_DEPTS
```

FREE

The `free.sql` script is a great way to quickly find out the storage attributes of the tablespaces in your database. `free.sql` takes one parameter, a number indicating which column to sort the results of the report by. The following columns are displayed in the result set of the `free.sql` report:

- ❏ **Tablespace** name.

- ❏ **Kbytes**. This is the size of the tablespace, in kilobytes.

- ❏ **Used**. This is the number of kilobytes that have been consumed by the tablespace in comparison to the size of the tablespace.

- ❏ **Free**. This is the number of kilobytes available for data in the tablespace.

- ❏ **% Used**. This is the percentage of the tablespace that has been consumed already.

- ❏ **Largest**. This is the largest extent available in the tablespace (in KB).

- ❏ **MaxPoss Kbytes**. This is the maximum size the tablespace can possibly be. This can be different from the `Kbytes` column in the case of files that can autoextend, or grow.

- ❏ **% Max Used**. This is the percentage of the tablespace that has been consumed compared to the maximum possible size of the tablespace (held in the `MaxPoss Kbytes` column).

Administrators will find this script useful for reporting space consumption in the tablespaces of the database.

Script

`FREE.SQL` is a somewhat elaborate script, so we will investigate each section of the script to understand what is happening at each stage. The header of the script sets the linesize to be wide enough to accommodate all the data that will be output from the script and to set the heading separator character. By default this is '|', but we set it to this explicitly since we rely on it in the output of the query.

We then go on to use `COLUMN` commands to format each column that will be displayed in the query results. We specify the column name (which will be matched up to the columns selected in the query), the format for the column's output, and a heading to be used in the query results.

```
set linesize 85
set headsep '|'
column dummy            noprint
column pct_used         format 999.9        heading "%|Used"
column name             format a10          heading "Tablespace"
column Kbytes           format 99,999,999   heading "KBytes"
column used             format 99,999,999   heading "Used"
column free             format 99,999,999   heading "Free"
column largest          format 99,999,999   heading "Largest"
column max_size         format 99,999,999   heading "MaxPoss|Kbytes"
column pct_max_used format 999.9            heading "%|Max|Used"
```

Now that the columns are set up we're just about ready to run the query. First though, let's use a BREAK ON REPORT command along with COMPUTE SUM commands to provide totals for each of the three listed columns below:

```
break on report
compute sum of kbytes on report
compute sum of free on report
compute sum of used on report
```

Now that the SQL*Plus environment is established, let's run the query. We perform a select statement using two nested select statements. Inside the first nested select statement (identified as A below), we retrieve the amount of free space and the largest segment of free space available in each tablespace from the DBA_FREE_SPACE view. In the second nested select statement (identified as B below), we are querying the amount of space allocated to, and the maximum number of bytes in, the data files for the tablespaces. This is a union between the DBA_DATA_FILES and the DBA_TEMP_FILES views. These two nested queries are then joined together in the outer join statement to provide a number of useful space consumption statistics about the tablespaces in your database.

```
select nvl(b.tablespace_name,
         nvl(a.tablespace_name,'UNKNOWN')) name,
         kbytes_alloc kbytes,
         kbytes_alloc-nvl(kbytes_free,0) used,
         nvl(kbytes_free,0) free,
         ((kbytes_alloc-nvl(kbytes_free,0))/kbytes_alloc)*100 pct_used,
         nvl(largest,0) largest,
         nvl(kbytes_max,kbytes_alloc) Max_Size,
         decode( kbytes_max, 0, 0, (kbytes_alloc/kbytes_max)*100) pct_max_used
   from ( select sum(bytes)/1024 Kbytes_free,
                max(bytes)/1024 largest,
                tablespace_name
           from sys.dba_free_space
          group by tablespace_name ) a,
        ( select sum(bytes)/1024 Kbytes_alloc,
                sum(maxbytes)/1024 Kbytes_max,
                tablespace_name
           from sys.dba_data_files
          group by tablespace_name
          union all
         select sum(bytes)/1024 Kbytes_alloc,
                sum(maxbytes)/1024 Kbytes_max,
                tablespace_name
           from sys.dba_temp_files
          group by tablespace_name ) b
  where a.tablespace_name (+) = b.tablespace_name
  order by &1
/
```

Try It Out

1. In the example, we call the free.sql script and pass a single numeric argument, indicating the column to sort on. We'll use the script twice just to see the ordering happening. The first time we call it, we'll order by 1 (the tablespace name). The second time we'll order by 2 (the kilobytes allocated to the tablespace).

```
sdillon@SLAPDB.US.ORACLE.COM> @free 1
```

Tablespace	KBytes	Used	Free	% Used	Largest	MaxPoss Kbytes	Max Used
CWMLITE	20,480	64	20,416	.3	20,416	33,554,416	.1
DRSYS	20,480	7,936	12,544	38.8	12,544	33,554,416	.1
EXAMPLE	37,760	37,504	256	99.3	256	33,554,416	.1
INDX	25,600	640	24,960	2.5	24,768	33,554,416	.1

				%		MaxPoss	Max
SYSTEM	332,800	308,224	24,576	92.6	23,592	33,554,416	1.0
TEMP	40,960	40,960	0	100.0	0	0	.0
TEMPSMALL	10,240	10,240	0	100.0	0	0	.0
TOOLS	10,240	2,688	7,552	26.3	7,488	33,554,416	.0
UNDOTBS	204,800	1,344	203,456	.7	199,808	33,554,416	.6
USERS	76,800	5,440	71,360	7.1	51,136	33,554,416	.2
	----------	---------	--------				
sum	780,160	415,040	365,120				

10 rows selected.

```
sdillon@SLAPDB.US.ORACLE.COM> @free 2
```

Tablespace	KBytes	Used	Free	% Used	Largest	MaxPoss Kbytes	Max Used
TOOLS	10,240	2,688	7,552	26.3	7,488	33,554,416	.0
TEMPSMALL	10,240	10,240	0	100.0	0	0	.0
CWMLITE	20,480	64	20,416	.3	20,416	33,554,416	.1
DRSYS	20,480	7,936	12,544	38.8	12,544	33,554,416	.1
INDX	25,600	640	24,960	2.5	24,768	33,554,416	.1
EXAMPLE	37,760	37,504	256	99.3	256	33,554,416	.1
TEMP	40,960	40,960	0	100.0	0	0	.0
USERS	76,800	5,440	71,360	7.1	51,136	33,554,416	.2
UNDOTBS	204,800	1,344	203,456	.7	199,808	33,554,416	.6
SYSTEM	332,800	308,224	24,576	92.6	23,592	33,554,416	1.0
	----------	---------	-------				
sum	780,160	415,040	365,120				

10 rows selected.

How It Works

The numeric argument you pass matches the column number in the results of the query. The numbers 1-8 inclusive correspond to tablespace name, kilobytes allocated to the tablespace, used space in the tablespace, free space in the tablespace, percentage of space used in the tablespace with respect to its allocated size, largest segment of free space in the tablespace, maximum size the tablespace can extend to, and percentage of space used in the tablespace with respect to its maximum size respectively.

INDEX

This is a very useful script for retrieving index data for all the tables owned by the current user. Index names and indexed columns (up to the first 16 columns) are returned in the result set. For developers who are writing queries against tables, index definitions are very important. Anybody tuning SQL in an application will also need this information. This is a great way to do a fast lookup of indexes defined.

Script

Note that the column formatting in this script uses the third COLUMN command to set the width of the COLUMNS column to 40. This is to format query results for the purpose of displaying data in this book, not necessarily for real-world usage. To think that 16 columns could possibly fit into 40 characters is unrealistic. The actual setting for this column should be more like 80 or 100, depending upon your terminal type.

```
column table_name format a15 word_wrapped
column index_name format a25 word_wrapped
column columns format a40

break on table_name skip 1

select table_name,
       index_name,
rtrim(
     max( decode( column_position,  1, column_name, '' ) )||','||
     max( decode( column_position,  2, column_name, '' ) )||','||
     max( decode( column_position,  3, column_name, '' ) )||','||
     max( decode( column_position,  4, column_name, '' ) )||','||
     max( decode( column_position,  5, column_name, '' ) )||','||
     max( decode( column_position,  6, column_name, '' ) )||','||
     max( decode( column_position,  7, column_name, '' ) )||','||
     max( decode( column_position,  8, column_name, '' ) )||','||
     max( decode( column_position,  9, column_name, '' ) )||','||
     max( decode( column_position, 10, column_name, '' ) )||','||
     max( decode( column_position, 11, column_name, '' ) )||','||
     max( decode( column_position, 12, column_name, '' ) )||','||
     max( decode( column_position, 13, column_name, '' ) )||','||
     max( decode( column_position, 14, column_name, '' ) )||','||
     max( decode( column_position, 15, column_name, '' ) )||','||
     max( decode( column_position, 16, column_name, '' ) ), ',' )
     columns
from user_ind_columns
group by table_name,index_name
/
```

Example

In this example, we use the HR schema from the Oracle 9*i* Sample Schemas, though you could use any account that has tables with indexes defined.

```
sdillon@SLAPDB.US.ORACLE.COM> @connect hr/hr
Connected.
hr@SLAPDB.US.ORACLE.COM> @index

TABLE_NAME        INDEX_NAME                     COLUMNS
---------------   ------------------------       ------------------------------------
COUNTRIES         COUNTRY_C_ID_PK                COUNTRY_ID

CUSTOMER_TAB      CUSTOMER_PK                    CUSTOMER_NO

DEPARTMENTS       DEPT_ID_PK                     DEPARTMENT_ID
DEPARTMENTS       DEPT_LOCATION_IX               LOCATION_ID

EMPLOYEES         EMP_DEPARTMENT_IX              DEPARTMENT_ID
EMPLOYEES         EMP_E-MAIL_UK                  E-MAIL
EMPLOYEES         EMP_EMP_ID_PK                  EMPLOYEE_ID
EMPLOYEES         EMP_JOB_IX                     JOB_ID
EMPLOYEES         EMP_MANAGER_IX                 MANAGER_ID
EMPLOYEES         EMP_NAME_IX                    LAST_NAME,FIRST_NAME
```

```
JOBS              JOB_ID_PK                    JOB_ID

JOB_HISTORY       JHIST_DEPARTMENT_IX          DEPARTMENT_ID
JOB_HISTORY       JHIST_EMPLOYEE_IX            EMPLOYEE_ID
JOB_HISTORY       JHIST_EMP_ID_ST_DATE_PK      EMPLOYEE_ID, START_DATE
JOB_HISTORY       JHIST_JOB_IX                 JOB_ID

LOCATIONS         LOC_CITY_IX                  CITY
LOCATIONS         LOC_COUNTRY_IX               COUNTRY_ID
LOCATIONS         LOC_ID_PK                    LOCATION_ID
LOCATIONS         LOC_STATE_PROVINCE_IX        STATE_PROVINCE

LOCATIONS_INC     SYS_IOT_TOP_31741            REGION_ID, COUNTRY_ID, LOCATION_ID
LOCATIONS_IOT     SYS_IOT_TOP_31736            REGION_ID, COUNTRY_ID, LOCATION_ID
LOCATIONS_IOT_C   SYS_IOT_TOP_31738            REGION_ID, COUNTRY_ID, LOCATION_ID

REGIONS           REG_ID_PK                    REGION_ID

23 rows selected.
```

SHOWSQL

showsql.sql is an informative overview of all the sessions that exist in the database at the time the script is executed. It is in two parts, the overview and the detail.

In the overview, the following columns are selected from the V$SESSION view:

- ❑ USERNAME. The user that is connected to the database for this session.

- ❑ SID_SERIAL. The session identifier and the session serial number.

- ❑ STATUS. The status of the session. Possible values include ACTIVE, INACTIVE, KILLED, and CACHED.

- ❑ MODULE. This is the name of the currently executing *module* (see SET_APPLICATION_INFO below, for more information).

- ❑ ACTION. This is the name of the currently executing *action* (see SET_APPLICATION_INFO below, for more information).

- ❑ CLIENT_INFO. This is the content of the CLIENT_INFO. (see SET_APPLICATION_INFO below, for more information).

SET_APPLICATION_INFO is a PL/SQL-supplied package that can be used to provide useful information in the V$SESSION view. The MODULE, ACTION, and CLIENT_INFO fields can be set with procedures in the package.

In the detailed output from showsql.sql, there is more data to be found from the V$SESSION view. A PL/SQL block uses an implicit cursor to loop over the V$SESSION view and output data for each row found. There are three DBMS_OUTPUT.PUT_LINE lines spooled for each row of the V$SESSION view. In those rows is the following data:

- ❏ Line #1, session identifiers. Included in this column is the username of the session, the session identifier, the session serial number, the operating system process identifier (OSPID), and the program that initiated the session.

- ❏ Line #2, time information. The time the session began followed by the current time and the time the last command was executed (multiple commands can be executed within a single session).

- ❏ Line #3, SQL text. The SQL found in the V$SQLTEXT_WITH_NEWLINES is spooled out on the third line of output, for each row.

Using this script in your tuning, testing, and debugging efforts will save you time and energy when it comes to figuring out what is going on in your database. Additionally, it should encourage you to instrument your code with DBMS_APPLICATION_INFO calls. Setting the MODULE, ACTION, and CLIENT_INFO columns of this package throughout your code, so as to be able to use this script, will make it easier for you to tell what is happening inside the database and your application.

Script

```
column username format a15 word_wrapped
column module format a15 word_wrapped
column action format a15 word_wrapped
column client_info format a15 word_wrapped
column status format a10
column sid_serial format a15
set feedback off
set serveroutput on

select username, ''''||sid||','||serial#||'''' sid_serial,
       status , module, action, client_info
  from v$session
 where username is not null
/

column username format a20
column sql_text format a55 word_wrapped

set serveroutput on size 1000000
declare
  x number;
  procedure p ( p_str in varchar2 )
  is
    l_str    long := p_str;
  begin
    loop
      exit when l_str is null;
      dbms_output.put_line( substr( l_str, 1, 250 ) );
      l_str := substr( l_str, 251 );
    end loop;
  end;
begin
  for x in (select username||'('||sid||','||serial#||
                   ') ospid = ' || process ||
                   ' program = ' || program username,
                   to_char(LOGON_TIME,' Day HH24:MI') logon_time,
                   to_char(sysdate,' Day HH24:MI') current_time,
                   sql_address, LAST_CALL_ET
```

```
                  from v$session
                where status = 'ACTIVE'
                  and rawtohex(sql_address) <> '00'
                  and username is not null
                order by last_call_et)
    loop
      dbms_output.put_line( '--------------------' );
      dbms_output.put_line( x.username );
      dbms_output.put_line( x.logon_time || ' ' || x.current_time||
                    ' last et = ' || x.LAST_CALL_ET );
      for y in ( select sql_text
                   from v$sqltext_with_newlines
                  where address = x.sql_address
                  order by piece )
      loop
        p( y.sql_text );
      end loop;
    end loop;
end;
/
```

Try It Out

1. Open one SQL*Plus session and use an administrative account to run the following script:

```
sdillon@SLAPDB.US.ORACLE.COM> begin
  2     for i in 1 .. 60 loop
  3        dbms_lock.sleep(2);
  4     end loop;
  5   end;
  6   /
```

2. In *another* SQL*Plus session, while the above process is still running, run the showsql.sql script:

```
sdillon@SLAPDB.US.ORACLE.COM> @showsql

USERNAME        SID_SERIAL       STATUS     MODULE          ACTION
CLIENT_INFO
--------------- ---------------- ---------- --------------- --------------- -
SDILLON         '9,5354'         ACTIVE     SQL*Plus
OE              '12,261'         INACTIVE
SDILLON         '15,6169'        ACTIVE     SQL*Plus
--------------------
SDILLON(15,6169) ospid = 310 program = sqlplus@slaphappy.us.oracle.com (TNS V1-V3)
Friday    10:43  Friday    11:55 last et = 0
select username||'('||sid||','||serial#||
                    ')
ospid = ' || process ||
                ' program = ' || pro
gram username,
            to_char(LOGON_TIME,' Day HH24:
MI') logon_time,
```

```
                        to_char(sysdate,' Day HH24:M
    I') current_time,
                    sql_address, LAST_CALL_ET

    from v$session
                where status = 'ACTIVE'

                and rawtohex(sql_address) <> '00'

    and username is not null
                order by last_call_et
    --------------------
    SDILLON(9,5354) ospid = 356 program = sqlplus@slaphappy.us.oracle.com (TNS V1-V3)
    Friday    11:18   Friday    11:55 last et = 3
    begin
      for i in 1 .. 60 loop
        dbms_lock.sleep(2);
      end loop
    ;
    end;
```

How It Works

In our first SQL*Plus window, we run a script which takes just over two minutes to execute, using DBMS_LOCK.SLEEP as a means to 'pause' the PL/SQL code. We loop sixty times and pause for two seconds in each iteration of the loop. While this is executing we run the showsql.sql script to see the PL/SQL block we have running in the other SQL*Plus session in action. This session is the first one we see, namely SDILLON(9,5354). There are two other sessions that exist in the database; one for the OE user and another for the SDILLON user. The SDILLON session represents the second SQL*Plus session that ran the showsql.sql script.

> In applications that have large numbers of users or large numbers of concurrent transactions, the output from this script can become formidable in no time. **DBMS_OUTPUT** has a fixed-size buffer, and it could very easily fill up when you spool a great deal of **SHOWSQL** data to the buffer.

SHOWSPACE

The showspace.sql script is for calling the database and displaying physical space information about segments in the database. The script creates a procedure called SHOW_SPACE that is basically a wrapper around the DBMS_SPACE PL/SQL supplied package. The three arguments submitted to the procedure are:

❑ **Segment name**. This is the name of the segment. If you were to query USER_SEGMENTS, you will find all those segments that belong to you (DBA_SEGMENTS and ALL_SEGMENTS exist as well). Segment names are usually the name of the table, index, lob, or whatever the object is that is stored in that particular segment.

❑ **Segment owner**. This is the owner of the segment, or the owner of the object that is stored in the segment. If you find segments using USER_SEGMENTS, the owner name is your own username. If you look in ALL_SEGMENTS or DBA_SEGMENTS, the OWNER column will give you this information. This argument to SHOW_SPACE is defaulted to your own username, so it is unnecessary to pass this information for segments you own.

❑ **Segment type**. This is the type of the segment. This parameter is defaulted to TABLE. In the ALL, DBA, and USER_SEGMENTS views the SEGMENT_TYPE column will give you this information. SHOW_SPACE is valid for the following types of segments:

   ❑ Tables
   ❑ Table partitions
   ❑ Table subpartitions
   ❑ Indexes
   ❑ Index partitions
   ❑ Index subpartitions
   ❑ Clusters
   ❑ LOBs

This procedure will display data that comes from the DBMS_SPACE package.

❑ **Free blocks**. The total number of free blocks in the segment.

❑ **Total blocks**. The total number of blocks in the segment.

❑ **Total bytes**. The total number of bytes in the segment.

❑ **Unused blocks**. The number of blocks that have not been used.

❑ **Unused bytes**. The number of bytes that have not been used.

❑ **Last used extent file identifier**. This is the file identifier for the last extent that contains data.

❑ **Last used extent block identifier**. This is the block identifier for the last extent that contains data.

❑ **Last used block**. This is the last block within the extent that contains data.

Script

```
create or replace procedure show_space(
  p_segname in varchar2,
  p_owner   in varchar2 default user,
  p_type    in varchar2 default 'TABLE')
as
  l_free_blks               number;

  l_total_blocks            number;
  l_total_bytes             number;
  l_unused_blocks           number;
  l_unused_bytes            number;
  l_lastusedextfileid       number;
```

781

```
    l_lastusedextblockid            number;
    l_last_used_block               number;

    procedure p( p_label in varchar2, p_num in number )
    is
    begin
      dbms_output.put_line( rpad(p_label,25,'.') ||
                            p_num );
    end;
begin
  dbms_space.free_blocks(
    segment_owner      => p_owner,
    segment_name       => p_segname,
    segment_type       => p_type,
    freelist_group_id  => 0,
    free_blks          => l_free_blks );

  dbms_space.unused_space(
    segment_owner      => p_owner,
    segment_name       => p_segname,
    segment_type       => p_type,
    total_blocks       => l_total_blocks,
    total_bytes        => l_total_bytes,
    unused_blocks      => l_unused_blocks,
    unused_bytes       => l_unused_bytes,
    last_used_extent_file_id => l_lastusedextfileid,
    last_used_extent_block_id => l_lastusedextblockid,
    last_used_block => l_last_used_block );

  p( 'Free Blocks', l_free_blks );
  p( 'Total Blocks', l_total_blocks );
  p( 'Total Bytes', l_total_bytes );
  p( 'Unused Blocks', l_unused_blocks );
  p( 'Unused Bytes', l_unused_bytes );
  p( 'Last Used Ext FileId', l_lastusedextfileid );
  p( 'Last Used Ext BlockId', l_lastusedextblockid );
  p( 'Last Used Block', l_last_used_block );
end;
/
```

Try It Out

1. We begin by creating a sample table with 1000 rows from the USER_OBJECTS view.

```
sdillon@SLAPDB.US.ORACLE.COM> create table my_objects as
  2   select *
  3     from user_objects
  4    where rownum < 1001
  5   /

Table created.
```

2. Now the table is created, let's use the SHOW_SPACE procedure to see what kind of space the object is consuming:

```
sdillon@SLAPDB.US.ORACLE.COM> exec show_space('MY_OBJECTS')
Free Blocks.............0
Total Blocks............8
Total Bytes.............65536
Unused Blocks...........6
Unused Bytes............49152
Last Used Ext FileId.....8
Last Used Ext BlockId....2185
Last Used Block.........2

PL/SQL procedure successfully completed.
```

3. Now we'll create an index on the MY_OBJECTS table we just created, and look at the space consumption for the index. First create the index as follows:

```
sdillon@SLAPDB.US.ORACLE.COM> create index my_objects_idx
  2  on my_objects( object_name, subobject_name )
  3  /

Index created.
```

4. Now that the index is created, run the SHOW_SPACE procedure by passing the index name and the value of INDEX for the P_TYPE parameter:

```
sdillon@SLAPDB.US.ORACLE.COM> exec show_space( 'MY_OBJECTS_IDX', p_type => 'INDEX'
)
Free Blocks.............0
Total Blocks............8
Total Bytes.............65536
Unused Blocks...........6
Unused Bytes............49152
Last Used Ext FileId.....8
Last Used Ext BlockId....2193
Last Used Block.........2

PL/SQL procedure successfully completed.
```

How It Works

You can see here, that space consumption was the same for both the table and the index. This is because they are both in the same tablespace and, since neither the table nor the index have their own storage clause, will inherit their storage attributes from that tablespace. In the tablespace the initial extent is 64KB, and each of the segments (MY_OBJECTS and MY_OBJECTS_IDX) took up less than that 64KB.

Summary

In this chapter, we have explored the notion of a 'SQL toolkit', a repository of useful SQL scripts and PL/SQL code to use in your database administration and application development. As you start to get comfortable with the Oracle environment, the data dictionary, and SQL*Plus, you will find your toolkit will become more and more valuable and that the time you save by having these scripts at your immediate disposal, rather than having to rewrite them every time you need them, will be invaluable.

Over time you will find that these scripts are only the beginning. You will create new scripts, modify existing scripts, and, as a result, become more and more efficient in your use of the database. Keep in mind that these are your tools to play with. Copy them, change them, delete them, do whatever you can in order to fully utilize everything that your Oracle database has to offer.

Case Study 1 – Debugging PL/SQL

Throughout this book you have been introduced to a wide range of features of the Oracle database. Now we are going to use many of those features to build a debug utility (called DEBUG), which I hope you will find useful when developing your own PL/SQL applications. We will bring together tables, triggers, built-in packages, SQL, PL/SQL, security, and user-defined types to build a flexible and extremely useful tool.

In the course of this Case Study we will:

❑ Explore what other debug options currently exist, why they do not give us the flexibility we need, and how the DEBUG package addresses those needs

❑ Walk through the requirements, design, implementation, and deployment phases of the development process of a PL/SQL package called DEBUG

❑ Learn how to effectively use this utility in both the development and deployments phases of your application

History

Debugging PL/SQL has always been difficult, mainly due to the limited options available to developers. One of the most commonly used tools is the Oracle-supplied package DBMS_OUTPUT, which allows the developer to spool text strings from an executing PL/SQL block back to the SQL*Plus command prompt or other third-party tools like TOAD.

Appendix B, Supplied Packages, has more information on DBMS_OUTPUT and its uses.

Limitations of DBMS_OUTPUT

For the simplest of debugging, DBMS_OUTPUT is sufficient, but it has some limitations that make it less than useful in many situations:

❑ The first limitation of DBMS_OUTPUT is that the application that is executing your PL/SQL needs to know how to retrieve DBMS_OUTPUT messages. DBMS_OUTPUT queues up the messages and waits for someone to ask for them. If your application or tool does not or cannot ask, then you will not see the messages. In web-based applications, for example, the application is a browser and the PL/SQL performs business logic on the server side. Some PL/SQL code – triggers, for example – cannot even be called directly.

❑ DBMS_OUTPUT can only spool up to 1,000,000 characters, which while it sounds a lot, is actually quite restrictive in practice. Consider a cursor-for loop looping over one hundred thousand records. If you wanted to debug each iteration of the loop, then this would leave you only 10 characters per record to print with DBMS_OUTPUT.PUT_LINE().

❑ Lines printed by DBMS_OUTPUT can only be 255 characters in length. This is not a major limitation (since you can work around it by breaking up your debug messages into 255 character lines), but it is a hassle. It is much easier not to have to worry about whether or not your debug messages are less than 255 characters.

❑ Lastly, DBMS_OUTPUT spools back your messages only after the process ends.. That means that there is no real-time feedback from DBMS_OUTPUT. If you have a long running process, and want feedback on its progress as it executes, DBMS_OUTPUT is not going to be useful to you.

Other Debug Messaging Options

There are other options available for real-time debugging. You can use DBMS_APPLICATION.SET_CLIENT_INFO to set a limited amount of information that can then be queried out of the database in real-time, but you cannot see a history of your debug messages, only the most recent one.

Another option for debugging is writing the messages to a debug message table in the database and committing those writes via an autonomous transaction. This will only work if you are running a version of the database that supports autonomous transactions, namely version 8.1.5 and higher. Even if your version supports autonomous transactions, the writes to the database cause rollback to be generated leading to unnecessary database activity. Not only that, but the messages still need to be queried continually to see the most current additions to the table.

You could use DBMS_TRACE but the information you get is limited. It can track line-by-line movement through your code but does not give you the ability to include your own messages. Oracle also supplies a package called DBMS_DEBUG but I have found it very hard to use. It requires you to use two sessions, one to control the session you are debugging as well as the session itself.

Although some of these approaches fall short of what we are looking for, the ideas they present have merit, and we will use them in the design of the DEBUG debugging utility. Let's now consider the other requirements we have for our DEBUG tool.

Requirements

Having thought about this debugging tool, and polled the other PL/SQL developers in my office to get their feedback, here is a wish list of features that we would like to have in a debugging utility:

- ❏ Useable in any PL/SQL

- ❏ No limit on the amount of debug that can be generated

- ❏ No limit on the length of a line of debug

- ❏ Real-time feedback

- ❏ Self aware – know what line and package it is in

- ❏ Ability to turn it on and off easily

- ❏ Selectively debug packages/procedures/functions

- ❏ Acts differently depending on who runs the process

- ❏ Easy to use

Having outlined what we require of our DEBUG tool, let's begin to look at how we can create it.

Database Design and Setup

Since this is a PL/SQL utility, it lives in the database, and we will need to have a schema to own it. This schema can be owned by any user with the CONNECT, RESOURCE, and CREATE PUBLIC SYNONYM roles granted to them. I would suggest that you create a schema to hold this DEBUG package and grant EXECUTE on the DEBUG package to PUBLIC. That way we have one copy of the package and everybody shares it. In my database, I usually have a schema called UTILITY that owns utilities like DEBUG so I will use UTILITY in our example:

```
SQL> create user utility identified by utility;
User created.

SQL> grant connect, resource, create public synonym to utility;
Grant succeeded.
```

Now we are ready to create the schema objects we will need to support the DEBUG utility.

Tables

What we want to do now is to set up the DEBUG package, so that it will act according to how each user has set up their environment. Instead of storing that information in the environment, we will store it in a database table called DEBUGTAB. The code to create this table is as follows:

```
create table debugtab(
    userid      varchar2(30),
    filename    varchar2(1024),
    modules     varchar2(4000),
    show_date   varchar2(3),
    date_format varchar2(255),
    name_length number,
```

789

```
    session_id  varchar2(3),
    --
    -- Constraints
    --
    constraint debugtab_pk
      primary key ( userid, filename ),
    constraint debugtab_show_date_ck
      check ( show_date in ( 'YES', 'NO' ) ),
    constraint debugtab_session_id_ck
      check ( session_id in ( 'YES', 'NO' ) )
)
/
```

As you can see by the column names, I store all the information for each user who wants to use DEBUG. Options, like which procedures generate debug messages, what the date-time stamp format is, and whether to show the session ID or not, are all stored in this table.

Indexes and Constraints

There is only one index on this table, namely the primary key DEBUGTAB_PK. It was created in the CREATE TABLE statement. I use the USERID and FILENAME combination to uniquely identify a record. That might seems a bit strange, since you might think that USERID would be sufficient. However, consider applications in which every user connects as the same login, and the user's true identity is retrieved by some other means (such as cookies in the case of a web-based application for example). If I had only used USERID as the primary key, then one debug profile would have had to suffice for the entire application. That would not be very friendly, or useful, especially if you have several developers working on the application simultaneously.

The check constraints on the DEBUGTAB table ensure that the values entered are correct, and that when reading data out of the DEBUGTAB table, we can assume those columns will only have YES or NO as their value.

Triggers

We use a trigger on the DEBUGTAB table to ensure that the profile data is formatted correctly when entered.

```
create or replace
trigger biu_fer_debugtab
before insert or update on debugtab for each row
begin
   :new.modules := upper( :new.modules );
   :new.show_date := upper( :new.show_date );
   :new.session_id := upper( :new.session_id );
   :new.userid := upper( :new.userid );
```

Here the trigger formats the data, uppercasing the values supplied.

```
  declare
    l_date varchar2(100);
  begin
    l_date := to_char( sysdate, :new.date_format );
  exception
    when others then
      raise_application_error(
        -20001,
        'Invalid Date Format In Debug Date Format' );
  end;
end;
/
```

This portion of the trigger validates the date format supplied. It attempts to create a string with the supplied mask. If the mask is invalid, an application error is raised and the insert is aborted.

This makes coding the DEBUG package much easier since we can assume that all the data in the DEBUGTAB table is valid.

UTL_FILE_DIR

UTL_FILE_DIR is a database parameter. It is set in the init.ora parameter file. When set, it lets Oracle know which directory or directories it can write to using the UTL_FILE-supplied package. This parameter is important as a security tool. Imagine if a PL/SQL developer wrote a routine that could write or erase data from files, and used it to open the database's data files (which is quite possible since the Oracle process is doing the writing and also has permission to write to its own data files). If this happened, your database would be corrupt. The variable UTL_FILE_DIR safeguards against such things. To set it, you need to include it in the init.ora parameter file and set it equal to the directory you want the database to be able to write to, using PL/SQL. I suggest that you set it to a temporary directory on the server. An example on UNIX might look like:

```
utl_file_dir = /tmp
```

and on a Windows machine, it might be defined as:

```
utl_file_dir = C:\Temp
```

There is more information about setting this parameter in Appendix B, Supplied Packages.

Package Layout

Let's now explore what the DEBUG package looks like. There are four main procedures that the DEBUG package must implement:

❑   Initialize the profile

❑   Generate debug messages

- ❏ List the current debug profile
- ❏ Clear the profile

The initialization procedure, `INIT()`, should take in all the options that one can set for the debug profile:

```
procedure init(
  p_modules     in varchar2 default 'ALL',
  p_file        in varchar2 default '/tmp/' || user || '.dbg',
  p_user        in varchar2 default user,
  p_show_date   in varchar2 default 'YES',
  p_date_format in varchar2 default 'MMDDYYYY HH24MISS',
  p_name_len    in number   default 30,
  p_show_sesid  in varchar2 default 'NO' );
```

The procedure, `F()`, that will generate the debug message should take in the parameterized message and a list of the variables to substitute:

```
procedure f(
  p_message in varchar2,
  p_arg1    in varchar2 default null,
  p_arg2    in varchar2 default null,
  p_arg3    in varchar2 default null,
  p_arg4    in varchar2 default null,
  p_arg5    in varchar2 default null,
  p_arg6    in varchar2 default null,
  p_arg7    in varchar2 default null,
  p_arg8    in varchar2 default null,
  p_arg9    in varchar2 default null,
  p_arg10   in varchar2 default null );
```

I'm sure a few of you have noticed that we have a hard limit for the number of substitutions into the debug message. There are two options if you wish to get around this limitation. You can either use || to build the debug string (giving you an unlimited number of values to substitute in), or you can use the `DEBUG.FA()` routine. Its specification is as follows:

```
emptyDebugArgv Argv;

procedure fa(
  p_message in varchar2,
  p_args    in Argv default emptyDebugArgv );
```

I'll explain later what the `ARGV` type is and how you use it. Suffice to say that it removes the 10 parameter limitation of the `F()` implementation.

Once the profile is set we need a way to review it. We need a status routine:

```
procedure status(
  p_user in varchar2 default user,
  p_file in varchar2 default null );
```

And finally we need a way to clear our debug profile when we no longer want to generate debug messages:

```
procedure clear(
  p_user in varchar2 default user,
  p_file in varchar2 default null );
```

Both STATUS() and CLEAR() take in P_USER and P_FILE. Remember the primary key to the debug profile is both of those values. The user will need to supply them both in order to access the correct record. As a shortcut, we allow P_FILE to be passed in as NULL. In that case all debug profiles for the supplied user will be affected.

Implementation

Now it's time to start coding. We will need to implement the four procedures in our specification but there are also some private procedures in the DEBUG package body that need to be implemented as well. Let's break up the private debug processes into logical units of work. We need to:

❑ Determine what code called DEBUG – WHO_CALLED_ME()

❑ Build the debug header info – BUILD_IT()

❑ Parse the debug message and perform substitutions – PARSE_IT()

❑ Write the debug message to a file – FILE_IT()

We will write a private procedure/function for each of these.

Let's start though with the public interfaces used to generate a debug message, F(), FA(), and DEBUG_IT().

F()

The procedure F() is the most commonly used procedure in the DEBUG package. You can use this anywhere in your code to generate a message to a file and so allow yourself to see (in real-time) what is going on. Its implementation is quite simple.

```
1    procedure f(
2      p_message in varchar2,
3      p_arg1    in varchar2 default null,
4      p_arg2    in varchar2 default null,
5      p_arg3    in varchar2 default null,
6      p_arg4    in varchar2 default null,
7      p_arg5    in varchar2 default null,
8      p_arg6    in varchar2 default null,
9      p_arg7    in varchar2 default null,
10     p_arg8    in varchar2 default null,
11     p_arg9    in varchar2 default null,
```

```
12        p_arg10   in varchar2 default null ) is
13     begin
14       debug_it( p_message,
15                   argv( substr( p_arg1, 1, 4000 ),
16                         substr( p_arg2, 1, 4000 ),
17                         substr( p_arg3, 1, 4000 ),
18                         substr( p_arg4, 1, 4000 ),
19                         substr( p_arg5, 1, 4000 ),
20                         substr( p_arg6, 1, 4000 ),
21                         substr( p_arg7, 1, 4000 ),
22                         substr( p_arg8, 1, 4000 ),
23                         substr( p_arg9, 1, 4000 ),
24                         substr( p_arg10, 1, 4000 ) ) );
25     end f;
```

As you can see it does nothing but repackage the ten P_ARGS up into an ARGV and passes it to a routine called DEBUG_IT().

The ARGV Type

ARGV is a type that we define in the DEBUG spec. It is defined as:

```
type argv is table of varchar2(4000);
```

We created the ARGV type to support the FA() implementation. Using this ARGV type, we can pass in any number of parameters into a procedure. Consider it as an array.

The procedure F() was included for simplicity while the procedure FA() was included for completeness. It is much easier to type this,

```
l_var varchar2(5) := 'World';
debug.f( 'Hello %s', l_var );
```

than to call this:

```
l_var varchar2(5) := 'World';
debug.fa( 'Hello %s', debug.argv( 'World' ) );
```

Secondly, in terms of how it is called, DEBUG.F() is closer to the C printf() function than DEBUG.FA() and I was trying to mimic printf().

If you have over 10 variables you need to substitute, then using FA() or || are your two options.

FA()

The `FA()` implementation is even simpler than `F()`.

```
1    procedure fa(
2      p_message in varchar2,
3      p_args    in Argv default emptyDebugArgv ) is
4    begin
5      debug_it( p_message, p_args );
6    end fa;
```

As you can see it makes a straight call to `DEBUG_IT()` without doing any work at all. You might wonder why we did not have `F()` call `FA()` and have `FA()` do the work. That will become clearer later on. For now, all I'll say is that it has something to do with calculating who called the `DEBUG` routine.

DEBUG_IT()

This procedure is the coordinator of the debug package. Both `F()` and `FA()` call it and it in turn calls the four private procedures that we mentioned briefly above. Any time that we have a package like `DEBUG`, a package with multiple entry points to common functionality, we should make a private controlling procedure to do all the real work. That way, if we need to make a change to the logic of the package, we make it in one place. All the entry points, `F()` and `FA()` in this case, stay synchronized in terms of their common functionality.

Let's take a look at the implementation of the coordinator of the `DEBUG` package.

```
1    procedure debug_it(
2      p_message in varchar2,
3      p_argv    in argv ) is
4      --
5      l_message long := null;
6      l_header long := null;
7      call_who_called_me boolean := true;
8      l_owner varchar2(255);
9      l_object varchar2(255);
10     l_lineno number;
11     l_dummy boolean;
12   begin
13
```

We knew by the way `F()` and `FA()` called `DEBUG_IT()` that it took in the debug message string and the `ARGV` type. We have also set up a few local parameters.

The first thing we want to do is to check whether the current user has `DEBUG` enabled. That is accomplished by selecting out any records in the `DEBUGTAB` table where the `USERID` is the current user. In this case we check it against the pseudo-column `USER`, which is set to the username of the user currently executing the procedure.

```
14         for c in ( select *
15                     from debugtab
16                     where userid = user )
17         loop
18
```

Next we need to make a call to the first of our four private procedures WHO_CALLED_ME(). The call is wrapped in the IF-THEN structure for performance reasons. If there are two records with the same USERID and different FILENAMES, then there is no reason to call WHO_CALLED_ME() the second time through the loop (since it will come up with the same results). This reduces CPU processing time.

```
19         if call_who_called_me then
20            who_called_me( l_owner, l_object, l_lineno );
21            call_who_called_me := false;
22         end if;
23
```

Now we want to check to see if the L_OBJECT variable returned by WHO_CALLED_ME() is in the comma-delimited list of object names that are currently being debugged.

```
24         if instr( ',' || c.modules || ',',
25                      ',' || l_object || ',' ) <> 0 or
26            c.modules = 'ALL'
27         then
28
```

Finally, if it is determined that the debug message should be written, we call the other three private procedures which will handle the work.

```
29            l_header := build_it( c, l_owner, l_object, l_lineno );
30     l_message := parse_it( p_message, p_argv, length(l_header) );
31            l_dummy := file_it( c.filename, l_header || l_message );
32
33         end if;
34      end loop;
35
36   end debug_it;
```

Notice that we do not check the return value from FILE_IT(). That's because there is nothing we can do if the message has failed. We don't want to stop execution of the application just because DEBUG could not write the message. The developer will have to troubleshoot why no messages are being written (see the *Troubleshooting* section later on).

Searching for Matches in Strings

Another thing you might be wondering is why both search strings in the INSTR() on lines 23 and 24 are padded with commas. That was done to ensure that no mistaken debugging of a routine takes place. Consider the case of two procedures, A() and AA(). If the developer only wanted to debug the procedure AA(), and a debug call was initiated from the A() procedure, then without the addition of the commas, the debug message would be printed mistakenly. Let's look at how the INSTR() function works.

```
SQL> select instr( 'Samantha', 'man' ) position from dual;

   POSITION
----------
         3
```

INSTR() looks for the second parameter within the first parameter and if it finds it, returns the index of it. In this example, INSTR() found the string man in the string Samantha starting at position 3.

Getting back to the example of the two procedures A() and AA(), the string 'A' is in the string 'AA', but we do not want to debug A() so we put a comma on each side of the strings and now search for ',A,' within the string ',AA,'. Since there is no match, no debug is generated, which is the desired effect. Here's an example to show this point.

```
SQL>  declare
   2      debug_procedure_name long := 'A';
   3      list_of_debuggable_procs long := 'AA';
   4  begin
   5      if instr( list_of_debuggable_procs,
   6                 debug_procedure_name ) <> 0 then
   7        dbms_output.put_line( 'found it' );
   8      else
   9        dbms_output.put_line( 'did not find it' );
  10      end if;
  11      if instr( ',' || list_of_debuggable_procs || ',',
  12                 ',' || debug_procedure_name || ',' ) <> 0 then
  13        dbms_output.put_line( 'found it' );
  14      else
  15        dbms_output.put_line( 'did not find it' );
  16      end if;
  17  end;
  18  /
found it
did not find it
```

WHO_CALLED_ME()

The first of the four procedures that we encounter in the DEBUG_IT() procedure is WHO_CALLED_ME(). This procedure will determine from what line of code in what procedure the debug message was called. What we want to do in this procedure is use the Oracle-supplied function DBMS_UTILITY.FORMAT_CALL_STACK() to get the call stack.

The **call stack** is the listing of the procedures and function that we have currently traversed. If I initially called procedure A() and it in turned called procedure B() which called procedure C() the call stack indicates to me where I currently am in the code and what procedure(s) I went through to get to that point. It also includes other information like current line numbers.

We can then use the string manipulation functions, SUBSTR(), INSTR(), LTRIM(), and RTRIM() to parse out the information we are interested in. Let's take a look at how that will work.

The first part of the code defines the procedure and the local variables. Notice the three OUT parameters. Since this procedure needs to return multiple pieces of information, we need to use Out parameters instead of making this a function (which could only return a single value).

```
1    procedure who_called_me(
2       o_owner   out varchar2,
3       o_object out varchar2,
4       o_lineno out number ) is
5    --
6       l_call_stack long default dbms_utility.format_call_stack;
7       l_line varchar2(4000);
8    begin
9
```

Included in the comments, lines 10 through 19, is an example of what the output to DBMS_UTILITY.FORMAT_CALL_STACK() might look like. The first three lines are heading information. Each subsequent line is a line in the call stack. The information in each line includes the owner, object name, and line number, among other things. It is those three pieces of information that I will need to parse out and return.

```
10   /*
11       ----- PL/SQL Call Stack -----
12       object      line  object
13       handle    number  name
14       86c60290      17  package body UTILITY.DEBUG
15       86c60290     212  package body UTILITY.DEBUG
16       86c60290     251  package body UTILITY.DEBUG
17       86aa28f0       1  procedure OPS$CLBECK.A
18       86a9e940       1  anonymous block
19   */
20
```

The primary task that WHO_CALLED_ME() needs to carry out is to skip the first 6 lines of the call stack. The first three, as we know, are just the heading information and the next three are calls from inside the DEBUG package itself. Those three calls in the debug stack are, in reverse order:

❏   The call to F() or FA() (line 16)

❏   The call to the controller procedure DEBUG_IT() (line 15)

❏   The call to the procedure WHO_CALLED_ME() (line 14)

If we had had F() call FA() and then have FA() do the work of DEBUG_IT(), the stack would have a different number of levels depending on which of the two we called, making it much harder to write WHO_CALLED_ME().

Let's consider the next section of code:

```
21       for i in 1 .. 6 loop
22         l_call_stack := substr( l_call_stack,
23                       instr( l_call_stack, chr(10) )+1 );
24       end loop;
25
```

Now the local variable L_CALL_STACK starts with the line we are interested in. For ease of use, let's set a local variable to just that line, ignoring anything after it:

```
26      l_line := ltrim( substr( l_call_stack,
27                       1,
28                       instr( l_call_stack, chr(10) ) - 1 ) );
29
```

If the call stack looked like the example above, then L_LINE will look like this:

```
86aa28f0           1  procedure OPS$CLBECK.A
```

Now let's begin to parse L_LINE. First we remove the object handle, 86aa28f0, by reassigning L_LINE to equal the SUBSTR() of itself starting at the first whitespace. This is wrapped within an LTRIM() that removes all leading whitespace.

```
30      l_line := ltrim( substr( l_line, instr( l_line, ' ' )));
31
```

L_LINE now looks like this:

```
1  procedure OPS$CLBECK.A
```

Now L_LINE starts with the line number of the code where this occurrence of DEBUG.F() or DEBUG.FA() was called from. We want to save that information and include it in the debug message, so that the developer can easily find exactly where in their code this message originated from. We assign it to the OUT parameter O_LINENO and then strip it from L_LINE.

Note that we use the same technique to remove the next word from L_LINE as we did to remove the object handle in the previous step.

```
32   o_lineno := to_number(substr(l_line, 1, instr(l_line, ' ')));
33   l_line := ltrim(substr(l_line, instr(l_line, ' ')));
34
```

Next we want to remove the kind of object that called DEBUG. The tricky part here is that there may be either one or two words to strip off. If DEBUG was called from,

❑   a procedure or function in a package body

❑   a member routine in a type body

❑   an anonymous block

then we need to remove the word body or block from L_LINE too, using the code shown below.

```
35        l_line := ltrim( substr( l_line, instr( l_line, ' ' )));
36
37        if l_line like 'block%' or
38           l_line like 'body%' then
39           l_line := ltrim( substr( l_line, instr( l_line, ' ' )));
40        end if;
41
```

Now the only thing left in the line is the *OWNER.OBJECT_NAME*. We now set the other two OUT parameters to the appropriate values using all four of the string manipulation functions:

```
42        o_owner := ltrim( rtrim( substr( l_line,
43                                  1,
44                                  instr( l_line, '.' )-1 )));
45        o_object  := ltrim( rtrim( substr( l_line,
46                                   instr( l_line, '.' )+1 )));
47
```

Finally, if DEBUG was called from an anonymous block, the call stack does not supply an *OWNER.OBJECT_NAME*, so the assignment of O_OWNER and O_OBJECT causes them to be set to NULL. We check to see if O_OWNER is NULL. If it is then we need to set O_OWNER to equal the user connected in the current session and set O_OBJECT equal to ANONYMOUS BLOCK.

```
48        if o_owner is null then
49           o_owner := user;
50           o_object := 'ANONYMOUS BLOCK';
51        end if;
52
53     end who_called_me;
```

BUILD_IT()

Once we determine that this call to DEBUG should generate a debug message, we call the second internal package procedure, BUILD_IT(), to build and return the header of the debug message. The header contains all the information about the call to DEBUG, formatted according to the debug profile set up with INIT(). It may include the timestamp of when it was called, the owner and object name from which it was called, and the line number of that object. We determined that information in WHO_CALLED_ME() and forwarded it to BUILD_IT(), along with other information for formatting the header.

```
1     function build_it(
2        p_debug_row in debugtab%rowtype,
3        p_owner     in varchar2,
4        p_object    in varchar2,
5        p_lineno number ) return varchar2 is
6        --
7        l_header long := null;
8     begin
9
```

There are just three steps in BUILD_IT(). First we want to check and see if we should include the SESSION_ID in the header information. If so, we assign the global variable, G_SESSION_ID, to the local variable L_HEADER. We use a global here for performance reasons. The session does not change once this DEBUG package is instantiated, so we don't need the overhead of getting the session ID on every call. Instead of this, we can simply set the global variable once in the instantiation block of DEBUG and then just reference it when necessary. I'll show you what that looks like later on; for now just assume that G_SESSION_ID is set correctly.

```
10        if p_debug_row. session_id = 'YES' then
11           l_header := g_session_id || ' - ';
12        end if;
13
```

Next, we want to determine if the message formatting wants to include the date and time. If so, we append the correctly formatted timestamp to L_HEADER.

```
14        if p_debug_row.show_date = 'YES' then
15           l_header := l_header ||
16                   to_char( sysdate,
17                          nvl( p_debug_row.date_format,
18                          'MMDDYYYY HH24MISS' ) );
19        end if;
20
```

Finally, we append the owner, object name, and line number to L_HEADER and return it to the caller DEBUG_IT().

```
21        l_header :=
22          l_header ||
23          '(' ||
24          lpad( substr( p_owner || '.' || p_object,
25               greatest( 1, length( p_owner || '.' || p_object ) -
26               least( p_debug_row.name_length, 61 ) + 1 ) ),
27               least( p_debug_row.name_length, 61 ) ) ||
28          lpad( p_lineno, 5 ) ||
29          ') ';
30
31        return l_header;
32
33     end build_it;
```

There is some tricky stuff here with GREATEST(), LEAST(), and SUBSTR() used to size the owner and object name correctly. The reason we allow the developer to control the size of the name display is that if we always use the maximum space to display the OWNER.OBJECT, then there is usually quite a bit of whitespace in it. Identifiers in Oracle can be a maximum of 30 characters, meaning that the OWNER.OBJECT can be as large as 61 characters. Since this is not usually the case though, we give developers a way to control that display length.

Another thing to note is the parameter type of P_DEBUG_ROW(DEBUGTAB%ROWTYPE). Since we call this routine from within a cursor-for loop in DEBUG_IT(), and the query for that loop is a SELECT * query, we can pass the entire row to the BUILD_IT() routine in one variable. This makes defining the procedure cleaner, which in turn makes the call to it shorter.

PARSE_IT()

Once the message header is complete, we may need to modify the message itself. In PARSE_IT() substitutions of %s to appropriate values are carried out. We need to pass not only the message string, but also the values to substitute into it (in the form of the ARGV type), and the length of the header string to PARSE_IT().

```
1    function parse_it(
2      p_message       in varchar2,
3      p_argv          in argv,
4      p_header_length in number ) return varchar2 is
5      --
6      l_message long := null;
7      l_str long := p_message;
8      l_idx number := 1;
9      l_ptr number := 1;
10   begin
11
```

You'll see why we need the header length later on.

The first thing to do is check and see if there is anything that needs substituting. If a % or a \ are not found in the message, then we can just return the P_MESSAGE unaltered.

```
12     if nvl( instr( p_message, '%' ), 0 ) = 0 and
13        nvl( instr( p_message, '\' ), 0 ) = 0 then
14        return p_message;
15     end if;
16
```

Now we loop, looking for instances of %, and exit the loop when no more are found.

```
17     loop
18
19       l_ptr := instr( l_str, '%' );
20       exit when l_ptr = 0 or l_ptr is null;
```

If a % is found, then we append all characters prior to it to the local variable L_MESSAGE.

```
21       l_message := l_message || substr( l_str, 1, l_ptr-1 );
22       l_str :=  substr( l_str, l_ptr+1 );
23
```

Next we examine the character immediately following the %. If it is an s then we've found where a substitution needs to happen and carry it out.

```
24          if substr( l_str, 1, 1 ) = 's' then
25             l_message := l_message || p_argv(l_idx);
26             l_idx := l_idx + 1;
27             l_str := substr( l_str, 2 );
28
```

If the character immediately following the % is another %, we add one % to L_MESSAGE and continue. In Oracle, if you have two single quotes together in a string, the first one escapes the second one and only one is displayed; that same logic is true here for percent symbols.

```
29          elsif substr( l_str,1,1 ) = '%' then
30             l_message := l_message || '%';
31             l_str := substr( l_str, 2 );
32
```

Or else if the character immediately following the percent we initially found was not a s or a %, then it's just a % in the string and should be appended to L_MESSAGE so it will be displayed.

```
33          else
34             l_message := l_message || '%';
35          end if;
36
37       end loop;
38
```

Now we make a second pass over the message to look for \n and \t. Those familiar with coding in C or Java know that to put a new line or a tab into a printed string, you use \n and \t respectively. Since we are copying the C style of using %s for placeholders in variable substitution, we include the new line and tab formatting also. The logic here is exactly the same as in the previous loop. First we reset the local variables:

```
39       l_str := l_message || l_str;
40       l_message := null;
41
```

Now we loop, looking for a \ and exit when no more are found.

```
42       loop
43
44          l_ptr := instr( l_str, '\' );
45          exit when l_ptr = 0 or l_ptr is null;
```

If a \ is found, we append everything prior to it to L_MESSAGE.

```
46          l_message := l_message || substr( l_str, 1, l_ptr-1 );
47          l_str :=  substr( l_str, l_ptr+1 );
48
```

Now we examine the character immediately following the \. If it is an n then we add a new line to the message, which is where the length of the debug header comes into play. I want the new line to start right below where the first line did, which is immediately following the header. So the new line must be padded with spaces the length of the header in order to line up properly.

```
49        if substr( l_str, 1, 1 ) = 'n' then
50            l_message := l_message || chr(10) ||
51                        rpad( ' ', p_header_length, ' ' );
52            l_str := substr( l_str, 2 );
53
```

If the next character is a t, we append the tab character to L_MESSAGE.

```
54        elsif substr( l_str, 1, 1 ) = 't' then
55            l_message := l_message || chr(9);
56            l_str := substr( l_str, 2 );
57
```

If the next character is another \, we handle it just as above with the double percents.

```
58        elsif substr( l_str, 1, 1 ) = '\' then
59            l_message := l_message || '\';
60            l_str := substr( l_str, 2 );
61
```

Or else it is just a \ and we print it.

```
62        else
63            l_message := l_message || '\';
64        end if;
65
66     end loop;
67
```

All that is left to do is return the parsed and formatted string.

```
68     return l_message || l_str;
69
70   end parse_it;
```

There is nothing extremely hard in this procedure. The only thing to watch is that, in using SUBSTR() and INSTR(), you do not lose a character in the process.

FILE_IT()

Finally, the header and message are parsed and formatted and are ready for display. We can now attempt to write the information to the desired file using the fourth and final private function in the DEBUG package called FILE_IT(). Its definition and local variables are pretty straightforward. This function will return TRUE or FALSE depending on whether or not it was successful in writing the message to the file.

```
1    function file_it(
2      p_file   in debugtab.filename%type,
3      p_message in varchar2 ) return boolean is
4      --
5      l_handle utl_file.file_type;
6      l_file long;
7      l_location long;
8    begin
9
```

Notice that we define P_FILE as DEBUGTAB.FILENAME%ROWTYPE. This ensures that the data types for this variable stay in sync with the table DEBUGTAB. If you recall, FILE_IT() is called with the filename stored in the database, and that information is retrieved using a cursor-for loop in DEBUG_IT(). To avoid a type mismatch, we define this parameter as type DEBUGTAB.FILENAME%TYPE, which will keep the input parameter the same type as the column filename in the table.

The first thing we want to do is determine the file name and the directory passed in. To do this we use SUBSTR() and INSTR() to manipulate a VARCHAR2. The parameter P_FILE is the fully qualified path and file name that we should write the message to.

Notice we also do a REPLACE(), swapping all the back slashes for forward slashes.

```
10   l_file := substr( p_file,
11                     instr( replace( p_file, '\', '/' ),
12                            '/', -1 )+1 );
13
14   l_location := substr( p_file,
15                         1,
16                         instr( replace( p_file, '\', '/' ),
17                                '/', -1 )-1 );
18
```

Once that is done, we use the Oracle-supplied package UTL_FILE to open the file:

```
19   l_handle := utl_file.fopen(
20                   location => l_location,
21                   filename => l_file,
22                   open_mode => 'a',
23                   max_linesize => 32767 );
24
```

then write the message into the file:

```
25   utl_file.put( l_handle, '' );
26   utl_file.put_line( l_handle, p_message );
```

and then close the file and return TRUE:

```
27        utl_file.fclose( l_handle );
28
29        return true;
30
```

You might think it would be easier and more efficient if we left the file open and only wrote the message each time and you would be right. But, since we don't know when the last call to DEBUG is going to be made, we can't know when to finally close the file. So yes, opening and closing the file is a performance hit but a necessary one.

> *Remember, DEBUG is normally used during the development phase of your application, so a slight performance increase is fine. I'll show you later on how to remove most of the overhead of DEBUG during deployment without changing a single line of your application code.*

The last block of code is the exception handler for FILE_IT():

```
31    exception
32      when others then
33        if utl_file.is_open( l_handle ) then
34          utl_file.fclose( l_handle );
35        end if;
36
37        return false;
38
39    end file_it;
```

We use the UTL_FILE package and so need to catch and handle any exceptions which may be raised. UTL_FILE can throw many different exceptions, and anyone of them will leave us unable to write the message. We don't want DEBUG to cause the routine calling it to fail, so we capture all exceptions with the WHEN OTHERS clause and quietly close the file and return FALSE, never having written the debug message.

> *That can cause confusion for the developer who is expecting debug to be generated. See the section on troubleshooting for the most common problems when using DEBUG.*

INIT()

Now we have finished all the code for writing the debug message to a file but we haven't given the developer a way to initialize DEBUG. This is where the INIT() procedure comes into play. It takes in as parameters all the attributes that a developer can set in their debug profile. All the parameters are defaulted so you can just call DEBUG.INIT() to set up your profile.

```
1    procedure init(
2      p_modules    in varchar2 default 'ALL',
3      p_file     in varchar2 default '/tmp/' || user || '.dbg',
4      p_user       in varchar2 default user,
5      p_show_date   in varchar2 default 'YES',
```

```
 6        p_date_format in varchar2 default 'MMDDYYYY HH24MISS',
 7        p_name_len    in number   default 30,
 8        p_show_sesid  in varchar2 default 'NO' ) is
 9        --
10        pragma autonomous_transaction;
11        debugtab_rec debugtab%rowtype;
12        l_message long;
13     begin
14
```

The first thing to do is delete any profiles that conflict with the one that we will insert.

```
15        delete from debugtab
16         where userid = p_user
17           and filename = p_file;
18
```

Now we perform the insert, using the RETURNING-INTO clause of the INSERT statement to capture the values that were inserted.

```
19        insert into debugtab(
20           userid, modules, filename, show_date,
21           date_format, name_length, session_id )
22        values (
23           p_user, p_modules, p_file, p_show_date,
24           p_date_format, p_name_len, p_show_sesid )
25        returning
26           userid, modules, filename, show_date,
27           date_format, name_length, session_id
28        into
29           debugtab_rec.userid, debugtab_rec.modules,
30           debugtab_rec.filename, debugtab_rec.show_date,
31           debugtab_rec.date_format, debugtab_rec.name_length,
32           debugtab_rec.session_id;
33
```

Remember we created a trigger, BIU_FER_DEBUGTAB, on the DEBUGTAB table that could change the data on the way into the table. The trigger uppercases a few of the columns. I might have supplied yes as the value for SESSION_ID, but the trigger will uppercase the value and store YES. We want to know exactly what the row that was inserted looked like, and so we return its values. We store those returned values in DEBUGTAB_REC, which is defined as a DEBUGTAB%ROWTYPE, so we know the types will match.

Next we want to write to the debug file the current debug profile settings. To do this we build up a message string that includes all the values inserted into the DEBUGTAB table

```
34        l_message := chr(10) ||
35                   'Debug parameters initialized on ' ||
36        to_char( sysdate, 'dd-MON-yyyy hh24:mi:ss' ) || chr(10);
37        l_message := l_message || '            USER: ' ||
```

```
38          debugtab_rec.userid || chr(10);
39    l_message := l_message || '         MODULES: ' ||
40          debugtab_rec.modules || chr(10);
41    l_message := l_message || '        FILENAME: ' ||
42          debugtab_rec.filename || chr(10);
43    l_message := l_message || '       SHOW DATE: ' ||
44          debugtab_rec.show_date || chr(10);
45    l_message := l_message || '     DATE FORMAT: ' ||
46          debugtab_rec.date_format || chr(10);
47    l_message := l_message || '     NAME LENGTH: ' ||
48          debugtab_rec.name_length || chr(10);
49    l_message := l_message || 'SHOW SESSION ID: ' ||
50          debugtab_rec.session_id || chr(10);
51
```

Finally, we attempt to write the message by calling FILE_IT(). This time we do care about the return code from FILE_IT(), since, in the event of our being unable to write to the file, then there is no reason why we should allow the initialization to occur. If FILE_IT() is unsuccessful, we roll back the insert and raise an application error:

```
52    if not file_it( debugtab_rec.filename, l_message ) then
53      rollback;
54      raise_application_error(
55        -20001,
56        'Can not open file "' ||
57        debugtab_rec.filename || '"' );
58    end if;
59
```

Otherwise we commit and return.

```
60      commit;
61
62    end init;
```

You might think that it is a bad thing to commit or roll back in this procedure because it could affect open transactions. But remember line 10:

```
pragma autonomous_transaction;
```

This makes the INIT() procedure run in its own transaction space. Committing or rolling back in it will have no effect on the transaction that called it.

CLEAR()

Having generated a way to create a debug profile, we need to create a way to remove it as well. CLEAR() is that procedure, and it is very simple. It just deletes from the DEBUGTAB table any record that matches the inputted parameters. Again we use the PRAGMA AUTONOMOUS_TRANSACTION directive to ensure the commit called will not affect the calling transaction.

```
1    procedure clear( p_user in varchar2 default user,
2                      p_file in varchar2 default null ) is
3      pragma autonomous_transaction;
4    begin
5      delete from debugtab where userid = p_user
6              and filename = nvl( p_file, filename );
7      commit;
8    end clear;
```

> **Note that in this procedure, if the caller does not supply a filename, all the profiles for the specified user will be deleted.**

STATUS()

Lastly, we supply a routine to display the current debug profile. Just like CLEAR(), the user supplies the username and an optional filename. Since it displays its output using DBMS_OUTPUT.PUT_LINE, the developer needs to call this routine from SQL*Plus or some other DBMS_OUTPUT-aware client.

```
1    procedure status(
2      p_user in varchar2 default user,
3      p_file in varchar2 default null ) is
4      --
5      l_found boolean := false;
6    begin
7
```

Now we print the header of the listing and display the output using DBMS_OUTPUT.PUT_LINE.

```
8       dbms_output.put_line( chr(10) );
9       dbms_output.put_line( 'Debug info for ' ||
10                     p_user );
```

Loop over any rows that satisfy the cursor-for loop query.

```
11      for c in ( select *
12                    from debugtab
13                    where userid = p_user
14                        and nvl( p_file, filename ) = filename )
15      loop
16        dbms_output.put_line( '---------------' ||
17                         rpad( '-', length( p_user ), '-' ) );
```

Set a local Boolean variable, L_FOUND, to TRUE so that we'll know that we found at least one matching record.

```
18        l_found := true;
```

Next we use DBMS_OUTPUT.PUT_LINE to write the output to the developer's screen.

```
19        dbms_output.put_line( 'USER:              ' ||
20                               c.userid );
21        dbms_output.put_line( 'MODULES:           ' ||
22                               c.modules );
23        dbms_output.put_line( 'FILENAME:          ' ||
24                               c.filename );
25        dbms_output.put_line( 'SHOW DATE:         ' ||
26                               c.show_date );
27        dbms_output.put_line( 'DATE FORMAT:       ' ||
28                               c.date_format );
29        dbms_output.put_line( 'NAME LENGTH:       ' ||
30                               c.name_length );
31        dbms_output.put_line( 'SHOW SESSION ID:   ' ||
32                               c.session_id );
33        dbms_output.put_line( ' ' );
34     end loop;
35
```

Finally, if we do not find any records, we notify the caller of that fact with this message.

```
36     if not l_found then
37        dbms_output.put_line( 'No debug setup.' );
38     end if;
39
40  end status;
```

Finishing Touches

The only code left that we have not yet shown you is the instantiation code of DEBUG. If you recall, we used a global variable called G_SESSION_ID to store the session ID. We told you that we populated that value once on the first call to DEBUG. The variable is defined as:

```
package body debug as

  g_session_id varchar2(2000);
```

and the code that initializes it is this:

```
begin
   g_session_id := userenv('SESSIONID');
end debug;
```

There you go – the entire DEBUG utility. Now let's see how you can use it.

1. The first thing that you want to do is set up your DEBUG profile using INIT():

```
SQL> exec debug.init( 'all', '/tmp/myDebug.dbg' );

PL/SQL procedure successfully completed.
```

That's it. You are now debug enabled. Any code that you execute as the user, in this case BOOK, that has a call DEBUG.F() or DEBUG.FA() will cause a message to be written to the file /tmp/myDebug.dbg.

2. Let's look at that file right now.

```
Debug parameters initialized on 28-OCT-2001 21:29:51
                USER: BOOK
             MODULES: ALL
            FILENAME: /tmp/myDebug.dbg
           SHOW DATE: YES
         DATE FORMAT: MMDDYYYY HH24MISS
         NAME LENGTH: 30
     SHOW SESSION ID: NO
```

If you remember, the INIT() procedure writes to the file the current working profile's attributes and that is what you see above. We only supplied INIT() with the name of the file and which modules we wanted DEBUG active for, and it used defaults for the rest of the values.

1. You can use the procedure STATUS() from the SQL*Plus command prompt to see the current profile enabled.

```
SQL> exec debug.status
Debug info for BOOK
-------------------
USER:                    BOOK
MODULES:                 ALL
FILENAME:                /tmp/myDebug.dbg
SHOW DATE:               YES
DATE FORMAT:             MMDDYYYY HH24MISS
NAME LENGTH:             30
SHOW SESSION ID:         NO

PL/SQL procedure successfully completed.
```

Try It Out – Generating Messages

1. Now let's make a call to DEBUG.F().

```
SQL> exec debug.f( 'my first debug message' );

PL/SQL procedure successfully completed.
```

2. Pretty anti-climactic wasn't it. There was no indication that anything happened. Go check line 7 of the debug file now or use STATUS() to see what's changed.

```
10282001 213953(          BOOK.ANONYMOUS BLOCK     1) my first debug message
```

There it is! There is your message. But what is all this extra stuff? That is the header information that was created and added to the message.

❑   The first set of numbers is the date in the format of MMDDYYYY and the second set of numbers is the time in the format of HH24MISS. That is the date format just as the profile says it should be.

❑   The next piece of information is the owner and object that initiated that call. We see that it says that the anonymous block owned by the user BOOK made the call and it was at line 1 of that object.

Remember how WHO_CALLED_ME() parsed that information from the call stack? This is where it becomes very useful.

Try It Out – Modifying Your Profile

1. Let's change our profile and generate another message.

```
SQL> begin
  2      debug.init( p_file => '/tmp/myDebug.dbg',
  3                  p_date_format => 'HH:MI:SSAM',
  4                  p_name_len => 20 );
  5  end;
  6  /
PL/SQL procedure successfully completed.

SQL> exec debug.f( 'another message' );
PL/SQL procedure successfully completed.
```

2. Inspecting the debug file will reveal the following.

```
Debug parameters initialized on 28-OCT-2001 21:51:04
            USER: BOOK
         MODULES: ALL
        FILENAME: /tmp/myDebug.dbg
       SHOW DATE: YES
     DATE FORMAT: HH:MI:SSAM
```

```
            NAME LENGTH: 20
       SHOW SESSION ID: NO

       09:53:19PM(BOOK.ANONYMOUS BLOCK    1) another message
```

3. We now have a new date format and the name length is shorter. You can play with the formatting until it's right for you. I like the default myself so I am going to put it back.

```
SQL> begin
  2     debug.init( 'all', '/tmp/myDebug.dbg' );
  5  end;
  6  /
PL/SQL procedure successfully completed.
```

4. Let's now explore how the substitution works. Recall that the DEBUG utility allows the caller to pass in a string, and values to be substituted into it. For every %s found in the message, DEBUG will try and substitute the next parameter. If you execute the following:

```
SQL> exec debug.f( '%s %s!', 'hello', 'world' );
```

5. the resulting debug message will be:

```
10282001 224317 (           BOOK.ANONYMOUS BLOCK    1) hello world!
```

Try It Out – Using FA()

1. Using F() is only good when you have 10 parameters or fewer. If you have more you can use the FA() call. Recall that this procedure takes in a message and a user-defined type, ARGV. Here's an example of calling it.

```
SQL> exec debug.fa( 'The %s %s %s', debug.argv( 'quick','brown','fox' ) );
```

2. And the result is:

```
10282001 225121(           BOOK.ANONYMOUS BLOCK    1) The quick brown fox
```

ARGV can take any number of values so now we have a facility to pass in an unlimited number of values to substitute.

Try It Out – Formatting

1. You can also use \n and \t to format the message.

```
SQL> exec debug.f( 'The %s\n%s fox', 'quick', 'brown' );
```

2. Again, the resulting message:

```
10282001 225630(        BOOK.ANONYMOUS BLOCK    1) The quick
                                                   brown fox
```

Try It Out – Removing the Profile

1. When you are done debugging, you can remove your profile using the following call to DEBUG.CLEAR():

```
SQL> exec debug.clear;

PL/SQL procedure successfully completed.

SQL> exec debug.status

Debug info for BOOK
No debug setup.

PL/SQL procedure successfully completed.
```

Any subsequent calls to DEBUG.F() or DEBUG.FA() will not generate debug messages for the user BOOK.

Try it Out – Making the Package Executable By PUBLIC

1. To make the DEBUG package executable by PUBLIC, execute the following:

```
SQL> grant execute on debug to public;

Grant succeeded.
```

2. Now connect as another user, for example, SCOTT, and use the DEBUG package. You need to prefix all references to DEBUG's procedures with UTILITY.DEBUG:

```
SQL> connect scott/tiger
Connected.
SQL> exec utility.debug.init('all', 'C:\Temp\MyDebug.dbg');

PL/SQL procedure successfully completed.

SQL> exec utility.debug.status;

Debug info for SCOTT
--------------------
USER:             SCOTT
MODULES:          ALL
FILENAME:         C:\Temp\MyDebug.dbg
SHOW DATE:        YES
DATE FORMAT:      MMDDYYYY HH24MISS
NAME LENGTH:      30
SHOW SESSION ID:  NO

PL/SQL procedure successfully completed.
```

Now, let's move on to the really impressive feature of DEBUG, the ability to selectively display debug messages depending on what procedure it is called from.

Try It Out – Selective Debugging

1. Again, let's initialize our debug profile but this time let's give it a list of procedures to debug.

```
SQL> exec debug.init( 'A,C,E', '/tmp/myDebug.dbg' );

PL/SQL procedure successfully completed.

SQL> exec debug.status

Debug info for BOOK
-------------------
USER:                 BOOK
MODULES:              A,C,E
FILENAME:             /tmp/myDebug.dbg
SHOW DATE:            YES
DATE FORMAT:          MMDDYYYY HH24MISS
NAME LENGTH:          30
SHOW SESSION ID:     NO

PL/SQL procedure successfully completed.
```

2. That says that we only want to see debug messages if they are generated from an object called A, C, or E. Now let's write a few simple procedures that generate debug. We'll make them call one another too.

```
SQL> create procedure a as
  2  begin
  3    debug.f( 'chris' );
  4  end;
  5  /

Procedure created.

SQL> create procedure b as
  2  begin
  3    a;
  4    debug.f( 'joel' );
  5  end;
  6  /

Procedure created.

SQL> create procedure c as
  2  begin
  3    b;
  4    debug.f( 'sean' );
  5  end;
```

```
  6  /

Procedure created.

SQL> create procedure d as
  2  begin
  3    c;
  4    debug.f( 'tyler' );
  5  end;
  6  /

Procedure created.

SQL> create procedure e as
  2  begin
  3    d;
  4    debug.f( 'tom' );
  5  end;
  6  /

Procedure created.
```

3. We have 5 procedures, E(), which calls D(), which calls C(), and so on. Each procedure also makes a call to DEBUG.F(). Run E() and then examine the file /tmp/myDebug.dbg

```
SQL> exec e;

PL/SQL procedure successfully completed.

        Debug parameters initialized on 28-OCT-2001 22:09:19
                    USER: BOOK
                 MODULES: A,C,E
                FILENAME: /tmp/myDebug.dbg
               SHOW DATE: YES
             DATE FORMAT: MMDDYYYY HH24MISS
             NAME LENGTH: 30
         SHOW SESSION ID: NO

        10282001 222118(                   BOOK.A    3) chris
        10282001 222118(                   BOOK.C    4) sean
        10282001 222118(                   BOOK.E    4) tom
```

Only the debug messages from the procedures A(), C(), and E() were written to the file. That is because, when we initialized our profile, we only asked for debug message in those 3 procedures. It did not matter that D(), which is not being debugged, called C(), which was. DEBUG did exactly what we wanted.

This is the power of DEBUG. Imagine if you were debugging an application that called 100+ different procedures, and you wanted to debug messages from only two of them. You could wade through the mounds of code that create debug messages in your application and comment out all the debug messages you are not interested in and then recompile. Or you can use DEBUG, and simply configure your profile to give you exactly the messages that you want without changing a single line of application code.

Using DEBUG

There are many places where you can use DEBUG.

❑ First you can use it in any PL/SQL application. Just sprinkle calls to F() and FA() wherever you want to. And when you want them to become active, initialize a debug profile. When you are not debugging an application, just clear your profile and the calls to DEBUG won't produce any output.

❑ Consider a PL/SQL application or routine that is not called from SQL*Plus. How about a Forms application that calls some server-side PL/SQL? How can you easily get any feedback from your code? You can't. You need DEBUG.

❑ If you are familiar with row-level security (RLS) in Oracle 8i (see the *Fine-Grained Access Control* section in Chapter 13, *Security*), then you know about the policy procedure you need to implement to enable that feature. But that procedure cannot be called directly. Oracle calls it itself when a SELECT is performed on the table with RLS enabled. Good luck getting feedback from that without using DEBUG.

❑ Triggers are another example of a PL/SQL routine that is not directly called by a user or an application and DEBUG is a great way to monitor what the trigger is doing.

❑ Using the timestamp of each debug message, you can determine how long it takes to get from debug messages to debug messages in your code. This can aid you in finding performance bottlenecks in your code. If you have the following,

```
...
debug.f( 'before calling my_proc' );
my_proc;
debug.f( 'after calling my_proc' );
...
```

and the time between messages is long, you know that the procedure MY_PROC() is taking significant time to execute and you might want to look into increasing its performance.

Troubleshooting DEBUG

We saw that DEBUG was coded to quietly fail if it could not write the message to the file. Here are some things to look for if you are not getting DEBUG messages or are getting errors initializing your profile.

You Get an Error Initializing the Profile – File Does Not Exist

Check to see if Oracle has privilege to write to the directory. That can be accomplished by logging into SQL*Plus as a DBA and running this.

```
SQL> show parameter utl_file_dir

NAME                                  TYPE        VALUE
------------------------------------- ----------- ----------------
utl_file_dir                          string      /tmp
```

817

Verify that the value is the same as the directory that you are passing in. This value is case-sensitive on UNIX so double-check to ensure it's an exact match.

An alternative way to check is to review the `init.ora` file and see what the value is set to. Remember, even though it says one thing in the `init.ora` file, the value may be different because the value may have been changed after the database was started.

> **Values in the `init.ora` are only read at startup.**

You Get an Error Initializing the Profile – File Exists

Check the privileges on the file. The Oracle process owner needs write permission on the file.

No Message is Written To the Debug File

- ❑ Verify that your debug profile for the appropriate user is in fact enabled by using `DEBUG.STATUS()`.

- ❑ Verify that the Oracle process owner has write permission to the directory specified in the profile. It's true that, when the profile was initialized, the directory and file were valid but things might have changed since then.

- ❑ Verify that the Oracle process owner has write permission on the file itself. Again, things may have changed since the profile initialization.

- ❑ Verify that the directory is still a valid value of the `init.ora` parameter `UTL_FILE_DIR`.

Debug In-Production Code

Once you have completed the development process and want to move the application into production, you may well still have hundreds and hundreds of lines of debug. You want to avoid the overhead of calling DEBUG to maximize performance. While working through each message and removing them all will do the trick, there is an alternative solution. All you need do is modify the `F()` and `FA()` procedures, adding `return;` as the first line of each. This way, when either is called, they immediately return, doing no work whatsoever. It's true that there is still a bit of overhead with this method, but the benefit outweighs that overhead.

To test the timing of calls to `DEBUG.F()` you can use a simple PL/SQL procedure, such as the one shown below. In this case we default the test to perform 1000 `DEBUG.F()` calls, sending in 3 substitution variables for each call. We do that 20 times and then calculate the average time it took for 1000 calls:

```
create procedure debug_timer(
  p_test_cnt number default 20,
  p_iterations number default 1000 ) as
  --
  l_start timestamp;
  l_end timestamp;
  l_timer number := 0;
```

```
begin
   for i in 1 .. p_test_cnt loop
      l_start := current_timestamp;
      for j in 1 .. p_iterations loop
         debug.f( 'A %s C %s E %s G', 'B', 'D', 'F' );
      end loop;
      l_end := current_timestamp;
      l_timer := l_timer +
                 to_number( substr( l_end-l_start,
                            instr( l_end-l_start, ':', -1 )+1 ));

   end loop;
   dbms_output.put_line( 'In ' || p_test_cnt || ' tests ' );
   dbms_output.put_line( 'it took an average ' ||
                         l_timer/p_test_cnt   || ' seconds' ||
                         '/' || p_iterations || ' calls to f().');
end debug_timer;
```

Note that this procedure will only work in Oracle 9*i* and up. I use the new data-type **TIMESTAMP**, which measures sub second time, to a default precision of 6 decimal places.

Try It Out – Timing Debug Statements

1. Now let's run this procedure and see the results.

```
SQL> exec debug_timer
In 20 tests
it took an average 1.83848415 seconds/1000 calls to f().

PL/SQL procedure successfully completed.
```

As you can see, in this case it took on average 1.83 seconds to perform 1000 DEBUG.F() calls. Of course your results will vary depending on your processor.

2. Let's now run the same test against the modified version of DEBUG. All we do is add a return; as the first line of F() and FA() as shown below:

```
procedure fa(
   p_message in varchar2,
   p_args    in Argv default emptyDebugArgv ) is
begin
   return;
   debug_it( p_message, p_args );
end fa;

procedure f(
   p_message in varchar2,
   p_arg1    in varchar2 default null,
```

```
        p_arg2    in varchar2 default null,
        p_arg3    in varchar2 default null,
        p_arg4    in varchar2 default null,
        p_arg5    in varchar2 default null,
        p_arg6    in varchar2 default null,
        p_arg7    in varchar2 default null,
        p_arg8    in varchar2 default null,
        p_arg9    in varchar2 default null,
        p_arg10   in varchar2 default null ) is
    begin
        return;
        debug_it( p_message,
                argv( substr( p_arg1, 1, 4000 ),
                      substr( p_arg2, 1, 4000 ),
                      substr( p_arg3, 1, 4000 ),
                      substr( p_arg4, 1, 4000 ),
                      substr( p_arg5, 1, 4000 ),
                      substr( p_arg6, 1, 4000 ),
                      substr( p_arg7, 1, 4000 ),
                      substr( p_arg8, 1, 4000 ),
                      substr( p_arg9, 1, 4000 ),
                      substr( p_arg10, 1, 4000 ) ) );
    end f;
```

3. Now let's rerun the timing test, and look at the results:

```
SQL> exec debug_timer
In 20 tests
it took an average .04530185 seconds/1000 calls to f().

PL/SQL procedure successfully completed.
```

Forty-five thousandths of a second on average to execute 1000 calls to DEBUG.F() is not very much time. So it would seem that leaving the debug calls in your production application is not going to dramatically impair performance.

> Note that these figures are simply for comparison, and do not constitute absolute debug timing. The figures you get back in performing these tests will naturally vary depending upon how your system is configured.

A further benefit is that you can remove the return; from the two procedures and debug your production application at any time. We all know that errors come up in production applications that are difficult or impossible to reproduce in a development environment. Leaving the calls to DEBUG in your code gives you the ability to witness the error in real-time and more quickly track down and fix the problem.

Summary

In this chapter we have looked at the DEBUG utility, and seen how useful it is compared to DBMS_OUTPUT for debugging your code. We have looked at how the DEBUG application was built. We looked at what features we wished to implement, and used this to help design the schema and implement the package. We then looked at how to effectively use the utility in your development process.

The code presented in this chapter represents a 'cut-down model' of the full version of DEBUG, and copies of both routines will be available for download at www.apress.com. The full version may well prove useful to those of you who wish to enhance the version given here, to include features such as support for %#.#s formatting and increased header formatting options.

We hope that, by walking through this process, you will have learned a few tricks and techniques that you can use in your daily PL/SQL development.

Case Study 2 – Finding People

In this Case Study, we will review an application built to solve a problem we experienced at Oracle, involving employee contact information. While this may seem somewhat simple and rudimentary, there is more to it than mere code and SQL. You will find the application code itself is very easy to consume, reproduce and modify to fit your own data. What's more, you can change the source data for this application and apply the principles you learn in this case study to any number of other problems you might encounter in your own day-to-day operations.

Please note: all the code used in this case study is available to download from the Apress web site (http://www.apress.com/), in the code download for the book.

History

Back in the early 1990s, Oracle used to distribute an Employee Handbook every year. Amongst other things, the handbook had an employee directory that listed each employee, with their e-mail address and their phone number. When employees needed to communicate with each other, the Employee Handbook was their friend. Simply looking the people up in an alphabetical listing meant that you were 'connected'. There were a few problems with this model, however:

❑ The information wasn't complete. Yes all the employees were listed, but what if you wanted to know somebody's fax number? Or somebody's manager? Or the employees that reported to somebody? Or addresses? There was so much simple information that should have been included, but wasn't, in order to ensure that the book was small, paperback, and relatively easy to carry around.

❑ The information was likely to change. As soon as somebody moved from one office to another, a person was hired, or a person was fired, you were waiting for that information to be published in next year's Employee Handbook.

❑ Although the handbook was paperback and not all that large (a few hundred pages or so), carrying it around along with your laptop, paperwork, and other required gear while traveling was not very convenient.

Surely there was a better solution to getting phone numbers and information about the company's personnel? What we needed was a utility enabling us to quickly look up contact details of employees in the company, which could also be updated quickly when information changed.

PHONE

In the early to mid 1990's, Oracle Corporation had a number of UNIX e-mail servers, with each employee being given an operating system user account on one of them. This facilitated sharing of information between large numbers of employees. Manipulating it was our first attempt to provide the utility we knew we needed.

A database report was written that queried all the employees' names and phone numbers from the Human Resources database (since that had the most up-to-date information available). The data returned from the database report was written to a flat file that could then be used to search for employees' names. The database report would be run every night, collecting updated data and writing the file to the file system. This process took place on every e-mail server, so that the information was available to all our employees.

A UNIX shell script called `phone` was then written to search the file (using `grep`) for the search string passed to the script. The phone shell script was also placed on each e-mail server and public execution privileges given to any employee with a user account. Every employee now had access to the latest employee information using a simple interface that was very fast. Calling the `phone` script was as simple as follows:

```
$ phone sdillon
Sean M. Dillon, sdillon@us.oracle.com, (703)123-4567
```

PHONE pretty much eliminated the need to use the Employee Handbook for looking up phone numbers and e-mail addresses. The problem of carrying around the handbook while traveling or having outdated information had been solved.

Enabling the Information Age – PEOPLE

With the release of **Oracle Internet Server** (OIS) version 1.0 came **Oracle Web Agent** (OWA), a `cgi-bin` program that accepted a URL request from a web browser, and executed a PL/SQL procedure based on that URL. PL/SQL packages were supplied that wrote HTML text into a buffer that would be returned to the user's web browser once the procedure had finished executing. This model became popular very quickly, and people began writing dynamic PL/SQL-based web applications using OIS and OWA.

With this in mind, it was decided that we should take the file used in the PHONE application and web-enable the search. The web made this data even more accessible than the original PHONE application, letting users query the PHONE data from any web browser on any computer in the company. If e-mail servers were shut down for upgrades or enhancements, the web-based search was still available. Many employees didn't feel comfortable using a UNIX login, so they never used PHONE anyway. The web browser alternative was very attractive.

We wanted to extend the capabilities of the PHONE application, which meant that we had to draw up a specification for what we wanted our new application, named PEOPLE, to do. Our key targets were:

❏ To provide a wide range of employee information, such as name, phone number, e-mail address, hire date, line manager, and so on. This meant that the source file for the PHONE application was no use to us, and we would have to extract the information directly from the Human Resources database.

❏ To create a simple web-based search facility. Any employee should be able to type in a search string, and a search of the employee directory should return up to 50 results.

❏ To make this application as fast and scalable as possible. It was a sure bet that everyone in the company would want to use it as some stage, so it would have to be able to deal with the possibility of large volumes of requests.

The key premise here was that we should make the search engine fast. To achieve this, we had to come up with a solution that not only satisfied our functional requirements, but also met our performance needs. We used an iterative approach in coming up with this solution, as satisfying the functional requirements was easy... but meeting our performance needs was extremely difficult. We needed to know just how well or how poorly our approach would perform under pressure. We knew we had many thousands of users that could potentially call this application, many times throughout a business day. We didn't want to write an application that people didn't use because it was too slow or worse, broke under heavy loads.

The route we took was to implement a candidate solution, then test it to *destruction*. This meant that we wrote testing tools to simulate loads on the server that would emulate an operating environment under peak load conditions. When you write an application and test it at your desk, you are testing in solitude. Single-user tests rarely show performance problems because you typically have all the resources of your application and the database to yourself. When you run a complex query, and it takes one-fifth of a second to execute, is that good? Is it bad? Why? The answer is, it really depends. What are your requirements? How do you measure good versus bad? What happens if you do the same query four or five times in a row? How about one thousand times? What if one thousand users do the query at the same time? Ten thousand? What does it take to make the application fail? How many users can the application support, and what kind of response times can users expect to receive when there is this much of a load on the system?

These are the types of questions we asked ourselves for each and every solution we tried. Time and again, we found that our performance was unsatisfactory for one reason or another, and we had to go back to the design to change things around to get it to work faster, or smarter, or more efficiently. Once we had made the design changes, we would implement them and do it all over again. This was our iterative testing/development cycle. This was testing to destruction.

This application now receives 250,000 hits per day. That's about 3 hits per second. Since the application is international and our employees live around the world, this load is fairly constant throughout the day. Many people believe that once they have built a program that answers the question correctly, they are done. As long as the application 'does the right thing', tuning is left as an afterthought. The 'buy-bigger-hardware' approach is a common misunderstanding of tuning, and this crushes IT budgets around the world. People would rather add processing power than change a solution that works to improve its performance. This is the key to performance testing. This is a critical step in the life cycle of the product development approach.

Throughout this case study, we're going to look at why we made the decisions we made. We'll discuss not only how the application is implemented, but why doing it this way was best for satisfying our functional and performance requirements.

The Application

We've talked about this application quite a bit; let's get into the code. Even though the application is fairly simple, there are still a considerable number of moving parts that make up its infrastructure. There are DDL scripts to create objects, PL/SQL packages for interfacing with the application, and a number of other components to understand. In the course of this section, we'll review each of the following:

❑ The application schema

❑ The objects we require. These are the EMPLOYEES and FASTEMP tables

❑ Populating the staging tables

❑ The PL/SQL packages PPL_UTILITY and PEOPLE

❑ Adding the data to the application and maintaining it

We'll begin by taking a look at the creation of the schema that is necessary for the application.

Creating the Schema

We'll create a user called PPL that will be the owner of all the objects and code in our application (PPL is short for PEOPLE). We'll do this in the first part of a script that we'll call ppl_main.sql. This script will eventually encompass everything we need to do to get our application up and running. It will be our 'master installation script'.

In this part of the script, we use SQL*Plus to prompt the user for values that will be used in the installation. This allows us to personalize it by using variables, and have the user supply the values to those variables before the script executes. The variables we will ask for are as follows:

❑ Application user password. The PPL schema's password, which is whatever the user chooses to specify.

❑ Default tablespace. The application user's default tablespace (most likely USERS).

❑ Temporary tablespace. The application user's temporary tablespace (most likely TEMP).

❑ ORACLE_ADMIN user password. We need to be connected as a user with appropriate permissions for creating the application user account at the beginning of our process. ORACLE_ADMIN is the name of the user we showed you how to create in Chapter 2, to which we gave the DBA role and therefore appropriate permissions. You could also choose to give the SYS or SYSTEM password here, but you'll need to remember to give the correct username as necessary in the script too.

❑ Spool file. An audit of the entire installation will be stored in this spool file.

- ❏ Path. The path on the file system where the spool file will be created.

- ❏ Connect string. The database service name that the PPL user will need to supply when connecting to a database over a network, for example, if my database has a database service name of slapdb, this is what I would need to enter here. Yours will be different.

Try It Out – Master Installation Script 1

1. Let's get started then by placing the following SQL*Plus commands at the top of the ppl_main.sql file. When the file is executed from SQL*Plus these commands will prompt the values for the settings listed above.

```
PROMPT
PROMPT specify password for PPL as parameter 1:
DEFINE pass     = &1
PROMPT
PROMPT specify default tablespeace for PPL as parameter 2:
DEFINE tbs      = &2
PROMPT
PROMPT specify temporary tablespace for PPL as parameter 3:
DEFINE ttbs     = &3
PROMPT
PROMPT specify password for ORACLE_ADMIN as parameter 4:
DEFINE pass_sys = &4
PROMPT
PROMPT specify log path (WITH trailing slash) as parameter 5:
DEFINE path = &5
PROMPT
PROMPT specify connect string for PPL as parameter 6:
DEFINE connectstr = &6
PROMPT
```

2. Once we have accepted the parameters, we need to open a spool file so as to capture everything that happens during the installation. The spool file will record any messages in our scripts, errors we encounter, and the results of our installation actions. We add the appropriate commands to the script:

```
DEFINE spool_file = &path.ppl_main.log

SPOOL &spool_file
```

3. Now that we have set up SQL*Plus to spool to a file we can review later, we connect to the database as the ORACLE_ADMIN user and drop any existing PPL user with the cascade option to ensure all schema objects are deleted as well. This ensures that we create our schema from scratch every time we run the script.

Remember, you'll need to alter the ORACLE_ADMIN in the CONNECT command to the username of the account you wish to use for creating the application user.

```
CONNECT ORACLE_ADMIN/&pass_sys@&connectstr


Prompt ****** Dropping PPL User ....


DROP USER PPL CASCADE;
```

4. Now we can begin building the PPL schema and granting appropriate privileges. That's exactly what the next section of the ppl_main.sql script does:

```
Prompt ****** Creating PPL User and granting privileges ....
CREATE USER ppl IDENTIFIED BY &pass;


REM setup the user's tablespaces
ALTER USER ppl DEFAULT TABLESPACE &tbs
               QUOTA UNLIMITED ON &tbs;


ALTER USER ppl TEMPORARY TABLESPACE &ttbs;


REM grant the user the privileges needed for the application
GRANT create session
     , create table
     , create procedure
     , create view
     , create synonym
     , create public synonym
     , drop public synonym
     , alter session
TO ppl;
```

5. Now that the user is created, assigned to the appropriate tablespaces, and has been granted all the privileges needed to create and maintain the application, we can proceed to making the required objects for our application. There is just one more thing we need to do before continuing. We need to log in as the application user (PPL) so that all the objects we're going to create will belong to the right schema! We can do this by adding the following to the ppl_main.sql script:

```
CONNECT ppl/&pass@&connectstr
```

This takes the variable values provided by the user as a result of our prompting (the PPL user password and the connect string).

Creating the Objects

Over the next few sections, we are going to look at a number of tables, PL/SQL packages, and other supporting database objects for our database. Different classes of objects are found in different files, in order to help organize the source code for the application. We will use these files during the initial installation of the application (eventually our `ppl_main.sql` script will call each of them in turn), and for maintenance of the application over time. Let's begin by looking at the tables we will use.

In the first of our object files, we'll create two tables that will be used in the PEOPLE application:

❑ EMPLOYEES table. We **denormalize** all the tables from our human resources tables, in this case, the HR schema and place the data we might want to look at in this table. Denormalizing means that we copy all the data from the tables but do not maintain any dependencies. That way we are not required to join any tables to show an employee's row.

❑ FASTEMP table. This will be used when we query for employee records using the search string. We will put three columns in this table. The first column is the EMPLOYEE_ID of the employee. The second column, EMPDATA, will be the one used by the application to search for employee records. The last column will be a ROWID pointing to the employee's corresponding record in the EMPLOYEES table. In this way we can query this table using the EMPDATA column and find corresponding records in the EMPLOYEES table using the resulting ROWIDs.

Rationale for the Tables

The FASTEMP table is very small compared to the EMPLOYEES table. When I say small, I am referring to the columns contained in the table and not the number of rows, which should be equivalent. There is one row in the FASTEMP table for each row in the EMPLOYEES table. This table is used as a custom-built index on the EMPLOYEES table. Let's look at how this is done.

The EMPDATA column in the FASTEMP table is the key to searching for employees in our application. We want to allow users to search for employees based on their employee IDs, names, e-mail addresses, phone numbers, job titles, or departments. We'll concatenate the user's id, name, e-mail address, phone number, job title, and department name together (separated by slashes), and convert the entire string to upper-case. This results in records that look something like this:

```
ppl@SLAPDB.US.ORACLE.COM> select empdata from fastemp where rownum < 6;

EMPDATA
-----------------------------------------------------------------------
206/WILLIAM GIETZ/WGIETZ/PUBLIC ACCOUNTANT/ACCOUNTING
145/JOHN RUSSELL/JRUSSEL/SALES MANAGER/SALES
147/ALBERTO ERRAZURIZ/AERRAZUR/SALES MANAGER/SALES
146/KAREN PARTNERS/KPARTNER/SALES MANAGER/SALES
149/ELENI ZLOTKEY/EZLOTKEY/SALES MANAGER/SALES
```

When we query on the row, we'll convert the search string to upper-case (yes the query is case *in*sensitive) and wrap it with Oracle's wildcard character, %. This results in a query that looks something like this:

```
select rowid
  from fastemp
 where empdata like '%' || upper('some search string') || '%';
```

When we pass a search string such as `Manager`, the resulting WHERE clause looks like this:

```
where empdata like '%MANAGER%';
```

...which from our result set listed above would retrieve rows 2 through 5. This is because their EMPDATA columns include the word MANAGER in them. This would return four ROWID's that point to the EMPLOYEES table rows that match those employees' records.

You will probably be thinking that Oracle cannot use an index when it queries a table with a WHERE clause of LIKE '%SOMEVALUE%'. If you were thinking that, you're absolutely correct! Oracle will not use an index with a LIKE operator and the first character of the search value being a wildcard. This is because it will have no idea where in the index the first character is, and would have to full scan the index anyway. This too, we did by design. Instead of using a B-Tree index for these values, we use this type of query, ensuring the entire FASTEMP table is read into the buffer cache. Every query that comes after this one simply full scans every block in the FASTEMP table (which are already in memory) for the value. Once the resulting ROWID's are found, they are used to probe into the EMPLOYEES table for the full record of data.

Denormalization

By denormalizing the EMPLOYEES table, we eliminate the need for Oracle to perform joins to retrieve data from other tables. We can afford to denormalize the EMPLOYEES table because it is primarily a reporting table, only used for reading rows during the life of the application. We break some of the traditional relational database rules because, for our requirements, the rules do nothing but slow down our query. By querying a limited number of records from the EMPLOYEES table using ROWIDs, we guarantee we are retrieving the rows in the fastest manner possible.

Now that we have an understanding of why the tables are constructed the way they are, let's write the script that will create them in our database.

Try It Out – Build the PEOPLE Tables

We'll call this script `ppl_cre.sql`. It will create the EMPLOYEES table to hold all the employee personnel information and the FASTEMP table for querying. Later in this *Try It Out*, we'll also create another script called `ppl_cmnt.sql` that will place comments on our two tables.

1. In the first part of the script we'll create the EMPLOYEES table. This table is wide, which means it is responsible for holding a fully denormalized employee row, resulting in all the data you could ever want on an employee being held in a single record.

```
Prompt ******  Creating EMPLOYEES table ....


CREATE TABLE employees
    ( employee_id         NUMBER(6)
```

```
    CONSTRAINT          emp_employee_id_pk PRIMARY KEY
,   first_name          VARCHAR2(20)
,   last_name           VARCHAR2(25)
    CONSTRAINT          emp_last_name_nn NOT NULL
,   name_last_first     VARCHAR2(50)
    CONSTRAINT          emp_last_name_first_nn NOT NULL
,   full_name           VARCHAR2(50)
    CONSTRAINT          emp_full_name_nn NOT NULL
,   email               VARCHAR2(25)
    CONSTRAINT          emp_email_nn NOT NULL
,   phone_number        VARCHAR2(20)
,   hire_date           DATE
    CONSTRAINT          emp_hire_date_nn NOT NULL
,   direct_reports      NUMBER(6)
,   total_reports       NUMBER(6)
,   job_id              VARCHAR2(10)
,   job_title           VARCHAR2(35)
    CONSTRAINT          emp_job_nn NOT NULL
,   job_start_date      DATE
,   mgr_employee_id     NUMBER(6)
,   mgr_first_name      VARCHAR2(20)
,   mgr_last_name       VARCHAR2(25)
,   mgr_full_name       VARCHAR2(50)
,   mgr_job_title       VARCHAR2(35)
,   mgr_email           VARCHAR2(25)
,   mgr_direct_reports  NUMBER(6)
,   mgr_total_reports   NUMBER(6)
,   department_id       NUMBER(4)
,   department_name     VARCHAR2(30)
,   street_address      VARCHAR2(40)
,   postal_code         VARCHAR2(12)
,   city                VARCHAR2(30)
,   state_province      VARCHAR2(25)
,   country_name        VARCHAR2(40)
,   region_name         VARCHAR2(25)
,   CONSTRAINT          emp_email_uk UNIQUE (email)
) ;
```

2. Now we'll add the section of our `ppl_cre.sql` script that will build the `FASTEMP` table. This table holds all the data that can be searched, in upper-case, along with `ROWID`s for the `EMPLOYEES` table.

```
Prompt ****** Creating FASTEMP table ....
CREATE TABLE fastemp
    ( employee_id      NUMBER(9)
    , empdata          VARCHAR2(2000)
    , employees_rowid  ROWID
    ) ;
```

3. Once the tables are created, we write some comments on them to help keep a record of what the tables and the tables' columns are for. This new script should be saved (or downloaded) as `ppl_comnt.sql`,

```
COMMENT ON TABLE employees
IS 'This table holds ALL the employee personnel information from the HR schema.
This table is WIDE... It is responsible for holding a fully denormalized row from
the EMPLOYEES, LOCATIONS, DEPARTMENTS, REGIONS, COUNTRIES and JOBS table';

COMMENT ON COLUMN employees.direct_reports
IS 'This is the number of people that report DIRECTLY to this person in the
company. This information should be rolled up on a recurring basis.';

COMMENT ON COLUMN employees.total_reports
IS 'This is the TOTAL number of people that report to this person in the company,
whether it be directly or somewhere in a nested chain of command. This information
should be rolled up on a recurring basis.';

COMMENT ON TABLE fastemp
IS 'The FASTEMP table is created to hold the data that will be used to search for
employee records. This table is considered a TALL, SKINNY table as its sole
purpose is to provide summary data to search from and a pointer into the fully
denormalized EMPLOYEES table.';

COMMENT ON COLUMN fastemp.empdata
IS 'EMPDATA is the column that we will search on. This table will be rebuilt on a
recurring basis as well, so the search information is kept up-to-date. This column
is made up of a number of columns UPPER cased and delimited by /''s. The columns
included are: EMPLOYEE_ID, FULL_NAME, EMAIL and PHONE_NUMBER';

COMMIT;
```

Staging Tables

As a part of this application, we use local staging tables to localize data from production systems such as a corporate Human Resources application or a global employees database into our own database. This is useful for a number of purposes.

- ❑ It relieves the production system from any ongoing procedural access. Copying the tables (as we will discuss below) is just like performing a single query on the tables. This minimizes resource consumption on production systems.

- ❑ If we need to rebuild the tables again for any reason, we do not have to reconnect to production systems and cause further performance overhead.

- ❑ The data is all copied locally, that way we do not have to worry about using serialized access to the tables in case things change while we are loading our application tables.

For this case study, we are going to use the Human Resources (HR) schema from the Oracle 9*i* sample schemas. (For more information on the Oracle 9*i* Sample Schemas, see Chapter 4, *The New 9i Sample Schemas* and Appendix D, *Installing Sample Schemas*.) If you want to use this application for your own company or group of users, you may find that some of the columns we have chosen in this case study are not applicable to your particular data source. Don't hesitate to modify the table designs for the EMPLOYEES and FASTEMP tables in order to facilitate your own data requirements. Just make sure you try the methodology we have used throughout this case study for your performance requirements (remember, test to **destruction**!).

Populating the Staging Tables

The next step in our application installation scripts is to create and populate the staging tables. To accomplish this, we use the SQL*Plus COPY command. SQL*Plus COPY lets us do a single scan of each table, copying every record of data from a Human Resources application into our own staging tables. This has minimal impact on the Human Resources application, and gives us all the source data to work against locally.

One thing you will notice is that we don't create these tables before we perform the COPY command. When you copy a table in SQL*Plus, the resulting table will be created if it doesn't already exist. In the script we'll create, we use this methodology to create and populate all of the local staging tables from the HR tables on another database (in this case, we are simply connecting to the HR schema in the local database). As an example of this COPY command, the first table we will copy is the REGIONS table. The COPY command looks like this:

```
copy from hr/hr@slapdb replace regions_stage using select * from regions;
```

This syntax tells SQL*Plus to copy data from the HR schema in the database identified by SLAPDB. The data will be used to create a staging table named REGIONS_STAGE. The keyword replace tells us that if the table does not exists, the COPY command should create it first and populate it using the query in using SELECT * FROM REGIONS. If the table does exist in the user's schema (the user that executes the COPY command) then we drop it, before creating and populating it.

Try It Out – Populating the Staging Tables

Let's create the appropriate script to achieve this now, and call it `ppl_popul.sql`:

You'll need to substitute your own database name wherever SLAPDB is used in this script if you connect via a network. If your database is local, you don't need the @ and the connect string at all.

```
Prompt ******  Populating REGIONS_STAGE table ....
copy from hr/hr@slapdb replace regions_stage using select * from regions;


Prompt ******  Populating COUNTRIES_STAGE table ....
copy from hr/hr@slapdb replace countries_stage using select * from countries;


Prompt ******  Populating LOCATIONS_STAGE table ....
copy from hr/hr@slapdb replace locations_stage using select * from locations;


Prompt ******  Populating DEPARTMENTS_STAGE table ....
copy from hr/hr@slapdb replace departments_stage using select * from departments;


Prompt ******  Populating JOB_STAGE table ....
copy from hr/hr@slapdb replace jobs_stage using select * from jobs;


Prompt ******  Populating EMPLOYEES_STAGE table ....
copy from hr/hr@slapdb replace employees_stage using select employee_id,
first_name, last_name, email,
phone_number, hire_date, job_id, manager_id, department_id from employees;


Prompt ******  Populating JOB_HISTORY_STAGE table ....
copy from hr/hr@slapdb replace job_history_stage using select * from job_history;
```

How It Works

In most all of the SQL*Plus COPY commands above, we SELECT * FROM <TABLE_NAME> in order to copy the data from the production (source) system to our local staging tables. The one exception is the EMPLOYEES_STAGE table. The reason we avoid selecting all the columns is because we do not want to query the SALARY or COMMISSION_PCT columns. This information is sensitive, and our application is for public consumption ('public' meaning that anybody in the company who has access to the application can query all the data). We not only *should not* have access to that data, but if we did have access we *should avoid* copying it locally. Having it in more than one place on the network increases the risk of security breaches and disclosure of sensitive data.

PL/SQL APIs

Now it is time to create the two PL/SQL packages for our application that will perform the majority of our work.

❑ The PPL_UTILITY package will do processing for us during the installation and data population phases of our application. In PPL_UTILITY, we provide procedures for **scrubbing** the data.

❑ The PEOPLE package will have procedures for performing the employee searches and returning REF CURSORS to the data. PEOPLE will be granted to PUBLIC so any user in the database is able to perform employee searches. PPL_UTILITY, on the other hand, is reserved for our PPL schema's use, only.

The term scrubbing refers to the process of selecting data from the staging tables and inserting rows into our application tables. In the production application at Oracle, we extract data from four different systems, not just one Human Resources database. This scrubbing process is used to merge these four data sets together.

The majority of Human Resources systems are not as simple as the Oracle 9*i* sample schema, HR. In general, Human Resource systems have a large amount of historical data that can be used by reporting tools to analyze the company's employee data. In the case of the PEOPLE application, this data is useless. There is no reason to store this historical data locally, as the scope of the application does not encompass it.

In the PPL_UTILITY package, we simply use one procedure to denormalize the HR tables into the EMPLOYEES table and another to query the EMPLOYEES table and populate the FASTEMP table.

Try It Out – Creating the Utility Package

Let's look at how this process is done. We'll step through the rest of the PPL_UTILITY package and explain snippets of code as we go. All the snippets should be added to a script which we'll call ppl_util.sql, or you can download the entire script from the Apress web site.

1. The first part of our script is the PPL_UTILITY package specification:

```
Prompt ****** Creating PPL_UTILITY PACKAGE ....

create or replace package ppl_utility as


  procedure load_employee;

  procedure load_fastemp;


end ppl_utility;
/
show error
```

This is simple enough. There are two procedures in this package; we use the first procedure (LOAD_EMPLOYEE) to load the EMPLOYEE table with data from the staging tables, and the second procedure (LOAD_FASTEMP) to populate the FASTEMP table using concatenated data from the EMPLOYEE table.

2. Next we need to begin the package body declaration:

```
Prompt ****** Creating PPL_UTILITY PACKAGE BODY....
create or replace package body ppl_utility as
```

3. Then we add the first of the procedures in the package, LOAD_EMPLOYEE. This procedure is used to select the data from the staging tables and insert it into the EMPLOYEES table. In this procedure, we use an implicit cursor to query all the rows from the staging tables. In the body of the loop, we insert the values into the EMPLOYEES table:

```
/* This procedure is used to normalize data from the HR staging tables
   into the EMPLOYEES table. */
procedure load_employee
is
begin
  for i in ( select e.employee_id
               , e.first_name
               , e.last_name
               , decode( e.first_name, null, '', e.first_name || ' ' ) ||
                 e.last_name full_name
               , e.last_name || decode( e.first_name, null, '', ', ' ||
                 e.first_name ) name_last_first
               , e.email
               , e.phone_number
               , e.hire_date
               , e.job_id
               , e.manager_id mgr_employee_id
               , ( select count(*)
                     from employees_stage e2
                    where e2.manager_id = e.employee_id )
                 direct_reports
               , ( select count(*)
                     from employees_stage e3
                    connect by prior e3.manager_id = e3.employee_id
```

```
        start with e3.employee_id = e.employee_id )
    total_reports
, mgr.first_name mgr_first_name
, mgr.last_name mgr_last_name
, decode(mgr.first_name, null, '', mgr.first_name || ' ') ||
    mgr.last_name mgr_full_name
, mgr.email mgr_email
, mgr.phone_number mgr_phone_number
, mgr.hire_date mgr_hire_date
, mgr.job_id mgr_job_id
, j2.job_title mgr_job_title
, ( select decode(max(jh.end_date),null,e.hire_date,
                  max(jh.end_date)+1) job_start_date
      from job_history_stage jh
     where e.employee_id = jh.employee_id(+))
    job_start_date
, ( select count(*)
      from employees_stage mgr2
     where mgr2.manager_id = e.employee_id )
    mgr_direct_reports
, ( select count(*)
      from employees_stage mgr3
     connect by prior mgr3.manager_id = mgr3.employee_id
     start with mgr3.employee_id = e.employee_id )
    mgr_total_reports
, e.department_id
, d.department_name
, d.manager_id dept_manager_id
, d.location_id
, l.street_address
, l.postal_code
, l.city
, l.state_province
, l.country_id
, c.country_name
, c.region_id
```

```
                , r.region_name
                , j.job_title
          from employees_stage e
                , employees_stage mgr
                , departments_stage d
                , locations_stage l
                , countries_stage c
                , regions_stage r
                , jobs_stage j
                , jobs_stage j2
        where e.department_id = d.department_id(+)
          and e.manager_id = mgr.employee_id(+)
          and e.job_id = j.job_id(+)
          and d.location_id = l.location_id(+)
          and l.country_id = c.country_id(+)
          and c.region_id = r.region_id(+)
          and mgr.job_id = j2.job_id(+)
      ) loop
      insert into employees ( employee_id
                            , first_name
                            , last_name
                            , full_name
                            , name_last_first
                            , email
                            , hire_date
                            , job_title
                            , job_start_date
                            , phone_number
                            , direct_reports
                            , total_reports
                            , job_id
                            , mgr_employee_id
                            , mgr_first_name
                            , mgr_last_name
                            , mgr_full_name
                            , mgr_job_title
```

```
                             mgr_email
                           , mgr_direct_reports
                           , mgr_total_reports
                           , department_id
                           , department_name
                           , street_address
                           , postal_code
                           , city
                           , state_province
                           , country_name
                           , region_name )
        values ( i.employee_id
               , i.first_name
               , i.last_name
               , i.full_name
               , i.name_last_first
               , i.email
               , i.hire_date
               , i.job_title
               , i.job_start_date
               , i.phone_number
               , i.direct_reports
               , i.total_reports
               , i.job_id
               , i.mgr_employee_id
               , i.mgr_first_name
               , i.mgr_last_name
               , i.mgr_full_name
               , i.mgr_job_title
               , i.mgr_email
               , i.mgr_direct_reports
               , i.mgr_total_reports
               , i.department_id
               , i.department_name
               , i.street_address
               , i.postal_code
```

```
                      , i.city
                      , i.state_province
                      , i.country_name
                      , i.region_name );
          end loop;
      end load_employee;
```

4. The next procedure in the PPL_UTILITY package is LOAD_FASTEMP. This procedure, which is constructed in much the same way as the LOAD_EMPLOYEE procedure, is responsible for querying all the rows from the EMPLOYEES table and inserting them into the FASTEMP table. The only bit of code here that might need some explanation is the INSERT statement. In the VALUES clause of the INSERT INTO FASTEMP statement, we are concatenating the searchable columns together into the EMPDATA column of the FASTEMP table.

```
/* This procedure used to concatenate data from the EMPLOYEES table
   into the FASTEMP table */
procedure load_fastemp
is
begin
  for i in ( select rowid
                    , employee_id
                    , full_name
                    , email
                    , job_title
                    , department_name
             from employees
           ) loop
      insert into fastemp ( employee_id
                          , empdata
                          , employees_rowid )
      values ( i.employee_id
             , i.employee_id || '/' ||
               upper( i.full_name ) || '/' ||
               upper( i.email ) || '/' ||
               upper( i.job_title ) || '/' ||
               upper( i.department_name )
             , i.rowid );
  end loop;
end load_fastemp;
```

```
end ppl_utility;
/
show error
```

The SHOW ERROR statement at the end of the package will output any database errors that occur in the compilation of the PPL_UTILITY package.

The PEOPLE package will be used as the interface to this application. When a user wants to use the functionality offered in the PEOPLE application, they use this package. Let's walk through the PEOPLE PL/SQL package to get an understanding of how to build it and why we used this approach.

Try It Out – Creating the PEOPLE Package

Let's call the script we'll create here ppl_api.sql.

1. The first line is the CREATE OR REPLACE statement for the package:

```
Prompt ****** Creating PEOPLE Package ....
create or replace package people as
```

2. Next, we will declare a REF CURSOR type that can be used by users wanting to interface to these packages (for a reminder on REF CURSORs, check out Chapter 10, *PL/SQL*). A REF CURSOR provides a convenient way for developers writing PL/SQL to call this package and retrieve a set of records without having any access to the tables or knowing anything about how the records are retrieved. This gives us a way, as the application provider, to ensure that anybody that wants to query the data in our application tables will have to use this application as their interface.

```
type employees_ref_cursor_type is ref cursor return employees%rowtype;
```

3. Then we declare two functions: GET_EMPLOYEE() which retrieves a single employee record by providing a single EMPLOYEE_ID, and GET_EMPLOYEES() to retrieve a set of records by providing a search string:

```
function get_employee( p_employee_id in number )
  return employees_ref_cursor_type;

function get_employees( p_search in varchar2 )
  return employees_ref_cursor_type;

end people;
/
show error
```

841

4. Now that the package specification is created and complete, we can write the package body:

```
Prompt ****** Creating PEOPLE Package Body ....
create or replace package body people as
```

5. The first function in the package body we will implement is GET_EMPLOYEE(). This function is very simple. First, we declare a local REF CURSOR variable of type EMPLOYEES_REF_CURSOR_TYPE, which we declared in the package specification. In the body of the function, we open the REF CURSOR using a query from the EMPLOYEES table where the EMPLOYEE_ID equals the P_EMPLOYEE_ID argument passed to it. Either one or zero rows will be retrieved into the REF CURSOR, and then we return the REF CURSOR to the caller:

```
function get_employee( p_employee_id in number )
   return employees_ref_cursor_type
is
   l_emp employees_ref_cursor_type;
begin
   open l_emp for
     select *
       from employees
       where employee_id = p_employee_id;
   --
   return l_emp;
end get_employee;
```

6. The second function is GET_EMPLOYEES(). It is constructed in much the same way as the GET_EMPLOYEE function. A local REF CURSOR is declared and we open it using a query on the EMPLOYEES table. The primary difference in this function compared to GET_EMPLOYEE is the structure of the query. Instead of doing a single record query using the EMPLOYEE_ID column, we are going to do a query that selects many rows from the EMPLOYEES table by ROWID. In order to find out which ROWIDs we should retrieve, we perform a nested query on the FASTEMP table that selects all the ROWIDs where the EMPDATA column is like the P_SEARCH parameter (the search string).

```
function get_employees( p_search in varchar2 )
   return employees_ref_cursor_type
is
   l_emps employees_ref_cursor_type;
begin
   open l_emps for
     select *
       from employees
       where rowid in ( select fe.employees_rowid
                          from fastemp fe
                          where fe.empdata like upper( '%' || p_search || '%' )
                          and rownum < 52 )
       order by employee_id;
   return l_emps;
end get_employees;
```

One other detail you will notice about the query is that we constrain the query to 51 records. One of our application requirements states that if a user provides a search string that returns more than 50 records, they must provide a more specific search string to constrain the number of rows selected to 50 or less. The reason why we return 51 rows instead of only 50 is to provide a 'poor-man's' row counter. If a user saw 50 records returned to the screen, they would not know if there were any more records to be shown. If they retrieve 51 records, we still only show them 50, but because there is a remaining record we know there are more than 50 records available, and can instruct the user appropriately.

7. Finally, we end the package body with the END PEOPLE code and use the SHOW ERROR SQL*Plus command to display any errors that Oracle may encounter. After the SHOW ERROR, we GRANT EXECUTE privilege on the PEOPLE package to the PUBLIC role. This means any user can call this application using the PEOPLE package. We then drop any public synonym named PEOPLE and recreate it for the package we just made.

```
end people;
/
show error

grant execute on people to public;
drop public synonym people;
create public synonym people for people;
```

Adding the Data To the Application

Now that we have reviewed the procedural code, we can talk about the ongoing maintenance of the application. Once the EMPLOYEES and FASTEMP tables are created, they need to be populated. Our PPL_UTILITY package is created for that sole purpose, so we will use a script to call this PL/SQL package to load up the EMPLOYEES and FASTEMP tables.

Try It Out – Populate the Tables

To do this we place the following SQL*Plus commands in a script called ppl_load.sql:

```
Prompt ****** Populating EMPLOYEES and FASTEMP tables from staging tables..

truncate table employees;
truncate table fastemp;

begin
  ppl_utility.load_employee;
  ppl_utility.load_fastemp;
end;
/

COMMIT;
```

This script truncates our application tables and then calls the two PL/SQL procedures in the PPL_UTILITY package. The two procedures are used for loading the application with data from the staging tables. Whenever we change or update the staging tables, we should rerun this script in order to repopulate the EMPLOYEES and FASTEMP tables.

Maintaining the Data

If you remember our original PHONE application, which was nothing more than a shell script on an e-mail server, we reran the database report nightly in order to have the most up-to-date information available the next day. We'll continue this trend in the PEOPLE application, by using the operating system job scheduling systems AT (on Windows platforms) and CRON (on UNIX platforms).

In the AT and/or CRON jobs, we use the ppl_popul.sql script to SQL*Plus COPY the original Human Resources tables to the application's staging tables, again. This will give us the latest and greatest information directly from the HR schema. These staging tables will then be used to reload the EMPLOYEES and FASTEMP tables using the ppl_load.sql script that we just created above.

For the Human Resources system, we perform this 'reload' every night. New employees are getting hired all the time; people get married and their names change; people move to a new office or decide to start working out of a home office instead of the office complex where they once worked. All these changes and more will happen on a daily basis at the company, and each of these people will wonder why their data isn't current if our PEOPLE application does not reflect the up-to-date information within a day or two of the change.

Let's look at how we can set up nightly updates on both a Windows system and a UNIX system.

Try It Out – Repopulating the Tables Nightly – Windows

To schedule this process on a Windows machine, we make a command file that performs the reload, a SQL*Plus script to perform the entire reload, and an AT command to schedule the command file to be run.

1. The command file that is responsible for executing this SQL*Plus script once connected to the database is called ppl_reload.cmd (the -S in the SQL*Plus command line is for 'silent mode'. SQL*Plus will login as PPL/PPL, run the reload.sql script, and never spool any data):

```
sqlplus -S ppl/ppl @reload.sql
```

2. The SQL*Plus script for this process is named ppl_reload.sql. It calls the necessary scripts for repopulating the tables:

```
@ppl_popul.sql
@ppl_load.sql
exit
```

3. And the AT command you can issue to schedule the job is as follows:

```
at 00:00 /every:M,T,W,T,F,Su ppl_reload.cmd
```

For users using Windows XP, the AT command is considered a thing of the past and a new GUI interface has been provided to schedule tasks to be run. This new GUI is called Scheduled Tasks. You can still use AT commands in Windows XP, but they will show up in the Scheduled Tasks folder after they have been specified.

Try It Out – Repopulating the Tables Nightly – UNIX

The files are much the same on a Unix machine. We can use the same `ppl_reload.sql` script as above. We can also reuse the `ppl_reload.cmd` file by just naming it `ppl_reload` and granting execute permissions on the file. The only notable difference is the way you submit a job to the `cron`. We need to make a `crontab` entry for the user that owns the `ppl_reload` script. An example of your user's `crontab` entry might look like this:

```
00 0 * * * /u01/app/oracle/Oracle 9i/sqlstuff/reload
```

This would mean that on the 00'th minute of the day, the 0'th hour of the day, every day of the month, every month of the year, every day of the week, we run the script located at the fully qualified filename `/u01/app/oracle/Oracle 9i/sqlstuff/reload`.

Using this model, you can update your tables entirely every few hours, every day, as often as you'd like. Using the operating system is necessary because we need to invoke the SQL*Plus COPY command in the `ppl_popul.sql` script, and that must happen from SQL*Plus rather than from within the database.

Master Installation Script

At this point we have created all the objects that make up the application, populated our tables with staging data, scrubbed the staging data to make our denormalized employee records and created a process to schedule the recurring data loading process on our operating system. What we can do now is finish off the installation script we began earlier so that it can be used to create the entire application. Earlier in the chapter, we made a script called `ppl_main.sql`, in which we included a number of SQL commands in order to create the user, assign the user's tablespaces, and grant the appropriate privileges to the user to create and maintain the application. We'll use that script as our baseline, and add SQL*Plus commands at the bottom of that file. The commands will invoke the other files involved in the creation of the application. This means we will be able to run the `ppl_main.sql` script to create the entire application with minimal installation instructions.

Try It Out – Master Installation Script 2

The last line of our `ppl_main.sql` script should presently read as follows:

```
CONNECT ppl/&pass@&connectstr
```

1. We'll simply append the following SQL*Plus commands to the end of this file to invoke the other files we have built so far:

```
-- create tables and constraints

@ppl_cre

-- add comments to tables and columns

@ppl_comnt

-- populate staging tables
```

```
@ppl_popul

-- create procedural objects

@ppl_util
@ppl_api

-- load application tables

@ppl_load.sql
```

2. The very end of our master installation script is where we switch the spool to the log file off:

```
spool off
```

When this entire script is run, it will prompt the user for the answers to a number of questions. These answers are passed as variable values at appropriate times to the SQL*Plus commands and other PL/SQL scripts that are invoked as we move further down. All activity is logged in the log file that is created at the location specified by the user, so that it can be reviewed in order to find any errors or issues that may have been encountered throughout the installation.

User Interface

The PL/SQL API we built in the PEOPLE package is one of the most versatile ways to build applications in the database. By offering a REF CURSOR that will return a set of records, we have effectively encapsulated access to our application's base tables and ensured any access to the data will come through our PL/SQL packages. By offering these PL/SQL packages to the PUBLIC role in the database, we make it available to a number of types of applications. In this case study, we'll build a simple SQL*Plus interface that we can either use directly from SQL*Plus itself or from our operating system command line. Let's take a look at the steps involved.

SQL*Plus/Command Line Interface

In this section, we will write a couple of scripts that access the PEOPLE package; the first is a high-level script that allows us to search employee records, and the second is a detailed employee lookup that shows all the data for an employee. The scripts will be available to be run by any valid database user, because the PEOPLE package is granted to PUBLIC.

Try It Out – Employee Search

The first script is called people.sql, and is used to do a search for employees whose data matches the specified search string.

1. Firstly, we use a few SQL*Plus commands to ensure the data returned from our PL/SQL block will be spooled to the display, check the LINESIZE to make sure it can handle the output data on single lines, turn off verify so replacement variables are not displayed, and turn off feedback to suppress the PL/SQL procedure successfully completed message we receive after executing a PL/SQL block.

```
set serveroutput on size 100000
set linesize 100
set verify off
set feedback off
```

2. We then declare some variables to use in our script. L_EMPS_REFCUR will be used to contain the results of the PEOPLE.GET_EMPLOYEES() function call. L_EMP is a row of the REF CURSOR type and will be used to fetch and display the records from the REF CURSOR. L_INDEX is used as a counter later in the script.

```
declare
   l_emps_refcur people.employees_ref_cursor_type;
   l_emp         l_emps_refcur%rowtype;
   l_index       pls_integer := 1;
begin
```

3. Next, we call PEOPLE.GET_EMPLOYEES() and pass the parameter &1 which is the first parameter passed into the script (you will see how the parameter is passed below). Once the function has been executed and L_EMPS_REFCUR is assigned to the results, we fetch the first record from the REF CURSOR into the L_EMP row variable.

```
l_emps_refcur := people.get_employees('&1');
fetch l_emps_refcur into l_emp;
```

4. Then we have two DBMS_OUTPUT.PUT_LINE calls that output the headings we need for the output to come:

```
dbms_output.put_line(
   lpad('|  Id', 6) || ' ' || rpad('Name', 18) || ' ' ||
   rpad('Number', 20) || ' ' || rpad('Email', 12) || ' ' ||
   rpad('Title', 30) );
dbms_output.put_line(
   rpad('|-', 5, '-') || ' ' || rpad('-', 18, '-') || ' ' ||
   rpad('-', 20, '-') || ' ' || rpad('-', 12, '-') || ' ' ||
   rpad('-', 30, '-') );
```

5. Now we have output the headers, we will enter a loop to output the rows returned from the PEOPLE.GET_EMPLOYEES() function. As soon as we evaluate the cursor attribute %FOUND and there are no rows remaining in the cursor, this loop will exit. If PEOPLE.GET_EMPLOYEES() returns no rows, this will happen before we actually enter the loop.

Inside the loop, we use LPAD and RPAD to format the output to ensure each row lines up in columns. We increment L_INDEX on each iteration of the loop, and then check the value of L_INDEX to see if we get more than 50 rows in our return (remember what was said earlier about the GET_EMPLOYEES() function, it will return up to 51 rows to tell calling applications there are more than 50 results for the search string provided). If there are more than 50 rows, a message is displayed informing the user that their search string needs to be further constrained.

```
      while l_emps_refcur%found loop
        dbms_output.put_line(
          lpad('| ' || l_emp.employee_id, 6) || ' ' || rpad(l_emp.name_last_first, 18)
|| ' ' ||
          rpad(l_emp.phone_number, 20) || ' ' || rpad(l_emp.email, 12) || ' ' ||
          rpad(l_emp.job_title, 30) );

        l_index := l_index + 1;
        if l_index = 51 then
          dbms_output.put_line('');
          dbms_output.put_line('| There were more than 50 rows returned, you might
want to try to further ' ||
                               'constrain your search string.');
          exit;
        end if;
        fetch l_emps_refcur into l_emp;
      end loop;
```

6. Once the loop is complete, we will check the %ROWCOUNT. If it is zero, we will output a message indicating that there were no rows found. If we don't do this, the script will output column headers for a result set, but no rows, and the user will have no message to indicate that their search was unsuccessful.

```
      if l_emps_refcur%rowcount = 0 then
        dbms_output.put_line('');
        dbms_output.put_line('No rows found.');
      end if;
```

7. Once we have checked the %ROWCOUNT on the REF CURSOR, we can close it.

```
      close l_emps_refcur;
    end;
    /
    set feedback on
    set verify on
    exit
```

At the end of the script, we set the SQL*Plus values back to their defaults and exit SQL*Plus. The EXIT statement may be removed in cases where users want to call this script from SQL*Plus and not a command line. In this case, the SQL*Plus environment will be restored once the script has completed its execution.

Now that we have a SQL*Plus script that does the query and displays the results, we can write a command file or shell script (depending on your operating system) to log in to SQL*Plus for us, execute this script, and disconnect from SQL*Plus so the user is effectively shielded from having to use a database tool.

848

Try It Out – PEOPLE Search Command File

1. For Windows users, copy the following text into a file named `people.cmd` on your operating system:

```
sqlplus -S scott/tiger@slapdb @people.sql %1
```

For UNIX users, copy the following text into a file named `people` on your operating system:

```
sqlplus -S scott/tiger@slapdb @people.sql $1
```

UNIX users will also have to grant execute to the file (this particular `chmod` command allows any user to execute the `people` script):

```
chmod a+x people
```

This script assumes a number of things, however:

❑ You have a user named SCOTT with the password TIGER in your database. If you do not have this user in your database, you can replace `scott/tiger` with a user/password that does exist.

❑ You have the `sqlplus` command in your PATH environment variable in your UNIX session or your CMD prompt (on Windows). If `sqlplus` is not in your PATH, this script will fail because it can't find `it`.

❑ The database is local. If the database is on the network somewhere or you connect to it using Oracle Net Services, you will have to modify the login information with a connect string (ie `scott/tiger@<your connect string>`).

2. Once this script is created, you can run it from your command prompt as follows:

```
$ people john
| Id Name                Number              Email        Title             | 110
|---- ------------------- ------------------- ------------ -----------------|
Chen, John          515.124.4269        JCHEN        Accountant
| 139 Seo, John          650.121.2019        JSEO         Stock Clerk
| 145 Russell, John      011.44.1344.429268  JRUSSEL      Sales Manager
| 179 Johnson, Charles   011.44.1644.429262  CJOHNSON     Sales Representative
```

Some security-minded system and database administrators might have heart failure at the thought of putting a valid database username and password in a shell script on the operating system, though. If you wanted to make the PEOPLE search available to you when you were logged into SQL*Plus (thereby eliminating the need to hardcode a username/password), you can put the `people.sql` script in your $SQLPATH directory. If you do this, you also need to remove the last line of the script (EXIT) or every time you call it from SQL*Plus your session will end. In SQL*Plus we would do the same search like this:

```
SQL> @people john
| Id Name                Number                Email           Title
|---- ------------------- --------------------- --------------  ------------------
| 110 Chen, John          515.124.4269          JCHEN           Accountant
| 139 Seo, John           650.121.2019          JSEO            Stock Clerk
| 145 Russell, John       011.44.1344.429268    JRUSSEL         Sales Manager
| 179 Johnson, Charles    011.44.1644.429262    CJOHNSON        Sales Representative
```

Now that we can find the overview information for employees in our PEOPLE application, let's create another script for getting the detailed information for an employee.

Try It Out – Individual Employee Details

The primary key in our application is the EMPLOYEE_ID, so we'll pass the EMPLOYEE_ID value to a script called people_detail.sql in order to retrieve all the information about a particular person. In this script, we pass the EMPLOYEE_ID of the employee you want more information about, and the script calls the PEOPLE.GET_EMPLOYEE() function to get all the information about that employee. Using DBMS_OUTPUT, the information in the cursor is displayed in a vertical format for easy readability.

1. As with the people.sql script, we prepare the SQL*Plus environment for outputting data to the display:

```
set serveroutput on size 100000
set linesize 100
set verify off
set feedback off
```

2. Now we declare the L_EMPS_REFCUR variable in this script along with a %ROWTYPE variable of the L_EMPS_REFCUR variable type. We also declare a L_EMP_ID in this script to hold the parameter passed in for the employee's ID.

```
declare
  l_emps_refcur people.employees_ref_cursor_type;
  l_emp         l_emps_refcur%rowtype;.
  l_emp_id      number;
```

3. Next we declare a local procedure in the header of this script to send data to the display. This procedure quite simply does a DBMS_OUTPUT.PUT_LINE of the name and value passed in as parameters to the procedure.

```
procedure put( p_name in varchar2, p_value in varchar2 )
is
begin
  dbms_output.put_line( '|' || lpad( p_name, 23 ) || ' : ' || p_value );
end put;
```

4. We cast the first parameter to a number value into our L_EMP_ID variable. This is an important step because if the user passes in a character value such as A or something that will not cast to a number, a VALUE_ERROR exception will be thrown. We catch this exception toward the end of the script.

```
begin
  l_emp_id := to_number('&1');
```

5. Next, we call PEOPLE.GET_EMPLOYEE and pass the employee ID to the function. This retrieves the record for that employee (if there is one) and the next line fetches that record into the l_emp row variable.

```
l_emps_refcur := people.get_employee(l_emp_id);
fetch l_emps_refcur into l_emp;
```

6. In the following IF...THEN...ELSE statement, we see if a row was returned from the GET_EMPLOYEE function or not. If no row was returned, we output an appropriate message. If a row was returned, we call the local PUT procedure to output the employee's details:

```
if l_emps_refcur%rowcount = 0 then
  dbms_output.put_line('');
  dbms_output.put_line('No rows found for employee id ' || l_emp_id);
else
  put( 'Employee ID', l_emp.employee_id );
  put( 'Name', l_emp.full_name );
  put( 'E-Mail', l_emp.email );
  put( 'Phone Number', l_emp.phone_number );
  put( 'Hire Date', to_char( l_emp.hire_date, 'DD Month YYYY' ) );
  put( 'Direct Reports', l_emp.direct_reports );
  put( 'Total Reports', l_emp.total_reports );
  put( 'Job ID', l_emp.job_id );
  put( 'Job Title', l_emp.job_title );
  put( 'Job Start Date', to_char(l_emp.job_start_date, 'DD Month YYYY' ));
  put( 'Department ID', l_emp.department_id );
  put( 'Department Name', l_emp.department_name );
  put( 'Street Address', l_emp.street_address );
  put( 'Postal Code', l_emp.postal_code );
  put( 'City', l_emp.city );
  put( 'State Province', l_emp.state_province );
  put( 'Country Name', l_emp.country_name );
  put( 'Region Name', l_emp.region_name );
  put( '-', '-' );
  put( 'Manager Employee Id', l_emp.mgr_employee_id );
  put( 'Manager Name', l_emp.mgr_full_name );
  put( 'Manager Title', l_emp.mgr_job_title );
  put( 'Manager E-Mail', l_emp.mgr_email );
  put( 'Manager Direct Reports', l_emp.mgr_direct_reports );
  put( 'Manager Total Reports', l_emp.mgr_total_reports );
end if;
```

7. Now that the appropriate data has been output to the calling user, we close the REF CURSOR. After the REF CURSOR is closed, we have an exception block. Earlier in the code, we had to assign a command-line parameter to a number value. If an invalid number is passed in as the command-line parameter, the VALUE_ERROR exception will be thrown. In this exception block, we catch the VALUE_ERROR exception and display an appropriate message:

```
    close l_emps_refcur;
exception
  when value_error then
    dbms_output.put_line('You have entered an invalid number.');
end;
/

set feedback on
set verify on
exit
```

8. Calling the `people_detail.sql` script from the command line or SQL*Plus requires the same process as for `people.sql`. Here is the Windows command file (`people_detail.cmd`):

```
sqlplus -S scott/tiger @people_detail.sql %1
```

and its UNIX shell script equivalent (`people_detail`):

```
sqlplus -S scott/tiger @people_detail.sql $1
```

Try It Out – Searching for a Person's Details

Now as an example of using these two scripts together, we'll look for somebody named David.

1. First we do a search for all the employees who have the string `Dav` in their records:

```
$ people Dav
| Id Name               Number               Email        Title
|---- ------------------ -------------------- ------------ ------------------------
-------
| 105 Austin, David      590.423.4569         DAUSTIN      Programmer
| 142 Davies, Curtis     650.121.2994         CDAVIES      Stock Clerk
| 151 Bernstein, David   011.44.1344.345268   DBERNSTE     Sales Representative
| 165 Lee, David         011.44.1346.529268   DLEE         Sales Representative
```

2. We can then see the ID number of the one we're interested in (in this case David Lee), and use that as the search string in `people-detail`:

```
$ people_detail 165
|         Employee ID : 165
|                Name : David Lee
|              E-Mail : DLEE
|        Phone Number : 011.44.1346.529268
|           Hire Date : 23 February  2000
|      Direct Reports : 0
```

```
|            Total Reports : 3
|                   Job ID : SA_REP
|                Job Title : Sales Representative
|           Job Start Date : 23 February  2000
|            Department ID : 80
|          Department Name : Sales
|           Street Address : Magdalen Centre, The Oxford Science Park
|              Postal Code : OX9 9ZB
|                     City : Oxford
|           State Province : Oxford
|             Country Name : United Kingdom
|              Region Name : Europe
|                        - : -
|      Manager Employee Id : 147
|             Manager Name : Alberto Errazuriz
|            Manager Title : Sales Manager
|           Manager E-Mail : AERRAZUR
| Manager Direct Reports : 0
|  Manager Total Reports : 3
```

Summary

This case study has taken a look at the approach that a development team at Oracle Corporation took to building a useful and worldwide employee search. We used the database for as much of the functionality as possible, and kept the code and logic as close to the data as we could. Access to the application is filtered through a PL/SQL stored procedure and therefore the functionality is highly reusable. As you can see in the SQL*Plus scripts above, PL/SQL stored procedures were used to perform the queries necessary to retrieve the desired data. Using these PL/SQL stored procedures, we could embed the API calls in a PL/SQL Web Toolkit application or call these stored procedures using Java and JDBC, as in a Java Server Page, a Java Servlet, or a Java application on somebody's desktop.

The case study illustrates how the team achieved its two goals of speed and scalability. It is worth noting here that the application has grown in scope and capability over time. From its simple beginning it grew so as to incorporate a page for querying the PEOPLE repository for employees, a page that showed the results of that search, and an organization chart that showed who an employee reported to (their manager) and all of the employees that reported to them.

This shows the importance of design, since the original design allowed for increasing functionality, as the popularity of the application increased. Providing a fast, easy-to-use application ended up with this application's server being one of the top ten network traffic generating servers within the whole corporation!

Using the design ideas discussed throughout this case study, you can build applications to use in your organizations to help share information with your peers in a fast, efficient, useful manner. Remember, all the code included in this case study as well as other application ideas (web-based interfaces in PL/SQL and Java) will be available for download from the Apress web site.

©2000 by Lauren Ruth Wiener (http://www.verbing.com

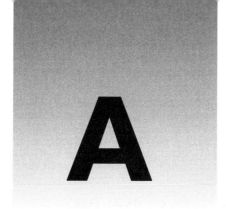

SQL Function Reference

This appendix outlines various functions you will encounter in the Oracle database, the syntax used to call the function, and an example or two for each to help provide context to the explanation.

Many of the examples use a table called DUAL to query against, so we'll explain that first, and then go on to look at:

- ❑ NUMBER Functions
- ❑ DATETIME Functions
- ❑ CHARACTER Functions
- ❑ CONVERSION Functions
- ❑ AGGREGATION Functions

DUAL

There is a table defined in the Oracle data dictionary named DUAL. This table is provided so a developer performing a query or writing a function can guarantee a known result. The table has one column named DUMMY of type VARCHAR(1), and there is one row in the table with the value X.

```
SQL> select * from dual;

DUMMY
----------
X
```

You might be asking yourself how one column, one row, and one table equate to guaranteeing a known result. Well, if you select a constant value (such as a string literal) or an expression from any table, the result will be returned once for each row of the result set. In the case of DUAL, this means that we always return one result:

```
SQL> select 'BLAH'
  2    from dual;

'BLA
----
BLAH

1 row selected.
```

As you can see, when we select a string literal value from the table, the literal value is returned once.

You can use the DUAL table to do math, using SQL queries to return one value. We'll see many examples of how this is done in this appendix.

> **DUAL is used extensively by Oracle, so care should be taken to never insert, update, or delete from DUAL. Violating this rule is very dangerous for your database, as there are many internal operations that Oracle performs which are dependent on DUAL. User-written PL/SQL and stored queries may also be dependent upon DUAL, and errors or wrong answers may be uncovered if the DUAL table is modified.**

NUMBER Functions

Oracle has a variety of functions to process and manipulate number values in the database. The following table lists some of the more common number functions available in the Oracle database:

ABS()	MOD()	SIGN()
CEIL()	POWER()	TRUNC()
FLOOR()	ROUND()	

ABS()

The ABS() function is used to get the absolute value of the parameter passed to the function.

```
number_value := ABS( number_value )
```

```
SQL> select abs(13.4)
  2    from dual
  3  /

ABS(13.4)
----------
     13.4
```

```
SQL> select abs(-4.5)
  2     from dual
  3  /

ABS(-4.5)
----------
       4.5

SQL> select abs(-70 * 415) "Using an expression"
  2     from dual
  3  /

Using an expression
-------------------
              29050
```

CEIL()

This function returns the next smallest integer value greater than or equal to the parameter passed in.

```
number_value := CEIL( number_value )
```

```
SQL> select ceil( 10.00000000001 )
  2     from dual;

CEIL(10.00000000001)
--------------------
                  11

SQL> select ceil( -1.99 )
  2     from dual
  3  /

CEIL(-1.99)
-----------
         -1
```

FLOOR()

The opposite of CEIL(), FLOOR() returns the largest integer value less than or equal to the parameter passed in.

```
number_value := FLOOR( number_value )
```

```
SQL> select floor( 10.00000000001 )
  2     from dual
  3  /
```

```
FLOOR(10.00000000001)
---------------------
                   10

SQL>
SQL> select floor( -1.99 )
  2     from dual
  3   /

FLOOR(-1.99)
------------
          -2
```

MOD()

MOD() returns the remainder of a division operation.

```
number_value := MOD( numerator, denominator )
```

```
SQL> select mod( 11,2 )
  2     from dual
  3   /

 MOD(11,2)
----------
         1

SQL> select mod( 150.12, 2.6 )
  2     from dual
  3   /

MOD(150.12,2.6)
---------------
           1.92
```

POWER()

POWER() returns the first number, raised to the power of the second number.

```
number_value := POWER( base_number, to_the_power_of )
```

```
SQL> select power( 10, 5 )
  2     from dual
  3   /

POWER(10,5)
-----------
     100000
```

```
SQL> select power( -5, 3 ) "Using Negatives"
  2     from dual
  3  /

Using Negatives
---------------
          -125

SQL> select power( 5.2, 2.7 ) "With Reals"
  2     from dual
  3  /

With Reals
----------
85.7450441
```

ROUND()

The ROUND() function rounds a number up either to the left or right of a decimal point, depending on the sign of the second parameter. The second parameter must be an integer. If the second parameter is negative, the first number is rounded up to that many digits to the left of the decimal point. A positive second value means the first number is rounded up to that many digits to the right of the decimal.

```
number_value := ROUND(base_number [, integer_indicating_number_of_digits ])
```

```
SQL> select round( 12345.67890 )
  2     from dual
  3  /

ROUND(12345.67890)
------------------
             12346

SQL> select round( 12345.67890, 2 )
  2     from dual
  3  /

ROUND(12345.67890,2)
--------------------
            12345.68

SQL> select round( 12345.67890, -2 )
  2     from dual
  3  /

ROUND(12345.67890,-2)
--------------------
               12300
```

SIGN()

`SIGN()` takes one parameter, and returns either a –1, 0, or 1 depending on whether the parameter is less than zero (-1), zero (0), or greater than zero (1).

```
number_value := SIGN( number_value )
```

```
SQL> select sign( 123 )
  2     from dual
  3  /


 SIGN(123)
----------
         1

SQL> select sign( 100 - ( 50 * 2 ) ) "Using expressions"
  2     from dual
  3  /

Using expressions
-----------------
                0

SQL> select sign( 123 * -1 + 122) "Using expressions"
  2     from dual
  3  /

Using expressions
-----------------
               -1
```

TRUNC()

The `TRUNC()` function drops all digits a number up either to the left or right of a decimal point, depending on the sign of the second parameter. The second parameter must be an integer. If the second parameter is negative, the first number is truncated to that many digits left of the decimal point. A positive second value means the first number is truncated to that many digits right of the decimal.

```
number_value := TRUNC(base_number [, integer_indicating_number_of_digits ])
```

```
SQL> select trunc( 12345.67890 )
  2     from dual
  3  /

TRUNC(12345.67890)
------------------
             12345

SQL> select trunc( 12345.67890, 2 )
```

```
 2    from dual
 3  /

TRUNC(12345.67890,2)
--------------------
          12345.67

SQL> select trunc( 12345.67890, -2 )
 2    from dual
 3  /

TRUNC(12345.67890,-2)
--------------------
             12300
```

DATETIME Functions

In order to process and manipulate dates, Oracle provides a number of functions that operate on the various date-related data types in Oracle.

ADD_MONTHS()	LAST_DAY()	NUMTOYMINTERVAL()
CURRENT_DATE()	LOCALTIMESTAMP()	ROUND()
CURRENT_TIMESTAMP()	MONTHS_BETWEEN()	SYSTIMESTAMP()
DBTIMEZONE()	NEXT_DAY()	SYSDATE()
EXTRACT()	NUMTODSINTERVAL()	TRUNC()

ADD_MONTHS()

This function is used to add or subtract a number of months to/from a date value.

```
date_value := ADD_MONTHS( date_value, number_of_months )
```

If today is 3rd November 2001 then:

```
SQL> select add_months( sysdate, 12 ) "Next Year"
 2    from dual
 3  /

Next Year
---------
03-NOV-02

SQL> select add_months( sysdate, -12 ) "Last Year"
 2    from dual
```

```
  3  /

Last Year
---------
03-NOV-00
```

CURRENT_DATE()

The CURRENT_DATE() function returns the current date in the current session's time zone (which can be altered).

```
date_value := CURRENT_DATE
```

```
SQL> column sessiontimezone for a15
SQL> select sessiontimezone, current_date
  2    from dual
  3  /

SESSIONTIMEZONE CURRENT_DATE
--------------- --------------------
-05:00          03-nov-2001 09:03:56

SQL> alter session set time_zone = '-08:00'
  2  /

Session altered.

SQL> select sessiontimezone, current_date
  2    from dual
  3  /

SESSIONTIMEZONE CURRENT_DATE
--------------- --------------------
-08:00          03-nov-2001 06:05:16
```

CURRENT_TIMESTAMP()

The CURRENT_TIMESTAMP() function returns the current date in a TIMESTAMP WITH TIME ZONE data type in the current session's time zone (which can be altered). The precision of the TIMESTAMP value returned can optionally be specified as a parameter to the CURRENT_TIMESTAMP() function.

```
timestamp_with_time_zone_value := CURRENT_TIMESTAMP([timestamp_precision])
```

```
SQL> column sessiontimezone for a15
SQL> col current_timestamp format a36
SQL> select sessiontimezone, current_timestamp
  2    from dual
  3  /
```

```
SESSIONTIMEZONE CURRENT_TIMESTAMP
--------------- -------------------------------------
-08:00          03-NOV-01 06.10.45.000000 AM -08:00

SQL> alter session set time_zone = '-11:00'
  2  /

Session altered.

SQL> select sessiontimezone, current_timestamp(3) current_timestamp
  2     from dual
  3  /

SESSIONTIMEZONE CURRENT_TIMESTAMP
--------------- -------------------------------------
-11:00          03-NOV-01 03.11.53.000 AM -11:00
```

DBTIMEZONE()

This function returns the time zone that was specified in the CREATE DATABASE statement, or the most recent ALTER SYSTEM SET TIMEZONE statement.

```
varchar_value := DBTIMEZONE
```

```
SQL> select DBTIMEZONE
  2     from dual
  3  /

DBTIME
------
-05:00
```

EXTRACT()

The EXTRACT() function is used to find out the value of a field of a datetime or interval value. There are a variety of date fields available to the EXTRACT() function, including:

SECOND	YEAR
MINUTE	TIMEZONE_MINUTE
HOUR	TIMEZONE_HOUR
DAY	TIMEZONE_REGION
MONTH	TIMEZONE_ABBR

```
date_value := EXTRACT( date_field FROM [ datetime_value | interval_value ])
```

```
SQL> select extract( month from sysdate ) "This Month"
  2    from dual
  3  /

This Month
----------
        11

SQL> select extract( year from add_months(sysdate,36) ) "3 Years Out"
  2    from dual
  3  /

3 Years Out
-----------
       2004
```

LAST_DAY()

The LAST_DAY() function returns the date of the last day of the month containing the date parameter.

```
date_value := LAST_DAY( date_value )
```

```
SQL> select last_day( date'2000-02-01' ) "Leap Yr?"
  2    from dual
  3  /

Leap Yr?
----------
29-FEB-00

SQL> select last_day( sysdate ) "Last day of this month"
  2    from dual
  3  /

Last day
---------
30-NOV-01
```

LOCALTIMESTAMP()

This function returns the date and time in the current session's time zone in a TIMESTAMP value.

```
timestamp_value := LOCALTIMESTAMP
```

```
SQL> column localtimestamp format a28
SQL> select localtimestamp
  2    from dual
  3  /
```

```
LOCALTIMESTAMP
----------------------------
03-NOV-01 10.40.20.000001 AM

SQL> select localtimestamp, current_timestamp
  2    from dual
  3  /

LOCALTIMESTAMP                    CURRENT_TIMESTAMP
----------------------------      ------------------------------------
03-NOV-01 10.42.30.000000 AM 03-NOV-01 10.42.30.000000 AM -05:00

SQL> alter session set time_zone = '-08:00'
  2  /

Session altered.

SQL> select localtimestamp,
  2          to_char(sysdate, 'DD-MON-YY HH:MI:SS AM') "SYSDATE"
  3    from dual
  4  /

LOCALTIMESTAMP                    SYSDATE
----------------------------      ---------------------
03-NOV-01 08.02.10.000000 AM 03-NOV-01 11:02:10 AM.
```

MONTHS_BETWEEN()

The MONTHS_BETWEEN() function determines the number of months between two dates. The value returned is a real number indicating the whole months and a fraction of the month between the two dates. If the first date is earlier in time than the second date, the value returned is a negative number.

```
number_value := MONTHS_BETWEEN( date_value, date_value )
```

```
SQL> select months_between( sysdate, date'1971-05-18' )
  2    from dual
  3  /

MONTHS_BETWEEN(SYSDATE,DATE'1971-05-18')
----------------------------------------
                              365.534266

SQL> select months_between( sysdate, date'2001-01-01' )
  2    from dual
  3  /

MONTHS_BETWEEN(SYSDATE,DATE'2001-01-01')
----------------------------------------
                              10.0826695
```

NEXT_DAY()

Given a datetime value, the NEXT_DAY() function returns a date value of the first occurrence of the day indicated in the second parameter (a character string of the name of the day that should be returned).

```
date_value := NEXT_DAY( date_value, day_of_the_week )
```

```
SQL> select next_day( date'2001-09-11', 'SUNDAY' )
  2    from dual
  3  /

NEXT_DAY(
---------
16-SEP-01

SQL> select next_day( date'2002-01-01', 'FRI' )
  2    from dual
  3  /

NEXT_DAY(
---------
04-JAN-02
```

NUMTODSINTERVAL()

NUMTODSINTERVAL() accepts a number and a character value representing which part of the INTERVAL DAY TO SECOND should be populated by the function. Valid character values are SECOND, MINUTE, HOUR, and DAY.

```
interval_day_to_second_value := NUMTODSINTERVAL( number, type_of_interval )
```

```
SQL> column current_timestamp format a38
SQL> select current_timestamp
  2    from dual
  3  /

CURRENT_TIMESTAMP
--------------------------------------
03-NOV-01 01.05.57.000001 PM -08:00

SQL> select current_timestamp + numtodsinterval( 2, 'hour' ) current_timestamp
  2    from dual
  3  /

CURRENT_TIMESTAMP
--------------------------------------
03-NOV-01 03.06.25.000001000 PM -08:00
```

NUMTOYMINTERVAL()

NUMTOYMINTERVAL() accepts a number and a character value representing which part of the INTERVAL YEAR TO MONTH should be populated by the function. Valid character values are YEAR and MONTH.

```
interval_year_to_month_value := NUMTODSINTERVAL( number, type_of_interval )
```

```
SQL> select current_timestamp
  2     from dual
  3  /

CURRENT_TIMESTAMP
-------------------------------------
03-NOV-01 01.10.48.000001 PM -08:00

SQL> select current_timestamp + numtoyminterval( 3, 'month' ) current_timestamp
  2     from dual
  3  /

CURRENT_TIMESTAMP
-------------------------------------
03-FEB-02 01.11.22.000000000 PM -08:00
```

ROUND()

ROUND returns a datetime value formatted to the next highest part of a date, optionally indicated by a character-based format parameter. (Valid formats can be found at the end of this section.)

```
date_value := ROUND( date_value [, format_mask ] )
```

```
SQL> select round( sysdate )
  2     from dual
  3  /

ROUND(SYS
---------
04-NOV-01

SQL> select round( sysdate, 'year' )
  2     from dual
  3  /

ROUND(SYS
---------
01-JAN-02

SQL> select round( sysdate, 'month' )
  2     from dual
```

```
  3   /

ROUND(SYS
---------
01-NOV-01

SQL> select round( sysdate, 'q' ) "Quarter"
  2    from dual
  3   /

Quarter
---------
01-OCT-01
```

SYSDATE()

This function returns the current date and time in a DATE value, based on the database's time zone.

```
date_value := SYSDATE
```

```
SQL> select sysdate
  2    from dual
  3   /

SYSDATE
---------
03-NOV-01

SQL> select to_char(sysdate,'DD-MON-YY HH24:MI:SS' ) "Right Now"
  2    from dual
  3   /

Right Now
-----------------
03-NOV-01 16:44:50
```

SYSTIMESTAMP()

This function returns the current time and date in a TIMESTAMP WITH TIME ZONE value, based on the time zone of the database.

```
timestamp_with_time_zone_value := SYSTIMESTAMP
```

```
SQL> select systimestamp
  2    from dual
  3   /

SYSTIMESTAMP
-------------------------------------
03-NOV-01 04.46.24.000000 PM -05:00
```

TRUNC()

The TRUNC() function returns a DATE value truncated to the value optionally specified in the format mask parameter. For more information about format masks, see the section below entitled '*Date Format Models for ROUND() and TRUNC()*'.

```
date_value := TRUNC( date_value [, format_mask ] )
```

```
SQL> select trunc( sysdate )
  2     from dual
  3   /

TRUNC(SYS
---------
03-NOV-01

SQL> select to_char( trunc( sysdate, 'HH' ),
  2                  'DD-MON-YY HH24:MI:SS' ) "The Current Hour"
  3     from dual
  4   /

The Current Hour
------------------
03-NOV-01 16:00:00
```

Date Format Models for ROUND() and TRUNC()

The following format masks are available for use in the date-related ROUND() and TRUNC() functions:

❏ Year: YYYY, YYY, YY, Y, YEAR

❏ Quarter: Q

❏ Month: MONTH, MON, MM, RM

❏ Day: DDD, DD, J

❏ Starting day of the week: DAY, DY, D

❏ Hour: HH, HH12, HH24

❏ Minute: MI

Some rules regarding the various dimensions of the date field when used with ROUND():

❏ Years round up on July 1.

❏ Quarters round up on the 16th day of the second month in the quarter.

CHARACTER Functions

Oracle provides plenty of functions for working with string values in SQL and PL/SQL. The following table lists all those functions that are described below:

CHR()	LPAD()	TRANSLATE()
INITCAP()	REPLACE()	TRIM()
INSTR()	RPAD()	UPPER()
LENGTH()	SOUNDEX()	
LOWER()	SUBSTR()	

CHR()

The CHR() function is used for retrieving a character in the database character set, or the national character set identified by the binary number parameter. This is especially useful for characters that cannot be identified using a keyboard. In order to use the national character set, you may optionally use the USING NCHAR_CS clause.

```
character_value := CHR( number_value [ USING NCHAR_CS ] )
```

```
SQL> select chr(71)||chr(114)||chr(111)||chr(111)||chr(118)||chr(121) "Cool!"
  2      from dual
  3  /

Cool!
------
Groovy
```

INITCAP()

The INITCAP() function is for making the first word in each word of the character string passed to the function upper case, and the rest of the letters lower case.

```
character_value := INITCAP( character_value )
```

```
SQL> select initcap('THESE WORDS will be INITcapped')
  2      from dual
  3  /

INITCAP('THESEWORDSWILLBEINITC
------------------------------
These Words Will Be Initcapped

SQL> select initcap( table_name )
```

```
  2     from user_tables
  3  /

INITCAP(TABLE_NAME)
------------------------------
Bonus
Casepartyaddress
Courses
Dept
Emp
Employees
Salgrade
Subjects

8 rows selected.
```

INSTR()

INSTR() is useful when you are trying to determine the numeric position of a particular search string within a character string, or iterating through a document looking for multiple instances of a character string. In the syntax below, you will see you can tell Oracle to look for the *n*th instance of a particular search string, instead of simply the first iteration. You can also give Oracle a position from which to begin its search.

```
numeric_value := INSTR( character_value, search_string
                         [, start_position [, occurrence ] ] )
```

```
SQL> select instr( 'Where is the fourth letter E in this sentence?', 'e', 1, 4 )
  2     from dual
  3  /

INSTR('WHEREISTHEFOURTHLETTEREINTHISSENTENCE?','E',1,4)
-------------------------------------------------------
                                                     22
```

LENGTH()

Passing a character string to the LENGTH() function returns the number of characters in the string.

```
number_value := LENGTH( character_value )
```

```
SQL> select ename, length( ename )
  2     from emp
  3  /

ENAME       LENGTH(ENAME)
----------  -------------
SMITH                   5
```

```
ALLEN              5
WARD               4
JONES              5
MARTIN             6
BLAKE              5
CLARK              5
SCOTT              5
KING               4
TURNER             6
ADAMS              5
JAMES              5
FORD               4
MILLER             6

14 rows selected.
```

LOWER()

Passing a character string to the LOWER() function causes every character in the string to be converted to lower case.

```
character_value := LOWER( character_value )
```

```
SQL> select lower( table_name )
  2     from user_tables
  3  /

LOWER(TABLE_NAME)
----------------------------
bonus
casepartyaddress
courses
dept
emp
employees
salgrade
subjects

8 rows selected.
```

LPAD()

The LPAD() function takes the first character-based argument, and pads out the left-hand side for n number of characters (the second parameter) with either spaces or characters in the optional character-based third parameter.

```
character_value := LPAD( character_value, number_of_characters_to_pad
                        [, characters_to_pad_with ] )
```

```
SQL> select lpad( '*', 5, '*' )
  2      from dual
  3  /

LPAD(
-----
*****


SQL> column empname format a15
SQL> select lpad( '.', 2*level, '.' ) || e.ename empname,
  2          d.dname, e.job
  3    from emp e, dept d
  4   where e.deptno = d.deptno
  5   start with e.mgr is null
  6   connect by prior e.empno = e.mgr
  7  /

EMPNAME          DNAME          JOB
---------------  -------------- ---------
..KING           ACCOUNTING     PRESIDENT
....JONES        RESEARCH       MANAGER
......SCOTT      RESEARCH       ANALYST
........ADAMS    RESEARCH       CLERK
......FORD       RESEARCH       ANALYST
........SMITH    RESEARCH       CLERK
....CLARK        ACCOUNTING     MANAGER
......MILLER     ACCOUNTING     CLERK
....BLAKE        SALES          MANAGER
......ALLEN      SALES          SALESMAN
......WARD       SALES          SALESMAN
......JAMES      SALES          CLERK
......TURNER     SALES          SALESMAN
......MARTIN     SALES          SALESMAN

14 rows selected.
```

LTRIM()

The LTRIM() function trims leading spaces, or a designated character, off the front of a character string.

```
character_value := LTRIM( character_value [, character_to_trim ] )
```

```
SQL> select '"' || ltrim( '    Some String' ) || '"' "A String"
  2      from dual
  3  /

A String
-------------
"Some String"
```

REPLACE()

The REPLACE() function allows you to replace a sequence of characters with a different sequence of characters. The third parameter, the replacement value, is optional. Not passing a replacement value will simply strip the search string from the original string.

```
character_value := REPLACE( character_value,
                            search_string [, replacement_value ] )
```

```
SQL> select replace( 'Oracle is great!', 'great', 'awesome' )
  2     from dual
  3  /

REPLACE('ORACLEISG
------------------
Oracle is awesome!
```

RPAD()

The RPAD() function takes the first character-based argument, and pads out the right-hand side for n number of characters (the second parameter) with either spaces or characters defined in the optional (character-based) third parameter.

```
character_value := RPAD( character_value, number_of_characters_to_pad
                         [, characters_to_pad_with ] )
```

```
SQL> select rpad( '*', 5, '*' )
  2     from dual
  3  /

RPAD(
-----
*****

SQL> select rpad( ename, 10, ' ' ) || '(' || job || ')' "Responsibilities"
  2     from emp
  3     order by ename
  4  /

Responsibilities
--------------------
ADAMS      (CLERK)
ALLEN      (SALESMAN)
BLAKE      (MANAGER)
CLARK      (MANAGER)
FORD       (ANALYST)
JAMES      (CLERK)
JONES      (MANAGER)
KING       (PRESIDENT)
```

```
MARTIN      (SALESMAN)
MILLER      (CLERK)
SCOTT       (ANALYST)
SMITH       (CLERK)
TURNER      (SALESMAN)
WARD        (SALESMAN)

14 rows selected.
```

RTRIM()

The RTRIM() function trims trailing spaces, or a designated character, off the end of a character string.

```
character_value := RTRIM( character_value [, character_to_trim ] )
```

```
SQL> select '"' || rtrim( 'Some String      ' ) || '"' "A String"
  2     from dual
  3   /

A String
-------------
"Some String"
```

SOUNDEX()

This function returns a character string that represents the way a word or character string 'sounds'. This function can then be applied to two character strings that are not spelt the same, but 'sound the same'.

```
character_phonetic_representation := SOUNDEX( character_value )
```

```
SQL> select e.employee_id, e.last_name, e2.employee_id, e2.last_name
  2     from employees e, employees e2
  3    where e.employee_id != e2.employee_id
  4      and soundex( e.last_name ) = soundex( e2.last_name )
  5   /
```

EMPLOYEE_ID	LAST_NAME	EMPLOYEE_ID	LAST_NAME
156	King	100	King
153	Olsen	132	Olson
154	Cambrault	148	Cambrault
132	Olson	153	Olsen
148	Cambrault	154	Cambrault
100	King	156	King
161	Sewall	157	Sully
194	McCain	158	McEwen
171	Smith	159	Smith
157	Sully	161	Sewall

```
          159 Smith                    171 Smith
          180 Taylor                   176 Taylor
          199 Grant                    178 Grant
          176 Taylor                   180 Taylor
          192 Bell                     185 Bull
          206 Gietz                    190 Gates
          185 Bull                     192 Bell
          158 McEwen                   194 McCain
          178 Grant                    199 Grant
          190 Gates                    206 Gietz

      20 rows selected.
```

SUBSTR()

SUBSTR() is used to extract a piece of a character string. Parameters include the source string to extract from, the position where Oracle should begin extracting, and an optional length parameter. The position parameter can be positive or negative. A negative position parameter indicates to count back from the end of the string for that many characters, rather than counting forward from the beginning of the string.

```
character_value := SUBSTR( character_string, position [, length ] )
```

```
SQL> select substr( '1234567890', 5 )
  2     from dual
  3   /

SUBSTR
------
567890
```

TRANSLATE()

The TRANSLATE() function modifies a character string by converting all those characters in the search string with the corresponding characters in the translation string. If the search string has no corresponding value in the translation string parameter, NULL is used to replace that character in the result. If NULL is passed as the search string, the return value is NULL.

```
character_value := TRANSLATE( character_value, search_string,
                                    translation_string )
```

```
SQL> select translate('1910 Oracle Way',
  2
'1234567890ABCDEFGHIJKLMNOPQRSTUVWXYZabcdefghijklmnopqrstuvwxyz',
  3                    '1234567890') "Number Portion Only"
  4     from dual
  5   /
```

```
Number
------
1910

SQL> select length(
  2            translate('how many consonants are there?',
  3                      'bcdfghjklmnpqrstvwxzaeiouy? ',
  4                      'bcdfghjklmnpqrstvwxz')
  5          ) "# of consonants"
  6    from dual
  7  /

# of consonants
---------------
             15
```

TRIM()

The TRIM() function trims leading and/or trailing characters from the beginning and/or end of a character string.

```
character_value := TRIM( [ { { LEADING | TRAILING | BOTH }
                         [character_to_trim ] |
                          character_to_trim } FROM ] character_value )
```

```
SQL> select '"' || trim( ' ' from '    This is a string    ' ) || '"' "Result"
  2    from dual
  3  /

Result
------------------
"This is a string"

SQL> select trim( trailing ' ' from 'This is a string    ' ) "Result"
  2    from dual
  3  /

Result
----------------
This is a string
```

UPPER()

The UPPER() function is used to convert all the characters in a string to upper case.

```
character_value := UPPER( character_value )
```

```
SQL> connect hr/hr
SQL> select department_name, upper( department_name )
  2    from departments
  3    where rownum < 11
  4    order by department_name
  5  /

DEPARTMENT_NAME                    UPPER(DEPARTMENT_NAME)
------------------------------     ------------------------------
Administration                     ADMINISTRATION
Executive                          EXECUTIVE
Finance                            FINANCE
Human Resources                    HUMAN RESOURCES
IT                                 IT
Marketing                          MARKETING
Public Relations                   PUBLIC RELATIONS
Purchasing                         PURCHASING
Sales                              SALES
Shipping                           SHIPPING

10 rows selected.
```

CONVERSION Functions

Oracle provides plenty of functions for working with string values in SQL and PL/SQL.

CAST()	TO_NCLOB()	TO_TIMESTAMP()
CHARTOROWID()	TO_DATE()	TO_TIMESTAMP_TZ()
TO_CHAR()	TO_DSINTERVAL()	TO_YMINTERVAL()
TO_NCHAR()	TO_LOB()	TRANSLATE ... USING()
TO_CLOB()	TO_NUMBER()	

CAST()

The CAST() function converts a value of one data type into a value of another data type. Oracle is very good about performing this functionality for you for standard scalar types, but this is especially useful for collection types. Used with the MULTISET() function, collection objects can be constructed from queries.

```
return_value := CAST( [ expression | subquery | MULTISET ( subquery ) ] AS type )
```

```
SQL> create type vc2tab as table of varchar2(4000)
  2  /
Type created.
```

```
SQL> declare
  2    l_enames vc2tab;
  3  begin
  4    select cast( multiset ( select ename from emp ) as vc2tab )
  5      into l_enames
  6      from dual;
  7
  8    for i in 1 .. l_enames.count loop
  9      dbms_output.put_line(l_enames(i));
 10    end loop;
 11  end;
 12  /
SMITH
ALLEN
WARD
JONES
  . . .
JAMES
FORD
MILLER

PL/SQL procedure successfully completed.
```

CHARTOROWID()

This function is for creating a ROWID value from a character-based representation of a ROWID.

```
rowid_value := CHARTOROWID( character_value )
```

```
SQL> select empno, ename, job, hiredate
  2    from emp
  3    where rowid = chartorowid('AAAHqXAABAAAR74AAI')
  4  /

    EMPNO ENAME      JOB       HIREDATE
---------- ---------- --------- ---------
     7839 KING       PRESIDENT 17-NOV-81
```

TO_CHAR()

There are three types of TO_CHAR() functions.

TO_CHAR(character)

The character-based TO_CHAR() function is for transforming a CLOB, NCLOB, or NCHAR value into the database character set.

```
character_value := TO_CHAR( clob_value | nclob_value | nchar_value )
```

```
SQL> create table xmldata(
  2     xmldoc clob )
  3  /

Table created.

SQL> insert into xmldata
  2  select dbms_xmlquery.getxml('select * from emp')
  3     from dual
  4  /

1 row created.

SQL> select to_char( xmldoc )
  2     from xmldata
  3  /

TO_CHAR(XMLDOC)
-----------------------------------------------------------
<?xml version = '1.0'?>
<ROWSET>
   <ROW num="1">
      <EMPNO>7369</EMPNO>
      <ENAME>SMITH</ENAME>
      <JOB>CLERK</JOB>
      <MGR>7902</MGR>
      <HIREDATE>12/17/1980 0:0:0</HIREDATE>
      <SAL>800</SAL>
      <DEPTNO>20</DEPTNO>
   </ROW>
   <ROW num="2">
      <EMPNO>7499</EMPNO>
      <ENAME>ALLEN</ENAME>
      <JOB>SALESMAN</JOB>
      <MGR>7698</MGR>
      <HIREDATE>2/20/1981 0:0:0</HIREDATE>
      <SAL>1600</SAL>
      <COMM>300</COMM>
      <DEPTNO>30</DEPTNO>
   </ROW>

. . .

   <ROW num="14">
      <EMPNO>7934</EMPNO>
      <ENAME>MILLER</ENAME>
      <JOB>CLERK</JOB>
      <MGR>7782</MGR>
      <HIREDATE>1/23/1982 0:0:0</HIREDATE>
      <SAL>1300</SAL>
      <DEPTNO>10</DEPTNO>
   </ROW>
</ROWSET>
```

TO_CHAR(*datetime*)

The datetime-based TO_CHAR() function is for transforming a DATETIME value into a VARCHAR2 value, optionally using a specified date format. (Date formatting options can be found at the end of the *Conversion Functions* section.)

```
character_value := TO_CHAR( datetime_value [, date_format ] )
```

```
SQL> select to_char( sysdate, 'DD/MM/YY HH24:MI:SS' ) "Right Now"
  2    from dual
  3  /

Right Now
-----------------
04/11/01 19:28:31

SQL> select to_char( hiredate, 'Day Mon, YYYY' )
  2    from emp
  3    where empno = 7839
  4  /

TO_CHAR(HIREDATE,'D
-------------------
Tuesday   Nov, 1981
```

TO_CHAR(*number*)

The number-based TO_CHAR() function is for transforming a numeric value into a VARCHAR2 value. (Number formatting options can be found at the end of the *Conversion Functions* section.)

```
character_value := TO_CHAR( number_value [, number_format ] )
```

```
SQL> select ename, to_char( sal, '$9,999.99' ) "Salary"
  2    from emp
  3  /

ENAME      Salary
---------- ----------
SMITH         $800.00
ALLEN       $1,600.00
WARD        $1,250.00
JONES       $2,975.00
MARTIN      $1,250.00
BLAKE       $2,850.00
CLARK       $2,450.00
SCOTT       $3,000.00
KING        $5,000.00
TURNER      $1,500.00
ADAMS       $1,100.00
JAMES         $950.00
FORD        $3,000.00
MILLER      $1,300.00

14 rows selected.
```

TO_NCHAR()

TO_NCHAR() provides the same functionality as the TO_CHAR function. There are three flavors, TO_NCHAR(character), TO_NCHAR(datetime), and TO_NCHAR(number). The only difference is that the return values are in the database's national character set. See the TO_CHAR() function above for syntax and examples.

TO_CLOB()

The TO_CLOB() function transforms either an NCLOB value or other character-based data types (VARCHAR2, VARCHAR2, CHAR, NCHAR) to CLOB values.

```
clob_value := TO_CLOB( character_value )
```

```
SQL> create table xmldata(
  2     xmldoc clob )
  3  /

Table created.

SQL> insert into xmldata values
  2  ( to_clob( '<?xml version="1.0"?>
  3  <ROWSET>
  4     <ROW num="1">
  5        <EMPNO>7369</EMPNO>
  6        <ENAME>SMITH</ENAME>
  7        <JOB>CLERK</JOB>
  8        <MGR>7902</MGR>
  9        <HIREDATE>12/17/1980 0:0:0</HIREDATE>
 10        <SAL>800</SAL>
 11        <DEPTNO>20</DEPTNO>
 12     </ROW>
 13  </ROWSET>' ) )
 14  /

1 row created.
```

TO_NCLOB()

TO_NCLOB() provides the same functionality as the TO_CLOB() function. The only difference is that the return values are in the database's national character set. See the TO_CLOB() function above for syntax and examples.

TO_DATE()

The TO_DATE() function is for converting a character string to its date equivalent. A date format string can be provided to tell Oracle how to interpret the character string. (Date formatting options can be found at the end of the *Conversion Functions* section.)

```
date_value := TO_DATE( character_value [, format_string ] )
```

```
SQL> create table author_log(
  2      activity clob,
  3      completed date
  4  )
  5  /

Table created.

SQL> insert into author_log values (
  2      'Began SQL Functions appendix',
  3      to_date( '04-NOV-2001 08:00', 'DD-MON-YYYY HH24:MI' )
  4  )
  5  /

1 row created.
```

TO_DSINTERVAL()

This function creates an INTERVAL DAY TO SECOND value.

```
interval_day_to_second_value := TO_DSINTERVAL( character_value )
```

```
SQL> alter session set nls_date_format = 'DD-MON-YYYY HH24:MI:SS';

Session altered.

SQL> select sysdate
  2      from dual
  3  /

SYSDATE
--------------------
11-NOV-2001 10:58:13

SQL> select sysdate - to_dsinterval( '1 00:00:00' ) "US Marines
Birthday"
  2      from dual
  3  /

US Marines Birthday
--------------------
10-NOV-2001 10:58:13
```

TO_LOB()

The TO_LOB() function is used for converting LONG and LONG RAW values to CLOBs and BLOBs, respectively. The function can only be used in a subquery of an INSERT statement.

```
INSERT INTO table ( clob_or_blob_column )
SELECT TO_LOB( long_or_long_raw_column )
   FROM table
```

```
SQL> create table old_log(
  2      activity long,
  3      completed date
  4  )
  5  /

Table created.

SQL> insert into old_log values (
  2      'Completed chapter 1', sysdate - 60 )
  3  /

1 row created.

SQL> insert into old_log values (
  2      'Completed chapter 2', sysdate - 30 )
  3  /

1 row created.

SQL> create table author_log(
  2      activity clob,
  3      completed date
  4  )
  5  /

Table created.

SQL> insert into author_log
  2  select to_lob( activity ), completed
  3      from old_log
  4  /

2 rows created.
```

TO_NUMBER()

The TO_NUMBER() function is used to convert a character value to a number value.

```
number_value := TO_NUMBER( character_value )
```

```
SQL> select to_number( '15' )
  2      from dual
  3  /

TO_NUMBER('15')
```

```
    ---------------
               15
```

TO_TIMESTAMP()

This function creates a TIMESTAMP value.

```
timestamp_value := TO_TIMESTAMP( character_value )
```

```
SQL> select to_timestamp( '2001-NOV-11 08:00:00', 'YYYY-MON-DD
HH:MI:SS' )
  2      from dual
  3    /

TO_TIMESTAMP('2001-NOV-1108:00:00','YYYY-MON-DDHH:MI:SS')
-----------------------------------------------------------------------
-----
11-NOV-01 08.00.00.000000000 AM
```

TO_TIMESTAMP_TZ()

This function creates a TIMESTAMP WITH TIME ZONE value.

```
timestamp_with_time_zone_value := TO_TIMESTAMP_TZ( character_value )
```

```
SQL> select to_timestamp_tz('2001-NOV-11 08:00:00 -05:00',
  2                          'YYYY-MON-DD HH:MI:SS TZH:TZM') "TS w/ TZ"
  3      from dual
  4    /

TS w/ TZ
-----------------------------------------------------------------------
-----
11-NOV-01 08.00.00.000000000 AM -05:00
```

TO_YMINTERVAL()

This function creates an INTERVAL YEAR TO MONTH value.

```
interval_year_to_month_value := TO_YMINTERVAL( character_value )
```

```
SQL> declare
  2      l_hiredate timestamp := to_timestamp('1996-11-04 07:00:00',
  3                                            'YYYY-MM-DD HH24:MI:SS');
  4      l_oneyr    interval year to month := to_yminterval('01-00');
```

```
  5      l_18mos     interval year to month := to_yminterval('01-06');
  6      l_threeyrs interval year to month := to_yminterval('03-00');
  7      l_fiveyrs  interval year to month := to_yminterval('05-00');
  8   begin
  9      dbms_output.put_line('One Year: '||(l_hiredate + l_oneyr));
 10      dbms_output.put_line('One + 1/2 Year: '||(l_hiredate +
l_18mos));
 11      dbms_output.put_line('Three Years: '||(l_hiredate +
l_threeyrs));
 12      dbms_output.put_line('Five Years: '||(l_hiredate + l_fiveyrs));
 13   end;
 14   /
One Year: 04-NOV-97 07.00.00.000000000 AM
One + 1/2 Year: 04-NOV-97 07.00.00.000000000 AM
Three Years: 04-NOV-99 07.00.00.000000000 AM
Five Years: 04-NOV-01 07.00.00.000000000 AM

PL/SQL procedure successfully completed.
```

TRANSLATE USING()

This function is for converting character values from the database character set to the database's national character set and vice versa.

```
character_value := TRANSLATE(character_value USING { CHAR_CS | NCHAR_CS } )
```

```
SQL> create table nchar_samples(
  2      char_data  char(100),
  3      nchar_data nchar(100)
  4   )
  5   /

Table created.

SQL> insert into nchar_samples( nchar_data )
  2   values ( N'Some text' )
  3   /

1 row created.

SQL> update nchar_samples
  2      set char_data = translate( nchar_data using char_cs )
  3   /

1 row updated.
```

Date and Number Format Strings

When converting character values to dates and numbers, or vice versa, Oracle offers some flexibility. Instead of having a fixed format that must be followed to convert a character value representing a date into a date format, you can provide a format string that tells Oracle how to interpret your data.

The same flexibility is offered when converting date and number values to strings, so you can do things like only show the name of the month, or the abbreviation of the month, or the numeric value of the month; or for a number, you might want to use a dollar sign ($) in front of the number to indicate a monetary value, or you may want to convert your number into Roman numerals. In this section, we will outline some of the formatting options available for date formats and number formats.

Date Formatting

The following list describes those formatting options for the TO_DATE() and the TO_CHAR(datetime) functions:

- ❏ AD, A.D. – AD indicator
- ❏ AM, PM, A.M., P.M. – The meridian indicator
- ❏ BC, B.C. – BC indicator
- ❏ RM – Roman numerals of month
- ❏ CC, SCC – The century indicator (1999 resolves to 20, 2001 resolves to 21, etc.)
- ❏ Y, YY, YYY, YYYY – Numeric value of the year (1, 2, 3, and 4 digits, respectively)
- ❏ YEAR – Character representation of year ("Two thousand one")
- ❏ YY – Numeric value of the month (1-12)
- ❏ RR – Given a two-digit year, this date format returns a year based on the second two digits of the current year. If the two digits are < 50, the first two digits become the current year's two digits. If they are >= 50, the first two digits are the current year minus one. (RR('99') = 1999, RR('00') = 2000)
- ❏ MON – Abbreviated character value of month (JAN, FEB, etc.)
- ❏ MONTH – Character value of month (JANUARY, FEBRUARY, etc.)
- ❏ MM – Numeric value of the month (1-12)
- ❏ WW – Numeric value of week of the year (1-53)
- ❏ W – Numeric value of week of the month (1-5)
- ❏ D – Numeric value of day of the week (1-7)
- ❏ DD – Numeric value of day of the month (1-31)
- ❏ DDD – Numeric value of day of the year (1-365)
- ❏ Day – Text value of day of the week

❑   HH, HH12 – Hour of the day (1-12)

❑   HH24 – Hour of the day (0-23)

❑   MI – Minute of the hour (0-59)

❑   SS – Seconds of the minute (0-59)

❑   SSSSS – Seconds of the day (0-86399)

Number Formatting

❑   9 – Returns a digit from the numeric value, by position (TO_CHAR(111,999) = 111)

❑   9,999 – Places a comma in the designated position (TO_CHAR(1234, '9,999') = 1,234)

❑   999.99 – Places a decimal point in the designated position (TO_CHAR(123, '999.99') = 123.00)

❑ $9999 – Returns the numeric value preceded by a dollar sign

❑   FM99 – Strips all leading and trailing blanks from the returned character value

❑   RN, rn – Returns the roman numeral representation for the number given (in upper and lower case, respectively)

❑   X – Returns the hexadecimal value for the number given. (TO_CHAR(20, 'XX') = 14)

AGGREGATION Functions

Oracle provides plenty of functions for working with values in SQL and PL/SQL.

AVG()	MIN()
COUNT()	SUM()
MAX()	

AVG()

The AVG() function returns the average of all the non-NULL values provided. If NULL values are included in the set of records passed to AVG(), those values are ignored completely.

```
SELECT AVG( number_column )
  FROM table
```

```
SQL> select avg( sal )
  2    from emp
  3  /

  AVG(SAL)
----------
2073.21429
```

COUNT()

COUNT() returns the total number of non-NULL values in a set of records. NULL values are not counted, unless COUNT (*) is used.

```
SELECT COUNT(column )
  FROM table
```

```
SQL> select count( * )
  2    from emp
  3  /

  COUNT(*)
----------
        14

SQL> select empno, ename
  2    from emp
  3  where mgr is null
  4  /

    EMPNO ENAME
---------- ----------
     7839 KING

SQL> select count( mgr )
  2    from emp
  3  /

COUNT(MGR)
----------
        13
```

MAX()

MAX() is used to determine the maximum value in a set of records.

```
SELECT MAX(column )
  FROM table
```

```
SQL> select max( sal )
  2    from emp
  3  /

  MAX(SAL)
----------
      5000
```

MIN()

MIN() is used to determine the minimum value in a set of records.

```
SELECT MIN(column )
  FROM table
```

```
SQL> select min( sal )
  2      from emp
  3  /

  MIN (SAL)
----------
       800
```

SUM()

The SUM() function is responsible for determining the sum of all the values in a set of records.

```
SELECT SUM(column )
  FROM table
```

```
SQL> select sum( sal )
  2      from emp
  3  /

  SUM(SAL)
----------
     29025
```

MISCELLANEOUS Functions

Oracle provides plenty of functions for working with string values in SQL and PL/SQL.

COALESCE()	LEAST()	SYS_CONNECT_BY_PATH()
DECODE()	NULLIF()	UID()
DUMP()	NVL()	USER()
GREATEST()	NVL2()	VSIZE()

COALESCE()

The COALESCE() function is for returning the first value in a list of values that is non-NULL. If all the values passed to the COALESCE() function are NULL, the return value is NULL. COALESCE() works for any data type, but all the data types passed in a single call must be either NULL or the same data type.

```
value := COALESCE( value {, value }... )
```

```
SQL> select coalesce( null, '', 'A' )
  2     from dual
  3  /

C
-
A

SQL> select coalesce( null, sysdate )
  2     from dual
  3  /

COALESCE(
---------
04-NOV-01
```

DECODE()

DECODE() is a comparison function, used for comparing a base value against up to 255 evaluation values in a single function call. Optionally, a default value can be passed at the end of the function to be returned in the case where the base value does not equal any of the evaluation values.

```
value := DECODE( base_value, evaluation_value1, return_value1
                       {, evaluation_value2, return_value2 }...
                       {, default_value } )
```

```
SQL> select dname, decode( loc, 'BOSTON', 'Red Sox fans',
  2                              'CHICAGO', 'White Sox fans',
  3                              'DALLAS', 'Astros fans',
  4                              'NEW YORK', 'Mets fans' ) "Baseball Team"
  5     from dept
  6  /

DNAME          Baseball Team
-------------- --------------
ACCOUNTING     Mets fans
RESEARCH       Astros fans
SALES          White Sox fans
OPERATIONS     Red Sox fans


SQL> select decode( ename, 'KING', 'KING OF THE HILL', ename ) "ENAME"
  2     from emp
  3  /

ENAME
----------------
SMITH
```

```
ALLEN
WARD
JONES
MARTIN
BLAKE
CLARK
SCOTT
KING OF THE HILL
TURNER
ADAMS
JAMES
FORD
MILLER

14 rows selected.
```

DUMP()

The DUMP() function provides meta data about the first parameter (expression) passed to the function, including data type code, length in bytes, and an internal representation of the expression. The data type codes are as follows:

- ❑ 1 – VARCHAR2, NVARCHAR2
- ❑ 2 – NUMBER
- ❑ 8 – LONG
- ❑ 12 – DATE
- ❑ 23 – RAW
- ❑ 24 – LONG RAW
- ❑ 69 – ROWID
- ❑ 96 – CHAR, NCHAR
- ❑ 112 – CLOB, NCLOB
- ❑ 113 – BLOB
- ❑ 114 – BFILE
- ❑ 208 – UROWID
- ❑ 180 – TIMESTAMP
- ❑ 181 – TIMESTAMP WITH TIME ZONE
- ❑ 182 – INTERVAL YEAR TO MONTH
- ❑ 183 – INTERVAL DAY TO SECOND
- ❑ 231 – TIMESTAMP WITH LOCAL TIME ZONE

Optional parameters to the DUMP() function are as follows:

❏ Return format. Allows you to specify the format of the return value. Valid return formats are as follows:

  ❏ 8 – Octal

  ❏ 10 – Decimal

  ❏ 16 – Hexadecimal

  ❏ 17 – Single-digit characters

❏ Start position. Specifies the position to start evaluating the expression.

❏ Length. Specifies the amount of data to evaluate.

```
value := DUMP( expression {, return_format {, start_position {, length } } } )
```

```
SQL> select dump( ename, 8 )
  2      from emp
  3  /

DUMP(ENAME,8)
------------------------------------
Typ=1 Len=5: 123,115,111,124,110
Typ=1 Len=5: 101,114,114,105,116
Typ=1 Len=4: 127,101,122,104
Typ=1 Len=5: 112,117,116,105,123
Typ=1 Len=6: 115,101,122,124,111,116
Typ=1 Len=5: 102,114,101,113,105
Typ=1 Len=5: 103,114,101,122,113
Typ=1 Len=5: 123,103,117,124,124
Typ=1 Len=4: 113,111,116,107
Typ=1 Len=6: 124,125,122,116,105,122
Typ=1 Len=5: 101,104,101,115,123
Typ=1 Len=5: 112,101,115,105,123
Typ=1 Len=4: 106,117,122,104
Typ=1 Len=6: 115,111,114,114,105,122

14 rows selected.

SQL> select dump( ename, 16 )
  2      from emp
  3  /

DUMP(ENAME,16)
------------------------------------
Typ=1 Len=5: 53,4d,49,54,48
Typ=1 Len=5: 41,4c,4c,45,4e
Typ=1 Len=4: 57,41,52,44
Typ=1 Len=5: 4a,4f,4e,45,53
Typ=1 Len=6: 4d,41,52,54,49,4e
Typ=1 Len=5: 42,4c,41,4b,45
Typ=1 Len=5: 43,4c,41,52,4b
```

```
Typ=1 Len=5: 53,43,4f,54,54
Typ=1 Len=4: 4b,49,4e,47
Typ=1 Len=6: 54,55,52,4e,45,52
Typ=1 Len=5: 41,44,41,4d,53
Typ=1 Len=5: 4a,41,4d,45,53
Typ=1 Len=4: 46,4f,52,44
Typ=1 Len=6: 4d,49,4c,4c,45,52
```

GREATEST()

The GREATEST() function is for returning the greatest value in a list of values, based on the database character set. A character is greater than another if it has a higher value in the database character set.

```
value := GREATEST( value {, value }... )
```

```
SQL> select greatest( 'A', 'a' )
  2    from dual
  3  /

G
-
a

SQL> select greatest( 'ONE', 1 )
  2    from dual
  3  /

GRE
---
ONE

SQL> select greatest( 1, 5, 10 )
  2    from dual
  3  /

GREATEST(1,5,10)
----------------
              10
```

LEAST()

The LEAST() function is for returning the smallest value in a list of values, based on the database character set. A character is less than another if it has a lower value in the database character set.

```
value := LEAST( value {, value }... )
```

```
SQL> select least( 'X', 'x' )
  2    from dual
  3  /
```

```
L
-
X

SQL> select least( 'A', 'B', 'C' )
  2      from dual
  3  /

L
-
A
```

NULLIF()

This function evaluates two expressions and determines if they equal each other or not. If they equal each other, NULL is returned. If they do not equal each other, the first expression is returned. The first expression cannot be a NULL value, or an error is raised.

```
value := NULLIF( expression1, expression2 )
```

```
SQL> select nullif( 1, 1 )
  2      from dual
  3  /

NULLIF(1,1)
-----------


SQL> select nullif( 1, null )
  2      from dual
  3  /

NULLIF(1,NULL)
--------------
             1
```

NVL()

NVL() is used for evaluating an expression, and returning a given value if the expression evaluates to NULL.

```
value := NVL( expression, alternative_return_value )
```

```
SQL> select nvl( '', 'Yes '''' is null' ) "Evaluate"
  2      from dual
  3  /
```

```
Evaluate
-------------
Yes '' is null


SQL> select e.ename, nvl( e2.ename, 'NO BOSS! PARTY TIME!' ) "MGR"
  2     from emp e, emp e2
  3   where e.mgr = e2.empno(+)
  4   /

ENAME        MGR
----------   -------------------
SMITH        FORD
ALLEN        BLAKE
WARD         BLAKE
JONES        KING
MARTIN       BLAKE
BLAKE        KING
CLARK        KING
SCOTT        JONES
KING         NO BOSS! PARTY TIME!
TURNER       BLAKE
ADAMS        SCOTT
JAMES        BLAKE
FORD         JONES
MILLER       CLARK

14 rows selected.
```

NVL2()

NVL2() takes the NVL() function one step further. If the first expression in NVL2() is not NULL, the second parameter is returned. If the value is NULL, the third parameter is returned.

```
value := NVL2( expression, not_null_return_value, null_return_value,)
```

```
SQL> select e.ename, nvl2( e2.ename, 'BACK TO WORK!', 'NO BOSS!' ) "MGR"
  2     from emp e, emp e2
  3   where e.mgr = e2.empno(+)
  4   /

ENAME        MGR
----------   -------------
SMITH        BACK TO WORK!
ALLEN        BACK TO WORK!
WARD         BACK TO WORK!
JONES        BACK TO WORK!
MARTIN       BACK TO WORK!
BLAKE        BACK TO WORK!
CLARK        BACK TO WORK!
```

```
SCOTT       BACK TO WORK!
KING        NO BOSS!
TURNER      BACK TO WORK!
ADAMS       BACK TO WORK!
JAMES       BACK TO WORK!
FORD        BACK TO WORK!
MILLER      BACK TO WORK!

14 rows selected.
```

SYS_CONNECT_BY_PATH()

This function works with the CONNECT BY condition in a hierarchical query to show the entire path in a single return value. Until Oracle 9*i*, this functionality was only accomplished programmatically. The first parameter is the column that should populate each level of the 'hierarchy' in the return value, the second parameter is the value delimiter.

```
character_value := SYS_CONNECT_BY_PATH( column_name, value_separator )
```

```
SQL> select lpad('*', 2*level, '*' ) || ename empName,
  2          dname, job, sys_connect_by_path( empno, '.' ) cbp
  3    from scott.emp emp, scott.dept dept
  4   where emp.deptno = dept.deptno
  5   start with mgr is null
  6   connect by prior empno = mgr
  7   order siblings by ename
  8  /
```

EMPNAME	DNAME	JOB	CBP
**KING	ACCOUNTING	PRESIDENT	.7839
****BLAKE	SALES	MANAGER	.7839.7698
******ALLEN	SALES	SALESMAN	.7839.7698.7499
******JAMES	SALES	CLERK	.7839.7698.7900
******MARTIN	SALES	SALESMAN	.7839.7698.7654
******TURNER	SALES	SALESMAN	.7839.7698.7844
******WARD	SALES	SALESMAN	.7839.7698.7521
****CLARK	ACCOUNTING	MANAGER	.7839.7782
******MILLER	ACCOUNTING	CLERK	.7839.7782.7934
****JONES	RESEARCH	MANAGER	.7839.7566
******FORD	RESEARCH	ANALYST	.7839.7566.7902
********SMITH	RESEARCH	CLERK	.7839.7566.7902.7369
******SCOTT	RESEARCH	ANALYST	.7839.7566.7788
********ADAMS	RESEARCH	CLERK	.7839.7566.7788.7876

```
14 rows selected.
```

UID()

UID() returns a number that uniquely identifies the connected user.

```
number_value := UID
```

```
SQL> select uid "Current UID"
  2     from dual
  3  /

Current UID
-----------
         54
```

USER()

The USER() function returns the name of the currently connected user.

```
character_value := USER
```

```
SQL> select user "Current User"
  2     from dual
  3  /

Current User
------------------------------
SCOTT
```

```
SQL> select object_name, object_type
  2     from all_objects
  3   where owner = user
  4  /

OBJECT_NAME                       OBJECT_TYPE
--------------------------------- -------------------
ADDRESS_TYP                       TYPE
AUTHOR_LOG                        TABLE
BONUS                             TABLE
CASEPARTYADDRESS                  TABLE
COURSES                           TABLE
DEPT                              TABLE
EMP                               TABLE
EMPLOYEES                         TABLE
GETCASEXML                        FUNCTION
GET_TRANSPOSED                    FUNCTION
NCHAR_SAMPLES                     TABLE
OLD_LOG                           TABLE
PK_COURSES                        INDEX
PK_DEPT                           INDEX
PK_EMP                            INDEX
PK_SUBJECTS                       INDEX
SALGRADE                          TABLE
SUBJECTS                          TABLE
SYS_LOB0000031587C00001$$         LOB
T                                 TABLE
TRANSPOSE                         FUNCTION

21 rows selected.
```

VSIZE()

This function returns the number of bytes the internal representation of the expression parameter consumes.

```
number_value := VSIZE( expression )
```

```
SQL> create table nchar_test (
  2     ename    varchar2(20),
  3     n_ename  nvarchar2(20)
  4  )
  5  /

Table created.

SQL> insert into nchar_test
  2  select ename, ename
  3    from emp
  4  /

14 rows created.

SQL> select ename,
  2         vsize( ename ) "Char Size", vsize( n_ename ) "NChar Size"
  3    from nchar_test
  4  /

ENAME                  Char Size NChar Size
-------------------- ---------- ----------
SMITH                          5         10
ALLEN                          5         10
WARD                           4          8
JONES                          5         10
MARTIN                         6         12
BLAKE                          5         10
CLARK                          5         10
SCOTT                          5         10
KING                           4          8
TURNER                         6         12
ADAMS                          5         10
JAMES                          5         10
FORD                           4          8
MILLER                         6         12

14 rows selected.
```

Supplied Packages

In this appendix, we will look at some of the more common supplied packages. These PL/SQL packages are usually installed in the database when it is created and are available to all schemas users (though they are owned by the SYS user). Their names are prefixed with either DBMS_ or UTL_. We will discuss the following seven supplied packages.

- ❏   DBMS_OUTPUT

- ❏   DBMS_RANDOM

- ❏   UTL_FILE

- ❏   DBMS_JOB

- ❏   UTL_RAW

- ❏   DBMS_LOB

- ❏   DBMS_SQL

This is in no way a complete list though. You can get a full listing of each package in the Oracle documentation *Supplied PL/SQL Packages Reference*.

For any given package you can use the DESCRIBE command to return a list of all the procedures and functions it contains, as well as the parameters available to it and its data types. Further information can be found in the specification (spec). The specs are stored in clear text and are usually quite well documented with comments. We could either query a spec out of the database, or just go look for it on the file system. They are located in $ORACLE_HOME/rdbms/admin. You will see many files in that directory. The ones you will be most interested in are those prefixed with dbms or utl and ending with the .sql extension. For example, the DBMS_RANDOM spec is located in the file dbmsrand.sql. The .plb files are the wrapped package bodies. Viewing the dbmsrand.sql file, you will see that it is nicely documented and that there are even examples on how to use it.

DBMS_OUTPUT

DBMS_OUTPUT allows the developer to return text messages from their PL/SQL routines to any client that is DBMS_OUTPUT aware. You can view the file containing the specification located at $ORACLE_HOME/rdbms/admin/dbmsotpt.sql.

The spec of DBMS_OUTPUT is fairly simple. There are only a few procedures defined:

DISABLE	NEW_LINE
ENABLE	PUT
GET_LINE	PUT_LINE
GET_LINES	

DBMS_OUTPUT is only useful for relatively small debugging tasks, since the buffer (where the messages are cached) is only 1,000,000 characters long, and each line only 255 characters. The package works by buffering your text messages into an array of VARCHAR2(255). Then a DBMS_OUTPUT aware client will spool that information when the procedure is successfully completed. We have all seen DBMS_OUTPUT.PUT_LINE() in action in SQL*Plus, but remember we needed to enable SQL*Plus to spool the messages back to us upon successful completion of the PL/SQL routines. With SQL*Plus, that was accomplished with the SET SERVEROUTPUT ON command. Without that command, you will not see any of your output.

ENABLE() / DISABLE()

SQL*Plus is a DBMS_OUTPUT aware client. But what if you wanted to display these messages from your C or Java program? You will need to enable the DBMS_OUTPUT package and then fetch and display the cached row programmatically. The syntax is as follows:

Usage

```
procedure enable (buffer_size in integer default 20000);
procedure disable;
```

The first thing your client will need to do is issue a call to DBMS_OUTPUT.ENABLE(). You supply it with a buffer size between 2,000 and 1,000,000 bytes (the default is 20000). This allows Oracle to allocate that much room for your messages. Attempting to store more information than space provided will cause an exception to be raised. Once enabled, the application can then make calls to PUT() and PUT_LINE() to cache the messages for later retrieval.

If at any time you want to turn off DBMS_OUTPUT message caching and clear the cache, a call to DBMS_OUTPUT.DISABLE() will accomplish that.

```
SQL> set serveroutput on
SQL> begin
  2    dbms_output.put_line( 'One' );
  3    dbms_output.disable;
  4  end;
```

```
  5   /

PL/SQL procedure successfully completed.
```

Here we enabled the SQL*Plus client to spool back any DBMS_OUTPUT messages with the call to SET SERVEROUT ON. This makes the call to DBMS_OUTPUT.ENABLE(), setting up the buffer, and prepares the client to spool the messages back. In the block itself, we cached one message but then invoked the DISABLE() procedure which cleared any previous messages in the cache. When the block completed, no messages were displayed. Until we enable DBMS_OUTPUT, either programmatically, DBMS_OUTPUT.ENABLE(), or manually with another call to SET SERVEROUT ON, we will not see any messages:

```
SQL> begin
  2     dbms_output.put_line( 'One' );
  3     dbms_output.put_line( 'Two' );
  4     dbms_output.put_line( 'Three' );
  5   end;
  6   /

PL/SQL procedure successfully completed.

SQL> begin
  2     dbms_output.put_line( 'One' );
  3     dbms_output.put_line( 'Two' );
  4     dbms_output.enable;
  5     dbms_output.put_line( 'Three' );
  6   end;
  7   /

Three
```

Alternatively, we could disable the SQL*Plus client from spooling back the messages by issuing the command SET SERVEROUTPUT OFF. We can still cache the messages if we enable DBMS_OUTPUT programmatically, but they will never be displayed because SQL*Plus is not currently displaying the cached messages. This is bad since you are sure to fill up the buffer as nothing is cleaning it up after every successful procedure completion. Unless you have a real reason to do so, do not enable DBMS_OUTPUT in your PL/SQL. Let the client running your procedure manage that.

PUT() / PUT_LINE() / NEW_LINE()

The procedures PUT() and PUT_LINE() allow you to put messages into the DBMS_OUTPUT cache. PUT() places your message just as it was sent. PUT_LINE() will add a new-line character to the end of your text string. The procedure NEW_LINE() adds a new line to the buffer. Calling PUT_LINE() is equivalent to calling PUT() and then NEW_LINE(). Any line cannot be longer than 255 characters.

Usage

```
procedure put(a varchar2);
procedure put(a number);
```

```
procedure put_line(a varchar2);
procedure put_line(a number);

procedure new_line;
```

Example

```
SQL> set serverout on
SQL> begin
  2      dbms_output.put( 'One' );
  3      dbms_output.put( 'Two' );
  4      dbms_output.new_line;
  5      dbms_output.put_line( 'Three' );
  6      dbms_output.put( 'Four' );
  7   end;
  8   /

OneTwo
Three

PL/SQL procedure successfully completed.
```

You can see that the calls to PUT() on lines 2 and 3 caused the messages to be displayed on the same line after the call to NEW_LINE() on line 4. Also notice that the message 'Four' was not displayed. Any message that does not end with a new line will not be returned or displayed.

GET_LINE() / GET_LINES()

The procedures GET_LINE() and GET_LINES() are used for clients that want to retrieve the DBMS_OUTPUT messages that have be queued up. SQL*Plus handles that for us when we initialize it to do so with the SET SERVEROUTPUT ON command. (Other clients would need to fetch the rows cached and display them using whatever means available.) The client can fetch one line at a time with GET_LINE() or fetch multiple lines with one call using GET_LINES().

Usage

```
procedure get_line(line out varchar2, status out integer);
procedure get_lines(lines out chararr, numlines in out integer);
```

Summary

Do not rely exclusively on DBMS_OUTPUT for generating debug messages. The line-size restriction and the relatively small buffer size do not make it a great solution for large scale application debugging. For simple small procedures and quick message retrieval from the SQL*Plus client, it works just great.

DBMS_RANDOM

DBMS_RANDOM is a package that generates random numbers or strings. It will generate a sequence of 38-digit Oracle numbers. You can view the specification in the file $ORACLE_HOME/rdbms/admin/dbmsrand.sql.

Here are the available procedures and functions:

Procedures	Functions
INITIALIZE()	VALUE() – returns NUMBER
SEED()	NORMAL() – returns NUMBER
TERMINATE()	RANDOM() – returns BINARY_INTEGER
	STRING() – returns VARCHAR2

VALUE()

The overloaded function VALUE() is used to request a random number from the DBMS_RANDOM package. The function VALUE() with no parameters will return a number with 38 digits of precision. It will be in the range of 0.0 up to but not including 1.0.

Usage

```
FUNCTION value RETURN NUMBER;
FUNCTION value (low IN NUMBER, high IN NUMBER) RETURN NUMBER;
```

Example

To generate 10 integers between 1 and 100, you could do the following:

```
SQL> begin
  2    for i in 1 .. 10 loop
  3      dbms_output.put_line( round( dbms_random.value*100 ) );
  4    end loop;
  5  end;
  6  /
13
19
64
99
48
7
7
5
83
32

PL/SQL procedure successfully completed.
```

Notice how 7 came up twice in a row. There is no guarantee that the same number will not come up twice, just that the numbers will be in a random order.

The second version of VALUE() takes in two parameters, an upper and lower bound. The possible values returned by using this call will be in the range of these bounds. Passing in LOW => 10 and HIGH => 50 will generate numbers between 10 and 49. To generate 10 integers again between 1 and 100 we could do this instead:

905

```
SQL> begin
  2    for i in 1 .. 10 loop
  3      dbms_output.put_line( trunc( dbms_random.value( 1, 101 ) ) );
  4    end loop;
  5  end;
  6  /
10
40
74
77
67
10
91
58
34
29

PL/SQL procedure successfully completed.
```

STRING()

The STRING() function will generate a random string. STRING() takes two required parameters. The first parameter is a key to tell STRING() the characteristics of the value you want returned. The keys include:

❑   U or u – The string can only contain uppercased alpha characters.

❑   L or l – The string can only contain lowercased alpha characters.

❑   A or a – The string can only contain upper and lowercased alpha characters.

❑   X or x – The string can only contain upper alpha-numeric characters.

❑   P or p – The string can contain any printable character.

The second parameter, LEN, dictates how long the string will be.

Usage

```
FUNCTION string (opt char, len NUMBER);
```

Examples

```
SQL> exec dbms_output.put_line( dbms_random.string( 'A', 20 ) );
qGkAKXPXswvrzwznvDDJ

PL/SQL procedure successfully completed.

SQL> exec dbms_output.put_line( dbms_random.string( 'x', 20 ) );
SJALDSAJKTCV5JBKIY45

PL/SQL procedure successfully completed.
```

```
SQL> exec dbms_output.put_line( dbms_random.string( 'P', 20 ) );
]*2OB'.^nf9b)Ztlv~Sh

PL/SQL procedure successfully completed.

SQL> exec dbms_output.put_line( dbms_random.string( 'l', 20 ) );
hriamgknxcxoehreplge

PL/SQL procedure successfully completed.

SQL> exec dbms_output.put_line( dbms_random.string( 'u', 20 ) );
NOGRKGBCNWIUQLEDIPAG

PL/SQL procedure successfully completed.
```

This is useful when you are populating a table with a bunch of dummy data to test how your application will run against a table with many rows of data.

SEED()

The procedure SEED() is an overloaded procedure that takes in either a BINARY_INTEGER or a VARCHAR2. This is the starting point for the random values to be returned. You should always attempt to seed with some unique value so your random values will truly be random. If the DBMS_RANDOM package is seeded with the same value, it will produce the same results in the same order.

Usage

```
PROCEDURE seed(val IN BINARY_INTEGER);
PROCEDURE seed(val IN VARCHAR2);
```

Examples

```
SQL> connect scott/tiger
Connected.

SQL> set serverout on
SQL> exec dbms_output.put_line( dbms_random.value );
.67332071470366751538704187176222262172

PL/SQL procedure successfully completed.

SQL> connect scott/tiger
Connected.

SQL> set serverout on
SQL> exec dbms_output.put_line( dbms_random.value );
.64740754965940299586220325260648615694

PL/SQL procedure successfully completed.
```

Notice that we connected twice and, without seeding the DBMS_RANDOM package, received different results. That is because the package was seeded with the time and session id, which were different for each connection.

```
SQL> connect scott/tiger
Connected.

SQL> set serverout on
SQL> exec dbms_random.seed( to_char( sysdate, 'YYYYMMDD' ) );

PL/SQL procedure successfully completed.

SQL> exec dbms_output.put_line( dbms_random.value );
.143971258442084442635154458208625507 54

PL/SQL procedure successfully completed.

SQL> exec dbms_output.put_line( dbms_random.value );
.032833540763035020233284426951425484 24

PL/SQL procedure successfully completed.

SQL> connect scott/tiger
Connected.

SQL> set serverout on
SQL> exec dbms_random.seed( to_char( sysdate, 'YYYYMMDD' ) );

PL/SQL procedure successfully completed.

SQL> exec dbms_output.put_line( dbms_random.value );
.143971258442084442635154458208625507 54

PL/SQL procedure successfully completed.

SQL> exec dbms_output.put_line( dbms_random.value );
.032833540763035020233284426951425484 24

PL/SQL procedure successfully completed.
```

This time we chose to seed the DBMS_RANDOM package ourselves, but we chose a poor value to seed with. The value of the function TO_CHAR(sysdate, 'YYYYMMDD') is going to be the same for everyone and we can see we get the same random numbers each time.

It is normally best practice to accept the default seeding of the package, which is the current username, the current time down to the second and the current session id. Those three values combined make for a pretty unique key to seed by.

NORMAL()

The NORMAL() function simply returns a random number from a normal distribution. The same rules apply to this function as to VALUE() and STRING() with regards to how the package was seeded.

Usage

```
FUNCTION normal RETURN NUMBER;
```

908

Examples

```
SQL> begin
  2      for i in 1 .. 10 loop
  3          dbms_output.put_line( dbms_random.normal );
  4      end loop;
  5  end;
  6  /
-1.19503152622542500144888406874463873571
.73757837518705841324141525632971728158503
-.79376461283381002164152267067227602982202
.57652109213861726502189172054765328577619
-.71107204029417139804692702947432603444575
.44569027724203224252098907553479992887892
-.09182639691334360488406813552197656533005
-1.08462420404879076083328769627598888086
1.33394747019616122501366949844410068467
.16216631183915359384825332431940891355786

PL/SQL procedure successfully completed.
```

INITIALIZE() / RANDOM() / TERMINATE()

These three routines are obsolete as of Oracle 9i. They have been left in for backward compatibility. They are mapped to the new procedure and functions we have already talked about.

Usage

```
PROCEDURE initialize(val IN BINARY_INTEGER);
FUNCTION random RETURN BINARY_INTEGER;
PROCEDURE terminate;
```

Old Function/Procedure Call	New Function/Procedure Call
INITIALIZE(seed_value)	SEED(seed_value)
RANDOM()	VALUE(-power(2,32), power(2,32))
TERMINATE()	N/A

Summary

DBMS_RANDOM is a great little utility for generating random numbers and strings. Make sure you seed the package uniquely or DBMS_RANDOM.VALUE() will not be as random as you think.

UTL_FILE

The UTL_FILE package gives the PL/SQL developer the ability to read an ASCII file from, or write it to, the server's file system. The spec is in the file $ORACLE_HOME/rdbms/admin/utlfile.sql.

UTL_FILE's procedures and functions are:

Procedures	Functions
FCLOSE()	FOPEN() – returns RECORD
FCLOSE_ALL()	FOPEN_NCHAR() – returns RECORD
FFLUSH()	IS_OPEN() – returns BOOLEAN
TERMINATE()	
GET_LINE()	
GET_LINE_NCHAR()	
NEW_LINE()	
PUTF()	
PUTF_NCHAR()	

Setup

In the init.ora file, you set the parameter UTL_FILE_DIR equal to the directory where PL/SQL can write files. You may have multiple entries for this parameter, each set to a directory that is writable by the instance owner. On UNIX they might look like this:

```
UTL_FILE_DIR = /tmp
UTL_FILE_DIR = /d0/users/clbeck/sql/stage
```

On Windows-based machines, entries may look like:

```
UTL_FILE_DIR = C:\Temp
UTL_FILE_DIR = E:\SQL\stage
```

> **Even though directories are not case-sensitive on Windows, the directories listed for UTL_FILE_DIR are. Take note as to how they are defined on your Windows machine and use the exact case. UNIX is always case-sensitive.**

Files can only be opened if they are in the specified directories. UTL_FILE will not open files in any sub directories.

UTL_FILE_DIR can also be set to "*" giving PL/SQL access to write to any directory that the Oracle instance owner can write to. This overrides the safeguards that this parameter was designed for. Be careful if you choose to set this value to * for the reasons described above.

Process

The process for using UTL_FILE is quite simple:

- ❑ Open a file with mode of Read, Write or Append.
- ❑ Read or write the file with the procedures supplied.
- ❑ Close the file when you are done.

A sample of that code may look like this:

```
declare
  l_file utl_file.file_type;
begin
  l_file := utl_file.fopen( '/tmp', 'debug.txt', 'w' );
  utl_file.put_line( l_file, 'One.' );
  utl_file.put( l_file, 'Two' );
  utl_file.fflush( l_file );
  utl_file.close( l_file );
exception
  when others then
    if utl_file.is_open( l_file ) then
      utl_file.fclose( l_file );
    end if;
..raise;
end;
```

This sample code opens a file /tmp/debug.txt with the mode of write. It then writes two lines to the file and closes it. The exception handler catches any exception that can be thrown and closes the file handle if it is open.

Exceptions

The UTL_FILE package can throw many different exceptions. They include:

Exception	Description
INVALID_PATH	Attempted to open a file in a path not defined in the init.ora parameter file.
INVALID_MODE	Attempted to open a file with a mode other than r, w, or a.
INVALID_MAXLINESIZE	Raised when a supplied MAXLINESIZE is out of range.
INVALID_FILEHANDLE	The file handle supplied to the package was invalid.
INVALID_OPERATION	The attempted request to open the file failed.
READ_ERROR	OS error occurred during the reading of the file.

Table continued on following page

Exception	Description
WRITE_ERROR	OS error occurred during the writing of the file.
INTERNAL_ERROR	Unspecified PL/SQL error.
CHARSETMISMATCH	A file is open using the FOPEN_NCHAR() function but then non-NCHAR operations are attempted on the file.

Types

UTL_FILE defines a package-level record type, FILE_TYPE. This record type is used as the handle to your file once it is opened. Although it is defined in the spec and is public, you should not attempt to read or modify any values in the type.

The record type is defined as:

```
TYPE file_type IS RECORD (id BINARY_INTEGER, datatype BINARY_INTEGER);
```

FOPEN() / FOPEN_NCHAR()

The overloaded functions FOPEN() (pronounced *F-Open*, not *fop-en*) and FOPEN_NCHAR() are usually the first call to UTL_FILE. You cannot operate on a file in PL/SQL unless you use one of these functions to first open the file.

Usage

```
FUNCTION fopen(location  IN VARCHAR2,
              filename   IN VARCHAR2,
              open_mode  IN VARCHAR2) RETURN file_type;

FUNCTION fopen_nchar( location  IN VARCHAR2,
                      filename   IN VARCHAR2,
                      open_mode  IN VARCHAR2) RETURN file_type;

FUNCTION fopen(location     IN VARCHAR2,
              filename      IN VARCHAR2,
              open_mode     IN VARCHAR2,
              max_linesize  IN BINARY_INTEGER) RETURN file_type;

FUNCTION fopen_nchar(location     IN VARCHAR2,
                     filename      IN VARCHAR2,
                     open_mode     IN VARCHAR2,
                     max_linesize  IN BINARY_INTEGER) RETURN file_type;
```

ID and DATATYPE are the elements or the record type returned. Each version of FOPEN() is overloaded. The difference is that the one version takes in an additional parameter, MAX_LINESIZE. That is the maximum length any line of the file can be. By default the length is 1023 and the OS dictates that. To specify a different max line size, call the version which accepts the MAX_LINESIZE parameter.

FOPEN()'s sister function is FOPEN_NCHAR() allows you to open the file and read or write Unicode, and not the database's default character set.

Example

```
declare
  l_file_handle utl_file.file_type;
begin
  l_file_handle := utl_file.fopen( '/tmp', 'tom.data', 'w' );
end;
```

Mode

Along with a location and a filename, you need to supply the mode you would like to open the file in:

r	Read-Only
w	Write / Overwrite If the file exists it will be overwritten
a	Append. If the file exists, all writes will be appended. If the file does not exist, it will be opened in the w mode

Exceptions

INVALID_PATH, INVALID_MODE, INVALID_OPERATION, and INVALID_MAXLINESIZE.

IS_OPEN()

The function IS_OPEN() is used to determine if a file handle is valid and pointing to an open file. It is useful in exception handling to determine if you should close the file. It takes in a UTL_FILE.FILE_TYPE and returns a Boolean. No exceptions are raised from this function.

Usage

```
FUNCTION is_open(file IN file_type) RETURN BOOLEAN;
```

Example

```
...
if utl_file.is_open( l_file_handle ) then
-- Do some work with the file
end if;
...
```

GET_LINE() / GET_LINE_NCHAR()

When a file is opened with the mode of r, (read mode), you can use the GET_LINE() and GET_LINE_NCHAR() functions to fetch one line of data at a time from the file. Each procedure takes in the file handle and populates an OUT parameter with the next line of the file. The GET_LINE_NCHAR() procedure is used when a file is opened with the FOPEN_NCHAR() function. A NO_DATA_FOUND error is raised when the end-of-file is hit. A VALUE_ERROR is raised if the buffer is too small.

Usage

```
PROCEDURE get_line(file   IN file_type,
                   buffer OUT VARCHAR2);

PROCEDURE get_line_nchar(file   IN file_type,
                         buffer OUT NVARCHAR2);
```

Example

Read every line of a file and store it in a database table:

```
declare
  l_file_handle utl_file.file_type
  l_buffer varchar2(4000);
begin
  utl_file.fopen( '/tmp', 'chris.data', 'r' );
  Loop
    get_line( l_file_handle, l_buffer );
    insert into file_table( seq, data )
    values ( file_sequence.nextval, l_buffer );
  end loop;
exception
  when NO_DATA_FOUND then
    utl_file.fclose( l_file_handle );
end;
```

Exceptions

INVALID_FILEHANDLE, INVALID_OPERATION, READ_ERROR, NO_DATA_FOUND, and
VALUE_ERROR.

PUT() / PUT_NCHAR()

These procedures are used to write data to the current line of the file. A new-line character is not added
to the end of the line. Two subsequent called to PUT() will write the data on the same line of the file.

Usage

```
PROCEDURE put(file   IN file_type,
              buffer IN VARCHAR2);

PROCEDURE put_nchar(file   IN file_type,
                    buffer IN NVARCHAR2);
```

Example

Writes Hello World to one line of the file:

```
...
utl_file.put( l_file_handle, 'Hello' );
utl_file.put( l_file_handle, ' ' );
utl_file.put( l_file_handle, 'World' );
...
```

Exceptions

INVALID_OPERATION, INVALID_FILEHANDLE, and WRITE_ERROR

NEW_LINE()

The procedure NEW_LINE() is used in conjunction with PUT() and PUT_NCHAR(). Calling NEW_LINE() will write a new-line character into the file ensuring that the next call to PUT() or PUT_NCHAR() will start in the next line.

Usage

```
PROCEDURE new_line(file  IN file_type,
                   lines IN NATURAL := 1);
```

Example

This writes Hello on the first line of the file and World on the next line:

```
...
utl_file.put( l_file_handle, 'Hello' );
utl_file.new_line( l_file_handle );
utl_file.put( l_file_handle, 'World' );
...
```

Exceptions

INVALID_OPERATION, INVALID_FILEHANDLE, and WRITE_ERROR.

PUT_LINE() / PUT_LINE_NCHAR()

The procedures PUT_LINE() and PUT_LINE_NCHAR() are exactly the same as their PUT counterparts except that a new-line character will be automatically appended to each buffer put.

Usage

```
PROCEDURE put_line(file   IN file_type,
                   buffer IN VARCHAR2);

PROCEDURE put_line_nchar(file   IN file_type,
                         buffer IN NVARCHAR2);
```

Example

Write three lines to a file:

```
...
utl_file.put_line( l_file_handle, 'One' );
utl_file.put_line( l_file_handle, 'Two' );
utl_file.put_line( l_file_handle, 'Three' );
...
```

Exceptions

INVALID_OPERATION, INVALID_FILEHANDLE, and WRITE_ERROR

PUTF() / PUTF_NCHAR()

The procedures PUTF() and PUTF_NCHAR() are similar to the PUT procedures except that they take optional formatting. It works like PRINTF() in C, but only in a limited fashion.

The buffer to be written can contain special sequences of characters that will be substituted prior to being written to the file, called **tokens**. Those tokens are:

- ❑ %s – The token will get substituted with the next value in the argument list.

- ❑ \n – This token will be replaced with a new line character.

If the formatted buffer contains more %s than arguments supplied, all additional %s will be replaced with NULL.

Usage

```
procedure putf(file    IN file_type,
               format IN VARCHAR2,
               arg1   IN VARCHAR2 DEFAULT NULL,
               arg2   IN VARCHAR2 DEFAULT NULL,
               arg3   IN VARCHAR2 DEFAULT NULL,
               arg4   IN VARCHAR2 DEFAULT NULL,
               arg5   IN VARCHAR2 DEFAULT NULL);

procedure putf_nchar(file    IN file_type,
               format IN NVARCHAR2,
               arg1   IN NVARCHAR2 DEFAULT NULL,
               arg2   IN NVARCHAR2 DEFAULT NULL,
               arg3   IN NVARCHAR2 DEFAULT NULL,
               arg4   IN NVARCHAR2 DEFAULT NULL,
               arg5   IN NVARCHAR2 DEFAULT NULL);
```

Example

Write two lines to a file, Chris was here as the first line and and so was Sean as the second:

```
utl_file.putf( l_file_handle, '%s was here\nand so was %s',
               'Chris',
               'Sean' );
```

Exceptions

INVALID_OPERATION, INVALID_FILEHANDLE, and WRITE_ERROR

FFLUSH()

The procedure FFLUSH() physically writes pending data to the file. For performance reasons, the data is usually buffered and written in large chunks. FFLUSH() forces the physical write to happen immediately. The data must be terminated with a new-line character.

Usage

```
PROCEDURE fflush(file IN file_type);
```

Exceptions

```
INVALID_OPERATION, INVALID_FILEHANDLE, and WRITE_ERROR
```

FCLOSE() / FCLOSE_ALL()

The FCLOSE() procedure is called to physically close the file handle itself. If there is pending buffered data to be written, you could receive a WRITE_ERROR exception. It is good practice to call FFLUSH() prior to calling FCLOSE().

The FCLOSE_ALL() procedure should only be called in an emergency. It closes every file handle open in a session but it does not change the state of the handles currently held. Calls to IS_OPEN() will still return TRUE but you will receive a WRITE ERROR if you attempt to write to the file. You would only use this procedure when exiting a program from an exception.

Usage

```
PROCEDURE fclose(file IN OUT file_type);

PROCEDURE fclose_all;
```

Example

Close the current file:

```
utl_file.fclose( l_file_handle );
```

Exceptions

```
INVALID_FILEHANDLE and WRITE_ERROR
```

Summary

UTL_FILE gives you the ability to read and write ASCII and Unicode files from within PL/SQL. You just need to be mindful of the file's mode and state when passing around its handle and make sure you properly handle the possible exceptions that can be raised.

DBMS_JOB

The DBMS_JOB package allows the developer to schedule PL/SQL routines to run unattended at some time in the future. Those familiar with the at or cron UNIX commands, or task scheduling with Windows, will see that DBMS_JOB is basically the same thing.

Configuration

You need to configure your database to support jobs. You need to set up the following database initialization parameters:

❑   JOB_QUEUE_PROCESSES – this tells Oracle how many processes should be started to handle the jobs in the queue.

❑   JOB_QUEUE_INTERVAL – this tells Oracle, in seconds, how often it should scan the queue for jobs that need to be executed (Note that this parameter is obsolete in Oracle 9*i*).

Example

```
JOB_QUEUE_PROCESSES = 2
JOB_QUEUE_INTERVAL = 300
```

This tells Oracle to start to process and scan the queue every 5 minutes for jobs ready to run.

Procedures	Functions
BROKEN()	BACKGROUND_PROCESS() – returns BOOLEAN
CHANGE()	IS_JOBQ() – returns BOOLEAN
INSTANCE()	
INTERVAL()	
ISUBMIT()	
NEXT_DATE()	
REMOVE()	
RUN()	
SUBMIT()	
USER_EXPORT()	
WHAT()	

Listing Your Jobs

Job definitions, like everything else in the database, are stored in the data dictionary. You can view your jobs and the status of each using the dictionary view USER_JOBS:

```
SQL> desc user_jobs
 Name                                      Null?    Type
 ----------------------------------------- -------- ----------------------------
 JOB                                       NOT NULL NUMBER
 LOG_USER                                  NOT NULL VARCHAR2(30)
 PRIV_USER                                 NOT NULL VARCHAR2(30)
 SCHEMA_USER                               NOT NULL VARCHAR2(30)
 LAST_DATE                                          DATE
 LAST_SEC                                           VARCHAR2(8)
 THIS_DATE                                          DATE
 THIS_SEC                                           VARCHAR2(8)
 NEXT_DATE                                 NOT NULL DATE
 NEXT_SEC                                           VARCHAR2(8)
```

```
TOTAL_TIME                                    NUMBER
BROKEN                                        VARCHAR2(1)
INTERVAL                           NOT NULL   VARCHAR2(200)
FAILURES                                      NUMBER
WHAT                                          VARCHAR2(4000)
NLS_ENV                                       VARCHAR2(4000)
MISC_ENV                                      RAW(32)
INSTANCE                                      NUMBER
```

You can get all the information about each job. You can see what jobs you have, what they will run (the WHAT column), when they are scheduled to run next (the NEXT_DATE column), how long it took them to run (the TOTAL_TIME column), and even find out if they were successfully run on their last attempt (the BROKEN column will tell you if the job failed).

Never attempt to change the values in the USER_JOBS view manually via SQL. Always use the DBMS_JOBS supplied package to manage your jobs.

It is important, if you have recurring database jobs, to regularly monitor them to make sure that they are all running successfully. Using the following query:

```
select job, what
   from user_jobs
 where broken = 'Y';
```

will tell you if you have any jobs that need your attention. Oracle will attempt to run a job 16 times. If it is not successfully after 16 attempts, it will no longer attempt its execution. You will then need to manually run the job. Once it has been executed successfully, Oracle will then manage its execution again.

SUBMIT() / ISUBMIT()

These procedures are how you get a job into the queue. SUBMIT() returns the job ID via an OUT parameter. Using ISUBMIT(), you would supply your own ID number.

Usage

```
PROCEDURE submit      ( job        OUT BINARY_INTEGER,
                        what       IN  VARCHAR2,
                        next_date  IN  DATE DEFAULT sysdate,
                        interval   IN  VARCHAR2 DEFAULT 'null',
                        no_parse   IN  BOOLEAN DEFAULT FALSE,
                        instance   IN  BINARY_INTEGER DEFAULT 0,
                        force      IN  BOOLEAN DEFAULT FALSE );

PROCEDURE isubmit     ( job        IN  BINARY_INTEGER,
                        what       IN  VARCHAR2,
                        next_date  IN  DATE,
                        interval   IN  VARCHAR2 DEFAULT 'null',
                        no_parse   IN  BOOLEAN DEFAULT FALSE);
```

919

Parameters

- ❑ JOB – This is the ID of the job in the queue. You can use this ID to modify and remove the job.

- ❑ WHAT – This is the block of PL/SQL that will be executed by the job.

- ❑ NEXT_DATE – This is the next time Oracle will attempt to run the job. Leave it NULL to only have the job run once then remove itself.

- ❑ INTERVAL – This is the formula to determine when is the next time the job will schedule itself.

- ❑ NO_PARSE – A Boolean flag to tell Oracle to either parse the block of code when the job is submitted (FALSE, the default) or when the job is first run (TRUE).

- ❑ INSTANCE – In a multi-instance environment, this tells Oracle which instance should handle the job execution. The default is 0.

- ❑ FORCE – A Boolean flag that when set to TRUE, tells Oracle to accept the instance ID regardless of whether or not the instance is currently running. FALSE is the default.

Example

Create a job to insert the date and time into a table every 5 minutes:

```
declare
    l_job number;
begin
    dbms_job.submit(
        l_job,
        'insert into T values ( to_char( sysdate, 'DD-MON-YYYY HH24:MI:SS' ) );',
        sysdate,
        'sysdate+(5/1440)' );
end;
```

There are a few things to note in this example. Firstly, we only supplied 4 parameters to the SUBMIT() procedure, but it takes 7. The last three parameters are defaulted so we do not need to supply values for them. Secondly, this job is scheduled to run the next time the job queue is processed. We know that because it was submitted with a NEXT_DATE of sysdate, which says, run it right now. Lastly, the interval was set to the string sysdate+(5/1440) and not the value of that expression. Understand that the interval is a formula to determine the next run-time, not the actual next run-time value.

Slipping Interval Problem

Over time, intervals can seem to slip. That means that the jobs will continually take more time in between runs than the interval allows. This is not a bug in Oracle. It is a function of how often the job queue is scanned, the number of jobs that need executing, and how your interval is defined.

In our example above, we tell the job to run every 5 minutes. But what if the database parameter JOB_QUEUE_INTERVAL is set to 600, or every 10 minutes. It is impossible for Oracle to execute that job every five minutes if it only scans the queue every 10 minutes. It will be run, in this example, but only every 10 minutes or so.

Even if the queue was scanned every five minutes, there is no guarantee that this job will run every five minutes on the nose. Consider, the job queue wakes up at 12:00:00 exactly and finds our job to run. It first calculates the next run-time, which in our case would be 12:05:00. Next, it runs our job, which takes some amount of time. There may also be other jobs that need executing. The database then runs each of them in turn, first calculating their next run date and then running them. This too takes some amount of time.

Let's say 2 minutes have passed since the job queue process awoke. It is now 12:02:00. The database now rests for 5 minutes before again scanning the queue for jobs to run. It wakes up again at 12:07:00. Our job was scheduled to run at 12:05:00. Herein lies the slipping interval problem. The NEXT_TIME attribute of a job is not when exactly the job will run, but rather the earliest date which the database will consider running the job.

To minimize the "slipping" you can lower the sleep time between job queue scans. If you have a lot of jobs in the queue that run frequently, you might consider adding more processes to handle the workload. And writing a more exact INTERVAL formula will help minimize the slipping. If you want a job to run at 3AM every day, don't schedule the job like this:

```
dbms_job.submit(
  l_job,
  'my_proc',
  trunc(sysdate+1) + (3/60),
  'sysdate+1' );
```

The next date will slip. Instead code your interval like this

```
dbms_job.submit(
  l_job,
  'my_proc',
  trunc(sysdate+1) + (3/60),
  'trunc(sysdate+1) + (3/60)' );
```

This ensures that no matter what time your job runs, it will schedule itself to run tomorrow at 3AM. If it does not run until 03:04AM, no big deal, it will still be scheduled to run at 03:00 tomorrow.

RUN()

The procedure RUN() will cause the database to execute the job immediately. The NEXT_DATE is recomputed. Even if a job is broken, its execution will be attempted. If, upon your frequent checks of the job queue, you find a broken job that the database is no longer attempting to run, you can fix it, and then using DBMS_JOB.RUN(), run the job and get the database to manage its execution again.

If you are running multiple instances, then you need to need to either set FORCE to TRUE, which will allow the job to run in the foreground process or set to FALSE if you are connected to the appropriate instance for running that particular job. An exception will be raised if you attempt to execute the job from the wrong instance and FORCE was set to FALSE.

Usage

```
PROCEDURE run      ( job      IN   BINARY_INTEGER,
                     force    IN   BOOLEAN DEFAULT FALSE);
```

Example

```
dbms_job.run( 12345 );
```

REMOVE()

Use this procedure to remove a job from the queue. Any job in the queue not currently running can be removed using this procedure.

Usage

```
PROCEDURE remove      ( job      IN  BINARY_INTEGER );
```

Example

```
dbms_job.remove( 12345 );
```

CHANGE()

The CHANGE procedure allows you to modify the user-set table attributes for a given job. The downside to using CHANGE() is that you must supply the WHAT, NEXT_DATE, and INTERVAL whether or not you wish to change their values.

Usage

```
PROCEDURE change      ( job      IN  BINARY_INTEGER,
                        what      IN  VARCHAR2,
                        next_date IN  DATE,
                        interval  IN  VARCHAR2,
                        instance  IN  BINARY_INTEGER DEFAULT NULL,
                        force     IN  BOOLEAN DEFAULT FALSE);
```

Example

```
dbms_job.change( 12345,
                 'insert into t values ( sysdate );',
                 sysdate,
                 'sysdate+1' );
```

WHAT()

The procedure WHAT() allow you to just change the WHAT of the given job.

Usage

```
PROCEDURE what      ( job      IN  BINARY_INTEGER,
                      what      IN  VARCHAR2 );
```

Example

```
dbms_job.what( 12345, 'update t set cnt = cnt + 1;' );
```

NEXT_DATE()

The procedure NEXT_DATE() allows you to just change the NEXT_DATE attribute of the given job.

Usage

```
PROCEDURE next_date ( job IN  BINARY_INTEGER, next_date IN  DATE    );
```

Example

Change the NEXT_DATE to 5 hours from right now:

```
dbms_job.nex_date( 12345, sysdate + 5/60 );
```

INSTANCE()

The INSTANCE() procedure allow you to change the INSTANCE attribute of the given job. If FORCE is TRUE, then the instance ID that you are setting need not be up, but if it is FALSE (the default) then the instance ID must currently be up and running.

Usage

```
PROCEDURE instance ( job      IN BINARY_INTEGER,
                     instance IN BINARY_INTEGER,
                     force    IN BOOLEAN DEFAULT FALSE);
```

Example

Change the instance ID to 3 even though instance 3 is not currently up.

```
dbms_job.instance( 12345, 3, TRUE );
```

INTERVAL()

The INTERVAL() procedure allows you to change the INTERVAL attribute of the given job.

Usage

```
PROCEDURE interval  ( job      IN  BINARY_INTEGER,
                      interval IN  VARCHAR2 );
```

Example

Change the interval to be every hour, on the hour.

```
dbms_job.interval( 12345, 'trunc(sysdate,''HH'')+(1/24)' );
```

BROKEN()

The BROKEN() procedure allows you to set the BROKEN status of the given job. BROKEN jobs are never run. You can use this procedure to disable a job but keep it in the queue. Setting the BROKEN parameter to TRUE sets the job's BROKEN status to Y. If you are re-enabling a job, then you can use the NEXT_DATE parameter to set its next scheduled run-time.

923

Usage

```
PROCEDURE broken      ( job       IN   BINARY_INTEGER,
                        broken     IN   BOOLEAN,
                        next_date  IN   DATE DEFAULT SYSDATE );
```

Example

Enable a broken job to run 15 minutes from now.

```
dbms_job.broken( 12345,
                 FALSE,
                 sysdate + (15/1440) );
```

UTL_RAW

The supplied package UTL_RAW is for work with the database type RAW. It is, as the name suggests, a utilities package for manipulating RAWs. Since PL/SQL does not allow the overloading of RAW and VARCHAR2, this package is required. This package contains all the standard procedures and functions that you would expect. Using the RAW data type is useful when working with binary data. Also the RAW data type is not affected by characterset conversions if it is transferred between databases with alternative charactersets. The specification can be found in $ORACLE_HOME/rdbms/admin/utlraw.sql.

Here are the functions in this package (there are no procedures):

Functions	
BIT_AND() – returns RAW	COMPARE – returns NUMBER
BIT_COMPLEMENT() – returns RAW	CONCAT() – returns RAW
BIT_OR() – returns RAW	CONVERT() – returns RAW
BIT_XOR() – returns RAW	COPIES() – returns RAW
CAST_FROM_BINARY_INTEGER() – returns RAW	LENGTH() – returns NUMBER
CAST_FROM_NUMBER() – returns RAW	OVERLAY() – returns RAW
CAST_TO_BINARY_INTEGER() – returns BINARY_INTEGER	REVERSE() – returns RAW
CAST_TO_NUMBER() – returns NUMBER	SUBSTR() – returns RAW
CAST_TO_NVARCHAR2() – returns NVARCHAR2	TRANSLATE() – returns RAW
CAST_TO_RAW() – returns RAW	TRANSLITERATE() – returns RAW
CAST_TO_VARCHAR2() – returns VARCHAR2	XRANGE() – returns RAW

CONCAT ()

The CONCAT() function concatenates up to 12 RAWs into a single RAW. If the resulting RAW is over 32K, a VALUE_ERROR is raised.

Usage

```
FUNCTION concat(r1  IN RAW DEFAULT NULL,
                r2  IN RAW DEFAULT NULL,
                r3  IN RAW DEFAULT NULL,
                r4  IN RAW DEFAULT NULL,
                r5  IN RAW DEFAULT NULL,
                r6  IN RAW DEFAULT NULL,
                r7  IN RAW DEFAULT NULL,
                r8  IN RAW DEFAULT NULL,
                r9  IN RAW DEFAULT NULL,
                r10 IN RAW DEFAULT NULL,
                r11 IN RAW DEFAULT NULL,
                r12 IN RAW DEFAULT NULL) RETURN RAW;
```

Example

```
SQL> select utl_raw.concat( '9', '0102', 'ff', '0a2b' ) from dual;

UTL_RAW.CONCAT('9','0102','FF','0A2B')
--------------------------------------------------------------------------
090102FF0A2B
```

CAST_TO_RAW()

The CAST_TO_RAW() function converts a VARCHAR2 of N data bytes into a RAW with the same number of data bytes.

Usage

```
FUNCTION cast_to_raw(c IN VARCHAR2 CHARACTER SET ANY_CS) RETURN RAW;
```

Example

```
SQL> select utl_raw.cast_to_raw( 'Cameron' ) from dual;

UTL_RAW.CAST_TO_RAW('CAMERON')
--------------------------------------------------------------------------
43616D65726F6E
```

CAST_TO_VARCHAR2() / CAST_TO_NVARCHAR2()

The CAST_TO_VARCHAR2() function is the opposite of the CAST_TO_RAW(). It will convert a RAW of N data bytes into a VARCHAR2 with N data bytes. If the characterset of the database is different then the result will probably be garbage. The CAST_TO_NVARCHAR2() function works just like the CAST_TO_RAW() function except that it returns a NVARCHAR2 data type value.

Usage

```
FUNCTION cast_to_varchar2(r IN RAW) RETURN VARCHAR2;
FUNCTION cast_to_nvarchar2(r IN RAW) RETURN NVARCHAR2;
```

Example

```
SQL> select utl_raw.cast_to_varchar2( '43616D65726F6E') from dual;

UTL_RAW.CAST_TO_VARCHAR2('43616D65726F6E')
---------------------------------------------------------------------------
Cameron
```

LENGTH()

The function LENGTH() returns the length of the imputed RAW value.

Usage

```
FUNCTION length(r IN RAW) RETURN NUMBER;
```

Example

It we take our raw value from the above example, we should get 7 since 'Cameron' has a length of 7.

```
SQL> select utl_raw.length( '43616D65726F6E') from dual;

UTL_RAW.LENGTH('43616D65726F6E')
--------------------------------
                               7
```

SUBSTR()

The SUBSTR() function returns a RAW starting from position POS of the length LEN. If LEN is omitted or NULL, the RAW starting at POS to the end of the RAW will be returned. If POS = 0, or LEN < 1 then a VALUE ERROR exception is raised.

Usage

```
FUNCTION substr(r   IN RAW,
                pos IN BINARY_INTEGER,
                len IN BINARY_INTEGER DEFAULT NULL) RETURN RAW;
```

Example

```
SQL> select utl_raw.substr( '0102030405', 3, 2 ) from dual;

UTL_RAW.SUBSTR('0102030405',3,2)
---------------------------------------------------------------------------
0304
```

TRANSLATE()

The TRANSLATE() function, given a RAW R, will replace every occurrence of each byte in FROM_SET with the corresponding positional byte in TO_SET. If a byte in FROM_SET is not present in R, it is skipped. Any byte in FROM_SET without a matching positional byte in TO_SET will be removed from R.

Usage

```
FUNCTION translate(r        IN RAW,
                   from_set IN RAW,
                   to_set   IN RAW) RETURN RAW;
```

Example

In the following example, we want to replace every 0x02 byte with 0x06. Since 0x03 does not have a positional match in TO_SET, it is removed.

```
SQL> select utl_raw.translate( '0102030405', '0203', '06' ) from dual;

UTL_RAW.TRANSLATE('010203040502','0203','06')
----------------------------------------------------------------------
0106040506
```

TRANSLITERATE()

This works similar to TRANSLATE() except that the result will always be the same length as the input R. If TO_SET is shorter than FROM_SET then those values in TO_SET without a positional match in FROM_SET will be replaced by either the first byte in PAD, if PAD is not NULL, or 0x00 if PAD is omitted or NULL;

Usage

```
FUNCTION transliterate(r        IN RAW,
                       to_set   IN RAW DEFAULT NULL,
                       from_set IN RAW DEFAULT NULL,
                       pad      IN RAW DEFAULT NULL) RETURN RAW;
```

Example

```
SQL> select utl_raw.transliterate( '010203040502', '0809', '01020304', '0a' )
     from dual;

UTL_RAW.TRANSLITERATE('010203040502','0809','01020304','0A')
----------------------------------------------------------------------
08090A0A0509
```

OVERLAY()

The function OVERLAY() returns a raw with the specified portion of TARGET replaced with ORVERLAY_STR. It will start at POS and replace LEN bytes of TARGET with LEN bytes of OVERLAY_STR.

If this occurs...	... this is the result
Length of OVERLAY_STR < LEN	OVERLAY_STR padded out to LEN bytes with the first PAD byte
Length of OVERLAY_STR > LEN	Extra bytes in OVERLAY_STR are ignored
POS + LEN > length of TARGET	TARGET is extended to contain the entire length of OVERLAY_STR
POS > length of TARGET	TARGET is extended to length POS with PAD and then extended LEN bytes of OVERLAY

Usage

```
FUNCTION overlay(overlay_str IN RAW,
                 target      IN RAW,
                 pos         IN BINARY_INTEGER DEFAULT 1,
                 len         IN BINARY_INTEGER DEFAULT NULL,
                 pad         IN RAW            DEFAULT NULL) RETURN RAW;
```

Example

Replace the first two bytes of 0x'010203' with 0x'AABB':

```
SQL> select utl_raw.overlay( 'aabb', '010203' ) from dual;

UTL_RAW.OVERLAY('AABB','010203')
--------------------------------------------------------------------------
AABB03
```

Replace two bytes of 0x'010203' with 0x'AABB', starting at the second byte:

```
SQL> select utl_raw.overlay( 'aabb', '010203', 2 ) from dual;

UTL_RAW.OVERLAY('AABB','010203',2)
--------------------------------------------------------------------------
01AABB
```

Replace two bytes of 0x'010203' with 0x'AABB', starting at the fifth byte. Since there is no fifth byte in that string and no PAD was supplied, 0x00 is used as the PAD.

```
SQL> select utl_raw.overlay( 'aabb', '010203', 5 ) from dual;

UTL_RAW.OVERLAY('AABB','010203',5)
--------------------------------------------------------------------------
01020300AABB
```

Replace the second byte of 0x'010203' with the first byte of 0x'AABB'.

```
SQL> select utl_raw.overlay( 'aabb', '010203', 2, 1 ) from dual;

UTL_RAW.OVERLAY('AABB','010203',2,1)
-----------------------------------------------------------------------------
01AA03
```

Replace the fifth byte of $0x'010203'$ with the first byte of $0x'AABB'$. Since there are only three bytes in $0x'010203'$, it will be padded out with PAD.

```
SQL> select utl_raw.overlay( 'aabb', '010203', 5, 1, 'FF' ) from dual;

UTL_RAW.OVERLAY('AABB','010203',5,1,'FF')
-----------------------------------------------------------------------------
010203FFAA
```

Exceptions

A VALUE_ERROR exception raised when:

❑ OVERLAY is NULL

❑ Length of result is longer than max length of a RAW

❑ LEN < 0

❑ POS < 1

COPIES()

The COPIES() function returns N copies of R concatenated together.

Usage

```
FUNCTION copies(r IN RAW,
                n IN NUMBER) RETURN RAW;
```

Example

```
SQL> select utl_raw.copies( '010203', 4 ) from dual;

UTL_RAW.COPIES('010203',4)
-----------------------------------------------------------------------------
010203010203010203010203
```

Exceptions

A VALUE ERROR exception is raised when:

❑ R is NULL

❑ R is 0 length

❑ N < 1

❑ Resulting RAW value is longer than the max length of a RAW

929

XRANGE()

The XRANGE() function returns a RAW starting at the START_BYTE and including every byte in succession to END_BYTE. If END_BYTE is less than START_BYTE, the range will wrap from 0x'FF' to 0x'01' and continue on to END_BYTE.

Usage

```
FUNCTION xrange(start_byte IN RAW DEFAULT NULL,
                end_byte   IN RAW DEFAULT NULL) RETURN RAW;
```

Example

```
SQL> select utl_raw.xrange( '01', '11' ) from dual;

UTL_RAW.XRANGE('01','11')
--------------------------------------------------------------------------------
0102030405060708090A0B0C0D0E0F1011

SQL> select utl_raw.xrange( 'fa', '06' ) from dual;

UTL_RAW.XRANGE('FA','06')
-------------------------------------------------------------------------------
FAFBFCFDFEFF00010203040506
```

REVERSE()

The REVERSE() function will reverse the RAW from end to end; the first byte becomes the last, the second byte becomes the second to last, and so on.

Usage

```
FUNCTION reverse(r IN RAW) RETURN RAW;
```

Example

```
SQL> select utl_raw.reverse( '0102030405' ) from dual;

UTL_RAW.REVERSE('0102030405')
-------------------------------------------------------------------------------
0504030201
```

Exception

A VALUE_ERROR is raised when the input R is Null.

COMPARE()

The COMPARE() function compares R1 and R2. If they differ in size, the shorter parameter will be padded out with PAD. It will return 0 is they are the same, otherwise it will return the index of the first mismatched byte.

Usage

```
FUNCTION compare(r1  IN RAW,
                 r2  IN RAW,
                 pad IN RAW DEFAULT NULL)  RETURN NUMBER;
```

Example

```
SQL> select utl_raw.compare( '010203', '01020304', '04' ) from dual;

UTL_RAW.COMPARE('010203','01020304','04')
-----------------------------------------
                                        0

SQL> select utl_raw.compare( '01050304', '01020304' ) from dual;

UTL_RAW.COMPARE('01050304','01020304')
--------------------------------------
                                     2
```

CONVERT()

The CONVERT() function will convert the raw R from the character set FROM_CHARSET to TO_CHARSET.

Usage

```
FUNCTION convert(r             IN RAW,
                 to_charset    IN VARCHAR2,
                 from_charset  IN VARCHAR2) RETURN RAW;
```

Exceptions

A VALUE_ERROR exception is raised when:

❑ R is NULL or 0 length

❑ TO_CHARSET or FROM_CHARSET NULL or 0 length

❑ TO_CHARSET or FROM_CHARSET is not supported by the Oracle server

BIT_AND()

The BIT_AND() function returns the bitwise logical AND of the supplied raws R1 and R2. If R1 and R2 are not of the same length, then bit for bit they are ANDed and the remaining bits of the longer are appended. If either parameter is NULL, NULL is returned.

Usage

```
FUNCTION bit_and(r1 IN RAW,
                 r2 IN RAW) RETURN RAW;
```

Example

Bitwise AND 0x01 and AND 0x0302. Remember 01 is 1 in binary and 03 is 11 in binary. Using AND should get you 01.

```
SQL> select utl_raw.bit_and( '01', '0302' ) from dual;

UTL_RAW.BIT_AND('01','0302')
--------------------------------------------------------------------------------
0102
```

BIT_OR()

The BIT_OR() function returns the bitwise logical OR of the supplied parameters R1 and R2. If R1 and R2 are of different lengths, the OR'ing is terminated at the last byte of the shorter and the extra bytes are appended to the result. If either parameter is NULL, NULL is returned.

Usage

```
FUNCTION bit_or(r1 IN RAW,
                r2 IN RAW) RETURN RAW;
```

Example

```
SQL> select utl_raw.bit_or( '01', '0302' ) from dual;

UTL_RAW.BIT_OR('01','0302')
--------------------------------------------------------------------------------
0302
```

BIT_XOR()

The BIT_XOR() function returns the bitwise exclusive OR of two RAW values, R1 and R2. If either parameter is longer than the other, the exclusive OR is terminated after the last byte of the shorter parameter and the remaining bytes are appended to the result. If either parameter is NULL, NULL is returned.

Usage

```
FUNCTION bit_xor(r1 IN RAW,
                 r2 IN RAW) RETURN RAW;
```

Example

```
SQL> select utl_raw.bit_xor( '01', '0302' ) from dual;

UTL_RAW.BIT_XOR('01','0302')
--------------------------------------------------------------------------------
0202
```

BIT_COMPLEMENT()

The BIT_COMPLEMENT() function returns the bitwise complement of the parameter R. It will return NULL if R was NULL.

Usage

```
FUNCTION bit_complement(r IN RAW) RETURN RAW;
```

Example

```
SQL> select utl_raw.bit_complement( '010203' ) from dual;

UTL_RAW.BIT_COMPLEMENT('010203')
--------------------------------------------------------------------------------
FEFDFC
```

CAST_FROM_NUMBER()

The CAST_FROM_NUMBER() function returns the binary representation of a number as a RAW.

Usage

```
FUNCTION cast_from_number(n IN NUMBER) RETURN RAW;
```

Example

```
SQL> select utl_raw.cast_from_number( 123.45 ) from dual;

UTL_RAW.CAST_FROM_NUMBER(123.45)
--------------------------------------------------------------------------------
C202182E
```

CAST_TO_NUMBER()

The CAST_TO_NUMBER() function casts the binary representation of a number in a raw to a number.

Usage

```
FUNCTION cast_to_number(r IN RAW) RETURN NUMBER;
```

Example

```
SQL> select utl_raw.cast_to_number( 'c202182e' ) from dual;

UTL_RAW.CAST_TO_NUMBER('C202182E')
----------------------------------
                            123.45
```

CAST_FROM_BINARY_INTEGER()

The CAST_FROM_BINARY_INTEGER() function returns the binary representation of a binary integer as a RAW.

Usage

```
FUNCTION cast_from_binary_integer(n IN BINARY_INTEGER,
                                  endianess IN PLS_INTEGER DEFAULT 1)
                                  RETURN RAW;
```

Example

```
SQL> select utl_raw.cast_from_binary_integer( 12345 ) from dual;

UTL_RAW.CAST_FROM_BINARY_INTEGER(12345)
--------------------------------------------------------------------------
00003039
```

CAST_TO_BINARY_INTEGER()

The CAST_TO_BINARY_INTEGER() function casts the binary representation of a binary integer in a raw to a binary integer.

Usage

```
FUNCTION cast_to_binary_integer(r IN RAW,
                                endianess IN PLS_INTEGER DEFAULT 1)
                                RETURN BINARY_INTEGER;
```

Example

```
SQL> select utl_raw.cast_to_binary_integer( '00003039' ) from dual;

UTL_RAW.CAST_TO_BINARY_INTEGER('00003039')
-----------------------------------------
                                    12345
```

DBMS_LOB

Since Oracle 8, Oracle has supported Large Objects, LOBS. Initially, there was no native support for these objects. The DBMS_LOB package was created to allow developers to manipulate LOBs. In Oracle 9, native support exists for some of the features in this package but the package still exists to provide both the additional functionality for BFILES and backwards compatibility. The spec for DBMS_LOB can be found in $ORACLE_HOME/rdbms/admin/dbmslob.sql.

Here are its functions and procedures:

Procedures	Functions
APPEND()	COMPARE() - returns NUMBER(38)
CLOSE()	FILEEXISTS() - returns NUMBER(38)
COPY()	FILEISOPEN() - returns NUMBER(38)
CREATETEMPORARY()	GETCHUNKSIZE() - returns NUMBER(38)
ERASE()	GETLENGTH() - returns NUMBER(38)
FILECLOSE()	INSTR() - returns NUMBER(38)
FILECLOSEALL()	ISOPEN() - returns NUMBER(38)
FILEGETNAME()	ISTEMPORARY() - returns NUMBER(38)
FILEOPEN()	SUBSTR() - returns RAW
FREETEMPORARY()	SUBSTR() - returns VARCHAR2
LOADFROMFILE()	
OPEN()	
READ()	
TRIM()	
WRITE()	
WRITEAPPEND()	

We saw LOBs introduced in Chapter 3, and more information can be found in the Oracle documentation *Application Developer's Guide - Large Objects*. LOBs are good for storing unstructured data like images, video, music, and when you want to store your data outside the database on the file system.

The DBMS_LOB package acts upon the LOB locator. This locator can point to either:

❏ Internal LOB – These are LOBs that are defined in SQL and are columns of database tables.

❏ External LOB – These are locators to physical external files located in a DIRECTORY object. These LOBs are knows as BFILES.

❏ Temporary LOB – These LOBs are defined in some programming interface like PL/SQL or OCI (Oracle Call Interface for C). These are mainly for performing transformations on LOB data.

LOBs can be up to 4 Gb in size but PL/SQL VARCHAR2s and RAWs can only be 32767K. This can be an issue if you are attempting to convert a LOB into a VARCHAR2 or a RAW.

Dealing with LOBs can be a bit tricky. An empty LOB and NULL is not the same thing. You will get an error if you attempt to perform LOB operations on a NULL. There is a built-in function EMPTY_CLOB() that will allow you to create an empty LOB to avoid this error:

```
SQL> create table my_lob(
  2     id number,
  3     c clob )
  4  /

Table created.


SQL> insert into my_lob values ( 1, empty_clob() );

1 row created.
```

Most of the CLOB manipulations are now, as of 9*i*, supported directly in SQL. SUBSTR(), INSTR() and TRIM(), now work on LOBs as well as VARCHAR2s. BFILES still need to be accessed and manipulated through the DBMS_LOB package. If you want to store your .pdf files on the filesystem but modify and maintain them in the database you can do the following.

First create a DIRECTORY.

```
SQL> connect system/manager as sysdba
Connected.

SQL> create or replace directory wrox_dir as 'C:\Temp';

Directory created.

SQL> grant read, write on directory wrox_dir to public;

Grant succeeded.
```

Now, create a table to store the BFILE locator and insert a row.

```
SQL> connect chris/chris
Connected.

SQL> create table bfile_table(
  2     name varchar2(255),
  3     the_file bfile );

Table created.

SQL> insert into bfile_table values ( 'doc 1', bfilename( 'WROX_DIR', 'my_doc.pdf'
) );

1 row created.

SQL> commit;

Commit complete.
```

There is no guarantee that the file `my_doc.pdf` exists. Oracle cannot manage files not in the database. To see if it is a valid file we could run the following:

```
SQL> declare
  2    l_bfile bfile;
  3    l_dir_alias varchar2(2000);
  4    l_filename varchar2(2000);
  5  begin
  6    select the_file
  7      into l_bfile
  8      from bfile_table
  9     where name = 'doc 1';
 10    dbms_lob.fileopen( l_bfile, dbms_lob.file_readonly );
 11    if dbms_lob.fileexists( l_bfile ) = 1 then
 12      dbms_output.put_line( 'Valid file' );
 13    else
 14      dbms_output.put_line( 'Not a valid file' );
 15    end if;
 16    if dbms_lob.fileisopen( l_bfile ) = 1 then
 17      dbms_lob.fileclose( l_bfile );
 18    end if;
 19  end;
 20  /

Valid file

PL/SQL procedure successfully completed.
```

That ensures that the file is on the file system.

Exceptions

The following is a list of the DBMS_LOB exceptions that the package can raise:

Exception	Error Code	Description
INVALID_ARGVAL	21560	An argument passed in was NULL, invalid or out of range.
ACCESS_ERROR	22925	You are attempting to write more that 4 Gb to the LOB.
NOEXIST_DIRECTORY	22285	The directory does not exist.
NOPRIV_DIRECTORY	22286	Oracle does not have permission to write to the directory or the file.
INVALID_DIRECTORY	22287	The DIRECTORY object being accessed is not valid.
OPERATION_FAILED	22288	The operation attempted failed.

Table continued on following page

Exception	Error Code	Description
UNOPENED_FILE	22289	The file is not opened.
OPEN_TOOMANY	22290	The maximum number of files has been opened.
NO_DATA_FOUND		Attempt was made to read a NULL LOB or read past the end of the LOB.
VALUE_ERROR	6502	Invalid argument type passed into a procedure.

Just like in UTL_FILE, it is important to close all of your LOB locators. By default, they will be all closed at the end of a session, but you should make an effort to manually close them in your program.

Most of the procedures and functions in this package are overloaded to support both CLOBs and BLOBs.

Let's take a look at the APIs.

APPEND ()

The APPEND() procedure appends the SRC_LOB to the end of the DEST_LOB. It is overloaded for both BLOBs and CLOBs.

Usage

```
PROCEDURE append(dest_lob IN OUT NOCOPY BLOB,
                 src_lob  IN            BLOB);

PROCEDURE append(dest_lob IN OUT NOCOPY CLOB CHARACTER SET ANY_CS,
                 src_lob  IN            CLOB CHARACTER SET dest_lob%CHARSET);
```

CLOSE()

The procedure CLOSE() will close any previously opened internal or external LOBs. It is overloaded for BLOBs, CLOBs, and BFILEs.

Usage

```
PROCEDURE close(lob_loc IN OUT NOCOPY BLOB);

PROCEDURE close(lob_loc IN OUT NOCOPY CLOB CHARACTER SET ANY_CS);

PROCEDURE close(file_loc IN OUT NOCOPY BFILE);
```

COMPARE()

The COMPARE() function will compare two similar LOBs, or part of them as defined by the input ranges. If equal, zero is returned. Otherwise a non-zero value is returned. If you are comparing BFILEs, they must already have been opened. It is overloaded for as, CLOBs, and BFILEs.

Usage

```
FUNCTION compare(lob_1    IN CLOB CHARACTER SET ANY_CS,
                 lob_2    IN CLOB CHARACTER SET lob_1%CHARSET,
                 amount   IN INTEGER := 4294967295,
                 offset_1 IN INTEGER := 1,
                 offset_2 IN INTEGER := 1)
  RETURN INTEGER;

FUNCTION compare(lob_1    IN BLOB,
                 lob_2    IN BLOB,
                 amount   IN INTEGER := 4294967295,
                 offset_1 IN INTEGER := 1,
                 offset_2 IN INTEGER := 1)
  RETURN INTEGER;

FUNCTION compare(file_1   IN BFILE,
                 file_2   IN BFILE,
                 amount   IN INTEGER,
                 offset_1 IN INTEGER := 1,
                 offset_2 IN INTEGER := 1)
  RETURN INTEGER;
```

Example

```
SQL> declare
  2    c1 clob := 'chris';
  3    c2 clob := 'sean';
  4  begin
  5    dbms_output.put_line(
  6      dbms_lob.compare( c1, c2 ) );
  7    dbms_output.put_line(
  8      dbms_lob.compare( c1, c2, 1, 5, 1 ) );
  9  end;
 10  /
-1
0

PL/SQL procedure successfully completed.
```

COPY()

The COPY() procedure will copy the AMOUNT of the SRC_LOB starting at SRC_OFFSET to the DEST_LOB starting at the DEST_OFFSET. If the DEST_OFFSET is beyond its end, non-Null padding will be appended before the copy takes place. The procedure is overloaded to copy both BLOBs and CLOBs.

Usage

```
PROCEDURE copy(dest_lob    IN OUT NOCOPY BLOB,
               src_lob     IN            BLOB,
               amount      IN            INTEGER,
               dest_offset IN            INTEGER := 1,
               src_offset  IN            INTEGER := 1);
```

939

```
PROCEDURE copy(dest_lob    IN OUT NOCOPY   CLOB CHARACTER SET ANY_CS,
               src_lob     IN              CLOB CHARACTER SET dest_lob%CHARSET,
               amount      IN              INTEGER,
               dest_offset IN              INTEGER := 1,
               src_offset  IN              INTEGER := 1);
```

CREATETEMPORARY()

The CREATETEMPORARY() procedure creates a temporary BLOB or CLOB in your default temporary tablespace. The CACHE parameter tells whether or not the LOB should be saved into the buffer cache. The DUR parameter tells Oracle when the LOB should be cleaned up at the end of the session or call. Use the global constants DBMS_LOB.SESSION and a for DUR's value.

Usage

```
PROCEDURE createtemporary(lob_loc IN OUT NOCOPY   BLOB,
                          cache   IN              BOOLEAN,
                          dur     IN              PLS_INTEGER := 10);

PROCEDURE createtemporary(lob_loc IN OUT NOCOPY   CLOB CHARACTER SET ANY_CS,
                          cache   IN              BOOLEAN,
                          dur     IN              PLS_INTEGER := 10);
```

ERASE()

The erase procedure erases some or all of a BLOB or CLOB. It starts at OFFSET and erases AMOUNT bytes/characters. If a + OFFSET is greater than the length of the LOB, then everything from OFFSET is erased and the exact number of bytes/characters erased are returned in the IN OUT parameter AMOUNT. The length of the LOB remains the same. The erased bytes/characters are zeroed out with Null-bytes or spaces.

Usage

```
PROCEDURE erase(lob_loc IN OUT NOCOPY   BLOB,
                amount  IN OUT NOCOPY   INTEGER,
                offset  IN              INTEGER := 1);

PROCEDURE erase(lob_loc IN OUT NOCOPY   CLOB CHARACTER SET ANY_CS,
                amount  IN OUT NOCOPY   INTEGER,
                offset  IN              INTEGER := 1);
```

Example

```
SQL> declare
  2     l_c clob := 'Hello World!';
  3     l_a number := 9;
  4  begin
  5     dbms_lob.erase( l_c, l_a, 6 );
  6     dbms_output.put_line( 'The clob now = *' || l_c || '*' );
  7     dbms_output.put_line( 'The amount that was erased was: ' || l_a );
  8  end;
  9  /
```

```
The clob now = *Hello        *
The amount that was erased was: 7

PL/SQL procedure successfully completed.
```

Notice that L_C is still as long as it was; just the string 'World!' was erased. And we asked to erase 9 characters, but given the offset we supplied, only 7 were actually erased.

FILECLOSE()

The FILECLOSE() procedure will close a previously open BFILE.

Usage

```
PROCEDURE fileclose(file_loc IN OUT NOCOPY  BFILE);
```

FILECLOSEALL()

The FILECLOSEALL() procedure will close all BFILES opened in a session.

Usage

```
PROCEDURE filecloseall;
```

FILEEXISTS()

The FILEEXISTS() function is used to determine if the FILE_LOC points to a valid file on the file system. It returns 0 if the file does not exist, 1 if it does.

Usage

```
FUNCTION fileexists(file_loc IN BFILE)
  RETURN INTEGER;
```

FILEGETNAME()

The FILEGETNAME() procedure returns via OUT parameters, DIR_ALIAS and FILENAME, the directory alias and the filename of the FILE_LOC. Not the physical directory and filename but rather that of the FILE_LOC.

Usage

```
PROCEDURE filegetname(file_loc  IN  BFILE,
                      dir_alias OUT VARCHAR2,
                      filename  OUT VARCHAR2);
```

Example

```
SQL> declare
  2    l_bfile bfile;
  3    l_dir_alias varchar2(2000);
```

941

```
    4    l_filename varchar2(2000);
    5  begin
    6    select the_file
    7      into l_bfile
    8      from bfile_table
    9     where name = 'doc 1';
   10    dbms_lob.fileopen( l_bfile, dbms_lob.file_readonly );
   11    if dbms_lob.fileexists( l_bfile ) = 1 then
   12      dbms_lob.filegetname( l_bfile, l_dir_alias, l_filename );
   13      dbms_output.put_line( 'Directory alias: ' || l_dir_alias );
   14      dbms_output.put_line( 'Filename: ' || l_filename );
   15    end if;
   16    if dbms_lob.fileisopen( l_bfile ) = 1 then
   17      dbms_lob.fileclose( l_bfile );
   18    end if;
   19* end;
SQL> /
Directory alias: WROX_DIR
Filename: my_doc.pdf

PL/SQL procedure successfully completed.
```

FILEISOPEN()

The FILEISOPEN() function determines if the supplied BFILE was previously opened. It returns 0 if the file is not open, 1 if it is open.

Usage

```
FUNCTION fileisopen(file_loc IN BFILE)
  RETURN INTEGER;
```

FILEOPEN()

The FILEOPEN() procedure is used to open an external BFILE.

Usage

```
PROCEDURE fileopen(file_loc  IN OUT NOCOPY  BFILE,
                   open_mode IN      BINARY_INTEGER := file_readonly);
```

FREETEMPORARY()

The FREETEMPORARY() procedure will free a previously allocated temporary LOB.

Usage

```
PROCEDURE freetemporary(lob_loc IN OUT NOCOPY  BLOB);

PROCEDURE freetemporary(lob_loc IN OUT NOCOPY  CLOB CHARACTER SET ANY_CS);
```

GETCHUNKSIZE()

The GETCHUNKSIZE() function returns the amount of space used in the LOB chunk to store the LOB value. It helps performance if you read and write LOBs by this amount. Writes are versioned by the chunk so if you write a chunk at a time there is no extra or duplicated versioning done. The function is overloaded for both CLOB and BLOB.

Usage

```
FUNCTION getchunksize(lob_loc IN BLOB)
   RETURN INTEGER;

FUNCTION getchunksize(lob_loc IN CLOB CHARACTER SET ANY_CS)
   RETURN INTEGER;
```

Example

```
SQL> select dbms_lob.getchunksize( c ) from my_lob;

DBMS_LOB.GETCHUNKSIZE(C)
------------------------
                    4036
```

Notice, it is a little less than 4K, the database block size. That is because there is little system-related information stored with the LOB.

GETLENGTH()

The GETLENGTH() function returns the length of the LOB locater. It is overloaded for all three LOB types, CLOB, BLOB, and BFILE. In 9*i*, the built-in function LENGTH() will also work.

Usage

```
FUNCTION getlength(lob_loc IN BLOB)
   RETURN INTEGER;

FUNCTION getlength(lob_loc IN CLOB CHARACTER SET ANY_CS)
   RETURN INTEGER;

FUNCTION getlength(file_loc IN BFILE)
   RETURN INTEGER;
```

INSTR()

The INSTR() function returns the position of NTH occurrence of PATTERN in the LOB starting at the position OFFSET. It is overloaded for CLOBs, BLOBs, and BFILEs. In 9*i*, the built-in function INSTR() will work on LOBS as well as VARCHAR2.

Usage

```
FUNCTION instr(lob_loc IN BLOB,
               pattern IN RAW,
               offset  IN INTEGER := 1,
               nth     IN INTEGER := 1)
   RETURN INTEGER;

FUNCTION instr(lob_loc IN CLOB     CHARACTER SET ANY_CS,
               pattern IN VARCHAR2 CHARACTER SET lob_loc%CHARSET,
               offset  IN INTEGER := 1,
               nth     IN INTEGER := 1)
   RETURN INTEGER;

FUNCTION instr(file_loc IN BFILE,
               pattern  IN RAW,
               offset   IN INTEGER := 1,
               nth      IN INTEGER := 1)
   RETURN INTEGER;
```

ISOPEN()

The ISOPEN() function is used to determine if a LOB was previously opened. It returns 1 if the LOB is open, 0 otherwise. The function is overloaded to support BLOB, CLOB, and BFILE.

Usage

```
function isopen(lob_loc in blob)
   RETURN INTEGER;

function isopen(lob_loc in clob character set any_cs)
   RETURN INTEGER;

function isopen(file_loc in bfile)
   RETURN INTEGER;
```

ISTEMPORARY()

The ISTEMPORARY() function is used to determine if a locator was created with the CREATETEMPORARY() procedure. It will return 1 if it is True, otherwise 0. The function is overloaded to support CLOB and BLOB.

Usage

```
FUNCTION  istemporary(lob_loc IN BLOB)
   RETURN INTEGER;

FUNCTION istemporary(lob_loc IN CLOB CHARACTER SET ANY_CS)
   RETURN INTEGER;
```

LOADFROMFILE()

The LOADFROMFILE() procedure allows the developer to copy the data from a BFILE into a BLOB or CLOB. The AMOUNT and OFFSETs can be specified for both the LOB and the BFILE.

Usage

```
PROCEDURE loadfromfile(dest_lob   IN OUT NOCOPY   BLOB,
                       src_lob    IN              BFILE,
                       amount     IN              INTEGER,
                       dest_offset IN             INTEGER := 1,
                       src_offset  IN             INTEGER := 1);

PROCEDURE loadfromfile(dest_lob   IN OUT NOCOPY   CLOB CHARACTER SET ANY_CS,
                       src_lob    IN              BFILE,
                       amount     IN              INTEGER,
                       dest_offset IN             INTEGER := 1,
                       src_offset  IN             INTEGER := 1);
```

OPEN()

The OPEN() procedure allows the developer to open both internal and external locators with the mode supplied. The modes are LOB_READONLY and LOB_READWRITE. External LOBs, BFILEs, can only be opened in LOB_READONLY mode.

Usage

```
PROCEDURE open(lob_loc   IN OUT NOCOPY BLOB,
               open_mode IN      BINARY_INTEGER);

PROCEDURE open(lob_loc   IN OUT NOCOPY CLOB CHARACTER SET ANY_CS,
               open_mode IN      BINARY_INTEGER);

PROCEDURE open(file_loc  IN OUT NOCOPY BFILE,
               open_mode IN      BINARY_INTEGER := file_readonly);
```

READ()

The READ() procedure reads AMOUNT of characters/bytes into the OUT parameter BUFFER, starting at the position OFFSET. The procedure is overloaded to support all three LOB types.

Usage

```
PROCEDURE read(lob_loc IN              BLOB,
               amount  IN OUT NOCOPY   BINARY_INTEGER,
               offset  IN              INTEGER,
               buffer  OUT             RAW);

PROCEDURE read(lob_loc IN              CLOB      CHARACTER SET ANY_CS,
               amount  IN OUT NOCOPY   BINARY_INTEGER,
               offset  IN              INTEGER,
               buffer  OUT             VARCHAR2 CHARACTER SET lob_loc%CHARSET);

PROCEDURE read(file_loc IN             BFILE,
```

```
        amount   IN OUT NOCOPY   BINARY_INTEGER,
        offset   IN              INTEGER,
        buffer   OUT             RAW);
```

SUBSTR()

The SUBSTR() function will return the AMOUNT of characters/bytes starting at the OFFSET. This function is overloaded to support all three LOB types. In 9*i*, the built-in function SUBSTR() also works on LOBs.

Usage

```
        FUNCTION substr(lob_loc IN BLOB,
                        amount  IN INTEGER := 32767,
                        offset  IN INTEGER := 1)
           RETURN RAW;

        FUNCTION substr(lob_loc IN CLOB CHARACTER SET ANY_CS,
                        amount  IN INTEGER := 32767,
                        offset  IN INTEGER := 1)
           RETURN VARCHAR2 CHARACTER SET lob_loc%CHARSET;

        FUNCTION substr(file_loc IN BFILE,
                        amount  IN INTEGER := 32767,
                        offset  IN INTEGER := 1)
           RETURN RAW;
```

TRIM()

The TRIM() procedure will shorten the supplied LOB to the length NEWLEN. It is overloaded to support CLOBs and BLOBs. The built-in function TRIM() now works with LOBs directly in 9*i*.

Usage

```
        PROCEDURE trim(lob_loc IN OUT NOCOPY  BLOB,
                       newlen  IN             INTEGER);

        PROCEDURE trim(lob_loc IN OUT NOCOPY  CLOB CHARACTER SET ANY_CS,
                       newlen  IN             INTEGER);
```

WRITE()

The WRITE() procedure writes the AMOUNT of characters/bytes in the BUFFER into the LOB starting at the position OFFSET. It is overloaded to support both CLOBs and BLOBs. If there is less data in BUFFER than AMOUNT specified, an error is raised. If there is more data in BUFFER, then only AMOUNT is written. If the OFFSET is greater than the LOB's length, the LOB is padded out and then the BUFFER is written. The procedure is overloaded to support CLOB and BLOB.

Usage

```
        PROCEDURE write(lob_loc IN OUT NOCOPY  BLOB,
                        amount  IN             BINARY_INTEGER,
                        offset  IN             INTEGER,
                        buffer  IN             RAW);
```

946

```
PROCEDURE write(lob_loc IN OUT NOCOPY  CLOB      CHARACTER SET ANY_CS,
                amount   IN             BINARY_INTEGER,
                offset   IN             INTEGER,
                buffer   IN             VARCHAR2 CHARACTER SET lob_loc%CHARSET);
```

Example

```
SQL> declare
  2     l_clob clob := '12345';
  3  begin
  4     dbms_lob.write( l_clob, 2, 3, 'AB' );
  5     dbms_output.put_line( l_clob );
  6     dbms_lob.write( l_clob, 2, 9, 'CD' );
  7     dbms_output.put_line( l_clob );
  8  end;
  9  /
12AB5
12AB5    CD

PL/SQL procedure successfully completed.
```

Notice the CLOB was padded out with spaces to accommodate the larger OFFSET.

WRITEAPPEND()

The WRITEAPPEND() procedure writes the AMOUNT of the BUFFER to the end of the LOB_LOC supplied. If the BUFFER is smaller than the AMOUNT supplied, an error occurs. If the BUFFER is greater, then only the AMOUNT is written.

Usage

```
PROCEDURE writeappend(lob_loc IN OUT NOCOPY  BLOB,
                      amount   IN      BINARY_INTEGER,
                      buffer   IN      RAW);

PROCEDURE writeappend(lob_loc IN OUT NOCOPY CLOB      CHARACTER SET ANY_CS,
                      amount   IN             BINARY_INTEGER,
                      buffer   IN      VARCHAR2 CHARACTER SET lob_loc%CHARSET);
```

Example

```
SQL> declare
  2     l_clob clob := '12345';
  3  begin
  4     dbms_lob.writeappend( l_clob, 5, 'ABCDEFGHIJK' );
  5     dbms_output.put_line( l_clob );
  6  end;
  7  /
12345ABCDE

PL/SQL procedure successfully completed.
```

DBMS_SQL

The DBMS_SQL package allows the developer to execute DML and DDL SQL dynamically. This might not sound like that much of a deal, but consider writing a search procedure which selects values based on the users inputs. Using DBMS_SQL you can, at run-time, build the WHERE clause and execute the query. You can write a generic routine that prints the result to any query. That would be impossible using straight PL/SQL. SQL defined in a PL/SQL routine is parsed and verified at compile time. SQL executed with DBMS_SQL is not parsed until run-time.

Procedures	Functions
BIND_ARRAY()	EXECUTE() – returns NUMBER(38)
BIND_VARIABLE()	EXECUTE_AND_FETCH() – returns NUMBER(38)
CLOSE_CURSOR()	FETCH_ROWS() – returns NUMBER(38)
COLUMN_VALUE()	IS_OPEN() – returns BOOLEAN
COLUMN_VALUE_CHAR()	LAST_ERROR_POSITION() – returns NUMBER(38)
COLUMN_VALUE_LONG()	LAST_ROW_COUNT() – returns NUMBER(38)
COLUMN_VALUE_RAW()	LAST_ROW_ID() – returns ROWID
COLUMN_VALUE_ROWID()	LAST_SQL_FUNCTION_CODE() – returns NUMBER(38)
COLUMN_VALUE_ROWID()	OPEN_CURSOR() – returns NUMBER(38)
DEFINE_ARRAY()	
DEFINE_COLUMN()	
DEFINE_COLUMN_CHAR()	
DEFINE_COLUMN_LONG()	
DEFINE_COLUMN_RAW()	
DEFINE_COLUMN_ROWID()	
DESCRIBE_COLUMNS()	
DESCRIBE_COLUMNS2()	
PARSE()	
VARIABLE_VALUE()	
VARIABLE_VALUE_CHAR()	
VARIABLE_VALUE_RAW()	
VARIABLE_VALUE_ROWID()	

Before Oracle 8*i*, DBMS_SQL was the only way to perform dynamic SQL. With the introduction of the EXECUTE IMMEDIATE PL/SQL command, issuing some dynamic SQL became much easier. But DBMS_SQL is still required when you do not know the number of items in the select list, their types or the number of bind variables. You need to programmatically inspect and react to the query being executed. DBMS_SQL gives you the API to do just that. Any valid SQL can be executed using DBMS_SQL.

The flow is as follows:

1. Open a cursor. Every DBMS_SQL statement executed must first be associated with a DBMS_SQL cursor.

2. Parse the statement. This is the point in which Oracle verifies that the statement about to be executed is valid SQL.

3. If the statement requires values to be supplied via bind variables, then bind those values.

4. If it is not a query, execute the statement.

5. If the statement returns a value then associate those values with local variables.

or

4. If the statement was a query, specify the variables in your procedure that will accept the select list values.

5. Execute the query.

6. Fetch the row.

7. Read the resulting values into local storage.

Finish with

8. Close the cursor in either case.

DBMS_SQL allows for both single value and array binding, as well as single row and array fetching. Array processing is important because it allows you to process multiple rows/values at a time, making just a single network round trip to the server, so saving time and network bandwidth. Let's look at a few examples.

The PRINT_TABLE() procedure is an excellent example of using DBMS_SQL. This procedure will print the results of any SQL statement that is valid for the user executing it. It runs with AUTHID CURRENT_USER, which means that the SQL is parsed as executing the procedure and not the procedure owner himself.

949

```
SQL> create or replace
  2  procedure print_table( p_query in varchar2 )
  3  AUTHID CURRENT_USER is
  4      l_theCursor      integer default dbms_sql.open_cursor;
  5      l_columnValue    varchar2(4000);
  6      l_status         integer;
  7      l_descTbl        dbms_sql.desc_tab;
  8      l_colCnt         number;
  9  begin
 10      dbms_sql.parse( l_theCursor, p_query, dbms_sql.native );
 11      dbms_sql.describe_columns
 12        ( l_theCursor, l_colCnt, l_descTbl );
 13
 14      for i in 1 .. l_colCnt loop
 15        dbms_sql.define_column
 16          (l_theCursor, i, l_columnValue, 4000);
 17      end loop;
 18
 19      l_status := dbms_sql.execute(l_theCursor);
 20
 21      while ( dbms_sql.fetch_rows(l_theCursor) > 0 ) loop
 22        for i in 1 .. l_colCnt loop
 23          dbms_sql.column_value
 24            ( l_theCursor, i, l_columnValue );
 25          dbms_output.put_line
 26            ( rpad( l_descTbl(i).col_name, 30 )
 27            || ': ' ||
 28            substr( l_columnValue, 1, 200 ) );
 29        end loop;
 30        dbms_output.put_line( '------------------' );
 31      end loop;
 32
 33  end print_table;
 34  /

Procedure created.
```

And executing the procedure yields the following result:

```
SQL> exec print_table( 'select * from emp where empno like ''778%''' );
EMPNO                         : 7782
ENAME                         : CLARK
JOB                           : MANAGER
MGR                           : 7839
HIREDATE                      : 09-JUN-81
SAL                           : 2450
COMM                          :
DEPTNO                        : 10
------------------
EMPNO                         : 7788
ENAME                         : SCOTT
JOB                           : ANALYST
```

```
MGR                        : 7566
HIREDATE                   : 19-APR-87
SAL                        : 3000
COMM                       :
DEPTNO                     : 20
-----------------

PL/SQL procedure successfully completed.
```

The PRINT_TABLE() procedure, at run-time, dynamically executed a query, determined the columns selected, and printed the results. Don't worry too much about the implementation yet, just realize that using this package you can run any query or perform any valid SQL not known until run-time.

OPEN_CURSOR()

The OPEN_CURSOR() function returns a DBMS_SQL cursor. This cursor, or handle, is the reference to the SQL being executed. It will be passed into every other procedure and function in the DBMS_SQL API.

Usage

```
function open_cursor return integer;
```

PARSE()

The PARSE() procedure is called to verify that the SQL about to be executed is valid. Since SQL executed by DBMS_SQL is not validated when the procedure is compiled (it can't because the SQL is usually not known at that time), the PARSE() procedure checks the syntax of the SQL. If the SQL is invalid, an exception is raised.

Usage

```
procedure parse(c in integer,
                statement in varchar2,
                language_flag in integer);

procedure parse(c in integer,
                statement in varchar2s,
                lb in integer,
                ub in integer,
                lfflg in boolean,
                language_flag in integer);
```

There are two versions of parse. One that takes in a VARCHAR2 and on that takes in DBMS_SQL.VARCHAR2s. The VARCHAR2s is defined as:

```
type varchar2s is table of varchar2(256) index by binary_integer;
```

If your statement is larger than 32K you need to break it up into 256 character pieces and populate a VARCHAR2S type and use the alternative parse procedure. The LB and UB parameters tell Oracle the lower and upper bound of the VARCHAR2S entries. You need not start at index 1 but all the entries must be contiguous. LFFLG, line feed flag, tells Oracle whether or not to insert a new line at the end of each entry in the VARCHAR2S type. LANGUAGE_FLAG is a constant that defines how Oracle should handle the SQL statement. The values are:

❑ DBMS_SQL.V6 – Specifies version 6 behavior.

❑ DBMS_SQL.V7 – Specifies version 7 behavior.

❑ DBMS_SQL.NATIVE – Specifies current version behavior.

Example

Create a table FOO using the VARCHAR2S style of PARSE().

```
SQL> declare
  2      l_cursor number := dbms_sql.open_cursor;
  3      l_stmt dbms_sql.varchar2s;
  4  begin
  5      l_stmt(3)  := 'junk';
  6      l_stmt(4)  := 'create table foo';
  7      l_stmt(5)  := '( n numb';
  8      l_stmt(6)  := 'er, v varchar2(100)';
  9      l_stmt(7)  := ')';
 10      l_stmt(8)  := 'more junk';
 11      dbms_sql.parse( l_cursor,
 12                      l_stmt,
 13                      4,
 14                      7,
 15                      FALSE,
 16                      dbms_sql.native );
 17      dbms_sql.close_cursor( l_cursor );
 18  end;
 19  /

PL/SQL procedure successfully completed.


SQL> desc foo
 Name                                      Null?    Type
 ----------------------------------------- -------- ---------------------------
 N                                                  NUMBER
 V                                                  VARCHAR2(100)
```

Notice that the statement is broken up into pieces and stored in the VARCHAR2S type. Lines 7 and 8 break the word NUMBER up and lines 5 and 10 put junk into our variable yet the statement still processed. That is because we parsed only entries 4 through 7 (lines 13 and 14) and did not insert a line feed after each entry (line 15). Since the entire statement is not longer than 32K we could have passed it as a single VARCAHR2, but we chose to use the alternative to demonstrate how it works.

Also notice that we did not execute the statement, we only parsed it. DDL is automatically executed when the statement is parsed.

BIND_VARIABLE()

The BIND_VARIABLE() procedure allows the developer to programmatically populate placeholders, or bind variables, in the statement about to be executed. Bind variables are extremely important for performance. Bind variables allow you to parse a query once and reuse it, changing just the bind variable's value.

Usage

```
procedure bind_variable(c in integer, name in varchar2,
                        value in number);

procedure bind_variable(c in integer, name in varchar2,
                        value in varchar2 character set any_cs);

procedure bind_variable(c in integer, name in varchar2,
                        value in varchar2 character set a
                        out_value_size in integer);

procedure bind_variable(c in integer, name in varchar2, value in date);

procedure bind_variable(c in integer, name in varchar2, value in blob);

procedure bind_variable(c in integer, name in varchar2,
                        value in clob character set any_cs);

procedure bind_variable(c in integer, name in varchar2, value in bfile);

procedure bind_variable(c in integer, name in varchar2,
                                     value in urowid);

procedure bind_variable(c in integer, name in varchar2,
                        value in time_unconstrained);

procedure bind_variable(c in integer, name in varchar2,
                        value in timestamp_unconstrained);

procedure bind_variable(c in integer, name in varchar2,
                        value in TIME_TZ_UNCONSTRAINED);

procedure bind_variable(c in integer, name in varchar2,
                        value in TIMESTAMP_TZ_UNCONSTRAINED);

procedure bind_variable(c in integer, name in varchar2,
                        value in TIMESTAMP_LTZ_UNCONSTRAINED);

procedure bind_variable(c in integer, name in varchar2,
                        value in YMINTERVAL_UNCONSTRAINED);

procedure bind_variable(c in integer, name in varchar2,
                        value in DSINTERVAL_UNCONSTRAINED);

procedure bind_variable_char(c in integer, name in varchar2,
```

```
                                    value in char character set any_cs);

        procedure bind_variable_char(c in integer, name in varchar2,
                                     value in char character set any_cs,
                                     out_value_size in integer);

        procedure bind_variable_raw(c in integer, name in varchar2,
                                    value in raw);

        procedure bind_variable_rowid(c in integer, name in varchar2,
                                      value in rowid);
```

Notice that the bind variable procedure is heavily overloaded. That is because we need to be able to bind in any SQL database into our statement. Notice too that the last 4 BIND_VARIABLE() procedures end with _TYPE. That is because Oracle will autocast RAW and ROWID to VARCHAR2 so we need to explicitly call a correct procedure so the casting will not occur.

Example

```
SQL> select * from foo;

no rows selected

SQL> declare
  2      l_cursor number := dbms_sql.open_cursor;
  3      l_ignore number;
  4  begin
  5      dbms_sql.parse( l_cursor,
  6                      'insert into foo values ( :n, :c )',
  7                      dbms_sql.native );
  8      dbms_sql.bind_variable( l_cursor, ':N', 1 );
  9      dbms_sql.bind_variable( l_cursor, ':C', 'Chris' );
 10      l_ignore := dbms_sql.execute( l_cursor );
 11      dbms_sql.bind_variable( l_cursor, ':N', 2 );
 12      dbms_sql.bind_variable( l_cursor, ':C', 'Sean' );
 13      l_ignore := dbms_sql.execute( l_cursor );
 14      dbms_sql.close_cursor( l_cursor );
 15  end;
 16  /

PL/SQL procedure successfully completed.

SQL> select * from foo;

         N V
---------- ----------------------------------------
         1 Chris
         2 Sean
```

Here we parsed the statement only once, but executed it twice with different values. Parsing a statement is usually an expensive procedure so we use bind variables to cut down on the number of times we need to do it. Not only can we benefit from this, but the next user who executes this code can too. The query is stored in the shared SQL area of the database. When Oracle first attempts to parse this statement, it looks to see if the statement has already been parsed. If so, then it can use that parsed statement instead of re-parsing it thus saving processing time.

BIND_ARRAY()

The BIND_ARRAY() procedure allows the developer to bulk bind many values at a time. When executed the statement will be executed multiple times for each set of bind variables. Again, this procedure is heavily overloaded to support all SQL types.

Usage

```
procedure bind_array(c in integer,
                     name in varchar2,
                     <VARAIBLE_NAME> in <VARIABLE_TYPE>);

procedure bind_array(c in integer,
                     name in varchar2,
                     <VARIABLE_NAME> in <VARIABLE_TYPE>,
                     index1 in integer,
                     index2 in integer);
```

where the VARIABLE_TYPE is of one of the following types defined in the DBMS_SQL spec:

```
type Number_Table is table of number
  index by binary_integer;
type Varchar2_Table is table of varchar2(2000)
  index by binary_integer;
type Date_Table is table of date
  index by binary_integer;
type Blob_Table is table of Blob
  index by binary_integer;
type Clob_Table is table of Clob
  index by binary_integer;
type Bfile_Table is table of Bfile
  index by binary_integer;
type Urowid_Table is table of urowid
  index by binary_integer;
type time_table is table of time_unconstrained
  index by binary_integer;
type timestamp_table is table of timestamp_unconstrained
  index by binary_integer;
type time_with_time_zone_table is table of time_tz_unconstrained
  index by binary_integer;
type timestamp_with_time_zone_table is table of
  timestamp_tz_unconstrained index by binary_integer;
type timestamp_with_ltz_table is table of
  timestamp_ltz_unconstrained index by binary_integer;
```

955

```
   type interval_year_to_month_table is table of
     yminterval_unconstrained index by binary_integer;
   type interval_day_to_second_table is table of
     dsinterval_unconstrained index by binary_integer;
```

The alternative version of BIND_ARRAY() allows you to define the start and stop indexes of the appropriate table types. It works the same way as the lower and upper bound parameters in the PARSE() procedure.

Example

Rewrite the BIND_VARIABLE() example above to use bulk binds.

```
SQL> declare
  2      l_cursor number := dbms_sql.open_cursor;
  3      l_ignore number;
  4      l_num dbms_sql.number_table;
  5      l_var dbms_sql.varchar2_table;
  6  begin
  7      dbms_sql.parse( l_cursor,
  8                      'insert into foo values ( :n, :c )',
  9                      dbms_sql.native );
 10      l_num(1) := 3;
 11      l_num(2) := 4;
 12      l_var(1) := 'Tom';
 13      l_var(2) := 'Joel';
 14      dbms_sql.bind_array( l_cursor, ':N', l_num );
 15      dbms_sql.bind_array( l_cursor, ':C', l_var );
 16      l_ignore := dbms_sql.execute( l_cursor );
 17      dbms_sql.close_cursor( l_cursor );
 18  end;
 19  /

PL/SQL procedure successfully completed.


SQL> select * from foo;

         N V
---------- ------------------------------------------
         1 Chris
         2 Sean
         3 Tom
         4 Joel
```

DEFINE_COLUMN()

The DEFINE_COLUMN() procedure allows the developer to define a column being selected from a query. It is only used for SELECT statements. Columns in the select list are referenced by their position. This allows us to set up local variables to handle the values from a select statement.

Usage

```
procedure define_column(c in integer,
                        position in integer,
                        column in <DATATYPE>);
```

where <DATATYPE> is one of the following:

DATE	TIMESTAMP_UNCONSTRAINED
BLOB	TIME_TZ_UNCONSTRAINED
CLOB	TIMESTAMP_TZ_UNCONSTRAINED
BFILE	TIMESTAMP_LTZ_UNCONSTRAINED
UROWID	YMINTERVAL_UNCONSTRAINED
TIME_UNCONSTRAINED	DSINTERVAL_UNCONSTRAINED

For VARCHAR2, RAW, ROWID, and LONG data types, use the following:

```
procedure define_column(c in integer, position in integer,
                        column in varchar2 character set any_cs,
                        column_size in integer);

procedure define_column_char(c in integer, position in integer,
                             column in char character set any_cs,
                             column_size in integer);

procedure define_column_raw(c in integer, position in integer,
                            column in raw,
                            column_size in integer);

procedure define_column_rowid(c in integer, position in integer,
                              column in rowid);

procedure define_column_long(c in integer, position in integer);
```

DEFINE_ARRAY()

The DEFINE_ARRAY() procedure allows the developer to set up bulk fetching of values from a SELECT statement. It tells Oracle where it will store the values returned from a SELECT statement once COLUMN_VALUE() is called. This will allow you to fetch multiple rows with a single call to FETCH_ROWS(). It saves on network round trips since many rows can be returned from the server with a single call. It is overloaded to support all base SQL types. The CNT parameter tells Oracle how many rows to return with a single fetch and the LOWER_BOUND parameter defines the starting index The values will be saved in the supplied type.

Usage

```
procedure define_array(c in integer,
                       position in integer,
                       <VARIABLE_NAME> in <VARIABLE_TYPE>,
                       cnt in integer,
                       lower_bound in integer);
```

where <VARIABLE_TYPE> is written as:

```
Type <table type> is table of <data type>
```

Table Type	Data Type
NUMBER_TABLE	NUMBER
VARCHAR2_TAble	VARCHAR2(2000)
DATE_TABLE	DATE
BLOB_TABLE	BLOB
CLOB_TABLE	CLOB
BFILE_TABLE	BFILE
UROWID_TABLE	UROWID
TIME_TABLE	TIME_UNCONSTRAINED
TIMESTAMP_TABLE	TIMESTAMP_UNCONSTRAINED
TIME_WITH_TIME_ZONE_TABLE	TIME_TZ_UNCONSTRAINED
TIMESTAMP_WITH_TIME_ZONE_TABLE	TIMESTAMP_TZ_UNCONSTRAINED
TIMESTAMP_WITH_LTZ_TABLE	TIMESTAMP_LTZ_UNCONSTRAINED
INTERVAL_YEAR_TO_MONTH_TABLE	YMINTERVAL_UNCONSTRAINED
INTERVAL_DAY_TO_SECOND_TABLE	DSINTERVAL_UNCONSTRAINED

EXECUTE()

The function EXECUTE(), as the name suggests, executes the given cursor. It returns the number of rows affected by either an INSERT, UPDATE, or DELETE. For any other statement, the return value is undefined and should be ignored.

Usage

```
function execute(c in integer) return integer;
```

EXECUTE_AND_FETCH()

The function EXECUTE_AND_FETCH() allows the developer, in one call, to execute a SELECT statement and fetch the rows. It is the same as calling EXECUTE() and then FETCH_ROWS() but it could reduce the number of network round trips. The return value is the actual number of rows fetched. The EXACT parameter, when set to TRUE, will cause an exception to occur if the number of rows fetched is not 1.

Usage

```
function execute_and_fetch(c in integer,
                            exact in boolean default false)
return integer;
```

FETCH_ROWS()

The FETCH_ROWS() function does just that, it fetches rows for a parsed and executed SELECT statement. It returns the rows into a buffer that can only be accessed by calls to the procedure COLUMN_VALUE(). The function returns the actual number of rows fetched.

Usage

```
function fetch_rows(c in integer) return integer;
```

COLUMN_VALUE()

The COLUMN_VALUE() procedure retrieves the fetched values into the local variables defined in the DEFINE_COLUMN() and DEFINE_ARRAY() procedures. The value references are determined by the POSITION in the select list of the query previously parsed and executed. An error is raised if the data type does not match the data type set up in the DEFINE_COLUMN() and DEFINE_ARRAY() procedures.

Usage

```
procedure column_value(c in integer,
                        position in integer,
                        value out <DATATYPE>);
```

where <DATATYPE> data type is one of the following:

NUMBER	TIME_UNCONSTRAINED
VARCHAR2 CHARACTER SET ANY_CS	TIMESTAMP_UNCONSTRAINED
DATE	TIME_TZ_UNCONSTRAINED
BLOB	TIMESTAMP_TZ_UNCONSTRAINED
CLOB CHARACTER SET ANY_CS	TIMESTAMP_LTZ_UNCONSTRAINED
BFILE	YMINTERVAL_UNCONSTRAINED
UROWID	DSINTERVAL_UNCONSTRAINED

You can also do bulk COLUMN_VALUE() operations.

```
procedure column_value(c in integer,
                       position in integer,
                       <VARIABLE_NAME> in <VARIABLE_TYPE>);
```

Where the VARIABLE_TYPE can be one of the following types defined in the DBMS_SQL specification.

NUMBER_TABLE	TIME_TABLE
VARCHAR2_TABLE	TIMESTAMP_TABLE
DATE_TABLE	TIME_WITH_TIME_ZONE_TABLE
CLOB_TABLE	TIMESTAMP_WITH_TIME_ZONE_TABLE
BFILE_TABLE	TIMESTAMP_WITH_LTZ_TABLE
BLOB_TABLE	INTERVAL_YEAR_TO_MONTH_TABLE
UROWID_TABLE	INTERVAL_DAY_TO_SECOND_TABLE

For those types that might be autocast, the following COLUMN_VALUE() procedures have been provided:

```
procedure column_value_char(c in integer,
                            position in integer,
                            value out char character set any_cs);
procedure column_value_char(c in integer,
                            position in integer,
                            value out char character set any_cs,
                            column_error out number,
                            actual_length out integer);

procedure column_value_raw(c in integer,
                           position in integer,
                           value out raw);
procedure column_value_raw(c in integer,
                           position in integer,
                           value out raw,
                           column_error out number,
                           actual_length out integer);

procedure column_value_rowid(c in integer,
                             position in integer,
                             value out rowid);
procedure column_value_rowid(c in integer,
                             position in integer,
                             value out rowid,
                             column_error out number,
                             actual_length out integer);
```

```
procedure column_value_long(c in integer,
                            position in integer,
                            length in integer,
                            offset in integer,
                            value out varchar2,
                            value_length out integer);
```

Example

Here is an example of using array binding and fetching:

```
SQL> declare
  2     l_cursor number := dbms_sql.open_cursor;
  3     l_num dbms_sql.number_table;
  4     l_var dbms_sql.varchar2_table;
  5     l_ignore number;
  6     l_cnt number;
  7  begin
  8     dbms_sql.parse( l_cursor,
  9                     'select n, v from foo',
 10                     dbms_sql.native );
 11     dbms_sql.define_array( l_cursor, 1, l_num, 100, 1 );
 12     dbms_sql.define_array( l_cursor, 2, l_var, 100, 1 );
 13
 14     l_ignore := dbms_sql.execute( l_cursor );
 15     loop
 16       dbms_output.put_line( 'About to attempt a fetch of 100 rows.' );
 17       l_cnt := dbms_sql.fetch_rows( l_cursor );
 18       dbms_output.put_line( 'Fetched ' || l_cnt || ' rows.' );
 19
 20       exit when l_cnt = 0;
 21
 22       dbms_sql.column_value( l_cursor, 1, l_num );
 23       dbms_sql.column_value( l_cursor, 2, l_var );
 24
 25       for i in 1 .. l_num.count loop
 26         dbms_output.put_line( 'N = ' || l_num(i) || ' V = ' || l_var(i) );
 27       end loop;
 28
 29       exit when l_cnt < 100;
 30
 31     end loop;
 32     dbms_sql.close_cursor( l_cursor );
 33  end;
 34  /

About to attempt a fetch of 100 rows.
Fetched 4 rows.
N = 1 V = Chris
N = 2 V = Sean
N = 3 V = Tom
N = 4 V = Joel

PL/SQL procedure successfully completed.
```

We only made one call to FETCH(), but got back all 4 rows. This will save network round trips when making calls to remote databases.

VARIABLE_VALUE()

The procedure VARIABLE_VALUE() allows the developer to retrieve the value or values returned by the RETURNING clause by passing in the name of the bind variable.

Usage

```
procedure variable_value(c in integer,
                         name in varchar2,
                         value out <DATATYPE>);
```

where the VALUE parameter can have one of the following types:

NUMBER	TIME_UNCONSTRAINED
VARCHAR2 CHARACTER SET ANY_CS	TIMESTAMP_UNCONSTRAINED
DATE	TIME_TZ_UNCONSTRAINED
BLOB	TIMESTAMP_TZ_UNCONSTRAINED
CLOB CHARACTER SET ANY_CS	TIMESTAMP_LTZ_UNCONSTRAINED
BFILE	YMINTERVAL_UNCONSTRAINED
UROWID	DSINTERVAL_UNCONSTRAINED

Or you can bulk retrieve the values using the following:

```
procedure variable_value(c in integer,
                         name in varchar2,
                         value in <DATATYPE>);
```

where VALUE can be one of the following DBMS_SQL defined types:

NUMBER_TABLE	TIME_TABLE
VARCHAR2_TABLE	TIMESTAMP_TABLE
DATE_TABLE	TIME_WITH_TIME_ZONE_TABLE
CLOB_TABLE	TIMESTAMP_WITH_TIME_ZONE_TABLE
BFILE_TABLE	TIMESTAMP_WITH_LTZ_TABLE
BLOB_TABLE	INTERVAL_YEAR_TO_MONTH_TABLE
UROWID_TABLE	INTERVAL_DAY_TO_SECOND_TABLE

If you are retrieving a VARCHAR2, RAW, or ROWID type, use the following:

```
procedure variable_value_char(c in integer,
                                name in varchar2,
                                value out char character set any_cs);

procedure variable_value_raw(c in integer,
                                name in varchar2,
                                value out raw);

procedure variable_value_rowid(c in integer,
                                name in varchar2,
                                value out rowid);
```

Example

```
SQL> create sequence my_seq;

Sequence created.

SQL> declare
  2     l_cursor number := dbms_sql.open_cursor;
  3     l_n number;
  4     l_ignore number;
  5     l_cnt number;
  6  begin
  7     dbms_sql.parse( l_cursor,
  8                    'insert into foo values ( my_seq.nextval, ''MARK'' ) ' ||
  9                       'returning n into :n',
 10                       dbms_sql.native );
 11
 12     dbms_sql.bind_variable( l_cursor, ':N', l_n );
 13
 14     l_ignore := dbms_sql.execute( l_cursor );
 15
 16     dbms_sql.variable_value( l_cursor, ':N', l_n );
 17
 18     dbms_output.put_line( 'Inserted the value "' || l_n ||
 19                            '" for the column N' );
 20
 21     dbms_sql.close_cursor( l_cursor );
 22  end;

Inserted the value "1" for the column N

PL/SQL procedure successfully completed.

SQL> select * from foo;

        N V
---------- ----------------------------------------
        1 MARK
```

```
1 Chris
2 Sean
3 Tom
4 Joel
```

IS_OPEN()

The IS_OPEN() function is used to test whether or not a DBMS_SQL cursor was previously opened. It returns TRUE if the cursor is open, FALSE otherwise. It is useful to use in the exception handler to determine if you should close the cursor or not.

Usage

```
function is_open(c in integer) return boolean;
```

Example

```
begin
  l_cursor := dbms_sql.open_cursor;
  ...
exception
  when others then
    if dbms_sql.is_open( l_cursor ) then
      dbms_sql.close_cursor( l_cursor );
    end if;
    raise;
end;
```

DESCRIBE_COLUMNS() / DESCRIBE_COLUMNS2()

The DESCRIBE_COLUMNS() procedure allows the developer to determine information about the select list of the query that was just parsed. It returns via OUT parameters, the number of columns, COL_CNT, and a table of records containing information for each column of the query, DESC_T. The DESC_T type is of DBMS_SQL.DESC_TAB, which is defined as:

```
type desc_tab is table of desc_rec index by binary_integer;
```

and the record is defined as:

```
type desc_rec is record (
        col_type             binary_integer := 0,
        col_max_len          binary_integer := 0,
        col_name             varchar2(32)   := '',
        col_name_len         binary_integer := 0,
        col_schema_name      varchar2(32)   := '',
        col_schema_name_len  binary_integer := 0,
        col_precision        binary_integer := 0,
        col_scale            binary_integer := 0,
        col_charsetid        binary_integer := 0,
        col_charsetform      binary_integer := 0,
        col_null_ok          boolean        := TRUE);
```

Element	Description
COL_TYPE	The data type of the column.
COL_MAX_LEN	The maximum length of the column.
COL_NAME	The name of the column.
COL_NAME_LEN	The length of the column's name.
COL_SCHEMA_NAME	The schema owner of the column if the column is a user-defined object type.
COL_SCHEMA_NAME_LEN	The length of the COL_SCHEMA_NAME value.
COL_PERCISION	The column's precision if the return type of the column is a number.
COL_SCALE	The column's scale of the return type of the column is a number.
COL_CHARSETID	The character set of the column value.
COL_CHARSERFORM	The character set form of the column.
COL_NULL_OK	A Boolean value indication if NULLs are allow as a value of the column.

The DESCRIBE_COLUMNS2() procedure is identical to DESCRIBE_COLUMNS() with one exception. It returns a DBMS_SQL.DESC_TAB2. That is a table of records of DESC_REC2. The structure of the records differs slightly from its counterpart. The COL_NAME attribute is defined as a VARCHAR2(32767), instead of a VARCHAR2(32). That gives you the ability to select a non-aliased expression that is longer than 32 characters.

Both DESCRIBE_COLUMNS() and DESCRIBE_COLUMNS2() can describe the following query:

```
select to_char( sysdate )
  from dual
```

whereas only DESCRIBE_COLUMNS2() can describe the query:

```
select to_char( sysdate, 'DD-MON-YYYY' ) ||
       to_char( sysdate, 'HH24:MI:SS' )
  from dual
```

CLOSE_CURSOR()

Usage

```
procedure describe_columns(c in integer,
                           col_cnt out integer,
                           desc_t out desc_tab);
```

965

```
        procedure describe_columns2(c in integer,
                                    col_cnt out integer,
                                    desc_t out desc_tab2);
```

Example

```
SQL> declare
  2      l_cursor number := dbms_sql.open_cursor;
  3      l_ignore number;
  4      l_desc dbms_sql.desc_tab2;
  5      l_cnt number;
  6  begin
  7      dbms_sql.parse( l_cursor,
  8                      'select to_char( sysdate, ''DD-MON-YYYY'' ) || ' ||
  9                          'to_char( sysdate, ''HH24:MI:SS'' ) ' ||
 10                          'from dual',
 11                      dbms_sql.native );
 12
 13      dbms_sql.describe_columns2( l_cursor, l_cnt, l_desc );
 14
 15      for i in 1 .. l_cnt loop
 16        dbms_output.put_line( 'Column ' || i || ' is "' || l_desc(i).col_name ||
'"' );
 17      end loop;
 18
 19      dbms_sql.close_cursor( l_cursor );
 20  end;
 21  /

Column 1 is "TO_CHAR(SYSDATE,'DD-MON-YYYY')||TO_CHAR(SYSDATE,'HH24:MI:SS')"

PL/SQL procedure successfully completed.
```

Using DESCRIBE_COLUMNS() in this script would produce the following error message:

```
declare
*
ERROR at line 1:
ORA-06502: PL/SQL: numeric or value error: dbms_sql.describe_columns overflow,
col_name_len=61. Use describe_columns2
ORA-06512: at "SYS.DBMS_SYS_SQL", line 1522
ORA-06512: at "SYS.DBMS_SQL", line 614
ORA-06512: at line 13
```

LAST_ERROR_POSITION()

The LAST_ERROR_POSITION() function will return the index into the statement where an error occurred after having parsed the statement. This is useful for giving feedback to the caller as to why his or her SQL statement failed the parse.

Usage

```
function last_error_position return integer;
```

LAST_ROW_COUNT()

The LAST_ROW_COUNT() function returns the total number of rows returned for a given statement.

Usage

```
function last_row_count return integer;
```

LAST_ROW_ID()

The LAST_ROW_ID() function returns the ROWID of the last row that was processed.

Usage

```
function last_row_id return rowid;
```

LAST_SQL_FUNCTION_CODE()

LAST_SQL_FUNCTION_CODE() returns the function code of the last OCI function that called it. The codes map as follows:

Code	Function	Code	Function	Code	Function
1	OCIINITIALIZE()	33	OCITRANSSTART()	65	OCIDEFINEBYPOS()
2	OCIHANDLEALLOC()	34	OCITRANSDETACH()	66	OCIBINDBYPOS()
3	OCIHANDLEFREE()	35	OCITRANS COMMIT()	67	OCIBINDBYNAME()
4	OCIDESCRIPTOR ALLOC()	36		68	OCILOBASSIGN()
5	OCIDESCRIPTOR FREE()	37	OCIERRORGET()	69	OCILOBISEQUAL()
6	OCIENVINIT()	38	OCILOBFILEOPEN()	70	OCILOBLOCATORIS INIT()
7	OCISERVERATTACH()	39	OCILOBFILECLOSE ()	71	OCILOBENABLE BUFFERING()
8	OCISERVERDETACH()	40		72	OCILOBCHARSETID()
9		41		73	OCILOBCHARSET FORM()

Table continued on following page

Code	Function	Code	Function	Code	Function
10	OCISESSIONBEGIN()	42	OCILOBCOPY()	74	OCILOBFILESET NAME()
11	OCISESSIONEND()	43	OCILOBAPPEND()	75	OCILOBFILEGET NAME()
12	OCIPASSWORD CHANGE()	44	OCILOBERASE()	76	OCILOGON()
13	OCISTMTPREPARE()	45	OCILOBGET LENGTH()	77	OCILOGOFF()
14		46	OCILOBTRIM()	78	OCILOBDISABLE BUFFERING()
15		47	OCILOBREAD()	79	OCILOBFLUSH BUFFER()
16		48	OCILOBWRITE()	80	OCILOBLOAD FROMFILE()
17	OCIBINDDYNAMIC()	49		81	OCILOBOPEN()
18	OCIBINDOBJECT()	50	OCIBREAK()	82	OCILOBCLOSE()
19		51	OCISERVER VERSION()	83	OCILOBISOPEN()
20	OCIBINDARRAYOF STRUCT()	52		84	OCILOBFILEIS OPEN()
21	OCISTMTEXECUTE()	53		85	OCILOBFILE EXISTS()
22		54	OCIATTRGET()	86	OCILOBFILE CLOSEALL()
23		55	OCIATTRSET()	87	OCILOBCREATE TEMPORARY()
24		56	OCIPARAMSET()	88	OCILOBFREE TEMPORARY()
25	OCIDEFINEOBJECT()	57	OCIPARAMGET()	89	OCILOBIS TEMPORARY()
26	OCIDEFINE DYNAMIC()	58	OCISTMTGET PIECE INFO()	90	OCIAQENQ()
27	OCIDEFINEARRAY OFSTRUCT()	59	OCILDATOSVC CTX()	91	OCIAQDEQ()

Code	Function	Code	Function	Code	Function
28	OCISTMTFETCH()	60		92	OCIRESET()
29	OCISTMTGET BINDINFO()	61	OCISTMTSET PIEC INFO()	93	OCISVCCTXTOLDA()
30		62	OCITRANSFORGET ()	94	OCILOBLOCATOR ASSIGN()
31		63	OCITRANS PREPARE()	95	
32	OCIDESCRIBEANY()	64	OCITRANS ROLLBACK()	96	OCIAQLISTEN()

Usage

```
function last_sql_function_code return integer;
```

Data Dictionary

The Data Dictionary is a collection of tables and views where Oracle stores all the information about the instance. The Oracle process maintains these tables and views in the SYS schema and users are granted read-only privilege on them. Just about all user access to the data dictionary is through user-accessible views, since the underlying base tables are very cryptic and complex. Each view is prefixed with either DBA, indicating that all objects will be shown regardless of execution privileges, ALL, indicating that all objects that you have privilege on will be shown, or USER, indicating that all objects owned by the user will be shown.

The following table lists each of the dictionary views that we'll look at. You need to understand that there are hundreds of data dictionary views in the Oracle database, and these are simply some of the more commonly used. For information about other views not covered here, refer to the *Oracle 9i Database Reference* documentation.

Topic	Data Dictionary Views
Dictionary meta data	DICTIONARY, DICT_COLUMNS, DBA_OBJECTS
Tables	DBA_TABLES, DBA_TAB_COLUMNS, DBA_TAB_PRIVS, DBA_COL_PRIVS, DBA_TAB_COMMENTS, DBA_COL_COMMENTS, DBA_CONSTRAINTS, DBA_CONS_COLUMNS, DBA_EXTERNAL_TABLES, DBA_EXTERNAL_LOCATIONS, DBA_OBJECT_TABLES, DBA_COLL_TYPES
Jobs	DBA_JOBS
Objects	DBA_TYPES, DBA_TYPE_ATTRIBUTES, DBA_TYPE_METHODS, DBA_METHOD_PARAMS, DBA_METHOD_RESULTS
Large Objects	DBA_LOBS
Views	DBA_VIEWS, DBA_UPDATEABLE_COLUMNS

Table continued on following page

Topic	Data Dictionary Views
Triggers	DBA_TRIGGERS, DBA_TRIGGER_COLS
PL/SQL	DBA_SOURCE, DBA_PROCEDURES, ALL_ARGUMENTS, DBA_DEPENDENCIES, DBA_ERRORS
Indexes	DBA_INDEXES, DBA_IND_COLUMNS
Security/Privileges	DBA_ROLES, DBA_ROLE_PRIVS, DBA_SYS_PRIVS
Miscellaneous	DBA_DIRECTORIES, DBA_USERS, GLOBAL_NAME
Short Names	CAT, CLU, COLS, IND, OBJ, DICT, SEQ, SYN, TABS

DICTIONARY

This view has a complete listing of all the views in the Data Dictionary along with a brief description.

Column Definitions and Usage

❑ TABLE_NAME [VARCHAR2(30)] – Name of the object

❑ COMMENTS [VARCHAR2(4000)] – Text comment on the object

You can use this view to get a count of classes of dictionary views like DBA_, USER_, ALL_, and the performance views.

```
SQL> column prefix format a6

SQL> select substr( table_name, 1,
  2                 case
  3                 when instr(table_name,'$') <> 0
  4                   then length( substr( table_name, 1, instr( table_name, '$' )
) )
  5                 when substr( table_name,1,3) in ('DBA','ALL' )
  6                   then 3
  7                 else
  8                   4
  9                 end ) prefix,
 10         count(*)
 11    from dictionary
 12   where table_name like 'DBA%'
 13      or table_name like 'USER%'
 14      or table_name like 'ALL%'
 15      or instr( table_name, '$' ) <> 0
 16   group by substr( table_name, 1,
 17                 case
 18                 when instr( table_name, '$' ) <> 0
 19                   then length( substr( table_name, 1, instr( table_name, '$' )
) )
 20                 when substr( table_name,1,3) in ('DBA','ALL' )
```

```
21                    then 3
22                    else
23                     4
24                    end )
25 /

PREFIX    COUNT(*)
------    ----------
ALL            172
DBA            244
GV$            226
SM$              1
USER           190
V$             230
X$               5

7 rows selected.
```

Or you can use it to get the description of any view in the dictionary.

```
set echo off
set verify off
set linesize 72
set pagesize 9999
set feedback off

Prompt Dictionary View Name &1

column table_name format a30
column comments format a200


select *
  from dictionary
 where table_name = upper('&1')
/
```

Save this to a file called `dlist.sql`. You execute it using the following:

```
SQL> @dlist dba_objects
Dictionary View Name dba_objects

TABLE_NAME
------------------------------
COMMENTS
----------------------------------------------------------------------
DBA_OBJECTS
All objects in the database
```

DICT_COLUMNS

Use this view to get a description of the columns in any dictionary table.

Column Definitions and Usage

Same as DICTIONARY with the addition of:

❑ COLUMN_NAME [VARCHAR2(30)] – Name of the column

This is a handy script to get a quick listing of the columns in any dictionary view and a brief description. Save the following into a file named dclist.sql:

```
set echo off
set verify off
set linesize 132
set pagesize 9999
set feedback off

Prompt Dictionary View Name &1

column columns format a30
column comments format a100

select dc.column_name,
       dc.comments
  from dba_tab_columns tc,
       dict_columns dc
 where tc.table_name = dc.table_name
   and tc.column_name = dc.column_name
   and dc.table_name = upper('&1')
 order by column_id
/
```

and execute it like this:

```
SQL> @dclist dba_users
Dictionary View Name dba_users

COLUMN_NAME                        COMMENTS
--------------------------------   ----------------------------------------------------
USERNAME                           Name of the user
USER_ID                            ID number of the user
PASSWORD                           Encrypted password
ACCOUNT_STATUS
LOCK_DATE
EXPIRY_DATE
DEFAULT_TABLESPACE                 Default tablespace for data
TEMPORARY_TABLESPACE               Default tablespace for temporary tables
CREATED                            User creation date
PROFILE                            User resource profile name
INITIAL_RSRC_CONSUMER_GROUP        User's initial consumer group
EXTERNAL_NAME                      User external name
```

DBA_OBJECTS

This view contains a listing of all the objects in the database.

Column Definitions and Usage

- ❏ OWNER [VARCHAR2(30)] – Username of the owner of the object

- ❏ OBJECT_NAME [VARCHAR2(128)] – Name of the object

- ❏ SUBOBJECT_NAME [VARCHAR2(30)] – Name of the sub-object (for example, partition)

- ❏ OBJECT_ID [NUMBER] – Object number of the object

- ❏ DATA_OBJECT_ID [NUMBER] – Object number of the segment which contains the object

- ❏ OBJECT_TYPE [VARCHAR2(18)] – Type of the object

- ❏ CREATED [DATE] – Timestamp for the creation of the object

- ❏ LAST_DDL_TIME [DATE] – Timestamp for the last DDL change (including GRANT and REVOKE) to the object

- ❏ TIMESTAMP [VARCHAR2(19)] – Timestamp for the specification of the object

- ❏ STATUS [VARCHAR2(7)] – Status of the object

- ❏ TEMPORARY [VARCHAR2(1)] – Can the current session only see data that it places in this object itself?

- ❏ GENERATED [VARCHAR2(1)] – Was the name of this object system generated?

- ❏ SECONDARY [VARCHAR2(1)] – Is this a secondary object created for domain indexes?

You can use it to get a quick account of the objects in your database. This query lists every object type and the number of objects of that type for the entire database.

```
SQL> select object_type, count(*)
  2    from dba_objects
  3    group by object_type
  4  /

OBJECT_TYPE          COUNT(*)
------------------- ----------
CLUSTER                    10
CONSUMER GROUP              4
CONTEXT                     2
DIMENSION                   5
DIRECTORY                   4
FUNCTION                   60
INDEX                     850
INDEX PARTITION           101
INDEXTYPE                   6
JAVA CLASS              11835
JAVA DATA                 290
JAVA RESOURCE             190
```

975

```
LIBRARY                   66
LOB                       66
MATERIALIZED VIEW          3
OPERATOR                  22
PACKAGE                  444
PACKAGE BODY             403
PROCEDURE                 51
QUEUE                     38
RESOURCE PLAN              3
SEQUENCE                 104
SYNONYM                13515
TABLE                    720
TABLE PARTITION           43
TRIGGER                   25
TYPE                     427
TYPE BODY                 46
VIEW                    2038
```

Or you can join it to another dictionary view and create a listing for an individual schema. Save the following script in a file called `dbls.sql`.

```
set echo off
set verify off
set pagesize 9999

column object_name format a30
column tablespace_name format a30
column object_type format a12
column status format a1

break on object_type skip 1

select object_type, object_name,
       decode( status, 'INVALID', '*', '' ) status,
       decode( object_type,
               'TABLE', (select tablespace_name
                           from dba_tables
                          where table_name = object_name
                            and owner = upper('&1')),
               'TABLE PARTITION', (select tablespace_name
                                     from dba_tab_partitions
                                    where partition_name = subobject_name
                                      and owner = upper('&1')),
               'INDEX', (select tablespace_name
                           from dba_indexes
                          where index_name = object_name
                            and owner = upper('&1')),
               'INDEX PARTITION', (select tablespace_name
                                     from dba_ind_partitions
                                    where partition_name = subobject_name
                                      and owner = upper('&1')),
               'LOB', (select tablespace_name
```

```
                          from dba_segments
                        where segment_name = object_name
                          and owner = upper('&1')),
                null ) tablespace_name
  from dba_objects a
 where owner = upper('&1')
 order by object_type, object_name
/
column status format a10
```

And run it supplying the schema you would like the listing for. For example:

```
SQL> @dbls scott

OBJECT_TYPE   OBJECT_NAME                            S TABLESPACE_NAME
-----------   ------------------------------------   - -----------------------
FUNCTION          ITE
              MY_UPPER
              NO_RETURN_TYPE                         *

INDEX         PK_DEPT                                  SYSTEM
              PK_EMP                                   SYSTEM
              SYS_C002499                              SYSTEM
              SYS_C002528                              SYSTEM

PACKAGE       EMPLOYEE_PKG
              VARIABLES

PACKAGE BODY  EMPLOYEE_PKG                           *
              VARIABLES

PROCEDURE     EMP_LOOKUP
              PRINT_TABLE

SEQUENCE      MY_SEQ

TABLE         ADDRESS_TABLE
              BONUS                                    SYSTEM
              DEPT                                     SYSTEM
              EMP                                      SYSTEM
              SALGRADE                                 SYSTEM

TYPE          CONSULTANT
              EMPLOYEE
              SALES_REP
              SHAPE
              SUB_TYPE                                *
              SUPER_TYPE

TYPE BODY     CONSULTANT
              EMPLOYEE
              SALES_REP
```

DBA_TABLES

This view shows all the relational tables in the database.

Column Definitions and Usage

❏ OWNER [VARCHAR2(30)] – Owner of the table.

❏ TABLE_NAME [VARCHAR2(30)] – Name of the table.

❏ TABLESPACE_NAME [VARCHAR2(30)] – Tablespace the table is stored in.

❏ CLUSTER_NAME [VARCHAR2(30)] – If the table is in a cluster, the cluster's name.

❏ IOT_NAME [VARCHAR2(30)] – If this row in DBA_TABLES is an index-organized table (IOT), IOT_OVERFLOW or IOT_MAPPING, this column is the name of the base IOT.

❏ PCT_FREE [NUMBER] – Percentage of the block that is available for updates only. Oracle will stop inserting rows into the block once the block reaches this percentage of free space in the block.

❏ PCT_USED [NUMBER] – Once PCT_FREE is reached, records will not be inserted into a block until the block falls below the PCT_USED percentage.

❏ INI_TRANS [NUMBER] – The initial number of transaction entries in a block set aside by Oracle in order to allow multiple transactions to simultaneously change rows within the same block for this table.

❏ MAX_TRANS [NUMBER] – The maximum number of transactions that can simultaneously change rows within the same block for this table.

❏ INITIAL_EXTENT [NUMBER] – The number of bytes of the first extent created for this table.

❏ NEXT_EXTENT [NUMBER] – The number of bytes of the next extent to be allocated for this table.

❏ MIN_EXTENTS [NUMBER] – The initial number of extents that are allocated for this table at creation time.

❏ MAX_EXTENTS [NUMBER] – The maximum number of extents that may be allocated for this table.

❏ PCT_INCREASE [NUMBER] – For each extent that is allocated for a table after the initial extent, the size of the next extent to be allocated grows by this percentage.

❏ FREELISTS [NUMBER] – The number of freelists for this table. Freelists track a list of data blocks that have room for new inserts into the table.

❏ FREELIST_GROUPS [NUMBER] – This is number of groups of freelists for the table. This is used with Oracle's Real Application Clusters.

❏ LOGGING [VARCHAR2(3)] – Specifies whether creation of this table, direct path load, and direct path inserts against this table are logged in the redo log (LOGGING vs. NOLOGGING).

❏ BACKED_UP [VARCHAR2(1)] – Whether this table has been backed up or not since the LAST_CHANGED column.

- ❑ NUM_ROWS [NUMBER] – The number of rows.

- ❑ BLOCKS [NUMBER] – The number of blocks used.

- ❑ EMPTY_BLOCKS [NUMBER] – The number of empty blocks.

- ❑ AVG_SPACE [NUMBER] – This attribute is the average amount of free space per data block.

- ❑ CHAIN_CNT [NUMBER] – The number of rows in the table that have been chained or migrated.

- ❑ AVG_ROW_LEN [NUMBER] – This is the average amount of space consumed by an individual row.

- ❑ AVG_SPACE_FREELIST_BLOCKS [NUMBER] – The average amount of free space in blocks per freelist.

- ❑ NUM_FREELIST_BLOCKS [NUMBER] – The number of blocks on a freelist.

- ❑ DEGREE [VARCHAR2(10)] – The number of threads used by the database to scan this table, per instance.

- ❑ INSTANCES [VARCHAR2(10)] – The number of instances that the table can be scanned in.

- ❑ CACHE [VARCHAR2(5)] – This attribute tells Oracle whether to try to keep this table's blocks in the buffer cache or not. (CACHE vs. NOCACHE).

- ❑ TABLE_LOCK [VARCHAR2(8)] – Whether table locking is enabled or disabled.

- ❑ SAMPLE_SIZE [NUMBER] – When this table is analyzed, Oracle can estimate statistics based on a percentage of the table instead of computing statistics based on the entire table. This saves time and processing, but is only as accurate as the amount of space used to estimate the statistics. SAMPLE_SIZE tells you what size was used to estimate the statistics.

- ❑ LAST_ANALYZED [DATE] – Identifies the date for the last time this table was analyzed.

- ❑ PARTITIONED [VARCHAR2(3)] – Indicates whether this is a partitioned table or not (YES/NO).

- ❑ IOT_TYPE [VARCHAR2(12)] – If this is an index-organized table (IOT), this will be either IOT, IOT_OVERFLOW or IOT_MAPPING. NULL if it is not an IOT.

- ❑ TEMPORARY [VARCHAR2(1)] – Indicates whether this is a temporary table or not (Y/N).

- ❑ SECONDARY [VARCHAR2(1)] – Whether the table was created by the Oracle 9i Data Cartridge.

- ❑ NESTED [VARCHAR2(3)] – Indicates whether this is a nested table or not (YES/NO).

- ❑ BUFFER_POOL [VARCHAR2(7)] – The default buffer pool for this table.

- ❑ ROW_MOVEMENT [VARCHAR2(8)] – Whether partitioned row movement is enabled for this table or not.

- ❑ GLOBAL_STATS [VARCHAR2(3)] – Indicates whether statistics were gathered on an entire partitioned table, or on partitions or sub partitions only.

- ❑ USER_STATS [VARCHAR2(3)] – Indicates whether the statistics for the table were specified instead of computed. Users can "create" statistics using the DBMS_STATS supplied package. If a user does this, this column will be YES. NO if not.

- ❑ DURATION [VARCHAR2(15)] – For temporary tables, this indicates the type of table (SYS$SESSION/SYS$TRANSACTION).

- ❑ SKIP_CORRUPT [VARCHAR2(8)] – Blocks of the database may be marked corrupt. Using the supplied package DBMS_REPAIR, you can tell Oracle to skip these blocks during table scans. This column will indicate whether the table will skip corrupt blocks or not.

- ❑ MONITORING [VARCHAR2(3)] – Whether MONITORING is enabled for this table or not.

- ❑ CLUSTER_OWNER [VARCHAR2(30)] – For clustered tables, the schema that owns the cluster that this table belongs to.

- ❑ DEPENDENCIES [VARCHAR2(8)].

This query results in a list of those tables belonging to the username passed into the script, along with various properties of these tables. The tables are ordered by table name, and grouped by their tablespace. The script below is named tableinfo.sql.

```
set verify off
set linesize 76
set pagesize 9999

break on tablespace_name skip 1
column tablespace_name  format a15
column table_name        format a30
column table_properties format a30 word_wrapped

select tablespace_name, table_name,
        decode( partitioned, 'YES', 'Partitioned ',
          decode( logging, 'NOLOGGING', 'Non-logging table ' ) ) ||
        decode( temporary, 'Y', 'Temporary (' ||
                decode( duration, 'SYS$SESSION', 'Session-based',
                                                 'Transaction-based' ) ||
                ')',
        '' ) ||
        decode( iot_type, null, '', 'Index-organized ' ) ||
        decode( nested, 'YES', 'Nested ', '' )
        table_properties
  from dba_tables
 where owner = upper( '&1' )
 order by 1, 2
/
```

In the following example, the HR schema from the Oracle 9i Sample Schemas is used:

```
SQL> @tableinfo.sql HR

TABLESPACE_NAME TABLE_NAME                      TABLE_PROPERTIES
--------------- ------------------------------ ---------------------------EXAMPLE
AUDIT_TBL
                CUSTOMER_TAB
                DEPARTMENTS
                EMPLOYEES
```

```
                    JOBS
                    JOB_HISTORY
                    LOCATIONS
                    REGIONS
                    SALES_PEOPLE
                    COUNTRIES                Index-organized
                    LOCATIONS_INC            Index-organized
                    LOCATIONS_IOT            Index-organized
                    LOCATIONS_IOT_C          Index-organized
                    SESSION_TAB              Temporary (Session-based)
                    TRANSACTION_TAB          Temporary (Transaction-based)
```

DBA_TAB_COLUMNS

DBA_TAB_COLUMNS contains information about all the columns of tables, views, and clusters.

Column Definitions and Usage

❑ OWNER [VARCHAR2(30)] – Owner of the table this column belongs to.

❑ TABLE_NAME [VARCHAR2(30)] – Name of the table this column belongs to.

❑ COLUMN_NAME [VARCHAR2(30)] – Name of the column.

❑ DATA_TYPE [VARCHAR2(106)] – Data type for the column.

❑ DATA_TYPE_MOD [VARCHAR2(3)] – Data type modifier for the column.

❑ DATA_TYPE_OWNER [VARCHAR2(30)] – Owner of the data type for the column.

❑ DATA_LENGTH [NUMBER] – Length specified for this column's data type.

❑ DATA_PRECISION [NUMBER] – Precision specified for this column's data type (NUMBERs and FLOATs).

❑ DATA_SCALE [NUMBER] – The scale of the column's data type. This indicates the digits to the right of the decimal place in a NUMBER.

❑ NULLABLE [VARCHAR2(1)] – Indicates whether this column can contain NULL values or not.

❑ COLUMN_ID [NUMBER] – Each column gets a sequence number when it is created.

❑ DEFAULT_LENGTH [NUMBER] – Length of the default value of the column.

❑ DATA_DEFAULT [LONG] – The default value assigned to the column in a new record if no value is given.

❑ NUM_DISTINCT [NUMBER] – The number of distinct values for this column. This data is kept for backward compatibility, and can now be found in the TAB_COL_STATISTICS view.

❑ LOW_VALUE [RAW(32)] –The lowest value for this column. This data is kept for backward compatibility. This data can now be found in the TAB_COL_STATISTICS view.

❑ HIGH_VALUE [RAW(32)] –The highest value for this column. This data is kept for backward compatibility. This data can now be found in the TAB_COL_STATISTICS view.

- ❏ DENSITY [NUMBER] –The density of the column. This data is kept for backward compatibility. This data can now be found in the TAB_COL_STATISTICS view.

- ❏ NUM_NULLS [NUMBER] – The number of NULL values for this column.

- ❏ NUM_BUCKETS [NUMBER] – The number of buckets for this column's histogram (if one exists).

- ❏ LAST_ANALYZED [DATE] – Identifies the date for the last time this column was analyzed.

- ❏ SAMPLE_SIZE [NUMBER] – When this column is analyzed, Oracle can estimate statistics based on a percentage of the table instead of computing statistics based on the entire table. This saves time and processing, but is only as accurate as the amount of space used to estimate the statistics. SAMPLE_SIZE tells you what size was used to estimate the statistics.

- ❏ CHARACTER_SET_NAME [VARCHAR2(44)] – The name of the character set for this column (CHAR_CS/NCHAR_CS).

- ❏ CHAR_COL_DECL_LENGTH [NUMBER].

- ❏ GLOBAL_STATS [VARCHAR2(3)] – Indicates whether column statistics were gathered on an entire partitioned table, or on partitions or sub partitions only.

- ❏ USER_STATS [VARCHAR2(3)] – Indicates whether the statistics for the column were specified instead of computed. Users can "create" statistics using the DBMS_STATS supplied package. If a user does this, this column will be YES – NO if not.

- ❏ AVG_COL_LEN [NUMBER] – Average length of the column in bytes.

- ❏ CHAR_LENGTH [NUMBER] –The length of the column in characters (only for CHAR, NCHAR, VARCHAR2, NVARCHAR2).

- ❏ CHAR_USED [VARCHAR2(1)] – Indicates whether the column's length was specified in bytes or characters.

- ❏ V80_FMT_IMAGE [VARCHAR2(3)].

- ❏ DATA_UPGRADED [VARCHAR2(3)].

In the following script, we write a query that emulates the SQL*Plus DESCRIBE command.

```
set verify off
set linesize 72
set pagesize 9999
set feedback off

Prompt Datatypes for Table &1

column data_type format a20
column column_name heading "Column Name"
column data_type   heading "Data|Type"
column data_length heading "Data|Length"
column nullable    heading "Nullable"

select column_name,
       data_type,
       substr(
```

```
            decode( data_type, 'NUMBER',
                    decode( data_precision, NULL, NULL,
                      '('||data_precision||','||data_scale||')' ),
                                data_length),
                1,11) data_length,
            decode( nullable, 'Y', 'null', 'not null' ) nullable
    from all_tab_columns
    where owner = USER
      and table_name = upper('&1')
    order by column_id
    /
```

In the example below, we use the desc.sql script on the DEPARTMENTS table:

```
SQL> @desc.sql DEPARTMENTS
Datatypes for Table DEPARTMENTS
```

Column Name	Data Type	Data Length	Nullable
DEPARTMENT_ID	NUMBER	(4,0)	not null
DEPARTMENT_NAME	VARCHAR2	30	not null
MANAGER_ID	NUMBER	(6,0)	null
LOCATION_ID	NUMBER	(4,0)	null

DBA_TAB_PRIVS

DBA_TAB_PRIVS displays all the privileges that have been granted on objects in the database.

Column Definitions and Usage

❑ GRANTEE [VARCHAR2(30)] – The user that the privilege was granted to.

❑ OWNER [VARCHAR2(30)] – The user that owns the object for which the privilege was granted.

❑ TABLE_NAME [VARCHAR2(30)] – The table the privilege was granted upon.

❑ GRANTOR [VARCHAR2(30)] – The user that granted the privilege to the grantee.

❑ PRIVILEGE [VARCHAR2(40)] – The privilege that was granted.

❑ GRANTABLE [VARCHAR2(3)] – Whether the GRANTOR can grant this privilege to other users or not (YES/NO).

❑ HIERARCHY [VARCHAR2(3)].

The following query is used to select all those object privileges for a particular user. The filename for this query is tabprivs.sql.

```
set verify off
set linesize 78
set pagesize 9999
set feedback off

Prompt &1.'s Object Privileges

column tab       format a24 heading "Schema.Object"
column privilege format a24 heading "Privilege"
column grantor   format a20 heading "Granted By"
column grantable format a6  heading "Admin?"

select owner || '.' || table_name tab,
       privilege,
       grantor,
       grantable
  from dba_tab_privs
 where grantee = upper( '&1' )
 order by owner, table_name, privilege
/
```

In the following example, we connect to the database as a user account with SELECT privileges on the DBA_TAB_PRIVS view, and run the tabprivs.sql script on the PM schema:

```
SQL> @tabprivs.sql PM
PM's Object Privileges


Schema.Object                 Privilege                Granted By           Admin?
----------------------------- ------------------------ -------------------- -----
OE.CUSTOMERS                  SELECT                   OE                   NO
OE.INVENTORIES                SELECT                   OE                   NO
OE.ORDERS                     SELECT                   OE                   NO
OE.ORDER_ITEMS                SELECT                   OE                   NO
OE.PRODUCT_DESCRIPTIONS       SELECT                   OE                   NO
OE.PRODUCT_INFORMATION        REFERENCES               OE                   NO
OE.PRODUCT_INFORMATION        SELECT                   OE                   NO
OE.WAREHOUSES                 SELECT                   OE                   NO
SYS.DBMS_STATS                EXECUTE                  SYS                  NO
```

DBA_COL_PRIVS

This view is used to display all privileges granted on particular columns in the database.

Column Definitions and Usage

❑   GRANTEE [VARCHAR2(30)] – The user who granted the privilege.

❑   OWNER [VARCHAR2(30)] – The user that owns the object for which the privilege was granted.

❑   TABLE_NAME [VARCHAR2(30)] – The table that contains the column the privilege was granted upon.

❑ COLUMN_NAME [VARCHAR2(30)] – The column the privilege was granted upon.

❑ GRANTOR [VARCHAR2(30)] – The user that the privilege was granted to.

❑ PRIVILEGE [VARCHAR2(40)] – The privilege that was granted.

❑ GRANTABLE [VARCHAR2(3)] – Whether the GRANTOR can grant this privilege to other users or not (YES/NO).

In the following code sample, connect to the database as the Oracle 9*i* Sample Schema HR, and run the following grants:

```
SQL> grant references ( employee_id ),
  2         update( first_name,last_name,job_id,manager_id,department_id )
  3  on hr.employees to scott;

SQL> grant references ( department_id ),
  2         update( department_name, location_id )
  3  on hr.departments to scott;

SQL> grant references ( job_id ),
  2         update( job_title )
  3  on hr.jobs to scott;

SQL> grant references ( location_id ),
  2         update( city, state_province )
  3  on hr.locations to scott;
```

Once the SCOTT user has a number of column privileges on HR's tables, use the colprivs.sql script to view the column privileges (and associated information) granted:

```
SQL> connect sdillon/sdillon
Connected.
SQL> @colprivs scott
Column Privileges For scott
```

Table	Column	Privilege	Granted By	Admin?
HR.DEPARTMENTS	DEPARTMENT_ID	REFERENCES	HR	NO
	DEPARTMENT_NAME	UPDATE	HR	NO
	LOCATION_ID	UPDATE	HR	NO
HR.EMPLOYEES	EMPLOYEE_ID	REFERENCES	HR	NO
	FIRST_NAME	UPDATE	HR	NO
	LAST_NAME	UPDATE	HR	NO
	JOB_ID	UPDATE	HR	NO
	DEPARTMENT_ID	UPDATE	HR	NO
	MANAGER_ID	UPDATE	HR	NO
HR.JOBS	JOB_ID	REFERENCES	HR	NO
	JOB_TITLE	UPDATE	HR	NO
HR.LOCATIONS	LOCATION_ID	REFERENCES	HR	NO
	CITY	UPDATE	HR	NO
	STATE_PROVINCE	UPDATE	HR	NO

DBA_TAB_COMMENTS/ DBA_COL_COMMENTS

Comments created on tables and views are displayed in these views.

Column Definitions and Usage

- OWNER [VARCHAR2(30)] – The owner of the object.

- TABLE_NAME [VARCHAR2(30)] – The object name the comment is for.

- COMMENTS [VARCHAR2(4000)] – Comment text for the object.

- TABLE_TYPE [VARCHAR2(11)] – The type of object the comment is for (DBA_TAB_COMMENTS).

- COLUMN_NAME [VARCHAR2(30)] – The column of the object that the comment is for (DBA_COL_COMMENTS).

Copy the following script into a file named `comments.sql`:

```
set linesize 10078
set verify off

variable tname varchar2(200)
begin
  :tname := upper('&1');
end;
/

column comments format a75 heading "Comments" word_wrapped

prompt Table comments for table &1

select comments
  from dba_tab_comments
 where table_name = :tname
/

column column_name format a20 heading "Column Name" word_wrapped
column comments format a55 heading "Comments" word_wrapped

prompt
prompt Column comments for table &1

select column_name, comments
  from dba_col_comments
 where table_name = :tname
 order by column_name
/
```

Comments are created for many of the tables and columns created during the installation of the Oracle 9*i* Sample Schemas. Using the `comments.sql` script, the table and column comments can be queried from the data dictionary:

```
SQL> connect hr/hr
Connected.
SQL> @comments EMPLOYEES

PL/SQL procedure successfully completed.

Table comments for table EMPLOYEES

Comments
-------------------------------------------------------------------------
employees table. Contains 107 rows. References with departments,
jobs, job_history tables. Contains a self reference.


Column comments for table EMPLOYEES

Column Name             Comments
--------------------    -------------------------------------------------
COMMISSION_PCT          Commission percentage of the employee; Only employees
                        in sales department eligible for commission percentage

DEPARTMENT_ID           Department id where employee works; foreign key to
                        department_id column of the departments table

EMAIL                   Email id of the employee
EMPLOYEE_ID             Primary key of employees table.
FIRST_NAME              First name of the employee. A not null column.
HIRE_DATE               Date when the employee started on this job. A not null
                        column.

JOB_ID                  Current job of the employee; foreign key to job_id
                        column of the jobs table. A not null column.

LAST_NAME               Last name of the employee. A not null column.
MANAGER_ID              Manager id of the employee; has same domain as
                        manager_id in departments table. Foreign key to employee_id
                        column of employees table. (useful for reflexive joins and
                        CONNECT BY query)

PHONE_NUMBER            Phone number of the employee; includes country code and
                        area code

SALARY                  Monthly salary of the employee. Must be greater
                        than zero (enforced by constraint emp_salary_min)

11 rows selected.
```

DBA_CONSTRAINTS

DBA_CONSTRAINTS shows information about constraints defined on tables in the database.

Column Definitions and Usage

- ❑ OWNER [VARCHAR2(30)] – The owner of the constraint.

- ❑ CONSTRAINT_NAME [VARCHAR2(30)] – The name of the constraint.

- ❑ CONSTRAINT_TYPE [VARCHAR2(1)] – A single character indicating the type of the constraint.

  - ❑ P – Primary Key
  - ❑ R – Foreign Key
  - ❑ U – Unique
  - ❑ C – Check
  - ❑ V – Check (on a view)
  - ❑ O – Read only (on a view)

- ❑ TABLE_NAME [VARCHAR2(30)] – The table or view the constraint is defined upon.

- ❑ SEARCH_CONDITION [LONG] – Text for a check condition.

- ❑ R_OWNER [VARCHAR2(30)] – For foreign keys, this is the table owner the foreign key refers to.

- ❑ R_CONSTRAINT_NAME [VARCHAR2(30)] – For foreign keys, this is the primary key constraint name the foreign key refers to.

- ❑ DELETE_RULE [VARCHAR2(9)] – For foreign keys, this is either CASCADE or NO ACTION.

- ❑ STATUS [VARCHAR2(8)] – Whether the constraint is enforced or not (ENABLED/DISABLED).

- ❑ DEFERRABLE [VARCHAR2(14)] – Whether the constraint can be deferred or not (DEFERRABLE/NOT DEFERRABLE).

- ❑ DEFERRED [VARCHAR2(9)] – Whether the constraint is deferred or not.

- ❑ VALIDATED [VARCHAR2(13)] – If all the rows in the table/view adhere to the constraint or not (VALIDATED/NOT VALIDATED).

- ❑ GENERATED [VARCHAR2(14)] – Indicates whether the constraint name is system-generated or user-specified.

- ❑ BAD [VARCHAR2(3)] – If you use the TO_DATE function with a two-digit year date format, this column will be YES. Otherwise, it will be NO. Constraints are said to be BAD if two-digit years are ambiguous.

- ❑ RELY [VARCHAR2(4)] – Indicates whether a constraint is enabled and enforced or not.

- ❑ LAST_CHANGE [DATE] – The last time the constraint was enabled or disabled.

- ❑ INDEX_OWNER [VARCHAR2(30)] – The user that owns the index.

❑ INDEX_NAME [VARCHAR2(30)] – The name of the index.

❑ INVALID [VARCHAR2(7)].

❑ VIEW_RELATED [VARCHAR2(14)].

See DBA_CONS_COLUMNS for usage information.

DBA_CONS_COLUMNS

DBA_CONS_COLUMNS shows detailed information about the columns that are a part of constraints defined on tables in the database.

Column Definitions and Usage

❑ OWNER [VARCHAR2(30)] – The owner of the constraint the column is a part of.

❑ CONSTRAINT_NAME [VARCHAR2(30)] – The name of the constraint the column is a part of.

❑ TABLE_NAME [VARCHAR2(30)] – The name of the table the constraint is defined upon.

❑ COLUMN_NAME [VARCHAR2(30)] – The name of the column.

❑ POSITION [NUMBER] – The position of the column relative to other columns that are a part of this constraint.

Pass a table name as the first argument to the following script to query constraint information from the data dictionary. This script only queries the first sixteen columns of any given constraint, so if there is a constraint with more columns than this then another query would be necessary:

```
set verify off
set linesize 78
set pagesize 9999
set feedback off

Prompt Column Constraints for Table &1

column constraint_name heading "Name" format a20
column constraint_type heading "Type" format a15
column columns format a25 word_wrapped
column invalid format a1 heading "V"
column deferred format a1 heading "D"
column status format a1 heading "S"

select substr(c.constraint_name,1,30) constraint_name,
       decode(c.constraint_type,
              'P','Primary Key',
              'R','Foreign Key',
              'U','Unique Key',
              'C','Check',
              'V','Check (on view)',
              'O','Read only (view)',
              'Unknown') constraint_type,
```

```
      max(decode( co.position,  1,
           substr(co.column_name,1,30), NULL )) ||
      max(decode( co.position,  2, ', '||
           substr(co.column_name,1,30), NULL )) ||
      max(decode( co.position,  3, ', '||
           substr(co.column_name,1,30), NULL )) ||
      max(decode( co.position,  4, ', '||
           substr(co.column_name,1,30), NULL )) ||
      max(decode( co.position,  5, ', '||
           substr(co.column_name,1,30), NULL )) ||
      max(decode( co.position,  6, ', '||
           substr(co.column_name,1,30), NULL )) ||
      max(decode( co.position,  7, ', '||
           substr(co.column_name,1,30), NULL )) ||
      max(decode( co.position,  8, ', '||
           substr(co.column_name,1,30), NULL )) ||
      max(decode( co.position,  9, ', '||
           substr(co.column_name,1,30), NULL )) ||
      max(decode( co.position, 10, ', '||
           substr(co.column_name,1,30), NULL )) ||
      max(decode( co.position, 11, ', '||
           substr(co.column_name,1,30), NULL )) ||
      max(decode( co.position, 12, ', '||
           substr(co.column_name,1,30), NULL )) ||
      max(decode( co.position, 13, ', '||
           substr(co.column_name,1,30), NULL )) ||
      max(decode( co.position, 14, ', '||
           substr(co.column_name,1,30), NULL )) ||
      max(decode( co.position, 15, ', '||
           substr(co.column_name,1,30), NULL )) ||
      max(decode( co.position, 16, ', '||
           substr(co.column_name,1,30), NULL )) columns,
      decode( invalid, 'YES', '*', '' ) invalid,
      decode( deferred, 'YES', '*', '' ) deferred,
      decode( status, 'INVALID', '*', '' ) status
  from dba_constraints c, dba_cons_columns co
 where c.owner = USER
   and c.table_name = upper('&1')
   and co.table_name = c.table_name
   and co.owner = c.owner
   and c.constraint_name = co.constraint_name
 group by substr(c.constraint_name,1,30), c.constraint_type,
          c.invalid, c.deferred, c.status
 order by c.constraint_type
/

prompt
prompt 'V' - * indicates constraint is INVALID
prompt 'D' - * indicates constraint is DEFERRED
prompt 'S' - * indicates constraint is DISABLED
```

At the bottom of the query, a legend is included to help the person performing the query to understand the output. The three final columns are abbreviated to a single character for each column, and an asterisk is output only in the case where the constraint is invalid, deferred, or disabled. Running the script on the HR schema's EMPLOYEES table produces the following results:

```
SQL> @cons EMPLOYEES
Column Constraints for Table EMPLOYEES

Name                 Type             COLUMNS                       V D S
-------------------  ---------------  ------------------------      - - -
EMP_EMAIL_NN         Check
EMP_HIRE_DATE_NN     Check
EMP_JOB_NN           Check
EMP_LAST_NAME_NN     Check
EMP_SALARY_MIN       Check
EMP_EMP_ID_PK        Primary Key      EMPLOYEE_ID
EMP_DEPT_FK          Foreign Key      DEPARTMENT_ID
EMP_JOB_FK           Foreign Key      JOB_ID
EMP_MANAGER_FK       Foreign Key      MANAGER_ID
EMP_EMAIL_UK         Unique Key       EMAIL

'V' - * indicates constraint is INVALID
'D' - * indicates constraint is DEFERRED
'S' - * indicates constraint is DISABLED
```

DBA_EXTERNAL_TABLES

This view provides information about the external tables created in the database.

Column Definitions and Usage

- ❑ OWNER [VARCHAR2(30)] – The owner of the external table.

- ❑ TABLE_NAME [VARCHAR2(30)] – The name of the external table.

- ❑ TYPE_OWNER [CHAR(3)] – The owner of the type of access driver used for the external table.

- ❑ TYPE_NAME [VARCHAR2(30)] – The type of access driver used for the external table.

- ❑ DEFAULT_DIRECTORY_OWNER [CHAR(3)] – The owner of the directory object where the external table exists.

- ❑ DEFAULT_DIRECTORY_NAME [VARCHAR2(30)] – The name of the directory object where the external table exists.

- ❑ REJECT_LIMIT [VARCHAR2(40)] – The number of conversion errors Oracle will allow before a query against this external table fails.

- ❑ ACCESS_TYPE [VARCHAR2(7)] – The type of access parameters for the external table.

- ❑ ACCESS_PARAMETERS [VARCHAR2(4000)] – The values of the access parameters for the external table.

See DBA_EXTERNAL_LOCATIONS for usage information.

DBA_EXTERNAL_LOCATIONS

This view provides information about the location of data for external tables in the database.

Column Definitions and Usage

- ❏ OWNER [VARCHAR2(30)] – The owner of the external table.

- ❏ TABLE_NAME [VARCHAR2(30)] – The name of the external table.

- ❏ LOCATION [VARCHAR2(4000)] – The name of the file that makes up the external table's data.

- ❏ DIRECTORY_OWNER [VARCHAR2(3)] – The type of access driver used for the external table.

- ❏ DIRECTORY_NAME [VARCHAR2(30)] – The name of the directory object where the external table exists.

Copy the following script to a file named exttabs.sql:

```
set verify off
set linesize 81
set pagesize 9999
set feedback off

Prompt External Table

column table_name format a22 heading "External|Table Name" word_wrapped
column src        format a54 heading "Source File"
column parms      format a54 heading "Access Parameters"

select t.table_name, d.directory_path || l.location src
  from dba_external_tables t, dba_external_locations l, dba_directories d
 where t.default_directory_name = d.directory_name
   and t.owner = l.owner
   and t.table_name = l.table_name
/

select table_name, access_parameters parms
  from dba_external_tables
 order by table_name
/
```

This script will first select the table name and the location of the source data for the external table. The next query in this script will query all the access parameters from the data dictionary view DBA_EXTERNAL_TABLES. The SH (shipping) schema, for example, has an external table named:

```
SQL> @exttabs
External Table

External
Table Name              Source File
```

```
--------------------- -------------------------------------------------------
SALES_TRANSACTIONS_EXT C:\Oracle\ora90\demo\schema\sales_history\sh_sales.dat

External
Table Name                 Access Parameters
--------------------- -------------------------------------------------------
SALES_TRANSACTIONS_EXT RECORDS DELIMITED BY NEWLINE CHARACTERSET US7ASCII
                         BADFILE log_file_dir:'sh_sales_ext.bad'
                         LOGFILE log_file_dir:'sh_sales_ext.log'
                         FIELDS TERMINATED BY "|" LDRTRIM
```

DBA_OBJECT_TABLES

DBA_OBJECT_TABLES contains information about all the object tables created in the database.

Column Definitions and Usage

This is the DBA_TABLES view with three additional columns as follows:

❑   OBJECT_ID_TYPE [VARCHAR2(16)] – This indicates whether the object ID this table is based on is user-defined or system-generated.

❑   TABLE_TYPE_OWNER [VARCHAR2(30)] – If this table is a typed table, this is the owner of the type.

❑   TABLE_TYPE [VARCHAR2(30)] – If this table is a typed table, this is the name of the type.

To see the object tables owned by the current user, copy the following script to a file named objtabs.sql. This is a query on the DBA_OBJECT_TABLES view that selects the tablespace name, table name, and some of the type information that was used in creating the table itself.

```
set verify off
set linesize 82
set pagesize 9999
set feedback off

Prompt Object Tables

column tablespace_name format a16 heading "Tablespace Name"
column table_name      format a25 heading "Table Name"
column type_name       format a30 heading "Type Name"

select tablespace_name, table_name,
       table_type_owner || '.' || table_type type_name
  from dba_object_tables
 where owner = USER
 order by tablespace_name, table_name
/
```

Using the PM schema, run the `objtab.sql` script to produce the following results:

```
SQL> @objtab
Object Tables

Tablespace Name   Table Name                  Type Name
---------------   ------------------------    ------------------------------
EXAMPLE           TEXTDOCS_NESTEDTAB          PM.TEXTDOC_TYP
```

DBA_COLL_TYPES

DBA_COLL_TYPES displays information about all the collection types in the database.

Column Definitions and Usage

❑ OWNER [VARCHAR2(30)] – Owner of the table containing the nested table.

❑ TABLE_NAME [VARCHAR2(30)] – Name of the nested table.

❑ TABLE_TYPE_OWNER [VARCHAR2(30)] – Owner of the type used to create the nested table.

❑ TABLE_TYPE_NAME [VARCHAR2(30)] – Name of the type used to create the nested table.

❑ PARENT_TABLE_NAME [VARCHAR2(30)] – Name of the table this nested table is a part of.

❑ PARENT_TABLE_COLUMN [VARCHAR2(4000)] – Name of the column in the parent table this nested table makes up.

❑ STORAGE_SPEC [VARCHAR2(30)] – The storage for the nested table can be user defined or left as the default. This column indicates which type of storage is used.

❑ RETURN_TYPE [VARCHAR2(20)] – Return type of the column.

In order to find out all those collections that a user owns, use the following script (named `colltypes.sql`):

```
prompt
prompt Collections

column type_name    format a35 heading "Collection Name"
column coll_type    format a8  heading "Type"
column element_type format a35 heading "Element Type"

select type_name,
       decode(coll_type,'TABLE','Table','Varray') coll_type,
       decode(elem_type_owner,null,'',
              elem_type_owner||'.') || elem_type_name element_type
  from dba_coll_types
  order by 1, 2
/
```

The OE user receives the following data when executing this script:

```
SQL> connect oe/oe
Connected
SQL> @colltypes

Collections

Collection Name                      Type      Element Type
------------------------------------ --------  ------------------------------
INVENTORY_LIST_TYP                   Table     OE.INVENTORY_TYP
ORDER_ITEM_LIST_TYP                  Table     OE.ORDER_ITEM_TYP
ORDER_LIST_TYP                       Table     OE.ORDER_TYP
PHONE_LIST_TYP                       Varray    VARCHAR2
PRODUCT_REF_LIST_TYP                 Table     NUMBER
SUBCATEGORY_REF_LIST_TYP             Table     OE.CATEGORY_TYP

6 rows selected.
```

DBA_JOBS

This view contains all the information about scheduled jobs in the database.

Column Definitions and Usage

❑   JOB [NUMBER] – Identifier of job.

❑   LOG_USER [VARCHAR2(30)] – USER who was logged in when the job was submitted.

❑   PRIV_USER [VARCHAR2(30)] – USER whose default privileges apply to this job.

❑   SCHEMA_USER [VARCHAR2(30)] – Default schema used to parse the jobs.

❑   LAST_DATE [DATE] – Date that this job last successfully executed.

❑   LAST_SEC [VARCHAR2(8)] – Same as LAST_DATE. This is when the last successful execution started.

❑   THIS_DATE [DATE] – Date that this job started executing (usually NULL if not executing).

❑   THIS_SEC [VARCHAR2(8)] – Same as THIS_DATE. This is when the last successful execution started.

❑   NEXT_DATE [DATE] – Date that this job will next be executed.

❑   NEXT_SEC [VARCHAR2(8)] – Same as NEXT_DATE. The job becomes due for execution at this time.

❑   TOTAL_TIME [NUMBER] – Total wallclock time spent by the system on this job, in seconds.

❑   BROKEN [VARCHAR2(1)] – If Y, no attempt is being made to run this job. See DBMS_JOBQ.BROKEN(JOB).

- INTERVAL [VARCHAR2(200)] – A date function, evaluated at the start of execution, becomes next NEXT_DATE.

- FAILURES [NUMBER] – How many times has this job started and failed since its last success?

- WHAT [VARCHAR2(4000)] – Body of the anonymous PL/SQL block that this job executes.

- NLS_ENV [VARCHAR2(4000)] – Alter session parameters describing the NLS environment of the job.

- MISC_ENV [RAW(32)] – A versioned raw maintained by the kernel, for other session parameters.

- INSTANCE [NUMBER] – Instance number restricted to run the job.

```
SQL> column priv_user format a15
SQL> column schema_user format a15

SQL> select priv_user,
  2          schema_user,
  3          this_date,
  4          next_date,
  5          decode( failures, null, 0, failures ) failures
  6     from dba_jobs
  7  /

PRIV_USER        SCHEMA_USER       THIS_DATE NEXT_DATE   FAILURES
---------------  ---------------   --------- ---------   ----------
SCOTT            SCOTT                       13-MAR-02          0
```

DBA_TYPES

This view contains information about all the object types in the database.

Column Definitions and Usage

- OWNER [VARCHAR2(30)] – Owner of the type

- TYPE_NAME [VARCHAR2(30)] – Name of the type

- TYPE_OID [RAW(16)] – Object identifier (OID) of the type

- TYPECODE [VARCHAR2(30)] – Typecode of the type

- ATTRIBUTES [NUMBER] – Number of attributes in the type

- METHODS [NUMBER] – Number of methods in the type

- PREDEFINED [VARCHAR2(3)] – Is the type a predefined type? (YES/NO)

- INCOMPLETE [VARCHAR2(3)] – Is the type an incomplete type? (YES/NO)

- FINAL [VARCHAR2(3)] – Is the type a final type? (YES/NO)

- ❏ INSTANTIABLE [VARCHAR2(3)] – Is the type an instantiable type?

- ❏ SUPERTYPE_OWNER [VARCHAR2(30)] – Owner of the supertype (NULL if type is not a supertype)

- ❏ SUPERTYPE_NAME [VARCHAR2(30)] – Name of the supertype (NULL if type is not a supertype)

- ❏ LOCAL_ATTRIBUTES [NUMBER] – Number of local (not inherited) attributes (if any) in the subtype

- ❏ LOCAL_METHODS [NUMBER] – Number of local (not inherited) methods (if any) in the subtype

- ❏ TYPEID [RAW(16)] – Type id value of the type

```
SQL> column name format a25
SQL> column extends format a29
SQL> column "# ATTRS" format a7
SQL> column "# METHS" format a7

SQL> select type_name name,
  2         decode( supertype_owner, null, null,
  3                 supertype_owner || '.' || supertype_name ) "EXTENDS",
  4         final,
  5         attributes "# ATTRIBUTES",
  6         methods "# METHODS"
  7    from dba_types
  8   where owner = upper( 'OE' )
  9  /
```

NAME	EXTENDS	FINAL	# ATTRS	# METHS
CUST_ADDRESS_TYP		YES	5	0
PHONE_LIST_TYP		YES	0	0
WAREHOUSE_TYP		YES	3	0
INVENTORY_TYP		YES	3	0
INVENTORY_LIST_TYP		YES	0	0
PRODUCT_INFORMATION_TYP		YES	12	0
ORDER_ITEM_TYP		YES	5	0
ORDER_ITEM_LIST_TYP		YES	0	0
CUSTOMER_TYP		NO	10	0
ORDER_TYP		YES	7	0
ORDER_LIST_TYP		YES	0	0
CATEGORY_TYP		NO	3	1
SUBCATEGORY_REF_LIST_TYP		YES	0	0
PRODUCT_REF_LIST_TYP		YES	0	0
CORPORATE_CUSTOMER_TYP	OE.CUSTOMER_TYP	YES	11	0
LEAF_CATEGORY_TYP	OE.CATEGORY_TYP	YES	4	2
COMPOSITE_CATEGORY_TYP	OE.CATEGORY_TYP	NO	4	2
CATALOG_TYP	OE.COMPOSITE_CATEGORY_TYP	YES	4	4

997

DBA_TYPE_ATTRS

Use the DBA_TYPE_ATTRS view to get information about the attributes of an object type.

Column Definitions and Usage

❑   OWNER [VARCHAR2(30)] – Owner of the type

❑   TYPE_NAME [VARCHAR2(30)] – Name of the type

❑   ATTR_NAME [VARCHAR2(30)] – Name of the attribute

❑   ATTR_TYPE_MOD [VARCHAR2(7)] – Type modifier of the attribute

❑   ATTR_TYPE_OWNER [VARCHAR2(30)] – Owner of the type of the attribute

❑   ATTR_TYPE_NAME [VARCHAR2(30)] – Name of the type of the attribute

❑   LENGTH [NUMBER] – Length of the CHAR attribute or maximum length of the VARCHAR or VARCHAR2 attribute

❑   PRECISION [NUMBER] – Decimal precision of the NUMBER or DECIMAL attribute, or binary precision of the FLOAT attribute

❑   SCALE [NUMBER] – Scale of the NUMBER or DECIMAL attribute

❑   CHARACTER_SET_NAME [VARCHAR2(44)] – Character set name of the attribute

❑   ATTR_NO [NUMBER] – Syntactical order number or position of the attribute as specified in the type specification or CREATE TYPE statement (not to be used as ID number)

❑   INHERITED [VARCHAR2(3)] – Is the attribute inherited from the supertype ?

```
SQL> column type format a30

SQL> select attr_name,
  2          decode( attr_type_owner, null, null, attr_type_owner || '.' ) ||
  3          attr_type_name ||
  4          decode( attr_type_name,
  5              'VARCHAR2', '('||length||')',
  6              'CHAR', '('||length||')',
  7              'NUMBER', '('||precision||','||scale||')',
  8              null ) type
  9    from dba_type_attrs
 10   where owner = 'OE'
 11     and type_name = 'COMPOSITE_CATEGORY_TYP'
 12   order by attr_no
 14  /

ATTR_NAME                           TYPE
----------------------------------  -------------------------------
CATEGORY_NAME                       VARCHAR2(50)
CATEGORY_DESCRIPTION                VARCHAR2(1000)
CATEGORY_ID                         NUMBER(2,0)
SUBCATEGORY_REF_LIST                OE.SUBCATEGORY_REF_LIST_TYP
```

DBA_TYPE_METHODS

This view contains information about the methods in object types.

Column Definitions and Usage

- ❑ OWNER [VARCHAR2(30)] – Owner of the type

- ❑ TYPE_NAME [VARCHAR2(30)] – Name of the type

- ❑ METHOD_NAME [VARCHAR2(30)] – Name of the method

- ❑ METHOD_NO [NUMBER] – Method number for distinguishing overloaded method (not to be used as ID number)

- ❑ METHOD_TYPE [VARCHAR2(6)] – Type of the method

- ❑ PARAMETERS [NUMBER] – Number of parameters to the method

- ❑ RESULTS [NUMBER] – Number of results returned by the method

- ❑ FINAL [VARCHAR2(3)] – Is the method final ?

- ❑ INSTANTIABLE [VARCHAR2(3)] – Is the method instantiable ?

- ❑ OVERRIDING [VARCHAR2(3)] – Is the method overriding a supertype method ?

- ❑ INHERITED [VARCHAR2(3)] – Is the method inherited from the supertype ?

```
SQL> clear breaks
SQL> break on num skip 1
SQL>
SQL> column method_name format a20
SQL> column param_name format a20
SQL> column num format 999
SQL> column "IN/OUT" format a6
SQL>
SQL> select tm.method_no num,
  2         tm.method_name,
  3         tm.method_type,
  4         tm.final,
  5         tm.instantiable,
  6         tm.overriding,
  7         tm.inherited,
  8         mp.param_name,
  9         mp.param_mode "IN/OUT"
 10    from dba_type_methods tm,
 11         dba_method_params mp
 12   where tm.owner = mp.owner
 13     and tm.type_name = mp.type_name
 14     and tm.method_name = mp.method_name
 15     and tm.method_no = mp.method_no
 16     and tm.owner = 'OE'
 17     and tm.type_name = 'COMPOSITE_CATEGORY_TYP'
 18   order by 1, 2, 3
```

```
  19  /

  NUM METHOD_NAME          METHOD FINAL INS OVE INH PARAM_NAME      IN/OUT
  ---- -------------------- ------ ----- --- --- --- -------------- ------
    1 CATEGORY_DESCRIBE     PUBLIC NO    NO  NO  YES SELF              IN
    2 CATEGORY_DESCRIBE     PUBLIC NO    YES YES NO  SELF              IN
```

DBA_METHOD_PARAMS

The view contains information about the parameters of methods of object types.

Column Definitions and Usage

- ❏ OWNER [VARCHAR2(30)] – Owner of the type

- ❏ TYPE_NAME [VARCHAR2(30)] – Name of the type

- ❏ METHOD_NAME [VARCHAR2(30)] – Name of the method

- ❏ METHOD_NO [NUMBER] – Method number for distinguishing overloaded method (not to be used as ID number)

- ❏ PARAM_NAME [VARCHAR2(30)] – Name of the parameter

- ❏ PARAM_NO [NUMBER] – Parameter number or position

- ❏ PARAM_MODE [VARCHAR2(6)] – Mode of the parameter

- ❏ PARAM_TYPE_MOD [VARCHAR2(7)] – Type modifier of the parameter

- ❏ PARAM_TYPE_OWNER [VARCHAR2(30)] – Owner of the type of the parameter

- ❏ PARAM_TYPE_NAME [VARCHAR2(30)] – Name of the type of the parameter

- ❏ CHARACTER_SET_NAME [VARCHAR2(44)] – Character set name of the parameter

See DBA_TYPE_METHODS for usage information.

DBA_METHOD_RESULTS

The DBA_METHOD_RESULTS view contains information about the return type from methods accessible to the caller.

Column Definitions and Usage

- ❏ OWNER [VARCHAR2(30)] – Owner of the type

- ❏ TYPE_NAME [VARCHAR2(30)] – Name of the type

- ❏ METHOD_NAME [VARCHAR2(30)] – Name of the method

- ❏ METHOD_NO [NUMBER] – Method number for distinguishing overloaded method (not to be used as ID number)

- ❏ RESULT_TYPE_MOD [VARCHAR2(7)] – Type modifier of the result
- ❏ RESULT_TYPE_OWNER [VARCHAR2(30)] – Owner of the type of the result
- ❏ RESULT_TYPE_NAME [VARCHAR2(30)] – Name of the type of the result
- ❏ CHARACTER_SET_NAME [VARCHAR2(44)] – Character set name of the result

```
SQL> clear breaks
SQL> break on num skip 1
SQL>
SQL> column method_name format a20
SQL> column param_name format a20
SQL> column result_type_name a25
SQL> column num format 999
SQL>
SQL> select tm.method_no num,
  2         tm.method_name,
  3         tm.method_type,
  4         tm.final,
  5         tm.instantiable,
  6         tm.overriding,
  7         tm.inherited,
  8         mr.result_type_name
  9    from dba_type_methods tm,
 10         dba_method_results mr
 11   where tm.owner = mr.owner
 12     and tm.type_name = mr.type_name
 13     and tm.method_name = mr.method_name
 14     and tm.method_no = mr.method_no
 15     and tm.owner = 'OE'
 16     and tm.type_name = 'COMPOSITE_CATEGORY_TYP'
 17   order by 1, 2, 3
 18  /

NUM METHOD_NAME          METHOD FINAL INS OVE INH RESULT_TYPE_NAME
---- -------------------- ------ ----- --- --- --- ------------------------
   1 CATEGORY_DESCRIBE    PUBLIC NO    NO  NO  YES VARCHAR2
   2 CATEGORY_DESCRIBE    PUBLIC NO    YES YES NO  VARCHAR2
```

DBA_LOBS

This view shows all the large objects, or LOBs, in the database.

Column Definitions and Usage

- ❏ OWNER [VARCHAR2(30)] – Owner of the table containing the LOB.
- ❏ TABLE_NAME [VARCHAR2(30)] – Name of the table containing the LOB.
- ❏ COLUMN_NAME [VARCHAR2(4000)] – The column of the table that is the LOB.

❑   SEGMENT_NAME [VARCHAR2(30)] – The segment that is storing the LOB.

❑   INDEX_NAME [VARCHAR2(30)] – The index of the LOB.

❑   CHUNK [NUMBER] – The size of the LOB chunk.

❑   PCTVERSION [NUMBER] – The maximum amount of space in a LOB block used for versioning.

❑   CACHE [VARCHAR2(10)] – The CACHE setting is how the cluster is cached in the database buffer cache.

❑   LOGGING [VARCHAR2(7)] – Whether changes to the LOB are logged.

❑   IN_ROW [VARCHAR2(3)] – Whether the LOB is eligible for in-line storage with the base row of the table.

In the following query, we will query DBA_LOBS to find out all the LOBS a particular owner owns, what tables and columns they are in, and the size of the LOB chunk.

```
set verify off
set linesize 80

prompt &1.'s LOBS
&1.'s LOBS

column table_column format a45 heading "Table and Column of LOB"
column lob_name format a25 heading "LOB Name"
column in_row format a6 heading "In?"

select table_name || '.' || column_name table_column,
       segment_name lob_name, in_row
  from dba_lobs
 where owner = upper( '&1' )
order by 1, 2
/
```

If we invoke this query using the OE schema, we get the following results:

```
SQL> @lobs OE
OE's LOBS

Table and Column of LOB                        LOB Name                  In? ------
---------------------------------------------  ------------------------- ---
CUSTOMERS."CUST_GEO_LOCATION"."SDO_ELEM_INFO"  SYS_LOB0000030851C00022$$ Yes
CUSTOMERS."CUST_GEO_LOCATION"."SDO_ORDINATES"  SYS_LOB0000030851C00023$$ Yes
WAREHOUSES."WH_GEO_LOCATION"."SDO_ELEM_INFO"   SYS_LOB0000030857C00012$$ Yes
WAREHOUSES."WH_GEO_LOCATION"."SDO_ORDINATES"   SYS_LOB0000030857C00013$$ Yes
WAREHOUSES.SYS_NC00003$                        SYS_LOB0000030857C00003$$ Yes
```

DBA_VIEWS

DBA_VIEWS contains information about all the views in the database.

Column Definitions and Usage

❏ OWNER [VARCHAR2(30)] – Owner of the view

❏ VIEW_NAME [VARCHAR2(30)] – Name of the view

❏ TEXT_LENGTH [NUMBER] – Length of the view text

❏ TEXT [LONG] – View text

❏ TYPE_TEXT_LENGTH [NUMBER] – Length of the type clause of the object view

❏ TYPE_TEXT [VARCHAR2(4000)] – Type clause of the object view

❏ OID_TEXT_LENGTH [NUMBER] – Length of the WITH OBJECT OID clause of the object view

❏ OID_TEXT [VARCHAR2(4000)] – WITH OBJECT OID clause of the object view

❏ VIEW_TYPE_OWNER [VARCHAR2(30)] – Owner of the type of the view if the view is an object view

❏ VIEW_TYPE [VARCHAR2(30)] – Type of the view if the view is an object view

❏ SUPERVIEW_NAME [VARCHAR2(30)] – Name of the superview, if view is a superview

We can use the following script to generate the CREATE VIEW command used to initially create the view. (Save it in a file called getaview.sql.)

```
set heading off
set long 99999999
set feedback off
set linesize 1000
set trimspool on
set verify off
set termout off
set embedded on

column column_name format a1000
column text format a1000

spool &2..sql
prompt create or replace view &2 (
select decode(column_id,1,'',',') || column_name   column_name
  from dba_tab_columns
 where table_name = upper('&2')
   and owner = upper('&1')
 order by column_id
/
prompt ) as
select text
```

```
   from dba_views
 where view_name = upper('&2')
   and owner = upper('&1')
/
prompt /
spool off

set termout on
set heading on
set feedback on
set verify on
```

You can execute it using `@getaview <user> <view_name>`. It will generate a file named `<view_name>.sql`.

DBA_UPDATABLE_COLUMNS

This view lists all columns of a join view and whether or not data can be modified through them.

Column Definitions and Usage

- ❏   OWNER [VARCHAR2(30)] – Table/View owner

- ❏   TABLE_NAME [VARCHAR2(30)] – Table/View name

- ❏   COLUMN_NAME [VARCHAR2(30)] – Column name

- ❏   UPDATABLE [VARCHAR2(3)] – Is the column updatable? (YES/NO)

- ❏   INSERTABLE [VARCHAR2(3)] – Is the column insertable? (YES/NO)

- ❏   DELETABLE [VARCHAR2(3)] – Is the column deletable? (YES/NO)

Use this script to get information about a join view. (Save it in a file called `viewrep.sql`.):

```
set echo off
set verify off
set linesize 72
set pagesize 9999
set feedback off

column view_name format a30
column column_name format a30
column i format a1
column u format a1
column d format a1

clear breaks
break on view_name

select table_name view_name,
       column_name,
```

```
        decode( insertable, 'YES', null, '*' ) i,
        decode( updatable, 'YES', null, '*' ) u,
        decode( deletable, 'YES', null, '*' ) d
   from dba_updatable_columns
  where owner = upper('&1')
    and table_name = upper('&2')
/

prompt
prompt
prompt '*' indicated action not permitted.
prompt
```

You can run it for any `<user>` `<view_name>` combination.

```
SQL> @viewrep hr emp_details_view

VIEW_NAME                          COLUMN_NAME                          I U D
-------------------------------    -------------------------------    - - -
EMP_DETAILS_VIEW                   EMPLOYEE_ID                          * * *
                                   JOB_ID                               * * *
                                   MANAGER_ID                           * * *
                                   DEPARTMENT_ID                        * * *
                                   LOCATION_ID                          * * *
                                   COUNTRY_ID                           * * *
                                   FIRST_NAME                           * * *
                                   LAST_NAME                            * * *
                                   SALARY                               * * *
                                   COMMISSION_PCT                       * * *
                                   DEPARTMENT_NAME                      * * *
                                   JOB_TITLE                            * * *
                                   CITY                                 * * *
                                   STATE_PROVINCE                       * * *
                                   COUNTRY_NAME                         * * *
                                   REGION_NAME                          * * *
```

Note that '*' indicates that the action is not permitted.

DBA_TRIGGERS

This view is a listing of all trigger-related information in the database.

Column Definitions and Usage

❑   OWNER [VARCHAR2(30)] – Owner of the trigger

❑   TRIGGER_NAME [VARCHAR2(30)] – Name of the trigger

❑   TRIGGER_TYPE [VARCHAR2(16)] – When the trigger fires. BEFORE/AFTER and STATEMENT/ROW

- ❑ TRIGGERING_EVENT [VARCHAR2(227)] – Statement that will fire the trigger. INSERT, UPDATE and/or DELETE

- ❑ TABLE_OWNER [VARCHAR2(30)] – Owner of the table that this trigger is associated with

- ❑ BASE_OBJECT_TYPE [VARCHAR2(16)] – Object type (TABLE, VIEW, SCHEMA, or DATABASE) that the trigger is attached to

- ❑ TABLE_NAME [VARCHAR2(30)] – Name of the table that this trigger is associated with

- ❑ COLUMN_NAME [VARCHAR2(4000)] – The name of the column on which the trigger is defined

- ❑ REFERENCING_NAMES [VARCHAR2(128)] – Names used for referencing to OLD and NEW values within the trigger

- ❑ WHEN_CLAUSE [VARCHAR2(4000)] – WHEN clause must evaluate to TRUE in order for triggering body to execute

- ❑ STATUS [VARCHAR2(8)] – ENABLED/DISABLED. If DISABLED then trigger will not fire

- ❑ DESCRIPTION [VARCHAR2(4000)] – Trigger description, useful for recreating trigger creation statement

- ❑ ACTION_TYPE [VARCHAR2(11)] – Action type of trigger's body (PL/SQL or CALL)

- ❑ TRIGGER_BODY [LONG] – Action taken by this trigger when it fires

You can use the following to produce a quick report on the trigger for the HR schema:

```
SQL> set linesize 77
SQL> column triggering_event format a30
SQL> column trigger_name format a20
SQL>
SQL> select trigger_name,
  2         triggering_event,
  3         trigger_type,
  4         status
  5    from dba_triggers
  6   where owner = 'HR'
  7  /

TRIGGER_NAME         TRIGGERING_EVENT            TRIGGER_TYPE      STATUS
-------------------- --------------------------- ----------------- --------
SECURE_EMPLOYEES     INSERT OR UPDATE OR DELETE  BEFORE STATEMENT  DISABLED
UPDATE_JOB_HISTORY   UPDATE                      AFTER EACH ROW    ENABLED
```

DBA_TRIGGER_COLS

Describes the use of all columns in triggers.

Column Definitions and Usage

- ❑ TRIGGER_OWNER [VARCHAR2(30)] – Owner of the trigger

- ❑ TRIGGER_NAME [VARCHAR2(30)] – Name of the trigger

❑ TABLE_OWNER [VARCHAR2(30)] – Owner of the table

❑ TABLE_NAME [VARCHAR2(30)] – Name of the table on which the trigger is defined

❑ COLUMN_NAME [VARCHAR2(4000)] – Name of the column or the attribute of the column used in trigger definition

❑ COLUMN_LIST [VARCHAR2(3)] – Is column specified in UPDATE OF clause?

❑ COLUMN_USAGE [VARCHAR2(17)] – Usage of column within trigger body

Here we show you a list of columns referenced in the trigger UPDATE_JOB_HISTORY in the HR schema.

```
SQL> clear breaks
SQL> break on table_name
SQL>
SQL> column table_name format a20
SQL> column column_name format a20
SQL>
SQL>
SQL> select table_name,
  2         column_name,
  3         column_list,
  4         column_usage
  5    from dba_trigger_cols
  6   where trigger_name = 'UPDATE_JOB_HISTORY'
  7     and trigger_owner = 'HR'
  8  /

TABLE_NAME           COLUMN_NAME          COL COLUMN_USAGE
-------------------- -------------------- --- -----------------
EMPLOYEES            DEPARTMENT_ID        YES OLD IN
                     EMPLOYEE_ID          NO  OLD IN
                     HIRE_DATE            NO  OLD IN
                     JOB_ID               YES OLD IN
```

We can see how these columns are referenced, by querying the DBA_TRIGGERS view:

```
SQL> set long 9999

SQL> select trigger_body
  2    from dba_triggers
  3   where owner = 'HR'
  4     and trigger_name = 'UPDATE_JOB_HISTORY'
  5  /

TRIGGER_BODY
--------------------------------------------------------------------------------
BEGIN
  add_job_history(:old.employee_id, :old.hire_date, sysdate,
                  :old.job_id, :old.department_id);
END;
```

DBA_SOURCE

This view contains the actual PL/SQL source code for the given object.

Column Definitions and Usage

- ❑ OWNER [VARCHAR2(30)] – Owner of the object

- ❑ NAME [VARCHAR2(30)] – Name of the object

- ❑ TYPE [VARCHAR2(12)] – Type of the object

- ❑ LINE [NUMBER] – Line number of this line of the source

- ❑ TEXT [VARCHAR2(4000)] – Source text

We can use the following script to retrieve PL/SQL from the database:

```
set feedback off
set heading off
set termout off
set linesize 1000
set trimspool on
set verify off

spool &2..sql

prompt set define off

select decode( type||'-'||to_char(line,'fm99999'),
               'PACKAGE BODY-1', '/'||chr(10),
               null) ||
       decode(line,1,'create or replace ', '' ) ||
       text text
  from dba_source
 where name = upper('&&2')
   and order = upper( '&&1')
 order by type, line;
prompt /

prompt set define on

spool off

set feedback on
set heading on
set termout on
set linesize 100
```

Save this script to a file called getcode.sql. To execute the script issue the following. @getcode <owner> <object_name>. It will produce a file named <object_name>.sql containing the source code of the object.

DBA_PROCEDURES

Use the DBA_PROCEDURES view to determine more information about procedures and functions.

Column Definitions and Usage

- ❏ OWNER [VARCHAR2(30)] – Owner of the object.

- ❏ OBJECT_NAME [VARCHAR2(30)] – Name of the object : top-level function/procedure/package name

- ❏ PROCEDURE_NAME [VARCHAR2(30)] – Name of the procedure

- ❏ AGGREGATE [VARCHAR2(3)] – Is it an aggregate function? (YES/NO)

- ❏ PIPELINED [VARCHAR2(3)] – Is it a pipelined table function? (YES/NO)

- ❏ IMPLTYPEOWNER [VARCHAR2(30)] – Name of the owner of the implementation type (if any)

- ❏ IMPLTYPENAME [VARCHAR2(30)] – Name of the implementation type (if any)

- ❏ PARALLEL [VARCHAR2(3)] – Is the procedure parallel enabled? (YES/NO)

- ❏ INTERFACE [VARCHAR2(3)]

- ❏ DETERMINISTIC [VARCHAR2(3)] – Is the procedure deterministic? (YES/NO)

- ❏ AUTHID [VARCHAR2(12)] – The AUTHID of the procedure (INVOKER/DEFINER)

```
SQL> select procedure_name,
  2          aggregate,
  3          pipelined,
  4          parallel,
  5          deterministic,
  6          authid
  7    from dba_procedures
  8   where owner = 'HR'
  9  /

PROCEDURE_NAME                  AGG PIP PAR DET AUTHID
------------------------------- --- --- --- --- -----------
ADD_JOB_HISTORY                 NO  NO  NO  NO  DEFINER
SECURE_DML                      NO  NO  NO  NO  DEFINER
```

ALL_ARGUMENTS

This view contains information about the parameters and return types of procedures and functions.

Column Definitions and Usage

- ❏ OWNER [VARCHAR2(30)] – Username of the owner of the object

- ❏ OBJECT_NAME [VARCHAR2(30)] – Procedure or function name

❏ PACKAGE_NAME [VARCHAR2(30)] – Package name

❏ OBJECT_ID [NUMBER] – Object number of the object

❏ OVERLOAD [VARCHAR2(40)] – Overload unique identifier

❏ ARGUMENT_NAME [VARCHAR2(30)] – Argument name

❏ POSITION [NUMBER] – Position in argument list, or null for function return value

❏ SEQUENCE [NUMBER] – Argument sequence, including all nesting levels

❏ DATA_LEVEL [NUMBER] – Nesting depth of argument for composite types

❏ DATA_TYPE [VARCHAR2(30)] – Data type of the argument

❏ DEFAULT_VALUE [LONG] – Default value for the argument

❏ DEFAULT_LENGTH [NUMBER] – Length of default value for the argument

❏ IN_OUT [VARCHAR2(9)] – Argument direction (IN, OUT, or IN/OUT)

❏ DATA_LENGTH [NUMBER] – Length of the column in bytes

❏ DATA_PRECISION [NUMBER] – Length: decimal digits (NUMBER) or binary digits (FLOAT)

❏ DATA_SCALE [NUMBER] – Digits to right of decimal point in a number

❏ RADIX [NUMBER] – Argument radix for a number

❏ CHARACTER_SET_NAME [VARCHAR2(44)] – Character set name for the argument

❏ TYPE_OWNER [VARCHAR2(30)] – Owner name for argument type in case of object types

❏ TYPE_NAME [VARCHAR2(30)] – Object name for argument type in case of object types

❏ TYPE_SUBNAME [VARCHAR2(30)] – Subordinate object name for argument type in case of object types

❏ TYPE_LINK [VARCHAR2(128)] – Database link name for argument type in case of object types

❏ PLS_TYPE [VARCHAR2(30)] – PL/SQL type name for numeric arguments

❏ CHAR_LENGTH [NUMBER] – Character limit for string data types

❏ CHAR_USED [VARCHAR2(1)] – Is the byte limit (B) or char limit (C) official for this string?

```
SQL> column object_name format a20
SQL> column data_type format a15
SQL>
SQL> clear breaks
SQL> break on object_name
SQL>
SQL> select object_name,
  2          argument_name,
  3          data_type
  4     from all_arguments
  5    where owner = 'HR'
  6    order by position
```

```
    7  /

OBJECT_NAME              ARGUMENT_NAME                 DATA_TYPE
-------------------      --------------------------    ---------------
ADD_JOB_HISTORY          P_EMP_ID                      NUMBER
                         P_START_DATE                  DATE
                         P_END_DATE                    DATE
                         P_JOB_ID                      VARCHAR2
                         P_DEPARTMENT_ID               NUMBER
```

DBA_DEPENDENCIES

The DBA_DEPENDENCIES view contains information about which objects are dependent on which other objects.

Column Definitions and Usage

❏ OWNER [VARCHAR2(30)] – Owner of the object

❏ NAME [VARCHAR2(30)] – Name of the object

❏ TYPE [VARCHAR2(12)] – Type of the object

❏ REFERENCED_OWNER [VARCHAR2(30)] – Owner of referenced object (remote owner if remote object)

❏ REFERENCED_NAME [VARCHAR2(64)] – Name of referenced object

❏ REFERENCED_TYPE [VARCHAR2(12)] – Type of referenced object

❏ REFERENCED_LINK_NAME [VARCHAR2(128)] – Name of DBLINK if this is a remote object

❏ DEPENDENCY_TYPE [VARCHAR2(4)] – Defines the dependency type (REF/HARD)

You can determine which objects your schema is dependent on with the following query:

```
SQL> set linesize 132
SQL> column referenced_object format a35
SQL> clear breaks
SQL> break on name on type
SQL>
SQL> select name,
  2         type,
  3         referenced_owner ||'.'|| referenced_name referenced_object
  4    from dba_dependencies
  5   where owner = 'HR'
  6  /

NAME                             TYPE           REFERENCED_OBJECT
-------------------------        ------------   --------------------------------
SECURE_DML                       PROCEDURE      SYS.STANDARD
UPDATE_JOB_HISTORY               TRIGGER        SYS.STANDARD
SECURE_DML                       PROCEDURE      SYS.DBMS_STANDARD
```

```
                                        SYS.SYS_STUB_FOR_PURITY_ANALYSIS
ADD_JOB_HISTORY          PROCEDURE      SYS.SYS_STUB_FOR_PURITY_ANALYSIS
EMP_DETAILS_VIEW         VIEW           HR.REGIONS
                                        HR.COUNTRIES
                                        HR.LOCATIONS
                                        HR.DEPARTMENTS
                                        HR.JOBS
EMP_DETAILS_VIEW         VIEW           HR.EMPLOYEES
SECURE_EMPLOYEES         TRIGGER        HR.EMPLOYEES
UPDATE_JOB_HISTORY       TRIGGER        HR.EMPLOYEES
ADD_JOB_HISTORY          PROCEDURE      HR.JOB_HISTORY
SECURE_EMPLOYEES         TRIGGER        HR.SECURE_DML
UPDATE_JOB_HISTORY       TRIGGER        HR.ADD_JOB_HISTORY
```

Or you can see which objects in the database are dependent on a particular object in your schema.

```
SQL> select owner || '.' || name name,
  2          type,
  3          dependency_type
  4     from dba_dependencies
  5    where referenced_owner = 'HR'
  6      and referenced_name = 'EMPLOYEES'
  7  /

NAME                                                    TYPE          DEPE
-----------------------------------------------------   ------------  ----
HR.MY_REPORTS                                           VIEW          HARD
HR.COMPANY_PHONE_BOOK                                   VIEW          HARD
HR.EMP_DETAILS_VIEW                                     VIEW          HARD
HR.SECURE_EMPLOYEES                                     TRIGGER       HARD
HR.UPDATE_JOB_HISTORY                                   TRIGGER       HARD
```

DBA_ERRORS

This is the view that SQL*Plus uses to return the current results from the SHOW ERRORS command on every object in the database.

Column Definitions and Usage

- ❏ OWNER [VARCHAR2(30)] – Owner of the object

- ❏ NAME [VARCHAR2(30)] – Name of the object

- ❏ TYPE [VARCHAR2(12)] – Type

- ❏ SEQUENCE [NUMBER] – Sequence number used for ordering purposes

- ❏ LINE [NUMBER] – Line number at which this error occurs

- ❏ POSITION [NUMBER] – Position in the line at which this error occurs

- ❏ TEXT [VARCHAR2(4000)] – Text of the error

If we compile a procedure and get an error we can query the DBA_ERRORS view to return the error, and allow other clients to mimic the SQL*Plus functionality.

```
SQL> connect system/manager
Connected.

SQL> set long 9999

SQL> select line || '/' || position "LINE/COL",
  2         text error
  3    from dba_errors
  4   where owner = 'SCOTT'
  5     and name = 'FOO'
  6  /

LINE/COL ERROR
-------- --------------------------------------------------------------
4/1      PLS-00103: Encountered the symbol "END" when expecting one of the
         following:
         ;
         The symbol ";" was substituted for "END" to continue.
```

DBA_INDEXES

Column Definitions and Usage

- ❑ OWNER [VARCHAR2(30)] – The user who created the index

- ❑ INDEX_NAME [VARCHAR2(30)] – The name of the index

- ❑ INDEX_TYPE [VARCHAR2(27)] – The type of index

- ❑ TABLE_OWNER [VARCHAR2(30)] – The owner of the table this index is built on

- ❑ TABLE_NAME [VARCHAR2(30)] – The name of the table this index is built on

- ❑ TABLE_TYPE [VARCHAR2(11)] – The type of the table this index is built on

- ❑ UNIQUENESS [VARCHAR2(9)] – Whether the index is unique or not

- ❑ COMPRESSION [VARCHAR2(8)] – Whether this index uses compression or not

- ❑ PREFIX_LENGTH [NUMBER] – Number of columns in the prefix of a compressed index

- ❑ TABLESPACE_NAME [VARCHAR2(30)] – Tablespace this index is stored in

- ❑ INI_TRANS [NUMBER] – The number of transaction entries in a block to allow multiple transactions to simultaneously change rows within the same block for this index

- ❑ MAX_TRANS [NUMBER] – The maximum number of transactions that can simultaneously change rows within the same block for this index

❑ INITIAL_EXTENT [NUMBER] – Number of bytes in the first extent created for this index

❑ NEXT_EXTENT [NUMBER] – Number of bytes in the next extent to be allocated for this index

❑ MIN_EXTENTS [NUMBER] – The minimum number of extents created for this index

❑ MAX_EXTENTS [NUMBER] – The maximum number of extents that can be created for this index

❑ PCT_INCREASE [NUMBER] – The percentage of the extent size that the next extent will grow by

❑ PCT_THRESHOLD [NUMBER] – Indicates the percentage of the block size that all non-key columns in the index must fit in, in order to not be broken out to the row overflow area

❑ INCLUDE_COLUMN [NUMBER] – The column number in the index that indicates the first column in the index (and all remaining columns) that will be stored in the row overflow area

❑ FREELISTS [NUMBER] – The number of freelists for this index. Freelists track a list of data blocks that have room for new inserts into the index

❑ FREELIST_GROUPS [NUMBER] – This is the number of groups of freelists for the index. This is used with Oracle's Real Application Clusters

❑ PCT_FREE [NUMBER] – Percentage of the block that is available for updates only. Oracle will stop inserting rows into the block once the block reaches this percentage of free space in the block

❑ LOGGING [VARCHAR2(3)] – Specifies whether creation of this index, direct path load, and direct path inserts against the table this index is built on are logged in the redo log (LOGGING vs. NOLOGGING)

❑ BLEVEL [NUMBER] – This is the depth of the index. A BLEVEL of zero indicates that the root blocks are the leaf blocks

❑ LEAF_BLOCKS [NUMBER] – The number of leaf blocks in the index

❑ DISTINCT_KEYS [NUMBER] – The number of distinct keys in the index

❑ AVG_LEAF_BLOCKS_PER_KEY [NUMBER] – This is the average number of blocks in which each distinct value in the index appears. For unique indexes, this number is always 1

❑ AVG_DATA_BLOCKS_PER_KEY [NUMBER] – This is the average number of data blocks pointed to by a distinct value in the index

❑ CLUSTERING_FACTOR [NUMBER] – This indicates how well the rows in the table are ordered, according to the index. If the value is near the number of blocks of the index, the table is well-ordered. Higher numbers indicate the table is randomly ordered

❑ STATUS [VARCHAR2(8)] – Whether the index is VALID or UNUSABLE

❑ NUM_ROWS [NUMBER] – The number of rows in this index

❑ SAMPLE_SIZE [NUMBER] – When this index is analyzed, Oracle can estimate statistics based on a percentage of the table instead of computing statistics based on the entire index. SAMPLE_SIZE tells you what size was used to estimate the statistics

❑ LAST_ANALYZED [DATE] – Identifies the date for the last time this index was analyzed

- ❑ DEGREE [VARCHAR2(40)] – The number of threads per instance for scanning the index

- ❑ INSTANCES [VARCHAR2(40)] – The number of instances that can scan an index simultaneously

- ❑ PARTITIONED [VARCHAR2(3)] – Whether the index is on a temporary table

- ❑ TEMPORARY [VARCHAR2(1)] – Whether the table this index is built upon or not

- ❑ GENERATED [VARCHAR2(1)] – The name of an index can be user-defined or system-generated. This column indicates how this index was named

- ❑ SECONDARY [VARCHAR2(1)] – Was the index was created by the Oracle 9*i* Data Cartridge?

- ❑ BUFFER_POOL [VARCHAR2(7)] – The default buffer pool for this index

- ❑ USER_STATS [VARCHAR2(3)] – Indicates whether the statistics for the index were "created" using the DBMS_STATS supplied package. If a user does, this column will be YES

- ❑ DURATION [VARCHAR2(15)] – For indexes built on temporary tables, this indicates the type of temporary table (SYS$SESSION/SYS$TRANSACTION)

- ❑ PCT_DIRECT_ACCESS [NUMBER] – If the index is on an IOT, this is the percentage of rows with valid guess

- ❑ ITYP_OWNER [VARCHAR2(30)] – For a domain index, the owner of the index type

- ❑ ITYP_NAME [VARCHAR2(30)] – For a domain index, the name of the index type

- ❑ PARAMETERS [VARCHAR2(1000)] – For a domain index, the parameter string

- ❑ GLOBAL_STATS [VARCHAR2(3)] – For partitioned indexes, indicates whether statistics were gathered on the entire index (YES) or on the index partitions (NO)

- ❑ DOMIDX_STATUS [VARCHAR2(12)] – Reflects the status of a domain index (NULL, VALID, IDXTYP_INVLD)

- ❑ DOMIDX_OPSTATUS [VARCHAR2(6)] – Reflects the status of an operation that was performed on a domain index (NULL, VALID, FAILED)

- ❑ FUNCIDX_STATUS [VARCHAR2(8)] – Indicates the status of a function-based index (NULL, ENABLED, DISABLED)

- ❑ JOIN_INDEX [VARCHAR2(3)] – Whether this is a join index or not

See DBA_IND_COLUMNS for usage information.

DBA_IND_COLUMNS

Column Definitions and Usage

- ❑ INDEX_OWNER [VARCHAR2(30)] – The user who created the index this column is a part of.

- ❑ INDEX_NAME [VARCHAR2(30)] – The name of the index this column is a part of.

- ❑ TABLE_OWNER [VARCHAR2(30)] – The owner of the table this column's index is defined on.

❏ TABLE_NAME [VARCHAR2(30)] – The name of the table this column's index is defined on.

❏ COLUMN_NAME [VARCHAR2(4000)] – The name of the column in the index.

❏ COLUMN_POSITION [NUMBER] – The position of the column in the index amongst the other columns.

❏ COLUMN_LENGTH [NUMBER] – The indexed length of the column.

❏ CHAR_LENGTH [NUMBER] – Maximum length of the column.

❏ DESCEND [VARCHAR2(4)] – Whether the column is sorted in descending order (Y) or not (N).

To get index information for a particular table, copy the following SQL*Plus script to a file named `indexes.sql`:

```
set verify off
set linesize 72
set pagesize 9999
set feedback off

variable tname varchar2(30)
begin
   :tname := upper('&1');
end;
/

prompt
Prompt Indexes on &1
column index_name heading "Index|Name"
column Uniqueness heading "Is|Unique" format a6
column columns format a32 word_wrapped

select substr(a.index_name,1,30) index_name,
       decode(a.uniqueness,'UNIQUE','Yes','No') uniqueness,
max(decode( b.column_position,  1, substr(b.column_name,1,30),
NULL )) ||
max(decode( b.column_position,  2, ', '||
substr(b.column_name,1,30), NULL )) ||
max(decode( b.column_position,  3, ', '||
substr(b.column_name,1,30), NULL )) ||
max(decode( b.column_position,  4, ', '||
substr(b.column_name,1,30), NULL )) ||
max(decode( b.column_position,  5, ', '||
substr(b.column_name,1,30), NULL )) ||
max(decode( b.column_position,  6, ', '||
substr(b.column_name,1,30), NULL )) ||
max(decode( b.column_position,  7, ', '||
substr(b.column_name,1,30), NULL )) ||
max(decode( b.column_position,  8, ', '||
substr(b.column_name,1,30), NULL )) ||
max(decode( b.column_position,  9, ', '||
substr(b.column_name,1,30), NULL )) ||
max(decode( b.column_position, 10, ', '||
```

```
    substr(b.column_name,1,30), NULL )) ||
  max(decode( b.column_position, 11, ', '||
    substr(b.column_name,1,30), NULL )) ||
  max(decode( b.column_position, 12, ', '||
    substr(b.column_name,1,30), NULL )) ||
  max(decode( b.column_position, 13, ', '||
    substr(b.column_name,1,30), NULL )) ||
  max(decode( b.column_position, 14, ', '||
    substr(b.column_name,1,30), NULL )) ||
  max(decode( b.column_position, 15, ', '||
    substr(b.column_name,1,30), NULL )) ||
  max(decode( b.column_position, 16, ', '||
    substr(b.column_name,1,30), NULL )) columns
from dba_indexes a, dba_ind_columns b
where a.owner = USER
and a.table_name = :tname
and b.table_name = a.table_name
and b.table_owner = a.owner
and a.index_name = b.index_name
group by substr(a.index_name,1,30), a.uniqueness
/
```

Running this script will generate a list of each index on the table along with related information:

```
SQL> connect hr/hr
Connected.
SQL> @indexes employees

Indexes on employees

Index                          Is
Name                           Unique COLUMNS
------------------------------ ------ --------------------------------
EMP_DEPARTMENT_IX              No     DEPARTMENT_ID
EMP_EMAIL_UK                   Yes    EMAIL
EMP_EMP_ID_PK                  Yes    EMPLOYEE_ID
EMP_JOB_IX                     No     JOB_ID
EMP_MANAGER_IX                 No     MANAGER_ID
EMP_NAME_IX                    No     LAST_NAME, FIRST_NAME
```

DBA_ROLES

DBA_ROLES displays all roles in the database, and whether a password is required to enable them.

Column Definitions and Usage

❏ ROLE [VARCHAR2(30)] – Name of the role

❏ PASSWORD_REQUIRED [VARCHAR2(8)] – Whether a password is required to enable them

```
SQL> select role, password_required
  2     from dba_roles
  3   order by role
  4   /

ROLE
------------------------------
CONNECT
RESOURCE
DBA
SELECT_CATALOG_ROLE
EXECUTE_CATALOG_ROLE
DELETE_CATALOG_ROLE
EXP_FULL_DATABASE
IMP_FULL_DATABASE
RECOVERY_CATALOG_OWNER
AQ_ADMINISTRATOR_ROLE
AQ_USER_ROLE
GLOBAL_AQ_USER_ROLE
OEM_MONITOR
PLUSTRACE
JAVAUSERPRIV
JAVAIDPRIV
JAVASYSPRIV
JAVADEBUGPRIV
JAVA_ADMIN
JAVA_DEPLOY

20 rows selected.
```

DBA_ROLE_PRIVS

This view displays what roles are granted to which users or roles in the database.

Column Definitions and Usage

❑   GRANTEE [VARCHAR2(30)] – Name of the user or role receiving the grant

❑   GRANTED_ROLE [VARCHAR2(30)] – Name of the role granted to the grantee

❑   ADMIN_OPTION [VARCHAR2(3)] – Whether the grantee has the ability to grant this role to other users or roles

❑   DEFAULT_ROLE [VARCHAR2(3)] – Whether the role is a default role for the user or not

In order to find out what roles have been granted to a particular user, use the following query:

```
set verify off

column grole format a20 heading "Role Granted"
column wadmin format a6 heading "Admin?"
```

```
prompt &1.'s granted roles

select granted_role grole, initcap(admin_option) wadmin
  from dba_role_privs
 where grantee = upper( '&1' )
 order by 1
/
```

If we were to pass the DBA role to this query, we would find all those object privileges granted to the DBA role:

```
SQL> @roleprivs DBA
DBA's granted roles

Role Granted          Admin?
-------------------- ------
DELETE_CATALOG_ROLE  Yes
EXECUTE_CATALOG_ROLE Yes
EXP_FULL_DATABASE    No
IMP_FULL_DATABASE    No
JAVA_ADMIN           No
JAVA_DEPLOY          No
SELECT_CATALOG_ROLE  Yes
WM_ADMIN_ROLE        No

8 rows selected.
```

DBA_SYS_PRIVS

This view shows all those system privileges that are granted to users or roles in your database.

Column Definitions and Usage

❑ GRANTEE [VARCHAR2(30)] – Name of the user or role receiving the grant.

❑ PRIVILEGE [VARCHAR2(40)] – Name of the privilege granted to the grantee.

❑ ADMIN_OPTION [VARCHAR2(3)] – Whether the grantee has the ability to grant this role to other users or roles.

In order to see all those privileges that have been granted directly to a user, use the following query:

```
set verify off

column priv    format a30 heading "Privilege"
column wadmin format a6 heading "Admin?"

prompt &1.'s Granted Privileges

select privilege priv, initcap(admin_option) wadmin
```

```
   from dba_sys_privs
 where grantee = upper( '&1' )
 order by 1
/
```

Calling this query using the HR user yields the following results:

```
SQL> @sysprivs HR
HR's Granted Privileges

Privilege                        Admin?
-------------------------------- ------
ALTER SESSION                    No
CREATE PROCEDURE                 No
CREATE SEQUENCE                  No
CREATE SESSION                   No
CREATE SYNONYM                   No
CREATE TABLE                     No
CREATE TRIGGER                   No
CREATE VIEW                      No

8 rows selected.
```

DBA_DIRECTORIES

This view is used to display information about directory objects created in the database.

Column Definitions and Usage

❏   OWNER [VARCHAR2(30)] – The user that created the directory.

❏   DIRECTORY_NAME [VARCHAR2(30)] – The name of the directory.

❏   DIRECTORY_PATH [VARCHAR2(4000)] – The path on the operating system this directory object refers to.

For a practical usage of DBA_DIRECTORIES see DBA_EXTERNAL_LOCATIONS.

DBA_USERS

This view provides information about all the users in the database.

Column Definitions and Usage

❏   USERNAME [VARCHAR2(30)] – Name of the user.

❏   USER_ID [NUMBER] – ID number assigned to the user.

❏   PASSWORD [VARCHAR2(30)] – The user's encrypted password.

- ACCOUNT_STATUS [VARCHAR2(32)] – Indicates whether the user's account is locked, unlocked, or expired.

- LOCK_DATE [DATE] – The date the account was locked (if ACCOUNT_STATUS is locked).

- EXPIRY_DATE [DATE] – The date the account expires.

- DEFAULT_TABLESPACE [VARCHAR2(30)] – Default tablespace for data.

- TEMPORARY_TABLESPACE [VARCHAR2(30)] – Default tablespace (temporary tables).

- CREATED [DATE] – User creation date.

- PROFILE [VARCHAR2(30)] – User resource profile name.

- INITIAL_RSRC_CONSUMER_GROUP [VARCHAR2(30)] – User's initial consumer group.

- EXTERNAL_NAME [VARCHAR2(4000)] – User external name.

In order to get an overview of user accounts in the database, save the following to a file named users.sql:

```
set define off
set echo off
set linesize 78

prompt User Information

column username format a20 heading "Username"
column default_tablespace format a14 heading "Default Tblspc"
column temporary_tablespace format a10 heading "Temp Tblspc"
column locked format a1 heading "L"

break on tblspc skip 1

select username, default_tablespace, temporary_tablespace,
       decode( account_status, 'EXPIRED & LOCKED', '*',
                               'OPEN', '' ) locked
  from dba_users
 order by username
/
set define on
```

Executing this file in SQL*Plus against a database should return information about the users in the database. The fourth column in the query results, L, is whether the account is locked ("*") or not.

```
SQL> @users
User Information

Username             Default Tblspc Temp Tblsp L
-------------------- -------------- ---------- -
AURORA$JIS$UTILITY$  SYSTEM         TEMP
AURORA$ORB$UNAUTHENT SYSTEM         TEMP
ICATED
```

CTXSYS	DRSYS	TEMP	*
CLBECK	USERS	TEMP	
DBSNMP	SYSTEM	TEMP	
HR	EXAMPLE	TEMP	
HR_AUDIT	USERS	TEMP	
LBACSYS	SYSTEM	TEMP	*
MDSYS	SYSTEM	TEMP	*
OE	EXAMPLE	TEMP	
ORACLE_DBA	USERS	TEMP	
ORDPLUGINS	SYSTEM	TEMP	*
ORDSYS	SYSTEM	TEMP	*
OSE$HTTP$ADMIN	SYSTEM	TEMP	
OUTLN	SYSTEM	TEMP	*
PM	EXAMPLE	TEMP	
PPL	USERS	TEMP	
QS	EXAMPLE	TEMP	
QS_ADM	EXAMPLE	TEMP	
QS_CB	EXAMPLE	TEMP	
QS_CBADM	EXAMPLE	TEMP	
QS_CS	EXAMPLE	TEMP	
QS_ES	EXAMPLE	TEMP	
QS_OS	EXAMPLE	TEMP	
QS_WS	EXAMPLE	TEMP	
SCOTT	USERS	TEMP	
SDILLON	USERS	TEMP	
SH	EXAMPLE	TEMP	
SYS	SYSTEM	TEMP	
SYSTEM	SYSTEM	TEMP	
TKYTE	USERS	TEMP	
WKSYS	DRSYS	TEMP	*

GLOBAL_NAME

This view is a one-row, one-column view that displays the global name of the current database.

Column Definitions

❑ GLOBAL_NAME [VARCHAR2(4000)] – The global name of the database.

GLOBAL_NAME can be used to find out the name of the database you are currently connected to. This is useful information for tools that connect to multiple databases. Place the following SQL*Plus command in a file named prompt.sql:

```
set termout off
column global_name new_value gname
select lower(user) || '@' || global_name global_name
   from global_name;
set termout on
set sqlprompt '&gname> '
```

Executing it from a standard SQL*Plus prompt is as follows:

```
SQL> @prompt.sql

GLOBAL_NAME
--------------------------------------------------------------------------
sdillon@SLAPDB.US.ORACLE.COM

sdillon@SLAPDB.US.ORACLE.COM> -- new sqlprompt!
```

Short Names

Some of the data dictionary views have synonyms as summarized here:

Synonym	Data Dictionary View
CAT	USER_CATALOG
CLU	USER_CLUSTERS
COLS	USER_TAB_COLUMNS
IND	USER_INDEXES
OBJ	USER_OBJECTS
DICT	DICTIONARY
SEQ	USER_SEQUENCES
SYN	USER_SYNONYMS
TABS	USER_TABLES

```
SQL> select table_name
  2     from user_tables
  3   /
```

is the same as...

```
SQL> select table_name
  2     from tabs
  3   /
```

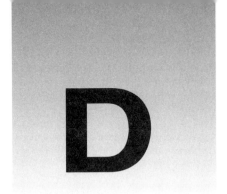

Installing Sample Schemas

In this appendix, we see how to install Oracle's sample schemas. We look at the familiar SCOTT schema as well as the new Oracle 9*i* sample schemas.

Installing the SCOTT Schema

The file used to install the SCOTT schema is utlsampl.sql, and can be found in the following directory:

Unix:
- ❑ 7 or earlier. $ORACLE_HOME/rdbms/admin/utlsampl.sql
- ❑ 8.0.0 – 8.0.6. $ORACLE_HOME/rdbms80/admin/utlsampl.sql
- ❑ 8.1.3 – 8.1.7. $ORACLE_HOME/rdbms/admin/utlsampl.sql

Windows:
- ❑ 7 or earlier. %ORACLE_HOME%/rdbms/admin/utlsampl.sql
- ❑ 8.0.0 – 8.0.6. %ORACLE_HOME%/rdbms80/admin/utlsampl.sql
- ❑ 8.1.3 – 8.1.7. %ORACLE_HOME%/rdbms/admin/utlsampl.sql

This script performs a number of operations:

- ❑ The users SCOTT, ADAMS, JONES, CLARK, and BLAKE are dropped.
- ❑ The user SCOTT is created with the password TIGER. SCOTT and is granted RESOURCE and UNLIMITED TABLESPACE privileges.
- ❑ The public synonym PARTS is dropped.
- ❑ The user SCOTT is connected, and this user is used to create the EMP, DEPT, BONUS, and SALGRADE tables.
- ❑ The tables are populated with sample data.

One noticeable difference between this script in Oracle 9*i* and previous versions is that the users ADAMS, JONES, CLARK, and BLAKE are not created. These users were created in previous versions to simulate employees from the EMP table having database accounts. In version 9.0.1, these users are removed for security reasons.

> *In Oracle 9i, a number of changes have been made to default user accounts created during installation to avoid security risks with default users and passwords. Now, many of the users that are created by default have their accounts locked.*

Some Oracle users would prefer to have these two tables created in a schema with their own username, rather than in the SCOTT schema. Instead of modifying the utlsampl.sql script, there is another script available named demobld.sql that helps do this. This script can be found in the following directory:

Unix:

❏ 8.0.0 – 8.0.6: $ORACLE_HOME/dbs/demobld.sql

❏ 8.1.3 – 9.0.1: $ORACLE_HOME/sqlplus/demo/demobld.sql

Windows:

❏ 8.0.0 – 8.0.6: %ORACLE_HOME%\dbs\demobld.sql

❏ 8.1.3 – 9.0.1: %ORACLE_HOME%\sqlplus\demo\demobld.sql

In order to use the demobld.sql script, connect to the database as a user with CREATE TABLE privileges and run the script. This creates the same tables and data as the utlsampl.sql script, but does so in the current user's schema. To remove the tables run the demodrop.sql script located in the same directory.

The SCOTT schema is not terribly complex. It was created many years ago and there haven't been many changes to this script throughout the years. To truly show off the capabilities of Oracle, our samples need to be stepped up considerably! With that in mind, let's move on to discuss the new sample schemas introduced in Oracle 9*i*.

Installing the Oracle 9i Schemas

There are two ways to install the sample schemas in Oracle 9*i*. The first and easiest way is to use the **Database Configuration Assistant** (**DBCA**). The other way is to run the installation scripts manually.

Using the DBCA

The sample schemas can be installed in a new or existing database. If you are using the DBCA to create a new database then you can simply allow the DBCA tool to install the sample schemas along with the new database, (see below for details). If you already have a database you want to install the sample schemas into, you can use the DBCA to generate the scripts you will use to perform the installation. Use the following steps to install the sample schemas with the DBCA tool:

1. Start up the DBCA from the command line (by typing dbca) or through the Windows **Start** menu. The file will be located in $ORACLE_HOME/bin/dbca on UNIX, and %ORACLE_HOME%\bin\dbca.bat on Windows.

2. Click the Next button to show the available tasks you can perform with the DBCA.

3. Select the Create a database radio button and click the Next button to continue.

4. Select the New database radio button and click the Next button to continue.

5. Choose a Global Database Name and SID, and click the Next button.

6. Click on the Example Schemas checkbox, and select the sample schemas you would like installed. You may want to review the guidelines below in the *Schema Dependencies* section when doing so.

7. Click on the Additional database configurations... button if you want to install the Oracle JVM and/or Oracle Intermedia (these are required for the Product Media schema).

8. Once you have selected the schemas and database configuration options to install, click on the Next button.

9. If you are only using the DBCA to install the sample schemas, you can simply click the Next button for the next three steps.

10. Select the server mode you want your database to operate in. If you are not sure, select Dedicated Server Mode, and click Next.

11. Configure the initialization parameters for your database instance. If you're not sure, select the Typical radio button, and select the Multipurpose option in Database Type. Click Next to continue.

12. Configure your database storage. If you wish to change the location of the data files from the default location, click on the Files Location Variables... button. Click Next to continue.

13. On the final page, what you do will depend on whether or not you are performing an installation or not. If you are really creating a database, select the Create Database checkbox and click Finish. The schema creation will be performed as a part of the database creation, and your work is done. If you are only using this wizard for the sample schema installation, click on the Generate Database Creation Scripts checkbox, select a destination directory for the files to be generated, and click on Finish.

14. Once you click Finish, you will be presented with an overview of all the options you selected for the database you wish to create. Simply click on OK to continue.

15. A dialog box will appear, which indicates your scripts are being created. Once the scripts are complete, you will be notified with a pop-up window telling you that the script generation was successful, and asking if you would like to perform another operation. Click No to close the DBCA.

16. Once the DBCA is closed, you can run the demoSchemas.sql file in the directory location specified in step 13 above.

> You will notice there are quite a few other files in that directory. This is because the DBCA has created all the scripts necessary for you to create an entire database, not just the sample schemas. Reviewing these files would be a good way to learn the steps involved in creating an Oracle database.

Manual Installation

Instead of using the DBCA, you can choose to perform a manual installation of the sample schemas, in one of two ways. The first and easiest way is by executing the following SQL*Plus script:

- ❏ UNIX: $ORACLE_HOME/demo/schema/mksample.sql

- ❏ Windows: %ORACLE_HOME%\demo\schema\mksample.sql

This file will create all of the sample schemas in the correct order, and will prompt you for all the information it needs for the installation (in other words, SYS, SYSTEM, and schema passwords, and so on). Since there are inter-schema dependencies there are grants that must be performed during the course of the installation between schemas. These grants are all handled in this single script. The default tablespace and temporary tablespace for each of the sample schemas is specified for you as EXAMPLE and TEMP respectively.

The other way to perform manual installations is to run each of the sample schemas' installation scripts individually. This takes longer, and is more work, but in the end you will have a better understanding of the schema objects, the inter-schema dependencies, and how to recreate data once you've been playing with it.

You do not have to install all the sample schemas if you don't want to. The problem then is that dependencies that exist between the schemas will prevent the successful installation of a schema if it is dependent on another schema that is not installed yet. An easy way to manage this is to install the schemas in the following order, until you have installed the schema(s) you want to install:

- ❏ Human Resources
- ❏ Order Entry
- ❏ Product Media
- ❏ Queued Shipping
- ❏ Sales History

In other words, if you wanted to install the Order Entry schema, you must first install Human Resources and then Order Entry. If you wanted to install Sales History, you need to install them all. We will talk more about inter-schema dependencies in a later section.

Human Resources Schema Installation

You will find that a manual installation of the schemas is relatively simple. The installation scripts are constructed so that one script can be run which will in turn run all the other scripts. The master script name is called <schema_name>_main.sql, and can be found in the schema's directory along with all the supporting installation scripts. The sample schema installation directories can be found in the following location:

❑   UNIX: $ORACLE_HOME/demo/schema/

❑   Windows: %ORACLE_HOME%\demo\schema\

For example, if we were to look for the Human Resources (HR) scripts we would find them in the following directory:

Unix:

```
$ ls $ORACLE_HOME/demo/schema/human_resources
./              hr_code.sql     hr_dn_c.sql     hr_idx.sql
../             hr_comnt.sql    hr_dn_d.sql     hr_main.sql
hr_analz.sql    hr_cre.sql      hr_drop.sql     hr_popul.sql
```

Windows:

```
C:\>dir/w/a/o %ORACLE_HOME%\demo\schema\human_resources
 Volume in drive C has no label.
 Volume Serial Number is 787E-5450

 Directory of C:\Oracle\ora90\demo\schema\human_resources

[.]             [..]            hr_analz.sql hr_code.sql   hr_comnt.sql
hr_cre.sql      hr_dn_c.sql     hr_dn_d.sql  hr_drop.sql   hr_idx.sql
hr_main.sql     hr_popul.sql
               10 File(s)           89,628 bytes
                2 Dir(s)        561,352,704 bytes free
```

As mentioned above, the hr_main.sql file is the master installation script for the Human Resources schema. This script performs the following steps:

1. Drops the HR schema and all its objects, if it already exists.

2. Creates the HR schema, and grants the appropriate privileges for the schema to create tables, procedures, sequences, triggers, views, and synonyms.

3. Grants the user the ability to execute the SYS.DBMS_STATS package.

4. Runs hr_cre.sql to create the HR tables, sequences, and constraints

5. Runs hr_popul.sql to insert all the data into the HR tables.

6. Runs hr_idx.sql to create indexes on the tables.

7. Runs hr_code.sql to create the procedural code owned by HR.

8. Runs hr_comnt.sql to add meta data comments to tables and comments.

9. Runs hr_analz.sql which uses the DBMS_STATS package to gather statistics for each table.

1029

Be sure to check the spool file which was generated in the script above for any errors you may have encountered but didn't see while you were running the scripts in SQL*Plus. The name of the spool file in the scripts above is `hr_mail.log`.

> One thing to note about the HR schema (but not the other schemas) is it is currently not Oracle 9*i*-dependent. There is nothing in the Human Resources installation scripts that prevents you from running the scripts on an Oracle 8*i* database (version 8.1.6 for example).

Order Entry Schema Installation

You will find the installation scripts for the Order Entry (OE) schema in the `order_entry` directory of the sample schemas directories. The files in this directory are as follows:

UNIX:

```
$ ls $ORACLE_HOME/demo/schema/order_entry
./                  oe_p_ar.sql     oe_p_itm.sql    oe_p_ru.sql
../                 oe_p_cs.sql     oe_p_iw.sql     oe_p_s.sql
oc_comnt.sql        oe_p_cus.sql    oe_p_ja.sql     oe_p_sf.sql
oc_cre.sql          oe_p_d.sql      oe_p_ko.sql     oe_p_sk.sql
oc_drop.sql         oe_p_dk.sql     oe_p_n.sql      oe_p_th.sql
oc_main.sql         oe_p_e.sql      oe_p_nl.sql     oe_p_tr.sql
oc_popul.sql        oe_p_el.sql     oe_p_ord.sql    oe_p_us.sql
oe_analz.sql        oe_p_esa.sql    oe_p_pd.sql     oe_p_whs.sql
oe_comnt.sql        oe_p_f.sql      oe_p_pi.sql     oe_p_zhs.sql
oe_cre.sql          oe_p_frc.sql    oe_p_pl.sql     oe_p_zht.sql
oe_drop.sql         oe_p_hu.sql     oe_p_pt.sql     oe_views.sql
oe_idx.sql          oe_p_i.sql      oe_p_ptb.sql
oe_main.sql         oe_p_inv.sql    oe_p_ro.sql
```

Windows:

```
C:\>dir/w/a/o %ORACLE_HOME%\demo\schema\order_entry
 Volume in drive C has no label.
 Volume Serial Number is 787E-5450

 Directory of C:\Oracle\ora90\demo\schema\order_entry

[.]              [..]             oc_comnt.sql    oc_cre.sql      oc_drop.sql
oc_main.sql      oc_popul.sql     oe_analz.sql    oe_comnt.sql    oe_cre.sql
oe_drop.sql      oe_idx.sql       oe_main.sql     oe_p_ar.sql     oe_p_ca.sql
oe_p_cs.sql      oe_p_cus.sql     oe_p_d.sql      oe_p_dk.sql     oe_p_e.sql
oe_p_el.sql      oe_p_esa.sql     oe_p_f.sql      oe_p_frc.sql    oe_p_hu.sql
oe_p_i.sql       oe_p_inv.sql     oe_p_itm.sql    oe_p_iw.sql     oe_p_ja.sql
oe_p_ko.sql      oe_p_n.sql       oe_p_nl.sql     oe_p_ord.sql    oe_p_pd.sql
oe_p_pi.sql      oe_p_pl.sql      oe_p_pt.sql     oe_p_ptb.sql    oe_p_ro.sql
oe_p_ru.sql      oe_p_s.sql       oe_p_sf.sql     oe_p_sk.sql     oe_p_th.sql
oe_p_tr.sql      oe_p_us.sql      oe_p_whs.sql    oe_p_zhs.sql    oe_p_zht.sql
oe_views.sql
               49 File(s)      3,286,640 bytes
                2 Dir(s)     561,377,280 bytes free
```

As you can see, there are quite a few more files involved for the installation of the Order Entry schema than there were for the Human Resources schema. You will notice, when we discuss using these scripts to install the sample schemas, that not all the files in this directory are used during the installation. This is because in this release of the database the default NLS_LANGUAGE and NLS_TERRITORY are "American". The unused files in this directory represent product descriptions and product information in other languages supported by the Oracle database.

As we saw in the Human Resources schema installation, you need only call the oe_main.sql file, which in turn calls all other necessary SQL*Plus installation files.

The oe_main.sql file is responsible for performing the following steps:

1. Dropping the OE schema and all its objects, if OE already exists.

2. Creating the OE schema, and granting the appropriate privileges for the schema to create tables, views, synonyms, materialized views, triggers, sequences, and perform query rewrite.

3. Granting the user the ability to execute the SYS.DBMS_STATS package.

4. Connecting as the HR schema, and granting object privileges on many of the HR tables.

5. Running oe_cre.sql in order to create the OE types, tables, sequences, synonyms, and constraints.

6. Running oe_p_pi.sql to populate the PRODUCT_INFORMATION table.

7. Running oe_p_pd.sql to populate PRODUCT_DESCRIPTION with a number of other language translations.

8. Running oe_p_whs.sql to populate the WAREHOUSES table, as well as the XMLType column warehouse_spec with XML data.

9. Running oe_p_cus.sql to populate the CUSTOMERS table.

10. Running oe_p_ord.sql to populate the ORDERS table.

11. Running oe_p_itm.sql to populate the ORDER_ITEMS table.

12. Running oe_p_inv.sql to populate the INVENTORIES table.

13. Running oe_views.sql to create various inventory, product, and product pricing views.

14. Running oe_comnt.sql to create meta data comments on tables and columns.

15. Running oe_idx.sql to create indexes.

16. Running oe_analz.sql which uses the DBMS_STATS package to gather statistics for each table.

17. Running oc_main.sql to create the OC subschema, which is basically a number of object types, object views, and inserts into those views.

The spool file is named oe_oc_main.log. This spool file contains the results of the entire installation. Be sure to review the file for any errors that may have occurred. Once this script is done and you have reviewed the spool file, the Order Entry schema is installed.

Product Media Schema Installation

You will find the installation scripts for the Product Media (PM) schema in the product_media directory of the sample schemas home directory. You will find many files in this directory that are not SQL files, but which are still necessary for the installation of the Product Media schema installation. The necessary files in this directory are as follows:

UNIX:

```
$ ls $ORACLE_HOME/demo/schema/product_media/pm_*
pm_analz.sql    pm_drop.sql    pm_p_lob.ctl    pm_p_ord.sql
pm_cre.sql      pm_main.sql    pm_p_lob.sql
```

Windows:

```
C:\>dir/w/a/o %ORACLE_HOME%\demo\schema\product_media\pm_*
 Volume in drive C has no label.
 Volume Serial Number is 787E-5450

 Directory of C:\Oracle\ora90\demo\schema\product_media

pm_analz.sql    pm_cre.sql      pm_drop.sql     pm_main.sql     pm_p_lob.ctl
pm_p_lob.dat    pm_p_lob.sql    pm_p_ord.sql
               8 File(s)         33,477 bytes
               0 Dir(s)     559,833,088 bytes free
```

Other files that are not mentioned are a variety of image, audio, and video files in the same directory that will be loaded into the database during the installation process. To install the entire Product Media schema, run the pm_main.sql file. This file will run all the necessary files for installing the Product Media schema.

The pm_main.sql file is responsible for performing the following steps:

1. Dropping the PM schema and its objects, if PM already exists.

2. Creating the PM schema, and granting the appropriate privileges for the schema to create tables, types, indexes, and procedures.

3. Connecting as the OE schema, and granting object privileges on many of the OE tables.

4. Granting the PM schema the ability to execute the SYS.DBMS_STATS package.

5. Running pm_cre.sql to create the OE types, tables, sequences, synonyms, and constraints.

6. Running pm_p_ord.sql to populate the PRODUCT_INFORMATION table.

7. Running pm_p_lob.sql to load the PRINT_MEDIA and TEXTDOCS_NESTEDTAB tables with documents in the product_media directory.

8. Running `pm_analz.sql` which uses the `DBMS_STATS` package to gather statistics for each table.

The spool file is named `pm_main.log`. This spool file contains the results of the entire installation. Be sure to review the file for any errors that may have occurred. Once this script is done and you have reviewed the spool file, the Product Media schema is installed.

Queued Shipping Schema Installation

The Queued Shipping (`QS`) schema installation is slightly more complex, due to the fact that we are creating eight schemas, not just one. Not only that but we are also configuring Oracle Advanced Queues. Getting your advanced queues installed, designed, configured, and working properly is an intermediate-to-advanced-level task. By installing the shipping schema(s) and analyzing the entire installation, you have a good baseline to work from when you want to start using Advanced Queues for your own projects.

All the files necessary for the installation are located in the `shipping` directory of the sample schemas' directories.

UNIX:
```
$ ls $ORACLE_HOME/demo/schema/shipping
./            qs_cre.sql    qs_main.sql    qs_ws.sql
../           qs_cs.sql     qs_os.sql
qs_adm.sql    qs_drop.sql   qs_popul.sql
qs_cbadm.sql  qs_es.sql     qs_run.sql
```

Windows:
```
C:\>dir /w/a/o %ORACLE_HOME%\demo\schema\shipping
 Volume in drive C has no label.
 Volume Serial Number is 787E-5450

 Directory of C:\Oracle\ora90\demo\schema\shipping

[.]           [..]          qs_adm.sql     qs_cbadm.sql   qs_cre.sql
qs_cs.sql     qs_drop.sql   qs_es.sql      qs_main.sql    qs_os.sql
qs_run.sql    qs_ws.sql
             10 File(s)         50,567 bytes
              2 Dir(s)     557,395,968 bytes free
```

To install all the shipping schemas, run the file `qs_main.sql`. This file performs the following steps:

1. Drops the `QS_ADM`, `QS`, `QS_WS`, `QS_ES`, `QS_OS`, `QS_CBADM`, `QS_CB`, and `QS_CS` schemas and their objects, if they already exist.

2. Alters the database instance to start up job queue processes if they aren't already running. These queue processes are responsible for managing queuing of messages.

3. Creates the `QS_ADM` schema, and grants all the appropriate privileges to this user. This user, as the schema name indicates, is the Queued Shipping Administration schema. This schema is granted the role `aq_administrator_role` as well as the queuing system privileges `ENQUEUE_ANY` and `DEQUEUE_ANY`. This indicates that this schema can enqueue and dequeue messages from any queue in the database.

1033

4. Creates the rest of the shipping schemas to represent various sections within the shipping department, as follows:

- ❑ QS – Queued Shipping schema.

- ❑ QS_WS – Western region shipping.

- ❑ QS_ES – Eastern region shipping.

- ❑ QS_OS – Overseas shipping.

- ❑ QS_CBADM – Customer billing administration. For security reasons, this schema is created to hold the customer billing queues and application tables.

- ❑ QS_CB – Customer billing.

- ❑ QS_CS – Customer service.

5. Once those schemas are created, they are granted appropriate privileges to perform the queuing tasks for which they will be responsible and create a variety of database objects, which are as follows:

- ❑ Clusters
- ❑ Database links
- ❑ Sequences
- ❑ Create sessions
- ❑ Synonyms
- ❑ Tables
- ❑ Views
- ❑ Index types
- ❑ Operators
- ❑ Procedures
- ❑ Sequences
- ❑ Triggers
- ❑ Types

They also have responsibility for executing the DBMS_AQ and DBMS_AQADM packages.

6. Connects as the OE schema and grants object privileges on the CUSTOMERS and PRODUCT_INFORMATION tables to QS_ADM.

7. Runs qs_adm.sql to create a few object types that will be used in the queues to pass data between the shipping subschemas. The appropriate privileges are granted to the other shipping subschemas to use these types.

8. Runs `qs_cre.sql` to create queues and queue tables for orders. A non-persistent queue is created to track the number of connections to the shipping application.

Queue tables are used to store queued messages and/or objects. These tables are created, managed, and removed through the Oracle Advanced Queues APIs.

9. Runs `qs_es.sql` to create queues and queue tables for the Eastern Shipping schema.

10. Runs `qs_ws.sql` to create queues, queue tables, and queue subscribers for the Western Shipping schema.

11. Runs `qs_os.sql` to create queues and queue tables for the Overseas Shipping schema.

12. Runs `qs_cbadm.sql` to create customer billing queues, queue tables, and queue subscribers.

13. Runs `qs_cs.sql` to create a customer status queue and queue table that is responsible for tracking the status of customer orders.

14. Runs `qs_run.sql` to create the `QS_APPLICATIONS` package. This package is for submitting orders to the collection of shipping subschemas for processing. Effectively, it is a front-end tool for the queues that have been created.

The spool file is named `qs_main.log`. This spool file contains the results of the entire installation. Be sure to review the file for any errors that may have occurred. Once this script is done and you have reviewed the spool file, the Queued Shipping schema and all the shipping subschemas are installed.

Sales History Schema Installation

The Sales History (`SH`) schema installation is fairly straightforward. It has a different installation process from the rest of the schemas, because it relies heavily on SQL*Loader to populate the vast relational tables that it consists of.

The files you will need for the sales history schema installation are located in two places. The `sales_history` directory under the sample schemas directories is where you will find the majority of the files needed:

UNIX:

```
$ ls $ORACLE_HOME/demo/schema/sales_history
./              sh_cremv.sql    sh_main.sql     sh_prod.ctl
../             sh_cust.ctl     sh_olp_c.sql    sh_prod.dat
sh_analz.sql    sh_cust.dat     sh_olp_d.sql    sh_promo.ctl
sh_comnt.sql    sh_drop.sql     sh_pop1.sql     sh_promo.dat
sh_cons.sql     sh_hiera.sql    sh_pop2.sql     sh_sales.ctl
sh_cre.sql      sh_idx.sql      sh_pop3.sql     sh_sales.dat
```

Windows:

```
C:\>dir /w/a/o %ORACLE_HOME%\demo\schema\sales_history
Volume in drive C has no label.
Volume Serial Number is 787E-5450

Directory of C:\Oracle\ora90\demo\schema\sales_history

[.]             [..]            sh_analz.sql    sh_comnt.sql    sh_cons.sql
sh_cre.sql      sh_cremv.sql    sh_cust.ctl     sh_cust.dat     sh_drop.sql
sh_hiera.sql    sh_idx.sql      sh_main.sql     sh_olp_c.sql    sh_olp_d.sql
sh_pop1.sql     sh_pop2.sql     sh_pop3.sql     sh_prod.ctl     sh_prod.dat
sh_promo.ctl    sh_promo.dat    sh_sales.ctl    sh_sales.dat
                22 File(s)      66,095,457 bytes
                 2 Dir(s)      556,748,800 bytes free
```

In addition to the sales history installation files, there are five files referenced from the $ORACLE_HOME/rdbms/admin directory (%ORACLE_HOME%\rdbms\admin on Windows). They are as follows:

UNIX:

```
$ ls $ORACLE_HOME/rdbms/admin/utlx*.sql
/export/home/Oracle 9i/rdbms/admin/utlxmv.sql
/export/home/Oracle 9i/rdbms/admin/utlxplan.sql
/export/home/Oracle 9i/rdbms/admin/utlxplp.sql
/export/home/Oracle 9i/rdbms/admin/utlxpls.sql
/export/home/Oracle 9i/rdbms/admin/utlxrw.sql
```

Windows:

```
C:\>dir /w/a/o %ORACLE_HOME%\rdbms\admin\utlx*.sql
Volume in drive C has no label.
Volume Serial Number is 787E-5450

Directory of C:\Oracle\ora90\rdbms\admin

utlxmv.sql      utlxplan.sql    utlxplp.sql     utlxpls.sql     utlxrw.sql
                5 File(s)           18,619 bytes
                0 Dir(s)        556,285,952 bytes free
```

To install the Sales History schema, run the file sh_main.sql. This file performs the following steps:

1. Drops the SH schema and its objects, if SH already exists.

2. Creates the SH schema, and grants all the appropriate privileges to this user. Privileges granted are as follows:

❑ Create session (connect to database)

❑ Alter session

❑ Create table

- ❏ Create dimension
- ❏ Create materialized view
- ❏ Query rewrite
- ❏ Create any directory
- ❏ Drop any directory

3. Grants execute on SYS.DBMS_STATS package to SH.

4. Runs sh_cre.sql to create the tables for the sales history schema.

5. Runs sh_pop1.sql to populate the COUNTRIES and CHANNELS tables.

6. Runs sh_pop2.sql to populate the TIMES table.

7. Runs sh_pop3.sql to populate the PROMOTIONS, CUSTOMERS, PRODUCTS, and SALES tables using SQL*Loader. The SALES_TRANSACTIONS_EXT external table is also created, and the data file is associated accordingly. The COSTS table is then populated with a INSERT INTO SELECT statement from the SALES_TRANSACTIONS_EXT table.

8. Runs sh_idx.sql to create all the Sales History schema's indexes.

9. Runs sh_cons.sql to enable the constraints on the SALES table.

10. Runs sh_hiera.sql to create all the Sales History schema's dimensions and hierarchies.

11. Runs sh_cremv.sql to create all the Sales History schema's materialized views.

12. Runs sh_analz.sql which uses the DBMS_STATS.GATHER_SCHEMA_STATS routine to analyze the entire Sales History schema.

13. Runs sh_comnt.sql to create meta data comments on tables and columns.

14. Runs utlxplan.sql to create the PLAN_TABLE table, which is used by the EXPLAIN_PLAN statement.

15. Runs utlxrw.sql to create the REWRITE_TABLE table that is populated by the DBMS_MVIEW.EXPLAIN_REWRITE procedure.

16. Runs utlxmv.sql to create the MV_CAPABILITIES_TABLE table that is used by the DBMS_MVIEW.EXPLAIN_MVIEW procedure.

The spool file is named sh_main.log. This spool file contains the results of the entire installation. Be sure to review the file for any errors that may have occurred. Once this script is done and you have reviewed the spool file, the Sales History schema is installed.

Schema Dependencies

In order to use the Oracle 9*i* sample schemas, there are inter-schema dependencies you need to understand:

❏ The Order Entry schema depends on the Human Resources schema

❏ The Product Media schema depends on the Human Resources and Order Entry schemas

❏ The Queued Shipping schema depends on the Order Entry schema

❏ The Sales History schema depends on the Order Entry schema

As indicated earlier in the chapter, if you are installing all the schemas you should do them in the following order: HR, OE, PM, QS, and SH. Creating the schemas in this order satisfies the schema dependencies.

In addition to inter-schema dependencies, there are technology dependencies to be aware of. Because the database can be configured with various options, you may or may not decide to include the Oracle Intermedia in your database installation. If you don't install this, you will not be able to use the Product Media schema, as it requires Intermedia to store and process image, audio, and video data. Use the following guidelines when choosing what database options to install:

❏ The Order Entry schema needs Oracle Spatial

❏ The Product Media schema requires Oracle Intermedia and the Oracle Java Virtual Machine

Installation Wrap Up

This completes the installation instructions for the Oracle 9*i* sample schemas. It is certainly more time-consuming and will take a greater number of keystrokes to complete the installation manually. On the other hand, once you perform a manual installation you have a much more intimate understanding of the sample schema architecture.

Options and Features

Not all of Oracle's options and features are available in every edition and release of the database. In this appendix, we will review the options and features available in the most recent releases of Oracle.

If you review the tables below, you may notice a trend in the way Oracle introduces features and options into the classes of the database. Typically, a new feature is introduced and made available only on the Enterprise Edition. It will stay this way for a number of releases until the functionality that the feature offers becomes mainstream in other vendors' products, at which time Oracle will make it available on the Standard Edition as well. For instance, in Oracle 8.0.4 object functionality was bundled in the "Objects Option". It was made available only to the Oracle Enterprise Edition database. In Oracle 8.1.5, "objects and extensibility" became a feature and was made available on both platforms, Standard and Enterprise. It stayed this way through 8.1.6 and 8.1.7, until Oracle 9*i* 9.0.1 was released. In 9.0.1, "objects and extensibility" isn't even mentioned; it's just a core feature of the database.

For the past few years, Oracle has published a document entitled "Getting To Know…" that provided a central resource of useful information about the new version. In this document you would find information such as:

- ❏   A summary of new features that were added
- ❏   Which features were no longer supported or were deprecated
- ❏   The titles of all the documentation
- ❏   Feature and option availability

The first one was published with Oracle 8 8.0.4, and the last one with Oracle 8*i* 8.1.7. In Oracle 9*i* 9.0.1, this information can be found in the RDBMS README documentation. For versions prior to Oracle 8 8.0.4, you can visit Oracle's Technology Network for new features by release and documentation at http://technet.oracle.com.

In the tables overleaf, we break down the option and feature availability by release.

Oracle 9*i* 9.0.1

Option Availability

Option	Personal	Standard	Enterprise
Advanced Replication	Y	N	Y
Oracle Advanced Security	N	N	Y
Oracle Change Management Pack	Y	N	Y
Oracle Data Mining	Y	N	Y
Oracle Diagnostics Pack	Y	N	Y
Oracle Label Security	Y	N	Y
Oracle Management Pack for Oracle Applications	N	N	Y
Oracle Management Pack for SAP R/3	N	N	Y
Oracle OLAP	Y	N	Y
Oracle Partitioning	Y	N	Y
Oracle Programmer	Y	Y	Y
Real Application Clusters	Y	N	Y
Oracle Spatial	Y	N	Y
Oracle Tuning Pack	Y	N	Y

Feature Availability

Features	Personal	Standard	Enterprise
Application Development			
AppWizard for Visual Studio (NT only)	Y	Y	Y
Autonomous Transactions	Y	Y	Y
COM cartridge (NT only)	Y	Y	Y
iSQL*Plus	Y	Y	Y
Java	N	Y	Y
JDBC drivers	Y	Y	Y
Microsoft Transaction Server Integration (NT only)	Y	Y	Y

Features	Personal	Standard	Enterprise
Application Development (Cont'd)			
Objects and extensibility	Y	Y	Y
PL/SQL native compilation	Y	Y	Y
PL/SQL stored procedures and triggers	Y	Y	Y
PL/SQL Server Pages	Y	Y	Y
User-defined aggregates	Y	Y	Y
XML	Y	Y	Y
Content Management			
Dynamic Services	Y	Y	Y
Oracle Database Workspace Manager	Y	Y	Y
Parallel Text Index Creation	Y	N	Y
Ultra Search	Y	Y	Y
Database Features			
Advanced Queuing	Y	Y	Y
Database event triggers	Y	Y	Y
DBMS_REPAIR package	Y	Y	Y
Drop column	Y	Y	Y
Flashback Query	Y	Y	Y
Globalization Support	Y	Y	Y
Index coalesce	Y	N	Y
Index-organized tables	Y	Y	Y
Instead-of triggers	Y	Y	Y
LOB support	Y	Y	Y
Locally-managed tablespaces	Y	Y	Y
LogMiner	Y	Y	Y
Online index build	Y	N	Y
Online table reorganization	Y	N	Y
Plan stability	Y	Y	Y

Table continued on following page

Features	Personal	Standard	Enterprise
Database Features (Cont'd)			
Quiesce database	Y	N	Y
Reverse key indexes	Y	Y	Y
Temporary tables	Y	Y	Y
Trial Recovery	Y	N	Y
Distributed Database Features			
Advanced Replication	Y	N	Y
Basic Replication	Y	Y	Y
Distributed queries	Y	Y	Y
Distributed transactions	Y	Y	Y
Heterogeneous services	Y	Y	Y
Integration			
Messaging Gateway to IBM MQ Series	Y	N	Y
Manageability			
Basic readable standby database	Y	Y	Y
Block-level media recovery	Y	N	Y
Database Resource Manager	Y	N	Y
Oracle Data Guard	Y	N	Y
Duplexed backup sets	Y	N	Y
Fast-start selectable recovery time	Y	N	Y
Global index maintenance during DDL operations	Y	Y	Y
Incremental backup and recovery	Y	N	Y
Legato Storage Manager	Y	Y	Y
Multiple block size	Y	Y	Y
Online backup and recovery	Y	Y	Y
Oracle Change Management Pack	Y	N	Y
Oracle Enterprise Manager	Y	Y	Y
Oracle Fail Safe for Oracle 9i on NT	Y	Y	Y
Oracle Managed Files	Y	Y	Y

Features	Personal	Standard	Enterprise
Integration (Cont'd)			
Parallel backup and recovery	Y	N	Y
Point-in-time tablespace recovery	Y	N	Y
Recovery Manager	Y	Y	Y
Resumable space allocation	Y	Y	Y
Standby Database GUI	Y	N	Y
Transparent application failover	Y	N	Y
Unused index identification	Y	Y	Y
Networking			
Connection pooling	Y	Y	Y
Oracle Connection Manager	Y	N	Y
Oracle Names	Y	Y	Y
Oracle Net Services	Y	Y	Y
Security			
Encryption toolkit	Y	Y	Y
Virtual Private Database	Y	N	Y
Fine-grained auditing	Y	N	Y
Password management	Y	Y	Y
Proxy authentication	Y	Y	Y
Warehousing/VLDB			
Analytic functions	Y	Y	Y
Automated parallel query degree	Y	N	Y
Bitmapped indexes and bitmapped joined indexes	Y	N	Y
Descending indexes	Y	Y	Y
Direct Path Load API	Y	Y	Y
Export transportable tablespaces	Y	N	Y
Import transportable tablespaces	Y	Y	Y
External tables	Y	Y	Y

Table continued on following page

Features	Personal	Standard	Enterprise
Warehousing/VLDB (Cont'd)			
Function-based indexes	Y	Y	Y
Long operations monitor	Y	Y	Y
Materialized views	Y	N	Y
MERGE (incremental refresh of tables)	Y	Y	Y
Optimizer statistics management	Y	Y	Y
Parallel analyze	Y	N	Y
Parallel bitmap star query optimization	Y	N	Y
Parallel DML	Y	N	Y
Parallel index build	Y	N	Y
Parallel index scans	Y	N	Y
Parallel load	Y	Y	Y
Parallel query	Y	N	Y
Pipelined table functions			
Sample scan	Y	Y	Y
Star query optimization	Y	Y	Y
Synchronous Change Data Capture	Y	N	Y

Oracle 8*i* 8.1.6, 8.1.7

Option Availability

Option	Workstation	Standard	Enterprise
Oracle Advanced Security	Y	N	Y
Oracle Change Management Pack	Y	N	Y
Oracle Diagnostics Pack	Y	N	Y
Oracle *inter*Media	Y	Y	Y
Oracle JServer	N	Y	N
Oracle JServer Enterprise Edition	Y	N	Y
Oracle Parallel Server	Y	N	Y
Oracle Partitioning	Y	N	Y

Option	Workstation	Standard	Enterprise
Oracle Programmer	Y	Y	Y
Oracle Spatial	Y	N	Y
Oracle Standard Management Pack	N	Y	N
Oracle Time Series	Y	N	Y
Oracle Tuning Pack	Y	N	Y
Oracle Visual Information Retrieval	Y	N	Y
Oracle WebDB	Y	Y	Y

Feature Availability

Features	Workstation	Standard	Enterprise
Application Development			
AppWizard for Visual Studio (NT only)	Y	Y	Y
Autonomous Transactions	Y	Y	Y
COM Automation Feature (NT only)	Y	Y	Y
JDBC drivers	Y	Y	Y
Microsoft Transaction Server integration (NT only)	Y	Y	Y
Objects for OLE	Y	Y	Y
ODBC Driver	Y	Y	Y
Oracle Call Interface (OCI)	Y	Y	Y
Pro*C	Y	Y	Y
SQLJ	Y	Y	Y
Database Features			
Advanced queuing	Y	N	Y
Database event triggers	Y	Y	Y
DBMS_REPAIR package	Y	Y	Y
Drop column	Y	Y	Y
Fine-grained access control	Y	N	Y

Table continued on following page

1047

Features	Workstation	Standard	Enterprise
Application Development (Cont'd)			
Index coalesce	Y	N	Y
Index-organized tables	Y	Y	Y
Indexes on NLS collating sequences	Y	N	Y
Instead-of triggers	Y	Y	Y
LOB support	Y	Y	Y
Locally-managed tablespaces	Y	Y	Y
LogMiner	Y	Y	Y
National language support (NLS)	Y	Y	Y
Objects and extensibility	Y	Y	Y
Online index build	Y	N	Y
Password management	Y	Y	Y
PL/SQL stored procedures, triggers	Y	Y	Y
PL/SQL Server Pages	Y	Y	Y
Plan stability	Y	N	Y
Reverse key indexes	Y	Y	Y
Temporary tables	Y	Y	Y
Distributed Database Features			
Advanced replication	Y	N	Y
Basic replication	Y	Y	Y
Distributed queries	Y	Y	Y
Distributed transactions	Y	Y	Y
Heterogeneous services	Y	Y	Y
Manageability			
Automated standby database	Y	N	Y
Readable standby database	Y	N	Y
Database resource management	Y	N	Y
Duplexed backup sets	Y	N	Y
Oracle DBA Management Pack	Y	Y	Y

Features	Workstation	Standard	Enterprise
Manageability (Cont'd)			
Fast-start fault recovery	Y	N	Y
Incremental backup and recovery	Y	N	Y
Legato Storage Manager	Y	Y	Y
Online backup and recovery	Y	Y	Y
Oracle Enterprise Manager	Y	Y	Y
Oracle Fail Safe for Oracle 8*i* on NT	Y	Y	Y
Parallel backup and recovery	Y	N	Y
Point-in-time tablespace recovery	Y	N	Y
Recovery Manager	Y	Y	Y
Server managed backup and recovery	Y	Y	Y
Transparent Application Failover	Y	N	Y
Networking			
N-tier authentication/authorization	Y	N	Y
Network access control	Y	N	Y
Connection pooling	Y	Y	Y
Multi-protocol connectivity	Y	N	Y
Multiplexing	Y	N	Y
Oracle Connection Manager	Y	N	Y
Oracle Names	Y	Y	Y
Net8	Y	Y	Y
Warehousing/VLDB			
Analytic functions	Y	Y	Y
Automated parallel query degree	Y	N	Y
Bitmap indexes	Y	N	Y
CUBE and ROLLUP	Y	Y	Y
Descending indexes	Y	Y	Y
Direct Path Load API	Y	Y	Y

Table continued on following page

1049

Features	Workstation	Standard	Enterprise
Warehousing/VLDB (Cont'd)			
Export transportable tablespaces	Y	N	Y
Import transportable tablespaces	Y	Y	Y
Function-based indexes	Y	N	Y
Long operations monitor	Y	Y	Y
Materialized views	Y	N	Y
Optimizer statistics management	Y	Y	Y
Parallel analyze	Y	N	Y
Parallel bitmap star query optimization	Y	N	Y
Parallel DML	Y	N	Y
Parallel index build	Y	N	Y
Parallel index scans	Y	N	Y
Parallel load	Y	Y	Y
Parallel query	Y	N	Y
Sample scan	Y	N	Y
Star query optimization	Y	Y	Y

Oracle 8*i* 8.1.5

Option Availability

Option	Workstation	Standard	Enterprise
Oracle Advanced Security	Y	N	Y
Oracle Change Management Pack	Y	N	Y
Oracle Diagnostics Pack	Y	N	Y
Oracle *inter*Media	Y	Y	Y
Oracle JServer	N	Y	N
Oracle JServer Enterprise Edition	Y	N	Y
Oracle JServer Enterprise Edition Accelerator (8.1.5 only)	Y	N	Y
Oracle Parallel Server	Y	N	Y

Option	Workstation	Standard	Enterprise
Oracle Partitioning	Y	N	Y
Oracle Programmer	Y	Y	Y
Oracle Spatial	Y	N	Y
Oracle Standard Management Pack	N	Y	N
Oracle Time Series	Y	N	Y
Oracle Tuning Pack	Y	N	Y
Oracle Visual Information Retrieval	Y	N	Y
Oracle WebDB	Y	Y	Y

Feature Availability

Features	Workstation	Standard	Enterprise
Application Development			
AppWizard for Visual Studio (NT only)	Y	Y	Y
Autonomous Transactions	Y	Y	Y
COM cartridge (NT only)	Y	Y	Y
JDBC drivers	Y	Y	Y
Microsoft Transaction Server Integration (NT only)	Y	Y	Y
Objects for OLE	Y	Y	Y
ODBC Driver	Y	Y	Y
Oracle Call Interface (OCI)	Y	Y	Y
Pro*C	Y	Y	Y
SQLJ	Y	Y	Y
Database Features			
Advanced Queuing	Y	N	Y
Database event triggers	Y	Y	Y
DBMS_REPAIR package	Y	Y	Y
Drop column	Y	Y	Y

Table continued on following page

1051

Features	Workstation	Standard	Enterprise
Database Features (Cont'd)			
Fine-grained access control	Y	N	Y
Index coalesce	Y	N	Y
Index-organized tables	Y	Y	Y
Indexes on NLS collating sequences	Y	N	Y
Instead-of triggers	Y	N	Y
LOB support	Y	Y	Y
Locally managed tablespaces	Y	Y	Y
LogMiner	Y	Y	Y
National language support (NLS)	Y	Y	Y
Objects and extensibility	Y	Y	Y
Online index build	Y	N	Y
Password management	Y	Y	Y
PL/SQL stored procedures, triggers	Y	Y	Y
Plan stability	Y	N	Y
Reverse key indexes	Y	Y	Y
Temporary tables	Y	Y	Y
Distributed Database Features			
Advanced replication	Y	N	Y
Basic replication	Y	Y	Y
Distributed queries	Y	Y	Y
Distributed transactions	Y	Y	Y
Heterogeneous services	Y	Y	Y
Manageability			
Automated standby database	Y	N	Y
Readable standby database	Y	N	Y
Database Resource manager	Y	N	Y
Duplexed backup sets	Y	N	Y
Oracle DBA Management Pack	Y	Y	Y

Features	Workstation	Standard	Enterprise
Manageability (Cont'd)			
Fast-start fault recovery	Y	N	Y
Incremental backup and recovery	Y	N	Y
Legato Storage Manager	Y	Y	Y
Online backup and recovery	Y	Y	Y
Oracle Enterprise Manager	N	Y	Y
Oracle Fail Safe for Oracle 8*i* on NT	Y	Y	Y
Parallel Backup and Recovery	Y	N	Y
Point-in-time tablespace recovery	Y	N	Y
Recovery Manager	Y	Y	Y
Server-managed backup and recovery	Y	Y	Y
Transparent Application Failover	Y	N	Y
Networking			
N-tier authentication/authorization	Y	N	Y
Network access control	Y	N	Y
Connection pooling	Y	Y	Y
Multi-protocol connectivity	Y	N	Y
Multiplexing	Y	N	Y
Oracle Connection Manager	Y	N	Y
Oracle Names	Y	Y	Y
Net8	Y	Y	Y
Warehousing/VLDB			
Analytic functions	Y	Y	Y
Automated parallel query degree	Y	N	Y
Bitmapped indexes	Y	N	Y
CUBE and ROLLUP	Y	Y	Y
Descending indexes	Y	Y	Y
Direct Path Load API	Y	Y	Y

Table continued on following page

Features	Workstation	Standard	Enterprise
Warehousing/VLDB (Cont'd)			
Export transportable tablespaces	Y	N	Y
Import transportable tablespaces	Y	Y	Y
Function-based indexes	Y	N	Y
Long operations monitor	Y	Y	Y
Materialized views	Y	N	Y
Optimizer statistics management	Y	Y	Y
Parallel analyze	Y	N	Y
Parallel bitmap star query optimization	Y	N	Y
Parallel DML	Y	N	Y
Parallel index build	Y	N	Y
Parallel index scans	Y	N	Y
Parallel load	Y	Y	Y
Parallel query	Y	N	Y
Sample scan	Y	N	Y
Star query optimization	Y	Y	Y

Oracle 8 8.0.4

Option Availability

Option	Standard	Enterprise
Objects Option	N	Y
Partitioning Option	N	Y
Advanced Networking Option	N	Y
Enterprise Manager Performance Pack	N	Y
Parallel Server Option	N	Y

Feature Availability

Option	Standard	Enterprise
Application Development		
Oracle Call Interface (OCI)	Y	Y
Objects for OLE	Y	Y
ODBC driver	Y	Y
Pro*C/C++	Y	Y
Database Features		
Advanced Queuing	N	Y
Reverse key indexes	Y	Y
Password management	Y	Y
Index-organized tables	Y	Y
PL/SQL stored procedures, triggers	Y	Y
Instead-of triggers	Y	Y
External procedures	Y	Y
National language support (NLS)	Y	Y
LOB support	Y	Y
Data Cartridges		
Context Cartridge	Y	Y
Video Cartridge	Y	Y
Image Cartridge	N	Y
Visual Information Retrieval Cartridge	N	Y
Time Series Cartridge	N	Y
Spatial Data Cartridge	N	Y
Distributed		
Distributed queries	Y	Y
Distributed transactions (2-phase commit, XA)	Y	Y
Heterogeneous Services	Y	Y
Basic Replication	Y	Y
Advanced Replication	N	Y

Table continued on following page

Option	Standard	Enterprise
Networking		
Oracle Names	Y	Y
Oracle Connection Manager	N	Y
Connection Pooling	Y	Y
Connection Multiplexing	Y	Y
Multiprotocol Connectivity	N	Y
Oracle Security Server	Y	Y
Object Features		
Object references (REFs)	Y	Y
Object collections (Nested tables, VARRAYS)	Y	Y
Object views	Y	Y
Manageability		
Enterprise Manager	Y	Y
Enterprise Manager Performance Pack	N	Y
Server Managed Backup and Recovery	Y	Y
Recovery catalog for online backup	Y	Y
Online recovery	Y	Y
Incremental backup and recovery	N	Y
Parallel backup and recovery	N	Y
Legato Storage Manager	Y	Y
Point-in-time tablespace recovery	N	Y
Fail Safe for Oracle 8 on NT	Y	Y
Warehousing/VLDB		
Bitmapped indexes	N	Y
Star Query optimization	Y	Y
Parallel Execution	N	Y
Parallel Load	N	Y
Parallel Query	N	Y

Option	Standard	Enterprise
Warehousing/VLDB (Cont'd)		
Parallel DML	N	Y
Parallel index scans	N	Y
Parallel bitmap star joins	N	Y
Parallel index build	N	Y
Parallel analyze	N	Y

V$ OPTION

The product installation media Oracle distributes includes all options available for that particular class of database. You must be licensed in order to use the options.

If you are interested in knowing what options have been installed in your database, you can query the dynamic view, V$OPTION, and you will find out the names of all the options available for your database, and a Boolean value indicating whether it is installed or not:

```
SQL> select parameter, value
  2    from v$option
  3    order by parameter
  4  /

PARAMETER                             VALUE
------------------------------------- ----------
Advanced replication                  TRUE
Application Role                      TRUE
Bit-mapped indexes                    TRUE
. . .
Spatial                               FALSE
Transparent Application Failover      TRUE
Visual Information Retrieval          TRUE

37 rows selected.
```

Index

A Guide to the Index

The index covers the numbered Chapters, the Case Studies and the Appendices. It is arranged alphabetically, word-by-word (that is, New York would be listed before Newark) with symbols preceding the letter A. Hyphens have been ignored in the sorting (so block terminator comes before block-based development) and acronyms have been preferred to their expansions as main entries.

O

S

salary calculation example
  implicit and explicit cursors, 377
Sales History see **SH sample schema.**
sales organization
  new sample schemas based on, 126
SALES table
  central role in SH sample schema, 137
SALES_REP object type
  company employees example, 650
sample schemas, 125
  comments created on installation, 148
  dependencies amongst the schemas, 1028, 1038
    technological dependencies, 1038
  gradual approach to learning, 138
  installing the schemas, 1025
    manual installation, 1028
    order of installing, 1028, 1038
    using the DBCA, 1026
  introduced, 13
  obtaining information about, 139
  stored procedures, 147
  using for simple queries, 31
SAVE command, SQL*Plus, 337
SAVEPOINT statement, 469
savepoints
  use recommended in modular code, 469
scalability
  benchmarking to scale, 708
  Oracle core competency, 153
scalar attributes
  stored in PL/SQL records, 358
scalar data types
  storing with objects and collections, 134
scale
  NUMBER data types, 90
Scheduled Tasks interface, 844
SCHEMA option
  CREATE TABLE statement, 106
schemas
  distinguished from users, 12, 500
  SCOTT and the new 9i sample schemas, 125
SCN (System Change Numbers), 467
scope
  ALTER SYSTEM statements, 164
  data dictionary views, 120
  PL/SQL variables and constants, 352
  REF data types, 655
  user-defined exceptions, 404
SCOTT sample schema
  dbls.sql script example, 770
  installing the schema, 1025
  relationship to 9i HR schema, 127, 128
  structure and relation to 9i samples, 125
SCOTT user accounts, 27
Scott, Bruce
  SCOTT sample schema and, 126
scripts, 339
  automating benchmarking with, 708
  availability as downloads, 139
  bigdate.sql script, 745
  calling from a web server, 315
  case.sql script, 389
  character string removal, 713
  colltypes.sql script, 994

colprivs.sql script, 985
comments.sql script, 148-149, 986
compbody.sql script, 752
compile_schema.sql script, 756-757, 759
compproc.sql, 754
comptrig.sql script, 755
compview.sql script, 755
connect.sql script, 745
controlling user input with ACCEPT, 325
createctl.sql script, 767, 769
create_tab_sync.sql script, 684
creating comments on sample schema
  installation, 148
dbls.sql script, 139, 769, 976
dblsl.sql script, 771
dclist.sql script, 974
demobld.sql script, 1026
deptemps.sql script, 330
desc.sql script, 141, 983
dlist.sql script, 973
example to list database objects, 139
example to list table details, 141
excprop.sql script, 402
exttabs.sql script, 992
flat.sql script, 746, 767
free.sql script, 772, 774
get*.sql scripts, 759
getallcode.sql script, 762
getallviews.sql script, 766
getaview.sql script, 1003
getcode.sql script, 761, 1008
getobject.sql script, 759
getview.sql script, 764
glogin.sql script, 34, 312, 744
hlpbld.sql script, 334
hrcomment.sql script, 148
hr_main.sql script, 1029
if_then_else.sql script, 386, 389
index.sql script, 775
indexes.sql script, 1016
invalid.sql script, 766
login.sql script, 34, 313, 336, 744
mksample.sql script, 1028
objtab.sql script, 994
oe_main.sql script, 1031
people.sql script, 846
people_detail.sql script, 850
plustrace.sql script, 719
pm_main.sql script, 1032
potential problems in using temporary files, 743
ppl_api.sql script, 841
ppl_comnt.sql script, 832
ppl_cre.sql script, 830
ppl_load.sql script, 843
ppl_main.sql script, 826, 845
ppl_popul.sql script, 834, 845
ppl_reload.sql script, 844
ppl_util.sql script, 835
print_table.sql script, 748, 751
prompt.sql script, 1022
qs_main.sql script, 1033
refex.sql script, 382
reverse engineering scripts, 759
running from a URI, 314
saving in files, 141
scope for documenting, 309
sh_main.sql script, 1036
showspace.sql script, 780

Notes

forums.apress.com

FOR PROFESSIONALS BY PROFESSIONALS™

JOIN THE APRESS FORUMS AND BE PART OF OUR COMMUNITY. You'll find discussions that cover topics of interest to IT professionals, programmers, and enthusiasts just like you. If you post a query to one of our forums, you can expect that some of the best minds in the business—especially Apress authors, who all write with *The Expert's Voice*™—will chime in to help you. Why not aim to become one of our most valuable participants (MVPs) and win cool stuff? Here's a sampling of what you'll find:

DATABASES

Data drives everything.

Share information, exchange ideas, and discuss any database programming or administration issues.

INTERNET TECHNOLOGIES AND NETWORKING

Try living without plumbing (and eventually IPv6).

Talk about networking topics including protocols, design, administration, wireless, wired, storage, backup, certifications, trends, and new technologies.

JAVA

We've come a long way from the old Oak tree.

Hang out and discuss Java in whatever flavor you choose: J2SE, J2EE, J2ME, Jakarta, and so on.

MAC OS X

All about the Zen of OS X.

OS X is both the present and the future for Mac apps. Make suggestions, offer up ideas, or boast about your new hardware.

OPEN SOURCE

Source code is good; understanding (open) source is better.

Discuss open source technologies and related topics such as PHP, MySQL, Linux, Perl, Apache, Python, and more.

PROGRAMMING/BUSINESS

Unfortunately, it is.

Talk about the Apress line of books that cover software methodology, best practices, and how programmers interact with the "suits."

WEB DEVELOPMENT/DESIGN

Ugly doesn't cut it anymore, and CGI is absurd.

Help is in sight for your site. Find design solutions for your projects and get ideas for building an interactive Web site.

SECURITY

Lots of bad guys out there—the good guys need help.

Discuss computer and network security issues here. Just don't let anyone else know the answers!

TECHNOLOGY IN ACTION

Cool things. Fun things.

It's after hours. It's time to play. Whether you're into LEGO® MINDSTORMS™ or turning an old PC into a DVR, this is where technology turns into fun.

WINDOWS

No defenestration here.

Ask questions about all aspects of Windows programming, get help on Microsoft technologies covered in Apress books, or provide feedback on any Apress Windows book.

HOW TO PARTICIPATE:

Go to the Apress Forums site at **http://forums.apress.com/**.

Click the New User link.